SOPHOCLES

Sophocles

....

A STUDY OF HIS THEATER IN ITS
POLITICAL AND SOCIAL CONTEXT

....

Jacques Jouanna

Translated by Steven Rendall

PRINCETON UNIVERSITY PRESS
PRINCETON AND OXFORD

Sophocle by Jacques Jouanna World Copyright © Librairie Arthème Fayard 2008

Copyright © 2018 by Princeton University Press

Requests for permission to reproduce material from this work should be sent to Permissions, Princeton University Press

Published by Princeton University Press,
41 William Street, Princeton, New Jersey 08540

In the United Kingdom: Princeton University Press,
6 Oxford Street, Woodstock, Oxfordshire OX20 1TR

press.princeton.edu

Jacket image: Marble head from a statue of the dramatist Sophocles, mounted on a modern herm. © The Trustees of the British Museum

LIBRARY OF CONGRESS CATALOGING-IN-PUBLICATION DATA
Names: Jouanna, Jacques, author. | Rendall, Steven, translator.
Title: Sophocles: a study of his theater in its political and social context/ Jacques Jouanna; translated by Steven Rendall.
Other titles: Sophocle. English
Description: Princeton; Oxford: Princeton University Press, 2018. | Includes bibliographical references and index.
Identifiers: LCCN 2017036423 | ISBN 9780691172071 (alk. paper)
Subjects: LCSH: Sophocles—Criticism and interpretation. | Greek drama—History and criticism.

Classification: LCC PA4417.J6913 2018 | DDC 882/.01—dc23 LC record available at https://lccn.loc.gov/2017036423

British Library Cataloging-in-Publication Data is available

This book has been composed in Adobe Garamond Pro

Printed on acid-free paper. ∞

Printed in the United States of America

10 9 8 7 6 5 4 3 2 1

TO HEINRICH VON STADEN,

IN MEMORY

OF PRINCETON

Why am I concerned with Sophocles?
Because there are new things that are very old
and old things that are very new.

—JEAN COCTEAU

CONTENTS

....

PART I

....

Sophocles the Athenian

Prelude

....

A SNAPSHOT OF SOPHOCLES

Finding the man behind the writer is a difficult, even impossible enterprise, especially when a man of the theater is concerned. This is even more true for an ancient author than for a modern one, because biographical information about the ancients seems questionable from the outset, especially if we don't take the trouble to look into its origin and assess its relative value. However, Sophocles is in this regard an exception among ancient authors, because we have a contemporary witness's report concerning him. It is a snapshot taken during a reception at which Sophocles, who had stopped off at the island of Chios, was the guest star. The report was composed by Ion of Chios, a writer born on the island who was younger than Sophocles, but like him a man of the theater. He had had the idea, which was very original at the time, of keeping a diary on the celebrities who passed through his homeland. Here is his account, as preserved in the work of a more recent author:

> I met the poet Sophocles on Chios when he was sailing to Lesbos as a *strategos*; he is a man who gets happy after having a few drinks and who is very astute. Hermesileos, his host and the Athenians' *proxenos*, seated him at his table. The boy assigned to pour the wine stood near the fire; he was clearly [red]. Sophocles spoke to him: "Do you want me to drink under agreeable conditions?" The boy said he did. "Then move slowly as you give me my goblet and take it away from me." When the boy blushed even more furiously, Sophocles said to his neighbor, who was lying on the same couch as he: "How beautiful it is, the verse composed by Phrynicus where he says: 'The light of love shines in scarlet cheeks.'" To which his neighbor, who was a grammar teacher from Eretria, replied: "Sophocles, I have no doubt that you are an expert in poetry. However, Phrynicus did not express himself well when he described the handsome boy's cheeks as 'scarlet.' For if a painter chose the color scarlet to represent this boy's cheeks, he would lose his beauty." When he heard these words spoken by the man from Eretria, Sophocles burst into laughter: "So, stranger, you are pleased by neither this verse of Simonides, which the Greeks nonetheless find so eloquent: 'the young girl making her voice heard from scarlet lips,' nor by the poet who speaks of Apollo with golden locks; for if a painter painted the god's hair in gold and not in black, the picture would be mediocre; nor by the poet

who says 'Rosy-fingered Dawn'; for if we took the color rose to paint her fingers, one would be representing a dyer's fingers, and not those of a pretty woman." This reply aroused laughter. And when the man from Eretria was stunned by this barrage, Sophocles resumed his conversation with the boy. As the boy tried to use his finger to remove a straw from the goblet, Sophocles asked whether he saw the straw clearly. The boy declared that he did. "Then blow it away, so as not to wet your finger." And when the boy tried to do so, Sophocles brought the goblet close to his own mouth, so that his head was closer to the boy's. And when he was very close to him, he seized him with his arm and gave him a kiss. Everyone present applauded, laughing and shouting to salute the cleverness with which Sophocles had taken the boy by surprise. "Gentlemen," Sophocles declared, "I have been training myself in strategy since Pericles claimed that although I knew poetry, I was ignorant of strategy. But didn't my stratagem succeed?" So there is one example among many others of the shrewdness of Sophocles' words and his acts when he took part in banquets.[1]

Here we are in the middle of the fifth century BCE, or more precisely, in the year 441/440. Sophocles was already over fifty years old. He had long been famous as a tragic poet and was occupying for the first time the political office of *strategos* along with Pericles. In this lively narrative in which Sophocles is sketched by a talented witness, we will point out, for the moment, only the overall impression.

It is a deliciously comic scene that shows two facets of Sophocles' character: in his conversation with the grammar teacher, it is the cultivated and brilliant poet who ridicules his interlocutor's professorial dogmatism and discreetly asserts the autonomy of poetry in contrast to painting: poetic technique must not be confused with pictorial technique! In the conversation between Sophocles and the young cupbearer, it is the strategist of love that we see at work. Here Sophocles, who was said to like boys, provides an example of his tactical skill by gradually drawing the victim into his trap. And there, he pretends to confuse military strategy and amorous strategy!

In the end, what unites these two facets of Sophocles' character is his power of seduction: by means of his great intelligence, full of irony and humor, he is able to win applause by mocking overly serious minds: that of the anonymous grammar teacher, but also that of Pericles, the master strategist. Sophocles, who was known for his ability to depict on the stage the misfortunes of the great, also knew how to make people smile in his private life, even when he was occupying a political office.

This report invites us to discover the man in all the diversity of his activities, not only literary, but also political and religious, and to assess the work of such an astute mind in all the wealth of its dimensions, while avoiding any dogmatism.

CHAPTER I

The Young Sophocles

....

Sophocles of the Athenian Deme of Colonus

Sophocles, whose life coincided with almost the whole of the fifth century BCE, was born in 497/496 or 495/494 in the city of Athens, where he died in 406/405. He was about a quarter of a century younger than Aeschylus, and about fifteen years older than Euripides. However, since he lived a long time, he died a year after Euripides.[1]

The city-state of Athens included more than the urban area; it extended to all Attica. Athens had freed itself from tyranny only a few years before Sophocles' birth. The new Athenian "civic space," which was the foundation of Athenian democracy, had been defined by Clisthenes: the basic unit was the deme. This was an administrative territorial district where every free Athenian had to be registered upon reaching majority in order to receive his civil and political rights. Each Athenian citizen thus belonged to a deme; and Sophocles' deme was Colonus, where he was born. In actuality, two demes bore the name "Colonus": one was called Kolonos Agoraios, the other Kolonos Hippeios. These two demes originally owed their names to a geographical peculiarity. "Kolonos" meant "hill." The first deme was in the city, near the public square or agora, as the adjective *agoraios* indicates. The second was outside the walls, northwest of the city, some distance from the ramparts of Athens and its acropolis. It was in this deme that Sophocles was born. It probably owed its qualifier "Hippeios" to a sanctuary of Poseidon Hippeios ("protector of horses") or to the eponymous hero Kolonos, who was a horseman.[2]

Each deme had been a district belonging to one of the ten tribes since Clisthenes' reform. The tribe to which Colonus belonged was the Aigeis tribe, which took its name from Aegeus, the former king of Athens. This tribe was second on the official list of the ten tribes.[3]

The Native Land: A Little Paradise

For every citizen, the deme was not only an administrative district; it was also his little homeland. Even though it was part of the great city of Athens, the deme was a community of citizens that had its own life, its assemblies, its magistrates, its cults; it was for everyone the native land, the place of childhood, the place whose memory was obscured by maturity's activities and then reemerged with all the more power when old age came. It is symbolic that at the end of his long career Sophocles brought the deme of his childhood back to life in his last work, and even in its title: *Oedipus at Colonus*.

All through the tragedy, Sophocles repeatedly mentions it. This attention is exceptional in his theater, because the tragic author does not usually appear behind his characters or his landscapes. Whether the deme is seen for the first time by foreign eyes, or presented by people familiar with it, we find the same awe before a luxuriant land blessed by the gods. Thus Antigone described the place where her blind old father has finally arrived after wandering in exile:

> Father, toil-worn Oedipus, the towers that ring the city, to judge by sight, are far off; and this place is sacred, to judge from its appearance: laurel, olive, and vine grow thick-set; and a feathered crowd of nightingales makes music within. So sit here on this unshaped stone; you have travelled a long way for an old man.[4]

These two first impressions—the sacred nature of the place and the richness of the land—are repeated and developed by the inhabitants of the deme. Here is how the first resident of Colonus met by Oedipus and Antigone presents his deme:

> This whole place is sacred; august Poseidon holds it, and in it lives the fire-bearing god, the Titan Prometheus. But as for the spot on which you tread, it is called the bronze threshold of this land, the support of Athens. And the neighboring fields claim Colonus, the horse-rider, for their ancient ruler; and all the people bear his name in common as their own. Such, you see, stranger, are these haunts. They receive their honor not through story, but rather through our living with them.[5]

From this first mention, which explains the name of the deme by the existence of a founding hero, emerges the sacred nature of the place. But it is to the song of the old men of Colonus that we owe the most vibrant and poetic praise of this paradisiacal land where it is good to live, even if one is a god:

> *Chorus:* Stranger, in this land of fine horses you have come to earth's fairest home, the shining Colonus. Here the nightingale, a constant guest, trills her clear note under the trees of green glades, dwelling amid the wine-dark ivy and the god's inviolate foliage, rich in berries and fruit, unvisited by sun, unvexed by the wind of any storm. Here the reveller Dionysus ever walks the ground, companion of the nymphs that nursed him. And, fed on heavenly dew, the narcissus blooms day by day with its fair clusters; it is the ancient crown of the Great Goddesses. And the crocus blooms with a golden gleam.

> Nor do the ever-flowing springs diminish, from which the waters of Cephi-
> sus wander, and each day with pure current it moves over the plains of the
> land's swelling bosom, bringing fertility. Nor have the dancing Muses
> shunned this place, nor Aphrodite of the golden rein.

All these details help make this deme where the Cephisus flows a land of
prosperity, made fertile by the pure water, protected from storms, rich in pas-
turelands in the valleys where horses graze, rich in flowers and fruits, and
covered with forests where nightingales nest and gods and goddesses abide. To
be sure, this enthusiastic description is that of old residents of the deme who
are a little chauvinistic. The "imitating" poet necessarily distances himself from
the characters he creates. But at the same time, the praise is sincere. It was not
only to please his deme, as one ancient critic suggested, that Sophocles composed such a eulogy to Colonus.[6] It was a way for the poet, who was approaching the end of his life, to immortalize his modest native land and probably to
express his gratitude to it. Is it unimportant to see him noting that the choruses
of the Muses do not despise this bit of earth? Perhaps as a child Sophocles saw
his vocation as a poet born there, like Hesiod who met the Muses on Mount
Helicon.

The Redoubtable Sanctuary of the Venerables

This deme was not only inhabited by familiar gods. It also was the home of redoubtable powers, "the daughters of Earth and Darkness,"[7] who were also called,
by antiphrasis, the Eumenides (i.e., "the Benevolent," to avert misfortune), or,
using an ambiguous term, the Semnai, that is, both the Venerable and the Redoubtable. It was their sanctuary in Colonus that Sophocles represented in his
Oedipus at Colonus. When the old men who form the chorus come to the sanctuary of these divinities, they express their fear of the invincible goddesses whose
name they are afraid to utter, and the holy terror they feel in passing by this
sanctuary they are forbidden to enter: "Their name we tremble to speak; we pass
them by with eyes turned away, moving our lips, without sound or word, in still
devotion."[8]

We can imagine, without much risk of error, that even in his childhood
Sophocles had felt that same sacred horror when he walked past the sanctuary
of the Erinyes while holding his father's hand.

Sophocles, the Son of Sophillos

The Athenian citizen drew his identity from his deme and, within the deme,
from his family and especially his father. Sophocles, of the deme of Colonus, was
the son of Sophillos (or Sophilos).[9] The information given by the ancients regard-

ing Sophocles' father diverges significantly. The *Life of Sophocles* mentions a discussion:

> Sophillos was not, as Aristoxenes says, a carpenter or blacksmith, nor, as Istros says, a dagger-maker by trade, but he did possess slaves who were blacksmiths or carpenters. For it is not likely that a man born of such a modest father would have been deemed worthy of the office of *strategos* along with Pericles and Thucydides, the most prominent men in the city.[10] And neither did he escape the barbs of the comic poets, who did not spare even Themistocles.[11]

To judge by this text, it is clear that the oldest evidence we have regarding Sophocles' father's trade presents him as a craftsman. The oldest source, Aristoxenes of Tarentum, one of Aristotle's pupils (fourth century BCE), says that he was a carpenter or a blacksmith; a source a century later, Istros, representing the erudition of the time of the Library of Alexandria,[12] attributes to him the trade of a dagger maker. These differences concerning Sophillos's trade, whether carpenter, blacksmith, or armorer, are of little importance. In any event, he practiced a trade that, in the society of the time, was in no way noble.

The modesty of Sophocles' origins later shocked biographers and scholars. We can admire the cleverness of the author of the *Life* in the first century BCE in arguing that Sophocles' father's status could not have been so humble. But Sophocles' later success cannot provide a basis for judging his origins. When modern writers present Sophocles as the son of a rich Athenian with slaves who were blacksmiths or carpenters, they are relying on the fallacious argument of a relatively recent biographer and not on the most ancient sources. This tendency to elevate Sophocles' father's status only increased in the course of antiquity. Pliny the Elder (first century CE) went so far as to claim that he was born into a prominent family.[13] In Pliny, as in Sophocles' biographer, though more implicitly, this high birth is related to the political role Sophocles played.

Let us be clear. Sophocles did not belong to an aristocratic family, as was assuredly the case for Pericles, and probably also for Aeschylus; but neither did he come from a low-class background, as Euripides did, if we believe the mockery of the comic poet Aristophanes, who claimed that Euripides' mother sold aromatic or medicinal herbs at the market in Athens.[14] He came from a class wealthy enough to qualify him to hold the office of strategos.[15] And it is certain that his father had the means to give his son a good education.

A Talented, Well-Trained Young Man

We have hardly any information about Sophocles' intellectual training and the way in which he acquired the immense culture that made him so brilliant at banquets.[16] He is supposed to have learned the tragic art from Aeschylus.[17] As a youth, he distinguished himself in two domains that played a capital role in the education of young Greek men, gymnastics and music. In these two disciplines, he won a prize and was rewarded with a crown of laurels. It is true that he received a good education: he studied music with a famous teacher, Lampros, who taught him to play the lyre and dance. It was probably due to this instruction and his natural talents that at the age of fifteen or seventeen, at the height of his attractiveness, he made his first public appearance during an exceptional ceremony held in the city in 480.[18]

Sophocles' Homeland in 480

At that time, the city of Athens and the Greek world in general witnessed, after the naval battle won at Salamis, the decline of the barbarian threat that had compromised its independence.

As we have seen, shortly before Sophocles' birth the Athenians had rid themselves of internal tyranny by driving out Hippias, the son and heir of the tyrant Pisistratos, and they had organized the administrative and political frameworks of their nascent democracy in such a way as to prevent the return of tyranny. But then they had been compelled to confront the threat of an external tyranny, that of the Persians. Moreover, the two dangers were partly linked, because as a result of the first Persian expedition sent by King Darius in 490 BCE, Hippias, who was advising the leaders of the expedition, Datis and Artaphernes, hoped to return to power in Athens. What was at stake in the battle of Marathon, where Athens repelled the twofold danger of external and internal tyranny, is clearly outlined in Herodotus by the man who played a crucial role at the beginning of the battle, the Athenian strategos Miltiades:

> Now the Athenians have come to their greatest danger since they first came into being, and, if we surrender, it is clear what we will suffer when handed over to Hippias. But if the city prevails, it will take first place among Hellenic cities.[19]

Sophocles was five or seven years old at the time of the victory won by the Athenians at Marathon with the help of the Plataeans—the triumph of the men who were later called the Marathonomachs ("the fighters at Marathon") and who remained, in the Greek imagination, the courageous defenders of freedom and democracy against tyranny and barbarian imperialism. Aeschylus fought in the battle, and for the rest of his life he remained proud of having repelled the "long-haired Persian."[20]

But ten years after this first Persian war, Xerxes, the son of Darius, personally led a powerful expedition by land and by sea that emerged from the whole of Asia with the intention of punishing Athens. It had already been the desire for vengeance that had moved Darius to launch the first expedition against Greece, and especially against the cities of Athens and Eretria in Euboea, which he accused of having helped the Greek colonies in Ionia, who paid him tribute, to rebel against his control. This attempt had failed at Marathon. This time, his son Xerxes intended to complete the punitive expedition. But his real goal was more ambitious: he wanted to secure a universal empire by joining Europe to Asia. The young Sophocles, who was old enough, or almost, to enter his name on the registers of the deme of Colonus and thus to acquire the title of citizen, could not help strongly resenting the threat that once again weighed on Athens.

The threat was in fact serious. While during the first Persian war the invaders had been defeated in northern Attica, at Marathon, and had not penetrated the city of Athens despite the barbarian fleet's incursion into the Athenian port of Phalerus, during the second Persian war Athens experienced the most dramatic hours in its history. Xerxes broke through the gate constituted by the pass at Thermopylae, despite the heroic resistance of a battalion of three hundred Spartans commanded by their king Leonidas. He then pushed on into Attica, which he ravaged, and occupied Athens, which had been almost completely deserted by its residents, who had taken refuge on the island of Salamis, and seized the Acropolis, whose temple was pillaged and burned. To the Athenians, the situation appeared hopeless, but the Greek fleet that had fallen back on Salamis succeeded in defeating the Persian fleet, which was too numerous to maneuver in the narrow strait separating the island of Salamis from the Attic coast. The Greek fighters saw clearly what was at stake in the battle. At dawn, when the attack began, they sang a song whose words the poet Aeschylus, who fought at Salamis as well as at Marathon,[21] reported in his tragedy *The Persians* produced eight years later:

> Now, sons of Hellas, now!
> Set Hellas free, set free your wives, your homes,
> Your gods' high altars and your fathers' tombs.
> Now all is on the stake![22]

In this war of liberation, the Greeks' naval victory was crushing. However, it was unhoped for, because the barbarians' forces were significantly superior to those of the Greeks. They had four times as many ships. Thus we can imagine what the Athenians must have felt after the naval battle, during the religious ceremony that took place around the trophy, that is, around the monument formed by the bodies of the enemies near the place where their rout had begun: relief regarding the threat that had retreated at least temporarily, pride regarding the Greeks' courage and wiliness, but above all gratitude to the gods to whom they spontaneously attributed this "divine surprise."

Sophocles must have shared such feelings with the rest of the Athenian community; but in his case, there was also the emotion and pride at having been chosen to dance and sing in honor of the victory, accompanying himself on his lyre. Here, in any case, is what Athenaeus reports:

> After the battle of Salamis, at any rate, he danced to the accompaniment of his lyre round the trophy, naked and anointed with oil. Others say he danced with his cloak on.[23]

Was he one performer among others in the chorus of young people? Or did he play, as the author of the anonymous *Life* suggests, the role of *exarch*, that is, the head of the chorus, singing as a solo the paean in honor of the victory before the chorus as a whole echoed it? In any case, Sophocles' grace and talent during this first performance before all the assembled Athenians are not in doubt. To confirm Sophocles' gifts as a musician and dancer, in this same passage Athenaeus recalls that later on, when he had become an author of tragedies, Sophocles acted in his own plays on two occasions:

> when he brought out the *Thamyris* he played the lyre himself. He also played ball with great skill when he produced the *Nausicaä*.

His tragedy entitled *Thamyris* (or *Thamyras*) is now lost, and the meager fragments still extant do not allow us to reconstruct the details of the action. But that does not prevent us from gauging the dexterity required to play the role of Thamyris, a cithara player from Thrace who belonged to the group of legendary musicians of whom Orpheus is the most illustrious. The best-known episode of the legend of Thamyris is the battle he fought against the Muses, as Homer already reported:

> the Muses met Thamyris the Thracian and made an end of his singing, even as he was journeying from Oechalia, from the house of Eurytus the Oechalian: for he vaunted with boasting that he would conquer, were the Muses themselves to sing against him, the daughters of Zeus that beareth the aegis; but they in their wrath maimed him, and took from him his wondrous song, and made him forget his minstrelsy.[24]

When Sophocles represented in the theater this competition between Thamyris and the Muses—which ended tragically for the singer—he had once again to prove before the Athenian people his talent as a musician.[25] And he showed off his talent as a dancer by playing ball in his play entitled *Nausicaa* or *The Washerwomen* (*Plyntriai*).[26] This play, whether it is a tragedy or a satyr play, is also lost. Its subject was the mythical sequence in the *Odyssey* in which Nausicaa, the daughter of the king of the Phaeacians, and her servants, who have come to wash their laundry in the river at the seaside, play ball and dance while the laundry dries, while Odysseus, shipwrecked on the Phaeacians' island, sleeps not far away, sheltered and hidden under a thick bed of leaves. Nausicaa leads the chorus of girls who sing and dance while throwing her the ball. One servant's clumsiness—provoked by the goddess Athena—causes the ball Nausicaa throws to fall into the river. The girls shriek. Odysseus wakes and sits up. The servants flee; only Nausicaa remains. This is their meeting.[27]

Although the extant fragments of this play are particularly few,[28] by referring to the *Odyssey* we can very well reconstruct the scene in which Sophocles, playing the role of Nausicaa, sings and dances and throws the ball to the fifty servant girls who form the chorus, which also sings and dances, until one servant misses the ball, the chorus's cry leads to Odysseus's appearance, and the latter provokes the terrified flight of the servants running off to hide.

Sophocles' Song at Salamis

To conclude this significant episode in Sophocles' youth in Salamis, we might mention that it inspired Victor Hugo to write a "Chanson de Sophocle à Sala-mine" ("Sophocles' Song at Salamis"), which he inserted into *La Légende des siècles*:

Here I am, a callow youth,
My sixteen years bathed in azure;
War, goddess of Erebus,
Somber war with outraged cries,

I come to you, the night is dark!
Since Xerxes is the stronger,
Take me for battle and for glory,
And for the tomb; but first

You, whom the sword obeys,
And the lightning bolt follows,
Choose me with your left hand
A beautiful girl with soft eyes,

Who knows nothing but how
To laugh an innocent laugh,
Who is divine, pink at the two
points of her naked breast.

Don't be harder on the man
Full of dark destiny
Than is on profound Neptune
The vivid morning star.

Give her to me, that I might quickly
Press her to my flaming heart;
I'm willing to die, oh Goddess,
But not before I've loved.

The poet, as we see, has taken great liberties with the ancient sources. He makes the young Sophocles a combatant, whereas at the time he was not yet old enough to fight. And he imagines him before the battle, and not afterward, at the time when the dark power of Xerxes is still threatening, when "the enormous blackness seeks to kill the star," and not when bright light of victory has shone forth and "restored hope to the convict universe."[29] In Hugo's work, the only light the young Sophocles hopes for before the battle, and perhaps before death, is that of love.

CHAPTER II

Sophocles the Politician

. . . .

Unlike Aeschylus and Euripides, Sophocles was not solely a man of the theater. To be sure, his life was regularly punctuated by the writing of tragedies, but he also held important political offices at times in his life that were also symbolic moments of Athens's most brilliant history, and then the most tragic. The fifth century BCE, which began so gloriously for Athens with its victory in the Persian Wars, and continued so splendidly with the years that have been called "the century of Pericles," ended with the fratricidal conflict between the two cities that had overcome the Persians, Athens and Sparta, leading to the humiliating defeat of Athens in 404. Sophocles died, however, before he learned the outcome of his city's tragedy.[1]

Sophocles the *Hellenotamias*

Sophocles was already in his fifties when he held his first public office. It had a technical name: it was the office of the "hellenotamias," or "Hellenic treasurer," an office that had been created during the levy of the Athenian Empire.[2]

The formation of the Athenian Empire was an indirect consequence of the Persian Wars. The victory at Salamis, which the whole city had celebrated, had put a stop to the Persian invasion, because Xerxes, rending his garments at the sight of his fleet's disaster, which he observed from a dominant point overlooking the bay of Salamis,[3] had decided to retreat. But the stigmata left by the passage of the barbarians through Athens were painful: all the houses, with the exception of those that had been used by Persian dignitaries, had collapsed; the Acropolis had been burned, and all that remained of the defensive ramparts were a few sections of wall. Besides, the Persian menace had still not been entirely averted after Salamis: the following year (in 479), Xerxes' brother-in-law, Mardonius, who had remained in Greece with a land army of three hundred thousand men, invaded Attica again. But Attica had been abandoned by its inhabitants, who once again took refuge on Salamis and on their boats; and faced with the Athenians' refusal to negotiate, Mardonius burned Athens and razed every remainder of the walls, houses, and temples that were still standing. What put a definitive end to the Persian Wars was two defeats of the barbarians, which, according to the ancients, took place on the same day: on land, in continental Greece, at

Plataea, the contingent commanded by Mardonius was routed and massacred, after its leader's death, by the combined army of the Greeks; and at sea, in Ionia, at Cape Mycale across from Samos, the Greek fleet blockaded the Persian fleet and burned it. This double battle corresponded to a double stake: the liberation of continental Greece and the liberation of the Greek islands.

But the fear of a possible return of the barbarians after the Persian Wars guided Greek policy, and particularly that of the Athenians, and led to the formation of what became the Athenian Empire. The primary concern of the Athenians after the Persian retreat was to reconstruct their city ravaged by the double invasion: they rebuilt their houses and especially their ramparts. Despite the anxiety of the Lacedaemonians and their allies in the Peloponnese on seeing the growing power of a city that, confident in its fleet, had shown so much audacity against the barbarians, the Athenians fortified their city in a short time, notably at the instigation of Themistocles. Above all, they completed the construction of a new port, Piraeus, which a few years later they connected with the city by means of ramparts, after having fortified it as well. This was an affirmation of the maritime vocation of Athens's power. This vocation took concrete form a little later in the hegemony that the Ionian allies and other peoples recently liberated from the Great King asked Athens to exercise. Sparta, immediately after the Persian Wars, had retained the command of the Greeks, even in the maritime domain: it is significant that the Greek fleets, sent to secure the barriers against the barbarians, Cyprus in the South and Byzantium in the North, were placed under the command of the regent of Sparta, Pausanias, even though the number of ships provided by the Athenians was greater than that provided by the Lacedaemonians. But the abuses of power committed by Pausanias, who behaved more like a tyrant than an ally, displeased the recently liberated partners: they asked for a change of hegemony. The Athenians found in this a pretext for obtaining command of the fleet that they had already wanted during the Persian Wars. It was during this change in hegemony that the office of the *hellenotamiae* was instituted, as Thucydides explains:

> The Athenians having thus succeeded to the supremacy by the voluntary act of the allies through their hatred of Pausanias, fixed which cities were to contribute money against the barbarian, which ships; their professed object being to retaliate for their sufferings by ravaging the king's country. Now was the time that the office of "Treasurers for Hellas" was first instituted by the Athenians. These officers received the tribute, as the money contributed was called. The tribute was first fixed at four hundred and sixty talents. The common treasury was at Delos, and the congresses were held in the temple.[4]

This new Athenian magistracy, created in 478/477, only two years after the Battle of Salamis, was collegial. A college of ten treasurers was made responsible for administering the product of the final revenues paid by the allies who did not want to participate directly in the struggle against the barbarians by sending ships. These treasurers were elected for a year by the popular assembly in Athens; they took office at the time of the Panathenaic Games, in July.

It is in the list of the tributes for 443/442, provided by an inscription, that "Sophocles of the deme of Colonus" appears as a hellenotamias.[5] Therefore it is not a literary testimony, but a testimony preserved on stone that is the source of our information, though what it tells us is nonetheless not as obvious as one might think.

An Epigraphic Puzzle

We have to imagine things very concretely, and restore a historical perspective to the discovery and reading of the inscription in order to grasp what is at stake in the problems concerning the identification of Sophocles. The inscription is in fact incomplete. Is the hellenotamias referred to by the inscription really Sophocles, and is this Sophocles really the tragic poet?

Let us go to the epigraphic museum in Athens, where we can see a large, quadrangular stele in Pentelic marble, more than 3.5 meters high, 1.1 meters wide, and almost 40 centimeters thick. This stele bears, inscribed on its four sides, the first fifteen lists, year by year, of the allies of Athens who paid tribute, starting in the year 454/453. Unfortunately, the stele has not been preserved whole; it is constituted of 180 fragments that do not all fit together and leave major lacunae. These fragments were found alongside the monumental gateway during excavations of the Acropolis carried out after Greece won independence in 1834.[6] The stele as we see it today was put back together in 1927. Several generations of epigraphists have gradually reconstituted the puzzle, starting from the discovery of the fragments in the early nineteenth century.

The learned publication (which is authoritative) in 1939 by scholars from the American school—a century after the discovery!—presents as follows the twelfth list, the one that concerns us, and that was constituted by assembling several fragments some of which were lost during the reconstitution of the stele in 1927. It represents the year 443/442.[7] The list properly so called of the allies paying tribute is divided into five columns, each comprising thirty-five lines: each line indicates the residents of a city preceded by the amount of the tribute they paid. The cities, which number 162, are grouped according to the five great geographical and administrative districts for collecting the tribute.[8] This list—which gives an idea of the magnitude of the task faced by the hellenotamiae responsible for collecting each of these tributes—is itself framed by two lines, one above, the other below the five columns, providing information regarding the year and the names of the secretary, the assistant secretary, and a hellenotamias. On the list for 443/442, the top line reads as follows: "During the twelfth years of the empire, Sophias, of the deme of Eleusis, was secretary." The bottom line, which is in fact a continuation of the top line, gives at the beginning, on a fragment now lost, the name of the assistant secretary ("Satyros of the deme Leuconone was assistant secretary"); then at the end, on an extant fragment, the name of the hellenotamias with his deme of origin. But this last part is unfortunately incomplete![9] The name of the hellenotamias as well as that of his deme are found, in fact, on a damaged part of the inscription. The American editors followed others in reading as the name of the hellenotamias the last seven letters OPHOKLES (the "PH" being a single Greek letter *phi*), which makes it possible to find, after restoring an initial "s," the name SOPHOKLES. As for the following name of the deme, the first four letters KOLO can be read without difficulty; but there the fragment breaks off. Like other editors, the Americans restored KOLO[NETHEN], "from the deme of Colonus." Who could this "Sophocles of the deme of Colonus" be, except Sophocles the great tragic poet? Let us recall that the Byzantine dictionary known as the *Suda* presented the latter this way: "Sophocles, son of Sophilos, of the deme of Colonus (KOLONETHEN)." This identification, which had not immediately established itself when the stone was first deciphered, now seems very likely, and the great majority of scholars consider it certain.[10] The inscription on stone remains lapidary in every sense. It reports the raw fact, without indicating why the popular assembly chose Sophocles. Nonetheless, since Sophocles' name appears as representing the college of the ten hellenotamiae we can infer that he was its chairman.[11]

The Transfer of the Treasury Managed by the Hellenotamiae from Delos to Athens

There is one detail on the stone that is revealing concerning the period in which Sophocles held this office of hellenotamias. The annual list of the tributes that the hellenotamiae managed is presented in the form of two series. Sophocles' name appears in the twelfth year of the second series. Between the two series a major event occurred concerning the location of the treasury that the hellenotamiae managed. This event reflects the transformation of the Delian League into the Athenian Empire, a transformation of which the historian Thucydides offers a remarkable analysis.

As we have seen, when the league was created in 478/477 the allies had willingly granted the Athenians hegemony. Although it was directed by the Athenians, the league's center was on the island of Delos. The sanctuary of Apollo on Delos, which was the Ionians' sanctuary, was the site of the league's meetings and especially that of the federal treasury constituted by the tribute paid by the allies. Thus the hellenotamiae, who were Athenian magistrates, had to manage a treasury that was on Delos. This somewhat paradoxical situation lasted a quarter of a century, until the treasury was transferred from Delos to Athens in 454/453, the most tangible sign of a transformation of the Delian League into an Athenian empire. In a way, it made the new era official. The numbering of the series of different colleges of hellenotamiae that followed was begun over starting with the transfer of the treasury to the temple of Athena in Athens. Sophocles' name appears in the second series, which extends from 454/453 to 405/404. This change of place was not merely symbolic. It led to changes in habits. Beginning in 454, the allies had to bring their tribute to Athens each year, where it was presented officially during the Dionysia, the great festival of Dionysus, on the dance floor of the theater, when all the tiers of seats were filled. The hellenotamiae now received each city's tribute in Athens and levied a sixtieth of it for the goddess Athena, and no longer for the Delian Apollo.

When Sophocles, acting as a hellenotamias, received officially the tribute paid by the representatives of the 162 cities who came to parade in the theater during the Dionysian Festival of 442, he was on familiar territory. In fact, he had been famous there as an author of tragedies for more than twenty years.[12]

Sophocles the Strategos: The First Mission (441/440)

It was also in the context of this transformation of the Delian League into an Athenian empire that Sophocles held his second public office. Only one year after the end of his first term as hellenotamias, in 441/440, he took part, as a strategos, in Athens's expedition against the island of Samos, which had revolted.

The transition from hegemony to empire was marked, in fact, not only by the concentration of financial means in Athens, but also, more profoundly, by the evolution of the relationships between the Athenians and their allies, which Thucydides points out immediately following his discussion of the establishment of the hegemony:

> Their supremacy commenced with independent allies who acted on the resolutions of a common congress. It was marked by the following undertakings in war and in administration during the interval between the Median and the present war, against the barbarian, against their own rebel allies, and against the Peloponnesian powers which would come in contact with them on various occasions.[13]

Thucydides goes on to analyze the general causes that led the Athenians to oppose their allies and to transform hegemony into empire: the allies' failure to deliver the right amount of tribute in money or ships, and in some cases their revolt. Once these revolts had been put down, the former allies were subjugated.

The first revolt the Athenians had to cope with was that of the island of Naxos, the largest of the Cyclades, around 470.[14] Naxos was the first to move from the status of an ally to that of a subject. Four years later, it was the turn of the island of Thasos, following a dispute over the trading posts and gold mines that the Thasians were operating on the Thracian coast across from the island. It took a siege lasting more than two years to force the Thasians to surrender to the Athenians, accepting very harsh conditions: their ramparts had to be destroyed, their fleet handed over, and tribute paid. Starting from the time when Pericles dominated Athenian policy, two other revolts took place before the Peloponnesian War, one on the island of Euboea in 446, and the other on the island of Samos five years later. Each time, Pericles intervened in person. In Euboea, he subjected the whole island and expelled all the residents of the city of Histiaea, where he established *cleruchs* (that is, Athenian military settlers). In this way he took revenge on the inhabitants of Histiaea, who, after capturing an Athenian ship, had massacred its crew.[15] The harshness of the repression marked people's memories: more than twenty years afterward, the comic dramatist Aristophanes still alluded to it in his plays.[16] It was during the other expedition, the one conducted against Samos, that Sophocles served as strategos alongside Pericles. This expedition took place in 441/440.

Pericles and the Revolt of Samos

For the Athenians, the revolt of Samos had a very special significance. While they acted rather despotically with regard to their allies in general, they had treated the three islands of Chios, Lesbos, and Samos more gently. As Aristotle says in his *Constitution of Athens*, they saw the inhabitants of these three islands as the guardians of their empire. The Athenians had therefore allowed them to retain their own constitution and the government of their possessions.[17] However, taking advantage of a war between Samos and the inhabitants of Miletus over the possession of Priene, in 441/440 (during the archontate of Timocles) the Athenians, under the command of Pericles, overthrew the established regime to establish democracy, took children as hostages whom they entrusted to the inhabitants of Lemnos, and set up a garrison. But the adversaries of democracy, supported by the satrap of Sardis, Pissosuthenes, reestablished the former regime, surreptitiously recovered the hostages, and broke with the Athenians after handing the Athenian garrison over to the barbarians.[18] Thus one of the three pillars of the empire was collapsing. Given Samos's naval power, it was control of the seas that was at stake;[19] the Athenians had to react. They did so rapidly, using exceptional means. Here is what Thucydides says about the beginning of their response:

> As soon as the Athenians heard the news, they sailed with sixty ships against Samos. Sixteen of these went to Caria to look out for the Phoenician fleet, and to Chios and Lesbos carrying round orders for reinforcements, and so never engaged; but forty-four ships under the command of Pericles with nine colleagues gave battle, off the island of Tragia, to seventy Samian vessels, of which twenty were transports, as they were sailing from Miletus. Victory remained with the Athenians.[20]

What shows the magnitude of the means employed is first of all the number of ships engaged: the fleet of sixty ships initially sent was twice reinforced, first by twenty-five ships coming from two of the most important other allies, Chios and Lesbos, and forty from Athens; then, the following year, sixty ships from Athens and thirty from Chios and Lesbos, which increased to 215 ships the total size of the allied fleet that besieged Samos.[21]

But the most exceptional measure was the number of generals sent. We know that since Clisthenes' reform the *strategoi* formed in Athens a college of ten magistrates (one for each of the ten tribes) elected annually among the wealthiest citizens; they could be reelected indefinitely.[22] As their name indicates (*strategos* means "he who leads the army"), they first had military functions, and it was not unusual for them to assume in turn the command of military expeditions by land or by sea. But they also played a political role. That was the case especially when a strategos was reelected repeatedly. At the time of the expedition to Samos, Pericles had already been a strategos several times. Having become the leader of the popular party after the death of Ephialtes (shortly after 461), he had first been elected strategos some fifteen years earlier (in 454/453)[23] and had been regularly reelected to that office for the past five years. Having eliminated not long before, by ostracism, his political adversary, Thucydides[24]—not the historian, but the head of the oligarchic party, Melesias's son—Pericles then reigned supreme in the city: "So, in what was nominally a democracy, power was really in the hands of the first citizen," the historian Thucydides says.[25] Thus it is natural that the historian, when he speaks of the generals sent to put down the Samians' revolt, mentions Pericles first and does not think it necessary to give the names of the other strategoi who accompanied him. But he does say how many of them there were, saying that Pericles was the tenth, which means that Pericles was accompanied by his nine colleagues.

Sophocles as Pericles' Colleague on the Samos Expedition

Sophocles was one of these nine colleagues. His presence is mentioned by the geographer Strabo: "The Athenians," he says, "formerly sent Pericles their general, and with him Sophocles the poet."[26] But it is to a fourth-century BCE historian of Attica, Androtion, that we owe the names of all the strategoi of the year 441/440. This Androtion, who studied under Isocrates, is better known as an orator and politician than as a historian. He has come down to posterity mainly for the political plea Demosthenes wrote against him, *Against Androtion*. But his local history of Attica was highly regarded in his own time. It served Aristotle as his principal source for everything in *The Constitution of Athens* that touches on the history of Athens. The list of strategoi given by Androtion felicitously supplements Thucydides' testimony. Here it is:

> Socrates of the deme Anagyronte, Sophocles of the deme Colonus, the poet, Andocides of the deme Cydathenaion, Creon of the deme Scambonides, Pericles of the deme Cholarges, Glaucon of the deme Kerameies, Callistros of the

deme Acharnes, Xenophon of the deme Melite, Lampides of the deme Piraeus (Hippothontis), Glauketes [Athenian], Clitophon of the deme Thorai.[27]

In this list, where the strategoi are designated by their names and their demes of origin, we see that Pericles does not appear first, detached from his colleagues, as he does in Thucydides. His name appears in the fifth position, after that of Sophocles, which is in the second position. The reason for this is that we are dealing with a list proceeding from an official document, in which the names of the generals are not arranged in a preferential order, but in the official sequence of the ten Athenian tribes, the ten strategoi having been elected at the rate of one per tribe. These ten tribes drew their names from ten Athenian "heroes" who are "eponymous" (literally, give their names), and whose statues were lined up on a long base in the middle of the central square in Athens, the agora.[28] Pericles appears in the fifth position because his tribe, the Acamantis, which owed its name to Acamas, one of Theseus's two sons, came fifth in the official order. Coming second, Sophocles was thus born in a deme that belonged to the Aigeis tribe, owing its name to Aegeus, king of Athens and father of Theseus.[29]

Reading this list, we understand that Sophocles incontestably belonged to the Athenian elite. In addition to the name of Pericles, we should note also that of Andocides. He was the grandfather of the orator Andocides, whom we know to have belonged to a noble line, the ancient family of the Kerykes. This grandfather had already played an important political role five years earlier: he had been one of the ten Athenians who had been chosen to negotiate, in 446, the thirty-year truce with the Lacedaemonians.[30] Under these conditions, we can see why the biographer of Sophocles revolted against the idea that the poet had a very modest origin, declaring: "For it is not likely that a man born of such a modest father would have been deemed worthy of the office of strategos along with Pericles and Thucydides, the most prominent men in the city."[31]

Why Was Sophocles Elected Strategos, and What Was His Role?

Regarding the reason for Sophocles' election as a strategos, one explanation was current as early as the Hellenistic period in the great scholarly center represented by the Library of Alexandria. At the beginning of the manuscripts of Sophocles' *Antigone* a presentation of the tragedy has been preserved that was written by one of the directors of that library, Aristophanes of Byzantium (third to second centuries BCE). It ends this way: "It is said that Sophocles was deemed worthy of his office as strategos at Samos because he had acquired fame as a result of the performance of his *Antigone*." Thus it is supposed to be Sophocles' literary success that justified his playing a political and military role.[32]

What was the role of the strategos Sophocles in this expedition against Samos? At first glance, it seems difficult to say, because our main sources on that expedition say nothing about this. Thucydides, as usual, goes right to the heart of the matter, without mentioning names. He distinguishes several stages in the campaign: first, the Athenians' initial naval victory off the coast of Samos, near the little island of Tragia located south of Samos; then the landing after the arrival of reinforcements and, following a victory on land, the siege of the city with its triple fortification; then the reversal of the situation: taking advantage of Pericles' departure at the head of a large part of the fleet, the Samians broke out toward the sea, making a sudden sortie that allowed them to destroy part of the besieging fleet and to gain access to the sea for a fortnight; then Pericles, having returned, closed off their access to the sea and renewed the siege; and finally, further reinforcements having arrived, the Samians surrendered after an eight-month siege and were forced to accept draconian terms: the destruction of the fortifications—which had been heavily damaged by siege machines—the surrender of the fleet, the provision of hostages, and war indemnities.[33]

In Thucydides, the protagonists of history are peoples and not individuals: the Athenians on one side, the Samians on the other. Only one individual emerges on the Athenian side: Pericles. In Diodorus Siculus, the second historian to report the facts, Pericles is also the only strategos mentioned.[34] Even in Plutarch, where history is more personalized—it is he who reports the role played by Pericles' companion Aspasia, a native of Miletus, in Pericles' decision to intervene on behalf of Miletus against Samos—the name of Sophocles does not appear.[35] But Plutarch nonetheless preserves clues, apropos of this crisis between Athens and Samos, one of which sheds light on the role of men of letters in the politics of the cities, and the other more precisely on the relationships between Pericles and Sophocles while they were both serving as strategoi.

The Poet Sophocles of Athens versus the Philosopher Melissus of Samos

Whereas Thucydides and Diodorus Siculus say nothing about the Samian leaders, Plutarch mentions the great man of the Samian resistance, a certain Melissus, whom historians of Greek philosophy know well as a student of Parmenides' and the last important member of the Eleatic school. Here is the passage from the "Life of Pericles" in which Plutarch discusses the role of the philosopher Melissus in the resistance, at the time when Pericles left to meet the Phoenician squadron:

> No sooner had he sailed off than Melissus, the son of Ithagenes, a philosopher who was then acting as general at Samos, despising either the small number of ships that were left, or the inexperience of the generals in charge of them, persuaded his fellow-citizens to make an attack upon the Athenians. In the battle that ensued the Samians were victorious, taking many of their enemy captive, and destroying many of their ships, so that they commanded the sea and laid in large store of such necessaries for the war as they did not have before. And

Aristotle says that Pericles was himself also defeated by Melissus in the sea-fight which preceded this. . . . When Pericles learned of the disaster which had befallen his fleet, he came speedily to its aid. And though Melissus arrayed his forces against him, he conquered and routed the enemy and at once walled their city in.[36]

In the two opposing camps, the strategoi were both men well known through their literary works, on the side of the Samians the philosopher Melissus, the author of a treatise on Being, and on the Athenian side the man of the theater Sophocles, who had just successfully staged his *Antigone*. No doubt Melissus's austere analyses of Being, both eternal and infinite, were, even in antiquity less well known than Sophocles' tragedies. But his work represents an indispensable chapter of the history of philosophy before Plato, and more exactly of the history of the monism called "Eleatic," in the heritage of Parmenides, who came from Elea, in southern Italy.[37] Here is how the historian of philosophy Diogenes Laertius (second century CE) presents the life and work of Melissus of Samos:

Melissus, the son of Ithagenes, was a native of Samos. He was a pupil of Parmenides. Moreover he came into relations with Heraclitus, on which occasion the latter was introduced by him to the Ephesians, who did not know him, as Democritus was to the citizens of Abdera by Hippocrates. He took part also in politics and won the approval of his countrymen, and for this reason he was elected admiral and won more admiration than ever through his own merit.

In his view the universe was unlimited, unchangeable and immovable, and was one, uniform and full of matter. There was no real, but only apparent, motion. Moreover he said that we ought not to make any statements about the gods, for it was impossible to have knowledge of them. According to Apollodorus, he flourished in the 84th Olympiad. [= 444–41].[38]

It is significant that Diogenes Laertius's chapter on Melissus, which appears between those on Parmenides of Elea and Zeno of Elea, also mentions in very laudatory terms the political and military role played by Melissus at Samos, particularly during the revolt of Samos in 441/440. It is probably not accidental that authors of chronographies make the philosopher's apogee coincide with the Olympiad that corresponds precisely to the most important event in his political career. To judge by all the testimonies that speak of his military and political role, during the revolt of Samos Melissus played, as a strategos, a role comparable to that of Pericles on the Athenian side, and not to that of Sophocles, which was undoubtedly much more modest. It is in fact the political and military opposition between Pericles and Melissus that is generally emphasized. "It was Pericles . . . whom Melissus opposed at the siege of Samos,"[39] says Plutarch. "As a politician, Melissus was opposed to Pericles," says the Byzantine encyclopedia, the *Suda*,[40] thus recalling the political dimension of the conflict between Athens and Samos. Whereas Pericles' first act was to establish a democratic regime in

Samos, Melissus, the man of the resistance, belonged to the aristocratic party. Nonetheless, the *Suda*, after mentioning the political contrast between Melissus and Pericles, goes on: "And Melissus, who was a general on the Samian side, fought a naval battle against Sophocles the tragic poet during the eighty-fourth Olympiad [= 444/441]."[41] That is the sole testimony to a naval battle in the war between Athens and Samos in which the two men of letters directly opposed each other during their tenure as strategoi.

The only occasion that really seems possible for such a naval battle is the one on which Melissus, taking advantage of the absence of Pericles when he went to meet the Phoenician squadron, made a sudden sortie during which he destroyed, as we have seen, part of the besieging fleet. It was then that he must have gone up against Sophocles (as well as the other strategoi who had remained). And since Melissus had convinced the Samians to make this sortie by emphasizing not only the small number of ships that were still there, but also the "inexperience of the strategoi"[42] who had remained, we can conclude that Melissus did not have a high opinion of the poet Sophocles' military talents. If in fact it is with this naval battle that the confrontation between Melissus and Sophocles should be connected, we have to recognize that it ended with a cruel defeat for the Athenians, who had, it is true, many fewer ships.

Military Strategy and Erotic Strategy

We have other echoes of the strategos Sophocles' conduct during this Athenian expedition to Samos that refer to his erotic strategy, an area in which he seems to have been expert. One of the rare witticisms uttered by Pericles, who was usually better known for his austerity than for his sense of humor, deals precisely with Sophocles' attraction to young men when he was his colleague as a strategos. In the Greek tradition, there is a story reported by Plutarch:

> Once also when Sophocles, who was general with him on a certain naval expedition, praised a lovely boy, he said: "It is not his hands only, Sophocles, that a general must keep clean, but his eyes as well."[43]

Pericles meant by that that a general must not allow himself to be corrupted by either money or love.[44]

This anecdote also appears in the Latin tradition, but in a more explicitly moralizing context. Here is how Cicero presents it in his treatise *On Duties*:

> it is unbecoming and highly censurable, when upon a serious theme, to introduce such jests as are proper at a dinner, or any sort of loose talk. When Pericles was associated with the poet Sophocles as his colleague in command and they had met to confer about official business that concerned them both, a handsome boy chanced to pass and Sophocles said: "Look, Pericles; what a pretty boy!" How pertinent was Pericles's reply: "Hush, Sophocles, a general should keep not only his hands but his eyes under control." And yet, if Sophocles had

made this same remark at a trial of athletes, he would have incurred no just reprimand. So great is the significance of both place and circumstance.[45]

Thus Cicero clearly sides with Pericles against Sophocles. Many modern scholars are instinctively skeptical regarding the historical foundation of such anecdotes. However, we have an authentic testimony concerning the relations between Pericles and Sophocles that more or less confirms this one. I refer to the words reported by Ion of Chios in his account of the banquet he attended when Sophocles, during his tenure as strategos, stopped off at Chios while he was sailing toward Lesbos. I have given this testimony in toto in the prelude to this part.[46] We recall that Sophocles ended his little scene of seducing the young cupbearer with these words: "I have been training myself in strategy since Pericles claimed that although I knew poetry, I was ignorant of strategy." With humor, Sophocles hints at his conflicts with Pericles, who seems not to have had a high opinion of the poet's competence in military matters. And his humor becomes still more piquant if we know that Pericles had earlier denounced one of his witty remarks about a young man's beauty. He was persisting in his mistake!

Sophocles' Visit to Chios: What Was He Doing There?

From the account given by Ion of Chios there emerges apparently surprising information regarding Sophocles' activity during his tenure as strategos. Ion says that he met Sophocles on Chios "when he was sailing as strategos toward Lesbos." One would expect instead: toward Samos, if the reference is in fact to the Athenian expedition against Samos in 441/440. Thus some scholars have tried to connect Sophocles' stopover with another mission that they invent for the purpose at hand. But if we compare this clue given by Ion with the account of the Athenian expedition to Samos given by Thucydides, we see that when Pericles won an initial battle against the Samians, he was without part of the fleet (sixteen ships, to be exact). Some of the ships sailed south, toward the Asian coast of Caria, to watch for the possible arrival of the Phoenician fleet, while the others sailed north, toward Chios and Lesbos, to demand reinforcements from those two members of the Athenian league. We need only look at a map to understand that the ships that went north passed by Chios before reaching Lesbos. Sophocles was therefore the strategos (or one of the strategoi) commanding this contingent of ships that went to seek reinforcements. It was when Sophocles landed on Chios, before reaching Lesbos, that the famous banquet described by Ion took place.

The mission entrusted to Sophocles was not in any way dangerous. In this context, we can understand all Sophocles' humor during the banquet, when he reported Pericles' disabused judgment concerning his inexperience as a strategos. Pericles had probably not wanted to entrust to Sophocles the more delicate command of the detachment that had sailed south toward a possible encounter with the Phoenician fleet.[47] However that may be, Sophocles' mission produced results, since a reinforcement of twenty-five ships provided by Chios and Lesbos arrived to strengthen the Athenian fleet and facilitate the siege.[48] Sophocles returned to Samos after the first naval battle had been fought by Pericles near the little island of Tragia, but before Pericles left to reinforce personally the detachment sent south to ward off the Phoenician fleet. And it was after Pericles' departure in command of sixty ships that Melissus of Samos, taking advantage especially of the inexperience of the remaining generals, made, as we have seen, a successful sortie, and that was when the confrontation between Melissus and Sophocles took place.

Thus the account of the banquet on Chios, although apparently a rather trivial subject, allows us to define more clearly the role of Sophocles the strategos during the earlier phase of the expedition, and to note how little confidence Pericles must have had in him in the domain of generalship, despite his admiration of his work as a writer. The relations between Sophocles and Pericles must not have been as idyllic as one might think. They differed, at least, in temperament. But Sophocles' feigned modesty should not deceive us regarding his prestige in the high society of the allies. To gauge this prestige, it may be useful to present the personality of the author of the account, who was present at the banquet where Sophocles was the star.

Who Was Ion of Chios?

This witness is not unimportant, because according to the geographer Strabo, Ion was a very prominent figure on the island of Chios.[49] His presence at this banquet given by his compatriot Hermesileos to Sophocles is in no way surprising. First of all, he belonged to an aristocratic family on Chios, and as a youth he had rubbed shoulders with eminent people from Athens. In particular, when he was very young he had attended, during a trip to Athens, a banquet at which the strategos Cimon, whom he still greatly admired, was present. He also knew Pericles but did not like his haughty character.[50] In addition, Ion of Chios was, like Sophocles, an author of tragedies. About fifteen years younger than Sophocles, he began his theatrical career in Athens about twenty years later.[51] Of course, Ion's dramatic production is not comparable to Sophocles' in magnitude.[52] But although he was a minor tragic poet, Ion of Chios was not negligible. He won a first prize and was so pleased by the honor that he sent free wine from Chios to the Athenians.[53] He was sufficiently well known to the Athenian audience for Aristophanes to have mentioned him by name in one of his comedies.[54] And as late as the period of the treatise on the Sublime, his tragedies were still compared with those of Sophocles, as Bacchylides was compared with Pindar, even if the faultless talent of Ion of Chios and Bacchylides did not achieve the uneven genius of Pindar and Sophocles:

> In lyric poetry would you prefer to be Bacchylides rather than Pindar? And in tragedy to be Ion of Chios rather than—Sophocles? It is true that Bacchylides

and Ion are faultless and entirely elegant writers of the polished school, while
Pindar and Sophocles, although at times they burn everything before them as
it were in their swift career, are often extinguished unaccountably and fail most
lamentably. But would anyone in his senses regard all the compositions of Ion
put together as an equivalent for the single play of the *Oedipus*?[55]

But unlike Sophocles, Ion of Chios had a varied work as both a poet and a
writer of prose. In addition to his tragedies, he composed dithyrambs and won
in the same year, as we have seen, the prize for both the dithyramb and tragedy
in Athens. The prelude to one of his dithyrambs ("Let us await the Morning Star
that travels through the heavens, preceding in its course the white wing of the
sun") was famous, since Aristophanes alludes to it in his comedy of 421 (*Peace*,
v. 835): Ion had just died, and Aristophanes imagines that, according to popular
belief, he has been transformed into a star and has been given the name "Morning Star."[56] But Ion was also known as a philosopher: he composed a treatise in
which he explained the formation of the universe on the basis of three principles,
fire, earth, and air. Isocrates, in a brief review of the philosophers in which he
emphasizes their contradictions, mentions Ion:

> As for the ancient wise men, one claimed that the number of the elements was
> infinite, Empedocles [that there were] four, with hatred and friendship in them,
> Ion not more than three, Alcmaeon only two, Parmenides and Melissus just
> one, and Gorgias none at all.[57]

It is an accident that we find side by side in this review the names of Ion (of
Chios) and Melissus (of Samos), which the events of 441/440 have led us to
mention.

Thus while on Samos Melissus was preparing, as strategos, the resistance of
the Samian people in revolt against Athens, on Chios Ion was attending, as an
eminent local figure, the banquet given in honor of a distinguished guest, the
strategos Sophocles on duty in the Athenian expedition against the rebellious
Samos. Ion wrote down his memories of this banquet in what is the first autobio-
graphical work in Western literature, entitled *Epidemiai*, or "Sojourns" (referring
to major figures' sojourns on Chios). The only long extant fragment of this au-
tobiographical work is precisely the account of the banquet with Sophocles. It
is a fortunate accident that not only offers a vivid and direct presentation of
Sophocles' person, but also allows us to gauge his prestige in the allies' high
society, of which he might have made use in negotiating help in the service of
the excessively serious Pericles.

Sophocles at the Beginning of the Peloponnesian War (431)

The revolt of Samos was harshly put down by Pericles: after eight months of
siege, he destroyed the ramparts, seized the fleet, and levied a high fine, taking
hostages to ensure that the total amount was paid. A historian of Samos in the

fourth century BCE, Douris, criticizes the extreme cruelty of Pericles, who is supposed to have had the Samian soldiers assembled on the square in Miletus, where their heads were smashed in with sledgehammers and their bodies left unburied. However, the ancients accused this historian of exaggeration.[58] In any case Sophocles, who had just defended, in his *Antigone*, the untouchable right of the dead to a ritual burial, could hardly approve of that kind of excess.

This was the last revolt on the part of the allies before the Peloponnesian War (431–404). This war opposed Athens, a democratic city, at the head of its maritime empire, to Sparta, an oligarchic city and a power on land, at the head of its allies in the Peloponnese and in Boeotia. It put an end to the Thirty Years' Peace to which these two powers had agreed in 446. It was Pericles, whose political authority in Athens was at its apex during his old age, who persuaded the Athenians to go to war against Sparta.[59]

We do not know how Sophocles felt about the beginning of the Peloponnesian War. Pericles, who resisted Sparta's demands abroad and the pacifism of aristocrats suspected of "laconism"—that is, sympathies with Sparta—within, had drawn the Athenians into the war and chosen a strategy that had a major effect on the Athenians' way of life: relying on Athens's naval superiority and rejecting any pitched battle with the Lacedaemonians, Pericles forced the peasants of Attica to leave their farms and take refuge inside the city's ramparts and the Long Walls that connected the city with the port of Piraeus. The city of Athens was thus transformed into a kind of unconquerable island supplied by its port. But this advantage was counterbalanced by the serious problems constituted by a large-scale displacement of the population and the overcrowding of refugees living in the city or in Piraeus in cramped quarters or temporary huts, or even camping in shrines or at the foot of the Long Walls. The residents of the deme of Colonus, where Sophocles was born, participated in this exodus like all the other residents of Athens's demes. As Thucydides notes, the inhabitants of the countryside were far from pleased at having to move with their entire households:

> Deep was their trouble and discontent at abandoning their houses and the hereditary temples of the ancient constitution, and at having to change their habits of life and to bid farewell to what each regarded as his native city.[60]

For their part, the inhabitants of Colonus had abandoned their sanctuaries of Poseidon and the Eumenides, as well as the *heroon* of Oedipus, even though it was supposed to protect them against enemy invasions. Like other inhabitants of the evacuated demes, they had transported their livestock to the island of Euboea and took the doors and windows when they left their houses. From the ramparts of Athens they could see their fields, just as they had earlier seen the ramparts from their deme.[61] And it was in fact toward their fields that their eyes turned, like Diceopolis in Aristophanes' *The Acharnians*.[62] What did Sophocles think about that? We would like to know.

The Plague in Athens and the Plague in *Oedipus the King*

We would also like to know how Sophocles got through the new trial that the Athenians endured starting the following year, the famous "plague" of Athens, which spread, according to Thucydides, from Piraeus, and which decimated the population, especially the refugees. An initial epidemic lasted two years (430–428), and then, after a short respite, a second epidemic afflicted the city for a year (427–426).[63] There may be an echo in the poet's work of this trial undergone by Athens.

Some scholars have seen in the reference to the plague that opens Sophocles' *Oedipus the King* an allusion to this epidemic. In fact the reference at the very beginning of the play to a scourge raging in Thebes, the site of the tragic action, has been seen as an allusion to this epidemic.[64] Zeus's priest is the first who explains the situation to the city's leader, Oedipus:

> For the city, as you yourself see, is now sorely vexed, and can no longer lift her head from beneath the angry waves of death. A blight has fallen on the fruitful blossoms of the land, the herds among the pastures, the barren pangs of women. And the flaming god, the malign plague, has swooped upon us, and ravages the town: he lays waste to the house of Cadmus, but enriches Hades with groans and tears.[65]

This picture of distress is repeated by the chorus of old men during its entrance song:

> Alas, countless are the sorrows I bear. A plague is on all our people, and thought can find no weapon for defense. The fruits of the glorious earth do not grow; by no birth of offspring do women surmount the pangs in which they shriek. You can see life after life speed away, like a bird on the wing, swifter than irresistible fire, to the shore of the western god. With such deaths, past numbering, the city perishes. Unpitied, her children lie on the ground, spreading pestilence, with no one to mourn them. Meanwhile young wives and grey-haired mothers raise a wail at the steps of the altars, some here, some there, and groan in supplication for their terrible woes.[66]

The chorus, after deploring the ravages of the plague and recognizing its inability to combat it, calls on the gods for help: Athena, the daughter of Zeus, then Apollo and his sister Artemis, and finally Dionysus.

Several characteristics in this description of the plague and in the conduct of the anxious residents might have reminded Athenian spectators of what they themselves had experienced: "so many deaths, numberless deaths on deaths": that is what the Athenians had endured for four years, with a one year's remission. The toll had been very heavy: according to Thucydides, in the army alone there were around forty-five hundred fatalities,[67] and in the rest of the population the number of deaths was incalculable.[68] "Generations strewn on the ground / unburied, unwept, the dead spreading death": that is what the Athenians had seen at the height of the epidemic. We can compare these verses with part of the magisterial description of the "plague" in Athens written later by Thucydides, who not only witnessed it, like Sophocles, but was also sick with the disease:[69]

> By far the most terrible feature in the malady was the dejection which ensued when anyone felt himself sickening, for the despair into which they instantly fell took away their power of resistance, and left them a much easier prey to the disorder; besides which, there was the awful spectacle of men dying like sheep, through having caught the infection in nursing each other. This caused the greatest mortality. On the one hand, if they were afraid to visit each other, they perished from neglect; indeed many houses were emptied of their inmates for want of a nurse: on the other, if they ventured to do so, death was the consequence. This was especially the case with such as made any pretensions to goodness: honor made them unsparing of themselves in their attendance in their friends' houses, where even the members of the family were at last worn out by the moans of the dying, and succumbed to the force of the disaster.

And further on, Thucydides emphasizes the additional offenses due to the piling up of the refugees:

> The bodies of the dying were heaped one on top of the other, and half-dead creatures could be seen staggering about in the streets or flocking around the fountains in their desire for water. The temples in which they took up their quarters were full of the dead bodies of people who had died inside them. For the catastrophe was so overwhelming that men, not knowing what would happen next to them, became indifferent to every rule of religion or of law. All the funeral ceremonies which used to be observed were now disorganized, and they buried the dead as best they could.[70]

What is comparable in Sophocles' description of the Theban plague and Thucydides' description of the plague in Athens is not only that the dead were abandoned without being ritually mourned, but also that they are dangerous because the disease is contagious. "The cadavers bring death," Sophocles says; and Thucydides, who stresses the importance of contagion among those who come close to the sick, notably physicians,[71] also notes that cadavers make even the birds of prey sick.[72]

Confronted by such a devastating scourge, humans are powerless. "A plague is on all our people, and thought can find no weapon for defense," Sophocles' chorus observes.[73] In a comparable way, Thucydides acknowledges the inefficacy of human means: "Nothing could be done, nor could the physicians, treating this disease for the first time, found themselves facing an unknown malady."[74] Thus the people turn toward the gods. In Sophocles,

> Meanwhile young wives and grey-haired mothers raise a wail at the steps of the altars, some here, some there, and groan in supplication for their terrible woes. The prayers to the Healer ring clear, and with them the voice of lamentation.

Thucydides also mentions the supplications in the sanctuaries. And if we wanted to take the comparison all the way, we could see an analogy between the two city leaders who have to cope with the scourge, Oedipus and Pericles. At the beginning of Sophocles' tragedy, the priest asks Oedipus to be the city's physician by treating the disease for which he will turn out to be responsible. And in reality, Pericles had to deal with criticisms that held him responsible for the plague, as Plutarch points out:

> They, in the delirium of the plague, attempted to do him harm, persuaded thereto by his enemies. These urged that the plague was caused by the crowding of the rustic multitudes together into the city, where, in the summer season, many were huddled together in small dwellings and stifling barracks, and compelled to lead a stay-at-home and inactive life, instead of being in the pure and open air of heaven as they were wont. They said that Pericles was responsible for this, who, because of the war, had poured the rabble from the country into the walled city, and then gave that mass of men no employment whatever, but suffered them, thus penned up like cattle, to fill one another full of corruptions, and provided them no change or respite.[75]

Certainly, it is not appropriate to try to find in a Greek tragedy an excessively direct transposition of reality and to draw forced conclusions from it. Oedipus is not Pericles,[76] and it is difficult to see the two historical epidemics of plague in the tragic plague.[77] We also have to take literary models into account: in Sophocles, the conception of the generalized scourge that attacked the city of Thebes in the three domains of life (vegetable, animal, and human) is not the reflection of a reality, but the heritage of an archaic conception that is already present in Homer's epic and in Hesiod.[78]

That said, the importance taken on by the theme of the plague at the beginning of *Oedipus the King* can be plausibly explained by the importance of the scourge that ravaged Athens during the first several years of the Peloponnesian War. An initial indication of this is that the theme of the plague is not traditional in the Oedipus myth before Sophocles, or for that matter, after him.[79] A second indication is provided by the comparison with *Antigone*, a tragedy by Sophocles that was produced ten years before the plague hit Athens. Between these two Theban tragedies there are analogies, despite the difference in their mythic subjects. In *Antigone* the prophet Tiresias already refers to the sickness when tells Creon: "And it is your will that is the source of the sickness now afflicting the city."[80] The cause of the disease is comparable in the two tragedies: it results from an offense committed by the leader of the city, Creon in *Antigone*, Oedipus in *Oedipus the King*. And the offense, twice denounced by the prophet, is of the same nature: it is connected with a dead person, in *Antigone* one who has not been ritually buried, and in *Oedipus the King* one who has not been avenged. But despite these analogies, there is a great difference: in *Antigone* the sickness of the city of Thebes appears only furtively toward the end of the tragedy, whereas in *Oedipus the King* it is front and center from the outset.

Why is the plague treated so differently? Probably because in the meantime Athens experienced its own tragedy. This real tragedy developed differently from a literary creation, but it ended with the death of its protagonist, Pericles, who was himself struck by the plague:

> The plague laid hold of Pericles, not with a violent attack, as in the case of others, nor acute, but one which, with a kind of sluggish distemper that prolonged itself through varying changes, used up his body slowly and undermined the loftiness of his spirit.[81]

Before falling sick himself, Pericles had seen, during the same epidemic, the deaths of a number of those close to him, notably his sister and his two legitimate sons.[82] Pericles died at the age of sixty-seven; Sophocles was about the same age but survived Pericles by almost a quarter of a century.

Another of Sophocles' Missions as Strategos: Sophocles as Nicias's Colleague

According to Thucydides, the death of Pericles marked a break in public leadership. None of the political leaders who followed Pericles in Athens had as much authority as he did. Thus when he assesses Pericles' work, Thucydides clearly contrasts his way of governing with that of his successors:

> So, in what was nominally a democracy, power was really in the hands of the first citizen. But his successors, who were more on a level with each other and each of whom aimed at occupying the first place, adopted methods of demagogy which resulted in their losing control over the actual conduct of affairs.[83]

Among Pericles' successors was Nicias, son of Niceratos, with whom Sophocles had also served as strategos. The sole testimony we have regarding this mission is a passage in Plutarch's "Life of Nicias." Here it is:

> It is said that once at the War Department, when his fellow commanders were deliberating on some matter of general moment, he bade Sophocles the poet state his opinion first, as being the senior general on the Board. Thereupon Sophocles said: "I am the oldest [*palaiotatos*] man, but you are the senior [*presbutatos*] general."[84] So also in the present case he brought Lamachus under his orders, although more of a general than himself.[85]

The anecdote Plutarch reports implies that Sophocles, when he was a strategos with Nicias, was the eldest of the ten strategoi, but Nicias was the most eminent.[86] It testifies to the mutual respect between Nicias and Sophocles, which contrasts with the less cordial relations between Sophocles and Pericles. Nicias must have been the chairman of the college of the strategoi, whether this chairmanship was annual or revolving. In one of their meetings, he invites Sophocles, who was his elder,[87] to give his opinion first; but Sophocles replies with clever courtesy, effacing himself before the prestige of Nicias. The affinity between these two men can be explained in part by Nicias's love of the theater. He had shown his generosity each time that he was assigned, as *choregos*, to finance a chorus. He outdid all his predecessors and all his contemporaries in the splendor of the productions. In his *Gorgias*,[88] Plato mentions the tripods that Nicias and his brothers won as prizes and "arranged in fine order" in the sanctuary of Dionysus, on the flank of the Acropolis, where the plays were performed. Five hundred years later, in the time of Plutarch, the aedicula Nicias had had erected to display them could still be seen.[89] Nicias's successes in the theater as a choregos and Sophocles' successes as a dramatic author are in one way analogous: they often won the first prize, occasionally came in second, but were never defeated, that is, they never came in third.[90]

Since this anecdote on Sophocles as a strategos and colleague of Nicias is known to us only through Plutarch, it has sometimes been questioned. Some have suggested that Plutarch or his source confused Sophocles the tragic author and Sophocles son of Sostratides, who had gone as a general on an initial expedition to Sicily in 426/425, and who, when he returned to Athens in 424/423, was banished along with one of his colleagues for not having realized the Athenians' dream, the conquest of Sicily.[91] But Sophocles' witty reply to Nicias ("I am the oldest [*palaiotatos*] man, but you are the senior [*presbutatos*] general"), this way of playing on words to efface himself modestly, is very much in the style of the tragic author as we have seen him at the banquet on Chios during his first stint as strategos.[92]

At What Point in Nicias's Career Did Plutarch Mention Sophocles as a Strategos?

The anecdote is recounted by Plutarch at a precise point in Nicias's career during the second part of the Peloponnesian War, during the expedition to Sicily (415–413 BCE).

In the first part of the Peloponnesian War, after Pericles' death, Nicias had played an important role. He had been elevated to the top rank by the wealthy and the notables to oppose the extremist demagogue Cleon, who was violent but had the people's ear. Compared with this demagogue, who advocated a repressive policy with regard to the subjects of the Athenian Empire and an aggressive policy with regard to Sparta, Nicias appeared as the representative of moderation, or even of indecision. After Cleon's death in 422 BCE he was the great negotiator, on the Athenian side, of the peace treaty that was concluded a year later between Athens and Sparta and put an end to ten years of conflict. In antiquity, this treaty was already called the "Peace of Nicias."

But the name of Nicias remains attached above all to the Athenian expedition to Sicily, where he died tragically in the disaster for which he was partly responsible. Hostile from the outset to this ambitious enterprise, which he considered inopportune and risky, he did not succeed in winning over to his view the popular assembly, which allowed itself to be seduced by his young adversary Alcibiades. The prospect of an empire in the West to complement the empire in the East excited people, and hopes for the future masked the immediate dangers of such a distant undertaking. Since Nicias had been chosen as a strategos with full powers, along with Alcibiades and Lamachos, to lead the expedition, he was, at the beginning, in command of one-third of the fleet. However, it was Alcibiades who in fact held the authority.[93] After Alcibiades' departure, everything changed. Called back to Athens to defend himself against the accusation that he had parodied the Mysteries, Alcibiades had preferred to go into exile and defect to the enemy. To be sure, the two remaining generals had, de jure, the same power, as is proven by the new division, by drawing lots, of the army into two corps, one of which was commanded by each of the two generals.[94] But according to Plutarch, Nicias now held all the power.[95] Plutarch explains this preeminence by Nicias's wealth and prestige, as opposed to Lamachos's the poverty and simplicity. His preeminence lasted a year, between the moment in the summer of 415/414 when the trireme *Salaminian* arrived in Catania to take Alcibiades back to Athens,[96] and the moment in the spring of the following year, 414/413, when Lamachos was killed in a battle against Syracuse, which the Athenian troops were beginning to enter.[97]

Now, it was precisely to illustrate Nicias's preeminence over Lamachos that Plutarch introduced the anecdote about Sophocles and Nicias. Nevertheless, the anecdote alludes to a different period, necessarily earlier, which is not specified.[98] Thus it becomes necessary to trace with greater precision Nicias's career as a strategos to try to determine the date of Sophocles' second mission as a strategos.

Nicias's Missions as a Strategos

Nicias's career seems to have begun before the death of Pericles in 429.[99] According to Plutarch, Nicias "was held in some repute even while Pericles was still living, so that he was not only associated with him as general, but frequently had independent command himself."[100] However, this vague statement leaves historians perplexed,[101] because Thucydides does not mention Nicias as a strategos at any time before Pericles' death in the year 427/426, when he seized the island of Minōa located across from Megara.[102] Later, Nicias was reelected strategos every year until 422/421, the date of the peace treaty that bears his name.[103] At that point he was at the height of his glory, after the death in Amphipolis of his rival Cleon, the belligerent demagogue, and before his overt rivalry with Alcibiades. In his "Life of Nicias," Plutarch offers this description of Nicias's popularity after the conclusion of the peace treaty:

Most men held it to be a manifest release from ills, and Nicias was in every mouth. They said he was a man beloved of God, and that Heaven had bestowed on him, for his reverent piety, the privilege of giving his name to the greatest and fairest of blessings. They really thought that the peace was the work of Nicias, as the war had been that of Pericles. The one, on slight occasion, was thought to have plunged the Hellenes into great calamities; the other had persuaded them to forget the greatest injuries and become friends. Therefore, to this day, men call that peace "The Peace of Nicias."[104]

During the period from the peace to the beginning of the Sicilian expedition, Nicias's career as a strategos is no longer as easy to determine as it is during the war years, when the leadership of operations was a sufficient criterion of *strategia*. Thucydides does not mention Nicias for the year 421/420. The following year, Nicias led an Athenian embassy to Sparta that was assigned to demand the application of the peace treaty.[105] The total failure of this embassy marked the end of the predominant position held by Nicias, who had been an advocate of the rapprochement with Sparta, and the beginning of Alcibiades' career as a strategos; he was an advocate of an alliance with Argos. Elected strategos in 419/418, the young Alcibiades led Athenian operations in the Peloponnese.[106] Nicias seems to have been less prominent until the Sicilian expedition, when he was to be a general and oppose Alcibiades.[107]

In short, it is not possible to arrive at a complete count of Nicias's strategia, but the ones of which we have certain knowledge are already very numerous.

When Were Nicias and Sophocles Strategoi Together?

These two conclusions make it doubly difficult to situate precisely the strategia during which Sophocles and Nicias were colleagues. However, modern historians have noted one particularity that results from the joint presence of Sophocles and Nicias in the same college of strategoi. We know that as a rule, there were ten strategoi in Athens and one representative for each tribe was elected for one year. Thus in theory there should not be two strategoi from the same tribe at the meeting of a council of strategoi. But modern historians have pointed out that Sophocles and Nicias belonged to the same tribe.[108] This is a case of double representation, already well attested in the time of Pericles,[109] where one of the two generals coming from the same tribe was a major figure in Athenian public life, representing not his tribe but the Athenians as a whole (a strategia called *ex hapantōn*).[110] In the case of Sophocles and Nicias, despite the author's literary prestige there is no doubt that it was the politician who represented the Athenians as a whole. Thus we cannot place this prestigious strategia at the beginning of Nicias's career. A year before 426/425 seems impossible.[111] The most plausible solution is to situate it during one of his reelections at the end of the first phase of the Peloponnesian War, when the armistice was being negotiated, or at the beginning of the Peace of Nicias, before Alcibiades' rise to power. At that time Sophocles was over seventy years old.[112] Being elected strategos at that age was not impossible; there were no age limits for exercising that office. We have the example, in the fourth century, of Phocion, who was a strategos at the age of eighty. When Phocion undertook a general mobilization of the Athenians under the age of sixty for an expedition to Boeotia, he replied to the recriminations of the oldest of them: " 'It is no hardship,' said Phocion, 'for I who am to be your general am in my eightieth year.' "[113] Here we must add that Sophocles' political career continued after 415, because he was a city commissioner after the disastrous Sicilian expedition.[114]

The scene in which Sophocles pays homage to Nicias took place in Athens, at the palace of the strategoi (the *strategion*), the place where the generals were accustomed to assemble and which Nicias, "when he was councilor, . . . was first to reach and last to leave."[115]

Sophocles' Strategia with Nicias and Aristophanes' Mockery in Peace

To confirm this date of Sophocles' strategia with Nicias, efforts have been made to make use of Aristophanes' sole mockery of Sophocles. In his comedy *Peace*, which dates from the Dionysia of 422/421 and thus precedes the Peace of Nicias by only a short time, Aristophanes, through the intermediary of his hero, the Athenian winemaker Trygaeus, tells Peace, who has returned after ten years of absence, news about what happened to the people she had known before her departure. The god Hermes serves as Peace's spokesman (vv. 695–99):

> *Hermes:* She wants to have news of a whole heap of old-fashioned things she
>   left here. [695] First of all, how is Sophocles?
> *Trygaeus:* Very well, but something very strange has happened to him.
> *Hermes:* What then?
> *Trygaeus:* He has turned from Sophocles into Simonides.
> *Hermes:* Into Simonides? How so?
> *Trygaeus:* Because, though old and broken-down as he is, he would put to sea
>   on a hurdle to gain an obolus.

The allusion is not to the poet's work, but to his life. Sophocles, despite his age, did not fear to risk his life for the love of money. This liking for money characterized the late poet Simonides (556–468 BCE), who was, it is said, the first Greek poet to get paid for his eulogies. So that is why Sophocles is transformed into Simonides! But it is not clear how Sophocles could negotiate a price for his tragedies. On the other hand, an ancient commentator reports that Sophocles enriched himself during his service as a strategos.[116] According to this commentator, this occurred during the strategia on Samos. That is impossible, because Peace had not yet departed at that time. The joke alludes to a more recent event, between 431 and 421, the period during which Peace had given way to War. That is why people thought of relating this joke with the strategia that Sophocles is supposed to have carried out with Nicias shortly before the performance of Aristophanes' comedy. Aristophanes would be mocking the thoughtless risks the old Sophocles ran during that strategia, not out of concern for the state, but out of his appetite for profit. Such an interpretation is not impossible, but the allusion is too vague for us to be able to arrive at any certainty regarding it.[117]

Was Sophocles a Strategos with Thucydides, Pericles' Rival?

The *Life of Sophocles* provides two additional bits of information that might suggest that Sophocles' political career was even fuller.

The first is given incidentally, right at the beginning, as a reason for contesting the opinion of those who attribute a modest origin to him:

> For it is not likely that a man born of such a modest father would have been deemed worthy of the office of *strategos* along with Pericles and Thucydides, the most prominent men in the city.[118]

Thus Sophocles would have been a strategos, not only with Pericles, but also with Thucydides. But which Thucydides? Insofar as he is presented on the same level as Pericles, as the first of the city, we think immediately, not of the historian, but of the great politician who was Pericles' rival, Thucydides son of Melesias. Since this Thucydides had been exiled by ostracism in 443 and 433, the reference may be to a strategia that preceded this exile, during the years between 450 and 445, when Thucydides had the most power and was in fact serving as a strategos, or, less plausibly, to a strategia he exercised after his return.[119] Nonetheless, this vague reference to a strategia exercised with Thucydides has aroused many doubts, even, it has to be recognized, among historians who are not naturally inclined to systematic skepticism in matters of biography. All the usual techniques for unpacking ancient testimonies have been employed. The most economical of these is to refer to a confusion between two homonyms in the sources. The author of the *Life of Sophocles* is said to have committed an "unfortunate confusion"[120] between Thucydides, son of Melesias, and another Thucydides who was also a strategos on the expedition against Samos.[121] Another technique consists in supposing that two names have been confused. Since the two most eminent figures in the group of strategoi who sailed against Samos with Sophocles were Pericles and Andocides, it has been proposed to substitute, in the testimony of the *Life of Sophocles*, Andocides for Thucydides.[122] In this way, the allusion would be solely to Sophocles' strategia against Samos.

Did Sophocles Exercise a Strategia in the War against the Anaians?

The second additional clue given by the *Life of Sophocles* concerning his strategia contrasts with the first in the precision of its details:

> And the Athenians chose him as a *strategos* at the age of sixty-five (or sixty-nine) in the war against the Anaians seven years before the Peloponnesian War.[123]

What strikes us first in this sentence is the reference to a little-known city. Now, this city is not unrelated to the revolt of Samos. After the latter's revolt against Athens, the city of Anaia, which was located on the mainland across from the island of Samos, served as a refuge for Samians who were die-hard enemies of Athens. They thus threatened to destabilize the Athenian Empire in Ionia.[124] In their desire to free the Ionian cities from the tyranny of Athens, they were de facto allies of the Lacedaemonians.[125] An example of their aggressiveness with regard to the Athenians is provided by an armed conflict that took place in 428, during the Peloponnesian War. Having to cope with the revolt of the island of Lesbos after that of Samos, the Athenians, who were searching for new financial resources, sent Lysicles with four other strategoi to collect the allies' contributions. But when Lysicles was crossing the plain of the Meander, he was attacked by the Anaians and the Carians, and he perished along with a large number of his men.[126] Thus if we accept the text of the *Life of Sophocles* as it stands, basing ourselves on the dating in relation to the Peloponnesian War, we can conclude that it alludes to a war between the Athenians and the people of Anaia that took place ten years earlier, in 438, shortly after the end of the revolt of Samos (439) and the arrival of Samian refugees in Anaia.

Thus Sophocles would have been a strategos on three occasions—if we do not include a strategia with Thucydides, son of Melesias—twice before the Peloponnesian War, during the revolt of Samos in 441/440, with Pericles; a few years later, in 438, at a time when the aftereffects of the revolt of Samos were still perceptible; and a third time with Nicias during the Peloponnesian War.

But all is not clear in the dates given by the *Life of Sophocles*. Seven years before the beginning of the Peloponnesian War, Sophocles was not sixty-five years old, but rather fifty-seven, if we take the date of birth given by the *Life of Sophocles* (495/494).

Thus scholars have tried to neutralize this testimony and to conflate this strategia of Sophocles either with the one he exercised with Pericles or with the one he exercised with Nicias.[127] But this passage can be neutralized only by making changes in the text of the *Life of Sophocles*. Those who want to identify the strategia with that of 441/440 replace the expression "against the Anaians" with "against the Samians."[128] As for those who advocate identifying this strategia with the one Sophocles exercised with Nicias, they modify the date of the war against the Anaians by replacing "seven years before the Peloponnesian War" (= 438) with "seven years before the Peloponnesian ceasefire" (= 428).[129] Without intending to enter into too technical discussions, we can note that whatever solution is adopted, it presupposes a modification of the text of the *Life of Sophocles*.

Nonetheless, Thucydides provides an important indirect testimony in favor of a war against the Anaians that took place shortly after the end of the revolt of

Samos. The revolts of the allied islands against the Athenian Empire were successive, but they resembled one another. The same causes seem to have produced the same effects. The revolt of Lesbos (429/427), which occurred thirteen years after that of Samos, led to a comparable situation. Once the revolt had been put down, exiles took refuge on the mainland across from the island. Just as the exiles from Samos had gone to Anaia, the exiles from Mytilene and other cities on Lesbos seized, in 424/423, a city on the mainland, Antandros. However, while the exiles were getting ready to fortify their base, the Athenian strategoi, who had gone to collect tribute in the Hellespont and Pontus Euxinus, learned of this takeover. And here is how they reacted, drawing on the Athenians' experience after the revolt of Samos:

> The same summer the Mitylenians were about to fortify Antandrus as they had intended, when Demodocus and Aristides, the commanders of the Athenian squadron engaged in levying subsidies, heard on the Hellespont of what was being done to the place (Lamachus their colleague having sailed with ten ships into the Pontus) and conceived fears of its becoming a second Anaia,—the place in which the Samian exiles had established themselves to annoy Samos, helping the Peloponnesians by sending pilots to their navy, and keeping the city in agitation and receiving all its outlaws. They accordingly got together a force from the allies and set sail, defeated in battle the troops that met them from Antandrus, and retook the place.[130]

The Athenian strategoi thus learned the lessons of history. If they acted so quickly and effectively against the exiles after the revolt of Lesbos, that was because they remembered what had happened after the revolt of Samos. We can conclude that when the Samian refugees established themselves in Anaia thirteen years earlier, the Athenian strategoi who were in charge of things did not react vigorously enough, because they had not become sufficiently aware of the threat to the Athenian Empire that these refugees might represent. And why shouldn't Sophocles have been one of those strategoi?[131]

The Elderly Sophocles in the Service of the State in Danger

Sophocles' political career did not end with the strategia when he was Nicias's colleague; he held a last political office at a very advanced age. But whereas those he had held up to that point were regular offices of the Athenian democracy at the height of its power, the last responsibility entrusted to him by the Athenians was exceptional, at a moment of crisis for the democracy, after the disastrous expedition to Sicily.

When in 413 the news of the complete destruction of the expeditionary corps, which had left for Sicily two years earlier with such pomp, finally reached Athens, the first reaction was incredulity. People could not believe that Nicias (who had almost succeeded in taking control of Syracuse just before the Syracusans received Lacedaemonian reinforcements commanded by Gylippus, and who had himself received considerable reinforcements sent from Athens under the leadership of the strategos Demosthenes) had in the end been forced, after the destruction of the whole Athenian fleet blockaded in the port of Syracuse, to make a dead-end retreat across Sicily. They could not believe this defeat that ended with an unconditional surrender, the survivors being imprisoned in Syracuse's rock quarries—the famous Latomia—and, to crown it all, with the execution of Nicias himself, the man who, in Thucydides' view, "of all the Hellenes in my time, least deserved such a fate, seeing that the whole course of his life had been regulated with strict attention to virtue."[132]

The second phase was that of dismayed reflection on the consequences of the disaster. Deprived of men, ships, and resources, the Athenians saw themselves at the mercy of their enemies. The first of these were the Lacedaemonians, who had for some months (since the spring of 414/413) held the fort of Decelea in Attica itself, only about twenty kilometers northeast of the city of Athens, and visible from the city's ramparts. Then there were the Syracusans; the Athenians worried that they would undertake, on the strength of their victory over the primary maritime power, an expedition against Piraeus. And finally, they feared—and the facts soon confirmed their fears—that the subjects of the empire would rapidly defect after such a setback for the dominant power. In short, the Athenians despaired of their fate: it was the homeland itself that was in danger.

The third phase was that of action. From their reflection on the gravity of the situation, the Athenians drew a sudden surge of energy and made decisions that they immediately put into application. Let us listen to Thucydides:

> Nevertheless, with such means as they had, it was determined to resist to the last, and to provide timber and money, and to equip a fleet as they best could, to take steps to secure their confederates and above all Euboea, to reform things in the city upon a more economical footing, and to elect a board of elders to advise upon the state of affairs as occasion should arise. In short, as is the way of a democracy, in the panic of the moment they were ready to be as prudent as possible.
>
> These resolves were at once carried into effect.[133]

Regarding these elders entrusted with proposing measures for public safety, who were called "commissioners" (in Greek, *probouloi*, literally "those who make propositions"), Aristotle provides supplementary information in his history *The Constitution of Athens*. He cites a decree of a certain Pythodorus that was issued two years after the constitution of the college of commissioners in 413 but alludes to the latter. Here it is:

> The resolution of Pythodorus was as follows: "That in addition to the ten Preliminary Councillors already existing the people choose twenty others from

those over forty years of age, and that these, after taking a solemn oath to draft whatever measures they think best for the state, shall draft measures for the public safety and that it be open to any other person also that wishes, to frame proposals, in order that they may choose the one that is best out of them all."[134]

The "existing ten members" referred to in the decree are, certainly, the ones Thucydides mentions in connection with the election of 413, held after the announcement in Athens that the Sicilian expedition had ended in disaster. They are therefore ten in number, like the strategoi. And we can add, thanks to a more recent testimony, that they were elected at the rate of one per tribe, as was the case for the college of the strategoi.[135] But Pythodorus's decree adds further information concerning the commissioners: in 411, the college was enlarged from ten to thirty members. It was this larger college that voted in 411 to establish the oligarchic regime known as that of "the Four Hundred," that is, a regime that gave the real power to a council of four hundred citizens. This amounted to a revolution, and according to Aristotle, "the chief movers having been Peisander, Antiphon and Theramenes, men of good birth and of distinguished reputation for wisdom and judgement."[136] In this way the appointment of the commissioners, which was an exceptional measure taken in an exceptional situation, led to the establishment of an oligarchic regime in Athens, after a century of democracy. Among the elders who voted to change the regime was Sophocles.

Sophocles the "Commissioner" Voted for the Oligarchic Revolution of the Four Hundred

Again, it is Aristotle who gives us this information, but this time in a work that is not a work of history, and in connection with a concrete example given to illustrate the teaching of rhetoric. Toward the end of book 3 of his *Rhetoric*, Aristotle discusses briefly the use of interrogation in the refutation, and the way in which questions must be asked or answered; and each time, he illustrates by a concrete example the right use of the question or the response. To illustrate the way to respond, he cites Sophocles' reply to a question asked by Pisander, one of the main architects of the oligarchic revolution:

> If a conclusion is put in the form of a question, we should state the reason for our answer. For instance, Sophocles being asked by Pisander whether he, like the rest of the Committee of Ten, had approved the setting up of the Four Hundred, he admitted it. "What then?" asked Pisander, "did not this appear to you to be a wicked thing?" Sophocles admitted it. "So then you did what was wicked?" "Yes, for there was nothing better to be done."[137]

From this lively exchange between Pisander and Sophocles, we can conclude that Sophocles was one of the commissioners who voted in 411 for the establish-

ment of the oligarchic regime of the Four Hundred. Thus Sophocles participated, as a commissioner, in the establishment of the regime for lack of a better
option, and he later openly opposed the most prominent official of this new
regime in a situation that we cannot determine.

Nonetheless, since Aristotle gives Sophocles' name without any further details
regarding his family or his deme, there have been skeptics—and there always
will be—who say that the reference might be to another, more obscure Sophocles.[138] However, the reader of Aristotle's *Rhetoric* can hardly have thought of an
obscure person. This brief dialogue, in which Sophocles' response to Pisander is
a model of the reply to be given to a conclusive question, comes after two examples of models for questions to be asked. These two examples are a question
Pericles asked his soothsayer Lampon and another Socrates asked his accuser
Meletos. How could the reader of the *Rhetoric* imagine for a moment that Aristotle is taking an obscure Sophocles as a model of rhetoric after taking a Pericles
or a Socrates? Isn't this little dialogue, in which Sophocles' reply is presented as
a rhetorical model, better suited to the man of the theater, who had to be a
consummate specialist in rhetoric to make his characters speak? In fact, in his
Rhetoric Aristotle himself often takes his examples from Sophocles' theater. Thus
advising the orator not to speak too much about himself, but instead to make
another person speak when he wants to refute his adversary, he gives the following example:

> Sophocles, also, introduces Haemon, when defending Antigone against his
> father, as if quoting the opinion of others.[139]

This reference to Sophocles precedes by only one page the reference to Sophocles engaging in dialogue with Pisander. What reader of Aristotle, reading the
Rhetoric in a continuous manner, would imagine that one page later Aristotle,
citing twice the name of Sophocles, and both times as a rhetorical model, might
be referring to two different persons? To suggest the hypothesis that the Sophocles who was speaking with Pisander was not the author of tragedies, one would
have to quibble outside of any context.[140]

> Among modern authors there is an instinctive repugnance to imagine the great
> tragic poet involved in partisan quarrels. . . . To posterity, it seems that Sopho-
> cles lived only to compose tragedies and that he did not know any struggles
> other than Dionysian competitions. The feelings of a fifth-century Athenian
> were completely different. He did not imagine that the poet or artist was a
> being apart, living differently from his fellow citizens; for him, as for others,
> public life was the main concern, and in his epitaph, Aeschylus did not men-
> tion his dramatic triumphs and mentioned only the bravery he had shown at
> Marathon.

This reflection by a scholar of the late nineteenth century is still valid today.[141]

When Was Sophocles a "Commissioner"?

What emerges from Aristotle's testimony is that Sophocles was part of the body of commissioners enlarged to the number of thirty that voted, in 411, to establish the oligarchic regime of the Four Hundred. But was he already one of the ten commissioners elected in 413? Sophocles' discussion with Pisander does not imply that. However, we have to think that if Pisander and his friends had the number of commissioners increased in 411, it was in order to include convinced supporters of oligarchy. But this was not the case for Sophocles, because he voted only reluctantly for the change in regime. Thus we can legitimately conclude that Sophocles was already part of the college of ten commissioners elected in 411 and that in it he represented his tribe, the Aïgeis, as he had represented it in his strategia. At this time, he was over eighty years old.

A College of Prestigious Old Men

Who were Sophocles' colleagues? The only other commissioner whose name we know is Hagnon, the father of Theramenes.[142] This Hagnon, son of a Nicias, came from the deme of Steiria.[143] He thus represented tribe of the Pandionids in the college of commissioners. Hagnon's political career presents analogies with that of Sophocles. Like Sophocles, Hagnon was a strategos during the revolt of Samos; but he was elected one year later and led, with two other colleagues, a reinforcing fleet from Athens to Samos.[144] Like Sophocles, he was a strategos again during the Peloponnesian War: once with Pericles, in the summer of 430,[145] and again after Pericles' death, in 429/428.[146] Like Sophocles again, he collaborated with Nicias: he was one of the sixteen Athenian notables who concluded the fifty-year peace treaty between Athens and Sparta in 421, as well as the treaty of alliance.[147]

Hagnon's merits were recognized by the people.[148] We can infer that Sophocles and Hagnon were more or less contemporary in age. This brief comparison of their political careers shows the prestige of the elderly men who were chosen as commissioners in these dramatic times. The city was becoming aware of the disastrous consequences of the young people's ambitions. In fact, earlier, when the popular assembly was discussing the Sicilian expedition, Nicias had vainly appealed to the wisdom of the elders to resist the young Alcibiades' projects. Now the city was relying on the experience of the elderly who had earlier rendered eminent services to their homeland.

To be sure, these prestigious old men could seem really very old. The advanced age of the commissioners was mocked—not without cruelty—by the comic authors. Aristophanes, in his *Lysistrata* (performed in 411, shortly before the oligarchic revolution of the Four Hundred) represented a commissioner who endures the gibes of women determined to make peace with Sparta . . . and to bury the old man before his time. Here is the end of the scene in which three women, Lysistrata, Calonice, and Myrrhine, are working on the ritual preparations for adorning the living corpse and send him off to Hades:

> *Lysistrata:* O why not finish and die?
>   A bier is easy to buy,
>   A honey-cake I'll knead you with joy,
>   This garland will see you are decked.
> *Calonice:* I've a wreath for you too.
> *Myrrhine:* I also will fillet you.
> *Lysistrata:* What more is lacking? Step aboard the boat.
>   See, Charon shouts ahoy.
>   You're keeping him, he wants to shove afloat.
> *Magistrate:* Outrageous insults! Thus my place to flout!
>   Now to my fellow-magistrates I'll go
>   And what you've perpetrated on me show.
> *Lysistrata:* Why are you blaming us for laying you out?
>   Assure yourself we'll not forget to make
>   The third day offering early for your sake.
>   (Exit the commissioner).[149]

Among the spectators during the performance of the comedy in the theater of Dionysus in Athens, and probably in the first rows, were the ten commissioners, who could easily recognize one another, and among them were Sophocles and Hagnon! They must have laughed along with the others, but somewhat nervously. It is true that these wise old men were beginning to feel the effects of age. Sophocles himself, from the age of eighty on, could not totally repress a senile trembling. In a trial in which his adversary accused him of trembling to seem old (and no doubt thus to attract pity), Sophocles replied that "he trembled, not, as the accuser said, in order to appear old, but from necessity, for it was against his wish that he was eighty years of age."[150]

The Commissioners' Energetic Effort to Reconstruct the Fleet

These commissioners, despite their advanced age, displayed an energy to which Aristophanes indirectly pays homage. In *Lysistrata*, the commissioner's concern is twofold: finding wood for the oars, and finding money![151] This concern is echoed in the passage in Thucydides where it is a question precisely of the commissioners' creation, to "provide timber and money, and to equip a fleet as they best could."[152] Thus these were the commissioners' two principal missions to recreate Athens's power. During the winter following the defeat in Sicily they worked actively on them. They tried to lighten the state's burden by suppressing useless expenses wherever they could and managed to procure the wood necessary to reconstruct a fleet. The Athenians, like the Lacedaemonians, were preparing for war again.[153] It was this belligerent policy adopted by the commissioners, and by men in general, that the women in Aristophanes' comedy condemned. But the commissioner's work was effective: the reconstruction of the Athenian fleet was spectacular. In the early spring of 412/411, the Lacedaemonians were full of scorn for the Athenians, because they had not seen the size of the Athenian fleet.[154] However, shortly afterward, the Athenians were able to line up twenty-one ships, and then thirty-seven, which were subsequently sent to blockade a Lacedaemonian fleet on the coasts of the Peloponnese.[155]

Nevertheless, the twofold task of Hagnon, Sophocles, and the other commissioners was complicated by the external situation, and then by the internal situation.

The Commissioners Confront External Problems

Externally, despite the vigilance of the Athenian authorities, the revolts of the allies multiplied with the help of the Lacedaemonians and possibly with that of Persia, and also at the instigation of Alcibiades, who had gone into exile first in Lacedaemonia and then in Persia. With each new bit of bad news, the Athenians had to intervene with their triremes, either to prevent a revolt or to contain it. Above all, the Athenians feared a revolt in Euboea; but it came instead in Chios in 412. It was the most important allied city. The situation was serious. So the Athenians, in order to accelerate the construction of the fleet, made an exceptional decision: they would use the reserve of a thousand talents that had been put aside at the beginning of the Peloponnesian War to ensure the defense of the city in the event of a maritime attack on Athens, and which it was forbidden, on pain of death, to propose spending for other reasons.[156] The decision was not easy to make: since it diverted this war treasury from its original purpose, it was necessary to abrogate the death penalty for which the original decree provided before proceeding to a vote on the use of the reserve. There is no doubt that this exceptional financial decision was made by these exceptional magistrates; it was they who administered the finances. It is significant that it was one of the commissioners who came, in Aristophanes' comedy, to get money at the Acropolis in order to pursue a war: that corresponds to reality.[157] On the other hand, what is fictitious is that the women barricaded the Acropolis and decided to substitute themselves for the commissioners to manage the state's treasury, not in order to pursue a war, but to make peace.[158]

Space does not allow me to discuss in detail here the multiple ups and downs of the Athenian interventions seeking to stop the epidemic of revolts during the years 412/411. After Chios there was Eurythrai, then Clazomenes, Teos, Lebedos, and Haïrii, and especially Miletus, which was located across from Samos.[159] To understand that the commissioners did not fail in their double mission of preserving the public safety under the gravest circumstances, we need only underline with Thucydides the extreme energy deployed by the Athenians after the revolt of Chios. And thanks to the use of the reserve of a thousand talents, they succeeded in assembling in the base on Samos a fleet of a hundred ships, approximately the equal of that of the Peloponnesians and their allies. They even tried to wage a decisive naval battle between Samos and Miletus, which the Lacedaemonian fleet avoided.[160]

The Commissioners Confront the Crisis of the Democratic Regime

Domestically, the commissioners who had taken office in 413 had to take sides in the crisis of the democratic regime that resulted in the establishment of the oligarchic regime of the Four Hundred. This was an internal crisis that could not fail to make a great impression on the minds of contemporaries. It was difficult to put an end to a century of democracy, as Thucydides splendidly reminds us:

> It was no light matter to deprive the Athenian people of its freedom, almost a hundred years after the deposition of the tyrants, when it had been not only not subject to any during the whole of that period, but accustomed during more than half of it to rule over subjects of its own.[161]

As a commissioner, Sophocles, as we have seen, voted for the establishment of this oligarchic regime, but he did so for lack of a better option. He must therefore not have belonged to the faction of the hard-line oligarchs, that of Pisander, Antiphon, Phrynicus, and Theramenes, the best-known advocates of oligarchy, whose intelligence Thucydides recognizes.[162] But at the same time, since he agreed to vote in favor of oligarchy, he refused to accept the excesses of democracy, that is, the demagogues' adventurist policy. Moreover, insofar as it deprived the established democratic institutions of the initiative,[163] the creation of commissioners after the disaster of 413 was already by itself a limitation imposed on the excesses of democracy. At the very least, the elders elected to this commission could be only moderate democrats.

But it would be a mistake to conclude, by a simplifying shortcut, that from the outset contemporaries saw the creation of this commission as a first step toward oligarchy. Democratic institutions persisted, and the commissioners were created in accord with democratic rules, with the election of one commissioner per tribe. Furthermore, the commissioners were responsible for the functioning of the democracy, since they were entrusted with bringing together the council and the popular assembly.[164]

That said, it is not possible to determine the attitude of each commissioner during this troubled period when the oligarchic conspiracy was being formed. Thucydides insists on the atmosphere of suspicion that reigned in Athens, even in the democratic party, where there were astonishing conversions to oligarchy.[165] Thus the conduct of a single commissioner might be judged in radically different ways depending on the light in which it was considered. That is the case for Hagnon, the only commissioner whose name we know in addition to that of Sophocles. He is presented sometimes as an oligarch conducting a policy later pursued by his son Theramenes,[166] sometimes as a man liked by the people. His son Theramenes is supposed to have benefited from his father's reputation to be a democrat himself before he converted to oligarchy.[167]

Nonetheless, the ten commissioners designated in 413 saw their power reduced when Pisander and his oligarchic friends actually installed the new regime. The measure that Pisander had the popular assembly adopt, and that consisted in adding another twenty younger members to the college of commissioners, made the older commissioners a minority on the enlarged commission that was entrusted with making better proposals for the safety of the state.[168]

This enlarged commission proposed, moreover, useful and relatively moderate measures for a period that was not supposed to last any longer than the war: the use of all assets for the war; drastic economies in the functioning of the state; a political regime including a popular assembly limited to five thousand citizens, four hundred members to be assigned to recruit these five thousand. Sophocles, in his capacity as a commissioner, participated in the drafting of these measures. The rest seems to have escaped the control of the ten old commissioners even more. For it was a commission of a hundred members chosen from within the assembly of the Five Thousand that finalized the oligarchic regime by instituting the leadership council consisting of four hundred members.

We understand better the conditions under which Sophocles thought he had to vote for the establishment of the regime of the Four Hundred. No doubt he did not see a better solution, as he later told Pisander. But in any event, it is not easy to see how the old commissioners could have opposed the realization of the conspiracy as soon as they had clearly lost the majority in the enlarged commission, and especially when the definitive drafting of the oligarchic constitution of the Four Hundred was entrusted to a still more numerous commission of a hundred members.

Thus Sophocles was powerless when he attended the final session of the popular assembly that endorsed the oligarchic constitution of the Four Hundred in May 411. Faced with Pisander's proposals, no one raised a protest. The irony of fate was that this assembly took place, exceptionally, in Sophocles' native deme.

The Extraordinary Session of the Popular Assembly in Colonus and Sophocles' *Oedipus at Colonus*

The popular assembly was ordinarily held within the city walls, on the little hill of the Pnyx west of the Acropolis; but Thucydides states that this last session took place outside the walls, in Colonus, in the sanctuary of Poseidon located ten *stadia* from Athens.[169] Thus it was at a sacred site in Sophocles' native deme that this extraordinary meeting occurred. Scholars have wondered what the reason for this choice was, without finding an explanation that can be regarded as conclusive. It has even been hypothesized that the commissioner Sophocles, who was proud of being born in Colonus, was asked to propose a site for the meeting and thereby provide the latter with the moral caution of a person held in high respect.[170] In any case, this last meeting soon left sad memories when the government of the Four Hundred, after having installed itself in the hall of the former council, showed its true face: it did not convoke the assembly of the Five Thousand and imposed itself by force, reducing to silence its principal adversaries by imprisoning or murdering them.[171]

Thus when Sophocles mentioned in his *Oedipus at Colonus* the sanctuary of Poseidon in Colonus, and inserted into the fabric of the myth a general meeting of the Athenian people in this sanctuary on the occasion of a sacrifice made by Theseus to Poseidon, it was difficult for the author or the spectators not to think of the sinister meeting of the assembly in 411. At the very spot where, in reality, the assembly of 411 had had on its agenda the burial of democracy, Sophocles represented in the myth an Athenian assembly meeting under the direction of King Theseus, who in the theater was, as we know, the symbol of Athenian democracy. In Sophocles' tragedy, this assembly meets to honor by a sacrifice the god of the sanctuary of Colonus, Poseidon, and the people gathered together rushes, in a general mobilization ordered by Theseus, to put an end to the kidnapping of Oedipus's daughters, Antigone and Ismene, whom the Theban Creon had abducted by force, violating the sovereignty of the Athenian territory. In short, the mythic image of a just and strong Athenian people, gathered together in the sanctuary of Poseidon in Colonus, seems to be intended to erase the real image of an Athenian people assembled a few years earlier in the same sanctuary to subject itself and resign itself to the violence of the oligarchy.

Sophocles' Opposition to the Oligarchic Regime

One of the consequences of holding the assembly in Colonus in May 411 was certainly—even if no testimony formally proves it—the end of the mission of the commissioners who had been elected in 413 to an unlimited term of office.[172] Now "the Four Hundred, together with the ten officers on whom full powers had been conferred, occupied the Council-house and really administered the government."[173] Sophocles, after devoting two years of his life to Athens's recovery, could now return more fully to literary creation. In fact, he staged his *Philoctetes* in 409. But for all that he did not lose interest in the political situation. The oligarchic regime of the Four Hundred whose abuses he discovered along with others lasted only a few months. The altercation between Pisander and Sophocles reported in Aristotle's *Rhetoric* probably occurred during this period, because after the fall of the Four Hundred Pisander, accompanied by the most active members of the oligarchic party, went over to the enemy, taking refuge in the fort at Decelea, which was the Lacedaemonians' most advanced position in Attica. Even if it is not possible to determine the precise circumstances of the conflict between Sophocles and the advocate of the oligarchic regime of the Four

Hundred, it took place in the period in which an internal opposition to this regime's abuses was becoming manifest.

The opposition did not take long to develop. However, at first it came from outside, from the Athenian fleet concentrated on Samos. At the very time when the oligarchic regime was established in Athens, the failure of the oligarchic conspiracy on Samos had strengthened the democratic regime on the island and reinforced the role of the strategoi with the Athenian expeditionary corps who were hostile to the oligarchy. As Thucydides puts it, "The struggle now was between the army trying to force a democracy upon the city, and the Four Hundred an oligarchy upon the camp."[174] Athenian power had become a bicephalic monster, each head (Samos and Athens) making its own decisions. While the Four Hundred tried to negotiate a peace treaty with the king of Sparta, Agis, who was posted in the fort of Decelea, and also directly with Sparta,[175] the Athenians on Samos were working to recall Alcibiades, whom they made a strategos in order to benefit from the help of Persia in the war against Sparta. If the fleet at Samos did not sail to Piraeus to overthrow the oligarchy, that was because of the intervention of moderates on Samos,[176] and then of Alcibiades, who avoided a civil war.[177]

Next, the opposition to the regime of the Four Hundred developed in the city itself. The abuses of the extremist oligarchs who were managing things, such as Pisander or Antiphon, alienated not only people who had accepted the oligarchy for lack of a better solution, like Sophocles, but even the moderate oligarchs of whom the best known is Theramenes, son of Hagnon. The moderates were calling for a more egalitarian regime that gave real power to the "assembly of the Five Thousand" that the Four Hundred had not convoked. While remaining wary of the Four Hundred's policy toward the Lacedaemonians, which they deemed too favorable, they feared the intervention of the army on Samos and especially Alcibiades, with whom, they thought, it would be necessary to come to terms in order to survive.[178] The opposition of the moderate oligarchs, which was initially secret and limited to a small number, grew after the failure of the embassy the Four Hundred sent to Sparta to negotiate a peace treaty. It became acute when a dispute arose regarding the construction of a fort at the entrance to Piraeus that would have turned into a civil war had not the elders intervened.

Another Intervention by the Elders to Save the City

This fort, which the Four Hundred were building at the entrance to Piraeus, was of capital strategic importance. Once the construction was completed, a handful of men would suffice to control any entry into Athens. The fort was constructed in principle to protect Athens from a possible invasion by the fleet at Samos. But it seemed to Theramenes and to the opposing oligarchs that it might be surrendered to the Lacedaemonians. The facts seemed to confirm these suspicions:

a Lacedaemonian squadron had advanced as far as the island of Aegina, whereas in principle it was supposed to go to Euboea. The hoplites assigned to the construction of the fort then took hostage a strategos of the oligarchic party in power and set about destroying the fort. The news of the strategos's arrest, which reached Athens during the council of the Four Hundred, inflamed the people, who spoke of taking up arms to march on Piraeus. Athenian power now seemed to be divided into three: not only between Athens and Samos, but in Attica itself there was a danger of civil war between Athens and Piraeus. This division into three parties corresponded, *grosso modo*, to the division of the armaments, which, as we know, had been based on a social division ever since Solon's reform: the sailors—who came from the poorest section of the people—based on Samos, remained faithful to democracy; the cavalry—recruited in the wealthiest social class—supported the extremist oligarchs in the city; while in Piraeus the hoplites—representing the intermediary class, rich enough to pay for armor but not a horse—were supporting the opponents of the regime of the Four Hundred. Here is how Thucydides describes this day of crisis that opposed Piraeus to the city:

> All was now panic and confusion. Those in the city imagined that Piraeus was already taken and the prisoner put to death, while those in Piraeus expected every moment to be attacked by the party in the city. The older men, however, stopped the persons running up and down the town and making for the stands of arms; and Thucydides the Pharsalian, Proxenus of the city, came forward and threw himself in the way of the rival factions, and appealed to them not to ruin the state, while the enemy was still at hand waiting for his opportunity, and so at length succeeded in quieting them and in keeping their hands off each other.[179]

At times when the city was in crisis, the elders recovered a decisive role. In the crisis of 413, the elders had worked within the institutional framework; here they acted spontaneously. But it is rather natural to think that those among them who had acquired prestige for having been part of the college of commissioners intervened here again in the first rank to reconcile the opposed parties. Perhaps it was under such dramatic circumstances that Sophocles intervened directly with Pisander to formulate criticisms of the Four Hundred and to make him understand the reasons for the opposition to the regime. To judge by the dialogue reported by Aristotle, Pisander seems to have been haughty, accusing Sophocles, in his famous conclusive question, of inconsistency and even of betraying the oligarchic regime for which he had voted as a commissioner, upon which Sophocles is supposed to have revealed what he really thought at the time of the vote, justifying at the same time his past conduct and his present conduct. Sophocles was one of the moderates whom Thucydides calls "those of the middle," as distant from the belligerent demagogues as from the pro-Lacedaemonian oligarchs. He was one of those who wanted to maintain the unity of the city by concord.

The intervention by the elders and the moderates was effective: it averted civil war and led to an assembly of reconciliation in the sanctuary of Dionysus in Athens.[180] But this assembly did not have time for deliberations. What momentarily reconciled the two parties was the presence of about forty enemy ships that were sailing along the Salamine coast. The Lacedaemonian fleet had never come so close to Athens before. Civil war yielded to external war. There was a general mobilization. We know what happened next: the defeat off the shores of Euboea of the Athenian fleet, which had hastily left Piraeus, the revolt of Euboea, an island so essential for supplying Athens, the fall of the Four Hundred, and the replacement of the oligarchic regime by a moderate regime founded on the assembly of the Five Thousand, before democracy was finally reestablished. Did Sophocles approve of this change in regime? We can think he did if we recall Thucydides' and Aristotle's praise of the regime of the Five Thousand. Thucydides declares:

> It was during the first period of this constitution that the Athenians appear to have enjoyed the best government that they ever did, at least in my time. For the fusion of the high and the low was effected with judgment, and this was what first enabled the state to raise up her head after her manifold disasters.

As for Aristotle, in his view:

> During this period the constitution of the state seems to have been admirable, since it was a time of war and the franchise was in the hands of those who possessed a military equipment.[181]

Did Sophocles also approve of the ancillary measure that consisted in beginning the reconciliation between the two heads of Athenian power by sending emissaries to Samos and recalling Alcibiades?

The Recall of Alcibiades and Sophocles' *Philoctetes*

After 411, we no longer have documents concerning any direct involvement in public affairs on Sophocles' part. But his tragedy *Philoctetes*, performed in the spring of 409 when Sophocles was eighty-seven years old, has been related by some scholars to Alcibiades' return. This interpretation does not go back to antiquity. It seems to have been first proposed in the second half of the eighteenth century by a French writer, M. Lebeau le cadet, in a memorandum written for the Académie des inscriptions et belles lettres. Adopted by some, criticized by others, the theory that there is a relationship between *Philoctetes* and the contemporary political situation remains debatable.[182] In any case, *Philoctetes* is the only tragedy by Sophocles performed during his lifetime that we can situate with certainty in the context of his life. And the question of the relations with contemporary reality arises all the more relevantly because Sophocles had just played an important role in the life of his city.

The Problems Raised by Alcibiades' Return

First let us recall the historical situation at the time when Sophocles was composing his *Philoctetes*. The advocates of the passage from the oligarchy of the Four Hundred to the moderate government of the Five Thousand, in particular Theramenes, faced with the urgency of the situation resulting from the revolt of Euboea, had issued a decree calling Alcibiades and other exiles back to Athens and sent emissaries to Samos to inform him of the decree.[183] However, Alcibiades had not yet returned to Athens at the time when Sophocles was composing and having his tragedy performed. He made his triumphal return to Athens two years after the performance of *Philoctetes*, in 407. Thus more than three years went by between the Athenians' decree and the exile's actual return to Athens.

We can only wonder at such a delay, and at the contrast between the rapidity with which Alcibiades had joined the Athenian army on Samos in 411[184] and the slowness with which he returned to Athens. Thucydides remains totally silent about all this. He says not a word about the effect the decree produced on Alcibiades himself. When he speaks again of Alcibiades for the last time, it is solely to mention his return to Samos after a mission to the Persian satrap Tissaphernes, along with a secondary maritime operation that he conducted toward the end of the summer of 411 at Halicarnassus and on the island of Cos.[185] Xenophon's silence is comparable; he continues Thucydides' account from that moment on. But he makes no mention of the question of Alcibiades' return to Athens before the year 407.

This silence on the part of the two historians is partly filled in by Plutarch, the biographer of Alcibiades. Here is how Plutarch presents Alcibiades' reaction to the news of his recall, which he received on Samos:

> After this the Four Hundred were overthrown, the friends of Alcibiades now zealously assisting the party of the people. Then the city willingly ordered Alcibiades to come back home. But he thought he must not return with empty hands and without achievement, through the pity and favour of the multitude, but rather in a blaze of glory.[186]

Let us leave aside Plutarch's shortcut regarding the evolution of the political situation in Athens at the time when the Athenians invited Alcibiades to come back. It was not democracy that had been established immediately after the fall of the Four Hundred, but rather the mixed regime of the Five Thousand. The return of democracy took place soon afterward, but it had not yet happened. What matters here is the motive Plutarch attributes to Alcibiades to explain his refusal to return immediately. The biographer suggests a noble motive: the desire for glory. Alcibiades wanted a triumphal return, and for that he had to come back crowned with victories and loaded down with booty taken from the enemy. With great consistency, Plutarch sees in the series of naval battles fought and the successes won the necessary condition that Alcibiades imposed on himself for his return.

This way of seeing things is no doubt coherent, but it is partial. First of all, we can ask whether the decree recalling Alcibiades issued by the Athenians was as spontaneous as Plutarch implies it was. We have a more complex version of the facts, that of the historian Diodorus Siculus.[187] According to Diodorus, Alcibiades himself was the instigator of an intervention by the Athenians of Samos with the new government of Athens to get it to ask for his recall. In this version of the facts, Alcibiades seems less idealistic and the question of his return more complicated. The decree concerning his return was probably the subject of meticulous and perhaps difficult negotiations. In any event, it was the result of an objective alliance between Theramenes and Alcibiades. One of the reasons that led Theramenes to oppose the regime of the Four Hundred, of which he was part, was precisely the fear of Alcibiades from the moment that he joined the fleet on Samos.[188] And once the oligarchic regime had been overthrown, the best way for Theramenes to establish his authority was to propose a reconciliation with a rival he feared. Alcibiades, for his part, seized the opportunity offered by the fall of the oligarchy, whose members had refused to vote for his return,[189] to take a step through the intermediary of the Athenians of Samos. Under these conditions, why did he wait so long before returning after he obtained the decree? Because he thought this return was not without risks. In fact, even when he returned in 407, accounts agree in recognizing Alcibiades' anxiety as he approached Piraeus.[190] He feared his enemies.

The Athenians had remained very divided with regard to him, and there was no lack of grievances. First of all, the accusation that he had parodied the Eleusinian Mysteries—which had led him to go into exile—had not been forgotten. In fact, the very first time that the question of Alcibiades' return was raised in the popular assembly, in 411, protests were made by the two great families among which the priests of the Eleusinian Mysteries were recruited.[191] Then he was blamed for all the harm he had done his country, both through his counsels and his acts, since his exile first among the Lacedaemonians, and then among the barbarians. What bothered the Athenians more directly was the presence of Lacedaemonians in the fort of Decelea not far from Athens, a strategic point that Alcibiades had advised the Lacedaemonians to occupy while he was in exile. Thirdly, Alcibiades' political opinions were fluctuating to say the least, though it is true that the times were very agitated and changing. He hated the democracy that had exiled him, and he had initially demanded the establishment of the oligarchy during the first negotiations (412/411) for his return.[192] But since the oligarchic revolution had ultimately taken place without him, it was the strengthened democracy on Samos that had recalled him.[193] And it was the moderate government of the Five Thousand that issued the decree recalling Alcibiades to Athens shortly before the reestablishment of democracy in the course of the summer of 410. This new change of regime must not have facilitated the conditions for his return, because its inevitable consequence was to give power back to the demagogues. But it was a demagogue who had been Alcibiades' principal accuser in the affair of the parody of the Mysteries, a certain Androcles, whom the supporters of the oligarchy had eliminated in Athens to please Alcibiades shortly before the oligarchic revolution in 411.[194] Under these conditions, we can assume that the new demagogues, such as Cleophon, must not have particularly desired his return. Weighing against these grievances there was the immense hope that his return would save the city. It was believed that he held the key to the way out of the conflict between Sparta and Athens, namely the possibility of detaching Persia from the Lacedaemonians and persuading it to ally itself with Athens, thanks to his privileged relations with the satrap of Ionia, Tissaphernes. But above all, through his victories over the enemy at the Hellespont, Alcibiades showed that he was the necessary condition for the salvation of the city. Thanks to his tactical daring he had just won, in 410, a decisive victory at sea and on land, at Cyzicus, a city on the south shore of the Black Sea, over the Lacedaemonians commanded by Mindaros, and over their Persian ally Pharnabazus. The distress message sent to Sparta reveals, in four short sentences, the extent of the disaster: "The ships are gone. Mindarus is dead. The men are starving. We know not what to do."[195] This message was intercepted and reached Athens. The hope of a final victory was reborn, thanks to Alcibiades.

Such was the Athenians' state of mind when Sophocles composed his *Philoctetes* and when the spectators attended its performance in 409. The question of Alcibiades' return was in everyone's thoughts.

Sophocles' *Philoctetes*

Let us now recall the main traits of the myth and the development of the tragedy to judge the relation that it has been possible to establish between Alcibiades' return and that of Philoctetes. The subject is taken from the epic cycle of the Trojan War. At the beginning of the play, the war has been going on for ten years. The Achaeans are besieging Troy without being able to take the city. At the beginning of their expedition, while they were crossing Greece on their way to Troy, they had abandoned Philoctetes on the unpopulated island of Lemnos. Although he was a redoubtable archer, a snake had bitten his foot, and the painful wound that had resulted gave off an unbearable odor. "Full soon," Homer says, "were the Argives beside their ships to bethink them of king Philoctetes."[196] "Full soon"? It took them ten years! Ten years of fighting, the death of prestigious heroes such as Patrocles, Ajax, Achilles, and Antilochus, and especially Odysseus's capture of the Trojan soothsayer Helenus, who revealed to the Argives an oracle on the taking of Troy. According to this oracle, the return of Philoctetes armed with his bow was indispensable for the Greeks' victory (and for his own healing). The Argive leaders then sent a mission to Lemnos to bring Philoctetes back. When he returned to Troy, Philoctetes' wound was healed by the doctors, and he used his bow to kill Paris, Helen's abductor.

It was from this epic sequence of the myth of Troy that Sophocles drew his tragedy. The choice of subject was not original. The other two great tragic authors had also written a play on Philoctetes. When Sophocles presented his play in 409, the oldest spectators certainly remembered having seen Aeschylus's *Philoctetes* more than forty years earlier, and that of Euripides twenty years earlier, in 431, at the very beginning of this Peloponnesian War that never came to an end, either! The dramatic sequence chosen by the three tragic authors in mythical history is identical: it concerns the dangerous and decisive moment when the embassy the Achaeans sent from Troy arrives on the island of Lemnos to find the unfortunate and redoubtable Philoctetes—presumably very ill disposed toward those who had abandoned him on his island!—and to try to bring him back, with his bow, to Troy. This way of taking up the same subject is frequent among the Greek tragic authors, who sought originality, as we know, more in the manner than in the subject matter.

In Sophocles' *Philoctetes*, the two emissaries sent from Troy by the Achaean leaders are the old Odysseus and the young Neoptolemus, the son of Achilles. At the beginning of the tragedy, they reach Philoctetes' cave, located on a solitary extremity of the island of Lemnos. Philoctetes is not in his cave. Odysseus takes advantage of his absence to explain his mission to Neoptolemus. The son of Achilles must act alone, because Odysseus, who had earlier abandoned Philoctetes on the island at the command of his leaders, would be recognized by Philoctetes and killed by his infallible arrows; moreover, the son of Achilles has to act by ruse, the only way of seizing the bow. Odysseus goes to wait at a distance while Neoptolemus is joined by the crew of his boat, which forms the chorus. Then we see the arrival of the hero Philoctetes, who is both wretched and redoubtable: he is an invalid who painfully drags his sore foot; but his bow, which he inherited from Heracles, invariably hits the target, and his character remains inflexible. The whole development of the play is based on the execution of the trick worked out by Odysseus—here we cannot follow all its twists and turns[197]—and its failure: it is to Greece, his homeland, that Philoctetes wants to return, not to Troy. However, the myth cannot be violated by the tragic author. Thus Philoctetes' return to Troy ultimately takes place thanks to the appearance of the god Heracles, who has come as an ambassador from Olympus, by air, to reveal Zeus's designs: Philoctetes and the son of Achilles must go to Troy to conquer the city and glory together.

The Analogies between the Myth and Reality

What analogies have been found between Sophocles' *Philoctetes* and the question of Alcibiades' return to Athens? There are, at the very least, general coincidences between the myth and reality. In both cases, a hero who is participating in an Achaean expedition in the context of a long war is forced to leave the expedition at the outset: Philoctetes had to let the Achaean expedition continue on its way to Troy without him; Alcibiades, recalled by the Athenians to be judged, had to abandon his command in Sicily and then go into exile to avoid being put on

trial. And then, in both cases, the war drags on and on, and those who are deprived of the help of the exiled hero become aware that his return is indispensable
for putting a victorious end to the war. Thus they want to call back from exile
the person who had to leave the expedition. Philoctetes is recalled by an embassy
that has come to Lemnos, composed of Odysseus and Neoptolemus in Sophocles' version; Alcibiades, recalled by a decree issued by the government of the
Five Thousand, has received an embassy from Samos. But the return does not
take place without difficulties. Philoctetes does not want to come back, and
Alcibiades delays his return. These general analogies incontestably lend a contemporary relevance to the myth of Philoctetes. The simple choice of this myth
in 409 could be interpreted as a way of drawing attention to Alcibiades who,
despite the decree recalling him issued in 411, still had not returned two years
later.

That a Greek tragic poet could reorient the meaning of a myth by an implicit
reference to contemporary reality is not in itself extraordinary. It was, moreover,
already the case in lyric poetry: the myth of Philoctetes itself had been used by
the poet Pindar—half a century before Sophocles—in the eulogy of Hieron, the
tyrant of Syracuse. Valiant, despite the kidney stones from which he suffered,
Hieron is compared by Pindar with Philoctetes in an allusion to contemporary
events:

> But now he has gone to battle in the manner of Philoctetes; and under compul-
> sion even a haughty man fawned on him for his friendship. They say that the
> god-like heroes went to bring from Lemnos that man afflicted with a wound,
> the archer son of Poeas, who sacked the city of Priam and brought an end to
> the toils of the Danaans; he went with a weak body, but it was fated. In such a
> way may a god be the preserver of Hieron for the time that is still to come,
> giving him the opportunity for all he desires.[198]

Unlike lyric poetry, tragedy cannot be as explicit in its use of myth to refer to
contemporary reality. However, encouraged by the precedent set by Pindar, one
might be tempted to refine the comparison between Sophocles' Philoctetes and
Alcibiades. If Philoctetes and Alcibiades both seem to be indispensable, it is not
only because of their persons, but also because of the "decisive" weapon they
alone can provide to change the power relationships. Philoctetes has the infallible
bow he inherited from Heracles; Alcibiades is the only person who can arrange
for the Athenians an alliance with the Persians. At least that is what was believed,
and the prospect that was held out by those who were working for Alcibiades'
return. Pisander and the envoys from Samos, who came in 411 to speak before
the popular assembly in Athens to urge Alcibiades' return, used this argument,

> giving a brief summary of their views, and particularly insisting that if Alcibi-
> ades were recalled and the democratic constitution changed, they could have
> the king as their ally, and would be able to overcome the Peloponnesians.[199]

Under these conditions, the hope of an imminent final victory announced toward the end of the tragedy by the prophecy of the soothsayer Helenus, on the condition that Philoctetes returns to Troy, might suggest an imminent victory of Athens if Alcibiades returns there.[200] What is more, the tragedy ends with the word "return," uttered by the chorus in the last verse: the chorus of sailors, at the moment it leaves the stage, addresses a prayer to the nymphs of the sea for "a saving return." An allusion to the current situation at the end of a tragedy would not be in any way extraordinary. At the end of Euripides' *Hippolytus*, performed in 428, the spectator, listening to the chorus praising Hippolytus, who has just died in an unexpected way, could not fail to think of Pericles, who had just died of the plague. Similarly, here, the return of Philoctetes might evoke the expected return of Alcibiades, just as Hippolytus's death evoked the unexpected death of Pericles.

That said, we should avoid adopting either of two excessive, opposed views. One consists in denying any possible allusion to Alcibiades on the pretext that there is no coincidence between the mythical character and the historical person. It is very clear that Philoctetes is not Alcibiades: the crippled, suffering tragic hero is not the brilliant victor at Cyzicus; and the opportunistic cleverness of the Athenian strategos does not correspond to the stubborn integrity of the Achaean leader.[201] But the obvious gap between myth and reality is not an obstacle to possible allusions to reality. From the moment that we become aware that allusions to current reality in Greek tragedy can occur, contrary to what happens in lyric poetry or in comedy, solely through a transposition into the logic of the mythical situation, further analogies may appear. Thucydides tells us that when Alcibiades addressed an assembly of Athenians on Samos for the first time since his twofold exile, he began by complaining about the misfortune that exile had been for him personally.[202] Now, these misfortunes in exile are the first thing Sophocles' listeners hear about when Philoctetes appears and tells Neoptolemus and the chorus of sailors, in long speech, how he was abandoned in a solitary place and how he had to fight to survive.[203] It would be excessive to deny any possibility of an analogy between Philoctetes and Alcibiades when both try to arouse the pity of their listeners by referring to the misfortunes of their exile. On the other hand, there is another view that consists in trying to force resemblances by nudging history. For instance, we cannot say that the analogy is evident because Alcibiades several times declined the offer to return to Athens, just as Philoctetes refuses on several occasions to return to Troy.[204] And we cannot draw from the tragedy a clear political message addressed by Sophocles to the spectators. No doubt we can see in the Odysseus of the *Philoctetes*, who notes the omnipotence of the word (vv. 98ff.), and for whom the end justifies the means (vv. 81–85), a criticism of demagogues like Celon who returned to power in 410 with the reestablishment of a democracy.[205] No doubt we can propose the plausible hypothesis that Sophocles, who was rather favorable to a moderate democracy, could be issuing in Heracles' final message both an appeal for Alcibiades' return, which was necessary for the final victory, and a warning to Alcibiades himself, who had to "observe the piety due the gods" (v. 1441).

However, it must be stressed that these possible allusions to contemporary reality have no impact on the general development of the tragedy. That is what Lebeau le cadet, who is considered the first modern scholar to propose the hypothesis of a relation between the return of Philoctetes and that of Alcibiades, straightforwardly posits: "I did not find in the course of the play any particular trait that could prove that conjecture."[206] In fact, it is significant that Sophocles did not adopt a variant of the myth that is already found in Euripides and that could have brought the myth even closer to reality: Odysseus, in Euripides' tragedy, announces an embassy of Trojans that is going to come get Philoctetes so that he might help them win a victory.[207] Was Philoctetes the exile going to contribute to the success of the Trojan enemies? That is precisely what Alcibiades did in reality, by collaborating with the Lacedaemonians against his own country. If Sophocles did not adopt this variant of his predecessor, that was because he was not seeking principally to establish a strict parallelism between myth and reality. Sophocles does not translate the reality into the myth; at most, he transposes it. Transposition has the advantage of presenting, in the form of reflections or ethical discussions of general significance in the scenes of the myth, questions that were being debated on the contemporary political scene. But by the same token it has the disadvantage of making allusions to current realities less legible and more uncertain. In the historical scene of the popular assembly of the people of Athens where Pisander tried to get Alcibiades' return accepted, the issue was above all safety and victory: but the price the democrats had to pay was giving up their own political convictions: after strong protests, the people allowed itself to be convinced. In the scene in the tragedy in which Odysseus shows Neoptolemus how to get Philoctetes' to return, the price Neoptolemus has to pay is giving up his own convictions to achieve this return by trickery; and after strong protests, Neoptolemus allows himself to be convinced, at least temporarily. In both cases, the return of the exile necessary for salvation raises problems of conscience for those who are calling him back. The importance of the theme of safety, problems of conscience raised by calling back an exile—these are themes of poetic fiction that might find an echo in the minds of Athenian audiences in 409. But we have to recognize that the more the transposition is elaborated, the less the allusion to current reality becomes discernible. Thus the evaluation of the share of reality in Sophocles' *Philoctetes* depends to a certain extent on the subjectivity of the ancient spectator, and also on that of the modern interpreter.[208]

In any event, Sophocles, who had been closely involved in the government of affairs from 413 to the establishment of the regime of the Four Hundred, no doubt found himself confronted, like his contemporaries, by this problem of Alcibiades' return. He certainly attended as a commissioner the popular assembly of 411 where this return proposed by Pisander was debated before the Four

Hundred was established. And he certainly later attended as a citizen the assembly of the Five Thousand where Theramenes had Alcibiades' return approved after the fall of the Four Hundred. What exactly was his position? We can only formulate hypotheses, basing ourselves on his earlier political career and on a reasonable interpretation of the role of current events in the *Philoctetes*. He probably wished, in a spirit of efficacy and concord, the return of Alcibiades; but he probably could not forget that the latter had been the political adversary of the person who was pursuing Pericles' policy, Nicias, to whom the tragic author had paid homage when he served as a strategos with him. Ultimately, Sophocles must have voted, for lack of a better choice, to approve Alcibiades' return, just as he had voted, for lack of a better choice, for the regime of the Four Hundred. And what makes his hesitations at the time of the vote for Alcibiades' return very plausible is less political considerations than religious ones; he could hardly forget the impieties that had earned Alcibiades his condemnation. Sophocles was, in fact, famous for his religious spirit.

CHAPTER III

Sophocles the Religious Man

....

"Sophocles was loved by the gods like no other," we read in the *Life of Sophocles*.[1] Being loved by the gods was a privilege. However, in a religion in which the gods were in the image of men and liked to be adored, it was impossible to be loved by the gods without taking part in their worship with the greatest piety.[2] One anecdote connects Sophocles with the cult of Heracles. It was especially in the worship of Asclepius, the god of medicine, that Sophocles played an important role. He helped introduce into Athens the worship of that divinity in the 420s BCE. And as a recompense, he was "heroized" after his death, that is, he was himself made the object of a cult, as were all the people whose status was intermediary between humans and gods, and whom the Greeks called "heroes."

Sophocles and the Cult of Heracles in Athens: Sophocles' Dream

To illustrate the fact that Sophocles was loved by the gods, the *Life of Sophocles* recounts the following anecdote:

> Sophocles was loved by the gods like no other, according to what Hieronymus says about the golden crown. When the latter was stolen from the Acropolis, Heracles revealed to Sophocles in a dream where it had been hidden, telling him the house where he should look by entering on the right. Sophocles made a "revelation" to the people regarding this crown and received a talent. That was, in fact, the reward that had been promised. Thus receiving this talent, he founded the sanctuary of Heracles "Revealer."[3]

It goes without saying that it is imprudent to trust anecdotes reported concerning ancient authors without any critical distance. Inversely, it is arbitrary to reject them en bloc without having gauged, as far as possible, the greater or lesser antiquity of the sources cited, the credibility of the authors who report them, or how widely they were diffused in antiquity. In the present case, it is indispensable for the reconstruction, if not of reality, then at least of a historical view of the image of Sophocles among the ancients. The source that the *Life of Sophocles* takes care to indicate is ancient. This Hieronymus, who came from the island of Rhodes, of which he has remained one of the glories, lived in Athens in the third century BCE. He was particularly well known for his works on literary history. He composed a work in several books entitled *On Poets*, from which this anecdote was probably taken. The source is thus ancient. Moreover, since this scholar belonged to the Peripatetic School, he transmitted a knowledge that may well have come from an older source.[4] Aristotle, the founder of the school, had already written a work in three books, the *Poets*, which is now lost.[5] We may thus be in contact with an Athenian learning preceding Alexandrian scholarship.

This anecdote was also known through Latin literature. In his *De divinatione* (*On Divination*) Cicero (first century BCE) quotes it as one example among others of the truthfulness of dreams. After giving examples of dreams in the Greek philosophers, Cicero comes to Sophocles' dream:

> To the testimony of philosophers let us add that of a most learned man and truly divine poet, Sophocles. A heavy gold dish having been stolen from the temple of Heracles, the god himself appeared to Sophocles in a dream and told him who had committed the theft. But Sophocles ignored the dream a first and second time. When it came again and again, he went up to the Areopagus and laid the matter before the judges who ordered the man named by Sophocles to be arrested. The defendant after examination confessed his crime and brought back the dish. This is why that temple is called "the temple of Heracles the Informer."[6]

If we compare the two versions of the anecdote, we can find a common core. In a dream, Sophocles saw the god Heracles, the very same he had made appear at the end of his *Philoctetes* to resolve the situation. It was a dream-message in which the god revealed to him how to find a precious object that had been stolen and to make an accusation with the Athenian authorities. But what is surprising is the number of divergences in such a short passage. The precious object stolen is not the same—in the *Life of Sophocles* it is a crown; in Cicero it is a cup. The place where the theft took place also differs: the treasury of the sanctuary of Apollo in one case, the sanctuary of Heracles in the other. Sophocles' revelation is not made to the same body: the popular assembly in the *Life*, the tribunal of the Areopagus in Cicero. But the most important divergence has to do with Sophocles' religious role. In the tradition going back to Hieronymus, Sophocles is not only beloved of the gods but honors them, and he founds the temple of Heracles Revealer. In Cicero's version, we do not see Sophocles' piety in action. The sanctuary of Heracles existed before Sophocles' dream, and the only consequence of the dream for the sanctuary is a slight change in its name: it takes the name of the Sanctuary of Heracles Revealer. Basically, the Greek tradition emphasizes the close and reciprocal ties between the man and the divinity. In the Latin tradition, on the contrary, these personal ties do not exist: the divinity acts and the man submits, obeying almost under constraint. To tell the truth, Cicero is interested only in the question of truth of dreams, and not in Sophocles, like the biographer.

Is the Anecdote Authentic?

Faced with such differences, scholars have debated which of the two versions was the more likely to be reliable. Opinions differ, as they do on all questions where the evidence is scant.[7] This Heracles Revealer provided revelations regarding other people, but he did not leave much about himself. We know only through the commentator Hesychius (fifth century CE) that the byname "Revealer" (Mènutes) designates Heracles in Athens; but we do not know where his sanctuary was.

Despite the paucity of evidence, it nonetheless seems reasonable to decide in favor of the version given by the *Life of Sophocles*, for two reasons. The first is the antiquity of the sources of this anecdote, which may go back, as we have seen, to the Aristotelian milieu.[8] The second reason is that in the Latin tradition itself there is another mention of the anecdote that tends to confirm the Greek version. In his treatise *On the Soul* the father of Latin theology, Tertullian, gives the example of Sophocles' dream to illustrate the idea that a dream can reveal a theft: "When a gold crown was taken from the Acropolis, Sophocles the tragic poet found it in a dream."[9]

Although the example is used, in Tertullian as in Cicero, to illustrate the veracity of a dream, the details Tertullian gives are in accord with those of the *Life of Sophocles*: it is a gold crown that has been stolen, not a gold cup, and it was stolen on the Acropolis and not in the sanctuary of Heracles. However, Tertullian left aside what principally interests us here, the reference to Heracles.

In short, the version given by the *Life of Sophocles* is likely to reflect the oldest state of the anecdote. But does this antiquity allow us to grant the story a basis in truth? It is impossible to arrive at certainty about this question. Nonetheless, it is significant that archaeologists have not neglected this anecdote. At the end of the nineteenth century, when excavations were being carried out on the Acropolis, four votive inscriptions to Heracles were found on the south flank and a small bust of Heracles on the west flank. These discoveries have been related to the sanctuary of Heracles "Revealer" that Sophocles is supposed to have founded on the south flank of the Acropolis in the middle of the fifth century, thus restoring a tradition of the presence of Heracles on the Acropolis that was well attested in the sixth century on the pediments of the temples, but which disappeared after the Persian Wars.[10] In any case, it is not unlikely that Sophocles played a role in the Athenian cult of Heracles, because it is undeniable that he played one in the introduction of the cult of Asclepius in Athens during the 420s BCE.

Sophocles and the Cult of Asclepius in Athens: Sophocles as the Host of the God

The second divinity with whom Sophocles had a privileged relationship is the god of medicine, Asclepius. It is Plutarch who, on two occasions, provides information about this tradition, once in one of his *Parallel Lives*, and again in one of his moral essays. The most explicit testimony occurs in the "Life of Numa," the second king of Rome after Romulus. What connection could there be between the second king of Rome and Sophocles? Toward the end of his life, Numa retired from society after losing his spouse. He liked to walk in the sacred woods and in solitary places, where he was, it was said, consoled by the nymph Egeria. This friendship between a man and a divinity leads Plutarch to expand on humans who have had a privileged relationship with the gods. First of all are the poets, like Hesiod and Pindar, and among them Plutarch mentions Sophocles:

> Again, there is a story, still well attested, that Sophocles, during his life, was blessed with the friendship of Aesculapius, and that when he died, another deity procured him fitting burial.[11]

In his moral essay entitled "That Epicurus Actually Makes a Pleasant Life Impossible," Plutarch alludes in comparable terms to the hospitality Sophocles gave Asclepius. In the course of this essay, which is a refutation of Epicurus's moral doctrine, Plutarch contrasts the Epicurean conception of religion, as a source of superstitious fears, with the joy of men beloved of the gods, like Pindar and Socrates. Then he comes to Sophocles: did he feel a only moderate joy

> when he entertained Aesculapius, as both he himself believed, and others too, that thought the same with him by reason of the apparition that then happened?[12]

In these two passages, it is said that Sophocles had a special relationship with Asclepius. The god did the man the honor of coming to his house as a guest. Moreover, each passage contributes additional information that does not intersect. The "Life of Numa" stresses the numerous testimonies that attested, still in Plutarch's time, to the veracity of this hospitality. The philosophical essay, on the other hand, suggests that the god's appearance was not merely private, but pleased everyone.

The privileged relationship between Asclepius and Sophocles is also well illustrated by the literary description of a painting that represented Sophocles between Melpomene, the Muse of tragedy, and the god Asclepius. Here is the last part of this description, which concerns the relationship between Sophocles and Asclepius. To make his description more vivid, the author, Philostratus the Younger, addresses Sophocles directly:

> In my opinion, Asclepius, who is there near you, is probably inviting you to compose a paean and does not find it unworthy to hear himself called by you "illustrious by wisdom," and his eyes turned toward you, in which there is the spark of joy, allow us to divine hospitable relations a little later.[13]

Here we find again the idea that Sophocles is loved by the god and that the god has chosen him to be his host at his home. The painter has discreetly represented the god's call, which can be seen in the joyous spark in his eyes.[14]

Receiving a God in One's Home

To our modern minds, this reception of the god Asclepius by Sophocles may seem strange. It is much less strange if we put it back in the context of the foundation of cults in Greece. Receiving a god as a guest in one's own home means in a very concrete way that Sophocles received a representation of the god in his house, whereas the god did not yet have a home, that is a sanctuary, in Athens. In other words, Sophocles participated in the introduction of the cult of Asclepius in Athens by receiving in his own home a representation of the god that came from one of his already existing sanctuaries, in this case the one most famous in the classical period, that of Epidaurus in the Peloponnese.[15]

What kind of representation of the god was it? We can formulate a reasonable hypothesis by comparison with foundations of the cult of Asclepius that proceeded from Epidaurus. Here, for example, is the form in which the god from Epidaurus reached Sicyone, another city in the Peloponnese:

> They [sc. the Sicyonians] say that the god was brought to them from
> Epidaurus in the likeness of a serpent, riding in a carriage drawn
> by mules, and that the person who brought him was a Sicyonian
> woman Nicagora, mother of Agasicles, and wife of Echetimus.[16]

It is thanks to this transportation of the sacred serpent that a sanctuary of Asclepius could be founded in Sicyone. Transported in this case by land, the god could also arrive by sea. Here is how the cult of Asclepius was introduced in Rome:

> When the state was troubled with a pestilence, the envoys dispatched to bring
> over the image of Aesculapius from Epidaurus to Rome fetched away a serpent,
> which had crawled into their ship and in which it was generally believed that
> the god himself was present. On the serpent's going ashore on the island of the
> Tiber, a temple was erected there to Aesculapius.[17]

The account of the foundation of the cult is a little more complex. At first, it was a representation of a god, namely a statue from Epidaurus, which was transported. But the presence in the ship of a serpent, Asclepius's sacred animal, took over and became the guide that was followed to choose the place to found the sanctuary.

By analogy with the way the cult of Asclepius spread from Epidaurus to Sicyone to Rome,[18] it is reasonable to suppose that the representation of the god received by Sophocles in his home was either a statue, or rather a sacred serpent brought to Athens from the sanctuary at Epidaurus. The arrival of the representation of the god constituted the epiphany that, according to Plutarch, gave not only Sophocles but also the Athenians great joy.

Sophocles Priest of Halon

We may wonder why it was Sophocles who received the god in his home when the cult of Asclepius was introduced in Athens. To be sure, Sophocles was beloved of the gods and loved them himself. But is that a sufficient reason? We might find an additional explanation in a hint given in the *Life of Sophocles*:

> He was also the priest of Halon, who was a hero (brought up) with Asclepius by Chiron.[19]

This sentence has caused much ink to flow. The healer-hero Halon, who is supposed to have been, along with Asclepius, the disciple of the good centaur Chiron on Mount Pelion in Thessaly, is not known from other sources. Hence various modifications of this name have been proposed.[20] What matters here is that Sophocles was the priest of a healer-hero close to Asclepius. It is not unusual to find a priest hosting a divinity in his own home.[21] As such, Sophocles could have received the new healing divinity in Athens before it had been definitively established in a sanctuary.

Sophocles Heroized

Sophocles did not limit himself to receiving the new divinity in his home but also participated in the establishment of the latter's cult. This information is given incidentally in a testimony that is of great importance for understanding the importance that Sophocles' role in the reception of Asclepius in Athens had in the eyes of his contemporaries. However, this document is only an article in a relatively recent (ninth century CE) Byzantine dictionary; but it contains very precise information:

> Dexion: that is what Sophocles was called by the Athenians after his death. It is said that at the death of Sophocles the Athenians, wanting to pay him homage, established for him a heroic sanctuary and called it Dexion, because of his reception (*dexeos*) of Asclepius. He had in fact received the god in his house and had constructed an altar. It is for that reason that he was called Dexion.[22]

Regarding the relations between Sophocles and Asclepius, this article confirms what we already knew from Plutarch and Philostratus the Younger, namely that Sophocles received the god in his home. But it adds something else: Sophocles constructed an altar for the god. This must refer to an altar set up not in his home, but in one of the sacred enclosures on the south flank of the Acropolis where the god Asclepius was honored.[23] Finally, what is completely new with respect to other testimonies is the recognition that the Athenians gave Sophocles for the role he played in the reception of the saving god. It was manifested, after his death, by his heroization under the name of Dexion, that is, "he who receives" the god. We have to imagine this heroization very concretely: a sanctuary was delimited to honor Sophocles, and he was worshiped there.

To be sure, many a modern may be surprised that the tragic poet was heroized not for his theatrical production but for the role he played in the introduction of the cult of Asclepius in Athens. Now we know the poet and too often ignore the man. But for Sophocles' contemporaries, the man's virtuous action was primary. That is also what the *Life of Sophocles* says (c. 17), citing as its source Istros, an Alexandrian scholar of the third century BCE, a disciple of Callimachus and a specialist in the history of Attica:

> Istros says that the Athenians, because of the virtue of the man, issued a decree deciding to make a sacrifice to him every year.

Thus Sophocles was not only heroized but received an official cult by the city's decree. This posthumous destiny of Sophocles is comparable to that of the physician Hippocrates, who received on his native island of Cos a heroic cult with sacrifices on his birthday each year.[24]

Confirmations and New Information Provided by Archeology and Epigraphy: The Sanctuaries of Amynos and Dexion

Strangely, it is the most recent source that provides the most precise information about Sophocles' heroization; and some critical minds might be tempted to doubt these details. But archeology and epigraphy have confirmed in the most striking way the information given by the literary source.[25]

At the end of the nineteenth century, German excavations led by Dörpfeld on the western part of the Acropolis unearthed a little sanctuary surrounded by walls that had a fountain at its center, near which there was a small temple.[26] The dedicatory inscriptions that could be read on the offerings first revealed that the sanctuary was that of a healer-hero named Amynos, unknown from other sources, to whom Asclepius was added, and then the goddess of health, Hygia. Up to that point, there was no connection with Sophocles. But the excavators found in a fountain a Pentelic marble stele bearing about twenty lines of writing in which they were surprised to read the name Dexion, that is, Sophocles heroized. Here is that inscription, which epigraphists date to the second half of the fourth century BCE:

> Cleainetos son of Cleomenes of the deme of Melite made the proposal. It was decided by the "orgeons," because Calliades son of Philinos of the deme of Piraeus and Lysimachides son of Philinos of the deme of Piraeus are men gener-

ous for the common affairs of the orgeons of Amynos, of Asclepius and Dexion, to pay them homage for their virtue and their justice toward the gods and the common affairs of the orgeons, to crown each of them with a gold crown worth five hundred drachmas, to accord them exemption from the *conge* in the two sanctuaries for themselves and their descendants, to give them, with a view to the sacrifice and the offering deemed appropriate by the orgeons, to inscribe this decree on two stone steles, and to erect one of them in the sanctuary of Dexion and the other in the sanctuary of Amynos and Asclepius, to give for the confection of these steles what is deemed proper by the orgeons, so that others might also compete in efforts for the common affairs of the orgeons, knowing that the orgeons will grant benefactors rewards commensurate with their good deeds.[27]

This stele, whose inscription is almost completely intact, gives the text of a decree that does not shine for its originality: a simple decree rewarding two persons who have rendered service. And yet, how much precise information about the heroized Sophocles, as soon as we compare the inscription with the article in the Byzantine dictionary!

The two texts illuminate one another. In the absence of literary testimony, we would not have known that Dexion, in the epigraphic text, corresponded to the heroized Sophocles. But for its part, the inscription definitively confirms the veracity of the Byzantine testimony: there was indeed a sanctuary of Dexion, since the decree was inscribed on two steles, one of which was erected in the sanctuary of Dexion! Unfortunately, the second stele has not been found; and neither has an ex-voto dedicated to Dexion. This makes it impossible to determine with certainty the location of the sanctuary of the heroized Sophocles.[28]

The inscription also confirms the ties between Asclepius and Dexion. In this respect, the inscription provides further information in relation to the literary text: what it tells us is that the sanctuary of Dexion was administered conjointly with another sanctuary, that of Amynos and Asclepius, by the same assembly of the faithful, the "orgeons" of Amynos, Asclepius, and Dexion.[29] The order of the divinities is probably not an accident. There must initially have been a sanctuary of Amynos, a healing hero of Attica. His name signifies his function: he is the divinity "who averts" (*amynei*) illness. And the hypothesis has been proposed that the healer-hero of whom Sophocles was the priest was this Amynos, and not Halon, as indicated by the *Life of Sophocles*.[30] As a priest of the healer-hero Amynos, Sophocles would have received Asclepius at his home when he was introduced into Athens, and the sanctuary of Amynos, after the reception of the new god, would have become the sanctuary of Amynos and Asclepius. Then, upon Sophocles' death, at the time of his heroization and the creation of the sanctuary of Dexion, the *orgeons* who administered the sanctuary of Amynos and Asclepius would have assumed responsibility for administering the new sanctuary of the heroized Sophocles.

The Asclepieion of Athens and Sophocles' Paean

All the same, the sanctuary of Amynos and Asclepius is not the main sanctuary where the new god was established. The great sanctuary, the Asclepieion, was located not far away, not on the west flank of the Acropolis, but on the south flank, on a rectangular terrace at the foot of the Acropolis's steep slopes, adjoining on the west the theater of Dionysus where Sophocles had his tragedies performed. The location is perfectly indicated by Pausanias: it is the first sanctuary one passes on leaving the theater to go to the Acropolis.[31] In this sanctuary, where Pausanias could still admire the statues of the god and his children as well as the paintings, it is not surprising that excavations have revealed traces of the presence of Sophocles and confirmed, here again, what we knew from literary sources.[32]

What the literary sources reveal concerning Sophocles' piety with regard to Asclepius is not only, as we have seen, his reception of the god in his home and the construction of an altar, but also the composition of a song in honor of the god, a "paean."

What is a paean?[33] Originally, "Paean" was a proper name. In the Mycenaean tables of Knossos, Paean was a healing divinity, and in Homer, he was the gods' physician.[34] In Hesiod, Paean is still a god of medicine distinct from Apollo.[35] Then, with the development of the cult of Apollo, the ancient healing divinity disappeared as such, but his name persisted as a title, and then as a name for Apollo himself, who thus inherited the healing powers of his predecessor. As for the common noun, "paean," it refers, already in Homer, to a song addressed to Apollo either to ask him to avert illnesses such as the plague, or to thank him for having done so.[36] This name comes from the fact that the divinity was invoked by the cry "Iè Paean" in a sort of refrain. The paean is thus a kind of cultic song, originally apotropaic, and executed by a chorus in the course of a religious ceremony in honor of Apollo. This cultic dimension was preserved even when the paean left the framework of the Apollonian religion and was addressed to other gods.

Sophocles had composed not only tragedies but also paeans.[37] In this respect, he was part of a poetic tradition made famous before him by the poets of the lyric chorale, Bacchylides and Pindar. The only paean of Sophocles that has remained famous is the one he composed in honor of Asclepius. It was sung by the Athenians at the celebration of the cult of Asclepius, as is also indicated, in the third century CE, by the sophist Philostratus in his *Life of Apollonius of Tyana*. The way in which this indication is inserted into the narrative proves that Sophocles' paean was well known to all of Philostratus's readers. In fact, recounting the visit of Apollonius, Philostratus, this curious, mystical neo-Pythagorean who wandered among the Brahmin sages of India, describes the rituals in which these sages engaged in their worship of the gods. Here is the passage that ends with the allusion to Sophocles' paean to Asclepius:

Thus they went close to a spring that Damis [Apollonius's companion], who saw it later, said resembled that of Dirce in Boeotia. First they undressed, then they anointed their heads with an unguent the color of amber, and this unguent warmed the Indians so much that their bodies began to smoke and rivulets of sweat ran down them, as when one takes a steam bath; then they jumped into the water; and then, after taking their bath in this way, they headed for the temple, crowned and all occupied singing a hymn. Standing, and forming a chorus, with Iarchas [the leader of the sages] as the head of the chorus, they took their sticks and struck the soil with them, and the latter swelled like a wave, lifting them two cubits in the air. Meanwhile they sang a song reminiscent of Sophocles' paean that is sung in Athens in honor of Asclepius.[38]

The savor of this narrative proceeds from the mixture of the fantastic and the real. So that the reader can imagine the scene in such a distant country, the comparisons with Greek realities are abundant: first the spring of Dirce in Thebes, then the steam bath, and finally Sophocles' paean to Asclepius. Thus Sophocles' paean was as well known to Philostratus's readers as the practice of the sauna![39]

The Rediscovery of Sophocles' Paean

Sophocles' paean must thus have been sung, still in the time of Philostratus, by an Athenian chorus with a chorus leader, on the occasion of the festival of Asclepius. Hence it is not surprising that excavations on the Acropolis uncovered fragments of a paean by Sophocles, fragments that were gradually assembled and published between 1876 and 1936. In 1876, the principal fragment, including the very legible name of Sophocles and the beginning of the paean, was published, and the editor proposed to see in it the beginning of the famous paean to Asclepius that was still sung during the Roman period.[40] This discovery immediately elicited interest: it was said that Sophocles' paean "was beginning to return from the underworld."[41] There was no doubt that the first verse of the poem was an invocation to the mother of Asclepius: "Very famous daughter [of Phlegyas] and the mother of the god who averts pains"; and in the second verse could be found the poetic adjective "long-haired," one of the usual epithets of Apollo, the father of Asclepius. The discovery of two other adjoining fragments in 1909[42] and three additional fragments published in 1936[43] allows us to read in the second verse, after the invocation of Asclepius's mother: "I am going to begin a hymn that elicits the cry" and a little further on an appeal to the god: "May you come!" Nonetheless, despite the ingenuity of the epigraphists in assembling the scattered fragments of the inscription, we have only a few bits and pieces of the first seven verses and a few letters of several other verses. It is impossible to produce a continuous translation. Thus the outcome is rather disappointing!

However, between 1927 and 1936 archeologists succeeded in reconstituting the monument where the inscription was found.[44] This is the monument called the Sarapion, which has a triangular base and was originally surmounted by a tripod. Thus it was originally a monument in honor of a choreographic victory. The base was inscribed on all three sides, but not necessarily at the same time. The front side (side A) includes, in addition to the original dedication, a second dedication in honor of Sarapion, a Stoic poet and philosopher who was a friend of Plutarch's, made by his grandson, priest of Asclepius, who had also had transcribed on this side two of his grandfather's works a medical poem and a paean.[45] The right lateral side (side B) gives a list of singers of paeans arranged by tribes that can be dated to the beginning of the third century CE.[46] It is on the left lateral side (side C) that Sophocles' paean is inscribed. Since the reconstruction of the monument in 1936, scholars have never ceased to debate the date, the different purposes of the monument, and the relation among the diverse inscriptions on the three sides.[47] The most certain conclusion is that this monument must be related to an influential family in Roman Athens of the second and third centuries CE, the Statii family of the deme of Cholleïdes, which was particularly connected with the Asclepieion.[48] Sophocles' paean, copied on side C, probably in relation to the list of the singers of paeans on side B,[49] testifies in any case to the currency of Sophocles' paean at the beginning of the third century CE, more than seven centuries after its composition.[50] The epigraphy of the Asclepieion in Athens thus confirms the role Sophocles played in the cult of Asclepius in the imperial period. It is natural to think that the fame of Sophocles' paean at that time, far from being a resurgence in a late period that was passionately interested in archaism, was a tradition that went back to the foundation of the cult of Asclepius, of which Sophocles was the instigator.[51]

What Was Sophocles' Real Role in the Introduction of the Cult of Asclepius in Athens?

Was Sophocles the sole instigator? The epigraphy of the sanctuary of the Asclepieion in Athens raises once again the problem of who was responsible for the introduction of this cult in Athens. Let us therefore stay with the Asclepieion. But let us leave the monument of Sarapion, where Sophocles' paean is inscribed, to go, in imagination, to the so-called monument of Telemachus.

This causes us to go back a rather long way in time, because if the inscription of Sophocles' paean on Sarapion's monument dates from the beginning of the third century CE, Telemachus's monument takes us back to the classical period, the beginning of the fourth century BCE. The latter is one of the most singular votive monuments in the sanctuary. Reconstituted by archeologists who were able to successfully piece together the fragments preserved in Athens and London, Telemachus's monument consists of a quadrangular column offering inscriptions on all four sides.[52] This column had on its summit a two-sided relief representing on one side Asclepius and his daughter Hygia (that is, Health) inside the temple of the Asclepieion, and on the other the entrance to the sanctuary seen from the outside, surmounted by the representation of four animals sacred to the god, two serpents on the pediment and two cocks on the roof. But what interests us here are the remains of the inscription engraved on the column, where one can read a version of the foundation and development of the sanctuary, which begins this way:

> Telemachus was the first to found the sanctuary and the altar for Asclepius, for Hygia, for the Asclepiades, and for the daughters of Asclepius. . . . [Asclepius] coming from Zea at the time of the Great Mysteries, stopped in the Eleusinion; and making him leave his home . . . , Telemachus brought him here on a chariot, [in accord with oracles]. With him came Hygia, and thus was founded this whole sanctuary under the archontate of Astyphilos of the deme of Kydantides.[53]

From the beginning of the inscription, a certain Telemachus firmly claims the foundation of the Asclepieion in Athens, asserting that he is "the first" to have founded the sanctuary and the altar when the god came from Epidaurus. Concretely, Telemachus solemnly conveyed the representation of the god (whether this was a statue or a sacred serpent) in a chariot to his new sanctuary.[54] The inscription then continues in the form of a chronicle of the foundation of the sanctuary, with its difficulties, and the improvements that Telemachus made from year to year over a decade. This chronicle is certainly very valuable for the history of the first developments of the Asclepieion in Athens, and also for the date and the circumstances of the introduction of the cult of Asclepius, which took place under the archontate of Astyphilos, that is, in the year 420/419, in connection with the Great Mysteries of Eleusis in honor of Demeter and Korè.[55] But it also raises an important problem regarding the introduction of the cult of Asclepius in Athens. Here we are in the presence of two different if not contradictory versions. Telemachus's version does not leave any room for a reception of Asclepius in Sophocles' home. How then can we account for this divergence between two versions, both of which are perfectly well attested?

Some scholars have seen here, plausibly, a rivalry between two private initiatives that might have initially been joint or contemporary, and that led to different developments. When the god coming from Epidaurus arrived by sea, as a priest of the healing divinity Sophocles might have received in his home a representation of the god before introducing it into the already existing sanctuary of the hero Amynos, which had become the sanctuary of Amynos and Asclepius, where he founded an altar for Asclepius. It has even been suggested that Sophocles' prestige might have played an important role in the necessary collaboration between the priests who came from Epidaurus and the Eleusinian priest belonging to the two great families of the Eumolpides and the Keryces, who were responsible for receiving the new god in the Eleusinion of Athens. That would

explain the importance of the reception of the god in Sophocles' house. Telemachus, for his part, arranged a new sanctuary for the god and his family, apparently independently of the Keryces, with whom he got involved in a lawsuit over
the delimitation of the terrain. The two individual initiatives to introduce a cult
that was not initially public are not incompatible. But Sophocles' celebrity, the
success of the paean he had composed in honor of the god, and finally his
heroization after his death (in 406), as "the one who received" Asclepius—all
that might have amplified Sophocles' role and put the founder of the Asclepieion
in the shade. So the latter might have felt the need to recall, in a long inscription
that is dated to the beginning of the fourth century, the role he had played in
the introduction of the god and in the foundation and development of his great
sanctuary.[56]

Whatever the details of the introduction of the cult of Asclepius in Athens in
420 may be, Sophocles' religious authority won out over Telemachus's generosity.
Even in the Asclepieion founded by Telemachus, it was the name of Sophocles
that was to remain attached to the sanctuary in late antiquity, probably because
of the renown of his paean to Asclepius. In this respect we have a concrete testimony that is all the more significant because it contains an incidental reference
to Sophocles. The Neoplatonist philosopher Marinos, who succeed Proclus at
the head of the Academy in 485 CE, speaks in his *Life of Proclus* about the very
agreeable situation of his predecessor's family home:

> The house Proclus owned was also very agreeable, a house that his father Syri-
> anos and Plutarch his grandfather, as he called him, had already lived. It was
> near the sanctuary of Asclepius, famous because of Sophocles, and the sanctu-
> ary of Dionysus with its theater. It was visible, and even, moreover, within
> earshot of Athena's Acropolis.[57]

Thus Proclus's house was on the south flank of the Acropolis, not far from
the theater of Dionysus and the sanctuary of Asclepius, which was located west
of the theater, on a terrace at the foot of the steep slopes of the Acropolis. It is
interesting to note that Sophocles appears here, in a way completely unexpected
by moderns, not in relation to the sanctuary of Dionysus where his theatrical
works were performed, but in relation to the nearby sanctuary of Asclepius.
Marinos's testimony, which is all the more precious because it seems paradoxical,
sheds new light on the image of Sophocles: ten centuries after his death, he was
still contributing to the fame of the sanctuary of Asclepius in Athens!

The Success of the Cult of Asclepius in Athens

Let us return to the year 420/419, when the cult of Asclepius was introduced in
Athens. Let us set aside the quarrel between Sophocles and Telemachus regarding
who established the cult and try to understand the importance of the religious
phenomenon in which they both participated. Asclepius's penetration into Ath-

ens constitutes a significant step in the completely exceptional development of the cult of a healing divinity whose origins are modest.[58]

In Homer, in the eighth century BCE, Asclepius, famed for his medical knowledge acquired from the centaur Chiron, was not a god but only the prince of Trikka in Thessaly, and the father of two of the most famous physicians of the Achaean army, Podalire and Machaon, who are called the "Asclepiades." After his death, Asclepius must have been the object of a heroic cult in his city. In fact, it was in this Thessalian city that the oldest sanctuary devoted to his cult was located.[59] The divine descent of the physician-hero, probably already attested in Hesiod, first appears in literary texts preserved in Pindar (first half of the fifth century): Asclepius is the son of Apollo and a mortal, Coronis, the daughter of the Thessalian Phlegyas: his medical knowledge made him a benefactor of men, but he died tragically, struck down by Zeus for having abused his knowledge by resuscitating a mortal.[60] This filiation is adopted by Sophocles in his paean in honor of Asclepius. In the fifth century, the most important sanctuary of Asclepius was the one in Epidaurus in the Peloponnese. It made a decisive contribution to the spread of the cult. For if the oldest sanctuary, that of Trikka in Thessaly, might have been the origin of the cult of Asclepius on the island of Cos, the homeland of the physician Hippocrates, it was the clergy of Epidaurus that played a determining role in the dissemination of the cult of Asclepius: first to Athens, in the late fifth century; then, starting in the fourth century, to Crete (in Lebena), to Asia Minor (in Pergamon), and even, as we have seen, to Rome.

The expansion of the Epidaurian cult beyond the Peloponnese had been preceded by a first step: the installation of a sanctuary of Asclepius on the island of Aegina, a natural stopping place on the way from Epidaurus to Athens. One of Aristophanes' comedies, *The Wasps*, performed in 422, provides certain testimony to this. We learn, during a discussion between servants at the beginning of the comedy, which takes place in Athens, that the old master, named Philocleon, is suffering from an incurable illness. His son has tried to heal him by all the means locally available: words, medical purgation, the religious medicine of the Corybantes. Everything has failed. His final recourse is to take his father to Aegina, so that he can sleep in the temple of Asclepius, see the god in a dream, and be cured.[61] But the invalid has slipped away to return to the tribunal in Athens. From this passage it clearly emerges, on the one hand, that in 422 there was still no sanctuary of Asclepius in Athens, and on the other hand, that the closest sanctuary of Asclepius was the one on Aegina. Thus we can see that the spread of the cult from Epidaurus to Athens in 420 was a natural consequence in the progression of the healing divinity from Epidaurus. Sophocles' or Telemachus's initiatives, which were apparently individual, are thus part of the overall expansion of the Epidaurian cult.

These individual initiatives might also correspond to a need felt by the Athenians, especially after the "plague" epidemic that had decimated the city at the beginning of the Peloponnesian War in 429/428, with a fresh outbreak in

427/426.[62] The Athenians turned toward the gods, such as Apollo, who averted ills, or Athena, who protected health.[63] But they did not have a special divinity for medicine. In the city itself, where the people had taken refuge, there were not many healer-heroes: in addition to the hero of whom Sophocles was the priest (if Halon is a defective form of Amynos), we know only one anonymous "physician-hero." No doubt rationalists like Thucydides had noted during the epidemic the complete impotence of religious medicine and traditional medicine. But the mass of the people, or religious people like Sophocles, did not share Thucydides' judgment. Humans' impotence when faced with the plague probably contributed to the introduction of the new healing god, even if there was no direct connection in time. During this period of war, favorable conditions had to be awaited. Then in 421/420 the Peace of Nicias put a temporary end to the hostilities, and this facilitated the god's journey from Epidaurus to Athens.

The cult, introduced in 420/419 right in the center of the city on the slopes of the Acropolis, was well integrated into the ancient cults, while adding its own mark. As we have seen, on the one hand it inserted itself into the sanctuary of the healer-hero Amynos, and on the other hand it benefited from a new sanctuary. There was also a sanctuary of Asclepius in Piraeus, founded shortly before the one in the city or simultaneously with it.[64] At the beginning of the fourth century, the cult of Asclepius was sufficiently well established for Aristophanes to accord it a major place on the stage of the theater of Dionysus. Whereas in 422, in *The Wasps*, the comic author, limiting himself to a simple allusion, was obliged to take his character afflicted with madness to the Asclepieion of Aegina, thirty years later, in his *Ploutos* of 388, he can have his character afflicted with blindness treated in Athens itself, whether it was in the sanctuary of Asclepius in the city, adjacent to the theater of Dionysus, or in the sanctuary in the port;[65] and he can linger at length and amusingly on the narrative of a scene of nocturnal healing in the temple of Asclepius, now that the rites are familiar to Athenian audiences. And whereas, in the first comedy, the god's treatment failed, in the second it is fully successful. The poet, while making people smile, can no longer question, before an Athenian audience, the miraculous powers of the healing god. At that time, the Athenian sanctuary of Asclepius was adorned with ex-votos given to the god by believers who had been miraculously cured.

The Presence of Asclepius in Sophocles' Theater

Sophocles also witnessed the success of the new cult that he had helped introduce; and he must have taken a certain pride in it. The importance acquired by Asclepius finds an echo even in his tragedies. Although tragedy is not, like comedy, a mirror of everyday life, in Sophocles' late tragedies there is one mention of Asclepius that stands out in particular when it is connected with the role

Sophocles played in the introduction of his cult in Athens. I refer to the *Philoctetes*, performed in 409.[66] Eleven years after receiving Asclepius in his home and after having erected an altar to him, Sophocles ended his *Philoctetes* in an exceptional way by having a divinity, Heracles, appear and urge Philoctetes to go to Troy, promising him victory and restored health. And who will provide the cure? Asclepius in person! "For the healing of your sickness, I will send Asclepius to Troy,"[67] says Heracles to Philoctetes.

This reference to Asclepius is all the more remarkable because it is an innovation with regard to the epic tradition and even with regard to the rest of the tragedy. In the epic tradition, Asclepius could not care for Philoctetes at Troy, because he was not yet a god, as we have seen, but a Thessalian prince endowed with medical knowledge. Not having taken part in the expedition against Troy, probably because of his age, he sent his two sons, the Asclepiades; and it was one of them, Machaon, who cured Philoctetes, as is indicated by the summary of this episode treated in a lost epic poem in the Trojan cycle, the so-called *Little Iliad*:

> After that, Odysseus seized Helenus in an ambush, and following one of the latter's oracles, Diomedes brought Philoctetes back from Lemnos. Philoctetes, cared for by Machaon, kills Alexander (= Paris) in single combat.[68]

Regarding Philoctetes' cure, Sophocles had followed the epic tradition in the rest of his tragedy. In fact, according to Helenus's prophecy that Neoptolemuoens reveals to Philoctetes, it was the two sons of Asclepius that were to cure him if he consented to go to Troy.[69] But Heracles' revelation at the end of the tragedy transports us into a different period and a different world: it is no longer the epic world where Asclepius was still a man; instead, it is Sophocles' contemporary world where Asclepius has become a healing god endowed with ubiquity and present in the different sanctuaries of Greece. Of course, for a spectator attending the performance in the fifth century BCE, this gap is minute; for Asclepius had come to the Asclepieion in Athens with his whole family and notably with his two sons, Podalire and Machaon:[70] for the Athenians, the cult of the two sons was thus inseparable from that of the father. Hence the replacement of the sons by the father must have looked to Athenians less like a break with the epic tradition than a progression in the certainty of the cure: the power of the healing god Asclepius is superior to that of his sons. And we thus understand better the sudden turnabout of Philoctetes who, after having remained deaf to the word of Helenus's oracle, immediately obeys Heracles. But in the tragic author, who chose to depart from the tradition, the substitution of Asclepius for the Asclepiades is full of meaning: Sophocles makes Asclepius enter into myth of Philoctetes, exactly as he had helped Asclepius enter the city of Athens.

Thus Sophocles served to glorify Asclepius the healing god not only in his life but also in his work, either directly, by composing the paean in honor of him, or indirectly, by introducing the new healing divinity into his theater.[71]

CHAPTER IV

Sophocles and Dionysus

....

THE THEATRICAL CAREER

Let us now leave the sanctuary of Asclepius on the south flank of the Acropolis, which can symbolize the religious role Sophocles played in his city, and return to the theater of Dionysus adjacent to it: that is where Sophocles especially distinguished himself through his long career as a man of the theater, over a period of more than sixty years. When Pausanias visited the theater of Athens more than six centuries later, he could still see, among the statues honoring the tragic poets, that of Sophocles.[1]

A Brilliant Debut in the Theatrical Career in 468

Sophocles' theatrical career began with a first attempt that was a masterpiece: he won his first victory the very first time he participated in the competition. At least that is what we are told by Plutarch, who reports the circumstances of that victory in his "Life of Cimon," Cimon having been one of the most important Athenian strategoi before Pericles:

> When Sophocles, still a young man, entered the lists with his first plays, Apsephion the Archon, seeing that the spirit of rivalry and partisanship ran high among the spectators, did not appoint the judges of the contest as usual by lot, but when Cimon and his fellow-generals advanced into the theatre and made the customary libation to the god, he would not suffer them to depart, but forced them to take the oath and sit as judges, being ten in all, one from each tribe. So, then, the contest, even because of the unusual dignity of the judges, was more animated than ever before. But Sophocles came off victorious, and it is said that Aeschylus, in great distress and indignation thereat, lingered only a little while at Athens, and then went off in anger to Sicily. There he died also, and is buried near Gela.[2]

This important testimony regarding the beginning of Sophocles' career, and his relations with his elder, Aeschylus, deserves close examination.

First, the precise year of the victory can be deduced from the name of the archon. In Athens, there were three magistrates called "archons" who, in the classical period, were chosen by lot each year: the *archon basileus* (king ruler), the *polemarch* (war ruler), and the *eponymos archon* (name ruler). The technical term *eponymos* means that this archon gave his name to the year in which he held office. Now, one of the functions of this archon was precisely to organize the Great Dionysia festival, which took place every year in the spring and included, among other events, a tragedy competition. Thus Plutarch, by giving the name of the archon who handled the tragedy competition, also tells us the name of the eponymous archon, allowing us to determine the date of the event. The archontate of Apsephion corresponds to the year 469/468. This date is, moreover, confirmed by a chronicle of Greek history dating from the Hellenistic period that is preserved on the stone known as the Marble of Paros. On it can be found, among the events related by this chronicle for the fifth century BCE:

> Sophocles, son of Sophillos, of the deme of Colonus, won the victory in the tragedy competition at the age of twenty-eight, under the archontate of Apsephion in Athens.[3]

The agreement between the two testimonies regarding the name of the archon is rather remarkable;[4] thus it was in 468 that Sophocles won his first victory.[5]

At that time, Aeschylus's first victory went back about fifteen years. This competition in 468 thus marked the victory of a talented young man over his elder. It was probably also a victory of a disciple over his master.[6] It is easy to imagine that the master was deeply affected by his defeat. But can we follow Plutarch when he claims that this failure was the direct cause of his departure for Sicily, to the court of Hieron?[7] In reality, Aeschylus did not permanently lose the favor of the Athenian audiences. On the contrary. At the following competition, he won again, though over two competitors neither of whom was Sophocles. That was the year in which he presented *Seven against Thebes*.[8] And he took his revenge in a later competition in which he won over Sophocles, when he had his *Suppliants* performed.[9] Finally, Aeschylus won a third victory in 458 with the three tragedies of the *Oresteia* that have come down to us.[10] All this information thus leads us to qualify seriously Plutarch's statements concerning the relation between Aeschylus's defeat by Sophocles in 468 and his departure for Sicily. Ten years had passed between the two events, ten years during which Aeschylus had won the competition at least three time, once over Sophocles.

An Exceptional Procedure for a Tragedy Competition

Nonetheless, it remains true that Sophocles' first victory was memorable, for two reasons: it marked the birth of a new talent challenging a confirmed authority; but especially the decision was made in accord with an exceptional procedure, by a very influential authority. To understand what was exceptional about it, let us recall the normal procedure, which will allow us to emphasize a point that is important, though little known, among the conditions for the success of any Greek tragic author.

Success was not measured, as it is today, by the number of performances of the same play before a series of different audiences. Tragic plays were written to be performed once, all before the same audience, composed chiefly of Athenian citizens, in the theater of Dionysus, during the god's festival. Success was measured by victory in a competition against two adversaries, during which each competitor presented three tragedies—forming what is called a trilogy—and a satyr play, that is, a shorter play tending toward the comic, and whose chorus was composed of satyrs. The whole set constituted a tetralogy. All that is well known.[11] What is less well known is the way in which the ranking of the three candidates was made. Who made the final decision? Although it occurred in a democracy that commonly voted by a show of hands in a popular assembly, the final decision was not for the audience to make directly and was not made by an "applause meter." It was entrusted to a jury of ten sworn judges belonging to each of the ten tribes and chosen in accord with an electoral principle in favor in Athenian democracy: drawing lots. Nonetheless, the effects of the drawing of lots were tempered insofar as the choice was made on the basis of a list of candidates drawn up in advance by each tribe and established by the council. After the performance of all twelve plays—which in the classical period took place over three days, with one day per author—each of the ten judges proposed his ranking by writing it on a tablet. The final decision depended, after another drawing of lots, on at least five judges. The jury was chosen anew for every competition.[12]

This, then, was the regular procedure. It is fairly complex and might seem somewhat singular to moderns insofar as the jury was not necessarily composed of experts. Nonetheless, it represented, ultimately, a happy medium between the finicky judgment of experts and the passionate judgment of the crowd, even though the crowd's reactions might have influenced the judges.[13]

This procedure was not applied during Sophocles first victory, or more exactly it was interrupted in its final phase by the eponymous archon entrusted with organizing the competition. That is what we have to understand when Plutarch says that the archon "did not appoint the judges of the contest as usual by lot." It was in fact just before the performance that lots were drawn to choose the members of the jury. Previously the preliminary list of candidates had been decided on by the council for each of the ten tribes; each name had been written on a tablet; and the tablets corresponding to each of the ten tribes had been placed in ten sealed urns, kept on the Acropolis under the guard of the treasurers of the public treasury. These ten urns were then brought down from the Acropolis to the theater of Dionysus, and it was when they were about to be opened to begin drawing lots to determine the ten members of the jury, and then to have them swear an oath, that the archon decided to interrupt the procedure in the face of a violent disagreement among the spectators. He probably feared that the judges would be too influenced by the crowd. He appealed to the authority of the strategoi, taking advantage particularly of the prestige of one of them, Cimon, who was surrounded by the aura of his crushing victory over the barbarians at Eion, in Thrace, and over pirates on the island of Scyros, from which he had brought back the ashes of the national hero of Athens, Theseus.[14] Despite its audacious character, the procedure respected the balance among the ten tribes, which were all represented in the college of the strategoi. However, because of its exceptional character, it gave the final decision an unforgettable luster. It is very likely that Aeschylus, without going so far as to withdraw into exile, felt a deep bitterness.

Nevertheless, there remains in Plutarch's testimony an obscurity concerning which questions have been raised. How did it happen that such a violent quarrel was able to divide Athenians into supporters of Aeschylus and supporters of Sophocles even before the audience had seen the tragedies, and even without yet knowing any work of Sophocles, if it is true that he was participating in the competition for the first time?

We might find the beginning of an answer in a ceremony that took place a few days before the performance. This ceremony bore in Greek the name of Proagōn, that is, "Prelude to the Competition." This was a sort of "parade" that took place at the Odeon situated near the theater,[15] where each of the three authors chosen for the tragic competition presented the subject of the plays that he was going to have performed. He also presented the chorus and the actors who were going to perform the plays. We can imagine that during this parade in which the authors tried to favorably impress the audience, the author's contribution had a certain importance for the outcome of the competition. In Plato's *Symposium*, Socrates mentions very concretely and vividly how a tragic author, Agathon, had impressed people during the parade before the crowd:

> "Nay, Agathon, how forgetful I should be," replied Socrates, "if after noticing your high and manly spirit as you stepped upon the platform with your troupe—how you sent a straight glance at that vast assembly to show that you meant to do yourself credit with your production, and how you were not dismayed in the slightest—if I should now suppose you could be flustered on account of a few fellows like us."[16]

Had Sophocles, on the occasion of his first presentation, shone in a very special way, and had he, benefiting from the attraction of novelty, unleashed the passions of his future spectators? That is not implausible when we know how clever he could be before the audience at banquets.[17] Nonetheless, we may wonder whether Plutarch is not giving Sophocles too much credit. Could the preliminary parade have had a decisive importance? Was Sophocles able to impress his audience so favorably on his first contact with it, when we know that his voice, too frail, did not allow him to be an actor in his own tragedies?[18]

Some scholars have therefore doubted that this victory corresponds to his first participation in the competition. They base themselves on another testimony—later, it is true—that of Eusebius, bishop of Caesarea in Palestine (third/fourth centuries CE). In his *Chronicle* this author distinguishes between the year in which Sophocles began to present tragedies and the year in which he won his first victory. According to him, they were separated by a gap of two years. Thus it would be in 471/470 that Sophocles began to enter the competition, whereas he won his first victory in 469/468.[19] But Eusebius's *Chronicle* is far from being free from errors. Scholars generally stick with Plutarch's version. The essential point remains that Sophocles' first victory is placed in 468 by all the known sources and that it had a completely exceptional impact. It was approved by a prestigious judge, Cimon, who was at that time the strategos the most admired and the best loved by Athenians. One would like to know at least the title of the tragedies that earned Sophocles such a success. But our sources are entirely silent on that point. That is to say that they are capricious and often deprive of us of what we most want to know.

Comparison of the Career of Sophocles with That of Aeschylus

This initial feat opened a brilliant theatrical career, fertile and full of successes. Of all the Greek tragic authors, Sophocles is the one who came the most often onto the stage after the announcement of the results of the competition to receive from the archon the crown of laurels, the symbol of victory, while his name was proclaimed amid the applause of the audience.

However, Aeschylus had a very brilliant career. He distinguished himself on the Athenian stage, from his first victory in 484 to his death in 456, winning thirteen victories in all. When he had to compete with Sophocles, although he was defeated in 468, he took his revenge a few years later, as we have seen, by outdoing him with a trilogy the first play of which was *The Suppliants*. Finally, after his death, the Athenians authorized by decree the revival of his tragedies. This constituted a first in the history of Greek theater. Never before, from the birth of dramatic competitions in Athens in the second half of the sixth century (535), had a revival been envisaged, whether for Thespis, the founder of tragedy, for his disciple Phrynichus, or for Aeschylus's other great predecessors or rivals, Choirilos and Pratinas. We have to wait until the beginning of the fourth century (386) for the revival of an ancient tragedy with different actors to appear on the program of the tragic performances at the Great Dionysia. And despite that, the homage paid Aeschylus remains unique; for the revivals of his plays in the fifth century were part of the tragic competition, whereas in the fourth century the revivals of earlier plays were programmed on the margins of the usual competition. Thus it happens that Aeschylus more often won the first prize after his death than during his lifetime.[20] Under such conditions, it is easy to see why

Aeschylus erased the memory of all his predecessors and was considered already in late antiquity the father of tragedy.

Compared with Aeschylus's career, that of Sophocles was, if not more brilliant, at least much more extensive. Aeschylus did not win first prize until 484, when he was forty, whereas he had begun to compete when he was thirty.[21] For his part, Sophocles won his first victory when he was much younger—in 468, he was not yet thirty.[22] Above all, he established himself more quickly: even if we adopt the most pessimistic hypothesis, according to which two years separate his first participation in the competition and his first victory, we are far from the ten long years during which Aeschylus awaited success. And starting from their respective first victories, Sophocles' career was twice as long as Aeschylus's: not quite thirty years for Aeschylus, a little over sixty years for Sophocles! Thus it is not surprising that Sophocles won more victories than Aeschylus during his lifetime: twenty-four victories, including eighteen at the Great Dionysia, and the rest in the Lenaia. Now since during a competition at the Great Dionysia an author presented four plays (three tragedies and a satyr play) and in the Lenaia only two tragedies, we see that Sophocles obtained the first rank for ninety of his plays out of a total of 123 (or 130)![23] His rate of success exceeds 70 percent. And when Sophocles did not win first place, he was never completely defeated; he always came in second.[24]

Comparison of Sophocles' Career with That of Euripides

Sophocles' success seems even more brilliant if we compare his theatrical career with that of his young contemporary Euripides, which began in 455 when he won third place with his tragedy *Peliades* (now lost).[25] Even though he was fifteen years younger than Sophocles, Euripides had a career that took place with the chronological framework of Sophocles' career. Euripides died just before Sophocles, in 407–406. The traditional view according to which Euripides succeeded Sophocles is therefore false. Euripides' career, which lasted almost fifty years, is strictly contemporaneous with that of Sophocles, even though it began thirteen to fifteen years later. Now, during this half century of activity, Euripides never had a success comparable to that of the two other great tragic authors. He waited about fifteen years, like Aeschylus, before having his first success, in 441.[26] But unlike Aeschylus and Sophocles, he only very rarely enjoyed victory: during his lifetime, he won first place only four times.[27] And when Sophocles and Euripides were competing against each other, the Athenians preferred Sophocles.[28] Thus it seems that Euripides had a real chance only when Sophocles was not participating in the contest. Thus in 428 Euripides won the first prize with his *Hippolytus*, when Sophocles was not competing.[29] Ahead of his time, Euripides, ridiculed by the comic authors, did not succeed in triumphing over Sophocles, who was more in conformity with the traditions. This does not mean that the theater of Euripides did not exercise a profound influence on his audience, and even perhaps on his more successful competitor. Some Athenians, according to what Plutarch reports in his "Life of Nicias," obtained their salvation, after the disaster of the Athenian expedition to Sicily, by reciting verses or singing the lyrical parts of Euripides to the Sicilians, who were fond of his theater.[30] As for Sophocles' esteem for his rival, it was publicly manifested when he learned the news of Euripides' death, which occurred in Macedonia, where he had gone into exile. During the parade that preceded the next Great Dionysia, in March 406, Sophocles walked wearing a dark robe and escorted by his chorus and actors without a crown, which made the people weep.[31] It is also reported that when Sophocles learned of Euripides's death he said, "The stone I used to sharpen my poetry has disappeared!"[32] Is this remark authentic? In any case, it is graceful and corresponds to a reality: the beneficial effects of competition among tragic authors, and perhaps the influence that Euripides' pathos may have exercised on Sophocles' last tragedies.

A Disappointment When a Masterpiece Was Produced

Sophocles' brilliant career did not exclude a few disappointments here and there. Being in second place behind Aeschylus was not a dishonor. But when Sophocles was beaten by a less prestigious rival, the defeat was harder to bear. That is what happened when he presented one of his masterpieces, *Oedipus the King*. This tragedy was considered the most beautiful even in antiquity. And yet Sophocles did not win first prize, being defeated by a certain Philocles. Six centuries later, this judgment still scandalized the rhetorician Aelius Aristides:

> Sophocles was defeated by Philocles at Athens for his *Oedipus*; O Zeus! O gods! Against that *Oedipus* even Aeschylus could have nothing to say. Does that make Sophocles less good than Philocles? In any case it would shame him, Sophocles, simply to hear it said that he is better than Philocles![33]

Without seeking to justify the jury that preferred Philocles to Sophocles, we can better understand its choice if we try to bring back to life Sophocles' competitors, who have fallen into almost total oblivion because their works have disappeared without a trace. When we recreate the microcosm of the tragic authors of the fifth century, using the set of testimonies available to us, this decision made by the judges of the competition may seem a little less astonishing. Philocles was not a nobody; he even belonged to a noble family of tragic poets, since he was Aeschylus's nephew.[34] He was thus well trained. To be sure, the nephew was not spared by the comic authors. Aristophanes mocks the sourness of his melodies and pronounced on his poetry this final judgment: "Philocles, being ugly, composed ugly poetry."[35] Nonetheless, the nephew produced an oeuvre that surpassed that of his uncle in its size: a hundred tragedies.[36] This means that Philocles was judged worthy of participating in competitions almost as often as

Sophocles. By crowning a nephew of Aeschylus, the judges no doubt felt they were not shaming themselves.

A Surprising Elimination during the Choice of Competitors

A second qualification that we need to make concerning Sophocles' success in his theatrical career is a surprising failure. He had the bitter misfortune of not even being included among the competitors for the prize.

This setback provides us with a reason to return to the conditions for selecting the participants in a tragic competition. We have already seen how the victor was selected among the three competitors. But we have to realize that this competition was in fact a final. At the beginning, there were many more candidates. To use the traditional expression, the competitors approached the organizer of the festival, the eponymous archon, and "asked for a chorus." The role of the organizer was to eliminate candidates, leaving only three finalists. He granted only three choruses, which were paid for by three *choregoi*.[37] A passage from Plato's *Laws* informs us indirectly regarding the way in which this preliminary examination was carried out. In his ideal regulation of the tragic competitions, which was inspired by the real one, Plato addresses tragic authors in these terms:

> So now, ye children and offspring of Muses mild, do ye first display your chants side by side with ours before the rulers; and if your utterances seem to be the same as ours or better, then we will grant you a chorus, but if not, my friends, we can never do so.[38]

This text suggests that the candidates competing in the Great Dionysia had to submit for examination by the eponymous archon the whole manuscript of their four plays (tragic trilogy and satyr play). What were the archon's criteria for selection? In reality, no testimony informs us as to the way in which he made his preliminary choice. Not being a specialist—since a new one was chosen every year—how could he avoid a kind of arbitrariness or injustice? In any event, Sophocles once underwent the painful experience of being eliminated during this preliminary examination. Our information is reliable, because it is provided by one of Sophocles' contemporaries, older than he, the poet Cratinos (520–423), who expresses his indignation in one of his comedies, entitled *The Cowherds* (*Boukoloi*). The three verses in which Cratinos challenges the archon's judgment are extant:

> Who did not grant Sophocles a chorus when he asked for it, but [did grant one to] the son of Cleomachus whom, for my part, I would not deem worthy of presenting a play even for the festival of Adonis.[39]

We do not know the name of the magistrate who failed to grant Sophocles a chorus, and that is too bad, because that would also tell us the exact date of his failure. The poet who was preferred to him, Cleomachus's son, was a certain

Gnesippus who was mocked for his effeminate and licentious inspiration.[40] Thus Sophocles experienced the same misfortune as so many other more or less obscure poets, such as Morsimos, Aeschlyus's great-nephew. The only difference is that a comic poet was indignant at the rejection of Sophocles, while another comic poet was delighted that Morsimos had been rejected![41]

If even the best authors could be rejected during the preliminary selection or in the final result, that is probably because the competition was in reality more lively than the selection of the three great tragedians made by posterity makes it seem, and as Aristophanes already suggests. In the Athens of the end of the fifth century, there was still a genuine passion for writing tragedies, and the poets had to fight to "ask for a chorus" from the archon, if we believe one of Aristophanes' characters:

> *Heracles:* Surely you must have some other youngsters,
> At least ten thousand tragic playwrights,
> All babbling miles further than Euripides.[42]

We must, of course, take comic exaggeration into account: in a city of about forty thousand citizens, one could hardly have thousands of authors of tragedies! But despite his scorn for this younger generation, Aristophanes is obliged to recognize that some of them were able to obtain a chorus and participate in the competition. The passion for tragic competition did not disappear with the death of the three great tragic authors.

How Can Sophocles' Theatrical Career Be Reconstructed?

We would like to be able to follow in detail the whole of Sophocles' long career, which lasted more than sixty years, from his first victory in 468 to his death in 406/405. We would like to know the exact rhythm of his participations in the tragic competitions, the chronology of the victories he won at the Great Dionysia or the less prestigious festival of the Lenaia, the plays presented at each of these completions, and also the number and names of the competitors he faced, along with the final ranking. But that is a history that cannot be written in its continuity.

The necessary documents did exist in antiquity. There were, for example, the archons' archives, where the results of the various competitions at the Great Dionysia and the Lenaia must have been recorded. There were also learned works written on the basis of these archives. Aristotle composed two documentary studies on the history of the theater, on the one hand the *Didascaliae*, that is, the results of the competitions, and on the other the *Victories at the Dionysia*. But these two works, which would have been so precious for the history of the Greek theater, are known only by their titles.[43]

Other documents that proceed directly or indirectly from these archives have come down to us, but in an extremely fragmentary form. They have been preserved on stone, on papyrus, and also at the beginning of manuscripts giving the tragedies. It is by examining these three types of material that we will reconstruct the still accessible elements of Sophocles' career.

The Inscriptions and Sophocles' Theatrical Career

It is the inscriptions on stone that reproduce the form of the archives the most faithfully. The excavations on the south flank and the north flank of the Acropolis, as well as the ones in the agora in Athens, on the north flank of the Areopagus, have brought to light fragments, scattered far and wide over the terrain, of three lists that archeologists have gradually reconstituted.

One of these, called *Fasti* by moderns, gave the victors for all the competitions at the Great Dionysia, year by year. The other two bore only on tragedy and comedy, but they concerned the two Athenian festivals at which there were theatrical performances, not only the Great Dionysia, but also the Lenaia. One, designated by the technical name *Didascaliae*, gives the ranking of the competitors, with the titles of the plays performed; the other, called "List of Victors," gives the victors classified by the date of their first victory and indicates the total number of their victories.[44]

The name of Sophocles appears twice, on two different lists: once on the list of the *Fasti*[45] at the Great Dionysia (ΔIIIII = 18).[46] Since the preserved fragments of these different lists are few in number and very scattered, it will be seen that our possession of these two bits of information about Sophocles is almost miraculous. They were not discovered, moreover, at the same time. The fragment of the list of the victors was known as early as the nineteenth century, but the name of Sophocles, which is missing its beginning, was not immediately identified, because it was initially thought that this list of the *Fasti* gave only the names of comic authors.[47] The fragment of the list of the *Fasti* was found only much later during the excavation of the north slope of the Areopagus, in 1937, and it was not published until 1943.

By chance, this new fragment, spanning two columns, contains in the first column the name of Sophocles, and in the second, two lines farther down, the name of his son Iophon. Thanks to this single stone, we learn of two victories in the Great Dionysia in Sophocles' family, the father's victory in 447 and the son's victory a decade later, in 435. The name of Sophocles appears, in fact, twice more in this same list of the *Fasti*, as the victor for the year 387 and for the year 375; but this time it refers to Sophocles' grandson, who bore the same name as his grandfather. Thus we can see a kind of family enterprise emerging.[48]

In the category of the inscriptions giving information on Sophocles' theatrical career, in addition to the inscriptions from the archives concerning the tragedy competitions, there are also the dedications on monuments erected by the choregoi. On one of these monuments celebrating two choregoi from Eleusis, the name of Sophocles appears as the victor in a tragedy competition, just after that of Aristophanes as the victor in a comedy competition. Here is a translation of the dedication:

> Gnathis, son of Timocedes [and] Anaxandrides, son of Timagoros,
> being *choregoi*, won the comedy competition;
> Aristophanes gave the performance.
> Second victory in the tragedy competition;
> Sophocles gave the performance.[49]

This dedication by two choregoi from Eleusis in honor of their double victory in the comedy competition (with Aristophanes as author) and in the tragedy competition (with Sophocles as author) has been interpreted in diverse ways. Does it refer to victories won during a festival of the Dionysia in Athens, when the choreography was organized by two choregoi, or rather to the "Dionysia in the fields" at Eleusis? On the last hypothesis, we would be dealing with revivals presented by the authors themselves.[50]

The inscriptions also provide information on the performances of Sophocles' plays after his death, either negatively or positively. We know that starting at the beginning of the fourth century, more exactly starting in 387–386, an old tragedy was performed *hors concours* at the Great Dionysia. But for the only years on which we have any information, namely the three consecutive years from 341 to 339, the name that appears is not that of Sophocles but that of Euripides. Is that an accident? Instead, it is the sign of the success of Euripides' theater in the middle of the fourth century.[51] However, in an inscription found during the excavation of the agora in 1933 and published in 1938, we learn that in the middle of the third century BCE an actor won an actors' competition by playing in one of Sophocles' tragedies.[52]

Papyruses and Sophocles' Theatrical Career

Information can also be drawn from another category of documents, papyruses. From stones yielded up by the soil of Attica, we now pass to the papyruses preserved by the sands of Egypt. A fragment of a papyrus from Oxyrhynchos, giving the remains of a *didascalia*, has preserved the results of a competition in which Sophocles won second place, behind Aeschylus, when the latter presented his tetralogy beginning with *The Suppliants*. A certain Mesatos came in third.[53] Here is a translation of the fragment:

> Under the ar[chontate of . . .] [or "under Ar(chemides)"]
> Aeschylus won a victory [with] The Suppliants, The Egyptians,
> The Danaïds, and Amy[mone as the satyr play].
> Sophocles was second, [and the third was]
> Mesatos with N[. . .] The Bacchae, The Fool[s],
> The Shepherds, [and] Cyc[nos]
> the satyr play.

Published in 1952, this papyrus made a great sensation.[54] It challenged what scholars thought they knew about the chronology of the first Greek tragedies that have been preserved: it was thought that the oldest tragedy was Aeschylus's *The Suppliants*, notably because of the importance of the chorus. This tragedy was placed before 472, the known date of *The Persians*.[55] But Sophocles' participation, revealed by the papyrus, in the competition that Aeschylus won forces us to invert the relative dates of *The Persians* and *The Suppliants*. In fact the very presence of Sophocles implies that the performance of Aeschylus's *The Suppliants* came after the beginning of Sophocles' career, which started, as we have seen, only in 468, with a victory.[56] *The Suppliants* can therefore not be later than 467. And since it was Aeschylus who won first place in 467 with *Seven against Thebes*,[57] we can conclude that *The Suppliants* is later than not only *The Persians* (472), but also *Seven against Thebes* (467). This competition, in which Sophocles came in second, thus cannot be earlier than 466; but it cannot be after 456, the date of the death of Aeschylus. Furthermore, we have to exclude the year 458, when Aeschylus won first place with another trilogy, the *Oresteia*.[58] Among the remaining years, it is impossible to choose, if we restore the beginning of the fragment "Under the ar[chontate of . . .]," since the name of the archon is missing. On the other hand, if we adopt the second restoration, namely, "Under Ar[chemenides]," who was the eponymous archon in 464–463, this competition would date the Great Dionysia of 463. Aeschylus, defeated by Sophocles in 468, took his revenge a few years later.

The Manuscripts and Sophocles' Theatrical Career

The third category of documents that could lead us back to the Athenian archives is formed by the clues possibly given in the medieval manuscripts at the beginning of the tragedies. The text of each of the extant tragedies, whether they are by Aeschylus, Sophocles, or Euripides, is generally preceded in the manuscripts by an introduction, and sometimes by several introductions. This introduction, which scholars call the hypothesis or argument, corresponds to what we would call a preface.

These prefaces, to limit ourselves to Sophocles, are not all of the same importance: some are only a summary without interest, while others yield precious clues regarding the circumstances of the performance. Unfortunately, such clues are rare in the forewords to Sophocles' plays. There is nothing important for four of the seven tragedies: *Ajax*, *The Women of Trachis*, *Oedipus the King*, and *Electra*. We lack any chronological landmark or any classification for three of them: *Ajax*, *The Women of Trachis*, and *Electra*. In one of the prefaces to *Oedipus the King*, we have a clue to the ranking: we learn that Sophocles "was defeated by Philocles, as Dicearchus says."[59] We have already seen how, in the second century CE, Aelius Aristides was scandalized by this unjust defeat of Sophocles.[60] But the preface given in the medieval manuscripts has the merit of citing a much older source that dates from the third to second centuries BCE. Dicearchus was a disciple of Aristotle and Theophrastus, whose encyclopedic knowledge was comparable to that of his masters. Thus we go back, thanks to this testimony, to a source earlier than Alexandrian erudition. Unfortunately, there is no indication regarding the absolute date if this is a competition in which Socrates did not win first place. All that has been determined concerning the date is that some people called the tragedy not *Oedipus the King* but rather "the first *Oedipus*," referring to the other tragedy about Oedipus (viz. *Oedipus at Colonus*), "because of the time of the *didasacaliae* and because of the events." That is, *Oedipus the King* is earlier than *Oedipus at Colonus* both in its date of production and in the sequence of the myth.

A Preface to Sophocles' *Antigone,* Written by an Alexandrian Librarian

More precise information regarding dates and rankings is provided by other prefaces. These are prefaces attributed, by name or not, to Aristophanes the Grammarian, that is, to Aristophanes of Byzantium. He was one of the directors of the Library of Alexandria in the Hellenistic period (c. 195–180) and the great editor of the classical poets, notably the tragedians.[61] Of the immense work done by this scholar on Greek tragedy there remain only a few brief, clear prefaces. They can be recognized by a schema of exposition that is quite stable, despite a few variants. The preface to *Antigone*, attributed expressly to Aristophanes of Byzantium, is presented this way:

1. subject of the tragedy
2. treatment of the same mythical sequence in two other tragic authors
3. site of the drama
4. composition of the chorus
5. indication of the first character who speaks
6. summary of the play
7. information on the performance

Of all these rubrics, the most important are the second and the last, because they provide information exterior to the text of the tragedy.

The second gives us information concerning the other tragedies of two other great tragic poets treating the same subject. Thus we learn, thanks to the preface to *Antigone*, that Euripides also composed a tragedy entitled *Antigone* and that it varies from Sophocles' in important ways. In Euripides, Antigone is not alone when she buries her brother Polynices. She is caught in the act with Hemon, the king's son. The tragedy has a happy ending, because Antigone marries Hemon and has, by him, a child named Memon. These few clues show how much Euripides' lost tragedy differs in its conception of the tragic: in Sophocles, the heroine acts alone and dies in total solitude; in Euripides she acts with the man she loves and marries him.[62]

The last rubric of the preface, concerning the conditions of the theatrical production (or *didascalia*) is, in theory, the most precious. When it is complete—but this is rare—it gives the date of the performance, the ranking obtained in the competition, the tragedies performed, and the name of the choregos. In the case of *Antigone*, however, this rubric does not take its traditional form. Here it is:

> It is said that Sophocles was deemed worthy of his generalship on Samos because he was admired when his Antigone was performed. This play is the thirty-second.

Since Sophocles was a strategos in 441/440,[63] the performance of the tragedy, which we can suppose won him a victory, would have occurred not long before. Nevertheless, it cannot have been performed at the Great Dionysia of 442/441, because that is the date at which Euripides won his first victory under the archontate of Diphilos.[64] The date 443/442 is thus the more plausible. We see the final notation of the play's order number, which presupposes an ancient classification of the play in Sophocles' tragic work, probably the order of the performances. This figure of thirty-two could correspond to the central place of the eleventh trilogy.[65] Thus Sophocles would have participated in eleven competitions out of twenty-seven possible ones between 468 and 442.[66]

Sophocles' Participation in Two Competitions According to the Prefaces to Euripides' Tragedies

If we follow the chronological order in the indications provided by the prefaces attributed or attributable to Aristophanes of Byzantium to retrace Sophocles' theatrical career, we will refer first to two prefaces to tragedies by Euripides; for they tell us indirectly that Sophocles twice defeated Euripides.

The first is the preface to *Alcestis*:[67] in his rubric on the performance, the Alexandrian scholar indicates first the date, both by the archon (Glaukinos) and by the Olympic year (85, 2), that is, 438. Then he gives the ranking: Sophocles was the victor, followed by Euripides. The author of the preface certainly knew the tetralogy that had earned Sophocles his victory. However, as he was writing an introduction to a play by Euripides, he limited himself to listing the four plays that Euripides presented at the competition.[68] And, as for the ranking, the name of the third competitor is not even mentioned. That information mattered little if Euripides was second.

The other preface is that to *Medea*.[69] The date is indicated in the same way, by the archon (Pythodoros) and by the Olympic year (87, 1), that is, 431. But this time the ranking is given in complete form, since Euripides came in third, behind Sophocles, who was himself preceded by Euphorion, the son of Aeschylus. Nevertheless, here too the preface mentions only the tetralogy presented by Euripides.

These prefaces, as can be seen, provide only the information necessary for the introduction to a particular play or author. The editor knew more: the director of the Library of Alexandria had all the information about all the competitions and could also read, in his library, all the plays that he mentioned . . . or almost all. One detail in the preface to *Medea* is very significant in that regard. After listing the four plays presented by Euripides in the competition of 432—three tragedies, *Medea*, *Philoctetes*, and *Dictys*,[70] along with a satyr play, *The Harvesters*—Aristophanes of Byzantium concluded with this remark concerning the satyr play: "It has not been preserved." If the director of the library takes care to mention what was already lost in his time, that is because he had everything else. Thus we can imagine the mass of texts and information that Alexandrian scholars had on Greek theater, and more generally on Greek literature at the beginning of the second century BCE.

This selection made in the information during the composition of the prefaces is all the more damaging because it deprives us of the bases for assessing the ranking. The fact that Sophocles was defeated by Euphorion, Aeschylus's son, can be interpreted in two ways: either Aeschylus's son presented his own tragedies, or he won the victory by presenting tragedies by his father, whether they had not yet been performed or were revivals.[71]

The Date of the Competition of *Philoctetes* and *Oedipus at Colonus*

For the rest of the theatrical career, we return to two prefaces concerning Sophocles' theater. The first is the preface to *Philoctetes*:

> It [sc. the subject] is the recall of Philoctetes from Lemnos to Troy by Neoptolemus and Odysseus, in accord with Helenus's prophecy. This Helenus, since he knew oracles related to the taking of Troy, in accord with the prophecy of Calchas, was captured by night in an ambush set up by Odysseus and taken in chains to the Greeks.
>
> > The scene is on Lemnos.
> > The chorus consists of old men sailing with Neoptolemus.
> > The subject is already found in Aeschylus.
> > The play was performed under Glaucippus. Sophocles won first place.

Even though the origin of this preface is not indicated,[72] its structure makes us think of Aristophanes of Byzantium. We recognize parts comparable to those in the preface to *Antigone*: the subject, the site of the action, the composition of the chorus, the treatment of the myth by predecessors, information about the performance. However, the order of the rubrics may vary. The information about the treatment of the myth does not come in the second position, as it does in the preface to *Antigone*. Moreover, the preface to *Philoctetes* is too short to be in conformity with the original. Parts are missing, such as the first person who speaks and the summary of the play. Others have been simplified. For example, the original preface must have mentioned, for the sequence of the myth dealt with by the two other tragic poets, not only Aeschylus but also Euripides. We have just seen in fact that in his preface to *Medea* Aristophanes of Byzantium had mentioned a *Philoctetes* by Euripides performed in 431. As for the last part regarding the conditions of the performance, it does not mention the other plays in Sophocles' tetralogy, as is done in the two preceding prefaces concerning Euripides' tetralogies. Nonetheless, this last part gives us two bits of important information: first, the date of the tragedy, indicated by the name of the eponymous archon who organized the competition, Glaucippus, which corresponds to the year 409;[73] second, the success of the tetralogy of which *Philoctetes* was part, since Sophocles won first prize.

The last preface is that to *Oedipus at Colonus*. In truth, as is rather often the case, several introductions of differing origins are read in the manuscripts, before or even after the tragedy. We have four prefaces for the tragedy *Oedipus at Colonus* alone, but they are not all equally important. The fourth is the only one that is attributed to a scholar. He is a certain Saloustios; we also have a preface by him placed at the beginning of *Antigone*.[74] Even though it is attributed to a scholar, this preface is of no use: it summarizes the beginning of the tragedy and ends with a laudatory judgment. The three other prefaces are anonymous. The third is in verse. It is no more useful than that of Saloustios, because it also limits itself to a summary, though a more complete one. There remain the first two prefaces that are found in current editions.[75] They seem to complement each other, as if a preface going back to Aristophanes of Byzantium had been cut in two. In the first preface, we recognize the principal rubrics characteristic of the Alexandrian scholar: the presentation of the myth, the site of the action, the composition of the chorus, and the first person who speaks. What we expect after that is the information on the performance. But the second preface begins precisely there. Here is how it begins:

> *Oedipus at Colonus*, it was Sophocles the grandson, the son of Ariston, when his grandfather was dead, who presented it under the archontate of Micon (= year 402/401).

The date of the performance of *Oedipus at Colonus* is therefore posthumous. It took place in March 401, when the eponymous archon Micon was the organizer of the Great Dionysia, and was arranged by Sophocles' grandson, who had the same name as his grandfather.[76] Nothing is said about the other plays that were in the competition or about the latter's result. However, other information provided by the end of this preface will lead us to discuss the date of Sophocles' death, the homage paid him, and his relations with his sons and grandsons.

An Assessment of Sophocles' Theatrical Career

Before 468 BCE: The first competition and the first victory at the age of twenty-eight in the Great Dionysia (literary sources: Plutarch, "Life of Cimon"; epigraphic sources: "Marble of Paros" *Chronicle*; the list of victors).

467: Sophocles does not participate in the competition. Aeschylus takes first prize, followed by Aristias, with the tragedies of his father Pratinas, and Polyphrasmon (papyrological source: *P. Oxy.* 2256.2; manuscript source: *Seven against Thebes*).

After 467 and before 456: Sophocles wins second prize in the Great Dionysia, behind Aeschylus presenting his trilogy beginning with *The Suppliants* (papyrological source: *P. Oxy.* 2256 fr. 3).

Unknown date: **Ajax**.

Unknown date: **The Women of Trachis**.

447: Sophocles wins at the Great Dionysia (epigraphic source: list of the *Fasti*).

442 (before Sophocles; strategia in 441–440): **Antigone**, the thirty-second play in an old classification (manuscript source: preface to the tragedy).

438: Sophocles victor at the Great Dionysia, ahead of Euripides, presenting his *Alcestis* (manuscript source: preface to *Alcestis*).

431: Sophocles takes second place at the Great Dionysia, behind Euphorion, Aeschylus's son, probably with plays by his father, and before Euripides, presenting his *Medea* (manuscript source: preface to *Medea*).

Unknown date: Sophocles, presenting **Oedipus the King**, is defeated by Philocles (literary source: Aelius Aristides; manuscript source: preface to *Oedipus the King*).

428: Sophocles does not participate in the competition. First place: Euripides, with *Hippolytus*. Second place: Iophon, Sophocles' son. Third place: Ion of Chios (manuscript source: preface to *Hippolytus*).

Unknown date: **Electra**.

Before 423: Sophocles "asks for a chorus" and does not receive one (literary source: Athenaeus citing Cratinos).

409: Sophocles victor at the Great Dionysia with his **Philoctetes** (manuscript source: preface to *Philoctetes*).

406: Sophocles takes part in the Great Dionysia competition and pays homage in the Proagōn to Euripides, who has died in Macedonia (literary source: *Life of Euripides*).

Toward the end of his life: Sophocles victor in a competition (in Athens? in Eleusis?) when two Eleusinians were choregoi (epigraphic source: IG II2 3090).

End of 406/beginning of 405: death of Sophocles. He had written a total of 123 plays (source: *Suda*) or 130 (source: *Life of Sophocles*), seven of which have been preserved (boldface in this list). He won 24 victories (source: *Suda*) or 20 (source: *Life of Sophocles*, 8), of which 18 in the Great Dionysia (epigraphic source: list of Victors). He never came in third (source: *Life of Sophocles*).

401: **Oedipus at Colonus**, presented after Sophocles' death, by his grandson, whose name was also Sophocles (manuscript source: preface to **Oedipus at Colonus**).

Middle of the third century BCE: an actor won first prize by playing in a tragedy by Sophocles (epigraphic source: inscription ed. B. D. Meritt, *Hesperia* 7, 1938, 116 = DID A 4 b 8 Snell).

CHAPTER V

Happy Sophocles

....

The Date of Sophocles' Death and the Literary Homage Paid Him

The end of the preface to *Oedipus at Colonus*, after mentioning the eponymous archon Micon who presided over the Great Dionysia of 401, where Sophocles' last tragedy was presented by his grandson, goes on this way:

> This archon is the fourth archon starting from Callias (= year 406/405), the archon under whom most people say Sophocles died. That is clear according to the following: on the one hand in *The Frogs* Aristophanes has the tragic authors return from the Underworld, and on the other Phrynicus, in the comedy entitled *The Muses*, which he presented at the same competition as *The Frogs*, expresses himself this way:
>
> > Happy Sophocles, who died after living
> > for a long time, a happy, clever man,
> > the author of many fine tragedies;
> > he had a happy end, without having suffered any trouble.

This end of the preface discusses the date of Sophocles' death. It cites two testimonies that clearly indicate that Sophocles was already dead in January 405 at the time of the Lenaia competition.

The least well known of these is the comic author Phrynicus, who, in his comedy entitled *The Muses*, performed during this competition, resoundingly praised Sophocles after his death. The great merit of the preface is that it cites the four verses of this eulogy, which is all the more exceptional because comic authors spent their time making fun of their contemporaries.[1] These verses also suggest that Sophocles' old age was not unhappy. Plato's testimony tends to confirm this.[2] Sophocles, who was not a bitter old man, was delighted to have escaped love, as if he had escaped a furious and savage master. But this witticism may have hidden part of the reality. Sophocles suffered from senile palsy,[3] and in his *Oedipus at Colonus* the chorus of old men devotes a whole song to the misfortunes of life that culminate in the miseries of "powerless, unsociable, inimical old age," in which personal overtones have been discerned.[4]

The second testimony concerning his death is well known. At the same competition, Aristophanes, under the name of Philonides, had presented his comedy *The Frogs*, whose subject is directly inspired by the deaths in quick succession of two great tragedians, Euripides and Sophocles, not to mention that of Agathon.[5] To be sure, Sophocles was definitely not central in the comedy;[6] it is Euripides who remains the comic author's target, after his death as during his life. But in several passages in his comedy Aristophanes pays incidental homage to Sophocles.

First, when the god of the festival, Dionysus, noticing that there are no longer any tragic authors worthy of the name in Athens, decides to go to the Underworld to look for Euripides and to ask Heracles for information about the journey to be made, Heracles is astonished that he is not going to look for Sophocles. Here is the relevant passage in the dialogue between Dionysus and Heracles:

> *Dionysus:* I want a clever poet, for the race
>   is now extinct—all who survive are bad.
> *Heracles:* What! Isn't Iophon alive?
> *Dionysus:* Well, he's the only good thing left, if he's good at all. I don't even
>   know for sure if that's the case.
> *Heracles:* Why don't you bring back Sophocles, Euripides' superior, if you've
>   really got to take one?
> *Dionysus:* Not before I take Iophon aside all by himself,
>   and test what he does without Sophocles. Besides, Euripides is such a
>   scoundrel,
>   he might well try to run away with me,
>   but Sophocles was easy going here, and easy going there as well.[7]

The setting aside of Sophocles is a way of paying him homage. The homage is twofold: it is paid to both the poet and the man. Dionysus is well aware of Sophocles' talent as a poet; but he wants to see what his son Iophon can do without his father's help. And he recognizes that as a man, Sophocles had a good character.

Next, in the middle of the comedy, there is a fine example of his good character, as opposed to Euripides' ambition. When the turbulent Euripides arrived in the Underworld, he tried to dislodge Aeschylus from his throne of tragedy. Sophocles, on the contrary, embraced Aeschylus, held out his hand to him, and left him the throne. However, he vowed to fight Euripides as a second-string athlete in the event that Aeschylus was defeated in the battle that was to oppose him to Euripides for the possession of the throne.[8]

At the end of the comedy, Aristophanes again pays homage to Sophocles: when Dionysus, after arbitrating the struggle between Aeschylus and Euripides, decides, against all expectations, to bring Aeschylus back to Earth, and not

Euripides, of whom he initially seemed so fond, Aeschylus advises Pluto, the god of the Underworld, to entrust his throne to Sophocles and not to Euripides:

> As for my chair of honour,
> give it to Sophocles to keep safe for me
> in case I ever come back here. He's the one
> whose talent I would put in second place.
> Bear in mind—the rogue right there, this clown,
> this liar, will never occupy my chair,
> not even by mistake.[9]

Not without a sense of humor, Aristophanes ends his comedy with a ranking of tragic authors in a fictive competition bearing not on a year, but on a whole century of the tragic genre. In the fifth century, the three finalists are already Aeschylus, Sophocles, and Euripides, and the ranking given clearly assigns the first place to Aeschylus, the second to Sophocles, and the third to Euripides. This selection seems to us natural. And yet it presupposes, on the part of a contemporary, a lucid choice among a considerable multitude of tragic authors who had participated in the annual competitions in the course of the fifth century. This list of winners had to please the audience. It accorded the first prize to Aristophanes' *Frogs* in the Lenaia comedy competition in 405, and the second prize to Phrynicus's *The Muses*. Aristophanes' comedy had that much success when it was performed again.[10]

The Circumstances of Sophocles' Death

Sophocles was thus already dead before the Lenaia festival of 405. How long had he been dead? If he died under the archontate of Callias, as the argument for *Oedipus at Colonus* suggests, he did so between July 406 and January 405. It is also under Callias's archontate that the historian Diodorus Siculus situates Sophocles' death, but he adds a detail concerning the cause of death and a comparison with the death of Euripides. Here is what he says:

> At this same time Sophocles the son of Sophilus, the writer of tragedies, died at the age of ninety years, after he had won the prize eighteen times. And we are told of this man that when he presented his last tragedy and won the prize, he was filled with insuperable jubilation which was also the cause of his death. And Apollodorus, who composed his *Chronology*, states that Euripides also died in the same year; although others say that he was living at the court of Archelaüs, the king of Macedonia, and that once when he went out in the countryside, he was set upon by dogs and torn to pieces a little before this time.[11]

Diodorus, referring to the chronographer Apollodorus of Athens (second century BCE), thus places the death of Euripides in the same year as Sophocles', a short time before. But another chronology, that of the Marble of Paros, situates Euripides' death in the course of the preceding year, under the archontate of Antigenes.[12] And that is the date usually adopted, because it is the only one that allows us to justify what the *Life of Euripides* says about Sophocles' behavior when he learned of Euripides' death:

> It is said that on hearing of Euripides' death, Sophocles led the chorus and the actors wearing mourning clothes and without a crown during the prelude to the competition, which made the people weep.[13]

This scene in Athens, in which Sophocles pays discreet but moving homage to his rival who has died in Macedonia, can have occurred only during the presentation of the Great Dionysia competition in March 406, under the archontate of Antigenes. Euripides had died shortly before.

Diodorus also reports the way in which the two great tragic authors died. He says that Sophocles died in Athens from the joy of his victory,[14] whereas Euripides died far away, in a less glorious way. The contrast probably says more about the image the ancients had of the two authors than the reality of their deaths. Furthermore, if Sophocles' death took place under the archontate of Callias, a death caused by the joy at the announcement of a victory is impossible, because there was no place for a performance between July 406, when the archon took office, and the Lenaia of 405, when Sophocles was already dead.[15]

This account of Sophocles' death reported by Diodorus is in fact only one of three versions that have come down to us, and it is not the most widespread. It has also been said that while declaiming his *Antigone*, Sophocles had strained his voice too much during a long passage without a pause and definitively lost his breath.[16] The most widespread version is the most prosaic one: Sophocles choked on a grape seed. The *Life of Sophocles* gives few details about this tragic mishap: the actor Callipides, returning from Opous after his work at the festival of the Conges, is supposed to have brought Sophocles a grape seed; the old man, taking a still-green seed in his mouth, is supposed to have suffocated on it, given his great age.[17]

The ancients were fond of these anecdotes about the death of famous men and liked to collect them. Here are three verses attributed to a lyric poet of the Hellenistic period in which the deaths of the three great tragic authors are brought together:

> On Aeschylus, while he was writing, a tortoise fell.
> Sophocles on swallowing a grapeseed suffocated.
> The Thracian dogs devoured Euripides.[18]

Regarding the circumstances of the deaths of the three tragic poets, the essential difference is not in these not very reliable stories. It resides in the fact that Sophocles the Athenian died in Athens, whereas the other two, who were also born in Athens, died far from their homeland: Aeschylus in Sicily, at Syracuse, and

Euripides in Macedonia, at Pella. Sophocles was too involved and established in the political, religious, and theatrical life of his country to leave it. After being closely involved in its recovery in the dramatic times that followed the failure of the Sicilian expedition, and probably having pinned his hopes on Alcibiades' return, he remained until the end an active dramatic author and an attentive observer of the Athenian situation.

The Situation of Athens in the Very Last Years of Sophocles' Life: From the Return of Alcibiades (407) to the Battle of the Arginusae (406)

Before mentioning Sophocles' death, the historian Diodorus Siculus reported what happened in Athens in 406/405. In that year during the Peloponnesian War, when the situation was becoming increasingly perilous for the Athenians, a great military event took place: the naval battle of the Arginusae, in which the Athenian fleet engaged the Lacedaemonian fleet in what was expected to be the decisive battle.

The hopes the Athenians had earlier pinned on Alcibiades' return in June 407 were short-lived. To be sure, Alcibiades, having been granted full powers, had secured the route by land to reestablish the ritual procession from Athens to Eleusis during the festival of the Mysteries, whereas before his return the fear of the Lacedaemonians had forced the Athenians to go directly by sea. Moreover, he had increased the forces on the ground and at sea to try to win back members of the Athenian confederation that had joined the dissidents. Thus he besieged Andros, which had defected, and then reached Samos, which he chose as a naval base. Meanwhile, the Lacedaemonian fleet, commanded each year by a different *navarch*, in this case Lysander, was based not far away on the Asian mainland, in the port of Ephesus.[19] However, taking advantage of a moonless night and the absence of Alcibiades, who had left on his long maritime expedition with the best soldiers, the Lacedaemonian king Agis, who was stationed with his troops in the fort of Decelea north of Athens, led his troops against Athens and tried to take the city. All the Athenians, old or young, appeared in arms on the ramparts. The panic was general. But the Athenian cavalry drove back the enemy cavalry, which consisted mainly of Boeotians. Agis then set up his camp in the gardens of the Academy, not far from Colonus, Sophocles' native deme, before making the next day an assault on the city that failed when the Athenians showered his troops with projectiles from the top of their ramparts. After ravaging Attica, the king of Sparta withdrew to the Peloponnese.[20] The warning had been chilling. The very existence of Athens was at stake.

Some have wanted to see in this dramatic event the point of departure for Sophocles' last tragedy, his *Oedipus at Colonus*. When he is about to die in Colonus, Oedipus promises the king of Athens that the site of his death, if it remains secret, will protect Athens against an invasion coming from Boeotia[21] as effectively as a large allied army. Did the hero Oedipus buried in Colonus keep his promise and play, in the minds of his contemporaries, a protective role in such a critical situation? When the chorus of the residents of Colonus praises horses in the tragedy,[22] is it indirectly praising the Athenian cavalry whose bravery had saved Athens? Such allusions to reality, while possible, are not demonstrable.

Alcibiades' expedition did not turn to his advantage. Having left Samos for a secondary operation toward the north, Alcibiades left his pilot Antiochos on Samos with the order to keep a low profile. However, Antiochos, through a clumsy provocation, triggered a naval battle with Lysander's fleet at Notion, not far from Ephesus, in which he was defeated and killed. Small cause, big effect. The situation was certainly not compromised, because Alcibiades' fleet remained superior to Lysander's. But the news of Alcibiades' defeat led to an immediate popular turnaround in Athens: the people dismissed Alcibiades for his negligence. He went into exile again, but this time without going over to the enemy. To replace him, the people promptly elected ten strategoi, thus returning to the democratic system.[23]

One of these was Conon. He succeeded Alcibiades as commander of the fleet at Samos but did no better. He found himself blockaded again by the fleet of the Lacedaemonian navarch Callicratidas, Lysander's successor, in the port of Mytilene on Lesbos. The announcement of this defeat produced an emergency reaction: the Athenians made an exception and mobilized slaves as freemen in order to send a rescue expedition. This fleet, augmented by the contributions of allies who remained faithful, met the Lacedaemonian fleet not far from Mytilene, off the Arginusae islands. We know what happened: the Athenians, after the Lacedaemonian navarch disappeared, drove off the enemies and saved Conon's fleet; but when the Athenians had lost fifteen ships, a storm arose and prevented them from saving the crews of the sinking vessels and collecting their dead. What should have been a victory turned into a national tragedy, because the people, stirred up by demagogues, reproached the strategoi for not having saved the crews, sentenced eight of them to death, and executed the six who came back to Athens. Among them was Pericles the Younger, the son of the great Pericles and Aspasia, though he had shone in the naval battle by resisting the Lacedaemonian navarch Callicratidas and causing his loss.[24]

This naval battle had already taken place when Aristophanes presented his *Frogs* at the Lenaia in 405, since in his comedy he twice alludes to what was exceptional in this battle: slaves fought alongside freemen and were emancipated.[25] Thus the event occurred long enough before the festival for Aristophanes to be able to insert the allusion to it into his text.

Was Sophocles still alive when this battle took place? Did he witness the internal disturbances that it triggered in the popular assembly, where only Socrates spoke against the demagogues' abuses?[26] It is impossible to say. In any case, Sophocles knew not only about the banishment of Alcibiades, but also about Conon's dramatic situation blockaded at Mytilene, for according to Diodorus the latter event occurred before Callias took office and gave his name to the year during which Socrates died, 406/405.[27]

Sophocles' Funeral and the Public Homage Paid Him

The critical situation of Athens had an impact on funerals.[28] The tombs of Sophocles' family were located outside the walls of Athens, at a distance of eleven stadia (about two kilometers), along the road to Decelea. Decelea is the town in Attica, north of Athens, that had been fortified by the Lacedaemonians on the advice of Alcibiades when he defected to the enemy. We can imagine that these family tombs were situated on the territory of the deme of Colonus where Sophocles was born.

For his funeral to take place, it was therefore necessary to go outside the walls, whereas since the beginning of the war, pursuing the strategy adopted by Pericles, the whole of the Athenian population had gathered together inside the ramparts, leaving the countryside to the enemy. Thus going outside the walls was not without danger. We recall that the Athenians had given up the traditional procession by land between Athens and Eleusis. After his return, Alcibiades had reestablished this procession in November 407, but at the price of an exceptional military escort. For funerals, the enemy's authorization was therefore required. It is said that the enemy leader, posted at Decelea, had a dream in which Dionysus, the god of tragedy, urged him to let the funeral cortege proceed. When he understood that it was Sophocles' cortege, he let it pass.[29] Such was the homage paid by the enemies.

The public homage paid by the Athenians was a decree by which the Athenians promised to make a sacrifice in his honor every year. The reason given in the *Life of Sophocles* is rather vague: "because of the man's merit."[30] In reality, it was the Athenians' gratitude, not for his tragedies, but for his reception of the cult of Asclepius in Athens, because he was heroized under the name of Dexion, "he who receives." It was his religious activity, not his theatrical work, that earned him this status as a hero.[31]

His tragedy performed after his death, *Oedipus at Colonus*, was a prefiguration of the fate that awaited him: the heroization of *Oedipus* foreshadows that of Sophocles in a kind of tragic irony that the author himself did not perceive when he was writing his tragedy. But when the spectators saw the tragedy in the theater at Athens after the author's death, this was obvious to them.

His tomb, it is said, was surmounted by a bronze siren.[32] This was an allusion to the seductive magic of his song.

In the Hellenistic period, a poet named Dioscorides composed a funerary epigram for Sophocles, whose tomb he imagined surmounted by a satyr holding in his hand a tragic mask of a woman in mourning. The satyr thus addressed the passerby who asked him a question to which he replied:

This tomb, man, is that of Sophocles, whom I have received from the Muses
as a sacred trust, being myself sacred. It is he
who took me away from Phlius, where I still walked among thistles
and transformed me from the wood that I was into gold
and covered me with fine scarlet fabric. At his death
I stopped here my foot well-made for the dance.

How fortunate you are, what a good post you have received! But this mask
with shorn locks that you hold in your hand, what play does it come from?

If you say either *Antigone* or *Electra*
You won't go wrong. For both plays are a highpoint of art.[33]

The satyr symbolizes the satyr play, which Sophocles caused to make progress
by transforming it. He comes from the city of Phlius in the Peloponnese and
holds in his hand a tragic mask of a woman with her hair shorn off as a sign of
mourning, thus paying homage to Sophocles' tragedy, which attained the summit of art in the representation of the two young women.

The Search for Sophocles' Skull

Archeologists set out in search of Sophocles' tomb by leaving from the ramparts
of Athens and traveling eleven stadia along the road to Decelea, following the
information in the *Life of Sophocles*. Without success. But at the end of the
nineteenth century an original spirit, a Danish government official, thought they
should have looked eleven stadia not from the ramparts of Athens but from the
walls of Decelea, and he claimed to have found Sophocles' tomb at that distance.
The skull he discovered, despite the very strong reactions of German philologists
to his interpretation of the *Life of Sophocles*, was sent to Berlin, and then to the
World's Fair in Chicago before being deposited in a museum in Copenhagen.
This skull from the fifth century BCE, even though there is no chance that it is
that of Sophocles, still interests specialists in paleopathology because of its
"plagiocephaly."[34]

Sophocles and the Family Heritage:
A Family of Authors of Tragedies

The fact that Sophocles' grandson arranged for the performance of his last tragedy is emblematic of the family heritage. Sophocles was a new man in the trade
of writing tragedies. But he had a kind of family workshop where he trained a
son and grandson who also won fame in the theater.

Sophocles had a legitimate son, Iophon, with his wife Nicostratè. It was this
son who followed in his father's footsteps. Sophocles also had a bastard son—
Ariston—with a courtesan from Sicyone, named Theoris, whom he loved in his

old age, when his temples were already white. "Dear is Theoris," Sophocles is supposed to have slipped into one of his songs for the chorus in homage to his companion.[35] It is the son of this Ariston, also named Sophocles, like his grandfather, who was the director of *Oedipus at Colonus* before beginning his own theatrical career.[36]

Why didn't Sophocles' legitimate son Iophon see to it that his father's tragedy was performed after his death? We can find an explanation in a quarrel between the legitimate son and the father toward the very end of the latter's life that the biographical sources like to relate. Iophon is supposed to have accused his father of senile dementia because he was neglecting the family's property. But the son did not win his case. Sophocles is supposed to have pled his own cause, notably with this sentence: "If I am Sophocles, I am not senile; if I am senile, I am not Sophocles." And he is supposed to have recited a passage from his *Oedipus at Colonus*, which he had just written, thus eliciting the enthusiastic admiration of his judges. This lucidity of Sophocles at a very advanced age is given as an example by ancient authors, both Greek and Latin, such as Cicero and Plutarch, when they want to vindicate old age.[37]

Such a quarrel between a father and his son, whether or not it corresponds to reality, must not mask the main thing that the father transferred to his son. Like his father, Iophon became an author of tragedies. Mutatis mutandis, this is comparable to what happened in the great families of doctors. The two sons of the famous physician Hippocrates, a contemporary of Sophocles, also became physicians. In both families, it is a sign that a technical knowledge was passed down from father to son. We could pursue the analogy further by noting that in both families the sons remained in the shadow of the father. Thessalos and Dracon, Hippocrates' sons, like Iophon, Sophocles' son, would not be known if their father had not been famous. Despite the initial advantage constituted by the excellent training received, the son is in danger of seeing his own merit attributed to his illustrious father. That is what happened to Iophon. When Dionysus, in Aristophanes' *Frogs*, complains about the shortage of tragic authors after the death of Euripides and Sophocles, Heracles replies that there are still a few, and he thinks first of Iophon. Dionysus, while recognizing that Iophon's tragedies are good, maliciously implies that it is necessary to wait and see what the son will produce without his father.[38]

This son nonetheless had a more than honorable career. He composed fifty tragedies, won the first prize at the Great Dionysia in 435, and was second at the Great Dionysia in 428, defeated by Euripides, but ahead of Ion of Chios.[39] He even had the honor of being chosen to compete against his father; on such an occasion, the Sophocles family won two places out of three in the competition.[40] Iophon had descendants. His son, called Sophocles son of Iophon of Colonus, as well as his grandson, Iophon son of Sophocles of Colonus, are attested by epigraphy, one as the steward of the treasury of the goddess Athena at the very end of the fifth century, the other as the adjunct secretary of a college of ten members, in the middle of the fourth century.[41] But it does not seem that these two following generations of the legitimate line continued in the theatrical career.

The transmission of the art of tragedy in the family was not limited to Iophon's legitimate son. The son of Ariston, called Sophocles like his grandfather, also had a theatrical career. Sophocles had a particular affection for this grandson;[42] he must have taught him the art of tragedy as carefully as he did his legitimate son. After being his grandfather's spiritual heir by having *Oedipus at Colonus* performed in 401, Sophocles the Younger began his own career in 396, at the beginning of the fourth century BCE. He composed forty tragedies and won at least seven victories, including two at the Great Dionysia in 387 and in 375.[43]

Thus it is clear that the art of tragedy was a subject taught in the family, with a transmission of knowledge over two generations; and it is also clear that the tragic genre was not extinguished, as is too often said, with the end of the fifth century, because the career of Sophocles' grandson began at the dawn of the fourth century.

We even find, two centuries later, a descendent of Sophocles, also called Sophocles, who was a tragic author and a lyric poet. He certainly did not have a career like that of Sophocles the Elder or even like that of Sophocles the Younger, and he composed only fifteen tragedies. But we know that one of his victories was won in a competition outside Athens, at the festival of the Charites at Orchomenus, a city in Boeotia, around 100 BCE.[44]

The Family Lineages of Tragic Authors of the Fifth and Fourth Centuries: The Comparable Example of Aeschylus

This transmission of the craft of the tragic author within a family is not peculiar to Sophocles. It is a rather remarkable, but also neglected feature of the transmission of the tragic art in the fifth century.[45] We will limit ourselves to the most striking example, that of Aeschylus's descendants.

Like Sophocles, Aeschylus was a new man in tragedy. He had two sons who embraced a theatrical career. The better known is Euphorion, the other Euaion.[46] These men of the second generation are not necessarily second-rate tragic authors. Euphorion, as we have seen, once defeated Sophocles and Euripides.[47] However, a doubt persists concerning the significance of this victory: did he present his own plays, or was he participating in the competition with tragedies written by his father, as the law authorized him to do?

In any case, Sophocles was defeated by another member of Aeschylus's family who was participating in the competition with his own plays. This was Philocles, the author of a hundred tragedies, who won the first prize when Sophocles presented his *Oedipus the King*, which, as we recall, made Aelius Aristides indignant.[48] Philocles was the son of Aeschylus's sister.[49] And especially—and it is important to stress this as characteristic of the tragic art—this nephew of

Aeschylus's was the origin of a whole lineage of tragic authors stretching over three generations: his son Morsimos, his grandson Astydamas, and his two grandsons, Philocles (the Younger) and Astydamas (the Younger).[50] It happens that the beginning of Astydamas the Elder's career coincides, to within two years, with the beginning of that of Sophocles the Younger.[51] Thus a grandson of Aeschylus and a grandson of Sophocles must have competed against each other in the first half of the fourth century, as had Aeschylus and Sophocles in the first half of the fifth century. This is a fine example of the continuity of the transmission of tragic knowledge in the family framework over at least a century.

What remains of this production by the descendants of Aeschylus or Sophocles? Names, titles of works, sometimes a few verses preserved in anthologies, or a few fragments resuscitated thanks to pieces of papyrus. Not much. It has to be admitted. But on the one hand this filiation in the transmission of art of tragedy makes us aware of the importance of the technical aspect of the composition of a Greek tragedy, and on the other hand, it asks us to divest ourselves of simplifying views: Greek tragedy did not begin with Aeschylus's *The Persians* in 472, and it did not end with Sophocles' *Oedipus at Colonus* in 401. It cannot be summed up in three great tragic authors. Tragedy did not die in the fifth century with the death of Euripides and Sophocles, or with the defeat of Athens in 404. Over several centuries new plays continued to be presented every year for competition.[52] Starting in the fourth century BCE, Greek tragedy simply lost everything in the great wreck of ancient literary works. Let us not take an accident for an ineluctable fate.

The Portraits of Sophocles

When Pausanias visited the theater of Athens in the second century BCE, he could still see portraits of the tragic and comic authors, among them that of Sophocles. Here is what he says about them (1, 21).

> In the theater the Athenians have portrait statues of poets, both tragic and comic, but they are mostly of undistinguished persons. With the exception of Menander no poet of comedy represented here won a reputation, but tragedy has two illustrious representatives, Euripides and Sophocles. . . . The likeness of Aeschylus is, I think, much later than his death.

The traveler's reaction is quite revelatory of the gap between the selection made by the literary tradition and the reality of things. This gap seems clearer for comedy than for tragedy. But the majority of those who were unknown to Pausanias were authors who were liked or celebrated in their own time.

We will take one example: Astydamas the Younger, who was, as we have seen, the last descendent of Aeschylus's family, and a prominent figure in the middle of the fourth century, winning at least seven victories in the Great Dionysia. He was the victor in 341 and 340, which is no small achievement, since it presupposes the presentation in two consecutive years of five tragedies esteemed by the Athenian audience.[53] It was then that the Athenians honored for the first time a descendent of Aeschylus's family, by decreeing to erect a bronze portrait of him inside the theater. Let us overlook the boastfulness of the author who wrote an inscription of four lines in which he praised himself in such an unbearable way that the council rejected his text. This bragging was later ridiculed by the comic authors, to the point that the expression "You boast like Astydamas" became proverbial.[54] But the bronze statue was made, and a fragment of the marble base bearing the first letters of his name was found inside the theater of Dionysus.[55] Did Pausanias consider such a portrait, which no doubt existed when he came to visit the theater, one of the mass of unknowns? Pausanias's knowledge of the theater, in the second century CE, was no longer comparable to that of a scholar at the Library of Alexandria like Aristophanes of Byzantium, in the second century BCE.

Thus as for the portraits of the authors of tragedies, Pausanias was ultimately interested only in the three great fifth-century Athenian authors of tragedies who had by then emerged from the mass of the others. In fact, they had emerged rather quickly in Athens itself. As early as the fourth century, the Athenian state had adopted two measures that concerned these three authors, and only them. They were due to the orator and statesman Lycurgus (c. 390–c. 325). The first of these measures concerns us here directly. Lycurgus had bronze statues of these three authors erected.[56] It was thus those statues that Pausanias saw four centuries later. His remark on the fact that the statue of Aeschylus was not erected during his lifetime is therefore valid also for the two others. It was not until the fourth century that tragic authors saw portraits of themselves erected within the theater enclosure during their lifetimes. Aeschylus did not have any reason to think of writing an inscription to place on the base of his statue, as was the case for the descendent of his family, Astydamas. In the famous draped marble statue in the Vatican, said to be a portrait of Sophocles as soon as it was discovered in 1839, we see a copy of the statue erected by Lycurgus in the Athens theater. But does this statue really represent Sophocles? The shade of Theodore Reinach, the erudite founder of the Villa Kerylos at Beaulieu-sur-Mer, where one can see a copy of the Vatican's statue, is there to remind us that the common opinion is not as solidly founded as one might think. According to Theodore Reinach, the posture of the man represented with his arm hidden underneath his cloak is not that of a poet, but that of an ancient orator.[57] The statue he had brought into his villa was not, in his view, that of Sophocles but that of Solon!

Concerning the iconography of Sophocles, we will end with the paintings. We have seen that even as a youth Sophocles was an excellent player of the lyre or cithara and that later on he played the cithara during the performance of his *Thamyris*.[58] To confirm this talent as an instrumentalist, the *Life of Sophocles* points out that he was represented with his lyre in a painting on the Puerile. This portico in Athens owes its name precisely to the paintings that adorned it on three sides. Pausanias described them in the same report on his journey to Athens in which he mentions the statues at the theater.[59] The frescos or paintings he mentions represent battles in ancient or modern history, notably Theseus's battle against the Amazons or the Athenians' battle against the barbarians at Marathon. However, in everything Pausanias describes, there is no reference to a representation of Sophocles. Does that mean that the *Life of Sophocles* is inventing things? Or should we think instead that in his description Pausanias limited himself to the great frescoes, without paying attention to the less important paintings?

There are other paintings representing Sophocles. Here is a lost painting that the words of an author of the imperial period, Philostratus the Younger, bring back to life:[60]

> Why, O divine Sophocles, do you delay receiving Melpomene's gifts? Why do you cast your eyes toward the earth? For I do not know if it is because you are already collecting your thoughts or because of your awe before the goddess. Come now! Have courage, old man! Receive the gifts. For one cannot reject gifts from the gods, you know that, I assume, because you have heard it from one of the members of Calliope's *thiase*.[61] Thus you see the bees, how they fly above you and hum sweetly and divinely, sprinkling the ineffable drops of their own dew. For that is what more than anything must come to life through your poetry. And no doubt people will soon cry out about you: "He's the hive of the good Muses." . . . You see also the goddess in person who holds in reserve elevation and sublimity of thought for you now and who, with a benevolent smile, dispenses her gift. In my opinion, Asclepius, who is there near you, is no doubt inviting you to compose a paean and does not find it unworthy to hear himself called by you "illustrious by wisdom,"[62] and his eyes turned toward you, in which there is the spark of joy, allow us to divine hospitable relations a little later.[63]

The composition of the painting is clear. In the center, Sophocles casts his eyes down. He is flanked by two divinities: on one side the Muse of song and tragedy, Melpomene, is about to offer him the presents of tragic inspiration and smiles at him benevolently; on the other Asclepius turns on him a bright and promising gaze. Above Sophocles, bees fly and sprinkle drops of honey, presumably on his mouth. This picture signifies that the painter did not see Sophocles solely as the author of tragedies. To be sure, that is an important part of the picture, given material form by the Muse of tragedy and by the bees. Moreover, the presence of the bees echoes a well-attested literary theme, that of poetry compared to bees' honey, and more particularly to a characteristic of Sophocles' art. The poet had been nicknamed "the bee" because of the sweetness of his songs, a sweetness recognized even by the comic poets, who were ordinarily more ferocious. The comic poet Aristophanes even speaks of Sophocles' mouth as being anointed with honey.[64] However, the painter, by representing Asclepius at Sophocles' side, was paying homage to another aspect of Sophocles too neglected by moderns, his religious work. He is the elect of the god Asclepius, as well as of the goddess of tragedy. This is an allusion to the role that Sophocles played in the cult of Asclepius in Athens: he had, we recall, the honor of receiving the god in his home, composed a paean sung by the Athenians in the god's enclosure, and was heroized after his death for having received the god.[65]

In the end, this picture, which shows Sophocles receiving, at the dawn of his life, the twofold divine inspiration of Melpomene and Asclepius, gives us a rather balanced image of the man and his work, even if there is in it no allusion to his political activity.

PART II

....

Sophocles the Tragic Poet

Prelude

....

A TRAGIC DISASTER

The tragedies of Sophocles that have been preserved are seven in number. The list, in what is probably a chronological order, is *Ajax, Women of Trachis, Antigone, Oedipus the King, Electra, Philoctetes*, and *Oedipus at Colonus*.[1] A detailed presentation of each of these tragedies will be found at the end of this volume in appendix I. These are all that remain of the 123 or 130 plays[2] that he wrote. The great majority were tragedies; his satyr plays necessarily constituted less than a quarter of the total.[3] In the medieval manuscripts containing all Sophocles' extant tragedies—they are relatively rare—the order of presentation is more or less arbitrary: *Ajax, Electra, Oedipus the King, Antigone, Women of Trachis, Philoctetes, Oedipus at Colonus*, with a possible inversion of the last three, *Oedipus at Colonus, Women of Trachis, Philoctetes*.[4] This first choice of seven tragedies was followed, during the Byzantine period, by a second, more limited choice that retained only the first three tragedies on this list, namely *Ajax, Electra*, and *Oedipus the King*. It was for this Byzantine triad that a considerable number of manuscripts has been preserved.[5]

Sophocles is not the only author many of whose works were lost. Much the same is true for Aeschylus, of whose ninety plays we have only seven tragedies. However, the losses are proportionally smaller for "the father of tragedy," since his work was less extensive from the outset. The figure of seven extant tragedies is not accidental. It is the result of a choice made in educational milieus at a date generally situated in the second century CE.[6] The success of this choice, which nonetheless preserves in their totality seven tragedies for each author, was responsible, at least in part, for the disappearance of the others. A selection of plays was also made for the third of the great tragic authors. But Euripides was luckier, even though he had less success during his lifetime. In addition to the plays selected, which were ten in number, nine more of his tragedies have survived, proceeding from a different edition in which the plays were presented in alphabetical order.[7] Survival is not always the result of a deliberate choice!

In addition to the plays preserved in toto, bits of other plays by the three great tragic dramatists, or even minor ones, have survived. These are fragments coming either from quotations made by ancient authors or from papyruses.[8] In a few cases, these data may be complemented by the iconography. For Sophocles, for example, since the middle of the last century we have known the fragments of a bowl called "Homeric" that represents a scene from a lost tragedy, the *Athamas*, with inscriptions in which we can read the name of Sophocles.[9] All the fragments of these lost plays, whether identified by their titles or not, have been collected by scholars.[10] In this way we know the names of 115 of Sophocles' lost plays, which are listed and presented at the end of this volume, in appendix II. If we add the seven extant tragedies, we obtain the figure of 122 plays, which corresponds more or less to the total of the plays attested in the *Suda*. Thus we can determine the titles of all Sophocles' plays. This gives us a very precise idea of the variety of the myths Sophocles chose. Nevertheless, the fragments are too few to allow us to reconstitute the whole of a play, with one exception, a satyr play entitled *The Searchers* (*Ikhneutai*), in which the chorus of satyrs sets out, like bloodhounds, to find a man who has stolen Apollo's flocks. At the end of the play, the person responsible for the theft is revealed to be the very young Hermes, a gifted child who is both a clever thief and the inventor of the cithara.

In addition to plays, Sophocles also wrote elegies, epigrams, and paeans, as well as a prose treatise on the chorus in which he opposed the views of his predecessors, and particularly Thespis, the first Athenian author of tragedies. These works have also been lost, except for the few fragments of the paean in honor of Asclepius that was discussed in connection with Sophocles' religious role in Athens.[11] It was perhaps in this treatise on the chorus that he characterized the evolution of his art in three phases in the course of his career: after imitating Aeschylus's bombastic style, and then adopting a bitter, studied manner of his own, he modified the form of the style by choosing the one best suited to the description of character.[12]

CHAPTER VI

The Mythic Imagination

·················

The Subjects of Greek Tragedies

All of Sophocles' tragedies, whether or not they have been preserved, have a mythic subject. With few exceptions, that was the rule in Greek tragedy.

The best-known exception is Aeschylus's tragedy *The Persians*, performed in 472, whose subject was a historical event: the defeat of the Persians in the second Persian war (480), in the course of which they had invaded Greece under the leadership of Xerxes. They penetrated as far as Athens before they were repelled, notably in the naval Battle of Salamis. The performance of the tragedy, only eight years after these events, must have greatly impressed Athenian spectators, a considerable number of whom had taken part in them, and could turn around and see, on the Acropolis behind them, the visible marks of the barbarians' burning of temples that had still not been rebuilt. But this exception is entirely relative, because during the contest of 472, where he triumphed with his tragic trilogy followed by a satyr play, Aeschylus had framed his tragedy on a modern subject between two others that dramatized a mythic subject: *Phineus*, about the king of Thrace who was blind and all whose food was being eaten by the well-named Harpies; Glaucus the son of Sisyphus, who came from Potniae in Boeotia and who had horses that fed on human flesh and devoured their owner one day when they were starving. Only an accident of tradition allowed this tragedy dealing with a historical subject to survive, whereas the two other tragedies in the trilogy were lost.

The exception constituted by *The Persians* was probably not the first. Before Aeschylus, one of his predecessors, Phrynichus, had already presented *The Capture of Miletus* in Athens. At the beginning of the fifth century Miletus, a Greek city on the coast of Asia Minor, had revolted against the Persians, to whom they were paying tribute, and drew other cities in Ionia into its revolt. But six years later the Persian king, Darius, put down the revolt and seized Miletus, which he razed in 494. According to Herodotus, the Athenians, who had supported Miletus's rebellion, showed in countless ways how painful the capture of Miletus was for them. The historian goes on:

> When Phrynichus wrote a play entitled "The Fall of Miletus" and produced it, the whole theater fell to weeping; they fined Phrynichus a thousand drachmas

for bringing to mind a calamity that affected them so personally, and forbade the performance of that play forever.[1]

Phrynichus, who was already a famed tragic author before the capture of Miletus, had thus decided to represent a contemporary subject. Not only was he made to pay a heavy fine, but his play was destroyed. Nonetheless, this was not because he had broken a rule that was supposed to oblige authors to choose mythic subjects. It was because he had represented misfortunes too close to the Athenians. They considered the misfortunes of Miletus their own, because they were Ionians like the inhabitants of Miletus. Aeschylus no doubt remembered that lesson, since the victory at Salamis, unlike the capture of Miletus, made it possible to represent the tragedy of the Persians defeated by the Greeks. His tragedy, whose intention was the opposite of Phrynichus's, also had an opposite effect on the audience: Aeschylus won the competition.

However, the choice of a contemporary subject remained entirely exceptional. During the theatrical performances at the Dionysia of Athens in the fifth century BCE, a kind of balance between the choice of subjects between tragedy and comedy had been established: comedy could deal with a contemporary subject, as was often the case in Aristophanes' work, whereas tragedy remained in the domain of myth. The choice of a mythic subject was better suited to the majesty of tragedy. Comedy, for its part, was closer to everyday life. But above all, there had to be a certain distance between the subject and the spectator if a misfortune was to be a source of pleasure. This could be clearly seen when Phrynichus's *The Capture of Miletus* was performed. By representing a misfortune that was too close to that of the spectators, Phrynichus failed by triggering a real pain, and not the emotion peculiar to tragedy.

What Does It Mean to Speak of the "Mythic Subject" of a Tragedy?

Nonetheless, we must not allow ourselves to be misled by the modern sense of the word "myth" and think that the Greek "myth" was necessarily opposed to reality and to history. In the time of Aeschylus and Sophocles, myth was not yet synonymous with fable or legend. In the context of a tragedy, the Greek word *mythos* refers to a "speech" or a "narrative" without implying a negative judgment concerning its relation to reality. Let us take the example of Sophocles' *Philoctetes*. When the god Heracles appears at the end of the tragedy, his speech, which is a speech of truth, is designated three times by the Greek word *mythos*, whereas the speech of humans has been previously designated by the Greek word *logos*. Thus we see a use that is the inverse of what we would expect, if we judge the meaning of the world in relation to a development that has not yet taken place in tragic poetry. In reality, in tragedy, the two Greek words *mythos* and *logos* are still synonymous, and the choice to use one or the other depends more on considerations of style and rhythm than on semantics. Let us take another very significant example from Aeschylus's *The Persians*. When the queen speaks to the resuscitated Darius and tells him what has happened—the defeat of his son Xerxes—she says: "You will learn all the mythos in a short logos."[2] The mythos in question here is the narrative of the facts that actually happened. Thus there is no opposition between the mythos, which is a mythic narrative, and the logos, which is a historical narrative. It is even a borderline case in which mythos is truly history. And if Aeschylus was able to represent, in a single trilogy, a drama that we call "historical" and two dramas that we would call "mythic," that is probably because the spectators must not yet have seen a radical difference between myth and history.

Therefore in reading the Greek tragic poets we should forget our modern conception of myth, just as we should forget modern medicine to properly understand Hippocrates' medicine. It was especially in the following century that the Greek word *mythos* acquired a pejorative connotation, chiefly under the influence of Plato. The term was probably already tending toward such a meaning in fifth-century prose, particularly in historians who were trying to discover in the past the reality of historical facts. Thucydides, in whose work an adjective derived from *mythos* appears for the first time, namely *mythōdes*, giving it the meaning of "mythic, marvelous." The word appears in the important passage where Thucydides defines his own historical method. He criticizes the poets who tend to inflate and embellish past facts in their songs and historians who seek more to give the reader pleasure than to inform him regarding the truth: "the subjects they treat of being out of the reach of evidence, and time having robbed most of them of historical value by enthroning them in the region of legend . . . (*mythōdos*)."[3]

But at the same time, even as he rejects the mythic, Thucydides recognizes its attraction. He notes that "the way that most men deal with traditions, even traditions of their own country, is to receive them all alike as they are delivered, without applying any critical test whatever."[4] This observation on the ease with which people accept uncritically narratives about the past, made by the man who was the first to apply such a rigorous rationalism to the establishment of past facts, is the most precious testimony we have for judging the way in which Athenian spectators received what we call the mythic subject of tragedies. For them, it was not something fabulous without relation to reality, but the history of ancient times that they accepted as such, because it proceeded from tradition. It is only in this sense that we can speak of myth in tragedy: a narrative belonging to ancient times bequeathed by tradition, whether that tradition was written or oral.[5]

The Great Tragic Families and the Power of Tradition

Thus tradition imposes itself on the tragic author, who takes his subjects from myths that are known to everyone and are drawn from a few great tragic families. "The best tragedies are written about a few families—Alcmeon for instance and Oedipus and Orestes and Meleager and Thyestes and Telephus and all the others whom it befell to suffer or inflict terrible disasters."[6] A little further on he returns to this same idea: "tragedies are about few families."[7]

This way of seeing the tragic myths in the framework of families and not cities, as we now have a tendency to do because of the predominance accorded to politics, should give us pause. Whereas we have a tendency to designate myths by the cities to which they are attached, Argos, Thebes, Troy, Athens, and so on, Aristotle speaks of families. He has a better grasp on the origin of the tragic, which arises from the relations among the members of a family, even if the political dimension is an inherent given in most of these families from the moment that they acquire power in a city. To limit ourselves to the extant tragedies of Sophocles, whereas we speak of the Theban myth (*Oedipus the King, Antigone*), the Argive myth (*Electra*), the Trojan myth (*Ajax, Philoctetes*), and the Attic myth (*Oedipus at Colonus*), not to mention a myth of Trachis (*Women of Trachis*), Aristotle would speak of five great tragic families: that of Oedipus (*Oedipus the King, Antigone, Oedipus at Colonus*), that of Orestes (*Electra*), that of Heracles (*Women of Trachis*), that of Ajax (*Ajax*), and that of Philoctetes (*Philoctetes*). With the exception of the latter, where the hero's isolation is total, all these tragedies present, in addition to the hero or heroine, what would now be called the cast, several members of the family who maintain relations of affection or hatred with the main character. These families are often designated by the name of an ancestor. The Theban family of Oedipus is that of the Labdacids, from the name of Labdacos, Oedipus's grandfather.[8] The family of Orestes and Electra is designated under two names, either the Pelopids, from the name of Pelops, the founder of the family, or, more frequently, the Atreids, from the name of Atreus, one of Pelops's sons, the father of Agamemnon and of Menelaus, and the grandfather of Orestes and Electra.[9]

The history of most of these families was so well known that the tragic authors could not change the most important elements. Let us listen once again to Aristotle:

> It is not right to break up the traditional stories, I mean, for instance, Clytemnestra being killed by Orestes and Eriphyle by Alcmeon.[10]

However, the weight of tradition does not exclude innovation. For Aristotle immediately goes on:

> But the poet must show invention and make a skillful use of the tradition.

Tragic Invention and Comic Invention

Since tragic invention deals with traditional data known to the audience, it is not comparable to comic invention, where the author creates his own subject. The resulting ease in setting forth a tragic subject was mocked by a comic author of the fourth century BCE, Antiphanes. To this ease, he opposes the difficulty faced by the comic author, who has to invent and set forth a new subject:

Tragedy is a marvelous genre
In every regard, for from the outset
its subjects are known to the audience
even before a character opens his mouth, so all
the poet has to do is remind them. If I name Oedipus,
they know all the rest of the story: the father is Laius,
the mother Jocasta, who are his sons and daughters,
what he is going to suffer and what he has done. If
Alcmeon is named, by that very fact they know
all his children, that he killed his mother who'd gone mad
and that Adrastes, outraged, will immediately come, and leave again. . . .
Then when the poets are no longer capable of saying anything
and completely give up in their plays,
they just crank up the theatrical machinery
and for the spectators that is enough.
On the other hand, we don't have those advantages,
We have to invent everything, new names,
the past, the present, the denouement,
the introduction. If any of these points is forgotten
by some Chremes or some Phidon, he is booed,
whereas a Peleus and a Teucer can do anything.[11]

Obviously, there is comic exaggeration in this presentation of the ease of composing a tragedy. But the convergence with Aristotle regarding the conception of
the tragic myth is remarkable. Like the philosopher, the comic author reasons
on the basis of families. On hearing the name of a tragic hero, the spectators'
memory spontaneously recreates the other members of the family.

Moreover, by showing to what extent the audience was aware of the great
tragic families, these two ancient testimonies provide us with an opportunity to
compare the culture of ancient spectators with our own. There is sometimes
convergence, sometimes divergence. Concerning the myths of Oedipus and
Orestes, our culture is comparable. On the contrary, the myth of Alcmeon,
which was just as famous in antiquity as that of Orestes because in both cases a
son killed his mother to avenge his father, is for the modern reader of Greek
tragedies a black hole. The reason is the great disaster mentioned in the prelude
to this part of our study. In fact, although we have preserved tragedies on the
families of Oedipus and Orestes, the tragedies on the family of Alcmeon have,
as the result of an unfortunate accident, totally disappeared.

Convergence between the Mythic Culture of the Spectators of Sophocles' Time and Our Own: The Families of Oedipus and Orestes

From the Oedipus family, which Antiphanes mentions first, we still have three
tragedies by Sophocles. Two tragedies draw their titles from the hero himself,

Oedipus the King and *Oedipus at Colonus*, and the title of a third is the name of his daughter, Antigone. Moreover, like the contemporary Athenian spectators, we know the name of his father, Laius, that of his mother, Jocasta, who was also his wife, those of his sons Eteocles and Polynices, and those of his two daughters, Antigone and Ismene. Several members of this Theban hero's family are characters in these two tragedies: Jocasta appears in *Oedipus the King*,[12] and at the end of that tragedy, when Oedipus leaves the palace after having blinded himself, he hears the weeping of his two daughters, who are present on the stage, and he speaks to them.[13] However, Sophocles doesn't even take the trouble to designate them by name, which confirms the pertinence of Antiphanes' observations. In *Oedipus at Colonus*, which is set many years after *Oedipus the King*, Antigone appears at the beginning with her blind father, whom she guides in his exile; in the middle of the tragedy we see the arrival from Thebes of her sister Ismene, and toward the end, of Oedipus's son Polynices. Finally, in *Antigone*, whose mythic sequence is after that of *Oedipus at Colonus*—since Oedipus is dead, as are his two sons Eteocles and Polynices—his two daughters, Antigone and Ismene, appear at the beginning of the tragedy.

As for the myth of Orestes, which Aristotle mentions immediately after that of Oedipus, its tragic treatment is very well known, because we have the three great tragedies in which Orestes, to avenge his father, Agamemnon, kills his mother, Clytemnestra: Aeschylus's *Libation Bearers*, Sophocles' *Electra*, and Euripides' *Electra*.[14] We can verify what Aristotle says about the impossibility of changing traditional myths. In all these tragedies Orestes kills his mother, and we can add, as another indispensable element, that Orestes kills his mother's lover, Aegisthus.

Thus four of Sophocles' extant tragedies (out of a total of seven) are devoted to these two myths. The selection made by scholars and by chance has thus resulted in our being very well informed about these two tragic families—almost as well informed about them as the contemporary Athenian spectators. We have to say "almost" because several tragedies bearing on these families have been lost. For example, Sophocles also composed a tragedy about Orestes' mother, entitled *Clytemnestra*, and another about his sister Iphigeneia, whom his father, Agamemnon, was obliged to sacrifice to secure the departure of the fleet for Troy.[15]

The Difference between the Mythic Culture of the Spectators in Sophocles' Time and Our Own: The Myth of Alcmeon

In antiquity, the myth of Alcmeon, quoted by both Aristotle and Antiphanes as a great tragic myth, was as popular as that of Orestes. Like Orestes, Alcmeon killed his mother (Eriphyle) to avenge his father, the seer Amphiaraus, who died because of his wife; after this murder he was pursued, like Orestes, by the goddesses of vengeance, the Erinyes, and he went into exile afflicted by madness. The dramatic schema was exactly the same.[16]

All the tragedies about Alcmeon's vengeance have disappeared. Sophocles wrote a play about Alcmeon gone mad after murdering his mother, but there remains only one verse and a half plus two words; he also wrote a play about his father, entitled *Amphiaraus*, and still another about his mother, entitled *Eriphyle*.[17] Thus three of Sophocles' plays bear the names of members of this tragic family. Euripides, for his part, composed two tragedies about Alcmeon at two different points during his exile.[18] Since fifth-century Greek theater cannot be reduced to the three great tragic authors, we have to take into account as well so-called minor authors. The tragic dramatist Agathon, represented by Aristophanes in one of his comedies and a guest in Plato's *Symposium*, composed an *Alcmeon*.[19] If we had complete texts of all these tragedies we would have a much more precise idea of how this myth was represented on the stage.

To get a sense of the richness and complexity of this ancient myth, which was already mentioned allusively by Homer and dealt with in epic poems after Homer but before the age of tragedy,[20] we have to make use not only of the iconography but also of the much more recent testimonies of mythographers and sometimes historians.[21] Let us say simply—and this is already complicated—that Alcmeon was the son of the seer of Argos, Amphiaraus, married to Eriphyle, the sister of the king of Argos, Adrastus. This Argive myth is connected with the Theban myth of the sons of Oedipus; and it is in this guise that it is indirectly present in the extant tragedies. Polynices, having taken refuge in Argos and married one of the king's daughters, plans to organize an expedition to take back power in Thebes, which is in the hands of his brother Eteocles. This expedition, conducted by seven leaders (including Polynices and Adrastus) is known in the theater chiefly through the extant tragedy by Aeschylus entitled *Seven against Thebes*.[22] It is also known, secondarily, through two tragedies by Sophocles that have been preserved: *Oedipus at Colonus*, which is set at the time when the Argive expedition was holding Thebes, and *Antigone*, which begins immediately after the failure of the Argive expedition and the fratricidal battle between Eteocles and Polynices. One of these seven leaders was the seer Amphiaraus. He participated in the expedition under duress. He knew, in fact, through his gift of prophecy, that he was to die during it, as would, moreover, all the other leaders with the sole exception of Adrastus. He was obliged to take part in the expedition because his wife, Eriphyle, had been persuaded by a gold necklace given her by Polynices, her nephew by marriage, the famous necklace of Harmonia. Before leaving, Amphiaraus asked his son Alcmeon to avenge him when he grew up. Ten years later, the sons of the seven Argive leaders, called the Epigoni, left to avenge their fathers on another expedition against Thebes. And Alcmeon, executing his father's orders, killed his mother.

One sign of the notoriety of this vengeance is found in the extant theater of Sophocles. When Electra, in the play of the same name, learns the (false) death of Orestes, the brother she has been waiting for to avenge her father, Agamemnon, killed by her mother, the chorus, which consists of women friends, reminds

her, to console her, of the case of Amphiaraus, which parallels that of
Agamemnon:

> *Chorus:* No, for I know that the prince Amphiaraus was ensnared by a wom-
>   an's chain of gold and swallowed up. And now beneath the earth—
> *Electra:* ah, me, ah, me!
> *Chorus:* —He reigns supreme with the wits of the living.
> *Electra:* ah, me!
> *Chorus:* ah, me, indeed! For the murderess—
> *Electra:* Was slain.
> *Chorus:* Yes.
> *Electra:* I know it; I know it. For a champion arose to avenge the grieving
>   dead. But for me no champion remains: he who yet remained has been
>   snatched clean away.[23]

All it takes is a single proper name, Amphiaraus, and allusions to a woman's
gold necklace and an avenger for the myth to return in all its detail to the mind
of the spectator. Sophocles doesn't even need to give the name of the murderess
or that of the avenger, so well known is the myth to the spectators and so great
is the parallel between the two myths of Alcmeon and Orestes.

The comic author Antiphanes alludes to the same myth of Alcmeon, but to
a later sequence. Struck by madness after murdering his mother, Alcmeon, like
Orestes, goes into exile. That is when he had sons. And contrary to Athenian
spectators who could, according to Antiphanes, name all the sons on hearing the
simple name of Alcmeon, we would find it very hard to call them up from
memory, or even their number. He had five sons by three women! In the course
of his wandering after killing his mother, Eriphyle, Alcmeon had with his first
wife, the daughter of Phegeus, king of Psophis in Arcadia, a son named Clytios;
the latter was later to leave Psophis for Elis after his father's treacherous assassination by the brothers of this first wife. With his second wife, Callirhoe, the daughter of the river Achelous, Alcmeon had two sons, Amphoterus and Acarnan.
Acarnan is the eponymous hero of the region of Greece known as Acarnania.
But we have still not listed "all his children" mentioned by Antiphanes. According to the mythographer Apollodorus, Euripides attributes to Alcmeon two
children whom he sired at the beginning of his madness, before going into
exile. The mother of these children was Manto, the daughter of the Theban seer
Tiresias, whom he had obtained as booty after the Epigoni's expedition. They
had a destiny that was both tragic and romantic. Let us cite the mythographer:

> Euripides says that in the time of his madness Alcmeon begat two children,
> Amphilochus and a daughter Tisiphone, by Manto, daughter of Tiresias, and
> that he brought the babes to Corinth and gave them to Creon, king of Cor-
> inth, to bring up; and that on account of her extraordinary comeliness Tisi-
> phone was sold as a slave by Creon's spouse, who feared that Creon might make

her his wedded wife. But Alcmeon bought her and kept her as a handmaid, not knowing that she was his daughter, and coming to Corinth to get back his children he recovered his son also. And Amphilochus colonized Amphilochian Argos in obedience to the oracles of Apollo.[24]

This simple summary of the Euripidean version that completes the development the mythographer devotes to the tragic story of Alcmeon gives us an idea of the richness of the mythic material that we have lost and that seems to have been well known to spectators, if we believe Antiphanes' testimony. But we can ask whether Antiphanes was not making a sly joke by attributing to spectators such a flawless memory of such a complicated story.

Tragic Myth and Local Reality: Alcmeon's Family and Foundations

All the same, the ancient audiences' familiarity with the myths also comes from the fact that the history that was the subject of Sophocles' tragedies was inserted into the geographical and religious realities of their time. What now appears to us to be a mythic imagination detached from any reality was connected with precise places where the memory of the heroes was concretely present.

Continuing to explore the great tragic family of Alcmeon before returning to the better-known myths of Oedipus or Orestes, we might see in it different ways of anchoring myth in a local reality: myths of foundation or heroic cults.

So far as foundations are concerned, three types are represented by Alcmeon's sons: the foundation of a family, the foundation of a city, and the foundation of a region.

1. The foundation of a family: His son Clytios, to whom Alcmeon's first wife gave birth, and who, as we have seen, left his native city for Elis after the death of his father, founded a family of seers there. We have proof that this myth was in fact part of the social reality of that city. A resident of Elis, a winner at Olympia, is proud to recall, in the inscription commemorating his victory, that he belongs to the illustrious family of the "Clytids with prophetic voices."[25]

2. The foundation of a city: According to Euripides, Amphilochus, the son of Alcmeon and Tiresias's daughter, founded the city of Argos in Amphilochia. This city, situated at the end of the gulf of Ambracia, was undoubtedly much less famous than Argolid Argos in the Peloponnese, which was the site of the tragic family of Agamemnon in part of the tragic tradition[26] and also the homeland of the seer Amphiaraus, the father of Alcmeon. Nonetheless, it was the most powerful city in Amphilochia, a region in the west of continental Greece. To show that this myth of the foundation of a city must have ultimately been considered historical by the spectators of fifth-century tragedies, it suffices to call on the testimony of the historian Thucydides, who presented the history of Amphilochian Argos in relation to an expedition led

by the Athenian strategos Phormion to rescue the city at the beginning of the Peloponnesian War:

> This Argos and the rest of Amphilochia were colonized by Amphilochus, son of Amphiaraus. Dissatisfied with the state of affairs at home on his return thither after the Trojan war, he built this city in the Ambracian gulf, and named it Argos after his own country. This was the largest town in Amphilochia, and its inhabitants the most powerful.[27]

Thucydides, who was not accustomed to report the histories of the founders of cities and whose skepticism regarding mythic narratives we have already noted, presents this foundation of Amphilochian Argos by Amphilochus on the same level as the rest of his account, and thus as history. To be sure, the version set forth by the historian is not exactly the same as that of the tragic author, because according to Thucydides, this Amphilochus was not the grandson of the Argive seer Amphiaraus, but rather his son, and consequently Alcmeon's brother rather than his son. There were thus two different versions, but they are connected with the same family. Is there a difference in nature between these two versions, on the pretext that one is reported by a historian and the other by a man of the theater?

3. The foundation of a region: according to the mythographer Apollodorus, Alcmeon's two sons born of his second marriage, Amphoterus and Acarnan, founded Acarnania. This is another good example showing that Athenian spectators in ancient times did not distinguish between myth and history. A second passage in Thucydides is relevant to this foundation, again in the context of the campaign being waged by the strategos Phormion in the western part of continental Greece. After a geographical description of the Achelous River, which dumps its alluvia into the sea near Oeniadae, as well as several of the Echinades Islands, which are situated across from the river's mouth, Thucydides mentions Alcmeon's exile:

> The islands in question are uninhabited and of no great size. There is also a story that Alcmeon, son of Amphiaraus, during his wanderings after the murder of his mother was bidden by Apollo to inhabit this spot, through an oracle which intimated that he would have no release from his terrors until he should find a country to dwell in which had not been seen by the sun; or existed as land at the time he slew his mother; all else being to him polluted ground. Perplexed at this, the story goes on to say, he at last observed this deposit of the Achelous, and considered that a place sufficient to support life upon, might have been thrown up during the long interval that had elapsed since the death of his mother and the beginning of his wanderings. Settling, therefore, in the district round Oeniadae, he founded a dominion, and left the country its name from his son Acarnan. Such is the story we have received concerning Alcmeon.[28]

This narrative about Alcmeon's exile after the murder of his mother, Eriphyle, is of exactly the same order as the myth of a tragedy. The murderer had to go into exile, fearing the Erinyes. He sought to put an end to the pollution resulting from his crime by consulting the oracle of Delphi, who gave him an answer that was enigmatic, but clear enough to allow him to find the place where he was to settle. Thucydides does add that this was a traditional story, but he considered it worth reporting. If a mind as rigorous as that of the historian takes myth into account, how could the Athenian audience of the tragedies not do the same? Geographical reality strengthens the belief in the myth. Ultimately, two major regions of western Greece west of the Achelous owe their names to two members of the family of the seer of Argos, Amphiaraus: Amphilochus gave his name to Amphilochia (whether this Amphilochus was the son or the grandson of Amphiaraus), and Acarnan, the son of Alcmeon, gave his name to Acarnania.

Tragic Myth and Local Reality: Alcmeon's Family and the Heroic Cults

But it could be objected that this geography is very distant for an Athenian spectator, and that it could hardly increase familiarity with the myth. It is here that we will discover a new dimension of the local implantation of the myths of tragedy. Tragic heroes are related to the local geography not only by the cities they may have founded (foundation myths), but also by the places where they died and where they may be the object of a cult (heroic cults).

First of all, Alcmeon, the victim of an ambush by his first wife's brothers, died in Psophis, on the upper reaches of the Erymanthos River, where he was buried. In the second century CE Pausanias was still able to see his tomb there. He describes it before recalling the myth. The tomb was distinguished neither by its height nor by its decoration, but it was surrounded by gigantic cypresses that were not trimmed because they were dedicated to the deceased.

If this tomb was not necessarily known to all Athenians, the same is not true for the sanctuary dedicated to his father, Amphiaraus, after he died in Boeotia. We know that the seer—presented at length in the famous shields scene in Aeschylus's *Seven against Thebes*, where his wisdom contrasts with the pride of the other Argive leaders—was swallowed up by the earth, along with his chariot, during the siege of Thebes.[29] Not far from the place where he disappeared, a sanctuary was built, where Amphiaraus was deified. It is near Oropos, in the border region between Boeotia and Attica. This sanctuary developed later than the tragic myth; it dates mainly from the fourth century. But the Athenians who went there, among other places, to be cured by Amphiaraus, who had become a healing god, found in it the confirmation of the myth. They were able to admire the great altar divided into parts reserved for the gods or particular heroes.[30] Some are clearly related to the history of the family: on the side of the father,

Amphiaraus, there is the son Amphilochus, the one who, according to Thucydides, founded Amphilochian Argos. His other, more famous son, Alcmeon, is not represented, because he was impure after having killed his mother. But his myth is perhaps not totally absent. Among the divinities worshipped on one of the parts of the altar is the River Achelous. It was the river god that purified him and gave him his daughter in marriage, who bore him two children. The religious reality of a famous sanctuary on the borders of Attica was thus in accord with the myth.

To conclude our discussion of the family of Alcmeon, let us add that in Athens there was also an altar to Amphilochus, Alcmeon's brother.[31] Thus one of the members of the Argive family whom the tragic authors Sophocles and Euripides had represented at the theater of Dionysus in the fifth century, and whom Aeschylus's descendant Astydamas continued to represent onstage in the fourth century,[32] had a cult presence even in Athens! The Athenian religious reality could only reinforce belief in this Argive myth.

Tragic Myth and Athenian Reality: The Myths of Orestes and Oedipus

Despite the multiplicity of places connected with Alcmeon's tragic destiny, his wanderings never put him in direct contact with Athens. On the contrary, the exiles of Orestes and Oedipus took them to Athens, one to be put on trial there, and the other to die there.

The use of this anchorage in reality may, however, vary from one tragic author to the next. Whereas the myth of Orestes was inserted into Athenian reality by Aeschylus and Euripides, insofar as the hero is tried for matricide before the tribunal of the Areopagus,[33] Sophocles ends the tragedy in which Orestes has completed his vengeance, namely his *Electra*, without the slightest allusion to his madness or his judgment by the tribunal.[34] So we will leave aside the Athenian version of the myth of Orestes in order to attend to the myth of Oedipus, because it is Sophocles who gives the fullest expression to the heroization of the Theban hero on Athenian territory.

In his *Oedipus at Colonus* Sophocles departs from Homer by having Oedipus die outside Thebes. In Homer, Oedipus, having probably died in battle, was buried in Thebes, where funeral games were held in his honor.[35] But Sophocles chose to dramatize a local version of the myth connected with the existence of a tomb of Oedipus in Attica. He situates it a few kilometers from the Acropolis, in the countryside outside the walls, at Colonos Hippios, the place where he was born. In this tragedy about the heroization of an Oedipus who, after a long exile, has come back to die in an Athenian deme, Athens is constantly present through its personages and its landscapes.

In actuality, two places in Attica must have claimed the tomb of Oedipus at one time or another. When Pausanias visited the region in the second century CE, it was not at Colonus that he saw Oedipus's tomb, but rather in the city of

Athens itself. It was precisely at the foot of the north flank of the areopagus, inside the sanctuary the Venerables, that is, the Eumenides (or Erinyes). Here is what he says about it:

> Within the precincts is a monument to Oedipus, whose bones, after diligent inquiry, I found were brought from Thebes. The account of the death of Oedipus in the drama of Sophocles I am prevented from believing by Homer, who says that after the death of Oedipus Mecisteus came to Thebes and took part in the funeral games.[36]

Reaching Colonus next, Pausanias returns to the myth of Oedipus, but he speaks simply of a heroic sanctuary and not of a tomb:

> There is also pointed out a place called the Hill of Horses, the first point in Attica, they say, that Oedipus reached—this account too differs from that given by Homer, but it is nevertheless current tradition—and an altar to Poseidon, Horse God, and to Athena, Horse Goddess, and a chapel to the heroes Peirithous and Theseus, Oedipus and Adrastus. The grove and temple of Poseidon were burnt by Antigonus when he invaded Attica, who at other times also ravaged the land of the Athenians.[37]

Between Homer's and Sophocles' versions of the death of Oedipus, Pausanias does not hesitate: he chooses Homer. His problem is only how to resolve the contradiction between the burial of Oedipus in Thebes, attested by Homer, and the presence of his tomb in Athens. He states that he has undertaken an in-depth investigation, from which it results that Oedipus died in Thebes, but his bones were transported to Athens. However, despite his effort to be precise, Pausanias overlooks another problem, that of the exact location of the tomb in Attica. He has not resolved the contradiction between what he says and what Sophocles says in his *Oedipus at Colonus*, for in that tragedy, Oedipus's tomb is not inside the walls of Athens, but outside them, in Colonus. Now, Sophocles could hardly claim Oedipus's tomb for the deme where he was born (surrounding with a certain mystery the exact spot where it was located)[38] if the spectators knew that it was in Athens, in the sanctuary of the Erinyes, not far from the theater of Dionysus. Despite the malleability of the myth, Sophocles cannot have invented or deformed a local version. If that is so, then the tomb Pausanias was shown in the sanctuary of the Erinyes must have been a more recent creation, probably through an assimilation of two sanctuaries dedicated to the same goddesses, the urban sanctuary in Athens and the rural sanctuary in Colonus.[39]

Moreover, this local version of the death of Oedipus at Colonus is not peculiar to Sophocles. It is also attested in Euripides' *Phoenician Women*, a tragedy performed a few years before Sophocles' play. At the end of the *Phoenician Women*, Oedipus, ready to leave Thebes and go into exile with Antigone, tells her that the oracle of Delphi will be fulfilled: after having wandered, he will die on Athenian soil, precisely at Colonus, the residence of Poseidon Hippios.[40] This coincidence between Euripides and Sophocles has caused much ink to flow.

Some have wanted to see in the end of Euripides' tragedy the source of Sophocles' inspiration. But did Sophocles need a literary source to think about what he had known since he was a child? Others have wanted to see in the passage at the end of the *Phoenician Women* an addition made after Euripides' death and inspired by Sophocles' tragedy, what is called an "actors' interpolation." However, relating the tragic myth to a local religious reality is characteristic of Euripides.[41]

In reality, the convergence between the two tragedies by two authors who knew the local traditions perfectly confirms that in the fifth century the tomb of Oedipus that the Athenians claimed was located in their city was in fact situated in Colonus and not, as in the time of Pausanias, in the sanctuary of the Erinyes in Athens. If there is a domain where the tragic author is not at liberty to change a mythic tradition, it is certainly the religious reality, which the Athenian spectators were capable of checking.[42] The anchoring of a myth in local reality does not, however, prevent several places from being able to claim the tomb of a single hero. A variant of the myth, not attested in the tragedy, mentions a place other than Thebes or Colonus for Oedipus's tomb, namely the Boeotian city of Eteonos.[43]

Tragic Myth and Time: The Two Great Wars of the Age of Heroes

Tragic myth is not situated in space alone; it is also situated in time. Although the tragic families belong to a distant past, history is organized less loosely than people think, in a development in which events are placed in a chronology that is relative, calculated by the number of generations, sometimes by years, and even by days. This traditional chronology is obviously not peculiar to the tragic poets. It goes back to the epic.

The tragic families are part of the age of heroes that Hesiod placed in the myth of races, after the golden, silver, and bronze races and before the current race, that of iron. Two great military exploits mark this period, which Hesiod describes this way:

> Grim war and dread battle destroyed a part of them, some in the land of Cadmus at seven-gated Thebes when they fought for the flocks of Oedipus, and some, when it had brought them in ships over the great sea gulf to Troy for rich-haired Helen's sake: there death's end enshrouded a part of them.[44]

Hesiod begins by referring to the war that owes its name to the seven leaders who attacked the seven gates of Thebes, the cause of which was Oedipus's heritage, poetically represented here by the flocks. Hesiod's allusive style supposes that the myth has been well known since time immemorial. He does not need to mention the quarrel between Oedipus's two sons, Eteocles and Polynices, the latter's exile, or the expedition he organized in Argos to reconquer power. Then

Hesiod turns to the expedition to Troy, which arose from the abduction of Helen by the Trojan Alexander-Paris, Priam's son, leading to a war that was the subject of great epics, only two of which have been preserved: the *Iliad*, devoted to a sequence of the battles, from the wrath of Achilles to the death of Hector, and the *Odyssey*, one of the epics about the tragic return of the survivors after the Trojan War.

The Relative Chronology of These Two Great Wars: One Generation Apart

The order in which Hesiod discusses these two wars is not an accident. In fact, they did not take place in the same period. They are separated by a generation. Several passages in the *Iliad*, although distant from one another and concerning different persons, provide very clear indications of this fact.

During the boxing contest that took place in connection with the funeral games in honor of Patrocles, Homer presents the only warrior who dared to challenge the indisputable champion, Epeius. He is Euryalus, an Argive leader and the son of Mecisteus. This Mecisteus "had come to Thebes for the burial of Oedipus, when he had fallen, and there had worsted all the sons of Cadmus."[45] This passage is generally used to say that Oedipus, according to Homer, died at Thebes. And it is in fact to these verses that Pausanias is referring when he opposes, as we have seen, Homer's and Sophocles' versions of Oedipus's death.[46] But this passage is also instructive regarding the relative chronology of myths. The death of Oedipus precedes the Trojan War by one generation, since Euryalus's father Mecisteus took part in the games in honor of Oedipus, whereas Euryalus himself took part in the games in honor of Patrocles, who died during the Trojan War.

As for the famous war of the Seven against Thebes fought over "Oedipus's flocks," it too took place one generation before the Trojan War. Let us return to Euryalus's boxing match. He was knocked out, defeated pitifully. But he had as an ardent supporter the supreme chief of the Argive contingent, "the son of Tydeus," that is, Diomedes. Now, who was Tydeus? He was precisely one of the seven leaders of the expedition against Thebes.[47] Thus one generation separates this Theban war from the Trojan War. The difference in time is such that Tydeus's son never knew his father, who left too soon for the war from which he never returned.[48] Even Agamemnon, the leader of expedition against Troy, did not meet Tydeus, but he heard about his exploits during the Argive expedition against Thebes.[49]

The Two Theban Wars and the Two Trojan Wars

The history of this period, which spans two generations that accomplished exploits and often suffered a tragic fate in wars, is in reality a little more complex than Hesiod suggests. During the first generation, there was a first Trojan war, and during the second generation, a second Theban war.

We know that the war of the Seven against Thebes resulted in the War of the Epigoni, in which the sons of the Seven returned to Thebes to avenge their fathers.[50] Thus this expedition took place in the same generation as the Trojan War. In fact, the sons of these leaders are present in Troy: not only Diomedes son of Tydeus, but also Sthenelus son of Capaneus.[51] Can these two expeditions be situated in accord with a relative chronology? Here again Homer is astonishingly precise. Sthenelus, son of Capaneus, present at Troy, alludes to the expedition of the sons who succeeded in taking Thebes, the city with seven gates, where their fathers had failed. Thus the second expedition against Thebes occurred shortly before the Trojan War.[52]

Just as there were two expeditions against Thebes, there were two against Troy. What we call the Trojan War was in reality a second war. One generation earlier, an initial expedition was conducted by Heracles against Troy. Again, it is Homer who gives us a relative chronology. Confronting Sarpedon, an enemy from Lycia, Tlepolemus, the head of the contingent from the island of Rhodes, points out that his father Heracles destroyed Troy because its king, Laomedon, Priam's father, refused him the horses he had promised him in exchange for a favor.[53] This first expedition was much more modest, since Heracles came with only six ships and a small number of warriors. However, it was more efficacious, since Heracles destroyed the city and widowed its streets.

According to Tlepolemus the reason for this efficacy is that the preceding generation was that of the true heroes who were sons of Zeus.[54] His father Heracles was in fact Zeus's son. Thus it is strange to note that a hero of the Trojan War felt that the generation that preceded him was more heroic. We have an analogous impression when the aged Nestor refers to the lost heroes of the preceding generation, whom he considers better, citing among them the king of Athens, Theseus,[55] one of the figures whom we will find in Greek tragedy and in particular, to limit ourselves to Sophocles, in *Oedipus at Colonus*.

Thus in this age of heroes that Hesiod sees as a whole, Homer draws a finer distinction between two generations: as a rule, the sons who take part in the Trojan War see more heroism in the preceding generation, that of their fathers who participated in the war of Seven against Thebes or the first expedition against Troy.[56]

Homeric Chronology and Tragic Chronology

The Greek tragic poets respected this chronology of the myth by generations that we have seen in the epic.

In both Sophocles and Homer a generation separates the two expeditions to Troy. In his *Ajax*, Sophocles made use of a situation analogous to that Homer describes. Just as Tlepolemus, fighting at Troy, refers in the past tense to the first expedition led by his father, Heracles, so Ajax, also fighting at Troy, refers to the participation of his father, Telamon, in the first expedition. Here is how Ajax, who has just understood his mad act—he has massacred animals thinking he was massacring the leaders on whom he wanted to take revenge because they unjustly deprived him of Achilles' arms—draws a parallel between his fate and that of his father:

> I am one whose father's prowess won him the fairest prize of all the army, whose father brought every glory home from this same land of Ida; but I, his son, who came after him to this same ground of Troy with no less might and proved the service of my hand in no meaner deeds, I am ruined as you see by dishonor from the Greeks. And yet of this much I feel sure: if Achilles lived, and had been called to award the first place in valor to any claimant of his arms, no one would have grasped them before me. But now the Atreids have made away with them to a man without scruples and thrust away the triumphs of Ajax.[57]

In Sophocles' tragedy, as in the *Iliad*, the warriors of the young generation are haunted by the comparison with the heroic conduct of their fathers. Telamon had won the prize for bravery for having been the first to enter Troy during the expedition led by Heracles.[58] But the tragic author, while adopting the Homeric theme of the comparison of generations, also renews it. For Ajax, unlike Tlepolemus, does not recognize his father's superiority. The younger generation, in the tragic perspective, is no less heroic than the preceding one. What emerges from the comparison of the father with the son is the injustice of the fate reserved for the son compared to that of his father. Whereas the father received the reward corresponding to his bravery—that is, Hesione, the daughter of the king of Troy—the son was deprived by the Atreids of the honor that his heroic conduct deserved, Achilles' arms. From one generation to the next, it is not the decline of heroism that emerges but rather that of the recognition of heroic values.

Sophocles' Tragedies Prior to the Trojan War: A Relative Chronology of the Sequences of the Oedipus Myth

The relative chronology of Sophocles' extant tragedies can be understood in two ways: either by the relative date of composition—and we have seen the degree of indetermination that prevents us from arriving at a strict classification—or by the relative date of the myth dramatized. In order to properly situate a tragedy in Sophocles' work and in the mythic imagination, we need to keep in mind this twofold meaning of "relative chronology."

Let us take the three tragedies related to the myth of Oedipus. In all likelihood, Sophocles composed them in the following order: *Antigone, Oedipus the King, Oedipus at Colonus*. But in the order of the mythic events, even though all three are prior to the Trojan War, the sequence dramatized in *Oedipus the King* precedes that of *Oedipus at Colonus*, which precedes *Antigone*. In fact, *Oedipus the King* begins when Oedipus is still the triumphant king, the man who has obtained the throne of Thebes for having delivered the city from the ravages of a monster, the Sphinx, by solving its enigma. However, he has to confront another scourge that has struck Thebes, and his efforts to put an end to it are this time to cause him to discover his own enigma, the murder of his father, the marriage to his mother, bringing into the world children who are also his brothers and sisters, a discovery that leads to his downfall, his blinding, and his desire to go into exile.

In the logical order of events, the sequence of *Oedipus at Colonus* follows after an extended interruption corresponding to the long duration of an exile. Sophocles seems to want to establish a continuity between the two tragedies or to attenuate the discordances. For example, he takes care to explain why the exile desired at the end of *Oedipus the King* has become an exile endured at the beginning of *Oedipus at Colonus*.[59] In the tragedy we will see not the passage from happiness to unhappiness, as in *Oedipus the King*, in accord with the most classic schema of Greek tragedy, but the inverse movement, the progressive rehabilitation of the old Theban, blind and exiled, his insertion, by means of supplication, into a new hospitable city, Athens, represented by its king, Theseus. We also witness Oedipus's heroization in the religious sense of the term, in Sophocles' native land, where his tomb will become that of a hero protecting against any Theban invasion. The mythic chronology of this tragedy is established precisely by reference to the expedition of the Seven against Thebes. The action takes place at the time of the siege of Thebes by the army of Argos,[60] before the assault, at the time when the two parties facing each other come to negotiate an alliance with Oedipus: first Creon, in the name of the Thebans and their leader Eteocles, and then Polynices himself, in the name of the whole army of Argos and its leaders—but in vain, despite the use of violence by one and supplication by the other.[61]

The mythic sequence dealt with in *Antigone* follows that of *Oedipus at Colonus*, though we need not suppose that there is a long interval between them. *Antigone* begins the day after the decisive battle that was won by the Thebans, but in the course of which the two brothers Eteocles and Polynices killed each other. It opens with a scene between Antigone and Ismene. Now, at the end of *Oedipus at Colonus*, Oedipus entrusts his daughters to Theseus, and after his death Antigone asks Theseus to send her and her sister back to Thebes so that they can try to stop the murder of their two brothers.[62] Theseus agrees to have them taken there. Thus little time needs to have elapsed between the two tragedies, just enough for Polynices to rejoin the attackers below the walls of Thebes, for his two sisters to return to the palace at Thebes, and for the assault on the city to take place during the night that precedes the beginning of *Antigone*. The connection between the two mythic sequences is all the better managed because in *Oedipus at Colonus* Polynices asks his sisters to ensure his own burial in the event that his father's curses are fulfilled, and this is precisely the main subject of *Antigone*.[63]

From the point of view of the myth, the continuity between the three tragedies seems so satisfying that it is tempting to speak of a trilogy. But that would be misleading, because there remains a great difference between a genuine trilogy composed of three tragedies meant to be performed in a single competition, like Aeschylus's *Oresteia*, and three tragedies dealing with the same myth that were performed in different competitions and in an order that does not necessarily correspond to the chronology of the myth. *Oedipus the King* and *Oedipus at Colonus* are sequential both in the order of composition and in the order of their subjects. On the other hand, it is certain that *Antigone*, which follows *Oedipus at Colonus* from the point of view of the mythic sequence, was composed long before. Thus what could be seen, in *Oedipus at Colonus*, as a foreshadowing of what will occur in *Antigone* according to the time of the myth is in fact only an allusion to a tragedy performed in the past.

In contrast to a true trilogy, each tragedy is thus only one part of a triptych, but it constitutes, like a painter's picture, an independent whole having its own dramatic logic, despite the continuity of the mythic sequences; and the same characters are not necessarily dealt with in the same way in all the tragedies.[64] The version of the myth chosen can even change. Thus there is a major divergence between the death of Oedipus in *Antigone* and his death in *Oedipus at Colonus*. In the first scene of *Antigone*, Oedipus's daughter speaks of the death of her father, who "perished in hatred and infamy,"[65] and toward the end of the tragedy, which is set in Thebes, she mentions that she herself buried her father, as she had her mother.[66] Thus when Sophocles wrote his *Antigone* nothing suggested what makes his *Oedipus at Colonus* original, namely a glorious death of Oedipus outside Thebes, after a long exile.

It is true that the allusions to Oedipus's death are fleeting in *Antigone*, and that about forty years elapsed between the performances of the two tragedies.

The Tragedies Whose Subjects Precede the Trojan War: The Myth of Heracles

In addition to the three tragedies about the myth of Oedipus, a fourth, among the seven that remain to us, is situated before the Trojan War: the one whose protagonist is Heracles. In fact, we have seen that Heracles undertook a first war against the Troy of Laomedon, Priam's father, and that one of his sons, Tlepolemus, was among the warriors in the *Iliad*.[67] The tragedy about him is entitled *Women of Trachis*: it owes its title to the chorus of young women of Trachis, the city where the drama takes place, situated at the foot of Mount Oeta, not far from Thermopylae.

However, this tragedy contains neither an explicit relative chronological indication with regard to the Trojan War, as is the case in the *Iliad*, nor an implicit one, as in *Ajax*. The first expedition against Troy is not one of the exploits of Heracles mentioned in the course of the tragedy. The legend of Heracles, the son of Zeus and the mortal Alcmena, is known above all through the many works accomplished in the service of others, and notably Eurystheus,[68] which kept him away from his home and his wife, the Etolian Deianira, daughter of Oeneus, to whom he sometimes returned to sire children.[69] Sophocles chose the final sequence, the hero's death after a victorious expedition. The death of Heracles is already mentioned in the *Iliad*. It is Achilles who refers to it when he accepts the idea of the death that awaits him once he has avenged Patrocles by killing Hector:

> For not even the mighty Heracles escaped death, albeit he was most dear to Zeus, son of Cronos, the king, but fate overcame him, and the dread wrath of Hera.[70]

This simple allusion to Heracles' death in Homer gives us no indication regarding its precise circumstances. Its cause is already a woman's jealousy, but it is the goddess Hera, Zeus's wife, who pursues with her hate a son born outside marriage.[71] In Sophocles' work, Heracles dies on returning from a victorious expedition to Oechalia, in Euboea, against the king of that city, Eurytus: he dies because of the jealousy of his wife, Deianira, who could not accept his returning with a captive woman, Iole.[72]

The tragedy's sequence includes analogies with a mythic sequence that is much better known but chronologically later, since it follows the Trojan War: Agamemnon, back from his victorious expedition to Troy, with his captive Cassandra, will be put to death by his wife Clytemnestra. Sophocles was aware of the analogy between the two situations, because in *Women of Trachis*, as in Aeschylus's *Agamemnon*, we witness a comparable scene in which the wife receives the captive woman, her rival, who has to enter the palace: the woman addresses her rival, but the rival does not respond.[73] However, this analogy is there the better to bring out the differences. Deianira is in fact the reverse of Clytemnestra. She kills out of love, whereas Clytemnestra kills out of hate. Deianira kills without knowing it, whereas Clytemnestra kills by trickery. Deianira's crime is not in fact a crime of passion in the traditional sense of the term. It is the tragic act par excellence, in which the heroine causes the opposite of what she wanted, the death of the dear one whose love she wanted to win back. She has him sent as a gift a tunic coated with a balm that she believes is a magic philter. It turns out to be a poisoned gift in the true sense of the term. As soon as Heracles puts the tunic on, the poison irremediably eats away his body. Deianira has been, in spite of herself, the instrument of a dead man's vengeance on Heracles. This balm had been treacherously given her by an unsuccessful rival who was dying from an arrow shot by Heracles. Thus Deianira's act had intentions opposite to those of Clytemnestra. The consequences were also opposed: after murdering Agamemnon Clytemnestra expresses her joy;[74] Deianira, learning from her son Hyllos the effect the poison has had on Heracles, leaves in silence to commit suicide.[75] *Women of Trachis* is first of all the tragedy of Deianira, who will die before seeing her husband again. Then comes the tragedy of Heracles, who appears borne on a litter, suffering from the pain of the poison that is devouring him and his anger at his wife whom he believes to be his murderer, before he discovers the vengeance taken on him by the centaur Nessos. He then tells his son his last wishes: to be cremated at the summit of Mount Oeta, winning, at the end of the tragedy, a last victory over a last monster, pain, at the time that he is led toward a death worthy of his heroic life. Sophocles remains very discreet regarding the heroization that this death will constitute. Nothing is expressly said concerning his life as an Immortal on Olympus, where, already according to the *Odyssey*,

> among the immortal gods [he] takes his joy in the feast, and has to wife Hebe,
> of the fair ankles, daughter of great Zeus and of Here, of the golden sandals.[76]

Sophocles, who was later to deal with the heroization of Oedipus in *Oedipus at Colonus*, wanted to preserve a human dimension in his tragedy, perhaps out of respect for Deianira.[77] In the choice of the mythic material a tragic author makes, silences are also revealing.

Nonetheless, Heracles reappears in all his divine splendor at the end of another of Sophocles' tragedies that was composed after *Women of Trachis* and whose mythic sequence dates from the following generation: *Philoctetes*. Philoctetes is connected with the myth of Heracles, because it is he who lit Heracles' funeral pyre on Mount Oeta. And as a reward he inherited Heracles' infallible bow. This development of the myth is not explicit in *Women of Trachis*. However, it is already present negatively at the end of the tragedy. When Heracles asks his son Hyllus to take him to the highest summit of Oeta, where there is a sanctuary of his father, Zeus, to build a funeral pyre and set it on fire, Hyllus cries out and does not want to become his father's murderer by lighting the pyre, to which his father replies: "If you fear that, at least perform the rest."[78] This answer leaves room for the myth of Philoctetes, who will light the pyre. Here too, silence is revealing.

The Tragedies about Troy: *Ajax* and *Philoctetes*

Although they belong to the Trojan War material, the tragedies *Ajax* and *Philoctetes* do not correspond to the same mythic sequence as the *Iliad*. They are chronologically later. And when we compare the two tragedies with each other, it seems that the mythic sequence of *Ajax* is earlier than that of *Philoctetes*.

In the *Iliad*, Homer takes as his subject the war from the quarrel between Achilles and Agamemnon to the death of Hector by Achilles' hand. Now, the origin of Sophocles' *Ajax* is the death of Achilles and the decision regarding the question as to whom his arms should be awarded. Being the best warrior after Achilles, Ajax, son of Telamon, thought the arms should be given to him. However, in a judgment that Ajax thinks was warped by intrigues involving the two heads of the army, Agamemnon and Menelaus,[79] the arms are awarded to Odysseus. In Sophocles, Ajax's anger against Odysseus and against the two Atreids mirrors Achilles' anger against Agamemnon in Homer. But whereas Achilles withdrew into solitude and inaction, Ajax meditated in solitude and then acted. He went off at night, sword in hand, to kill Odysseus and the two leaders. However, just when he was about to carry out his vengeance, the goddess Athena engulfed him in an access of madness and led him to attack the army's livestock. Ajax massacred part of it on the spot, thinking he was killing the two Atreids, and took part of it with him, thinking he had taken Odysseus prisoner. Sophocles' tragedy begins the next morning, with Odysseus looking for the person guilty of the massacre. It continues with the triumphant joy of an Ajax still prey to his madness, and then his awakening and the painful recognition of his dishonor and of the punishment inflicted by Athena.[80] It culminates in Ajax's suicide, far from everyone, and with the discovery of his body by his captive Tecmessa and her brother, Teucer. The tragedy ends with bitter debates concerning his body, which has become the stake in a struggle: the two Atreids successively forbid Teucer to bury a traitor, but the arrival of Odysseus, who had nonetheless been Ajax's rival, resolves the situation. Odysseus pays homage to the dead man's courage and finally persuades the king to allow his burial.

The sequence in *Philoctetes* is necessarily later than that of *Ajax*, because in the course of the action Philoctetes learns of the death of Achilles and then of that of Ajax.[81] At the beginning of the tragedy, Odysseus and Achilles' son Neoptolemus arrive, sent on mission by the Achaeans' army that has been besieging Troy for ten years without success. They have come to find Philoctetes, whom they abandoned on the island of Lemnos as they were sailing toward Troy. Here is how Odysseus explains this abandonment: Philoctetes was afflicted with an ulcer that was eating away his foot, and his cries of pain prevented the proper accomplishment of religious ceremonies.[82] What led the Achaeans to take a new interest in the son of Poeas, whom they had left for such a long time in a lonely place where he survived only thanks to his courage and his bow inherited from Heracles?[83] It was a prophecy made by the Trojans' seer, Helenus, who had been captured by Odysseus: Troy could not be taken without the help of Philoctetes with his bow and his collaboration with the son of Achilles.[84] But the spectator discovers the content of this prophecy only gradually, in the course of the tragedy. The mission is dangerous precisely because Philoctetes, despite his infirmity, has a bow with infallible arrows. Odysseus, not being able to act directly for fear of being recognized, orders Neoptolemus to win Philoctetes' confidence by trickery, which is contrary to the nature of Achilles' son. The tragedy consists first of the development of the plan to trick Philoctetes: a dramatic turnabout makes this easier, since Philoctetes' pain forces him to hand over his bow to Neoptolemus; but immediately afterward another turnabout hinders the plan: Neoptolemus's conscience forces him first to tell Philoctetes the truth, and then finally to give his bow back to him, despite Odysseus's opposition, all this culminating in a spectacular scene in which Philoctetes draws his bow against Odysseus, who beats a hasty retreat without saying a word. After the final failure of Odysseus's plan of trickery, Neoptolemus, who has now become Philoctetes' friend, tries to persuade him to leave for Troy. However, Philoctetes remains intransigent, and the mission would be jeopardized without the final appearance of a deity, Heracles, the bow's former possessor, who convinces Philoctetes to go to Troy, where he will first be healed by Asclepius, the god of medicine, and then win glory by fighting with the son of Achilles to conquer Troy.

A Tragedy after the Trojan War: *Electra*

The last of Sophocles' extant tragedies, if we follow the chronology of the myth, is his *Electra*. The action is supposed to have taken place several years after the Trojan War—six years after, according to Homer. But in the tragedy, the time Electra spends weeping over the death of her father Agamemnon and waiting for her brother Orestes to return to avenge the murder of the man whom her mother and her lover Aegisthus killed with an axe, "just as woodmen chop an oak,"[85] is a more subjective time: it is a large part of her life spent in the solitude of a hostile milieu,[86] the permanence of mourning, the eternity of waiting.

The subject of the tragedy belongs to the category of myths relating to the returns of the heroes after the Trojan War. Whereas the expedition leaving for Troy voyaged together from Aulis onward, the returns from Troy took place ten years later in a scattered order, some warriors choosing to travel by sea, as they had before, and others preferring to travel by land. And the fortunes of the heroes were diverse: some returned directly without problems, others died on the way, and still others reached their homes after a long detour. Those who reached their homelands also had differing fates: most resumed a normal life without difficulty, but one hero, Odysseus, had to win back his power by trickery and force, while another, Agamemnon, was the victim of the trickery of those who had remained behind.

The subject of the tragedy is the vengeance of Orestes after the murder of Agamemnon by Aegisthus and Clytemnestra, or rather this vengeance as experienced by Electra, because as the title of the tragedy indicates, she has become the main character, eclipsing Orestes. It is true that Orestes is the character the audience sees first, accompanied by Pylades and the tutor who has saved him and accompanied him in his exile; and it is the plan for revenge that is first set forth in this inaugural scene. The plan of action had to be established first, a revenge that will be carried out exactly according to plan. But from that point on, it is Electra who occupies the spotlight, first alone, and then confronted successively by her friends, the women in the chorus, her sister Chrysosthemis, and then, in a long sequence, by her enemy, her mother Clytemnestra. We are already almost at the midpoint of the tragedy. It is then that the vengeance begins to be carried out, in two phases: first the arrival of the tutor, in disguise, announcing the false death of Orestes in a chariot race in Delphi and then returning to the palace, then the arrival of Orestes, bringing with him an urn containing the ashes of the alleged dead man. Each time, Electra is there, lamenting the death of her brother and then the disappearance of the avenger, until she joyfully recognizes him. And when the tutor reminds the two young people that it is time to act, we are almost at the end of the tragedy. The execution of the vengeance takes place in record time: first the murder of the mother, then Aegisthus's return; the end comes so quickly that the tragedy is over before the second murder. Everything is centered on Electra.

From the Relative Chronology of Myth to the History of the Myth: The Example of the Myth of Oedipus

The mythic material from which tragic authors draw the sequence that they choose to dramatize is thus situated in accord with a relative chronology. Every tragic sequence of the myth is situated in the history of a tragic family and in the more general history of the great events constituted by wars between cities or the great catastrophes that strike cities independently of one another. This definition holds for all the extant tragedies of Sophocles. Thus we must rid ourselves of the notion that Greek mythology is an imaginary world situated outside time.

But each tragic myth also has its history. From Homer on, or more generally from epic poetry to tragic poetry by way of lyric poetry, myths were able to evolve and diversify.

One of the most striking examples is the case of Oedipus. As we have seen, in the *Iliad* he dies in battle and is buried with honor in Thebes, since his funeral was accompanied by games in which Mecisteus, Euryalus's father, participated, while Euryalus himself participated in the funeral games for Patroclus.[87] The point of mentioning this in the *Iliad* is to establish a correspondence between the two generations of the age of heroes, the past generation, that of Oedipus and the Seven against Thebes, and the present generation, that of Agamemnon and the Trojan War. The funeral games in honor of Patroclus, Achilles' friend who died heroically in battle, are thus implicitly compared to the games in honor of Oedipus in the preceding generation. Despite the brevity of this allusion to Oedipus, it is clear that the version popularized by tragedy, and particularly by Sophocles at the end of his *Oedipus the King* and the beginning of his *Oedipus at Colonus*, that of an Oedipus who blinded himself before going into exile, is completely unknown in the *Iliad*'s version, which is the oldest version of the myth available to us. And even if the *Odyssey*'s version, which is probably more recent, is much closer to that of tragedy, insofar as it mentions the murder of the father, the marriage with the mother, and the mother's suicide, it nonetheless remains that Oedipus continued, in spite of everything, to reign over Thebes after the death of the woman who was both his mother and his wife.[88] Thus there is no contradiction between the *Iliad*'s version and that of the *Odyssey* regarding Oedipus's destiny after the discovery of his twofold crime. He did not leave Thebes for exile, and nothing is said about his blinding.[89] On the other hand, Oedipus's destiny became more moving in tragedy: the laws of the genre required it.[90]

Thus myth, history transmitted by a tradition that was initially oral and later written, also has its history, which is perceptible for us through the literary redevelopment of it that took place from the eighth century, the date of Homer, down to the fifth century, the date of tragedy.

This historical perspective on the evolution of myth in the course of transmission is often obscured in the presentation of Greek myths, because the syntheses of the mythographers of the Roman period are taken as the basis. To be sure, they have the merit of organizing in a coherent way the abundant material of the Greek myths, but they have the disadvantage of presenting these myths as though they had emerged fully fledged from the Greek imagination, rather as Athena emerged from Zeus's head. If we want to assess the originality of the tragic poets in the way they were able to make choices or undertake redevelopments of the mythic material for dramatic or other purposes, it is indispensable to take into account the history of the mythic sequences before the time when tragic authors decided to adapt them for the theater.

The Gaps in the Prehistory of the Tragic Myth: The Myth of Oedipus Again

Here we collide with a gap between the author's culture and our knowledge of myth that is still greater than the gap we have already noted between the Athenian spectator's culture and ours. Most of the theatrical production has disappeared, and we must now add the fact that apart from a few fragments or late summaries most of the epic and lyric poetry that would allow us to reconstitute the prehistory of tragic myth has also been lost in the disappearance of the bulk of Greek literature.

To continue with the example of Oedipus: when Sophocles decided to write his *Oedipus the King*, and shortly afterward his *Oedipus at Colonus*, he was situating himself in a vast epic tradition whose scope we can gauge, but whose exact content we do not know. The state of the myth of Oedipus in the epic cannot be summed up with two quick allusions to the *Iliad* and the *Odyssey*. Two whole epic poems, more or less contemporary with Homer, were centered on Oedipus and his family. One, entitled *Oedipodeia*, was still known to Pausanias in the second century CE, but we have only two verses from it! The other, entitled *The Thebaid*, which was also known and admired by Pausanias, dealt with the quarrel between Oedipus's two sons—Eteocles and Polynices—over who would inherit their father's throne, a quarrel that led to the war of Seven against Thebes. But we still have only six fragments with a total of about twenty verses![91]

We must add that Sophocles was not the first tragic author to have put the story of Oedipus and his family on the stage. In 467, Aeschylus had successfully presented a trilogy connected with the history of the family over three generations, an *Oedipodeia* in which the first tragedy was entitled *Laius* (Oedipus's father), the second *Oedipus*, and the third *Seven against Thebes*, not to mention that the satyr play entitled *The Sphinx* must have been related to the tragic myth, since it was by solving the Sphinx's riddle that Oedipus had conquered this monster that was ravaging the city of Thebes. Of this tragic trilogy we have only the final tragedy, *Seven against Thebes*. Thus we lack the beginning of this great depiction of the Theban family, and in particular the central play that corresponds exactly to the mythic sequence dramatized by Sophocles in his *Oedipus the King*. This tragedy of Aeschylus's completely disappeared in antiquity; there remains not even one verse of it! In such a case, it is impossible to gauge with certainty Sophocles' originality with respect to his predecessor.[92]

We can still dream that some papyrus will be found that will provide us with new information about these lost texts. And sometimes dreams come true. Between the epic poems of the *Oedipodeia* and the *Thebaid*, which date from the end of the eighth century, and Aeschylus's *Oedipodeia* in the first half of the fifth century, lies the lyric poetry produced in the seventh and sixth centuries, and in particular that of Stesichorus of Himera, a poet of the first half of the sixth century whose choral poetry rehearsed the great myths of the epic, thus playing the role of a bridge between the epic and tragedy. In 1977, a papyrus preserved at the University of Lille revealed major fragments of a poem about the Theban myth that scholars plausibly attributed to Stesichorus. These fragments do not concern Oedipus directly, but rather his wife (Epicaste in the epic; Jocasta in the tragedy). She tries, after a prediction by the seer Tiresias, to reconcile her two sons Eteocles and Polynices when they are arguing over their father's heritage, by proposing that they share it by drawing lots.[93] Thus we find here a resuscitated version of the Theban myth dating from the sixth century! We are obliged to note that it is completely at odds with the version Sophocles chose in his *Oedipus the King*. The version attributed to Stesichorus assumes that Jocasta continues to live after Oedipus's death, whereas in Sophocles' tragedy, Jocasta, when she learns the terrible reality, leaves the stage in silence and goes off to commit suicide. Sophocles remained within the wake of the epic tradition of the *Odyssey*, in which Epicaste hanged herself when she learned the news, whereas Oedipus continued to live. From the knowledge of this new testimony it therefore results that there were, at the time when Sophocles composed his *Oedipus the King*, radically different variants of the myth, among which the tragic author had to choose.

Above all, this testimony casts new light on Euripides' treatment of the Theban myth. In *The Phoenician Women*, whose subject corresponds to the mythic sequence of Aeschylus's *Seven against Thebes*, that is, the quarrel between the two sons over their dead father's heritage, Jocasta tries to reconcile the two enemy brothers. Before the discovery of the papyrus, this scene was considered an invention on Euripides' part; in fact, it is inspired by the reelaboration of the myth in the choral lyric of the sixth century. How many surprising things we have learned about the prehistory of a tragic myth and the creation of the Greek tragic poets thanks to this simple fragment of papyrus! In fact, nothing in the mythographers led us to suppose such a variant of the myth before Euripides' tragedy.

From this we can draw a more general lesson concerning the complexity and malleability of the mythic tradition, the coexistence of different or even contradictory versions, the choice of different options available to the tragic poets, and especially our inability to judge, in the present state of our knowledge, the originality of a tragic author in the realm of what Aristotle calls "invention," when the gaps in the literary tradition that precede him are too great.

A Prehistory of a Tragic Myth with Fewer Gaps: The Myth of Orestes

When Sophocles decided to make Orestes' revenge the subject of his *Electra*, he was in the same situation as when he composed *Oedipus the King*. The mythic sequence had already been dramatized by Aeschylus in a linked trilogy, the *Oresteia*, which dated from 458, just as his *Oedipus the King* had been preceded by the linked trilogy of the *Oedipodeia* of 467. By accident, Sophocles' two tragedies correspond to the two central tragedies in Aeschylus's two trilogies. *Oedipus the King* corresponds, as we have seen, to Aeschylus's *Oedipus*, which was preceded by a *Laius* and followed by *Seven against Thebes*. Sophocles' *Electra* corresponds to the central play of the *Oresteia*, *The Libation Bearers*, which was preceded by *Agamemnon* and followed by *The Eumenides*.

However, for us the great difference is that the whole of the trilogy of the *Oresteia* has survived and that we therefore have Aeschylus's tragedy corresponding exactly to the mythic sequence of Sophocles' *Electra*. The situation is all the more favorable for assessing Sophocles' originality because Euripides' tragedy on the same mythic sequence, also entitled *Electra*, has been preserved as well. Thus we have a remarkably propitious situation that has often been used to bring out the choices peculiar to each of the authors or even the development of the theatrical genre, though it is particularly unfortunate that we cannot tell whether Sophocles' *Electra* preceded or followed that of Euripides.[94]

Of course, if we look into the mythic material available to Sophocles when he wrote his *Electra*, before this material was shaped by Aeschylus, we find ourselves in a state of uncertainty comparable to that we encountered regarding the myth of Oedipus. However, the uncertainty concerning either epic or lyric poetry is not quite as great.

Regarding epic, we already have the information Homer gives us in passing about Orestes, as he does about Oedipus. The "divine Orestes" returns seven years after the murder of his father to kill the assassin, Aegisthus, who had enslaved the people. Then when he has buried "his hated mother, craven Aegisthus too," he organizes a funeral meal for the Argives on the very day that Menelaus returns from Troy.[95] The epic Orestes, while he already kills his mother, does not yet have the destiny of a tragic hero who, at the very moment that he does good, does evil. Far from it. His revenge brings him universal glory; and he is mentioned by a goddess as a model of bravery and filial piety.[96] He appears as a righter of wrongs and as a liberator. Sophocles was able to make use of Homer's old version to conclude his tragedy *Electra* by presenting Orestes as a liberator and by eliminating everything that constituted the subject of the last tragedy of Aeschylus's *Oresteia*, namely the madness of Orestes pursued by the Erinyes, his exile, and his trial in Athens before the tribunal of the Areopagus.[97]

The epic poem that plays, for the myth of Agamemnon and Orestes, a role analogous to that played by the *Oedipodeia* and the *Thebaid* in the myth of Oedipus, is the poem known as *Returns from Troy*. It has also been lost, but its content is somewhat better known, because we have brief summary of it. Attributed to Agias of Troezen (seventh century BCE), this poem related in five books the adventures of the heroes returning from the expedition to Troy, with the obvious exception of Odysseus, who was already the subject of the *Odyssey*. The tragic consequences of Agamemnon's return occupy the last part of the narrative. Here is the sentence that sums up this final episode:

> Then, when Agamemnon is killed by Aegisthus and Clytemnestra, there is the vengeance by Orestes and Pylades, and Menelaus's return home.[98]

Despite the brevity of the summary, a new character appears who is not found in the *Odyssey*: Pylades, Orestes' friend who accompanies him to carry out the revenge. This character became a component of the tragic myth, because he is Orestes' companion in all three of the tragic poets. What is astonishing, however, is that Electra is mentioned neither in Homer nor in *Returns*, even though she is, like Pylades, an indispensable part of the tragic myth and her importance increases from Aeschylus to Sophocles and Euripides, as is already shown by the mere titles of the tragedies.[99] The three daughters of Agamemnon mentioned by Homer in the *Iliad* are Chrysothemis, Laodice, and Iphianassa.[100] Of these three sisters, only Chrysothemis passed directly from Homer to Sophocles' tragedy. The two other names were replaced in the tragic myth: Electra replaces Laodice, and Iphigeneia replaces Iphianassa, except that Sophocles does not confuse these two latter characters in his *Electra*, because he mentions an Iphianassa living in the palace after Iphigeneia has been sacrificed.[101] Such changes are not important in themselves, but they attest to the malleability of the names in the prehistory of the tragic myth, at least for secondary characters. Obviously, no change of name for Orestes or Oedipus is conceivable.

However, the gaps in our information threaten to lead us to draw erroneous conclusions. On the basis of this comparison between the epic and tragedy, we might tend to think that the name "Electra" did not yet exist in the older period. But papyrological discoveries shed new light on the myth of Orestes, as well as on that of Oedipus. In the present case, it is a matter of papyrus fragments giving a passage from the epic poem by Hesiod entitled *The Catalog of Women*, which allows us to reconstruct a complete passage on Clytemnestra and the children she had with Agamemnon.[102] There is also, of course, Orestes, the last born, "who, when of adult age, took revenge on the murderer of his father and killed his arrogant mother with a pitiless bronze." As for the daughters, there are only two, not three as in Homer. Chrysothemis is absent. And the two others have names different from those they have in Homer. Homer's Iphianassa, who in the tragic myth becomes Iphigeneia, is called Iphimede in Hesiod.[103] The new testimony thus reveals a third name for one and the same character! And there is no possible confusion. Hesiod's Iphimede is indeed the Iphigeneia of the tragic myth, because her sacrifice by the Achaeans when they depart for Troy and her rescue by Artemis, who makes her immortal, are discussed at length.[104] As for the second daughter, she is "Electra who rivals, by her beauty, the immortals." Thus we have, thanks to this new testimony, a new proof that what we would have spontaneously tended to interpret as an evolution of the myth sometimes merely reflects the coexistence of two ancient variants.

For the history of the myth of Orestes, as for that of Oedipus, between the epic literature and tragedy there is the transition of lyric poetry: notably Stesichorus, who we know composed an *Oresteia*,[105] but also an older lyric poet, Xanthos, from whom Stesichorus took his inspiration precisely in his *Oresteia*.[106] These two works have been lost. However, a few testimonies and a few quotations from Stesichorus's *Oresteia* allow a glimpse of the elements that were to be adopted in the tragic myth of Orestes' vengeance: the role of Apollo of Delphi, Clytemnestra's disturbing dream, and the recognition scene with the lock of hair.[107]

A last testimony by lyric poetry before the tragic myth, or perhaps contemporary with it, deserves to be mentioned here. It is an ode by Pindar in honor of a Theban boy who had won a race in the games at Delphi, "in the rich countryside of Pylades, the host of the Laconian Orestes." That is how the myth of Orestes is introduced.[108] The main elements of the tragic myths are known: the survival of the young Orestes, saved by his nurse on the tragic day when Agamemnon and Cassandra were killed by the "woman without pity,"[109] his exile in Phocis at the home of Strophius, Pylades's father, and then, many years later, his return to his homeland, where, with Ares' help, he kills his mother and "makes Aegisthus fall into his own blood." However, nothing is said about either Electra or the tragic destiny of Orestes after the murder of his mother. And Pindar, making Orestes a Laconian from Amyclae, directly contradicts everything that we know about his origin in epic and tragedy.[110]

This Pindaric version of the myth, while it confirms the extent to which a myth could be multiform even if it has a few stable elements, is not without importance in assessing the apparent isolation of the end of Sophocles' *Electra*, which, as we have seen, is completely opposed to the conclusions of Aeschylus's and Euripides' plays, through the absence of Orestes' madness, which, as we have said, might be based on Homer. To judge by Pindar's version, Sophocles was not the only author of the fifth century not to speak of the tragic consequences of a righteous vengeance. Another particularity of Sophocles' *Electra* concerns the order of the murders in the course of Orestes' vengeance: whereas Aeschylus and Euripides have Aegisthus die first, and then Clytemnestra, Sophocles adopts the reverse order; and that was already the order in Pindar. Sophocles' choices are thus not as isolated as one might have thought.

These main outlines of a comparative history, from Homer to tragedy, of two great myths that gave rise to the majority of Sophocles' extant tragedies have to be complemented by a more general development that makes it possible to differentiate tragic myth from epic myth, both from a religious point of view and from a political point of view.

From Epic Myth to Tragic Myth: The Growing Importance of Delphi

From the religious point of view, what characterizes tragic myth as compared with epic myth is the much more prominent presence of the oracle of Apollo at Delphi.

The sanctuary was already mentioned in Homeric epic, where Delphi is called by an older name, Pytho. Agamemnon knew the wealth retained by the stone threshold of Apollo in Pytho;[111] and he consulted its oracle before the expedition to Troy.[112] The existence of the sanctuary is confirmed by Hesiod. In his *Theogony*, Hesiod connects an episode of the struggle for power between Zeus and his father Chronos with one of the most famous objects in the temple of Apollo in Pytho, the conical stone, "a marvel to mortal men."[113] Chronos devoured all his children, but Zeus was spared because his mother, Rhea, caused Chronos to swallow a large stone in place of the child. Zeus later made Chronos regurgitate the stone and erected it at Pytho, at the foot of Parnassus. Nonetheless, even if the sanctuary of Apollo at Delphi was known in the epic age, it had not yet acquired the importance it assumed beginning in the seventh century, becoming in the sixth century a sanctuary known all over the world.[114] Above all, what it is important to note here is that neither of the two great myths of Oedipus and Orestes is connected in the epic with Apollo of Delphi. What proves that the myth of Orestes had no connection with Delphi in the time of Homer is the fact that to carry out his revenge, Agamemnon's son returned not from Phocis, where Delphi is located, but from Athens.[115] In the tragedy, everything is put under the aegis of Apollo of Delphi and his oracle.

Orestes' Vengeance in the Tragic Myth and Apollo of Delphi

In the tragic myth of Orestes' vengeance, the oracle of Delphi is a traditional element as indispensable as the son's murder of his mother. In Sophocles' *Electra*, Orestes mentions the oracle at the beginning of the tragedy, when he reveals his plan for revenge to the tutor who is accompanying him:

> When I went to the Pythian oracle to learn how I might avenge my father on his murderers, Phoebus gave me the commandment which you will now hear: that alone, and by stealth, without the aid of arms or large numbers, I should carry off my right hand's just slaughters.[116]

Phoebus is another way of designating Apollo.[117] The oracle of Delphi, while approving the vengeance it describes as "righteous," tells Orestes how he must avenge himself: not by force, but by trickery, with his own hand, slaughtering his victims. It is in conformity with these recommendations that Orestes prepares his plan for revenge. Everything takes place as he planned. Toward the end of the tragedy, after the murder of his mother, when Orestes leaves the palace he again refers to the oracle as the guarantor of his action: "All is well within the house, if Apollo's oracle spoke well."[118] Orestes alludes here to "the righteous vengeance" of which Apollo spoke in his oracle.

Clearly, the role accorded to the oracle at Delphi is not Sophocles' creation. In Aeschylus's trilogy, the god of Delphi played an important and even more decisive role than he does in Sophocles. The powerful oracle of Loxias—another name for Apollo—in Aeschylus's *Libation Bearers* gave Orestes the order to avenge his father and threatened him with terrible reprisals if he did not do so, whereas in Sophocles' *Electra* Orestes himself makes the decision to avenge his father, before consulting the oracle as to how to do it. The sanctuary in Delphi is even the site of the tragedy at the beginning of the third play in the Aeschylean tragedy *The Eumenides*, where Orestes, pursued by the goddesses of vengeance, has taken refuge as a supplicant in the temple of Apollo. On two occasions, the god even appears in person to defend him.[119] There is nothing comparable in Sophocles. However, the sanctuary at Delphi reappears in his *Electra* at a point where we do not expect to find it. Orestes, to obey the oracle that has asked him to act by trickery, will make indirect use of the god to realize his plan for revenge, since he justifies his fictive death, which the tutor is to announce, by a mortal accident during a chariot race in the games . . . in honor of the god of Delphi! This god, who seems to cause Orestes' death at the time that he is saving him, is a subtle invention of Sophocles'.

Tragic Myth in *Oedipus the King* and the Oracles of Delphi

The god of Delphi plays an even more important role in the play Sophocles devoted to another great myth, that of Oedipus, for it is not a single oracle that intervenes, but a succession of oracles. In fact, all through Sophocles' *Oedipus the King*, Phoebus Apollo is present through his old or new oracles.

At the beginning of the tragedy, the city of Thebes is prey to a terrible pestilence. Oedipus has already saved it from an earlier scourge by means of his intelligence alone, by solving the Sphinx's riddle; that is how he became king of Thebes. But confronted by this second scourge, Oedipus's intelligence is helpless. He has found no better solution than to send a messenger to consult the oracle at Delphi:

> I have made use of the only remedy which I could find after close consideration: I sent my relative Creon, Menoeceus' son, to Apollo's Pythian residence to learn what we might do or say to protect this city.[120]

And then Creon arrives to announce the god's reply:

> I will tell you what I heard from the god. Phoebus our lord clearly commands us to drive out the defilement which he said was harbored in this land, and not to nourish it so that it cannot be healed.[121]

Then Creon sets forth the content of the oracle: the corruption arises from the fact that the murder of the preceding king, Laius, has not been avenged; the guilty parties, who have remained in the city, must be expelled.

When he has learned the content of the oracle, Oedipus asks Creon about the site of the murder and the circumstances under which it took place: where and how was Laius killed? Well, he had left precisely to consult the oracle at Delphi. He was not seen to return; but Creon does not know what he was going to ask the god. Of course, everyone goes to Delphi and comes back from Delphi, or not. And if Oedipus undertakes to lead the police investigation regarding the assassin, it is the better to serve his country and the god of Delphi.[122] Then when the chorus of old men enters, anxiously waiting for the oracle's response, Oedipus asserts that he is putting himself in the service of the god of Delphi and of the dead man.[123] In short, the oracle's response, announced at the beginning of the tragedy, is the proximate cause of the investigation to save the city, avenge the dead king, and serve the god.

Furthermore, in the course of the investigation that will gradually lead Oedipus to discover the truth about himself, two ancient oracles issued by Apollo of Delphi are successively unveiled in the same scene. The first is revealed by Jocasta to Oedipus: it is the oracle Laius received, according to which he was to die at the hands of a son who would be born of him and Jocasta, which led Laius to abandon the newborn child, his ankles shackled, on a mountain where no one should have passed by.[124] The second oracle is revealed by Oedipus to Jocasta: when he was being brought up in Corinth by the king Polybus, he was insulted during a banquet by a drunken man who said he was not the king's child, and he went to the oracle at Delphi to learn the truth about his origin. It was there that the oracle, without replying directly to his question, predicted that he would marry his mother, would bring into the world abominable children, and would be the murderer of his father.[125] To avoid fulfilling the oracle's prediction, he decided, when he left Delphi, not to return to Corinth. And it was on the way, at a crossroads, that the fateful encounter took place: one of the men, Oedipus, was leaving the oracle for the reason we know; the other, Laius, was going to consult it, and we don't even know why.

At the end of the tragedy, it is still a matter of consulting the oracle. In fact, when Oedipus has learned his origin and the extent of his misfortunes, when he has blinded himself after Jocasta's suicide and wants to go into exile, Creon, the new king, does not want to make a decision before consulting the oracle of Delphi once again:

> *Oedipus:* Cast me out of this land with all speed, to a place where no mortal shall be found to greet me.
> *Creon:* This I could have done, to be sure, except I craved first to learn from the god all my duty.
> *Oedipus:* But his pronouncement has been set forth in full—to let me perish, the parricide, unholy one that I am.
> *Creon:* Thus it was said. But since we have come to such a pass, it is better to learn clearly what should be done.
> *Oedipus:* Will you, then, seek a response on behalf of such a wretch as I?
> *Creon:* Yes, for even you yourself will now surely put faith in the god.[126]

Then, when Oedipus tries once again to get Creon to arrange for him to leave the country, the new king's reply is the same: "You ask for what the god must give."[127] "The god," without further specification, suffices to designate the god of Delphi, so crushing is his presence throughout the tragedy.

The place accorded the god of Delphi, the god par excellence in the tragic myth of Laius and Oedipus, contrasts with the epic myth as it was known at the time of the *Odyssey*, in book 11, where Odysseus sees Oedipus's mother among the dead:

> And I saw the mother of Oedipodes, fair Epicaste, who wrought a monstrous deed in ignorance of mind, in that she wedded her own son, and he, when he had slain his own father, wedded her, and straightway the gods made these things known among men. Howbeit he abode as lord of the Cadmeans in lovely Thebes, suffering woes through the baneful counsels of the gods, but she went down to the house of Hades, the strong warder. She made fast a noose on high from a lofty beam, overpowered by her sorrow, but for him she left behind woes full many, even all that the Avengers of a mother bring to pass.[128]

Essential elements of the tragic myth of Oedipus are already present here: the murder of the father, the marriage with the mother, the discovery of the scandal, the mother's suicide. But concerning divine intervention, the difference between "the gods" in the epic myth and "the god" in the tragic myth is significant. In the interval, the development of the Delphic oracle in the seventh and sixth centuries considerably altered the myth, so that in the tragedy it was now centered on the oracle of Delphi and her god.

Obviously, it was not Sophocles who carried out that revolution. In Aeschylus the oracles of Apollo of Delphi already played an important role in the myth of the family of Oedipus, to which he had devoted a trilogy covering three generations, Laius, Oedipus, and Oedipus's sons.[129] To be sure, we cannot tell whether the presence of the oracle of Delphi was as invasive in Aeschylus's *Oedipus* as it is in Sophocles' *Oedipus the King*, because the former tragedy is lost; but the reflection on the past put into the mouths of the women in the chorus in the last play of the trilogy, *Seven against Thebes*, enables us to go back to the first offense, that of Laius, Oedipus's father, precisely because he did not listen to the oracle of Delphi:

> Indeed I speak of the ancient transgression, now swift in its retribution. It re-mains even into the third generation, ever since Laius—in defiance of Apollo who, at his Pythian oracle at the earth's center, said three times that the king would save his city if he died without offspring.
>
> Ever since he, overcome by the thoughtlessness of his longing, fathered his own death, the parricide Oedipus, who sowed his mother's sacred field, where he was nurtured, and endured a bloody crop. Madness united the frenzied bridal pair.[130]

The accusation made against Laius is unambiguous. The king of the city of Thebes transgressed Apollo's oracle, despite his threefold warning. His punishment for that is exemplary, because it is twofold: on the one hand, it affects the guilty person himself; on the other hand, it is passed down over two generations of his descendants. Thus we understand why the chorus, in its final assessment of the tragedy of *Seven against Thebes*, and therefore of the trilogy, cries: "Divine decrees do not lose their edge!"[131] These oracles need no more specification than "the god" does in Sophocles' *Oedipus the King*, so clear is it that the myth is henceforth attached to the oracles of Apollo of Delphi.

The Death of Oedipus in *Oedipus at Colonus* and the Apollo of Delphi

The oracular Apollo of Delphi became among the tragic poets such an obvious given that it enters into even the variants of the myth most distant from the common fund. That is the case for the Athenian variant of the death of Oedipus, which Sophocles put onstage in his *Oedipus at Colonus*.[132]

When the aged Oedipus, guided by his daughter Antigone, arrives in the course of his exile at a place in Attica where he sits down, he learns from a man of the country that he is seated in a forbidden place consecrated to the Eumenides. Far from leaving it, as this inhabitant of Colonus asks him to do, he decides to settle there as a supplicant. The decision is sudden and strange. The spectator understands only a few moments later, when Oedipus, once again alone with Antigone after the departure of the inhabitant of Colonus, reveals the oracle of Delphi whose fulfillment he sees. Addressing the Eumenides, he says:

> Ladies of dread aspect, since your seat is the first in this land at which I have bent my knee, show yourselves not ungracious to Phoebus or to myself; who, when he proclaimed that doom of many woes, spoke to me of this rest after long years: on reaching my goal in a land where I should find a seat of the Awful Goddesses and a shelter for foreigners, there I should close my weary life, with profit, through my having fixed my abode there, for those who received me, but ruin for those who sent me forth, who drove me away. And he went on to warn me that signs of these things would come, in earthquake, or in thunder, or in the lightning of Zeus.[133]

The oracle that Oedipus presents includes a first part mentioned allusively because it is well known. It is the oracle that Oedipus revealed to Jocasta in *Oedipus the King*.[134] he will marry his mother, produce a monstrous race, and be his father's murderer. All that has already happened, since Oedipus is now exiled. But the second part is entirely new with respect to *Oedipus the King*. The word of the god of Delphi is there to guarantee the Athenian variant of the death of Oedipus, which differs from the Homeric version. Did Sophocles invent this? That is not certain, because when Euripides adopted, before Sophocles, the Athenian version at the end of *The Phoenician Women*, he already put it under the aegis of the god of Delphi.[135] Here is how Euripides presents the oracle in the final dialogue between Oedipus and Antigone at the time when they are going into exile (vv. 1703–7):

> *Oedipus:* Now, my daughter, the prophecy of Loxias is being fulfilled.
> *Antigone:* What prophecy? Will you speak of misery on top of misery?
> *Oedipus:* That I must wander and die in Athens.
> *Antigone:* Where? What fort in Attica will receive you?
> *Oedipus:* Colonus the holy, the house of the god of horses. But come, serve
>   me, your blind father, since you are eager to share in my exile.

The convergence between Euripides and Sophocles is clear: the end of the exile and the death of Oedipus in the Attic deme of Colonus are foretold by the god of Delphi. Nonetheless, the content of the oracle is considerably different. Whereas according to Euripides, in an explicit oracle Apollo revealed to Oedipus the place where he would die, Sophocles indicated the end of his exile and his death only allusively. It is clear that this divergence is explained by dramatic reasons. At the end of the tragedy, Euripides could not let doubt hover over Oedipus's final destiny, whereas at the beginning of his tragedy Sophocles wanted to arrange for surprise and discovery. The dramatic function of the oracle in *Oedipus at Colonus* is all the more evident because it is twofold, bearing both on the past and on the future. At the point where Oedipus reveals it, it serves first to justify the immediate past, that is, his decision to remain where he as a supplicant in the sanctuary of the Eumenides in Colonus. It also anticipates a proximate future, the moment when Oedipus, near the end of the tragedy, hearing the thunder and seeing lightning, recognizes the divine signs of his approaching death announced by the oracle.

From this comparison it therefore results that the content of a single oracle of Apollo of Delphi could vary from one author to another for dramatic reasons. This literary use of oracular responses would be confirmed by a comparison with the god's responses as known from inscriptions. In no inscription will one find an oracle's answer as long and as complex as the one in *Oedipus at Colonus*.[136] In sum, following an approach to religion that will seem strange in the perspective of the religions of the Book, the god's word was at once religiously infallible and literarily malleable.

The Modern Myth of a Delphic *Oresteia*

We would like to know why and how this evolution of the myths of Oedipus and Orestes occurred between the epic and tragedy, where they are now closely connected with the oracle of Delphi. But literary testimonies are too rare or too fragmented for us to be able to satisfy our curiosity, unless we give free rein to an imagination that is all the more dangerous because it is hidden beneath erudite appearances. It has been claimed that there was a Delphic oracle between Homer and Aeschylus, and that its traces can be found in the lyric poetry of Stesichorus in the sixth century and that of Pindar in the seventh.[137]

It has certainly been established that in Stesichorus Orestes' vengeance was already related to Apollo.[138] And indeed, in Euripides' *Orestes*, whose mythic sequence is situated after the murder of Clytemnestra, Orestes is in the grip of a kind of delirium: he thinks he sees his mother's Erinyes and asks his sister Electra to give him the bow that Apollo accorded him to defend himself against them.[139] An ancient commentator notes that Euripides borrowed this detail from Stesichorus,[140] which implies that Apollo made his appearance in the myth of Orestes before Aeschylus. If Apollo gave Orestes a bow to defend himself against the Erinyes after the murder of his mother, that must at least mean that he has taken him under his protection. As early as the sixth century, Apollo thus enters the myth of Orestes for sure, but we cannot say whether he played an important role in it.

On the other hand, it is rather surprising that in Pindar's testimony—which, as we have seen, is the only one before Aeschylus that has been preserved in toto[141]—Apollo plays no part in Orestes' revenge. To be sure, at the beginning of his poem, Pindar refers to Loxias, that is, to Apollo of Delphi, to say that he loves the Theban sanctuary of the Ismenion, where the ceremony in honor of the young Theban winner of the footrace at the Pythian Games is supposed to take place. But when the poet comes to the myth of Orestes, which constitutes the central episode in his eulogy, he does not mention an oracle of Delphi to explain Orestes' vengeance. Pindar does mention a god, but it is Ares and not Apollo: "But with the help of Ares who was a long time in coming, he killed his mother and slew Aegisthus." The only connection that Pindar establishes between Orestes and Delphi is his exile with Strophius, Pylades' father, who lives at the foot of Parnassus. Thus there is no material for reconstructing a lost model of a Delphic *Oresteia*.

This, then, is the general development affecting the mythic material from the religious point of view: the development of the Delphic oracle over the centuries preceding the production of tragedies had a decisive influence on the givens of the mythic material the tragic poets put on the stage: the oracular utterances of the god of Delphi became an inherent given of the two great myths of Oedipus and Orestes, even if each tragic author retained the freedom to use these utterances for his own purposes in the choice of his dramatic construction and in all the meanings that flowed from it.[142]

From Epic Myth to Tragic Myth: The Evolution of Politics

Can the general evolution of myth from epic to tragedy be clearly seen in the political domain as well?

The great novelty in the political domain that is comparable to the novelty in the religious domain is the appearance and development of democracy. The comparison has its limits, however, because the renown of the oracle of Delphi extended to the whole of Greece, whereas the development of the democratic political system concerned only a few city-states, especially those under the influence of Athens. However, since the audience of the tragic authors was essentially Athenian, we can see that the development of democracy was occasionally accompanied by an adaptation of the traditional mythic material to eliminate from it anything that might seem to conflict too much with contemporary reality.

Modern historians define Homeric civilization, which largely corresponds to the subject matter of Greek tragedy, as a civilization of the *oikos*, that is, of the great estates managed on an autarkic basis by nobles who passed them down from father to son, and these nobles were precisely the great heroes of tragedy. To this civilization of the oikos historians oppose the classical civilization of the *polis*, that is, of the city defined as a community of citizens, which emerged after the Dark Ages in the archaic Greece of the eighth century BCE, and was the civilization of the spectators of tragedy. No matter how legitimate this distinction may be, it does not seem that the audiences of Greek tragedies in the fifth century, or even their authors, felt that they were dealing with two radically different worlds. The Homeric epic was part of their culture from childhood on. It was the foundation on which they forged their conception of the past, their imagination, and their value hierarchy. They were familiar with heroes like Ajax,

Odysseus, and the Atreids whom they encountered in Sophocles' tragedies. They did not raise the existential question regarding the continuity or discontinuity between two worlds, the old and the new. For them, the mythic material was part of the world of a living tradition. Whereas moderns emphasize a discontinuity between two civilizations, ancient spectators could see continuities.

The Continuities between the Homeric World and That of the Spectators of Tragedy

Although it is true that Homeric civilization did not have the city-state (polis) in the political sense of the term, that is, a community of citizens participating more or less directly in the administration of the city, fifth-century spectators already saw in the Homeric poems a world of cities and towns not unlike those they knew. The word *polis* existed. In this connection, the Catalog of Ships at the beginning of the *Iliad*[143] that enumerates the various leaders of the different contingents involved in the Greek expedition against Troy mentions an impressive number of localities from which the members of the force came. Twenty-nine contingents from various regions of continental Greece and the islands brought together men from about 180 localities, and still the poet has not mentioned all the cities he knew. In the case of Crete, for example, he lists seven well-populated cities—and uses the word *polis*—but calls Crete the country of a hundred cities.[144] Some of the cities mentioned in the catalog are described as "well-fortified," which is particularly the case for Mycenae and Athens.[145]

Whatever the debates of modern scholars on the problems raised by this catalog, and especially its date, it was, for the Athenian of the fifth century, the first great textbook of geography and sometimes of history as well. It was still that for a specialist in geography and history like Strabo, three centuries later.

So how could a fifth-century Athenian not conceive the Greece of the Homeric age as a country composed of regions including numerous towns or cities, exactly like the Greece in which he lived?

The Heroes Attached to Cities: Continuities and Deformations between Epic and Tragedy; The Image of Thebes

The great heroes were, already in epic literature, attached to cities. And in that way, too, the Athenian spectator could not fail to see a continuity between the Greece of the age of myth and the Greece that he knew. That was the case for the Theban Oedipus or Ajax of Salamis.

The myth of Oedipus was already connected with the city of Thebes in Homer[146] and Hesiod.[147] Thebes was already known as the city "with seven gates."[148] The myth was so well established in a city that a tragedy could not change a place with respect to epic. Thebes is the site of the scene in *Oedipus the King* and in *Antigone* even if *Oedipus at Colonus* is set in Attica, where Oedipus arrives after a long exile in the company of his daughter Antigone; several characters arrive successively from Thebes, first his other daughter Ismene, then his brother-in-law Creon, and finally his son Polynices. In his *Antigone* Sophocles mentions Thebes "with seven gates" exactly as in the epic. This traditional epithet was already used in Aeschylus's *Seven against Thebes*, and before it in the lyric poetry of Pindar and Bacchylides.[149] This kind of qualifier was not only a literary borrowing from epic, but also corresponded to the reality of the Thebes that Pausanias was to visit: he says that the seven gates of the city's ancient walls still remained in his time, that is, in the second century CE.[150] Thus Athenian spectators who went to Thebes must not have seen any discontinuity between the Thebes of the Seven Gates mentioned by tragedy after the epic, and the Thebes they themselves were able to see.

Of course, the image of Thebes conveyed by literary productions might vary from one author to the next.[151] The seven-gated city is naturally more present in the work of Pindar, who was born in Thebes, than in Athenian authors. It is also possible that the image of epic Thebes in the Athenian tragic authors was affected by the Athenians' limited affinities with the Thebans in the classical period. Both authors and spectators remembered that during the Persian Wars Thebes had collaborated with the invaders. Moreover, Athenian democracy was very different from the oligarchic regime in Thebes. Nevertheless, until the beginning of the Peloponnesian War, in the theater the contemporary image of Thebes does not seem to have affected the prestige of the mythic Thebes. In Aeschylus's *Seven against Thebes*, the city of Thebes resisting the Argives like a ship at the height of a storm is the model of the civilized world resisting the barbarian world in a mental scheme that is still influenced by the experience of the Persian Wars. And in Sophocles' *Antigone*, the chorus of Theban elders, in its first song, presents Aeschylus's view of the aggression of Polynices and the Argives against Thebes.[152]

However, when the Peloponnesian War began, the Athenians' image of Thebes deteriorated. Hostilities opened in 431 when the Thebans launched a night attack on the Plataeans, who had been Athens's allies for almost a century, followed by the Lacedaemonians' siege of Plataea, and then, in 427, by the total destruction of the city, whose territory was henceforth under Theban control. The memory of this destruction was all the more vivid in Athens because the women, children, and elderly of Plataea had been taken in by the Athenians, along with 212 Plataeans who had succeeded in escaping during the siege and who were even granted Athenian citizenship.[153] Three years later, the Athenians, in a vast conspiracy to establish democracy in Boeotia, were defeated at the Battle of Delium, where many of their troops were killed, and negotiations to recover the bodies were begun through the intermediary of Athenian and Boeotian heralds.[154] Scholars have long seen a connection between this event and Euripides' *The Suppliants*, in which, after the expedition of the Seven against Thebes, Adrastes, the king of Argos, demands that the Thebans return the bodies of the leaders, which the Thebans refuse to do. When in the most famous scene in that tragedy Euripides presents a Theban ambassador confronting the king of Athens, Theseus, it is not impossible that the aggressive Theban full of contempt for democracy is a literary transposition of reality.[155]

Is such a negative view of Thebes also found in Sophocles after the beginning of the Peloponnesian War? Some scholars think so. In his last tragedy, *Oedipus at Colonus*, we see a comparable meeting between a Theban ambassador, Creon, and the same Athenian king, Theseus.[156] The Theban is also characterized by violence. Creon's violence in *Oedipus at Colonus* contrasts, moreover, with his wisdom in *Oedipus the King*. But on closer inspection, Sophocles is subtler. Through King Theseus's voice, Sophocles takes care to dissociate the image of Thebes from that of its ambassador.[157] Creon's violence in *Oedipus at Colonus* is thus not explained essentially as a reflection of contemporary actuality. It takes on its meaning in the logic of myth. It serves as a foil not only to highlight the image of Athens, but also to increase Oedipus's stature and contribute to his rehabilitation.[158]

Heroes Attached to Cities: Continuities and Distortions between Epic and Tragedy; The Image of Salamis

Among the tragic heroes of the following generation, that of the Trojan War, the case of Ajax of Salamis is analogous to that of Oedipus. He is also attached to a city of the epic that still existed in the classical period. The man who proved to be the best fighter of all after Achilles' withdrawal was born on the island of Salamis, near Athens. He came at the head of a modest fleet of twelve vessels.[159] In his tragedy *Ajax*, Sophocles made direct use of these facts. As a chorus for his tragedy, he chose the members of the crew of Ajax's flagship vessel, who were transformed into warriors upon their arrival at Troy. Even though the tragedy is set at Troy, the memory of Salamis, the homeland of both the hero and the chorus, is present. When it addresses its master for the first time, the chorus recalls his origin and his country: "Son of Telamon, you who hold your throne on wave-washed Salamis." Then, at the beginning of its first song, it addresses Salamis directly the better to emphasize its misfortunes at Troy: "O famous Salamis, you, I know, have your happy seat among the waves that beat your shore, eternally conspicuous in the eyes of all men."[160]

This distant homeland, a lost paradise for the Salaminians of myth, was for the Athenian spectator a familiar horizon of his land and his history. The chorus's insistence on the celebrity of the island could, without obvious distortion on the author's part, invite the spectator to incorporate into the fame of the Salamis of myth the Salamis of history, the Salamis of the naval battle that had freed the Greeks from the Persian invasion by sea in 480 and that had been made the subject of a play by Aeschylus in his *Persians* of 472. It was a continuity that the spectator must have felt between the Greece of myth, that of past history, and that of the present time. In its eternal, paradisiacal luminosity, Salamis is outside time, that is, outside all times.

However, in a few discreet strokes, Sophocles was able to strengthen the ties between Salamis and Athens. In Homer, the two cities were independent and had sent separate contingents. A bond seems nonetheless to have existed. In the Catalog of Ships, we read that Ajax, who came with twelve vessels, placed himself alongside the Athenian battalions. This passage, whether authentic or not, was cited by the Athenians in the fifth century, in the time of Solon, during their conflict with Megara over the possession of Salamis.[161] From that time on, Salamis had been attached to Athens. But in the tragedy, when Tecmesse, Ajax's captive, speaks for the first time to the chorus of Salaminians, she addresses them with great solemnity: "Mates of the ship of Ajax, offspring of the race that springs from the Erechtheids, the soil's sons."[162]

Here it is certain that the epic myth has been subtly modified for political reasons. By calling them "Erechtheids"—that is, descendants of Erechtheus, the first king of Athens—Sophocles erases the distinction made in Homer's Catalog of Ships between the Athenians as descendants of Erechtheus and the Salaminians. He makes them share in the honors of the Athenians' prestigious origin, and thus in their autochthonous character. But at the same time he strokes the Athenian audience's patriotic feelings by discreetly annexing the exploits of the Salaminian Ajax. And in a further alteration toward the end of the tragedy he orients the shift of Salamis toward Athens when the chorus of Salaminians, full of nostalgia, exclaims: "O to be where the wooded wave-washed cape fences off the deep sea, to be beneath Sunium's jutting plateau, so that we might salute sacred Athens!"[163]

Sophocles cleverly presents this return as a desire to see Cape Sunium again and to salute sacred Athens, thereby flattering the Athenian spectators' vanity by this praise for their homeland.[164] Henceforth the Salaminians' eyes were turned more toward Athens than toward Salamis. Thus the epic myth is given a slight twist to adapt it to the contemporary situation and the conditions of the dramatic representation.[165]

The Site of Orestes' Vengeance: Mycenae or Argos?

Such continuities between the hero and his native city, even if inflected by slight distortions, are exemplary. They do not apply to all tragic myths, because all the cities to which a myth was attached did not have the same longevity. In the age of tragedy, Mycenae was no longer the splendid city it had been at the time celebrated by Homer.

In Homer, Mycenae was the site of Agamemnon's palace,[166] the place where he was murdered and where his son Orestes returned to avenge his death by killing his mother, Clytemnestra, and the usurper Aegisthus.[167] At that time, it was certainly a "well fortified city," as we have seen in the Catalog of Ships in the *Iliad*, but it was also a city "rich in gold," as was confirmed by the excavations conducted by Schliemann and his successors,[168] and it had "streets as broad as Troy's."[169] But in the classical age the jewel of Mycenaean civilization—as it is called by modern historians, who have given it the name of that city—had been destroyed.

After its destruction at the end of the twelfth century, corresponding to the arrival of the Dorians, by the end of the seventh century and in the sixth century the city had regained a degree of prosperity, as has been shown by archeological excavations.[170] At the beginning of the fifth century, it had been capable of sending, during the second Persian war, a contingent of troops to Thermopylae to help the Lacedaemonians, and then another to the Battle of Pharsalia.[171] Proud of its past, Mycenae was the only city of Argolis that refused to submit to Argos. It was against the Argives' opinion that it had sent its contingent to Thermopylae, and it was competing with Argos for the sanctuary of Hera, the famous Heraion located between Mycenae and Argos, as well for the right to organize the Nemaean Games. Argos, suspecting that Mycenae was trying to challenge its hegemony over Argolis, took advantage of a temporary weakness of the Lacedaemonians, who were preoccupied by the revolt of the Messinians and by an earthquake, to mount an expedition, along with its allies, against Mycenae. It besieged Mycenae, seized the city, destroyed it, and reduced the Mycenaeans to slavery. This occurred in 468, ten years before Aeschylus put the myth of Agamemnon and Orestes on the stage in his *Oresteia*.[172] Here, there is clearly a discontinuity between Homeric Greece and classical Greece.

Now, Aeschylus sets, without the slightest possible ambiguity, the first two plays of his trilogy, *Agamemnon* and *The Libation Bearers*, not in Mycenae, but in Argos.[173] These two cities, although near one another, were distinct in the Homeric age and according to the Catalog of Ships, the Argive troops did not belong, like those from Mycenae, to Agamemon's contingent, but instead to Diomedes' contingent. However, here the Homeric evidence is not entirely coherent: a passage in the *Iliad* states that Agamemnon's power extended to "all of Argolis," and Agamemnon can situate his palace "in Argos," that is, in Argolis.[174] Nevertheless, Aeschylus's choice is remarkable, because he does not mention Mycenae at any point. What is the reason for this change? A poetic license taking advantage of Homer's ambiguity on this point? A desire to eliminate a conflict between the myth and the political state of Greece in his time? Or a still more precise political intention? The absence of Mycenae and the insistence with which Orestes, at the end of the trilogy, after he has been acquitted by the Athenian tribunal of the Areopagus, says that he is a resident of Argos and promises Athens that it will be rewarded by an alliance with his city,[175] might reflect a political goal, namely to take note of the destruction of Mycenae, Sparta's ally, and to celebrate the alliance between Argos and Athens that took place a few years later. We should probably be wary of an excessively political reading of

Greek theater, because too often it leads to unverifiable hypotheses. But the change made by Aeschylus with regard to epic myth does not seem attributable to chance. Aeschylus was followed by Euripides in his *Electra* and his *Orestes*,[176] though Euripides also sometimes mentions the Mycenaeans or Mycenae, which is in his work a simple poetic variant of "Argives" or "Argos."[177]

Confronted by Aeschylus's innovation on this point, which was partially adopted by Euripides, what choice did Sophocles make in his *Electra*? He did not follow Aeschylus, but instead placed Agamemnon's palace in Mycenae. At the beginning of the tragedy, the tutor accompanying Orestes on his return to his homeland describes the landscape that Orestes cannot remember—because he was too young when he left it—thus also informing the spectator regarding the background of the tragedy:

> Son of him who once commanded our forces at Troy, son of Agamemnon!—
> now you may survey all that your heart has desired for so long. There is the
> ancient Argos of your yearning, that consecrated land from which the gad-fly
> drove the daughter of Inachus; there, Orestes, is the Lycean market place,
> named from the wolf-slaying god; there on the left is Hera's famous temple;
> and in this place to which we have come, know that you see Mycenae, the rich
> in gold, and here the house of Pelops' heirs, so often stained with bloodshed.
> Long ago from here, away from the murder of your father, I carried you for her
> whose blood is yours, your sister, and saved you and reared you up to manhood
> to be the avenger of your murdered father.[178]

The description is particularly long, despite the urgency of the situation, and it is a little disconcerting for anyone who demands too much realism. First there is the landscape seen from an elevated viewpoint: the city of Argos and its territory in the plain. It is initially mentioned in connection with its ancient history, with the wanderings of Io, Inachus's daughter, who has been seduced by Zeus, transformed into a heifer, and tormented by a gad-fly because of Hera's jealousy; then with the site of the Lycian Apollo's temple; and finally with the famous sanctuary of Hera. That is the distant landscape the tutor shows Orestes. As for the place at which they have arrived, there is no possible doubt: it is Mycenae's acropolis, which provides a view of the Argolid plain, even if it is impossible to discern either a marketplace in Argos, on the right, fifteen kilometers away to the southwest, or the Heraion, on the left, only three kilometers away to the southwest, but located on a mountainside. What is important is that like Homer, Sophocles locates Agamemnon's palace in Mycenae. And at the outset, the connection with the epic tradition is asserted with the greatest clarity by the use of the epithet "rich in gold," which Homer already used to qualify Mycenae. And when the chorus of local women considers Orestes' return, it says that "this famous realm of the Mycenaeans shall one day receive him."[179] Thus Aeschylus's innovation is not adopted by Sophocles, who returns to location in the epic myth, incorporating the territory of Argos in the kingdom of Agamemnon and Orestes, as some passages in Homer authorize him to do.[180] In fact, when Aegisthus returns at the end of the tragedy, thinking he will find Orestes' dead body in the palace—instead, he finds Clytemnestra's body—he wants to show everyone this spectacle so that he can establish his power definitively and discourage attempts at rebellion. He says precisely "all the Mycenaeans and the Argives,"[181] not lumping them together as Euripides does, and if he mentions the Mycenaeans first, that is because the royal palace is located on Mycenae's acropolis.

Thus Sophocles seems to be reacting against Aeschylus's placement of the action in Argos. And yet, when *Electra* was performed, Mycenae was still emptied of its inhabitants, as it had been when the *Oresteia* was performed. Is that a sign that Sophocles is more faithful to the tradition of the epic myth and that he is less inclined than Aeschylus or Euripides to twist the mythic material to adapt it to a contemporary political reality? That seems likely. We will find this view confirmed in his treatment of the mythic Athens.

From Mythic Athens to Tragic Athens: How Democracy Affected the Image of Athens

The greatest and most permanent discontinuity that Athenian spectators might have seen between this ancient story, which was the subject matter of the tragedy, and contemporary reality concerned their own history.

In the time of the great myths that they saw represented in the theater, heroes were kings who reigned over subjects, whereas they, the spectators, were proud to be citizens of a city that was now democratic and that had banned tyranny, a city where each Athenian participated in the administration of the city in the popular assembly and possibly in the council, in the dispensing of justice in the courts, designated by voting the principal officials who governed the city, monitored their governance, for which they had to answer, and could even bring suits against them or exile them in the middle of their terms of office. No doubt we should not exaggerate the opposition between the royal Athens of mythic times and the democratic Athens of modern times. If there is an opposition to be made between the two images of Athens in the minds of fifth-century Athenian spectators, it is between the tyrannical Athens of the sixth century, that of Pisistratos and especially of his sons Hippias and Hipparchus, and the Athens of Clisthenes, whose reforms at the end of the sixth century provided the framework for the democracy that the spectators of Greek tragedy in the fifth century knew.

To understand the distinction that Athenians contemporary with Sophocles drew mentally between the Athens of the kings and the Athens of the tyrants, it suffices to quote two drinking songs celebrating the young Harmodius and Aristogiton, who were said to have freed Athens from tyranny by killing one of Pisistratus's sons, Hipparchus:

Harmodius and Aristogiton, hail!
You will have eternal glory;
Because you laid the tyrant low,
And to Athens gave equality.[182]

Harmodius, hail! you did not die,
But stay in the islands of the blest,
Where swift-footed Achilles lives,
And Diomedes, Tydeus' brave son.[183]

One of these two drinking songs contrasts tyrannical Athens with democratic Athens, while the other likens the liberator from tyranny to the heroes of the Homeric epoch. The glory Harmodius won in a period that we would describe as "historical" raises him to the rank of heroes living in a period that we would call "mythic." The man who, in the popular mind, had become not only Athens's liberator from tyranny but also the founder of its democracy found his proper place in the pagan paradise, alongside the prestigious heroes of the *Iliad*, heroes that might also be found in tragedy.

So we can see why this people, which was nevertheless so suspicious of any tyrannical or oligarchical tendencies, had no trouble recognizing itself in the image of the Athens of its ancient kings crowned with the prestige of the epic dimension.

The Image of Theseus, King of Athens, in Aeschylus, Euripides, and Sophocles: A Comparison

The king of Athens who has the most important role in the extant tragedies is Theseus, son of Ægeus and descendent of Erechtheus.[184] With him arises the problem of the encounter between the image of royal Athens and the reality of democratic Athens. How is the image of the ideal king presented in a tragic myth intended for the audience of a democratic city-state?

In the relative chronology of the myth, Theseus belongs, as we have seen, to the generation that had experienced the war of the Seven against Thebes. He was a contemporary of Oedipus and also of Heracles.[185] Theseus belongs to the generation of the dead heroes that the aged Nestor lists in the *Iliad*, heroes whose strength was greater than that of the warriors at Troy.[186] In Troy, the leader of the Athenians was Menestheus, son of Peteos, an excellent general, to be sure, but one who left no trace on the tragic myth and was totally eclipsed by his predecessor Theseus and by his sons Demophon and Acamas.[187] Between the *Iliad* and tragedy, Theseus was, like Heracles, the subject of epic poems;[188] and Bacchylides' lyric poetry mentions several of the hero's exploits before he took power.[189]

The oldest tragedy in which Theseus appears is Aeschylus's *The Men of Eleusis*, which has unfortunately been lost. But it was devoted to an extremely famous service the Athenian king did the Argives after the war of the Seven against Thebes. When the Thebans refused to bury the bodies of the Argive attackers, Theseus intervened on behalf of the dead. This deed had remained so present to the minds of the Greeks that before the Battle of Plataea in 479 BCE the Athenian leaders referred to it during their rivalry with the Tegeans to obtain the honor of being placed on the left wing of the army opposite the Lacedaemonians on the right. This is ancient history, to be sure, but it is history, since it was possible to refer to such a service to obtain a place of honor in a battle; and the Athenians did obtain it. Here is this exploit as it is presented by the Athenians in their discourse at Plataea, according to Herodotus (Theseus's name is not uttered because the king recedes behind the Athenian community):

> When the Argives who had marched with Polynices against Thebes had there made an end of their lives and lay unburied, know that we sent our army against the Cadmeans [= the Thebans] and recovered the dead and buried them in Eleusis.[190]

Euripides used the myth in his extant tragedy *The Suppliant Women*, but he adopted the warlike version already attested in the Athenians' speech at Plataea.[191] This divergence in the treatment of the myth is not fundamental for the image of Athens, because it still confirms its glory.[192] Homer did not know this Athenian version, because Diomedes, Tydeus's son and one of the seven Argive leaders fighting Thebes, mentions that his father was buried in Thebes, which suggests that the Thebans did not forbid their burial.[193] In Sophocles, Theseus does not, as in Aeschylus and Euripides, intervene after the war of the Seven against Thebes, but before the hostilities begin, at the time when he is going to protect Oedipus, who has taken refuge on his territory, and he does so in *Oedipus at Colonus*.[194]

The loss of Aeschylus's *The Men of Eleusis* has deprived us of a comparison that would have been extremely interesting regarding the way in which Aeschylus and Euripides presented the king of Athens in the same mythic sequence. Nonetheless, to gauge the impact of Athens's democratic ideals on the mythic kingdom, it remains possible to compare three "mythic" kings represented by the three tragic poets in an analogous dramatic situation: the king of Argos, Pelasgus, in Aeschylus's *The Suppliant Women*; the king of Athens, Theseus, in Euripides' *The Suppliants*; and Theseus again in Sophocles' *Oedipus at Colonus*.

The pertinence of this comparison, despite the difference in the mythic subjects or the sequence chosen in a single myth, results from a fundamentally analogous situation, that of a tragedy of supplication.[195] A king intervenes to protect a suppliant who has taken refuge in his country at a time when his pursuer, who has come from outside, seeks to seize him by force or cause him to be expelled. In all three tragedies, the scene in which the king confronts the pursuer's emissary reveals his image.

Let us begin with Aeschylus's play, which is by far the oldest.[196] The daughters of Danaus, forming the chorus, have taken refuge as suppliants at an altar located on Argive territory to escape being married to Egyptus's sons, who have pursued them from Egypt. At the point when the herald of the sons of Egyptus is preparing to carry them off by force, the country's king, Pelasgus, hearing their cries of distress, hastens to aid them.[197] In a lively, brief dialogue between the two men, the "mythic" king denounces the violence of a barbarian who has come into a Greek country whose laws and gods he does not respect, and announces the city's decision:

> A decree has been passed by the unanimous resolve of the people of the State, never, under compulsion, to surrender this association of women. Through their resolve [945] the rivet has been driven home, to remain fixed and fast. Not on tablets is this inscribed, nor has it been sealed in folds of books: you hear the truth from free-spoken lips. Now get out of my sight immediately![198]

The king is not a barbarian despot who issues his orders by secret written messages. At the beginning of the tragedy he is presented as the leader exercising his power over a vast territory; here he becomes the spokesman for a decision made unanimously by his people. He is a very democratic king, and not only starting from this point when he reveals his innately democratic nature. As soon as Danaus's daughters have begged him to protect them against the sons of Egyptus, at the risk of war, the king refuses to make a decision before consulting his people; he convokes them, and it is the people that have issued a decree by a show of hands, even if this vote resulted from a persuasive discourse delivered by the king before the assembly. The vocabulary of democratic political life, with words like "people," "vote" and "show of hands," "decision," and "decree," is used along with the vocabulary of royal power. This conception of a democratic kingdom is all the more surprising because nothing in the mythic subject matter suggested this anachronistic representation of a king who is not even Athenian. In short, Pelasgus is, unexpectedly, the first democratic king in tragic mythology.

If Euripides used, some forty years later,[199] the same title that Aeschylus had given his play, even though he chose a different myth, that is because the fundamental situation is comparable. The suppliants forming the chorus are the Argive mothers of the leaders who died during the expedition known as the Seven against Thebes. Accompanied by the unfortunate leader of the expedition, Adrastus, king of Argos, they beg Theseus to get the Thebans to hand over the bodies of their sons. At that point a herald enters; he has been sent by the new king of Thebes, Creon, whom the king of Athens is going to oppose.[200] The scene between Theseus and the Theban herald, which is clearly another version of the scene between Pelasgus and the herald of the sons of Egyptus, develops the political theme much more extensively. When the Theban herald asks on arriving: "Who is the despot of this land?," Theseus gives him a reply that, coming from a mythic king, is rather stupefying:

> You have made a false beginning to your speech, stranger, in seeking a despot here. For this city is not ruled by one man, but is free. The people rule in succession year by year, allowing no preference to wealth, but the poor man shares equally with the rich.[201]

Compared with Aeschylus, this represents a significant change. Whereas Pelasgus said that he could not act without consulting his people, even though he was king, here Theseus speaks as if the monarchy had been abolished and replaced by democracy, because it is the people that governs. Thus even though in the myth Theseus is the king of Athens just as Creon was the king of Thebes, Euripides manages, by a sudden intrusion of the political reality of his time into the myth, to contrast Athenian democracy with the Theban regime. And this is the occasion for a political debate—which is, as Euripides humorously emphasizes, off the subject—in the two opposed speeches in which the representative of Thebes praises monarchy and criticizes democracy, whereas Theseus replies with a critique of monarchy and a paean to democracy. With a certain audacity, Euripides makes the Athenian king a spokesman for democracy.

This encouraged the average spectator to draw the conclusion that Theseus was the founder of democracy. To be sure, the ancient historians made King Theseus the source of political reforms. Thucydides attributes to him the union of the towns of Attica into a single city-state.[202] In his *Constitution of Athens*, Aristotle says that it was under Theseus that the first genuine constitution that deviated a little from the monarchical state was adopted.[203] But how could he be seen as the founder of democracy when his successor, who led the Athenian contingent at Troy, was also a king and a descendant of Erectheus?[204] Nevertheless, the popular view of Theseus as the founder of democracy was clearly attested in the fourth century. The painter Euphranor had represented him alongside Democracy and Demos on the portico of Zeus Liberator in Athens, a painting that Pausanias was still able to see six centuries later.[205] Pausanias mentions that the general opinion among the common people was that the democracy created by Theseus lasted until the tyranny of Pisistratus. Of course, he points out the falsity of such an idea held by a people that does not know history and that relies on what it has heard since childhood in lyric choruses and in tragedies. No doubt Euripides' tragedy *The Suppliants*, with its so singular representation of Theseus, counts among these poetic works that led the public to have an erroneous view of history.[206]

When Sophocles composed, fifteen year later, the scene in which Theseus hurries to respond to the chorus's appeal and collides with the Theban Creon, who has carried off the daughters of his protégé Oedipus, he was remembering the corresponding scene in Aeschylus's *The Suppliant Women*. He puts into the mouth of the king of Athens what the king of Argos said. "Do you think you have come to a land of women?" Pelasgus asked the herald.[207] "You are taking captives at will and subjugating them by force, as if you believed that my city was void of men," Theseus tells Creon.[208] This is not plagiarism, but rather an indirect homage Sophocles is paying to Aeschylus. On the other hand, there is no allusion to the scene in Euripides, which Sophocles nonetheless knew well. This silence comes from the fact that Sophocles created a Theseus very different from that of Euripides. He has restored his royal majesty.[209] Moreover, the image of the king in Sophocles is still less democratic than it is in Aeschylus. Whereas Pelasgus could not make the decision to accept the request made by the suppliants, the daughters of Danaus, without consulting his people, Theseus decides to receive the suppliant, Oedipus, without saying anything about consulting his people;[210] then, when he has to make a quick decision to arrest, before they cross the border, Creon's men who have abducted Oedipus's two daughters, he orders his whole people to assemble at the intersection of the two roads that they could have taken.[211] Theseus is, of course, the idealized king of a free city that respects the law and the gods. But the democratic vocabulary Aeschylus uses regarding his democratic king is absent. There is no question of a decree issued by the people or a show of hands. Moreover, Sophocles' Theseus has nothing in common with the Euripidean Theseus who is effaced behind the power of the people. In Sophocles, there is no conflation of the two political systems, monarchy and democracy. That is clear from the outset, when Oedipus questions the resident of Colonus to find out whether there is a ruler or it is the people who decides. The resident's response is unambiguous: it is a king who rules.[212]

On the basis of the comparison of these three tragedies, it is clear that in Sophocles the mythic tradition is less adapted to the political realities of democratic Athens than it is in Euripides, or even in Aeschylus. There is a certain paradox here: the tragic author who in his life was the most involved in the political history of his city is the one who in his work has transformed the myth the least to adapt it to the realities of his time.

The Wealth of the Mythic Tradition: The Great Tragic Families in Sophocles' Lost Plays

In this attempt to present the tragic myth and the problems it raises, my examples have been chosen chiefly from the great mythic subjects that concern the extant tragedies, with the exception of the myth of Alcmeon. However, let us avoid reducing Sophocles' theater to the seven extant tragedies, or even to the spoken parts of these tragedies alone. Instead, let us seek to broaden the picture by making use of the information provided by the tragedies that have come down to us in fragmentary form. We will begin with what these fragments tell us regarding the great tragic families, and then examine the myth of the Trojan War, the Trojan cycle that provided Sophocles with so much inspiration. Without this broadening, it is impossible to guess the prodigious wealth of the Greek mythic imagination.[213]

The contribution of the lost plays to our knowledge of the two great tragic families represented in the extant tragedies is uneven. All three of the tragedies concerning Oedipus's family have been preserved: *Oedipus the King, Oedipus at Colonus*, and *Antigone*. In these three texts, the family is called the Labdacids,[214] that is, the descendants of Labdacus, the founder of the line, whose son is Laius, Oedipus's father. On one occasion the reference to the history of the family goes much further back, when Oedipus, in his passionate desire to discover Laius's murderer, not only mentions Labdacus, the father of Laius, but goes three generations beyond the founder of the family: first to Polydorus, Labdacus's father, then to Cadmus, the founder of Thebes, and finally to Agenor, Cadmus's father.[215] But despite this prestigious lineage, Sophocles wrote no other plays about this family of the Labdacids.

On the other hand, only a small proportion of the plays that Sophocles devoted to the other great tragic family, that of Agamemnon and Orestes, are extant. Nine of his plays that were focused on this family have been lost; only one has come down to us, *Electra*, in which Orestes avenges the murder of his father, Agamemnon. The family also appears in a secondary role in *Ajax*, where Agamemnon speaks after his brother Menelaus in opposing Ajax's burial; nonetheless, the tragic destiny of the family is not involved. Of the nine lost plays two were about Orestes' relatives, one bearing the name of his mother, Clytemnestra, and the other the name of his sister sacrificed by Agamemnon before the departure for Troy, Iphigeneia. The seven others go back to earlier generations, thus illustrating the tragic history of this family much more amply than that of the Labdacids.

In *Electra*, there are fleeting references to this family going back in time.[216] At the beginning of the tragedy, the tutor shows Orestes the place where they have come: "Know that you see Mycenae, the rich in gold, and here the house of Pelops' heirs."[217] It is the family's palace called by the name of its ancestor, Pelops. Later on, when the girls' chorus, sensing that the hand of justice is about to fall on the family, sings of the first sin, that of Pelops, the founder of the house:

> O chariot-race of Pelops long ago, source of many a sorrow, what disaster you have brought upon this land! For ever since Myrtilus sank to rest beneath the waves, hurled to utter destruction from his golden chariot in disgraceful outrage, from that time to this, outrage and its many sorrows were never yet gone from this house.[218]

This kind of elliptical reference, in the style of the choral lyric,[219] assumes that the spectator has a knowledge of mythology that we find astonishing, in part because we have lost many of the tragedies these spectators knew. One of Sophocles' tragedies, performed before 414, was probably about this famous chariot race in which Pelops defeated Hippodamia's father. This tragedy is entitled *Oenomaus*, after Hippodamia's father. Oenomaus was the king of Pisa, who killed all his daughter's suitors, whom he defeated in chariot racing, down to the day when Hippodamia, having fallen in love with Pelops, bribed her father's coachman, Myrtilus, who loved her. Myrtilus replaces the bronze linchpins of Pelops's chariot with beeswax ones; the wheel comes off, the father dies, and Pelops wins the race. But Myrtilus, having tried to rape Hippodamia, is thrown into the sea by Pelops. However, before he dies, the coachman curses Pelops. According to the chorus in *Electra*, these curses were the source of the Pelopids' misfortunes.[220] Among the latter that persisted in the palace there is, of course, the most recent, the death of Agamemnon, killed by Clytemnestra and Aegisthus. However, in the preceding generation there was also the rivalry for power between Atreus, Agamemnon's father, and Thyestes, Aegisthus's father; its most famous episode is the banquet at which Atreus fed Thyestes his own sons' flesh.[221] Sophocles wrote a lost tragedy about Atreus and three tragedies about Thyestes.[222] And if we add that Sophocles also wrote a tragedy about Pelops's sister, entitled *Niobe*, and another about Pelops's father, entitled *Tantalus*, it is clear that we are going back into the mythic time of this family of the Pelopids as far as its origin and beyond, that is, over five generations from Orestes to Tantalus, who is Zeus's son. Thus the myth of the Pelopid family, represented by a single extant tragedy, recovers a broad historical perspective if we take into account all the lost tragedies devoted to Tantalus, to Pelops, and to his descendants in the generations preceding the Trojan War.[223]

Of the great tragic families that Sophocles treated in his work, the one that suffered the most from the loss of the tragedies is that of Alcmeon, whose myth parallels that of Orestes. We have already discussed this myth, along with those of the other great families, to show the difference between the culture of Sophocles' contemporaries and our own.[224] We have seen that four of Sophocles' lost plays were connected with this myth. Three derive their names from the three members of the family: Alcmeon, the avenging son, Amphiaraus, the avenged father, and Eriphyle, the mother on whom the vengeance is taken. The fourth tragedy, *The Epigones* (= descendants) owes its name to the sons of the Seven against Thebes, who have left on a new expedition to avenge their dead fathers. Alcmeon has doubly avenged his father, first by participating in a victorious expedition against Thebes, and again by killing his mother on his return. Thus taking the lost tragedies into account reveals the existence and the importance of this tragic family in Sophocles' production.

The Wealth of the Mythic Tradition: The Trojan Cycle in Sophocles' Lost Plays

However, the lost plays are most revealing with respect to the generation of the heroes of the Trojan War. We have seen that among the extant tragedies, two out of seven—Ajax and Philoctetes—deal with the expedition to Troy. But we must add at least thirty-odd plays—tragedies or satyr plays—for this mythic period that stretches from the causes of the war to the more or less turbulent return of the heroes to their homeland, Odysseus being the one who returned last.

Regarding this period, the tragic authors could draw their subjects from a body of epic material that was much richer than the one that has come down to us. In addition to the *Iliad* and the *Odyssey*, they had other epics with episodes that, put end to end, covered the whole of the mythic sequence, inserting the *Iliad* and the *Odyssey* into it at their appointed places. When they used them, the tragic authors of the fifth century were not concerned with the origin or date of all these poems, as was later scholarship, starting with Aristotle. For them, it was a body of Homeric lore, in the broad sense of the term, on which they drew. Aristotle drew a distinction between Homer, the author of the *Iliad* and the *Odyssey*, and other poets who wrote Trojan epics. Even though these epics have been lost, we have a valuable summary that indicates the content of the main episodes in each of them.[225] This material will be presented briefly here.

If we follow the chronological order of the myth, the first poem is the *Cyprian Songs*, a long epic in twelve books that covers the period from the causes of the war up to Achilles' withdrawal from the battle, that is, up to the beginning of the *Iliad*.[226] The other poems in the cycle, completing what happens after the *Iliad*, each cover a shorter period: three distinct poems, put end to end, form eleven books, which corresponds to the length of the *Cyprian Songs*. They relate the end of the Trojan War just as the *Cyprian Songs* relate the beginning: the *Aetheopis* takes as its subject the exploits of Achilles up to his death;[227] the *Little Iliad* goes from the consequences of Achilles' death to the cunning introduction of the wooden horse into Troy;[228] finally, *The Sack of Troy* (*Iliupersis*) describes the taking of Troy.[229] After the war comes the story of the returns. A poem on this subject was supposed to complement the *Odyssey*, which deals only with the return of Odysseus.[230] Finally, there is a sequel to the *Odyssey*, called the *Telegony*, from the name of the son of Odysseus and Circé, Telegonus, who is not mentioned in the Homeric poems. The best-known passage is the final episode, where Telegonus, going in search of his father, arrives in Ithaca, where he goes on a raid and kills his father without knowing it, as Oedipus had done.[231]

The length of mythic time covered by these epics of the Trojan cycle and the multiplicity of the episodes allowed them to provide the tragic poets with numerous subjects. A very important passage in Aristotle's *Poetics* can serve as a point of departure here. Aristotle notes that Homer's poems (the *Iliad* and the *Odyssey*), organized in accord with the unity of action around the wrath of Achilles or the return of Odysseus, did not provide the subject matter for many tragedies, whereas other epics, such as the *Cyprian Songs* or the *Little Iliad* that were composed of multiple parts, did:

> Out of an *Iliad* or an *Odyssey* only one tragedy can be made, or two at most, whereas several have been made out of the *Cypria*, and out of the *Little Iliad*

more than eight, e.g., *The Award of Arms, Philoctetes, Neoptolemus, Eurypylus, The Begging, The Laconian Women, The Sack of Troy*, and *Sailing of the Fleet*, and *Sinon*, too, and *The Trojan Women*.[232]

Aristotle had an immense advantage over us: he could read all the epic poems and all the tragedies he cited. What is important about the extent of the loss of the theatrical production is that of the ten tragedies listed here, only two have come down to us intact, Euripides' *The Trojan Women* and Sophocles' *Philoctetes*. The absence of the authors' names in this list does not make it easier to identify the lost tragedies. Which are the tragedies, preserved or lost, that Sophocles drew from the mythic sequence envisaged by Aristotle in his list, that is, the period between the death of Achilles and the taking of Troy?

The order of the enumeration of the tragedies in the *Poetics* is not insignificant. In general it follows the episodes of the *Little Iliad* in accord with the chronology of the myth. In any case, the first tragedy mentioned in the *Poetics*, *The Award of Arms*, corresponds to the first episode in the *Little Iliad*, summed up this way by Proclus: "The Award of Arms [of Achilles] takes place and Odysseus, in accord with Athena's wish, receives them. Ajax, become mad, damages the Achaeans' captive herds and commits suicide." It is Aeschylus who is the author of this tragedy. But from the beginning of this enumeration it is clear that the list of tragedies whose subject is drawn from the *Little Iliad* is not complete, for it is obviously from this same episode that Sophocles borrowed his extant tragedy *Ajax*.

As for his *Philoctetes*, it is taken from the following episode in the *Little Iliad*, which Proclus presents this way: "Afterward, Odysseus having set up an ambush, captures Helenus, and the latter having prophesied the fall of Troy, Diomedes takes Philoctetes back from Lemnos. Healed by Machaon, Philoctetes confronts Alexander in single combat and kills him." When Sophocles composed his *Philoctetes*, the myth had already been put on the stage by the two other great tragedians in plays that already bore the same title.[233] However, Sophocles differs from the other two tragedians because he wrote a second tragedy on Philoctetes entitled *Philoctetes at Troy*.[234] It corresponds to the second part of the episode in the *Little Iliad*, in which Philoctetes, his wound healed, performs deeds, the most remarkable of which is his single combat against Alexander-Paris, whom he kills with the bow he inherited from Heracles. But the few fragments that remain offer no clues regarding the details of the action.

Among the other tragedies cited in Aristotle's list, three are by Sophocles: *Eurypylus, The Laconian Women*, and *Sinon*.[235] Eurypylus is the son of Telephus who has unwillingly come to the aid of the Trojans, a victim like Amphiarius of "gifts to women."[236] His exploits and his death are presented this way in the summary of the *Little Iliad*: "Eurypylus, son of Telephus, comes to the aid of the Trojans and although he performs his high deeds, Neoptolemus kills him." In Sophocles' tragedy, a messenger relates the single combat in which Eurypylus and Neoptolemus confronted one another "without insults and without brag-gadocio," as self-possessed warriors.[237] The death of Eurypylus seems to have been decisive. After it the siege of Troy and the preparation for taking it begins, notably with the construction of the wooden horse. *The Laconian Women* is about Odysseus's mission when he secretly enters Troy to prepare to take it. The tragedy is named, as often happens, after the chorus, which is composed of the faithful servants that Helen took with her when she left her homeland in Laco-nia. The play was devoted to an episode at the end of the siege in which Odys-seus, probably accompanied by Diomedes, sneaks into Troy at night through a sewer. Although he is disguised as a beggar, Helen recognizes Odysseus.[238] Far from betraying him, Helen helps him. Odysseus, who had come to prepare the taking of Troy, seizes the statue of Athena, the famous Palladion, which he carries back to the ships, aided by Diomedes.

No one other than Sophocles seems to have composed a tragedy named *Sinon*. The role played by the Greek Sinon after the construction of the wooden horse is well known through the account of the taking of Troy in Virgil's *Aeneid*.[239] It is he who, having stayed alone with the wooden horse after the tactical retreat of the Greek forces to the island of Tenedos, got himself arrested by Trojan shepherds. Chained by them and taken before Priam, he succeeded, by means of a long, cunning speech, in arousing the Trojans' pity and persuading them to receive the wooden horse. It is not impossible that in the splendid speech he gives Sinon Virgil was inspired by Sophocles' lost tragedy, because this speech has a family resemblance with Neoptolemus's cunning speech in the *Philoctetes*.[240]

Thus eight of Sophocles' tragedies are drawn from the *Little Iliad*. If we add to the *Little Iliad* the epic poem that immediately follows it, *The Sack of Troy*, the list of Sophocles' plays ranges over an extremely short mythic time. It is true that the taking of Troy and its destruction constitute a sequence particularly suitable for tragic subjects.

Three of Sophocles' tragedies correspond to three episodes of the taking of Troy: Laocoon, Ajax the Locrian, and Polyxena.[241] In the summary of the epic poem *The Sack of Troy*, the first episode is that of Laocoon, the priest of Apollo and the victim of a portentous event after the Trojans had brought the wooden horse into Troy as an offering to Athena and were celebrating what they thought was the end of the war: "At this very time, two serpents appear and kill Laocoon and one of his two sons; disquieted by this portentous event, Aeneas and his men surreptitiously leave for Ida." This excessively curt summary should be comple-mented by the epic, moving account in Virgil's *Aeneid*. This episode was drama-tized by Sophocles in his tragedy entitled *Laocoon*. In Sophocles' work, Aeneas's father, Anchises, predicted the fall of Troy by comparing the ancient recom-mendations made by his mother Aphrodite with the recent misfortune that had struck Laocoon's family, and ordered his son to take him to Ida.[242]

The epic poem deals with three memorable episodes during the sack of the city itself: first, death of Priam, killed by Neoptolemus in his palace, when the king had taken refuge at the altar of Zeus; next, Menelaus's discovery of Helen, whom he takes back to the ships after killing her new husband, Deiphobus; and finally, the impious conduct of Ajax the Locrian, son of Oileus. This third episode is presented this way in the summary: "Ajax, son of Oileus, seeking to take Cassandra away by force, pulls down the statue of Athena to which she is clinging as a suppliant; angered by this impious act, the Hellenes want to stone him, but Ajax saves himself by taking refuge at the altar of Athena and thus escapes the danger that threatens him."[243] It is this last episode that Sophocles dramatized in his tragedy entitled *Ajax the Locrian*, in order to distinguish him from Ajax of Salamis. Athena was said to appear in the tragedy and address harsh reproaches to the Greeks.[244]

The epic poem *The Sack of Troy* ends with the tragic sacrifice of Polyxena, the daughter of Hecuba and Priam, demanded by Achilles' ghost, who appears over his tomb. Here is Proclus's summary: "Then, burning the city, the Hellenes sacrifice Polyxena on Achilles' tomb."[245] This episode was dramatized by both Sophocles and Euripides. The sacrifice of Polyxena occupies the first part of Euripides' tragedy entitled *Hecuba*. One ancient commentator notes on the first verse of this extant tragedy: "What concerns Polyxena can also be found in Sophocles." Sophocles' tragedy was entitled *Polyxena*.[246] In it, the shade of Achilles appeared over his tomb, as did that of Darius in Aeschylus's *The Persians*.[247] In antiquity, this appearance of Achilles was considered as impressive as the death of Oedipus at the end of *Oedipus at Colonus*.[248]

Thus we can count eleven tragedies by Sophocles on the short period concerning the end of the Trojan War, from the death of Achilles to the taking of Troy, the period that corresponds to the *Little Iliad* and *The Sack of Troy*. That is only one part of the epic sequence devoted to the Trojan myth. We must also count the period that precedes it, from the causes of the war to the death of Achilles, the period that was covered by the *Cyprian Songs*, the *Iliad* and the *Aethiopis*, and then the period that follows the taking of Troy, that is, the sequence of the heroes' returns to their homelands, corresponding to the epic poems *The Returns from Troy*, the *Odyssey*, and the *Telegony*.

Without being able to pursue in detail this inquiry whose origin was the passage from Aristotle's *Poetics* giving a list of the plays that the tragic poets drew from the *Little Iliad*, we must emphasize, in a synthetic way, that what Aristotle says in the same passage about the difference in inspiration between the *Iliad* and the *Cyprian Songs* is strikingly verified for Sophocles. From the *Iliad* Sophocles drew only one play, or perhaps two,[249] whereas—to repeat Aristotle's words—the *Cyprian Songs* gave rise to many tragedies, in fact to seven tragedies at least, to which must be added six satyr plays.[250] Let us mention, among these tragedies in addition to *Iphigeneia*—already cited regarding the great tragic families in the lost tragedies—*The Madness of Odysseus.*[251] This tragedy about Odysseus deserves special attention, because Sophocles alludes to it in his *Philoctetes.* At the moment when Philoctetes, under the control of the guards, spills his bile against Odysseus, he makes a brief allusion to a not very glorious event in his adversary's past: "You sailed with them only when brought under their yoke by trickery and compulsion."[252]

This simple allusion to the way in which Odysseus was compelled to take part in the expedition against Troy assumes that this past was well known to the spectators. In fact, it already constituted an episode of the *Cyprian Songs* that is presented this way by Proclus:

> Then they [Menelaus and Agamemnon, after Helen's abduction] gathered the leaders, going all over Greece. And since Odysseus pretended to be mad because he did not want to participate in the expedition, they caught him *in flagrante delicto* by abducting, at Palamedes' suggestion, his son Telemachus in order to punish him.

In his *Agamemnon,* Aeschylus already alluded to this recruitment of Odysseus by compulsion.[253] But Sophocles devoted an entire tragedy to it, entitled *The Madness of Odysseus.* The tragedy on Odysseus's madness was supposed to constitute a fine illustration of the allusive passage in *Philoctetes.* Under the single Greek word *klopè,* which means not only ruse but more precisely abduction by ruse, lies the whole implicit story of the abduction of Telemachus to confound Odysseus's simulation.[254] Unfortunately, this tragedy, whose subject we know well, has been totally lost except for two verses and a few words! A fine example of how inquiry into the lost plays of a tragic author, especially in the case of Sophocles, is simultaneously instructive and disappointing.

Odysseus never pardoned Palamedes. He planned his death, which took place at the beginning of the war, just before Achilles retired to his tent. Sophocles wrote a play on this subject, *Palamedes.*[255] As in the case of Philoctetes, each of the three great tragedians wrote a *Palamedes.* But unlike Sophocles' play, the others have been lost. The death of Palamedes, son of Nauplius, known for his ingenuity, is one of the last episodes of the *Cyprian Songs.* Proclus's summary mentions only the fact: "Then comes the death of Palamedes." But we know a little more about it thanks to Pausanias, who could still read this epic poem in the second century CE. Describing the famous fresco that Polygnotus, a contemporary of Sophocles, had painted on a wall of the treasury of Cnidus in Delphi, one part of which illustrates Odysseus descending into the Underworld, Pausanias lingers over a scene in which we see Ajax of Salamis, Palamedes, and Thersites playing dice—a game Palamedes invented—while the other Ajax, the Locrian, stands watching them play. According to Pausanias, Polygnotus brought together in this scene all of Odysseus's enemies. And concerning Palamedes, he notes he remembers reading about his death in the *Cyprian Songs*: he was killed by Diomedes and Odysseus during a fishing expedition.[256] This is the oldest version of the myth. But even while being inspired by the myth, the tragic poets could innovate. They privileged another of Odysseus's stratagems described by Polyaenus in his work *Stratagems in War* (second century CE): "There is also this stratagem that the tragic poets sang: Odysseus triumphed over Palamedes in the Achaeans' tribunal by surreptitiously putting gold in his home, and the most knowledgeable of the Greeks was thus accused of treachery." Moreover, Odysseus had forced a Phrygian prisoner to write a false letter sent by Priam to convict Palamedes of treason. Here again, the fragments are too few to reconstruct Sophocles' tragedy. This is also true of Aeschylus's and Euripides' *Palamedes*.[257]

The death of Palamedes, stoned by the Greeks, was not without consequences. Just as Odysseus took revenge on Palamedes, Nauplius, Palamedes' father, wanted to avenge his son. Sophocles wrote a tragedy on this vengeance entitled *Nauplius Lights a Fire*.[258] This vengeance allows us to jump from the *Cyprian Songs* to the epic poems about the warriors' returns, because it took place when the fleet returned.

In the summary of the epic poems about the returns from Troy, this episode is mentioned laconically: "Then the storm near the Capharean Promontory is described." The Capharean Promontory is south of Euboea, which one passes on returning from Troy. In Euripides' *Helen*, Menelaus, referring briefly to the hardships of his return, alludes to "Nauplius's fires in Euboea."[259] These events must thus have been well known to spectators in the fifth century BCE. They are explained by later mythographers: to avenge himself, during the storm suffered at night by the Greek fleet off the Capharean Promontory, Nauplius lit fires on the coast to attract the ships, which were wrecked there. The title of Sophocles' tragedy leaves no doubt about its subject.[260] The death of Agamemnon and the vengeance of Orestes was also mentioned at the end of *The Returns from Troy*. Here is Proclus's summary: "Then, while Agamemnon was killed by Aegisthus and Clytemnestra, there is the vengeance taken by Orestes and Pylades and the return of Menelaus to his home." Sophocles' tragedy *Electra* is thus connected to a certain extent with the epic of *The Returns*, because the vengeance occurs at the same time as the return of Menelaus, but it is related to it only indirectly and is situated rather in the history of the tragic family of the Pelopids.[261]

So far as the returns are concerned, Sophocles drew several plays from the *Odyssey*.[262] The most famous is entitled *Nausicaa* or *The Laundresses*. It was inspired by book 6, in which the daughter of the king of the Phaeacians is playing ball with her servants when she encounters Odysseus. Sophocles, as we have already seen, is supposed to have shown marvelous skill in throwing the ball as he played the role of Nausicaa.[263] Another play entitled *The Footwashing* (*Niptra*) is based on another famous scene in the *Odyssey*, in which the nurse, washing Odysseus's feet, recognizes him by a wound he had received while hunting.[264] However, Sophocles did not neglect the most romantic epic that provided a sequel to the *Odyssey*, the *Telegony*. The final episode, which deals with Odysseus's death, gave rise to the tragedy entitled *Odysseus Wounded by the Spine*.[265] Telegonus, the son of Circé and Odysseus, leaves in search of his father, whom he has never known. Landing in Ithaca, he carries out a raid. Odysseus arrives to repel the aggressor and is mortally wounded by his own son. The recognition comes when it is too late. In this play, the dying Odysseus appears on a litter and laments his fate as Heracles does at the end of *Women of Trachis*.[266]

In short, Sophocles often drew his inspiration from the epic cycle. This was noticed in antiquity. A learned guest at Athenaeus's Banquet (second century CE) remarked: "Sophocles loved the epic cycle to the point of composing whole plays following the way the myth was treated in it."[267]

The Wealth of the Mythic Tradition: Secondary Myths in the Extant Tragedies and Principal Myths in the Lost Tragedies

In the tragedies that have been preserved whole, it is not only the principal mythic subject of the tragedy that appears but also, through the mediation of the choruses, other myths that are more or less related to the principal subject. These secondary myths were often the principal myths of lost tragedies. This is therefore a final way to suggest the wealth of the mythic imagination in Sophocles' theater.

The technique that consists of inserting into a mythic framework references to other, older myths, evoked by analogy, is not an invention of the tragic genre.[268] It already appeared in Homer. The best-known example is that of the myth of Meleager in the *Iliad*. To try to convince Achilles to give up his anger against Agamemnon, an official embassy is sent to him. Phoenix, his old tutor, speaks second after Odysseus. In a long speech addressed to Achilles, he does not limit himself to references to the recent past, Achilles' childhood which he guided so carefully, but recalls, as he says himself, a "deed of old days and not of yesterday." Then Phoenix recounts, in more than seventy verses, the story of Meleager, a tragic myth par excellence from which Sophocles himself drew a tragedy.[269] Why such a long narrative in the *Iliad*? Because there are analogies between Meleager's wrath when he refuses to fight to defend his city under attack and the wrath of Achilles refusing to repel the assaults of the Trojans defending their city under attack. Meleager serves as an example, or rather a counterexample. Achilles must not act as Meleager did. He must not refuse the gifts the envoys offer and await the most critical moment to give up his anger and return to combat. The myth of Meleager thus already functions in the *Iliad* as a secondary myth in a context of persuasion.

Sophocles uses a secondary myth chiefly in a context of consolation. It is at the very moment when the heroine is at the nadir of her despair that the chorus takes examples from past history. Thus when Electra is desolate upon learning of her brother's (false) death, to console her the women in the chorus refer to the earlier, parallel myth of Alcmeon, as we have already seen in the presentation of the myth of the son of Amphiaraus.[270] This technique of evocation by analogy reaches its high point in a chorus in Sophocles' *Antigone*. Whereas Electra wept over the death of her brother Orestes, Antigone weeps over her own fate, because she has to enter the subterranean prison that will be her final resting place. She leaves lamenting her suffering, expressing her indignation against those who caused it, and finally, asserting her piety. The chorus of old Theban men then addresses the young woman, even though she has already left. It devotes a whole song to asking her to resign herself to her fate. To do so, it chooses in the past three exemplary destinies that are comparable to hers.[271] Here is the first one:

> So too endured Danaë in her beauty to change the light of the sky for brass-bound walls, and in that chamber, both burial and bridal, submitted her destiny's yoke. And yet was she of esteemed lineage, my daughter, and guarded a deposit of the seed of Zeus that had fallen in a golden rain. But dreadful is the mysterious power of fate—there is no deliverance from it by wealth or by war, by towered city, or dark, sea-beaten ships.

The evocation of Danaë takes the audience back several generations before Antigone.[272] Danaë had a destiny that was simultaneously prestigious and tragic. The prestigious side is emphasized by Zeus himself in Homer, who cites among his lovers "Danaë of the fair ankles, daughter of Acmsius, who bare Perseus, pre-eminent above all warriors."[273] Sophocles insists instead on the tragic aspect. But to understand the allusions, we have to recall the whole of the story. The king of Argos, Acrisius, having consulted the oracle at Delphi regarding the birth of a son, learned that he would not have any, but that of his daughter would be born a son who would kill him. To prevent her from having a son, he immediately imprisoned his daughter in an underground prison of bronze constructed under the courtyard of his palace. But Zeus, who was infatuated with Danaë, managed to unite with her in the form of a golden rain, and from this union was born the hero Perseus whose exploit was to decapitate Medusa, and who in the end accidentally killed his grandfather at Larissa in Thessaly. The oracle was ultimately fulfilled: Acrisius did not escape his destiny.[274] Sophocles had treated the story in several tragedies. One is entitled *Acrisius*, another *Danaë*, and a third *The Men of Larissa*. This latter play is about the death of Acrisius, who was killed at Larissa by a discus thrown by his grandson Perseus during a competition.[275]

The analogy between the fate of Danaë and that of Antigone is based essentially on the subterranean prison. Before Antigone, Acrisius's daughter had left the light of day to be imprisoned underground in a sepulchral chamber far from anyone's eyes, under constraint. But she was also a woman "esteemed for her birth." Antigone must therefore resign herself. The chorus even suggests that Danaë was a woman all the more esteemed because she bore within her Zeus's seed. Thus a fortiori Antigone must resign herself. There is a certain cruelty in reminding Antigone of Danaë's divine pregnancy, even if she is not present. Antigone had complained, at the moment of her departure, about not having experienced union with a husband. We must not expect too much delicacy from a chorus of men, especially since it had not spared the rebellious young woman its criticism as she was leaving. The analogy is thus a lesson in submission to the power of destiny, expressed by the image of the yoke.

It is this image of the yoke that serves as a link to the second secondary myth chosen by the chorus in *Antigone*, that of Lycurgus, son of Dryas:

> And Dryas's son, the Edonian king swift to rage, was tamed in recompense for his frenzied insults, when, by the will of Dionysus, he was shut in a rocky prison. There the fierce and swelling force of his madness trickled away. That man came to know the god whom in his frenzy he had provoked with mockeries. For he had sought to quell the god-inspired women and the Bacchanalian fire, and he angered the Muses who love the flute.[276]

This time Antigone's destiny is compared to that of a man, and no longer to that of a woman. The name of the man, Lycurgus, is not even mentioned by Sophocles, who is content with a periphrasis—Dryas's son—which is a sign of the fame of the myth. This Lycurgus, the king of the Thracian people the Edoni, opposed the god Dionysus when he came into his country, and was punished for it; a man cannot oppose a god, even unwittingly. Attested as early as the *Iliad*,[277] the myth had been popularized by Aeschylus's tetralogy entitled *The Lycurgeia*,[278] and also by a rival of Aeschylus who presented a tetralogy with the same title at the competition of 467 BCE.[279] It was Aeschylus's production that remained famous in the fifth century, to the point that Aristophanes cites it and parodies it in one of his comedies.[280]

From Homer to tragedy the meaning of the myth remains unchanged, but its form evolves. In Homer, Dionysus is still a child, and it is the god's nurses whom Lycurgus pursues, while Dionysus, frightened by the man's threats, plunges into the sea, and is saved by Thetis. From Aeschylus on, Dionysus is no longer a child, but a young man with an effeminate air, followed by the *thiasus* of the Bacchantes. Sophocles' allusion suggests that the king, who is of a choleric nature, mocked the god without knowing his identity, and that he wanted to stop the Bacchantes' excesses. But the god took revenge on him. In Homer, the gods' vengeance was first of all blindness. According to Sophocles, the king was imprisoned in a stone dungeon where he had time to get over his madness. The choice of such a punishment—a variant in the myth or an invention of the tragic author?[281]—establishes an obvious link with the destiny of Antigone, who is also condemned to a stone prison.[282] But we are still astonished by the choice of a secondary myth that compares a woman who declares her piety in her last words[283] with a man who is punished for his impiety. Why such a difference? The ancients saw simply a comparison bearing on the sameness of the misfortunes, without reference to the problem of guilt.[284] We can also see in this a way of combining consolation with a lesson: the chorus of old men, even though they felt pity for the young woman when she came out of the palace to go to her prison, has not ceased, all through the tragedy, to denounce the folly of her revolt. Just as Lycurgus discharged in prison his insulting anger against the god, Antigone will discharge in her prison her insulting anger against the king.[285]

We will deal more briefly with the third and final secondary myth evoked by the chorus to urge Antigone to resign herself, even though it occupies twice as much space as each of the other two myths. The chorus first transports the spectator to another region of Thrace, to Salmidessa, whose king was Phineus. His two sons had had their eyes put out by a cruel stepmother with "the point of a shuttle." They wept over their lamentable fate. Then comes the evocation of their mother. She was Cleopatra, Phineus's first wife who was repudiated and had to accept her sons' sad fate. Cleopatra was nonetheless the daughter of a god, Boreas (the north wind), and her mother was the daughter of the Athenian king Erectheus.[286] Sophocles is very allusive, not even giving the name of the woman whose fate is compared to that of Antigone. It is true that he dealt with this myth as a principal myth in several other tragedies.[287] Here is the conclusion of the last myth, and with it, the chorus's song:

> She was the child of Boreas, running swift as horses over the steep hills, a daughter of gods. Yet she, too, was assailed by the long-lived Fates, my child.[288]

The lesson that concludes the third myth repeats that of the first. It is a lesson of submission: Antigone must submit because women as noble as Danaë or Cleopatra had to do so. And from Danaë to Cleopatra, there is even a progression that must reinforce the reasons for submitting. Danaë had received a divine seed. Cleopatra had been born of a divine seed.

Such are the three secondary myths that offer the chorus in Sophocles' *Antigone* a reference point for putting into perspective the fate of the heroine who is heading for her underground prison. But Antigone herself, just as she is about to enter her final resting place, had already compared her deplorable end with that of another woman of whom she has heard, Niobe:

> I have heard with my own ears how our Phrygian guest, the daughter of Tantalus, perished in so much suffering on steep Sipylus—how, like clinging ivy, the sprouting stone subdued her. And the rains, as men tell, do not leave her melting form, nor does the snow, but beneath her weeping lids she dampens her collar. Most like hers is the god-sent fate that leads me to my rest.[289]

Thus four secondary myths are used to give an ample mythic orchestration of Antigone's destiny. And three of them have been the object of principal myths in other lost tragedies by Sophocles, whether they were earlier or later than their evocation in *Antigone*. There is an echo effect in the poet's immense work where these secondary myths are a reminder of old tragedies or the seed of new ones.

Taking the lost tragedies into account thus incontestably lends the extant tragedies a new dimension and offers a new perspective on the immensity of the mythic forest exploited by Sophocles, where there still remains something to be discovered. We can certainly not deny that an incursion into Sophocles' fragmentary plays is disappointing insofar as with the exception of the satyr play *The*

Searchers, none of the extant plays can be reconstituted in its dramatic progression. But the inquiry considerably broadens the palette of the mythic subjects treated in tragedy. And ultimately, when Aristotle declares in his *Poetics* that the tragedies do not have a large number of families as their subject, he already risks contributing to giving a simplifying view.[290]

The Elaboration of the Mythic Tradition in Sophoclean Tragedy: Tradition and Innovation

Faced with the wealth of the mythic material, even though it is perceived by the audience as an old, traditional story including the stories of the great families in the succession of the generations and of the great cities punctuated by civil wars between Greek cities or by distant expeditions across the seas, the spectators doubtless had a very malleable conception of the details, so rich and varied were the traditions. The complexity and variety of the different versions of the same myth, its development in literature from Homer to the tragic poets, passing by way of the rest of the epic tradition and lyric poetry, might authorize the tragic authors to adopt different perspectives on the same mythic sequences that they dramatized. The tragic authors did not fail to compete with their epic or lyric models and especially among themselves, to put their own stamp on the material and to win the favor of the audience.

Tragic production, when the subject is mythic, is never complete creation. It is a subtle mixture of tradition and invention in different degrees.

It goes without saying that the choice of a subject already implies options with respect to the tradition. When Sophocles chooses a subject like Sinon, which seems not to have been treated by any of his predecessors, or for that matter by any of his successors, he had a free hand to dramatize an episode from the taking of Troy on the basis of an epic model. The subject was completely original, at least in the tragic genre. This degree of originality is, generally speaking, the case when Sophocles is the first to dramatize a mythic sequence, even a better-known one. It seems that Sophocles was the first to dramatize the death of Heracles (in *Women of Trachis*)[291] and perhaps even Antigone's revolt.[292]

The originality may also consist in the choice of the mythic variant taken as the tragedy's principal subject. That is the case, as we have seen, in his *Oedipus at Colonus*. When Sophocles dramatizes the local variant of Oedipus's death in Attica, against Homer's authority, he chooses a subject that no tragic author of the fifth century had dealt with as a principal subject.[293] In this sense, we can say that the last tragic production of the fifth century deals with an original subject, even though its protagonist is one of the tragic heroes par excellence.

On the other hand, when Sophocles chooses a character and a mythic sequence that have already been treated before him by one or several of his predecessors, the subject seems less new if we judge it by modern criteria; but for the ancients, the challenge was greater and the play on the tragic models subtler and more exciting. Four of the extant seven tragedies by Sophocles take up subjects already treated by Aeschylus. Two of them concern the two great tragic families. We have seen, by studying the history of these myths, that *Oedipus the King* and *Electra* are inspired by the central plays in Aeschylus's two trilogies, the *Oedipodeia* and the *Oresteia*.[294] The other two tragedies in which Sophocles reworked a subject treated by Aeschylus belong to the Trojan cycle. Ajax's suicide had already been treated by Aeschylus in his play *The Thracian Women*.[295] And Sophocles' *Philoctetes* had been preceded by a *Philoctetes* by Aeschylus, and also by one by Euripides.[296]

The reworking of the same mythic sequences, insofar as the tradition offered variants, forced the tragic authors to make choices that might agree or disagree with those of their predecessors. Some of Aeschylus's innovations with respect to Homer were not challenged by Sophocles. We have seen, for example, how the role played by the Delphic oracles in the tragic destiny of Oedipus or Orestes is a new element in Aeschylean tragedy in relation to Homer, one that Sophocles adopted and used.[297] But other innovations in Aeschylus's tragic version were not adopted. By presenting Orestes as a liberator at the end of *Electra*, Sophocles returns to a Homeric conception of the vengeance and does away with the tragic repercussions of the matricide and Orestes' madness, which conclude the corresponding play by Aeschylus, *The Libation Bearers*, and then the exile and judgment in Athens that form the subject of the last play in the Aeschylean trilogy, *The Eumenides*.[298]

Sophocles' subtle play with the selected mythic material in relation to Aeschylus often escapes us when the corresponding tragedy by Aeschylus has not been preserved. This happens in three cases out of four (*Ajax*, *Oedipus the King*, *Philoctetes*). However, even then we can benefit from valuable clues provided by ancient readers who were able to compare the two tragedies. We will take the example of a variant of the Ajax myth on the question of the hero's invulnerability:

> It has been handed down from history that Ajax was invulnerable in every part of his body, except only in the armpit, because Heracles, having covered him with his lion's skin, had left that part uncovered because of the case that held his bow. Apropos of Ajax, Aeschylus says that he bent his sword—his skin did not yield to the blow struck to kill himself—, "as when one draws a bow," before a divinity, according to what he says, came to show him where he had to strike the blow. Sophocles, for his part, not wanting to compete with an Ancient, but thinking he could not fail to mention this, says simply "by rending my flank with this sword," without saying what part of his flank.[299]

This comparison, preserved in the scholia on *Ajax*, comes from an ancient commentator who could still read Aeschylus's tragedy on the subject, *The Thracian Women*. It seems that Aeschylus adopted a variant of the myth unknown to Homer. In fact, in the *Iliad*, Ajax is not invulnerable; when Hector confronts him and the arrow is about to pierce his chest, it is the armor that stops it, not some invulnerability.[300] Thus Aeschylus introduces a marvelous variant of which he was not necessarily the inventor: Heracles, the friend of Telamon, Ajax's father, is supposed to have made his son invulnerable by covering him with his lion's skin, except for a precise place on his side, in the armpit. This variant is exploited by the tragic author to introduce a *peripeteia* in what is supposed to be the story of Ajax's suicide reported by a messenger. Without ignoring this variant, because he does not mention the flank accidentally, Sophocles much more discreetly includes it in such a way that it does not seem to contradict the state of the myth in Homer. This subtle play of Sophocles on the Homeric model and the Aeschylean model would completely escape us without the clues provided by the scholiast.[301]

The play with models is even more complex when Sophocles has to take into account, not a single tragedy but several. When he decided to compose his *Philoctetes*, he had to compete not only with Aeschylus's *Philoctetes* but also with that of Euripides.[302] Even though these two tragedies have been lost, except for a few tiny fragments, here again an ancient reader serves us as a guide. The documentation is, moreover, much more favorable. It is no longer a matter of a punctual note written by an anonymous commentator but of a general comparison deftly written by an author of the first century CE, Dio Chrysostom (Dion of Prusa), who had all three *Philoctetes* in his library.

Innovation and Creation: The Myth in Sophocles' *Philoctetes*

When he was not feeling well, Dio Chrysostom spent his day composing a discourse on the comparison of the three books. It is a unique document—given here in appendix IV—that tells us about the comparative reading that a scholar of the Roman period could make of the tragedies by Aeschylus, Euripides, and Sophocles, about five centuries after their creation.[303]

For the problem that occupies us here—Sophocles' elaboration of the mythic material—we can use the precise clues that Dio's discourse contains regarding the two lost tragedies by Aeschylus and Euripides.[304] It is possible to gauge both the malleability of the tragic myth and the choices Sophocles made compared to his predecessors. The example of the men sent as envoys to bring Philoctetes back is enlightening. In Aeschylus's tragedy, the Achaeans sent a single man to find Philoctetes ill and abandoned on his island, following the prophecy of the Trojan seer Helenus: it was Odysseus, the very one who had captured the Trojan seer. By so doing, Aeschylus already made an important innovation with respect to the standard epic model, the *Little Iliad*. This epic poem dissociated the actors: it attributed to Odysseus the capture of the seer Helenus, but to another hero, Diomedes, the mission to bring Philoctetes back.[305] The motive for the innovation in Aeschylus is clear: the character of Odysseus was more suitable for a mission involving a ruse. As for Euripides, he innovates in relation to Aeschylus while retaining his predecessor's innovation with regard to the epic. In fact, he chooses Odysseus as Aeschylus did but has him accompanied by Diomedes. This innovation had the advantage of combining the form taken by the tragic myth with the ancient form of the epic. Dio Chrysostom clearly saw that Euripides' innovation with respect to Aeschylus was a return to the ancient. For him, this is a Homeric element, probably because he must have attributed the *Little Iliad* to Homer. However, Euripides innovated both with regard to the epic and to Aeschylus's tragedy by introducing a second Trojan embassy competing with the first, which made Philoctetes a stake between the two enemies.

Confronted by these innovations, what is Sophocles' position? He does not adopt Euripides' boldest innovation concerning the Trojan embassy. Concerning the Greek embassy, he keeps Aeschylus's innovation regarding Odysseus, while adopting the principle of two ambassadors introduced by Euripides. But he replaces Diomedes by a young hero, Neoptolemus, the son of Achilles. By doing so, he deviates from the *Little Iliad* by eliminating Diomedes, but he adheres to it in another way, by inverting, not without a certain audacity, the order of two episodes in this epic that are quite distant from one another. In the *Little Iliad*, Neoptolemus does not arrive before Philoctetes' return. Far from it: Philoctetes has time to return to Troy, to be treated by a physician, Machaon, the son of Asclepius, and to perform his exploits by killing Paris-Alexander, Helen's husband. Helen even has time to marry another man! It is only afterward that Odysseus goes to Scyros to look for Neoptolemus and gives him his father's arms once he has arrived at Troy. This rather extraordinary modification of the course of the epic story gives us an idea of the license the tragic authors could take concerning what seems to be a matter of detail, but which is of great consequence on the theatrical level, for this modification leads to a creation. The character of Neoptolemus is Sophocles' great creation in his *Philoctetes*, especially since Sophocles gives the ephebe the main role in the mission, pushing into the background the threatening character of Odysseus, who had held the main role in Euripides as he had in Aeschylus. But while deviating from his predecessors' choice, Sophocles manages astutely to bring it back into the imagination of the plan for a ruse. The episode of the false merchant, come to announce false news to trigger the realization of the planned ruse, alludes to the imminent arrival of a mission composed of whom? Of Odysseus and Diomedes, as in Euripides. This is a wink to Euripides' *Philoctetes*, performed twenty years earlier. While writing their plays, the tragic poets were sometimes able to have a little fun as well.

The elaboration of the mythic material is, of course, only a point of departure for a tragic poet's invention. What counts above all is the way it is shaped in the theatrical space and in the development of the action in which the characters encounter each other. And in this shaping, the authors had more freedom, in particular regarding the choice of the chorus or the secondary characters.[306] From this result all the effects liable to impress or seduce the public and to win over the judges in order to triumph in one day in a competition in which there is only one victor.

CHAPTER VII

Space and Spectacle

....

Unlike an epic or lyric poet dealing with mythic material, a dramatic author must represent that material in a given space at a given time before a given audience. This shaping of the mythic material inherited from tradition in the spatio-temporal frameworks of the spectacle constitutes one of the difficulties and also one of the originalities of the Greek theater. In this chapter we will study what relates to space and to spectacle, and in the following chapter what relates to time and to the development of the action.

The Theater of Dionysus in Athens

To reconstitute the theatrical dimension of Sophocles' drama (or that of Aeschylus or Euripides), we have to take into account the particularities of the ancient theater as compared to the modern theater. The best way to do this is first of all to become acquainted with the place where the fifth-century BCE spectator went to sit on the tiers of the theater where all Sophocles' tragedies were performed, the theater of Dionysus in Athens, situated on the southeast flank of the Acropolis.

The theater had completely disappeared in the Middle Ages, and it was not until the middle of the eighteenth century that its exact site was rediscovered (Chandler 1765). Investigations began only a century later, in 1838,[1] and the main excavations were conducted by Wilhelm Dörpfeld starting in 1882, on behalf of the German Archeological Institute.[2] Naturally, we have to consider the fact that the present remains of the theater built of stone do not go back beyond the fourth century BCE and that they were repeatedly rebuilt up until the Roman period. Consequently, what we see does not exactly correspond to the fifth-century theater where Sophocles' plays were performed for the first time. Nonetheless, the three fundamental elements of any ancient theater are still visible: the place where the spectators sat, the *theatrōn*, now forming a semicircle of tiers slightly extended by two wings; the dance floor or *orchestra*, now also semicircular, where the chorus was; and finally the *skene*, the space where the actors played, a complex including what we now call the stage and a stage building used as wings and as part of the setting.

Without taking up for the moment some rather delicate questions regarding the space that was visible in Sophocles' time, let us say simply that in the fifth century BCE, in place of the stone tiers where tourists now sit, there were wooden benches. This is attested by a detail in Aristophanes' comedy *The Thesmophoriazusae*, performed in 411: the women complain about Euripides because he spoke ill of them in the theater, and they claim that men, having become distrustful, look, "on returning from the theater," to see if there isn't a lover hiding in their homes. But the literal meaning of the expression that is translated that way is "on returning from the bleachers" (*ikria*), that is, the wooden benches on which the spectators sat and which required wooden scaffolding on the two sides, east and west, to support the benches.[3] Thus it was a wooden theater built on the south slope of the hill.

Among the elements of the ancient landscape, setting aside modern buildings, there remain: to the left, the mountain range Hymettus, and behind, the imposing wall of the Acropolis, where Athena, the protectress of the city, resides in her famous temples of the Erectheon and the Parthenon. If one has read Sophocles' tragedies before entering the theater, its details will immediately seem familiar. For example, when Athena appears to Odysseus at the beginning of *Ajax*, the reference is clearly to Athena the protectress of the Homeric hero; but the Athenian spectator of the fifth century also thought about Athena who protected him from the height of the Acropolis. The continuity between the ancient myth and contemporary reality operated spontaneously. Another example: when, at the end of *Philoctetes*, Heracles appears to foretell Philoctetes' future and to promise him that if he agrees to go to Troy the ulcer on his foot will be cured by Asclepius, the Athenian spectator immediately thought of the sanctuary of Asclepius adjacent to the theater at the foot of the Acropolis, where he could see tangible signs of gratitude to the healing god: ex-votos representing, among other things, legs that had been healed. Between the myth represented in the theater and reality, the connection was all the more obvious because the proximity in space reinforced the continuity in time.

Today there still subsist elements of the topography of the theater and its immediate environment that provide clues to the circumstances and conditions of dramatic representation in the time of Sophocles. The modern tourist, before going to sit on the tiers, passes near the two temples of Dionysus.[4] Accustomed as he or she is to theaters that are solely places of culture and entertainment, the tourist will have difficulty in realizing that the theater where the great Athenian tragedies were performed was a sacred space adjacent to the sanctuary of a god, Dionysus.[5] The tourist will understand a little better upon seeing on the first tier, facing the stage, the most prominent place of honor, the marble throne of the priest of Dionysus, identified by its inscription: "[throne] of the priest of Dionysus Eleutherius." It is true that this throne dates at the latest from the reconstruction of the theater in the second half of the fourth century BCE, as do all the other seats in the first row (*proedria*), which also bore inscriptions and were reserved mainly for the priests of the various divinities and magistrates. But this continued a custom that already existed in the time of Sophocles. Several blocks that were part of the stone tier of the first row, bearing the beginning of an inscription corresponding to a priest's seat, have been found. This inscription has been dated to the end of the fifth century BCE. This is one of the rare vestiges of the theater that existed toward the end of Sophocles' dramatic career.[6]

The Athenian theater was thus indissolubly connected with the cult of Dionysus, of this god who was considered a benefactor of humanity because he discovered wine, just as Demeter, honored in her sanctuary in Eleusis, had given humans bread.[7]

Theatrical Performances and the Festivals in Honor of Dionysus (the Lenaia and the Great Dionysia)

This connection with the god was manifest in the very circumstances in which theatrical performances took place. They were an integral part of the festivals in honor of the god. Thus tragedy was enacted in a sacred space and time. But at the same time these festivals of the god were officially organized by city magistrates who, during the theatrical performances, sat like the priests in the first rows; the member of the council had their reserved sector in the theater;[8] and the essential core of the audience was constituted by the citizens. Thus theatrical performances were, like the procession in honor of the god, both religious and political. When in the fourth century Demosthenes, who had been assigned to finance the performance of the chorus representing his tribe at the god's festival, was manhandled by the rich Midias while he was exercising his office in the theater, he saw in this both an impious act against the god and an attack on the city.[9]

These festivals were either the Lenaia or the Great Dionysia. The Lenaia probably owe their name to the Lenai, who were servants of Dionysus, like the Bacchantes.[10] This festival took place every year in the month of Gamelion, that is, in January, under the supervision of the archon-king. In the classical period, it included a procession and a tragedy and comedy competition.[11] The tragic competition involved only two tragic authors with two tragedies, without a satyr play.[12] Sophocles must have participated in this contest several times, even though we have no explicit testimony to that effect.[13] It was at this festival that the tragic poet Agathon won his first victory in 416, during his first participation in a contest: the event is well known, because Plato chose it as the framework for his *Symposium*.[14] The Lenaian festival was ancient, but the institution of a tragedy contest there was relatively recent; it probably did not yet exist when Sophocles began his career. Our information on the beginnings of this contest is incomplete. A date around 440/430 has been proposed, but nothing more precise. What is certain is that it already existed in 421/420, the date when the fragment of the inscription on the didaskalia for the performance of tragedies at the Lenaia begins.[15] At first, the performances must have taken place in the Lenaion, the sanctuary of Dionysus near the agora northwest of the Acropolis. Then they were transferred to the large theater located on the south flank of the Acropolis.[16] Nonetheless, people continued to speak of "contests in the Lenaion."[17]

The Lenaian festival in honor of Dionysos Lenaios is older than that of the Great Dionysia in honor of Dionysus Eleuthereus.[18] But the tragic competitions of the Great Dionysia were older than those of the Lenaia, and they had acquired more prestige. One of the signs that the Great Dionysia were relatively recent is that like the Lenaia, they were not organized by the archon-king, the heir of the king's religious powers, but by the eponymous archon, that is, by the archon who gave his name to the year.[19] This festival in honor of Dionysus Eleuthereus took place in the month of Elaphebolion, that is, March, at the end of winter and at the beginning of spring. In the fifth century, having become the most important festival of Dionysus in Athens, it had included tragic competitions since the second half of the sixth century, under Pisistratus. The first victory we know of is that of Thespis, in 535/531.[20] The tragic competitions of the Great Dionysia are thus more than a century older than those of the Lenaia. In addition, they involved more competitors, who entered more plays: three authors presented three tragedies followed by a satyr play. The term "trilogy" is used to refer to the tragedies, especially when they deal with the same subject, and the term "tetralogy" is used to refer to a set of four plays presented by an author. Aeschylus knew only the tragic contests of the Great Dionysia. By chance, the first extant reference in the (incomplete) inscription giving the results of the contest at the Great Dionysia records the victory Aeschylus won with the oldest extant tragedy, *The Persians*, in 472.[21]

The main event of the festival was a sacrificial procession, as it was in the Lenaia. And as in the Lenaia, the comic and tragic actors participated in it.[22] As for the contests, which were placed under the authority of the eponymous archon, they were four in number. According to an inscription on stone recording the annual results,[23] they were presented in the following order: first a contest of children's choruses and a contest of men's choruses in honor of Dionysus, in which representatives of the ten tribes competed by singing hymns in honor of the god, dithyrambs; then the tragedy contest among three competitors; and finally, a comedy contest. During the Peloponnesian War (431–404 BCE), when the comedy contest was reduced to three competitors presenting one comedy (instead of five competitors), the contests of tragedies and comedies must have taken place over three days (instead of five), each day being devoted to the performance of a tragic tetralogy (three tragedies and a satyr drama by a competitor), then a comedy in the evening. That is what emerges from Aristophanes in his comedy *The Birds*, performed at the Great Dionysia in 414 BCE, where the chorus of birds vaunts the privilege of having wings:

There's nothing better or merrier than sprouting wings. Say one of you spectators had wings, and got hungry, and grew bored with the tragic performances;
then he'd have flown out of here, gone home, had lunch, and when he was full,
flown back here to see us.[24]

The spectator's day must have been long, and it was continuous from the
morning on; without any opportunity to go home to eat lunch, he attended the
performance of three tragic plays before a satyr play that constituted the transition to the comedy. The comic author hinted, not without malice with regard
to his colleagues who wrote tragedies, that the spectator did not like tragedies as
much as comedies.

The Composition of the Audience at the
Lenaia and at the Great Dionysia

The audience that Aristophanes' comic chorus addressed was obviously the
same as that for the tragedies. Since the festivals in honor of Dionysus were a
city festival, each citizen could witness the show, on the condition, of course,
that he paid for his seat in the theater, like any other spectator.[25] But whereas
in the Lenaian festival the audience consisted only of Athenians and resident
foreigners ("metics"), the Great Dionysia also included foreigners, notably del-
egations of members of the Athenian Empire, whether they had come to solemnly pay the tribute on the occasion of this festival, or were allies provisioning
their ships. It is again Aristophanes who provides very precise indications regarding the composition of the audience, because unlike the tragic authors, a
comic author can allude to the audience directly or indirectly. During
the Lenaia of 425, in Aristophanes' comedy entitled *The Acharnians*, his hero
Diceopolis, giving a pacifist speech addressed to the spectators as much as to
the chorus, declares:

> We are alone, it's a Lenaian competition,
> the foreigners aren't yet here, nor tribute money
> nor allied troops from the cities of our empire,
> but now we are by ourselves, clean-hulled.[26]

The agricultural metaphor ("clean-hulled"), so familiar to the ancients, is
worth explaining here. The grain is separated from the chaff; once the grain has
been hulled, it is crushed to make flour, and the flour is sifted to separate out
the bran. The foreigners are compared to the husk, the residents of Athens to
the husked grain, with the distinction between two categories, the citizens representing the finest flour, the metics the bran. During the Lenaia, the audience
was thus limited to those who lived in Athens, citizens and metics, whereas the
audience at the Great Dionysia was broader. The Lenaian festival was more intimate, but that of the Great Dionysia was more prestigious. The various delega-

tions of the allies forming the Athenian Empire converged there, coming from the coasts and islands of the Aegean Sea at the time of spring sailing. The official deposit of the tributes at the theater during the Great Dionysia gave the citizens of Athens a concrete image of their wealth and power.[27]

Did Women Attend the Performances?

Citizens, metics, and even foreigners could attend the performances. But how about Athenian women? The question remains open.[28]

One thing is sure: they played no role in the contests, whether those for dithyrambs, comedies, or tragedies. The choruses representing each tribe at the Great Dionysia were choruses of men or children who did not wear masks. The choruses of the tragedies or comedies might, of course, be choruses representing women. Out of the seven extant choruses of Sophocles' tragedies, two are composed of young women who come from the place where the tragedy is set and are friends of the heroine: one consists of young women from Trachis who are friends of Deianira, Heracles' wife, and it gave the tragedy its name, *The Women of Trachis*;[29] the other consists of young noblewomen from Mycenae, friends of the heroine Electra, who gives her name to the tragedy.[30] However, these choruses of women are played by men wearing masks. The same goes for all the female characters in all the tragedies. They are played by male actors wearing masks. Hence no woman played a role in a tragedy.

Does that mean that women were not present in the audience in the classical period? Some have said it does, basing themselves on passages in Old Comedy or New Comedy that allude to the audience. When they discuss the audience they are addressing, Aristophanes (in *Peace*) and Menander (in *Dyscolos*) list children, young people, and men but do not mention women.[31] Nevertheless, in the *Gorgias* Plato contrasts the audience of tragedy, which includes children, women, freemen, and slaves, to that of the assemblies formed solely of freemen.[32] How could Plato have made such a contrast if women were not allowed to watch the tragedies? There must have been no legal prohibition. But it is likely that in reality, women were few in the audience, and slaves even fewer.[33] In Aristophanes, one passage indicates that the Athenian normally left his wife at home.[34] The comic author suggests that when the husband got home, after having attended Euripides' tragedies speaking evil of women, he considered his own wife with suspicion and looked around to see if she had not taken advantage of his absence during the whole day to bring in a lover. The joke is possible only if the Athenian citizen usually went to the theater without his wife. It has been asked whether the women present were not segregated from the men and relegated to the most distant seats, because in *Gynecocracy*, a comedy by Alexis, a comic poet of the four/third centuries, a woman addressing other women complains that in the theater they have to sit on the last benches to watch, as if they were foreigners.[35]

The Audience at the Great Dionysia:
A National and International Forum

At the Great Dionysia, not only those who participated in the contest but also citizens who wanted to promote themselves sought to take advantage of the privileged forum provided by the large audience assembled for the theatrical performances. There were abuses such as these, mentioned by fourth-century orator:

> It frequently happened that at the performance of the tragedies in the city proclamations were made without authorization of the people, now that this or that man was crowned by his tribe, now that others were crowned by the men of their deme, while other men by the voice of the herald manumitted their household slaves, and made all Hellas their witness; and, most invidious of all, certain men who had secured positions as agents of foreign states managed to have proclaimed that they were crowned—it might be by the people of Rhodes, or of Chios, or of some other state—in recognition of their merit and uprightness. And this they did, not like those who were crowned by your senate or by the people, by first obtaining your consent and by your decree, and after establishing large claims upon your gratitude, but themselves reaching out after the honor with no authorization from you. The result of this practice was that the spectators, the *choregoi*, and the actors alike were discommoded, and that those who were crowned in the theater received greater honors than those whom the people crowned. For the latter had a place prescribed where they must receive their crown, the assembly of the people, and proclamation "anywhere else" was forbidden; but the others were proclaimed in the presence of all the Hellenes; the one class with your consent, by your decree; the other, without decree.[36]

The various abuses are presented in an ascending order. But they are all based on the idea that the audience in the theater was a forum more prestigious than the popular assembly, and that it was possible, by means of intrigue, to have oneself crowned before this national and international audience without passing through institutional channels. These abuses were sanctioned by a law; but they must have existed as early as the fifth century. Regarding one of the abuses mentioned here, "the emancipation of a slave, taking the Greeks as witnesses," we know a famous example in Socrates' time, that of Nicias, reported by Plutarch:

> A story is told how, in one of his choral exhibitions, a house servant of his appeared in the costume of Dionysus, very fair to see, and very tall, the down of youth still upon his face. The Athenians were delighted at the sight, and applauded for a long time. At last Nicias rose and said he deemed it an unholy thing that one who had been acclaimed as a god should be a slave, and gave the youth his freedom.[37]

The theatrical performances at the Great Dionysia offered, to be sure, the best opportunity to reach the largest audience in Athens. It exceeded the context of the city, including, in addition to Athenian citizens and metics, representatives of all the cities of the Athenian Empire. From that to maintaining that this international audience represented the totality of Greece there is a rhetorical leap that must not have offended the Athenians, but rather flattered their self-esteem.

Even the authors found in this an opportunity to sell their works. That is revealed to us by a single but extremely reliable testimony. Plato alludes to it in the course of a fictive debate before the court between Socrates and his accuser Meletus:

> "That is what I say, that you do not believe in gods at all." You amaze me, Meletus! Why do you say this? Do I not even believe that the sun or yet the moon are gods, as the rest of mankind do? "No, by Zeus, judges, since he says that the sun is a stone and the moon earth." Do you think you are accusing Anaxagoras, my dear Meletus, and do you so despise these gentlemen and think they are so unversed in letters as not to know, that the books of Anaxagoras the Clazomenian are full of such utterances? And forsooth the youth learn these doctrines from me, which they can buy sometimes (if the price is high) for a drachma in the orchestra and laugh at Socrates, if he pretends they are his own, especially when they are so absurd![38]

The works of the philosopher Anaxagoras, who came from Clazomenae, one of the cities in Asia Minor allied with Athens, were thus sold in the theater "on certain occasions." What could these occasions have been (Plato does not explain—perhaps because it was too obvious in his time) except the theatrical performances, particularly those of the Great Dionysia where the allies joined the Athenians?

No Performance without Money: An Official Sponsorship

Before spectators whose numbers were more like those for a present-day soccer game than for a theatrical performance;[39] the stakes involved in the tragic contest exceeded by far those of modern plays. The three authors selected to compete at the Great Dionysia had to appeal to this large audience, immediately, during a single performance of their four plays. The spectacle was thus not the least factor in their success.

The spectacle depended not only on the inventiveness of the tragic author, but also on the generosity of the choregos, that is, the rich Athenian who had been chosen by the eponymous archon to pay the costs of the performance.[40] Demosthenes, who was a choregos at the Great Dionysia, not for a tragedy, but for his tribe's chorus, boasts of having had golden crowns made for the members of the chorus.[41] Moreover, in these choral contests in honor of Dionysus, the importance of the choregos was such that in the official inscriptions reporting the results his name appeared alone alongside that of the victorious tribe. As astonishing as it may seem, the name of the composer of the melody and the words of the dithyramb was not mentioned.[42]

Things were different for the tragedy contest. In the official inscriptions, the name of the author appears as well as the name of the choregos. Nonetheless, in the formal order the social prestige of the choregos superseded the author's talent. Thus in the inscription for 448–447 the (mutilated) name of the choregos appears before that of Sophocles, who won first place.[43] Moreover, when he won, the choregos received a larger prize than the author did, not a crown, but a tripod that he displayed at the top of a monument erected in memory of the victory. It was these choregic monuments that the spectators saw when they went to the theater, first in the street of "the Tripods," at the foot of the Acropolis, which led to the theater from the east,[44] and then inside the god's enclosure, where they saw in particular a monument in the form of a temple surmounted by a row of tripods erected by a single family, that of Nicias. Plato speaks about this in his *Gorgias*, and Plutarch says that the monument could still be seen in his time, in the second century CE.[45]

As a choregos, Nicias had a career that mirrored that of Sophocles as an author. He participated in numerous contests and often won without ever experiencing a defeat. That is a sign that the generosity of the choregos, and probably also his popularity, played more than a negligible role in his success. In his essay "On the Glory of the Athenians" Plutarch sketches a suggestive picture of the choregos' expenses and the splendor of the performances, though he considers this glory empty, compared with that of generals:

> What profit, then, did these fine tragedies bring to Athens to compare with the shrewdness of Themistocles which provided the city with a wall, with the diligence of Pericles which adorned the Acropolis, with the liberty which Miltiades bestowed, with the supremacy to which Cimon advanced her? If in this manner the wisdom of Euripides, the eloquence of Sophocles, and the poetic magnificence of Aeschylus rid the city of any of its difficulties or gained for her any brilliant success, it is but right to compare their tragedies with trophies of victory, to let the theatre rival the War Office, and to compare the records of dramatic performances with the memorials of valour. Is it, then, your pleasure that we introduce the men themselves bearing the emblems and badges of their achievements, and assign to each their proper entrance? Then from this entrance let the poets approach, speaking and chanting to the accompaniment of flutes and lyres. . . . Let them bring with them their equipment, their masks and altars, their stage machinery, their revolving changes of scene, and the tripods that commemorate their victories. Let their tragic actors accompany them, men like Nicostratus and Callippides, Mynniscus, Theodorus, and Polus, who robe Tragedy and bear her litter, as though she were some woman of

wealth; or rather, let them follow on as though they were painters and gilders and dyers of statues. Let there be provided also a bounteous outlay for stage furnishings, supernumeraries, sea-purple robes, stage machinery, as well as dancing-masters and bodyguards, an intractable crowd. It was in reference to all this that a Spartan not ineptly remarked that the Athenians were making a great mistake in wasting their energies on amusements, that is to say, in lavishing on the theatre what would pay for great fleets and would support armies in the field. For, if we reckon up the cost of each tragedy, the Athenian people will be seen to have spent more on productions of *Bacchae, Phoenissae, Oedipuses,* and *Antigones,* and the woes of Medea and Electra, than they spent in fighting for their supremacy and for their liberty against the barbarians. For the generals often ordered their men to bring along uncooked rations when they led them forth to battle; and the commanders, I can swear, after providing barley-meal and a relish of onions and cheese for the rowers, would embark them on the triremes. But the men who paid for the choruses gave the choristers eels and tender lettuces, roast-beef and marrow, and pampered them for a long time while they were training their voices and living in luxury. The result for the defeated choregoi was to be held in contumely and ridicule; but to the victors belonged a tripod, which was, as Demetrius says, not a votive offering to commemorate their victory, but a last oblation of their wasted livelihood, an empty memorial of their vanished estates. Such are the returns paid by the poetic art and nothing more splendid ever comes from it.[46]

No other ancient text gives such a broad and vivid account of the expenses that the performance of tragedies required in the time of Sophocles and Euripides.

The Role of the Choregos

Etymologically, the word *choregos* means "head of the chorus." Thus the choregos was in charge of the chorus, whatever the contest for which he had been named (dithyramb, comedy, tragedy).[47] Here we will limit ourselves to tragedy. Starting from the moment when, after the drawing of lots, the choregos formed a team with one of the three tragic authors selected,[48] he proceeded to recruit the members of the chorus, who were called *choreutes.* Sophocles had increased their number from twelve to fifteen.[49] Their main role was to sing and move on the dance floor of the theater, or orchestra, during the performance of the three tragedies and the satyr play.

Recruitment varied depending on the nature of the contest. Unlike the men's or children's choruses recruited in each of the ten tribes, the tragic or comic choruses were chosen from the whole body of Athenian citizens, no matter where they came from. The choregos's role in choosing the chorus seems to have been decisive. A choregos named Antisthenes always won, even though he was unable to sing and instruct the chorus, because he knew how to recruit competent people.[50] This example concerns the competition among the tribes' choruses. However, it is legitimate to think that the same was true for the tragic chorus. The most important choice was that of the leader of the chorus, the *coryphaeus*, because, as Demosthenes says, "if the leader is withdrawn, the rest of the chorus is done for."[51] It was not enough for the choregos to recruit the choreutes, to feed and lodge them. He also had to oversee their training. It was up to him to choose and pay an instructor for the chorus (*chorodidascalos*), or as we would say, a director, whose task was to prepare the fifteen *choristes* to sing and dance in the four plays that the author was presenting in the contest. This involved long and intensive rehearsals, because the whole of the performance consisted of about fifteen different passages sung and danced by the chorus. The role of the author, in this regard, had diminished in the time of Sophocles. Whereas the older tragic authors from Thespis to Aeschylus undertook themselves to instruct the chorus and to invent dance figures,[52] this task was later delegated to a specialist. That does not mean that Sophocles, who like his predecessors remained the composer of the music as well as of the words, did not sometimes intervene directly in the preparation of the chorus. We have seen that while still a child he had studied music and dance at the school of the famed musician Lampros.[53] Athenaeus, who tells us about Sophocles' musical training, adds that "when he brought out the *Thamyris* he played the lyre himself. He also played ball with great skill when he produced the *Nausicaä*."[54]

Since the choregos paid for everything concerning the chorus, he also had to finance the costumes for the various choruses of the three tragedies and the satyr play, which meant forty-five costumes with the corresponding masks. He might resort to renting costumes,[55] or have them made.

Did he also oversee the proper functioning of the rest of the show? We can presume that if we believe this anecdote reported by Plutarch about a performance of a tragedy in which an actor got into a conflict with the choregos, in the fourth century BCE, in the time of Phocion:

> And once when the Athenians were witnessing an exhibition of new tragedies, the actor who was to take the part of a queen asked the choregus to furnish him with a great number of attendant women in expensive array; and when he could not get them, he was indignant, and kept the audience waiting by his refusal to come out. But the choregus, Melanthius, pushed him before the spectators, crying: "Dost thou not see that Phocion's wife always goes out with one maid-servant? Thy vanity will be the undoing of our women-folk." His words were plainly heard by the audience, and were received with tumultuous applause.[56]

Thus the choregos was responsible not only for the chorus but also for the silent characters, whose number and costumes contributed to the success of the show. He had to take into account the author's requirements and sometimes also those of the actors, or to oppose them, as is the case here.

Law required the choregoi to expend a minimum amount. However, they could show generosity in order to please the audience by the magnificence of the spectacle and thus contribute to winning a victory, serving in this way their personal glory while at the same time gaining the people's gratitude by performing an office imposed by the state.[57] Thus one of Lysias's clients, accused of corruption, recalled among his past services, among other offices, a *choregia* for a tragedy that he paid for a year before the performance of Sophocles' *Philoctetes* and which had cost him thirty *minae*, or three thousand drachmas. He claimed that if he had limited himself to what the law required he would not have spent even a fourth of that amount.[58] A tragic choregia must have been more expensive than a comic one. This same client of Lysias's spent only sixteen minae, that is, one thousand six hundred drachmas, for a comic chorus, including the costs of the victory celebration.[59] However, the choregia for a tragedy was less burdensome than for a men's chorus. Under the archontate of Glaukippos, the same client of Lysias's financed, at the same festival in which Sophocles won a victory with his *Philoctetes*, a men's chorus that cost him five thousand drachmas, including the dedication of the tripod, thus much more than the tragic chorus he had paid for the preceding year. The main reason for this is that the men's chorus was much larger than a tragic chorus (fifty choreutes instead of fifteen[60]). The difference is also explained by the result of the contest. Not having won the preceding year with his tragic chorus—otherwise he would have mentioned it—he did not have to pay the supplementary costs associated with victory, "that final libation made from a dilapidated fortune," as Plutarch ironically put it.

The Author's Role

As for the tragic poet in the time of Sophocles, although he was no longer the main director of the chorus, he kept the title of "instructor" (*didascalos*): presenting a tragedy continued to be called "instructing" in the inscriptions reporting the results of the contests. The poet had to direct the three actors, choose their costumes and their masks, and finance, using the sum allotted him by the state, everything in the performance that did not concern the chorus and the extras. It is significant that the author's expenses during the preparation of the show are much less well known than those of the choregos.

The same goes for his reward after the victory. It was undoubtedly more modest than that of the choregos: the ivy crown was accompanied by a prize in money the amount of which was set by a decree of the popular assembly.[61] We have no evidence regarding the amount. In any case, the poet received nothing comparable to the tripod, which, once it was dedicated, remained in the people's eyes the sole monument immortalizing the victory.

In the end, the author's victory was in a way confiscated by the choregos, a little as the victory in the chariot races in the Olympic games was that of the owner of the team rather than that of the charioteer.

The Importance of the Spectacle

In a competition of this kind, in which the money spent was so important, in which the social prestige of the three choregoi chosen among the richest Athenians was in play, and in which most of the audience, even though it included all the Athenians and foreigners living in Athens, extended far beyond the framework of the city of Athens through the arrival of foreign allies and tribute payers, to the point that the orators could speak without too much implausibility of all the Greeks, how can we imagine that the spectacle in tragedy was not a major component of an author's success?

Aristotle's position has helped eclipse this essential aspect of Greek theater. In his discussion of tragedy that occupies the central part of his *Poetics*, Aristotle certainly recognizes that the organization of the spectacle, that is, what has to do with seeing (*opsis*), is one of the six constitutive parts of tragedy; but he depreciates this aspect and maintains that spectacle is the part of tragedy most external to art:

> Spectacle, while highly effective, is yet quite foreign to the art and has nothing to do with poetry. Indeed the effect of tragedy does not depend on its performance by actors, and, moreover, for achieving the spectacular effects the art of the costumier is more authoritative than that of the poet.[62]

To demonstrate that spectacle is the most external element of tragedy, Aristotle establishes two distinctions here: between tragedy performed and tragedy read; and between the costumier and the author. The second distinction corresponds to a reality that already existed in the time of Sophocles. To make the masks for their characters, the authors of tragedies or comedies called on craftsmen called *skeuopoioi*. The first mention of these craftsmen is made by Aristophanes in his *Knights*. The mask for his character, the Paphlagonian, resembled the face of the demagogue Cleon, but none of the skeuopoioi wanted the resemblance to be total, because Cleon was too dreadful.[63]

A little further on, qualifying his distrust with regard to spectacle, Aristotle says that the spectacle "needs the choregia."[64] That is to say the same thing in a slightly different way. The choice of a good mask maker must have depended on the expenditures the choregos agreed to make. The theoretical distinction Aristotle draws between the author and the choregos undoubtedly corresponds to a reality. Nonetheless, from the moment that the author and the choregos formed a team, the author's instructions given to the choregos for the performance of the spectacle must have been as important as the implementation, because it was usually following the poet's instructions that the choregos made the expenditures.[65] The author remained a director.

As for the distinction Aristotle makes between tragedy seen and tragedy read, it has little reality for the fifth century, when tragedy existed only in and through performance during a festival. In any event, no author of Sophocles' time wrote a tragedy to be read. Tragic writing was inseparable from the competition and performance by actors. Sophocles, like all his predecessors or rivals, wrote with a view to performance. His text necessarily has a theatrical dimension.

In Search of the Material Conditions of Performance in Sophocles' Time

Unlike a modern dramatist whose play is written to be performed in an undifferentiated theater, the Athenian author wrote his series of four plays with a view to their being performed in a given space, that of the theater of Dionysus in Athens. Thus we can imagine that the tourist who sits in the very place where the audience sat during the performance of Sophocles' tragedies—and who has in hand the text of the seven extant complete tragedies—is in a privileged position to understand the way in which the ancient dramatist used the theatrical space. In the presence of the text and the monument, the tourist seems to be in the best possible position to reconstruct what might well be the sole performance of each tragedy that the Athenian public witnessed during the author's lifetime. Nonetheless, the obstacles to such a reconstruction remain large, because what subsists is incomplete and sometimes misleading, even if we try to fill in the gaps with the help of other literary or iconographic evidence that can provide us with clues to the material organization of the performance.[66]

The first obstacle is connected with the fact that the text of each of Sophocles' seven extant tragedies gives only the words, without any indication concerning the dance figures or the choral song that was accompanied by a flute player.[67] To be sure, the metric analysis of the choral parts, that is, the parts sung by the chorus, provides some clues: it identifies the place of the tempi marked when the choreutes' feet struck the floor during the dance, it brings out the parallelisms between the pairs of strophes and antistrophes corresponding to the symmetrical movements of the chorus, and finally it offers an idea of the extreme diversity of rhythms liable to express the whole gamut of emotions and feelings. But what completely escapes us for Sophocles' choruses is the melody composed by an author who was as much a musician as a man of the theater. Thus in a performance in which the parts spoken by the characters alternated with the parts sung by the chorus, in a genre that combined what corresponds to our theater and our opera, the whole musical part has disappeared.

The tourist sitting on the tiers of the theater of Dionysus in Athens can nonetheless think that he or she is contemplating the dance floor where the choreutes moved, masked and costumed, to provide a plausible embodiment of the characters they represented in the tragic fiction. This is true, but only partly, because the marble-tiled, semicircular space that we now see belongs to a state of the theater after the classical period. It is the marble theater constructed under Lycurgus in the second half of the fourth century and later modified several times, in the Hellenistic and then in the Roman period, not only with a view to choral or theatrical performances, but also for gladiatorial combats, and even, later on, for *naumachia* (simulated naval battles).[68] The current marble tiling dates from the Roman period, as does the stone parapet separating the orchestra from the first rows of seats. One wonders whether this parapet was not built to protect the latter during gladiatorial combats. In fact, we have a literary testimony on these combats in which the honorific seats of the proedria were not spared. The orator Dio Chrysostom (first to second centuries CE), in his speech to the residents of Rhodes, mentions with scandalized irony the Athenians who watched gladiators fight in their theater of Dionysus:

> The Athenians look on at this fine spectacle in their theatre under the very walls of the Acropolis, in the place where they bring their Dionysus into the orchestra and stand him up, so that often a fighter is slaughtered among the very seats in which the Hierophant and the other priests must sit.[69]

Under these conditions, it is not surprising that in the time of Hadrian a (second century CE) an elevated loge for the emperor, as well as new honorific seats further from the orchestra were constructed.

The modern spectator thus sees nothing of the ancient orchestra, a flat surface of beaten earth, where the choruses of Sophocles' tragedies danced and which could be entered through two lateral passageways or *eisodoi*.[70]

What Was the Form of the Orchestra in the Time of Sophocles?

It may seem strange to inquire into the form of the dance floor in the theater of Dionysus in the time of the great tragic dramatists, so unanimous seems the agreement since the conclusions drawn by the first great excavator of the theater. The excavations conducted by the German Willhelm Dörpfeld in the theater of Dionysus in Athens unearthed as early as 1886 four elements, distant from one another, that led him to propose the hypothesis of a circular orchestra twenty-four meters in diameter.[71] This reconstruction by the German archeologist having been approved by a great German philologist U. von Wilamowitz-Moellendorff, in the same year,[72] a vulgate on the circularity of the dance space in the theater of Dionysus in Athens in the fifth century formed and has been adopted in all the academic syntheses on Greek theater, even the most recent. The orchestra is thus supposed to be circular in the time of Sophocles and to have in its center an altar of Dionysus on which the flute player stood.[73] It is true that the circular form of the orchestra in the theater at Epidaurus, which dates from the end of the fourth century, makes a great impression.

However, archeological evidence excavated in the theater of Dionysus and published in 1928 pointed to a new hypothesis: these are ten quadrangular blocks that were moved and reused, with inscriptions dating from the last quarter of the fifth century, bearing the marks of seats in the first row, which is called the proedria. In fact, one of the inscriptions designates the seat of a priest.[74] But this first row, which can be reconstructed over a length of ten meters, is not curved but rectilinear.[75] The consequence of this archeological observation seems thus to be that at the end of Sophocles' career, the first tier at least of the theater of Dionysus in Athens was in stone, and that the orchestra must not have been circular in form but rectangular, or rather trapezoidal, about thirty meters wide and fifteen meters deep.

Nonetheless, given the large number of theaters ranging from the fourth century BCE to the third century CE that have circular or semicircular dance floors and that are found throughout the Greco-Roman world from Asia to Gaul and Spain, it was unlikely that Dörpfeld's hypothesis would be successfully challenged in the 1930s. At that time the only rectangular orchestra that was known was the theater in Thorikos, in southern Attica, which was considered an exception.[76] But in the 1970s and 1980s other theaters with straight tiers were discovered, first the Odeon in Argos,[77] and then the theater of Isthmia,[78] which led to rethinking the question of the form of the orchestra in the fifth century.[79] In Attica itself the theater of Trachones, in the present-day suburbs of Athens, excavated between 1973 and 1977, revealed four groups seats comparable to those that were found in the theater of Dionysus, but this time they had remained in place.[80] Thus for the past twenty years, some archeologists have been challenging, with solid arguments, Dörpfeld's hypothesis regarding the circular orchestra.[81] There was a major modification of the theater in Athens between the period of Sophocles in the fifth century and that of Lycurgus in the fourth century; it seems not only that a theater made essentially of wood was replaced by a theater made of stone, but also that a theater with rectangular tiers of seats and a rectangular orchestra was replaced by a theater with circular tiers of seats and a circular orchestra.

In any case, the form of the orchestra has no direct relation with that of the dances, because the same place was used in the same festival for the dithyrambic choruses' circular dances,[82] whereas the tragic choruses were formed in a quadrangle.

The Chorus in the Orchestra in the Time of Sophocles: Entrance, Movements, Exit

In the time of Aeschylus, the chorus was composed of twelve members (or choreutes). Sophocles increased the spectacle by raising the number to fifteen.[83]

When the masked chorus, preceded by the unmasked flute player,[84] entered the orchestra through the side entrance on the right (with respect to the spectator), it was in a rectangular formation in three files (*stichoi*) of five choreutes each or five ranks (*zuga*) of three choreutes each. The left-hand file was composed of the five best singers in the group, because they were the closest to the spectators and directly in front of them once they were in place and had pivoted to face the audience.[85] The leader of the chorus or coryphaeus was in the third position in the left file, so that he was in the center of the five choreutes closest to the spectators after they had pivoted.[86]

In Sophocles' tragedies, the entrance of the chorus (or *parodos*) took place after one or two scenes of dialogue between the characters. It was followed by an initial song and an initial movement by the chorus, as is indicated by the presence of strophes and antistrophes. In six plays out of seven, the chorus's text began immediately with this system of strophes/antistrophes, which means that the chorus, coming in through the entrance on the right side, silently took its place and immediately began to dance and sing. In a single extant tragedy by Sophocles, *Ajax*, the system of strophes/antistrophes in lyric verses, that is, sung verses, is preceded by thirty-eight verses in a march rhythm that are uttered in recitative, that is, in a sustained tone, accompanied by the flute, either by the leader of the chorus, as is generally said, or by the chorus as a whole.[87] There is no doubt that this first part preceding a triad (the strophe/antistrophe pair followed by an epode) corresponds exactly to the moment when the chorus enters with a rhythmic step and takes its place in the orchestra before singing and dancing. This solemn entrance is a technique already attested in Aeschylus: in *The Persians* and *The Suppliants*, the tragedy begins directly with the rhythmic procession of the chorus; in *Agamemnon*, the rhythmic procession takes place only after a scene in which a character appears, the watchman on the roof of the palace. Thus it is to this last tragedy of Aeschylus's that Sophocles' *Ajax* is close. An attempt has been made to see in this Aeschylean structure of the chorus's entrance in *Ajax* the sign of a period in which Sophocles was still under Aeschylus's influence. In fact, according to Plutarch, Sophocles himself acknowledged that in the first phase of his career, he had been influenced by Aeschylus before detaching himself from him.[88] The hypothesis is thus plausible.[89]

As soon as the chorus of a tragedy had entered the orchestra, it usually remained there during the whole duration of the tragedy, intervening chiefly in songs with dance (*stasima*) that provided pauses in the development of the drama. The indications contained in the text of the stasima regarding the chorus's dance are rare. There is one in *Ajax*. When the hero leaves the stage to escape dishonor by committing suicide, deceiving those around him by a cunning speech in which he pretends to resign himself and go off to purify himself by bathing in the sea, the chorus formed by his companions, falsely relieved of fear concerning their leader's fate, begins, in the second *stasimon*, a song of happiness: it soars with joy, invokes the god Pan, the dancing teacher, and cries: "Now I want to dance!"[90] On the other hand, in *Oedipus the King*, the chorus of old men from Thebes, scandalized by the impious attitude of Queen Jocasta and King Oedipus, who now refuse to believe Tiresias's prophecies and the Delphic oracles, cries out in a burst of despair: "If such deeds are held in honor, why should we join in the sacred dance?"[91]

Since the custom was for the chorus to remain present in the orchestra during the whole play, the exceptional exits in the course of the tragedy are all the more striking. The sole exception in Sophocles' seven extant tragedies is again *Ajax*. A change in place justifies this exception.[92] The chorus's exit in the middle of the tragedy, as well as its reentry, offer a spectacle that the text allows us to reconstruct rather precisely. After Ajax's departure, the chorus's joy is of short duration. A messenger comes to give them the order not to allow Ajax to leave that day, if they want to see him again alive. It is too late. Understanding the tragedy of the situation, Tecmessa gives orders and will herself set out in search of Ajax to try to save him:

> *Tecmessa:* Ah, me! My friends, protect me from the doom threatened by fate! Hurry, some of you, to speed Teucer's coming; let others go to the westward bays, and others to the eastward, and there seek the man's disastrous path. I see now that I have been deceived by my husband and cast out of the favor that I once had with him. Ah, my child, what shall I do? I must not sit idle. I too will go as far as my strength will carry me. Move, let us be quick, this is no time to sit still, if we wish to save a man who is eager for death.
>
> *Chorus:* I am ready to help, and I will show it in more than word. Speed of action and speed of foot will follow together.[93]

All these words spoken by Tecmessa and the chorus are rich in information about the spectacle. In principle, Tecmessa gives orders to three groups. The first group is to go to Teucer, Ajax's half brother, whose return the messenger has just announced. It is generally supposed that this first group consists of silent servants. The two other groups are to set out in search of Ajax. They correspond to the two semichoruses that will go out through the two opposite side exits. The text's indications coincide admirably with the topography of the Athenian theater, because one of these exits leads toward the west and the other toward the east. The exit of the two semichoruses is rapid and silent. It contrasts with the slow, solemn initial entrance of the chorus as a whole in a rhythmic step.

The two semichoruses reenter just after Ajax's suicide. But this is not a return to their point of departure, because the place of the tragedy has changed. It is the endpoint of their search, which appears to have been in vain, but has in reality led them to the proximity of Ajax's body:

> *First Semichorus:* Toil follows toil yielding toil! Where, where have I not trudged? And still no place can say that I have shared its secret. [870] Listen! A sudden thud!
>
> *Second Semichorus:* We made it, we shipmates of your voyage.
>
> *Semichorus 1:* [875] What news, then?
>
> *Semichorus 2:* All the westward flank of the ships has been scoured for tracks.

Semichorus 1: And did you find anything?
Semichorus 2: Only an abundance of toil. There was nothing more to see.
Semichorus 1: Neither, as a matter of fact, has the man been seen along the
   path that faces the shafts of the morning sun.[94]

Naturally, the chorus's second entry[95] is made by semichoruses, like the first exit, and through each of the two lateral entrances. But the two groups do not enter at the same time.

The group that left through the eastern exit returns first, and its entrance contrasts with its departure. Whereas it had hurried quickly toward the exit, it returns with a heavy pace, out of breath after its long quest. At first it utters only short words (disyllables and monosyllables), and alliterations of words beginning with *p* express this breathlessness. Despite the eminently tragic context, by means of this spectacle unusual in a tragedy Sophocles elicits in the spectator a pity, tender or even amused, for these ordinary people who have come up empty after their hunt. Here we are not far from the tone of a satyr play. Immediately after the eminently emotional moment of Ajax's suicide, which has just occurred almost live, the break in the tone, deliberately sought by Sophocles, attenuates what might be unbearable in an excessively moving situation.

The encounter of the two semichoruses also makes the audience smile. After arriving all out of breath through the eastern entrance, the first semichorus suddenly stops on hearing a dull sound. The second semichorus, which has come in through the opposite entrance without being seen, then rushes forward to reassure it in a fleeting moment of joy at finding each other again after such a long ordeal. The chorus, once again united, returns to the norm.

At the end of every tragedy the chorus left the orchestra after making a final remark to conclude the drama, in a cortege preceded by the flute player.[96]

Such is thus the space in which the chorus moves, the orchestra of beaten earth that can be reached through two opposite lateral entrances oriented to the east and to the west. Uncertainties may remain regarding the form of this dance space in the classical period, which was more trapezoidal than circular, or regarding the presence or absence of an altar of Dionysus at its center.[97] The disappearance of any musical score makes it impossible to reconstitute the flute playing, and the metrical analysis of the choral parts provides only a sketchy image of the chorus's movements. Nevertheless, it remains that, in certain privileged cases, the chorus's movements can be constituted with precision thanks to stage directions that the author inserted into his text in a very natural way.

The Actors: What Is a Good Actor?

Whereas the choreutes played throughout the tragedy the same characters, which were part of a group, the actors were always fewer in number than the characters they played. Consequently, in the course of a single tragedy they played several characters, which obliged them not only to change costumes and masks, but also to change their voices and play characters both male and female, both young and old.

Given the dimensions of the theater, the qualities required in a good actor were first of all the clarity, power, and volume of the voice, which had to carry a long way. Next, since they embodied several characters, came the aptitude to modify with subtlety and accuracy the registers of their voices to adapt them to the different feelings of a single character or to different roles. These essential qualities were more difficult to acquire than the expressiveness of the gestures compensating for the impossibility of showing feelings by the face hidden behind a mask.

A good actor had to also be a good singer, insofar as he might play roles that the male or female characters sang at certain times, like the chorus. Those were exceptional moments where the song expressed an intense emotion. For example, the character of Ajax, overwhelmed by emotion, sings when, after his attack of madness, he sees again his companions that form the chorus. The situation is even completely reversed at the beginning of the dialogue, because Ajax sings whereas the chorus speaks.[98] Similarly, Electra, suffering from the constantly renewed pain of her father's murder, sings when she encounters for the first time the chorus of her friends in a dialogue in which, this time, the chorus's song responds to that of the character.[99] Antigone also sings under the impact of emotion; but it is toward the end of the tragedy, when she is going to her last resting place, the underground prison to which King Creon has condemned her.[100]

The attention the ancients gave to the virtues or defects of the actors' voices was very remarkable. "Actors have to be judged by their voices," Demosthenes is supposed to have said; and he added, because of his own well-known speech defect, "but we have to judge orators by their thought."[101] Later on, the lexicographer Pollux devoted most of his discussion of the actors' vocabulary to the voice.[102] An indication of the subtlety of the Greeks' analysis of the voice is the wealth of the vocabulary devoted to it: Greek includes about a hundred and thirty composite adjectives whose second element refers to the voice (*phonè*) and whose first element qualifies it.[103]

The Actors' Contest

Sophocles did not have the bronze voice of his Athena,[104] but rather a "small voice" (*mikrophonia*). Thus he had to break with the tradition that made the author also be a main actor, as was the case for Aeschylus.[105] This innovation itself later became a tradition. Actors acquired autonomy and importance as early as the middle of the fifth century, and they became professionals.

The official sign of the recognition of the actors was the addition of a tragic actors' contest alongside the author's contest, first in the Great Dionysia, and then in the Lenaia. The first tragic contest known from the inscription of the

Fastes, where it is attested in an actors' contest at the Great Dionysia, is that of the year 447, when it was precisely Sophocles who won the prize. A new line was added at the end of the results of the tragedy competition: it gives the name of the winning actor: "actor: Herakleides." This is, of course, the name of the main actor. Nothing indicates that this Herakleides was Sophocles' actor. He might also have been an actor for one of Sophocles' two unfortunate competitors. Since the results of the preceding years are lacking in this accidentally incomplete inscription, it is impossible to determine exactly the date at which this new contest was created. But it was necessarily instituted after the competition of 458, which Aeschylus had won with his *Oresteia*, because the results of that tragic contest, preserved in the same inscription of the *Fastes*, do not yet include the additional line relating to the actor. Thus it was in the decade 457–447 that actors were for the first time awarded a prize in the Great Dionysia, and probably only a few years before 447.[106]

On the actors' contest at the Lenaia, our information is fragmentary. What is certain is that it already existed in 421–420.[107]

Actors deserved to be rewarded, because their performance was significant, even if we do not base our view on a single tragedy, as people are too inclined to do, but rather on the whole set of four plays in which all the roles were played by the same team of actors in the course of a day. The task became even more complicated for them when, in the time of Sophocles, the disappearance of the linked tetralogy eliminated any continuity between the characters in one play and another and increased the diversity of roles.

We understand, under these circumstances, why the great tragic authors were eager to have good actors. We know the name of one actor who regularly worked for Sophocles, Tlepolemus.[108] After Sophocles' death, when in addition to new tragedies, old tragedies were revived at the contest of the Great Dionysia, an actor named Polos (c. 300 BCE) won fame for his skill in playing equally well the character of Oedipus when he was old, exiled, and begging (*Oedipus at Colonus*) and when he was a king in the prime of life (*Oedipus the King*).[109]

Sophocles Introduced the Third Actor

Sophocles put his mark on the evolution of the Athenian theater as regards both the actors and the chorus. The innovation concerning the actors is mentioned by Aristotle in a famous passage of the *Poetics* on the development of tragedy:

> It was Aeschylus who first raised the number of the actors from one to two. He also curtailed the chorus and gave the dialogue the leading part. Three actors and scene-painting Sophocles introduced.[110]

This innovation, if it is really due to Sophocles, had already been adopted by his elder, Aeschylus, at the end of his career, which situates the introduction of the third actor in the 460s.[111] It marked the final development of the tragic genre. The latter attained its definitive nature with Sophocles. In fact, during the whole history of the organization of tragic contests in Greece, the rule of three actors was maintained, with the practical consequence that even the most spectacular scenes could not bring together, if we leave the chorus aside, more than three speaking characters. And what was initially a constraint due to the necessity of limiting the expenses involved in organizing the performance became a norm that could not be violated. In his epistle to the Pisos (*The Art of Poetry*), at the end of the first century BCE, Horace advises the would-be dramatist: "Nor let a fourth actor essay to speak."[112] This view of things could not be shared by Sophocles. On the contrary, he tried to loosen the constraints by creating the third actor.

Sophocles' innovation relating to the actors is still more important than the one relating to the chorus. The increase from twelve to fifteen choreutes merely added an additional ring of three choreutes to give the song and dance more amplitude. This improvement of the spectacle had no impact on the literary creation. Whereas in continuing the work of Aeschylus—who had increased the number of actors invented by Thespis from one to two—by making the transition from two to three actors, Sophocles created more possibilities for introducing new characters and allowed the construction of scenes of greater scope by bringing together three speaking characters distinct from the chorus. This necessarily had an impact on theatrical writing.

Actors and Characters: The Distribution of Roles among the Three Actors

Despite the addition of a third actor, there were still more characters than actors. In constructing his action, the tragic author could not forget to insert pauses allowing the actor changing roles time to change his costume and his mask. In other words, to understand tragic creation in all its aspects, it is worthwhile to inquire into the manner in which the various characters of a tragedy could be distributed among the three available actors. Doing so will allow us to gauge the performance of the actors and especially to reflect on the way in which the tragic author overcame the constraints resulting from the smaller number of actors with respect to the number of characters. For Sophocles, the ratio is often eight characters for three actors (*Ajax, Oedipus the King, Oedipus at Colonus*). The maximum is nine characters in *Antigone*, and the minimum five characters in *Philoctetes*.[113]

In a troupe formed of three actors, there was a hierarchy corresponding to their respective degrees of competence. The technical terms designating each of the three actors (protagonist, deuteragonist, tritagonist) clearly imply a ranking. Officially, the only actor recognized was the protagonist or the head of the troupe, because his name alone appeared on the list of winners in the actors' contest. The term "tritagonist" is first attested in Demosthenes,[114] and in his work it has a pejorative meaning: in his attack on Aeschinus, his political adversary, Demosthenes makes fun of him not because he was an actor, but because he was always the tritagonist in the various troupes.[115] The caricature gives us a concrete idea of the lively reactions of the Athenian audience, even during the performance of a tragedy: it whistled and might attack a bad actor by throwing various things at him—figs, raisins, or olives.[116] However, the role of a tritagonist was unjustly depreciated by Demosthenes to make his case; even if there was a hierarchy among the three actors in the troupe, it goes without saying that a protagonist had to engage as deuteragonist and even as tritagonist actors who were as competent as possible.

The Roles of the Protagonist

To assign a character to the protagonist, the criterion of song must have been as crucial as that of the importance of the character in the tragedy.[117] And when the two criteria are joined, there is little chance of being mistaken. By virtue of these two criteria, the protagonist certainly played what we would now call the title role in *Ajax*,[118] *Electra*,[119] *Oedipus the King*,[120] *Oedipus at Colonus*,[121] and *Philoctetes*.[122]

If there were two characters who sang in the course of a tragedy and if these two characters could not be played by the same actor (that is, if they appeared onstage at the same time), one had to be assigned to the protagonist and the other to the deuteragonist. That is especially the case in *Antigone*. Antigone sings, and so does Creon;[123] thus these two roles would be assigned to the protagonist and the deuteragonist respectively, although one might still hesitate regarding which was considered the primary role, that of Antigone, the title character of the play, or that of Creon, who is onstage much longer.

In Sophocles' last tragedy, *Oedipus at Colonus*, where the lyricism of the characters is most developed, three characters sing at one time or another in the tragedy: Oedipus, Antigone, and Ismene. The character of Oedipus is played by the protagonist and that of Antigone by the deuteragonist. Does that mean that an exception was made and a singing role, that of Ismene, was entrusted to a tritagonist? In reality, Ismene's role at the end of the tragedy, when she sings, could be played by the protagonist, since at that point Oedipus has definitively left the stage.[124] The mask even made it possible to occasionally have a single character played by two different actors.

As a general rule, the protagonist played one role or possibly two. For example, he played a single role in *Philoctetes*, where the characters are few. He played two notably in the so-called diptych tragedies (*Ajax, The Women of Trachis*), where he played the main character in each of the two parts of the tragedy: Ajax in the first part of the tragedy of the same name, and Teucer, his half brother, in the second part; Deianira in the first part of *The Women of Trachis*, and Heracles in the second part. These two roles were relatively balanced. On the other hand, in the other tragedies where the protagonist played two roles, an imbalance was inevitable because the main role required a longer presence onstage. Thus in *Oedipus at Colonus*, there is no possible comparison between the crushing, continuous presence of the protagonist playing the role of Oedipus, during most of the tragedy, and his modest and short appearance with the mask and costume of Ismene to participate in the two girls' final *lamento* after the death of their father.

The Roles of the Two Other Actors

In the distribution of the other roles between the deuteragonist and the tritagonist, the same criteria must have applied. When two characters had an important part in a tragedy and could not be played by a single protagonist, the second was played by the deuteragonist. In *Philoctetes*, the deuteragonist plays Neoptolemus opposite the protagonist playing Philoctetes. As for the third actor, he was assigned the three other roles: Odysseus, the merchant, and Heracles. The tritagonist, even more than the deuteragonist, had to play several secondary roles.

The question of the distribution of roles among the actors nonetheless remains uncertain, because the oldest testimony we have regarding the assignment of the role of Creon to the tritagonist in Sophocles' *Antigone* is hard to reconcile with what modern scholars reconstitute on the basis of solid criteria. Here is what Demosthenes says in his diatribe against Aeschines, who was, as we have seen, a tritagonist in a troupe of actors more famous than he:[125]

> But the *Antigone* of Sophocles has often been acted by Theodorus and often by Aristodemus; and in this play there are some admirable and instructive verses, which he must know quite well by heart, since he has often delivered them himself, but which he has omitted to quote. For you know, I am sure, that in every tragedy it is, as it were, the special privilege of third-rate actors to play in the rôle of tyrants and sceptred kings. Consider, then, these excellent lines, placed by the poet in the mouth of our Creon-Aeschines in this play.[126]

It is clearly stated that Aeschinus, as a tritagonist, played the role of Creon in *Antigone*, and it is stated just as clearly that the roles of tyrants and kings were reserved as a privilege for the tritagonists. It can hardly be said that Demosthenes invented all this just to make his case.[127] In certain cases, the assignment of kings' roles to tritagonists was necessary: Agamemnon's role in the second part of Ajax was certainly played by the tritagonist, because that of Teucer was played by the protagonist and that of Odysseus by the deuteragonist. But in *Antigone* the assignment of the role of Creon to the tritagonist seems entirely surprising: he is the character who remains by far the longest onstage, and he has a role including a sung part. According to modern criteria, he can be played only by the deuteragonist, or even by the protagonist, certainly not by the tritagonist.

The only way to resolve the contradiction between the ancient testimony and the modern solution is to accept the fact that the distribution of the actors in the staging of *Antigone* might have varied over time. Demosthenes is not talking about the first performance of the play during Sophocles' lifetime, but rather about the revivals in the fourth century. The criteria of choice might thus have changed, on the one hand in relation to audience reactions that had become predictable in the course of the revivals, and on the other hand in relation to the requirements of actors who had become stars concerned about their popularity. It was better for a protagonist or a deuteragonist to play roles more appealing than Antigone, Haemon, or Tiresias, and let the tritagonist play tyrants whom the audience probably liked less well.

In the case of one of the two leaders of the troupe mentioned by Demosthenes, Aristotle provides in his *Politics* a complementary testimony that tends to confirm this:

> For perhaps the tragic actor Theodorus used to put the matter not badly: he had never once allowed anybody to produce his part before him, not even one of the poor actors, as he said that audiences are attracted by what they hear first; and this happens alike in regard to our dealings with people and to our dealings with things—all that comes first we like better.[128]

By "poor actors" we must obviously understand the tritagonists. Theodorus thus never let any other actor enter the stage before him, not even a tritagonist. If we apply this policy to the distribution of the roles in Sophocles' *Antigone*, it is clear that this famous fourth-century protagonist could give only himself the role of Antigone, because it is she who speaks first in the first scene with Ismene; and if we apply the same principle to the deuteragonist, he had to choose the role of Ismene, who speaks second in the tragedy. Given these conditions, Creon's role automatically falls to the tritagonist. That is what explains the "Creon-Aeschine" to whom Demosthenes refers. Aristotle's testimony thus indirectly confirms that of Demosthenes regarding the distribution of the roles in the revivals of *Antigone* after Sophocles' death. At the same time, it illustrates how the stardom of fourth-century actors was able to change the criteria of the assignment of the actors' roles as they can be reasonably reconstituted for the first performance in the time of the author.

The Silent Characters and the Spectacle

To give the spectacle greater scope, the tragic author used, in addition to the three actors and the chorus, extras called "mutes." Masked and costumed like the actors, they differed from them simply by the fact that they remained silent. Regarding the existence of silent extras in Greek tragedy, we can cite a little-known testimony preserved in a medical treatise attributed to Hippocrates, "the father of medicine" and a contemporary of Sophocles. Bad doctors are compared to silent extras in tragedy:

> Such persons are like the figures which are introduced in tragedies, for as they have the shape, and dress, and personal appearance of an actor, but are not actors, so also physicians are many in title but very few in reality.[129]

Scenes in which silent extras appear in tragedies without their presence being mentioned in the text are frequent. The Athenians could not imagine that a king would make a formal entrance without carrying his scepter and without being followed by his guard composed of several silent extras. This was so natural that the tragic author felt no need to mention it. For example, when Agamemnon, the head of the Achaian expedition to Troy, appears in the second part of *Ajax* to oppose his enemy's burial, he arrives accompanied by his royal escort, even though it is not mentioned in the text.[130] It is, in fact, the absence of an escort that is pointed out. Thus Antigone, announcing the entry of Polynices in *Oedipus at Colonus*, remarks that he comes "without attendants."[131] Ordinarily, the existence of guards or servants is mentioned only when they must act. When Creon, the new king, appears in *Antigone*, nothing is said about his escort. However, later on, the presence of servants is indirectly attested each time he gives an order: an order first to go find Ismene, then to take Antigone and Ismene prisoner in the palace, and finally to take Antigone to her underground prison.[132] Creon even addresses all his servants, present or absent, when he suddenly decides to leave to free Antigone: "Go, go, my servants, each and all of you! Take axes in your hands, and hurry to that place there in view!"[133] Also, when the king returns at the very end of the tragedy, bearing the body of his son Haemon, who has committed suicide on Antigone's corpse, he is clearly followed by the long funeral cortege of all his servants who had left with axes. This is a scene whose spectacular dimension we risk missing if we reason solely on the basis of the three actors without taking the extras into account.[134]

The reconstitution of the performance, in the case of the extras, certainly includes an unknown element; for as a rule, the number of servants is not specified. If it is not, that is simply because their number might vary depending on the greater or lesser generosity of the choregos during the performance. In any case, Creon left with all his servants. When he comes back, there must have been in the visible space a minimum of thirty costumed and masked characters, including the chorus.

Apart from the servants, the author might introduce children whose silence is not in any way implausible. In the two scenes where he appears, the blind seer Tiresias is guided by a boy. This child belongs to the category of servants.[135] But other children are closely linked with important characters: Ajax's son in *Ajax*[136] or Oedipus's daughters, Antigone and Ismene, at the end of *Oedipus the King*.[137] The presence of silent children may also provide a spectacular scene. At the beginning of *Oedipus the King*, the spectators see, like Oedipus when he comes out of his palace, a group of silent children holding branches and sitting in the posture of suppliants on the steps of the altar located in front of the palace.

A modern person will find stranger the idea of giving Orestes a companion, his friend Pylades, who says not a single word in the whole tragedy.[138] At the beginning of *Electra*, Sophocles takes care to mention Pylades' presence. The tutor, the first character to speak, addresses not only Orestes but also "you, best of allies, Pylades."[139] Pylades' presence will be discreetly recalled at every exit and entrance of Orestes. Once, Orestes even addresses his faithful friend, at the decisive moment when he goes into the palace to carry out his vengeance. Pylades obeys in silence. It is true that Sophocles, not without humor, has Orestes say that the situation no longer requires long speeches!

The Distribution of Roles between the Actors and the Extras

The use of such extras serves to connect various characters different from those that are played by the actors. It is a way for the author to give scope to the spectacle while compensating for the limited number of actors. However, the extras can also be used, in a subtler way, to allow more characters to speak. A single character may, in the same tragedy, be played sometimes by an actor, sometimes by an extra. The impact on the spectacle is not visible because two characters of the same size could wear the same costume and mask without the spectator noticing it. The only external sign—which could not be discerned by the spectator, so cleverly was the thing done—is that the character who spoke very naturally in one part of the tragedy is suddenly struck by a prolonged or definitive muteness. But seen from the wings, this is a perfectly demonstrable trick that reveals the tragic authors' constant effort to loosen the constraints of the limitation to three actors. By replacing the actor playing a character by an extra, the author could recuperate that actor to play another speaking character.

That is what happens in the case of Tecmessa, Ajax's companion. During the first part of the tragedy, so long as Ajax is still alive, she plays an important role. But once she has found Ajax's dead body, she leaves the scene at a curt order issued by Teucer in order to go seek her son who has remained alone in Ajax's residence.[140] But when she returns with her son to watch over the hero's body,[141] she remains constantly present until the end of the tragedy, but without saying a single word. By remaining silent next to Ajax's body, she applies literally the maxim that the hero, during his lifetime, had hurled at her when she asked him for explanations at the time of his mysterious nighttime exit: "Woman, silence graces woman"![142] The reason for this silence has in fact to do with the necessity of recuperating the deuteragonist, who has successively played, in the first part of the tragedy, the role of Odysseus, and then that of Tecmessa: Sophocles needs to make Odysseus reappear at the end of the tragedy to resolve the debate over the burial of Ajax. When Tecmessa returns with her son, she is therefore no longer played by the same actor; the latter has been replaced by an extra. The spectators have noticed nothing; the costume and the mask authorized such devices.

The case of Ismene in *Oedipus at Colonus* is still more complex: she is struck dumb during a large part of the tragedy but finds her tongue at the end to sing and lament with Antigone after their father's death. What happened?

The Constraint of Three Actors in *Oedipus at Colonus*: The Myth of the Fourth Actor

In *Oedipus at Colonus*, Sophocles engages in an unprecedented tour de force: he leaves two speaking characters continually present onstage during a large part of the tragedy: Oedipus and his inseparable guide, his daughter Antigone.[143] That is to say that during all this time he uses two actors, the protagonist playing the role of Oedipus and the deuteragonist playing that of Antigone. He has at his disposition only the tritagonist to play the other characters. The four characters who come in during the first half of the tragedy, before Antigone's departure— namely the resident of Colonus; Oedipus's second daughter, Ismene, who has come from Thebes; the king of Athens, Theseus; and Creon, Thebes's envoy— thus can be played only by the tritagonist. This also implies that starting with the arrival of the resident of Colonus, the entrance of any new speaking character presupposes the earlier departure of the preceding one and a pause sufficient to allow the tritagonist to change his costume and mask.[144] This is a cascade of problems that the poet had to cope with and that he was sometimes forced to resolve by using tricks.

These tricks consisted in dividing a role not only between an actor and an extra, as in *Ajax*, but even between two actors.

When the role is divided between two actors, nothing is in principle visible in the spectacle seen from the outside. The actors simply have to be of about the same size and assume the same voice. That is what the character of Theseus does. When he first enters, as we have just seen, he can be played only by the tritagonist. But when he hurries back after the chorus calls for his help against Creon's violence, he can no longer be played by the tritagonist, who is playing Creon. Only the deuteragonist, freed up by the abduction of Antigone, can play the role of Theseus returning in haste after changing his costume and his mask.[145]

Dividing a role between an actor and an extra leaves a mark on the spectacle, even if it is difficult to discern in the performance: the silence of a character. We have seen this with the character of Tecmessa in *Ajax*. But in *Oedipus at Colonus* Sophocles uses this device in a more sophisticated way. Ismene, when she first comes in, speaks, but she then remains silent when she comes back again; finally she recovers her voice when she enters the stage for the third time. It is not her silence that intrigues us. The reason is simple. When the two sisters reappear, freed by Theseus and Creon's guards, who had abducted them, Antigone speaks while Ismene remains silent, and she does so for almost five hundred verses, simply because three actors cannot play four characters present at the same time on the stage: Oedipus, Theseus, Antigone, and Ismene. The use of an extra is inevitable.

What perplexes us more is that Ismene recovers her voice and sings with Antigone in the final lamento. Modern scholars have long debated the distribution of the actors at the end of this tragedy, where four speaking characters return successively after accompanying Oedipus to his last resting place: the messenger giving the account of Oedipus's miraculous death, then Antigone and Ismene, whose arrival is announced by the messenger,[146] and finally Theseus. Some scholars have hypothesized a fourth actor to play these four speaking characters. But this hypothesis, which is not based on any ancient testimony, collapses of its own weight. If Sophocles had had a fourth actor, why would he have left Ismene silent for five hundred verses, even though Oedipus, as is natural, addresses both his daughters? Why wouldn't he have used the fourth actor as soon as Ismene returns the first time?

Since there are in fact only three actors for four speaking characters, two characters have to be played by the same actor. From the moment that the arrival of Oedipus's two daughters is announced by the messenger, these three characters are visible at the same time and are played by the three actors, whatever distribution is proposed. The only solution that remains for the arrival of Theseus is to make him played by the same actor who played the messenger. The latter, after the arrival of the two sisters, disappears during the funeral threnody sung by the two sisters and the chorus and reappears wearing the mask and costume of Theseus.

But what distribution should be adopted? The solution proposed by those who reject the hypothesis of the fourth actor is to assign to the protagonist the roles of the messenger and Theseus, to the deuteragonist the role of Antigone, and to the tritagonist the role of Ismene. But there are two problems with this distribution. The first is well known to the proponents of this solution. Theseus's role in the rest of the tragedy already has to be divided between the tritagonist and the deuteragonist. If at the end the role of Theseus is assigned to the protagonist, we end up with each of the three actors playing the same role. That is a record that hardly pleads in favor of Sophocles' cleverness. The second problem has gone unnoticed, because the criterion of song, though of capital importance, is not generally taken into consideration in examining the question of the distribution of roles. To assign the role of Ismene to the tritagonist is to give the latter a singing role, which is obviously not suitable for a third-rate actor. The simplest and most effective solutions must be found. Since the protagonist is freed up by the definitive disappearance of Oedipus, and since Ismene's final role is solely sung, why not give this role to the best of the troupe's singers, the protagonist? That means that the character of Ismene is played successively by the tritagonist when she has a speaking role, by an extra during her first return to the stage, when she has a silent role, and by the protagonist during her second return, when she has a singing role. The resources available to Sophocles—three actors and possibly silent characters—are used in accord with the skills of each. In this case, no problem is involved in assigning a single character to two different actors, because they operate in the two different registers of the voice, the spoken and the sung. Finally, if this solution is adopted, the role of Theseus, at the end of the tragedy as at the beginning, is played by the tritagonist. His role in the play as a whole is thus shared only between two actors.

This reading of Greek tragedy from the wings is neither arbitrary nor useless. On the contrary, it allows us to assess the increasingly sophisticated feats used to resolve technical problems, and especially to gauge the talent of the author who integrates them with the greatest naturalness into the plot of his tragedy. The deferred entrances of the characters or the exits required by the constraints of the distribution of actors are always justified in the context of the theatrical fiction. For example, at the end of *Oedipus at Colonus*, Theseus's tardy arrival, as compared with that of Oedipus's two daughters, which is necessary to give the tritagonist time to take off the messenger's costume and put on that of Theseus, is explained in the framework of the fiction. Oedipus, after listening to the messenger's account, sends away his daughters before he dies, whereas he asks Theseus to remain at his side. Thus it is logical that Theseus returns after the two women. In this way, the necessities of the fiction skillfully mask the constraints of the performance.

The Modalities of Communication in the Scenes with Three Speaking Characters

In Sophocles' work, scenes with three speaking characters exploit the new potentialities he had given the Athenian theater by creating the third actor. He makes use of these potentialities in the oldest of his extant tragedies. In *Ajax*, there are two scenes with three speaking characters that use three actors: one, near the beginning of the tragedy, is a little unusual because it brings together a goddess hovering in the air, Athena, and two men on the earth, Odysseus, who is already onstage, and Ajax, still in the grip of his madness, coming out of his house at the call of the goddess.[147] The second is the final scene, where three men meet, King Agamemnon, who violently opposes Teucer regarding the problem of Ajax's burial, and Odysseus, who comes in to arbitrate the conflict.[148] But for all that the meetings do not give rise to a dialogue among the three characters. In the first scene, Odysseus remains silent out of fear and witnesses, immobile, the dialogue between Athena and Ajax, who, in his madness, does not see Odysseus. In the second scene, it is Teucer who remains silent during the whole duration of the dialogue between Odysseus and Agamemnon. These scenes with three characters consist of a single dialogue. And when in this dialogue the third character present is mentioned, he is designated only by a third-person pronoun, as if he were not there.[149] Thus in this ancient tragedy there is still not a true scene with three speaking characters. The third character behaves as if he were an extra.[150]

Later, Sophocles wrote scenes in which three characters speak.[151] Thus in *Antigone*, after the conflict between King Creon, who has forbidden the burial of Polynices, and Antigone, whom a guard has caught burying her brother, Ismene comes in weeping. At the beginning of the scene, the three characters speak one after the other: Creon addresses Ismene, who answers him, then Antigone interrupts to contradict her sister's reply. This exchange among three characters nonetheless remains exceptional. The scene is then organized in two successive dialogues: the first between Antigone and Ismene, the second between Ismene and Creon. There is no discussion among the three characters. During these two dialogues, the third person remains momentarily silent: first Creon, then Antigone. When in the dialogue the third character present is mentioned, his name is used, as if he were not there. Antigone, in her dialogue with sister, speaks this way about the king: "Ask Creon. Your concern is for him."[152] The absence of an exchange among the three characters increases, in fact, the dramatic tension. After the preceding scene in which she violently opposed Creon, Antigone has broken off all communication with him.[153] An exchange of words among these two characters seems henceforth impossible. And it has not been sufficiently noticed that the last, famous reply in her collision with Creon—"It is not my nature to join in hate, but in love"[154]—is the last thing she says to him in the whole tragedy, henceforth showing only hatred and scorn for him. Even when she encounters him once again when he comes to hasten her departure to her underground prison,[155] she continues to ignore him and does not even answer when he addresses her for the last time.[156]

A final step is taken in the most recent tragedies. The flexibility of the exchanges and the rapidity of the speeches sometimes removes any solemnity from the three-character scene. In *Philoctetes*, performed in 409, we find the shortest, most intense, and most spectacular three-character scene in all of Sophocles' extant theater. This scene involves the three main characters: Philoctetes, Neoptolemus, and Odysseus.

They had already appeared in an earlier scene, but in a way that reminds us of the older type used in *Ajax*.[157] Philoctetes demands his bow. Neoptolemus, pitying him, hesitates to give it back to him. Odysseus emerges from the shadows to put an end to his hesitations and prevent him from returning the bow. For eighty verses, from Odysseus's arrival to his departure, the encounter among the three characters is reduced to a confrontation between Philoctetes and Odysseus that Neoptolemus witnesses as a silent spectator.

In the second scene, everything changes. Remorsefully, Neoptolemus returns the bow to Philoctetes. Odysseus emerges once more to oppose this, but it is too late. In a crisis situation, all three characters speak in bursts:

Neoptolemus (speaking to Philoctetes): Come, stretch out your right hand and
    be master of your bow! (As he hands the bow and arrows to Philoctetes,
    Odysseus suddenly appears, but is not seen by Philoctetes)

Odysseus: But I forbid it, as the gods are my witnesses, in the name of the Atreids and the entire army!

Philoctetes (speaking to Neoptolemus): Son, whose voice was that? Do I hear
   Odysseus?

Odysseus (closer, now visible to Philoctetes): Be sure of it, and you see him at
   your side, who will carry you to the plains of Troy by force, whether or not
   the son of Achilles is willing.

Philoctetes (to Odysseus, after having drawn his bow in his direction): But it
   will bring you no joy, if this arrow fly straight. *Odysseus flees from the stage.*

Neoptolemus (to Philoctetes, restraining his arm holding the bow): Wait—by
   the gods, no! Do not let it fly!

Philoctetes (speaking to Neoptolemus): Let go of me, in the name of the gods,
   dear boy!

Neoptolemus (speaking to Philoctetes): I will not.

Philoctetes (speaking to Neoptolemus, his bow still drawn): Alas! Why did you
   take from me the chance to kill my hated enemy with my bow?

Neoptolemus (speaking to Philoctetes): It would have been honorable neither
   for me, nor for you.

Philoctetes (speaking to Neoptolemus and no longer drawing his bow, because
   Odysseus has left without saying a word): Well, you may be sure of one
   thing, at least: the army's chiefs, the lying heralds of the Greeks, though
   bold with words, are cowards in the fight.[158]

All the stage directions, given here for the reader's convenience, follow from
the text itself. There is no longer any silent character, no succession of long dialogues between two characters. The three characters speak briefly in turns during
six exchanges; and each time the characters' gestures and movements can be
reconstituted with the most extreme precision. At the very moment when Neoptolemus returns Philoctetes' bow to him, Odysseus, still in the background,
cries out to forbid it. We have the impression that this second meeting is going
to take place like the first one, because Odysseus, at first far away and only heard
by Philoctetes, moves closer to be seen, as he had the first time, and makes threats
just as violent.[159] But everything changes because he acts too late. Philoctetes,
once again in possession of his bow, responds to Odysseus's violence by brandishing his infallible bow. Odysseus stands motionless. Neoptolemus, who has remained alongside Philoctetes, grasps his hand to prevent him from releasing his
arrow. Then Odysseus, even though he is a master of language, retreats and sinks
back into silence in the shadows from which he had emerged. Here Sophocles
exploits brilliantly the possibilities of a three-character scene that he had himself
created half a century earlier, but which had long remained the prisoner of the
rhetorical frameworks of dialogue. Here the dialogue between Philoctetes and
Neoptolemus is interrupted by Odysseus, the master of words, but the master
of words himself is reduced to a definitive silence. Rhetoric is deconstructed; life
takes its revenge.

Dialogic Communication between
Speaking Characters and the Chorus

The constraints imposed by the limitation of the number of actors are attenuated by the presence of the chorus. The chorus can enter into dialogue with the characters. In fact, this dialogic communication with the chorus was the only one that existed originally, when there was only one actor, in the time of Thespis, the founder of Athenian tragedy. No literary testimony from this first phase has been preserved, since the oldest tragedies we have date from the period when there were already two actors. Aristotle very rightly connects this doubling of the actors owed to Aeschylus with the development of dialogue between the characters and the regression of choral song. And if we pursue this line of reasoning, we can foresee that Sophocles' introduction of the third actor accentuated to a certain extent this twofold tendency. However, communication between the chorus and the characters remained very lively, especially in Sophocles, so that Aristotle could say that in his work the chorus played the role of a character.[160]

The dialogue between the chorus and the characters takes various forms (lyric, chanted, or spoken) and appears at various times (especially in moments of intense emotion at the beginning or at the end of the tragedy). However, the chorus's role is equivalent to that of a speaking character when it enters into dialogue with a single character present on the stage. Modern scholars are accustomed to assign these speeches solely to the leader of the chorus, the coryphaeus. But ancient testimonies, manuscripts and scholia, refer only to the chorus.[161] Such spoken dialogues between the chorus and a character are found especially after the entrance song. Traditionally, the chorus makes its entrance singing and dancing, when the visible space is empty. In this case, after the chorus's entrance song a character comes in, and the chorus, ceasing to sing, enters into dialogue with him until a second character appears (*Ajax, Antigone, Oedipus the King*). Sometimes a character is already present when the chorus enters. Its song is thus addressed to the character (*The Women of Trachis*) or takes the form of a lyric dialogue with him (*Electra, Philoctetes, Oedipus at Colonus*). Then it is normally followed, as in the preceding case, by a spoken dialogue before the arrival of a new character.[162] Whatever form it takes, this communication between the characters and the chorus raises the problem of the space where the actors move with respect to the chorus.

The Space Where the Characters Act: Defining the Problem

Did the characters act in the orchestra like the choreutes, or on a slightly elevated stage located behind the orchestra? How was the theatrical space constructed?

A tourist seated on the tiers of the theater of Dionysus in Athens can infer nothing of what he or she will see. Next to the current semicircular orchestra will be seen the base of a stage that is clearly elevated with respect to the orchestra and connected with it by a central stairway of which four steps remain. The tourist can see, to the right of the stairway, the remains of sculptures that ornament the base; they illustrate the birth and power of Dionysus and attest to the permanence of the bond between the god and the theater. But these remains threaten to mislead more than they guide. The sculpted frieze, which was probably part of an altar of Dionysus, dates from the Roman period, from the time of Nero or Hadrian. It has been reused in a new stage erected, after the destruction of Athens by the Herules in the third century CE, by an Athenian archon, Phaidros, whose name is inscribed on one of the steps of the stairway connecting the stage with the orchestra.[163] In any case, the significant difference in height of more than a meter that currently subsists between the stage and the orchestra could not have been suitable for the performance of tragedies in which the dialogue between the chorus and the characters was still so natural, not to mention that the stage has been extended so far forward that the side entrances no longer allow actors to enter the orchestra. Finally, the disappearance of this base, on the east side, frees up the space and makes it possible to rediscover the communication of one of the two side entrances with the orchestra and to see from the tiers of seats the foundation of the fourth-century stage building. These foundations are the oldest we can reach. Recent excavations have confirmed that none of the vestiges of the stage building in situ is attributable to the fifth century.[164]

The current remains thus can tell us nothing about the material organization of the theatrical space in time of Sophocles, which must have consisted of wooden structures. To try to form an idea of it, we are reduced to hypotheses. They all claim to be based on the text of the tragedies, but they diverge, notably regarding the space where the characters act. Let us begin with what is generally agreed on.

The Stage Building and the Movement of the Actors

In the time when Sophocles' tragedies were first performed, the actors played in front of a wooden building that is usually called by the Greek term *skēnē* (literally, "house"). The façade of this long building defined the visible space where the chorus and the characters appeared. Since the fifth-century building was made of wood, it has left no trace, and its dimensions are unknown. The stone building that replaced it in the fourth century was about fifty meters long and eight meters deep. The existence of such a stage building goes back at least to Aeschylus's *Oresteia* (458 BCE), in which we see the watchman, at the beginning of *Agamemnon*, on the roof terrace of this building representing the palace, which the characters could enter and leave, inaugurating frontal entrances and exits in the visible space, that is, facing the audience, whereas in Aeschylus's earlier plays all the characters' entrances and exits were made through the lateral passages.[165]

The essential function of this building, in addition to the quality of the acoustics, which must not be neglected in an open-air theater, and in addition to its integration into the dramatic fiction, notably as a palace,[166] was to serve as wings where the actors changed their masks and costumes each time that they had to change roles. The actors could reach it in two ways: either directly, from the visible space where they played, through a central door—a single door being necessary for the performance of Sophocles' tragedies[167]—or, once they had exited by one of the two lateral passageways, through entrances hidden from the audience, a central door in the rear, or rather two doors located on the small east and west sides of the building corresponding to the two lateral exits.[168] Once they were ready for their new role, they could appear to the spectators, depending on what was needed, either directly through the door in the façade of the stage building, or through one of the two lateral entrances.

This movement of the actors is essential for the performance of the spectacle. The author thus had to include in the conception of his tragedy the necessary time for the actors to make the changes in costume and mask within the stage building, so that the character that they had been playing could exit by the lateral passageways or through the door in the façade, and the new character they were to play could appear to the audience directly through the door in the façade or through the detour of the lateral entrances. Depending on the distance to be covered, the time it took to make these changes varied. We could easily find examples in Sophocles' theater to illustrate all these possibilities. The pauses in the action constituted by the chorus's songs were systematically exploited by the tragic author to carry out these changes. But changes were also necessary in the course of the action. Some of them required great nimbleness.

The tragedy *Oedipus at Colonus* can serve as an example to illustrate these changes, just as it was chosen to illustrate the distribution of roles among the actors. The two questions are connected. We have seen how Sophocles, by using the protagonist and deuteragonist in the first part of the tragedy, and by the continual presence of Oedipus and his daughter Antigone on the stage, forced the tritagonist to play during all that time each new speaking character who came in: the resident of Colonus, Ismene, Theseus, and Creon.[169] The tritagonist therefore had to make three changes in the course of this sequence. The first of these changes left plenty of time to the tritagonist, since between the exit of the resident of Colonus and the appearance of Ismene were intercalated a spoken scene (between Oedipus and Antigone), and then the arrival of the chorus (in the form of a long dialogue with Oedipus, sung and then spoken). The two other changes take place thanks to a choral song, the tritagonist leaving the visible space just before the chorus's song and reappearing just after it. Such changes were thus made under comfortable conditions. On the other hand, the change that corresponds to Theseus's second entrance is more acrobatic. The drama has grown more lively. Creon, who has come on behalf of the besieged Thebans to find Oedipus and obtain his protection, in conformity with the instructions of the oracles, resorts to violence when confronted by Oedipus's refusal. He has his guards abduct Antigone, manhandles Oedipus, and tries to take him away by force, to the point that the indignant chorus cries for help and the king of Athens, Theseus, comes running in response:

> *Theseus:* What is this shout? What is the trouble? What fear has moved you to stop my sacrifice at the altar to the sea-god, the lord of your Colonus? Speak, so that I may know the situation; for that is why I have sped here more swiftly than was pleasant.[170]

We have already seen, in the distribution of the roles, that Theseus could be played, when he makes this second entrance, only by the deuteragonist freed up by the abduction of Antigone. What has to be stressed here is how exceptional this change is in relation to the three changes that the tritagonist has previously made. It is much more rapid, because it takes place in the course of a single scene. The time at the actor's disposal is very brief: about forty verses, and that in a scene in which the dialogue exchanged between the chorus, Creon, and Oedipus is lively and thus swift.[171] While these verses are being delivered, the deuteragonist, who has exited through a lateral passageway, must go into the stage building, take off Antigone's costume and mask, put on Theseus's costume and mask, go out of the stage building and then enter through the lateral passage on the opposite side. We can understand, under these conditions, why Creon's guards had to hasten to take Antigone away, and why the king, coming to help, appears running faster than he would have liked. The violence of the former and the forced haste of the latter are explained in the same way when we consider the spectacle from the wings. There was no time to lose! And we cannot help seeing a certain humor when the author makes his Theseus say that he ran faster than he would have liked. The actor must have thought so as much as the character he was playing did.

Such then is the principal function of the stage building before which the actors played, a function unanimously recognized, because the development of the spectacle is impossible without a place where the actors can change hidden from the audience's eyes.[172]

But Where Did the Actors Play?

The space where the actors played in front of the stage building has been, on the other hand, the subject of interminable debates since the end of the nineteenth century. Two solutions are opposed. According to some scholars, the actors played on a wooden stage that was elevated with respect to the orchestra and was called the *logeion*.[173] According to other scholars, the actors played on the same level as the chorus in the orchestra. On the hypothesis of an elevated stage, the actors coming from the lateral entrances first entered the orchestra and climbed a central stairway to reach the stage, whereas direct communication with the stage building took place at the level of the stage. On the other hand, if the actors played on the dance space, the communication with the stage building took place at ground level.

The oldest theory is that of the elevated stage. It is based on the testimony of the lexicographer of the Greek language Pollux (second century CE), whose *Onomasticon* is full of information about the theater. It is he who says expressly that "the stage is the place peculiar to the actors, whereas the orchestra is the place peculiar to the chorus."[174] And it is he again who explains the movement of the actors entering the visible space through the lateral passageways: "When they enter through the orchestra, they climb onto the stage by a stairway; the steps of the stairway are called degrees."[175] This testimony is obviously much more recent than the performances during Sophocles' lifetime. But Pollux reflects an older tradition. The Roman architect Vitruvius (first century BCE), comparing the Greek theater with the Roman theater, said: "The Greeks have a roomier orchestra, and a 'scaena' set further back, as well as a stage of less depth. They call this the λογεῖον."[176] And if we go back in time, in his *Poetics* Aristotle already drew a topographical distinction between actors and chorus. When he is defining the lyric dialogue between the chorus and a character (a dialogue called commos), he designates the character by the expression "what comes from the stage," contrasting it with what comes from the orchestra.[177] These clues seem to be in accord with the existence of a stage preserved in the theater in Athens.

However, starting in the last twenty years of the nineteenth century, the opinion was expressed that certain scenes in the Greek theater in which the chorus was in close contact with the characters could be correctly performed only if the actors and the chorus played in the same space and on the same level.[178] Around the same time, the excavations that were beginning to be systematically made in the theaters, notably Dörpfeld's excavations in the theater of Athens, were shedding new light on the successive reconstructions and showing, in any case, that the material organization of the theater of Dionysus in the fifth century could not be deduced with certainty from the remains in stone. The fact that Dörpfeld adopted the thesis according to which the actors and the chorus played on the same level made this solution very influential. At the beginning of the twentieth century, it was endorsed in France by Bodin and Mazon in a work on Aristophanes that was read throughout the whole century and had an impact on teaching in French universities at least down to the 1960s.[179]

However, this new theory did not win universal approval in its own time. In late nineteenth-century Britain, there was a reaction against Dörpfeld's thesis. Although this reaction maintained the hypothesis of an elevated stage, it recognized that the stage was much lower in the fifth century than it had been in earlier periods.[180] This position is now generally adopted, because several passages in Euripides, whose theater was more realistic than that of Aeschylus or Sophocles, seems to allude, not without a slightly amused irony, to the difficult moments when the old men who had entered the visible space through the lateral entrances had to climb the few steep steps from the orchestra to the stage.[181]

The Stage and the Orchestra: The Limits of Dramaturgical Analysis

Nevertheless, the analysis of the tragic text, despite the numerous clues that it contains regarding the organization of the spectacle, has its limits for recreating the space of performance on the basis of the space represented in the tragic fiction. There remains a zone of uncertainty concerning the degree of the realism of these clues. In this respect, some interpretations of the tragic text that are used to strengthen the hypothesis of the elevated stage may have nothing to do with the material organization of the theater.

For example, an attempt has been made to see an indication of the existence of an elevated stage in the beginning of the scene in *Ajax* where the hero is about to address his son.[182] Here is the passage in which Ajax, after his fit of madness, asks to see his son and to speak to him, whereas Tecmessa, the mother, had sent him away out of prudence:

Ajax: Let me speak to him and see him face to face.

Tecmessa: Oh, yes—he is close by, watched by our servants.
Ajax: Then why is his presence delayed?
Tecmessa: My child, your father calls you. Bring him here, servant, whichever of you is guiding his steps.
Ajax: Is the man coming? Or has he missed your call?
Tecmessa: Here now one of the servants approaches with him.
Ajax: Lift him; lift him up here. Doubtless he will not shrink to look on this newly-shed blood, if he is indeed my true-born son and heir to his father's manners. But he must at once be broken into his father's harsh ways and moulded to the likeness of my nature. Ah, son, may you prove luckier than your father, but in all else like him. Then you would not prove base.[183]

The arrival of the son is full of dramaturgical indications. Tecmessa, for fear that in his madness her father might kill his son,[184] had sent him away, entrusting him to servants. But this place, although it was not visible for the spectators, is close, since the voice of a character in the visible space can reach it. Tecmessa announces the arrival of the servant, an extra, who leads the child by the hand as he enters the visible space through a lateral passageway.[185] What happens then, when Ajax asks Tecmessa to "lift" the child? Does that mean that she takes the child from the hands of a servant standing on the level of the orchestra and places him on the elevated stage?[186]

The text can be interpreted more naturally, whether or not there is an elevated stage. When the slave leading the child has approached Ajax and Tecmessa—

without leaving the orchestra, if the actors are playing at the same level as the chorus, or after having climbed with the child the few steps that lead to the stage—if there is a slightly elevated stage—Ajax orders Tecmessa to take the child and lift it to put it in his arms. That is what Tecmessa does during the first five verses of Ajax's speech. And when Ajax addresses his child directly, he is now holding him in his arms. Then, at the end of his speech to the child, Ajax gives him back to Tecmessa, saying "Come, take the child right away."[187] Thus nothing in the text obliges us to see here an allusion to the material conditions of the performance.

The limits of the dramaturgical analysis of the text of the tragedy are such that we might find in a single tragedy clues that can be used in contradictory ways in favor of the hypothesis of an elevated stage reserved for the characters or, on the contrary, in favor of an absence of separation between the characters and the chorus. That is the case in Sophocles' last tragedy, *Oedipus at Colonus*.

When the old men forming the chorus enter the orchestra for the first time, frightened because they have learned that a foreigner has entered the forbidden space of the sanctuary of the redoubtable Eumenides, they are looking for the man, resolved to stone him. Oedipus had hidden in the thick vegetation of the sacred wood at the fork in the road. Then he reveals himself. During a turbulent lyrical dialogue, the chorus, being far away from him but within earshot, forces him to leave the forbidden part of the sanctuary and come to sit down on a rock. It guides him orally as he advances, and at a certain moment it cries:

> *Chorus:* There! Do not incline your steps beyond that ledge of bedrock.
> *Oedipus:* This far?
> *Chorus:* Enough, I say
> *Oedipus:* [195] Shall I sit down?
> *Chorus:* Yes, move sideways, and crouch low on the edge of the rock.[188]

Oedipus, in his movement from the forbidden space of the sanctuary of the Eumenides to a profane space, stops where the chorus wants him to sit down. Having arrived at a rocky platform that he must not go beyond, he has to move along the extremity of the rock. One is tempted to think that the edge of this rocky platform corresponds to the edge of the elevated wooden stage where the actors are. This interpretation might be confirmed by another of Sophocles' tragedies in which the visible space also represents a natural landscape with rocks: *Philoctetes.* When Odysseus emerges the first time to prevent Neoptolemus from returning Philoctetes' bow to him, he is forced to make Philoctetes recognize him and orders him to leave, willingly or unwillingly, to go to Troy with his bow. But Philoctetes refuses:

> *Philoctetes:* No, never—even if I must suffer every torment, so long as I have this island's steep cliffs beneath me!
> *Odysseus:* What do you plan to do?

Philoctetes: Throw myself now from the rock and shatter my head on the rocks below!

Odysseus: Quick, seize him, both of you! Do not give him the chance![189]

It is difficult to imagine such a threat of suicide if the actor playing the role of Philoctetes was standing on the smooth floor of the orchestra. Between the tragic text and the performance space, the contradiction seems too flagrant to explain by theatrical conventions alone. On the other hand, if Philoctetes is standing on a stage that is elevated above the orchestra, even if the difference in height is not really very great, he can threaten, without too much implausibility, to leap over the edge of the stage to kill himself.

So there are two passages in *Philoctetes* and *Oedipus at Colonus* that suggest the existence of a stage reserved for the actors and a difference in elevation between the stage and the orchestra. However, a passage in *Oedipus at Colonus* puts the chorus and the actors in direct contact. Creon has come to find the exiled Oedipus and take him back to his homeland in order to benefit from his protection in the war of Seven against Thebes, exactly as Odysseus, in the scene in *Philoctetes* that we have just mentioned, has come to get Philoctetes with a view to winning the Trojan War. Like Odysseus, Creon ends up resorting to violence. This violence is manifested in the arrest order they both give their servants: the order to arrest Philoctetes in one case, and the order to take Antigone away in the other. But whereas the chorus in *Philoctetes* remains passive and silent—how could it behave otherwise, since its master, Neoptolemus, is also passive and silent?—the chorus in *Oedipus at Colonus* speaks up to protest against the violence. At the moment that Creon arrests Antigone, the chorus protests verbally, threatens to act, to call for help, but without success. Once the guards have taken Antigone away and Creon is preparing to leave, the chorus adds action to words:

Chorus: Stop there, stranger!
Creon: Hands off, I say!
Chorus: I will not let go, unless you give back the maidens.[190]

This moment of violence when the chorus struggles with a character is an exception in Sophocles' extant tragedies. It shows that the communication between the chorus and the characters is not merely verbal, but sometimes even physical. Those who argue against the presence of a stage have obviously found a supporting argument in this passage.[191]

The Most Plausible Solution: A Stage Where the Actors Played

The fact that we find in a single tragedy passages that can provide opposed arguments regarding the problem of the presence or absence of an elevated stage in the theater of Dionysus in the time of Sophocles will strengthen the position of skeptics for whom this question is of little importance.

However, the divergent testimonies do not all have the same weight. It is easier to have an angry chorus (or its leader) climb a few steps to seize the arm of a character who has just done something odious and is about to come down than to make a character standing at ground level say that he is going to throw himself off a cliff. There are degrees in conventions and plausibility.

Finally, one argument in favor of a stage that is slightly elevated in relation to the level of the orchestra remains quite strong, because it is based not on the texts but on the arrangement of the theater itself.[192] The absence of a difference in elevation between the chorus and the actors in no way harms the spectacle if the spectator is seated on the raised tiers of the theater of Dionysus; but when the spectator is at the same level as the orchestra, what could he see of the actors hidden behind the choreutes? The seats in the first row, which were not elevated in the time of Sophocles, would be the worst, especially the seats in the center. But it was just these seats that were the most honorific, with the seat reserved for the priest of Dionysus in the center.

In short, despite the uncertainty concerning the form of the orchestra, the presence or absence of a slightly raised stage, and the number of doors that opened on the façade of the stage building, it remains that the presence and arrangement of the fundamental elements necessary for the performance of Sophocles' tragedies is clear: a visible space that the chorus always entered through a side passageway and that the actors playing the characters reached either through the two side entrances or through the frontal entrance of the stage building. This performance space was the matrix on which the author modeled the space represented in his tragic fiction.

The Integration of the Stage Building into the Tragic Fiction: A Constructed Residence

The tragic author usually had no difficulty in using the stage building, because he integrated this structure into his tragic fiction. That is the case in five out of Sophocles' seven extant tragedies.

The stage building generally represents a royal place or its equivalent. In *Antigone* and *Oedipus the King*, it is the palace of the Labdacids in Thebes; in *Electra*, it is the palace of the Atreids in Mycenae. The residence of Deianira and Heracles in *The Women of Trachis* is that of a host in Trachis.[193] Its appearance must not have differed from that of a palace. Even Ajax's residence in the Greek camp at Troy must not have been very different in aspect from the other royal residences, except that it was supposed to be built of wood. That is why Sophocles designates it by the specific Greek term *skēnē* (in the singular or plural), which denotes a construction in wood (or canvas); in this case, it referred to both the stage building and the stage itself, both of which were constructed of wood. We can note the perfect match in this tragedy between the space of representation and the space represented.

The Transformation of the Stage Building
by the Sets: Rural Landscapes

In the other two tragedies, the stage building is transformed into a grotto (*Philoctetes*), or disappears completely and is replaced by a sacred wood without any structure (*Oedipus at Colonus*). The second part of *Ajax* also presupposes a rural landscape without any structure.

Such changes raise the problem of the sets. In this domain, as in others, Sophocles was famous for having made improvements. Aristotle, in the passage in his *Poetics* where he attributes to Sophocles the introduction of the third actor, adds that he also introduced *skenographia*, that is, painted sets.[194]

Philoctetes' grotto, which is located on a lonely promontory on the island of Lemnos, has two entrances, only one of which is visible. Not far from this grotto, on the left, there is a spring. However, this natural setting, which is very different from the palace tragedies, was in no way exceptional for the spectators. It corresponded to the traditional setting of the satyr play that they saw after the tragic trilogy. In fact, Sophocles' satyr play entitled *The Searchers* (*Ichneutae*) offers a setting comparable to his *Philoctetes*. The countryside is located in Arcadia, on Mount Cyllene: at the back of the stage one sees the grotto of the nymph Cyllene, who is secretly raising the very young, prodigious Hermes, who, before he was six days old, had already stolen Apollo's oxen and invented the lyre. The satyrs form the chorus, attracted by the reward Apollo has promised (gold and freedom), and leave in search of the thief like bloodhounds (whence the name of the satyr drama, *Ichneutae*). In *Philoctetes*, as in *The Searchers*, the door of the stage building corresponds to the entrance to the grotto and is used as a frontal entrance or exit. The only difference is that the grotto has a door in *The Searchers* whereas in *Philoctetes* it has none. The grotto of a man abandoned without resources is not comparable to that of a goddess. The panels of the stage building door must have remained open and invisible during the performance of *Philoctetes*.

While similar to the rural setting of *Philoctetes*, the setting of *Oedipus at Colonus* differed from it in that it included no structure of any kind, and hence no visible door. The text explicitly specifies that nothing can be built in the sanctuary.[195] The central door of the stage building was probably masked by a painted panel representing trees, because the setting is a sacred wood. However, this panel, placed at a certain distance from the opening, did not block it. The door retained its dramaturgical function as a passageway. To be sure, no character appears in the tragedy through the frontal opening. Thus we return to a situation more or less analogous to that Aeschylus's older tragedies, where there was no stage building, and where all the characters entered the stage from the side. But one character did go out through the masked central door: Ismene, when she goes to "the further side of this grove" to carry out the purifying sacrifice in the name of her father.[196] It was perhaps also behind this painted panel that Oedipus hid with Antigone when he left the road and plunged "into the sacred wood" at the time when the chorus is hurrying to find the intruder and sees no one.[197]

A Bold Change in Setting: An Inhabited Residence

It is also a painted panel of this kind that is used in one of the most spectacular scenes in Sophocles' theater, Ajax's suicide.

The peculiarity of this tragedy, from the point of view of space and setting, is that its performance requires a change of place. Whereas the whole first part of the play occurs in front of Ajax's home, the second, from Ajax's monologue preceding his suicide onward, is set in an isolated place in the Trojan countryside where he has gone. Such a change of place is already remarkable in itself. The only other example we have in the extant tragedies is a play by Aeschylus, *The Eumenides*, which begins in front of the temple of Apollo in Delphi and ends in front of the temple of Athena in Athens.[198] In both cases, the change of setting is preceded by the departure of the whole of the chorus: in *The Eumenides*, the chorus has left in pursuit of Orestes; in *Ajax* the chorus and Tecmessa have gone to look for Ajax. Thus in both tragedies there is a wholly exceptional moment when the visible space is empty, without characters or chorus.

The change in setting takes place thanks to this total break in the spectacle between the two parts of the tragedy; a genuine pause deliberately arranged by the author. Sophocles' technique is so close to that of Aeschylus that it seems to take its inspiration from the latter. But this technical similarity may be ultimately explained by the fact that the requirements for performance were the same. This pause must have been necessary for the change of setting, no matter how limited it might have been. Nonetheless, the change in setting is more extensive in *Ajax* than it is in *The Eumenides*. In Aeschylus's case, the setting remains the same in kind, a temple; thus the decoration of the stage building, if there was one, did not need to be modified. The only absolutely necessary new element is a statue of Athena that had to be placed in front of the temple (replacing the statue of Apollo); in fact, Orestes, coming in through one the lateral entrances, hurries up to this statue and adopts the posture of a suppliant.[199] On the other hand, in Sophocles, a change in the nature of the setting has to be made. We pass from the classic type of set with a residence in the background to a rural setting without structures, that is, to set in which the frontal entrance is masked and is no longer used to let a character make an exit.

How did this change take place? It is impossible to explain in detail what Sophocles contributed in the domain of the painting of sets. Were there already in his time interchangeable painted panels between the columns of the stage building's façade, as is attested in the Hellenistic period by both inscriptions and the vestiges of theaters other than that of Athens?[200] Did there already exist what is called in Greek *periaktoi*, that is, a sort of triangular revolving aedicule that could show three different painted panels that were used especially when there were changes in place in the course of a play?[201] Nothing allows us to affirm or deny it. If these panels existed, they had a purely decorative function. The case is different for the panel masking the entrance to the stage building. It had both a decorative and a dramaturgical function.

In every case, the change from a palatial to a bucolic setting, even if it was exceptional within a single tragedy, was not in itself exceptional. Such changes occurred regularly every time a tetralogy was performed, in passing from the last tragedy of the trilogy to the satyr play,[202] and would thus pose no technical problem.

From the dramaturgical point of view, the second setting in *Ajax* is not different in nature from that in *Oedipus at Colonus*. The movement of the characters now takes place solely through the lateral entrances, as in the whole of *Oedipus at Colonus*. Nonetheless, even though it is masked by a painted panel, the door in the stage building must remain an exit through which an actor can leave the stage without being seen by the spectators. This material organization of the spectacle is, as we have seen, implied by Ismene's exit in Sophocles' last tragedy. It is also necessary to understand the representation of Ajax's suicide in his earliest tragedy.

A Suicide Presented Live, Both Visible and Hidden

Ajax's suicide in the visible space is incontestably the most audacious scene Sophocles produced. He distinguished himself from his predecessor Aeschylus who, treating the same myth, had had Ajax's suicide related by a messenger.[203]

After the change in setting made while the visible space was completely empty, the beginning of the second part of the tragedy is presented as a tableau in which Ajax alone is present in the visible space.[204] He delivers a long monologue in which he announces, first, that he has solidly planted a sword in the earth with its point turned toward the sky. Then, after invoking the tutelary or avenging gods and addressed a moving final farewell to life, he commits suicide by leaping into the air and coming down so that the point of his sword penetrates his side. Did this suicide, though it happened in the visible space, happen in front of the spectator's eyes?

Some productions, even ancient ones, must have presented the suicide before the spectators. A sophist of the imperial period, a contemporary of Hadrian, alludes to a theatrical sword with a retractable blade that was used precisely in the performance of *Ajax*.[205] However, if we examine in detail the stage directions contained in Sophocles' own text, we see that the presentation of this scene was subtler.

The Three Categories of Stage Directions: Their Illustration in the Case of Ajax's Suicide

One of the paradoxes of the text written by the Greek tragic poets is that even though it was composed for a single performance, it included stage directions as if they were intended to guide a director for another performance, or a reader to help him imagine the spectacle. Among these stage directions, some are given in the scene where the action takes place (contemporary stage directions); these are the most obvious. Two other categories attract less attention, though they are just as important: the ones delivered in a preceding scene, before the action even takes place (progressive stage directions), and those that provide complements once the action has taken place (regressive stage directions).

We can illustrate this theoretical distinction by the scene of Ajax's suicide. The monologue preceding his suicide offers hardly any details regarding the place where he is. Thus there is no contemporary stage direction concerning the place. However, there has been a change in setting. In fact, these directions have been given earlier, at the time when Ajax departs. In his wily speech explaining why he is leaving his companions, Ajax has indicated the place where he is going, even though Tecmessa and the chorus are mistaken about his intention: he is going to an "untrodden" place where, after purifying himself, he will bury his sword in the prairies along shore.[206] Thus at the time of his suicide Ajax is in a lonely place not far from the sea. The progressive stage directions suffice to guide the spectator.

On the other hand, Ajax's monologue contains contemporary stage directions concerning the way Ajax commits suicide. The whole beginning explains how he has solidly buried the hilt of his newly sharpened sword in the earth to ensure a rapid death.[207] Even in the prayers that follow, a direction is cleverly inserted when Ajax invokes Hermes, asking that his death be quick: "I call also on Hermes, guide to the underworld, to lay me softly to sleep with one quick, struggle-free leap, when I have broken open my side on this sword."[208] But the most important direction is revealed after the action, when Tecmessa discovers Ajax's body lying behind a grove.[209] From this regressive stage direction, we can deduce what the spectators saw and what they did not see. They saw Ajax leap, but in doing so he disappeared behind the painted panel located across from the door in the stage building. The spectators thus did not see the sword buried in the earth that Ajax talks about in his monologue before committing suicide; it is supposed to be hidden by the grove. Once the protagonist playing the character of Ajax has plunged behind the panel, he can leave by the central opening in the stage building without being seen, as through this opening a mannequin representing his dead body is substituted for him. In this way, Tecmessa coming through this same masked door a little later, cries out in despair upon discovering the body, which will cause the chorus to say: "Whose cry broke from that nearby grove?" As for the protagonist who played Ajax, he was able to return a few moments later through a side entrance, playing the role of Teucer in the second part of the tragedy.

Thus without cultivating paradox, we can say that Ajax's suicide takes place in the visible space without the decisive instant of the suicide being seen by the spectators. The Greeks avoided representing the moment when blood was shed.

With audacity, but without transgressing the limits of decency, Sophocles represented a suicide "live," simultaneously heroic and pathetic, with a remarkable economy of means.

The Visible Tragic Place Is an Exterior Space

Let us leave these exceptional cases in which the central door of the stage building is masked and return to those in which the characters appear normally in the visible space, either by the door of the residence located at the back of the stage, or by the two lateral entrances.

The Greek theater is realistic in the sense that the space represented in the tragic fiction is of the same nature as the space of representation. Just as the stage building corresponds, in the theatrical fiction, to a residence, so the visible outdoor space in front of the stage building where the actors and the chorus are corresponds in the tragic fiction to the outdoor place in front of the residence, the two lateral entrances being opposite paths leading to this place. The tragic place is thus an exterior space that is in theory public, a meeting point for characters who may come from a nearby interior, the palace, or from the two opposed directions.

This topography is rather confusing for a modern spectator used to an interior tragic place. The notions of interior and exterior have been reversed. We can take as an example Racine's *Phèdre*, which is a reworking of Euripides' *Hippolytus*. In Racine, all the visible action takes place inside the palace, whereas in Euripides it takes place outside, in front of the palace. This inversion is particularly disturbing when a character in the Greek theater enters through the back of the stage. We are accustomed to say that a character enters the stage, whereas for Sophocles and his spectators, the character comes out of the palace. Thus at the beginning of *Oedipus the King*, we see Oedipus come out of his palace and address a group of children who have come there led by a priest. They are seated as suppliants on an altar located in front of the palace, holding suppliants' branches in their hands, because the city of Thebes is in the grip of a plague. The tragic place is thus definitely a public place.

The public nature of the tragic place is sometimes a constraint; but the authors knew how to cleverly integrate that constraint into their tragic fiction. The following scene from *Oedipus the King* is a good example of this. Creon, whom Oedipus had sent to Delphi to consult the oracle of Apollo regarding remedies for ridding his city of the plague, comes in through a lateral entrance representing one of the two roads leading to the palace. But before he reveals the oracle's response, Creon asks Oedipus, significantly, where he wants to hear it:

> *Creon:* If you want to hear in the presence of these people, I am ready to speak: otherwise we can go inside.
> *Oedipus:* Speak to all. The sorrow that I bear for these is more than for my own life.[210]

After these few words, it is clear that the characters are aware that they are outside. To "go inside" is to return to the palace, and consequently to leave the public space. Sophocles makes Creon envisage the possibility, which is a priori reasonable, of a secret report; but he makes Oedipus himself exclude it, by justifying it by noble reasons in the framework of the tragic fiction: Oedipus's life counts less than that of his subjects. In reality, Sophocles could not do otherwise, because no visible scene can take place inside the palace.[211] This is a fine example of a performance constraint that the author skillfully uses to characterize his character. Here he emphasizes the king's devotion to his people.

This constraint of an exterior tragic space may seem to us to become conventional when the characters are obliged to leave the palace to tell each other secrets. Thus in the first scene in *Antigone*, Antigone comes out of the royal palace of Thebes with her sister Ismene and asks her if she has heard an important bit of news, an edict issued by the head of state. Ismene replies that she has not. To which Antigone replies:

> I knew it well, so I was trying to bring you outside the courtyard gates to this end, that you alone might hear.[212]

Sophocles thought he should explain why the two sisters come out of the palace. They did so to escape indiscreet listeners! Thus Antigone has brought Ismene out into a public place so that she might be the only one to hear. The situation may seem paradoxical. A theatrical constraint is at the origin of this situation: since the scene has to take place outside, the author had to make his characters come outside so that the audience can listen to this secret conversation. But in the end the justification Sophocles gives is not completely implausible, if we consider that every Greek tragedy is supposed to begin at dawn. At that hour, the outside, being still deserted, is more suitable for a secret conversation than the inside of the palace, where it might be heard by servants who are already up and about.[213]

Virtual Spaces

In opposition to the visible space, by "virtual space" we mean the space that the spectators do not see, but have to imagine to understand the action.

In Greek theater, there are two virtual spaces, which differ in nature: a closed space, that of the residence that people enter and from which they emerge by the central door, and an open space that is also reached by the lateral paths. Since these two lateral paths lead in opposite directions, the open space is twofold and takes on different, or even opposed, meanings in the various tragedies.

Naturally, even when the tragedy does not include a residence at the back of the stage, the lateral entrances retain the same function, and the exterior virtual space that is reached is organized in the same way. Thus in *Oedipus at Colonus*, the lateral entrances represent the path that passes in front of the Eumenides' rural sanctuary and leads in opposite directions.

The Exterior Virtual Space

In the theater of Dionysus, the lateral passageways (sometimes called *parodos* or *eisodos* in the singular and *parodoi* or *eisodoi* in the plural) were oriented toward the west (the right-hand entrance with respect to the spectators) and toward the east (the left-hand entrance with respect to the spectators). Beyond each passageway a distinct virtual space extended. According to Pollux (second century BCE), these lateral entrances had a conventional meaning:

> So far as the lateral entrances are concerned, the one on the right led from the countryside, the port, or the city; all those who came from elsewhere by land passed through the other entrance.[214]

How far back did this codification establishing a distinction between the roads that came from within the city-state, whether from the city, the countryside, or the port, and those that came from abroad by land? It is hard to say. Pollux, while a valuable witness, describes the theater as if the performances had not changed between the fifth century BCE and his own time. Nevertheless, even if a codification of this kind is not valid for all periods and for all tragedies, it has the merit of drawing our attention to the fact that the entrances of the characters by the lateral paths were not accidental and that the tragic author organized the topography of his tragic fiction by basing it on the arrangement of the Athenian theater and making use of two virtual exterior spaces.

Sophocles' tragedy in which the codification given by Pollux is the most operative is *Oedipus at Colonus*, where the visible space represents part of the deme of Colonus not far from the city of Athens. From the right can come all the characters who arrive either from the Athenian countryside, namely from the deme of Colonus (the resident of Colonus, the chorus of officials from Colonus, Theseus, when he comes in the second time) or from the city of Athens (Theseus's first entrance). Through the left lateral entrance entered those who "came from elsewhere by land," to used Pollux's expression, namely, at the beginning, Oedipus and Antigone coming from abroad after a long exile whose point of departure was Thebes, then Ismene coming from Thebes, and finally Creon, also coming from Thebes. Thus there is a great coherence in the use of the lateral entrances, concerning which we might be tempted to say that one symbolizes the Athenian world and the other the Theban world. But there is never anything systematic in Sophocles' work. One entrance surprises us: Polynices, coming from abroad, enters from the right. To be sure, he is coming from Thebes, but he first went as a suppliant to a sanctuary in Colonus, the sanctuary of Poseidon, from which Theseus himself came in his second entrance. That is why Polynices comes, like Theseus, from the right. Then, driven away by his father, he leaves by the left exit. Thus he follows an itinerary opposite that of his father. Oedipus, coming from abroad through the left entrance, finds his last resting place in Colonus by going out on the right and will become Athens's protecting hero.

The Communication between the Exterior
Virtual Space and the Visible Space

The exterior virtual space reached by the lateral paths is sometimes close; but in general it is remote.

It is close when the communication can be made by voice. For example, when in *Oedipus at Colonus* Theseus comes running in through the right lateral entrance, he says that he interrupted the ceremony of the sacrifice of an ox on the altar of Poseidon, the protector of Colonus, when he heard the chorus's call for help.[215] Thus he is coming from a nearby virtual space that, while remaining invisible to the spectators, retains a possible connection with the visible space, that of the voice.

But most of the time, the virtual space that is reached or from which people come through the lateral entrances is a remote space that is not within earshot. Then all the phases of the tragic action that occur in this remote virtual space can be reported only through the intermediary of characters who have witnessed the action and have come to report it in the visible space.

The necessity of establishing communication between the remote virtual space and the visible space explains the existence in Greek tragedy of a certain category of characters, the messengers. To become aware of the astonishing presence of these anonymous characters, we need only read the list of dramatis personae given in the manuscripts at the head of each of Sophocles' tragedies and organized according to the moment when they appear onstage for the first time. The messenger (in Greek, *aggelos*) appears in the list of characters in six out of Sophocles' seven extant tragedies.[216] We must add that nonanonymous characters may also be messengers—that is the case for Lichas, Heracles's herald in *The Women of Trachis*—or play the role of a messenger—like Hyllos, Deianira's son, in *The Women of Trachis*. In the only tragedy in which there is no messenger as such, *Electra*, several characters play this role by reporting what happened in the virtual space of the eisodoi. In particular, the tutor, announcing Orestes' false death, uses the magic of words to provide a vivid account, extending over more than eighty verses, of the chariot race at the Olympic Games in which Orestes' chariot, having first escaped a general accident, crashed into a boundary stone just as he was about to win the victory. Thus if there is one tragedy by Sophocles that does not have a messenger, there is not a single one that does not have a messenger's report.

Recreating by means of all the resources of verbal art the action that occurred outside, the report of the messenger, faithful or fictive, becomes in tragedy a spectacle within a spectacle of which the audience was very fond. Of course, this is not peculiar to Sophocles' art. In the oldest tragedy we have, Aeschylus's *The Persians*, the messenger's report is a major element, the one that announces the disaster. Listening to the account of Xerxes' defeat at Salamis, we are astonished to note that its narrative technique has already achieved perfection.[217]

The Interior Virtual Space

In *The Persians*, as in Aeschylus's other oldest tragedies, the only virtual space known is the one reached through the lateral paths. The interior space of the residence at the back of the stage did not yet exist. The interior virtual space appeared only at the end of Aeschylus's career, after the *Oresteia*. It dates from the time when the stage building was created, or at least integrated into the tragic fiction.[218]

Between the frontal virtual space and the lateral virtual space, there are similarities and differences. The essential difference is that the actions carried out in the closed space of the private residence are of chiefly familial import. This is where families settle their scores. It is inside the palace that the Sophocles in *Electra*, following Aeschylus in the *Oresteia*, has Orestes wreak his vengeance, killing his mother to make her pay for the murder of his father.

On the other hand, the distinction between a nearby virtual space and a more distant virtual space is still valid.

Sometimes, the closed door of the palace lets a voice be heard, in both directions. A cry in the interior is heard outside. When Clytemnestra is murdered, in Sophocles, as in Aeschylus, those who remained in the street—the women of the chorus and of course also the spectators—perceive the cries or words of the victim. A private murder, to be sure, but one that overflows into the public space. In this case there is no need for a messenger. The messenger is the cry from the interior: "Someone shouts inside. Do you not hear, friends?"[219] Conversely, a character inside can hear voices from outside. In *Antigone*, here is how Eurydice, Creon's wife and the mother of Haemon, justifies coming out of the palace to address the old men in the chorus:

> People of Thebes, I heard your words as I was on my way to the gates to address divine Pallas with my prayers. At one and the same time I was loosening the bolts of the gate to open it, and the sound of a blow to our house struck my ear. In terror I sank back into the arms of my handmaids, and my senses fled. But repeat what your news was, for I shall hear it with ears that are no strangers to sorrow.[220]

Regarding the door of the stage building that in the tragic fiction is the door of the palace, the limit between the virtual interior space and the visible space, no other tragedy gives such a precise indication. It is a door with two panels that one opens when going out by pulling the panels toward the interior. If one is inside, near the door, sounds from outside can be heard. From the vestibule, Eurydice has heard the news of her son Haemon's death announced by the messenger. Going out, she is herself her own messenger relating what has happened to her inside. It is Eurydice, whom we did not know and about whom no one had spoken, who delivers three verses in which, with a physician's exactitude and concision, she describes the shock of the news, her collapse behind the door, and her fall into her attendants' arms. She has pulled herself together and now appears in the public space, asking courageously that she be told the news directly and pointing out that this is not the first misfortune she has suffered. These are the only words this wounded mother utters.

After the messenger has recounted her son's death, she turns on her heel and silently goes back into the palace. From that point on, the residence becomes a distant virtual space. It is the most secret place, hidden from the audience, the place where cries are no longer heard and where women, struck hard by misfortune, commit suicide. Thus three women go inside after having learned or understood their calamity: in addition to Eurydice in *Antigone*, Deianira in *The Women of Trachis* and Jocasta in *Oedipus the King*.[221] Communication with the visible space can henceforth take place only with the help of a messenger coming from the interior. In fact, on all three occasions a messenger comes out of the palace to report the women's deaths: a nurse in *The Women of Trachis* and a second messenger in both *Antigone* and *Oedipus the King*.[222]

The Topography of the Interior Virtual Space: The Microcosm of the Palace

All these reports delivered by messengers recounting family crises allow us to enter the interior world of the palace.

The messenger's brief account of Eurydice's death tells us only one thing: she killed herself near the family altar. The altar is also present in the account of Deianira's suicide. Like Eurydice, she had taken refuge there to grieve.[223]

Nevertheless, in the case of Deianira, the messenger's report, which is much fuller, reveals other details regarding this world of the interior. Following with the nurse's eyes Deianira's movements, the modern reader understands what was obvious to the ancients: the palace's double entry door, with its vestibule, opens first onto a courtyard around which the residence's rooms are arranged; thus everyone who comes from the exterior and enters the various parts of the palace has to pass through this space. In fact, a few moments after Deianira silently reenters the palace through this door, her son Hyllos, who has nonetheless disavowed her, also goes inside through it. Thus Deianira is able to see her son one last time in the courtyard as he is preparing a litter to leave again to meet his dying father. But the heart of the palace is Heracles' room, where she finally goes after having lingered at the altar and walked throughout the palace, meeting a servant here and there.

It is also in the nuptial chamber that Jocasta commits suicide. But unlike Deianira, she goes there directly after crossing the palace threshold. This nuptial chamber re-creates an invisible space within the interior world, a hidden space where the act of suicide is concealed from the eyes of the spectators sitting on the tiers. Jocasta closes the door of the bedroom behind her. This interior door ultimately has a function analogous to that of the door of the vestibule: it allows cries or words to be heard but prevents the act of suicide itself from being seen. Nonetheless, we penetrate privacy still more deeply. Whereas the door of the vestibule masked the familial murders, even though the spectators heard the victim's words, the door of the bedchamber allows sounds to be heard only by those inside and masks the suicide. Thus as we move further into the world of the interior, we also move from the tragedy of the family to the tragedy of the individual.

The topography of the enclosed virtual space behind the door at the back of the stage is thus more complex than it seems.

From the Open Space to the Enclosed Space

As a rule, the enclosed and private virtual space of the palace is opposed to the open and public virtual space of the lateral entrances. The scenes reported in the messengers' accounts that come from the interior contrast, in fact, with those of messengers coming from outside. What a contrast between, on the one hand, the account of Orestes' death in his chariot accident in front of the audience of all the Greeks at the Pan-Hellenic games in Delphi, and, on the other hand, the account of Deianira's death in her nuptial chamber, hidden from everyone's sight!

However, Sophocles' art was also able to create, in the exterior virtual space, a scene that resembles those of the enclosed world of the interior. In *Antigone*, a messenger, even though he comes from outside, reports tragic facts that have occurred in the enclosed space par excellence, the stone prison where Antigone has been incarcerated by the king to punish her revolt. The same Greek word, *thalamos*, is used to designate the nuptial chamber where Deianira kills herself and this stone chamber where Antigone commits suicide.[224] In both scenes, those who hasten to help arrive too late, when the act has already taken place. And the one who loves—in one case the son, in the other the fiancé[225]—can only throw himself on the dead woman. But the enclosed world of the underground chamber lacks the complex topography of a partitioned palace. In this palace of Hades with a single room in which everything is gathered together, the family confrontation reaches an unparalleled acuteness in the presence of servants: Haemon, the furious son, draws his sword against his father before Antigone's corpse, then turns it against himself and embraces the body of his beloved before breathing his last breath.[226] Through the messenger's words, the spectator's imagination experiences this family tragedy live, in an enclosed space far from the palace.

From the Enclosed Space to the Open Space

On the other hand, Sophocles does not hesitate to gradually lend scope to the account of scenes inside the palace that must eventuate in a public appearance. In *Oedipus the King*, the report given by the messenger who has come out of the palace to announce Jocasta's suicide and Oedipus's self-mutilation gradually moves from the enclosed world to the open world. While Jocasta's suicide takes place behind the closed door of the bedchamber, without anyone having been able to see or intervene, from the moment that Oedipus rushes forward to open this double door, all this becomes a spectacle for Oedipus and for the servants, of whom the messenger is the spokesman. The spectacle of Jocasta's hanged body, but also of Oedipus, who takes down the corpse and puts out his eyes with the golden pins taken from his wife and mother's clothing. And just as the spectator's imagination witnessed the sword penetrating Haemon's side and the spurt of blood, it witnesses Oedipus's repeated blows to his eyeballs and the flow of blood. The spectacle becomes even greater than in Haemon's case, where everything happens in a short time and ends in the silence of death in the underground grotto that has become Hades' realm. Here everything is amplified, first by the relentless blows struck, the prolonged description of the bloodshed, which is compared to a dark hail, and above all the cries and words of Oedipus who, from the moment when he no longer sees anything, tries to transform himself into a spectacle before the eyes of all the inhabitants of Thebes:

> He cries for someone to unbar the gates and show to all the Cadmeans his father's slayer, his mother's—the words must not pass my lips.[227]

The scene inside reported by the messenger will thus naturally flow into the visible space, which is the public space. In fact, immediately after mentioning Oedipus's desire to show himself in public, the messenger announces that the door of the palace is opening and that the spectacle will soon be seen. There follows one of the most impressive scenes in Sophocles' theater: through the spectacle of Oedipus's bloody face, the dramatist seeks expressly to inspire pity, but also terror, in the spectators.[228] The palace door opens like a ripe fruit after the spectator's imagination has made a round trip into the world of the interior: having taken as its point of departure the palace door that closes after Jocasta silently goes inside, and moving to the second door, that of the nuptial chamber, which opens and then closes again when Oedipus arrives in a storm, the imagination guided by the messenger's account has come back to the door of the palace, which opens and gives way to vision. The boundary between interior space and visible space is blurred by the magic of Sophocles' verbal art.

How Can an Interior Scene Be Represented Outside? The Machine Known as an *Eccyclema*

This passage from the interior space to the visible space does not always take place in such a subtle way. To transform the interior space into a visible space, tragic authors resorted to the ancient theatrical machine that is the strangest for a modern mind, the one called an eccyclema.[229] This low platform on wheels, which was slightly narrower than the door, and that was pushed open from the inside into the visible space, had as its purpose to show outside what was supposed to occur inside. The comic dramatists did not fail to mock such a rudimentary device. On two occasions, Aristophanes uses this theatrical machine to present the tragic authors he is ridiculing, thus deliberately breaking the theatrical illusion for comic purposes.[230] However, even the greatest tragic authors resorted to this device. In 458, in the *Oresteia*, in which the stage building was first used dramaturgically, Aeschylus also used the eccyclema three times.[231] Sophocles used it in the oldest tragedy by him that we have, *Ajax*. The proof of the use of the eccyclema comes from the fact that the door of the residence opens to reveal a spectacle, without any character having moved from the inside to the outside.

In this respect, Ajax's first two appearances are clearly opposed. When Ajax, in the grip of madness, emerges from his house the first time, at the call of Athena, he bursts out, addresses Athena, and then leaps back into his house.[232] The stage directions regarding how he comes out and goes back in are not given at the time of the scene, but a little later when Tecmessa, playing the role of a messenger from the interior, describes in the course of her account this exit of Ajax that the spectators saw from the outside.[233] This is probably the only time in Greek theater when the same scene is seen from the outside by the spectators and then described by a character who has seen it from the inside. The reader gains from this, because the regressive stage directions allow him or her to imagine what the fifth-century spectators saw during Ajax's first appearance: a mad Ajax, bursting out of his house, which he leaves open, shaken by an enormous laughter, and after his dialogue with Athena, leaping back inside and closing the door. During this first appearance of Ajax there is, of course, no need to use the eccyclema. But once Ajax has recovered his wits and become aware of his act of madness, as we learn in the rest of Tecmessa's account, he remains prostrated in his house, sitting amid the livestock he has massacred. From the outside, his laments are heard, and then reasonable words, without seeing him. Then the chorus asks that the door be opened. Tecmessa herself obeys the order:

> There, it is open. Now you can look on this man's deeds, and his true condition.[234]

This is the paradigm example of a situation where the use of the eccyclema is necessary, as the ancient commentators already noted.[235] It is clear that the door opens to let the chorus see the spectacle inside the house, without anything having in principle changed. Ajax is still in the same state of prostration. But simply opening the door does not suffice for the spectacle to be seen by the spectators on all the tiers of the theater. It is necessary that, by a displacement from the space where Ajax is to the inside of the house, he appear to all the spectators seated amid the animals he has massacred. It is the low platform heeled outside the open door that makes it possible to carry out that displacement. The eccyclema thus allows the spectacle to be viewed first in the form of a tableau, an eminently moving tableau in which we see the hero seated on the floor, covered with blood, amid the slaughtered and bloody animals, witnessing his disastrous error.[236] This displacement to the outside is all the more necessary because Ajax, on seeing the chorus of his companions for the first time after his fit of madness, is so moved that he begins to sing. How can we imagine that a character can sing while sitting on the floor inside the stage building, even if the door is open? The strange convention that allows the interior space—which is in principle enclosed and private—to be presented outside, in a visible space—which is in principle open and public—finds its sole justification in the necessities of performance.

The superimposition of spaces becomes so strange that the reader of a Greek tragedy has a tendency to forget it. In the lyric dialogue between Ajax, the chorus, and Tecmessa, we forget that each of the characters is in his or her own space, the chorus in the orchestra, Tecmessa onstage in front of the palace—if we agree that the actors played on a slightly elevated stage—and Ajax is on his low platform in front of the palace door. Even if we know that the eccyclema was used, we hardly wonder about the second time that the eccyclema is moved, when it is brought back inside.[237] However, the spectator who had seen the platform rolled outside also saw it later pulled back inside. And the actor could not ignore this second movement.

So at what point was the machine that had been rolled out to show Ajax pulled back inside? In other words, how long did Ajax remain on his platform? To gain a precise idea of this moment in the tragedy, it may be useful to glance at Aristophanes' comedy *The Acharnians*, which was performed in 425. In it, Aristophanes mocks for the first time the tragic dramatists' use of the eccyclema. By using it, he makes Euripides appear. He emphasizes the device with such clarity that one wonders neither about the means used nor the time when the machine is employed. Euripides, lying down at home on his bed, where he is writing with his feet in the air, is too busy to be able to go out and says that he is going to "have himself rolled outside."[238] Then we see him lying down, just as Ajax is prostrated here, and he is surrounded by his characters' rags just as Ajax is surrounded by his massacred animals. As for the moment when the machine is brought back inside in the comedy, it is when Euripides, annoyed by the importunate Diceopolis, asks his servant to close the door:

> Insolent hound! Slave, lock the door![239]

The point when the eccyclema is returned to its initial position corresponds to the point when the character orders the door closed. In the tragedy, in a completely analogous way, Ajax orders Tecmessa to close the door:

> Come, take the child right away, shut tight the doors and make no laments before the house. God, what a weepy thing is woman. Quick, close the house! It is not for a skillful doctor to moan incantations over a wound that craves the knife.[240]

Thus Ajax's order to Tecmessa to shut the door is the signal in the text indicating that the eccyclema is going to be brought back in. We have to know how to translate the character's words into dramaturgical terms. After a brief and lively exchange between Ajax and Tecmessa, the platform on which he is lying is rolled inside. Tecmessa, who was outside, comes back in the door and closes it from the inside. The stage is now empty, but the chorus is singing and dancing in the orchestra.

The determination of the precise moments when the eccyclema is rolled outside, and then back inside, has as its consequence that Ajax remains all during his second appearance that is, for more than two hundred verses,[241] lying on the eccyclema, whose surface is relatively small, still surrounded by slaughtered animals. This whole scene is thus static. It is from this central position, in front of the open door, that Ajax delivers two famous speeches, one on his misfortunes, the other addressed to his child, whom he his holding in his arms. The only change—but it is an important one—is that the hero, appearing seated amid the animals, is necessarily standing when he asks Tecmessa to "lift" the child up to him. This is the principal interest of this stage direction.[242] At what point did the prostrate hero stand up? The text does not say. It is very probably at the time when he moves from speaking to singing.[243] Having mastered his emotion, in his first long speech he is now going to make an organized list of his misfortunes. A change in the mode of expression, a change in posture, such are the audible or visible signs of the beginning of the hero's rebirth.

The Eccyclema and the Exposition of Corpses

The eccyclema made it possible to show a static tableau of what was inside the house, but the tragic dramatists also used it to show, after a murder or a suicide perpetrated in the palace, the visible proof of acts that decency did not allow them to show the spectators. The eccyclema was thus the platform where corpses were displayed.

The end of Sophocles' *Electra* is an example of this. After Clytemnestra has been murdered in the palace, Aegisthus returns from the city's suburbs, joyous, and asks that the palace door be opened so that all the Cadmeans can see what he believes to be Orestes' corpse.[244] The reference to the door that has to be opened to show everyone a spectacle inside the palace is the sign that the eccyclema will be used. Then there appears, on the eccyclema, a body accompanied by two characters, Orestes and Pylades. This way of presenting dramatic events was not in itself an innovation. In *The Libation Bearers*, Aeschylus had already dealt with the same mythical sequence that Sophocles chose for his *Electra*, the bodies of the victims appearing at the same time as the murderer, with the help of the eccyclema.[245] But in Sophocles the body is not just a moving spectacle that proves the act committed in the interior virtual space; it is also a way of producing a new turn in the action in the visible space by unveiling the corpse that Aegisthus recognizes as that of Clytemnestra and not Orestes. As for the moment when the eccyclema is rolled back inside and the door closed behind it, that occurs at the end of the scene that concludes the tragedy. Orestes orders Aegisthus to go into the palace. He has to go in first, and the eccyclema, still carrying Orestes, Pylades, and the body of Clytemnestra, is rolled inside; then the palace door is closed. It is in the shadowy interior of the palace, outside the time of the tragedy, that Orestes completes his vengeance by committing a second murder. With the palace door closed, the chorus remains alone in the orchestra: it concludes the tragedy with three verses before filing silently out, led by the flute player. This tragedy offers an exceptional conclusion because it ends in the middle of an action, during a tense dialogue between two characters. It closes with the prospect of a murder that is about to take place and whose victim's body will never be seen.

Ordinarily, all the deaths reported take place in the time of the tragedy, and the presence of the corpses in the final scene is the visible testimony to misfortunes and mistakes. Thus the end of *Antigone*, which focuses on Creon's tragedy, accumulates the successive reports of two deaths in his family, those of his son Haemon and his wife, Eurydice, two suicides that follow that of Antigone herself. The corpses converge toward the visible space, coming first from the exterior virtual space, and then from the interior virtual space. Through one of the lateral entrances, Creon appears carrying his son's body, over which he weeps.[246] He has hardly returned when he learns of his wife's death, and even before he is informed of the circumstances of her suicide, the body appears, coming this time from inside the palace:

> *Chorus:* The sight is at hand. It is no longer hidden inside.
> *Creon:* Ah, misery! There I see a new, a second evil! What destiny, ah, what,
>   can still await me? I have just now taken my son in my arms, and now I see
>   another corpse before me! Oh, tormented mother! Oh, my son![247]

Eurydice's body is certainly visible to the spectators at the point when the messenger refers to its presence. Was it brought out by means of the eccyclema, as is generally thought? It is true that the use of the eccyclema is mentioned by an ancient commentator.[248] However, unlike the other two passages in which Sophocles definitely used the eccyclema, there is no indication here regarding the opening of the door. Moreover, the body has been moved, because the messenger says that it is no longer hidden inside the palace.[249] Thus it has been brought outside by servants.[250] Is the visible body supposed to be in the palace or outside it? Nothing is completely sure, because even when the use of the eccyclema is proven, it can happen that the spectator is no longer certain whether what is made visible through the convention of the eccyclema is in the palace or outside it.

The Eccyclema and the Confusion of Spaces

In this regard, we can contrast the ends of the two scenes in which we have seen that the eccyclema was definitely used, in *Ajax* and in *Electra*. From a technical point of view, these two scenes resemble one another. Through dialogue, Sophocles links two characters who in theory belong to two distinct spaces: one brought in by the eccyclema, belongs to the interior space, while the other is located outside. Tecmessa, who has come out of the house, is addressed by Ajax from the eccyclema, just as Aegisthus, who has not gone inside, is addressed by Orestes from the eccyclema. But the two scenes differ in the degree of differentiation between the two spaces. In *Ajax*, Sophocles faithfully follows the conventional code: Ajax, from the inside of his house, reproaches Tecmessa for weeping outside the house;[251] and when he asks her to close the door, she goes in after the eccyclema has been rolled inside, and she closes the door from the inside. On the other hand, in *Electra*, the bitter dialogue between Orestes and Aegisthus ignores the conventional distinction between the two spaces:

> *Orestes* (to Aegisthus): Go in, and quickly. Words are not at stake here, but your life.
> *Aegisthus:* Why take me into the house? If this deed is just, what need is there of darkness? Why is your hand not quick to strike?
> *Orestes:* Do not give orders, but go to where you struck down my father, so that in that very place you may die.[252]

Although Orestes is on the eccyclema, that is, conventionally, inside the palace, Aegisthus seems to speak to him as if he were outside, since he is astonished that Orestes is not prepared to kill him where he is, outdoors. It is true that Sophocles' concern in this passage is to justify a more essential convention. A murder cannot take place in broad daylight in front of the spectators but must be committed in the shadows of the palace. At the end of the dialogue, the confusion of the two spaces is even greater. When Orestes cuts the conversation short and repeats his order to move forward, Aegisthus replies: "You lead," to which Orestes answers, "You must go first." This politely sinister exchange is in conflict with the convention of the eccyclema: how can Orestes precede Aegisthus in entering, since he is supposed to be inside the palace? However, the development of the spectacle is possible despite this twist given the convention. Aegisthus walks through the open door of the palace before the eccyclema bearing Orestes, Pylades, and Clytemnestra's body is rolled inside and the door is closed.

The Elevated Apparitions: The *Mechane* and the *Theologeion*

In addition to the eccyclema, the tragic dramatists had another theatrical machine that gave the visible space a supplementary dimension, that of height. The elevated space is the domain of the gods. In reality, they could appear in two ways, either by means of the theatrical machine par excellence, which is called in Greek a mechane (literally, "machine"), or by means of a raised stage called a theologeion ("the place where the gods speak"), as distinguished from the *logeion skēnē* where humans speak. These two resources are mentioned by Pollux (second century CE) in his discussion of the theatrical vocabulary:

> The *mechane* shows the gods and also the heroes in the air, like Bellerophon or Perseus. It is found near the left side entrance, and is higher than the *skēnē*.[253]

The mechane is a sort of crane whose erect mast made it possible to show actors floating in the air, hooked to cables by a harness, so that they could play gods or winged heroes. This crane, operated by a machinist, is well known because of Aristophanes' parodic use of it. In his comedy entitled *Peace*, he has his hero Trygaeus lifted, astride a dung beetle, from the earth to the sky with the help of the mechane, the same machine that had lifted Bellerophon riding his winged horse Pegasus in the tragedy by Euripides that Aristophanes is parodying. Though it did not transform actors into stuntmen, this device was not without risk: the tragic actor thus raised into the air had to trust his life to the machinist and say in petto what the comic hero could say out loud:

> Alas! how frightened I am! oh! I have no heart for jests. Ah! machinist, take great care of me.[254]

The second way of showing the gods above the stage is the theologeion. Here is what Pollux says about it:

> From the *theologeion*, which is higher than the stage, the gods appear, like Zeus and those who were with him in the weighing of souls.[255]

In Pollux's view, this elevated place was not to be confused with the roof terrace of the stage building, where Antigone climbed, accompanied by the tutor, in Euripides' *The Phoenician Women*, to contemplate the army that was besieging Thebes, because he calls that by a different name (*distegia*).[256] Modern scholars think that there were in fact two different names for the same secondary stage, formed by the roof terrace of the stage building, where men or gods could appear depending on the needs of the fiction. This secondary stage was reached by a ladder.

Theoretically, the gods could thus appear in two ways, either on the roof terrace of the stage building, or suspended in the air by the mechane. In Sophocles' extant theater two divinities appear, Athena at the beginning of *Ajax* and Heracles at the end of *Philoctetes*. How do they appear? On the theologeion or with the help of the mechane?

The Apparition of Athena at the Beginning of Ajax

The apparition of a divinity to begin a tragedy is not exceptional in the Greek theater of the fifth century. In Euripides, a divinity may appear to deliver an expository monologue: for example, Cypris, the goddess of love, in his *Hippolytus*. More rarely, two divinities speak to each other in an initial scene: for instance, Poseidon and Athena in *The Trojan Women*. It is generally thought that the divinities appeared on the secondary stage, the theologeion. In any case, they are at a distance from humans, and they do not enter into communication with them in Euripides.[257] In Sophocles, on the other hand, in the single case where a divinity is present at the beginning of a tragedy, she addresses humans. At the beginning of *Ajax*, Athena speaks first to Odysseus alone, and then to Ajax; then again to Odysseus after Ajax departs.

What spectators saw at the beginning of the tragedy was a tableau: in front of Ajax's house, Odysseus, silent and seeming very absorbed, has his head down, following footprints as if he were a hunter tracking prey. Then Athena, his tutelary goddess, who has appeared above him some time earlier, speaks to him:

> *Athena:* Always, son of Laertes, have I observed you on the prowl to snatch some means of attack against your enemies. So now at the tent of Ajax by the ships where he has his post at the camp's outer edge, I watch you for a long time as you hunt and scan his newly pressed tracks, in order to see whether he is inside or away. . . .
>
> *Odysseus:* Voice of Athena, dearest to me of the gods, how clearly, though you are unseen, do I hear your call and snatch its meaning in my mind, just as I would the bronze tongue of the Tyrrhenian trumpet![258]

The opening of this tragedy offers very precise clues for reconstituting part of the spectacle: humans' acts and their relations with the divinities. But regarding the question of where the divinity appears, the text is silent. This gap results in part from the fact that the human hears the goddess but does not see her. Sophocles, through the medium of his dialogue, could not have the man describe the goddess, as he has the goddess describe the man. The only precise indication regarding Athena Odysseus gives concerns the timbre of her voice, which is so recognizable by its sonority, and which is compared to a bronze trumpet. This is, moreover, a director's instruction regarding the way the actor playing the divinity should deliver his text. In any case, on the basis of what Athena herself says, we know that some time earlier she "came on the path as a lookout friendly to your hunt."[259] In the initial tableau, she observes, as an immobile spectator, the man's worried search. This static presence seems at first to justify the generally accepted modern view that she appears on a theologeion.

However, Athena, at first a spectator, becomes an actor when she organizes the spectacle by making Ajax come out completely mad. The apparition of the bloodied hero, leaping out with a whip in his hand, occasionally shaken by raucous laughter, a wild animal exhibited by Athena, who plays at taming it in front of an Odysseus reduced to the role of a helpless, dumbfounded spectator, is a spectacle of rare power. To understand the whole presentation of this scene, we have to take into account the subtle play of sight and hearing. The all-powerful goddess sees and hears everything.[260] As we have said, the sane man, Odysseus, hears the goddess but does not see her. On the other hand, when the madman comes out, Odysseus sees and hears him. And the madman—what does he see and hear? He hears the goddess, because he has emerged from his house at her summons. He does not see Odysseus, because Athena has promised Odysseus that she will ensure that he is not seen by Ajax. But does Ajax see the goddess? The answer to this question is probably to be found in his first words when he bursts out of his house at Athena's second call:

> Welcome, Athena! Welcome, daughter sprung from Zeus! How well have you stood by me! I will crown you with trophies of pure gold in gratitude for this quarry![261]

These first words Ajax addresses to the goddess contrast with those of Odysseus. Whereas Odysseus greets the goddess's voice ("Voice of Athena, dearest to me of the gods"), Ajax greets the goddess ("Welcome, Athena!"). And whereas Odysseus expressly acknowledges that he does not see the goddess, Ajax spontaneously addresses her without there being any distance between them. Thus Ajax hears the goddess and sees her. The madman, whose mind has been led astray by the goddess, does not see what he should see and sees what he should not see. He does not see the man, but he sees the goddess, who shows herself to him in full daylight the better to deceive him.

If Athena is made to appear on the roof terrace of the house, how could Ajax, bursting out of the door, perceive the goddess and greet her as rapidly as he does? Was the spectacle conventional to that point? Under these conditions, would the choice of the mechane be preferable? If the goddess appeared suspended above the stage in front of the house, Ajax could see her immediately when he comes out.

The Apparition of Heracles at the End of Philoctetes

The apparition of a divinity to put an end to a tragedy is facile procedure whose use was denounced by both the comic poets and the philosophers of the fourth century BCE.[262] Sophocles seems to have made use of it less often than Euripides did. In any case, in the extant tragedies the procedure is attested ten times in Euripides and only once in Sophocles.[263]

It is in his *Philoctetes* that Sophocles has a divinity appear to resolve a tragedy insoluble on the human level. Philoctetes has remained inflexible despite the whole range of means of pressure and persuasion used by the Achaians' emissaries, Odysseus and Neoptolemus, to convince him to go to Troy with his bow. In the tragic fiction, the mission succeeds, even though in a way opposite to the myth, because Neoptolemus finally agrees to take Philoctetes back to his homeland, whereas his mission was to take him to Troy. However, Heracles appears at the last minute to bring the tragedy back into agreement with the myth.[264] Although a god's intervention may seem artificial, the choice of the divinity is not, because Philoctetes is the heir of Heracles, who left him his bow. Philoctetes is about to leave when Heracles intervenes:

> *Heracles:* Not yet, not until you have heard my commands, son of Poeas. Know that your ears perceive the voice of Heracles, and that you look upon his face. For your sake I have left my divine seat and come to reveal to you the purposes of Zeus, and to halt the journey on which you are departing. Hearken to my words.[265]

The apparition of the two divinities in *Ajax* and *Philoctetes* is comparable. After listening to the divinity's words, the man begins with an analogous exclamation regarding the familiar or desired voice of the divinity, reflecting the bond of close intimacy that exists between the divinity and the man.[266] However, we note an essential difference, from the point of view of internal communication, that is, of the spectacle as it is seen by the characters themselves within the tragic fiction: whereas Athena was heard but not seen by Odysseus, Heracles is heard and seen by Philoctetes. Sophocles takes care to explain this very clearly in his characters' words.[267] This is an example of the subtlety with which Sophocles introduces variants into entirely comparable scenes. The fact that Odysseus hears Athena without seeing her in no way diminishes his relationship with the divinity. In Euripides' tragedy *Hippolytus* the eponymous hero, while asserting that he is the only man who has the privilege of living at Artemis's side, also recognizes that he does not see her, whereas he hears her voice.[268] However, the presence of Heracles, as soon as he is seen and heard, is all the more persuasive. This difference changes nothing, of course, in the spectacle seen by the spectators, because for them Athena is as visible as Heracles is.

Regarding Athena's itinerary before she appears, the text of *Philoctetes* is a little more explicit than the text of *Ajax* is about Heracles' itinerary. Heracles says that he has left his celestial abode, that is, Olympus, in order to descend to the world of men. How does he appear? On the mechane or on the theologeion?

It has been asked, in a general way, whether the use of the mechane and the theologeion did not correspond to apparitions that differed in nature, the mechane allowing moving apparitions, whereas the theologeion was reserved for more static apparitions. The examples Pollux chooses to illustrate the use of the mechane and the theologeion may tend in this direction. The heroes Bellerophon and Perseus, cited in connection with the mechane, move through the air thanks to their wings, one having a winged horse and the other winged sandals. On the other hand, the scene from Aeschylus's lost tragedy *The Weighing of Souls*, which took place on the theologeion, is a static scene, since the souls have to be weighed on a scale. Thus when the journey through the sky is expressly described, as it is for example at the end of Euripides' *Andromache*, when the chorus announces the arrival of the divinity crossing the luminous ether before she lands on the soil of Phthia,[269] the use of the mechane is considered certain. On the other hand, in the absence of precise indications regarding the divinity's movements, as is the case here, we think rather of the use of the theologeion.

But isn't the absence of precise indications a sign that the modalities of a divinity's apparition did not need to be specified, so traditional were they?[270] The abundance of testimonies to the mechane in the fourth century BCE and the absence of any reference to the theologeion at that period show that in the tragic performances of the fourth century the gods regularly appeared at the end of tragedies with the help of the mechane.[271] Why would the same not be true already in the fifth century?[272]

CHAPTER VIII

Time and Action

....

The Action Is the Drawing of a Tragedy;
the Characters Are Its Color

The way Aristotle orients his discussion of Greek tragedy in his *Poetics* is probably
not the way the tragic poets of the fifth century would have chosen. He mini-
mizes the role of the spectacle, whose importance in Sophocles' theater we have
just seen.[1] On the other hand, he grants primordial importance to the action.
Thus his definition of tragedy, despite its technical nature, deserves to be quoted
to begin this chapter:

> Tragedy is, then, a representation of an action that is heroic and complete and
> of a certain magnitude—by means of language enriched with all kinds of orna-
> ment, each used separately in the different parts of the play: it represents men
> in action and does not use narrative, and through pity and fear it effects relief
> to these and similar emotions. By "language enriched" I mean that which has
> rhythm and tune, i.e., song, and by "the kinds separately" I mean that some
> effects are produced by verse alone and some again by song.[2]

From this definition, which is famous above all for the tragic passions of pity
and terror and for their "purgation," we will focus here only on what concerns
the action.

Tragedy is the imitation, by means of art, of an elevated action, represented
by characters and not by means of a narrative. This definition distinguishes
tragedy from both epic and comedy. Like epic, tragedy is the imitation of a noble
action; in this respect, it is opposed to comedy, which imitates a vulgar action.
On the other hand, in its means of imitation, tragedy is opposed to epic and
closer to comedy. Whereas epic operates through the *aoidos* or singer, tragedy
operates, like comedy, through the intermediary of characters on a stage.

Aristotle's definition lists six constitutive parts of tragedy,[3] of which the most
important is "the arrangement of the incidents," to which Aristotle gives the
name of *mythos* (plot or action).[4] In Aristotle, mythos thus has nothing to do
with the degree to which the mythic subject matter is fictional but instead is
defined by the organization of the action, the use made of the mythic sequence
the author chooses as his subject. Later on in his discussion, Aristotle constantly

insists on this preeminence: "The incidents and the plot are the end at which tragedy aims, and in everything the end aimed at is of prime importance."[5]

This element of tragedy is even more important than the characters: "The plot then is the first principle and as it were the soul of tragedy: character comes second."[6] And to clarify his idea, Aristotle compares tragedy with painting: "If a man smeared a canvas with the loveliest colors at random, it would not give as much pleasure as an outline in black and white."[7] In a tragedy, the plot is comparable to a drawing and the characters to color. In his drawing, the tragic poet thus imitates "a noble action" drawn from the mythic subject matter and enhances it by depicting characters. This drawing has "a certain magnitude," forming a whole like a painting. But unlike a painting, the magnitude of the action is not static. The plot that the tragic poet organizes within the selected mythic sequence unfolds over a period of time. There is therefore a temporality peculiar to tragedy.

The Temporality of Tragedy: The Time of Representation or External Time

The temporality of tragedy can be understood in two different ways. Just as there is the space of representation and the space represented in the tragic fiction, there is the time of representation, or external time, and the time represented, or the internal time.

Aristotle considers that "the limit of length considered in relation to competitions and production before an audience does not concern this treatise. Had it been the rule to produce a hundred tragedies, the performance would have been regulated by the water clock, as it is said they did once in other days."[8]

The clepsydra or water clock made it possible to measure the relative time very precisely. It was regularly used in trials to measure the maximum time reserved for each of the parties involved. Was it also used at a certain period to measure the exact time reserved for each of the participants in the tragedies contest? That is what Aristotle suggests in this passage, referring to a source whose origin he does not specify.

In any case, the concern to respect the equality of the three selected candidates must have required a maximum length for the total time allotted to each of them during the performance of their tetralogy composed of three tragedies and a satyr play. It is impossible to evaluate precisely the total duration of such a performance, for the very good reason that not a single tetralogy is extant. But it was on the order of eight to ten hours. A tragic poet contemporary with Euripides, Aristarchus of Tegea, is thought to have been the first to set a limit to the length of the plays,[9] though we do not know exactly what that means. Does it refer to the length of each play or to that of the set of four?

Although the conditions of the contest required that each contestant be allotted the same overall amount of time, the amount allotted to each of the four plays was probably left to the discretion of each author. In fact, an examination of the length of each of Sophocles' seven extant tragedies shows a genuine inequality. Between the shortest play, *Women of Trachis*, and the longest, *Oedipus at Colonus*, there is a difference of five hundred verses, which is rather considerable, the average length of the seven tragedies being a little less than fifteen hundred verses.[10] That the author could vary the length of the tragedies within a single trilogy is clearly shown by the only intact trilogy we have, Aeschylus's *Oresteia*: between the first and longest tragedy in the trilogy, *Agamemnon*, and the third and shortest, *The Eumenides*, the difference is more than six hundred verses; that is, the difference is greater than the one separating Sophocles' shortest tragedy from his longest tragedy.[11]

Moreover, among the extant works of Aeschylus, Sophocles, and Euripides there are no two tragedies that have exactly the same length. Thus there is no period of time peculiar to the performance of a tragedy taken separately. As a general rule, the satyr play must have been much shorter than a tragedy. The only satyr play that has been preserved in its entirety, Euripides' *Cyclops*, consists of only a little more than seven hundred verses, or half the average duration of one of Sophocles' tragedies.[12] But even here there is no set length, because we know that Euripides' play *Alcestis*, which in performance certainly occupied the place reserved for a satyr play, is much shorter than *Cyclops*.[13]

Thus the three competitors in the tragedy contest at the Great Dionysia in the fifth century must have been subject to a limit on the total time of the performance, but they preserved a certain freedom to determine how much time was given to each of the four plays.[14]

Finally, we can ask whether the amount of time accorded to each candidate did not vary in the course of the fifth century. Aeschylus's tragedies are, on the whole, shorter than those of Sophocles and Euripides. Six out of seven of Aeschylus's tragedies are no longer than eleven hundred verses, whereas none of Sophocles' tragedies is shorter, and only one of Euripides' tragedies is.[15] It seems that toward the end of the fifth century, authors tended to write longer tragedies. However, it remains that the only two tragedies in the extant Greek theater that exceed seventeen hundred verses, Euripides' *The Phoenician Women* and Sophocles' *Oedipus at Colonus*, date from the last decade of the fifth century.[16] *Oedipus at Colonus*, which is the longest of the thirty extant tragedies from the fifth century, is also the last tragedy composed. That may not be entirely fortuitous.

The external time was therefore a matter of concern for the tragic poet, who had to arrange the relative length of each of his plays so as not to exceed an overall time limit. This constraint was in addition to the one that obliged the author to arrange, in the course of each play, the periods of time necessary for the actors to change their costumes and masks inside the stage building.[17] These are constraints relative to time that were peculiar to Greek tragedy. They cannot be ignored if we want to gauge the complex and meticulous requirements of the art of writing a tragedy in antiquity. In this sense, these constraints, although imposed from outside by the requirements of the contest or the material conditions of performance, are not external to art.

It has even been asked whether the tragic poets did not calculate in a much subtler way the proportional distribution of the architecture of their tragedies by respecting mathematical proportions between the number of verses accorded to each part, which would correspond to subtle proportions in the equilibrium of the real duration of the performance.[18] But even if we suppose that such proportions were sought—apart, of course, from strophic correspondences—they could hardly be perceived by spectators or even by the judges, and hence could not have had a major influence on the result of the contest.

The Temporality of Tragedy: The Time of the Tragic Fiction or Internal Time

By saying, in his definition of tragedy, that the action is "complete and of a certain extent," Aristotle translated into spatial terms an action that in fact unfolds in time.

These two terms qualifying the tragic action were not chosen accidentally. They correspond to the two necessary conditions for beauty, according to Aristotle: order and extent.[19] A "complete" action corresponds to what we call "unity of action." The mythic sequence chosen must be unified, and include a beginning, a middle, and an end; and the events of the action have to succeed in an orderly way such that all the parts, united by the plausible or the necessary, cohere. On the other hand, the "extent" of the action does not refer solely to what we call the unity of time in the classic sense of the term, that is, the unfolding of the action within the limits of a single day. According to Aristotle, the limit of the extent of the action is measured by the spectator's ability to remember. In this context, the action must include the succession of events that cause the hero to pass from unhappiness to happiness or from happiness to unhappiness.[20]

Nonetheless, Aristotle was well aware that unlike epic poets, tragic poets sought to reduce the duration of their tragedy to "a single revolution of the sun."[21] Sophocles' tragedies, like those of Aeschylus and Euripides, begin at the end of the night or at sunrise. To be sure, the notations of time are, on the whole, rather discreet. They are clearest at the beginning of the tragedy, especially when the preceding night has already been marked by an initial tragedy (as in *Ajax* with the massacre of the herds or in *Antigone* with the death of her two brothers), or when the end of the night was simply the occasion of a bad dream that made the character leap out of bed, like Deianira in *Women of Trachis* or Clytemnestra in *Electra*.[22] Indications regarding the passage of time become less frequent in the middle of the plays. In *Antigone*, after the rising sun, the noonday sun is mentioned.[23] Then, these indications disappear toward the end of the tragedies. The end of the day or the approach of night is never mentioned. The reason for this is that the tragedy concludes with an atemporal moral lesson.

Sophocles sometimes took advantage of this constraint relating to internal time to increase the density of the tragic. He transformed an ordinary day into a fateful day. This is the case in his two oldest tragedies *Ajax* and *Women of Trachis*. In *Ajax*, the seer Calchas tells us that Athena is pursuing Ajax with her vengeful anger during this single day, which allows hope for salvation if Ajax succeeds in surviving it.[24] In *Women of Trachis*, Heracles' calculation of the days of his absence, which he explains to Deianira as he is departing, ends up making that day the fateful day when his destiny is to be decided: either the end of his life or the end of his labors and the beginning of a happy life.[25] In these two tragedies the day becomes the critical day that decides what the hero's destiny as a whole will be, as an illness the day of crisis decides the fate of the patient, death or life. This technique is also used by Sophocles in his last tragedy, *Oedipus at Colonus*. The day when Oedipus arrives in Colonus seems to be a repetition of the countless and interminable days of wandering in exile accompanied by his daughter Antigone. But here too, a detail, which acquires its significance through the existence of an earlier oracle, transforms this ordinary day into a decisive day for the hero's destiny: on learning from a resident of Colonus that he has stopped in a sanctuary of the Eumenides, Oedipus suddenly realizes that Apollo's oracles are being fulfilled and that he has reached the end of his exile.[26]

This unity of time, which we consider, often in a banal way, as a limited period of time within which all the dramatic reversals must take place becomes, in this way, a significant instant in the overall duration of a life, or, to adopt a spatial and athletic (running) metaphor used by Sophocles himself, the turning point in the career of a destiny.[27]

The Alternation of Speech and Song in the Unfolding of the Performance

The unfolding of the performance of every tragedy is governed by a law that is an original feature of the Greek theater, the alternation of spoken parts and sung parts. Here again, it is appropriate to quote Aristotle. He is our primary source of information concerning the technical terms designating the different parts of a tragedy that result from this alternation:

> We have already spoken of the constituent parts to be used as ingredients of tragedy. The separable members into which it is spatially divided are these: Prologue, Episode, Exode, Choral Song, the last being divided into Parode and Stasimon. These are common to all tragedies; songs sung by actors on the stage and "commoi" are peculiar to certain plays.
>
> A prologue is the whole of that part of a tragedy which precedes the entrance of the chorus. An episode is the whole of that part of a tragedy which falls between whole choral songs. An exode is the whole of that part of a tragedy which is not followed by a song of the chorus. A parode is the whole of the first

utterance of the chorus. A stasimon is a choral song without anapaests or trochaics. A commos is a song of lament shared by the chorus and the actors on
the stage.[28]

This analysis of the different sequences of the performance has provided the
basis for modern specialists' study of Greek tragedy,[29] and it will serve as a
framework for the following developments. It has the merit of being precise and
clear. Aristotle considers the parts common to all tragedies before examining the
parts peculiar to some of them. Then he defines each of these parts.

Regarding the common parts, he draws a fundamental distinction by separating the spoken arts that essentially come from the stage, that is, from the characters played by the actors (prologue, episodes, *exodos*), from the parts sung and
danced by the chorus (parodos, stasima). This distinction is in fact essential
during the performance. The spectator's eyes are attracted, in one case, by the
characters who are speaking on the stage, and in the other case by the chorus
that is singing and dancing in the orchestra to the accompaniment of the "flute."
This distinction in kind is associated with a rule of alternation between the
spoken parts and the sung parts. The tragedy begins with a spoken part (prologue), followed by a sung part (parodos or entrance of the chorus). The body
of the tragedy is composed of an alternation between spoken parts (episodes)
and sung parts (stasima). After the chorus's final song comes a last spoken part
(exodos).

Aristotle's analysis is applicable to all of Sophocles' tragedies, as we can see in
the presentation of each of the tragedies given in appendix I. What is not fixed
is the number of stasima and, consequently, the number of episodes, which is
equal to the number of stasima. In Greek tragedy, there are from three to five
stasima, and in a few cases six.[30] So far as Sophocles is concerned, four tragedies
out of seven have four stasima (*Ajax*, *Women of Trachis*, *Oedipus the King*, *Electra*). Just one has only three stasima (*Philoctetes*). Two have more than four stasima: *Antigone* has five, and *Oedipus at Colonus*, which is exceptionally long, has
six. In these two tragedies, there is thus an alternation between seven or even
eight spoken parts (including the prologue, five or six episodes, and the exodos)
and six, or even seven sung parts (including the parodos and five or six stasima).
This is the maximum number of parts that can be found in a Greek tragedy.

This structure is the result of an evolution of the tragic genre. According to
Aristotle, tragedy emerged from a choral song in honor of Dionysus, with the
initial addition of a single actor, and then a second actor by Aeschylus, and finally a third by Sophocles.[31] According to Aristotle, this development of tragedy
corresponds to a diminution of choral song and an growth of speeches delivered
by characters. One of the signs of this development is the regular presence in
Sophocles and Euripides of a spoken prologue preceding the arrival of the chorus. Initially, the chorus entered first. The tragedy thus began with the parodos.

Traces of this older state are visible in Aeschylus, where two tragedies out of seven begin directly with the entrance of the chorus. However, this development did not take place in a linear fashion. The beginning of Aeschylus's extant work corresponds to an intermediary period in which the author could choose to begin with the direct arrival of the chorus or with a spoken prologue.[32] As for the regression of the choral parts, there is nothing systematic about it. The choral parts certainly diminished in length after Aeschylus,[33] but they did not decrease in number. On the contrary, the stasima are less numerous in Aeschylus's work than in that of Sophocles and Euripides.[34] Thus we see an evolution of Greek tragedy toward an acceleration of the rhythm of the alternation between spoken and sung parts, and thus toward an acceleration of the rhythm of the performance.

What Aristotle adds regarding the parts peculiar to certain tragedies qualifies the opposition between characters who speak and the chorus that sings. There are moments when the characters sing, either alone (monodies) or as a duet, or in a sung dialogue with the chorus (*commoi*).[35] Conversely, the chorus speaks when it intervenes as a character in the spoken parts, through the intermediary of its leader, the coryphaeus, as modern scholars suppose, or all together in unison, if we adhere to the indications in the manuscripts.[36] Thus nothing is completely rigid in the unfolding of the performance.

Modern scholars add to these two modes of expression—speech and song—an intermediary mode that is sustained declamation accompanied by a "flute." Thus in theory a passage in a tragedy can be sung, spoken, or recited. In this respect, we should be grateful to the French scholar Paul Mazon for having had the idea, in the early twentieth century, of giving these distinctions material form in his translations of Aeschylus's and then Sophocles' theater by putting the sung parts in italics to distinguish them from the spoken parts, and by indicating the parts in recitative with the word "melodrama."[37] Thus there are three modes of expression in Greek classical tragedy that seem also to correspond to three degrees in the expression of feeling: the spoken, the recited, and the sung. All the same, since recitative is a relatively rare mode of expression, the essential opposition is still that between song and speech.[38]

Speech and Song in the Greek Theater: The Criterion of Language

What criteria allow us to make these distinctions between speech and song, in the absence of musical scores (which we know were completely lost for Sophocles' theater)? Technical differences in language and versification. We will give the reader an idea of this without going into excessive detail.

The most obvious difference in language has to do with dialectal color. Whereas the language of the spoken parts is for the most part the same as that used by the Athenian spectators—what scholars call Ionian-Attic—one of the characteristics of the lyric language of Greek tragedy is its Dorian flavor, which is recognizable especially by the open pronunciation of long *o*'s corresponding to the long *e*'s of the Ionian-Attic dialect.[39] Consequently, there may be a certain paradox in imagining that in the theater Athenian spectators heard parts sung in a dialect that, during the Peloponnesian War, might remind them of their enemies, the Lacedaemonians. In reality, it is not even certain that the spectators made such a connection, because this Dorian dialect belonged to the tradition. The parts of the tragedy chanted by a chorus proceeded from the choral lyric, that is, from songs a chorus originally sang during religious ceremonies. But this choral lyric developed in the Dorian lands where the life of the community took precedence over that of the individual, particularly in Sparta, even if the great poets representing this genre, such as Pindar or Bacchylides, were not natives of cities where Dorian was spoken.[40] In addition to the dialectal coloring, the vocabulary, inherited from epic and lyric poetry in which rare words and compounds were abundant, contrasts with the vocabulary of the spoken parts, which is simpler and closer to everyday speech, especially in the dialogues.

The dialectal difference between the sung parts and the spoken parts reflects their separate origins. Tragedy was born from a choral poetry of Dorian origin through the addition of parts spoken by one, then two, then three actors playing characters who expressed themselves in Ionian-Attic. The addition of spoken parts was an Athenian innovation.

Speech and Song in the Greek Theater: The Criterion of Versification

The contrast between sung and spoken parts is due above all to the rhythm of the verse.[41] The regularity of the rhythm in the spoken parts contrasts with its great diversity in the sung parts. But here again this contrast can be explained historically. The meters of the sung parts are inherited from the Dorian choral lyric, whereas the meters of the spoken parts belong to the Ionian tradition.

In Sophocles' time, the rhythm of the spoken parts was regular. Of the two verse forms inherited from the Ionian tradition, there remained only one, "iambic verse" (*to iambeion*).[42] Aristotle explains the definitive choice of this verse form in the development of the tragic genre by its natural analogy with the rhythm of speech.[43] However, regularity does not mean monotony. The tragic poets, even in the oldest extant tragedies, introduced movement into the rhythm of the spoken parts by dividing the verses among the characters, playing on the alternation between the extent of the long speeches and the tension of more or less rapid dialogues. For a long time, the fastest form of exchange in the spoken parts of tragedies was the verse-for-verse dialogue that was given the name of *stichomythia*.[44]

However, tragic poets, always seeking to produce effects by varying the rhythm of the performance, moved on to still more rapid exchanges by dividing the verses among the interlocutors in moments of extreme tension. These dialogic exchanges, in which verses are divided among the interlocutors, are also designated by a technical term, *antilabai*.[45] This license, which alters the unity of the verse, appeared only gradually. It was exceptional in Aeschylus. Like Euripides, Sophocles made use of it, especially in his last two tragedies, *Philoctetes* and *Oedipus at Colonus*, and he did so with discernment, not dividing verses at the beginning of his tragedies.[46] Without according too much importance to statistics, we can make a comparative assessment: in *Antigone*, which dates from the 440s, there is no dialogic exchange in which verses are broken, whereas thirty years later, we count thirty-three verses divided in this way in *Philoctetes*, and Sophocles' last tragedy, *Oedipus at Colonus*, culminated with fifty-four broken verses.[47]

The goal of this new resource is clear: it offers a further stage in the change of rhythm in dialogue. And whereas the rare examples of it in the earliest tragedies present the verses divided into two parts, in the later tragedies where the examples are most numerous a single verse is sometimes divided into three or even four parts. At the end of *Electra*, when Orestes gives Aegisthus the final order to go into the palace where he is to die, a single verse is divided into three parts:

> *Orestes:* Move forward!
> *Aegisthus:*   You lead.
> *Orestes:*   You must go first.[48]

The record is set by a verse in *Philoctetes* that is divided into four parts, at the time when the hero is suddenly struck by a crisis in his disease in front of Neoptolemus, who does not understand what is happening to him:

> *Neoptolemus:* What new thing has come on you so suddenly that you wail for yourself with these loud shrieks?
> *Philoctetes:* You know, son.
> *Neoptolemus:*   What is it?
> *Philoctetes:*   You know, boy.
> *Neoptolemus:*   What ails you?
>   I do not know.
> *Philoctetes:*   How could you not know? Oh, oh![49]

With this example, we reach the limit of rapidity in spoken dialogue in Sophocles. Of the four verses quoted, two are divided between the interlocutors, one into four parts, the other into two. What justifies this exceptional rapidity of the dialogue is the intensity of the physical pain, which Philoctetes tries to stifle and which Neoptolemus does not understand. The rapidity of the exchanges and the intensity of the feeling combine in these extreme effects sought by dislocating the verse.

Despite these exceptional moments, the tragic poets could not find in the metrics of spoken exchanges a source of endless variations of rhythm. On the other hand, the choral parts are characterized by a diversity of rhythms that a modern reader can hardly imagine. A great range of substitutions allows a diversity of possibilities even within a single rhythm. The complexity of lyric metrics is such that genuine specialists are rare and tend to use a technical vocabulary that is often arbitrary, so that the metrical schemas offered in editions frequently mask more than they illuminate the effects produced by the recurrence or interruption of basic rhythmic elements.[50] Confronted by this complexity, even the general reader can draw the most important conclusion: the composition of the text and the musical score for the choral parts required extensive technical knowledge. Being a tragic poet was not something that could be improvised.[51]

This technical knowledge incorporated the whole heritage of the Dorian choral lyric. What was inherited was not only the majority of the lyric meters, but also their organization into wholes that corresponded to each other. Starting in the sixth century BCE, the choral poem was composed of triads, that is, of three strophic elements, the ode (commonly called a *strophe*), the antode (commonly called an *antistrophe*), and the epode. Strophe and antistrophe responded strictly to each other, because they were composed in accord with the same metrical scheme, whereas the epode added a complement in a related rhythm. This is the composition that we find, for example, in the poems Pindar wrote in honor of the victors at the Pan-Hellenic games. The system was adopted in the choral songs of Greek tragedy. The metrical correspondence between the strophe and the antistrophe remains the rule.[52] In performance, it took the form of symmetrical movements by the chorus, with the same number of paces, corresponding to the same number of stresses in the verse. This echoing of the rhythm of the song, on which repetitions of sound, words, or themes could be grafted, remained the foundation of the lyricism. But the tragic poets introduced more flexibility and freedom into the frameworks of the Dorian lyric. The triad was no longer the rule. In other words, the presence of the epode had become optional. Some tragedies, such as *Antigone* and *Oedipus the King*, no longer included a single triad. We find only one triad in most of the other tragedies (*Ajax, Philoctetes, Oedipus at Colonus*).[53] And there are never two triads in succession in any single choral song by Sophocles, whereas the succession of triads was regular in Dorian lyric.[54] The tragic poet's freedom is also shown by the number of strophic elements, which varies. What is dominant in Sophocles' work is the song composed of two systems of strophes and antistrophes that are generally alone or sometimes terminated by a single epode. But some shorter songs contain only one pair of strophes and antistrophes, while others have, very exceptionally, three couples of strophes and antistrophes, terminated or not by an epode.

This autonomy of tragic lyric poetry with respect to the great Dorian choral lyric is also seen in the lyric verse. In addition to the inherited verse forms, the tragic poets developed a lyric verse that was peculiar to them, the *dochmiac*. This verse, which is frequently associated with other verses, is emblematic of the freedom sought by tragic poets in the expression of feeling, because it is characterized by the multiplicity of possible substitutions. This multiform verse, whose variants attain a record number of about twenty, is the best suited to express the disorders of the most violent emotion, whether it is pain or joy.[55] Already well attested in Aeschylus, the dochmiac is an extreme means of expression that Sophocles does not use randomly: he does not introduce it into the beginning of his tragedies, but only starting at the point where the tragic action has reached a certain degree of tension and emotion.[56] For example, in *Ajax*, this verse appears when the hero sings his feeling on seeing the chorus again after his fit of madness, in which he has dishonored himself; it reappears when the chorus, having left to look for Ajax, returns all out of breath without having found anything, and anxiously wonders what has happened to him, and finally when it laments once the body has been found. The use of this verse obviously corresponds to two apexes of feeling in this tragedy. It also appears, massively, in Creon's lamentations at the end of *Antigone*.[57]

The conditions peculiar to the theater led to additional freedoms through the dialogue's penetration into the lyric. The traditional choral songs were sometimes replaced by sung dialogues between the chorus and a character. This innovation took place during Sophocles' career, in his last tragedies.[58] The first of Sophocles' tragedies where it is present is *Electra*. Two out of five of the chorus's songs are replaced by sung dialogues between the chorus and the main character. The chorus's entrance is the occasion for an initial dialogue, entirely lyric and very long, in which the chorus seeks to console Electra.[59] Once again, when Electra has just heard of Orestes' false death, the chorus tries to support her in an entirely lyrical dialogue that replaces a choral song.[60] Of course, in these lyric dialogues, the strophic structure remains.[61] Moreover, the dialogue is shaped by the rules of lyric, because the correspondence between each pair of strophes and antistrophes holds not only for the metrics, but also for the distribution of the speeches between the two speakers.[62]

As an example, here is the beginning of the second lyric dialogue replacing the second stasimon in *Electra*. It perfectly illustrates these symmetries in the sung replies. Electra, who has just learned of Orestes' false death, laments after the departure of Clytemnestra and the tutor, who have gone into the palace, and she no longer has any desire to live. The chorus, to console her, refers to the myth of the seer Amphiaraus, who died like Agamemnon, as a result of his wife Eriphyle's perfidy, and was then avenged by his son Alcmeon:[63]

> *Chorus:* Where are the thunderbolts of Zeus, or where the shining Sun, if they
>   look upon these things and quietly cover them over?
> *Electra:* Ah, me, ah, me!
> *Chorus:* My child, why do you weep?
> *Electra:* Oh!

Chorus: Give no cry of bad omen!

Electra: You will break my heart!

Chorus: How do you mean?

Electra: If you suggest that I keep hope for those who have surely passed to Hades, you will trample even harder upon me as I waste away.

Chorus: No, for I know that the prince Amphiaraus was ensnared by a woman's chain of gold and swallowed up. And now beneath the earth—

Electra: Ah, me, ah, me!

Chorus: —He reigns supreme with the wits of the living.

Electra: Ah, me!

Chorus: Ah, me, indeed! For the murderess—

Electra: Was slain.

Chorus: Yes.[64]

The symmetry between the strophe and the antistrophe in the organization of the replies is perfect: three verses at the beginning for the chorus, four at the end for Electra, all of them enclosing four verses divided in the same way between two interlocutors. The division of three verses between the two interlocutors, comparable to the division of verses in the spoken dialogues, corresponds to the maximum rapidity of exchange in lyric dialogue.

This innovation in *Electra*, where two choral songs out of five are replaced by lyric dialogues, contrasts with the older tragedies. *Ajax*, *Women of Trachis*, *Antigone*, and *Oedipus the King*, where all the choral parts are sung solely by the chorus—if we except the very special case of the chorus's return in *Ajax*. The innovation seems then to have progressed between *Electra* and *Philoctetes*. The proportion rises from one tragedy to the next: from two songs in dialogue out of five, we move to three out of four in *Philoctetes*. Moreover, while the chorus entered twice into dialogue with Electra, Sophocles introduces variety into *Philoctetes* by having the chorus sometimes converse with Neoptolemus, sometimes with Philoctetes.[65] And whereas the dialogues replacing the choral songs were purely sung in *Electra*, they mix recitative with song in *Philoctetes*.[66]

To be sure, it would imprudent to seek to establish a systematic relationship between the innovations in the sung parts and the tragedies' chronology.[67] In fact, the proportion in Sophocles' last tragedy, *Oedipus at Colonus*, is smaller than in *Philoctetes*: it has only three lyric dialogues out of seven: the parodos, the first stasimon, and the fifth stasimon.[68] However, the dialogue of the parodos, while it retains the mixture of song and declamation, as in *Philoctetes*, has a new freedom. It brings three characters into dialogue: the chorus, Oedipus, and Antigone.[69]

Thus in the course of tragedy's development, the details are made more flexible in order to give more spontaneity to a theater that was constantly seeking to move closer to the spontaneity of life.[70]

Speaking and Singing in Their Relationships with the Plot

The distinction between spoken parts and sung parts is essential, not only from the point of view of the spectacle, but also from that of the plot. As a general rule, it is in the spoken parts that the plot progresses before the spectators' eyes, whereas the choral songs mark a pause and provide time for reflection.

In the sung parts, the chorus has no crucial dramatic role, as is shown in particular by the fact that when it enters at the beginning of the tragedy, it never provides news that might initiate the action or make it advance; and a fortiori, it does not do so later on, because then it normally remains where it is. Nevertheless, the tragedy often begins with news that sets it in motion. Let us take the case of *Oedipus the King*. The tragedy of the city is present from the outset, with the plague that is ravaging Thebes, but it is not yet the tragedy of its king, which is the essential subject of the play. What sets the action in motion is the Delphic oracle's response demanding the punishment of the assassins of the late King Laius as a condition for the plague's end. But it is not the chorus that brings this news. It has been preceded by the person whom Oedipus had sent to consult the oracle, Creon. The spectator is already informed when the chorus formed of elderly Theban men enters, asking itself questions. In Greek tragedy, the chorus does not provide information. Instead, it comes to know things because it has heard people talk about them.[71] The lack of a dramatic role for the chorus in the choral parts is confirmed by the exceptional case in which the chorus has been sent to get information. In *Ajax*, right in the middle of the play, the chorus is ordered by Tecmessa to go look for the hero, who has disappeared. But when it returns to the orchestra it has seen nothing, heard nothing; and it is a character, Tecmessa herself, who will discover the body of the hero, who has committed suicide.

Despite all that, the tragic action does not stop during the parts sung by the chorus. On the contrary, the author takes advantage of the pause in the action in the visible space to have crucial acts take place in the virtual space, whether exterior or interior. For example, all Antigone's acts that flow from her decision to bury Polynices occur during a choral song. It is during the first choral song— to which a spoken part is added—that Antigone buries Polynices' body the first time, without being seen by the guards; and it is during the second choral song—and only during it—that she covers him up again and is caught in the act.[72] As for Creon's ritual burial of Polynices, it also takes place during a choral song, the last one. During this final song another important act occurs: the suicide of Haemon, Antigone's fiancé.[73] In general, the time when the chorus's songs take place is the time of suicides, that of Deianira or that of Jocasta.[74]

Thus we cannot say that the chorus's songs have no role in the unfolding of the plot; but it is chiefly a negative role.[75] It allows the tragic poet to maintain, thanks to the alternation of the spoken and sung parts, the continuity of an action that unfolds in different places, sometimes in the visible space and sometimes in virtual spaces.

In this way tragic poets skillfully took advantage of the alternation of the actors' speech and the chorus's song to ensure, above and beyond the apparent discontinuity of the spectacle, the continuity of the action.

The Different Sung Parts in Their Relationship to the Plot: The Parodos and the Stasima

Although the fundamental opposition is that between the spoken parts and the sung parts, we must not neglect the various subdivisions that have been distinguished since Aristotle, because they allow us to refine the relation between the different parts of a tragedy and the plot. All the parts, whether spoken or sung, do not have the same role. Even for the sung parts, the relationship with the plot is different in the parodos from what it is in the stasima.

The first reason for distinguishing between the parodos and the stasima has to do primarily with space and spectacle. That is what is indicated by the words themselves that are used to designate these two types of sung sequences. The word *parodos* refers to a movement of arrival, while the word *stasimon* refers to a stationary state. The parodos is the thus the chorus's song of arrival when it comes into the orchestra through a lateral entrance,[76] whereas any other song, once the chorus has come in, is called a stasimon.[77] However, the distinction is also pertinent from the point of view of the plot. By its nature, the parodos is more closely connected with the plot than the stasima are.

In fact, the arrival of the chorus has to be justified in the parodos, but in the stasima there is no longer any reason to justify it. The ancients paid close attention to the skill with which the tragic poets chose their chorus and integrated it into the plot. To make the chorus's entrance seem natural, Sophocles often chose a group of men or women close to the hero or the heroine, whether this relation was personal or political.[78] When the relation is personal, the chorus comes to learn the news on its own initiative; on the other hand, when the relations are political, it comes when summoned.[79] Whatever the reason for its coming there, the chorus is obliged to introduce itself and justify its arrival, because normally it enters an empty space. These indications are distributed with art during the parodos.[80]

Secondly, the parodos usually contributes to the exposition of the action, which is no longer the case with the stasima. In this respect we can contrast the chorus's first two songs in *Antigone*, the parodos and the first stasimon. From its very first verse, the parodos is integrated into the time of the action and into the place of the drama:

> Shaft of the sun, fairest light of all that have dawned on Thebes of the seven gates, you have shone forth at last, eye of golden day, advancing over Dirce's

streams! You have goaded with a sharper bit the warrior of the white shield, who came from Argos in full armor, driving him to headlong retreat.[81]

After the spoken prologue, in which the secret meeting of Antigone and Ismene probably occurs at the end of the night,[82] the entrance of the chorus, making this vibrant appeal to the sun, corresponds to the beginning of the day. Moreover, the light of the rising sun makes it possible to reveal in a natural way the site of the action, the city of Thebes, which is named for the first time and evoked by two significant details, its seven gates and its river, the Dirce. Above all, the parodos contributes to the exposition of the situation. After the spoken prologue presenting the new family tragedy that has occurred during the night, namely the fratricidal single combat between Eteocles and Polynices, the sung parodos celebrates Thebes' victory and its liberation from the enemy invasion that had proceeded from Argos. Sophocles has shown the spectator two successive tableaus that serve to present the two sides of the situation.

Thus the parodos is integrated, as was the initial spoken part, into the place and time of the action, and it contributes to the exposition, even if the chorus has not yet been told what will bring about the tragedy: that the new king, Creon, refuses to allow the body of Polynices, the invader, to be buried.

In contrast with the parodos, the first stasimon of *Antigone* makes a break with the time and place of the tragedy. It begins with a eulogy for humans in general; here is the first strophe:

> Wonders are many, and none is more wonderful than man. This power spans the sea, even when it surges white before the gales of the south-wind, and makes a path under swells that threaten to engulf him. Earth, too, the eldest of the gods, the immortal, the unwearied, he wears away to his own ends, turning the soil with the offspring of horses as the plows weave to and fro year after year.[83]

This hymn to the grandeur of man seems unrelated to the tragedy. When the spectators have just witnessed the tense discussion between the king and the guard who has come to announce, unwillingly, the attempt to bury the dead man, and when they have just heard the last words of this ordinary man who is chiefly concerned with his own safety,[84] their astonishment is complete as soon as the chorus starts speaking. There is an abrupt leap between the guard, a very down-to-earth representative of humanity, and this ethereal reflection on the grandeur of man, who dominates nature by discovering the arts. We move not only from the particular to the general, but also from the inferior to the superior.[85] This flight of thought, intended by Sophocles, is a sudden escape far from the tension of the tragedy. More generally, thanks to song, dance, and the magnitude of their poetic evocation, the stasima are moments allowing the spectator to breathe and transcend, through thought and imagination, the particular context of a family and a city, and be immediately transported toward the universal.[86]

However, for all that the stasima are not without any relation to the plot. Despite the initial impression of a break, Sophocles arranges—in the course of the chorus's song, generally in the second half—an explicit and allusive return to the dramatic situation. Here, the attractiveness of a fresco depicting the human adventure must not make us forget the question that is really fundamental for the economy of the tragedy: what is the place and the role of this hymn to human power in the dramatic plot? We have to pay attention to the end of the stasimon, where the chorus defines the good and the bad use of this power. Humans have to respect the laws of their cities and the justice of the gods. It is no accident that the chorus ends its song with an imprecation against the man whose audacity gets him exiled from his city. Because who is seen coming immediately after this stasimon? Not a man but a woman who has broken the laws of her city. The chorus's stupefaction is all the greater, but its condemnation remains irrevocable. In the chorus's eyes, Antigone, by burying Polynices, has violated "the King's laws."[87]

Thus the stasimon does not have a solely negative dramatic function by allowing the action to take place in the virtual space—it is, in fact, during this stasimon that Antigone is caught in the act of burying Polynices a second time;[88] here, it indirectly prepares Antigone's entrance while at the same time making it a surprise.

The Spoken Parts: The Beginning of the Tragedy or Prologue

All the spoken parts distinguished by Aristotle—prologue, episodes, and exodos—are more involved in the plot than the sung parts are. However, they do not all have the same role. The prologue, a spoken part that precedes the chorus's entrance, functions to set forth, through the intermediary of the characters, the initial situation dramatic situation.

The fact that the prologue always has the same function did not prevent authors from creating their own styles. Around the same time, Sophocles and Euripides took rather different paths. Euripides chose clarity, and perhaps also ease, by regularly beginning his tragedies with a speech by one of the characters expounding the past, the present, and the future. Instead, Sophocles chose naturalness and liveliness, beginning his tragedies with a dialogue between two characters.[89]

The best way to show how these two techniques are opposed is to compare two tragedies in which Sophocles and Euripides deal with the same mythic sequence, their *Electra*s. Sophocles' *Electra* begins with a dialogue between Orestes and the tutor; after a long exile in Phocis, they are returning together to Argos to take revenge. Euripides introduces a single character, a peasant from Argos to whom Electra has been married off. The expository technique thus diverges in method. It is easy for Euripides to present an exposition intended to inform the audience by tracing the story and making it a kind of history lesson, beginning in the distant past, with Agamemnon's departure for Troy, and ending in the present, with Orestes' return to Argos. His intention was undoubtedly to refresh the audience's memory, and also to set forth his version of the facts, which often deviates from the beaten path. No one knew that Electra had been driven out of the palace and married to a poor peasant, and still less that this affable peasant had respected Electra's virginity. It took a detailed presentation by this man of the people, who emerged from Euripides' imagination, to explain his entrance into the dark history of the noble family of the Atreids. At the end of his speech, the tragedy has still not begun, even if the peasant vaguely foresees Orestes' return.

In Sophocles' play, on the contrary, the exposition is already action. Orestes, ready to take revenge, arrives accompanied by his friend Pylades and the old servant who, in the past, had rescued him. Since Sophocles begins his tragedies with a dialogue between two characters, we might have expected a dialogue between Orestes and his friend Pylades. Pylades is in fact there, but he remains stubbornly silent. Sophocles preferred to allow a humbler character to speak. Why? The constraints involved in an expository dialogue were certainly involved in this choice. In order for an expository dialogue to seem natural, one of the two characters has to have knowledge that the other lacks. Returning to his native land, Orestes cannot recognize the places he sees because he was too young when he left. Pylades, a foreigner, does not know them. Only the old servant who saved Orestes when his father was murdered is capable of presenting them. Thus it is he who naturally speaks, addressing both Orestes and his friend Pylades.

Sophocles later adopted the same technique in the beginning of *Philoctetes*, where two characters arrive in a place known to only one of them: Odysseus knows the cavern where Philoctetes was abandoned during the Argives' expedition to Troy, whereas Achilles' young son Neoptolemus, who is accompanying Odysseus, does not know it, because he joined the expedition only later on. Thus it is Odysseus who opens the dialogue by describing the place to Neoptolemus, just as the tutor described it to Orestes. The analogy between the beginning of the two tragedies does not stop there. In both cases, the dialogue continues with the passage from preparation to action; and in both cases, there is a dangerous mission to be accomplished. Here again what justifies the dialogue is that one character knows something the other does not. Orestes tells the tutor about the cunning plan he has developed to take revenge, and assigns him the role that he is to play, just as Odysseus tells Neoptolemus about the cunning speech he must make to Philoctetes to get his bow away from him. The only difference is that in Sophocles' *Electra* knowledge of the plan of action and the situation is shared by both characters, the old one who provides the information and the young one who commands, whereas in *Philoctetes*, both knowledge and power are concentrated in Odysseus, the leader of the mission. However, the dialogue at the beginning of *Philoctetes* is enriched by a dramatic tension, by a nascent conflict between the two characters as to how to act, a conflict that appears to have been nipped in the bud by Odysseus, but which will later explode in the course of the tragedy.

This dramatic tension is even more manifest in the beginning of *Antigone*. The dialogue between Antigone and Ismene with which the tragedy opens already contains the same elements as the prologue in *Philoctetes*, although the situation is very different. First of all, the expository dialogue is justified by the knowledge of one character who informs another: Antigone tells her sister about Creon's edict forbidding the burial of Polynices. Next, one character explains his or her plan of action to the other: Antigone informs Ismene of her decision to bury Polynices, no matter what, and asks for her help. Finally, a dramatic tension arises concerning the ways of acting: should they avoid betraying a brother or submit to the established authority? However, unlike *Philoctetes*, the tension leads, right from the start, to a break between the two sisters. Ismene cannot make up her mind to commit an act of insubordination and madness, and Antigone, disappointed and scornful, breaks with her. No other prologue in extant Greek tragedy reaches such a degree of dramatic and tragic intensity.

The first dialogue between two characters, in which the initial situation is set forth, may constitute the whole of the prologue as it is defined by Aristotle, namely the whole spoken part preceding the entrance of the chorus. This is in fact the case when the discussion becomes tense (*Philoctetes*) or leads to a break (*Antigone*). In his other tragedies, Sophocles makes the prologue more extensive by having a third character speak after the initial dialogue and thus already using the third actor in the prologue. Sometimes this is a secondary character whose arrival is fortuitous, but occurs at the right time: in *Women of Trachis*, Deianira's son Hyllus turns up just when his mother, already conversing with a slave woman, wants to send him away to look for his father, a little like Telemachus in the *Odyssey*. In *Oedipus at Colonus*, a resident of Colonus enters when Oedipus and Antigone are wondering about the place to which they have come. The new character is sometimes much more important. In two tragedies, it is the title character who makes his or her first appearance. When he is summoned by the goddess Athena, Ajax, in the grip of madness, leaps out of his hut to proclaim his illusory victory. Electra, tormented by her pain, comes out of the palace at the call of the sun to sing about her grief.[90] From the point of view of the plot, the most important arrival is Creon's in *Oedipus the King*, because he brings news that determines the drama's orientation: the Delphic oracle's response connecting the city's salvation with the investigation into the murder of Laius, the former king.

Usually, the arrival of a character bearing news from the outside does not take place in the prologue, but rather after the chorus's entrance, at the beginning of the first episode.

The Spoken Parts: The Middle of the Tragedy or the Episodes

Aristotle defines episodes as the spoken parts located between two songs sung by the chorus. These correspond to the acts in French classical tragedy; but by adopting a fixed number of five acts the tragic authors of the seventeenth century followed a rule in Horace's *Art of Poetry*[91] that is foreign to the flexibility of Greek tragedy. The number of songs sung by the chorus was not fixed in the Greek tragedies of the fifth century BCE, and the number of episodes varies as well.[92] The number of five acts is equivalent to a Greek tragedy including three episodes, because we must add the prologue and the exodos, which correspond to the first act and the fifth act, respectively. Just one of Sophocles' tragedies has this structure, *Philoctetes*. The other tragedies have four episodes (*Ajax, Women of Trachis, Oedipus Rex, Electra*), five (*Antigone*), or even six (*Oedipus at Colonus*).

The length of the episodes is not constant, either. Here again there is no obvious rule. The rhythm of the alternation within a tragedy can vary considerably. In *Ajax*, the imbalance between the first episode, which consists of almost four hundred verses, and the second episode, which consists of less than fifty verses, is spectacular.[93] The first episode is entirely dominated by the various stages in the hero's gradual return to lucidity after his fit of madness and by the new fears that this new state elicits in his entourage: we hear him spoken of, then we hear his groans, then we see him and hear him, first lamenting and openly desiring death, then reasoning in a long speech and honorably getting a grip on himself in the face of his dishonor, and finally addressing another long speech to his son, but remaining unmoved by the pity of those close to him who fear that he will commit suicide. Following this first episode, the chorus's song in the first stasimon is a song of despair. On the other hand, the second episode consists of a single speech, Ajax's unexpected conversion. Having come back apparently completely transformed by the time he has spent reflecting, Ajax, moved by his loved ones' pity, respectful of the gods, and submitting to the Atreids' power, decides to go off to purify himself. In the second stasimon, the chorus, trusting Ajax's words too much, engages in a frenetic dance of joy. Thus Ajax's speech, which by itself forms an episode, is framed by two songs sung by the chorus, which passes almost instantaneously from sorrow to joy. The bold imbalance Sophocles introduces between the length of the two episodes emphasizes the dramatic turn of events and accelerates the passage from despair to joy. But the chorus's joy is as short-lived as it is intense, because the following episode begins with the entrance of a messenger whose message slices through the chorus's joy like a razor.[94] In a few moments, through the imbalance in the length of the episodes, the chorus moves from despair to joy, and then from joy to fear. It is not imbalance in the length of episodes that is exceptional, but rather balance. Only one of Sophocles' tragedies has episodes of almost comparable length: *Antigone*.[95]

The acceleration of the rhythm by abridging episodes reaches an exceptional degree in Sophocles' last tragedy, *Oedipus at Colonus*. Whereas the third episode consists of three hundred verses, the two following episodes have only about two hundred verses each, and the last episode only fifty-eight.[96] The reason for this is that events move very quickly after Creon has abducted Oedipus's daughters in the course of the third episode (324 verses long). Theseus brings the young women back, then leaves again (fourth episode of 215 verses). Next, Polynices comes to beg his father to speak to him, but in vain, and leaves again (fifth episode, 198 verses long). Finally, Theseus, alerted by Oedipus's appeals and those of the chorus, returns to learn of the imminence of Oedipus's death, and the benefits the city will receive by being the site of his tomb (sixth episode, 56 verses long). At the end of this episode, everyone leaves—Oedipus with his daughters, and Theseus with his servants—for Oedipus's last resting place. The end of the tragedy (exodos of 224 verses) becomes slower and ampler again. The general departure at the end of the sixth episode is opposed to the subtly dissociated returns in the exodos, which extend the time of the tragedy by multiplying its effects: the return first of just one of Theseus's servants, who comes as a messenger to give a detailed account of Oedipus's last moments—an account that is by itself longer than the whole preceding episode (81 verses vs. 56 verses); the return of the two young women in tears, escorted by Theseus's other servants, who are themselves weeping, and the funereal lament sung by the young women with the chorus; finally, Theseus returns alone and puts an end to the threnody before the chorus concludes the tragedy with the traditional brief remark.

The alternation of the spoken parts and the sung parts in a tragedy is thus not regular and pendular. The absence of any rule regarding the length of the episodes gives authors the freedom to modify the rhythm of the performance.

What Does the Word "Episode" Mean?

By defining an episode as "that [spoken] part of a tragedy which falls between whole choral songs," Aristotle clearly situates the place of this part in the alternation of speaking and singing. But his definition is solely descriptive. It does not refer to the concrete meaning of the word "episode" (*epeisodion*) and offers no indication of the episode's role in the plot.

The meaning of the word "episode" has evolved considerably. If we consult a modern dictionary, the first meaning given is "a brief unit of action in a dramatic or literary work." The word seems to have left the domain of use it had in Aristotle. We are in fact more likely to speak of an episode in a novel than in a play. We no longer find the reference to the technical meaning of the term in Aristotle, which was still adopted in the seventeenth century by Pierre Corneille in his *Discours du poème dramatique*. Enumerating the parts of ancient tragedies, Corneille says:

> The prologue is what is recited before the chorus's first song; the episode what
> is recited between the chorus's songs, and the exodos what is recited after the
> chorus's last song.

This is a translation pure and simple of Aristotle's definition. To tell the truth, even though for us this passage in the *Poetics* represents the first use of this technical terminology, Aristotle himself does not seem to be innovating. He states the definitions without justifying them, which he would not have failed to do had they not been customary.

How did this technical meaning of "episode" emerge from the concrete meaning of the Greek word *epeisodion*? We are in the habit of starting out from the meaning "something inserted as an addition." In this case, an episode is a secondary action inserted into the primary action.[97] But taking that route we arrive at a definition that is absolutely not suited to episodes in Greek tragedy. There is nothing secondary about them, because they form the very heart of the action. To understand the technical meaning, we have to go back beyond Aristotle in the history of the Greek language, back to the tragedies of the classical period themselves. The Greek word *epeisodos* (from which *epeisodion* is derived) is first attested in one of Sophocles' tragedies, *Oedipus at Colonus*. Creon, who has come as a Theban ambassador to bring Oedipus back whether he wants to return or not, enters the visible space through a side entrance and addresses these words to the chorus of old men from Colonus:

> Gentlemen, noble dwellers in this land, I see from your eyes that a sudden fear has troubled you at my coming [*epeisodou*].[98]

The Greek word *epeisodos* refers to nothing other than the arrival of a person coming from the exterior. Although the stage is considered an outside place, a character who comes into it through a lateral passageway seems to be entering. The word that a character in a tragedy uses to refer to his own entrance into the visible space is found precisely at the beginning of what Aristotle calls in technical terms an "episode," in this case the second episode.

On the basis of this concrete meaning of *epeisodos*, denoting a character's arrival, it is possible to understand how the word *epeisodion*—"episode"—could acquire a specialized meaning in the theatrical vocabulary to denote the spoken part of a tragedy, where a character arrives after a choral song.[99]

The Action in the First Episode: The Role of Information Coming from the Outside

The absence of a norm regarding the length and number of episodes prevents us seeking to discern a function peculiar to each of the episodes of a Greek tragedy in the unfolding of the plot. Nonetheless, we can try to identify a few tendencies in the way Sophocles used each episode to complicate and resolve the plot.[100]

After the initial situation has been set forth in the prologue, and possibly in the parodos, the beginning of the first episode is marked by the arrival of a character. This first arrival, whether it occurs immediately after the beginning of the episode or is slightly deferred,[101] occupies a privileged position. Generally speaking, it is a new character who appears. Then there are two possibilities: it can be a character central to the tragedy or a character whose importance depends not on social status but rather on the crucial information that he or she provides and that changes the initial situation.

In three tragedies, the first arrival is that of an important character. In *Antigone*, the new king, Creon, comes to announce to the chorus his principles of governance and his first decisions. And in *Philoctetes*, it is the hero himself, who is simultaneously powerful because of his infallible bow and miserable because of his ravaged body and his diseased foot that he drags behind him. Creon and Philoctetes both appear for the first time. On the other hand, in *Oedipus Rex*, when Oedipus comes out of the palace after the parodos because he has heard the chorus's prayers, he is already well known to the spectators, having come out the first time at the very beginning of the tragedy.

To illustrate the second case, the arrival of a character who brings news that produces a turning point in the plot, the clearest example is provided by *Women of Trachis*. At the beginning of the first episode, when Deianira, who has remained onstage after the prologue, comes to tell the chorus of young women about her fear concerning her husband's absence, a first messenger arrives wearing a crown on his head, the sign of good news.[102] His announcement that Heracles has returned alive and victorious makes joy succeed fear. Moreover, the arrival is twofold. After this first anonymous messenger, Heracles' official herald, Lichas, arrives.[103] He confirms the good news, but he brings with him, among the captive women, the one who will provoke Deianira's jealousy and cause the tragedy.

In other tragedies, the messenger's role is less conspicuous, because it is played by a character not identified as a messenger. Thus in *Electra* it is the heroine's sister, Chrysothemis, who brings news at the beginning of the first episode. It is no longer apparently good news for the heroine, as in *Women of Trachis*, but a threat:

> I will tell you all that I know. If you will not cease from your mourning, they intend to send you where you will never look upon the sun's brilliance, but passing your life in a covered chamber beyond this land's borders you will make hymns of your calamity.[104]

The threat, which increases the tragic nature of the situation, is to be carried out the same day, when Aegisthus has returned from the fields. In this punishment envisaged for Electra we recognize the same punishment to which Antigone is subjected. But the threat is not carried out. That does not mean, however, that it is completely pointless. It allows us to gauge Electra's determination not to yield to the powerful and to remain faithful to her people:

> Then for this, may he arrive quickly!

The same role as a messenger is played by Ismene, Antigone's sister, at the beginning of the first episode in *Oedipus at Colonus*. But whereas Chrysothemis came out of the palace, Ismene comes from far away, from Thebes, to bring news to her father. This role as messenger is clearly stressed by Oedipus:

> And you, my child, in former days came forth, bringing your father, unknown to the Cadmeans, all the oracles that had been given concerning Oedipus. [355] You became a faithful guardian on my behalf, when I was being driven from the land. Now, in turn, what new tidings have you brought your father, Ismene? On what mission have you set forth from home? For you do not come empty-handed, I know well, [360] or without some cause of fear for me.[105]

The news takes on more scope than in *Electra*, and it is crucial, this time, for the development of the plot. It informs the hero regarding what is happening in Thebes: Oedipus's two sons are on the point of fighting over the possession of power in what is called the war of the Seven against Thebes; but in light of new oracles, the Thebans want to make Oedipus come back, in order to obtain his protection, without, however, agreeing to bury the parricide on Theban soil. This news arouses Oedipus's anger at his sons and foreshadows what will happen in the course of the tragedy. Oedipus will have to cope first with the violence of Creon, Eteocles' emissary, and then with Polynices' supplications.

The arrival, in the course of the first episode, of a character bearing news is so indispensable that it survives even in the tragedies in which the first arrival is that of a tragic hero. Then it occurs only after a delay. That is the case in *Antigone*, *Oedipus the King*, and *Philoctetes*.

In *Antigone*, after Creon enters and gives his speech from the throne justifying, before the royal council, his refusal to allow Polynices' burial, a guard arrives to reveal, after many hesitations, that the dead man has just been buried by some unknown person.[106]

A comparable delayed entrance occurs in the first episode of *Oedipus the King*. After Oedipus arrives and issues before the chorus his royal edict regarding the murder of Laius, Tiresias comes in with his revelations concerning the identity and the fate of Oedipus. What can there be in common between two characters situated at opposite ends of the social scale, between a humble guard in *Antigone* and a great seer in *Oedipus the King*? It is their dramatic function that makes them comparable. In both tragedies, the king's power, at the very moment when it is expressed with solemnity before the chorus, is shaken by the revelations that the new arrivals have brought.

Finally, in *Philoctetes*, the arrival of a supposed merchant plays a role analogous to that of Ismene in *Oedipus at Colonus*.[107] The false merchant is spreading the latest news from Thebes. The schema is identical; and the information, in both cases, implies new dangers for the hero. In fact, the merchant reveals, among other things, that Odysseus and Diomedes are coming to find Philoctetes, a very long time after he was abandoned, in order to take him where he does not want to go, just as Ismene announces the arrival of Thebans who, long after having expelled Oedipus, intend to take him back where he no longer wants to return. To be sure, the great difference is that the news announced by the merchant falsifies reality, because it is part of Odysseus's plan to trick Philoctetes. But the effect of this news on Philoctetes is very real, making worry and a feeling of emergency take the place of joy.[108]

In short, in the first episode of one of Sophocles' tragedies we usually find, in addition to the appearance of the main characters, the arrival of a secondary character who brings news that changes the initial tragic situation, either by making it worse by new threats (*Antigone*, *Oedipus the King*, *Electra*, *Philoctetes*, *Oedipus at Colonus*), or by temporarily attenuating or eliminating it by good news that will soon prove to be the source of a new tragedy (*Women of Trachis*).

The Action in the Second Episode: The Role of Changes That Proceed from Within

When we compare the second episodes in Sophocles' tragedies, we are struck by the disproportion of their lengths. Some are short or even very short (*Ajax*, *Women of Trachis*, *Philoctetes*, *Oedipus at Colonus*), while others are two or three times longer (*Antigone*, *Oedipus the King*, *Electra*). The shortest second episode is in *Ajax* and consists of a single speech forty-seven verses long addressed by Ajax to the chorus;[109] the longest is that in *Oedipus the King*, which runs to three hundred and forty-nine verses and includes the successive arrival of three characters, Creon, Oedipus, and Jocasta, and the departure of one of them, Creon.[110] This contrast clearly shows that we cannot claim to find rules in the organization of this episode.

However, despite these obvious differences, it is possible to oppose the second episode to the first in certain tragedies. Whereas the first episode is the site of a change coming from outside, in three tragedies the second episode is the site of a change that comes from inside. It is the hero himself who changes. This change, whether real or feigned, willed or suffered, brings about a dramatic reversal in the action.

The most famous such reversal is that of Ajax announcing his decision not to commit suicide out of respect for his people and to submit to the gods and the leaders in conformity with the law of alternation in the world (night and day, winter and summer, sleep and waking, etc.). This reversal, taken literally by an excessively credulous chorus, is in reality feigned by Ajax in order to escape the vigilance of his companions and to allow him to be alone and commit suicide.

The second episode of *Women of Trachis* begins with an analogous but very real change. Deianira, who at the end of the first episode claimed to understand her rival and not want to fight against the gods, declares the situation unbearable when she returns at the beginning of the second episode. Jealousy has done its work. Wisdom has disappeared. Deianira has decided to smear the tunic to be given Heracles with what she thinks is a love philter, but which will turn out to be a deadly poison.

Finally, the second episode of *Philoctetes* also begins with the hero in crisis. This time it is not a moral but a physical crisis. Leaving the grotto where he had gone before the Argives' departure, to seek the plant that could ease his pain and to see if he still has some arrow to his bow, Philoctetes is suddenly gripped by excruciating pains that force him to give his bow to Neoptolemus before going off to sleep at the end of a crisis that coincides with the end of the second episode. The dramatic reversal seems to favor Neoptolemus's mission, since he now has the bow.

The Action in the Other Episodes: The Preparation and Accomplishment of Catastrophes

In two tragedies, the third episode is the point where the catastrophes are already feared, and then realized. These are the two so-called diptych tragedies (*Ajax, Women of Trachis*), where the construction of the episode is analogous.

At the beginning of the episode, a bit of news arouses fears that the worst is about to occur. In *Ajax*, a messenger, the spokesman for a seer, comes to tell the chorus, and then Tecmessa, that Ajax must not be allowed to leave: in *Women of Trachis*, Deianira comes to tell the chorus that the philter, left in the sun, has eaten away the cotton that was used to smear the tunic sent to Heracles as a present. These two signs excite alarm regarding the hero's fate. Whether or not they allow time to react in an attempt to avoid the catastrophes, they appear too late. The catastrophes occur: in one case, Ajax's death, in the other, Heracles' fatal disease. However, Sophocles varies the means of presentation. The spectators witness Ajax's last moments, whereas they learn from Hyllus, the son of Heracles and Deianira, the effect of the poison on Heracles. In *Ajax*, only the spectators hear the hero's last words and witness his suicide; in *Women of Trachis*, they are not the only ones who hear Hyllus's account. His mother Deianira also hears it and leaves without saying a word.

A third episode that ends with a character leaving in silence is not peculiar to *Women of Trachis*. That is also how Sophocles ends the third episode in two other tragedies, *Antigone* and *Oedipus the King*.

In *Women of Trachis*, Deianira, after learning, through her son's report that rings like an indictment, the terrible effect of the philter on Heracles, silently goes back into the palace. The chorus comments on her exit, addressing her directly, but she does not reply:

> Why do you leave without a word? Do you not know that your silence pleads your accuser's case?

Similarly, at the end of the third episode of *Antigone*, after the quarrel between Creon and his son over the fate to be reserved for his fiancée, Haemon's abrupt exit is commented on by the chorus, addressing Creon:

The man is gone, King Creon, in anger and haste. A young mind is fierce when stung.[111]

Again, at the end of the third episode of *Oedipus the King*, when Jocasta, after the arrival of the Corinthian messenger, has understood everything about Oedipus's origin and has gone back into the palace without explaining her departure, the chorus addresses Oedipus:

Why has this woman gone, Oedipus, rushing off in wild grief? I fear a storm of sorrow will soon break forth from this silence.[112]

On each occasion, the chorus stresses the anxiety elicited by this silence. And in fact this silence is the sign of a catastrophe: "A storm of sorrow will soon break forth from this silence." The two women, Deianira and Jocasta, will commit suicide inside the palace. The man, Haemon, will commit suicide next to the body of his fiancée.

In this way, the end of the third episode prepares the way for what will provide tragic moments in the following spoken parts. In *Women of Trachis*, the nurse's announcement of Deianira's suicide occupies the fourth episode. In *Antigone*, Haemon's suicide is announced by a messenger much later, at the beginning of the exodos.[113] In *Oedipus the King*, the announcement of Jocasta's suicide is also delayed almost to the beginning of the exodos, where it is also reported by a messenger.[114] The difference in composition between *Women of Trachis*, on the one hand, and *Antigone* and *Oedipus the King*, on the other, is that *Women of Trachis* is a diptych tragedy. In this tragedy, the exodos is devoted to Heracles' tragedy after that of Deianira.

Starting with the fourth episode, catastrophes occur one after the other, and lamentations become numerous. Thus the beginning of the fourth episode in *Ajax*, a diptych tragedy like *Women of Trachis*, is occupied by the arrival of Teucer, who has been assured of Ajax's death and is grieving, just as the fourth episode of *Women of Trachis* is occupied as a whole by the lamentations over Deianira's disappearance and the account of her death. And the fourth episode of *Antigone* once again begins with tears, those of the young woman over her own impending death, at the moment when she is leaving for her underground prison. In the fourth episode of *Oedipus the King*, there is also a discovery of the catastrophe, but it takes place at the very end of the episode, coinciding with the end of the investigation, when Oedipus learns with horror his true identity.

Even when the tragedy does not end in misfortune, the fourth episode is the time of discovery and deep feeling. Holding the funeral urn in her arms, Electra first laments Orestes' false death before the recognition scene between the brother and sister that makes joy succeed suffering.

The Spoken Parts: The End of the Tragedy or Exodos

Technically, the word *exodos* refers to the spoken part that ends with the exit of the characters and the chorus. It corresponds to the last act of a modern tragedy.

The word does not reflect its meaning very well, because the exodos, insofar as it is preceded by a choral song, has to begin with the entrance of a character, just as an episode does. And sometimes it even happens that a major character enters for the first time. In this respect, the exodos of *Women of Trachis* is the best example we can give of the mismatch between the traditional denomination and the actual content of the part. It is, in fact, at the beginning of this part that Heracles, whose return was announced in the first episode, appears for the first time. This last part of the tragedy is essentially reserved for the announcement of deaths, for the spectacle of bloodshed and weeping. The exodos in *Antigone* is the most complete example: a messenger coming from outside announces Haemon's death and thus also that of Antigone, who has hanged herself in her cell; Haemon committed suicide over his fiancée's body after a violent quarrel with his father. When her son's death is announced, Eurydice, Creon's wife, goes silently back into the palace. This silent departure is analogous to those that end, as we have just seen, the third episode in three other tragedies.[115] It foretells a suicide. In fact, when Creon returns from the outside virtual space carrying his son's body and bemoaning his pain and his mistakes, a second messenger, coming this time from the interior virtual space, tells him of the death of his wife. Three suicides, announced by two messengers, thus succeed one another and crush a man who realizes his errors too late.

In the exodos of *Oedipus the King*, Sophocles adopts, in a way, the same technique of presentation he used in *Antigone*, even though the deaths are less numerous. A single messenger suffices, but he seems to have inherited the function of the two messengers in *Antigone*. Coming from inside, like the second messenger in *Antigone*, he announces the death of Jocasta, Oedipus's wife (and mother), just as the second messenger in *Antigone* announced the death of Eurydice, Creon's wife. But his arrival opens the exodos, like that of the first messenger in *Antigone*, who comes from outside; and the narrative technique is the same: a death is immediately announced (Haemon in one case, Jocasta in the other), but in the detailed account of the suicide we learn about a second catastrophe connected with the first. Haemon's death is caused by Antigone's suicide by hanging, whereas Jocasta's death by hanging is the cause of Oedipus's self-mutilation when he plucks out his eyes with the dead woman's pins. And in *Oedipus the King*, as in *Antigone*, the spectacle confirms the narrative: what corresponds, from the theatrical point of view, to Haemon's corpse is Oedipus, who appears alive, of course, but with his face stained with blood.

The exodos of *Oedipus at Colonus* also belongs to the same category: it begins with the arrival of a messenger who announces immediately the death of Oedipus, as the messenger in *Antigone* announced the death of Haemon, or the messenger in *Oedipus the King* announced the death of Jocasta,[116] and the announcement is followed by a long, detailed report, as in the other two tragedies.[117] However, in *Oedipus at Colonus* the account of the death takes on a magnitude that it did not have in the other two tragedies, and it is not followed by a sight that confirms it. The reason for this is that the death is of a different nature. It is not the suicide of one of the hero's family, which is only one of the misfortunes that have driven people away from him: it is death wrapped in the mystery of the hero himself that has made him rise to a different status, that of a demigod, the protector of a city.

The Final Ritual of the Exodos

The end of the first spoken part in all of Sophocles' tragedies is distinguished from the episodes by two formal characteristics that justify the term "exodos."

The first of these is well-known: the exodos ends with a brief reflection by the chorus, which concludes the drama before it makes its exit. This technique begins to appear in Aeschylus and becomes traditional and sometimes artificial in the other two tragic poets. To stay with Sophocles, this final speech by the chorus is from three to seven verses long. If it sometimes mentions the chorus's departure,[118] it is above all a reflection on what the play has shown the spectator[119] about the human condition[120] and the role of the gods.[121] It sometimes takes a didactic turn to recommend wisdom and respect for the gods.[122] However, in the later tragedies it seems to lose this reflexive and didactic function regarding humans in general and be reduced to a speech that concludes the tragedy.[123] This means that the final interpretation of a tragedy cannot be reduced to a closing speech. We have seen that at the end of his tragedies Sophocles makes more or less veiled allusions to the future. But their meaning for the interpretation of the tragedies is hotly debated.[124]

The second characteristic is no less real, but it is subtler, because it consists in a change of rhythm in the final section. Thus it requires a little more explanation.

As Aristotle said in his definition of tragedy cited at the beginning of this chapter, in Greek tragedy speech is adorned by rhythm. In the spoken parts, this rhythm is usually iambic, as we have seen.[125] However, the rhythm changes not only in the chorus's final remarks but usually also in the last section of the dialogue between characters.[126] In general, the rhythm changes from iambic (short-long) to anapaestic (short-short-long), or more rarely, to trochaic (long-short).[127] This change in rhythm corresponds to a change in diction. The characters abandon speech to adopt a diction intermediary between speech and song, what moderns call recitative. The characters are then accompanied by the "flutist."[128]

Finally, this change in rhythm and diction marks the last turning point in the play, the one where we pass from discussing or deploring misfortunes to a final action, that of departing. For example, in *Ajax*, the change in rhythm comes when Teucer, after thanking Odysseus for intervening in favor of Ajax's burial, moves on to the arrangements for carrying out this burial and taking the corpse away.[129] In *Women of Trachis*, the change occurs at a comparable moment: Heracles, still lying on his litter, is getting ready to leave for this funeral pyre on Mount Oeta, and his son orders his servants to carry him away.[130]

Sometimes, a transitional formula emphasizes this turning point in the course of the plot at the moment the rhythm changes. Thus in *Oedipus the King*, after a long, moving speech addressed by Oedipus to his children, the first words Creon utters at the moment of the change in rhythm are these:

Your grief has had a sufficient scope: move on into the house.[131]

This change in rhythm is accompanied by an entirely exceptional acceleration of the final dialogue between Creon and Oedipus, in which the repartee is so rapid that the interlocutors share verses. Then the chorus concludes the tragedy in its final speech.

All these changes contribute to a sort of ritual for concluding the tragedy. But in one of his tragedies, *Philoctetes*, Sophocles very subtly uses an expected ending to create surprise. The final scene in dialogue, between Philoctetes and Neoptolemus, has, from the point of view of rhythm and theme, all the characteristics of a tragic ending. Neoptolemus, even though he has regained Philoctetes' confidence by giving the bow back to him, does not succeed in persuading him to go to Troy and has to resign himself to honoring the promise he had made Philoctetes to take him back to his homeland in continental Greece. But from the moment that Neoptolemus suggests that they leave, the rhythm changes exactly as it does at the end of *Oedipus the King*. A lively dialogue begins between the two characters in the same rhythm as that of the final dialogue between Oedipus and Creon.[132] The spectator is expecting nothing further except the chorus's speech intended to conclude the tragedy with this departure. But the surprise comes from the sudden intervention of a divinity that has descended from the heavens. Sophocles has deliberately led the spectator astray all the way to the end, making him think he has reached the end of the tragedy the better to surprise him with a new development. And the scene added after this false departure for continental Greece will end with the true departure to Troy, with the expected change in rhythm and the chorus's final speech.[133] That is why we can speak of a double ending to *Philoctetes*. Sophocles has played on the traditional codes of the end of the exodos to surprise the spectator.

The Parts Peculiar to Certain Tragedies: Songs Proceeding from the Stage

With the exodos ends the exposition of the main parts that constitute the "extent" of a Greek tragedy, to adopt Aristotle's vocabulary, or rather that punctuate the temporal unfolding of the performance: prologue, parodos, the alternation of episodes and stasima, exodos. To complete his analysis, Aristotle adds parts peculiar to certain tragedies, namely lyrical pieces within the spoken parts, which he calls "songs sung by actors on the stage and 'commoi.'"[134]

The phrase "songs sung by actors on the stage" is clear in itself. These are songs that come from characters without the participation of the chorus, a manifestation of the characters' most intense emotion. They may be presented in two forms: solos or duets.

A single lyrical duet is attested in Sophocles' extant tragedies. It occurs after the recognition scene between Orestes and Electra. Lyric duets are particularly appropriate in moments of recognition. We also find them in several of Euripides' tragedies, but not in his *Electra*.[135] In Sophocles, it is placed in a triadic framework (strophe, antistrophe, epode), which it is not in Euripides, where the recognition duets are outside the strophic framework. Delighted to find Orestes, whom she had long awaited, Electra begins to sing. Her irresistible joy is expressed by an agitated rhythm, including dochmiacs. However, it is not a duet in unison. Whereas Electra sings, Orestes speaks in the strophe and the antistrophe. This contrast can be explained in part by feminine sensibility. In Euripides, we find an analogous tendency in recognition duets, where the men are less inclined to express their feelings passionately than the women are. But there is another explanation, as well. While witnessing Electra's explosion of joy, Orestes seeks to control his emotions, for fear that they might compromise the realization of his vengeance. The lyrical duet thus remains within the dramatic situation.[136]

As for the solos, which are also called "monodies,"[137] Sophocles resorted to them much less often than Euripides did. We can cite only one or two examples in the extant tragedies. The sole uncontested instance is a solo by Antigone in the last tragedy, *Oedipus at Colonus*. At a crucial moment early in that play, when the chorus, discovering Oedipus's identity, tries to drive him out of Colonus, Antigone addresses to it a plea on her father's behalf in the form of a song, the better to arouse its pity.[138] This song is free of the constraints of the strophic framework. Aristotle saw in a song without a strophe an opportunity for actors to "imitate," in a more artistic way, in song and in words, the characters they played.[139]

The second monody is again that of a young woman who passionately defends her father, but this time a dead father. It is, in fact, her eternal mourning that Electra expresses to the morning sunlight, like a nightingale, when she appears for the first time before the spectators. Here is the beginning of her monody:

> O you pure sunlight, and you air, light's equal partner over earth, how often have you heard the chords of my laments and the thudding blows against this bloodied breast at the time of gloomy night's leaving off![140]

The rhythm (whose basic foot is the anapaest) has been interpreted differently by specialists. According to some, it is a section in recitative, accompanied by the "flute"; according to others, it is a plaintive song. This second solution is probably the better one, because in addition to technical reasons founded on versification,[141] the harmony between form and content is perfect if Electra sings. Thus these "songs" of lamentation to which she herself refers, and the comparison she then makes between her complaints and those of the nightingale, are completely comprehensible.[142] In the corresponding sequence of Euripides' *Electra*, that is, the one that immediately precedes the chorus's entrance, the heroine also sings a solo about her misfortunes. The lyricism is clearer in Euripides.[143] Since monodies are more frequent in Euripides' theater, we might be tempted to see an influence of Euripides' *Electra* on that of Sophocles. But apart from the fact that the relative chronology of the two *Electras* has not been established,[144] plaintive lyrical anapaests are attested as early as the oldest extant tragedy, Aeschylus's *Persians* (472 BCE).[145]

The Parts Peculiar to Certain Tragedies: The Dialogues Coming from the Stage and the Chorus (Commoi)

The scarcity of songs sung as solos or duets in Sophocles does not mean that characters did not sing in his tragedies. On the contrary, there is not a single tragedy by Sophocles in which the main character does not sing at some time or another. It is just that this song, inserted into the spoken parts, comes chiefly in the course of a dialogue with the chorus. That is the particular part of tragedy that Aristotle calls a commos.

Aristotle defines the commos as a shared "lamentation" (threnody) coming from the chorus and from the stage. The Greek word *commos* does not in itself include the idea of a sung dialogue. It denotes, in fact, a detail of the rite of funereal lamentation, the action of striking (*koptein*) one's breast and head, the rite to which Electra alludes in her lamentation that we have just quoted.[146] It is in this sense that the word *commos* is used in Aeschylus's *The Libation Bearers* during the funeral song over the tomb of Agamemnon in which the characters, Orestes and Electra, as well as the chorus, sing in alternation.[147] It was probably from this passage that the technical term *commos* used in Aristotle's *Poetics* was derived, because the word does not appear anywhere outside these two passages. The commos was thus originally a song of mourning.

In Sophocles' tragedies, there is a commos that corresponds particularly well to this definition. It is found in his last tragedy, *Oedipus at Colonus*. It is a lamentation, all in song, proceeding from the stage (Antigone and Ismene) and from the chorus after Oedipus's death, at the end of the tragedy. It is a threnody.[148] Here is a passage from it:

> *Antigone:* He died on the foreign ground that he desired; he has his well-shaded bed beneath the ground for ever; and he did not leave behind unwept sorrow. With these weeping eyes, father, I lament you; nor do I know how in my wretchedness I must still my grief for you that is so immense. Alas! You wanted to die in a foreign land, but you died without me near.
> *Ismene:* Wretched me! What fate awaits you and me, dear, orphaned as we are of our father?

Chorus: Cease from your grief, dear girls, since his end is blessed. No one is beyond the reach of evil.[149]

This commos plays the role of a ritual lamentation. For a dead person to be buried in accord with the ritual, he has to have a tomb and tears. Oedipus, who was born in Thebes, found a tomb in the foreign land of Colonus. For the rite to be complete, members of his family had to shed their tears; in this case, his two daughters.

When Aristotle uses the term *commos* to designate a particular part of tragedy, he has to empty the term of its original content in order to denote, in a broader sense, the whole dialogue sung by a character and the chorus within the spoken parts, and not only the songs of mourning. That is, in any case, the sense in which the term will be used here.[150]

Most of the sung dialogues between a character and the chorus that are inserted into the spoken parts are constructed in accord with the rules of the choral lyric, that is, in a strophic framework.[151] In this case, the passage in song is explained by the degree of emotion of the character who sings it, and not by any tradition. The proof of this is that the commoi in which the chorus sings are rare, even thought the chorus's traditional mode is song. In the major commoi, it is the heroines and heroes who sing their tragic destiny, whereas the chorus expresses itself in recitative or in speech. Given that these commoi are explained above all by the emotion of one of the two interlocutors, they are generally what are called semilyrical dialogues, that is, dialogues in which a single interlocutor sings.[152]

The Chorus's Song in the Commoi

When it receives bad news or finds itself in moving situations, the chorus may begin to sing in the course of an episode or the exodos, whereas the character on the stage expresses himself or herself in a lower register. For example, when at the beginning of the first episode it learns from Tecmessa the truth regarding its leader's madness, the chorus of Ajax's sailors begins to sing in a commos, while Tecmessa expresses herself in recitative.[153] Or again, in the exodos of *Electra*, when the women of the chorus hear Clytemnestra's cries coming from inside the palace as Orestes is killing her, they sing under the impact of emotion in a commos, whereas Electra continues to speak.[154] Here, the contrast emphasizes the chorus's agitation as much as Electra's bitter hatred. Such commoi, composed of a single strophe/antistrophe pair, are brief and stress an emotional moment in the action.[155]

Women's Song in the Commoi

Sung dialogues inserted into the spoken parts occur especially when the main character is suffering intense pain and is lamenting. It may seem to us more natural for a woman to sing her pain. Thus Antigone, when she appears for the last time before going to the underground prison where she will die, sings in a dialogue with the chorus of old men, at the beginning of the fourth episode. Here is the beginning of this commos:

> Citizens of my fatherland, see me setting out on my last journey, looking at my last sunlight, and never again. No, Hades who lays all to rest leads me living to Acheron's shore, though I have not had my due portion of the chant that brings the bride, nor has any hymn been mine for the crowning of marriage. Instead the lord of Acheron will be my groom.[156]

The fact that Antigone is singing is indicated not only by the lyrical rhythm and the Dorian coloring of the language; the text itself says that she is. In fact, when Creon leaves the palace to hasten Antigone's departure, he implicitly refers to her song when he tells the guards to take her away:

> Do you not know that dirges and wailing before death would never be given up, if it were allowed to make them freely? Take her away—now! And when you have enshrouded her, as I proclaimed, in her covered tomb, leave her alone.[157]

It is no accident that Creon uses the word "dirges." Being inside the palace, he heard Antigone's song, which resembles a swan song. And that explains why he rushes out to hasten the movement.

The chorus, for its part, does not at first sing but instead expresses itself in recitative during the first half of the commos. This difference highlights the character's song and her emotion by contrasting it with the less emotional diction of the chorus. Nonetheless, in the second part of the commos, both Antigone and the chorus sing. Thus there is a growth of the chorus's emotion and a passage from a semilyrical dialogue to a lyrical dialogue.[158] The chorus's growing emotion is not, however, a sign of pity for Antigone, but rather a sign of its rising indignation against the young woman's bold disregard of established authority.

Antigone's last sung complaints, sung in an epode in which she laments her solitude, are suddenly interrupted when Creon comes out of the palace. That is how the commos ends.

Men's Song in the Commoi

Commoi are not the prerogative of the heroines alone, quite the contrary. Heroes, even the most intransigent, such as Ajax or Heracles, sing when they have been overcome by an intense pain. This pain is physical in Heracles' case, and psychological in Ajax's case. The effect of the pain is comparable. The two heroes are depressed, this state being perceptible even in their posture. One of them, Ajax, is sitting on the ground, while the other, Heracles, is lying on a stretcher.

In the course of the first episode, as soon as Ajax sees his companions who form the chorus, he is overwhelmed by emotion and addresses them directly by singing in a commos.[159] As in the commos in *Antigone*, the main character's emotion is emphasized by the contrast between his singing and the chorus's diction. The contrast is even greater here, because the chorus speaks, whereas the character sings. Thus there is an inversion of the normal modes of diction. This example shows how the alternation of words and song can be employed against the convention to strengthen the expression of emotion. Nevertheless, the flexibility of the way it is performed gives this semilyrical dialogue between Ajax and the chorus the peculiarity of bringing in a third character. Although Ajax addresses only the chorus, Tecmessa sometimes speaks in the chorus's place.[160] In this commos, the dividing line runs not between what comes from the stage and what comes from the orchestra, to adopt Aristotle's terms, but rather between Ajax on the one hand, and his entourage, including the chorus and Tecmessa. The Aristotelian definition of the commos, in its generality, cannot account for the flexibility with which authors insert dialogue into lyrical frameworks depending on the particular situations.

Heracles' physical pain, like Ajax's psychological pain, is expressed through song. However, this song is adapted to the type of pain. Ajax's psychological pain remains constant throughout the lyrical dialogue. Heracles' physical pain, on the other hand, varies in intensity. At first, his pain is dormant, because the hero arrives asleep. Then it awakens, and awakens him. Thereupon he expresses himself in recitative.[161] Finally, when it becomes too excruciating, he cries out and sings in a rhythm that expresses the greatest agitation: two attacks of physical pain determine two sung passages that correspond to one another.[162] The sick man writhes in pain and expresses contradictory desires: first he asks his entourage to leave him alone, then to help him; but at the height of his pain, he twice expresses a wish to die. This is not, strictly speaking, a commos in accord with Aristotle's definition, because the chorus of young women—devastated by the appearance of the suffering hero whose return at the beginning of the tragedy had been announced as triumphal—does not say a word, except at the end of the commos to express its dismay at the hero's misfortunes.[163] The dialogue takes place with the two other characters present on the stage, the old man, whom some have suggested might be a doctor, and the young Hyllus, Heracles' son. Between Heracles' two sung parts, they speak about how to care for the sick man.[164] And yet it is not really a dialogue between Heracles and the two other characters, because although the sick man addresses his entourage, the two caregivers do not answer him but speak to each other, too preoccupied as they are to calm his agitation and to keep him there. Here, the contrast is thus between the hero who is writhing in pain and the two men who are watching over him and express themselves in a less emotional register, while the chorus remains silent.[165]

The structure of the commoi is thus malleable enough to be adapted to particular situations, so that general classifications cannot explain the subtlety of the way they are used in detail to "imitate" reality.

The Place of the Commoi in the Spoken Parts:
From Song to Speech or from Speech to Song

In these moments when the hero sings, the tragic poet plays on registers of diction (song, recitative, speech) not only in the commos between characters in dialogue with each other, but also in the evolution of the hero's state. We can observe two inverse developments. There are the heroes who sing and lament at the beginning before regaining their self-control and expressing themselves in speech; and there are, on the other hand, those who move from speech to song and lament at the end, after having lost an apparent self-control.

Ajax and Heracles belong to the first category. Ajax does not, of course, sing when he appears the first time. In reality, being in the grip of madness, he is no longer himself. His first real appearance comes when he has recovered his lucidity after having massacred the herds instead of his enemies, and it is then that he sings and laments in a commos with the chorus. This moving moment thus occurs at the beginning: a moment of resignation, of a desire to die to escape suffering and shame. Then, after the moans of pain that overwhelm him, the hero slowly and gradually regains his self-control. Then he moves from song to speech.[166] This shift is a reliable signal. Ajax's song in dialogue with the chorus is followed, after the lamentations, by two verses spoken by the chorus, and a long speech of about fifty verses, a sort of monologue in which the hero, now depending only on himself, moves from moaning to reflecting on his moaning, from a list of his misfortunes to a return to heroic values, that is, to his true nature, as the chorus notes at the end of his speech.

We find an analogous evolution in Heracles, even though the pain is not of the same kind and moves through stages corresponding to all the registers of diction. As we have seen, Heracles begins by expressing himself in recitative before beginning to sing when he is in the grip of two attacks of raging suffering caused by the poison that is eating away his flesh, and like Ajax, he calls for death to take him. The sung passage is ended by a formal procedure identical to that in *Ajax*. Two verses spoken by the chorus are followed by a long speech of more than sixty verses[167] in which Heracles enumerates with bitter irony his past and present trials, and at the very end recovers his nature as a hero who rights wrongs.[168] The only difference is that it is more difficult to master a physical pain than a psychological one. A third attack of the illness strikes Heracles in the course of his speech, which leads him to cry out and make a short change in rhythm that corresponds to a brief return to song within the speech,[169] as well as a brief desire for an immediate death. The choice of the rhythm and the mode of expression correspond, *grosso modo*, to the patient's temperature chart! We see how the tragic poet, while respecting the traditional codes, skillfully adapts the modalities of diction to the rhythms of the body and the mind.

Finally, the two heroes, Heracles and Ajax, go off to meet a freely accepted death.

Conversely, other heroes sing at the end of the tragedy when they are shattered by misfortune. In the tragedies in which the heroes move from happiness to unhappiness, to revert to Aristotle's expression,[170] they sing during their last appearance. The most famous example is Oedipus at the end of *Oedipus the King*. When he appears, his face bloody after putting out his eyes with the golden pins from Jocasta's robe, the spectacle is unbearable to see—the chorus begins to turn away with dread; it is also unbearable to hear. Oedipus's cries, which Tiresias had predicted at the beginning of the tragedy, ring out in a commos.[171] Everything elicits pity. The blood and song recall the scene in which Ajax, prostrated, faces the chorus, even though the scene in *Oedipus the King* is more moving because the hero is covered, not with the blood of the animals he has slaughtered in a moment of madness, but with the blood that is flowing from his own eyes, which he has deliberately put out. The sung cries of the two heroes echo each other. "Ah, Darkness, my light!" (*Ajax*, v. 394); "Oh horror of darkness that enfolds me" (*Oedipus the King*, vv. 1313ff.). The commos between the hero and the chorus is aimed at the same effect: highlighting the hero's emotion. Contrary to the usual case, the hero sings, and the chorus speaks.[172]

Even when the hero sings at the end of the tragedy, the intensity of the emotion may decrease. Oedipus's song is followed by a long speech in which the hero, exactly like Ajax,[173] reflects on his destiny before the plot takes over again in the form of a final dialogue between the hero and Creon.

On the other hand, at the end of *Antigone*, Creon—illustrating, like Oedipus, the hero who has fallen from happiness into unhappiness—remains overwhelmed by an increasing emotion. The dialogue in which he sings of his misfortunes occupies the whole last part of the tragedy.[174] This is a commos that is close to the etymological meaning of the term, because it takes place in the funereal context of intense lamentation.[175] He is lamenting the death of his son, whose body he is carrying, and he laments anew when he hears the news of the death of his wife, whose body he then sees. The construction of this commos is greatly admired by specialists in metrics. "We are stunned by an art that combines so much balance with an apparent freedom," Alphonse Dain declares.[176] Part of this apparent freedom comes from the fact that the commos includes the arrival of a new character emerging from the palace to announce a second death, which sets Creon to lamenting again. But this new arrival does not disturb the strophic framework of the commos, even though it is made more flexible by the insertion of brief spoken dialogues within the semilyrical dialogue.[177] Thus in his dialogue, Creon speaks three times in a single verse, addressing either the messenger or the chorus.[178] But the rest of the time he sings, and his song, in which the most emotional lyric rhythm is already dominant,[179] is highlighted by the continuous spoken verses of its two interlocutors. It is significant that the commos and also the tragedy—with the exception, of course, of the chorus's final reflection—ends with a final increase in Creon's emotion. After a spoken verse, he sings in the most agitated rhythm to signal his departure:

Lead me away, I beg you, a rash, useless man. I have murdered you, son, unwittingly, and you, too, my wife—the misery! I do not know which way I should look, or where I should seek support. All is amiss that is in my hands, and, again, a crushing fate has leapt upon my head.[180]

Unlike the true Sophoclean hero, who always emerges after a plunge into despair, Creon, who at the beginning of the tragedy appeared as a captain who has saved the ship of state tossed by the storm of war, notes the shipwreck of his family and his own shipwreck. He comes out staggering, crushed by a fate too heavy for him to bear.

This finale is all the more remarkable because *Antigone* is the only one of all Sophocles' extant tragedies that ends with a lyric dialogue in which emotion does not decline. Even in *Oedipus at Colonus*, where after Oedipus's death his two daughters sing their long threnody with the chorus, the emotion calms when Theseus enters for the last time. His first words are significant: "Cease your lament, children!"[181]

Such are the commoi inserted into the spoken parts that Aristotle defines as songs coming from the stage and from the chorus. From the examination of concrete examples it emerges that the Aristotelian definition, which is too general, cannot account for the subtlety and inventiveness with which Sophocles, starting from a relatively simple strophic architecture and dialogic structure, adapts the effects to each particular situation by means of multiple variations.[182] Nonetheless, these effects usually converge to highlight the suffering and desperate hero's emotional song to his or her entourage.

From Aristotle's Parts of the Tragedy to the Division into Scenes

More generally, although Aristotle's division of Greek tragedy into parts has its merits, it also has its limits. This traditional division, beyond which too few scholars venture, should not prevent us from analyzing tragedy by scenes; because the scene, which in French criticism is delimited by the entrance or exit of a character, is the minimal unit of any theatrical work. Even if in ancient Greek there is no word designating this reality, the tragic poet's instinct, better than Aristotle's philosophical perspective, organized the play into scenic sequences. The Greek tragic poet was all the more inclined to regard this division as important because the entrance and exit of characters were in part conditioned, as we have seen, by a constraint peculiar to Greek theater, namely its limitation to three actors. Thus in the presentation of the structure of each tragedy given here in an appendix, we have taken into account not only the Aristotelian divisions but also the division into scenes.[183]

Analysis by scenes, when it is performed on Greek theater, is often considered a complement inserted into the frameworks of Aristotelian analysis. This is justified when the frameworks are regular, that is, in the oldest of Sophocles' tragedies where the spoken parts—prologue, episodes, and exodos—form autonomous wholes separated from each other by sung parts, which are themselves autonomous, and in which the chorus remains alone in the visible space, with no characters onstage. Then the spoken parts form acts that can be divided into scenes. But the break between the spoken parts and the sung parts introduced a discontinuity that was sometimes awkward. In certain cases, the poet had to find a reason for making a character exit before the chorus's song and making him return immediately afterward. Thus in *Ajax*, Sophocles has Teucer leave at the end of the fourth episode on the pretext that he is going to prepare the burial of Ajax. Why? In reality, it is because room has to be made for the chorus, which is going to sing its fourth stasimon. In fact, immediately after the chorus's song, Teucer returns in a panic because he has seen Agamemnon hurrying toward them. The poet thus adds a small reversal in the action. In reality, it is a clever way of masking a constraint. In his following career, Sophocles would not hesitate to do away with the obstacle by having a character remain onstage during a sung part.[184] This happened gradually. In that respect, the comparison of the parodos in *Ajax*, *Women of Trachis*, and *Electra* is instructive. In *Ajax*, when the chorus enters the visible space, there is no one onstage. At the end of the prologue, the three characters leave: Ajax goes back into his house, Athena flies into the heavens, and Odysseus leaves through a lateral exit. When the chorus of sailors returns to the visible space to listen to the rumors spread by Odysseus, according to which their master is supposed to have massacred the Greeks' herds, it is alone and uneasily looks around for Ajax. Then the first episode begins with the arrival of Tecmessa, Ajax's concubine, who comes out of the house and confirms the rumors. Thus there is a clear scenic separation between the prologue, the parodos, and the first episode. The move from speech to song and from song to speech is thus accompanied each time by a change of scene, if the latter is defined as the sequence delimited by the entrance or exit of a character,

On the other hand, when the chorus of *Women of Trachis* enters the orchestra to find Deianira, who it knows is worried by Heracles' long absence, the stage is not empty. At the end of the prologue, Hyllus, Deianira's son, has gone to look for his father, but Deianira herself has remained on the stage. Nonetheless, during the whole duration of the chorus's song, Deianira remains silent, even though the chorus naturally addresses her in the second half of the parodos, offering her advice and asking her not to lose hope. It is only after the end of the song that Deianira addresses the chorus in speech, thus inaugurating the first episode. The song of the parodos continues to keep its autonomy, because the character who has remained onstage is still not participating in the action. But there is no break in scene between the parodos and the first episode, because no character enters between the two. Hence the Aristotelian division no longer corresponds to the division into scenes. The parodos and the beginning of the first episode form one and the same scene.[185]

The situation in *Electra* is entirely comparable, but an additional step is taken in the continuity between the prologue, the parodos, and the first episode. When the chorus of young women comes in, the heroine is already present, like Deianira in *Women of Trachis*. However, unlike *Women of Trachis*, no character exits at the end of the prologue, before the parodos. And especially, the chorus's song is no longer autonomous, because it has been replaced by a lyrical dialogue between the chorus and Electra. The character present onstage is no longer on the sidelines. The chorus becomes the equivalent of a character. It enters and addresses the character already onstage, who answers it. The dialogue, already lyrical in the parodos, becomes spoken at the beginning of the first episode. The continuity of the scene is thus even more remarkable than in *Women of Trachis*. The Aristotelian division between the parodos and the beginning of the first episode is blurred. It corresponds to a simple difference in diction in a long scene of dialogue between a character and the chorus. More generally, in Sophocles' tragedies from *Electra* on, the replacement of a choral song by a dialogue between the chorus and a character seeks to integrate the sung parts into the action, whether they are a parodos or a stasimon, and to establish scenic continuities over and above the Aristotelian divisions.[186]

Conversely, there are breaks in the action that escape Aristotelian analysis because they are situated within spoken parts considered as a whole. Then only scenic analysis allows us to perceive these breaks. There are in fact moments when the visible space remains empty for an instant during the performance of the spoken parts. These breaks occur when the chorus is not there, that is, when it has not yet entered or (and this is exceptional) when it has left. In *Electra*, the prologue, presented as continuous in the Aristotelian analysis, is characterized by an important break between two scenes. In the first scene, Orestes, Pylades, and the tutor enter from outside by the left-side entrance. Before the character whose laments they have heard comes out of the palace, they leave, on the advice of the tutor, even though Orestes is tempted to stay to find out who has been making these laments.[187] Thus between the exit of the characters at the end of the first scene and the beginning of the second scene marked by the entrance of Electra, the visible space remains empty for a brief period of time. This break in the middle of the prologue symbolizes the separation between the exterior world and the interior world.[188] The encounter between these two worlds will occur only much later in the tragedy, during the recognition scene between Orestes and Electra. A much more important break takes place during the third episode of *Ajax*, at the time when the chorus has abruptly left with Tecmessa to look for the hero. Between verses 813 and 814, in which the chorus announces its departure, and verse 815, when Ajax's last monologue begins, the Aristotelian analysis does not make it possible to discern the slightest discontinuity. We are in the middle of a spoken part without any change in the meter. And yet it is there that we find the break that is essential from the theatrical point of view. An exceptional change of place and setting occurs between the two segments: the spectator is transported from the place in front of Ajax's house to a deserted place where Ajax has buried his spear in the ground in order to commit suicide.[189]

So that is why the reading of a tragedy in terms of its scenes is an indispensable complement to the Aristotelian analysis.

Scenes, from Epic to Tragedy

Aristotle sees these tragic poets as the successors of the epic poets, while at the same time noting the differences between the two genres. According to him, the continuity consists in the imitation in verse of a serious subject, whereas the differences proceed above all from the mode of imitation: the epic proceeds by narrative; tragedy by representation. Aristotle adds a difference in the way time is used: the epic is not limited in time, whereas tragedy seeks to limit itself to a twenty-four-hour period. But there is another continuity that Aristotle did not point out, because he did not analyze the division of tragedies into scenes. In Sophocles, the clearest example is the sequence in *Ajax* where the hero, resolved to die in order to escape dishonor, refuses to be moved by his companion Tecmessa's pleas, and then addresses to his son what will be his last words.[190] Ever since antiquity, similarities have been seen with the passage in book 6 of the *Iliad*, commonly called "the farewells of Hector and Andromache," where Hector, before leaving for the combat that he will ultimately not survive, cannot allow Andromache to persuade him to remain, and addresses to his child what will also be his last words.[191] The ancient commentators were sensitive to parallels in expression.[192] But such reminiscences take on all their meaning only within an overall situation that is comparable: a man must leave to go toward death; a woman asks him to stay so as not to abandon her or his young child; the man cannot grant her request because he rejects dishonor; he then addresses his son (even though the child does not speak) because it is his son who must perpetuate the family's honor. The transposition from epic to tragedy is all the more natural because the characters' speeches are related to the direct style of the epic. Thus there is a parallelism between Andromache's speech to Hector in the epic and that of Tecmessa to Ajax in the tragedy. Even in gestures, the parallel is perceptible: the man takes the child in his arms when he addresses him and then hands him back to his wife, asking her to go inside. The epic model is present only to make the tragic poet's deliberate deviations more evident: a less human hero, who treats his wife more roughly, and who is also more prideful with his son. In vying with Homer, Sophocles shows a great deal of ingenuity. But isn't epic sweetness ultimately more attractive than tragic roughness?

The Typical Scenes in Greek Theater: The Messenger Scene

As a craftsman, Sophocles knows how to vary the rhythm of the performance by using scenes of differing length, and within scenes, by the rhythm of the communication. Let us set aside transition scenes and concentrate instead on the structure of the most important scenes. We will not discuss here the spectacular aspect of certain great scenes that were dealt with in the preceding chapter[193] but will instead emphasize the structure and rhythm of two major scenes typical of Greek theater, a scene providing information, the messenger scene, on the one hand, and a scene of action, the *agōn* scene, on the other hand.

The messenger scene is necessary to communicate to those who have remained in the visible space, and consequently also to the spectators, information about parts of the action that have taken place outside the visible space.[194] From the spatial point of view, these scenes can be divided into two large categories, depending on the place from which the messenger comes: those in which the character arrives through a side entrance to recount what is supposed to have occurred outside, and those in which the character comes through the frontal entrance to recount what has occurred inside the palace.[195] A single tragedy can belong to both of these categories. For example, in *Women of Trachis* Hyllus comes through a lateral entrance to inform his mother Deianira of the destructive effect of the tunic she has given Heracles, whereas the nurse comes out of the palace to announce Deianira's suicide.[196] But from the temporal point of view these two categories of scenes develop in accord with the same rhythm, that is, they have the same structure. It is in this sense that we can speak of a scene typical of tragedy.

The messenger scene begins with a rapid and relatively brief dialogue in which the personage who has remained in the visible space, whether it is the chorus or a character, questions the new arrival. Then the messenger relates, in one or two verses, the essence of the news. For example, Hyllus addressing Deianira:

Hyllus: Listen to me! You have killed your husband, my father—my father![197]

Or later on the nurse announcing to the chorus Deianira's suicide:

Deianira has departed on the last of all her journeys, departed without stirring a foot.[198]

In the introductory dialogue, the messenger also explains how he learned the news, to make his message credible. Thus Hyllus regarding Heracles' misfortune:

I have seen my father's overwhelming misfortune with my own eyes. I did not learn of it by hearsay.[199]

Similarly, the nurse regarding Deianira's suicide:

Chorus: Did you witness that violent deed, poor helpless one?
Nurse: I did, yes, since I was standing close by.[200]

Then in response to a last question by the person receiving him, the messenger develops his message in a long speech before the scene ends with the reaction of the person who has heard the news.

Making the spectators relive through verbal art an action that took place elsewhere, the messenger's account becomes a play within a play of which the audience was very fond. It assumed an epic dimension, especially when the event reported took place in the exterior space in the presence of a crowd. In this respect, we can contrast the account of Heracles' illness in *Women of Trachis* with the account of Deianira's suicide. Whereas Deianira commits suicide inside the palace, in the solitude of the nuptial bedchamber, it is during a solemn sacrifice before his whole army that Heracles is struck by the poisoned tunic his wife has given him.

The bravura scene constituted by the messenger's report is not a peculiarity of Sophocles' art. The oldest extant tragedy, Aeschylus's *The Persians*, includes the messenger's report announcing to the Persian queen Xerxes' defeat in the naval battle at Salamis and then on land on an island in harbor, and finally his disastrous retreat over the River Strymon in Thrace. In three long speeches, the messenger reports with epic amplitude and realistic precision the series of catastrophes that struck the Persian expedition. There is no doubt that the technique of the messenger's account had already reached perfection.[201] This observation usefully reminds us that Greek tragedy was not born at the time of the first extant tragedies. What is for us a beginning was then already a fulfillment.

But one of Sophocles' originalities is to have developed with great daring what can be called the "misleading report." This kind of report appears chiefly in tragedies where a character is entrusted with a mission that involves deception. The most famous one is that of the tutor in *Electra* recounting the death of Orestes.[202] In the corresponding tragedy by Aeschylus, *The Libation Bearers*, Orestes' death is falsely announced, but it is not the subject of a narrative. We have no idea how this death was produced.[203] Neither is there any deceptive report in Euripides' *Electra*. But in Sophocles the tutor, whom Orestes had briefly instructed regarding how to announce his death—"Tell them, and affirm it with your oath, that Orestes has perished by a fatal chance, hurled at the Pythian games from his speeding chariot" (*Electra*, vv. 46–50)—vividly develops, in a speech of exceptional length (more than forty-eight verses), a little tragedy in which the hero moves from happiness to unhappiness: having won all the contests on the first day of the Delphian games, the following day Orestes seeks to complete his triumph by winning the chariot race. It is an exciting race in which the hero miraculously escapes a general smash-up before colliding with a boundary stone on the last turn and suffering a fatal fall. Why such a long account? The spectator is well aware that the speech is deceptive, because he has already seen Orestes. Is it so that the audience can better appreciate the contrasted reactions of the mother and the sister? Isn't it also because Sophocles knows that the spectator may feel a purer pleasure in responding to a moving and tragic account, even though he knows that it is fictitious? And isn't it also, for a sophisticated part of the audience, a pure intellectual pleasure to savor the tutor's brilliant inventiveness . . . and that of his creator? Even as he innovated with respect to Aeschylus, Sophocles connected up with a tradition, that of the *Odyssey*, in which Odysseus's deceptive speech given to avoid being unmasked when he learns that he has returned to his homeland delights a privileged auditor, the goddess

Athena.[204] This is also an observation that makes us aware of the nature of innovation in the Greek tragic poets: it often consists in distinguishing oneself from one's rivals by associating one's work with a an older literary model. The innovation is at the same time a return to tradition.

After the central nucleus constituted by the messenger's report, the last part of the scene concerns the effects of the message on the characters. Two main cases can be distinguished. Sometimes there is temporary good news: for example, the announcement of Heracles' victorious return in *Women of Trachis*. It leads those present, Deianira and the young women in the chorus, to rejoice;[205] but this joy is short-lived. Most of the time, it is bad news that is announced. In *Women of Trachis*, after Heracles' victory, we learn about his illness, and then Deianira's death. Each time, the news elicits intense pain, which is manifested either in lamentations, or conversely, by silent departure. Deianira goes away without saying a word after listening to the account of Heracles' illness,[206] whereas the chorus sings in a commos after the news of Deianira's suicide.[207] A third case is subtler: the news announced is ambiguous, because some people see it as good and others see it as bad. In *Electra*, the announcement of Orestes' death provides Sophocles with an opportunity to contrast the reactions of the mother and the sister: Clytemnestra's triumphant relief on learning that her son, whose return she had been fearing, is dead, and Electra's irremediable despair at losing a brother whose return she had been awaiting. And since the news is false, the contrast is accompanied by a powerful effect of tragic irony.[208]

The Typical Scenes in Greek Theater: The Agōn Scene

Unlike the messenger scene, the scene representing a struggle between two characters, called an agōn scene (*agōn* is a Greek word meaning "confrontation") does not yet appear in Aeschylus in its definitive form. These conflictual scenes are not peculiar to Sophocles. They are also found in Euripides. However, since it is used by Sophocles in his oldest tragedy, *Ajax*, he is generally regarded as its true creator.[209]

This kind of scene is nonetheless part of an intellectual context in which agonistic rhetoric developed in the course of the fifth century under the influence of trials (judicial rhetoric) and oratorical competitions in the popular assembly (political rhetoric). It was theorized by professors of eloquence called "sophists," particularly by one of them, Protagoras, who was known for having said that there were two opposite theses for every subject. This technique of the agōn invaded literary genres, not only the theater, but also history, notably in Thucydides' work, where politicians' antilogical speeches present the same situation from an opposite point of view. In the theater, the agōn scene also exists in comedy, but it assumes a different form and another meaning. In comedy, it is a struggle between the chorus and a character, in which the oratorical contest is often preceded by a physical brawl, whereas in tragedy it is a confrontation between two characters, the chorus serving as judge or witness.

Although the organization of these scenes in tragedy is not as formal as the scenes in comedy, an agōn scene in tragedy is constructed around a kernel uniting two movements with contrasting rhythms: a first movement that is slow and rhetorical, in which two interlocutors confront one another in two lengthy speeches, each of which is followed by a short reflection by the chorus, and a second movement that is more rapid, in which the confrontation is transformed into a lively dialogue that usually leads to replies verse by verse (stichomythia) or even half verses (antilabai). As early as *Ajax* we already find a typical example. On the question of Ajax's burial, an initial debate opposes Teucer, the dead man's half brother, representing the family, and Menelaus, representing public authority.[210] The confrontation has all the characteristics of an agōn scene. When Teucer tries to take Ajax's body away to bury it, Menelaus comes to prevent him from doing so. After a brief exchange of five verses, in which Menelaus forbids the burial and Teucer asks him why, Menelaus sets forth his point of view in a speech thirty-nine verses long. The chorus punctuates this speech with two verses. Teucer replies in a speech twenty-five verses long, which is also punctuated by a two-verse remark by the chorus. The rhythm abruptly accelerates in a second part, where the confrontation between the two characters takes place in a verse-for-verse dialogue twenty-two verses long, then is broadened at the end of the scene by two longer replies of eight and nine verses before concluding with speeches of two verses. We are counting verses here only to give an idea of the quest for balances and breaks in the rhythm. This is a face-to-face encounter between two characters, the chorus intervening only twice with two verses to render its judgment after each opposing speech. The chorus's judgment is, moreover, balanced not only in its form but also in its content. It brings out, for one party as for the other, what is wise or just in each, and what is excessive. But the two characters pay hardly any attention to the chorus's intervention, apart from a subtle difference: Menelaus proudly ignores the Ajax's sailors, whereas Teucer addresses them when they criticize his adversary, but does not mention their criticisms when he is the object of them.[211] The two adversaries are thus essentially confined in their confrontation. Within this collision, Sophocles, while varying the rhythm, maintains the balances, even if it is pointless to seek too systematically to find mathematical proportions. In fact, the two speeches are not of equal length, but the dialogue that follows them is almost perfectly balanced. The essential effect is produced by the break in the rhythm at the center of the scene, where after the two long speeches, the tension is suddenly increased in a dialogue in which the characters oppose one another verse for verse. At the point where the change takes place, there is no transition; and this is deliberate.

These agōn scenes in which each character presents his point of view on an important issue lead never to a reconciliation, but instead to an exacerbation of sensibilities and increasing anger before a break and a departure. Thus it is not only the formal structure that characterizes the agōn scenes in Sophocles, but also a crisis within a world that should be united. Here, the quarrel between Teucer and Menelaus opposes allies in the Greek camp at Troy, with the result that the internal divisions make people forget the external enemy, who is ultimately less odious than the internal enemy. Elsewhere, the discord is within the family itself. For example, in *Antigone*, it sets a father, Creon, and his son, Haemon, at odds in an exactly analogous formal framework in which the symmetries are even clearer. After an initial exchange of two sets of four verses, there are two long opposing speeches of almost the same length (forty-two verses for Creon's speech, forty-one verses for Haemon's speech). Each of the two speeches is punctuated by two verses by the chorus, and the whole is followed by a rapid dialogue in the form of a long stichomythia that ends with a final exchange of two sets of four verses. Thus the correspondence between the initial exchange and the final exchange introduces an additional symmetry. On the other hand, the change between the two parts is somewhat less abrupt in the scene in *Antigone* than it is in the scene in *Ajax*. Two exchanges of two verses precede the stichomythia.[212] Such resemblances in the composition, even if variations in detail are always possible, are obviously not a matter of chance. As for the cycle of anger, it is even more spectacular in *Antigone* than it is in *Ajax*. The outcome of the two scenes is identical: the discussion ends with a departure in the grip of anger, that of Menelaus in *Ajax* and that of Haemon in *Antigone*. But the beginning is different: in Ajax, relations were tense from the moment Menelaus arrived. The latter addresses Teucer brusquely, whereas in *Antigone* Haemon presents himself humbly before his father. The conflict therefore does not flare up at the same time in the two scenes. In *Ajax*, the rising anger and violence are already visible in each of the speeches, and the chorus stresses what was excessive on both sides. In *Antigone*, on the other hand, the father's speech is an affirmation of authority in which the chorus finds nothing objectionable. The son's reply, which is clever but courteous, is also approved by the chorus. It is only starting with the rapid dialogue that the latent conflict is revealed and violence explodes, leading once again to a break between father and child. Thus the second agōn scene makes explicit not only a conflict, but also its genesis.

To this basic schema Socrates added elements that lent more scope to the agōn scene without changing its dramatic profile. That is the case in the scene between the seer Tiresias and Oedipus in *Oedipus the King*.[213] At its center, we recognize the two elements that constitute the nucleus of an agōn scene: first the two speeches of the king and the seer, separated by a four-line comment by the chorus; then the rapid-fire dialogue, partly in the form of stichomythia.[214] But instead of being preceded by a brief introductory dialogue, as in the two preceding scenes, the two speeches come when the scene is already well underway. Oedipus has received Tiresias with great respect in a long speech of sixteen verses;[215] then, Tiresias's refusal to speak during a long, sixty-four verse speech makes the king's anger rise, generating in turn the seer's anger and a first wave of revelations.[216] The opposed speeches thus correspond to the culmination of Oedipus's wrath. As for the rapid dialogue that follows the two speeches, it does not conclude the scene, even though Tiresias decides to leave and Oedipus does not hold him back. Then comes a final, sixteen-line speech in which the seer, before departing, makes a second wave of revelations. The nucleus of the agōn scene is thus inserted into a larger whole.

Certain modifications of the expected schema also create surprises. For instance, the scene in *Women of Trachis* in which Hyllus, Deianira's son, comes to tell his mother about Heracles' illness can be seen as a truncated agōn scene. Of course, as we have seen, it is first of all a messenger scene. Like a messenger, Hyllus delivers a long speech about the effect of the poison on Heracles' body and mind. But this speech is not solely informative; it is also, from the outset, an indictment. The son accuses his mother of murdering his father through the effect of her poisoned gift. After the son's speech, we therefore expect the accused to answer the accusation. That is the significance of the chorus's questions when Deianira exits without making any reply:

> Why do you leave in silence? You must know
> that silence pleads the cause of your accuser.[217]

Deianira's silent departure thus produces a surprise that is all the more impressive because it breaks off a scene that could have been developed by a clash between the son and the mother, like the scene in *Antigone* in which the son clashes with his father. Cutting it short upsets all the rhetorical frameworks by doing away with the second speech and the rapid dialogue. But Deianira's silence will turn out to be beneficial for her memory. After her suicide, Hyllus will realize his mistake and defend his mother when he speaks to his father.

Another surprise effect can proceed from an outcome contrary to expectations, for instance, from a conflict that does not lead to a break. That is what happens in the last agōn scene in *Ajax*. One particularity of the end of this tragedy is the succession of two agōn scenes. This is unique in Greek tragedy. We have already chosen the first scene in which Teucer and Menelaus come to grips as a typical example of an agōn scene. It is followed by a second agōn scene after a pause introduced by a choral song. Formally, the organization of the second agōn scene seems identical to the first: it begins with two long speeches, one by Agamemnon, the other by Teucer, each speech being followed by a two-line comment by the chorus, and then a rapid dialogue including a series of verse-for-verse exchanges. But what differs in the second case is that at the expected turning point between the two major parts of an agōn scene, namely the long speeches and the rapid dialogue, an event occurs, the arrival of a new character, Odysseus. We can admire the way Sophocles has inserted this arrival into the very structure of the agōn. He takes advantage of the two verses of the chorus's ritual intervention after the second long speech to mention Odysseus's arrival:

Lord Odysseus, you arrive at the right time, if mediation, not division, is your purpose in coming.[218]

The rapid dialogue that follows is also given a new twist. It does not continue, as expected, the face-to-face encounter between the two adversaries; instead, one of the two interlocutors continues to speak and addresses the new arrival. The dialogue then takes place between Agamemnon and Odysseus, Teucer remaining silent. This change ought in principle to lower the tension, because Odysseus is a friend of Agamemnon's. But at the same time Odysseus unexpectedly defends the dead man and thus appears as Teucer's ally. The argument will thus retain a lively, rapid rhythm before arriving at a resolution. Odysseus finally succeeds in persuading Agamemnon to authorize Ajax's burial, though Agamemnon is not reconciled with his enemy.

Thus we have an example of an agonistic structure that ends not with a break but with a placation. Such a change in the dramatic profile was possible only because the entrance of a character was inserted into a preestablished framework. The character's arrival is all the more unexpected. By dissociating in an unusual way the agonistic framework from the scenic division, Sophocles creates surprise by having the character who resolves the drama intervene at the moment when he is least expected to do so.[219]

From the Structure of the Scene to the Structure of the Tragedy

The analysis of messenger scenes and agōn scenes has provided us with an example showing that there are structures based on a change of rhythm that can be used to produce typical scenes (these structures not being peculiar to Sophocles), that these structures can be varied to adapt them to particular situations, and finally that they are sometimes deliberately twisted by Sophocles to create unexpected situations.

The analysis of the typology of scenes could be transposed to the whole of tragedies. Just as certain scenes include a basic structure that remains recognizable despite the variations, there are also whole tragedies that develop through major stages that can be compared on the basis of an analogous initial situation. Just as we speak of agōn scenes and messenger scenes, we can also speak of supplication tragedies and return tragedies.

The Supplication Tragedies

The oldest extant supplication tragedy is by Aeschylus and is entitled precisely *The Suppliants*.[220] The fifty Danaids, who have come from Egypt accompanied by their father, Danaus, take refuge in a sanctuary in the Argive countryside. They are pursued by the fifty sons of Egypt, who want to marry them by force. Before the arrival of their enemies, the Danaids supplicate the king of Argos,

Pelasgus; struggle to resist the aggressors' violence; and are finally rescued by the king of the country, who drives off the intruders and welcomes the Danaids in his city. This tragedy has the major stages of what constitutes a supplication tragedy. These major stages correspond to the relations between the three elements that compose the tragedy, the suppliant, the person supplicated, and the pursuer. At the outset, the suppliant is a foreigner—or a group of foreigners—who comes into a city from outside, takes refuge in a sacred space, asks the residents for their hospitality, and begs to be protected and integrated into that city. The supplication gives rise to a dramatic tension between the suppliant and the person supplicated until the latter agrees to become the suppliant's protector. But what changes the situation is the arrival of a representative of the pursuers who has come to tear the suppliant away from the sacred place. The situation is very tense and generally ends with a threat of violence or with the aggressor's use of violence against the suppliant. Finally the protector hurries in to oppose the aggressor, first through words, then through action. The tragedy ends with the aggressor's defeat and the integration of the suppliant into the city of his or her protector.

Sophocles returns to this schema in his last tragedy, *Oedipus at Colonus*.[221] This tragedy retraces the progressive steps in the heroization of Oedipus, but this heroization takes place in the context of a supplication tragedy. The suppliant element is represented by Oedipus accompanied by Antigone. They are foreigners exiled from Thebes who have come to the deme of Colonus, a territory of the city of Athens. The supplicated group is constituted by the successive representatives of Colonus and of Athens. They appear in accord with a subtle gradation: first a simple resident of Colonus, then the elderly administrators of the deme of Colonus forming the chorus, and finally the king of the city of Athens, Theseus. It is with the chorus that the scene of supplication proper takes place, the scene in which the suppliant's request arouses the reticence of the group supplicated and leads to a tension that has ultimately to be overcome by the suppliant's arguments. The element of the aggressor is represented by Creon, who has come from the city of Thebes as its ambassador. His task is to take Oedipus away and bring him back to the boundary of Theban territory, where, according to new oracles, he is to ensure the triumph of the side that he joins in the struggle for power being waged between his two sons. The scene of violence in which the aggressor attacks the suppliant sees Creon carry off Antigone, after having abducted Ismene, and then threaten Oedipus himself. The chorus's call for help causes the most important of the persons supplicated, King Theseus, to intervene. He confronts the pursuer verbally in an agōn scene[222] and then with his effective action puts an end to the pursuer's violence and returns Oedipus's two daughters to him. The suppliant then expresses his gratitude to his protector. A new development is produced by the arrival of Polynices, who has come, like Creon, to persuade Oedipus to return and support his party. This sequence inverts the roles. Polynices presents himself as a suppliant and Oedipus becomes the one who is supplicated. But the father remains intransigent and rejects his son, whom he sends away. The end of the tragedy comes about through the exile's integration into his new city. This integration takes the particular form of Oedipus's heroization in a death in which, in accord with a reversal announced by the oracles, the suppliant becomes a protector of the city. Far from being artificially imposed from outside, this dramatic schema sheds considerable light on the development of *Oedipus at Colonus*.

The Return Tragedies

In the case of return tragedies, the situation is a little more complex. Any tragedy in which a hero returns to his homeland after a more or less lengthy absence should be considered a return tragedy. However, we must distinguish between two different types of return tragedy: the return of the victorious king after a long absence that ends tragically, and the return of the young prince who has come to avenge his dead father and reconquer power.

The oldest extant tragedy illustrating the first type is Aeschylus's *Agamemnon*, in which the king, having returned to Argos after his victory at Troy, falls into the trap laid by his wife, Clytemnestra, and her lover Aegisthus. The spectator sees the triumphant hero move suddenly from happiness to unhappiness. In Sophocles' theater, one tragedy belongs to this type: *Women of Trachis*, where the hero Heracles, after a long absence, returns following his victory over Eurytus and also falls victim to his wife, Deianira's, ruse—whose fatal result is this time involuntary. A comparison of these two tragedies is pertinent, even though they do not belong to the same myth.[223] To be sure, the development of *Women of Trachis* differs from that of *Agamemnon* in several ways. However, the obligatory stages or scenes are comparable. On the one hand, the absent hero's return does not take place at the beginning of the tragedy, but after a period of waiting.[224] On the other hand, the arrival of a messenger who announces the victorious return precedes the arrival of the victor himself.[225] Finally, the victor does not return alone. He is accompanied by a captive whom the queen has to accept into her home. The scene where Deianira allows her rival Iole to enter is a memory of the scene in which Clytemnestra brings her rival Cassandra into her home.[226] But Sophocles dissociated the captive's return from that of the king. In Aeschylus, the king returns triumphant with his captive, and both of them fall victim to a trap laid by his wife with the help of her lover. In the end, the murderers are triumphant, despite the chorus's opposition. For his part, Sophocles has Heracles' captive arrive at the same time as the messenger and delays the warrior's arrival: he does not appear until his wife's trick has already done its unintended damage far away. Thus it is a hero who is mortally wounded but still alive whom the spectator sees. Nevertheless, his wife, far from being exultant, commits suicide after learning of the disaster that she has involuntarily caused. As for the captive, she escapes the tragedy. Several of these variations, despite an identical initial situation, are due to the fact that the character of the unfaithful wife in Aeschylus is transformed by Sophocles into a faithful wife. Nonetheless, in Sophocles' *Women of Trachis* as in Aeschylus's *Agamemnon*, the victorious hero who has come home with a captive after a long absence dies a victim of his wife's ruse—even though Deianira is the opposite of Clytemnestra. Doesn't the permanence of the structures allow us to understand that an excess of good feelings can lead to the same tragic result as bad feelings?

The second large group of return tragedies groups together the tragedies in which the hero's mission is to avenge his father and to regain the power that has been confiscated by usurpers. In the extant tragedies, the typical example is Aeschylus's *The Libation Bearers*. In Sophocles' theater, the play that belongs to this group is his *Electra*.[227] The comparison of the structure of these two tragedies is all the more appropriate because this time they deal with the same myth. Whereas, in the first group of return tragedies, the king's return is delayed and first announced by a messenger, in the second group the legitimate prince appears at the very beginning of the tragedy. Orestes, accompanied by his friend Pylades, is already present in the prologue in both *Electra* and in *The Libation Bearers*. Since it is given that Orestes returns secretly, the tragic poet must present successively and separately those who come from outside and those who live in the palace. But in the palace there is a contrast between the friends who are awaiting Orestes' return and the enemies on whom vengeance must be taken. The encounter with the friendly party takes place in the form of a recognition scene, whereas the encounter with the enemy party leads to the avenging murder. In *Electra*, as in *The Libation Bearers*, a recognition scene between Orestes and Electra takes place before vengeance is taken.[228] As for the vengeance itself, it takes place through a ruse that is fundamentally identical: the false news of Orestes' death. And once Orestes has in this way been able to get into the palace, he acts and kills his mother. Of course, unlike the recognition scene, the murder scene is not witnessed by the audience. It occurs inside the palace.

Nevertheless, Sophocles made variations even when he was reworking these general schemas.[229] Sophocles presents the exterior world and the interior world separately and then establishes a disequilibrium by privileging the interior world. In fact, after a single scene introducing Orestes, he prolongs the introduction of Electra over four scenes. First we see her alone, then in her relations with her entourage in the course of a triptych that begins with her relations with her sister Chrysothemis, whose position is intermediary between the friends and the enemies, and ends with the conflict with her enemy, her mother, Clytemnestra. The result is not only that interest is focused on the character of Electra, as has often been pointed out, but also that the interior world is dramatized. In Aeschylus, Electra never meets Clytemnestra. On the other hand, Sophocles eliminates the unbearable face-to-face encounter between the son and the mother in the visible space before the murder.[230] Sophocles' tragedy is thus more intimate in that it unveils incessant family quarrels inside the palace.

This imbalance also results in the recognition scene and the revenge being delayed. Moreover, these two moments, which are so clearly distinguished in Aeschylus, who begins with the recognition scene before setting forth the plan for revenge and its realization, are more subtly mixed in Sophocles. The plan for revenge is presented at the outset, long before the recognition scene, and the beginning of its realization, by having the tutor enter the palace to announce the false news of Orestes' death, also precedes the recognition scene. Such changes are connected with what might be called the technique of doubling.

The Technique of Doubling and New Developments in the Plot

As compared with Aeschylus, Sophocles doubled the characters coming from the outside in his *Electra*. Aeschylus still had only one active character, Orestes, because his friend Pylades remained silent except for one brief, exceptional remark.[231] While retaining Pylades as a silent character, Sophocles doubles the active element by introducing the tutor, who has accompanied Orestes during his exile. From the outset, Sophocles asserts his originality with respect to Aeschylus and creates a surprise by allowing this new character to speak at the beginning of the tragedy. We know how important the person who speaks first in a tragedy was considered, at least by some actors.[232]

This doubling of characters leads to a doubling of the action. The realization of the vengeance takes place in two stages. Whereas in Aeschylus characters coming from the outside enter the palace all at once, in the form of two Phocian travelers who report Orestes' death, in Sophocles they enter in two stages, because he has two active characters. First the tutor enters and announces the death of Orestes in a long speech; then Orestes enters, accompanied by Pylades, bringing concrete proof—the funerary urn that is supposed to contain Orestes' ashes—to confirm the news. This twofold arrival necessarily leads to a doubling of the Electra's reactions of despair, because she is present each time, and consequently to a doubling of emotion.

We can speak of a technique here, because the doubling also applies to the interior world. Just as Sophocles added a new character accompanying Orestes, he gives Electra a sister, Chrysothemis, in accord with a technique that he had already perfected in his *Antigone*, where Ismene was both the double and the opposite of Antigone. The introduction of this new character not only makes it possible to establish a striking contrast between the two sisters in two scenes in which they confront one another, but also to double the recognition scene. In Aeschylus, Electra's discovery of signs of Orestes on the tomb leads to the recognition. Sophocles transposes this discovery to Chrysothemis in an initial scene where the Aeschylean idea of recognition by means of a lock of hair on the tomb is adopted, but fails: Chrysothemis's true deduction regarding Orestes' presence is rejected by Electra, who has already been deceived by the false news of Orestes' death. The actual recognition takes place in a second original scene, the one with the urn that is supposed to contain Orestes' ashes. This doubling leads to a new development in the plot with Chrysothemis's passage from joy to despair, followed by Electra's passage from despair to joy. These reversals serve above all to increase the surprise of the spectator, and especially the cultivated spectator who, remembering Aeschylus, shares in Chrysothemis's joy before being dismayed to see error triumph, while at the same time being amused by the cleverness with which Sophocles pays tribute to Aeschylus . . . and bids him farewell. For Sophocles, it is ultimately a way of enriching the microcosm of his characters.

CHAPTER IX

The Characters

....

In Aristotle's definition of tragedy, though the action is the essential part, because tragedy is defined first of all as the imitation of an elevated action that forms a whole, the characters come immediately afterward in order of importance, because this action is realized not through the intermediary of a narrative, as in epic, but through that of characters who act. That is the originality peculiar to theater as a genre. However, still according to Aristotle, the characters in action are necessarily defined by what they are and what they think, by their character (*ethos*) and their intelligence (*dianoia*),[1] because these are the two causes that determine their actions and therefore their success or failure. But these two fundamental aspects of the characters are not given in advance, as might be possible in a narrative; in the theater, they can be revealed only through characters' decisions and declarations. And since in his *Poetics* Aristotle does not limit himself to analyzing the tragic genre but instead seeks to offer advice to future authors of tragedies, he issues rules regarding the ethos of the characters: they must be superior to ordinary mortals, in conformity with their natural or social condition, and lifelike and coherent from one end of the tragedy to the other. This kind of abstract analysis may not be the best way to approach Sophocles' characters; but it was one of the ways of interpreting Greek theater and one of the points of reference for the creation or the criticism of French theater in the classical period.[2]

Characters as They Should Be

It is in Aristotle's poetics that we find the famous formula in which Sophocles, speaking of his characters, said that "he portrayed people as they ought to be and Euripides portrayed them as they are."[3] La Bruyère transposed this formula in his comparison between Corneille and Racine:

> Corneille enthralls us by his characters and ideas; Racine's coincide with ours; the one represents men as they ought to be, the other as they are. There is in the first more of what we admire and what we ought even to imitate; and in the second more of what we perceive in others or feel within ourselves. Corneille elevates, surprises, controls and instructs us; Racine pleases, affects, moves

and penetrates us. The former employs the most beautiful, the most noble, and the most commanding arguments; the latter depicts the most praiseworthy and the most refined passions. . . . Corneille is more moral, Racine more natural. The one seems to imitate Sophocles, the other Euripides.[4]

Even though La Bruyère makes no reference to Aristotle's *Poetics*, he owes to it the best-known formula in his famous parallel between Corneille and Racine, or more exactly he ultimately owes it to Sophocles, since Aristotle is reporting Sophocles' judgment on his characters as compared to those of Euripides. La Bruyère's sentence seems to be a simple translation, even though the Greek verb *poiein*, which means "create" or "represent," is rendered as *peindre* ("paint"); but the translation is easily understood in the Aristotelian perspective, in which tragic creation is imitation and "the poet represents life, as a painter does or any other maker of likenesses."[5]

The context in the *Poetics*, where Aristotle reports Sophocles' judgment on his characters as compared with those of Euripides, is worth examining more closely. In that way we can respond to what might be seen as errors on the part of the authors; Sophocles' statement is given by Aristotle as an example of a response to a criticism. This criticism is that Sophocles' representation of his characters is not in accord with the truth.[6] It is based on the idea, probably widespread in the second half of the fifth century BCE, according to which the work of art should conform to reality. Euripides himself, in Aristophanes' comedy *The Frogs*, where he defends the merits of his theater as compared with that of Aeschylus, boasts of having represented people of all social statuses and ages, and of having introduced onstage affairs of everyday life that everyone is in a position to assess.[7] Art exists because it can be compared with reality. It is in a response to such a realist conception of art that Sophocles' formula is situated. It asserts a gap between art and reality in the creation of characters, a gap that is justified by reference to an ideality. But in Aristotle this reference to an ideality becomes a requirement for any creation of a tragic character, which must, according to him, be better than reality. "Tragedy," he declares, "is a representation of men better than ourselves."[8] Even characters consumed by anger must be remarkable. For that very reason, a tragic character is defined by opposition to the comic character, who is worse than people are in reality. Aristotle has transformed into a rule what was in Sophocles only a response to an objection. The philosopher's admiration for Sophocles' conception of his characters is founded on reason. It is therefore not surprising that when Aristotle chose concrete examples to point out the flaws in the realization of characters he took them from Euripides' works, and not from those of Sophocles.[9]

Sophocles' reputation for having composed characters superior to the average human has remained intact since antiquity. Aelius Aristides, a Greek rhetorician of the Second Sophistic, in a speech in which he defends Pericles against Plato's unjust accusation of having make Athenians loquacious,[10] sees Sophocles as being to theater what Pericles was to politics, in contrast to Euripides, who was accused, notably by Aristophanes, of having accustomed the Athenians to talking too much:

> I see that Sophocles, whose words are so sweet, has never had the reputation of exciting Athenians to loquacity, because, in my opinion, he sought above all majesty and presented characters [ethe] superior to the majority of men.

In this assessment made five centuries after Aristotle, whatever might have been subjective in Sophocles' judgment of his own characters has disappeared. It has even become the defining feature of the characters in his theater. In Aelius Aristides, even more clearly than in Aristotle, the point under discussion is clear: the creation of characters is not solely an ethical question; it is not limited to the conformity or deviation between the picture and the reality, as in painting, but also implies a moral and political choice insofar as the creation of characters has, for the spectators assembled in the theater of Dionysus, consequences comparable to those that politicians' speeches have for the people assembled on the Pnyx. The analogy is all the more natural because the audience was substantially the same.

The Characters in Their Context

This Aristotelian approach to the characters is in danger of giving priority to heroes and heroines—for instance, Philoctetes, Oedipus, Antigone, and Electra—of seeing them and nothing else. It may tend to emphasize what is remarkable in them, their energy and their solitude in misfortune, whether that solitude is imposed on them or desired by them, ignoring all the ties woven with their entourages, ties of friendship or of hate, and their accidental meetings with so-called minor characters. In short, it may tend to ignore everything that is familiar or everyday but is not necessarily trivial. The tragic character does not exist in isolation but is revealed through his or her relations with other characters. It is not that Aristotle's analysis completely neglects this relational perspective. But the passage in the *Poetics* where it is discussed has not attracted much attention. Here it is:

> As to the question whether anything that has been said or done is morally good or bad, this must be answered not merely by seeing whether what has actually been done or said is noble or base, but by taking into consideration also the man who did or said it, and seeing to whom he did or said it, and when and for whom and for what reason; for example, to secure a greater good or to avoid a greater evil.[11]

The assessment of a tragic character does not depend solely on the absolute value of the character's words or his or her acts outside of any context. That is a way of setting aside criticisms in the name of absolute moral criteria, as Plato did. Poetics is not identical with either ethics or politics.[12] Assessment must take into account variables, some of which are related to the tragic action: the point in the action when the character speaks or acts has its importance, and so does the impact of his or her conduct on the course of the action. But other variables are more directly connected with the characters: we have to take into account the character who speaks or acts and the character to whom he or she speaks or on whom the character acts; today, we would refer to these as the sender and the receiver. It is too bad that Aristotle limited himself to enumerating all these variables without providing a commentary or an example. Nonetheless, regarding the relation between a character's words and his or her nature, another passage in the *Poetics* can shed light on what Aristotle meant, even though the problem is not exactly the same. In his theory, inherited from Sophocles, that tragic characters must be better than they are in reality, Aristotle remarks that "even a woman is 'good' and so is a slave, although it may be said that a woman is an inferior thing and a slave beneath consideration."[13] When Sophocles had a slave speak he took precautions to avoid offending against social conventions, while at the same time showing how the slave he had created as a tragic character might be worthy of esteem. For example, at the beginning of *The Women of Trachis*, the noble Deianira, Heracles' wife, is accompanied by a slave whom the list of dramatis personae identifies as a "slave nurse." Here are her first words, after Deianira has described, in a long initial speech, her fears concerning the prolonged absence of her husband, about whom she has received no news:

> Queen Deianira, many times have I seen you bewailing Heracles' departure and weeping bitter tears of lamentation. But now, if it is proper that a slave should teach free people, I will speak up for you: since you have such a multitude of children, why not send one of them to seek your husband? Hyllus should be the first to go, if he has any care about his father's welfare. But here he is, running fast toward the house! If you believe my words were spoken rightly, now is the time to try them on your son.[14]

Before giving her mistress advice, the slave woman takes every precaution by referring to her state as a slave. She does not want to be accused of the pretension that consists in forgetting her own condition, whatever it might be. Deianira indirectly congratulates her slave on her advice when she addresses her son, who arrives immediately afterward:

> My child, my son, wise sayings sometimes come even from humble people like this woman. She is a slave, but what she says rings free.[15]

This old slave woman corresponds to the definition of the tragic character according to Aristotle and Sophocles. She is what a real person should be, taking into account her social status. Devoted to her mistress, she shows wisdom while at the same time remaining within the limits of her condition. Through this example, we can understand better what Aristotle means when he recommends that in judging acts and words in tragedy, we consider who is producing them.

To conclude this analysis of a neglected passage in the *Poetics* we must note that although statements in tragedy are adapted to the character who utters them, they also have a relation to the person to whom they are addressed. Nothing in the rest of the *Poetics* illuminates this statement. But since the situation of speech in the theater quite often coincides with that of persuasive speech, whether it is political or judicial, we can find in Aristotle's *Rhetoric* an example taken from Sophocles to show the impact that the presence of the person addressed may have on a character's speech. I refer to the speech Haemon addresses to his father, Creon, in defense of Antigone. Here is the text from the *Rhetoric*, where the example is cited in the context of a development on refuting the adversary:

> In regard to moral character [ethos], since sometimes, in speaking of ourselves, we render ourselves liable to envy, to the charge of prolixity, or contradiction, or, when speaking of another, we may be accused of abuse or boorishness, we must make another speak in our place, as [do] Isocrates . . . and Archilochus. . . . Sophocles, also, introduces Haemon, when defending Antigone against his father, as if quoting the opinion of others.[16]

Aristotle alludes to the agōn scene in Sophocles' *Antigone*, where Haemon, even though he has previously proclaimed his obedience to his father, Creon, opposes the vehement indictment in which Creon sentences his fiancée, Antigone, to death. And to refute his father temperately, without clashing with him directly, Haemon first reports what he has heard said among the common people in the city of Thebes, which is mourning:

> I can hear these murmurs in the dark, how the city moans for this girl, saying: "No woman ever merited death less—none ever died so shamefully for deeds so glorious as hers, who, when her own brother had fallen in bloody battle, would not leave him unburied to be devoured by savage dogs, or by any bird. Does she not deserve to receive golden honor?" Such is the rumor shrouded in darkness that silently spreads.[17]

According to Aristotle, Haemon's words are explained by his consideration for the person to who he is speaking. The son, to avoid conflict with his father, adopts the rhetorical strategy of attributing to others his own opinions. A modern reading may be less skeptical regarding Haemon's sincerity. Can we really say that Haemon is inventing the rumor by transposing his own argument to a fictive voice? But whether or not Haemon invents this rumor—which is mentioned nowhere else in *Antigone*, it remains that Aristotle is right about the rhetorical move. Haemon first borrows the voice of another, the city of Thebes, to persuade his father to abandon his plan. Then he borrows the voice of maxims.

Finally, when he introduces his own view in the first person, he takes the same oratorical precaution, mutatis mutandis, as the slave in *The Women of Trachis* when she addresses her mistress Deianira:

> Father, give way and allow a change from your rage. For if even from me, a younger man, a worthy thought may be supplied, by far the best thing, I believe, would be for men to be all-wise by nature. Otherwise—since most often it does not turn out that way—it is good to learn in addition from those who advise you well.[18]

Wisdom may come from the mouth of a young freeborn man, just as it can come from the mouth of an old slave woman. But in both cases, the expression of wisdom has its limits. We can ultimately see in Haemon's case an example of the double variable that Aristotle recommends considering in the characters' speech as well as in their acts. Haemon's speech cannot be understood without reference to the character who is speaking and to the character being addressed.

A Microcosm of Characters

From this Aristotelian analysis, unburdened of its theoretical apparatus, there remains the insight that every tragedy forms a microcosm in which the characters, who are visible to the spectators through words and acts, are not defined solely as entities acting and reacting to events in accord with their nature or social status, but are instead constantly embedded in a relational fabric with other characters in the meeting place constituted by the stage, and in the period of time corresponding to the day of the tragedy. The characters unify what might be separate in the space of representation, for example, the orchestra and the stage. Through its words, the chorus is one of the characters, especially in Sophocles, where, as Aristotle notes, the chorus is an actor that contributes to the action.[19] The gods themselves are sometimes characters, even though their presence is exceptional in Sophocles' work; and the voice is here again the bond that connects the heights where they appear in the heavens with the earth where humans live. Unlike Euripides, in whose work the gods may intervene at the beginning of the tragedy without having any contact with the humans, in Sophocles the voice of the god who appears is recognized by humans, whether at the beginning or at the end of the tragedy. And it is no accident that both times when a divinity appears, whether it is visible or not, the first word uttered by the man to whom it speaks is "Voice of Athena, dearest to me of the gods," or "Ah, friend whose voice I have longed to hear."[20] Thus the word is the link that unites in each tragedy a microcosm of characters in which the scenic differences between chorus and actors fade away, where individuals, whether they are different or similar in social rank or nature, live side by side, where the hero can realize his or her ethics of excellence only through the judgment of others, and where, despite the tensions and clashes between friends and enemies that dominate the stage, the solidarity between the small and the great is affirmed.

The chorus of sailors in *Ajax* offers, beyond the gap between the heroes and ordinary folk, a fine metaphor of the necessary solidarity between the great and the small:

> Point your shaft at a noble spirit, and you could not miss; but if a man were to speak such things against me, he would win no belief. It is on the powerful that envy creeps. Yet the small without the great are a teetering tower of defence. For the lowly stand most upright and prosperous when allied with the great, and the great when served by less.[21]

The metaphor here is that of the rampart constituted by large and small stones, and in reality it is based on an experiential truth drawn from the technique of building walls. Plato recalls this principle in the *Laws*:

> for even masons say that big stones are not well laid without little stones.[22]

This principle, which is essential for the construction of stone walls built without mortar and is employed metaphorically in the *parados* of *Ajax*, emphasizes the social solidarity between the small and the great. And later in the tragedy we find a continuation of this truth when great Ajax, having collapsed among the animals he slaughtered in his madness, sees, when he recovers his reason, the sailors who have become his only support:

> Ah, good sailors, you alone of my friends who alone still abide by the true bond of friendship, see how great a wave has just now crested over and broken around me, set on by a murderous storm![23]

The metaphor of the wall has disappeared, replaced by the image of a storm at sea. But the idea remains. The loyalty of the small is the only support that remains to the great in the collapse caused by misfortune.

This "mason proverb"[24] used by Sophocles in a social context is taken up by Plato in his *Laws* to show that attention to small things is just as necessary as attention to great ones in man's various technical activities, and to transpose this truth to the divinity's activity. Contrary to what a young atheist might think, the gods are not indifferent to small things, human affairs, and concerned only with great things, the functioning of the universe. Among these human techniques, Plato cites, as he usually does, medicine, the art of piloting ships, and also strategy, economics, and politics. And it is then that he uses the example of a humbler activity, that of the mason. He could just as well have chosen poetics. In the construction of his microcosm of the characters peculiar to each of his tragedies, Sophocles, like a mason or a god, accords no less attention to minor characters than to major ones; it is by a careless simplification that modern readers tend to confound characters and heroes.

Of course, this microcosm in which the great and the small live side by side does not resemble the society of Sophocles' time. Unlike comedy, which plunges into the contemporary political and social life of democratic Athens in the fifth century BCE, tragedy—and not only Sophocles' tragedy—is situated in a heroic world closer to the Homeric world than to the contemporary world. But the spectators, although familiar with Homer since childhood, had no feeling of foreignness and immediately perceived the perennial nature of the problems and feelings.

The World of the Humble

The sailors in the chorus of *Ajax* who use the metaphor of the solidarity between the great and the small offer the best way to enter this world of the humble that Sophocles brought to life. Necessarily, the members of a chorus are anonymous and have no individuality. But the ease with which a Greek tragic chorus passes from "we" to "I"[25] suggests that the collectivity, while existing as such, forms an individuality. And in the course of the tragedy, by means of details given here and there in both the lyrical and the spoken parts, Sophocles succeeds in raising to the status of characters these sailors from the crew who had come from Salamis to Troy not only to sail Ajax's ship, but also to fight alongside him, and who had already been doing so for ten years.

To be sure, at first they seem to exist only through their sovereign:

> Son of Telamon, you who hold your throne on wave-washed Salamis near the open sea, when your fortune is fair, I rejoice with you. But whenever the stroke of Zeus, or the raging rumor of the Danaans with the clamor of their evil tongues attacks you, then I shrink with great fear and shudder in terror, like the fluttering eye of the winged dove.[26]

And in fact during the whole first part of the tragedy, the chorus reacts in accord with Ajax's destiny, intensely experiencing feelings ranging from fear to despair and even including the joy of false hope, depending on what it sees, believes, or discovers. Even outside the tragic moments, the humble have no strength when it is deprived of its leader, especially when this impetuous leader resembles a great bird of prey.[27] Even within the crowd of the humble, there is a hierarchy; and these men who form the chorus in *Ajax* are not just random individuals. When Tecmessa, Ajax's war captive and wife, emerges in response to the chorus's call and greets them in these terms: "Mates of the ship of Ajax, offspring of the race that springs from the Erechtheids,"[28] she introduces them with a certain formality. Even though they remain nameless, they belong to an illustrious race, the descendants of Erectheus, that is, the mythical king who emerged from the earth and who is the ancestor of the people of Athens. Thus they belong to the same family as the Athenian spectators who are witnessing the tragedy in the theater of Dionysus in Athens, at the foot of the Acropolis, where the tomb of Erectheus is located. Through this genetic bond, Sophocles cleverly connects still more closely the spectators with the characters in the tragedy and further increases their empathy. And these sailors were not just another group among the men who took part in the Salaminian expedition to Troy, either.[29] Ever since Homer, it has been known that Ajax commanded the Salaminian contingent and left with twelve ships.[30] The sailors in the chorus are those who served on Ajax's ship; they are therefore part of the group closest to the leader. This explains the community of feeling that Tecmessa spontaneously attributes to them by using the pronoun "us" immediately after greeting them:

> Cries of grief are the portion of us who care from afar for the house of Telamon. Ajax, our terrible, mighty lord of untamed power, now lies plagued by a turbid storm of disease.[31]

The hero's tragedy strengthens the union of those who are devoted to him; and in the absence of his half brother Teucer, who will not return until after his death, the group of friends is formed by his wife and war captive, Tecmessa, along with his most prominent soldiers. Only the small stones remain now that the storm has destroyed the rampart. But they are bound together by the mortar of trust and compassion. Sophocles uses this understanding between the wife and the soldiers to justify in a natural way the story of the nighttime expedition and Ajax's madness as seen from inside:

> *Chorus:* In what way did the plague first swoop down on him? Tell us who share your pain how it happened.
> *Tecmessa:* You will hear all that took place, since you are involved.[32]

Confronted by the misfortune of the great, the humble share the pain. And they seek to help them as much as they can. In fact, Tecmessa, who fears that Ajax will commit suicide, asks the chorus, his friends, to reason with him: "Men of his kind can be won over by the words of friends."[33] All through the first part of the tragedy, from Ajax's second entrance after he has regained his wits to the discovery of his corpse, the collaboration between Tecmessa and the men of the chorus as they try to save Ajax continues to be the indissoluble bond that remains despite all the reversals. We see them trying, one after the other, to convince Ajax, each with his or her own means of persuasion. We see them immediately act together when the messenger informs them that Ajax's departure to seek an alleged redemption was a ruse. Tecmessa gives the order to leave: "Move, let us be quick, this is no time to sit still, if we wish to save a man who is eager for death." "I am ready to help," the chorus replies.[34] We see them end up, after a long search in the areas of the countryside along the sea, in the same place; and when Tecmessa discovers the body behind a thicket, she cries to the chorus: "I am lost, destroyed, razed to the ground, my friends!"[35] This macabre discovery is the occasion for another dialogue between Tecmessa and the chorus, in which the chorus's suffering is in harmony with that of Tecmessa . . . or almost. For ultimately each person, even among the humble, experiences his or her own tragedy.

To Each His or Her Own Tragedy

The only time when Tecmessa is in conflict with the chorus is when, hearing her groans, it thinks it knows the pain she feels when she loses Ajax. She corrects them: "It is for you to analyze my troubles, but for me to feel them too fully." And the chorus replies: "I must agree."[36] A subtle difference in the way those close to the hero mourn is thus fleetingly acknowledged. Despite their understanding and compassion, each person experiences misfortune in relation to his or her identity and his or her past. The spectator has learned the woman's tragedy in a long speech in which she speaks about it to save the hero who has caused her misfortune in the past and to whom she is now attached.[37]

The spectator learns about the tragedy of the men in the chorus chiefly in the lyrical parts, which provide the sole occasion for the humble to speak about themselves. Here is the beginning of the first stasimon, where, after lauding its native island as a lost paradise, the chorus of Salaminians deplores its misfortunes:

> But I, miserable, have long been delayed here, still making my bed through countless months in the camp on the fields of Ida. I am worn by time and with anxious expectation still of a journey to Hades the abhorred, the unseen.[38]

This is the complaint of soldiers stuck where they are, eaten away by an endless passage of time, and worried about death in combat. Their ordinary tragedy is overwritten by the hero's tragedy, which is also their own. After Ajax's death, the fourth and last stasimon echoes this beginning of the first stasimon. The whole song is detached from the present issue of Ajax's burial, which occupies the second part of the play, and refocused again on the chorus itself: in it we find once again the complaint about the endless time spent fighting in the damp Troad; but it broadens into a curse on the inventor of war, who is responsible for the loss of happiness:

> No delight in garlands or deep wine-cups did that man provide me, no sweet din of flutes, that miserable man, or pleasing rest in the night. And from love—god!—from love he has totally barred me. Here I lie uncared for, while heavy dews constantly wet my hair, damp reminders of joyless Troy.[39]

This is a memory of the lost happiness of a peaceful life, with its banquets and love affairs, contrasted with the hard life of the warrior, further aggravated by the death of the man who was their rampart against the fears of a nighttime attack. Thus the chorus ultimately wants to return to its homeland.[40]

Thus for a few moments, in a kind of interlude in the middle of the argument between the great figures over Ajax's body, the humble are given an opportunity to sing about their misfortunes. And in doing so they almost forget what the great have told them to do. Just before this fourth stasimon, Teucer had ordered them to behave like men, not women, and protect during his absence the woman and child who had remained as suppliants near Ajax's corpse.[41] In its complaint, which represents both the culmination and the conclusion of this focus on the chorus, the latter says nothing about the mission Teucer gave it. During the whole first part of the tragedy, the chorus has been an important and lively character in the drama, not only in its desire to save Ajax with Tecmessa's help, as we have seen, but also because it has experienced, in counterpoint to Ajax's tragedy and in a displaced way, its own tragedy. A tragedy of the humble, in four stages: first bewilderment, then the mad, frenetic joy the chorus shows after Ajax's departure when, deceived by ambiguous words, it thinks he has returned to good intentions;[42] immediately afterward, the painful awakening caused by the messenger's revelations, which slice through its joy and make anguish succeed joy;[43] then the abrupt action with Tecmessa to catch up with a fate that is always fulfilled too quickly and in which humans always arrive too late;[44] and finally the discovery of the irreparable and reflection on its own error:

> Ah, what blind folly I have displayed! All alone, then, you bled, unguarded by your friends! And I took no care, so entirely dull was I, so totally stupid. Where, where lies inflexible Ajax, whose name means anguish?[45]

It is after this crisis experienced in a way that is displaced with respect to the hero's tragedy that the chorus moves to the center of attention with its complaint that covers the whole of its fourth stasimon and last song before becoming once again, in the exodos, a very ordinary chorus, limiting itself to punctuating the long speeches of the great characters with its moral approbative or disapprobative judgments, announcing the arrival of a new character, and concluding the tragedy. If in his tragedies Sophocles ever treated the chorus as a character in the full sense of the term, it was certainly in this one. And thanks to the scholiast, we have the good fortune to be able to gauge the originality of Sophocles' creation with respect to the tragedy in which Aeschylus had already dramatized the same mythic sequence:

> It is in a convincing way that in Sophocles' *Ajax* the chorus is composed of men from Salamis who, on the one hand, can express themselves freely, given that they are freemen and, on the other hand, feel compassion [for Ajax] because they are his compatriots, and speak with respect, because they are his subordinates. For it would not be convincing to introduce a chorus of Achaians, both because they could not feel compassion [for Ajax] and because they could not oppose the king. The solution of a chorus of war captives is well-suited for taking charge of a dead man, like Aeschylus in *The Thracian Women*, but it is not well-suited to the character; see how the captives could reproach Menelaus.[46]

Whereas in his *Thracian Women* Aeschylus had chosen a chorus of women war captives, which was uniquely appropriate for mourning, Sophocles created a character whose roles are more balanced, not only moving but also dramatic.

The scholiast provides a good analysis of the components of the character and of their consequences for relationships with other characters in the play; but we must add that Sophocles gave these subordinate characters a soul.

The Personality of the Humble

Other modest and anonymous characters move like phantoms through Sophocles' tragedies. However, they do not lack personality. It is worthwhile to compare Antigone's guard with these soldiers of Ajax's.

This guard belongs to the group the new king, Creon, has assigned to watch over Polynices' body, whose burial he has just forbidden. He makes only two appearances: one reluctant, to announce bad news to the king (the violation of the edict he has just promulgated, the dead man having been covered with soil by some unknown person, despite the guards' surveillance), the other triumphal, to bring in the guilty party, Antigone, who has been caught in the act of burying her brother again after the soil on the body had been cleared away by the guards. In these two opposite scenes Sophocles created a character belonging to the common people who, in addition to his function as a messenger, speaks to us about himself and the group of guards to which he belongs. It is thus possible to compare him with Ajax's sailors.

Setting aside the obvious differences resulting from the contrast between the brevity of the guard's appearance and the almost constant presence of the chorus, we can see that these humble characters have traits in common. They speak of their sufferings with realism and spontaneity. The evocation of sailors/soldiers who must cope with the dampness of the dews corresponds to that of the guards who must endure a cloud of dust. Two evocations are based on lived experience of what subordinates may have to endure during their assignments outside the theatrical space. And when these humble characters enter the visible space, they recount in great detail what they have done.

Having hurried off in opposite directions to look for Ajax, the soldiers, all out of breath when they begin to reappear, can at first only repeat short words:

> Toil follows toil yielding toil! Where, where, where have I not trudged? And still no place can say that I have shared its secret.[47]

When he appears for the first time, the guard in *Ajax* notes humorously that he is not out of breath, as a messenger worthy of the name ought to be:

> My king, I will not say that I arrive breathless because of speed, or from the action of a swift foot. For often I brought myself to a stop because of my thoughts, and wheeled round in my path to return. My mind was telling me many things: "Fool, why do you go to where your arrival will mean your punishment?" "Idiot, are you dallying again? If Creon learns it from another, must you not suffer for it?" So debating, I made my way unhurriedly, slow, and thus a short road was made long.[48]

What is characteristic of these two entrances, which nonetheless contrast in rhythm, is the same use of the first person by the humble person to speak about himself. This procedure is obviously more striking in the guard's entrance, which is famous. Deviating from the traditional image of the messenger, this character even emphasizes this difference. His subtle mixture of cunning and naïveté makes the spectator smile. If the guard expatiates at such length about himself and about his hesitations first seen from the outside, and then from the inside through the contradictory injunctions of his conscience, it is in order to delay as much as possible the announcement of the bad news: the guards have failed in their mission; at the end of the night Polynices' body was covered with soil despite their surveillance. And when, in finally making his announcement, this chance messenger uses the conventional formula, "I want to tell you first," it is, against all expectation, to speak again about himself:

> I want to tell you first about myself—I did not do the deed, nor did I see the doer, so it would be wrong that I should come to any harm.[49]

The king has to promise that he will not be harmed before he will finally agree to speak and become a traditional messenger, that is, brilliant.

A final analogy may be drawn between these humble sailors in the chorus of *Ajax* and the guard in *Antigone*: their ability to move abruptly from the greatest despair to the greatest joy. To contrast these two moments Sophocles employed a comparable dramatic technique, although the ways of using the alternation of spoken and sung parts are reversed.[50] In *Ajax*, the contrast occurs between two songs by the chorus (the first stasimon and the second stasimon), separated by a brief spoken scene; in *Antigone*, the contrast is between two spoken scenes, separated by a choral song. In the interim a reversal takes place: in *Ajax*, the hero's feigned decision not to commit suicide and his revolt; in *Antigone*, the heroine's arrest. Before the reversal, the chorus in *Ajax* was all gloom. Then, immediately after the departure of the hero, whom it believes has been cured and saved, it leaps with joy in a frantic dance:

> I shiver with rapture; I soar on the wings of sudden joy! O Pan, O Pan, appear to us, sea-rover, from the stony ridge of snow-beaten Cyllene. King, dance-maker for the gods, come, so that joining with us you may set on the Nysian and the Cnosian steps, your self-taught dances. Now I want to dance. And may Apollo, lord of Delos, step over the Icarian sea and join me in his divine form, in eternal benevolence![51]

Similarly, the guard in *Antigone* passes from a hesitant entrance to an assertive one, moving from fear for his own life to triumphal joy, because he brings with him the proof that saves him, Antigone, the guilty party:

> My king, there is nothing that a man can rightly swear he will not do. For second thought belies one's first intent. I could have vowed that I would not ever come here again, because of your threats by which I had just been storm-

tossed. But since this joy that exceeds and oversteps my hopes can be compared in fullness to no other pleasure, I am back—though it is contrary to my sworn oath—bringing this girl who was caught giving burial honors to the dead. This time there was no casting of lots. No, this piece of luck has fallen to me, and me alone. And now, my king, as it pleases you, take her yourself, question her and convict her. But justice would see me released free and clear from this trouble.[52]

Like the chorus, the guard is suddenly overwhelmed by an unhoped-for, boundless joy. But the analogies stop there, because this joy has a very different meaning. In the case of the guard, it is a selfish joy of being sure of his own salvation without worrying about others; in that of the chorus, it is an altruistic joy at the idea of the salvation of others. The humble character's relation to the hero is opposite in nature in the two cases. Whereas the chorus is constantly focused on Ajax, even when he is absent, the guard pays no attention to Antigone, whose eyes continue to be cast down,[53] and does not speak to her. It is not that the guard is completely insensitive to the young woman's misfortune, of which he is the instrument, but his personal safety takes priority. Here are the concluding words of his account of Antigone's arrest:

> She made no denial of anything—at once to my joy and to my pain. For to have escaped from trouble one's self gives the greatest joy, but it stings to lead friends to evil. Naturally, though, all such things are of less account to me than my own safety.[54]

In the end, the guard remains the prisoner of his own universe, as does Antigone herself. There is no possible communication here between the world of the humble and the world of the great. Thus we see emerge within the common people represented by Sophocles a difference between those who participate in the values of solidarity and those who remain closed up in their universe of mediocrity. The metaphor of the small stone that is useful to the large for the construction of a rampart is thus not valid for all.

Conflict among the Humble

Not only may humble characters react differently from one another in different situations, but they may also do so in the same situation and consequently enter into conflict with one another. Sophocles took advantage of this dramatic resource in two tragedies, *The Women of Trachis* and *Oedipus the King*.

In *The Women of Trachis*, the scene where the humble characters confront one another results from Sophocles' doubling of the announcement of Heracles' return. In a return tragedy,[55] that is, one in which people are waiting for the return of the hero, who has gone off on an expedition, it is usual for this return to be preceded by the arrival of a messenger who announces it. For example, the

return of the victorious hero in Aeschylus's *Agamemnon* is preceded by a messenger's report. Here Sophocles innovated by doubling the announcement.[56] He
has Lichas, Heracles' official messenger, preceded by a resident of Trachis who
wants to be the first to announce the good news to Heracles' wife, Deianira.
Lichas himself, bombarded by questions, has been delayed by the crowds of the
people of Trachis. This doubling of the messengers multiplies the reversals: first
there is Deianira's total joy upon hearing the first messenger's news; then, when
Lichas arrives accompanied by the captives, a joy tempered by pity for the captives in general and especially for one of them, the only one who can control her
pain. Above all, this doubling is an opportunity to draw a new development
from the second messenger's announcement, when it is learned that he has
twisted the truth to spare Deianira. The first messenger, who has remained alone
with Deianira, reveals to her the contradiction between the information he has
just heard from Lichas and the information he had heard earlier from the same
messenger: it was not to seek vengeance that Heracles undertook the expedition
from which he is returning victorious, but because he was in love with the king's
daughter, the captive for whom Deianira spontaneously felt pity and whom she
allowed to enter her home. Stunned, in a scene of interrogation, Deianira questions Lichas in the presence of the first messenger to determine the facts.[57] Even
though she appeals to Lichas's sense of truth, the latter avoids the question regarding the identity of the captive he has brought back, feigning ignorance. It is
then that the first messenger brusquely intervenes, without introducing himself,
in order to contradict Lichas:

> Look here: to whom do you think you are speaking?[58]

There ensues a confrontation between the two messengers in a lively and familiar dialogue thirty-five verses long: the two men of the people face off against
one another in front of Deianira, one of them trying to confound the other by
recalling what he has just heard from him, the other evading the question by
drawing an unconvincing distinction between opinion and assertion, and especially by scorn. On closer inspection we see that these two men of the people do
not have exactly the same social status. The first messenger is only a nameless
man, probably a slave serving Deianira, who has put a crown on his head to
announce good news, hoping thereby to obtain a reward and advantage from
his mistress.[59] Lichas, in contrast, is a freeman.[60] He has a social function: he is
Heracles' herald, that is, his official messenger, his spokesman.[61] His function
gives him a certain importance. He is surrounded by a crowd when he arrives in
Trachis, whereas the first messenger was simply an individual in that crowd. This
difference in social status is perceptible in the confrontation itself. When the
anonymous man confronts him without showing respect, Lichas is indignant
and seeks to break off the conversation ("Farewell. I was a fool to listen to
you"[62]), questions his mistress regarding this individual whom he does not know,
describing him using the scornful term "stranger" ("In God's name, my dear

mistress, tell me, I pray you, who this stranger is"[63]), and breaks off the dialogue by suggesting that his interlocutor is mad:

> Madam, let this man be dismissed. To prate
> with such a madman suits not my discretion.[64]

From the difference in social status between the two characters, we can also deduce a clue to their destiny. After helping reveal the truth, the anonymous messenger disappears forever. Like Antigone's guard, he leaves the drama at the point where the tragedy of the great, of which he has been an instrument, begins; but unlike Antigone's guard, he goes away without his departure even being mentioned. Deianira says not a word to send him on his way or thank him. Will he have his reward and his mistress's gratitude? No one knows. On the other hand, Lichas continues to be a character in the drama, and he will have the privilege, if we can call it that, of participating in the tragedy, because we will learn of this messenger's pitiful death as an innocent victim of Heracles' furious anger:

> [Heracles] seized Lichas where the ankle joins the foot
> and dashed him on a rock swept by the sea
> so that the white brain seeped among his hairs,
> and all his shattered skull was bloodied over.
> At this the people raised a mournful cry
> that one was maddened and the other slain.[65]

Lichas, who had lied on his own initiative in his first message to avoid being the instrument of Deianira's tragedy, and then recognized his mistake, becomes, for having scrupulously done his duty as a messenger this time, the instrument of Heracles' tragedy and the involuntary cause of his own death. This is a further example of the fact that the tragic destiny affects even the humble.

Whereas in *The Women of Trachis* the conflict between the two men of the people takes place at the moment when Deianira's tragedy is being woven, in *Oedipus the King* it takes place in the denouement, in the scene in which Oedipus discovers the truth about himself.[66] The two men of the people who confront each other in this scene are not as alien to one another as are their counterparts in *The Women of Trachis*, and they are not the result of a simple doubling for the occasion. They have already met and have long been part of Oedipus's destiny, because they both played a role in the survival of the child when he was abandoned by his father and mother in the mountains near Thebes. One was the servant of Laius who was supposed to leave the child to die, the other the Corinthian servant who took in the child.

Mutatis mutandis, the Corinthian servant corresponds to the messenger in *The Women of Trachis*, while Laius's servant corresponds to Lichas. Beyond the considerable differences due to very different myths, the resemblances show that Sophocles took up an analogous dramatic framework by creating these pairs of

humble characters. The Corinthian servant, like the anonymous messenger in
The Women of Trachis, arrives spontaneously to announce good news. He does
not present himself as an official messenger sent by the city of Corinth to announce Oedipus's appointment as king following Polybus's death. Instead, it was
by trusting a rumor circulating at the time when the decision was imminent that
he left Corinth to go to Thebes. Thus he arrived before an official messenger, just
as the resident of Trachis arrived before Lichas, the official spokesman. These
two unofficial messengers have the same motive: they rush to be the first to announce the news in the hope of gaining some advantage.[67] It is a commonplace
that every messenger carrying good news expects a reward; but this is not the
only way the two men resemble one another. They are characterized above all by
the pride they take in their knowledge and their irrepressible need to reveal the
whole truth. In addition, the first announcement of good news is followed by a
second report that astounds the great personages: just as the first messenger in
The Women of Trachis reveals to Deianira the truth regarding Heracles' love for
Iole, the Corinthian messenger in *Oedipus the King* reveals to Oedipus part of
the truth about his origin: he is not the son of the king of Corinth, Polybus, and
his wife, Merope; it was he, the messenger, who brought him from the Cithaeron
mountains, where he was guarding Polybus's flocks, having received him from
another shepherd who was Laius's servant.

This new revelation leads in both cases to a scene of investigation with three
characters and a confrontation between the two minor characters. Everything is
organized in an analogous way. The character who is to be the object of the investigation arrives just when he is needed after the revelation: in *Oedipus the
King*, he is Laius's shepherd, who corresponds to Lichas in *The Women of Trachis*.
Nevertheless, in *Oedipus the King* the Corinthian messenger's revelation has in
the meantime led to Jocasta's departure, because she has now understood. Even
as he makes use of analogous dramatic schemas, Sophocles enriches them with
variations. But the scene of investigation and confrontation unfolds in a comparable way: first, there is an intense questioning of the humble character by his
master or mistress, who is all the more eager to confirm the truth because it is
the sign of disaster. Then, since the character questioned conceals the truth out
of concern for the questioner, the humble character takes over, the one who has
already told what he knows. Thus the two humble characters face off while their
superiors remain silent.[68]

This confrontation does not lead, in either *Oedipus the King* or *The Women of
Trachis*, to a result, because faced with difficult questions, the person questioned
reacts with violence. But what was verbal violence in *The Women of Trachis* begins
to verge on physical violence in *Oedipus the King*. Here is the end of the dialogue
between the Corinthian messenger and the Theban servant:

> *Messenger:* Come, tell me now: do you remember having given me a boy in
> those days, to be reared as my own foster-son?

Servant: What now? Why do you ask the question?
Messenger: This man, my friend, is he who then was young.
Servant: Damn you! Be silent once and for all!
Oedipus: Do not rebuke him, old man. Your words need rebuking more than
  his.[69]

Faced by the revelations made by the Corinthian messenger, who insists, with
a heedless jubilation, on making the truth known, the Theban servant reacts with
violence, striking him with his stick. It has to be said that this servant was probably the only person who had known these terrible secrets for years.

This servant's past has been reconstructed in detail by bits of information
distributed all through the tragedy before he arrives. He was the only person
who escaped when Laius was murdered. He returned to Thebes to announce the
news, but his account falsified the number of killers, probably to mask his cowardice.[70] A loyal servant born in the palace of Laius and Jocasta, he asked the
queen's permission to return from the palace to the countryside when he recognized that the new king of Thebes was Laius's murderer.[71] He wanted to keep
his distance in order to remain loyal to Laius, to avoid seeing the latter's wife in
the arms of his murderer, and the better to keep his dark secret by isolating
himself. On Oedipus's orders, Jocasta summons him to be a witness for the
defense, but although he maintains that Laius was killed by a band of robbers
and not by a lone man,[72] he becomes, after the Corinthian messenger's revelations, the object of a second investigation that takes him back to a still more
distant past, that of Oedipus's birth. From that moment on, he was already the
holder of another dark secret that he had revealed to no one, and this time, he
was responsible: asked by Jocasta to abandon the infant, he took pity on him
and gave him to a Corinthian shepherd.[73] The old man has kept these two secrets
for a long time. When he comes in response to Jocasta's summons, he is at first
dominated by mistrust, which is increased by the presence of the Corinthian,
whom he feigns not to recognize. And when the Corinthian messenger triumphantly announces that the child he received from him is none other than
Oedipus himself, the old man suddenly understands: the two secrets are connected. The man he knew was the murderer of Laius becomes the murderer of
his father, and also the husband of his mother. The old Theban's violence against
the man who has revealed the truth without being able to gauge all its consequences corresponds to the horror of what he has just realized. Thus he will try
even harder to conceal the truth in order to spare Oedipus, just as in *The Women
of Trachis* Lichas tries to disguise the truth to spare Deianira.

In both tragedies, the scene in which the altercation between the two members of the common people takes place ends in an analogous way. After the
quarrel, the man who reveals the truth says not another word and disappears
without a trace, whereas the one who disguised the truth becomes the object of
new pressures on the part of his mistress or his master. However, the methods

used vary and are adapted to the nature of the character conducting the investigation. In a long speech, the woman begs and gives persuasive arguments, while the man resorts to threats and violence in a rapid, tense dialogue. Both methods arrive at the same result: the total revelation of the truth and, in Oedipus's case, the hero's realization of the real extent of his misfortune. But the spectators are also shown that the humble characters indirectly caused the catastrophe that has befallen their betters, and precisely as a result of their good intentions. For in *Oedipus the King* it was they who saved the child: the Corinthian messenger proudly reminds Oedipus that he is the one who rescued him;[74] and when Oedipus, who now knows everything, asks the Theban servant a final question, the responsibility of the common people is clearly emphasized:

> *Oedipus:* Why, then, did you give him to this old man?
> *Servant:* Out of pity, master, thinking that he would carry him to another
> land, from where he himself came. But he saved him for the direst woe. For
> if you are what this man says, be certain that you were born ill-fated.[75]

The oracle of Apollo at Delphi, according to which Laius was to be killed by his son, has been fulfilled, even though the great personages have done all they could to avoid it. Its accomplishment was made possible by the humble people's attempts to save a child's life: one of them did not do what he was commanded to do and the other did more than he was asked to do. Thus it is ultimately through the commoners' good intentions that the gods fulfill their oracles and sooner or later cause the tragedy of the great. Here little lies are little stones useful for the construction of the gods' edifice.

The Fundamental Components of a Dramatic Character: Nature

When the tragic poet puts characters onstage, whether they are humble or great, he creates them on the basis of fundamental components that are visible especially when these characters are introduced. They are defined by a nature, a social function, and a role in the drama.

By nature, we must understand first the character's origin or birth. It is above all origin that establishes the distinction between the humble and the great. In the confrontation between Menelaus and Teucer concerning Ajax's burial, Ajax's half brother begins his speech in response to Menelaus with the following general remark, which he addresses to the chorus:

> Never again, my fellow Salaminians, will I be amazed if some nobody by birth
> does wrong, when those who are reputed to be born of noble blood employ
> such wrongful sentiments in their arguments.[76]

The dividing line due to origin seems to be a basic given that structures the opposition between the humble and the great. There are those who are nothing by birth, and those who are noble by birth. Those who are nothing by birth generally remain nameless in the theater—not to mention the bit players who are necessary in theater. Among the characters who speak, several are anonymous: this is clearly the rule for members of the chorus, and it is very often the case for messengers. In *Ajax*, out of eight speaking characters, only one is anonymous, and he is the messenger. Sent by Teucer to announce his return and transmit an instruction to Ajax, this character appears without being announced and then disappears without any special mention once his mission has been accomplished.[77] Tecmessa does not even turn to him when she wants to send someone to warn Teucer. No one has any idea what his name, his origin, or his personality is. The messenger is completely coterminous with his role in the drama. This is the proof that a character can exist dramatically without existing socially or psychologically. But this is a minimal treatment. The presentation of humble characters has shown us that a character, even if anonymous and of obscure birth, can have a strong presence that gives a particular aspect to his role—that is the case for the guard in *Antigone*—or successive details may give him a destiny, specific even though obscure, on the margins of the world of the great, but with points of contact that are decisive for the main articulations of the hero's destiny—and that is the case for the Corinthian messenger and especially the Theban servant in *Oedipus the King*.

Within each of these groups, a subtler hierarchy appears. Among the characters of obscure origin, we have already seen, in *The Women of Trachis*, the distinction between slaves and freemen. Deianira's nurse is a slave, which does not prevent her, despite her slavish thoughts, from speaking as if she were free.[78] On the other hand, the herald Lichas, though in Heracles' service, is a freeman.[79] That is what we learn when Deianira tries to convince him to tell the whole truth:

> Tell me the truth! It is a foul disgrace for a free man to be known as a liar.[80]

Deianira thus does not address the same kind of argument to a slave and a freeman. Here she appeals to the freeman's self-respect and his sense of honor.

A distinction within the category of slaves itself is perceptible. It is delicately noted by Sophocles at the beginning of Oedipus's close questioning of the Theban servant in the scene in which he will learn the whole truth.[81] To Oedipus's question as to whether he was in Laius's service, the servant replies, not without pride:

> I was—not a bought slave, but reared in his house.[82]

Thus in the category of slaves we can perceive a subtle hierarchy between those who were born in the palace and those who come from outside. The former enjoy more than the latter their masters' confidence and goodwill.[83]

Even among the great, there is a distinction within the order of birth between those who are of legitimate birth and those who are bastards. This is used dramatically in *Ajax*.[84] Like Ajax, Teucer is the son of the famed Telamon, prince of Aegina, who had distinguished himself in the first Trojan war conducted by Heracles.[85] But whereas Ajax was born of Telamon's legitimate wife, Eriboia,[86] Teucer is the son of a war captive. Teucer himself points this out, shortly after his first appearance, when he is assessing his misfortune as he contemplates the body of Ajax, which he has just discovered. Sophocles drew a parallel between Ajax's assessment of his destiny after he has become aware of his madness and that Teucer makes after becoming aware that Ajax has really died. Where should he go? The temptation to return to their father is instinctively felt by both sons.[87] But both also reject the idea, imagining how an inflexible hero would receive them—one a dishonored son, the other a son who could not save his brother. Teucer imagines what Telamon might say to him:

> What will a man like him leave unsaid? What insult will he forego against "the bastard offspring of his spear's war-prize," against your "cowardly, unmanly betrayer," dear Ajax [?][88]

The word "bastard" has been used. It is the supreme insult when it comes from the father. This insult will be found again in Agamemnon's mouth during Teucer's second confrontation with the leaders of the army to safeguard Ajax's corpse. Agamemnon calls Teucer the "son of the captive," and even a "slave" and a "barbarian."[89] In Agamemnon's insult the true violence of his anger goes even further than Telamon's imagined violence. At first, Teucer replies in the same register, finding barbarians in Agamemnon's noble ancestry—his paternal grandfather, Pelops, was a barbarian from Phrygia, and his mother was from Crete—and praising his own mother, the daughter of Laomedon, the king of Troy; she was chosen by Heracles as a reward for Telamon's bravery.

Unlike those who are nothing by birth, the great are part of a family history. However, this history has dark areas or scandals that could be conveniently brought out—already at that time—when one wanted to tarnish a hero's reputation. Odysseus is a good example of this. Those who did not like him called him the son the Sisyphus, king of Corinth, and not the son of Laertes, king of Ithaca. That is how Ajax's sailors or Philoctetes refer to him.[90] This insult is the consequence of a dark story about great tricksters that is recounted, with precise details not known elsewhere—in a scholium on *Ajax*:

> It is said that Anticlea, sent [by her father Autolycus] from Arcadia to Laertes' palace in Ithaca to marry him, met along the way Sisyphus, and from their encounter Odysseus was born. Sisyphus, king of Corinth, was a man capable of anything, whom Homer called "the trickiest of men"; it was he, in fact, who had had his own name and monogramme engraved on the claws and hooves of his animals. Autolycus, who "excelled in theft and perjury," stole the animals from him and changed their form; the theft of the animals, despite their transformation, did not escape Sisyphus; he recognized them by the monograms. Afterward, Autolycus, wanting to win Sisyphus's favor, treated him to a banquet

and put his daughter Anticlea in his bed; and when the girl was with child by Sisyphus, he gave her in marriage to Laertes. That is why Odysseus is the son of Sisyphus. Sophocles usually calls Odysseus the son of Sisyphus.[91]

It is not entirely true that Sophocles usually calls Odysseus the son of Sisyphus. He knew how to subtly vary the appellation depending on the development of the judgment concerning the character. This is clear in *Ajax*. At the beginning, the sailors of the chorus call Odysseus the son of Sisyphus when they see in him the enemy of Ajax, on the same level as the Atreids; but at the end of the tragedy, once Odysseus has played the role of mediator, obtaining from Agamemnon the authorization to bury Ajax ritually, he becomes a sage in the eyes of the chorus and "good Odysseus" in the eyes of Teucer. Thus it is no accident that Teucer, in the last words he addresses to Odysseus, calls him "progeny of aged Laertes."[92]

Finally, nature can manifest itself in the great not only by the transmission of hereditary qualities attached to the nobility, but also by hereditary maledictions attached to the family. This constitutes at least a theoretical dividing line between the heroes who belong to accursed families and the others. In Sophocles' extant tragedies, two great families are traditionally accursed, that of the Labdacids (Oedipus and his daughter Antigone) and that of the Atreids (Orestes and Electra). This corresponds to four plays out of seven. In the three other plays (*Ajax*, *Heracles*, *Philoctetes*), tragedy emerges for the first time in a family with a glorious past. The most beautiful expression of this malediction attached to successive generations of a family doomed to suffer the hatred of a divinity appears in Sophocles in a song of the chorus in *Antigone*:

> Blest are those whose days have not tasted of evil. For when a house has once been shaken by the gods, no form of ruin is lacking, but it spreads over the bulk of the race, just as, when the surge is driven over the darkness of the deep by the fierce breath of Thracian sea-winds, it rolls up the black sand from the depths, and the wind-beaten headlands that front the blows of the storm give out a mournful roar.[93]

The ill fortune sent by the gods is compared to a wave whipped by the winds. In each generation, it rolls over the weak and makes the great groan, as a wave rolls over the sand and strikes the whitecaps. This general reference to accursed families is then applied by the chorus to the family of the Labdacids, in which disaster strikes the last descendant, Antigone.

But despite the beauty of this poetic evocation, the weight of the past is not as great in Sophocles as it is in Aeschylus. In his *Oedipus the King* Sophocles does not emphasize the crimes committed by Laius of which Oedipus is supposed to be the victim. What is particularly significant is that in his *Electra* the curse on the family of the Atreids is considerably attenuated. At the end of the tragedy, Orestes is not in the grip of misfortune once he has taken his revenge, as is the case in Aeschylus's *The Libation Bearers*.[94]

The origin of the characters also explains to a certain extent their nature. On nature as inherited, the most famous commentary is that of the chorus speaking of Antigone, whose nature is inherited from her father Oedipus:

> She shows herself the wild offspring of a wild father, and does not know how to bend before troubles.[95]

But here there is nothing systematic, either. The two pairs of sisters born of the same father do not resemble on another. Ismene lacks the wild nature of Antigone; and Chrysothemis lacks that of Electra.[96]

The Fundamental Components of a Dramatic Character: The Social Function

A character's social function is related more or less directly with his or her origin. Low-born people, when they appear as speaking characters in tragedy, are servants, whereas the high-born are leaders or kings.

Among the servants who are slaves, the ones closest to their masters, even though they remain anonymous, are those who grew up in the palace and have been entrusted with raising the royal family's children or with an important mission concerning them. The Theban shepherd in *Oedipus the King* and the tutor in *Electra* are good examples of this.[97] They both helped save the child who was entrusted to them, either by accomplishing the mission in the case of the tutor, who received the infant from Electra's hands to take him far away from the murderers of Agamemnon,[98] or, on the contrary, by inverting it, in the case of the Theban shepherd who saved the child he was supposed to kill.[99] And in the case of Orestes' tutor, this function led to a familiarity between the servant and the hero, since they shared long years of exile in Phocis, where the servant raised the prince before returning with him to Mycenae to take revenge. Thus the servant can plausibly not limit himself to receiving orders, but also give his master advice[100] and even lecture him rather tartly for his imprudence at the time of the recognition.[101] His importance is further signaled by the fact that his arrival leads to a second recognition scene and a second effusive response from Electra, though she has not a word for Pylades![102]

In the social organization of Sophocles' tragedies, we can draw a distinction between those whose framework is the Achaian expedition to Troy (*Ajax* and *Philoctetes*) and those that take place in the royal palace of a city, whether it is Mycenae (*Electra*) or Thebes (*Oedipus the King*, *Antigone*).

Within the framework of the Achaian expedition, the social function of the leading figures owes a great deal to the hierarchy inherited from the epic tradition, whether in the form of the Homeric poems or the poems of the epic cycle. But although the tragic poet has the freedom to choose the characters he presents or does not present, and can even vary the presentation of a character as malleable as Odysseus, the configuration of power remains the same from one tragedy to the next. At the summit of the hierarchy are the two Atreids, that is, the sons of Atreus, Agamemnon and Menelaus. They are recognized as the leaders of the expedition. Even Ajax, their adversary after they have given Achilles' arms to Odysseus, declares, when he feigns submission to them:

> And so hereafter I shall, first, know how to yield to the gods, and, second, learn to revere the Atreidae. They are rulers, so we must submit.[103]

In both *Philoctetes* and *Ajax*, the two sons of Atreus are spoken of as an almost inseparable couple. The only time they are mentioned separately is in *Ajax*, where they appear in succession to oppose the burial of the hero's body. And it is only there that a hierarchy is established: Menelaus is the cause of the expedition, while Agamemnon is its leader.[104] Menelaus himself implicitly recognizes that Agamemnon is the one who commands the army. When he announces to Teucer the decision to leave the body where it is, he presents this decision as being his own and that of the man who "commands the expedition."[105] From that point on, the successive appearance of the two Atreids takes place in a crescendo, Agamemnon holding the supreme decision-making power. The couple of the Atreids is closely associated with Odysseus to form a trio that is hated by both Philoctetes and Ajax: Ajax attributes to the Atreids' intrigues the decision to award Achilles' arms to Odysseus,[106] while Philoctetes attributes to the Atreids and to Odysseus the decision to abandon him alone on the island of Lemnos.[107] Alongside the great—embodied by the two rulers of the expedition and the leaders of the contingents, such as Odysseus, Ajax, and Philoctetes—the soldiers are represented in both tragedies by the chorus: the chorus of Neoptolemus's sailors in *Philoctetes* reminds us of the chorus of sailors in *Ajax*. Faced by the rivalries and quarrels of the great, the humble are characterized by their loyalty to their leader. Thus the two tragedies about the Trojan myth are constructed on a comparable use of the social organization of the Achaians' expeditionary corps at Troy. We might add that the role of women in these tragedies about the expeditionary corps is rather discreet. To be sure, Tecmessa, Ajax's captive wife, plays an important role in the first part of the tragedy, but in the second part she is relegated to the rank of a silent character when the quarrel over Ajax's corpse becomes a battle among men.[108] As for *Philoctetes*, it has no female characters.

In the tragedies that take place in the framework of a city, Thebes or Mycenae, the duality of the commanders in chief is replaced by a single royal authority. And whereas the heroes in the Trojan tragedies were chosen, on the model of the *Iliad*, among the leaders of the contingents in conflict with the expedition's commanders in chief, in the framework of the city the main character or one of the main characters is the leader himself. This is obvious in *Oedipus the King*, where from beginning to end everything is centered on a single character, the king of Thebes; in *Antigone*, another king of Thebes, Creon, is also a tragic character, on the same level as the title character. Since the king plays a primordial or essential role in these two tragedies, it is not surprising that the composition of the chorus is related to the royal function: in *Antigone* it is composed of elderly citizens of Thebes who form the royal council, and in *Oedipus the King* it represents more broadly the people of the city. There is too great a tendency to blur the social status of the chorus by using vague descriptions, even when its status is relatively clear. Thus in the list of dramatis personae placed at the head of the manuscripts of *Antigone*, the chorus is designated by the vague expression "elderly Thebans." But if King Creon has convoked them, he has a precise reason for doing so. He is bringing the traditional royal council together at the time when he takes power after the death of Eteocles and Polynices.[109] Moreover, the tragedies focused on a king naturally include a royal family residing in the palace. The queen is regularly present: Jocasta in *Oedipus the King*, Eurydice in *Antigone*. And what is possible, though it was excluded in the Trojan tragedies, is especially the presence of young women of royal blood: Antigone and Ismene in *Antigone*, Electra and Chrysothemis in *Electra*. The conflicts that occur among the leaders in the Achaian camp at Troy arise within the royal family, between the king and his relatives, whether they belong to the same generation—like Oedipus's brother-in-law, Creon, in *Oedipus the King*—or to the following generation—like Creon's son, Haemon, in *Antigone*. Sophocles even exploited the presence of young women of royal blood to produce a far more exceptional scene in which the king has to face up to the rebellion of his niece. From then on, the same ethical problem, namely whether one can ritually bury a warrior who has turned against his own people, is embodied in a conflict between characters who are rather different depending on whether we are in framework of the expeditionary corps or that of the city. What was in *Ajax* a conflict between the two Atreids and the dead man's half brother becomes in *Antigone* a struggle between the king and the dead man's sister. Finally, in both tragedies where the king is the center of the drama, Sophocles enriched the conflicts between the king and his entourage by adding an opposition of a different kind proceeding from a character who has a separate social status, the seer. The seer opposes Oedipus at the beginning of *Oedipus the King*, as he opposes Creon at the end of *Antigone*. He is the sole citizen to escape the sovereign's power, insofar as he is the servant of the god, and consequently the only one who can claim to speak on equal terms with him in moments of tension.[110] The characters' social function is thus a parameter whose importance must not be underestimated.

The Fundamental Components of a Dramatic Character: His or Her Role in the Action

The third component of a character in a tragedy, his or her role in the action, is less directly connected with the nature of the character than his or her social function is. An example will show this clearly: the choice to use dramatically the two characters who arrive with Orestes at the beginning of *Electra*, namely Pylades and the tutor. Even though Pylades is a friend of noble origin, while the tutor is a simple servant, Sophocles relegated Pylades to the role of a silent character, whereas the tutor is Orestes' interlocutor and his auxiliary in taking revenge. One of the reasons for this assignment of roles is that the tutor is the only one who knows the place to which the avengers have come, and is thus the only one of the three who is capable of serving as a guide and offering a natural presentation of the site of the tragedy when they arrive. Thus Sophocles can choose to give an important role in the action to a character who is not of illustrious birth. On the other hand, he can give a character of high birth a dramatic function that usually falls to a modest character. Whereas the role of messenger is generally attributed to anonymous characters, in *The Women of Trachis* it takes on an exceptional importance when it is attributed to Hyllus, Heracles' son, coming to tell his mother, Deianira, about the tragic effects of the tunic smeared with a philter that she had given her husband as a present.[111] Although it retains the traditional qualities of an ordinary messenger's report, Hyllus's account becomes a son's indictment accusing his mother of having killed his father. Consequently, the messenger's report leads to an exceptional dramatic situation: the silent departure of the addressee of the message, the mother, who has gone, as we soon learn, into the palace to be alone and there commit suicide.

The assignment of dramatic roles and their moment of action is thus one of the great domains in which the dramatic author's freedom to create is exercised beyond the constraints of the givens of the myth. Under these conditions, the author's choice to give characters a greater or a lesser dramatic presence is not without impact on the orientation he wants to give to his drama's meaning.

The Dramatic Presence of Virtual Characters

There are several degrees of the dramatic presence of characters, and these degrees have thresholds. The most important threshold is the one that separates virtual characters from visible characters. Virtual characters are the ones who are spoken about but never seen. By definition, their dramatic presence is weak. But they can nonetheless have an important impact on the unfolding of the drama, as is particularly the case for seers and the deceased.[112]

Seers whose prophecies are conveyed by a messenger are no doubt less spectacular than seers present on the stage, but they can nonetheless have a major influence on the action: as soon as it becomes known, the prophecy made by the Greek army's seer Calchas in *Ajax* triggers the departure of the chorus and Tecmessa in search of Ajax; the prophecy of the Trojan seer Helenus in *Philoctetes* triggers, as soon as the merchant informs Philoctetes of it, his departure to escape Odysseus.[113] Moreover, this latter prophecy is the origin of the whole action because it is the Trojan seer, who has been captured by Odysseus, who has revealed that Philoctetes' return to Troy with his bow is indispensable for a Greek victory.

Even the invisible dead have a strong dramatic presence in several tragedies: this is obvious in *Antigone*, where the burial of Polynices, even though his corpse remains invisible, is the essential issue in the first part of the tragedy;[114] it is also obvious in *Electra*, where the death of Agamemnon is for his daughter Electra the reason for living and acting, as in *Antigone* the death of Polynices was for his sister Antigone the imperious reason for acting; and in *Electra*, when revenge is taken by murdering Clytemnestra, the chorus exclaims:

> The curses bring fulfillment: those who are buried live. For men long dead are draining their killers' blood in a stream of requital.[115]

The murdered dead reawaken after a long period of latency, ultimately leading to the destruction of their murderers. In the two tragedies, it is the hero himself on whom the deceased's vengeance is taken. In *Oedipus the King*, the murdered Laius's reawakening manifests itself, after Oedipus's triumphant reign, in the plague that rages throughout the city.[116] The cause of this plague, which has been partially revealed by the Delphic oracle, sets in motion the king's investigation that leads to his recognition of his parricide and his self-mutilation.[117] Nevertheless, the dead man's presence remains very unobtrusive. It is more assertive in *The Women of Trachis*. Heracles returns triumphant from an expedition to Euboea; but his past, as in Oedipus's case, catches up with him: when he arrives moribund on a litter, he believes he has been killed by his wife, who gave him a poisoned tunic; but when he learns from his son that Deianira has committed suicide, having been deceived by the alleged philter that the centaur Nessus had given her, he finally realizes that he is the victim of a delayed vengeance taken by the dead centaur, which Heracles had killed after it tried to rape Deianira. Then we hear Heracles utter these extraordinary words:

> And now this beast the Centaur, as the god
> foretold, though dead, has torn my life away.[118]

This is the proof that the dead are present in Greek tragedy, not only in the form of corpses shown, especially at the end of tragedies, to increase the emotion by visual display,[119] but also as characters that are all the more powerful because their presence is obscure. Their action is all the less predictable because it can take place through the intermediary of animate or inanimate instruments. Ajax's sword is the most famous inanimate instrument: before committing suicide by falling on his sword planted in the earth, Ajax recalls that it is a gift from Hector who, in this way, long after his death, is taking his revenge.[120] When the instrument of vengeance is an animate being, it may be either an auxiliary who acts deliberately in the deceased's interest, like Orestes in *Electra*, or in a more tragic way, an involuntary helper, like Deianira in *The Women of Trachis*. This latter tragedy remains the most striking example of action by a dead person taking revenge on his murderer with the help of two instruments, one animate and the other inanimate. Deianira is ultimately only the unwilling agent of the dead centaur's vengeance on his murderer—a delayed vengeance, by ruse: deceived by the centaur's last recommendations, Deianira has preserved and transmitted the instrument of vengeance, the blood of the dead centaur mixed with the venom of the Lernaian Hydra, which seemed to be a force for union but was in reality a force for destruction.[121]

The Dramatic Presence of Visible Characters

For the visible characters, the threshold is the one that separates characters who are silent, simple bit players, from those who speak, though a single character can, in the course of a single tragedy, be both speaking and silent. We have seen that the character of Tecmessa changes in status in the course of the play, ceasing to speak when the tragedy moves from the private sphere to the public sphere.[122]

On the other hand, within the category of speaking characters, there is no longer a threshold differentiating their greater or lesser dramatic presence. Nevertheless, it is possible to establish degrees depending on the length of time they are present onstage. For example, it is significant that Antigone, the title character of the tragedy, is onstage for a much shorter time than is Creon, and this is one of several signs that the tragedy is as much the king's as it is the young woman's. But apart from any statistical consideration—because statistics cannot be substituted for the impression made on the spectator—what is characteristic of Sophocles' theater is the concentration of attention on characters constituting a nucleus around which turn, like electrons, those whom we usually call "tragic heroes." They are either at the center of the tragedy as a whole (like Oedipus in *Oedipus the King* or *Oedipus at Colonus*, or again Electra and Philoctetes in the tragedies bearing their names) or dominate by their presence half of the tragedy, in the case of what we call "diptych" plays, *Ajax* and *The Women of Trachis*. The clearest example of this second option is *The Women of Trachis*, where the focus is on Deianira's tragedy until the account of her suicide, whereas the end of the play is dominated by the tragedy of Heracles, the two characters never being present together onstage. In a comparable way, the first half of *Antigone* is dominated mainly by the character of Antigone until she leaves for her underground prison, never to return, while the character of Creon, who is struck by a series of misfortunes, becomes the tragic hero. However, unlike *The Women of Trachis*, the two characters meet and enter into conflict onstage. Whether they dominate with their presence a part or the whole of the tragedy, these tragic heroes often reveal themselves when they have to cope with disasters in scenes where they are put in confrontation with friends or enemies. It is this world of the great personages that we now have to examine.

Epic Heroes in Tragedy: Ajax and Philoctetes

More than in the case of humble characters, nature is a major basic component in the construction of the heroes. The latter's conduct depends not only on a prestigious origin, but also on everything that is attached to that origin, notably a moral character and an ethical requirement. In this respect, a great family relationship is established between the two heroes who are at the center of the two tragedies connected with the myth of the expedition to Troy, Ajax and Philoctetes.

The importance of the notion of nature in the construction of the character of Ajax is spectacular. It is visible first of all in the strong presence of the theme of filiation. The chorus calls Ajax "son of Telamon."[123] Although that is a common periphrasis, it is flattering for the son, because it associates the father's glory with him. Here we must avoid an error in perspective. Since Ajax is now better known than his father Telamon, we might be tempted to see in the appellation "son of Telamon" merely a rhetorical figure. But Telamon, Ajax's father, had distinguished himself during the first expedition conducted against Troy, that of Heracles, and as a reward for his exploits he received Laomedon's daughter Hesione, who bore him a son, Teucer, Ajax's half brother. This was well known to the Athenian audience. The fate of this father is recalled by small allusions in several passages of the tragedy where the two half brothers Ajax and Teucer refer to him.[124] In particular, when Ajax, regaining lucidity after his act of madness, reflects on his misfortunes, his father's glorious destiny immediately occurs to him:

> Look, I am one whose father's prowess won him the fairest prize of all the army, whose father brought every glory home from this same land of Ida; but I, his son, who came after him to this same ground of Troy with no less might and proved the service of my hand in no meaner deeds, I am ruined as you see by dishonor from the Greeks.[125]

Thus there is an apparent injustice in the destiny of the son as compared with that of his father. But the son knows very well that despite that, his father will not pardon him:

> How shall I face my father Telamon, when I arrive? How will he bear to look on me, when I stand before him stripped, without that supreme prize of valor for which he himself won a great crown of fame?[126]

For Ajax, it is impossible to return to his father, which amounts to saying that a return to his homeland of Salamis is out of the question.

But the theme of filiation does not stop there, because Ajax himself is a father. After listing his misfortunes, he asks to see his son, who is still very young. From a long speech in which he addresses by turns the mother and the child, the child and the chorus, it emerges that the son, the family's heir, must perpetuate the father's nature. He must be "moulded to the likeness of my nature":[127]

> Ah, son, may you prove luckier than your father, but in all else like him. Then you would not prove base.[128]

The only way Ajax's son can resemble him is to distinguish himself by bravery in combat, for Ajax's nature, which he inherited from his father and is transmissible to his son, can be expressed only in exceptional conduct in battle. That is the only way out, for the son of the man who was the best in combat. Telamon had already doomed his son Ajax to excellence.

Ajax has in fact fully realized his nature by becoming the equal of his father, since after Achilles' death he was the best of the Achaians. Far from being a marginal hero, as some like to say because he was posted on the edge of the Achaian camp, he was in reality the rampart that protected the Achaians at one end of the line of ships, following the Homeric geography well known to the audience: it is there that the best warrior must be posted. Achilles, before his death, was at the other end.[129] The extremities of the line are the place of danger, and being there is a sign of bravery and honor. It is the choice place for the epic hero. But in the tragic perspective, achieving exploits is not the center of the subject as it is in the epic perspective. In tragedy, the nature of the hero is not revealed in his exploits, but in a crisis. This crisis, in Ajax's case, is the result of a twofold rupture: the first, caused by men, was the unjust attribution of Achilles' arms, not to the best warrior after him, namely Ajax, but to another, Odysseus; and the second, caused this time by a goddess, when he tried to take revenge for the affront: Athena plunged him into madness and into the worst of dishonors at the very time when he was trying to avenge his honor. How will the hero's nature manifest itself and react when he emerges from his madness? That is the fundamental question that guides the presentation of the character and his relations with others.

Thus Sophocles presents the character in a dynamic, not static, manner. It is the story of reawakening after a nightmare that is, in fact, reality. And thanks to the subtle mixture of narratives and spectacle, the audience is in a position to reconstruct, as in a puzzle, its various stages. Ajax's joy in taking revenge on his enemies in the unawareness of insanity has been followed, with his return to reason, by pain. But the awakening was long and gradual. The first steps are described lucidly and in detail in Tecmessa's report to the chorus: first there were gestures of despair and cries, the hero's collapse, sitting among the slaughtered animals, and then a long period of prostration. In the first stage, Ajax seems himself to have been reduced to the state of animal. The fall of the hero in the scale of values is impressive. Then, in a second stage, he begins to return to humanity: he is able to speak and threatens Tecmessa in order to find out the truth concerning what he has done; when he learns it, it causes another fit of moaning, followed by another period of calm. But during this second crisis, Tecmessa notes that Ajax seems to have lost his heroic nature:

> He immediately groaned mournful groans, such as I had never heard from him before. For he had always taught that such wailing was for cowardly and low-hearted men.[130]

Tecmessa's astonishment at the apparent change in the Ajax's nature is accompanied by the fear that some disaster might occur, as her remarks suggest;[131] and even if, out of modesty or superstition, Tecmessa does not define this disaster, the first of Ajax's statements heard by the spectator makes it clear that she is referring to suicide. The whole rest of the tragedy up to the death of Ajax will consist in showing how the hero recovers his nature and overcomes his misfortune by committing suicide.

One of the essential phases is constituted by the long speech in which Ajax lists his misfortunes and deliberates concerning what he should do. After rejecting a dishonoring return to his homeland or a heroic death in combat that would give pleasure to his enemies the Atreids, he decides to seek a solution that will show his father that he is not in nature unworthy of him:

> That must not happen. Some enterprise must be sought whereby I may prove to my aged father that in nature, at least, his son is not gutless.[132]

The word "nature" takes on a great importance; it includes all the noble qualities inherited from his father. They must be expressed in glorious acts, even if they put his life in danger. But since a heroic death in combat is excluded, the only remaining option is suicide, which is implicit in the final maxim:

> The options for a noble man are only two: either live with honor, or make a quick and honorable death.[133]

And it is no accident that the chorus, after such a speech, emphasizes, in a metaphorical way, that Ajax's words do not resemble those of a child substituted for another at the time of birth, but have issued from his own mind:

> No man shall say that you have spoken a bastard word, Ajax, or one not bred of your own heart.[134]

The chorus's judgment, far from being an anodyne remark intended to fill the gap between Ajax's and Tecmessa's speeches, is an important stage in Ajax's evolution. Whereas Tecmessa no longer recognized Ajax when, overcome by despair, he gave himself over to a moaning and groaning incompatible with the way he spoke in the past, the chorus notes that his present words are in accord with his deep nature. Having broken down under the impact of his misfortune, Ajax has just triumphed over it by making a decision that will permit him to safeguard his nature. But at the cost of his life.

After overcoming the assaults of misfortune, he must resist the pressure of those close to him who are trying to save his life: first of all, the chorus, which asks him to abandon these thoughts, that is, to abandon his nature;[135] and especially Tecmessa, who, in a long speech paralleling Ajax's, appeals to his pity but also to his sense of duty to his family—his son, his wife, his relatives. In a final formulation, Tecmessa skillfully turns Ajax's argument against him by giving a definition of nobility in which the demands of a personal ethics of excellence are replaced by the duties of gratitude to his people:

Whoever lets the memory of benefits seep from him, he can no longer be a noble man.[136]

Will Ajax hear this appeal? Will he yield to his companions' entreaties? The answer is delayed by his insistence on seeing his son. However, the lengthy speech that he delivers as he holds his son in his arms is at once a reaffirmation of his nature and preparation for his fateful decision. The reassertion of his own nature is expressed in his wish that his son be his equal in his nature:

> But he must at once be broken into his father's harsh ways and moulded to the likeness of my nature.[137]

Ajax has recovered his dignity because he has to be a model for his son. But this recovery supposes as its condition sine qua non that he will commit suicide. That is how we must understand Ajax's counsels to the chorus and to his son regarding the future: they are, in fact, his last will and testament. Thus he rejects Tecmessa's tears and supplications with a certain brutality. Because this scene resembles in many ways the famous scene in the *Iliad* known as "Hector's farewell to Andromache,"[138] the insensitivity of Ajax, who brusquely orders his captive go back inside, is opposed to the delicate sensitivity of Hector, who takes pity on his wife at the moment when he asks her to go home.[139] The contrast is obviously intended by Sophocles. However, underneath the warrior's harshness, a controlled sensitivity was revealed for a moment when he spoke to his son. Even Tecmessa's words were not completely ignored, because in his last advice Ajax is taking care of his family: he counts on Teucer to protect his son, and on his son to protect his aged parents. But he stiffens when people try to soften his resolve:

> You have foolish hope, I think, if you plan so late to begin schooling my temper.[140]

Those are the last words Ajax says to Tecmessa before the house's door closes behind her. They are the clearest evidence of the inflexibility of his nature. During a single choral song, an extraordinary turnabout seems to have occurred. Ajax, followed by Tecmessa, reappears. Under pressure from his family, he seems to have lost his inflexibility, just as he has momentarily lost it under the impact of his misfortune. Tecmessa's emotional appeals seem at last to have had an effect on him:

> For even I, who used to be so tremendously strong—yes, like tempered iron— felt my tongue's sharp edge emasculated by this woman's words, and I feel the pity of leaving her a widow and the boy an orphan among my enemies.[141]

This change appears to be the result of meditation, because Ajax justifies it by more general considerations on the passage of time, which can produce the unexpected, on the alternation of natural powers in the universe, and on the instability of human relationships. He resisted but is now going to yield. He will move from heroism to wisdom. At least that is what he says, and that is what those around him, Tecmessa and the chorus, believe. But the ambiguity of his words is such that this speech is in reality nothing but a ruse to allow him to go away without arousing suspicions and to implement the only decision that is in conformity with his nature, suicide.

In tragedy, in contrast with epic, the touchstone of heroism is no longer behavior in combat with external enemies, but one's attitude with regard to the dishonor and misfortune brought about by an unjust decision made by internal enemies. The hero, momentarily unnerved, seems to lose his nature, but he recovers it by overcoming not only the misfortune but also his entourage's call for wisdom. His lonely death fully realizes his unchanged nature. That is the meaning of the hero's final words, in which he refers to himself in the third person as he bids farewell to the sun, his homeland, and Troy:

> This is the last word that Ajax speaks to you.[142]

Toward the end of his career, Sophocles took up once again the problem of the constructing an epic hero whose nature has to cope with the misfortune caused by internal enemies; and these internal enemies are the same ones. Philoctetes shares Ajax's hatred for the trio formed by the two Atreids and Odysseus. Like Ajax, he feels himself to be the victim of their unjust decision. In both tragedies, the hatred of internal enemies feeds the hero's energy, and the idea that they might be laughing at his misfortunes is the cruelest of his sufferings. The tragedy erupts into Philoctetes' destiny, as it does into Ajax's, through two breaches: one is also due to men's unjust decision, and the other to a divinity, but in the reverse order. Philoctetes fell victim to a human decision after having had an illness sent by the gods. Suffering from an ulcer that was eating away his foot and that was caused by the bite of a sacred serpent guarding the open sanctuary of a divinity,[143] he was, on the Atreids' order, was left behind by Odysseus because his cries of pain disturbed the regular performance of sacrifices. Despite his illness, he was ignobly abandoned in a lonely place on the island of Lemnos while he was sleeping after a particularly painful crisis in his disease.[144] However, the great difference between these two destinies is that in the case of Ajax, these two breaches are recent—the madness caused by the divinity occurred during the night preceding the tragedy—while in the case of Philoctetes they occurred ten years earlier. Whereas in *Ajax* the hero's awakening to discover the extent of the disaster happens during the time of the tragedy, in *Philoctetes* it is part of a distant past. But this past surges up in the present of the tragedy as a result of the arrival of Neoptolemus accompanied by his sailors. The account of this that Philoctetes himself gives clearly distinguishes the stages in his self-recovery after a moment of helplessness:

> Can you imagine, boy, what kind of awakening I had when they had gone, and
> I rose from sleep that day?—what stinging tears I wept, and what miseries I

bewailed when I saw that the ships with which I had sailed were all gone, and that there was no man in the place, not one to help me, not one to ease the sickness that afflicted me, when looking all around me, I could find nothing at hand, save agony—but of that a ready store?[145]

This awakening is still more moving that than of Ajax, because the sick man cannot count on help from anyone. But it may be less painful, because Philoctetes' conscience is not tortured, like Ajax's, by a dishonoring act. His recovery of himself consisted not in saving his honor but in surviving thanks to his bow and his willpower. Confronted by this high-born hero doomed to lead a solitary life in a hostile environment, prey to hunger and illness, the chorus spontaneously feels pity, but it also feels admiration for his incredible resolution.[146] Philoctetes himself is aware that his misfortune has revealed his nature:

> Let us be going, my son, when we two have made a solemn farewell to my homeless home inside, so that you may also learn by what means I sustained my life, and how stout of heart I was born. For I believe that the mere sight would have deterred any other man but me from enduring these sufferings. But I have been slowly schooled by necessity to endure misery.[147]

This reference to his nature, to his enduring courage, reminds us of Ajax's references to his own nature. The comparison is all the less arbitrary because the same rare adjective, *eukarios*, "with a steadfast heart," is used by both heroes.[148] However, Philoctetes' "savageness," which he himself asks the strangers to disregard,[149] must not be overemphasized; it is an appearance that has not changed his deep nature, even if at the end of the tragedy Neoptolemus uses the same word to refer to Philoctetes' wild nature.[150]

For Philoctetes, son of Poeas, the only hope of escaping this miserable life is to return to his father in his homeland, at the foot of Mount Oeta.[151] Unlike Ajax, he can do so because he has done nothing contrary to his honor. And he believes that in Neoptolemus he has finally found not only a friend who shares his hatred for the internal enemies but also someone who will help him return to his homeland. Sophocles introduces multiple reversals to accelerate or retard this return, which is greatly desired from Philoctetes' point of view,[152] but not from that of the success of Odysseus's mission: what makes this departure so urgent is the intervention of the false merchant, in the course of which Philoctetes learns for the first time about Odysseus's (imminent) arrival to take him to Troy; what delays this departure is first of all a crisis of his disease, in which the spectator witnesses directly part of the difficulties that Philoctetes has had to surmount in his ten years of solitude, and during which he is forced to give his bow to Neoptolemus; then Neoptolemus's moral crisis, which is, for Philoctetes, the starting point for a further tragedy reproducing the first one, because he is once again the victim of a betrayal, and aggravating it, because he finds himself without his bow and doomed to no longer be able to survive if he refuses to leave for Troy. How will he confront this new misfortune?

When he is overwhelmed by despair, like Ajax he begs the chorus to help him commit suicide.[153] And again like Ajax, he shows an exceptional resistance to those who try, either by force or by persuasion, to make him yield. One scene is new with respect to *Ajax*: the face-to-face encounter between the hero and his enemy Odysseus. Even though he is extremely disadvantaged physically compared with his triumphant enemy, and even though he is handicapped by his illness and now deprived of his bow, Philoctetes displays an extraordinary determination in refusing to go to Troy:

Odysseus: Now our march must begin.
Philoctetes: Never!
Odysseus: Now, I say. You must obey.
Philoctetes: Ah, misery! Clearly, then, my father sired me to be a slave and no free man.[154]

Like Ajax, so far as he can see the only way to remain faithful to his nature is to commit suicide. In fact, immediately after uttering these words, Philoctetes tries to retain his freedom to kill himself. But this reduces him to a still greater powerlessness, because Odysseus gives the order to tie his hands. Thus the hunter with his infallible bow and arrows has become his worst enemy's prey.[155] But even though he is without a weapon, he does not give up. Words are the ultimate weapon he has to draw up a lucid and passionate indictment of his oppressor's baseness and cowardice, and to curse his three enemies, Odysseus and the Atreids, who are laughing at him in his misery, in much the same way that Ajax cursed them.[156] Like Ajax, Philoctetes has to cope with the efforts to persuade him to yield. Just as Ajax seemed to be impervious to the arguments given by the chorus and by Tecmessa, Philoctetes seems impervious to those of Neoptolemus. And both heroes are reproached by others for being too arrogant in misfortune.[157] This imperviousness is merely apparent; Philoctetes also reveals for a moment his sensitivity to what others say: "Ah, me, what shall I do? How can I ignore this man's words, when he has advised me with good will?"[158]

But ultimately, Philoctetes will yield to others' advice no more than Ajax did. Neither of them is capable of yielding when doing so would put them in conflict with themselves. In both of them, the hatred of the internal enemies who have attacked their honor is stronger than the desire for glory in combat. It is true that the outcome of their destiny will be very different, because one of them, abandoned by the divinity, will meet the demands of his nature by committing suicide, while the other will finally hear the call of the divinity that will take him to Troy, healing, and glory. But despite the misfortunes they have suffered, neither of the two has yielded to human beings in such a way as to put in danger the ethical imperatives inherited from their fathers. What they have had to discover is the paths that must be followed to continue to put into practice, amid misfortunes that prevent them from engaging in combat, the aristocratic values that are naturally connected with it. And if they have not yielded, that is because the wave of disasters has struck them at a time when their heroic nature was already well established.

That is how it is with these seasoned heroic natures (Ajax, Philoctetes) who are suddenly torn away from their natural domain of action and find, with pain but without a moral crisis, the paths to persevere in their being despite enemies or friends.

A Budding Epic Hero in Tragedy: Neoptolemus in *Philoctetes*

But what happens when the heroic nature inherited from the father is first put to the test of reality. This is the question that Sophocles raises in *Philoctetes*—and which is new with respect to *Ajax*—by introducing a young hero of the following generation, of that second generation that was not part of the first contingent of the expedition against Troy. The idea comes from Sophocles himself, since the character of Neoptolemus does not appear in this mythic sequence in the works of his predecessors.[159]

Of all the characters created by Sophocles, Neoptolemus is the one whose nature is the most prestigious, since he is the son of Achilles, the best of the Achaians of the first generation that left to fight the second Trojan war. This filiation is highlighted at the beginning of the tragedy—when Odysseus addresses him for the first time, calling him the "child bred of the man who was the noblest of the Greeks, Neoptolemus son of Achilles"[160]—and is recalled throughout the tragedy.[161] Neoptolemus introduces himself to Philoctetes as the son of Achilles.[162] When he arrives at Troy after the death of his father, the Achaians see in him his father's double.[163] His young heroic nature should, like that of his father, find its natural home in combat, where his strength and bravery could express itself. But from the beginning of the tragedy he sees himself in a role that is not in conformity with his nature. Odysseus, when he sets forth his mission and imposes it on him, knows this perfectly well:

> Son of Achilles, you must be loyal to the goals of your mission—and not with your body alone. Should you hear some new plan unknown to you till now, you must serve it, since it is to serve that you are here.[164]

This new assignment consists in deceiving Philoctetes in order to seize his bow. Odysseus tries to overcome Neoptolemus's objections while at the same time expressly acknowledging that the mission is contrary to his nature:

> Well I know, my son, that by nature you are not apt to utter or contrive such treachery.[165]

And in fact Neoptolemus begins by refusing to use this method, in the name of his natural ethics, in conformity with that of his father:

It is not in my nature to achieve anything by means of evil cunning, nor was
it, as I hear, in my father's. But I am ready to take the man by force and without
treachery, since with the use of one foot only, he will not overcome so many of
us in a struggle. And yet I was sent to assist you and am reluctant to be called
traitor. Still I prefer, my king, to fail when doing what is honorable than to be
victorious in a dishonorable manner.[166]

Nonetheless, Neoptolemus finally allows himself to be convinced by the rhetorical skill of Odysseus, who demonstrates the impossibility of using force because of Philoctetes' infallible bow and the impossibility that Neoptolemus can
win at Troy without the presence of that bow:

> *Odysseus:* You will be celebrated in the same breath as clever and as noble.
> *Neoptolemus:* So be it! I will do it, and cast off all shame.[167]

It is clear that this decision, obtained by Odysseus by means of his power of
persuasion, is contrary to Neoptolemus's nature. This first scene contains in germ
all the basic givens that explain the development of the son of Achilles from the
moment when he encounters another character who resembles him by nature,
Philoctetes. This resemblance is confirmed by the latter in his curses against
Odysseus when he is at his mercy:

> And you, who cannot think one healthy or one noble thought, how stealthily
> you have once more ambushed and trapped me, taking this boy for your screen,
> because he was a stranger to me. He is too good for your company, but worthy
> of mine, since he had no thought but to execute his orders, and he already
> shows remorse for his own errors and for the wrongs done me.[168]

At the very moment when Philoctetes utters these words, Neoptolemus's
evolution has already begun. He had first embroidered on Odysseus's deceptive
canvas with such skill that he had no difficulty in winning Philoctetes' trust by
pretending to feel the same hatred for the Atreids, and he had pretended to
agree to take Philoctetes back to his homeland. Is Neoptolemus going to turn
out to be a clever man, a *sophos* like Odysseus? The mission seems to be advanc-
ing with a disconcerting ease when Philoctetes' fit of pain suddenly contributes
to the mission's success and also to its failure: success insofar as Philoctetes is
obliged to entrust his bow to Neoptolemus, failure insofar as Philoctetes' physical crisis helps trigger a moral crisis in Neoptolemus. In fact, whereas Neoptolemus could leave, taking Philoctetes and his bow with him, he suddenly stops,
just as Philoctetes had stopped just as he was departing, struck down by the fit
of pain. Sophocles dramatically put these two crises in parallel and prepared the
second by the first; for Philoctetes' suffering had already awakened Neoptolemus's pity.[169] This awakening of pity prepares for the revival of the feeling of
shame.[170] During this moral crisis, Neoptolemus becomes aware that he has lost
his nature.

All is offense when a man has abandoned his true nature and does what does not suit him.[171]

Remorse obliges him to tell the truth, first with the firm intention of continuing his mission by keeping the bow and taking Philoctetes away by force, and then, after Philoctetes' violent and desperate reaction, with hesitation and the temptation to return his bow to him. But Sophocles multiplies dramatic reversals. First Odysseus intervenes to prevent Neoptolemus from returning the bow and to save the mission; then Neoptolemus returns, this time having made the firm decision to return the bow. Thus the young man's decisive evolution has taken place offstage. From that point on, Neoptolemus, who has completely freed himself from his fear of Odysseus, dares to confront and defy him, then he calls Philoctetes and returns his bow to him. This time, Odysseus arrives too late. This is when Neoptolemus wins back his true nature and becomes Philoctetes' sincere friend. Sophocles uses Philoctetes to emphasize Neoptolemus's recovery of his nature:

> You have revealed the true stock, my son, from which you spring. You are no child of Sisyphus, but of Achilles, whose fame was the fairest when he was among the living, as it is now with the dead.[172]

For all that, Neoptolemus has not abandoned the idea of taking Philoctetes to Troy, now using not ruse or force, but persuasion. He advances two essential arguments based on Helenus's prophecy: the curing of his illness by the son of Asclepius and the greatest of glories to be won by conquering Troy. Neoptolemus speaks as a friend speaking in the interest of a friend, seeking to reawaken in him the aristocratic ideal of glory in combat. But he does not succeed in overcoming the bitter hate that Philoctetes nourishes for his enemies. Thus, having run out of arguments, he finds himself forced by Philoctetes to honor a promise he had made him during his mission of deception—to take him back to his homeland. By accepting his failure, Neoptolemus ultimately realizes the maxim that he had formulated at the beginning when he defined his nature for Odysseus:

> I prefer, my king, to fail when doing what is honorable than to be victorious in a dishonorable manner.[173]

Thus we arrive at the most paradoxical situation. Two heroes have an opportunity to express themselves together in the domain of action natural to them, glory in combat. However, they forgo doing so precisely in order not to be in contradiction with their nature, one not wanting to yield to his enemies, the other not wanting to be disloyal to his friend. Only a divinity could reconcile their heroic nature with the natural domain where it is supposed to flourish.

That is how it is with this young man of heroic nature (Neoptolemus) who, involved in a deceptive mission contrary to what he is, succeeds, after a moral crisis, in regaining his harmony with himself.

Epic Heroes as Counterpoints in Tragedy: The Atreids and Odysseus

Facing these heroic figures, the Atreids and Odysseus act in counterpoint. The Atreids, whether they are speaking characters in *Ajax* or virtual characters in *Philoctetes*, retain the same negative image. From start to finish, they are pursued by the hatred of the heroes (Ajax, Philoctetes); and when they appear, the result is hardly to enhance their image: they seem to be defined by scornful violence accompanied by cowardice in the exercise of a power that they fiercely claim over all others, no matter what their merit.[174]

On the other hand, Odysseus, whose origin is contested—is he the son of Laertes or Sisyphus?[175]—and whose nature is unstable, is treated very differently in *Ajax* and in *Philoctetes*.[176] In the older play, his image is initially negative, like that of the Atreids, at least as Ajax sees it, but it is transformed after Ajax's death: the spectator sees Odysseus oppose one of the Atreids, defend the worth and memory of the man who was his enemy, and thus become the representative of wisdom.[177] But in the later play, in Philoctetes' mind Odysseus's image remains constantly associated with that of the Atreids, and in this case his conduct does not change it. He presents himself to Neoptolemus as a man of experience who has evolved since his youth and has discovered that words are more powerful than acts,[178] while to Philoctetes he presents himself as a man who can play every role and always win.[179] Thus his nature is opposite that of Neoptolemus, who prefers, as we have just seen, an honorable failure to a dishonorable victory. But the facts will contradict his claims. Odysseus, despite his skill, fails, and he leaves the stage defeated and silent.[180] Nonetheless, his image is not totally negative in *Philoctetes*. It must not be forgotten—though it often is—that he finds an advocate in the chorus, when Philoctetes makes excessive accusations against him. According to the chorus, Odysseus is not reprehensible: the mission he is carrying out is desired by the gods, and he is the envoy of a collectivity in the service of which he is acting.[181] This subtle rehabilitation constitutes a counterpoint to the unflattering portrait of Odysseus that emerges from the tragedy as a whole.[182]

Scholars have long seen this change in the treatment of the character of Odysseus between an early and a late tragedy by Sophocles as reflecting the intellectual and political evolution of Athens in the second half of the fifth century, a change that was due to the influence of the sophists on intellectual life—especially after Gorgias of Leontini's embassy to Athens in 427—and the appearance of demagogues in political life after the death of Pericles. In fact, the development of new rhetorical techniques to which contemporaries were responsive[183] may justify the importance Odysseus now accords to speech. It is also possible that the same words had in the meantime taken on a different connotation. This is the case for the word *sophos*. At first it meant both "wise and knowledgeable," because there was originally no antinomy between knowledge and wisdom. But with the discovery of techniques of persuasion that made it possible to make a weak thesis win out over a strong one, the word *sophos* took on a pejorative connotation and designated cleverness more than wisdom. In both *Ajax* and *Philoctetes*, the word *sophos* is used to qualify Odysseus. Nevertheless, the connotation of its use is not the same. In *Ajax*, which preceded the influence of sophistic in Athens, the chorus of Salaminians congratulates Odysseus on having obtained from Agamemnon the authorization to bury Ajax:

> Whoever denies, Odysseus, that you were born wise in judgment [*gnōmè sophon*] is a total fool.[184]

The word *sophos* is in no way ambiguous in this passage. It refers to wisdom and is opposed to foolishness. In *Philoctetes*, a later play written after the development of sophistic, the word is used once again to qualify Odysseus. Here is how Neoptolemus presents Odysseus to Philoctetes at the beginning of the tragedy:

> The man is a clever wrestler. But even clever schemes, Philoctetes, are often blocked.[185]

It is not possible to translate the same words in the same way in the two tragedies. Odysseus, who is wise in *Ajax*, has become clever in *Philoctetes*. Then, during his final confrontation with Odysseus, Neoptolemus, who is resolved to return his bow to Philoctetes, uses the same word to describe Odysseus during his final confrontation with him:

> *Neoptolemus:* You who are clever by nature [*sophos*] say nothing that is clever [*sophon*],
> *Odysseus:* And your words are not clever, nor is that which you want to do.
> *Neoptolemus:* And yet if they are just, they are better than clever.
> *Odysseus:* And how is it just for you to give up what was won by means of my plans?
> *Neoptolemus:* My error was to my dishonor, and now I must try to retrieve it.[186]

Consistency within a tragedy requires us to continue to translate *sophos* as "clever" to qualify Odysseus. Cleverness cannot be confused with wisdom, because Neoptolemus contrasts a just behavior with a clever one. To designate wisdom, he uses another word. When the verbal confrontation looks like it will turn into a test of strength, Odysseus suddenly yields, while at the same time threatening to make a report to the army, which will punish Neoptolemus. It is then that Neoptolemus recognizes, not without irony, Odysseus's wisdom:

> Now you're being wise [*esōphronèsas*]. And if you are so wise [*houtō, phronès*] hereafter, perhaps you may steer clear of trouble.[187]

Hence to account for the evolution of the meaning of words and Odysseus's character between two tragedies that were composed at an interval of about thirty years, we can say that "the heroes from the distant past look different in light of the political and intellectual reality."[188] Nevertheless, Sophocles' creations are much less marked by current events than those of Euripides.[189]

Political Heroes in Tragedy: Creon in *Antigone* and Oedipus in *Oedipus the King*

The epic heroes who took part in the expedition to Troy were far away from the cities they led, and they experienced their tragedy in an unusual political structure where the hierarchy of heroic values they stood for could conflict with that of a central authority that was simultaneously recognized and contested. These epic heroes became tragic heroes the moment they entered into conflict with the central power. On the other hand, in the mythic sequences in which the heroes are situated in their city-states, the problem changes, because the heroes themselves exercise power there. It is in this sense that we can speak of political heroes, because tragedy then develops not against the background of the hero's challenge to the government, but against that of the challenge others pose to their own power. This challenge may arise within their family itself, which introduces inextricable ties between political tragedy and family tragedy.[190] In this respect, two heroes deserve to be compared: Creon in *Antigone* and Oedipus in *Oedipus the King*.

The character of Creon in *Antigone* is often neglected, because Antigone's rebellion occupies center stage during the first part of the tragedy. Creon is often seen as playing the role of a foil by being the oppressor of a just cause. But if we examine him more closely and consider the tragedy as a whole, things become more complex. Without engaging in futile disputes about who is the main hero in the tragedy or at what point a character in a tragedy has to be considered a tragic hero—because these issues are artificial and do not correspond to the reality of the dramatic performance—we see that Creon obviously experiences, like Oedipus, a tragedy connected with his social function as king. And whereas Oedipus is an experienced king when the tragedy opens, Creon is a novice who has just assumed his office the night preceding the tragedy, after the unexpected death of his predecessor. The city has just escaped an assault by the enemy army, but King Eteocles and his brother Polynices have died in a fratricidal single combat. In accord with the law of succession by blood, Creon has succeeded Eteocles.[191] When he first appears, Creon does not act at all like a tyrant, but like a good king. In his first statements, which might be called his speech from the throne, he refers to the legitimacy of his succession as king and shows his determination to follow the royal tradition of the city. He declares irreproachable principles of government that were in antiquity considered models of the genre: the king must confine himself to the best decisions that are in city's interest, without hiding, out of cowardice, what must be condemned, and without giving personal friendship priority over love of country.[192] And even his famous decree including the twofold decision to bury Eteocles with all honors because he defended his homeland, and to reject Polynices' burial because he sought to destroy his homeland and its gods, is clearly presented by Creon as the direct consequence of his political principles.[193] To Sophocles' spectators this edict must not have appeared as astonishing as a modern reader might think, because in Athens itself it was possible to refuse to bury in the soil of Attica a traitor to his homeland or a thief who had stolen sacred objects.[194] Invested with his new royal office, Creon identifies himself with it, or more precisely he sees in it the touchstone that will reveal his true nature, as it must reveal the nature of any man:

> Now, it is impossible to know fully any man's character, will, or judgment, until he has been proved by the test of rule and law-giving.[195]

This general maxim, inspired by the maxim of a sage, whether he was Bias or Chilon,[196] places Creon squarely in line with traditional wisdom. But at the same time it takes on, if we resituate it in the context of the tragedy as a whole, an involuntary tragic irony.[197] The reactions to the unexpected prohibitions that the new king immediately encounters in the exercise of this power will reveal his deep nature by showing how the passion with which wise principles are applied can obscure reason.

It must be acknowledged that Creon has to cope with an unprecedented opposition: the transgression of the edict, not by a man, but by a young woman; and this young woman is very close to him: she lives in the royal palace, is his niece, and moreover, is the fiancée of his son. That is enough to disconcert a king whose policy consists entirely in putting the interest of the city above that of his family.

But Creon's true nature had already begun to reveal itself earlier, when he encountered the first obstacle as king, that is, the news that his edict has been violated, though no one yet knows by whom. He becomes angry, suspicious, and threatening: angry when the chorus suggests that the mysterious way in which Polynices' body has been covered with soil might suggest divine intervention;[198] suspicious, because he sees in the violation of his edict the sign of a conspiracy against him fomented secretly by people who have bribed the guards; and he threatens the guards, whom he promises to kill after torturing them, if the guilty party is not found.

All these feelings seem to be revealed in the exercise of monarchical power. Nature and social function are intimately connected in this kind of great figure; and scholars have not failed to compare this change in Creon with the law of the evolution of the king into a tyrant that Herodotus highlights in his famous discussion of the comparative merits of monarchy, democracy, and oligarchy.[199]

This scene is followed by other scenes of conflict in which we see the king confront, first, young members of his own family: Antigone the rebel, then Ismene, her sister, and finally his son Haemon. In this whole part, the tragedy is both political and familial. Each confrontation ends in violence, and the king's growing wrath is reflected in his increasingly irreparable decisions.

The last confrontation is of another nature. It brings the king and the seer together and makes clearer the blindness of the king, who is as impervious to the warning issued by an old man endowed with divine knowledge as he is to the young people's arguments. But the chorus, which up to that point has not condemned the king's decrees, except his decision to put Ismene to death, strongly exhorts Creon to reconsider this decision. Reluctantly, Creon yields, but too late. The catastrophes accumulate: Antigone's death leads to his son's suicide, and the death of his son leads to the suicide of his wife, Eurydice. All these disasters make him understand his errors.[200] Thus between the beginning and the end, the character of Creon has evolved considerably: at the outset he spoke only in political terms, but now, confronted by the misfortunes that are striking his family, he has abandoned any reference to the city and gained access, by becoming aware of his mistakes, to a broader wisdom beyond politics and the family. At the end, he recognizes what he angrily rejected at the beginning: the gods' intervention.[201]

A little later in his career, Sophocles returned to the study of a political hero whose nature is revealed through his function as king. Once again, it is in a play set in Thebes, but the mythic sequence it deals with is earlier than that of *Antigone*. I refer to Oedipus in *Oedipus the King*. Despite what seem to be major differences in the situation, we can recognize convergences in the evolution of the royal character.

In *Oedipus the King*, as in *Antigone*, the character is initially merged with his function as king, and he devotes himself wholly to being a good king. Oedipus is facing a crisis in the city that he has to cope with, just as Creon was at the outset emerging from a crisis that he had to settle. But whereas Creon has just become king, Oedipus has reigned for a rather long time. And if Oedipus is king, it is not by any right of legitimate succession, but because he has saved, by his intelligence, the city of Thebes from an initial crisis, the ravages of the Sphinx. Confronting this second crisis, a devastating plague,[202] the king appears to the people as the supreme recourse, the one who must save the city. In fact, his first concern is the city: "My soul is in pain at once for the city, for myself, and for you."[203] And after reflecting on the impossibility of resolving the this second crisis by his intelligence alone, as he had done for the first one, he has decided to resort to divine knowledge: first to the Delphic oracle, following his own initiative, and then to the city's seer, Tiresias, on the advice of his brother-in-law Creon. In all this, the king's conduct is exemplary. Such is the initial situation.

But as in *Antigone* and in a still subtler way, the king, in his desire to do too much good, will reveal, notably when confronting others, feelings that might be called tyrannical, or at least analogous to those of Creon: anger and suspicion leading to blindness. Sophocles has deliberately repeated the confrontation between the king and the seer that he had already used in his *Antigone* and that drew its initial inspiration from a scene in Homer's *Iliad*.[204] Oedipus's reactions to Tiresias are comparable to Creon's. At first full of respect for the seer, the two kings get angry when faced with revelations that challenge them and react like kings whose power is threatened, accusing Tiresias and threatening him, and this leads the latter to offer new revelations as they are caught up in a cycle of anger on both sides. To be sure, Sophocles made changes, notably in the place of the scene in relation to the course of the action: the meeting between the king and the seer, which was the last major scene of conflict in *Antigone*, becomes the first major scene in *Oedipus the King*. It is there that Oedipus shows for the first time his tyrannical feelings. It is there that the word "anger" appears for the first time in the tragedy. And it is there that the king begins to develop his fear of a conspiracy, which he will express more fully in the second scene of conflict, confronting his brother-in-law Creon, exactly as the Creon in *Antigone* had begun to develop the thesis of a conspiracy as soon as someone opposed his power.

Thus there is a kind of natural fatality in the exercise of power that results from wanting to exercise it too well. The Oedipus of *Oedipus the King* falls into the same excesses and the same mistakes as does the Creon of *Antigone*. In Sophocles' theater only the king of Athens, Theseus, escapes this mechanism leading royal power to transform itself into a tyrannical power.[205] The origin of anger in the case of Oedipus subtly displays this mechanism whose source is often an excess of goodness. If Oedipus begins to get angry at the seer, it is because he is reacting as a responsible king: in Tiresias's refusal to reveal what he knows, Oedipus sees a lack of civic spirit; and that is what seems to him intolerable and triggers his wrath. Then this anger, feeding on the imagination, leads to unfounded accusations against the seer, which elicit the seer's well-founded accusations, which in turn provide more material for the king's anger and for the thesis of a conspiracy organized by Creon, of which Tiresias would be an instrument. Thus we see how concern for the state ends up distorting the king's judgment through anger. This distortion is lucidly emphasized by the chorus when Creon arrives, scandalized by the unjust accusations Oedipus has made against him:

> But perhaps this taunt came under the stress of anger [*orgè*], rather than from the purpose of his reason [*gnome*].[206]

This antithesis between "anger" (*orgè*) and "reason" or "judgment" (*gnome*) is very remarkable. Extremely rare in the fifth century, it is unique in Greek theater. But it is found in the historian Thucydides, notably in the relations between Pericles and the people of Athens. The comparison is instructive. In Thucydides, "anger" is a reaction of the crowd that Pericles fears and that he tries to contain in order to lead the people to act with "judgment."[207] On the other hand, in Sophocles "anger" defines the leader's reaction. And it is all the more surprising because Oedipus had become king of Thebes precisely thanks to his "judgment," which allowed him to solve the Sphinx's riddle.[208] This anger will reach its apex in the encounter between the king and the supposed creator of the conspiracy; the king's violence makes him deaf to Creon's justifications, deaf to the counsel of the chorus, which supports Creon, and the grip of anger on him leads him to condemn to death without judgment the alleged creator of the conspiracy, just as the Creon of *Antigone* threatened with death all his opponents real or imaginary, without making any distinctions among them; but by doing that they both thought they were acting in the city's interest. It is at the end of the scene in which Oedipus wants to condemn Creon to death that he utters his famous exclamation: "Hear him, O city, O city of Thebes!"[209]

Thus despite the differences between these two tragedies with regard to the conduct of the action, we find the same evolution in the royal personage: like Creon, at the beginning Oedipus merges with his function as king and then allows himself to be misled by anger and the fear of a conspiracy.

However, the tragedy of *Oedipus the King* later takes a turn different from that in *Antigone*, because Jocasta intervenes to put an end to the quarrel between her brother and her husband and to reassure her husband regarding the seer's accusations. This scene of intimacy contrasts with the preceding scenes, in which the king confronted presumed political enemies. But in trying to reassure Oedipus, Jocasta reveals to him a bit of information that will cause the king to move from an investigation undertaken to identify the murderer of Laius in order to save the city to an investigation into himself. It is in fact a detail that Jocasta mentions in passing, the intersection of three roads where Laius was killed, that suddenly causes a detail of his past to rise up in Oedipus's mind, arousing the worry that he might himself be the murderer he is seeking. Henceforth he thinks only about himself:

O Zeus, what have you decreed for me?[210]

The hero will continue to pursue his research with the same passion, but his preoccupation with the city will disappear completely. The distribution of the uses of the word "city" in the tragedy as a whole is significant. Virtually all the uses of this word (eighteen out of nineteen) are found in the first half of the tragedy, and the word appears nine times in Oedipus's speeches. From that point on, he utters the word "city" only once. This change corresponds exactly to the passage from political scenes to the private scene in which the spouses reveal to each other a part of their pasts. Henceforth Oedipus floats between concern and hope, depending on the information that comes in, until he finally discovers the truth about who he is: the murderer of his father, the husband of his mother, and the brother of his children.[211]

Then, when he returns to the stage at the end of the tragedy after having put out his eyes, the reflection on misfortunes, the hero's as well as the chorus's, broadens to include humanity as a whole.[212] It is not only the Cadmeans, but mortals in general who become the spectators of his sufferings,[213] and his exceptional destiny exceeds, in the order of misfortune, that of all other mortals.[214]

Tiresias had already predicted this level of exception in misfortune.[215] This is a kind of inversion of epic exemplarity, in which the hero was the best of all the warriors of all the contingents. In his misfortune, the fallen political hero reaches an exemplarity that goes beyond the context of the city and becomes the focal point for all humanity.

Women's Silence

A final analogy between Creon's destiny in *Antigone* and Oedipus's destiny in *Oedipus the King* proceeds from the fact that these kings indirectly cause their wives' death. Unlike an epic hero like Ajax, whose catastrophe does not lead to other deaths, the political heroes suffer not only from their own misfortunes but from the deaths that result from them. The analogy between the fate of the two queens is all the more striking because they disappear in the same way, in silence, in order to commit suicide inside the palace.

In Ajax's epic universe, the ideal assigned to women is silence. When Ajax was silently preparing to leave alone on his nighttime expedition to take revenge on those who had attacked in his honor, Tecmessa tried to find out what was going on, and according to her, the only reply she received was a formula she had often heard but which she obeyed:

"Woman, silence graces woman."[216]

This maxim is obviously not peculiar to Ajax or to the epic universe. It must already have been proverbial in Sophocles' time. It is found elsewhere in the tragedies of Sophocles and Euripides,[217] as well as in a form that is similar but a little less excessive, in a contemporary philosopher, Democritus:

Speaking little adorns a woman.[218]

In Athens, a woman's silence was a sign of a good education, at least in matters external to the household, such as politics and war. However, in one of Aristophanes' comedies set during the Peloponnesian War women complain about the silence that is imposed on them by their husbands every time they want to speak up, even discreetly, in favor of peace.[219] Nonetheless, Ajax's maxim must not have seemed scandalous to spectators during the performance of the play: in the fourth century, Aristotle still cites it in his *Politics* as a maxim applicable to women, but not to men.[220]

This reticence imposed on women by men is different from the "excessive silence" of several of Sophocles' female characters who leave the stage and enter the palace without saying a word.[221] This is a tragic silence, presaging a suicide.

When, in *Antigone*, Creon's wife, Eurydice, emerges from the palace[222] and hears from the messenger the whole truth about her son's suicide, she goes back into the palace without a word. The chorus notes this silent departure and expresses its concern to the messenger. Although he, too, is struck by it, the messenger hopes that the present silence is a form of the "silence that adorns a woman": Eurydice, he thinks, must want to avoid lamentations outside, in the public space, and has left to organize mourning inside the palace, in the space that is her own. He bases this view on her discretion.[223] The chorus, for its part, remains more circumspect:

> I do not know. But to me, in any case, a silence too strict seems to promise trouble just as much as a fruitless abundance of weeping.[224]

Then the messenger, adopting these words, considers another possible meaning of this silence: an idea hidden in a shattered heart. The spectator soon learns that this was the right diagnosis. In fact, Creon had hardly returned carrying the body of his son in his arms before he learned of his wife's suicide. Of Eurydice, a queen-for-a-day who had left in silence, we have no more than a limited sketch; but the few details provided are all significant. Pious, she came out to make a sacrifice to Athena. Emotional, when she hears the sound of the bad news she faints inside her home, into the arms of her servants; she gets a grip on herself when she is outside, in order to listen to the messenger's report; then she goes away in silence. From the few words that she utters when she enters, we are already aware that she has known misfortune.[225] A little later on, we learn that this misfortune was the loss of her first son, who died gloriously.[226] Before committing suicide by stabbing herself in the chest at the foot of the altar, this woman who is so reasonable but overwhelmed by pain moans over the death of her first son, and then of her second son, and finally curses her husband, whom she accuses of having murdered her children. This death probably has a primarily dramatic role: it serves to strengthen the emotional dimension of the tragedy that has befallen Creon, struck by one misfortune after another. But Eurydice is not a passing shadow. She has her own tragedy, that of a woman who is essentially a mother.[227] Her final hatred of her husband echoes the son's final hatred of his father.

Sophocles used this character of the king's wife in his *Oedipus the King*, giving her more presence. Jocasta also leaves in silence when she understands Oedipus's misfortune—which is also hers—and once again, it is the chorus who draws attention to this silence:

> Why has this woman gone, Oedipus, rushing off in wild grief? I fear a storm of sorrow will soon break forth from this silence.[228]

But before she departs, Jocasta plays, with respect to her husband, an essential role that Creon's wife, who did not even encounter her husband, did not have in *Antigone*. As soon as she makes her entrance onstage, Jocasta acts in a remarkable way, as a woman who does not limit herself to the silence that adorns women. It is she who reduces to a simple private dispute the conflict that the men presented as a governmental quarrel, by reminding them of the essential concern: the tragedy of the city.[229] However, after Creon's departure, the scene becomes private: it is a long interior scene—which takes place outside for scenic reasons—in which the wife assures her husband of her devotion.[230] She is in fact devoted to him; she lives in sync with his fears and constantly tries to calm them. But despite themselves, good intentions reveal the tragedy. By trying to calm his concerns, she reveals an initial clue that feeds new worries;[231] and by trying to reassure him, she awakens his concern until her efforts to conceal the truth, when she has discovered it, lead to Oedipus's failure to understand and to the break at the very moment when her only remaining option is to leave in silence. Like Eurydice, she leaves to commit suicide, but not with a sword, at the foot of the altar, but in her bedroom, by hanging herself. She does not blame her husband, who is also her son. For him, she feels no hate, only pity.[232] Oedipus, on the other hand, explodes with anger when she goes away in silence, irritated by her attitude, which he considers haughty, and irritated also by the chorus's worried remark:

> Break forth what will! Be my race ever so lowly, I crave to learn it. That woman perhaps—for she is proud with more than a woman's pride—feels ashamed of my lowly origin.[233]

This is a scene in which a woman goes away in silence, in which the chorus worries about this departure, and in which the man, who has remained onstage, does not understand and explodes with anger. Sophocles had already used this kind of scene in his *Women of Trachis*, when he presented the most loving of women, Deianira, Heracles' wife. Once her son Hyllus has told her about the disastrous effects of the tunic she gave her husband, and concluded by indicting and cursing her, Deianira, understanding the whole magnitude of the catastrophe, goes away:

> *Chorus: To Deianira.* Why do you leave without a word? Do you not know
>   that your silence pleads your accuser's case?
> *Hyllus:* Let her leave. May a fair wind speed her far from my sight! Why
>   should she falsely keep the dignity of the name "Mother," when she is all
>   unlike a mother in her deeds? No, let her go—farewell to her. May such
>   delight as she gives my father become her own![234]

Of the three scenes in which a woman goes away in silence, this is the most dramatic, because the chorus speaks up not after her departure, but at the time when she is leaving. This only makes her silence all the more striking. The violence of her son's accusation that she murdered his father redoubles the pain of a woman who, out of love, has caused the death of the man she loves.

In Sophocles' extant tragedies, no other character who is a married woman has received a treatment as attentive and as subtle. The whole first part of the tragedy, before the arrival of the messenger announcing Heracles' victorious return, is devoted to a presentation of her life, either by Deianira herself or by the chorus, even if this presentation is inseparably connected with Heracles' destiny. From the beginning of the tragedy, we hear a woman speak at length about herself in the first person, recount her life as in a story, a cruel story. After a carefree, happy youth in her father's home, her life has been a series of fears. Fears of different kinds: first the horrible prospect of being given in marriage to a monstrous suitor attracted by her beauty; then the dread of being present at Heracles' battle against this monster, though she was too distraught to watch it; and finally, after the joy of rescue, the perpetual fear for a husband who was too often absent, returning from time to time to engender children.

In her reply to the young women of the chorus who have come to give her hope, Deianira moves beyond her own case to speak about the condition of women in general, about the hiatus constituted by marriage, which she sees not as the fulfillment of woman's nature through maternity, but as the loss of the paradise of childhood and the entry into nights of anxiety about members of her family, her husband and her children. But this particular morning, when she awoke with a start, fear is at its height: after fifteen months of absence this day is decisive for her husband's destiny, according to the oracles he left behind when he departed.

The tragedy will present, in a condensed form, what Deianira has experienced in her past destiny: a brief moment of joy upon learning that her husband has returned safe and victorious, then an anxiety, but one entirely different in kind from those she had known earlier. At first, her meeting with the captive brought by Lichas, Heracles' herald, spontaneously elicits her pity, but then arouses in her, when she learns the truth about Heracles' love, a new feeling, the jealousy of the mature woman who has been left for a younger rival.

But just when is this jealousy manifested? When is the plan to remedy the situation formed? Is it as soon as she learns the truth from Lichas, and when, at the same time that she promises him to accept the captive and not to resist the god of love, she takes him inside to give him a gift? Or is it only once she has gone back into the palace, during the chorus's song, that the rise of jealousy produces a turnaround and leads her to make her decision before going out again to tell the chorus about it? Answers to this question differ and lead to quite different judgments of the character. Did she deceive Lichas from the outset, feigning first to understand, in order to draw the truth out of him, and then to get him to take a gift smeared with a love philter? Or was her initial self-control and wisdom sincere, reminding us of her earlier attitude when she had already shown understanding concerning Heracles' infidelities? The second explanation is preferable for reasons both psychological and theatrical.

Deianira's speech to Lichas to encourage him to tell the truth includes words of a profound sensitivity that do not seem to be part of a trick:

> I felt a profound pity when I saw her because her beauty has destroyed her life, and she, unfortunate one, has against her will devastated her fatherland and enslaved it.[235]

Deianira can feel the greatest pity only because she herself has experienced this inescapable link between beauty (*kallos*) and pain (*algos*), two words that are close to one another in Greek and that Sophocles deliberately juxtaposes.[236] At first, pity strengthens Deianira's wisdom. There is no reason to doubt her sincerity when she promises Lichas to show understanding, even after the revelation of the truth.[237]

Taking Sophocles' theatrical technique into account leads in the same direction: it is not at the very end of an episode that a reversal takes place in a character, but rather in the interval between two episodes, offstage, during the chorus's song, to produce a powerful effect of surprise, between a character's departure and return. The model of this surprise technique is found in *Ajax*. Having gone into his home at the end of the first episode, Ajax comes out of it at the beginning of the second episode. In the interval, as in *The Women of Trachis*, there has been only a choral song. But Ajax emerges totally changed, at least apparently. This is a surprise for the chorus. The same surprise effect is repeated later in *Antigone*, when the guard, who had left swearing he would never return, comes back triumphant, after the chorus's song, bringing Antigone with him. But it is especially in *Philoctetes* that this surprise effect is greatest: it is in the offstage space, during a stasimon, that Neoptolemus makes the final decision to return Philoctetes' bow to him, and thus to escape Odysseus's grip; his sudden return to the stage followed by Odysseus produces the greatest of surprises. Thus major decisions are made offstage, provoking surprise in the spectator and, we must add, a decisive turning point in the action, because the decision is always followed by action.

It is inside the home, in the solitude of her bedchamber, while she is preparing the welcome-home present for her husband, that Deianira becomes aware of the unbearable nature of the situation and decides to act. She comes out, without being seen, to tell the chorus about it. She confides in the young women at length, expecting them to have compassion for her fate and to advise her regarding her decision. She analyzes the situation lucidly—as a fading beauty, can she compete with a beauty in the bloom of youth?—and reacts with moderation. Unlike Sophocles' other great characters, she does not fly into a rage—is it dignified to get angry with a sick person, even if he is sick with love? Is it dignified to get angry when one is a sensible woman?[238] The controlled suffering of a woman who understands too well contrasts with the impulsive anger of men who understand nothing until it is too late—first her son, and then, after his death, her husband.

But against the intolerable, she is offered a liberating relief: she recalls, like a tale from the depths of her memory, a miraculous substance that has long been preserved in a locked bronze casket. It is an ancient present given her by an old centaur. And we are thrown back years, back to the time when she was a flourishing beauty, when Heracles had just married her after freeing her from a monster.

Now she is threatened by another monster, the centaur Nessus, who carries her on his shoulders over the Evinos River. At the midpoint of the river, he tries to rape her. The young woman cries out, the young husband turns around and shoots an arrow at the old centaur, who has time before dying to tell Deianira how to collect his blood, which will provide a remedy against infidelity. His instructions have remained graven on the young woman's memory: she is capable, so many years later, of quoting them verbatim. And she does it! The tunic is smeared with the magic substance. Finally, it will be said, an act by this woman who up to this point has only known how to wait or to act at the suggestion of others. And yet the very idea of acting already elicits concern:

> May deeds of wicked daring always be far from my thoughts and from my knowledge, as I detest the women who attempt them![239]

Deianira is the diametrical opposite of a woman with men's thoughts like Clytemnestra in Aeschylus.[240] However, she still hopes to win back her husband's love and triumph over her rival. But nothing is yet definitive: whether she sends Heracles the tunic depends on the chorus's opinion. A strange situation for an experienced woman whose act has caused her to lose her confidence, and who is asking young women to tell her what to do. Then things happen very fast. The chorus's opinion is not unfavorable. Next, a chance event settles everything: the appearance of the messenger Lichas as he leaves to rejoin Heracles. The hesitant woman now disappears beneath the official personage. She gives Lichas instructions of a diabolical precision to ensure that the substance produces its effect. Thus irreparable decisions are made in an instant.

Now, once Lichas has left, the infernal mechanism has gone into operation. First, as soon as Deianira goes back into the palace, she discovers a disturbing event that she hastens to report to the chorus: the sun's heat has destroyed the bit of wool she used to smear the philter on the tunic, and in its place, blood is boiling up; then comes the confirmation of her fears when Hyllus arrives to report the reality of the catastrophe, the terrifying effect of the destructive poison on Heracles, and finally, Deianira's menacingly silent departure.

But despite the effect it produces after her son's accusations, Deianira's silent departure is less surprising than the others, because the significance of the silence was announced in advance. In fact, the prodigy Sophocles inserts here was not only a way of preparing, by means of a wordless messenger, the announcement of Heracles' tragic destiny, but also an opportunity to reveal Deianira's profound character when she is confronted by the approaching catastrophe. Sophocles has used a little bit of wool reduced to ashes not only to cause the collapse of his character's great illusion, but also to unveil the tragic nature of her own destiny: too much naïve confidence in other people's goodwill, a belated recognition of the significance of an act whose consequences threaten to reduce intentions to nothing.[241]

And yet at the very moment that this destiny is escaping her control, Deianira takes it in hand by making an irrevocable decision:

> Nevertheless, I am resolved that, if he is to be brought down, at the same time
> I too will die along with him in the selfsame fall. No woman could bear to live
> with a reputation for evil, if she cares above all that her nature is not evil.[242]

These are the closing words of Deianira's last speech. They recall the heroic ideal formulated by Ajax, also at the end of a speech.[243] The victim of a destiny that transcends her, she decides to prefer death to dishonor. Henceforth the silence of her departure is eloquent. Later on, neither the announcement of her death nor the way she commits suicide—by using a sword, like Ajax—will be a complete surprise.[244]

The Heroism of Young Women: Antigone and Electra

The silence of married women who abruptly leave the stage and head voluntarily toward death contrasts with the song and speech of the young woman who lingers before leaving under constraint for the underground prison that is to be her last home. As she is taken away by Creon's guards, Antigone calls on the citizens of her homeland embodied in the chorus to witness her fate, at the beginning of a long scene of lamentation and protest—a commos.[245] Here is the sung beginning:

> Citizens of my fatherland, see me setting out on my last journey, looking at my
> last sunlight, and never again. No, Hades who lays all to rest leads me living
> to Acheron's shore, though I have not had my due portion of the chant that
> brings the bride, nor has any hymn been mine for the crowning of marriage.
> Instead the lord of Acheron will be my groom.[246]

And here is the end in recitative:

> O city of my fathers, land of Thebes, and you gods, our ancestors! I am led
> away now; there is no more delay! Look at me, you who are Thebes' lords—
> look at the only remaining daughter of the house of your kings. See what I
> suffer, and at whose hands, because I revered reverence![247]

At both the end and the beginning of the long scene in which she is led away from the palace to her underground prison, the young woman not only complains and protests but also wants to show herself to the whole city in order to protest against the scandal or to make a scandal. To be sure, like the women who disappeared silently, Antigone will commit suicide. This will also be learned from a messenger, and it will be discovered that she has hanged herself, like Jocasta. But she speaks her moving words onstage, before she goes off to her prison and death, whereas the older women's final words are reported by a messenger. However, we know nothing about the young woman's suicide; it takes place in the solitude of the prison, without any witness.

Sophocles did not neglect the dramatic power of silence, even for Antigone. But here again he made a change. Her silence occurs not at the end, but at the beginning, when the guard brings her before the king. The triumphant babble of the man of the people presenting his catch, which is a surprise—a woman and not a man!—contrasts with the young woman's silence. Sophocles even gave a hint as to the silent young woman's bearing: she remains immobile, with her eyes cast down.[248] This silence is clearly not of the same nature as that of the women overwhelmed by a mute suffering. It is the sign of the tension of her whole being, of the immobile resistance after the act has been accomplished, a prelude to the speech in which she will confront the representative of the established power. From the outset, this speech, following a silence, takes on a force unusual in a young woman, a depth that seems to have come from elsewhere, a little like that of seers, a height where the world of mortals is observed from the world of the gods above, but also from that of the gods below:

> *Creon:* And even so you dared overstep that law?
> *Antigone:* Yes, since it was not Zeus that published me that edict, and since not of that kind are the laws which Justice who dwells with the gods below established among men. Nor did I think that your decrees were of such force, that a mortal could override the unwritten and unfailing statutes given us by the gods. For their life is not of today or yesterday, but for all time, and no man knows when they were first put forth.[249]

These words are no doubt the most famous in Sophocles' theater.[250] Put back in their context, these verses are for Antigone the basis for the public justification of her transgression of the king's edict forbidding Polynices' burial; because the ritual burial of the dead is one of these divine laws that are "unwritten and unfailing." Later on, the spectator will find, in the words of the seer Tiresias, a partial confirmation of the well-foundedness of the young woman's statement: the dead man does not fall within the jurisdiction of the king; he belongs to the gods below.[251]

Thus it is a religious duty that Antigone has fulfilled. Right to the end, she will proclaim the piety of her act: her last remarks, which we have quoted, end with the word "piety."[252] But from the start she was aware of the tragic nature of the situation: even before she committed it, she knew that this act of piety was also an act of transgression. Sophocles put in her mouth the boldest of verbal juxtapositions: she says she is "a pious criminal."[253] This lucidity regarding the consequences of her act—an act that will lead to incomprehension and death—does not affect her decision. To her sister who evades giving Antigone the help she asks for, she replies:

> I will bury him—it would honor me to die while doing that.[254]

With such words, the young woman elevates herself to the level of heroism, to use a convenient term that has no counterpart in the Greek of Sophocles' time. And unlike women who leave in silence to move toward a heroism imposed by misfortune, the young woman has freely chosen to act for a just cause at the cost of her life. Her heroism rivals that of the men who go to war to die a noble death. Facing Creon as well, she asserts her heroism:

> How could I have won a nobler glory than by giving burial to my own brother?[255]

The choice of words is important. Glory (*kléos*) is usually that of epic heroes, of Ajax, Philoctetes, or even Orestes.[256] The use of this word to qualify a woman is completely exceptional in Sophocles' theater. It is found only in the mouth of two young women, Antigone and Electra.[257]

But unlike epic heroes, whose glory corresponds to the values of the society in which they live, the young woman demands a glory that does not fail to pose a problem for the society in which she lives, insofar as it leads her to leave the place reserved for women. This emerges clearly from the scene in which her sister Ismene refuses to follow her in deciding to violate the royal edict by burying their brother. It would be an oversimplification to see in Ismene only a foil whose cowardice brings out by contrast Antigone's heroism. Ismene's submission to the established order is not that of a fearful young woman but instead results from a lucid observation of the relations between the sexes and between the king and his subjects:

> No, we must remember, first, that ours is a woman's nature, and accordingly not suited to battles against men; and next, that we are ruled by the more powerful, so that we must obey in these things and in things even more stinging.[258]

To these sensible remarks, Antigone responds by refusing dialogue and by breaking with her sister. She goes off alone.

Although Antigone's heroism isolates her from the living, it brings her closer to the dead. Immediately after having told Ismene that she intends to bury her brother and emphasized the nobility of a death resulting from that act, she goes on:

> I shall rest with him, loved one with loved one.[259]

This love for her brother is, along with piety and glory, what drives her decision. It is a promise of reunion with him in the beyond and more broadly the promise of reunion with her family.[260] In the conflict with Creon, whereas the king wants to show her that an enemy of the city (in this case, Polynices), even if dead, cannot become a friend, Antigone inserts her love for her brother into a maxim by which she defines her nature:

> It is not my nature to join in hate, but in love.[261]

This is once again spoken by a young woman who seems to have come from elsewhere. The formula is striking by the rarity of its expression and the originality of its thought.[262] This moral maxim, which may seem to us familiar since the appearance of Christianity, runs counter to the Greeks' traditional moral beliefs, according to which friendship consists not only in having the same friends as one's friends, but also the same enemies. That is, moreover, the traditional conception to which Creon refers in speaking to his son.[263]

If we limit ourselves to these striking and profound words spoken by the young woman, we will retain the image of an exceptionally gifted and heroic young woman who sacrifices herself out of piety and love for her brother. And it is hardly astonishing that, faced with such originality and determination, all the characters present on the stage—her sister, the king, and the chorus of old men, the king's councilors—show such incomprehension and accuse her of madness—all of them save the king's son, the young man who loves her.

And this young man brings a new point of view to the agōn scene in which he confronts his father. In order to warn his father, he discusses the rumors he has heard in the city criticizing the decision to sentence Antigone to death, and, on the contrary, praising Antigone's behavior unreservedly:

> In any case, it is my natural duty to watch on your behalf all that men say, or do, or find to blame. For dread of your glance forbids the ordinary citizen to speak such words as would offend your ear. But I can hear these murmurs in the dark, how the city moans for this girl, saying: "No woman ever merited death less—none ever died so shamefully for deeds so glorious as hers, who, when her own brother had fallen in bloody battle, would not leave him unburied to be devoured by savage dogs, or by any bird. Does she not deserve to receive golden honor?" Such is the rumor shrouded in darkness that silently spreads.[264]

This rumor in the city presupposes that news spreads quickly. The agōn scene is located at the beginning of the third episode. Now, it was at the end of the preceding episode that the spectators learned of Creon's decision to put Antigone to death, even though she is his son's fiancée, as Ismene tells us at this very point. We have to assume that during the choral song intercalated between the two episodes, the news of Antigone's death sentence has spread like wildfire and that Haemon has come because he has learned about it, and has heard the Thebans' unfavorable reactions to this decision. But this vibrant eulogy of Antigone is spoken by someone who loves her. Hasn't Haemon attributed to others, at least in part, his own enthusiasm, as Aristotle suggests?[265] How can he speak for the city? It remains that the chorus, in its song situated immediately after this scene, sees in the quarrel between father and son the destructive work of Eros, the god of love.[266]

In other words, does the young woman's ideal vision have to be qualified?

First of all, what is clearest is that Antigone does not limit herself to formulating fine principles and applying them but also does all she can to provoke Creon. Her attitude contrasts not only with that of Ismene, but also with those of Haemon and Tiresias. At the very moment when she is stating the great principles that have made her speech immortal, she attacks Creon even before she has been attacked:

> And if my present actions are foolish in your sight, it may be that it is a fool who accuses me of folly.[267]

Confronted by such an aplomb that breaks all the rules—not political but social rules—that Ismene mentioned in the first scene of the tragedy, it is not surprising that the chorus, whose reaction is expected after the first speech in an agōn scene, concentrates on the Antigone's conduct and not on her argumentation:

> She shows herself the wild offspring of a wild father, and does not know how to bend before troubles.[268]

This remark is not anodyne, because even if the chorus is incapable of understanding the loftiness of Antigone's argument, it offers a way of explaining her behavior by reference to her nature. The chorus comes back to this theme, amplifying it in the stasimon that follows this episode.[269] Antigone is not only the daughter of a wild father but also belongs to the family of the Labdacids, one of the accursed families whose malediction pursues them from generation to generation.[270] She was born under the sign of misfortune. Then the chorus returns to this idea a final time in the lyric dialogue it exchanges with Antigone before her departure. Even though it is deeply moved for a moment when the young woman enters, it continues to reproach her:

> You have rushed headlong to the far limits of daring, and against the high throne of Justice you have fallen, my daughter, fallen heavily. But in this ordeal you are paying for some paternal crime.[271]

Once again, the chorus resumes its explanation by family descent. But it varies its point of view. It no longer emphasizes the hereditary character of natural qualities, but rather the transmission of crimes. And this time Antigone's response may seem surprising in such an indomitable young woman:

> You have touched on my most bitter thought and moved my ever-renewed pity for my father and for the entire doom ordained for us, the famed house of Labdacus. Oh, the horrors of our mother's bed! Oh, the slumbers of the wretched mother at the side of her own son, my own father! What manner of parents gave me my miserable being! It is to them that I go like this, accursed and unwed, to share their home. Ah, my brother, the marriage you made was doomed, and by dying you killed me still alive![272]

This is the only moment in the tragedy when the armor of heroism is breached. Antigone, for just an instant, recognizes her wound, the destiny of an accursed race, which has ended up haunting her as it did Ismene, but which she wanted to forget at the moment of deciding and acting. And this cherished brother, whom she has defended at all costs, she now accuses of ultimately being her murderer; for he is not exempt of responsibility, either, because of his marriage to the daughter of Adrastus, the king of Argos, thanks to which he was able to mount his expedition against his homeland. Once again a dead man indirectly kills a living one.[273] Then this confession leads to the most desperate lament, the admission that she is utterly alone. Antigone's exit could have taken place right then. But Sophocles, by making Creon enter to put an end to the lamentations, restored to the young woman her heroic tension. Ignoring the king, because she is no longer speaking to him, in his presence Antigone rediscovers her justifying, provocative voice that continues to scandalize the chorus:

Still the same tempest of the soul grips this girl with the same fierce gusts.[274]

Finally, there remain shadowy areas that make this character the most mysterious that Sophocles created. These shadowy areas have to do with a strange line of reasoning in this last scene and especially with silences.

When Antigone gives her ultimate justification for her action, addressing herself to Polynices, she engages in a calculation that, while having a parallel in contemporary literature, disconcerts us: she has done for her brother what she would not have done for a husband or a son, because it would always be possible for her to have another husband or another son, whereas it is impossible to have another brother, because her parents are dead.[275] This argument is also made in Herodotus, by the wife of Intaphernes, one of the great personages of Persia. To punish Intaphernes, who has failed to show respect for him, Darius has him imprisoned, along with all his sons and all the men of his family. By coming to beg Darius to spare them, Intaphernes's wife is able to get him to agree to spare *one* of them. To Darius's great astonishment, she chooses her brother. The justification she gives is exactly the same as that given by Antigone.[276] But we are astonished to find Antigone making such an argument: this discrimination between individuals is hardly in accord with the universal demands of the unwritten law she throws in Creon's face at the beginning of their first confrontation. And we are also astonished by this calculation presented in the hypothetical mode, since Antigone is neither married nor a mother, whereas in Herodotus Intaphernes's wife is actually forced to choose among her husband, son, and brother. Therefore since Goethe,[277] some modern writers have been strongly tempted eliminate a passage that tarnishes the heroine's image.

But the text was already read this way by Aristotle, who cites two verses of this passage in his *Rhetoric* and who, far from being surprised by the argument, chooses this sole example to illustrate the necessity of providing, in a defensive plea, a justification of the cause, when the act appears incredible.[278] Must we see in the lack of agreement between Antigone's two lines of argumentation the proof that Sophocles did not take care to make his characters coherent from one scene to another? Isn't this rather another indication of the scandalous attitude of Creon, even if the paths seem different?

In any case, this new line of argument reinforces Antigone's silence. Her devotion to her brother Polynices seems to eclipse the rest. To be sure, she complains that Creon's decision has deprived her of marriage and motherhood. But she never says a word about Haemon, the fiancé whom she had been promised. It is her sister Ismene who, defending him before Creon, tells the spectators about the engagement:

> *Ismene:* What? You will kill your own son's bride?
> *Creon:* Why not? There are other fields for him to plough.
> *Ismene:* But not fitted to him as she was.
> *Creon:* I abhor an evil wife for my son.
> *Antigone:* Haemon, dearest! How your father wrongs you![279]

Antigone's silence regarding this fiancé promised her has seemed to some so shocking that they tried to attribute to Antigone Ismene's fine invocation concerning the beloved Haemon. But Antigone never speaks of her love for Haemon. Is this simple modesty? or a focus of her love on this brother, since she has chosen the world of the dead? By dying in solitude, Antigone hopes to rejoin her father. And when Haemon commits suicide over her dead body in order to rejoin her, this proves his love for her: in reporting this scene, the messenger interprets it as a tragic marriage.[280] But hadn't Antigone already left?

A second silence reinforces Antigone's focus on Polynices: when she speaks of the dead in her family whom she is going to rejoin and who she hopes will love her because she has carried out the burial rites for them, she mentions her father, her mother, and her brother. She does not say *brothers*. This silence, once again, has seemed so shocking that some scholars have tried to see in it a reference to Eteocles, even though it can refer only to Polynices.[281] In reality, although Eteocles is her brother by both her father and her mother, she has excluded him from her horizon. Why? Because he treated her brother Polynices as a slave?[282] Because he was honored by Creon? In any event, it is a curious lapse on the part of someone who obeys only the imperative of the family law.[283] Confronting Creon, she defines herself as someone who shares love and not hate. However, she did not hesitate to pass abruptly from love to hate in the scene in which her sister Ismene felt incapable of opposing the city and tried to persuade her to give up an impossible aim:

> If you mean that, you will have my hatred, and you will be subject to punishment as the enemy of the dead.[284]

As soon as Ismene refuses to help her, she disappears from the circle of Antigone's friends, and when Ismene wants to support her again after she has committed the act, Antigone sarcastically rejects her even though she is suffering, refusing a love that is manifested in words and not in acts. Despite Ismene's effort to plead her sister's cause with Creon, she will definitively disappear from her horizon. Antigone's deepest statement about herself is perhaps in her second and last discussion with Ismene:

> Your choice was to live, it was mine to die.[285]

This loyalty to a dead person can also define the other young heroine in Sophocles' extant tragedies: Electra. But whereas the first was loyal to a brother, the second is loyal to a father. As soon as the young Electra appears onstage, she begins to lament the murder of her father, who was killed in a cowardly way upon his return from the Trojan War; the murderers were his wife, Clytemnestra, and her lover Aegisthus. In composing his *Electra*, Sophocles clearly had in mind Aeschylus's *The Libation Bearers*, which dealt with the same sequence in the myth in which the young Orestes comes to Argos after many years in exile to avenge his father and reestablish his power. From a comparison with *The Libation Bearers* it clearly emerges that Sophocles gave the character of the young Electra a central place that she did not have in Aeschylus's play. It is well known that whereas in Aeschylus the character Electra disappears completely after the recognition scene in the second part of the tragedy, which is devoted to the vengeance,[286] Sophocles delayed as much as he could the moment of recognition and vengeance in order to make Electra preeminent; moreover, she remains present during the vengeance.[287]

The consequence is that the character of Orestes goes almost unnoticed. He merges with his role as avenger, sure of his right to exact vengeance and sure of his method, after consulting the Delphic oracle.[288] He shows decisiveness when he lays out his plan for revenge, despite a moment's hesitation when he hears a cry inside the palace.[289] He speaks laconically to both the gods and humans, is not insensitive to his sister's misfortunes, and feels pity for her, but he remains moderate in his joy during the recognition scene.[290] He acts calmly when he kills his mother, without feeling any remorse,[291] or when he confronts Aegisthus at the end of the tragedy. The paradox is that the imaginary Orestes created by the tutor in his narrative is more attractive than the real Orestes.[292]

Sophocles' originality consists not only in centering the tragedy on Electra, but also adopting a technique of doubling the characters.[293] He borrowed from his own tragedy *Antigone* the idea of a pair of sisters who are close, because they have the same father and mother,[294] and distant in their conduct and the motivation of their action. The Electra-Chrysothemis pair repeats, about fifteen years later, the Antigone-Ismene pair. The submission and resignation of one sister is contrasted with the revolt of the other and her loyalty to a dead man. The dramatic use made of this opposition is comparable: the two sisters confront one another in two scenes of the tragedy and come to a definitive break, after which Chrysothemis, like Ismene, disappears completely and falls into oblivion.[295] This repetition is probably an index of the success won during the performance of *Antigone* by the scenes in which the two sisters face off against one another. Sophocles also seems to have been fascinated by a problem to which he returns on this occasion: how a decisive event can elicit different reactions from individuals despite their common origin. Here he seems to give a more complex explanation. In *Antigone*, the chorus noted, as we have seen, that Oedipus's daughter had inherited her father's character, but it went no further than that.[296] This idea of heredity, adopted by Electra, is applied to the pair of sisters. These are the first words Electra addresses to Chrysothemis when they first meet:

> It is strange, indeed, that you, the daughter of our father from whom you grew, should forget him and instead show concern for your mother! All your admonitions to me have been taught by her; you speak no word of your own. . . . But now, when you could be called the child of the noblest father among men, be called instead your mother's daughter.[297]

Electra's words imply that family descent normally passes through the father; young women who behave heroically are imitating the paternal model. However, a character can forget his or her nature by following bad teachings. Thus Electra explains her sister's behavior and their divergences by reference to the problem of the relations between nature and nurture, a problem that Sophocles deals with on a larger scale in *Philoctetes*, where he shows the nature of Neoptolemus, son of Achilles, momentarily obscured by Odysseus's teachings.[298] But Electra's partial explanation reduces Chrysothemis to what she is not. The repeated opposition between the two sisters suggests, more profoundly, that in an exceptional situation there are two fundamental ways of reacting. Chrysothemis and Ismene react in conformity with the social rules in accord with which they were brought up and in relation to a realistic conception of wisdom. That is what explains a certain relatedness between their arguments: the weakness of women's nature compared with the strength of a man;[299] submission to the existing authority, no matter what the cost;[300] the absurdity of attempting the impossible;[301] the belief that the dead understand that the living cannot help them.[302] In opposition to that both Electra and Antigone assert the duty of piety: indefectible loyalty to the deceased man who has not been ritually buried and who must be avenged;[303] also, loyalty to oneself, that is, to the decision made, even if it means losing one's life in an impossible mission; a conception of the nature of women which is defined by the origin of the family and not by the opposition of the sexes. Women, like men, must act in accord with the family's code of honor. And in the case of Antigone and Electra one can rightly speak of heroism. They are in fact the only female characters in Sophocles' theater who use the expression "a well-born woman" (*eugenes gunè*)[304] and refer to the ethical demand attached to it: to live honorably or die.[305] This female heroism, invented by Sophocles, is distinguished from male heroism in the sense that it does not correspond to the standard of society and is met with incomprehension. Nonetheless, the chorus's lack of understanding is much less radical in *Electra* than in *Antigone*. Moreover, it is a chorus composed not of men but of women, friends of Electra. Nonetheless, in the confrontation between the two sisters, when Electra announces her decision to kill Aegisthus, her father's murderer, the chorus sides with Chrysothemis's prudence.[306] That does not prevent it, however, from expressing its admiration for Electra's heroism and piety in the song that follows this quarrel.[307]

Despite the spiritual kinship between Antigone and Electra, there are differences between them that have to do in part with the technique of presentation, and in part with the diversity of the situations resulting from the myth.

The importance of the character of Electra in the tragedy is shown not only by the comparison with Aeschylus's *The Libation Bearers*, as we have just seen, but also by Antigone's place in the play. Antigone disappears relatively early in the tragedy, and even before she does, she speaks for less time than Creon does—despite her strong presence when she is onstage with her sister or Creon, or when she departs for her underground prison. From the point of view of dramatic technique, even in the part of the tragedy in which Antigone is present, Creon is the central character: he is confronted successively with the chorus, the guard, Antigone, and then his son. In *Electra*, on the other hand, it is the young woman who occupies the main role. She is confronted successively with the chorus, her sister Chrysothemis, her mother, and then with her sister again before the great recognition scene with her brother Orestes, and then with the tutor. Even at the moment of vengeance, Electra is present outside the palace to watch for Aegisthus's arrival, and she remains visible until the end of the tragedy. Electra's time onstage is thus much longer than that of Antigone; and the same goes for her speaking time. We must not make the mistake of imagining that every title character has, as such, an equivalent dramatic role. If by the dramatic role of a character we mean his or her place, relative to the other characters, in the development of the action, it is clear that Electra's dramatic role is more important than Antigone's. In fact, of all the female characters in Sophocles' theater, Electra is the only one who occupies a central place during most of the tragedy. So much for the differences having to do with dramatic technique.

The differences emerging from the situation are more important, whether the initial situation or its development is concerned. Antigone's heroism is practically coeval with the tragedy. On the other hand, Electra has a long past of resistance behind her. Her father's death, which Electra wants to avenge, occurred about ten years earlier; the death of Polynices, whom Antigone wants to bury, dates from the night preceding the tragedy. It would be a mistake to see in Electra's incessant lamentations a merely passive and verbal resistance. They not only proceed from a loyal attachment to the dead man but also constitute a permanent challenge to the murderers' authority and an ardent appeal addressed to the gods below for vengeance and for the return of her brother, her only hope. The proof that these lamentations are subversive is that the established power in the palace has reduced Electra to the status of a starving slave.[308] The chorus emphasizes Electra's rebellious attitude but recommends prudence:

> You have far excelled in achieving misfortune, ever breeding wars in your hardhearted soul. But such strife should not be pushed into a conflict with the powerful.[309]

The additional misfortunes that result from this challenge are made visible for the spectators themselves. Electra is dressed in a shabby robe.[310] And when Chrysothemis appears richly dressed, the sight offers a concrete idea of the consequence of choices: one of the young women enjoys social freedom and a life of luxury, at the price of submission to the powerful; the other has loyalty to a dead man at the price of a social death. The contrast between the two opposite ways of life embodying two opposite ethical choices renews, by giving it a temporal dimension, the contrast between the two sisters as it was presented in *Antigone*.[311]

The power of Electra's dissenting words can be gauged by the ruler's reprisals, which he has just exacerbated by deciding to incarcerate Electra in an underground prison: that is what Chrysothemis announces to her.[312] Here, Sophocles established, in a sort of wink to himself, an additional connection with Antigone, whom Creon put in a prison of the same kind.[313] Against rebels, the powerful, whoever they may be, pursue the same policy of repression. Although Creon's threat is quite real,[314] there would probably not be time to execute it. But this first new event in Electra's life serves only to strengthen her will not to yield to the powerful and her loyalty to her dead father, this time not only at the price of her social life, but at the price of her life itself.

The young woman's words of protest will be actualized precisely in her confrontation with the powerful, represented by her mother, Clytemnestra, whom she hates.[315] This agōn scene corresponds to the scene in which Antigone defies Creon: the two rebellious young women challenge the established power. However, we must not expect to find in Electra's arguments all the brilliance of Antigone's, because the political dimension is absent. The scene between the daughter and her mother has a family dimension. Nonetheless, the confrontation is situated on the ethical and religious level, because Justice (Dikè) appears at the heart of the debate.[316] Clytemnestra is the first to mention the goddess Justice in the first speech in the antilogy. Clytemnestra does not deny that she killed Agamemnon but insists that she did not act alone. It was Justice who killed him! To defend herself, Clytemnestra accuses. She accuses Agamemnon of having sacrificed his own daughter Iphigeneia. Thus she takes up the defense of the dead girl and feels no remorse for her act. In the second speech of the antilogy, Electra turns her mother's argument against her, while remaining on the terrain of justice. It was, she says, not out of a concern for justice that Clytemnestra killed Agamemnon; she acted under the influence of her lover Aegisthus. She exonerates her father by pointing out that he acted under duress. However, she moves beyond arguments based on justice by denouncing the dishonorable conduct of her mother, who lives with her father's enemy and has borne him a child.[317] Then she concludes her speech with a violent attack on her mother, going so far as to imply that she would kill her if she were strong enough.

The confrontation with the powerful reveals a kinship between the two young women: the same appeal to justice, the same fidelity to a dead man, and above all the same passionate violence that overthrows hierarchies, to the indignation of their powerful opponent who denounces their insolence, and also to the astonishment of the chorus.[318] Clytemnestra is scandalized, obviously! But the fact that the chorus, which consists of Electra's friends, denounces her fury—that deserves attention. These young heroines go beyond the bounds of the socially acceptable.

However, Electra does not attain the supreme degree of heroism at the same pace as Antigone does. She has long practiced a verbal resistance, reinforced by an initial threat, but she will make a heroic decision comparable to that of Antigone a little later, when she learns of Orestes' supposed death, during the unfolding of his plan of deception. And it is then that the second confrontation between the two sisters, Electra and Chrysothemis, will play the same dramatic role as the first confrontation between Antigone and Ismene in *Antigone*.[319] The delay signifies the difference in pace in the evolution of the two young heroines: a difference that has to do not with their character but with the difference in their situation. Electra waits for Orestes before taking action to avenge their father. Now she is alone with her sister, just as Antigone was. And just like Antigone, Electra will ask her sister to help her. To be sure, there is more rhetoric and less energy in the scene of confrontation in *Electra* than in that in *Antigone*. But faced by their sisters' refusals, Electra and Antigone show the same decisiveness in acting against all opposition.[320]

That is where the similarity of the respective destinies of Electra and Antigone stops. Because of the way events develop, from that point on the destinies of the two young women take opposite paths: whereas Antigone acts alone and assumes all the consequences, including suicide, Electra does not even have to have to consider how to implement her decision, because her brother's arrival will put an end to her solitude. Nonetheless, Sophocles momentarily delays the joy of the recognition by prolonging Electra's mourning, by means of the ruse preparing the way for vengeance: holding in her arms the urn that is supposed to contain Orestes' ashes, Electra reveals through her moving despair her love for her dead brother. This feeling reminds us again of Antigone, who sacrificed herself for her dead brother. But whereas Antigone simply asserted this fraternal love, Electra lives it with the carnal sensitivity of a big sister and nurse talking fondly about the past. After the long joy of the recognition scene, which is prolonged by the recognition of the tutor, there no longer remains much time for action. In a very surprising way, Sophocles delays Orestes' entrance into the palace, which marks the beginning of the execution of the vengeance. But once he has gone in, accompanied by Pylades, the tutor, and Electra, things go very fast: while Clytemnestra, who has received the urn from Orestes' hands, prepares it for the funeral, Electra, who has once again come out of the palace to watch for Aegisthus's return, shows a liberating violence after so much accumulated hatred when she hears the cries of her mother, who has been struck a first time, and even encourages her brother to strike her again. After the matricide she feels hardly any remorse, any more than Orestes does when he comes out with Pylades, his bloody sword in his hand. This is an important difference from Euripides' *Electra*.[321]

When Aegisthus, who had left at dawn, returns to the palace joyful and triumphant after hearing of Orestes' death, it is once again Electra who undertakes to receive him. She participates masterfully in the plan of deception by confirming Aegisthus in his error, using language full of double entendres,[322] and pretends now to submit to his tyrannical power. But when Aegisthus discovers the truth by lifting the cadaver's shroud, Electra urges her brother to kill him without further delay and to hand over the usurper's body to the gravediggers he deserves, that is, dogs and birds. That is the only way she can obtain deliverance from her ills.[323] But does that show piety? It is noteworthy that at the moment of carrying out the two murders, Electra thinks less about avenging her father than about her own deliverance. And echoing Electra's words, the chorus concludes the tragedy by announcing that the house of Atreus has recovered its freedom.[324]

The Repetition of the Same Characters in Different Tragedies

Given the small number of myths and families dramatized in Sophocles' seven extant tragedies, a phenomenon occurs fairly often that is rather surprising for a modern reader: the repetition of the same character in two or even three different tragedies. Leaving aside individuals who appear as characters in one tragedy and are spoken about in one or two other tragedies—as is notably the case for Agamemnon and Menelaus, or again Polynices[325]—four characters return in two different tragedies and three even reappear in three tragedies.

In the case of the myth of the Labdacids, the characters who appear twice are Oedipus and the seer Tiresias. But this doubling does not occur in the same two tragedies: Tiresias appears in *Antigone* and in *Oedipus the King*, whereas Oedipus is the central character in *Oedipus the King* and in *Oedipus at Colonus*.[326] In the case of the Trojan myth, it is Odysseus who plays a role in each of two tragedies (*Ajax* and *Philoctetes*). Finally, Heracles appears twice: in the second part of *The Women of Trachis* and at the end of *Philoctetes*.

The characters who appear three times are the two daughters of Oedipus, Antigone and Ismene, who are presented in three tragedies: *Antigone*, *Oedipus the King*, and *Oedipus at Colonus*. However, in *Oedipus the King*, the two sisters appear only as silent characters at the end of the tragedy, because they are still children.[327] Ultimately, the only character who appears three times in a speaking role is Creon: he is present in the three tragedies about the family of the Labdacids.

This outline of the repetitions would be much richer if we took into account the lost tragedies. For example, Odysseus, who appears twice in the extant tragedies, was also the title character of two lost tragedies: *Odysseus Wounded by the Spine* and *The Madness of Odysseus*.[328] Philoctetes, the title character of an extant tragedy, *Philoctetes*, was also the title character of a second tragedy that is lost: *Philoctetes at Troy*.[329]

In these repetitions, Sophocles sought to vary the given material in several ways, usually by modifying the moments in the lives of the characters' social status or even their nature. In any case, the extant tragedies retain their autonomy, to the point that the characters could be treated in very different ways. We have already studied the most striking example of this, that of Odysseus: presented as a sage at the end of *Ajax*, at the beginning of *Philoctetes* he is defined as a disillusioned realist.[330] Creon is another good example of this diversity in the ways of treating characters.

A Character Present in Three Tragedies: Creon

It seems possible to reconstitute the character's curriculum vitae, as seen by Sophocles, on the basis of various elements contained in each of the three tragedies, if we put them in the chronological order of the myth (*Oedipus the King, Oedipus at Colonus, Antigone*), and not in that of the composition of the tragedies (*Antigone, Oedipus the King, Oedipus at Colonus*). In *Oedipus the King* Creon is first of all, as Queen Jocasta's brother, Oedipus's devoted friend. The king has entrusted him with a secret mission to consult the oracle at Delphi, before unjustly suspecting him of conspiracy; at the end of the tragedy, after the king's collapse, Creon serves as regent. In *Oedipus at Colonus*, he appears again as a Theban envoy who has come to seek, in conformity with the oracles, the support of the exiled Oedipus, at the time when Eteocles is reigning over Thebes and Polynices is besieging the city with the help of the Argives in an attempt to seize power. Flashbacks provided by Ismene or Oedipus himself even tell us what happened to Creon during the interval between the two tragedies: Creon served as regent, first keeping Oedipus in Thebes when he wanted to go into exile, and then exiling him when he no longer wanted to leave; at first he reigned with the assent of the two brothers, Eteocles and Polynices, until they began to fight for power. Finally, in *Antigone*, he has just taken power, immediately after Eteocles and Polynices have killed each other in single combat, but this time not as regent, but as the legitimate successor to the throne after the death of all the males in the Labdacid line. His one-day reign ends in a family catastrophe comparable to that of Oedipus. Even though Sophocles did not compose the different parts of this career in the chronological order of the myth, the three tragedies display a quite obvious overall coherence in the character's career.

But that does not mean that Sophocles imagined a single character with a fixed nature whom we see in episodic sequences. The "technique of recurrent characters" in Sophocles has nothing in common with that of the French novelist Balzac. The three creations of the character of Creon are independent of each other: it is in the last tragedy, *Oedipus at Colonus*, the one that corresponds to the middle of Creon's career, that he appears most debased: he represents trickery and violence when he arrives as Thebes's envoy to convince Oedipus to return to his homeland.[331] Such an image hardly corresponds to that of the much younger Creon of *Oedipus the King*, who is neither politically ambitious nor bitter,[332] or to the Creon of *Antigone*, who is aware of the responsibilities of royal power when he takes control of Thebes after the fratricidal duel of Eteocles and Polynices.[333]

Some differences have to do in part with the different social situation in which Creon finds himself in each of the tragedies: initially, royal majesty cannot put up with the violence, and still less the trickery, of a mere ambassador. But the differences also have to do with the dramatic role assigned to the character of Creon: the Creon of the end of *Oedipus the King* serves as a positive foil emphasizing Oedipus's fall, whereas conversely, in *Oedipus at Colonus*, Creon serves as a negative foil emphasizing Oedipus's rehabilitation.[334] Should we also take into account the creator's development? Between the creation of King Creon in *Antigone* and Ambassador Creon in *Oedipus at Colonus*, there is an interval of thirty years in Sophocles' career. In the meantime, the author has aged . . . and his character, though a little younger in *Oedipus at Colonus* than he is in *Antigone*, is also feeling the effects of age![335]

Oedipus Ten Years Later: Evolution and Continuity

The change in age and status is even more obvious in the case of Oedipus. The collapse of the "political hero" that constituted the last phase of Creon's destiny constitutes the first phase in the case of Oedipus. After the fall of the triumphant monarch in *Oedipus the King*[336] we witness in *Oedipus at Colonus* the rehabilitation of the old man who, after a long exile, attains through his death a heroic cult. And this time, the chronology of the composition of the tragedies corresponds to the chronology of the myth. The reappearance of the same character is here all the more remarkable because he plays the main role in both tragedies. This is the only example of such a reappearance in Sophocles' extant theater. Nonetheless, it is not unique in his production as a whole.[337]

Oedipus in *Oedipus at Colonus* is, in comparison to what he was in *Oedipus the King*, a man changed by time, by the misfortunes of exile, but he retains the nobility of his nature. This is masterfully illuminated in the first words by which he presents himself at the beginning of *Oedipus at Colonus*, addressing his daughter Antigone, his companion in exile:

Child of a blind old man, Antigone, to what region have we come, or to what city of men? Who will entertain the wandering Oedipus today with scanty gifts? Little do I crave, and obtain still less than that little, and with that I am content. For patience is the lesson of suffering, and of the long years upon me, and lastly of a noble mind.[338]

The contrast between the two views of Oedipus at the beginning of the two tragedies is theatrically striking for the spectators, or at least for those who had the privilege of attending, at an interval of thirty years, the two performances. The king of the city of Thebes used to emerge from his palace at the call of a crowd that begged him almost as a divine savior. Now he has become a blind and lonely wanderer without a homeland.[339] He is a "poor ghost" of the old Oedipus.[340] The spectator immediately sees an Oedipus that the reader learns to know only later, when Polynices describes his father: he is clad in dirty rags, while above the sightless eyes his unkempt hair flutters in the breeze.[341] But the changes are more profound than the sight of the character onstage reveals. It is not only an external change in social status, but also an internal change. The man whom Creon accused, at the end of *Oedipus the King*, of always wanting to be the master, even in misfortune,[342] is presented, at the beginning of *Oedipus at Colonus*, as a sage who has learned to be content with little and to put up with his condition; in short, a Stoic *avant la lettre*. Oedipus does not even mention this internal transformation, but he specifies its causes, which are three in number: first he has become wise by learning from his misfortunes; second, time has done its work. These are the external causes of his internal change. In conclusion, he adds a third cause, which is, this time, internal: the nobility of his nature.[343] This last explanation is of capital importance, because it constitutes the link between the first two stages of Oedipus's destiny: despite the visible contrast between the two Oedipuses that we see at the beginning of these two tragedies, the same internal flame continues to burn beneath the ashes. Oedipus has been brought low, but he has not been broken. This new wisdom, the result of an interaction between the innate and the acquired, remains a form of heroism.

From this point of view, Oedipus must be compared with Philoctetes. Two heroes who have to face suffering over a long period of time and alone—is it an accident that they are the heroes of Sophocles' last extant tragedies?—have arrived at the same wisdom. The same Greek word (*stergein*) is used by both to designate this wisdom.[344] It is a mixture of endurance and resignation, but the complete opposite of an abdication. As for the explanation, it is comparable from one tragedy to the next: it is a wisdom learned in the school of necessity, but it also presupposes a courageous nature.[345]

This nature is manifested in these two heroes not only by their astonishing power of resistance to adversity, but also by the violence of their resentment against those whom they hold responsible for their unjust exile from society. Just as throughout the tragedy Philoctetes shows an inextinguishable hatred for the two Atreids and Odysseus, in *Oedipus at Colonus* Oedipus nourishes a pitiless hatred for his two sons and Creon. Sophocles drew great effects from scenes in which the hero finds himself facing his enemies, whom he is seeing again after such a long time. Moreover, the situation in these scenes is analogous: it is those who are responsible for banishing the exile who come to seek him, even if they have to resort to violence, because an oracle has revealed the necessity of the exile's presence in order to win a victory. From the hero's point of view, these scenes serve to reveal his deep nature: even if the hero has been wise enough to adapt, with time, to his external circumstances, time has had no effect on his inner life, on the resentments that explode, so many years later, like a torrent of lava that has emerged from the depths of the soul.[346] Sophocles even doubled the effects in his *Oedipus at Colonus*, since Oedipus has to confront successively the two opposed parties who come to obtain his help: first Creon, Eteocles' representative, who corresponds to Odysseus in *Philoctetes*, and then Polynices, his own son, whose petition he rejects first by remaining silent, and then with maledictions. Ultimately, we find in the curse made by the old Oedipus near the end of *Oedipus at Colonus* the same impetuous violence as that of the curse he makes at the beginning of *Oedipus the King* against the murderer of Laius, that is, against himself. Despite the changes, from one tragedy to the other the hero seems to remain, from a human point of view, fundamentally self-identical.[347]

But in Sophocles a person's destiny is not explained solely by the interplay of human powers. Oedipus at Colonus ends with the heroization of Oedipus, who is promoted, after his death, to a status intermediary between humans and gods. Enjoying a cult in the deme of Attica, he uses his power to protect the city where he has been received. The verse that best sums up this decisive presence of the gods in his destiny is spoken by Ismene when she comes to bring Oedipus news of Thebes:

The gods now raise you up; but before they worked your ruin.[348]

Heracles in *The Women of Trachis* and in *Philoctetes*

This change in the status of a character who appears twice in Sophocles' tragedies is even clearer in the case of Heracles. At the end of *The Women of Trachis*, he is suffering and moribund, while at the end of *Philoctetes* he appears as a god.[349]

In *The Women of Trachis*, after Deianira's suicide is announced and the chorus sings a song that marks the transition between the Deianira's tragedy and that of Heracles, the whole last third of the play is occupied by a long scene in which Heracles, borne on a litter, arrives accompanied by an old man and his son. At first, we witness the hero's awakening and the attacks of his illness. A frightening and moving image of the monster killer defeated by an internal monster, a "wild, uncombatable plague" that is devouring him in repeated crises,[350] at each of which he cries out and begs to be killed to escape his pain. His nature as a hero seems to be damaged. He himself ironically emphasizes this transformation under the impact of his disease:

> Pity me moaning and weeping like a girl! No one could say that he had ever seen this man do that before. No, always without complaint I used to pursue my troubles. But now in my misery I have been found a woman, instead of the man I used to be.[351]

This reminder of his past exploits and his prestigious descent, as the son of Zeus and Alcmena, only reinforces the paradoxical situation of a hero who sees himself reduced by pain to the status of a woman. And the height of the irony is that it is the result of a gift from a woman, his own wife. But does that mean that he has lost his nature? The violence of his own anger against Deianira is the sign, as paradoxical as it may seem, of what the hero has not abdicated: in his desire to punish the woman he believes to be his murderer, he continues, in spite of everything, the battle against monsters that he has waged throughout his life. At the end of his long speech about his past and present trials, he declares:

> But you may be sure of one thing: though I am nothing, though I cannot move a step, yet she who has done this deed shall feel my heavy hand even so. Let her but come to me so that she may learn to proclaim this message to all the world, that in my death, as in my life, I punished the guilty![352]

After such a display of violence, a modern spectator would be tempted to point out Heracles' brutality and compare it with his wife's gentleness. But that is not the effect it produces on the chorus, even though the latter consists of Deianira's friends. After Heracles' long speech, what the young women emphasize is what an immense loss for Greece it would be to lose such a hero.[353] Thus it is the image of "the best of mortals" (*pantōn ariston andra*) that seems to predominate.[354] And in the *Tusculanes* Cicero quotes the whole of this speech to show how difficult it is to scorn pain, when we see Hercules so incapable of mastering his own.

Violent feelings are an initial way of clinging to life while resisting pain. But his son's plea on behalf of his mother, whose innocence he learned too late, makes Heracles realize, in light of the oracles he knows concerning his own destiny, the true cause of his illness, the centaur's vengeance, on the one hand, and on the other, the gravity of his own condition, which will certainly cause his death. After a brief moment of intense emotion in which he wants to summon his whole family, Heracles gives Hyllus, his eldest son, his final instructions. Now he resumes an imperious, solemn tone, imprisoning Hyllus in the implacable logic of the duties of descent reinforced by the religious constraint of an oath sworn in advance.[355]

The first instruction concerns the preparations for his death: Hyllus must take his father to the highest summit of Mount Oeta, where there is a sanctuary of Zeus, construct a funeral pyre of oak and olive wood, and burn him alive on it, without weeping or moaning. And to forestall Hyllus's objections, Heracles concludes this initial instruction by threatening his son with an eternal paternal curse if he fails to obey. Confronted by such imperatives, Hyllus complains, protesting against a requirement that could make the son the murderer of his father. Heracles reassures him by seeing in his son not a murderer but a physician, and he makes a slight concession by allowing him to entrust the task of lighting the pyre to someone else, so long as he takes care of all the rest.

The second instruction concerns the fate of Iole: the son, after the father's death, must take her as his wife. In Heracles' view, this second demand is less important than the first. And yet he imposes it with the same ardor when confronted by the stronger reluctance of a son who is on the brink of rebelling, protesting against an idea that seems to him that of a sick man; in any case, a horrible and impious idea that would couple him with the woman who caused his mother's death and the destruction of his father. And this time, to make him obey, the father no longer invokes his own curse, but that of the gods.[356] The son ultimately yields:

Hyllus: I can never be condemned for obeying you, Father.
Heracles: Your words make a fair ending.[357]

Why does the father make such demands with such intransigence? In no other scene in Sophocles' theater do we see a father impose on his son respect for the father as a categorical imperative, and the son yield.[358] The question has often been asked, and moral judgments, sometimes severe, have been passed on Heracles, describing him as egocentric, brutal, violent, the representative of a savage world that contrasts with the sensitivity of his son, whom he tramples on, or the gentleness of his wife, whom he does not know. But such criteria are probably outside the codes of the heroic world. What Heracles demands from his son is to be his "ally."[359] By entrusting his concubine to his eldest son after his death, Heracles ensures that his heritage won in battle will be transmitted. And by demanding that his son carry out the cremation rites, Heracles ensures his passage into the beyond. What is more, Heracles knows that in that way he is testing Hyllus to see if he is a son worthy of his father. The son's definitive submission to the father at the time of death is the guarantee of the continuity of the family's heroism.

The final image of Heracles is that of a hero who goes bravely into death, giving the order for the convoy to leave as soon as possible. He who had shortly before compared himself to a woman is now going to master this savage illness that is eating him away from inside, the hero's final victory over a monster, no longer in physical combat, but in a burst of his soul's energy. Here are his last words:

Come, then, before you awaken this plague, O my hardened soul, give me a bit of steel to bind my lips like stone to stone! Stop any cry, since the task you accomplish, though by constraint, gives cause for joy.[360]

This Heracles who leaves lying on a litter, but not defeated, at the end of *The Women of Trachis* descends in glory from the heavens at the end of *Philoctetes*. Even though there is probably a long interval of time between the composition of these two tragedies, if we juxtapose these two images of Heracles we are struck first by the contrast between them. After the last words of the human Heracles, here are the first words of the divine Heracles, addressing Philoctetes as he is getting ready to return to his homeland with Neoptolemus:

> Not yet, not until you have heard my commands, son of Poeas. Know that your ears perceive the voice of Heracles, and that you look upon his face. For your sake I have left my divine seat and come to reveal to you the purposes of Zeus, and to halt the journey on which you are departing. Hearken to my words. First I would tell you of my own fortunes—how, by toiling through and enduring so many toils to the end, I have won the glory of deathlessness, as you witness. And for you, be sure, this fate is ordained, that through these toils of yours you will make your life far-famed.[361]

The contrast in the dramatic representation could be made concrete by examining the representation in vase paintings. The suffering Heracles is shown bearded, whereas the divine Heracles enjoys an eternal youth.[362] It is probably the latter to which Sophocles alludes when he has his character say that his "deathlessness" can be witnessed. The contrast in the representation is accompanied by a contrast in Heracles' relation to his father. At the end of *The Women of Trachis*, Zeus's instructions were revealed to the human Heracles through ambiguous oracles, but he did not yet know Zeus's intentions. He was preparing himself for death, not for immortality. In *Philoctetes*, Heracles is the spokesman for Zeus's intentions, which up to that point were known only through the intermediary of an oracle. But beyond this contrast there is a continuity between the two images. The divine Heracles of *Philoctetes* has not forgotten his trials and his suffering. He begins by recalling them, which is also Sophocles' internal allusion to his own theater. These past trials are part of his destiny, which has become glorious, just as Philoctetes' present trials will be followed by a glorious future. The divine Heracles also recalls the funeral pyre on which he was cremated at the summit of Mount Oeta, when he asks Philoctetes to bring part of the booty won with his bow;[363] this refers to a cult of Heracles at the summit of Mount Oeta, which had been joined with that of his father, Zeus, mentioned at the end of *The Women of Trachis*.[364]

Conversely, *The Women of Trachis* presents a reversed image of the privileged relationship between Heracles and Philoctetes that concludes *Philoctetes*. As we have seen, in *The Women of Trachis* Heracles, faced with Hyllus's protests, allows him not to light the pyre himself.[365] What in the tragedy is a concession made by Heracles to his son is at the same time a way of preserving, without saying so, an indispensable element of the myth: it is in fact Philoctetes who will light the funeral pyre and thus inherit Heracles' infallible bow.[366] That is an example, among others, of these implicit allusions that were probably understood by the audience—or part of it—whose culture in the domain of mythology was superior to our own. This is probably not the only such allusion in the conclusion of *The Women of Trachis*. The marriage of Hyllus and Iole imposed by Heracles is connected with the story of the return of the Heracleides, in which Hyllus was to play an important role and also to be killed.[367] Finally, and above all, the Athenians were well aware that after having been cremated on Mount Oeta, Heracles, far from being abandoned by his father, had reached Olympus.[368] The Athenians were the first to honor Heracles as a god, and at the time of the Battle of Marathon sanctuaries already existed in Attica where Heracles was worshipped.[369] To be sure, Sophocles makes no explicit allusion to the divinization of Heracles at the end of *The Women of Trachis*, and the characters are not aware of it. But it is difficult not to take it into account in interpreting the tragedy, especially since Sophocles establishes in *Philoctetes* an implicit link between the divinization of Heracles and his cult at the pyre on Mount Oeta.[370] Sophocles probably makes a discreet allusion to this in Hyllus's last words, when he recognizes, despite his violent indignation at Zeus's indifference, the inability of humans to predict the future.[371] This leaves open the gods' hidden intentions. There is room for the heroization of Heracles.

Nonetheless, by this deliberate general silence at the end of *The Women of Trachis* Sophocles further emphasizes Heracles' heroism in accepting his destiny and gives its full meaning to Hyllus's desperate questioning of the indifference shown by Zeus, Heracles' father, regarding his son's suffering. Just as humans understand too late the signs sent by the gods, don't they doubt their silence too soon?[372]

CHAPTER X

Humans and the Gods

....

The Voice of the Gods: Heracles at the End of *Philoctetes*

The appearance of the deified Heracles at the end of *Philoctetes* is exceptional in two ways: on the one hand, this is the only divine apparition at the end of a tragedy in Sophocles' extant theater; on the other hand, and especially, it is the only time when a divinity descends from the heavens to clearly reveal "Zeus's designs"[1] to a mortal.

A god's presence, despite the surprise that Sophocles arranged, is in no way arbitrary. For a divinity to descend from the heavens and manifest himself or herself to a mortal, the latter has to be particularly beloved by that divinity; and for Heracles, Philoctetes is indeed one of the elect, because it was he who consented to light his funeral pyre and received his bow in return. This appearance of Heracles recalls that of Athena in the *Iliad*:[2] just as Athena, sent by Hera, appears to prevent Achilles from drawing his sword despite his anger at Agamemnon, so Heracles, Zeus's spokesman, appears to prevent Philoctetes from returning to his homeland. In both cases the divinity intervenes to prevent the mortal from making a bad decision, and in both cases the mortal takes the god's advice. A divinity less exalted than Athena, Heracles delivers a message that nonetheless has prestige, because he comes from Zeus.

This message consists first of predictions regarding the future of Philoctetes and Neoptolemus: the curing of Philoctetes' ulcer by Asclepius, the death of Paris, who was responsible for the war, pierced by arrows from Heracles' bow, and the destruction of Troy by the joint action of Philoctetes and Neoptolemus. The bow constitutes the link between the god and the man: having conquered Troy a first time in the hands of Heracles, the bow must now conquer the same city again, a generation later, in the hand of Philoctetes. But the message is not solely a prediction of the future; it also makes recommendations concerning the conduct to be adopted. Here is the end of Heracles' speech:

> But of this be mindful, when you plunder the land—that you show reverence towards the gods. Do this because Father Zeus regards all else as of less account, and because Piety does not die along with mortals. Whether they are alive or dead, their piety does not perish.[3]

On hearing such a beloved voice, Philoctetes, who had so long resisted human persuasion, immediately submits: he gives up his plan to return to his homeland and goes to Troy.[4] Such is the power of the divine word, even if Neoptolemus's friendly talk had already paved the way.[5] Thus in his last words Philoctetes will pay homage to the "all-taming God who has brought these things to pass," that is, Zeus. By describing Zeus as the "all-taming God," Sophocles innovates by transposing to Zeus the qualifier that Homer applied to sleep.[6] This affirmation of Zeus's power reminds us of a chorus in *Antigone* in which Zeus is called the supreme power that even sleep cannot conquer, any more than time can.[7]

But Philoctetes says nothing in particular about the warning contained at the end of the divine message. It is true that the advice given regarding the conduct to be adopted is not connected with the present of the action. This merely makes still more remarkable the insistence with which Zeus's spokesman solemnly affirms the necessity of humans respecting piety.[8] Piety must have priority over everything else, even heroic values. The moral lesson takes on all its meaning by reference to an event that is left unsaid and will take place after the time of the tragedy, but which the spectators knew well. One of the two characters who listen to the divine message, Achilles' son Neoptolemus, will not take this warning into account, because during the destruction of Troy he kills King Priam when the latter takes refuge at the altar of a god, and as if by chance this altar happens to be Zeus's.[9] The warning is also an a posteriori condemnation of the behavior of Odysseus, who at the beginning of the tragedy urged Neoptolemus to abandon piety for a day, and boasted that he could win a piety contest, except for missions where the end justifies the means.[10] The piety that Zeus demands of humans is not divisible. It exists or it does not.

The Voice of the Gods: Athena at the Beginning of *Ajax*

When the voice of a familiar god is heard, there is reason to rejoice. Philoctetes' joyful interjection when he hears Heracles' voice recalls that of Odysseus when he hears Athena's voice at the beginning of *Ajax*.[11] Compared with Heracles' apparition, we note one difference in the relationship between the man and the divinity. Whereas Heracles is heard and seen by the men to whom he appears, Athena, although seen by the audience, is heard only by Odysseus. This mode of apparition is probably of no significance concerning the degree of closeness between the human and the god, even if the relations between humans and gods lost in tragedy the familiarity they could attain in the epic.[12] In Euripides as well, Artemis, even though Hippolytus worships her exclusively, is heard by her protégé only when she appears at the end of *Hippolytus*.[13] But in *Ajax* this mode of appearance allows Sophocles to vary effects to show different aspects of the goddess's power, first in a dialogue with Odysseus alone, then in a dialogue with Ajax in Odysseus's presence, and finally once again in a dialogue with Odysseus alone.

The divinity's power has to do first of all with the superiority of her knowledge. Now, knowing is first of all seeing. Athena sees what humans do not see: she sees the inside, the inside of houses—and is thus able to reveal that Ajax is inside his house—but also the inside of hearts—knowing full well what Odysseus is seeking in his hunt at daybreak. She also sees in the dark and can recount in detail what no mortal has seen—not even Tecmessa, who witnessed Ajax's departure: the hero's nighttime expedition, sword in hand, from his house at the outskirts of the Achaian camp to the center, where he found the leaders on whom he wanted to take vengeance. The goddess shares her knowledge with her protégé, accusing the guilty party.

Her omniscience is accompanied by omnipotence. The goddess intervened in the course of human affairs just before the time of the tragedy. It was she who abruptly interrupted, at the last moment, Ajax's vengeance, by diverting his action to the flocks. She takes responsibility for her intervention and torments her victim ruthlessly:

> It was I who prevented him, by casting over his eyes oppressive notions of his fatal joy. . . . I kept urging him on, kept hurling him into the snares of doom.[14]

The goddess reverses the course of things: Ajax, who has left on a solitary hunt for his enemies, becomes, at the very moment when he is reaching his prey, the prey of the goddess, who has pushed him into her nets. Moreover, the goddess is not content to talk about her past action; she will show its present effects. That is what is involved in the scene in which Athena, like a bear tamer, has Ajax come out of his house in the grip of his madness, before an Odysseus petrified with fear. We have seen the impression made by the spectacle of this blood-spattered madman, leaping about with his whip in his hand and shaken by bursts of laughter.[15] But we now have to bring out its meaning. It is the goddess herself who takes care to state the moral as soon as Ajax has gone back into his house:

> Do you see, Odysseus, how great is the strength of the gods? Whom could you have found more prudent than this man, or better able to do what the situation demanded?[16]

This moral lesson, whose scope is general, is not imposed from outside. It arises from the spectacle of Ajax's madness, whose paradigmatic import the goddess emphasizes. The madman is not just anybody, but the man who was, after Achilles' death, the best of the Achaians by his intelligence and his courage. The gods' omnipotence is shown by their ability to lead even the best of men astray.

That is the significance of the spectacle as seen from the point of view of the goddess, who was an actor in it. And now, with Odysseus's response,[17] the same spectacle seen from the point of view of the man who witnessed it:

> I know of no one, but in his misery I pity him all the same, even though he hates me, because he is yoked beneath a ruinous delusion—I think of my own

lot no less than his. For I see that all we who live are nothing more than phantoms or fleeting shadows.[18]

Confronted by the extent of his rival's misery, Odysseus, moving beyond the traditional moral code that consists in laughing at one's enemy's misfortune,[19] experiences a new feeling, a feeling of pity. This is already a way for Sophocles to increase the emotional impact of the spectacle, because a misfortune that can elicit pity even from an enemy corresponds to the ultimate degree on the scale of catastrophes. The messenger in *Oedipus the King*, after telling how Oedipus put out his eyes, ends his report, at the very moment when Oedipus is about to reappear with blood on his face, by making the following remark to prepare the audience for the intensity of the spectacle:

Soon you will behold a sight which even he who abhors it must pity.[20]

But what is, in this passage from *Oedipus the King*, only a way of gauging the intensity of a misfortune is in *Ajax* a feeling experienced by a character in the tragedy as he confronts his enemy. Obviously, this is not the only passage in which a character expresses pity for another person's misfortune. Confronted by the misery of another epic hero, *Philoctetes*, the chorus also admits its pity.[21] It is not even the sole example in Sophocles' work of an enemy who feels pity on contemplating a hero brought low. In *Oedipus the King*, Creon had every reason to resent Oedipus because at the beginning of the tragedy he had accused him of conspiracy and had threatened to have him killed. However, at the end of the tragedy, he does not come to laugh at him[22] when he knows that he is defeated and blind; instead, he takes pity on him,[23] by giving him a pleasure amid his misfortunes, the presence of his daughters.[24] The feeling of pity at the tragic fate of great men is sufficiently natural for Aristotle to consider pity one of the two tragic feelings par excellence, alongside fear.[25] But what is exceptional in Odysseus's expression of pity in *Ajax* is that it is accompanied by a justification that goes beyond the particular case. Echoing Athena's words that show how the spectacle demonstrates the gods' power, Odysseus, in a brilliant formulation, demonstrates human weakness. These are the two sides of the same reality. The spectacle of Ajax leads Odysseus to move beyond his enmity to find a common denominator linking all mortals, the fragility of the human condition. The actual misfortune of the other is the sign of one's own possible misfortune. The spectacle effects, through the intermediary of reflection on the human condition, a process of soul-searching. It is in this sense that Odysseus says that he feels pity for Ajax, thinking about himself as much as about Ajax. Pity is not seen as an altruistic feeling, but it is rooted in the awareness that the other's misfortune could one day be one's own. Pity for others is not a matter of forgetting oneself, but of realizing that one's own condition is fragile.

Contemplating the spectacle of Ajax's madness, the goddess does not limit herself to asserting the power of the gods; before disappearing, she conveys to her protégé, who is now aware of the fragility of the human condition, a final message on how he is to behave:

> Therefore since you witness his fate, see that you yourself never utter an arrogant word against the gods, nor assume any swelling pride, if in the scales of fate you are weightier than another in strength of hand or in depth of ample wealth. For a day can press down all human things, and a day can raise them up. But the gods embrace men of sense and abhor the evil.[26]

The human wisdom advocated by the goddess is primarily negative: never show arrogance with regard to the gods; don't boast about being superior to other men, no matter in what way. She grounds her injunction in the awareness of the instability of human affairs.

Sophocles was not the first to connect the themes of divine power and the fragility or instability of human affairs with a morality of moderation. In the context of lyrical poetry, Pindar, particularly in his eighth Pythian, already gave the victor whom he was celebrating advice connected with the same themes:

> These things do not depend on men. It is a god who grants them; raising up one man and throwing down another. Enter the struggle with due measure. . . .
> The delight of mortals grows in a short time, and then it falls to the ground, shaken by an adverse thought. Creatures of a day. What is someone? What is no one? Man is the dream of a shadow.[27]

Not only by his themes, but also by the way he formulates them, Sophocles resembles Pindar. Notably, Pindar's definition of man as "the dream of a shadow," which is a hyperbole for unreality, corresponds to Odysseus's definition of humans as a "phantoms or fleeting shadows." Thus it is very likely that when Sophocles wrote this exchange between Athena and Odysseus he had Pindar's *Pythian Ode* in mind, paying homage to it and competing with it at the same time.[28] In any event, these are two embellished formulations of the traditional morality summed up in two laconic formulas attributed to the Seven Sages and inscribed on the temple of Apollo at Delphi: "Know thyself," and "Nothing too much."[29] In Athena's speech, as in Pindar, this wisdom is clearly reinserted into the relations between humans and gods. If the gods love those who are wise, they hate those who are not.

The place of this moral lesson in the tragedy is rather exceptional. It usually appears not at the beginning but at the end, in a reflection by the chorus that concludes the tragedy.[30] And in fact a comparable eulogy of wisdom and a warning against excess can be found at the end of *Antigone*, where the chorus draws the lesson from Creon's tragic destiny:

> Wisdom is provided as the chief part of happiness, and our dealings with the gods must be in no way unholy. The great words of arrogant men have to make repayment with great blows, and in old age teach wisdom.[31]

The lesson in morality situated at the beginning of *Ajax* is nonetheless not a substitute for what we expect at the end of the tragedy, because the chorus of Salaminians, before joining the cortège that is to convey Ajax's body to its last home, concludes the tragedy with the following reflection:

> Many things, I tell you, can be known through mortal eyes; but before he sees it happening, no one can foretell the future, or what his fate will be.[32]

Between the chorus's final reflection on humans' inability to foresee the future and the moral lesson drawn by Athena at the beginning of the tragedy, there is nonetheless a connection. It is precisely the instability of human affairs emphasized at the beginning that explains the unpredictability highlighted at the end.

This coming to awareness of the instability of the human condition, shown at the beginning and recalled at the end, is an invitation not only to reflect but also to experience new feelings regarding other people's misfortune, and also to act differently. We have seen how at the beginning of the tragedy Odysseus, far from laughing at his enemy's suffering, in conformity with a way of behaving common in the epic world, felt pity for him upon witnessing his misfortunes, via the medium of a reflective consideration of his own fragility as a man. But at that time he felt only a new emotion, paralyzed as he was by the fear elicited by the sight of Ajax's madness. However, at the end he will reappear as an actor in the tragedy. And if he returns, it is not to plant his foot on his enemy's body, as one might expect,[33] but to plead in favor of the dead man and to convince Agamemnon of the necessity of authorizing his burial. The argument he uses shows that he has learned the goddess's lesson and that he has not forgotten his realization that human destinies are fragile: he first speaks in the name of the gods, urging the king to respect their laws;[34] then, in conclusion, he returns to his own moral condition to justify his position. When Agamemnon asks: "Then do you truly urge me to allow the burying of the dead?," Odysseus replies: "Yes, for I too shall come to that necessity."[35]

This reflexive soul-searching on Odysseus's part is comparable to that triggered by his feeling of pity for his enemy.[36] In both cases, his soul-searching involves a recognition of what is universal in his fellow man and consequently of what binds them together, even if the other is an enemy. But whereas Odysseus's first bout of soul-searching envisaged a possibility—given the fragility of the human condition, I can fall into a misfortune similar to Ajax's—the second bout is based on a certainty. Odysseus knows that he is doomed, like Ajax, to die, and that the question of burial will arise for him as well, sooner or later. Agamemnon yields to Odysseus's arguments, but he retains his hatred for Ajax. That means that the king has not understood Odysseus's position in depth. In fact, he interprets Odysseus's reflective soul-searching as a banal manifestation of egoism: "How true it is that in all things alike each man works for himself!"[37] Agamemnon has not had the privilege of hearing the goddess's voice, as Odysseus has, or as the audience has. On the other hand, immediately after Agamemnon departs the chorus emphasizes Odysseus's wisdom:

> Whoever denies, Odysseus, that you were born wise in judgment is a total fool.[38]

This spontaneous recognition of Odysseus's wisdom by the chorus, which speaks for traditional morality, lends no support to those who would like to see in the character of Odysseus the representative of new values of solidarity that contrast with the goddess's vindictive and archaic attitude toward Ajax.

It remains that at the beginning of the tragedy the spectators may react rather violently to the disquieting element in the presentation of Athena, even if at the end of her speech she asserts that the power of the gods is not exercised in a random way. She gives the impression of playing with humans. She treats Odysseus, her protégé, with an amused irony when she wants to make Ajax come out: she accuses Odysseus of cowardice and pretends to be surprised that he is depriving himself of the pleasure of laughing at his enemy's misfortune.[39] Above all, she shows a cruel irony in dealing with Ajax, presenting herself at first as his ally, whereas the spectator is well aware that it is she who has cast him into his madness.[40] As the scholiast says with a certain spontaneity: "The spectator is on Ajax's side because of his misfortune, and is almost irritated with the poet."[41] Nevertheless, the poet has taken care, as the scholiast also remarks, to put in the last words that Ajax addresses to the goddess a sign of the hero's excessive character, a human offense against the divinity: when Athena is pleading in favor of the imaginary Odysseus so that he might not be whipped like a slave, Ajax categorically opposes her on this point. However, the spectator is in danger of not moving beyond the impression of a gap between the severity of the punishment inflicted by the goddess and this simple offense on the part of a man who, moreover, is in the grip of madness. But can one oppose a goddess, even for a moment? Sophocles leaves the question open at the end of the prologue. Later in the tragedy, he returns to it. Athena's attitude toward Ajax will be justified, no longer by the goddess's voice, but by that of an interpreter of the gods, a seer.

The Voice of the Gods and the Prophecy of the Seers

The gods appear directly only twice in Sophocles' extant theater. On both occasions, their presence is accompanied by the prophecy of a seer. In *Ajax*, the seer Calchas's prophecy comes after the divinity Athena's appearance; its function is to explain the latter. In *Philoctetes*, the prophecy of the Trojan seer Helenus comes before Heracles' epiphany and prepares it. However, a balance is established in the interplay of presences. When the divinity is visible, the seer does not appear: his prophecy is reported. Neither Calchas in *Ajax* nor Helenus in *Philoctetes* is seen by the spectators. On the other hand, when a seer is present onstage—and that is the case for Tiresias in *Antigone* and in *Oedipus the King*—no divinity appears.

In *Ajax*, the prophecy made by the Greek army's seer, Calchas, is reported by the messenger who has come to announce Teucer's return. Whereas Teucer, on returning from Mysia, is the target of a general hostility on the part of the soldiers, who want to stone "the madman's brother," the seer Calchas alone receives him warmly and advises him not to let Ajax come out of his house, because Athena's wrath will pursue him only on that particular day. First, this prophecy has a dramatic function: it immediately leads to the sending of a messenger, who will arrive too late, because Ajax has already left; and it triggers the hasty departure of the chorus and Tecmessa, who will themselves arrive too late, because they will find Ajax dead. But the prophecy also has an ethical function. What is remarkable in the messenger's faithful report of the prophecy is the number of lines accorded to the explanation of the goddess's wrath. This explanation occupies twenty verses, that is, more than half the messenger's speech.[42] This long development, which plays no role in the development of the action, begins with general reflections of an ethical nature on the severe punishment inflicted by the gods on humans whose thoughts rise above the human condition:

> Lives that have grown too proud and no longer yield good fall on grave difficulties sent from the gods, especially when someone born to man's estate forgets that fact by thinking thoughts too high for man.[43]

As often happens in Sophocles' theater, general reflections serve to introduce a particular case. Here, it is Ajax who is the illustration. The seer, through the messenger's report, refers to two decisive moments when Ajax's words have revealed his illusion that he can triumph without the gods' help. The first time was when Ajax was leaving on the expedition to Troy:

> Ajax, even at the time he first set out from home, showed himself foolish, when his father advised him well. For Telamon told him, "My son, seek victory in arms, but always seek it with the help of god." Then with a tall boast and foolishly he replied, "Father, with the help of the gods even a worthless man might achieve victory; but I, even without that help, fully trust to bring that glory within my grasp."[44]

On hearing Ajax reply so impudently to his father's wise advice, the spectator grasps, after the fact, the reason for the difference in their destinies. It is recalled that Ajax, drawing up a list of his misfortunes as he emerges from his fit of madness, contrasted his own infamy with the glory won by his father, whereas he had shown no less bravery than he.[45] At the time, this contrast merely strengthened the spectator's sympathy for the fallen hero and elicited a feeling of injustice with regard to this inequality of treatment. But now that the seer's prophecy has explained the past, what seemed inexplicable is justified. The man has paid the price for having claimed to be able to act without the gods. This presentation of the character of Ajax is all the more remarkable because it does not conform to the Homeric tradition. In Homer, Ajax, the son of Telamon, recognizes the intervention of the gods in the battle.[46] But with great subtlety, Sophocles has transposed to Ajax, son of Telamon, what Homer had said about Ajax, son of Oileus. The latter owed his death, upon his return from Tory, to an imprudent remark made during a storm, when Poseidon had saved him from drowning: "He declared that it was in spite of the gods that he had escaped the great gulf of the sea."[47] After this prideful remark, Poseidon split with his trident the rock on which the impious survivor had taken refuge and swallowed him up.

The second occasion on which Ajax uttered impious words was still more serious, because this time the words were addressed not to a man but to a divinity:

> Then once again in answer to divine Athena—at a time when she was urging him forward and telling him to turn a deadly hand against the enemy—he answered her with words terrible and blasphemous, "Queen, stand beside the other Greeks; where Ajax stands, battle will never break our line."[48]

By seeking to show his superiority over all others, Ajax commits the supreme impiety, that of refusing the divinity's aid. After the revelation of these two impious remarks, the spectator inevitably casts a new, retrospective eye on the scene between Athena and Ajax in the prologue. What might appear to be arbitrary cruelty on Athena's part is revealed to be, after the seer's prophecy, the goddess's justified wrath punishing, at an unforeseeable time, the man who tried to raise himself above the human condition. At first, Sophocles deliberately misled the spectators regarding the goddess's conduct so that he could enlighten them later on. It was a way of warning them against making hasty judgments concerning the gods. To understand, one has to know how to wait. But one must not await the gods' punishment before acting well.

Ajax learned too late; it was only after his act of madness that he became aware of the goddess's intervention and the impossibility of men being able to resist the gods:

> If a god sends harm, it is true that even the base man can elude the worthier.[49]

This general reflection placed in Ajax's mouth at the time he is listing his misfortunes also takes on its full meaning only in the new perspective provided by the seer's prophecy reporting Ajax's earlier remarks concerning the gods. It marks an evolution of the character in his relations with the gods. It is a recognition of what he refused to recognize up to that point; he had sought, despite his father's warning, to win a victory without the gods' help. The madness provoked by the goddess is a source of lucidity. Nevertheless, this lucidity does not lead to wisdom. To be sure, Ajax knows well what the path of wisdom is: yielding to the gods.[50] For a moment, he claims to adhere to this wisdom, but he does so in a wily discourse intended to deceive his entourage and enable him to make the only remaining exit that allows him to remain faithful to his nature: suicide. In the end, the hero will not submit. One silence is characteristic in the monologue he delivers before his suicide. At the moment he dies he invokes the help of several divinities, including Zeus, but says not a word about Zeus's daughter Athena. The goddess's speech, though justified by the seer's prophecy, has not had an impact on Ajax; although he recognizes her power after the misfortune she has inflicted on him, he does not recognize his own offense against her. The goddess's anger, which is supposed to end when the day is over, is ultimately less tenacious than the human's perseverance in his error. But the divinity's speech has not been useless: it awakened the wisdom of Odysseus, who will be the advocate of the hero's rehabilitation after his death.

In *Philoctetes*, as in *Ajax*, the seer's prophecy is known indirectly; but in contrast to *Ajax*, it precedes the goddess's speech. This inversion of the order leads to changes in meaning. In *Philoctetes* the prophecy no longer explains the god's speech; instead, the god's speech confirms the prophecy. And this prophecy is not that of the Greek seer, Calchas, but that of the Trojan seer, Helenus. The prophecy is gradually revealed all through the tragedy.

The first revelation is by the false merchant sent by Odysseus. He explicitly reveals part of the prophecy made by the Trojan seer, whom Odysseus captured by night: the destruction of Troy will not be possible unless Philoctetes is persuaded to leave his island for Troy; Odysseus is assigned to bring Philoctetes to Troy, by force if necessary; and he is on his way with Diomedes.[51] This initial revelation of the prophecy, in which truth and lie are inextricably interwoven, has a precise dramatic function. In Odysseus's plan of deception, it is intended to hasten his victim's departure: Philoctetes, believing he is escaping Odysseus by leaving for his homeland with Neoptolemus, is in reality to fall into his snares. But this first revelation also sheds light, retroactively, on the real cause of Odysseus and Neoptolemus's mission: it is only a human affair, but an enterprise dictated by the seer's prophecy.

The second explicit mention of the prophecy is made by Neoptolemus, toward the end of the tragedy. It is now stripped of any context of trickery. Neoptolemus, after regaining Philoctetes' confidence by returning his bow to him, now seeks, by genuine persuasion, to convince him to go to Troy. His argument is twofold; on the one hand, in Troy his ulcer will be cured by the son of Asclepius, and the other hand, his bow will allow him to conquer the Trojan citadel. And Neoptolemus reveals to Philoctetes that this twofold prediction has its origin in Helenus's prophecy.[52] This second explicit mention of the prophecy confirms the first by making Philoctetes the destroyer of Troy,[53] but it complements it, notably with regard to everything concerning Philoctetes' illness, its divine cause, and its healing.[54]

Moreover, Sophocles varies the point of view depending on the function of the character who is speaking. Whereas in his presentation of the prophecy the false merchant emphasized the person who captured the seer—the wily Odysseus, who swore he would bring back Philoctetes—Neoptolemus highlights the author of the prophecy, the worthy seer, who agrees to die if his prophecy is not fulfilled.[55] The fact that these changes in viewpoint complement each other, while at the same time being adapted to each situation, is obviously no accident. As he constructs each scene, Sophocles takes into account the dramatic progression as the whole and the characters' point of view.

We are nonetheless astonished that Neoptolemus, who at the end of the tragedy knows so much about Helenus's prophecy, seems not to know it at all at the beginning of the tragedy, when in speaking with Odysseus he makes objection after objection before finally allowing himself to be persuaded to act by means of trickery.[56] Should we conclude that his character is inconsistent, a sign of an imperfection in the dramatic construction? Or should we interpret this alleged ignorance retrospectively, as a strategy adopted by the young man who is pretending to be naïve in talking with his elder? In any case, it would be inappropriate to transform by interminable discussions a mere detail into an affair of state. The imperfection, if there is one, is hardly perceptible in performance. On the other hand, what is noticeable is the ultimate failure of Neoptolemus's effort at genuine persuasion. He had won Philoctetes' trust by lying but is unable to convince him to leave for Troy, despite the warrant of the seer's prophecy. It is not that the seer's veracity can be questioned. In fact, the god's speech will confirm the seer's prophecy: as we have seen, Heracles' message also promises healing and glory.[57] But between the reported prophecy of a seer and the voice of a god who shows himself, there is a great difference.

However, since the gods appear to humans directly only on exceptional occasions, humans, left to their own devices, may question what the gods' interpreters say.

When Humans Challenge the Gods' Interpreters

It is chiefly in the two tragedies in which the hero is the king of the city, *Antigone* and *Oedipus the King*, that divine interpreters are challenged or even contradicted. Among these interpreters we must distinguish between oracles issued by the gods in their sanctuaries and prophecies made by seers.

From the theatrical point of view, the situation is inverted in *Antigone* and *Oedipus the King* as compared to the two tragedies where the gods appear to epic heroes. Whereas the prophecies of the seers Calchas and Helenus are reported in *Ajax* and in *Philoctetes*, in *Antigone* and *Oedipus the King* it is the seer Tiresias who comes in person to make a prophecy. On the other hand, the god's speech is reported in the form of oracles. That is what happens in *Oedipus the King* when, faced by the crisis in the city and the impossibility of finding a solution by using his own human faculties, the king mobilizes all the resources of divine knowledge, the oracle of Apollo at Delphi and the city's seer in Thebes. Apollo's response is announced by a messenger—as was the prophecy of the seer Calchas in *Ajax*—whereas the seer Tiresias arrives in person. Thus Sophocles, even though he did not hesitate to combine the voice of the gods and seers' prophecies, seems to have avoided piling up theatrical effects, retaining a kind of balance between the direct presence of some and the indirect presence of others.

In Sophocles' theater, humans challenge seers principally in two parallel scenes in *Antigone* and *Oedipus the King*, in which the king of Thebes—Creon in one case, Oedipus in the other—confronts the seer Tiresias.[58] These two scenes, which are justly famous, are comparable, though they do not have the same position in the action and though Sophocles varied the effects. Tiresias arrives toward the end of the tragedy in *Antigone*, whereas in *Oedipus the King* he arrives at the beginning; and whereas in *Antigone* the seer presents himself spontaneously to deliver his knowledge to the king, in *Oedipus the King* he comes at the king's summons and does not want to reveal what he knows. But the dramatic progression of the two scenes is governed by an analogous psychological mechanism. At first the king receives the seer with courtesy and respect, and then, under the influence of anger, he makes violent accusations against the seer who, piqued, makes a series of threatening predictions against the king before breaking off the conversation. One of the accusations made by the king in the two scenes is that of venality;[59] and in *Antigone* the accusation is extended beyond the person of the seer Tiresias himself and applied to all seers: "The prophet-clan was ever fond of money," Creon declares.[60] But in the corresponding scene in *Oedipus the King* the accusations are graver. Whereas in *Antigone* Creon attacked only the person of the seer, while continuing to recognize his divinatory abilities,[61] in *Oedipus the King* the accusation of venality is accompanied by an accusation of incompetence. Tiresias, Oedipus says, "has eyes only for profit, but is blind in his art."[62] In this attack on the blind seer, Oedipus plays with scathing irony on the antithesis between "seeing" and "not-seeing." The seer recovers his sight when money is involved, but he is blind when it is a matter of his art. The violence of the king's attack on the seer is such that he insults him by calling him a "magus" and a "mendicant priest."[63]

Moreover, whereas in *Antigone* the accusations made against the interpreters of the gods are limited to the scene between the king and the seer, in *Oedipus the King* they are prolonged by a questioning of oracles. All through the investigation into the murder of Laius, depending on the hopes or fears, prophecies and oracles are met with either denial or horror by Oedipus and Jocasta. First it is Jocasta who, to calm Oedipus's anxiety regarding the seer Tiresias's prophecies, denies the existence of any mantic art: "Nothing of mortal birth shares in the science of the seer."[64] This challenge is already very serious, because it bears not only on the seers' prophecies but even on the oracle of Delphi itself. To justify her condemnation of any human art of prophecy, Jocasta reveals to Oedipus a first oracle of Apollo that was issued long before and that she thinks has not been fulfilled, because she believes that her son died shortly after his birth: this is the oracle issued to her husband Laius, according to which he was to die by his son's hand. However, in this first stage of her criticism, Jocasta still shows restraint. She draws a distinction between the god and his interpreters,[65] implying that it is the human interpreters of the oracle who are responsible for the fallibility of the god's utterance. But a final step in the questioning of the seers and oracles is taken when the Corinthian messenger arrives to announce the death of old Polybus, Oedipus's alleged father. It is Jocasta who learns this news, and she immediately sees in it a proof that the second old oracle of Apollo that Oedipus revealed to her, namely that he was to kill his father, was fulfilled no more than the first one. She immediately cries out: "Oracles of the gods, where do you stand now?"[66] Now it is the "oracles of the gods" themselves that are directly put in doubt: the distinction between the interpreters and the god is forgotten. And when Oedipus learns the news a few moments later, his questioning, which echoes Jocasta's, is a total condemnation of both oracles and seers: "Why indeed, my wife, should one look to the hearth of the Pythian seer, or to the birds that scream above our heads?"[67] Thus in *Oedipus the King*, from scene to scene the spectator witnesses, from the arrival of the seer Tiresias to the arrival of the messenger from Corinth, a slow but regular increase in Oedipus's and Jocasta's questioning of oracles and seers.

The Criticism of Seers and Oracles in the Literary Tradition and in Contemporary Thought

This questioning of seers and oracles by certain characters in Sophocles' theater can be better understood if we resituate it in the literary tradition and also in the rationalist movement of Pericles' century.

It was from Homer that Sophocles drew the idea of a scene in which a seer and a king opposed one another; he transposed the confrontation between King Agamemnon and the seer Calchas at the beginning of the *Iliad*.[68] Each of the two scenes in Sophocles contains elements that implicitly refer to Homer. Just as Calchas publicly denounces Agamemnon's offense in Homer, in *Antigone*, Tiresias openly denounces Creon's offense, thereby arousing the king's anger, just as Calchas did in Homer. In *Oedipus the King*, the consultation of the seer is justified, as in Homer, by the presence of a pestilence that is ravaging the whole community; and Tiresias hesitates to reveal his prophecy because he fears the king's reprisals, just as in Homer Calchas demanded Achilles' protection before speaking, in order to defend himself against the king's anger and resentment. But Sophocles made the conflict between the seer and the king more dramatic in both these scenes than it is in Homer, notably by accentuating the king's accusations against the seer. In Homer, although Agamemnon insults Calchas by calling him "prophet of evil,"[69] no attack puts in question the seer's honesty or competence. There is an accusation of cupidity in the Homeric scene, but it is made by Achilles against the king.[70] It is not impossible that Sophocles might have taken pleasure in transposing, by a subtle play of deliberate intertextuality, the accusation made against the king in the *Iliad* into an accusation made by the king against the seer in his two tragedies. But this transposition is not a simply literary game, because the accusation of venality made against the seer in Sophocles is part of what might be called the conspiracy syndrome: the king becomes obsessed with an alleged conspiracy and imagines that the conspirators are using, to achieve their ends, the venality of his subordinates. In both *Oedipus the King* and *Antigone*, the seer Tiresias is accused by the king of having been bribed in the context of a political conspiracy.[71]

In Homer, Sophocles may have found another scene where the mantic art is put in question. In book 12 of the *Iliad*, a fateful omen occurs at the moment when the Trojans are getting ready to make an assault on the Achaian wall: an eagle appears on the left, carrying a serpent in its talons. The Trojan Polydamas, who knows the art of divination, sees in this an omen of disaster; but Hector rebuffs him and questions divination by birds:

> Thou biddest us be obedient to birds long of wing, that I regard not, nor take thought thereof, whether they fare to the right, toward the Dawn and the sun, or to the left toward the murky darkness.[72]

This sharp attack on divination by birds made by Hector may have served Sophocles as a model when he has Oedipus make his sarcastic remark about "birds that scream above our heads."[73]

Thus the expression of skepticism with regard to the seers' art already appears in the literary tradition before Sophocles.[74] But this criticism was taken up and renewed by the rationalism that developed after Homer. The first Greek thinker known for having criticized divination while at the same time affirming the existence of the gods is the philosopher Xenophanes (sixth to seventh centuries BCE). This information is conveyed by Cicero in *De divinatione*,[75] but we know nothing about the arguments that the philosopher gave. On the other hand, a brief but important criticism of prophecy has been preserved in Hippocrates, who was Sophocles' contemporary. The physician, concerned about the discords that might exist in the treatment of acute illnesses, feared that the art of medicine might fall victim to the same criticisms as the art of divination. Here is what he says:

> And one might almost say against physicians that their art is comparable to the mantic art, since seers think that the same bird is a good sign if it appears on the left and a bad sign if it appears on the right, whereas there are seers who think the contrary; and in examining victims the same holds, opinions varying depending on the case.[76]

This is the first known text that bases the criticism of divination on internal contradictions among the seers' diverse methods, long before Cicero's *De divinatione*. Still, even though the attacks made by fifth-century scientists on seers could be frank and unsparing, it is very important to note that they never engage in polemics against the oracles of the great sanctuaries. This silence allows us better to gauge the scope of the criticism Sophocles puts in Oedipus's mouth when he places oracles and seers on the same level. It is unusually audacious, and Sophocles emphasizes it in an unusual way, through the indignant reaction of the chorus. In the following stasimon, the old men cry out in alarm at immoderation and impiety in general, a cry of alarm that is actually aimed at the audacity of the king and queen's rejection of the oracles:

> The old prophecies concerning Laius are fading; already men give them no value, and nowhere is Apollo glorified with honors; the worship of the gods is perishing.[77]

Human Error and the Veracity of Seers and Oracles

But at the same time that Sophocles has some of his characters make such irreverent remarks about seers or oracles, he does all he can to show that they are in error. Despite the ambiguity inherent in the meaning of words in the theater, since the tragic author can never express his feeling directly, but must reveal it through the mediation of signs that the spectator interprets like a seer, Sophocles' message is clear.

Each time a character puts seers or oracles in question, the facts rapidly show the truth of the predictions and the error of the character who challenged them. This holds for both *Antigone* and *Oedipus the King*. In *Antigone*, the seer's prophecy announcing the punishment of Creon's double offense by a death in his own family is fulfilled almost immediately with the suicide of his son Haemon, which the messenger comes to announce. And as soon as the messenger has announced Haemon's death, Sophocles has the veracity of the seer's prophecy emphasized by the exclamation the chorus addresses to the absent seer: "Ah, prophet, how true, then, you have proved your word!"[78] In *Oedipus the King*, the seer's prophecy and all three of the oracles turn out to be true in the end. It is Oedipus himself who recognizes this at the end of his investigation:

> Oh, oh! All brought to pass, all true. Light, may I now look on you for the last time—I who have been found to be accursed in birth, accursed in wedlock, accursed in the shedding of blood.[79]

Furthermore, this final revelation of the veracity of the prophecies and oracles by the man who denied them is preceded by provisional recognitions that Sophocles skillfully combines with questioning. In the course of the investigation, moments of delusion in which prophecies and oracles are denounced and moments of lucidity in which their fulfillment is feared follow one another and are connected on two occasions. Here are the two moments of lucidity:

> I have dread fears that the seer can see.[80]

> Fearing indeed lest Apollo's prophecy come true in me.[81]

With much art, Sophocles has arranged things so that one of these two parallel recognitions, which mark the stages in the dramatic progress toward the final revelation, bears on the seer's prophecy, and the other bears on one of the god's oracles. Ultimately, Sophocles' originality consists in his steady and unbroken confidence in both the seer's prophecies and the god's oracles.

The Comparative Status of Seers and Oracles in Sophocles' Theater

If in Sophocles' theater the message of the seers who are mortals is ultimately revealed to be as true as that of the gods' oracles, it is because there is no incompatibility between the art of the seer and divine inspiration, as we can see through the reflection on the sources of the seer's knowledge, notably in *Antigone* and in *Oedipus the King*. In *Antigone*, the art of divination by signs serves to formulate, at the beginning of the scene, the prophecy about the past and about the present—the diagnosis of the cause of the disease that is attacking the city, and Creon's edict forbidding Polynices' burial.[82] But at the end of the scene, when the seer reveals in a fit of anger his prophecy regarding the future—an impending death in the royal family—it is no longer a question of divination by signs.[83] It is a question of inspired divination, supposing that this distinction might already be pertinent in Sophocles' time. From *Antigone* to *Oedipus the King*, the image of the seer evolves and becomes even more prestigious: his prophecies, both about the past and about the present and the future, are no longer related to the interpretation of signs. They all emerge under the influence of anger and seem to belong to the order of inspired divination. What is particularly new with respect to the Tiresias of *Antigone* is the close relation established between the seer and the divine. When the chorus of *Oedipus the King* sees Tiresias coming, it calls him "the godlike prophet . . . in whom truth lives."[84] And during the confrontation between the seer and the king, Tiresias declares that he is the slave, not of Oedipus, but of Apollo Loxias.[85] That amounts to saying that the possession of the mantic art does not exclude natural knowledge inspired by the god. The alliance of what seem to us to be contraries gives the seers' prophecies a validity analogous to that of the god's oracles. This Sophoclean conception of the seer's status is ultimately not different from that of Homer, for whom the seer's knowledge proceeded from the divinity.[86] The nascent technological thinking of Sophocles' time had not yet structured clear oppositions between art and nature, between human knowledge and inspired knowledge. Art could still be a gift of the gods. Thus for Sophocles there was no difference in nature between the seer's prophecy and the god's oracle.

But from a theatrical point of view, there was still a great difference. The god's oracle is a disembodied speech expressed in the form of a response that the inquirer registers without engaging in any real dialogue with the god or looking into the god's motivations. On the contrary, the seer's prophecy, at least when it is made in the visible space, comes from a man whose human nature is not abolished by technical or inspired knowledge. Thus the prophecy is revealed through the play of human feelings in a dramatic conflict between the prophet and the inquirer in which the anger seems equal on both sides, even if it is not. The seer's message then becomes more indecipherable for the inquirer, who goes astray all the more rapidly because he interprets as a human motive what is actually a divine message.

By juxtaposing in a single tragedy, on the one hand, gods who express themselves either directly or through the intermediary of their oracles, and on the other hand, seers who prophesy onstage or whose prophecies are reported, Sophocles has presented divine speech in two forms and ultimately demonstrated that these two categories of messages converge. This is the case, as we have just seen, in four tragedies out of seven.

Old Oracles and New Oracles

Sophocles engaged in a further doubling within the oracles themselves. He introduced into a single tragedy two oracles given to one and the same person but at different times: the old and the new oracles given to Heracles in *The Women of Trachis*. When Heracles learns from his son Hyllus that the magic balm with which his wife, Deianira, smeared the tunic was given her by the centaur Nessus, he suddenly understands that he is surely doomed to die, because two oracles proceeding from Zeus, his father, are being fulfilled:

> It was foreshown to me by my father far in the past that I would perish by no creature that had the breath of life, but by one already dead, a dweller with Hades. So this savage Centaur in death has killed me alive, just as the divine will had been foretold. And I will show you how later oracles tally with the first and testify to the old prophecy. I wrote them down for myself from the mouth of my father's oak of many tongues in the grove of the Selli, who dwell on the hills and sleep on the ground. The tree said that, at the time which lives and now is, my release from the toils laid upon me would be accomplished. And I expected prosperous days, but the meaning, it seems, was only that I would die. For toil comes no more to the dead.[87]

Heracles now understands everything, because he interprets the present by the past that he has suddenly recalled. First there is an old oracle. Zeus, Heracles' father, had told him that he would die because of someone dead. In light of this oracle, Heracles now grasps the true import of his wife's gift. Deianira has served as a relay allowing the poison that issued from the lethal wound of the centaur Heracles killed with a poisoned arrow to give the dead centaur a delayed vengeance on the living man. For Heracles, this old oracle illuminates the ambiguous meaning of a second, more recent oracle. The old oracle had not been mentioned earlier in the tragedy. Hyllus and the spectators are hearing about it for the first time. On the other hand, the new oracle, which Heracles thinks he is also revealing for the first time, was already known to Hyllus and especially to the spectators. It is on the tablet Heracles left before departing, and Deianira revealed its contents first to Hyllus, then to the chorus, with further details.[88] It bears on Heracles' destiny and includes the oracle that was given him in Zeus's sanctuary at Dodona. This oracle was characterized both by its precision and its ambiguity: precision regarding the date of the decisive moment in Heracles' destiny, which corresponds exactly to the day of the tragedy itself;[89] ambiguity, on the other hand, regarding the outcome of the crisis: death or life without sorrows? Sophocles had already made use of this ambiguity at the beginning of the tragedy, for emotional and dramatic purposes. On the one hand, the oracle increased Deianira's anxiety concerning Heracles' absence; and on the other hand, it transformed an ordinary day into a fateful day for the hero's destiny.[90] Everything was supposed to be resolved during the day, but everything still remained open when the first messenger arrived to announce Heracles' victorious return. At the end of the tragedy what is remarkable is the convergence of the two oracles, one of which sheds light on the meaning of the other. They are both true, but humans were mistaken about the interpretation of one of them. The god's voice is sometimes equivocal, but the god does not make mistakes. Sooner or later, humans discover the meaning and the truth of the oracle. And what matters is that this discovery is made in an instant, on the basis of a detail mentioned by another person for whom it is meaningless, though it is filled with meaning for those who receive it. Even when the validity of oracles is not questioned by the characters—as is the case in *The Women of Trachis*, unlike *Oedipus the King*—their fulfillment leads the person involved to become aware, often painfully, of the reality of his destiny.

Is Apollo's Oracle Advising Orestes to Take Revenge Just?

It remains that modern commentators differ regarding the meaning to be attributed, in Sophocles' *Electra*, to the oracle of Apollo that Orestes consulted in Delphi before taking revenge on his father's murderers. Of course, no one will deny that the oracle is fulfilled here, as elsewhere in Sophocles' theater. But is it just?

Orestes reveals the content of the oracle at the beginning of the tragedy, when he explains to the tutor, who has returned with him, his plan for taking revenge:

> When I went to the Pythian oracle to learn how I might avenge my father on his murderers, Phoebus gave me the commandment which you will now hear: that alone, and by stealth, without the aid of arms or large numbers, I should carry off my right hand's just slaughters.[91]

Orestes recalls this oracle because it connects his plan for deception directly with the god's injunctions. Following the god's instructions, Orestes will carry out a vengeance in remarkable conformity with them. His plan for deception has three stages: first, in order to gain entry to the palace, the tutor announces Orestes' death in a chariot race at Delphi; then Orestes himself arrives bearing a funerary urn to confirm his own death, after having first deposited libations and offerings on his father's tomb; and finally the tutor comes out of the palace to inform Orestes as to what is happening inside it. These three stages govern the actual execution of the vengeance.[92] Nothing will disturb this development, not even the recognition scene between Orestes and Electra. There was only one moment of hesitation at the beginning, when Orestes, hearing lamentations inside the palace, suggests to the tutor that he remain to listen to them. But the tutor firmly sets Orestes back on the right path to vengeance:

> No, no; before all else, let us strive to obey the commands of Loxias and from them make a fair beginning by pouring libations to your father. For such actions bring victory within our grasp and give us mastery in all our doings.[93]

This call to order is placed under the sign of the oracle of the god at Delphi, designated here under the name of Loxias. It therefore further stresses the importance of the presence of the god, who, in the rest of the tragedy, will silently help Orestes. The total absence of an obstacle to the fulfillment of Orestes' enterprise is a clear sign of the veracity of the divine word. The tragedy is elsewhere; it is Electra's.

Thus the god's word is efficacious. But is it just? Here, vengeance involves matricide. Can the god, in all justice, advise a son to kill his mother? The question was clearly asked by Euripides in his *Electra*, which he wrote at about the same time, though we cannot determine the precise relative chronology of the two plays. After the parricide, Orestes and Electra are stunned by the magnitude of both their misfortune and their crime. It is in this context of high emotion, in which the characters sing with the chorus, that Orestes addresses Apollo in these terms:

> Ah, Phoebus! you proclaimed in song unclear justice, but you have brought about clear woes.[94]

To be sure, the man, even as he blames the god for the consequences of his oracle, is merely wondering about the meaning of a justice he does not understand. However, the judgment rendered by the Dioscuri, Clytemnestra's deified brothers who appear immediately after this sung dialogue to conclude the tragedy, intensifies the accusation that man makes against the god:

> Phoebus, Phoebus—but I am silent, for he is my lord; although he is wise, he gave you oracles that were not.[95]

The Dioscuri's questioning of the oracle is both audacious and prudent: prudent, because the condemnation bears on only one particular oracle rendered by the god at Delphi; and audacious, because Euripides has a divine oracle condemned by gods.

What about Sophocles? In his oracle, as it is presented by Orestes at the beginning of the tragedy, Apollo did not limit himself to urging Orestes to carry out the vengeance himself, by using trickery. He also approved this vengeance, since he described it as "just slaughters." That is the reason why Orestes, when he approaches the palace, can say that he is coming "by divine mandate to cleanse you as justice demands."[96] Thus in Orestes' first words the justice of his vengeance is guaranteed by the gods.

But at the end of the tragedy, Orestes alludes a second time to the oracle when he tells Electra that he has carried out the murder of their mother:

All is well within the house, if Apollo's oracle spoke well.[97]

Judgments concerning the meaning of this remark differ considerably. The traditional interpretation sees in it an expression of the confidence of Orestes, who once again takes refuge behind the god's authority. Some modern commentators see in it, on the contrary, an expression of the anxiety of the son who doubts the oracle's well-foundedness after his mother has committed her crime. A few even go so far as to emphasize the irony of Orestes' use of the word "well." And since this reference to the oracle comes at the end of the tragedy, it could be seen as casting doubt on the legitimacy of the oracular pronouncement.[98]

If we want to properly assess the end of the tragedy from the point of view not of a scholar sitting in his or her study and seeking the meaning of the whole ending of the play on the basis of one or two isolated verses, but rather from that of a spectator who is witnessing the performance and who is sensitive to the convergence of dramatic effects, everything points to an end radically different from that of Aeschylus's *The Libation Bearers* and from that of Euripides in his *Electra*. In Sophocles' work, there is no explicit reference to the Erinyes who in Aeschylus pursue the son after he murders his mother and drive him mad. If the Erinys is mentioned, it is in the context of the vengeance of Agamemnon, where the chorus associates it with Justice.[99] It is as if Apollo were helping tacitly but effectively to carry out the vengeance. The prayer that Electra addresses to Apollo asking him to show humans the punishment that the gods reserve for impiety is immediately granted through the murder of the impious woman.[100] And when the avengers come out again, the chorus comments: "I cannot blame the deed."[101] How, under these conditions, should we interpret the next words Orestes utters, which, following this commentary, sound like a kind of defiance of the oracle?

Nothing that precedes authorizes this abrupt change. And if there were a change, it would have to be perceptible in what comes afterward. But what does Orestes say about his mother? That her arrogance no longer dishonors Electra.[102] This is a condemnation without the slightest trace of doubt or remorse. If there were a change, how could we explain the fact that Orestes pursues masterfully the completion of the vengeance? For Sophocles, inverting the traditional order of the murders no longer makes the vengeance culminate in the matricide.[103] This inversion reinforces the well-foundedness of the vengeance. In his last words, Orestes can condemn Aegisthus's crime unreservedly, broadening his condemnation to the category of those who fear neither god nor man, to which his mother's lover belongs.[104]

It is not impossible that Sophocles was able, despite this convergence of dramatic effects, to slip a reference to the possible intervention of the Erinyes into what Aegisthus says when he speaks of the present and future misfortunes of the family of the Pelopids.[105] But can one rely on this sole allusion to question the interpretation of the whole of a tragedy? Isn't it rather Sophocles' amused and ironic wink as he puts Aeschylus's interpretation into the mouth the most abominable criminal ever?[106]

As for the chorus's last words, they stress the happy consequences of a vengeance that puts an end to the family's trials and brings liberation. The last word of the tragedy is carefully chosen: it designates a complete accomplishment (*teleōthen*) and marks a closure.[107]

By deviating from the tragic tradition regarding the consequences of matricide, and even the order of the murders, Sophocles was not totally innovating. He was returning, as we have seen, to the epic tradition and even to the lyric tradition.[108]

Therefore *Electra* does not constitute an exception to the confidence in oracles and seers that Sophocles shows in his other tragedies.

Oracles That Destroy and Oracles That Save

The importance Sophocles accords to oracles may have led him to adapt their traditional content to eliminate what in the obscure paths of divine justice might have seemed too inhuman. That is the case for the myth of Oedipus, in which Sophocles modified, from *Oedipus the King* to *Oedipus at Colonus*, the content of the oracle that Oedipus receives from Apollo.

To judge by *Oedipus the King* alone, we might see in the fulfillment of Apollo's oracles the disturbing destruction of an innocent man who, though he has not committed a clear past offense, is struck by misfortune, the victim of an "infernal mechanics" whose first cause goes back to the preceding generation. However, that is not the orientation that Sophocles chose when he developed his tragedy. So far as the oracles are concerned, he wanted to show how Oedipus, and Jocasta as well, were wrong to doubt them. The gradual and belated recognition of their fulfillment is there to refute their skepticism in the most flagrant way and to confirm the chorus's indignant rejection of that skepticism. Addressing the chorus at the end of the tragedy, Oedipus fully acknowledges the presence of Apollo:

> It was Apollo, friends, Apollo who brought these troubles to pass, these terrible, terrible troubles.[109]

Apollo's oracles do not back off, and the divine does not go away. The triumphs of human intelligence are transitory. The divine word remains. And what is significant at the end of the tragedy is that at no time is there any protest against the injustice and misfortune of Oedipus's fate. His entourage, whose compassion is quite moderate, does not spare the poor man its criticisms. The chorus reproaches him for blinding himself, while Creon always claims to know better.[110] As for the chorus's final remark, which is inspired by Oedipus's destiny, it draws from the contrast between his past grandeur and his present misfortune a general observation regarding the instability of the human condition, but it discusses neither the causes of Oedipus's fall nor the problem of his responsibility.

That problem will be taken up later in *Oedipus at Colonus*, a tragedy in which the gods, after humiliating a man, raises him up again. Sophocles returned to the oracle given by the Delphic Apollo predicting to Oedipus his well-known misfortunes, but he added a new dimension concerning the end of his destiny: on entering a last country after a long exile, Oedipus will be received by venerable goddesses, and he will see the course of his life change, bringing benefits to those who welcome him and ravages to those who drive him away. Signs will announce this change: an earthquake, thunder, or Zeus's lightning bolt.[111] In this way the oracle, which was solely destructive, becomes a means of salvation. Sophocles' manipulation is a way of restoring the intelligibility of divine justice and preparing the reconciliation between Oedipus and the gods. Moreover, Oedipus's experience has taught him that oracles are fulfilled. At the beginning of the tragedy, a single, apparently insignificant detail revealed by a third party suffices to make Oedipus suddenly realize that the second part of the oracle is being fulfilled. On learning from the resident of Colonus that he is in the Eumenides' sanctuary, he identifies it with the sanctuary of the venerable goddesses mentioned in the oracle.[112] The part of the oracle that refers to saving powers will in fact be fulfilled in the tragedy and produce signs announcing a new destiny. The oracle's function is thus both dramatic and religious.

However, the obstacles to receiving Oedipus in the place where he is supposed to find his tomb momentarily compromise this fulfillment. First, the chorus of residents of Colonus learns the identity of the newcomer and tries to drive him away. This reversal provides Oedipus with an opportunity to review his past and to take up the problem of his responsibility. He pleads not guilty, because "it was all unknowing I went where I went."[113] The second obstacle comes from outside. It is Creon, the Theban envoy, who comes to bring Oedipus back to the boundary of Thebes in order to benefit from his support. To justify the existence of this new obstacle, Sophocles introduces new oracles of Apollo of Delphi that Ismene has come to announce to her father: the Thebans will come to get Oedipus, dead or alive, for their own safety.[114] These oracles also have a twofold function: a theatrical function insofar as they have an impact on the development of the action; and a religious function because they are also the sign of the gods' rehabilitation of a man. "The gods now raise you up; but before they worked your ruin," Ismene declares when she announces these new oracles.[115] Nonetheless, the dramatic function and the religious function seem this time to work in opposite directions. Although the new oracles' religious meaning points in the same direction as the old oracle, their dramatic role threatens to compromise their fulfillment, because their result is on the one hand to encourage Creon, the emissary of Thebes—that is, of Eteocles—to do everything he can to get Oedipus away from his new adopted homeland, and on the other hand, to encourage Oedipus's other son Polynices to come and beg Oedipus to return to take part in the war of the Seven against Thebes.[116] Once these two obstacles have been removed, the signs of the fulfillment of the old oracle—thunder, lightning, and an earthquake—appear.[117] When the chorus hears and sees them, it spontaneously recognizes the presence of Zeus: "The sky resounds! Zeus!" But for Oedipus, who knows an oracle the chorus does not, the meaning is more precise: "This winged thunder of Zeus will soon take me to Hades."[118] Oedipus can now leave for his last home, where he will protect Attica's territory against any Theban invasion. The blind man's departure, without any human guide, and the account of his marvelous death given by the messenger, are the most tangible signs of his heroization. Before dying, Oedipus even hears the call of a god.[119] The accursed king has become a chosen hero.[120]

The Dream, a Message from Elsewhere

In addition to the messages the gods convey to humans directly or indirectly through the intermediary of their oracles or seers, Sophocles' tragedy presents other messages that come from beyond: dreams.[121]

This was obviously not an innovation on Sophocles' part. Since every Greek tragedy begins at daybreak, the arrival of a character is not infrequently justified by a dream that has made him leap out of bed. In the oldest extant tragedy, Aeschylus's *The Persians*, the arrival of the queen, who is worried about the lack of news about her son Xerxes, who had left long before on an expedition against Greece, is justified by a particularly impressive dream that she had during the night preceding the tragedy. She recounts her dream to the chorus: in it, she saw her son fall from a chariot drawn by two women representing Asia and Europe, a premonitory vision of Xerxes' defeat.[122] In an analogous situation, that is, in the initial situation of a return tragedy, Sophocles also uses a dream to justify a person's departure. Deianira, in *The Women of Trachis*, is worried about her husband, Heracles, who left long before on an expedition, but she has not had any news of him. She confides her concern to the chorus. And at the end of her speech, she reveals that she leapt out of bed, suddenly awakened by anxiety, even though she had been sound asleep.[123] Sophocles does not say precisely what this anxiety is about, but the dream can only have been a frightening one. Thus Deianira's arrival, her exit from the palace at the beginning of the tragedy, without any explanation having been given at that time, is justified after the fact. The dream not only has a theatrical function; it is also a premonitory sign. It points in the same direction as the oracle of Zeus at Dodona that Deianira has just been talking about. The dream occurs on the very day when, according to the oracle,

Heracles' destiny is to be decided: either death or life freed of sorrows. The dream and the oracle thus combine to increase the anxiety.

The mention of the dream nonetheless remains fleeting in this tragedy. Nothing is said about its content, nor about who is sending the message. It is especially in *Electra* that the dream plays an important role in the action,[124] a woman's frightening dream, once again. Clytemnestra, following a nightmare, has gone outside to be in the sunlight. This time, the content of the dream is given. It is reported by Chrysothemis to her sister Electra:

> It is said that she saw the father of you and of me restored to the sunlight and to her company once more. Then he took the scepter—once his own, but now carried by Aegisthus—and planted it at the hearth. From it branched upward a flourishing limb, by which the whole land of the Mycenaeans was overshadowed. Such was the tale that I heard told by one who was present when she revealed her dream to the Sun-god.[125]

For Electra, this dream is a premonitory sign sent by the dead Agamemnon to his murderer, Clytemnestra.[126] This interpretation is adopted and enlarged by the chorus in its subsequent song. It sees in "this sweet-blowing dream" a prediction of the avenging goddesses' arrival. Otherwise, the chorus maintains, all the means of predicting the future available to mortals, whether dreams or oracles, would have to be questioned. To its mind, that is obviously unthinkable.[127]

This profession of faith on the part of the chorus can be contrasted with Jocasta's attitude in *Oedipus the King*. To dispel Oedipus's anxiety regarding the fulfillment of the oracle predicting that he would marry his mother, Jocasta questions any kind of foresight in a world that is, in her view, governed by chance. She takes the example of dreams, to which one must accord no significance if one wants to live a tranquil life:

> Fear not that you will wed your mother. Many men before now have slept with their mothers in dreams. But he to whom these things are as though nothing bears his life most easily.[128]

This passage is famous, not only for its tragic irony,[129] but also because it has given rise to abusive psychoanalytic interpretations: not only has an Oedipus complex been invented (desiring to sleep with one's mother, whereas Oedipus would do anything to avoid it), but also, on the basis of this passage, a Jocasta complex (toying with the idea that Oedipus is her son, whereas in reality she is trying to calm her husband's anxieties).[130] Put back into its context, this conception of dreams as meaningless imaginings is used by Jocasta as an argument for nullifying the oracle Oedipus fears. However, the spectator, who could not have been ignorant of the myth, knew that the oracle had already been fulfilled. Hence the argument about the meaninglessness of dreams collapses by itself. Does that mean that for Sophocles, as for the chorus and Electra, every dream is, like every oracle, a significant message proceeding from the gods? The question remains open.[131]

In any case, in *Electra* Clytemnestra's dream is premonitory. Its presence in the myth is not Sophocles' creation. In *The Libation Bearers*, Aeschylus's tragedy dealing with the same mythic sequence, Clytemnestra had already been awakened by a frightening dream. Aeschylus himself borrowed the theme from the lyric poet Stesichorus's *Oresteia*, composed a century earlier.[132] It was a traditional literary theme. The poet's whole art consisted in distinguishing himself from his predecessors. Aeschylus gave the content of the dream in a scene that Sophocles recalls here: but Sophocles transposes it.[133] The interlocutors are different. In Aeschylus, it is the chorus that tells Orestes about the dream, in the presence of Electra, when the recognition scene between the brother and sister has already taken place. In Sophocles, it is Chrysothemis, a new character in relation to Aeschylus, who informs her sister Electra, before the recognition scene. The change in interlocutors proceeds from the fact that Sophocles has refocused his tragedy on Electra, and no longer on Orestes. The transposition involves not only the choice of interlocutors but also the content of the dream. Here is the content of the dream in Aeschylus:

> *Chorus:* She dreamed she gave birth to a serpent: that is her own account.
> *Orestes:* And where does the tale end, and what is its consummation?
> *Chorus:* She laid it to rest as if it were a child, in swaddling clothes.
> *Orestes:* What food did it crave, the newborn viper?
> *Chorus:* In her dream she offered it her own breast.
> *Orestes:* Surely her nipple was not unwounded by the loathsome beast?
> *Chorus:* No: it drew in clotted blood with the milk.
> *Orestes:* Truly it is not without meaning: the vision signifies a man![134]

The symbolic, premonitory vision of the serpent wounding Clytemnestra's breast and sucking in a clot of blood along with the milk is immediately interpreted by Orestes. He identifies with the serpent and sees in it an announcement of his murder of his mother:

> I, turned serpent, am her killer, as this dream declares.[135]

The vision of the serpent was not invented by Aeschylus. It is already found in Stesichorus. But in the lyric poet the serpent represented Agamemnon; the descendant of Plisthenes, that is, Orestes, emerged from the wounded head of the serpent. While preserving the animal vision, Aeschylus thus reoriented it toward the matricide. Sophocles, on the other hand, substitutes a marvelous horticultural vision for Aeschylus's monstrous animal vision: Agamemnon plants his scepter in his courtyard and from it miraculously grows a tree with immense foliage.[136] The blood that was present in the vision of Sophocles' two predecessors has completely disappeared. However, the idea of a miraculous birth, already attested in Stesichorus by the generation of a living being from a serpent's wound, was adopted by Sophocles in a different register. In the dream in Sophocles, the new shoot that grows miraculously from dead wood—but not from just any dead wood, because it is a scepter—symbolizes the unhoped-for rebirth of legitimate royalty. To be sure, in *Electra* the characters who favor taking revenge do not explain the precise meaning of the dream, as Orestes has done in Aeschylus. As for Clytemnestra, she still wants to believe in the ambiguity of her dream.[137] But the transformations of the dream that Sophocles makes with regard to Aeschylus are very significant. They end up eliminating from the dream any mention of the murder of the mother and retain only the rebirth of legitimate power, the new growth symbolizing Orestes. This change in perspective is coherent with the interpretation that Sophocles sought to give the vengeance as a whole: ultimately, he presents it as a restoration of the freedom of the Atreids and erases the traditional consequences of the matricide.[138]

From the Message to the Rite: Libations after a Frightening Dream

Religion is present in Greek tragedy, not only in the appearance of the gods and the presence of their mediators or their messages, but also in all the religious rites intended to regularly establish links between humans and gods, or to reestablish them when the gods' signs do not seem favorable. These rites take the form of prayers, libations, and sacrifices,[139] following a dream, primarily libations, that is, liquids poured on the earth. These libations are accompanied by prayers.

A frightening dream represents a threat to the dreamer; and so he or she tries to ward off the danger by carrying out a rite. This is what is called an apotropaic rite. In Sophocles' *Electra*, after her nightmare Clytemnestra sends her daughter Chrysothemis to pour libations on Agamemnon's tomb.[140] Here again, Sophocles adopts a theme that was found in the Aeschylean model.

When it tells Orestes the content of the dream, the chorus in *The Libation Bearers* reminds him that when Clytemnestra was awakened by her dream, she cried out in fright and had torches lit in the dark, and "then she sent these libations for the dead in the hope that they might be an effective cure for her distress."[141] The theme was even more important in Aeschylus, because the tragedy takes its title from this rite. *Choephoroi* means "libation bearers." These are the women of the chorus whom we see filing by, as they enter, carrying libations. The rite also had a greater theatrical presence. In Aeschylus, the libations are poured in front of the spectators, on Agamemnon's tomb, by Electra herself, but only after she has followed the chorus's advice and inverted the meaning of the rite by calling on the dead man, in her prayer, not to calm down, but instead to avenge himself.[142]

Sophocles did not borrow this scene of libations directly, because he located Agamemnon's tomb out of the spectators' sight. However, he frequently recalled Aeschylus's scene when Chrysothemis, telling Electra the content of the dream, prepares to take, on her mother's behalf, libations to the tomb of her father. Electra intervenes, not so that the prayer might be reversed, as in Aeschylus, but so that the mother's impious libations will be replaced by pure offerings made by the two young women. And, with the chorus's help, she succeeds in persuading her sister. Does Electra's argument that these libations for the dead man are intolerable[143] represent a criticism of the solution Aeschylus adopted, which, even though it inverts the meaning of the rite by the prayer, has the dead man sprinkled with his murderess's libations? It is not impossible. In Sophocles, the dead man will receive only the libations made by his son who has come to avenge him and the pure offerings of his daughters.[144]

Murders and the Deities of Vengeance

Calming the dead individual's anger is the goal of the rite of libations sent by the woman who has seen him in a dream. But the first cause of this anger goes back to the murder. Any bloodshed is a defilement. It arouses the wrath not only of the victim, but also of the deities of vengeance. The tragedy is the place where the dead man's friends pray the gods to take vengeance, and where his enemies seek to protect themselves by carrying out purification rites.

Two of these deities of vengeance are associated several times in Sophocles' theater. They are Justice and Erinys (plural *Erinyes*). Their arrival is announced by the chorus of women when Clytemnestra's dream is interpreted in *Electra*:

> If I am not a deranged prophet and one who lacks wise judgments, Justice, the sender of the omen, will come, winning the just victory of her hands' might. . . . She, too, will come, she of many hands and many feet who lurks in her terrible ambush, the bronze-shod Erinys.[145]

These two divinities are also associated in *The Women of Trachis* when Hyllus, Deianira's son, who has come to tell her about the devastating effects of the tunic she has given her husband Heracles, accuses her of having murdered his father. He ends his account, which is also an indictment, with the following wish:

> Such, Mother, are the designs and deeds against my father of which you have been found guilty. May Punishing Justice and the Erinys punish you for them![146]

Teucer already makes a comparable wish at the end of *Ajax* when he calls for revenge to be taken on the Atreids who sought to deprive Ajax's body of its tomb. The pair of the two avenging deities is, however, enlarged to form a triad by the addition of Zeus, king of the gods, in this passage:

> Therefore may the Father supreme on Olympus above us, and the unforgetting Fury and Justice the Fulfiller destroy them for their wickedness with wicked deaths, just as they sought to cast this man out with unmerited, outrageous mistreatment.[147]

However, no preestablished catalog of the avenging deities exists. Sophocles introduces variety even in analogous situations. Thus in *Electra*, when the chorus predicts, as we have just seen, the arrival of two avenging deities, Justice and

Erinys, Electra had earlier named five deities to urge them to come and avenge her father's murder:

> O House of Hades and Persephone! O Hermes of the shades! O potent Curse, and you fearsome daughters of the gods, the Erinyes, who take note when a life is unjustly taken, when a marriage-bed is thievishly dishonored, come, help me, bring vengeance for the murder of my father and send me my brother.[148]

These two catalogs have a single divinity in common, Erinys, who is mentioned once in the singular and once in the plural. This constant presence is normal. Since the epic, the Erinys or Erinyes had been concerned with avenging murders.[149] The other deities in Electra's prayer belong to the world below: Hades, the god of the Underworld, and his companion Persephone;[150] Hermes, described as "subterranean," is invoked because he serves as a guide in darkness, notably for the souls of the dead going to Hades.[151] There remains a deified abstraction, Imprecation (*Ara*). She represents the dead man's curse on his murderers. At the end of the tragedy, echoing Electra's initial prayer, the chorus evokes in its turn the Imprecations when she hears the last cries of Clytemnestra as she is struck down by her son:

> The curses [Arai] bring fulfillment: those who are buried live. For men long dead are draining their killers' blood in a stream of requital.[152]

Between the initial prayer and the final accomplishment of the vengeance, a decisive moment is the avengers' entrance into the palace. In the fourth stasimon, after Orestes, accompanied by Pylades and the tutor, has just managed to get inside, and Electra is following them after addressing a prayer to Apollo, the chorus, left alone, offers a visionary commentary on this entrance, because it also sees the avenging deities slip into the palace:

> Behold how Ares stalks onward, breathing bloody vengeance that is hard to oppose. Just now have the hunters of wicked crimes passed beneath that roof there, the hounds which none may flee. And so not long shall the vision of my soul hang in suspense. The champion of the spirits infernal is ushered on guileful feet into the house, the rich, ancestral palace of his father, and he bears keen-edged death in his hands. Maia's son Hermes, who has shrouded the guile in darkness, leads him right to his goal and delays no longer.[153]

By recalling the interpretation that it had given of the dream in the first stasimon, the chorus establishes a continuity between its foresight and the accomplishment of the vengeance. Its prediction that the avenging deities would arrive is fulfilled, even though their presence is invisible. They enter the palace with the men. However, the divinities vary from one song to another. Justice has disappeared. But two additional divinities appear: Hermes, who had already been invoked by Electra in her initial prayer, and Ares, the god of war. The only thing the chorus's two songs have in common is the Erinys. However, even while retaining this element, Sophocles introduces a variation. First, he now envisages several Erinyes: then he designates, using a poetic metaphor already employed by Aeschylus in *The Libation Bearers*,[154] that of hunting hounds pursuing game that cannot escape them. Does this twofold variation reflect a concern to adapt the evocation to the stage? Orestes, accompanied by two companions, is going hunting with his hounds to capture his prey. The metaphor is in situation. As for the plural, it may have a precise meaning. The avengers are three in number. Now, although the number of Erinyes was not set at an early date, they are also three in number, according to one tradition.[155] In a reference in which the borderline between reality and the imaginary is vague, such a correspondence in number increases the symbiosis between humans and gods in the realization of the vengeance.

Despite these references, the Erinyes are far from playing in Sophocles' *Electra* the important role they had in the same mythic sequence in Aeschylus. The essential reason has to do with the fundamentally different conception of Orestes' vengeance. At the end of Aeschylus's *The Libation Bearers*, the murder of the mother, imposed on Orestes by Apollo, leads to a new intervention on the part of the Erinyes, who drive Orestes mad. As for the last play in the trilogy, *The Eumenides*, where the Erinyes appear onstage and form the chorus, it opposed the ancient law of the Erinyes to the law of Apollo, before a resolution of the conflict through the acquittal of Orestes by the Athenian tribunal of the Areopagus, which was founded by and presided over by Athena; moreover, the fierce Erinyes are transformed into the benevolent Eumenides. In Sophocles, the vision of the divine world is very different. The Erinyes are not the divinities of the blind vengeance of bloodshed, and there is no opposition between Apollo and the Erinyes.[156]

As Electra stresses in her initial prayer, the Sophoclean Erinyes "take note when a life is unjustly taken." The important word here is "unjustly." We can now see why, when the chorus in *Electra* interprets Clytemnestra's dream, it can predict the arrival of both Justice and Erinys. The idea of justice is inseparable from that of vengeance. The Erinyes watch over Agamemnon because he died unjustly. This implies that the Erinyes do not avenge those who die justly. That is why they do not persecute Orestes for having killed his mother. Moreover, in Sophocles' *Electra* the Erinyes are designated, in an uncommon way, by the expression "the venerable Erinyes." The surprising aspect of this expression, which is peculiar to Sophocles, has not been noted.[157] Usually, the Erinyes are designated by the euphemism "the venerable Goddesses," "the Venerables," or "the Eumenides," but never "the venerable Erinyes." Sophocles respects the Athenian usage of the euphemism in the case of tragedies that take place on Athenian territory: in *Oedipus at Colonus*, they are not called Erinyes, but rather Eumenides or venerable Goddesses.[158] In *Electra*, on the other hand, where the Athenian usage of the euphemism is not necessary; the Erinyes are described as "venerable" because they are deities who uphold the law and are in no way dangerous to those who are defending a just cause and who call on them for help. They are dangerous for those who have committed an unjust murder, and particularly for those who, like Clytemnestra. do not fear them.[159]

Hence in Sophocles there is no contradiction between the action of the Erinyes and that of Apollo, who recognized in his oracle that Orestes' vengeance was justified.[160] Justice is the common factor that unites them. It is significant that at the decisive moment when the avengers go back into the palace, Sophocles introduces two successive complementary speeches: on the one hand Electra addresses a prayer to Apollo, and on the other hand the chorus announces the entrance of the Erinyes.[161] Thus the union of the gods is manifested in the execution of just vengeance, whether they are gods of the heavens or gods of the Underworld.

The Dead, the Gods Below, and Gods Above

Sophocles' gods thus do not experience the same conflicts as Aeschylus's gods did. But is there a conflict between what the gods above and the gods below demand from humans? This question arises apropos of the problem of burying a dead person who has been judged a traitor to the community. Must his burial be forbidden, or must the rite be carried out? Sophocles, who was very attentive to this problem in which politics and religion intersect, made his characters confront each other regarding this kind of subject on two occasions: first in the second part of *Ajax*, and then in the whole of his *Antigone*.

In the second part of *Ajax*, after the discovery of Ajax's dead body, his half brother Teucer wants to prepare the burial. But the two Atreids, Menelaus and Agamemnon, come successively to prohibit it. The dead man's representative confronts the representatives of the community in two clashes before Odysseus arrives to put an end to the conflict. In the first encounter with Menelaus and Teucer, the gods are invoked by each of the two parties. Menelaus sees in the protection of the divinity, who has diverted Ajax's madness to the flocks, a condemnation of his treachery and a justification for the interdiction of his burial.[162] Teucer, on the contrary, sees in the interdiction of the burial an insult to the gods. It is in the course of a stichomythic dialogue that the two adversaries confront each other over the gods:

> *Teucer:* When right is with him, a man's thoughts may be grand.
> *Menelaus:* What, is it right that the man who murdered me should prosper?
> *Teucer:* Murdered you? It is truly a strange happening, if in fact you live after being killed.
> *Menelaus:* A god rescued me. So far as that corpse is concerned, I am in Hades.
> *Teucer:* Then since it was the gods who saved you, do not dishonor the gods.
> *Menelaus:* What, would I find fault with divine law?
> *Teucer:* Yes, if by your presence here you prevent burial of the dead.

Menelaus: Prevent it I do, since he was at war with me and I with him. Burial in such a case would not be right.[163]

According to Teucer, divine law requires a dead person to be buried. According to Menelaus, this law does not apply to all the dead: it excludes enemies, that is, traitors to the community.

Menelaus's reply, despite its personal cast, must not have seemed to an Athenian audience completely out of place. In Athens itself, a law forbade burying a traitor to his homeland if he had been convicted in a court, not only on the Athenian territory, but even in Athenian possessions.[164] The most famous case is that of Themistocles. Despite his outstanding services to his homeland during the Persian Wars, notably at Salamis in 480 BCE, Themistocles had been ostracized ten years later. Banned from Athens, and then convicted of treason, his burial in Athens was prohibited by virtue of this law. After his death, which occurred in Asia in 459 BCE, his family brought his remains back to Attica. But it is noteworthy that this initiative on the part of his family was undertaken without the knowledge of the Athenian people.[165] The family's solidarity could thus conflict with the city's laws. That is the problem that Sophocles raised in his oldest extant tragedy, *Ajax.* Whereas the Atreids, Menelaus and Agamemnon, represent governmental power, even if this power appears in a violent and tyrannical form, Teucer, for his part, represents the family, even if he is a bastard. He feels himself invested with the duty to defend the honor of a man who is his blood relative.[166]

The problem was solved in this first tragedy thanks to the wisdom of Odysseus, who, even while being Ajax's enemy since their rivalry for the award of Achilles' arms, interceded with Agamemnon on the dead man's behalf.[167] His plea is based on both human and divine arguments. Humanly, being deprived of burial is a mark of dishonor. Odysseus recognizes the bravery of Ajax, who was the best of the Greeks after Achilles. A brave man therefore does not deserve this dishonor. Not only human but also divine justice demands that Ajax be buried. It is significant that in addressing Agamemnon Odysseus uses the argument based on divine laws that had already been used by Teucer in addressing Menelaus:

It would not be just, then, that he should be dishonored by you. It is not he, but the laws given by the gods that you would damage. When a good man is dead, there is no justice in doing him harm, not even if you hate him.[168]

In this passage the "laws given by the gods" echo the "divine law" Teucer had already mentioned. It thus seems that the burial of a dead person is a right demanded by the gods. Odysseus then adds that it is a right recognized by all the Greeks.[169]

The problem is taken up again in *Antigone,* but with greater breadth and depth. Instead of occupying only the end of the tragedy, the question of burial dominates the whole of the play. In fact, we learn in the first scene that Creon, the new legitimate king of the city of Thebes, has decided to forbid Polynices' burial.[170] The initial situation is also more complex. Unlike in *Ajax*, there is no sharp distinction between the representatives of the dead man's family and those in power. Political drama and family drama are interwoven in *Antigone*: Creon, who holds power, forbids his nephew Polynices' burial, and he is the uncle of Antigone, the sister and advocate of the dead man. The ties of blood are even further strengthened by ties of love: Antigone is the fiancée of the king's son, Haemon. Finally, the problem has been radicalized. If the deceased could be quite easily rehabilitated in *Ajax*, on the basis of his past bravery preceding his act of madness, Polynices in *Antigone* has deliberately committed an act of treason against his homeland by besieging it.

This kind of radicalization entails a difference regarding the place of the gods in the debate. In *Ajax* the gods were invoked especially by those who opposed the prohibition. In *Antigone*, they are adduced by both sides, and first of all to justify the interdiction. Here, in fact, is how Creon, the new king, addressing his council for the first time, presents the prohibition on burying Polynices:

> As for his brother, Polyneices, I mean, who on his return from exile wanted to burn to the ground the city of his fathers and his race's gods, and wanted to feed on kindred blood and lead the remnant into slavery—it has been proclaimed to the city that no one shall give him funeral honors or lamentation, but all must leave him unburied and a sight of shame, with his body there for birds and dogs to eat.[171]

In Creon's view, treason is accompanied by impiety. Polynices has tried to destroy his homeland and the gods of his people. As we have seen, in Athens these two charges would justify a prohibition on burying the dead man on the territory of his city. Creon's edict thus would not have seemed scandalous to the audience, even if the transposition in the myth explains a crueler form of interdiction. Moreover, Creon changes his mind about the accusation of impiety when the chorus, learning that Polynices' body has been mysteriously covered with earth, wonders if this isn't the work of the gods. The king reacts indignantly against that hypothesis:

> You say what is intolerable when you claim that the gods have concern for that corpse. Was it in high esteem for his benefactions that they sought to hide him, when he had come to burn their columned shrines, their sacred treasures and their land, and scatter its laws to the winds? Or do you see the gods honoring the wicked? It cannot be.[172]

The accusation of impiety is not without force. The ancients thought that like mortals, the gods lived in the city, each god inhabiting the temple dedicated to him or her. To invade a territory was therefore impious. We recall that in Aeschylus's *The Persians*, Darius severely condemned the impiety of his son Xerxes, who had burned temples in Greece.[173] The crime is all the more serious in this case because Polynices wanted to invade his own city. Creon presents himself here as the defender of his city's gods and their laws. It is not laws in general that Creon refers to here, contrary to what some interpreters think, but the laws of the gods, because that is what this is about. We thus find the expression "divine laws," which was already used in *Ajax* by the dead man's defenders; but what is notable is that the argument has changed sides: here it is put in the mouth of the very person who advocates prohibiting the burial. The problem is complex. The collision between Creon and Antigone cannot be reduced to a simple opposition between politics and religion.

Even before Creon's arrival, Antigone had already incidentally referred to the gods to justify her decision to bury her brother, despite the city's interdiction. She accused her sister, who had just refused to join her, of dishonoring "what the gods in honor have established."[174] But it is especially after her arrest, in her face-to-face encounter with Creon, that she develops with unparalleled force the idea of the superiority of divine laws over human laws to justify her transgression of the latter by her obedience to the former:

> *Creon:* And even so you dared overstep that law?
> *Antigone:* Yes, since it was not Zeus that published me that edict, and since not
>   of that kind are the laws which Justice who dwells with the gods below es-
>   tablished among men. Nor did I think that your decrees were of such force,
>   that a mortal could override the unwritten and unfailing statutes given us
>   by the gods. For their life is not of today or yesterday, but for all time, and
>   no man knows when they were first put forth. Not for fear of any man's
>   pride was I about to owe a penalty to the gods for breaking these.[175]

These words, which were already famous in antiquity, are considered the most forceful in Sophocles' theater. Aristotle, for instance, cites two verses from this passage in his *Rhetoric* to illustrate what he means by the "general law" common to all humans, as opposed to the "particular law" that varies depending on the states. However, Aristotle rationalizes the statement by seeing in the unwritten law of *Antigone* a natural law, and not a divine law.[176] In the earliest interpretations, the thought of Sophocles' characters was used, deformed, even betrayed. The religious aspect is essential here. No other text in Greek literature of the classical period contrasts with such power the transitory laws of mortals, even when they are inscribed on steles, with the unshakeable and immortal laws of the gods, even though they remain unwritten. This is the first time that the expression "unwritten law" appears in the extant Greek texts, an expression that was to come to designate the laws valid for everyone, as opposed to the particular laws of each city.[177] And if Antigone draws the distinction between the gods above, represented by Zeus, and the gods below, represented by Justice, it is the better to show the agreement of all the gods concerning the necessity of ritually burying the dead. Thus the tribunal that judges humans after their deaths and before which Antigone will have to answer for her conduct does not depend solely on the gods below. It is quite simply the gods' tribunal.

We cannot fail to mention here the reaction of the chorus and Creon after what was considered out of context as an anthology piece. On hearing these words, the elders of the royal council are sensitive, not to the depth of the argumentation, which is beyond them, but to the hardness of the daughter born to a hard father, whereas for her, wisdom would have consisted in yielding to misfortune.[178] In fact, Antigone's determination to reduce the king's decree to a personal decision, without any reference to the city, was probably excessive.[179] Creon has no answer, either, on the fundamental issue. He emphasizes Antigone's twofold insolence: committing a crime against the established laws and boasting about having committed it. Out of anger, he makes the decision to put her to death. But this new decision, as he implicitly recognizes, puts him in conflict with the Zeus of the family, even if he tries, confronting his son, to justify his decision by rejecting anarchy in the family as well as in the state.[180]

The confrontation between Creon and Antigone gradually leads, as we know, to a break and Antigone's incarceration, first in the palace, and then in an underground prison. Sophocles then brings in a mediator, as he did in *Ajax*. In *Antigone*, this mediator has an even more elevated status: after the wise Odysseus, it is the seer Tiresias. But unlike what happens in *Ajax*, in *Antigone* the mediator arrives when the rupture between the two parties is definitively consummated. Despite his status as a seer, Tiresias is not able to produce the reversal Creon seeks before it is too late. The king remains impervious to the bad omens that the seer has collected by his art and to his explanation of these signs as the result of a generalized pollution of the gods' altars by the flesh of the dead man carried by birds and dogs. To this conception of generalized pollution Creon even replies with another conception of the relations between gods and humans to justify his intention not to yield:

> You shall not cover that man with a grave, not even if the eagles of Zeus wish to snatch and carry him to be devoured at the god's throne. No, not even then, for fear of that defilement will I permit his burial, since I know with certainty that no mortal has the power to defile the gods.[181]

At the height of his anger against the seer, Creon uses a line of argument that he has not invented, even if he uses it in an extremely provocative context. It is based on the idea that there is an incommensurable distance between human weakness and divine power. Thus human pollution cannot contaminate the gods. Although we cannot determine with certainty the origin of this purified conception of divinity, it seems to have proceeded from intellectual milieus seeking to combat popular superstition.[182] In fact, in Euripides' *Heracles* Theseus uses the same theory to reassure Heracles, who is hesitating to uncover his head after his crime, for fear of contaminating the Sun: "You, a mortal, cannot pollute what is of the gods."[183] This formulation is very close to the one in Sophocles' *Antigone*, but it is used in the opposite way. Whereas Euripides attributes it to an idealized king, Sophocles puts it in the mouth of a king at a time when he is raving. Doesn't this reflect Euripides' and Sophocles' extremely different positions regarding religion?

Faced with Creon's blindness, there remains nothing for the seer to do but to predict an imminent future of disasters—the death of his son—and to explain it by denouncing the king's offenses against the gods. This denunciation constitutes the tragedy's third major development on the problem of burying the dead considered in relation to the gods. According to Tiresias, Creon's offense is two-fold. It consists of having buried a living person after having refused to bury a dead one:

> You have thrust below one of those of the upper air and irreverently lodged a living soul in the grave, while you detain in this world that which belongs to the infernal gods, a corpse unburied, unmourned, unholy. In the dead you have no part, nor do the gods above, but in this you do them violence. For these crimes the avenging destroyers, the Furies of Hades and of the gods, lie in ambush for you, waiting to seize you in these same sufferings.[184]

Thus Creon has confused the high and the low. He has kept a living person under the ground and kept a dead man above it. This confusion does not respect the division between these two distinct domains reigned over by different gods: on earth the gods above, underground the gods below. This division of jurisdictions presents a view of the world and of the gods that seems to resolve the latent conflicts between Creon's conception and that of Antigone concerning the question of the burial of a dead man who betrayed his country and his gods. It is perhaps the only solution that can respond to Creon's initial objections based on the impossibility of the gods honoring bad citizens. From the moment that a citizen dies, the justice of the gods above no longer applies to him. This position taken by the seer confirms the objection Antigone had already made to Creon when he tried to justify his prohibition on burying Polynices by referring to the latter's attack on his own country:

> Hades craves these rites, nevertheless.[185]

The consequence of such a position is that Sophocles probably considered the famous Athenian law on the impossibility of burying traitors or the impious on Athenian soil unjustified. Once humans have breathed their last, their bodies are no longer under the jurisdiction of the city, no matter how they behaved while they were alive. They belong to the gods below. Any decision to prohibit burial is ultimately impious.[186]

Human Prayer and the Silence of the Gods:
The Chorus's Hymn to Dionysus in *Antigone*

After making his prophecy, launched like the arrow of an expert archer, Tiresias goes away. He leaves the chorus speechless, and Creon as well. It is said that the chorus in Greek tragedy has no dramatic role. That is not the case here. In a brief but intense dialogue, the chorus, after emphasizing the frightening element in the predictions of an infallible seer, plays its full role as counselor. It asks Creon to repair the two offenses pointed out by the seer: he must free the woman who has been kept alive underground and bury the man whose body has remained above the earth. Adopting an imperious tone, it leads Creon to change his mind; he decides to leave immediately with all his servants to execute the chorus's counsels. Left alone, the chorus sings a hymn to Dionysus asking him to come to their aid. This hymn is one of the most accomplished and most fervent prayers in Sophocles' theater.[187] And yet the god remains silent. Sophocles' art, and the questioning to which the prayer leads, deserve special attention, especially since Dionysus is the god who presides over the theatrical contest. Here is this prayer sung and danced by the chorus:

> Strophe 1
> [1115] God of many names, glory of the Cadmeian bride and offspring of loud-thundering Zeus, you who watch over far-famed Italy and reign [1120] in the valleys of Eleusinian Deo where all find welcome! O Bacchus, denizen of Thebes, the mother-city of your Bacchants, dweller by the wet stream of Ismenus on the soil [1125] of the sowing of the savage dragon's teeth!
>
> Antistrophe 1
> [1126] You appear in the smoky glare of torches above the cliffs of the twin peaks, where the Corycian nymphs move inspired by your godhead, [1130] and Castalia's stream sees you, too. The ivy-mantled slopes of Nysa's hills and the shore green with many-clustered vines send you, when accompanied by the cries of your divine words, [1135] you watch over the avenues of Thebes.
>
> Strophe 2
> [1137] Thebes of all cities you hold foremost in honor, together with your lightning-struck mother. [1140] And now when the whole city is held subject to a violent plague, come, we ask, with purifying feet over steep Parnassus, [1145] or over the groaning straits!
>
> Antistrophe 2
> [1146] O Leader of the chorus of the stars whose breath is fire, overseer of the chants in the night, son begotten of Zeus, [1150] appear, my king, with your attendant Thyiads, who in night-long frenzy dance and sing you as Iacchus the Giver!

On a first reading, many allusions may appear mysterious. But they soon become clear if we are willing to allow ourselves to be guided. After examining this prayer, explaining its allusions, and showing the art with which Sophocles makes use of a ritual prayer, we will look into its place in the tragedy, because this prayer is not only a religious act obeying ritual customs; it is also a spectacle that produces an effect on the spectators, arousing their emotion and making them think.

In its structure, the prayer to Dionysus has all the ritual characteristics of a hymn in which the divinity is invoked at length before it is asked to provide help and to appear. But it is also artfully inserted into the usual strophic structure of the tragic lyric chorale, setting the pace of the chorus's dance.[188]

The ritual of the invocation consists in summoning the god and flattering him by recalling his power. First comes the name or the names of the divinity who is being invoked. The initial expression "of many names" (v. 1115) is a clever way of not forgetting anything. One of these names will be indicated a little farther on: "O Bacchus" (v. 1121); another name will appear at the end of the hymn: "Iacchus the Giver" (v. 1152). We do not find the name, so familiar to us, of Dionysus! Even before the first name expressly identifies the god, hints as to his origin allow him to be discovered. He is "glory of the Cadmeian bride," that is, his mother, Semele, the daughter of Cadmus, is proud of the son whom she bears in her. Given that Cadmus is the founder of Thebes, the god is, from the outset, rooted in the site of the tragedy. The hymn is thus in no way artificial. It is in its place in a Theban play, because Dionysus is the divinity par excellence of that city.[189] If Cadmus's daughter is proud of the son she is carrying, that is because his father is a god. He is "loud-thundering Zeus" (v. 1116). This epithet is in situation. It refers to Dionysus's tragic birth, after Semele, deceived by the jealous Hera, had asked Zeus to appear to her in all his glory. She was struck down by lightning, but Zeus saved the infant she was carrying by placing him in his thigh.

Then comes, in conformity with the ritual syntax in a hymn, a long relative clause introduced by "you who" (v. 1117), in which the mortal reminds the god of his share of honor. In it Sophocles develops a brilliant catalog of a sacred geography and thus reveals the extent of the god's power. First southern Italy, then the sanctuary of Deo (i.e., Demeter) in Eleusis on Athenian territory, and finally Thebes, the site of the tragedy, evoked geographically by its river, the Ismenus, and historically by an episode from its foundation, Cadmus sowing the dragon's teeth. Thebes is not only the homeland of the god Bacchus, but also that of his worshippers, the Bacchantes. We might think that the invocation will conclude at the end of the strophe.[190] But the antistrophe begins instead with a new departure marked by the initial personal pronoun "you" (v. 1126), addressing the god, and continues to use second-person pronouns and possessive adjectives throughout. It also continues the evocation of sacred sites—the twin peaks of the Phedriades, the Corycian cave, and the Castalian spring—but also a nocturnal celebration that took place every three years on the plateau, near the Corycian cave where Dionysus was supposed to appear amid the smoke of the Bacchantes' torches. The second area mentioned in the antistrophe, which is also connected directly to the god through the two plants that characterize him, ivy and the grapevine, is less easy for us to locate, because the name "Nysa" refers to a dozen possible regions, according to the geographer Stephanus of Byzantium.[191] All the same, it is thought that the reference is to Euboea, because Stephanus points out the existence at Nysa in Euboea of a miraculous vine that produces flowers and grapes every day. Sophocles knew of this miraculous vine; we know that from a fragment of his *Thyestes*.[192] The identification is therefore more or less certain. We return, finally, to Thebes, at the end of the strophe. But the reference to the various places where the god is worshipped does not end like a simple enumeration. With great skill, Sophocles sends Dionysus from Euboea to Thebes (v. 1133, "send you"). The enumeration thus ends like a journey by the god who comes back from Euboea to watch over Thebes. From one mention of Thebes to the other we can note a progression in the relation between the god and the place. The god was presented in the strophe, in a static way, as a "dweller" in Thebes (v. 1123). At the end of the antistrophe, he is mentioned in a dynamic way, returning as a tutelary god to "watch over" the avenues of Thebes. This progression in the image of the god within the invocation prepares the request that will be made in the following strophe.

However, the request is not made immediately. It does not correspond to the passage from antistrophe 1 to strophe 2. Although the strophic form is of clear importance for structuring the traditional parts of the hymn, it is not a framework without flexibility. The enjambments from one strophe to another can add variety. The invocation to the god is prolonged over three verses of strophe 2, by means of an addition on the privileged relations between the god and Thebes. Thebes is the god's preferred city, because it includes the sacred precinct commemorating the place where his mother was struck down. The mention of the mother's death, which concludes the evocation (v. 1139) is symmetrical with the beginning of this invocation, where the mother was already mentioned (v. 1115). This is a kind of echoing return known as annular composition. But in lyric poetry an echoing return is rarely a repetition. In the initial expression "glory of the Cadmeian bride" (v. 1115), it is the mother who was proud of her son about to be born, whereas in the final expression "with your lightning-struck mother" (v. 1139), it is the son who honors his dead mother.

After such a long invocation to the god (twenty-three verses) comes a very short request (four verses). The disproportion is very remarkable. This request, introduced by "and now" (v. 1140), returns the spectator to the present time of the tragedy. A few words suffice to recall the illness from which the city suffers and to call on the god for help. The whole city is prey to a violent disease (vv. 1140–41). These words refer to what the chorus has heard from the seer Tiresias, who told Creon that his decision was "the source of the sickness now afflicting the city" (v. 1015). This decision, as we know, is the refusal to bury Polynices, which has led, in accord with a process well explained by the seer, to a general pollution of the city. It is thus normal that the chorus should appeal to Thebes' tutelary divinity, asking him to come to deliver the city from the illness by purifying it.[193] The request "come, we ask" (v. 1144) presupposes that the god is not in Thebes at that time, but must come from one of the other countries mentioned in the antistrophe, either from Parnassus or from Euboea, crossing the turbulent Strait of Euripus.

The prayer could end there. But instead it makes a new departure. The second antistrophe constitutes, all by itself, a miniature hymn, a little jewel that forms a whole and offers, in a condensed form, the two parts expected in a hymn, the invocation and the plea. It is still the son of Zeus who is invoked; but the god takes on a cosmic dimension, because he directs the chorus of the stars. He is the god of dances and nocturnal processions. The request "appear" (v. 1149) continues the first request and presents it in a livelier fashion. After the arrival comes the epiphany. Dionysus, unlike other divinities such as Athena, Artemis, or Apollo, is not imagined arriving alone. He is inseparable from his cortege of servants. At the beginning of the hymn, Thebes is called "the mother-city of your Bacchants" (v. 1122); and at the end, the god's companions are called "Thyiads" (v. 1151), proof that the servants also have several names, like the god they serve.[194]

This, then, is the hymn's framework. Why such a long prayer to Dionysus at this point in the tragedy? Why such an imbalance between the invocation of the divinity and the final request?

The effect Sophocles sought in his long invocation of Dionysus is first of all a break with the rapid pace of the drama. The ampleness of the lyrical style at the beginning of the hymn contrasts with the tense energy of the spoken style in the preceding dialogue between the chorus and the king, and in Creon's final appeal to his servants. After a moment of extreme tension, Sophocles provides some breathing space in the drama and also allows the spectator's imagination a moment of escape. It is in this sense that we can say that in its beginning, this hymn is for the spectator, through its particularly long and sometimes picturesque invocation of the different places in the world where Dionysus is worshipped, an invitation to travel. Sophocles' desire to produce this effect of escape and breaking away with respect to the dramatic part that precedes is manifest in the choice of the first place mentioned. At the outset, it is the most distant country, Italy (v. 1119). The spectator is suddenly transported as far as possible from the site of the tragedy, without noticing at first the link between the hymn and the action. But the break, as is often the case in Sophocles' stasima,[195] is only apparent. At the end of each of the two invitations to travel contained in each of the first two strophes and antistrophes, we already return to Thebes, the site of the tragedy, but this is not yet the return to the tragedy. Both times, Thebes is referred to by familiar places, far from the noise and cries of the tragedy. It is only starting with the request introduced by "now when the whole city is held subject to a violent plague" that we come back to the actuality of the drama.

The plea refers, as we have just seen, to the very words that Tiresias had addressed to Creon in the preceding episode. Thus it is indeed the dramatic situation that fundamentally justifies the choral song. Through its prayer, the chorus wants to contribute to the success of the king's attempt to do away with every trace of pollution.

But it must be acknowledged that this reference to the dramatic situation in the hymn is minimal. The second hymn, crowning the first, no longer makes any reference to the dramatic situation. The spectator is invited to take a different kind of journey, one less terrestrial and more aerial. The spectator's imagination flies off again, but still further, as far as the stars that breathe fire. And in the whole of this second hymn, the allusion is especially to the dance: the god leads the dance of the stars; the god's companions dance frenetically to celebrate the god; the chorus also dances, imitating the god's companions. The spectator is also caught up in this Dionysian whirlwind. He awaits the appearance of the god who is able to conclude as the "Giver." Why this last movement? What is its function?

It is a way of giving the spectator renewed hope. Creon is supposed to go, following the chorus's advice, to bury Polynices and to free Antigone. And everyone awaits his return. But in the end of the hymn everything is done to see to it that an atmosphere of trust and hope, if not of joy, allays the anxiety that gripped the spectator when Creon left and creates the illusion that a happy end is possible. It is a somewhat perfidious art of the poet that will allow him to plunge the spectator still more brutally into the tragedy, eliciting, after illusion, consternation.

There is, however, one arrival that corresponds to the chorus's prayer. But the new arrival is not a god who will save the city; it is a man, the messenger, discoursing on the reign of chance and the instability of the human condition before he announces Creon's misfortune.[196] From that point on, the end of the hymn where the chorus aspires to the god's epiphany takes on, after the fact, a tragic irony. The prayer seems to have provoked an epiphany, but not the kind that was expected. In the end, the prayer to the god, even though it was so long and so fervent, turns out to be totally without effect.[197]

What conclusion should be drawn from this failure of the hymn and the prayers? Certainly not that all prayers are useless in a world in which chance reigns. Sophocles, beloved of the gods, the author of a famous paean to Asclepius, the healing god whose worship in Athens he helped establish, cannot have adhered to such a philosophy. It is probably a way of denouncing human illusion, when the offense has been committed by a mortal and the god's punishment is underway. Henceforth, nothing can forestall it, neither action on the part of those who repent nor the prayers of others who are concerned. In *Antigone* the punishment was already in motion when the hymn was sung. It had been in motion since the moment that the king refused to listen to the seer Tiresias's advice and the seer announced his punishment. Human instability exists, but contrary to what the messenger suggests, it is not a result of chance, and prediction is not impossible. The messenger has not had, like the chorus, the privilege of hearing the soothsayer Tiresias.

In such a dramatic context, the hymn to Dionysus could therefore not have the desired effect. It was not to have it. It is not one of the smallest paradoxes of Sophocles' art of tragedy that he gives such length, such attractiveness, and such fervor to the most successful hymn in all his extant theater, and yet he places it in a dramatic situation such that the god must remain silent. The god does not appear, but what does appear, through the arrival of the messenger, is the execution of divine punishment, and consequently the epiphany of the gods' power. The tragic irony of the end of the hymn can thus be interpreted on two levels: either superficially, as the ridiculous apparition of a man, the messenger, instead of the apparition of a god, an inopportune apparition, or more profoundly, as the epiphany of divine power through the announcement of the punishment of a man who, because he has committed offenses against gods, falls from happiness into unhappiness. And ultimately the end of the hymn, which closes with the expression "Iacchus the Giver," does not tell us what Iacchus gives. Nothing or everything? Nothing and everything? Sophocles' silence, which is analogous to that of the god, leaves the spectator free to discover and to realize.[198]

CHAPTER XI

Seeing, Hearing, and Understanding

....

The Gods' View and Humans' Indignation

Confronted by the silence of the gods, humans may have doubts. Thus at the very end of *The Women of Trachis*, Hyllus, seeing the sufferings of his father, Heracles, who is being eaten away by the lethal tunic his wife gave him, accuses the gods of indifference. Here is what he tells his servants at the moment when Heracles, mastering his pain, gives the order to carry him on a litter to the funeral pyre, where he will find the end of his sufferings and his life:

> Lift him, attendants! Grant me ample forgiveness for this, but also recall the great cruelty of the gods in the deeds that are being done. They beget children and are hailed as fathers, and yet they can let such sufferings pass before their eyes. No man foresees the future; the present is full of mourning for us, and of shame for the powers above, and indeed of hardship beyond compare for him who endures this disaster.[1]

Such a cry of revolt against the gods is unusual in one of Sophocles' characters, especially when it comes at the end of a tragedy. Beyond the generality of the indictment, one god in particular is targeted: Zeus, the father of Heracles. What Hyllus accuses him of is insensitivity. The god views from on high the spectacle of his son's suffering, but he does so with indifference. The mortal's cry of revolt goes so far as to denounce the god's shameful behavior. How should this accusation be understood? Is it a final message concerning the distance between humans and the gods, between humans' anxiety and the tranquility of the gods? Or is it, on the contrary, an all-too-human expression of the excess of pain? The spectator may also have doubts regarding the meaning of Sophocles' message, which is conveyed by his characters while he remains concealed behind them. One of the most disconcerting characteristics of his theater is precisely this way of raising questions without clearly indicating the answers. Or, to put the point more positively, the richness of his theater consists in showing all sides of situations in their reality, that is, in their complexity.

Does that mean that Sophocles leaves the spectators in complete uncertainty? Aren't there signs to guide them? At the end of *The Women of Trachis*, the most obvious sign is the chorus's final remark immediately following Hyllus's speech. The chorus of young women, addressing itself, is also about to leave to join the group accompanying Heracles to his last abode:

> Maidens, you must not stay by the palace,
> where you but lately have seen dreadful deaths
> with many sorrows unheard of before—and none of these things without
>   Zeus.[2]

The chorus's final judgment of the situation and Hyllus's last speech are marked by convergence and divergence. They converge in their analysis of the situation: it is pathetic in the etymological sense of the term, because it involves great suffering (*pathè*). In fact, the Greek word *pathè* returns as an echo at the end of one of the chorus's verses, as it does in one of Hyllus's.[3] But they diverge in their distance from these sufferings. Hyllus is suffering because he sees and feels his father's suffering,[4] whereas the chorus experiences both as spectators, almost as the audience does. Such a distance allows more room for reflection. From this first divergence follows a second one regarding the position with respect to the gods. It is certainly no accident that the god that Hyllus accuses of indifference is the same one whom the chorus sees as the cause of everything. And as Lichas tells Deianira, speaking about Heracles' servitude, there is no reason to be offended when Zeus is the master.[5]

Hence it seems to be the intensity of the pain that leads the man astray and causes him to be indignant at divine behavior that he no longer understands. Moreover, the conclusion shows a contrast between the father mastering his pain without protest and the son who is overcome by pain. A confirmation of this interpretation can be found in an earlier moment when the roles of Heracles and Hyllus were reversed. When he awakens, Heracles begins to invoke Zeus and to indignantly reproach him for having cast him into such a misfortune.[6] The son, who is at that point helping the old man control the sick hero struggling with an initial attack of pain after sleeping, declares:

> My hands are upon him,
> yet they cannot avail, in themselves, or with others' assistance,
> to bring relief to his anguished life: so Zeus has ordained it.[7]

Hyllus's position at that moment was no different from that of the chorus at the end of the tragedy: a recognition of Zeus's power and, implicitly, submission to that power.

The finitude of mortals may also be an additional cause of his incomprehension. One index of that kind of explanation is discernible, in reverse, in the very words of Hyllus that have just been cited. When Heracles' son expresses his indignation at the god looking on with indifference (*ephorōsi*), he also recognizes that human eyes are incapable of seeing the future: "There is none who sees (*ephora*) what the future may hold."[8] Thus the same Greek word (*ephoran*) is used to designate the gods' seeing and that of humans in two successive verses! But the gods' eyes see, and humans' do not. What role should be given to this recognition of the finitude of the human view? Despite the man's indignation at the divinity's present behavior, the possibility of a future action by the divinity that remains unknown to the man is left open. To be sure, Hyllus's remark on the finitude of the human view is fleeting. It occurs to him only in counterpoint, to accentuate the certainty of the present indignation. But it is probably Sophocles' invitation to the spectator to draw on his knowledge of myth and fill in what will happen in the immediate future. Although the end of *The Women of Trachis*, as we have said,[9] includes no allusion to what will happen to Heracles, the spectator is thus invited to recall that Heracles' funeral pyre on Mount Oeta will be not only the end of Heracles' suffering, but also his passage into the world of the gods. Thus the human view, blurred by the present pain and limited by its natural finitude, misinterprets the gods' view. Hyllus's revolt against the gods is the sign of his emotion and his finitude.

The God Who Sees Everything and Human Faith in Divine Justice

The Greek word used to denote the gods' view in *The Women of Trachis* reappears in *Electra* apropos of Zeus. It is found, no longer at the end of the tragedy, but at the beginning, when the chorus formed of Electra's women friends, trying to console her, urges her to moderate her sorrow, and gives her reasons to hope:

> Courage, my daughter, courage; Zeus in the sky is still mighty, and he sees [*ephora*] and rules all. Leave your oversharp anger to him; be neither excessively hostile to those you hate, nor forgetful of them.[10]

This time, the god, far from being indifferent, watches over the smooth functioning of human affairs. This reminder of all-seeing and all-powerful Zeus is there to denounce the excessive nature of Electra's sorrow. She must trust the supreme god whose prerogative it is to choose the punishment for criminals and, consequently, maintain more moderation between two excesses, the excess of hatred for those who have killed her father, and forgetting her father, who must be avenged.

Describing Zeus as a god "who sees everything" is new with respect to the Homeric tradition. It is well-known that the god "who sees everything" in Homer is the Sun. In fact, in the *Iliad*, Menelaus, to guarantee a pact between the Trojans and the Achaians, invokes several gods in a prayer, the first of which is Zeus, and the second is the Sun "who sees all and hears all." Here, Sophocles has transposed to Zeus what was said in Homer about the Sun, though he takes over only the reference to sight.[11]

However, later in the tragedy Sophocles combines the view of the two divinities, Zeus and the Sun, in a further comment made by the chorus with the intention of consoling Electra. The situation has gotten worse for Agamemnon's daughter. The tutor has just informed her, at the same time as her mother, of the (false) death of Orestes. Left alone with the chorus, she expresses her indignation at her mother's joy, loses all hope of vengeance, refuses to go back into the palace to continue to be the slave of her father's assassins, and no longer wants to live. The chorus intervenes at that point in a lyrical dialogue with Electra. Here is the first strophe:

> *Chorus:* Where are the thunderbolts of Zeus, or where the shining Sun, if they look upon these things and quietly cover them over?
> *Electra:* Ah, me, ah, me!
> *Chorus:* My child, why do you weep?
> *Electra:* Oh!
> *Chorus:* Give no cry of bad omen!
> *Electra:* You will break my heart!
> *Chorus:* How do you mean?
> *Electra:* If you suggest that I keep hope for those who have surely passed to Hades, you will trample even harder upon me as I waste away.[12]

In the chorus's first inquiry regarding Zeus and the Sun, Sophocles does not limit himself to transposing the Homeric tradition into this passage by speaking of Zeus's view; he also makes use of it in speaking about the Sun's view. What is the meaning of this inquiry? Not, as one might think outside of any context, a cry of despair on the part of the chorus when it is confronted by the indifference of the gods' view, comparable to Hyllus's cry at the end of *The Women of Trachis*. Such an interpretation would make the rest of the dialogue with Electra incomprehensible. What the chorus is trying to suggest is, on the contrary, a hope, as Electra recognizes at the end of the strophe. In the chorus's view, it is impossible to think that two divinities assigned to uncover crimes and to punish the perpetrators might not be able to act. That would be tantamount to saying that these divinities do not exist. That is the meaning of the inquiry: the chorus has faith in the gods' action and warns Electra against a despair so excessive that it threatens to become an offense against the gods and, consequently, to turn back against her. One ancient commentator even indicates how the scene should be played when Electra cries "Oh!" (in Greek, *pheu*!):

> The actor, at the same time as he cries out, should lift his eyes toward the heavens and hold out his hands, which the chorus interrupts by saying "Give no cry of bad omen!"[13]

Thus is the chorus's faith in the intervention of Zeus, who sees all and is not shaken, despite the worsening of the situation after the announcement of Orestes' death.

In the tragedy, this theme of the god's total vision acquires a particular weight, because in the interval between the two passages where the chorus refers to it, there is another mention of it, but this time in the adverse camp, that of the murderers. Having come out of the palace to make offerings and pray to Apollo that he might free her from the fear aroused by her dream, Clytemnestra, after a long altercation with her daughter, addresses a prayer to Apollo. Since her daughter is present, she does not tell the god everything but ends her prayer this way:

> As for all my other prayers, though I am silent, I judge that you, a god, must know them, since it is appropriate that Zeus's children see all.[14]

In a prayer, it is diplomatic to flatter the god. And that is what Clytemnestra does by ending her prayer to Apollo with a reminder of his prestigious lineage and his prestigious power. Like his father, Zeus, Apollo sees everything, even the most hidden thoughts. Seeing, for god, is thus deciphering, unveiling what is hidden. This "way of seeing" is completely Greek. The Greek word denoting truth (*a-letheia*) refers, essentially, to an unveiling of what is hidden.

The God's View and the Spectator's View

Comparing the last two passages encourages the spectator to see, to decipher, as well. Throughout this tragedy Sophocles places the spectator in a situation comparable to that of a god who sees everything. In fact, insofar as the development of the tragedy is the precise execution of the plan of deception set forth at the beginning, the spectator has everything he needs to distinguish between the true and the false at every moment of the action. But what does the spectator see as the consequence of the words the characters utter about the gods who see everything?

Immediately after Clytemnestra's prayer, which ends by mentioning the god who sees everything, and without any transition, what the spectator sees—and what he hears—is a messenger bringing news: the tutor announcing Orestes' death. For Clytemnestra, this is fundamentally the deliverance from all her fears, the realization of the very thing that she had desired at the secret heart of her prayer, but which she had not dared say. Clytemnestra thus can interpret the news only as the fulfillment of the prayer that she has just addressed to Apollo. She believes that the god has seen everything and that he has accomplished everything. But because he has seen Orestes at the beginning of the tragedy, the spectator can gauge the error of the character whose interior joy is illusory, and understand the tragic irony of the situation.[15] Clytemnestra is not only a victim of men's tricks; she is also a plaything in the hands of the gods. At the moment that she believes she enjoys Apollo's favor, the god is using her to destroy her. Or, to put the point more prudently—for the gods' action retains its element of mystery—everything happens as if the god were acting in this way. The joy of the good news leads the criminal to participate in the process of her own punishment. It is she, in fact, who spontaneously offers to welcome the tutor as a guest in the palace, to reward him for bringing good news.[16]

And immediately after the lyrical dialogue in which the chorus expresses its confidence in the view of Zeus and the Sun, what does the spectator see? The sudden arrival of a messenger bearing further news about Orestes. Chrysothemis rushes forward full of joy because she has seen on Agamemnon's tomb signs of Orestes' presence. The spectator knows that what Chrysothemis says is true and is led to see in this arrival the intervention of the gods. But Electra's despair—which is mistaken, because she is deceived by the false news—rejects her sister's report with commiseration and this time delays the accomplishment of the vengeance even as she wants to take it on herself alone. The spectator sees the tragic irony once again, but it has an inverse effect. Whereas Clytemnestra, in her error, accelerates her punishment, Electra, in her despair, delays her deliverance. It is as if the all-seeing eyes of Apollo and Zeus were making the just cause triumph, but were unveiling only gradually what is hidden, accelerating here, delaying there, in accord with an unpredictable progress in which the gods' irony seems to toy with human blindness.

The Paths of Tragic Irony: A Woman's Prayer to Apollo in *Oedipus the King* and in *Electra*

In the diverse paths taken by tragic irony, variety does not prevent certain paths from being analogous. The sequence from *Electra*—in which, as we have just seen, Clytemnestra's prayer to Apollo is immediately followed by a joy that will later prove illusory—had already been employed by Sophocles in his *Oedipus the King*, where Jocasta's prayer to Apollo is also followed by the arrival of a messenger. As in *Electra*, this messenger brings news that seems to free the woman from the anxieties expressed in her prayer to the god.

An attentive comparison between the two sequences could show how Sophocles constructed, in different circumstances but making use of the same framework, the tragedies of two women who are victims of the same tragic irony. The initial situation is already comparable: two worried queens come out of the palace to pray to Apollo Lyceus in the visible space.[17] Of course, the two women do not resemble one another; their motivations are different: Jocasta, is worried about her husband, while Clytemnestra fears for herself. Then the messenger's arrival is comparable. Coming immediately after the end of the prayer, without being announced, the messenger questions the chorus—a chorus of men in *Oedipus the King*, a chorus of women in *Electra*[18]—to find out if he has in fact come to the palace that he is looking for. Then, through the intermediary of the chorus, the messenger enters into contact with the queen and tells her the news he has brought from far away—one from Corinth, the other from Phocis. In both cases, the news is the announcement of a man's death: that of the king of Corinth in *Oedipus the King*, that of Orestes in *Electra*. This death will cause the queen to rejoice. Jocasta sees in it deliverance from her fears about Oedipus: his father is dead, and he did not kill him! Then the reversal will be comparable: the joy turns out to be based on an illusion. However, in *Oedipus the King* the news is not false, as it is in *Electra*. Unlike Orestes, old Polybus, the king of Corinth, has in fact died. The death announced is true; but the identity of the deceased is false. The man Jocasta believed to be Oedipus's true father turns out to be, in a second revelation made by the same messenger from Corinth, only his adoptive father. Finally, the reversal of the situation leads, in both cases, to the woman's death, a voluntary death in Jocasta's case, and an involuntary death in Clytemnestra's. There is no doubt that in his *Electra* Sophocles deliberately reworked a schema of tragic irony he had already used in his *Oedipus the King*.

The Perception of Tragic Irony: The Different Statuses of the Spectator

However, despite the analogy, the spectator's perception of tragic irony in these two cases is not of exactly the same nature, because the spectator does not have exactly the same status.

The status of the spectator is not often discussed in analyses of tragedy. The question does not, of course, concern his social status, but rather the degree of knowledge he has when he witnesses the performance of a given tragedy or a given scene within a tragedy. Sophocles makes the spectator's status vary. Sometimes he makes the spectator an equal of an omniscient god, sometimes a man who doubts himself, sometimes a man who has doubts, or is even ignorant.

The spectator is omniscient when the author fully informs him about the situation. Then he knows for sure what certain characters involved do not know. This kind of gap in knowledge is necessary to gauge with precision the reaction of characters who do not know. This is the case, as we have seen, for Clytemnestra's reaction, and also Electra's, to the news of Orestes' death, which both characters believe to be true, but which the spectator knows is false. He knows, as does the creator, of the trick, that Clytemnestra's joy, like Electra's despair, are based on an illusion; thus he perceives the tragic irony at work. At the same time, this false news reveals the true nature of the characters, who unveil themselves, and whom the spectator discovers. The spectator's omniscience continues throughout this tragedy, whereas the characters' knowledge may change. In fact, starting with the recognition scene between the brother and sister, Electra—and with her, the chorus—changes in status. She goes over to the side of those who know, and at the end of the tragedy the spectator will witness a reversal of the situation. The victim of tragic irony at the beginning, Electra becomes the agent of tragic irony at the end, when she deceptively receives Aegisthus.[19]

This kind of omniscience on the part of the spectator occurs particularly in tragedies where a plan of deception is carried out, not only in *Electra*, but also in *Philoctetes*. In these two tragedies, Sophocles sees to it that the plan for deception—along with the assignment of roles, including the deceptive speeches that are to be made—is announced in the first scene in dialogue. The scenario is thus set out at the beginning of the tragedy, before it is implemented in any way.[20] To be sure, in *Philoctetes*, unlike in *Electra*, the application of the plan includes several unforeseen events that alter or compromise the forecast: Philoctetes' physical crisis, and then Neoptolemus's moral crisis. Nonetheless, the scenes planned in the initial scenario take place in both *Philoctetes* and *Electra*. During all these scenes, the spectator is an omniscient witness to the deceptive speeches and savors in every detail tragic irony's subtle effects on the characters who fall victim to the trick.[21]

Except for those involving trickery, the only one of Sophocles' tragedies where the spectator has the status of a god is precisely the one where a divinity appears at the beginning: *Ajax*. In that play, Athena reveals to Odysseus—and to the spectator—everything that happened during the night: Ajax's solitary sortie driven by anger and the desire to avenge himself for not having received Achilles' arms, the intervention of the goddess herself to craze Ajax and direct his sword against the flocks and not the troops. The spectator is even superior to Odysseus in one respect: not only does he hear the goddess, as Odysseus does, but he also sees her. From that point on, the spectator can witness like a god two scenes of tragic irony: first, he sees Ajax's distraction and all Athena's irony with regard to him, and there again he has a certain superiority over Odysseus: whereas the latter is a witness paralyzed by terror, the spectator observes the scene with a fear purified by the distance inherent in drama. Then, after Odysseus's departure, the spectator can still discern with the greatest precision what is true and what is false in the chorus's questions about the rumor according to which Ajax is the one who massacred the flocks. The spectator knows that the chorus is deluded when it hopes that the rumor is false. But he knows that the chorus is right in assuming that Ajax would be capable of acting in this way only under the influence of a god-sent madness.[22] But he is aware of the tragic irony when the chorus, wondering which divinity is responsible for this madness, considers two possibilities—Artemis and Enyalius—neither of which is the right one.

On the other hand, in *Oedipus the King* the spectators do not have the same certainty in gauging all the manifestation of tragic irony. Their knowledge cannot be compared to that of the gods.[23] In fact, the true identity of Oedipus is not revealed at the beginning of the tragedy by a character who knows the truth. The only person who knows it is Laius's old servant. However, he appears not at the beginning of the tragedy, but toward the end, where his forced revelations provoke Oedipus's final recognition. The structure of *Oedipus the King* is thus not comparable to those of *Ajax*, *Electra*, or *Philoctetes*. To be sure, we have to take into account the fact that the myth of Oedipus was well known to the spectators, not to mention that the presentation of the tragedy had taken place in the ceremony preceding the *proagōn*. Of course, Sophocles took care to provide signs to guide the spectator by introducing early on the scene in which the seer Tiresias makes his prophecies. Nonetheless, the spectators' lack of complete certainty keeps them in suspense and makes them experience the various reversals with greater emotion and less distance. The tragic irony is immediately perceptible only in the tragedies where the spectator has divine knowledge. To show this, let us go back to the comparison between the two sequences in *Oedipus the King* and *Electra* where the two queens, after their prayers to Apollo, rejoice upon receiving the messenger's news. The spectators of *Electra* know immediately after the messenger's report of Orestes' death that Clytemnestra's joy is based on an illusion, whereas all the spectators do not necessarily understand immediately after the announcement of Polybus's death that Jocasta's joy, along with that of Oedipus, is also ill founded. Sophocles has set up a reversal by making the messenger's news have a twofold effect, transforming Oedipus's joy into concern and Jocasta's joy into certainty regarding her disaster. Once she has understood everything, the queen silently goes back into the palace to commit suicide.

Finally, in some cases the spectators, far from knowing everything or even suspecting, may be completely uncertain about a reversal, because Sophocles has given them nothing preliminary that would allow them to decipher in advance the tragic irony it includes. This is the case in the sequence in which Ajax announces, in the presence of the silent Tecmessa and the chorus, his total change in attitude with regard to mortals and gods, and his desire to leave to purify himself in order to escape the goddess's wrath. After his departure, this announcement triggers the chorus's enthusiastic joy, which is abruptly interrupted by the arrival of a messenger denouncing the chorus's illusion, because he has knowledge derived from a seer's prophecy. Did the listeners understand, upon hearing Ajax's speech, that it was meant to trick them? In any case, none of the characters present deciphered the ruse, not the chorus, and not even Tecmessa. What about the spectators? Here it is appropriate to use the plural rather than the singular, because unlike at the beginning of the tragedy, when every spectator, insofar as he was completely enlightened by the goddess, was capable of immediately perceiving the tragic irony when Ajax or the chorus entered, here the spectators' comprehension of the situation must have depended on the intelligence and sensitivity of each of them. Of course, Sophocles provided a few signs within Ajax's own speech that might awaken doubt regarding the sincerity of his conversion, certain intentionally ambivalent words in which, beneath the apparent meaning, a hidden sense lurks. Imperceptible for the characters (Tecmessa and the chorus), this hidden sense is meant to be understood by the audience. But which members of the audience? Certainly not by all, even if they know the what happens to Ajax in myth. Sophocles, even though he wrote for the whole of the audience, was well aware that the pace of comprehension varies from one spectator to the next. Some, absorbed in the play, will understand at the same time that the characters do. They will not perceive Ajax's irony and will rejoice with the chorus before being gripped by the messenger's warnings. They will then understand, belatedly, Ajax's equivocal language. Others—a minority?— will immediately perceive what is going on. Here are the last words that Ajax addresses to the chorus before leaving:

I am going to where my journey inexorably leads. But you do as I say, and before long, perhaps, though I now suffer, you will hear that I have found rest and peace.[24]

The double meaning of the last words ("found rest and peace") sum up the ambiguity of the whole speech: the chorus understands that Ajax will find rest and peace because he has agreed to change and decided to submit to the leaders and the gods, whereas Ajax means that he will find rest and peace in death, thus escaping dishonor.

The Signs of Tragic Irony: Consciously Ambivalent Language

Ambivalent language is often the sign of a situation of tragic irony. Two forms of such language can be distinguished. Sometimes a character uses it deliberately in speaking to another character who does not know something essential and does not understand the hidden meaning; sometimes it is used unconsciously by a character who does not know the hidden meaning and does not realize how right he or she is. In the first case, we speak of conscious or voluntary tragic irony, and in the second case we speak of unconscious or involuntary tragic irony.

Ajax's monologue is a case of conscious irony. The situation is rather exceptional: Ajax uses irony in addressing people he loves. If he deceives them by using irony, it is not in order to injure them but rather to be able to escape their grip and gain the freedom to commit suicide. The irony, in this case, is more a bitter irony with regard to his own destiny than an aggressive irony with regard to other people.

Ordinarily, conscious irony is used with joy against an enemy whom one has in one's power without the enemy knowing it, and in the most tragic cases, before he or she is put to death. This kind of irony is considered one of the characteristics of Aeschylus's art. In fact, the scene in *Agamemnon* in which Clytemnestra greets Agamemnon upon his return from Troy, before he is killed, is a model of conscious tragic irony in which certain ambivalent expressions allow us to discern, beneath the sweet words she speaks to the man who is officially her husband, an adumbration of the murder of the man who has become, in fact, her enemy, now that she has been seduced by Aegisthus.[25] Thus people have spoken about Aeschylean tragic irony. But Sophocles also created a comparable scene in the same myth, at the point where the murder of Agamemnon is avenged.

After the murder of Clytemnestra, Electra receives Aegisthus upon his return home, before he is put to death. She uses the same irony as the Aeschylean Clytemnestra had with regard to Agamemnon, even if the situation of the victim of the irony is different: in Aeschylus, the king does not know that Clytemnestra is his enemy, whereas in Sophocles Aegisthus is well aware that Electra hates him. Moreover, this irony is more accessible to the spectator than it is in Aeschylus,

because it is, as we have said, one of the scenes in which Sophocles has placed
the spectator in the position of an omniscient god.[26] The author has even taken
care to draw the spectator's attention to Electra's deception through the intermediary of the advice that the chorus gives her just before Aegisthus arrives:

> It would be well to whisper into this man's ear some few words of seeming
> gentleness, so that he may rush blindly upon his trial before Justice.[27]

Here the chorus indicates the sly tone that Electra should, and does, adopt
when she receives Aegisthus, in order to confirm his false joy and help him fall
by himself into Orestes' trap. It is not a matter of ambivalent language, to be
sure, but the spectator has all the necessary information to understand the ironic
meaning hidden under the surface of the dialogue between Electra and Aegisthus
that follows:

> *Aegisthus:* Which of you can tell me where those Phocian strangers are, who
> are said to have brought report for us that Orestes passed away amidst the
> shipwrecked chariots? You, you I ask, yes, you, who were in former days so
> bold. It seems to me that this concerns you most, so you must know best,
> and can best tell me.
> *Electra:* I do know. How could I not? Otherwise I would be an alien to the for-
> tune of my nearest kinsmen.
> *Aegisthus:* Where, then, may the strangers be? Tell me.
> *Electra:* Inside. They have found a way to the heart of their hostess.
> *Aegisthus:* Have they in fact reported him truly dead?
> *Electra:* No, not reported only. They have shown him.
> *Aegisthus:* Then I can identify the corpse myself?
> *Electra:* You can, indeed, though it is no enviable sight.
> *Aegisthus:* You have indeed given me a joyful greeting, beyond your custom.
> *Electra:* May joy be yours, if joy is what you find in these things.

From her first statement, "I do know," Electra answers Aegisthus by playing
on the extent of her knowledge. According to an apparent meaning, she knows
everything about Orestes' death because she has heard the details the tutor gave
in his report. But in a hidden meaning, she knows everything about this death,
which was no more than a ruse to carry out the vengeance. It is significant that
Electra's first ambivalent statement bears on knowledge. It is precisely the differences in the degree of knowledge that make tragic irony possible. The hidden
meaning is not perceptible by the hearer, because he does not have the information necessary to understand it, but it is understood by the spectator, who knows
everything, just as Electra does. Enjoying a superiority based on her knowledge,
Electra uses it as a weapon against her adversary to lead him still further astray
and to push him, like a beater, into Orestes' nets.[28] She does so with consummate skill when she answers Aegisthus's questions: she invents nothing that is

contrary to what has happened, but she uses sufficiently general expressions to misled her interlocutor. For example, when Aegisthus questions her as to how credible the news of Orestes' death is, she replies that the foreigners from Phocis did not limit themselves to words, but also showed evidence of the death. She is referring to the urn brought by Orestes himself, but Aegisthus thinks of Orestes' body. This makes possible a theatrical effect when Aegisthus uncovers the cadaver that he believes to be that of Orestes. He discovers that it is in fact that of Clytemnestra. This unveiling corresponds to the moment when Aegisthus discovers the hidden truth, recognizes Orestes, and suddenly passes from triumphant joy to the certainty of the tragic destiny that awaits him.

The most famous scene in Sophocles' theater where a character uses conscious tragic irony is that in which the goddess Athena makes the mad Ajax come out of his home to display him before Odysseus. Here is the dialogue between the man and the divinity:

> *Athena:* You there, Ajax, once again I call you! Why do you show so little regard for your ally?
>
> Enter Ajax, holding a blood-stained whip in his hand.
>
> *Ajax:* Welcome, Athena! Welcome, daughter sprung from Zeus! How well have you stood by me! I will crown you with trophies of pure gold in gratitude for this quarry!
>
> *Athena:* A fine pledge. But tell me this—have you dyed your sword well in the Greek army?
>
> *Ajax:* I can make that boast. I do not deny it.
>
> *Athena:* And have you launched your armed hand against the Atreidae?
>
> *Ajax:* Yes, so that never again will they dishonor Ajax.
>
> *Athena:* The men are dead, as I interpret your words.
>
> *Ajax:* Dead they are. Now let them rob me of my arms!
>
> *Athena:* I see. And the son of Laertes, how does his fortune with respect to you? Has he escaped you?
>
> *Ajax:* That blasted fox! You ask me where he is?
>
> *Athena:* Yes, I do. I mean Odysseus, your adversary.
>
> *Ajax:* My most pleasing prisoner, mistress, he sits inside. I do not wish him to die just yet.
>
> *Athena:* Until you do what? Or win what greater advantage?
>
> *Ajax:* Until he be bound to a pillar beneath my roof—
>
> *Athena:* What evil, then, will you inflict on the poor man?
>
> *Ajax:* —and have his back crimsoned by the lash, before he dies.
>
> *Athena:* Do not abuse the poor man so cruelly!
>
> *Ajax:* In all else, Athena, I bid you take your pleasure, but he will pay this penalty and no other.
>
> *Athena:* Well, then, since it delights you to do so, put your arm to use; spare no portion of your plan.

> *Ajax:* I go to my work. And I give you this commission: be always for me the
> close-standing ally that you have been for me today![29]

Voluntary tragic irony presupposes, as we have said, a gap between the knowledge of the person using it and the ignorance of the person he is addressing. Without this gap, there would be only a simple irony, which can obviously exist in tragic dialogues where two persons having the same knowledge confront one another. The ironic duel is then fought on equal terms.[30] But here the gap becomes an extreme opposition. The scene is based on the greatest distance one can imagine between knowledge and blindness, divine knowledge and the blindness of a man who has been deprived of rationality by the divinity who is exercising her irony on him.

Thus the dialogue takes an exceptional form as well. Here we have, as in the dialogue examined earlier, a dialogue of information. Is there any need to remind the reader that in every dialogue of this type, the person who does not know asks the questions and is therefore in charge of the dialogue, orienting its course by his or her questions? In conformity with the general rule, Aegisthus asks Electra questions, whereas Electra uses her conscious tragic irony in her answers, maneuvering Aegisthus to lead him to his death, even though she is not the leader of the dialogue. But in *Ajax* it is the omniscient Athena who asks the questions, because she feigns ignorance. She thus controls both the dialogue and the tragic action. Her irony draws attention, when she wishes, to the madness of the man proud of his imaginary triumph. At first, she congratulates him, and at the end she encourages him to continue to "do what [he] has in mind."[31] Addressed to a man who has lost his mind, this phrase is a particularly cruel form of irony. The scene is a kind of blueprint in which the power of the gods and the finitude of humans is shown. The meaning of the scene not only emerges from the dialogue between the ironic divinity and the crazed man but is also explained by the divinity herself after Ajax has gone back into his house. Thus for the spectator, there is no ambiguity regarding the meaning of this scene, even if he wonders about the causes of the goddess's determined persecution of the man whom she has driven mad. These causes will be revealed to the spectator only later, thanks to the knowledge of a seer, a man intermediary between mortals and the gods. Ajax is, in fact, being punished for the pride he showed in the past with regard to the goddess, a pride that a well-informed spectator could already discern at the very heart of Ajax's madness.[32] The man has lost his mind, but not his temperament.

The Signs of Tragic Irony: Unconsciously Ambivalent Language

Conscious tragic irony is thus an expression of a superior knowledge. Unconscious tragic irony is a sign of limited knowledge. We can already see this in the two preceding dialogues. We have already shown the ambivalent language of the character who is deliberately using tragic irony and his or her interlocutor's inability to understand the hidden meaning. But if we now examine the way the victim of voluntary tragic irony expresses him- or herself, it appears that the victim also uses ambivalent words during his or her illusory triumph preceding his or her recognition of the truth, whether it comes early or late; but the great difference is that the hidden meaning of the victim's own words escapes him or her. This hidden meaning bearing on the future inscribes itself on the victim's words by itself. Thus language is also the bearer of a truth regarding the destiny of the person who speaks.

Let us return first to the case of Ajax. As soon as he addresses Athena, he thanks her for having helped him and promises to crown her "with trophies of pure gold in gratitude for this quarry!"[33] Ajax understands the word "quarry" in a metaphorical sense. He is thanking the goddess for having helped him to kill the Atreids and to capture Odysseus. But his words are truer than he thinks. The hidden meaning is in fact the literal sense of the word, which denotes a hunted animal. And in fact Ajax has just hunted animals. He discovers that only later. But his language bears a sign that comes from elsewhere. The ambivalent language of an unconscious irony also suggests that humans can express desires that turn against them. Ajax's final request to Athena, to remain forever at his side as a "close-standing ally" amounts, in fact, to wishing that the goddess never cease to contribute to his own ruin.

Let us next return to the comparable dialogue in which Electra uses conscious tragic irony in receiving Aegisthus. The latter, for his part, also uses irony. In fact, he is the one who begins using it, when he enters. It is apparently the simple irony of the man who is triumphing after learning that Orestes is dead and addressing the loser in a haughty and mocking way, while Electra pretends to be despairing and humiliated. We recall the first words Aegisthus spoke to Electra:

> You, you I ask, yes, you, who were in former days so bold. It seems to me that this concerns you most, so you must know everything, and can best tell me.[34]

In these first ironic words a hidden meaning already glimmers underneath Aegisthus's simple irony, transforming it into involuntary tragic irony. When he says that Electra knows everything, he thinks she knows all about the consequences of Orestes' death. But what he says is truer than he thinks. Electra knows more about a death that is only fictive. So when Electra replies "I do know," her voluntary tragic irony is naturally grafted onto Aegisthus's involuntary tragic irony. And when Aegisthus continues to use irony, notably by complimenting Electra—"You have indeed given me a joyful greeting, beyond your custom"—it is an ill-timed irony, which escapes neither Electra nor the spectator. Aegisthus's illusory and ridiculous triumph recalls that of Ajax. Involuntary tragic irony intensifies the spectator's awareness of human finitude by suggesting that in his blindness he is the bearer of a truth he does not understand.

The ambivalent language of involuntary tragic irony finds its most frequent and most accomplished expression in Oedipus's discourse in *Oedipus the King*.[35] Starting when Creon returns with the Delphic oracle's reply asserting that the plague in Thebes will end only after the pollution resulting from the murder of Laius, the former king, has been purged, and when Oedipus questions Creon concerning the murder and decides to pursue the investigation himself, Oedipus's words take on a particular resonance, given the exceptional gap that exists between what he believes to be the case and what it really is, between what he believes he has done and what he has in fact done. He thinks he is the son of the king of Corinth, Polybus, and his wife Merope; in reality, he is the son of the king of Thebes, Laius, and his wife Jocasta. When he learns from the Delphic oracle that he is to kill his father and marry his mother, he believes he can escape the oracle by leaving Corinth for Thebes. On his way, he meets a man whom he kills because he has not shown him proper respect. Then, having freed Thebes of the scourge of the Sphinx by using his intelligence to solve its riddle, he becomes the king, believing he is a foreigner, whereas in fact he is a Theban, and he marries the former king's wife, who is, unbeknownst to him, his mother, with whom he has children. All these gaps between belief and reality—which will disappear only at the moment when Oedipus finally becomes aware of his true origin after the Theban shepherd's revelations—lead to statements that seem obvious to Oedipus, but which do not coincide with reality. Many of these sincere statements are falsehoods. They merely emphasize Oedipus's ignorance regarding his origin and the significance of his acts. For example, when Creon reminds Oedipus that Laius was king of Thebes before he (Oedipus) became king of the city, Oedipus replies: "I know it well—by hearsay, for I never saw him."[36] He did see Laius, in reality, when he met him before killing him; but he did not know he was his father. These examples of falsehoods become more numerous when Oedipus addresses the chorus to make his official proclamation asking all Thebans to help him find Laius's murderer. He justifies his proclamation by the fact that he is a foreigner, putting great stress on that idea:

> These words I will speak publicly, as one who was a stranger to the report, a stranger to the deed. I would not go far on the trail if I were tracing it alone, without a clue. But as it is—since it was only after the event that I was counted a Theban among Thebans.[37]

Oedipus's logic is that of an intelligent man who still reasons perfectly well. Having arrived in Thebes after Laius's death, and having been made a citizen after the murder, he is foreign to the matter and cannot, by himself, carry out the full investigation. However, all these statements are false. He is not a new citizen, because he was born in Thebes. He is not foreign to what was done, because he is the one who did it. Reasoning well on the basis of false assumptions thus amounts to logically imprisoning oneself in error.

At the same time, his statements may amount to the dissimulation of a meaning or a truth that Oedipus does not understand. And that is where we can truly speak of tragic irony. The body of his official proclamation to the Thebans itself offers examples of this. First, there are the statements that conceal a meaning that Oedipus does not grasp. His desire to serve the god and the dead man leads him to call down curses on the criminal.[38] His good intentions turn against him, because he is the murderer. And, to show once again his goodwill, he goes even further by cursing himself in the event that he should receive the criminal in his home:

> And for myself I pray that if he should, with my knowledge, become a resident of my house, I may suffer the same things which I have just called down on others.[39]

Such curses will thus turn doubly against him. Once Oedipus discovers his true identity, he will become aware of the aggravating circumstances that he has added by issuing this edict addressed to all Thebans. Thus he justifies to the chorus, after the fact, his decision to blind himself in order not to be obliged to lower his eyes before the Thebans.[40]

Now here is a speech in which Oedipus comes close to the truth without realizing it. In the rest of his edict, he accuses the Thebans of having been negligent at the time of their former king's death, of not having conducted the investigation at that time, without waiting for Apollo's injunction. Then he takes responsibility for conducting the investigation himself and gives his reasons for doing so:

> But now, since I hold the powers which he once held, possessing his bed and the wife who bore his children, and since, had his hope of offspring not been unsuccessful, children born of one mother would have tied us with a common bond—as it was, fate swooped upon his head—I will uphold this cause, as though it were that of my own father, and will leave no stone unturned in my search for the one who shed the blood.[41]

In his ardent desire to act on behalf of the dead man, the comparison "as though it were that of my own father" comes naturally to his lips. But it seems to be attracted by a truth that emerges without the speaker being aware of it. Oedipus expresses the truth here, but in a metaphorical form. More generally, throughout the passage, the truth is very near, because Oedipus already envisages in the mode of unreality what is true in reality: there are in fact children born of the same mother, Oedipus born from Laius's seed, and the sons and daughters born from Oedipus's own seed. Certain words take on the true meaning only by reference to the hidden reality.[42]

Why This Involuntary Tragic Irony?

How did the ancients explain the latent presence of truth in the words of someone who does not recognize it? Where does this truth come from? No hint is given in Sophocles' theater. This phenomenon can, however, find its general explanation in the belief according to which the gods can manifest themselves, among many other ways, in and through sounds. To continue with examples taken from Sophocles' theater, these are the sounds made by the foliage of the oak forest "with a thousand voices" at Dodona, which are interpreted by Zeus's oracles;[43] or the unknown cries of the birds that worry the seer Tiresias;[44] or the god at Delphi, who speaks through the voice of the Pythia.[45] Outside Sophocles' work, we can cite a curious oracle that gives a prophetic value to everyday words. This is the oracle of Hermes Agoraios (Hermes of the Agora) in Pharai, a small city in Achaia, in the northern Peloponnesus, not far from Patras. The functioning of this oracle is described by Pausanias (second century CE):

> In the middle of [the agora] is an image of Hermes, made of stone and bearded. Standing right on the earth, it is of square shape, and of no great size. . . . In front of the image is placed a hearth, which also is of stone, and to the hearth bronze lamps are fastened with lead. Coming at eventide, the inquirer of the god, having burnt incense upon the hearth, filled the lamps with oil and lighted them, puts on the altar on the right of the image a local coin, called a "copper," and asks in the ear of the god the particular question he wishes to put to him. After that he stops his ears and leaves the marketplace. On coming outside he takes his hands from his ears, and whatever utterance he hears he considers oracular.[46]

Nonetheless, on the basis of these examples one might think that the presence of the divinity in or through sounds or words is related to sacred spaces, either the oracular sanctuaries (Dodona, Delphi, Pharai) or the traditional seat of augury in Thebes.[47] But as early as Homer we find the belief according to which the gods may manifest themselves to humans outside of any sacred space, not only in dreams, but also in some of their words. Uttered apparently at random, these words are in fact inspired by the gods and have a prophetic meaning for those who are capable of deciphering them. In the *Odyssey*, on the morning of the day when Odysseus is preparing to massacre the suitors, he addresses a prayer to Zeus asking him to show himself not only by his thunder and lightning, but also by the voice of a person who is awakening. Zeus then manifests himself by his thunderbolt in a clear sky, which gives Odysseus great joy, and then by a servant who is herself praying to Zeus to ask that his day mark, for her, the end of her labors, and for the suitors their last meal. It is the simple voice of a weak servant hoping, very naturally, to escape her hard life of toil. However, for Odysseus her voice has a hidden value that that the servant obviously does not perceive: he knows that it is a prophetic statement inspired by Zeus, and he rejoices in it.[48] In the theater, the clearest testimony concerning these prophetic words is found in Aeschylus's *Prometheus Bound*. Listing the arts that he has revealed to humans, among the diverse forms of divination Prometheus mentions, after dreams, the interpretation of words whose meaning is prophetic:

> Voices baffling interpretation I explained to them.[49]

It is in this overall religious and cultural context that we fully understand involuntary tragic irony in Sophocles' theater, even if the literary use made of it presupposes a sophistication comparable to the literary elaborateness of oracular responses rather than to the more prosaic responses known through inscriptions. In tragic irony, unlike ordinary prophetic utterances, the hidden truth unconsciously expressed by words always refers to the speaking subject. It is a sign regarding the person who utters the words, a bad sign indicating a catastrophe to come.[50] Even as it bears on the person speaking, this sign, perceptible to the spectators, or at least to the most expert among them, does not emanate from the deep self, as moderns since Freud might be inclined to think, but rather from the gods who are thus discreetly manifesting their presence and their power. In Sophocles, is it an anonymous divine intervention, or can we identify in each tragic situation—as in the passage from the *Odyssey* where it was clearly a matter of a particular god, Zeus—the divinity who gives human language a double meaning? What gods inspire such words?

In the case of Ajax, the answer seems simple enough, given that the hero enters into dialogue, in an exceptional way, with Athena, the goddess who made him mad. We can explain the presence of unconscious irony in Ajax's speech by the action of the goddess, who is capable not only of making Ajax believe that she is his ally, but of guiding his language, so that it conceals a hidden meaning of which he is not aware. It is perhaps no accident that the word "ally," used regarding Athena's relation to Ajax, is used first by the goddess in the form of voluntary tragic irony when she summons Ajax, and then by Ajax himself in the form of involuntary tragic irony when he leaves the goddess.[51] The repetition of the same word at the beginning and the end of the dialogue emphasizes the goddess's complete control over the man, both his language and his distracted mind.

But when involuntary tragic irony is manifested in a tragedy where a divinity does not appear, what then? There is no obvious answer, but Oedipus's involuntary tragic irony, like that of Aegisthus, occurs in a tragedy in which the dominant divinity is Apollo. Orestes carries out his revenge on Aegisthus under the sign of the Delphic oracle. As for Oedipus's destiny, from his birth to his discovery of his identity it is marked by the oracles issued at Delphi. There are three of them in Sophocles' play. Isn't it already Apollo who silently manifests himself in the hidden meaning of ambivalent words? Isn't it he who manages in *Oedipus the King* to give, already in the proclamation of the edict, signs of the truth about Oedipus, before his prophet Tiresias reveals other, more explicit signs?

The god's ingenuity in showing himself through silences is found elsewhere in Sophocles' own tragedies, and in particular in *Oedipus the King*. When Oedipus, alerted by a drunken man who had told him he was not his father's true son, went to consult the oracle at Delphi to find out if he was in fact the son of Polybus, the king of Corinth, and his wife Merope, the god remained silent on the question asked but revealed what the man did not ask, namely that he would kill his father and marry his mother.[52] This silence was tragically effective. It led the man to go away from those whom he believed to be his parents and, in so doing, to fall victim to a kind of trap that the god had set for him so that he would kill his father. A supreme irony: the god's silence thus served to realize his oracle.

Even before Oedipus reveals this oracle, the chorus has already expressed its astonishment that, in the oracle stating that Thebes will be delivered from the scourge that is destroying it only after the corruption caused by the murder of Laius has been purged, the god remained silent on a crucial point. Why didn't he give the murderer's name? Oedipus replies to this question with a great deal of wisdom and resignation:

> Justly said. But no man on earth can force the gods to do what they do not want.[53]

This time the god's silence is dramatically effective. Without it, there would be no suspense and no tragedy. Apollo's silence is also Sophocles' silence.

The Effect of Involuntary Tragic Irony on the Spectators

Without raising too many metaphysical questions about the origin of this ambivalent language, the spectators could savor the subtlety of the allusions and feel the emotions aroused by this glimpse of the misfortune to come. An ancient commentator mentions the spectators' reactions in connection with the most famous example of involuntary tragic irony, the one in which Oedipus is about to launch into the search for the murderer, "as if Laius were his father":

> Such thoughts are not part of the majesty, but they move the "theater" [the spectators]. Thoughts of this kind are frequent in Euripides. Sophocles makes use of them only briefly to move the "theater" [the spectators].[54]

Beyond the classical conception of the tragic genre defined by majesty, the commentary is surprising in its modernity, because in its analysis of the tragic text the dimension of representation—that is, the effect the text produces on the spectator—remains essential. What the commentary brings out is the emotional effect of what we call unconscious tragic irony. Earlier, when Oedipus uttered against himself the curse that made him his own prisoner, the ancient commentator had already made a remark along the same lines:

> It was in ignorance that he uttered a curse against himself if he knows the murderer. That is why the speech becomes more moving.[55]

According to the scholiast, the spectators feel pity for Oedipus, given his ignorance of the misfortunes that he suggests without understanding them. And what is also surprising in this commentator is his reticence with regard to this kind of excessively easy effect, which the tragic author must use in moderation.

We are far from most moderns' admiration for Sophocles' skill in handling what they call tragic ambiguity.[56] Other times, other judgments.

From Involuntary Tragic Irony to the Consequences of Tragic Reversal: The Three Main Stages

The ambivalent language of involuntary tragic irony is thus a sign of ignorance in a character. It is also a foreshadowing of the eventual revelation of a hidden truth that the character expresses without understanding it, and that will lead to a tragic reversal in his destiny.

The exemplary destiny in this regard is that of Aegisthus in *Electra*. To be sure, Aegisthus is a character whom Sophocles left in the shadows for a long time, because he had him travel to the countryside and remain there for most of the tragedy, up to the murder of Clytemnestra.[57] He is in no way central in the tragedy. But from the moment Aegisthus appears, he has a more prominent presence than he does in Aeschylus.[58] What is exemplary about his destiny is that the different stages are clearly distinguished from one another and succeed each other at an accelerated pace.

The first stage is that of joy proceeding from ignorance and distraction. When he arrives, he is very happy because he has already heard the news of Orestes' death. The spectator witnesses the usurper's brief, illusory triumph; in his short dialogue with Electra, he shows his joy at what he thinks is the confirmation of Orestes' death, asserts his consolidated power, and threatens those who might try to resist him. Then, asking that the doors of the palace be opened, he wants to display, in a theatrical manner, before the whole people, what he thinks is Orestes' corpse.

The second stage, after his error, is his discovery of reality, through the unveiling of the corpse, which is not that of Orestes but that of Clytemnestra, and through his recognition of Orestes, whose enigmatic statement about the living man who speaks to the dead he now understands.[59]

The third stage is the reaction after the discovery. It is surprising by the brevity of its despair and by the self-control with which Aegisthus faces up to misfortune in a short verbal contest with Orestes, where, even though he is doomed to die, he even goes so far as to make use, this time with full awareness of what he is doing, of a remorseless sarcastic irony that responds to Orestes' triumphant irony.[60]

Aegisthus's destiny is thus exemplary, because Sophocles condenses the major stages of a tragic destiny into a few instants, abbreviating even the end, since Aegisthus's murder is cast outside the time of the tragedy.

These three major stages—ignorance, discovery, the effects of that discovery—are found again in the destiny of two other characters whose ambivalent language we have examined, Ajax and Oedipus, and of course more generally in the other characters who are the victims of a tragic destiny of which they become aware, such as Deianira and Heracles in *The Women of Trachis* or Creon in *Antigone*. Nonetheless, the length of time devoted to each of these three stages may vary considerably from one tragedy to the next. The first stage, that of the period of blindness, may be rather quickly passed in order to arrive at the period of coming to awareness. That is the case, for example, in *Ajax*, where the crisis of madness caused by the goddess does not extend beyond the prologue, because at the beginning of the first episode we learn from Tecmessa that Ajax has gradually recovered his wits before we see, with Ajax's second entrance, the effects of this discovery of the truth on the part of the dishonored hero. On the other hand, in *Oedipus the King* the period of ignorance, before he definitively recognizes his misfortune, extends over most of the play. Only the end of the play is devoted to the effects of this recognition.

In all that, the most important thing is the discovery that marks the dividing line between the two sides of destiny. And it is, without any doubt, a moment of extreme importance in Sophocles' theater. But before we examine this moment, which tells us who the man really is, not only by the knowledge of the truth that he learns about himself, but also by the reactions that it elicits in him, we have to examine the preceding stage, that of ignorance.

From Ignorance to Blindness and Distraction: The Prism of Feelings

The tragic situation par excellence is that in which a character, the victim of ignorance, commits with complete lucidity an act that runs counter to what he intended, and does so in a context that is beyond his control, because oracles are being fulfilled. In this respect, there are analogies between Deianira's destiny in *The Women of Trachis* and that of Oedipus in *Oedipus the King*.

On the subject of Deianira's ignorance, the chorus of young women engages in lucid reflections after her silent departure, when she has learned from her son the catastrophic effects on Heracles of her gift to him. The chorus sees in this the fulfillment of the oracle left by Heracles before his departure. Then it speaks about Deianira:

> Our wretched mistress could not foretell this pain.
> She only saw what grief was coming upon her
> from Heracles' new marriage; she acted;
> and now, because she has heeded
> the words of a stranger in fatal converse,
> surely she groans in anguish;
> surely soft droplets moisten
> her cheeks with numerous tears.
> And the fate which is coming foreshadows a fall,
> mighty, and born of deception.[61]

Such lucidity may seem astonishing on the part of the chorus of young women, even though it is not lucid about everything. The young women grasp only part of the truth when they imagine Deianira in tears. They have not foreseen her suicide. Sophocles has to arrange a surprise. But when they say "the fate which is coming foreshadows a fall, mighty, and born of deception," they bring out a twofold aspect of her destiny (*moira*): the fulfillment of the oracle about Heracles, the tragic meaning of which is revealed, and the deception that is none other than that of the centaur taking revenge on Heracles, long after his death. This is the context in which Deianira's destiny is inscribed. To be sure, the young women of the chorus do not yet know—and neither do the spectators—that the centaur's trick is also the fulfillment of an oracle, a different oracle that Heracles will reveal later on, when he suddenly becomes aware of his destiny. But they can nonetheless put Deianira's act back into the context that is beyond her comprehension. Deianira has seen, but she has not understood. What she has seen is the disaster caused by the arrival of the new wife. What she has not understood is the trick played by the centaur, who has avenged himself through his intermediary. She has been the instrument of destiny, or one might say, of the fulfillment of the oracles. But she would not have been able to act in that way had she not been driven by her own feelings—love for her husband and jealousy of a rival whom he has won in a combat fought for love. Human feelings are the intermediaries of destiny. But we must still take into account the fact that for the ancients, a feeling such as love is inspired by a divinity. The chorus ends its song by evoking the goddess of love, Cypris: "The Goddess of Love has been present among us, working these deeds in silence."[62] The gods act silently.

Thus Oedipus and Deianira both act, thinking they are doing the right thing, in a web of oracles that have to be fulfilled. Their acts turn against them and end tragically, for the person they love and for themselves. There is an analogy between Deianira's suicide after Heracles falls ill and Oedipus's self-mutilation after Jocasta's suicide. However, this comparison has its limits. The relation to the oracle is not the same: Oedipus is directly concerned by an oracle; Deianira is only an instrument for fulfilling oracles that concern her husband. In fact, in Sophocles' theater oracles act directly only on the fate of men, not of women. Moreover, Oedipus's ignorance is different from that of Deianira. She does not know what she is doing; he does not know what he has done and what he is.

In this respect, Oedipus's ignorance is exceptional. In this first stage that precedes his coming to awareness he passes through phases that range from lucidity to blindness and distraction, and he does so during the time of the tragedy, before the premonitions and the discovery of the truth.

So long as his past has not caught up with him, Oedipus is a model of lucid intelligence. It was by his intelligence that he came to the pinnacle of his power and glory by solving the Sphinx's riddle. And it was this king at the height of his abilities that we see at the beginning of the tragedy. At the head of a state in full crisis, he seeks to act as an intelligent leader responsible for the salvation of his people, even though his intelligence recognizes its limits, since he has found no better remedy for the scourge than to appeal to the god at Delphi. But from the moment that the Delphic oracle, brought back to Thebes by Creon, leads him to launch the investigation into Laius's murder, he falls into blindness and distraction.

First, his lucidity weaves, in a moment of tragic irony when he issues the edict, the net in which he will be caught. Second, he refuses to see the truth when he confronts the person who knows it, the seer Tiresias, and quarrels with him. This is the pivotal scene in which he sinks into blindness, the scene in which Sophocles plays most on seeing and knowing, on hearing and understanding. The seer is blind, but he makes subtle use of the vocabulary of seeing.[63] At the height of the conflict, when the seer has just revealed to Oedipus that he is the murderer sought and implies that he is living in shame with people dear to him, Oedipus launches a blind, violent attack on the seer at the very moment that he has just told the truth:

> You do not have that strength, since you are maimed in your ears, in your wit, and in your eyes.[64]

This is the sign of the king's blindness. And he subsequently continues his violent and ironic remarks, accusing the seer of having eyes only for money and of being blind regarding his art.[65] In a later passage, Tiresias replies to these insults:

> I tell you, since you have taunted my blindness, that though you have sight, you do not see what a state of misery you are in.[66]

Among the misfortunes Oedipus does not see is his impending blindness. which Tiresias foretells:

> With darkness upon those eyes of yours which now can see.[67]

The chorus sees in this confrontation a collision of two equally angry men.[68] But their wrath is not of the same nature. In the seer, it is a lucid wrath that tells the truth. Such anger is the privilege of seers. In the king, it is human wrath that leads the mind astray and makes it lose contact with reality. We have seen that in Sophocles, as in the historian Thucydides, anger (*orgè*) is the antithesis of reason (*gnōmé*)—with the great difference that in Thucydides it is the leader (Pericles) who fears that the people (the Athenians) might act "more out of anger than out of reason," whereas in Sophocles, it is the chorus, representing the people, that notes that the accusation of a conspiracy made by the king is due "more to anger than to reason."[69] The comparison brings out the degree of the tragic king's madness. This madness reaches its highpoint when Oedipus and Jocasta challenge not only the seer but also the oracles. This time, the chorus no longer seeks to excuse its king by referring to his anger but is shocked and despairs: "The worship of the gods is perishing."[70]

Anger is a feeling that leads people astray, especially kings. A comparable analysis would apply to Creon in *Antigone*.[71] But what also disturbs King Oedipus's lucidity—and this is something new with respect to the Creon of *An-*

tigone—it is not only anger but also anxiety. This anxiety comes over him at the moment when Jocasta, led by good intentions to vent her indignation after the seer's accusations, gives an example of an oracle that was not fulfilled: Laius did not die at his son's hand, as Apollo's servants predicted, but at those of highwaymen at the intersection of three roads. Immediately after this account intended to reassure him, Oedipus exclaims:

> What restlessness of soul, lady, what tumult has come upon me since I heard you speak![72]

Why is he so worried? A detail in the story, the intersection of three roads, suddenly reminds him of a moment in his past, the murder of a man at an intersection of this kind. He is gripped by uneasiness. What if that man was Laius? What has to be emphasized here is Sophocles' extraordinary insistence on expressing the psychological shock. According to the archaic representation of feelings, it is not the human who experiences the feeling; it is the feeling that takes hold of the human. Moreover, the words used to designate Oedipus's anxiety are of an entirely exceptional scope and rarity. The expression "restlessness of soul" (*planèma*) denotes, literally, the wandering of a traveler, and it is in this sense that it is used in Aeschylus's *Prometheus Bound*.[73] But the transposition to psychological vocabulary that we find here is unique. As for the noun "tumult" (*anakinèsis*), it is not attested elsewhere in Greek tragedy, either in the literal or the psychological sense. There is no doubt that Sophocles wanted to use these exceptional means of expression to mark the decisive moment that brings about the beginning of the reversal, the passage where anxiety and doubt begin to substitute themselves for certainty and anger, where Oedipus's extroverted feelings reconstructing the conduct of others are swept away by introverted feelings forcing him to question himself.

This shock has consequences. When Jocasta returns, after this scene and the chorus's song, to pray to Apollo, she does so because she finds Oedipus's state alarming:

> Oedipus excites his soul excessively with all sorts of grief, as he does not judge the new things from the old, like a man of sense, but is under the control of the speaker, if he speaks of frightful things. Since, then, I can do no good by counsel, to you, Lycean Apollo—for you are nearest—I have come as a suppliant with these symbols of prayer, that you may find us some escape from uncleanliness. For now we are all afraid, like those who see fear in the helmsman of their ship.[74]

Thus Oedipus's state has worsened since he retired to the palace. This is another example in which a major psychological change in the hero has taken place offstage, between two episodes.[75] In fact, before exiting, Oedipus had ended on a note of hope, which he drew from another detail given by Jocasta regarding Laius's murder: the plural "the murderers." If there were several murderers, as said, then he is not the murderer! In mathematics, one is not equal to several![76] Now, in the report Jocasta gives to the chorus, she no longer mentions that glimmer of hope. Oedipus is in the grip of anxiety; he has lost his lucidity, he is allowing himself to be influenced by pessimistic arguments, and he no longer listens to Jocasta when she tries to comfort him. The scope of Jocasta's concern has to be acknowledged when she compares Oedipus to a ship's pilot. She fears—and she is not the only one—that the king, in the crisis he is going through, might no longer be capable of guiding the ship of the city. It is remarkable that it is the queen who continues to be concerned about the political responsibility, whereas Oedipus, obsessed by his multiple fears about himself, has forgotten the city. But at the same time Jocasta, whose lucidity seems intact, resorts in her desperation to the god about whom she dared to say, at the end of the preceding episode, to the great indignation of the chorus, that the oracle given Laius had not been fulfilled. Just as Oedipus, in his inability to control the city's illness, had appealed to the Delphic Apollo, Jocasta, in her inability to control Oedipus's depression, calls on Apollo near the palace. And she also makes this decision in the interval between two episodes, a decision that is a reversal powerfully stressed by Sophocles. Whereas the chorus, commenting again on the preceding scene in which Jocasta questioned Apollo's prophecies, concludes its song by expressing its dread upon seeing that Apollo has been deprived of all honor, the spectator sees Jocasta coming to say a prayer to Apollo. The contrast is striking, but Jocasta's reversal can be explained psychologically as a reaction after the worsening of Oedipus's anxiety.

If we have taken the time to examine closely several "psychological" passages in Oedipus's development during the first stage, in which he gradually passes from lucidity to distraction under the impact of two feelings, anger and anxiety, it is in order to forestall two possible objections that have different origins.

Here is the first: can the theater still be explained by psychology? Doesn't that amount to psychologism? The answer is that for the ancients, in any case—and the texts are there to prove it—emotions or feelings are the human motor of theatrical action, and of action period, far more than reason is. The agreement we have shown between the man of the theater Sophocles and the historian Thucydides is illuminating in this respect. Feelings lead reason astray, even if anger and anxiety have inverse effects. But the sophistication of the psychology in Sophocles' work goes beyond this opposition. Reason can be at the very origin of the birth of feeling. If Oedipus's anger begins with the seer, that is reasonable because the seer refuses to speak for the welfare of the city. In Sophocles, there is no contradiction between dramatic effects and psychological analyses. They are often the two sides of single reality. Spectacular dramatic reversals may occur without any new event coming from outside: here, for example, the change in Jocasta's attitude with respect of Apollo. But these reversals find their explanation in the relational psychology of the characters: here, Oedipus's anxiety, which has become, in Jocasta's view, pathological, and as a result, Jocasta's decision, faced with her inability to reason with the sick man, to say a supplicating prayer to the god. In the theater, of course, the dramatic takes priority over the psychological. It is the effects that are shown. But even if the effects are shown first, they subsequently explained.

Here is the second objection: to interpret these psychological passages, why not use the advances made by the science of psychology since Freud and his successors, especially when Oedipus is involved? In fact, just as for the history of medicine, it is appropriate to examine the differences between the ancient and modern descriptions of illnesses before making any retrospective diagnosis, so in the domain of psychology it is appropriate to emphasize first the gap between the ancients' conception and that of moderns before making what might be called a retrospective psychological diagnosis. Now, the passage on the beginning of the anxiety is instructive regarding the most archaic Greek representation of the feelings. They are—like illnesses, in fact—forces that come from outside and take the individual in their grip. This is the opposite of depth psychology. In the second passage concerning anxiety, the "various anxieties" that obsess Oedipus are the fear of being the murderer, of living with the wife of his victim, of being punished in accord with his own edict, and of being exiled, but not yet of being his father's murderer and the husband of his mother. At his point, for the ancients Oedipus's depressed state has nothing to do with the modern concept of the "Oedipus complex."[77]

Coming to Awareness in *Oedipus the King*: Doubling and Orchestration

In order for Oedipus to definitively realize what he is, new information from outside is necessary. Aristotle sees in Oedipus's coming to awareness the combination of what he calls peripeteia and discovery. He defines peripeteia as a reversal in the plot and gives Oedipus (that is, Sophocles' *Oedipus the King*) as his example:

> A "reversal" is a change of the situation into the opposite . . .—like the man in the *Oedipus* who came to cheer Oedipus and rid him of his anxiety about his mother by revealing his parentage and changed the whole situation.[78]

Then he defines discovery as the passage from ignorance to knowledge, bringing about a passage from hatred to friendship or from friendship to hatred, between people destined for good fortune or ill. And he adds:

> Discovery is most effective when it coincides with reversals, such as that involved by the discovery in the *Oedipus*.[79]

Aristotle thus sees both peripeteia and discovery in the scene with the Corinthian messenger, or more precisely in the second part of that scene. In the first part, the messenger has just announced the death of Polybus, Oedipus's alleged father, which rejoiced Jocasta and then Oedipus, who thinks that the oracle of Apollo according to which he would kill his father has not been fulfilled. But immediately after his joy, Oedipus's anxiety emerges anew, like a hydra's head. The oracle also told him he would marry his mother. He tells the messenger about this fear, and it is then that the messenger gives him the second bit of information to which Aristotle refers. To calm Oedipus's fresh anxiety, the messenger hastens to reveal to him that he is not the son of Polybus and his wife Merope; instead, he himself saved his life by sheltering him in the Cithaeron mountains after having received him from one of Laius's shepherds. Thus we do in fact have a peripeteia in this scene, as Aristotle says, insofar as the two bits of information provided by the messenger bring first joy, then stupefaction. But contrary to what Aristotle says, Oedipus's discovery is not contemporary with this peripeteia. It is Jocasta's discovery that is contemporary. To understand, she had information that Oedipus was to receive only from Laius's servant, whose assignment had been to abandon the infant Oedipus in order to avoid the fulfillment of the oracle given to Laius, according to which he was to die at his own son's hands.

Thus Jocasta and Oedipus make discoveries at different times, producing the kind of doubling of effects that we have seen is characteristic of Sophocles' art. In this way, he can oppose to the woman's silent discovery the man's more theatrical discovery, and at the same time make the woman leave terribly misunderstood. She endures in silence this misunderstanding, in addition to the revelation that she has been her own son's wife. When at the end of the scene Oedipus questions the shepherd who gave Laius the child, she responds evasively, now that she has understood. But Oedipus, angry at Jocasta for being evasive, just as he had been angry with the seer who did not want to reveal the truth, will misunderstand Jocasta's intentions. In Sophocles, human anger is by nature the feeling that sets the imagination on the wrong track. It is the source of incomprehension of the other and of error about oneself. Oedipus will imagine that it is a feeling of shame about his obscure origin that dictates the attitude of Jocasta, who he thinks too proud of her nobility. Tragic irony calls for him to be at the opposite pole from the truth in this final moment of error.

It is only after the meeting with the Corinthian messenger and the Theban shepherd that Oedipus finally understands. Here is the moment of the discovery:

> Oh, oh! All brought to pass, all true. Light, may I now look on you for the last time—I who have been found to be accursed in birth, accursed in wedlock, accursed in the shedding of blood.[80]

With a striking and yet rhetorical brevity, Oedipus assesses a whole life under the sign of the forbidden. Now that what was hidden has been brought to light, Oedipus wants to flee this light, and he rushes into the palace.

Oedipus's discovery is immediately orchestrated by that of the chorus in a magnificent stasimon entirely devoted to reflection on Oedipus's fate. From the

outset, the chorus generalizes in an exclamation on humanity based on Oedipus's
example:

> Alas, generations of mortals, how mere a shadow I count your life! Where,
> where is the mortal who attains a happiness which is more than apparent and
> doomed to fall away to nothing? Your fate warns me—yours, unhappy Oedi-
> pus—to call no earthly creature blessed.[81]

In this first strophe, the chorus reflects both mathematically and poetically
on the value of human destiny. Mathematically, because the life of a man is equal
to zero. And the chorus explains by considering the question of happiness. It
continues to speak mathematically, but it adds a cosmic metaphor. A man would
have to have a quantity of happiness superior to that which makes him appear
and decline like a star. But having before its eyes the destiny of Oedipus, who
was the most fortunate and the most unfortunate—a subject it develops in the
rest of its song—the chorus concludes that this quantity of good fortune necessary to escape change does not exist among humans. What is implicit here is that
this quantity of fortune exists only among the gods. This reflection on human
destiny, drawn from the spectacle of Oedipus's fate, is not disembodied. The
chorus ends by turning its attention back to itself:

> Alas, child of Laius, would that I had never seen you. I wail as one who pours
> a dirge from his lips. It was you who gave me new life, to speak directly, and
> through you darkness has fallen upon my eyes.[82]

This reflection on oneself is the last stage in the recognition of the misfortune
of the other. From awareness of the destiny of the other arises first a general view
of the human condition, and then a reflection on itself. The chorus's destiny
mirrors, mutatis mutandis, that of Oedipus. It has lived at the hero's pace, re-
covering its life when he freed the city from the Sphinx and then became its king,
and it is now cast into the sleep of death by the reversal of the destiny of the man
who was its king. Finally, the self-reflection is accompanied by pity for the other.
This double reflexive movement when faced by a paradigmatic spectacle is comparable to that we have already observed in Odysseus after the spectacle of Ajax's
madness.[83] But although the double movement of generalization on human
fragility and self-reflection is comparable, the situation is different, because the
characters are not the same: the great Odysseus in *Ajax* feels a reasonable pity
for his enemy, while the modest chorus in *Oedipus the King* feels a frightened
and desperate pity. It would have preferred not to know Oedipus in order to
escape such pain!

Discoveries in Sophocles' Theater: The Example of *The Women of Trachis*

Jocasta's silent discovery, Oedipus's laconic but impressive discovery of himself,
and the chorus's simultaneously ample and desperate discovery—they all react

in accord with their nature and social position in the framework of the structures of the tragedy. There is thus not a single discovery but several. To identify in *Oedipus the King* Oedipus's discovery alone, as Aristotle does, would be an over-simplification. If we want to grasp the Sophoclean world in all its complexity and nuances, we must therefore situate the hero's discovery in the multiplicity of discoveries that each tragedy offers.

We will take *The Women of Trachis* as another example. As in *Oedipus the King*, separate discoveries have already been made by the wife and the husband, and their manifestations are comparable, even though the situation is very different. Deianira's discovery takes place in two stages: the first is the interpretation of a sign concerning the destructive power—and not the seductive power, as she thought—of the ointment with which she smeared the gift sent to Heracles; the second is her son Hyllus's report confirming that the gift prepared to win back her husband's love has led to consequences opposed to the ones she sought. She then becomes definitively aware of her tragic act and goes off in silence, like Jocasta.[84] As for Heracles, he will later learn the meaning of the two oracles that concerned him.[85] Here is the moment when the hero discovers the truth about his destiny:

> Oh oh! Wretch that I am! Oh, I am dying!
> I perish; I can see the light no longer!
> Alas, I understand my plight too well.[86]

We recall the moment when Oedipus becomes aware of the reality of his fate:

> Oh, oh! All brought to pass, all true. Light, may I now look on you for the last time—I who have been found to be accursed in birth, accursed in wedlock, accursed in the shedding of blood.[87]

These two discoveries are formally very close. They are preceded by the same doubled interjection of despair: "Oh! Oh!" In Sophocles, this double cry is a kind of signal of the discovery.[88]

In *The Women of Trachis*, in addition to these two discoveries made by the wife and the husband, we must not forget a third discovery inserted between the two others, that of the son, Hyllus. It is less visible, because it takes place in the virtual space of the palace, during the discovery of his mother's corpse. However, it is fully brought to light in the nurse's account. When she sees that her mistress intends to commit suicide, the nurse runs to find Hyllus. But when she returns with him, they find the woman's body pierced by a two-edged dagger thrust between the liver and the diaphragm:

> Her son screamed when he saw her, for he knew
> that he had driven her to this in anger,
> learning too late from servants that her deed
> was done in ignorance, at the Centaur's bidding.[89]

Hyllus's discovery arises from a spectacle: the suicide of Deianira. Seeing it instantly leads to understanding it: the son feels responsible for his mother's death, because in his anger he had wrongly accused her of being his father's murderer. Understanding thus leads to self-reflection, the perception of one's own errors and their cause, that infamous anger of which it was said that it is the source of blindness regarding the other. Here, comprehension is manifested not in words, but by the expression of pain: Hyllus explodes in groans; then, in the rest of the account, the nurse describes in great detail Hyllus's acts of desperation and affection for his mother. Pathos is one of the effects of the tragic discovery.

But the discovery could not take place without new information coming from the outside. Seeing Deianira's dead body would not, by itself, lead to understanding. One of the servants has just told Hyllus that Deianira was an involuntary killer who was the victim of the centaur Nessus's advice. That is the new information that comes from the outside and makes the discovery possible.

However, this new information arrives too late. That is one of the essential characteristics of the tragic discovery: it takes place when the acts have already occurred. Hyllus comes too late to save his mother. The dagger has already pierced her body. The same holds true for his mother's discovery. When Deianira discovers the sign that the ointment is dangerous, it is already too late. The gift has already been sent. Deianira analyzes the situation clearly:

> And so I know not what to think. I see
> only that I have done a dreadful deed.
> Why—for what reason—should the beast whose death
> I caused have shown me kindness as he died?
> It cannot be! No, wishing to destroy
> his slayer, he deceived me. I have learned
> too late, when learning can avail no longer![90]

The mother's and the son's discoveries thus resemble one another—both come too late. Even though they are independent of each other, the spectator can connect these discoveries and draw lessons by comparing them, especially in their partial and subjective aspects. As we have just seen, the son accuses himself of ultimately being his mother's murderer, just as he had accused his mother of being his father's murderer. But the spectator, because he has heard Deianira, knows that even without her son's anger, she would have committed suicide.[91] Thus he understands that the son is exaggerating when he accuses himself of murdering his mother. But he cannot yet understand how partial his mother's discovery was. During most of *The Women of Trachis* Sophocles does not place the spectator in the position of a god. The complete knowledge that transcends human limitations is discovered by the spectator only at the moment when Heracles himself becomes aware of his destiny.

As we have seen regarding Hyllus and Deianira, a discovery supposes a trigger, a sign or knowledge coming from outside. This also holds true for Heracles.

Despite having long known the two oracles, he has not understood their current relevance. He lacks an additional bit of knowledge. It is here that we can savor the subtlety with which the son's and the father's discoveries are connected in *The Women of Trachis*. Hyllus's discovery, as we have seen, came too late to enable him to save his mother. Nonetheless, his remorse will not be completely useless. If Hyllus has not been able to save his mother's life, he can try to rehabilitate her after her death. That is what he will do in speaking to his father. The task is a hard one, because Heracles' violent anger at his wife is at its height. But Hyllus takes advantage of a silence to act, both timidly and courageously, as his mother's advocate. First he tells his father about his mother's death and then exonerates her:

> *Hyllus:* The truth is this: she erred, yet she meant good.
> *Heracles:* Base villain! was it good to kill your father?
> *Hyllus:* When she beheld your new bride she endeavored
> to win you with a love charm, but she erred.
> *Heracles:* What man of Trachis deals in drugs so strong?
> *Hyllus:* The Centaur Nessus long ago convinced her
> to use this potion to inflame your passion.[92]

It is at this point that Heracles suddenly becomes aware of his misfortune and cries out *Iou! Iou!* For the spectator, the surprise is total, because the information that provokes Heracles' discovery is the same information that triggered Hyllus's discovery: the centaur Nessus's trick. But the effects of this information are radically different. Through it, the son discovers his mother's innocence, while the father discovers his own destiny. Their natures differ, but especially the knowledge preceding the information differs. A little further on, Heracles reveals the content of the old oracle that he alone knew:

> My father prophesied to me of old that none who breathed would ever take my life, but one already dead and gone to Hades. And now this beast, the Centaur, as the god foretold, though dead, has torn my life away.[93]

The spectators discover this last bit of information at the same time as Hyllus does, and it allows them to make a final discovery of all the forces that rule the characters' destiny. Only at that moment do they acquire the status of omniscient spectators. And, even though their attention is focused on the character of Heracles, they can, by a retrospective reflection, gauge the partial aspect of Deianira's discovery and pursue further her exoneration already begun by Hyllus. In the end, she has been merely the instrument of the vengeance taken by the dead centaur that was foreseen and even programmed. By whom? Certainly by Zeus, the source of the oracles. Why? The answer to that question is less clear. The spectators, even when omniscient, are ultimately not gods. However, their understanding of the spectacle becomes more refined along with that of the characters.

The Effects of Tragic Discovery: Lamentation, Reflection; The Case of Creon in *Antigone*

We now come to the third and last stage in the tragic reversal, the one that precedes the discovery. What effects does the discovery have on the characters? Here we should distinguish the characters who discover their own tragic reality from those who discover someone else's tragic reality. In fact, even if the other is the most cherished person, it seems that a distance remains. Ajax discovers his dishonor and ends up committing suicide. Tecmessa discovers Ajax's corpse and does not commit suicide, even though she has declared that he was everything for her. However, the distinction is sometimes difficult to draw. In *Antigone*, Eurydice, Haemon's mother, commits suicide after learning of her son's death.

It seems possible to draw a distinction between those who are struck dumb by the revelation and those who cry out in despair. The paradox is that the heroes lament, whereas the women fall silent. We have seen three women leave in silence: Deianira, Eurydice, and Jocasta. On the other hand, we hear the men exclaim: "Oh, I am destroyed, undone! (*olōla*)." This is the case for Aegisthus, and for Heracles, who even repeats the exclamation.[94] Nevertheless, the opposition must be qualified. We also hear another woman, Tecmessa, make the same exclamation when she discovers Ajax's body.[95] And Jocasta, even though she leaves silently without explaining her departure, cries out *Iou! Iou!* on learning Oedipus's fate.[96] Moreover, the women, once they have retreated into silence, lament inside the palace, as we learn from the messengers' accounts.[97] Nonetheless, the men's lamentation seems more spectacular than that of the women, even inside the palace. Oedipus, whose discovery was so impressive in its restraint when he was onstage, shrieks like a madman once he has gone back into the palace, where he is surrounded by his servants and occupies their whole attention.[98]

The longest lamentation in the visible space is that of Creon in *Antigone*, when he returns with the body of his son at the head of a funeral cortege formed by all his servants.[99] Sophocles, by choosing to insert this lamentation into the framework of a long, semilyrical dialogue in which Creon sings and the chorus speaks, has given it all the possible pathos. Here is the beginning of it:

> *Creon:* Ah, the blunders of an unthinking mind, blunders of rigidity, yielding death! Oh, you witnesses of the killers and the killed, both of one family! What misery arises from my reasonings! Haemon, you have died after a young life, youngest and last of my sons! O God! You have departed not by your foolishness, but by my own!
> *Chorus:* Ah, how late you seem to see the right!
> *Creon:* God, I have mastered the bitter lesson! But then, then, I think, some god struck me on my head with a crushing weight, and drove me into sav-

age paths,—ah!—and overthrew my joy to be trampled on! Ah, the labors men must toil through![100]

Despite the seer Tiresias's clear warnings and his urging to be wise, Creon allowed himself to be led astray by his anger and obstinacy. It took the chorus's intervention to get him to take the seer's revelations into account and revoke two decisions: the first to prohibit Polynices' burial and the second to confine Antigone in an underground prison. But the reversal came too late, as the messenger reports: Antigone has committed suicide by hanging herself; Haemon, after seeking to kill his father, has turned his weapon against himself. Creon returns and laments. Everything contributes to the expression of the intensity of the emotion: the abundance of exclamations, the echoing repetitions, the juxtaposition of contraries, the metaphors, and especially the rhythm chosen, the rhythm that corresponds to the strongest degree of emotion in Greek tragedy;[101] the musical score is all that is lacking to restitute the whole effect produced by Creon's sung lamentation.

In this discovery, lamentation and reflection are intimately connected. Creon repeatedly acknowledges his mistakes arising from bad decisions and the consequences of his errors. The semantic field of error is the richest of all Sophocles' tragedies.[102] Even before abruptly leaving to liberate Antigone, Creon had already sensed where the right path lay:

> I am held by the fear that it is best to keep the established laws to life's very end.[103]

Now he feels responsible for his son's death, and the errors that he henceforth acknowledges had already been lucidly denounced by his son during their confrontation:

> *Haemon:* Because I see you making a mistake and committing injustice.
> *Creon:* Am I making a mistake when I respect my own prerogatives?
> *Haemon:* Yes. You do not respect them, when you trample on the gods' honors.[104]

Creon had also remained deaf to Tiresias's warnings when the seer pointed out his mistakes still more clearly and urged him to reconsider his decision to prohibit the dead man's burial:

> Think, therefore, on these things, my son. All men are liable to err. But when an error is made, that man is no longer unwise or unblessed who heals the evil into which he has fallen and does not remain stubborn. Self-will, we know, invites the charge of foolishness.[105]

This reminder of the warnings previously addressed to Creon merely makes his change of mind more striking, even if it comes belatedly when he is facing the tragic consequences of his folly. For in *Antigone* Creon was not a hero who is the victim a destiny he does not understand, as was Oedipus in *Oedipus the King*. He seems to be the master of his fate, not being subject to an oracular prediction. This difference between Creon's destiny and that of Oedipus can be seen in the seer's remarks in the two tragedies. In *Antigone*, they are made when there is still time: "Realize that once more now you are poised on fortune's razor-edge";[106] in *Oedipus the King*, they occur when it has long been too late: "The future will come of itself, though I shroud it in silence."[107] Oedipus's fate was already sealed before the tragedy began. In contrast, the shift in Creon's destiny takes place within the time of the tragedy. It occurs at the very center of the scene with the seer, at the moment when Creon remains deaf to Tiresias's appeals urging him to atone for his crime, and just before the seer predicts the misfortunes to come. From that point on we understand that Creon is taking responsibility for the deaths that have occurred, the death of his son, and then, a few moments later, that of his wife, when the messenger is about to emerge from the palace to inform him of them.

However, even as he acknowledges his own responsibility, Creon attributes his error to a divinity who has struck him a heavy blow, pushed him along the wild paths of madness, and overturned his happiness. This is one more proof of the continued importance of the ancients' simultaneously objective and subjective conception of what we call inner life. It depends on a causality that was inextricable but not contradictory in fifth-century Athens, except for rationalists like Thucydides or the Hippocrates of the Sacred Disease. Creon is responsible for his madness, but the madness comes from a god, a god who is all the more dangerous because he is anonymous.

The chorus is there to provide a frame for Creon's lamentation and to comment on it. It introduces it by announcing Creon's arrival, in recitative, and to state the theme that Creon will elaborate at the beginning of his lamentation: the king arrives, the chorus says, bearing in his arms the clear sign of his own errors.[108] The theme of error is thus stated and immediately echoed in Creon's song. Then, the first time that the chorus speaks in the middle of Creon's song, it is calmly to recall—the chorus speaks in this semilyrical dialogue!—his belated lucidity.[109] But we know that for the Greeks, even information received belatedly is a source of wisdom.[110] Deaf to warnings, humans learn through suffering. In conclusion, the chorus crowns Creon's lamentation with a moral lesson given in recitative, which generalizes Creon's particular case.

Thus everything seems clear in this tragic conclusion whose moral is traditional and analogous to that of *Ajax*: wisdom is the first condition of happiness: it consists in not committing any impiety with regard to the gods. For those who have not understood this, punishment is there to teach them wisdom belatedly. Hence everything seems to be clear! And yet there is a silence astonishing to the spectator. Antigone is not even mentioned in this conclusion. Creon does not lament his fate. His lamentation is limited to the narrow circle of his family, his son and his wife. He says nothing at all about rehabilitation! And what will be done with Antigone's body? The young woman who sacrificed herself for the burial of her brother remains an anonymous corpse. What a strange paradox! This complete silence can only be oppressive for the spectator. Sophocles' treatment of Antigone is ultimately as mysterious as the character.

The last words of Creon's lamentation are words of deep despondency—one might even say they reflect the crushing weight of an excessively heavy destiny. His lamentation has always been accompanied by reflection. But it leads to neither a decision nor a promise of action or an action. It is an annihilation endured passively, without suicide:

> Lead me away, my servants, lead me from here with all haste, who am no more than a dead man![111]

The Effects of Tragic Discovery: The Case of Oedipus in *Oedipus the King*

The effects of Oedipus's discovery in *Oedipus the King* are comparable to Creon's in *Antigone*, even if Oedipus's despondency is reflected not only in lamentation but also in an act, that of self-mutilation.

In studying the characters, we have already had occasion to compare the initial development of these two "political heroes" who, seeking to exercise the office of king as well as they can, come to be distracted by anger in their confrontation with others and by the fear of a conspiracy. We have also seen how, when these two heroes pass from happiness to unhappiness, the political dimension fades away when they are faced by personal misfortunes whose significance becomes universal.[112] Let us now complete the comparison by showing that the final dramatic sequences, starting with the moment when the two heroes become aware of their errors or their misfortunes, have important analogies. In the two tragedies, the discovery is located at the very end of the episode preceding the chorus's last song.[113] The only difference is that the discovery is completed in the case of Oedipus, whereas it is beginning in Creon's case.[114] These discoveries are followed by the heroes' abrupt departures. Then comes the chorus's last song, during which is the tragic development of what happens in the virtual space, outside in *Antigone*, and inside the palace in *Oedipus the King*.[115] This song by the chorus is followed, at the beginning of the exode, by the arrival of a messenger coming to report the tragedy experienced by each of the two heroes, after they abruptly leave the stage and enter the virtual space.[116] One of the heroes, Creon, sees his son's suicide, while the other, Oedipus, sees Jocasta, his mother and at the same time his wife, after her suicide. But whereas Creon has escaped his son's sword, Oedipus has put out his eyes with Jocasta's pins. In both tragedies, the spectators witness the hero's appearance. Both heroes lament in semi-lyrical dialogues with the chorus, composed of two strophe/antistrophe pairs in which the emotional effect sought is technically the same, through the contrast between the part spoken by the chorus and the hero's song in the same jerky rhythm.[117] Given the similarity of these dramatic and lyrical structures, it is not surprising that the two heroes' confusion leads to almost identical requests addressed to the chorus at a comparable point in the dialogue: "Lead me away, my servants, lead me from here with all haste, who am no more than a dead man!" Creon sings to the chorus in the second strophe, "lead me from the land, lead me from here, the utterly lost, the thrice-accursed, the mortal most hateful to the gods!" Oedipus sings, also in the second stophe.[118] Even though they want to flee, the heroes will end up, in fact, going back into the palace.

The analogous lyrical and dramatic structures thus emphasize the analogy of situations and reactions. Of course, within these same structures, the characters' reactions, while coinciding remarkably in the desire to escape, are oriented differently. Creon bemoans what he decided and what he did, taking responsibility for his errors, because he is to blame for a destiny that was still open. Oedipus, for his part, bemoans what he is, because his destiny was closed. On the other hand, what he takes responsibility for is the act he has just committed, his self-mutilation. When the chorus asks Oedipus which divinity led him to put out his eyes, his reply is significant:

> *Chorus:* Man of dread deeds, how could you quench your vision in this way?
>   What divinity urged you on?
> *Oedipus:* It was Apollo, friends, Apollo who brought these troubles to pass,
>   these terrible, terrible troubles. But the hand that struck my eyes was none
>   other than my own, wretched that I am![119]

Oedipus discovers not only his misfortunes, but also their cause. He now recognizes Apollo's work, which the seer had predicted to him and which, in his folly, he had denied, to the great indignation of the chorus.[120] He acknowledges the gods' power, without making any protest or claim against them. That is an essential message of *Oedipus the King*. But Oedipus takes sole responsibility for the act he has just committed, just as Creon took responsibility for his errors. All the same, with regard to the gods, Oedipus's position is different from Creon's. Whereas Creon admitted a twofold causality to explain his acts, saying that he was responsible and at the same time recognizing the intervention of a nameless deity, Oedipus rejects this conception, which is implicit in the chorus's question: he makes a clear distinction between his destiny, which is determined by an identified god, and his act, for which he alone is responsible.

The importance attributed to this act leads to a variant in the dramatic structures. The semilyrical dialogue concludes the tragedy *Antigone* before the chorus's traditional speech: it ends with Creon's sung lamentation expressing once again his desire to go far away ("Lead me away, I beg you, a rash, useless man").[121] On the other hand, in *Oedipus the King* the semilyrical dialogue ends with a remark by the chorus that will provoke a new turn in the action.[122] The chorus expresses its perplexity: why did he blind himself rather than committing suicide? Oedipus justifies his act in a speech delivered with an astonishing vivacity, in spite of his misfortune. This new development adds, with respect to *Antigone*, an additional perspective on the hero. A person's true nature is also revealed in his reaction to misfortune. The annihilation for which Oedipus takes responsibility contrasts with that to which Creon is subjected.

The Effects of Tragic Discovery: A Decision and a Reconquest of the Self through Suicide; Deianira in the *Women Of Trachis* and Ajax in *Ajax*

In Oedipus's case, the hero does not simply endure misfortune. He responds with an act that is apparently impulsive, but is in reality claimed and justified after the fact. Nonetheless, the hero does not control his destiny. Confronting the new leader of the city, Oedipus has to submit by going into the palace and separating himself from his daughters. And he is no longer spared humiliation. He, who was initially the all-powerful king, compared to a god, has finally to hear, not even a word of consolation, but rather a stern reminder: "Do not wish to be master in all things."[123]

In the case of other Sophoclean heroes, the tragic discovery leads, in accord with decisions made in advance, to a total annihilation, suicide, the only solution considered to preserve honor. The clearest case is that of Deianira, but the most famous is that of Ajax.

Deianira's case is the most explicit because the moments when she becomes aware, decides, and acts follow one another in a relatively short span of time in the tragedy. We have seen that Deianira's discovery takes place in two stages.[124] As soon as she perceives the first sign, the disintegration of the bit of wool, she becomes completely aware of the gravity of her act. The account of Heracles' suffering merely provides confirmation. But what is remarkable is that as soon as she sees the first sign, after gauging her act's consequences, which seem to her ineluctable, she announces her decision to die with Heracles to save her honor:

> I am resolved that, if he is to be brought down, at the same time I too will die along with him in the selfsame fall. No woman could bear to live with a reputation for evil, if she cares above all that her nature is not evil.[125]

When did she decide? That is not made explicit. Probably inside the palace, before coming out, once she had weighed the consequences of the marvel she had just witnessed.[126] In any case, this is a definitive decision.[127] And it will be put into effect immediately after the confirmation, by the account of Heracles' suffering, of what Deianira had foreseen. There is no longer any place for words. After a silent departure, the act occurs inevitably, because Deianira has determined her own destiny in advance.

In the case of Ajax, the discovery occurs gradually starting from the moment when Tecmessa announces to the chorus his return to rationality after his fit of madness.[128] The main stages in the reconquest of the self, from the return to reason to the suicide, have been traced in our study of the character, and there is no need to return to them here.[129] But in a comparative perspective on the effects of the discovery, we can now take up the initial scene in which Ajax appears after he has recovered his wits.[130] This is once again a semilyrical dialogue between the hero and the chorus, exactly as in *Antigone* or *Oedipus the King*: the hero sings in a jerky meter, and the chorus speaks.[131] It is no accident that this type of emotional scene appears in three tragedies in which the heroes reappear after becoming aware of their disaster. The difference has to do with the place of the commos. In *Antigone* and *Oedipus the King* it comes at the end of the tragedy, whereas in *Ajax* it comes near the beginning.

Like Oedipus, Ajax laments his misfortunes and becomes aware of the cause, a divinity's intervention:

> Ah, Darkness, my light! O Gloom of the underworld, to my eyes brightest-shining, take me, take me to dwell with you—yes, take me. I am no longer worthy to look for help to the race of the gods, or for any good from men, creatures of a day. No, the daughter of Zeus, the valiant goddess, abuses me to my destruction.[132]

Behind the periphrasis "the daughter of Zeus" stands Athena. Having recovered his wits after his fit of madness, Ajax is the first in his group—Tecmessa, the chorus—to understand Athena's role. His enemy Odysseus knows it already, and so do the spectators, even though they still do not know the reasons for the goddess's attitude. The spectators' complete discovery occurs later, when a messenger reports the seer Calchas's revelations regarding the hero's offenses against the goddess. Thus when he bemoans his fate, Ajax recognizes Athena's power, just as Oedipus recognizes Apollo's. The lyrical dialogue continues, moreover, in *Ajax*, as it does in *Oedipus the King*, with a long speech in which the hero, passing from song to speech, reflects on his destiny. The themes of the lyrical part are reworked in the spoken remarks. Ajax returns to the goddess's intervention:

> As it was, the daughter of Zeus, the grim-eyed, unconquerable goddess, tripped me up at the instant when I was readying my hand against them, and shot me with a plague of frenzy so that I might bloody my hands in these grazers. And those men exult to have escaped me—not that I wanted their escape. But if a god sends harm, it is true that even the base man can elude the worthier.[133]

Ajax has recognized, with astonishing lucidity, the goddess's intervention. His explanation corresponds exactly to the one given by Athena herself when she was speaking to Odysseus.[134] Ajax fully acknowledges the goddess's power. In this sense, the misfortune teaches a lesson in wisdom. But no reconciliation will follow. In his monologue before committing suicide, Ajax says not a word about the goddess, even though he addresses other gods. The silence is revelatory.

The Effects of Tragic Discovery: The Acceptance of Death

Starting with the moment when Heracles suddenly becomes aware of his destiny,[135] he does not lament at length, despite a brief moment of despair. He gives instructions to his son, then asks to be carried to his funeral pyre. And as he is about to leave, he addresses his soul:

> Come, then, before you awaken this plague, O my hardened soul, give me a bit
> of steel to bind my lips like stone to stone! Stop any cry, since the task you ac-
> complish, though by constraint, gives cause for joy.[136]

These are Heracles' last words. They reflect a superhuman effort to confront his last moments with dignity, remaining master over his pain. We might be astonished by the absence in the semilyrical dialogue of a spoken lamentation analogous to those we find in *Ajax*, *Antigone*, and *Oedipus the King* after the discovery. In truth, the discovery of the meaning of Zeus's oracles is only the confirmation of what Heracles suspected, namely that his illness was fatal. The intensity of the pain that he felt was already a sign of that. In fact, as soon as he arrives, he accuses his wife of having killed him.[137] In addition, his lamentation began at the outset, facing the violence of the crises of his illness and the explosion of his anger against his wife. It is at that moment that the hero sings in the course of a semilyrical dialogue that eventuates in a spoken declamation, following a lyrical and dramatic sequence that is entirely comparable to the one in *Ajax*.[138] Thus the final discovery takes place when Heracles has passed from singing to speaking. In Sophocles' older tragedies, that is, those preceding *Electra*, we do not find a single character who plunges twice into a despair that would justify two dialogues in which he would sing. The laws of technique and conception of characters work in the same direction. The heroes can have one period of weakness when faced by the intensity of physical or mental pain, but not two!

Reversed Discoveries: *Electra* Compared with *Antigone*

On the other hand, starting with *Electra*, changes occur. The most obvious of these—but it is not the only one—is that the last three tragedies do not end tragically for the heroes. It is one of the paradoxes of Greek tragedy that the reversal may move not only toward misfortune but also toward good fortune.[139] Electra's destiny is opposed to that of Antigone, even though their initial situations are analogous.[140] Both of them, out of loyalty to a dead man, violently oppose their entourage, and they are threatened with the same punishment, confinement in an underground prison. But one sees this punishment realized, because it is imposed by the established power, whereas the other escapes it, because the established power is overthrown. It goes without saying that such a divergence in fates elicits very different reactions. In the case of Antigone, who had decided to bury her brother, even without her sister's help, the discovery of her destiny can only be tragic, from the moment that she understands that she is condemned to an underground prison. Sophocles then uses the same technical framework as for Ajax: a lamentation in a semilyrical dialogue in which the character initially overwhelmed by emotion sings, while the chorus speaks, and then delivers a long speech reflecting on his destiny.[141] The same framework is used for Oedipus at the end of *Oedipus the King*.

On the other hand, in *Electra* we witness two inverse discoveries, which constitute an innovation with respect to the earlier tragedies; and from the technical point of view, they are both highlighted by the two dialogues in which Electra sings.

The first discovery is tragic, when the tutor informs Electra of Orestes' death. This news initially increases her despair, which is now justified not only by the absence but also the death of the avenger she has so long awaited. Her despair is expressed in a dialogue sung with the chorus.[142] However, this tragic discovery cannot be experienced by the audience in the same way as those in the preceding tragedies in which the hero became aware of an actual misfortune. Since the spectators know, because they have seen Orestes, that the news of his death is false, their distance from the tragedy that Electra experiences is of a different kind. To the distance usual in any play is added the distance connected with the spectators' knowledge that Electra's tragic discovery is erroneous. But Electra's error nonetheless reveals her true nature. In fact, after her sung lamentation, Electra reacts by making a decision intended to cope with the new situation. Deprived of her brother's help, she decides, despite her sister's refusal to join her, to carry out the vengeance herself. We find here a tragic discovery/decision sequence comparable to Deianira's.[143]

Electra's second discovery occurs when she and Orestes recognize each other. It is the inverse of a tragic discovery. To use Aristotle's terms, it is a change from ignorance to knowledge for two characters destined for good fortune.[144] In order to accentuate the revelation, the recognition scene is skillfully inserted in continuity with the first tragic discovery. In fact, when Orestes arrives carrying an urn that is supposed to contain his ashes, this leads to a further aggravation of Electra's despair. As Electra sees it, the account of Orestes' death has now been confirmed by concrete proof.[145] But it is the lamentation over the urn that will be the origin of the recognition, first of the sister by the brother, then of the brother by the sister.[146] This second discovery gives rise to a semilyrical dialogue in which Electra sings, but this time with joy. Her interlocutor is not, as in the dialogues in the earlier tragedies, the chorus, but Orestes. Still, the same contrast remains between Electra's singing and Orestes' speaking. This contrast continues to highlight the emotion of the character who sings in a jerky rhythm, here Electra's irrepressible joy, which Orestes tries to restrain to avoid compromising the execution of the vengeance.[147]

Sophocles, by adopting for his recognition scene a schema that he regularly used for his heroes' discoveries, produces by Electra's song an emotional intensity that we do not find in the corresponding scenes in either Aeschylus's *The Libation Bearers*[148] or Euripides' *Electra*.

Multiple Discoveries: Philoctetes' Awakenings and Deaths

Like *Electra*, *Philoctetes* is a tragedy about trickery. But the two characters who give their names to the two tragedies do not have analogous relationships to the plan for trickery.

Electra, while being the central character of the tragedy, is marginal with respect to Orestes' plan for vengeance. The proof of this is that her name is not even mentioned when Agamemnon's son gives the tutor his instructions at the beginning of the tragedy. Thus it is by accident that Electra will be involved in carrying out the ruse. She happens to be present when the tutor comes to tell her mother the news of Orestes' death. Then, after the recognition scene with her brother, Electra moves over into the camp of the originators of the ruse. Philoctetes, on the other hand, is central to the plan of deception. He is the one whom Odysseus has been assigned to bring back from Lemnos to Troy, because the presence of his bow with its infallible arrows is indispensable for taking the besieged city. He has planned to act using Neoptolemus as an intermediary, to avoid being recognized, and to proceed by trickery in order to get around the obstacle of the bow. Although he is very reluctant, Neoptolemus is assigned to win Philoctetes' trust by means of a deceptive story. Odysseus reserves the option of sending a false merchant, if he deems that best. Thus Philoctetes will react depending on the development of the ruse.

As in *Electra*, false discoveries arise from the execution of the ruse. In *Philoctetes*, the ruse is set up in two successive scenes, following a doubling that recalls that in *Electra*. First there is Neoptolemus's deceptive speech, which is comparable to that of the tutor in *Electra*, and then the arrival of the false merchant, which parallels Orestes' arrival.[149] Nonetheless, whereas the effect of the doubling of the trick merely reinforced the false discovery of Electra's misfortune by confirming Orestes' death, Sophocles multiplied the effects in *Philoctetes* by making the hero's false hopes and fears alternate. In fact, during the first stage of the ruse, Neoptolemus, through his deceptive report, gives Philoctetes the illusion that he has found a companion in misfortune and fills him with joy by agreeing to take him back to his homeland. But at the very moment that Philoctetes exclaims "O day of joy unsurpassed! Most delightful man,"[150] the false merchant arrives. This is the second stage of the ruse prepared by Odysseus. Mixing the true and the false, the alleged merchant tells Philoctetes that an expedition led by Odysseus and Diomedes has been sent to take him, willingly or unwillingly, to Troy. He therefore casts Philoctetes into anxiety after a short moment of joy. At the end of this second stage, Philoctetes' cry of despair ("Alas!")[151] contrasts with his cry of joy in the first stage.

However, unlike *Electra*, where the ruse is carried out in accord with the plan made in advance, the novelty introduced by Sophocles in his *Philoctetes* consists of two unforeseen events, one of which is Philoctetes' physical crisis, and the other Neoptomelus's moral crisis. These two events can be viewed in two ways, depending on whether the spectator considers them in the objective perspective of the execution of the ruse or in the subjective perspective of Philoctetes' coming to awareness.

Let us take Philoctetes' physical crisis first. It seems objectively to be an advance in the realization of the ruse, since Philoctetes, forced to entrust his bow to Neoptolemus so that he can guard it for the duration of the crisis, loses in fact what continued to be his strength. And yet, when Philoctetes awakes after the end of his crisis and recovers consciousness, he is very happy to see that Neoptolemus is still there with his bow. For Philoctetes, this awakening upon emerging from the crisis takes on all its significance by reference to the awakening that occurred ten years earlier, when he discovered the Atreids' betrayal, under analogous circumstances, after a sleep upon emerging from a crisis. The comparison is obvious, not only because Philoctetes had earlier recounted this awakening to Neoptolemus,[152] but because he clearly alludes to it by contrasting the young hero's noble and compassionate attitude with the Atreids' behavior:

> The Atreids, certainly, those valiant generals, had no heart to bear this burden so lightly.[153]

Hope is thus reborn in Philoctetes' heart after this awakening. But the spectator sees all the tragic irony in Philoctetes' blind trust in Neoptolemus. And yet, Sophocles' subtlety is such that the naïve terms in which Philoctetes praises Neoptolemus's noble nature, by contrasting it with that of the Atreids, are not entirely illusory. They have a dramatic effect and help trigger Neoptolemus's moral crisis.

Let us now examine that moral crisis. Objectively, it puts a premature end to the plan of deception and threatens to compromise the mission, since Neoptolemus, full of pity and remorse, is about to reveal the truth to Philoctetes. But from Philoctetes' point of view, this is the first contact with the reality of the situation. To pursue the comparison with *Electra*, this moment corresponds to Electra's discovery of the end of the ruse, that is, to Orestes' and Electra's mutual recognition. We see that from that point on, the destinies diverge. For what was for Electra the end of a long nightmare becomes for Philoctetes the beginning of a new tragedy.

In reality, when Philoctetes learns that he must leave for Troy, he makes a doubly painful discovery: the loss of any hope of returning to his homeland, and betrayal by a man whom he thought his friend. This discovery is expressed first in the cry "I am destroyed—ah, misery!—betrayed!"[154] And then, in the following scene, this first cry is echoed by a second: "Ah, me, I am sold, destroyed!"[155]

This is the signal for a second discovery, when Philoctetes sees Odysseus coming to prevent Neoptolemus from returning the bow. Finally, when Philoctetes, falling victim to his fierce resistance, sees his bow being taken away—because Odysseus has decided to leave and ordered Neoptolemus to follow him—he realizes that what is happening is what he feared at the very moment when he discovered Neoptolemus's betrayal. He finds himself abandoned once again, but this time he is separated from his bow, without which he cannot survive. This is when Sophocles inserts a lyrical dialogue between the hero and the chorus, which is characteristic of the most painful discoveries in his theater.[156] In this third tragic discovery, Philoctetes echoes the complaints he had already addressed to nature at the time when he learned of Neoptolemus's treachery, but his lamentation, which he now sings, acquires an unequaled amplitude and becomes a lamentation on his impending death, since he is deprived of any means of survival.[157] As for the reaction expected after the lamentation, it is elicited by the chorus's attempt to make him change his mind. The rapidity of the exchanges in the final lyric dialogue correspond to a moment of crisis in which superficial versatility and emotivity cannot shake his deep will to resist: Philoctetes first refuses to leave, and then, when the chorus pretends to be going away, he begs it to return, using an argument we have already heard Ismene make: "There is no reason for indignation when the words of one crazed by a storm of pain are senseless."[158] And when finally the chorus, having returned, asks him to follow it, Philoctetes, using his remaining energy, refuses to leave. His last word before returning to the cave is "I am nothing now, nothing anymore!"[159] Philoctetes' return to his cave resembles an acceptance of death.

Thus in the series of discoveries, those that belong to the time of the ruse are contrasted with those that follow it. Whereas during the period of the ruse, Philoctetes' three discoveries caused an alternation of hope, fear, and then hope again, from the moment that Neoptolemus puts an end to the ruse, Philoctetes' three other discoveries all go in the same direction, toward the perception of an increasingly tragic situation.

These tragic moments are dispelled by a new reversal; Neoptolemus's definitive change of mind, leading him suddenly to return the bow, despite Odysseus's opposition. Now that he has regained possession of the source of his strength, Philoctetes can first threaten with his infallible arrows Odysseus (who disappears in silence), and then recognize the real nature of Neoptolemus (who resumes his true identity).[160] Then one might expect the true persuasion of his new friend Neoptolemus, which is moreover guaranteed by a seer's prophecy, to convince Philoctetes. The surprise is that Philoctetes, despite an instant of hesitation, does not change. It therefore seems that we have returned to the initial situation: Neoptolemus, the victim of his promise to take Philoctetes home, will obey. But in a final reversal, the former possessor of the bow, Heracles, suddenly appears. It takes a god to definitively persuade the intractable Philoctetes to leave for Troy.

None of Sophocles' other tragedies contains such a series of discoveries and recognitions. From one new development to the next, it is as though we have fallen into a theater of intrigue. However, despite the spontaneity, what remains stable in the end is the vivacity, even the violence of Philoctetes' reactions to the diverse situations, the astonishing constancy of this character who has been— ever since his first recognition, the recognition of his first abandonment, which might be called foundational—filled with an inveterate resentment against those who cravenly betrayed him, a resentment stronger than death, but not stronger than the gods.

Oedipus at Colonus: A Discovery of the Future and a Justifying Reflection on the Past

In *Oedipus at Colonus*, as in *Oedipus the King*, there is a special moment when Oedipus becomes aware of his destiny. These two crucial moments deserve to be compared. They are very different. In *Oedipus the King*, this moment occurs toward the end of the tragedy, when Oedipus finally realizes all the horror of his past.[161] On the contrary, in *Oedipus at Colonus*, this moment is located at the beginning of the tragedy, when Oedipus is made aware, in an unexpected way, of his future. It is apparently a very ordinary moment, when Oedipus encounters the first resident of the place where he has come. Whereas the resident of Colonus courteously asks him to leave the stone on which he has just sat down, because it is in the forbidden part of a sanctuary, Oedipus, learning that the sanctuary is that of the Eumenides, far from obeying, brusquely replies:

> Then graciously may they receive their suppliant! Nevermore will I depart from my seat in this land.[162]

It is exactly at that moment that Oedipus, after being given an apparently insignificant piece of information, becomes aware of his destiny in a sort of sudden illumination that neither the resident of Colonus or the spectator can understand. The spectator's status is thus different in Oedipus's two discoveries. In *Oedipus the King*, the spectator was prepared for Oedipus's sinister discovery, at least by Jocasta's earlier discovery. In *Oedipus at Colonus*, Oedipus's reaction is a total surprise for the spectators. They cannot understand, because they do not yet have any information to build on. They have to wait until the following scene, after the resident of Colonus's departure, so that Oedipus, who has remained alone with Antigone, can say everything in a long prayer to the divinities, in which Sophocles explains his hero's discovery to the audience:

> Ladies of dread aspect, since your seat is the first in this land at which I have bent my knee, show yourselves not ungracious to Phoebus or to myself; who, when he proclaimed that doom of many woes, spoke to me of this rest after long years: on reaching my goal in a land where I should find a seat of the

Awful Goddesses and a shelter for foreigners, there I should close my weary life, with profit, through my having fixed my abode there, for those who received me, but ruin for those who sent me forth, who drove me away. And he went on to warn me that signs of these things would come, in earthquake, or in thunder, or in the lightning of Zeus. Now I perceive [*egnōka*] that in this journey some trusty omen from you has surely led me home to this grove.[163]

In *Oedipus at Colonus*, as in *Oedipus the King*, this discovery is connected with the Delphic oracle. But whereas in *Oedipus the King* the oracle predicts only misfortunes, in *Oedipus at Colonus* Sophocles has added the part of the oracle that foresees the end of these misfortunes.[164] And whereas the discovery in *Oedipus the King* bore on the oracles that had been fulfilled, in *Oedipus at Colonus* it bears on predictions that are to be fulfilled. The spectator learns the content of these predictions: having arrived in the sanctuary of the venerable goddesses, Oedipus must find the end of his misfortunes by being received by hosts to whom he will bring benefits. To be sure, the predictions remain somewhat ambiguous, because they do not say exactly what this end of misfortunes and this turning point in destiny will consist in. But the oracle makes sufficiently clear the signs that will announce the moment of its fulfillment: an earthquake, a thunderclap, or a thunderbolt sent by Zeus, all of which will in fact occur toward the end of the tragedy. Finally, the essential difference between *Oedipus the King* and *Oedipus at Colonus* proceeds from the fact that Oedipus's attitude toward the oracles has changed between the two tragedies. Oedipus now knows by experience that oracles are fulfilled. He no longer doubts their truth.

The way in which Oedipus suddenly recognizes the imminent realization of oracles relating to his own destiny in *Oedipus at Colonus* reminds us of the way in which Heracles understands the imminence of his final destiny in *The Women of Trachis*.[165] In both cases, even though the subjects and the characters are very different, the technique is the same. The discovery depends on a triggering element, an apparently insignificant answer given by a third party to a question asked by the hero. The name of the Eumenides mentioned here by the resident of Colonus in response to Oedipus's question about the identity of the divinities of the sanctuary that he has reached plays the same role as the name of the centaur Nessus mentioned by Hyllus in response to Heracles' question about the magician who created the alleged love philter that Deianira smeared on the tunic. These names immediately cause a buried memory to surge up in both heroes, an oracle whose meaning and relevance they now fully grasp. To the surprise of their interlocutors—and to that of the spectators—they both react instantaneously. The explanation of their reaction comes only in a second stage, through the oracle's utterance, whose content and meaning they explain: an imminent end for both of them. But despite these deep resemblances, the discovery in *Oedipus at Colonus* remains original, at least in its dramatic role, because it is not situated at the end of the tragedy, as in *The Women of Trachis*, but at the beginning. In the latter play, the discovery of the fulfillment of the oracles merely accelerates the denouement of the tragedy, which ends before their actual fulfillment: the spectator does not witness Heracles' death, even through the mediation of a messenger. In contrast, in *Oedipus at Colonus*, the fulfillment of the oracles takes place in the time of the tragedy and ends with Oedipus's heroization. We have already seen, in the discussion of oracles, how the signs of the oracle are manifested and fulfilled.[166] But what must be added here is that there is originality in the place and function of Oedipus's discovery of their fulfillment. This is Sophocles' only tragedy where a hero's discovery occurs at the beginning of the tragedy, and it is probably also the only one where this discovery is, in a way, a privileged experience of contact with the divine. Thus it becomes, from the outset, a driving force behind the character's action as he confronts the human obstacles that will rise up before him before the oracle's fulfillment, which will in fact be announced by signs. It even provides a new strength for examining within himself his own past.

The first obstacle Oedipus encounters is the chorus. And to overcome this obstacle, he is obliged to justify his past. We know that the elders who administer the deme and who form the chorus arrive in haste, because they have been informed of the presence of a stranger in the forbidden part of the sanctuary. They begin by forcing Oedipus to leave this forbidden precinct, where he was in fact under the protection of the divinities. As soon as they learn who he is, they immediately order Oedipus and his daughter to leave. Despite a sung supplication that moves the old men, the latter do not revise their decision, for religious reasons: they fear that Oedipus's presence will pollute the city and provoke the gods' wrath. That is when Oedipus, in a passionate speech, delivers a plea justifying his past and affirming his new status acquired through his discovery.

First, here is the justification of his past conduct addressed to the chorus:

> You then drive me from the land, afraid of my name alone? Not, surely, afraid of my person or of my acts; since my acts, at least, have been in suffering rather than doing—if I must mention the tale of my mother and my father, because of which you fear me. That know I full well. And yet how was I innately evil? I, who was merely requiting a wrong, so that, had I been acting with knowledge, even then I could not be accounted evil. But, as it was, all unknowing I went where I went—while they who wronged me knowingly sought my ruin.[167]

Facing a criminal whose acts they have heard about, the members of the chorus react out of fear, even though he has not yet spoken. It is now Oedipus himself who explains their fears by alluding vaguely to his conduct toward his mother and his father. Over time, Oedipus has developed considerably with regard to this past. This is part of what is to be learned from the comparison between Oedipus's reaction in *Oedipus the King* and *Oedipus at Colonus*. In *Oedipus the King*, at the moment when he becomes aware of his true origin and

the acts he has committed—parricide and incest—Oedipus felt a fear of himself
not unlike the fear the chorus feels now. He never dreamed of exonerating himself on the basic issues, and this has not failed to astonish modern readers. The
only justification he gives the chorus for his acts concern his self-mutilation, for
which he firmly asserts his responsibility.[168] Now that a long period of time
separates him from his past acts, now that he has learned from suffering and
time,[169] he can plead not guilty in a logical argument from which emotion is
absent. The argument is situated on two levels. First, on the level of traditional
justice, the murder of his father is not a criminal offense because he merely reacted to a provocation;[170] then, on the level of intentional justice, neither his
parricide nor his incest are criminal offenses, because he acted without knowing
what he was doing. From this twofold argument it emerges that his nature is not
evil. But in justifying himself, Oedipus has remained vague regarding the details
of his crimes. The chorus, even though it is convinced by the argument, is still
curious. Thus at the end of the first episode, in the first stasimon, which is a sung
dialogue, the chorus once again expresses to Oedipus its desire to know more.[171]
This time, the theme that occupies the whole stasimon is taken up again in the
mode of emotion.[172] But Oedipus's line of argument remains the same. The last
verse of the stasimon, in which Oedipus asserts his innocence ("Pure before the
law, without knowledge of my act, I have come to this!"), is fully comprehensible
by reference to his first plea. In each of the two parts of the verse, we find the
two levels of argumentation presented earlier: he is not guilty with respect to the
law, because he only responded to violence;[173] he is not responsible because he
acted in ignorance.[174] He could have stopped there. But Sophocles once again
gives an unprecedented scope to the theme in a plea made by Oedipus to demonstrate his innocence with respect to the accusations made by Creon on his
arrival from Thebes. The length of the speech (forty-three verses) is all the more
surprising because Creon's references to the parricide and the incestuous marriage are brief (only two verses).[175] The plea is dominated, as it was the first time,
by the argument, but it is inflated by the breath of indignation. The argument
remains the same: the accent is put on the involuntary character of his two acts,
the murder of his father and the marriage to his mother;[176] the supplementary
argument that the murder was provoked by a preceding aggression is not omit-
ted. But a new element appears, the explanation by the gods, mentioned briefly
at the beginning and at the end: the gods were angry at the family; it is they who
pushed Oedipus to murder.[177] These two references remain discreet and vague.
They are there only to reinforce the absence of culpability in the man who was
not the personal target of the gods' anger.

On the contrary, what emerges from his initial discovery is his conviction that
his status has now changed: he is no longer an exile without resources and de-
pendent on the charity of others; he has become someone capable of benefitting
others. This is probably the most original discovery in Sophocles' theater. Ordinarily, discovery involves recognizing a fatal error or a limitation. Here, what is

exceptional is the discovery of a new power granted by the gods, even if it is implicitly linked with death. Oedipus alludes to this in the first scene with the resident of Colonus, when he asks that a messenger be sent to bring the king of the country, Theseus, "so that by a small service he may find a great gain,"[178] and he does this even before the spectator can understand why. It is only in the following scene, when he learns the terms of the oracle, that the spectator understands that Oedipus will benefit those who accept him.[179] The theme reappears when Oedipus is in the presence of the chorus. And it is there that his formulation is most striking:

> I have come to you as one sacred and pious, bearing comfort for this people.[180]

Nowhere else in Sophocles' theater does a character call himself "sacred." This word was used at the beginning of *Oedipus at Colonus*, to designate the "sacred" place where Oedipus had come.[181] After his discovery, Oedipus has become sacred like the place, now that he has placed himself under the protection of the divinities of the sanctuary and that he believes the fulfillment of Apollo's oracles is imminent. He is to have a special destiny, a heroization that will take place gradually in the course of the tragedy. And it is no accident that Oedipus uses the word "sacred" again at the final moment when he leaves to go, at the god's summons, to his final resting place, the blind man asking his daughters to follow him:

> Children, follow me. For now in turn it is I that shine forth wondrously as a leader for you, as you were your father's. Onward. Do not touch me, but allow me unaided to find the sacred tomb where it is my fate to be buried in this land.[182]

It would be impossible to represent more clearly in the theatrical space the reversal of the destiny of a man whom the gods have caused to fall and whom they raise up again because they have chosen to make of him, after his death, a tutelary hero of the city of Athens. His tomb becomes a sacred site. And that is what Theseus, the king of Athens, confirms when he returns after having been the sole close witness to the miraculous disappearance reported by the distant witness, the messenger. When Oedipus's daughters express the wish to go see his tomb, Theseus replies:

> Children, he told me that no one should draw near that place, or approach with prayer the sacred tomb in which he sleeps. He said that, so long as I saw to this, I would always keep the country free from pain.[183]

Oedipus's tomb is a sacred but forbidden place, like the sanctuary of the Eumenides at the beginning of the tragedy. That is the necessary condition for the protection of the territory promised by the hero in the full sense of the term. The hero is not, in the end, closer to mortals than to goddesses. The same holy fear surrounds them both.

By the time that the Athenian spectators witnessed the miraculous disappearance of Oedipus at Colonus, the author of the tragedy, who had been born in Colonus, had himself disappeared, and had himself been heroized. The spectators could not have failed to perceive an analogy between the author's destiny and that of his character. The fact that this was, as it turned out, the end of Sophocles' work seemed to coincide with the end of the man and thus to contain a kind of premonitory message. However, for contemporaries, it was impossible to conflate the man and his theater. If Sophocles was heroized, we must insist that it was not for his literary work, but for his religious work, the introduction of the cult of Asclepius in Athens.

Deus ex Machina

....

TIME AND NATURE

The Nature of Sophocles in His Time

When poets have nothing more to say
and give up entirely in their dramas,
they resort to the theatrical machine,
and for the spectators that suffices.[1]

Like the tragic author, I need to resort to the theatrical machine to conclude this sequence chosen in the myth of Sophocles. Let us invoke a deity who is not absent from Sophocles' theater, even if he did not serve as a deus ex machina in the Greek tragic authors: Time. Sophocles had one of his characters, Ajax, express a magnificent thought about Time, which is a power both creative and destructive: "Long and incalculable Time brings all things to light and then buries them in darkness."[2] This maxim is applied to cosmic time as well as to biological and human time: to the alternation of the seasons, of day and night, of sleep and waking, but also to feelings, friendship, and hatred. However, this maxim on Time, a power of change, is only a deception when spoken by the character. Ajax will not change; he prefers to remain loyal to himself, to his nature, at the cost of his life, even though those around him urge him to change. And the poet is there to bring back to life, in the moment of a performance before spectators that took place more than twenty centuries ago, what remains, despite the vicissitudes of time, what the historian Thucydides would call "an everlasting possession." Just as the tragic poet chose in his hero's mythic sequence the moment when his true nature is revealed in a crisis, I had to choose, in Sophocles' long history, which stretches from the fifth century BCE to the most modern performances of his plays, the sequence that seemed to me most suitable to reveal his nature. To me, the choice was clear: I decided to resituate the man and his work in his own time. At a time when the emphasis is on the history of the different interpretations of works over the centuries, interpretations that escape their authors, it has seemed to me neither impossible nor arbitrary—indeed, salutary—to immediately place readers in Sophocles' time by guiding them through the multiple aspects of his political and religious activity within the city of Athens, and through the multiple facets of his theatrical work resituated in the everyday political, religious, and intellectual life of his age, while at the same time respecting the autonomy of artistic creation. To do this one does not need a time machine, but only a critical, fresh reexamination of the many primary testimonies—literary, epigraphic, archeological—that allow us to bring back to life the various aspects of the man and the work. However, just as the dramatic author conceals the theatrical constraints he must cope with, it has seemed appropriate to leave in the wings, that is, in the notes at the end of this volume, many of the references to testimonies the direct study of which has served as the basis for each reconstruction. What remains primary is the encounter with what puts us in direct contact with Sophocles. That is the justification for the presence of numerous passages translated from Sophocles' seven extant tragedies and the place given to the exceptional document constituted by the firsthand report of a banquet at which Sophocles was the star. Here, scholarship serves only to put into perspective what is admirable in the destiny of a man who succeeded in maintaining a balance between his role as a citizen and his activity as a writer.

One might say, adapting Plato, that it is impossible to know Sophocles' nature without knowing the whole, that is, the totality of what he was. And to examine the whole, we must not give priority to one part of his work or neglect his life on the pretext that the biographical elements are tainted by a few implausible and contradictory stories, such as the three versions of his death. Throughout his life, Sophocles did in fact play a sufficiently significant role in his city for his name to appear several times in the city's inscriptions, not only as a dramatic author, but also as a politician. Unlike Euripides, who was above all an intellectual, Sophocles had important responsibilities in Athens, on at least four occasions. Let us recall that he was first a Hellenic treasurer for a year, then a strategos, first with Pericles, then with Nicias, and that he was one of the administrators of the city in peril after the defeat of the Athenian expedition to Sicily. He also played a religious role by contributing to the worship of Asclepius in Athens and by composing a paean in his honor. Does his success as a tragic author explain, at least to a certain extent, why his fellow citizens trusted him to administer their affairs? That is not impossible. The performance of his *Antigone* is thought to have played a role in his election as strategos along with Pericles. All through his career he was so well integrated into his city that he never considered leaving it, as did the other two great tragic authors, who died abroad, Aeschylus in Sicily and Euripides in Macedonia. After his death, Sophocles even had the privilege of being heroized, that is, of becoming the object of a cult with a sanctuary in Athens. However, this heroization is explained neither by his political role nor by his theatrical work, but rather by his religious activity, his reception in Athens of the healing god Asclepius, whose sanctuary was adjacent to the Athenian theater. It is necessary to put all this in historical perspective in order to avoid misunderstandings.

Nonetheless, in his own lifetime Sophocles was already famous, above all for his theatrical career and his successes. He had an exceptionally long career of some sixty years from his first victory the first time he participated in the contest in 468 to his death in 406–405, and he had the most brilliant record of achievement of all the tragic authors of the century of Pericles. He was never defeated and won about twenty victories, eighteen of them during the most important performances, those of the Great Dionysia. To see just how brilliant his success was we can recall that his rival Euripides won the contest only three times.

Historical perspective is also necessary to gauge the amplitude of his work and the diversity of his inspiration. We should not limit ourselves to the seven extant plays and still less make a selection among them to retain only *Antigone*, *Electra*, and *Oedipus the King*. We must remember that his work included from 120 to 130 plays (including the satyr plays), which corresponds to an average of two plays a year for sixty years. The volume of his work is more impressive than that of Aeschylus and Euripides, whose works were already quite extensive but did not reach a hundred plays. This presupposes, of course, not only great rapidity in writing but also a technical mastery and an extraordinary talent not only as a writer as subtle in detail as in the construction of the whole, but also as a musician and a choreographer, since every Greek dramatist was also the composer of the music for the chorus that was an integral part of the play. Is there any other famous dramatist who can rival him? Aristotle did not always contribute to the understanding of the Greek tragedy that preceded him. When he says that Greek tragedy concentrated on a small number of families from the Greek historical and mythic heritage, Aristotle helped conceal the almost unimaginable richness and diversity of Sophocles' inspiration. In addition to the seven plays that have come down to us complete, we have fragments of or testimonies to a 115 lost plays, the titles and often also the subjects of which are known to us. By taking these lost tragedies into account in the chapter on the mythic imagination and especially by giving in appendix II a presentation of everything that we can say about these lost tragedies without yielding to the desire to imagine what we do not know, I have sought to react against the tendency to simplifying oblivion that accelerates the work of Time. It then becomes possible to recognize the incredible diversity of the subject Sophocles treated and the enormous gaps that increase the distance between the mythological culture of Sophocles' contemporaries and our own. Let us recall the most flagrant example. Everyone know the myth of Orestes who avenged the death of his father, Agamemnon, by killing his mother, Clytemnestra. But who knows the myth of Alcmeon, which parallels that of Orestes? Alcmeon also killed his mother, Eriphyle, to avenge the death of his father, Amphiaraus, and he, too, was driven mad and had to go into exile. But Sophocles wrote four plays on this family, whose members give their names to three of these plays. The loss of these tragedies concerning this tragic family has deprived Western literature of a whole myth. Resituating Sophocles in his time thus consists in recognizing the brilliant culture of an audience or a part of an audience and especially of an author, a culture that we can rediscover through a better knowledge of the lost plays that form the greater part of his work. Reading the appendix on the lost plays will lead us far away from the beaten paths, in an attempt not to reconstruct lost edifices by using our imagination, but rather to discover, with archeological rigor, the scattered remains that testify to a gigantic oeuvre. There is ample material for a very fine presentation on the myths of the lost tragedies. And even if we limit ourselves to the seven extant tragedies, there again we should avoid simplifying or monopolistic interpretations. First of all, we must resist the temptation to blithely skip over the choral passages on the pretext that the language is more difficult, and thus to continue the simplifying work of Time. These choral songs are an integral part of the tragedy's continuity, either negatively, by making it possible for the action to continue elsewhere, or positively, by allowing the spectators to catch their breath. Moreover, the chorus, especially in Sophocles, is a character like the others, especially in the dialogues, whether spoken or sung, with other characters, even if the chorus retains, through its generalizing reflections, a special status as a commentator on the action.

We must also resist interpretations of Sophocles' work that start out from excessively contemporary schemas or concepts, instead of from ideas or structures that emerge from the text itself. The ambition to discover in—or rather to impose on—the most remarkable works of antiquity a so-called social relevance does not advance their cause. Sophocles does not need to be defended. He needs to be known.

Finally, we must resist abusive generalizations that lend priority to a single aspect, whether it is political, social, or religious. To be sure, tragedy is a manifestation of the city of Athens; and the authors undeniably played a role in educating the citizen, as Aristophanes reminds us in his fictive duel between Aeschylus and Euripides.[3] But political or moral education is not primary, and we have seen how, in the tragedies that might be called political (the ones in which the main character is a king) the government of the city seems central at the outset but then gradually disappears as the tragedy of the city becomes the tragedy of an individual whose misfortunes or errors broaden into a vision of and a reflection on the human condition.

Of course, tragedy was performed in a religious festival in honor of Dionysus. But everything is not on the same level. The plays were not part of a religious ritual honoring Dionysus, even if Dionysus's priest had a central place among the spectators. In the classical period theatrical productions enjoyed a clear autonomy with respect to the festival in which they took place. The proof of this is that Dionysus, despite a very beautiful prayer in his honor sung by the chorus in *Antigone*,[4] is not central in Sophocles' theater. In any case, we cannot put the religious rite and an alleged ritual of dramatic performance on the same level. In the performance, the spontaneity of artistic creation does not submit to inherited constraints; it incorporates them.

What must never be forgotten is that the tragic author wrote his text to be performed. The goal was first of all performance before an audience that was national or international, depending on the festival, in order to win a victory in a final competition among three competitors during one single performance. Therefore all the effects sought by the author had to help the author gain the approval of the audience and the judges. By relegating performance to the last rank, Aristotle grasped the essence of Greek tragedy of the fifth century BCE less well than did the comic dramatist Aristophanes, who knew, as a man of the theater, the importance of performance, and mocked the grand scenes of Euripides' tragedy while carefully avoiding any injury to the untouchable Sophocles. Aristophanes, who knew his audience's tastes, also wanted to win its approval.

Thus it is not appropriate to judge Sophocles' plays by giving priority to a microscopic analysis without subordinating the examination of the details to the convergence of overall effects that have to be taken into account in order to bring out the message or messages that were likely to be perceived by the audience during a single performance. Naturally, subtlety of detail exists as well, and to an exceptional degree. It shows that Sophocles, while addressing a single audience, sought to reach several audiences at once, an educated audience as well as a humbler audience, which did not seem to him incompatible. He did not think it useful, however, to adopt Euripides' easy way of setting forth his subjects in a long speech at the beginning of the play.

If there is a Greek miracle, it resides in the fact that what was written for a single performance has been preserved and crossed the centuries down to the current performances. That shows that this text had all the qualities that allowed it to continue to be performed, and dealt with human relationships, political, moral, and religious problems, from a point of view that is both terribly concrete and powerfully abstract, so that it is still capable of moving a modern mind, despite the disappearance of the pagan divinities.

But the miracle is also that over the twenty-five centuries that separate us from the author, despite the destructive work of Time, whole tragedies have been preserved, even if they represent only 6 percent of Sophocles' total production.

Sophocles' Work and the Test of Time: From the Death of Sophocles to the Renaissance

Thus it is worthwhile to follow the main lines of the major stages that explain both the preservation and the loss of Sophocles' work over time during a period of about twenty centuries.[5]

The first great step toward the preservation of these texts was taken by a fourth-century Athenian statesman, Lycurgus, who promoted the theater. He remodeled the theater of Dionysus, had bronze statues of the poets Aeschylus, Sophocles, and Euripides made, as we have seen, and (of special interest to us here) prescribed by decree that "their tragedies, being fairly engrossed, should be preserved in the public archive, and that the public clerks should read these copies as the plays were acted, that nothing might be changed by the players."[6]

This decree is a preservative measure, but not in the sense in which one would spontaneously be inclined to understand it. It was not issued to preserve texts likely to disappear but rather to preserve the authentic text, which was likely to be altered by the license taken by actors during performances. But the interventionism of the actors has probably been exaggerated.[7]

What performances are referred to here, since we have seen that the text was written for a single performance? In reality, from the fifth century BCE on, the plays presented during a single official competition in the theater of Dionysus in Athens must have been performed again in the theaters of the demes of Attica and elsewhere. Then, starting in the early fourth century, or more precisely in 386 under the archontate of Theodotus, it was decided to add to the traditional contest of the Great Dionysia the revival of an older play. It was in this context that the tragedies of Sophocles and Euripides were officially performed again.[8] In this way Sophocles' tragedies continued to be familiar to the Athenians of the fourth century. The orator Demosthenes testifies to this. In his polemic against Aeschines, he reports that Aeschines, when he was the third actor in known troupes, played the role of Creon in Sophocles' *Antigone*[9] and accuses him of not having applied to his life the wise political program that the character formulated when he entered onstage.[10]

The goal of Lycurgus's decree was thus less to preserve the texts than to preserve their authentic version. Let us imagine these public archives in which the plays were copied on papyrus scrolls, one scroll to a play. For three tragedians, we thus arrive at a total of about three hundred scrolls!

This measure was crucial for the preservation of part of the production of Greek tragedy in the fifth century, but it had as an indirect consequence: the elimination of the rest. Choosing the three great tragedians eliminated all the other authors, at least in the long run, even those who had won first prize and whose names were included in the inscriptions. In fact, no fifth-century tragedy, except for those of Aeschylus, Sophocles, and Euripides, has come down to us complete. Of course, the rest of the dramatic production continued to circulate. In the fourth century, Aristotle had other tragedies by fifth-century authors in his library. For example, Agathon, who appears in Plato's *Symposium* just after winning first prize at the Lenaian festival of 416, was still read in the fourth century by Aristotle, who mentions him several times in his *Poetics* and gives the title of one of his tragedies.[11] It is even very probable that the tragic plays of Ion of Chios, the poet who described the banquet where Sophocles was the star, were still extant in the first century CE. In fact, the author of the treatise *On the Sublime*, comparing Sophocles with Ion of Chios, asks, "would anyone in his senses give the single tragedy of *Oedipus* for all the works of Ion in a row?"[12] The formulation presupposes that all the works of the minor tragic author were still extant at that time.[13]

Despite its long-term negative consequences, Lycurgus's measure had a decisive influence on the preservation of the theater of the three great Athenian tragic authors, because we have had the exceptional good fortune to be able to follow the fate of these scrolls preserved in the state's archives. During the following stage, they were transported from Athens to Egypt.

We know that after Alexander's conquests a new era began, the Hellenistic period, in which the intellectual center of the ancient world shifted from Athens to Alexandria, a city Alexander himself had founded in Egypt. Let us recall that Alexander was not only a great conqueror but also a great reader who was fascinated by medicine and literature. During his expedition to Upper Asia, since he could not procure books, he had his treasurer Harpalus send him a stock of books from Pella, the capital of Macedonia. Among these books were a large number of tragedies by Euripides, Sophocles, and Aeschylus.[14] For their part, Alexander's successors, the sovereigns of Egypt, pursued a far-ranging cultural policy by creating and developing a research center, the Museum and a library, the famous Library of Alexandria, where their ambition was to collect the whole of the Greek world's literary and scientific production. Thus Ptolemy III, byname Euergetes, that is, Benefactor (ruled 247–221 BCE), obtained from the Athenians, in exchange for a major security deposit, a loan of all the scrolls constituting the official version of the great tragedians that Lycurgus had ordered made. The result was a luxurious copy, but the king of Egypt preferred to keep the original and sent the copy to the Athenians, forfeiting the security deposit.[15] Thus the work of the three great tragedians passed directly from Athens to Alexandria.

Even before acquiring this treasure, the preceding king, Ptolemy II Philadelphus (ruled 285–246), starting with a large collection that had already been acquired, had asked a scholar, Alexander of Aetolia, who was himself a tragic author belonging to the group of seven poets known as the Pleiade, to undertake an edition of the tragedians.[16] However, the editing project on the tragic poets in Alexandria took a different turn after the acquisition of the Athenian collection. The new edition was prepared by the head of the library, Aristophanes of Byzantium (c. 257–180). In this monumental work based on a collection of about three hundred items, each of the latter was given a short introduction in accord with a preestablished plan, traces of which are still found in our medieval manuscripts.[17] In his presentation of Sophocles' text, Aristophanes of Byzantium emphasized metrics and shed light on the arrangement of the choral songs. This was the standard edition on which his successors worked, adding commentaries. That was notably the case for Didymus of Alexandria in the first century BCE. He was nicknamed Chalcenterus ("man with bronze entrails") because he devoured books. In his commentaries, this indefatigable worker collected the notes of earlier grammarians. Thus he became the standard commentator. Whereas the name of Aristophanes of Byzantium appears only once in the scholia in the margins of our medieval manuscripts of Sophocles, Didymus is cited dozens of times. In this way he transmitted the Hellenistic heritage he had collected.

After Athens, and then Alexandria, it was Rome that became the new capital of Hellenism. However, it was not Caesar's conquest of Alexandria (48 BCE) that led to the burning of the Museum's Library and the disappearance of the official editions of the tragedians, as some have maintained.[18] Egypt became a Roman province (30 BCE). Rome henceforth attracted Greek authors and scientists who went to reside there. Caesar founded the first Greek and Latin libraries, whose direction he entrusted to Varro, a scholar who resumed the tradition of the Alexandrine philologists.[19] But there was no transmission of the tragic text comparable to the one that took place between Athens and Alexandria.

To tell the truth, Greek tragedy had already exercised its influence on Rome before that time. As early as the second half of the third century BCE, starting in 240, and during the second century, poets, most of them from southern Italy, where Hellenism was flourishing, translated or adapted Greek tragedies (or comedies) performed at the Roman Games. Only fragments of these now remain. Thus Sophocles' influence is all the more difficult to determine because comparisons based on the titles of plays often concern myths that Sophocles was not the only one to have dramatized and, moreover, concern plays by Sophocles that are themselves very fragmentary.[20] In the first century CE the situation changed. because we have preserved, under the name of Seneca, nine tragedies inspired by Greek models.[21] Euripides' influence on Seneca is preponderant,[22] but that of Sophocles is particularly clear on *Oedipus* and on another tragedy attributed to Seneca, *Hercules on Oeta*.[23] In this period, despite the Latin adaptations, the works of the great tragic authors were still directly accessible not only in public libraries but also in private libraries. The most famous testimony to this is that of Dio (John) Chrysosotom (c. 40–111 CE). Born in Prusa, Bithynia, he came to Rome before being exiled. One day, being ill, he stayed home and took from his bookshelves the three *Philoctetes*, that of Aeschylus, that of Sophocles, and that of Euripides. To amuse himself, he wrote up a comparison of the three tragedies. He published it, and it has come down to us.[24] The paradox is that two of these three tragedies have disappeared. Only one has been preserved whole, that of Sophocles. Why his rather than that of Aeschylus or Euripides? The reason is the choice of tragedies that was made later, probably in the context of university teaching. *Philoctetes* was one of tragedies by Sophocles chosen for inclusion in the curriculum, whereas the corresponding plays by Aeschylus and Euripides were not chosen. When was this choice made? Although we have no precise testimony, it is traditionally placed in the course of the second century CE, in the age of the emperors Hadrian (ruled 117–38), Antoninus (ruled 138–61), and Marcus Aurelius (ruled 161–80).[25] It was a period of renaissance in which the ancients were studied. It is thought that the choice was made in educational circles where a program of seven plays by Aeschylus, seven plays by Sophocles, and ten plays by Euripides was drawn up.[26] The differing treatment of the three tragedians is the sign that the youngest of them was the most favored in the circles where the choice was made. This success of Euripides' corresponds, moreover, to a more general tendency that is confirmed by the comparison of many papyruses of the three great tragedians that have been found in the sands of Egypt. Euripides very clearly takes the prize with 169 papyruses as compared with 35 for Sophocles and 32 for Aeschylus.[27] However, this general tendency needs to be qualified. Sophocles might be preferred to Euripides. For example, the treatise *On the Sublime* (first century CE) notes that Euripides was not naturally inclined to the sublime, whereas Sophocles' genius, like that of Pindar, attained grandeur, even if he committed errors.[28]

The selection of tragedies made by the Roman period played in the history of the afterlife of the tragedians a role comparable to Lycurgus's choice. Just as the first choice had as an unintentional result the disappearance of what was not chosen, namely the numerous authors of tragedies in the fifth century BCE in addition to the three great ones, an indirect result of the second choice was to cause the disappearance of all of Sophocles' work that was not chosen.[29]

Attempts have been made to relate this choice made during the Roman period to a revolution in the presentation of the ancient book, that is, a change in matter and form. We know that the book, presented first in the form of scrolls of papyrus, was gradually replaced by the parchment codex, that is, by leaves of parchment bound together, inaugurating our modern book. The consequence was that a parchment codex could contain many more texts than a papyrus scroll. Whereas a papyrus scroll contained only a single play, a parchment book could contain several plays, which led to forming groups. Thus a choice of several plays could be made.[30] But we must not give too much weight to the question of the material form taken by the text. Even if we agree that the selection of tragedies was made in the course of the second century, it took place before the generalization of the transition from the papyrus scroll to the parchment codex, a transition that took place in the third to fourth centuries. At most, one can say that the transition from the scroll to the codex might have facilitated the transmission and generalization of an ancient choice to our medieval manuscripts.[31]

It is legitimate to ask what the criteria for this second choice were, but the truth is that we have no evidence allowing us to answer the question. We can imagine that such a choice was governed by a criterion of quality. But it would groundless to believe that we have preserved Sophocles' best plays. In fact, we have only a very small proportion of the fifty-four tragedies that contributed to Sophocles' eighteen success in the competitions of the Great Dionysia. But we must be grateful to those who made the choice for having chosen *Oedipus the King*, since that tragedy, as we have seen, did not win first prize.[32] It has to be said that shortly after Sophocles' death, Aristotle, in his *Poetics*, already considers *Oedipus the King* a masterpiece.[33] And in the century in which this choice was made, Aelius Aristides was still scandalized by the Athenians who, when *Oedipus the King* was performed, dared to prefer Sophocles' rival Philocles.[34]

Did the choice of the seven plays lead to the loss of the rest of Sophocles' work as rapidly as has been claimed?[35] Unlike the first choice, which was a decree by the city of Athens, the second was in no way official. The knowledge of Sophocles' work in the second century CE was not limited to the plays selected by this choice. His reputation was the same throughout the Greek world. Despite Roman domination and the attraction of Rome, the great intellectual centers of the classical period (Athens) or of the Hellenistic period (Pergamon, Alexandria) remained vital. Thus after having traveled about, Lucian (second century CE), who was born in Samosata on the Euphrates in Syria, settled in Athens and not in Rome. On several occasions, he cites Sophocles with Euripides or Aeschylus. For example, when he describes a luxurious room where one of the paintings represents Orestes' vengeance, he sees it as inspired by Euripides or by Sophocles.[36] One might think this is an allusion to two tragedies preserved by the choice. But when Lucian cites two verses from Sophocles, the tragedy from which they are drawn is not one of those chosen: it is *Meleager*.[37] Even at the end of the second century and at the beginning of the third, Sophocles' work was still accessible long after a restricting choice. Athenaeus's *Deipnosophistae* ("The Dinner Sophists," second/third centuries CE) is a striking testimony to this fact. We know that many authors of Greek literature are mentioned or quoted in the course of the discussions among the guests. Among the tragic authors, Sophocles has a special place. If we had to rank them by the number of quotations made by Athenaeus, Sophocles would clearly win out over Euripides and even more clearly over Aeschylus.[38] So here is a further testimony that provides a few nuances with respect to the traditional view of Euripides' popularity during the imperial period. But what interests us most in this testimony is that it attests to the ample knowledge of Sophocles' work in Rome, after the date traditionally given for the choice. In fact, Athenaeus mentions many more plays that were not chosen than plays that were chosen, and among these plays, there are not only tragedies but also satyr plays. The total is thirty-six lost plays cited by Athenaeus as compared to four extant tragedies.[39] This is undeniable proof that six centuries after Sophocles' death a large part of his work was still extant. All the plays that Athenaeus cites are obviously only a selection from the corpus of plays that he knew.[40] Thus if the choice of seven of Sophocles' tragedies was already made in an academic milieu in the course of the second century CE, at the turn from the second to the third century it had not yet led to the disappearance of his work. And yet six to seven centuries later, the oldest parchment manuscripts extant contain only the seven chosen tragedies. The loss took place in the interval.[41] However, it does not seem that it took place as early as has been thought. In the fifth and sixth centuries CE, Sophocles' work was not forgotten. To be sure, this was the period of the epitome makers such as Stobaeus and of lexicographers such as Hesychius. They collected sententiae and expressions drawn from the tragedies. But a choice seems to have had no effect on them. In his *Anthology* of Greek literature, the Macedonian Joannes Stobaeus still cites about forty tragedies by Sophocles.[42] As for Hesychius, in his *Lexicon* he cites twice as many! This lexicographer accorded an exceptional place to Sophocles with respect to the other two great tragic poets, and he cites Sophocles' plays with astonishing precision, because he develops a possible distinction between plays that appear to bear the same title.[43] Moreover, we must add that we read these two works by Stobaeus and Hesychius in a simplified form.[44] Should we assume that these compilers or lexicographers no longer had direct contact with the texts? We must not minimize their culture. Stobaeus was an astonishing scholar, gigantically learned, who wanted to instruct his son and improve his taste for reading and his memory! Thus in the end it was after the fifth to sixth centuries that the losses took place. Even the famous choice that is traditionally placed in the second century CE, but of which we still find no trace two or three centuries later, may also have occurred later.

Nonetheless, it remains that starting in the tenth century the number of Sophocles' tragedies is ineluctably reduced to seven. In fact, the oldest manuscript, which dates from the middle of the tenth century, has only these seven plays. This treasure, which comes from Constantinople, is preserved in the Laurentian Library in Florence. It offers the seven tragedies accompanied by marginal notes issuing from the oldest continuous commentaries, which are called the ancient scholia.[45]

Finally, there was a last stage in the reduction of the work of the tragic poets. After the choice of the three great tragedians made by the Athenian Lycurgus in the fourth century BCE, there was a third selection that retained only the first three of the seven plays (*Ajax, Electra, Oedipus the King*).[46] Academic programs were narrowing further! This is what is called the Byzantine triad. It gave rise to the most recent scholia, the product of the philologists of Byzantium and Thessalonica under the dynasty of the first Paleologues (thirteenth to the fourteenth centuries CE) before the final fall of Constantinople in 1453.[47]

But this new selection, which gave rise to the great mass of Sophocles manuscripts, result in new losses. When Sophocles was printed for the first time in Venice by Alde Manuce in August 1502, the edition included the seven tragedies.[48]

Sophocles from the Renaissance to the Modern Era: A History to Be Written

Thus began a new era, that of modernity, in which Sophocles became accessible to a much larger number of readers, especially in the Greek editions that multiplied in the course of the sixteenth century,[49] in Latin translations,[50] and finally, much more rarely, in translations into modern languages. In fact, in the course of that century, for eight Greek editions and three Latin translations of the whole of Sophocles' extant work, there were, in France, only two translations of two tragedies published in French. They were produced by the same family of scholars, the Baïfs. The father, Lazare de Baïf, who had learned Greek in Italy precisely from Janus Lascaris, was the first to translate into "French verse" one of Sophocles' tragedies, *Electra*, in 1537.[51] His son Jean-Antoine de Baïf, one of the seven poets of the "Pléiade" along with Ronsard and du Bellay, published Sophocles' *Antigone* in French alexandrines in 1572.[52] A third tragedy was not translated into French until more than a century later, when the philologist André Dacier translated *Oedipus the King* in 1692. Dacier, who was chiefly concerned with fidelity, abandoned any poetic ambition: he translated the text into prose, foregoing *les belles infidèles*.[53]

With these three first tragedies translated into French we have—is this an accident?—the trio that was to have the greatest influence on the imagination, thought, and creation of moderns from the Renaissance down to the present. It constitutes the modern trilogy that succeeded the Byzantine triad with the substitution of a single play, *Antigone*, taking the place of *Ajax*. Henceforth *Antigone*, *Oedipus the King*, and *Electra* replace *Ajax*, *Electra*, and *Oedipus the King*.

Retracing the history of Sophocles' influence on Western literature and thought is a subject for another book. A synthesis remains to be written even though we are currently seeing an explosion of studies on the three Greek tragic authors in the domain that is now called "reception" from the Renaissance to the present.[54] Such a synthesis would have to follow several parallel paths that sometimes cross, but often run alongside each other without knowing it.

First of all, there is the path of the *grammatikoi*, that of the "grammarians," who are now called "philologists." Let us recall that Sophocles did not much like them; at his banquet in Chios, he mocks the sententious interpretation of a grammarian. However, it was the descendants of this finicky grammarian who helped safeguard the ancient texts, and particularly Sophocles' work. From the Renaissance down to modern editions, the philologists have sought, in the wake of the Alexandrian scholarship rediscovered during the Renaissance, to use the manuscripts to edit, translate, and also comment on Sophocles' extant works.[55] This path, of philological origin but enlarged by the historical dimension, is currently being ramified into multiple approaches in which several interpretive models have come in from other horizons: philosophical, especially since Hegel (1770–1831),[56] psychoanalytic, starting with Freud (1856–1939),[57] structuralist, and anthropological.[58] The collision between these diverse approaches cannot be left unnoticed. The quarrel between an interpretation based on respect for the (Greek!) text and a freer interpretation crosses the generations, one side denouncing easiness and arbitrariness, and the other myopia and a lack of imagination. But despite the current crisis of Hellenic studies, the attraction of Greek theater in general, and of Sophocles in particular, is still so lively throughout the world that it is no longer possible for a single individual to master the mass of articles on Sophocles that appear every year in scholarly journals.

The second path, which is less crowded but still present, is that of the "directors" who have adapted Sophocles' plays for the stage and now also for film, starting with the first performance of Greek theater in modern times, that of Sophocles' *Oedipus* translated into Italian, in Vicenza in 1585, in connection with the inauguration of the theater constructed there by Palladio.[59] For the past twenty years modern studies have greatly advanced knowledge of the history of the performances of Greek tragedies from the sixteenth to the end of the twentieth century.[60] This also corresponds to the desire to recover the theatrical dimension obscured by Aristotle, whose shadow had weighed too long on scholarship. From this point of view, new translations of Sophocles were written for the theater. Antoine Vitez (1930–90) began his career as a director with Sophocles' *Electra*, in his own translation, at the Maison de la Culture in Caen in 1966.[61] In this respect, the collaboration between philologists and theatrical directors has been fruitful. It gave rise to Jean and Mayotte Bollack's translation of *Antigone* (1999), which was made for the stage and directed by Marcel Bozonnet at the Maison de la Culture in Bourges, January 8, 1999. This translation by an eminent Hellenist was clearly made on the basis of the most recent philological research.[62] However, a new translation written for the stage may follow more indirect paths. Thus the philosopher Philippe Lacoue-Labarthe wrote for the stage translations of *Antigone* and *Oedipus the King* that were performed by the Théâtre national de Strasbourg at the Avignon festival in 1979 and 1998 respectively. These are French translations of the "interpretive" German translations of these two tragedies that Hölderlin made at the end of his intellectual life (1804). Hölderlin had taken as the model for his translation Juntes's sixteenth-century Greek edition (1555). A curious choice! Thus we return to a state of Sophocles' text earlier than the first performance of Sophocles in the Renaissance. Despite that, Hölderlin's translation, which was initially not well received by Goethe or Schiller, gained great importance in thinking about hermeneutics from the beginning of the twentieth century on.[63]

These first two paths sought in principle to serve Sophocles' text and to bring it back to life, even if directors produced more an adaptation than an "archeological" performance, too often doing away, regrettably, with the chorus, whose role, ill-perceived, seemed annoying, thus mutilating Sophocles' work even more gravely than the destructive work of Time. Why is there such infatuation with the slightest fragment of a statue excavated by archeologists and such indifference to the mutilation of parts of a tragedy whose poetic and even dramatic power converged in the effect on the spectators desired by the author?

French translations intended for performance onstage could also take as their basis an *Electra* more distant from Sophocles, the result of a rewriting and not a translation. Thus the *Electra* by the Austrian writer Hugo von Hofmannsthal (1903), inspired by Sophocles' *Electra*, was recently translated for a performance given in 2006 at the Théâtre national de Bretagne.[64] Thus we encounter the third path, that of the creators, theatrical authors.

Like ancient tragic authors, modern authors have competed to write plays on the same myths, starting with Garnier's *Antigone* at the end of the sixteenth century. Here too, what I have called the "modern trilogy" functions. It is in fact these three tragedies by Sophocles that have given rise to the largest number of tragic creations in which the moderns compete with the ancients, as the ancients competed among themselves. There are three lineages.

The oldest lineage, if we refer to the date of the first play that took up a Greek myth, is that of *Antigone*. The first creation inspired by the Greek myth dates from the end of the sixteenth century. It is *Antigone ou la Piété* by Robert Garnier (1580).[65] For this lineage, I refer the reader to George Steiner's remarkable study *Antigones*,[66] the best introduction to this flourishing series from Garnier's *Antigone* down to Bertolt Brecht's (1962),[67] passing by way of many others, including that of Jean Cocteau, which is a sort of faithful condensation of Sophocles' play enhanced by sets designed by Picasso and accompanied by the music of his friend Arthur Honegger (1922), before that music was transformed into an opera (1927),[68] and finally Anouilh's *Antigone* (1944), whose unprecedented success eclipsed the other reworkings of the ancient myth in France.[69]

The lineage of Oedipus, which began with Corneille's *Oedipe* (1559), continued with Voltaire's *Oedipe* (1718), if we confine ourselves to the great productions of the French classical theater.[70] In Corneille's time, *Oedipus* was considered the masterpiece of antiquity, but no distinction was made between the two ancients who dealt with the subject, Sophocles and Seneca. In fact, in the *Examen* of his *Oedipe* Corneille mentions them side by side and calls them the "great geniuses who preceded." Thus it is not surprising that Corneille borrowed elements from both of his predecessors, while at the same time making changes, notably by introducing a pair of lovers, a modification he explains in his *Examen*.[71] In Voltaire, on the other hand, Seneca, whose influence becomes indirect through the intermediary of Corneille's play, is no longer mentioned. Voltaire's assessment of Sophocles is very reserved. A partisan of the moderns, Voltaire "respects the French tragedian much more than the Greek." Nonetheless, he acknowledges his debt to his ancient predecessor: "I admit that without Sophocles I might never have finished my *Oedipus*; I would never have even set out to write it."[72] In the twentieth century, the myth was dramatized several times by Cocteau. Urged on by Igor Stravinsky, who had admired his *Antigone*, Cocteau wrote the libretto of *Oedipus Rex*, a very condensed version of Sophocles' play, translated into Latin in accord with the composer's preference, with a view to the opera-oratorio performed in Vienna in 1928;[73] and in parallel he used once again the technique of contraction he had used for his *Antigone* in writing an *Oedipe Roi* (1928/1937);[74] finally, he deviated more freely from his model in his tragedy most inspired by the myth, *La Machine infernale*, in which only the last act corresponds to the sequence in Sophocles' *Oedipus the King* (1934).[75] In all these works, Cocteau tried to bring the myth into the rhythm of his time. In the interim, Gide had staged his *Oedipus* (1930/1932).[76] Jean Anouilh, long after the success of his *Antigone*, composed an *Oedipe ou le Roi* that was published in 1986 and is much less well known.[77] The fascination of the Oedipus myth, to which psychoanalytic interpretations have incontestably given a new attractiveness since the end of the nineteenth century, is still powerful a century later. Jacqueline Harpmann, a Belgian psychoanalyst and novelist, has just published a trilogy entitled *Mes Oedipe* ("My Oedipuses").[78] The myth has even given rise to novels, two superb novels by the Belgian author Henri Bauchau, who viewed psychoanalysis from the inside, *Oedipe sur la route* (1990) and *Antigone*.[79] I hesitate to put on the same level a crime novel by Didier Lamaison, *Oedipe Roi*, which has nothing to do with psychoanalysis. However, it is well written, is based on an intelligent understanding of Sophocles' tragedy, and is not without charm.[80]

The third lineage, that of *Electra*, commences in France at the beginning of the eighteenth century, notably with Crébillon's *Electre* (1708), followed by Voltaire's *Oreste* (1750), and it reaches its apogee in the middle of the twentieth century from Jean Giraudoux's *Electre* (1937) to Jean Anouilh's *Tu étais si gentil quand tu étais petit* (1972), passing by way of Jean-Paul Sartre's *Les Mouches* (1943), Marguerite Yourcenar's *Electre ou la Chute des Masques* (1944), and Jean-Jacques Varoujean's *La Ville en haut de la colline* (1969). This is the most complex lineage because of the interplay of models, since Sophocles' play is not the only one involved; a role is also played by Aeschylus's *Libation Bearers* and especially by Euripides' *Electra*, which is so different from that of Sophocles, especially in its introduction of a marriage (of convenience) between Agamemnon's daughter and a peasant.[81] The modern trilogy is also verified by films: *Antigone* by Yorgos Javellas, with Irène Papas (1961), and more recently *Antigone* by Jean-Marie Straub and Danièle Huillet (1991); *Électre* by Michael Cacoyannis (1962); and *Œdipe Roi* by Pier Paolo Pasolini (1967).[82] Outside this trilogy, adaptations of Sophocles' work are rarer.[83] Gide composed, in addition to his *Oedipe*, a *Philoctète ou le Traité des Trois morales* (1898). Obviously, it is in Greece that Sophocles' work lives on most broadly. Among Yannis Ritsos's works, in addition to his *Orestes* (1966), his *Chrysothemis* (Electra's sister), and his *Ismene* (Antigone's sister), which correspond to the modern trilogy, we can mention his *Philoctetes* (1965) and his *Ajax* (1969). A rewriting of *Ajax* in modern times is exceptional. And yet, in the Byzantine period, *Ajax* was not only part of the triad, as we have seen, but was the only tragedy that had never ceased to be studied.[84] Other times, other views of the Sophoclean landscape!

Finally, among the artists inspired by Sophocles' theater, in addition to dramaturges and composers, there are also painters and sculptors.[85] What vast museum opens up at closing time? Toward the end of the nineteenth century, the sculptor Jean-Baptiste Hugues painted the blind Oedipus sitting on a bench hugging his daughter Antigone, whose head rests delicately on her father's shoulder. The sculpture, inspired by Sophocles' last tragedy, is in the Musée d'Orsay. When we consult the modern oracle—not the Delphic oracle but the "Internet" oracle—we can contemplate in our own homes an excellent image of this statue, though we may be surprised to find in it a new Sophoclean tragedy: *Oedipe à la colonne*! ("Oedipus at the Column"). Is this the column on which the Sphinx was perched when Oedipus triumphed over her by his intelligence?

Return to Colonus

Let us now return to Colonus, to the deme of Sophocles' childhood, which is also the site of his last tragedy, in which the blind Oedipus, after giving his last instructions to Theseus, the king of Athens, utters his final words:

> Light of day, no light to me, once you were mine, but now my body feels you for the last time! For now I go to hide the end of my life in the house of Hades. But you, dearest of strangers, may you yourself be prosperous, and this land, and your followers. In your prosperity, remember me in my death, and be fortunate evermore.[86]

When the Athenian spectators heard these words, Sophocles had already joined Oedipus in death. His contemporaries thus listened, as it were, to the voice of Sophocles speaking from beyond the tomb. The author already lived again through his character, and some of the spectators thought they were listening to his last will and testament. Since that single official performance at the end of the fifth century BCE, presented by his grandson, whose name was also Sophocles and who was also a playwright, continuing the family tradition, Time "that hides what is visible" has not succeeded, over twenty-five centuries, in erasing his memory. Despite the mutilations of his work, despite religious, social, economic, and, to a lesser degree, political changes—because democracy already existed!—the nature of Sophocles, who wanted to bring back to life all the aspects of human nature through the great or the humble, remains, just as human nature remains. From a full political, religious, and intellectual life there remains only one snapshot of the man, at a fashionable party; of an immense work of more than a hundred and twenty plays there remains only an anthology of seven tragedies preserved intact. Very little, one might say! But it is dazzling if we take everything into account, not forgetting the setting, the acts of a man whom we can revive, and the lost works whose foundations we can restore. Through the account of a banquet, oddly forgotten, or through a reading of the tragedies, or better yet through a performance of them, each of us can experience an immediate, singular, and living encounter with Sophocles and his characters, because "Time also makes the invisible grow."[87]

Appendix I

. . . .

PRESENTATION OF SOPHOCLES'
EXTANT TRAGEDIES

Ajax

1. The subject of the tragedy and the site of the action
   a) The tragedy is drawn from a sequence of the Trojan myth that follows the death of Achilles, that is, from a sequence later than the *Iliad*: After Achilles' arms have been awarded to Odysseus, Ajax, considering that these arms should have been awarded to him because he was the best warrior after Achilles, decides to take revenge on the leaders of the expedition, Agamemnon and Menelaus, as well as on Odysseus, during a nocturnal sortie that takes place on the night preceding the action. But when he has already reached the center of the camp where the leaders are sleeping, Athena turns his hand against the armies' flocks and their guards. Ajax takes part of the animals in chains to his house, in the belief that he has killed the Atreids and taken Odysseus prisoner.
   b) The tragedy begins in the part of the Greek camp at Troy where Ajax's house (represented by the building at the back of the stage) is located—that is, at one of the extremities of the camp (opposite the one where Achilles was before his death), whereas the leaders of the expedition and Odysseus are in the center. The sequence of the tragedy moves from the exposition of what happened during the night to the preparations for burying Ajax. The first part of it is occupied by Ajax's tragedy, from his madness, which Odysseus witnesses for a moment, to his suicide, by way of various phases: his painful awakening and his desire to die in order to escape dishonor, his decision to escape by deceiving his entourage (his companion Tecmessa and the chorus formed of his marines), and his departure. The second part of the tragedy takes place in a secluded area on the Trojan plain, beyond the Greek camp and not far from the sea. This is the place where Ajax commits suicide by impaling himself on his sword buried in the soil, where his body will be found by Tecmessa and the chorus. Ajax's body, present on the stage, will be the stake in the second

part of the action. Ajax's half brother, Teucer, who has returned too late to save Ajax's life, seeks to defend the dead man's interests by opposing the two leaders, first Menelaus, then Agamemnon, who want to prohibit the ritual burial because of Ajax's act of rebellion and treachery, until Odysseus finally intervenes as a mediator and obtains Agamemnon's authorization for the burial. Teucer, declining Odysseus's help, proceeds alone with his men to prepare for the burial.

c) This sequence in the Trojan myth was dealt with in two poems in the epic cycle that have been lost, but we have a summary of them in Proclus's *Chrestomathy*. The first of these is the *Aetheopis* (attributed to Arctinus of Miletus, end of the eighth century BCE), which ends with the funeral of Achilles and the quarrel between Ajax and Odysseus for the possession of Achilles' arms. We know from a scholium on Pindar that the author of the *Aethiopis* said that Ajax committed suicide at dawn. But it is especially at the beginning of the *Little Iliad* (attributed to Lesches of Pyrrha, seventh century) that the sequence is dealt with. Here is the summary given in Proclus's *Chrestomathy* (ed. Bernabé, 74, 3–5): "The award of arms took place and Odysseus, in accord with Athena's will, received them. Ajax, who had become mad, slaughtered the flocks the Achaians had taken as booty and committed suicide." The question of Ajax's burial must have already been part of the epic tradition. The author of the *Little Iliad*, according to Porphyry, quoted by Eustathius of Thessalonica, a commentator on the *Iliad* (285, 30 = frag. 3 Bernabé), says that Ajax's body was not burned in accord with the rite, because of the anger of the king (Agamemnon), but that he was the only one of the warriors who died at Troy to have been put in a coffin.

Though the *Iliad* does not deal with this sequence and makes no allusion to it, Sophocles found information about the character of Ajax in this poem and was able to transpose some famous scenes from the *Iliad*: in particular, the scene of Hector and Andromache's "farewells," where their son is present (*Iliad* 6), was transposed in the spoken part of the scene between Ajax and Tecmessa, partially in the presence of their son Eurysaces (vv. 430–95). On the other hand, the *Odyssey* alludes directly to this sequence in the *Nekyia* (book 2, vv. 453–60): when all the shades of the dead approach Odysseus to ask him for news of the living, Ajax, still angry at Odysseus, keeps his distance: beyond death, he does not pardon Odysseus for the victory he won in the attribution of Achilles' arms thanks to the favorable judgment made by the young women of Troy and of Pallas Athena; Ajax does not deign to reply to Odysseus's words, even though the latter pays homage to his bravery and asks him to overcome his wrath.

In lyric poetry, the mythic sequence is presented in Pindar's *Nemean Ode* 8, where the poet cites Ajax as an example of merit that has fallen victim to envy (v. 23: "Envy devoured the son of Telamon, throwing him onto his own sword"), and sides with Ajax against Odysseus, deploring the triumph of trickery over bravery: "In a secret vote the Danaans favored Odysseus; and Aias, robbed of the golden armor, wrestled with death" (vv. 26ff.).

Sophocles was not the first tragedian to have put this sequence on the stage. The scholia on *Ajax* that Aeschylus had already dealt with the same mythic sequence in a lost play entitled *The Thracian Women* (*TrGF* 3, frag. 83–87 Snell). This tragedy must have been the central play in a trilogy of which *The Award of Arms* must have been the first. These scholia allow us to specify Sophocles' innovations with regard to Aeschylus: the choice of the chorus, of Ajax's marines instead of the Thracian captive women (see above): the choice to present Ajax's suicide directly, whereas in Aeschylus's play it was recounted by a messenger (see above); greater discretion regarding a version of the myth later than Homer concerning Ajax's invulnerability except at one spot under the armpit; see above.

2. Chorus, characters, and actors

The chorus is constituted by the marines from Ajax's ship. The characters are, in order of entrance: Athena, Odysseus, Ajax, the chorus, Tecmessa, a messenger, Teucer, Menelaus, Agamemnon.

The protagonist plays successively the role of Ajax, then that of Teucer. The deuteragonist plays Odysseus, then Tecmessa (until v. 989; when she returns at v. 1168, Tecmessa is played by a mute actor. The tritagonist plays Athena, then the messenger, and then Menelaus and Agamemnon. Ajax's son Eurysaces is played by a child who does not speak. Another mute character (designated in the text): a servant guiding Eurysaces (vv. 541ff.).

3. Structure of the tragedy

A. The location of the scene in the first part of the tragedy: in front of Ajax's house.

* **Prologue** (or part of the tragedy situated before the chorus's entrance: vv. 1 to 133): three scenes.

1. Athena-Odysseus (vv. 1–88). Odysseus is in front of Ajax's house, looking for the person who massacred the army's flocks and their guardians. Athena, who has made her entrance by the *mechanè*, addresses him, though she remains invisible to him; she reveals to him everything that happened during the night: the guilty party is Ajax, who, driven by his anger at not having obtained Achilles' arms, undertook alone a nocturnal sortie to kill those responsible, and first of all the two leaders of the Achaian expedition (Agamemnon and Menelaus). Athena led him astray at the last moment by striking him with madness and sending him to attack the livestock that he took for his enemies.

2. Athena-Ajax, Odysseus as a spectator (vv. 91–117). The entrance of Ajax who, at the goddess's second summons, leaps out his house, sneering (cf.

vv. 301–5, regressive stage directions) and probably brandishing a whip (cf. v. 110 and the title of the tragedy, "Ajax bearing a whip" in the *Hypothesis*; cf. also v. 242). Dialogue between the mad hero and the goddess, who through her questions illustrates Ajax's distraction; he thinks he has achieved part of his vengeance by killing the Atreids and he wants to complete the second part of his vengeance by tying Odysseus to a column and whipping him before killing him. Ajax goes back into his house.

3. Athena-Odysseus (vv. 118–33). The goddess draws a moral lesson from the spectacle in the preceding scene: the just power of the gods; the man also draws a moral lesson: the fragility of the human condition. Famous verses: "I see that all we who live are nothing more than phantoms or fleeting shadow" (vv. 125ff.). Athena disappears into the sky by means of the mechanè; Odysseus, on Athena's orders (cf. v. 67), leaves by the side exit (on the right) to announce to the Argives what Athena has revealed to him.

* **Parados** (the chorus's entrance and its first song: vv. 134–200).
   1. Anapaestic part (in recitative) (vv. 134–71): the chorus enters (traditionally, from the right) and takes its place. It is composed of fifteen marines belonging to Ajax's ship. The chorus addresses Ajax. He is concerned, because he has heard the rumor, spread by Odysseus, that Ajax has killed the livestock. Ajax has to appear to put a stop to this rumor.
   2. Lyrical part composed of a triad (vv. 172–200): for the metrical analysis, see A. M. Dale, *Metrical Analyses of Tragic Choruses*, fasc. 1: Dactylo-Epitrite, BICS, supp. 21, 1, 1971, p. 14 sq. The chorus speculates on the divinities who might have been able to lead him astray (Artemis, Enyalius), in the event that he had attacked the flocks. But if this rumor was invented by the great kings (Agamemnon and Menelaus) and by Sisyphus's son (Odysseus), Ajax will have to rise up, instead of letting himself burn with anger at his misfortune, whipped into flame by the hurricane of rumor.

* **First episode** (vv. 201–595): three scenes.
   1. Tecmessa and the chorus (vv. 201–347). At the chorus's summons, it is not Ajax who comes out of his house at the back of the stage but his captive and wife, Tecmessa, to tell the sailors the news of Ajax's madness and to ask their help. From a formal point of view, the scene is divided into three parts:
      a. vv. 201–62: a dialogue between Tecmessa and the chorus, first in recitative (vv. 201–20), then semilyrical (vv. 221–62): commos in which the chorus begins to sing, whereas Tecmessa continues to express herself in recitative; a single strophe/antistrophe pair; metric analysis in A. M. Dale, *Metrical Analyses of Tragic Choruses*, fasc. 1: Dactylo-Epitrite, BICS, supp. 21, 1, 1971, p. 16. The chorus learns of the madness of Ajax, who has dishonored himself by bringing home the animals he

massacred or whipped (the ram attached to a column representing Odysseus). His madness has waned, but the return to lucidity is painful.

b. vv. 263–332: a spoken dialogue in which Tecmessa, at the chorus's request, describes Ajax's affliction from its origin to the present moment; the description of Ajax's behavior in his home before and after his expedition complements the description of the expedition itself given outside his home by Athena. The stages in Ajax's madness and of his return to sanity are subtly noted. The height of the crisis corresponds to Ajax's sortie, seen by the spectators (cf. prologue, scene 2) and evoked here from the internal point of view (vv. 301–5). After the crisis, there is a gradual return to reason: a period of silent stupor followed by a renewal of his contact with Tecmessa, who, at his request, reveals to him what he has done: cries of pain; then a new period of calm and a refusal to eat or drink, but his words and laments suggest the worst, the desire to commit suicide.

c. 333–47: the end of the scene is oriented by Ajax's cries calling for his son and then his half brother Teucer. The chorus asks to see Ajax, hoping its presence will reawaken his self-regard.

2. Ajax, the chorus, Tecmessa (vv. 348–544). Another appearance of Ajax, but one that contrasts with the first one (cf. prologue, scene 2): instead of an Ajax leaping about in madness, this is an Ajax who has collapsed among the animals he has slaughtered; it is an image of Ajax as he is inside the house, shown through the artifice of the eccyclema. An appearance less frightening than the first one, but more moving.

a. 348–429: commos between Ajax, who sings, and the chorus, which speaks (with Tecmessa's intervention; she, too, speaks): three strophe/antistrophe pairs (metrical analysis in A. M. Dale, *Metrical Analyses of Tragic Choruses*, fasc. 1: Dactylo-Epitrite, BICS, supp. 21, 1, 1971, pp. 17–19). Ajax's emotion increases when he sees his friends (whence the actor's agitated song, including dochmiacs, that contrasts with the chorus's spoken words).

b. vv. 450–544: scene between Ajax and Tecmessa. Having overcome his emotion, Ajax no longer sings but speaks. In a long speech, he sums up his unfortunate destiny and deliberates about what he must do. In the final maxim: "either live honorably or die honorably, that is what a man of noble birth must do," he hints at his final decision. In the second speech in the agōn, Tecmessa discreetly tries to convince Ajax to give up his plan by begging him not to abandon her, not to abandon his relatives or his son. She appeals not only to his pity, but also to his sense of duty toward his family. Ajax wants to see his son and talk to him.

3. Ajax and his son (vv. 545–95). Ajax, holding his son in his arms, first addresses him to give him his (last) counsels and then addresses the marines

who form the chorus, telling them to entrust to Teucer the mission of taking care of his son. Then he bequeaths his shield to his son and rather brusquely orders Tecmessa to close the door. At the end of the scene, the eccyclema on which Ajax stood is wheeled inside; Tecmessa goes back in with the child, then closes the door.

* **First stasimon** (vv. 596–645): consists of two strophe/antistrophe systems (for the metrical analysis, see A. M. Dale, *Metrical Analyses of Tragic Choruses*, fasc. 2: Aeolo-Choriambic, BICS, supp. 21, 2, 1981, pp. 16–17). Addressing its homeland, Salamis, a distant lost paradise, the chorus contrasts it with the hard life in the Troad, which is made harder by Ajax's tragedy. Ajax is a patient difficult to care for, who has been the victim of a fit of madness caused by a divinity. He has turned inward on himself and is a source of great pain for his family and friends. The chorus imagines Ajax's mother's suffering and his father's misfortune when they are informed of his mad act.

* **Second episode** (vv. 646–92): consists of a single scene. Ajax comes out of his house, followed by Tecmessa, who remains silent (her presence is indicated by the expression "this woman," v. 652). First there is a long monologue (vv. 646–84). Then Ajax addresses his wife and the chorus, one after the other. This is apparently a totally unexpected peripeteia (cf. v. 715). Ajax suggests that he has changed his mind, belatedly persuaded by his wife's arguments (cf. the speech in vv. 485ff.). He declares that he is going to purify himself by washing himself in the sea and by burying the corrupting object, his sword, in a deserted place. In the future, he will submit to the gods and respect the leaders. He sees a commitment to wisdom in the operation of the forces of the universe that submit (winter gives way to summer, night to day; storms end and sleep loosens its grasp). This law of change is also observed in human relations: neither hatred nor friendship is eternal. But these words have a double meaning and constitute a deceptive discourse that allows him to go off to kill himself without being followed by his family and friends, and also without worrying them. At Ajax's command, Tecmessa goes back into the house (after v. 686). Before leaving by the left-side exit (used for the first time in the tragedy), Ajax gives the chorus of marines his last instructions. The last word he speaks, namely "saved," sums up the ambiguity of the speech as a whole: the chorus understands that the Ajax, having changed his mind and renounced his hatred of the Atreids, will be saved (cf. vv. 715–17); but Ajax means that he will find salvation in death, thus escaping dishonor (cf. vv. 470ff.).

* **Second stasimon** (vv. 693–718): a single strophe/antistrophe pair (for the metrical analysis see A. M. Dale, *Metrical Analyses of Tragic Choruses*, fasc. 2: Aeolo-Choriambic, BICS, supp. 21, 2, 1981, pp. 18–19). The chorus begins a joyful dance, brief but lively. It invokes Pan, calling on him to come from Arcadia to dance with it, and Apollo, calling on him to come from Delos. The reason for this joy is the repentance of Ajax, who, forgetting his pain, is

going to be reconciled with gods and men. But the chorus's illusion will not last long. The messenger's arrival will bring it back to reality.

* **Third episode** (vv. 719–86): three scenes.

1. Messenger and chorus (vv. 719–86). The messenger enters without being introduced. First, he tells the chorus about Teucer's return from Mysia and the unenthusiastic welcome given the "madman's brother" by the army. Then he asks to speak to their master, Ajax. Learning that he has just left, he cries out in pain "iou, iou" (v. 737), which contrasts with the chorus's cries of joy, "io, io" in the preceding stasimon (v. 694). He has come too late, because Teucer had ordered him not to let Ajax leave before he (Teucer) has returned. The chorus tries to reassure the messenger by telling him about Ajax's good intentions; he has gone to reconcile himself with the gods. Then the chorus is accused of being foolish, because Calchas, the army's seer, has issued a prophecy on this subject. In a long narrative, the messenger reports the seer's prophecy: he advised Teucer to keep Ajax in his house all day long, because Athena is pursuing Ajax with her hatred only during the single day to punish him for two offenses he has committed: with regard to the gods before the expedition to Troy (he did not listen to the lessons of moderation given him by his father, who advised him to triumph with the gods' help), and with regard to Athena herself during a combat (in which he refused the goddess's help). After the messenger's speech, the chorus, understanding the gravity of the situation, summons Tecmessa.

2. Messenger, Tecmessa, and the chorus (vv. 787–814). Tecmessa comes out, accompanied by her son (cf. v. 809), probably led by a servant. The messenger conveys to her the essence of the situation; she understands that Ajax has deceived her and gives the order, on the one hand, to go find Teucer, and on the other hand, to look for Ajax on both the west and the east coasts. She decides to go as well to look for Ajax. But she leaves her son behind (cf. v. 984). Tecmessa's departure, and that of the chorus (which divides into two semichoruses, one of which runs out of the westside exit and the other out of the east-side exit). Change of place and setting.

B. Setting in the second part of the tragedy: a deserted place not far from the sea.

3. Ajax alone (vv. 815–65). Monologue before his suicide. Ajax first indicates the preparations for his suicide: the freshly sharpened sword is planted in the ground, the blade pointing up. The rest of the speech is occupied by invocations to the gods: first to Zeus, that Teucer might be forewarned and protect his body against his enemies; then to Hermes, that he might grant him a rapid death; then to the Erinyes, the goddesses of vengeance, that they might cause the Atreid's destruction; then to the Sun, that it might announce his death to his relatives. Mastering his emotion, Ajax

decides to act. He calls for death and says a last farewell to the light, to the distant land (his homeland, the illustrious Athens), and to the land of Troy, where he is. After this monologue, he falls on his sword, which is hidden behind a bush (cf. v. 892). The suicide, although it takes place in the visible space, is thus hidden from the spectators.

* **Epiparados** corresponding to the **third stasimon** (vv. 866–973): a first semichoruses enters, out of breath after a fruitless search, immediately followed by the second semichorus, which enters through the opposite side entrance; it has seen nothing, either. After this new entrance of the chorus in a lyric iambic rhythm (vv. 866–78), the rest is a semilyric dialogue between the chorus and Tecmessa. It consists of a single strophe/antistrophe system with epirrhema (strophe: vv. 879–914 + epirrhema vv. 915–24; antistrophe vv. 925–60 + epirrhema vv. 961–73); for the metrical analysis of the parts sung by the chorus, see A. M. Dale, *Metrical Analyses of Tragic Choruses*, fasc. 3: Dochmiac, BICS, supp. 21, 3, 1983, pp. 30–31. While the chorus is wondering how to find clues, it hears a cry behind a bush. It is Tecmessa, who has found Ajax's body pierced by the sword. Alternating lamentations of the woman and the marines. Tecmessa covers the body with a veil.

* **Fourth episode** (vv. 974–1184): four scenes.
    1. Teucer, the chorus, in the presence of Tecmessa (vv. 974–91). Teucer enters (cf. v. 804). The chorus confirms Ajax's death. Teucer's lamentations; he worries about the fate of Ajax's son. Learning that he has been left alone, he orders Tecmessa to find him as soon as she can. Tecmessa leaves.
    2. Teucer, the chorus (vv. 992–1046). A long speech by Teucer that summarizes the situation after Ajax's death, comparable to the summary that Ajax made after his fit of madness. In particular, the same theme of the impossible return to the father. Reflection on the deaths of Ajax and Hector, victims of their respective gifts (the sword was a gift from Hector, who had received a belt in exchange).
    3. Teucer, Menelaus, the chorus (vv. 1047–162). Agōn scene composed of two speeches punctuated by a traditional intervention by the chorus, two verses long, and followed by a stichomythic dialogue. With the arrival of Menelaus begins the great question that occupies the end of the tragedy: must Ajax be buried or not? As soon as he arrives, Menelaus violently opposes the burial and wants the body to be left where it is to be devoured by birds, because of Ajax's treachery, which would have succeeded without the gods' intervention. Full of hatred for Ajax, over whom he can triumph now that he is dead, Menelaus criticizes his lack of discipline, points out that the fear of leaders is indispensable for a state's survival. At the end of his speech he repeats his prohibition on burying the dead man and threatens to have Teucer killed if he disobeys. The chorus emphasizes not only the wisdom of Menelaus's principles, but also his violence toward the dead man. Teucer, in reply, questions the assumption that Ajax

took part in the expedition under Menelaus's orders. He asserts his intention to bury Ajax, despite Menelaus's or Agamemnon's prohibition, and ends by recalling Ajax's scorn for "nobodies" (v. 1114) and by showing his own scorn for Menelaus. In the final dialogue, where insults are combined with discussions of legal points, each party maintains his positions: one prohibiting Ajax's burial, the other insisting on its necessity. Menelaus's departure.

4. Teucer, the chorus, the entrance of Tecmessa and the child, who will remain present until the end of the scene, but without speaking (vv. 1163–84). After Menelaus leaves, the chorus asks Teucer to proceed to bury the body as soon as possible. Teucer announces the arrival of Ajax's wife and son. He asks the boy to approach the body as a suppliant, holding in his hand hair cut off as a sign of supplication. Teucer cuts off a lock of hair and gives it to the child. He advises the chorus to watch over the body while he leaves to arrange for the grave to be dug.

* **Fourth stasimon** (vv. 1185–222): consists of two strophe/antistrophe pairs (for the metrical analysis see A. M. Dale, *Metrical Analyses of Tragic Choruses*, fasc. 2: Aeolo-Choriambic, BICS, supp. 21, 2, 1981, pp. 20–21). While the group formed by the child and the mother (probably accompanied by servants) remains in the same position during the whole last part of the tragedy, until the final departure, the chorus laments its own sufferings resulting from the war that has deprived it of the pleasures of peace—banquets and love-making—which it contrasts with the hard life in the camp, which will be even more harrowing now that the protection provided by Ajax has been lost. The chorus ends its lament by expressing the wish to return to its homeland, to see Cape Sounion and salute sacred Athens.

* **Exodos** (vv. 1223–420): four scenes.

1. Teucer, Agamemnon, the chorus (vv. 1223–315). Teucer abruptly returns, because he has seen Agamemnon approaching (he has been alerted by Menelaus; cf. v. 1226). An agōn scene with two antithetical speeches separated, as is usual, by a remark made by the chorus; but the two speeches are not followed by a stichomythic dialogue. Agamemnon begins with a torrent of insults directed against Teucer, whom he calls the son of a war captive and a slave, and he shows his contempt for Ajax, not recognizing even his valor while he was alive. Condemning the attitude of Teucer and Ajax, who did not respect the decision of the majority of the judges in the award of arms, he intends to force respect for the law. He ends with further scornful comments on Ajax's physical strength and on the birth of Teucer, whom he calls a barbarian.

2. Odysseus, Agamemnon, the chorus, in the presence of Teucer, who does not speak (vv. 1316–73). Odysseus enters, having heard from far away the Atreids' shouts. He addresses Agamemnon as a friend and asks him not to dishonor the dead man by forbidding his burial, because this interdiction

is contrary to the law, to divine laws, and to the valor of the warrior whose bravery Odysseus recognizes even though he had become his worst enemy since the award of arms. Agamemnon resists in a stichomythia before finally yielding, against his will. He goes off, leaving Odysseus free to do what he wants, but repeats his hatred for Ajax.

3. Odysseus, Teucer, the chorus (vv. 1374–401). Odysseus, whose wisdom is saluted by the chorus, even goes so far as to offer to help Teucer bury the dead man. Teucer also pays homage to Odysseus's magnanimity, while at the same time cursing the two Atreids, but he declines Odysseus's proposal, out of respect for the dead man. Odysseus submits to Teucer's will and goes away.

4. Teucer, the chorus (vv. 1402–20). This is the finale with a change in rhythm and diction (passage from spoken iambic trimeter to anapaestic dimeter in recitative). Teucer gives his servants orders in preparation for Ajax's burial with his armor (in conformity with his last wishes; cf. v. 577); he asks Ajax's son to help him lift the body and asks all the friends to follow him. After a final comment on humans' inability to foresee the future, the chorus joins the cortege behind Ajax's body carried by Teucer and Ajax's son. We should note that Teucer does not even mention Tecmessa, who was nonetheless at her son's side (cf. vv. 1169 and 1174). She is reduced to silence in the second part of the tragedy, and finally her name is not even mentioned.

4. Date

There is no testimony regarding the date. It is generally thought that *Ajax* is one of Sophocles' older extant tragedies, and may even be the oldest. But there is no conclusive proof of this. Attempts to date it are based either on alleged allusions to current events, on possible literary influences (Aeschylus, *Niobe*; Pindar, *Nemean Ode* 8, Euripides, *Telephus* or *The Women of Crete*), on iconography, or especially on analyses relating to dramatic technique, structure, and style: the so-called diptych tragedy with the role of protagonist shared by two heroes who do not meet; little use of antilabai.

5. Iconography

See T.B.L. Webster, *Monuments Illustrating Tragedy and Satyr Play*, 2nd ed., London (BICS, supp. 20), 1967, p. 146.

6. Editions with notes; or commentaries

R. C. Jebb, Cambridge, 1896 (Greek text, English translation, and notes in English), rpt. with an introduction by P. Wilson, gen. ed. P. E. Easterling, London, 2004; A. Dain and P. Mazon, Paris: CUF, 1st ed. 1958 (Greek text, French translation and notes); compare the translation by P. Masqueray, Paris: CUF, 1922; A. Willem-Ch. Josserand, Liège, 1940 (Greek text, notes in French); J. C. Kamerbeek, Leiden, 2nd ed. 1963 (commentary in English); W. B. Stanford, London, 1963, rpt. New York, Arno, 1979 (Greek text, notes in English); J. de Romilly, Paris, PUF, 1976 (Greek text, notes in French); H.

Lloyd-Jones and N. G. Wilson, *Sophoclea: Studies on the Text of Sophocles*, Oxford, 1990, pp. 9–41 (notes in English); J. C. Hogan, *A Commentary on the Plays of Sophocles*, 1991; H. Lloyd-Jones and N. G. Wilson, *Sophocles: Second Thoughts*, Göttingen, 1997, pp. 11–29 (notes in English); A. F. Garvie, *Sophocles, Ajax* (edited with introduction, translation, and commentary), Warminster, 1998; J. Hesk, *Sophocles: Ajax*, London: Duckworth, 2003 (monograph in English).

Antigone

1. Subject of the tragedy and the site of the action
   a) The tragedy belongs to the Theban myth and more particularly to the story of the noble family of the Labdacids (cf. vv. 594 and 861). The sequence begins at the end of the night after the Argive assault on Thebes. The assailants who came with Polynices to displace his brother Eteocles and seize power in Thebes have been repelled, and the two brothers have killed one another (in the war traditionally called the war of the Seven against Thebes; cf. v. 141 and see Aeschylus's tragedy *The Phoenician Women*, c. 410). This sequence had been preceded by a past that is referred to allusively in the tragedy: Oedipus had married, without knowing it, his mother, Jocasta, and had with her two sons, Eteocles and Polynices, and two daughters, Antigone and Ismene; he blinded himself upon learning of his origin, and his wife committed suicide (see also the sections below on *Oedipus the King* and *Oedipus at Colonus*).

   Whereas Creon has just taken power and decided to forbid the burial of Polynices, who had come to attack his city and its gods, Antigone decides to ignore this prohibition and to bury her brother, despite her sister Ismene's prudent advice to the contrary. Caught in the act during her second attempt to bury him, Antigone is brought before Creon by a guard. Creon condemns her to be incarcerated in an underground prison, despite the intervention of Haemon, Creon's son, who is also Antigone's fiancé. After receiving the seer Tiresias's revelations and the chorus's advice, Creon changes his mind and abruptly leaves to bury Polynices and free Antigone. But he arrives too late to save Antigone; a messenger tells Eurydice, Creon's wife, that Antigone has hanged herself and that Haemon has committed suicide over his fiancée's body. Creon returns carrying his son's body and learns of his wife's suicide.
   b) This sequence of the myth was also dramatized by Euripides in his *Antigone*. Euripides' tragedy, whose date is unknown, is considered, on the basis of the criterion of metrics (free style: 416–409 BCE), later than that of Sophocles, which dates from the 440s (see below, 4. Date). The extant fragments of Euripides' tragedy are too few to allow a reliable reconstitution (see H. Van Looy, *Euripides*, vol. 8, CUF, *Fragments*, part 1, 1998, pp.

191–210), and *TrGF* 5.1, pp. 261–312 Kannicht). Nonetheless, argument no. 1 of Sophocles' *Antigone*, attributed to Aristophanes of Byzantium (see also the scholium on v. 1350) indicates changes made by Euripides: Antigone is not alone when she begins to bury her brother; she is caught in the act with Haemon; and in the end, she marries him and has a child named Maemon (or Maeon). Before Sophocles' *Antigone*, Aeschylus's *Seven against Thebes* (date 467 BCE) had, in the medieval manuscripts, a final scene in which the herald comes to announce the city's edict prohibiting Polynices' burial and in which Antigone opposes this edict and promises to bury her brother (vv. 1005–53), whereas the chorus is divided regarding which side it should support (vv. 1054–78). However, the authenticity of this ending is hotly debated. Sophocles may thus be the first to have dramatized Antigone's revolt.

2. Chorus, characters, and actors

The chorus consists of old men from the Theban aristocracy; they form the royal council devoted to the kings of Thebes (Laius, Oedipus, his sons, and now Creon); cf. vv. 165–74.

The protagonist plays the role of Creon, the new king of Thebes (with a sung part, vv. 1261–346), and perhaps that of Eurydice. The deuteragonist plays the role of Antigone, Oedipus's daughter and Creon's niece (with a sung part, vv. 806–82), and those of Haemon and Tiresias. The tritagonist plays the roles of Ismene, the guard, and the messenger. Such a distribution of roles is likely. However, certain roles might technically be played by another actor: for example, Eurydice might be played by the deuteragonist.

3. Structure of the tragedy

* **Prologue** (vv. 1–99): a single scene between Antigone and Ismene. Antigone has asked her sister Ismene to come out of the palace, even though the sun has not yet risen. It is the end of the night when the Argive army that was besieging Thebes has just left after the single combat in which their two brothers, Eteocles and Polynices, have died. Antigone has just heard news that she shares with her sister: Creon has made a distinction between the two brothers regarding burial: he has granted Eteocles full honors but has forbidden, by an edict to the residents of Thebes, the ritual burial of Polynices. This edict is addressed first of all to members of Polynices' family. Antigone asks her sister to help her bury the dead man, despite the prohibition. Ismene, in a speech (vv. 49–68), justifies her refusal to disobey the edict, reminding her sister of the family's misfortunes, their condition as women, and their submission to a leader. Antigone then decides to act alone as a "holy criminal," out of love for her brother (v. 74). After a brusque exchange in which Ismene's advice merely increases Antigone's resolve, the two sisters separate. Ismene goes back into the palace, while Antigone departs.

* **Parodos** (vv. 100–161): consists of two strophe/antistrophe pairs (vv. 100–154); for the rhythmic analysis see A. M. Dale, *Metrical Analyses of Tragic*

Choruses, fasc. 2: Aeolo-Choriambic, BICS, supp. 21, 2, 1981, pp. 22–23. The chorus, composed of fifteen elderly, white-haired men (cf. vv. 1091–92) forming the traditional council of the kings of Thebes, arrives at the palace, because it has been summoned by the new king, Creon (cf. vv. 159–61). It celebrates, with the rising sun, the victory that Thebes has just won over the Argive assailants who had come to lay siege to the city, led by Polynices who sought replace his brother as king. The enemy army has been routed; its assaults have been repelled with Zeus's help; the seven besieging leaders are all dead. The two brothers, Eteocles and Polynices, have killed each other, leaving Thebes without a king; but the city has won a victory, and the gods must be thanked by going to their temples and celebrating them with choruses. An announcement, in recitative, of Creon's arrival (vv. 155–61: anapaestic dimeters).

* **First episode** (vv. 162–331): two scenes.

1.   Creon and the chorus (vv. 162–222). This scene might be called the speech from the throne. In a long speech, the new king, who has come out of the palace, addresses the chorus, which has been the royal council since Laius. After recalling the legitimacy of the succession (he is Oedipus's nearest relative), the king announces his principles of government and the edict that he has just issued in accord with these principles. This is the edict the spectator has already heard discussed by Antigone. But it is not officially presented by its author: because Eteocles died fighting for his homeland, he is to be buried with all the honors due his bravery, whereas Polynices, who sought to destroy his homeland by coming back from exile, will be left unburied, to be devoured by birds and dogs. The councilors note this decision, recognizing the kings' power, but they show great prudence facing a king determined to put to death anyone who violates the decree.

2.   Creon, the guard, the chorus (vv. 223–331). One of the guards assigned to watch over the body comes in as a messenger. After many hesitations, he reveals his message: Polynices' body has been buried. Faced by the king's stupefaction, the guard makes a long speech (vv. 249–77) from which it emerges that the culprit is unknown. The crime was discovered by the guard who took over at dawn. But there was no trace either of the use of a tool or of the passage of a wild animal or a dog. The body has been covered by a thin layer of dirt, as though someone had sought to avoid soiling it. The guard then describes the effects produced by the news on the guards as a whole, the quarrels, the decision to report to the king, the drawing of lots to decide who would carry out this fearful mission. After the long account given by the guard, who insists that he and the other guards are innocent, the chorus, in a brief, two-verse interjection (vv. 278–79), proposes the hypothesis that the act is the work of the gods. This remark unleashes the king's irritation. In a speech even longer than the guard's, he denounces the absurdity of such an explanation by showing

that the gods cannot honor men who have just burned their temples. To this explanation given by the chorus, Creon opposes his own: the existence of a conspiracy, whose perpetrators are supposed to have paid the guards to carry out this act; he bases his hypothesis on the general observation of the power money has over humans. The king, once again addressing the guard (v. 305), threatens the guards with death by hanging if they do not find the guilty party. The scene ends, as it began, with a dialogue between the guard and the king, but the situation is reversed: the guard, who hesitated to announce his news at the beginning, becomes too talkative at the end. He goes away promising never to return, happy and surprised to escape with his life.

* **First stasimon** (vv. 332–83): consists of two strophe/antistrophe pairs (vv. 335–75); for the rhythmic analysis, see A. M. Dale, *Metrical Analyses of Tragic Choruses*, fasc. 2: Aeolo-Choriambic, BICS, supp. 21, 2, 1981, pp. 24–25. This is one of the most famous stasima in Sophocles' theater, because it begins with a superb paean to human beings in general. There is nothing more amazing in the world than human beings. They have been able to protect themselves and extend their power over nature (the sea, land, living beings, the environment) through the discovery of the arts. The chorus alludes to numerous arts, such as navigation, agriculture, hunting and fishing, animal taming, politics, architecture, and medicine. It is human beings themselves who have discovered all these arts through their resourceful intelligence. The only limit to this power it human mortality. This eulogy of human beings is an indirect echo of the theories of progress characteristic of the period (cf. Aeschylus, *Prometheus Bound*, vv. 442ff.; Euripides, *Suppliants*, vv. 201ff.; Thucydides, *History of the Peloponnesian War*, 1; Hippocrates, *On Ancient Medicine*). But this eulogy has, at the end of the stasimon, a counterpart that indirectly connects it with the action. Technical discoveries can be used in the city for both good and evil. The chorus praises the citizen who respects the laws and divine justice but excoriates the citizen who excludes himself from the city by his audacity. It alludes to what it has just learned in the preceding scene, namely that some audacious person has violated the king's edict.

But a dramatic turn of events occurs (vv. 376–83; recitative, anapaestic dimeters): the appearance of Antigone, whom the chorus sees with stupefaction. Thus it is not a man who appears to be the guilty party, but rather Antigone, the unfortunate daughter of an unfortunate father, who has, in the chorus's view, gone mad.

* **Second episode** (vv. 384–581): three scenes. The guard who had promised never to return comes in, triumphant, this time announcing his news immediately. Antigone is the guilty party; she has been caught in the act. Creon, who has conveniently come out of the palace, questions the guard, whose arrival contrasts with his previous appearance. The first time he had come

against his will, but he now returns willingly, describing the situation as a "piece of luck" for him (v. 397). The discovery of the culprit frees him from any accusation. Creon questions him regarding the circumstances of Antigone's arrest. This is an opportunity for the messenger to give another speech of about thirty verses (407–40). The guard recounts what has happened since he returned to his fellows: increased surveillance from a point overlooking the body, which has been cleared of the dirt covering it, a long rainstorm at midday that forced the guards to loosen their surveillance, and then the discovery, after the storm, of Antigone moaning over the bared body and beginning to bury it again; the capture of the young woman, who denies nothing. This confession causes the guard both joy and pain: but the pain of being the cause of the young woman's distress is less strong in him than the joy of finding his own salvation. Since her entrance, Antigone has remained silent, her head bowed. At Creon's first question, she admits being the perpetrator of the act. Creon can then send the guard away.

2. Creon, Antigone, the chorus (vv. 446–525). This is the face-to-face confrontation between the king and the young woman. It takes place in the form of an agōn scene with two opposed speeches separated by a judgment made by the chorus in two verses and followed by a sharp dialogue that increases the tension between the two antagonists. Creon questions the young woman. She admits that she acted deliberately and justifies her violation of the edict in a speech of twenty verses (vv. 450–70) that is of a surprising depth coming from a young woman. To the edict of a man, she opposes the unwritten but eternal divine laws that are those of Zeus and of the justice of the gods of the Underworld. It is these laws that she has obeyed, knowing full well that her revolt against the human edict will lead to her death. Antigone's justification then takes on a more personal tone: for her, death is less painful than leaving a son of her mother unburied. Her decision is thus in conformity, not only with justice, but also with her own interest. Antigone ends her speech with a provocation with regard to Creon, rejecting the accusation of madness and turning it against the king. The chorus, far from noting the profundity of Antigone's position, is critical of her: she has a bitter character, like that of her father, and is incapable of yielding in misfortune (vv. 471–72). Faced with Antigone's provocative attitude, Creon explodes in anger in a speech opposed to that of Antigone (vv. 473–96). But he is so outraged that he addresses the chorus to speak about the young woman. He accuses her of a twofold offense: after committing a crime, she boasts of having done it. He reserves for her, even though she belongs to his family, the worst of punishments, as well as for her sister, whom he accuses of have plotted with her. Antigone speaks up again, defying this new king by urging him to execute his sentence, taking note of the total lack of comprehension between the two of them, justifying her act, which she now presents as

glorious (v. 502), and denouncing the arbitrary element in a king's power. The confrontation ends in a stichomythia that reinforces the opposition of the points of view: the law of the family and of the dead to which Antigone appeals is opposed to the law of the state defended by Creon. It is in her last words uttered during the stichomythia that Antigone gives her famous definition of her nature: "It is not my nature to join in hate, but in love" (v. 523). It is noteworthy that after this stichomythia Antigone no longer says a word to Creon. The rupture between the young woman and the king is definitive.

3. Creon, Antigone, Ismene, the chorus (vv. 526–81). The chorus announces the arrival of Ismene, who emerges from the palace in tears. Creon had ordered her entourage to make her come (vv. 491ff.) because he suspected her of having participated in the act of rebellion. As soon as she arrives, Creon approaches her and questions her. She admits being guilty, like her sister. But Antigone does not accept this lie. The two sisters face off once again. Antigone scornfully rejects Ismene's belated help and increases the opposition between their choices: "Your choice was to live, it was mine to die" (v. 555). Despite that, Ismene tries to plead in favor of Antigone, pointing out in particular that she is the fiancée of Haemon, Creon's son, but Creon does not want to hear about it and seems determined to make her die. He orders her servants to imprison the two women in the palace.

* **Second stasimon** (vv. 582–625): two strophe/antistrophe pairs (metrical analysis in A. M. Dale, *Metrical Analyses of Tragic Choruses*, fasc. 1: Dactylo-Epitrite, BICS, supp. 21, 1, 1971, pp. 20–21). The chorus reflects on the misfortune that, under the influence of the gods, has shaken the different generations of a single family, as the waves of the sea are buffeted by a storm. That is the case of the family of the Labdacids to which Antigone belongs. She was the last descendant of the family, but she has been cut down by an act, a bit of dirt offered to the gods of the Underworld (that is, the burial of Polynices), by ill-considered words (addressed to Creon in the preceding scene), and by the Erinys, or goddess of vengeance (probably of the family) that has attached itself to her mind. In this way the chorus, broadening the perspective, resituates Antigone's destiny in that of her family. Then the chorus addresses a hymn to Zeus, the all-powerful, who leaves no human offense unpunished.

* **Third episode** (vv. 626–780): two scenes of unequal length.
    1. Creon, Haemon, the chorus (vv. 626–765). The chorus announces the arrival of Haemon, Creon's youngest son (probably coming from the city, where he has learned of Antigone's death sentence), and it wonders whether it is the pain occasioned by his fiancée's fate that explains his arrival. The encounter between the son and the father takes place in the context of an agōn scene of the regular type, including two antithetical speeches punctuated by a two-line judgment by the chorus, and ending

in a rapid dialogue in which verse-for-verse responses (stichomythia) are dominant. The father speaks first: mixing general maxims with references to the particular situation, he advises his son to submit to paternal authority and to respect the decision by giving up his fiancée, who has been condemned to death for an act of rebellion; but since the father is also the king, Creon broadens his reflection from the family to the city, condemning anarchy as the worst of scourges for the city, as it is for the family, and praising discipline. The chorus approves the king's position. In the opposing speech, the son initially responds diplomatically: he does not confront his father directly but reports to him, in his interest, the obscure rumbling in the city that is siding with the young woman. And still in the father's interest, the son offers counsels of wisdom and moderation, taking examples from nature (trees) or art (a ship) to urge his father to yield by letting go of his anger against Antigone. To conclude his speech, the son suggests that despite his youth, his advice is useful to his father. But the son's lessons irritate the father. In the dialogue that follows the two speeches, Creon and Haemon confront each other with increasing violence over Antigone's act, over the exercise of power, and over religion, to the point of rupture: the father, beside himself over the lack of respect shown by his son, whom he thinks the slave of a woman, orders Antigone to be brought out so that she might die in front of her fiancée, and the son, faced by his father's madness, departs, breaking definitively with him.

2. Creon, the chorus (vv. 766–80). Faced with Haemon's brusque departure, the chorus is worried; but Creon, still in the grip of his anger, pays it no mind and decides to put the two sisters to death. At the chorus's intervention, however, he abandons his decision to punish Ismene, recognizing that she did not participate in the act. In conclusion, he makes explicit the punishment he has in mind for Antigone: she will be imprisoned alive in an underground cavern and left just enough food to avoid corrupting the city. Creon goes back into the palace.

* **Third stasimon** (vv. 781–805): the chorus, remaining alone, sings a brief hymn to Love consisting of a single strophe/antistrophe pair (761–800; for the metrical analysis, see A. M. Dale, *Metrical Analyses of Tragic Choruses*, fasc. 2: Aeolo-Choriambic, BICS, supp. 21, 2, 1981, p. 26). He praises the invincible power of the god whose power extends over the sea as well as over the land, over animals as over humans and the gods. But this praise turns into a criticism of those who are under a divinity's power: they are struck with madness and fall into injustice, to their ruin. These general remarks are, in fact, a reflection on the preceding scene. The chorus sees in the quarrel between the father and the son an effect of Haemon's love for Antigone. Announcement, in recitative (vv. 801–5: anapaestic dimeters) of Antigone's departure for her prison.

* **Fourth episode** (vv. 806–943): two scenes.

   1. Antigone, the chorus (vv. 806–82). Antigone comes out of the palace led by Creon's servants, on her way to her last home. This scene is a sung dialogue (commos) between Antigone and the chorus, consisting of two strophe/antistrophe pairs and a short epode; for the metrical analysis, see A. M. Dale, *Metrical Analyses of Tragic Choruses*, fasc. 2: Aeolo-Choriambic, BICS, supp. 21, 2, 1981, pp. 26–29. The dialogue is initially semilyric, then lyric. In the first strophe/antistrophe pair, Antigone sings while the chorus expresses itself in recitative, whereas in the second, the chorus sings and so does Antigone. The heroine, in contrast with her severity when facing Creon, is overwhelmed by emotion as she confronts death. She calls on the chorus to witness her final departure to Hades, without having experienced marriage, except to death itself; she compares her fate to that of Niobe, who, mourning the death of her children, was turned to stone on Mount Sipylus in Lydia; she wants to protest, facing the residents of Thebes and its country, against the fate that awaits her in a prison far from the living and the dead. The chorus's attitude is rather enigmatic. On seeing Antigone, for a moment it is gripped by emotion, in spite of itself, and cannot hold back its tears. At first, it seems to want to console the young woman by showing the extraordinary nature of her death, which appears to irritate Antigone. However, subsequently the chorus does not spare her its criticism. It denounces her audacious behavior, emphasizes the burden of heredity, and, while recognizing her piety, attributes her impending death to her independent character. This position taken by the chorus ultimately leaves Antigone in total solitude. She will leave without friends shedding tears for her.

   2. Creon, Antigone, the chorus (vv. 883–943). Having heard Antigone's songs and moans, Creon comes out of the palace to order his servants to take the young woman to her underground prison as quickly as possible. This puts an end to Antigone's sung complaints. She now expresses herself in a long speech. She has turned her attention to the dead whom she will join, toward her father, her mother, and her brother Polynices, adding a further justification for her act: she did for her brother what she would not have done for a husband or for children, because she would have been able to have another husband or children, but not another brother, since her parents are dead (on this argument, compare Herodotus III, 119). She thus protests against the decision made by Creon, to whom she no longer speaks, but for whom she wishes the same fate as hers. The chorus maintains its criticism of Antigone, and Creon hastens the departure. In a final appeal, Antigone, being led away by the guards, declares her total piety (v. 943; cf. v. 74). Creon remains onstage, but he is silent during the rest of the chorus's song.

* **Fourth stasimon** (vv. 944–87): two strophe/antistrophe pairs: for the metrical analysis see A. M. Dale, *Metrical Analyses of Tragic Choruses*, fasc. 2: Aeolo-Choriambic, BICS, supp. 21, 2, 1981, pp. 30–31. Although Antigone has left, the chorus continues to address her (v. 949 and v. 987). To encourage her to submit to her fate with resignation, it recalls other destinies comparable to hers that illustrate the power of fate: first, Danaë imprisoned in a subterra-nean chamber, even though she came from a noble family and had received Zeus's seed in the form of a shower of gold (strophe 1); then Lycurgus, the king of the Edonians in Thrace, who was imprisoned by Dionysus for having opposed his cult (antistrophe 1); and finally Cleopatra, the daughter of Boreas: the two sons she had had with the king of Thrace Phineas were blinded by their stepmother; even though she was the daughter of a god, she had to undergo her destiny (strophe and antistrophe 2).

* **Fifth episode** (vv. 988–1114): two scenes.

  1. Creon, Tiresias (vv. 988–1090). This is the last scene in which the king confronts a character who has come from outside. This last character con-trasts with the earlier ones (the guard, Antigone, Haemon) by his age, his social status, and his moral authority because of his knowledge as a seer. Tiresias comes spontaneously to tell Creon that his destiny is on the ra-zor's edge (v. 996). In a long speech, the seer describes to the king, like a messenger, the unfavorable signs he has noted in the exercise of his art by observing the cries of birds (ornithomancy) and by examining the flame in sacrifices (pyromancy). Then he delivers his diagnosis, which is compa-rable to that of a physician: the city is sick because of the king's decision (cf. v. 1015); since the guards have left Polynices' body uncovered, the birds of prey, by carrying bits of flesh, have soiled the gods' altars, and the gods are angry and no longer accept the sacrifices made by mortals. The seer ends his speech with a therapeutic prescription: he asks Creon to undo his crime by yielding to the dead man. These counsels given by the seer in the king's interest trigger a blind and hyperbolic anger in Creon, who replies in a shorter speech. It is the specter of a conspiracy that re-turns (cf. vv. 289ff.) along with the accusation that Tiresias is acting in the hope of gain (cf. vv. 294ff.). The king imagines that the seer has been paid to contest his power. He clings to his prohibition on burying the dead man and does not believe that humans have the power to soil the gods. He ends his speech by predicting ruin for those who act out of an appetite for gain (cf. already vv. 221ff. and vv. 313ff.). The confrontation between the king and the seer becomes more intense in a verse-for-verse (sticho-mythic) dialogue. This confrontation triggers the anger of the seer, who in a final speech delivers veiled prophecies regarding the misfortunes to come, as a punishment for clearly denounced crimes: the death of one of his family for having imprisoned a living person in the world of the dead

and for having kept on earth a dead man who belongs to the gods of the Underworld; the moans of men and women in his home. These prophecies signal the death of his son Haemon and also of his wife, Eurydice.

2. Creon, the chorus (vv. 1091–114). The chorus has remained silent during the whole preceding scene, which is exceptional. It had spoken, in fact, in all the other scenes in which Creon confronted another character. It now speaks to express its concern regarding Tiresias's brusque departure, as it had after Haemon's hasty departure. Creon is also shaken by the seer's revelations. In a brief but intense dialogue, the chorus's counsels persuade the king to reverse himself, even though up to that point he had remained deaf to all counsels of prudence. Creon will rush off with all his servants to bury Polynices and free Antigone. His last words show that he is beginning to recognize his mistakes (vv. 1113ff.).

* **Fifth stasimon** (vv. 1115–54): the chorus sings a hymn to Dionysus in two strophe/antistrophe pairs; for the metrical analysis, see A. M. Dale, *Metrical Analyses of Tragic Choruses*, fasc. 2: Aeolo-Choriambic, BICS, supp. 21, 2, 1981, pp. 32–33. It celebrates the god's powers and asks him to appear to cure the city; see above.

* **Exodos** (vv. 1155–353): the announcement of the catastrophes accumulates in this brief ending to the tragedy.

1. A messenger, the chorus (vv. 1155–82). It is not the divinity who appears after the chorus's appeal, but rather a messenger, one of Creon's servants, who has come to announce his misfortunes: his son has committed suicide in a fit of anger against his father, the murderer of Antigone. The chorus emphasizes the truth of the seer's words (v. 1178; cf. vv. 1066–67).

2. The messenger, Eurydice, the chorus (vv. 1183–243). Having heard through the door the misfortune of her family, Eurydice, Creon's wife, has come out of the palace, after having felt ill. She asks to be informed. The messenger then delivers a detailed account of Creon's expedition: he has buried Polynices' body, but he arrived too late to free Antigone; he found her hanged and his son embracing his fiancée. The encounter between father and son turns into a tragedy. The son draws his sword against his father, and then, as he escapes him, he turns his sword against himself and once again embraces the body of his fiancée (now lying on the ground). After the messenger's report, Eurydice silently goes back into the palace.

3. The messenger, the chorus (vv. 1244–56). The chorus worries again about a silent departure; this is the third one in the tragedy. The messenger, equally surprised, goes back into the palace to discover Eurydice's intentions.

4. Creon, the chorus, then the messenger who comes back out of the palace (vv. 1257–353). The chorus announces Creon's arrival in recitative (vv. 1257–60). Creon's return, carrying his son's body in his arms, gives rise to

a sung dialogue between the character and the chorus (commos) consisting of two strophe/antistrophe pairs. The commos is semilyric. The agitated song of Creon in despair (dochmiacs; metrical analysis in A. M. Dale, *Metrical Analyses of Tragic Choruses*, fasc. 3: Dochmiac, BICS, supp. 21, 3, 1983, pp. 32ff.) contrasts with the spoken words of the chorus. The particularity of this commos is that the character onstage engages in dialogue not only with the chorus, but also with the messenger who comes out of the palace to announce Creon's wife's suicide (v. 1277). This lyric ensemble thus consists in fact of two scenes. Creon laments his errors, feels responsible for his son's death, and sees in his misfortune the mark of a god. The news of his wife's death (v. 1282), the appearance of her body (v. 1293), and the way in which she committed suicide (vv. 1301–5) lead to new waves of lamentation on the part of the hero, who wishes for death and vacillates under the weight of the disaster. The commos is followed by the conclusion in recitative by the chorus, which draws the moral lesson from what has been witnessed (vv. 1347–53).

4. Date

We do not know the date of the play's first performance. However, at the end of argument no. 1, attributed to Aristophanes of Byzantium, we read the following: "It is said that Sophocles was deemed worthy of his strategia in Samos because he was admired for the presentation of his *Antigone*. This play is the thirty-second." Since Sophocles was strategos in 441/440 (see above), the performance of the tragedy, which we can assumed won him a victory, would be slightly earlier. It cannot have been performed in 441, because that is the date when Euripides won his first victory, under the archontate of Diphilus (*Marble of Paros* A 60, *FGrHist.* 239 Jacoby). The date 442 is thus more plausible. The tragedy is the thirty-second in the order of the performances (cf. arguments no. 1 and no. 2). This figure of thirty-two may correspond to the central play of the eleventh trilogy, if Sophocles competed only in the Great Dionysia, which is very likely at that period.

5. Iconography

See L. Séchan, *Études sur la tragédie grecque dans ses rapports avec la céramique*, Paris, 1967 (1926), pp. 141ff.; T.B.L. Webster (cited in chapter V, "Happy Sophocles"), p. 147 sq.; A. D. Trendall and T.B.L. Webster, *Illustrations of Greek Drama*, London, 1971, p. 65; see also above.

6. Editions with notes; or commentaries

R. C. Jebb, 3rd ed., Cambridge, 1900 (Greek text, English translation and notes); rpt. with introduction and notes by R. Blondell, gen. ed. P. E. Easterling, London, 2004; A. Dain and P. Mazon, Paris: CUF, 1st ed. 1955 (Greek text, French trans., notes); compare the French translation by Masqueray, Paris: CUF, 1922; J. C. Kamerbeek, Leiden, 1978 (commentary in English); G. Müller, *Sophokles, Antigone*, Heidelberg, 1967; H. Rohdich, *Antigone: Beitrag zu einer Theorie des sophokleischen Helden*, Heidelberg, 1980; J. Wilkins and M. MacLeod, *Sophocles' Antigone and Oedipus the King*, Bristol Classical, 1987 (commentary in English); A. L. Brown, *Sophocles: Antigone*, Warminster, 1987 (Greek text, English translation, and notes in English); H. Lloyd-Jones and N. G. Wilson, *Sophoclea: Studies on the Text of Sophocles*, Oxford, 1990, pp. 115–49 (notes in English); H. Lloyd-Jones and N. G. Wilson, *Sophocles: Second Thoughts*, Göttingen, 1997, pp. 66–86 (notes in English); J. C. Hogan, *A Commentary on the Plays of Sophocles*, 1991; M. Griffith, Cambridge, 1999 (Greek text, notes in English).

Electra

1. Subject of the tragedy and history of the myth
   a) The tragedy belongs to the history of the Agamemnon family after the Trojan War. The sequence deals with the revenge taken by Orestes, Agamemnon's son. His father, who had been forced to sacrifice his daughter Iphigenia during the expedition's departure from Aulis, was killed, upon his return, by his wife, Clytemnestra, and her lover, Aegisthus. On that day, Orestes escaped being massacred thanks to his sister Electra, who made him leave (cf. vv. 1130ff.). His tutor took him to Phocis, the home of Strophis, Pylades' father. Long afterward, he has returned, when Electra is giving up hope that he will come back, because the messages she has received have proven false. At the beginning of the tragedy Orestes, accompanied by his friend Pylades and the tutor who had saved him, returns to Argos. He is coming to take revenge after having consulted the Delphic oracle regarding what he should do. He must act alone, by trickery. Orestes' vengeance will be carried out exactly in accord with the plan set forth at the beginning. The tutor will announce his death in an accident during a chariot race and will therefore be able to enter the palace. Orestes will come later, carrying an urn that is supposed to contain his ashes. It is at that point that Orestes and Electra recognize each other. The execution of the plan for revenge will then proceed very rapidly: first the murder of Clytemnestra, then, at the end of the tragedy, Orestes has Aegisthus enter the palace in order to kill him. But after Electra's second emergence from the palace in the second scene of the prologue, everything is centered on her. Haunted by mourning for her father, she is presented in her solitude, then in her relations with her entourage (her women friends forming the chorus, her sister Chrysothemis, and her mother Clytemnestra), before she reveals her heroic nature when she is faced by the death of her brother, and decides to carry out the vengeance by herself, despite her sister's advice, until she recognizes her brother and makes her contribution to the vengeance.
   b) The myth of Orestes' vengeance was already known through epic and lyric poetry. It is mentioned several times at the beginning of the *Odyssey*

(1, v. 40; 3, vv. 306–10; 4, vv. 546ff.; cf. vv. 263ff.). What is central in these passages is the just vengeance taken by the "divine Orestes" on Aegisthus, who has seduced Clytemnestra, at first against her will, and who killed Agamemnon by trickery when he returned from Troy, in order to seize power. The murder of the "odious mother" (3, v. 310) is mentioned in a secondary, indirect way. Electra is not mentioned. Neither is Pylades (Orestes' exile took place in Athens). Clytemnestra's responsibility for Agamemnon's murder is accentuated in song 11, vv. 410ff.: Aegisthus killed Agamemnon with Clytemnestra's complicity, and it is Clytemnestra who killed Cassandra.

Orestes' vengeance is also mentioned in Hesiod's *Catalog of Women* (frag. 23, vv. 28–30 Merkelbach-West). When he achieved majority, the "divine Orestes" avenged his father by killing his murderer and his "insolent mother." This time the mother's murder is put on the same level as that of Aegisthus.

The final mention of Orestes' vengeance in epic literature comes at the end of the *Returns from Troy*, known through Proclus's summary (ed. Bernabé 95, 5–7). Orestes avenges Agamemnon, who has been killed by Aegisthus and Clytemnestra. The sole innovation is the presence of Pylades, who takes part in the vengeance. This presupposes that Orestes was in exile in Phocis rather than in Athens, as in the *Odyssey*.

Lyric poetry served as a transition from epic to tragedy. The myth was dealt with by a lyric poet, Xanthos, and then by Stesichorus (sixth century BCE), whose *Oresteia* was inspired by Xanthos. We know the works of these two poets only through a few fragments (ed. Page, frag. 699–700 for Xanthos, and frag. 210–19 for Stesichorus's *Oresteia*). Some aspects of Stesichorus's *Oresteia* were borrowed by Aeschylus: Clytemnestra's dream, the recognition scene involving a lock of hair, and the character of the nurse (with a change of name: Laodamia in Stesichorus, Kilissa in Aeschylus). In the fifth century (474?–454?), Pindar chose the myth of Orestes in his *Pythian Ode* 11, vv. 11ff., connecting it with Delphi through the intermediary of Pylades, the son of Strophios, who lived at the foot of Mount Parnassus. It is thus at the foot of Parnassus that Orestes spent his exile. Thanks to his nurse (named Arsinoé in Pindar), he escaped the massacre of Agamemnon and Cassandra that was orchestrated by Clytemnestra, that "pitiless woman." Orestes came late, but he returned to avenge his father by killing his mother, and then Aegisthus. No mention is made of Electra. Contrary to the preceding tradition, Orestes is not from Argos, but rather from Laconia.

The first tragic author who adopted this sequence is Aeschylus, in *The Libation Bearers*, the central play in his trilogy the *Oresteia* (458 BCE). Euripides dealt with the same sequence in his *Electra*. These three tragedies are extant. Even though the three tragic authors treated the same subject several times (cf., for example, *Philoctetes*), this is the only case where the three tragedies were transmitted to us in their entirety. They have often been compared. But the chronological order is not certain: though Aeschylus's play is the oldest, the relative chronology of the two *Electras* is not known (cf. above, 4. Date). Sophocles' tragedy has innovations with respect to that of Aeschylus: in the staging (in Aeschylus, Agamemnon's tomb is in the visible space in front of the palace, whereas in Sophocles it is no longer visible but is accessible through one of the two side entrances); in the order of the murders (Aegisthus, then Clytemnestra in Aeschylus; Clytemnestra and then Aegisthus in Sophocles and in Pindar); in the replacement or addition of secondary characters (the replacement of Electra's nurse in Aeschylus by the tutor in Sophocles; the addition of Electra's sister, Chrysothemis); in the importance accorded to the main characters (Orestes in Aeschylus, Electra in Sophocles); in the end of the tragedy (the madness of Orestes after the matricide that ends Aeschylus's *Libation Bearers* is not mentioned in Sophocles). The innovations are even greater in Euripides.

2. Chorus, characters, and actors

The chorus consists of women from the Mycenaean nobility who are Electra's friends; cf. v. 128. The protagonist plays Electra, who, starting at v. 86, is present continuously throughout the tragedy (this is exceptional), even during the parts of the tragedy reserved for the chorus, the parados and the stasima, with the exception of the fourth stasimon. Several of these choral parts are replaced by lyric dialogues between the chorus and Electra (parodos, second stasimon). The character of Orestes is played by the deuteragonist, while the tutor is played by the tritagonist. Clytemnestra can be played only by the deuteragonist (cf. Clytemnestra's encounter with Electra played by the protagonist, and with the tutor played by the tritagonist), whereas the role of Chrysothemis is played either by the deuteragonist or by the tritagonist (she meets neither Orestes nor the tutor). Pylades, who does not speak, is acted by a bit player.

3. Structure of the tragedy

* **Prologue** (vv. 1–120): two scenes.

1. The tutor and Orestes (v. 185): in this return tragedy, in an initial scene the prologue presents those who come from outside to carry out the vengeance. Orestes, accompanied by his friend Pylades and his old tutor, arrives at dawn before the ancestral palace in Mycenae. Only two characters speak, the tutor and Orestes, because Pylades is played by a silent actor. The tutor (vv. 1–22) describes the landscape that Orestes is viewing, because he was too young when he left to remember it. Orestes describes his plan for vengeance (vv. 23–76). It is inspired by the oracle of Apollo at Delphi, whom Orestes consulted before returning, and who recommended acting alone, by trickery and not by force. Orestes tells his tutor

to announce his death, inventing a mortal accident during a chariot race at the games in Delphi. Following the god's instructions, Orestes himself, accompanied by Pylades, will first visit Agamemnon's tomb to make libations and deposit a lock of hair. He will then return to the palace, carrying a funerary urn that allegedly holds Orestes' ashes. The tutor concludes his speech with a prayer for the success of the enterprise. A plaintive cry is heard coming from inside the palace.

2. Electra comes out alone from the palace (vv. 87–120). A monologue in anapaestic dimeters. According to some scholars, this is a monody; according to others, it is a declaimed monologue. Electra has just confided her lamentations to the morning sunlight after nocturnal laments in the secrecy of her bedchamber. She recalls the cause, the unjust and pitiless murder of her father, who was killed by her mother and her lover Aegisthus. She will not cease her lamentations until revenge has been taken, and she addresses a prayer to the divinities of the Underworld that they might carry out this vengeance and above all make Orestes return. Though she does not know it, her wishes have been fulfilled even before she expressed them.

* **Parados**: vv. 121–250. Entrance of the chorus of women, members of the Mycenaean nobility who are Electra's friends. The song takes the form of a purely lyric dialogue between the chorus and Electra. It consists of three strophe/antistrophe pairs, with the whole concluded by an epode (rhythmical analysis in A. M. Dale, *Metrical Analyses of Tragic Choruses*, fasc. 3: Dactylic, BICS, supp. 21, 3, 1983, pp. 272–76). Each strophe or antistrophe is divided into remarks by the chorus and remarks by Electra. While espousing Electra's cause against her mother, who has committed an impious murder, the women of the chorus encourage her to temper her pain, seek to console her, and urge her to be prudent, out of friendship for her. But Electra, out of respect for her father, cannot listen to them, in the name of piety.

* **First episode** (vv. 251–471).

1. The continuation of the parados (vv. 251–327). There is no entrance or exit of characters. The parados and the beginning of the first episode thus form only a single scene. The only change is the passage from the sung to the spoken, and also an imbalance in the length of the remarks made by the characters. Whereas the sung dialogue was divided equally between Electra and the chorus, here, in the spoken part, the chorus is effaced by Electra, who gives a long speech of fifty-six verses (vv. 254–309) before engaging in a brief final dialogue with the chorus (vv. 310–27). In her speech, Electra justifies her attitude in a more organized way than in the sung part. She is aware that her perpetual lamentations are tiresome for her friends, but a woman of a noble nature (v. 257) is obliged to act that way when confronting the sufferings of a father that are also her own. Her everyday life is unbearable: like a slave, she must obey the murderers

whom she sees living without remorse. She is subject to their violence, especially when they reproach her for having saved Orestes. In the final dialogue, we learn that Aegisthus is not in the palace, but has already gone to the fields. This detail is important for carrying out the vengeance. Aegisthus does not return until the end of the tragedy (v. 1442).

2. Scene between the two sisters (vv. 328–471). The entrance of Chrysothemis, Electra's sister, who comes out of the palace. As the chorus indicates, she is carrying funeral offerings. The two sisters, though born from the same father and mother, have adopted different modes of behavior. One has chosen resignation, the other permanent revolution. Chrysothemis brings two bits of news: the first is that Electra is threatened by a punishment that resembles the one that Creon had planned for Antigone. As soon as Aegisthus returns, she must be incarcerated in an underground prison to put an end to her lamentations. This threat will not be carried out, because Aegisthus, when he returns, will not be able to implement his plans. But the announcement of this news makes it possible to gauge Electra's determination. She flinches neither before the threats of the powerful nor before her sister's recommendations. The second bit of news is the mission that her mother Clytemnestra has entrusted to her: pouring libations on her father's tomb in order to erase the frightening dream she has had during the night. In her dream, she saw Agamemnon thrusting his former scepter in the earth; from it has sprung a young shoot that covers the whole land of Mycenae with its foliage. Electra dissuades her sister from performing this mission and advises her to substitute their own offerings for their mother's, no matter how modest they may be (locks of their hair and a belt), to ask the dead man for a triumphal return of his son. The chorus approves this recommendation. Chrysothemis endorses this proposal, asking the chorus to be discreet. She leaves through the side exit that leads to Agamemnon's tomb.

* **First Stasimon** (vv. 472–515): Electra remains present on the stage. The chorus addresses her once (v. 479). However, she remains silent. Thus we have a traditional choral song. It is brief, consisting of a single strophe/antistrophe pair followed by an epode (metrical analysis in A. M. Dale, *Metrical Analyses of Tragic Choruses*, fasc. 3: Iambic, BICS, supp. 21, 3, 1983, pp. 214–16). The chorus sees in the dream a prophetic sign of the arrival of Justice and of the avenging Erinys. The crime will not remain unpunished. Violence has inhabited the palace ever since Pelops, the founder of the family, murdered his coachman, Myrtilus.

* **Second Episode** (vv. 516–822): three scenes.

1. Scene between the mother and the daughter (vv. 516–659). Clytemnestra emerges from the palace. The structure is the one expected in an agōn scene. First two speeches, in which each of the two characters present sets forth his point of view: Clytemnestra's speech (thirty-six verses: vv. 516–

51); Electra's speech (fifty-four verses: vv. 558–609). Then a more rapid dialogue (vv. 610–33). Clytemnestra defends herself, refuting in advance her daughter's accusations and justifying the murder of Agamemnon in the name of Justice, because he sacrificed her daughter (Iphigenia) without any valid reason. Electra replies by denouncing the injustice of Agamemnon's murder. First, she defends her father by showing that the divinity Artemis forced him to sacrifice his daughter at Aulis to allow the Achaians' fleet to leave for Troy, and she then accuses her mother of using this pretext of vengeance to live with the man who helped her kill Agamemnon. In conclusion, she vehemently rebels against her mother, going so far as to tell her that she would not hesitate to avenge her father's death if she could. The violence of these remarks leads to a dialogue in which each party maintains its position. This dialogue ends before the end of the scene. A last part (vv. 634–59) is occupied by what justified Clytemnestra's emergence from the palace. She has come, accompanied by a servant, to make offerings and prayers to Apollo that he might free her from the fear her dream has aroused in her, either by fulfilling it if it is favorable to her, or by turning it against her enemies in the opposite case.

2. The arrival of the tutor announcing to Clytemnestra and Electra the (false) news of Orestes' death. This is the beginning of the fulfillment of the vengeance by means of a ruse. The scene is typical of a messenger scene. First the news is announced, followed by an initial reaction on the part of those who hear it (Electra's despair; Clytemnestra's desire to be sure it is true), then the detailed account in an exceptionally long speech by the messenger (eighty-four verses: vv. 680–763), with a second, more developed reaction by the auditors. The (fictive) account of Orestes' death in the chariot race at Delphi develops with brio the depiction Orestes himself had given in his description of the vengeance (vv. 47–50). This is a tragedy within the tragedy: the account presents first an Orestes triumphant in the foot races and all the other competitions on the first day of the Pythian games; then, the next day, the catastrophe during the chariot race. All the details of the race bring it to life: ten competitors; the start, the first dramatic turnaround: an accident leading to a general collision from which only two contestants emerge, the Athenian and Orestes; the second dramatic turnaround: on the last lap, Orestes' chariot strikes a boundary stone and Orestes takes a fatal fall. This narrative, which is simultaneously epic, tragic, and pathetic, arouses opposed reactions in the characters: the chorus's despair at the death of the family of its masters; Clytemnestra's initially ambiguous reaction, apparently divided between relief and the pain of losing a son, but ultimately glad to be freed from the fear of vengeance; Electra, in a further manifestation of despair, attacks her mother again in a brief stichomythia. The scene ends when the tutor goes back into the palace. The plan for vengeance is carried out eas-

ily, despite a moment of hesitation when Clytemnestra reacts ambiguously to the news of her son's death.

3. Electra, who has remained alone with the chorus (vv. 804–22), denounces the behavior of her mother, who is outwardly distressed by her son's death, but internally delighted by it. In an emotional apostrophe, the young woman addresses Orestes, whose death has put an end to all her hopes and made her solitude even greater. She no longer wants to go into the palace and has no further desire to live.

* **Second stasimon** (vv. 823–70): this is the continuation of the preceding scene, insofar as there is neither an entrance nor an exit of the characters. It is a stasimon in the form of a dialogue between the chorus and Electra. The dialogue is purely lyric, consisting of two strophe/antistrophe pairs (metrical analysis in A. M. Dale, *Metrical Analyses of Tragic Choruses*, fasc. 1: Dactylo-Epitrite, BICS, supp. 21, 1, 1971, pp. 36ff.). Electra laments, and in spite of everything, the chorus seeks to restore her hope by envisaging a divine intervention and by comparing allusively the comparable vengeance of Amphiaraus, who was betrayed by his wife, Eriphyle, for a gold necklace. Eriphyle was in fact punished. But Electra cannot allow herself to be convinced: Amphiaraus was avenged by his son Alcmeon, who killed his mother, whereas for Agamemnon that is no longer possible, because Orestes is dead. The chorus, feeling compassion, also tries to console Electra by using another commonplace about death. But there again, Electra, in the depths of despair, cannot be convinced. Orestes' death is not ordinary, and he died far away, without his sister being able to give him a ritual burial.

* **Third episode** (vv. 871–1057): this episode includes only a single scene demarcated by Chrysothemis's entrance and exit. This long scene is composed of two parts. In the first, Chrysothemis runs in, happy to announce to Electra Orestes' return (vv. 871–937); in the second, Electra tries to involve her in her decision to carry out the revenge (vv. 938–1057).

1. The entrance of Chrysothemis constitutes an initial peripeteia. After the tutor's message announcing Orestes' death, here is Chrysothemis's message announcing that he is alive. Having returned from Agamemnon's tomb, where she has deposited offerings, Chrysothemis says that she saw there signs of Orestes' return: (1) libations and floral offerings; (2) on top of the burial mound, a lock of hair left by some close relative, who could only be Orestes. To Chrysothemis's interpretation of the signs she saw, Electra opposes the testimony of the person who said he had witnessed Orestes' death. Chrysothemis, despite the correctness of her reasoning, passes from intense joy to pain when she discovers the new misfortunes that have been added to the old ones. It is an aborted recognition scene. However, Chrysothemis now seems in phase with Electra: the death of Orestes appears to have united them in sorrow.

2. But this rapprochement between the two sisters is short-lived. They will confront one another in an agōn scene including two speeches followed by a stichomythia. Electra requests the aid of her sister, who grants her agreement in principle. In a long speech (vv. 947–89) Electra sets forth her new decision: she wants her sister to help her kill Aegisthus, the murderer of their father, because they are now the only ones who can do so. She tries to convince Chrysothemis by showing her what her life would be like if Aegisthus remains alive—a life without patrimony and without marriage—and what she will gain if she endorses her decision: a reputation for piety, a life that is once again free, the possibility of marriage and glory. But Chrysothemis, in an opposing speech (vv. 992–1014), denounces Electra's lack of prudence and her fury. She is only a woman, and the power relationships are too unequal. The attempt can lead only to disaster. She asks Electra to have the wisdom to yield to the powerful. After the two opposed speeches, the struggle continues in a rapid dialogue with a long stichomythic series. Confronted by Chrysothemis's refusal, Electra decides to act alone (vv. 1019ff.). The two sisters cannot understand or convince one another: the one's intransigence collides with the other's foresight. Chrysothemis goes back into the palace but does not reveal anything.

* **Third stasimon** (vv. 1058–97): the chorus, which has remained with Electra, begins a choral song composed of two strophe/antistrophe pairs; for the metrical analysis, see A. M. Dale, *Metrical Analyses of Tragic Choruses*, fasc. 2: Aeolo-Choriambic, BICS, supp. 21, 2, 1981, pp. 42ff. It finds its inspiration in the action, reflecting on the preceding scene in which the two sisters chose different paths. Whereas in the preceding scene (vv. 1015ff.) the chorus seemed to prefer the path of wisdom advocated by Chrysothemis, here it emphasizes the heroism and piety of Electra, whose choice is to defend her father, even at the price of her life, and it expresses its hope that she will win out over her enemies.

* **Fourth episode** (vv. 1098–383): the second phase of the execution of the plan for vengeance. Entrance of Orestes, accompanied by Pylades (cf. v. 1373), with the servants carrying the urn that is supposed to contain Orestes' ashes (cf. v. 1123). Two scenes.

   1. The recognition scene between Orestes and Electra (vv. 1098–325). Electra asks to take the urn in her arms. Then she laments in a long, emotional speech (vv. 1126–70) addressed to her dead brother. But at the same time, she indirectly reveals his identity (cf. v. 1137, "your sister"). The speech thus constitutes the first part of the recognition (Electra recognized by Orestes). In the following dialogue (vv. 1174–223), Orestes, overcome by emotion and pity, makes himself known and provides proof, his father's seal. The dialogue, with a series of antilabai (vv. 1220ff.), reaches an apex.

The most intense joy then takes the place of the deepest pain in a "song from the stage," a duet composed of a triad, that is, strophe/antistrophe/epode (vv. 1232–87). The duet is semilyric: Electra sings her happiness, while Orestes speaks (metrical analysis in A. M. Dale, *Metrical Analyses of Tragic Choruses*, fasc. 3: Dochmiac, BICS, supp. 21, 3, 1983, pp. 36–38). Orestes has to contain Electra's emotion and urges her to be prudent. Finally, once Electra's emotion is under control, the last part of the scene (vv. 1288–325) reverts to speech. Orestes cuts short in advance Electra's explanations of the conduct of her mother and Aegisthus in order not to delay the moment for acting. He merely asks her for the information necessary for the present moment and advises her to conceal her joy and shed pretend tears when she is around her mother. Electra agrees to do so. She tells him that Clytemnestra is in the palace, whereas Aegisthus has gone out. And she will not show her joy to her mother, whom she hates, even though she once again expresses her inextinguishable joy at seeing Orestes alive when she had thought him dead.

2. The tutor comes out of the palace (vv. 1326–83). From inside, he has heard them and comes to put an end to these "long speeches" and "insatiable shouting for joy." It is the moment of the second, much more rapid recognition. After Orestes, Electra recognizes the tutor, thanks to her brother's hints. Electra's cry of delight, "O joyous day!" (v. 1354) echoes her same cry in the first recognition (v. 1224). The tutor tells them that it is time to act: Clytemnestra is alone; there is no man in the palace. Orestes, accompanied by Pylades, bows down before the statues of the ancestral gods located in front of the palace. Then Orestes, Pylades, and the tutor enter the palace, along with the servants carrying the urn. Electra follows them after saying a prayer to Apollo Lyceus. This prayer without an offering, which is opposed to that of her mother (cf. the end of scene 1 of the second episode), will be heard by the god.

* **Fourth stasimon** (vv. 1384–97): the chorus remains alone (for the first time); it has time to sing only one strophe/antistrophe pair (metrical analysis in A. M. Dale, *Metrical Analyses of Tragic Choruses*, fasc. 1: Dactylo-Epitrite, BICS, supp. 21, 1, 1971, p. 38 sq.). It will be interrupted by Electra's abrupt exit. The tragedy accelerates at the time of vengeance. The chorus imagines that the divinities of vengeance—Ares and the Erinyes—enter the palace at the same time as the men. And it is Hermes who guides Orestes' crafty entrance armed with his sword.

* **Exodos** (vv. 1398–510): four scenes. The first two are inserted into the structure of a sung dialogue between the characters and the chorus (commos). The dialogue is semilyric; only the chorus sings.

1. Electra, the chorus (vv. 1398–421). Electra comes out of the palace and addresses the chorus. Like a messenger coming from inside the palace, she provides information regarding the preparations: Clytemnestra is ready-

ing for burial the urn that is supposed to hold Orestes' ashes, while Orestes and Pylades are near her. Electra has rushed out of the palace because her role is to watch for Aegisthus's arrival. But from the moment that Clytemnestra's first scream is heard, the spoken dialogue is transformed into a commos (vv. 1407–41). Clytemnestra's cries are heard several times, coming from inside the palace and mixed with the reactions of Electra and the chorus. Clytemnestra's cries and words make it possible to reconstruct the scene inside the palace: before dying, the mother has recognized her son; she is struck twice. Electra and the women of the chorus react in opposite ways: Electra remains calm; the chorus is frightened. The contrast is emphasized by the diction. Electra speaks; the chorus sings.

2. Once Clytemnestra has been murdered, Orestes and Pylades come out of the palace (vv. 1422–41). Orestes holds the bloody sword in his hand. He confirms that Clytemnestra is dead and that all is in order in the palace, "if Apollo's oracle spoke well." But they almost immediately go back into the palace, because the chorus announces Aegisthus's arrival in the antistrophe of the commos.

3. Aegisthus returns from the countryside (vv. 1442–65). He is joyful, because he has heard the news of Orestes' death. He is met by Electra, who ironically confirms Orestes' death and the presence of his body. Aegisthus is exultant and orders the door of the palace to be thrown open so that all the residents of Mycenae can witness the sight and henceforth accept his despotic power.

4. A final scene between Aegisthus and Orestes (vv. 1466–1510). A body covered with a sheet appears on the eccyclema, with Orestes and Pylades on each side of it. When he draws back the sheet, Aegisthus finds Clytemnestra's body, then recognizes Orestes and realizes that he has fallen into a trap. He tries to gain time, but Electra passionately intervenes one last time with her brother, urging that Aegisthus be rapidly put to death and left unburied. After a rapid exchange in which Aegisthus stands up to Orestes, he is forced to be the first to go back into the palace, where Orestes kills him in the very place where he killed Agamemnon, so that the vengeance might be complete. The tragedy ends with a reflection by the chorus on the fate of the tragic family: after many misfortunes, it has finally been set free thanks to Orestes' present action. The end is no way comparable to that of Aeschylus's *Libation Bearers*. However, some commentators have sought see in Aegisthus's last words (v. 1498) an allusion to the Pelopids' future misfortunes, namely Orestes' madness.

4. Date

The precise date of the tragedy is not known, because we have no documents concerning it. It is traditionally considered to be one of the last tragedies, particularly because of the rapidity and flexibility of the dialogue. In it we find twenty-five examples of *antilabè* (the division of one verse between two characters), with one verse divided into three parts (v. 1502). What is also remarkable is the way the dialogue penetrates into the lyricism. This tragedy, unlike *Ajax*, *The Women of Trachis*, *Antigone*, and *Oedipus the King*, has a parodos in dialogue. This is an innovation that is found again in the last tragedies, *Philoctetes* and *Oedipus at Colonus*. In addition, it also has a stasimon in dialogue (the second stasimon). This is also an innovation with respect to the series of four tragedies named above. This innovation also appears in *Philoctetes* (the second and third stasima). There is debate about the relative chronology of Sophocles' *Electra* and that of Euripides.

5. Iconography

See L. Séchan (cited in chapter X, "Humans and the Gods"); T.B.L. Webster (cited in chapter V, "Happy Sophocles"); A. D. Trendall and T.B.L. Webster (cited in chapter X, "Humans and the Gods").

6. Editions and commentaries

R. C. Jebb, Cambridge, 1894 (Greek text, English translation, notes); rpt. with introduction by J. March, gen. ed. P. E. Easterling, London, 2004; G. Kaibel, 1896, rpt. Stuttgart, 1967 (Greek text, notes in German); A. Dain and P. Mazon, Paris: CUF, 1st ed. 1958 (Greek text, French translation, notes in French); for the French translation, compare P. Masqueray, Paris: CUF, 1922; J. C. Kamerbeek, Leiden, 1974 (notes in English); J. H. Kells, *Electra*, Cambridge, 1973 (Greek text, notes in English); H. Lloyd-Jones and N. G. Wilson, *Sophoclea: Studies on the Text of Sophocles*, Oxford, 1990, pp. 42–78 (notes in English); H. Lloyd-Jones and N. G. Wilson, *Sophocles: Second Thoughts*, Göttingen, 1997, pp. 30–47 (notes in English); J. C. Hogan, *A Commentary on the Plays of Sophocles*, 1991; J. R. March, *Sophocles: Electra*, Warminster, 2001 (Greek text, English translation, and notes in English); M. Lloyd, *Sophocles: Electra*, London: Duckworth, 2005 (monograph in English).

Oedipus the King

1. Subject of the tragedy and history of the myth

a) The tragedy belongs to the Theban myth, like *Antigone* and *Oedipus at Colonus*. But even though Sophocles composed *Oedipus the King* after *Antigone* (see below, 4. Date), the subject of *Oedipus the King* comes earlier in the chronology of the myth than that of *Antigone*. In fact, at the beginning of *Oedipus the King* Oedipus, king of Thebes, is at the height of his glory, whereas at the time when *Antigone* begins he is already dead. On the other hand, the tragedy of *Oedipus at Colonus*, which is about Oedipus's death, is later than *Oedipus the King*, both in the chronology of the myth and in the date of its composition (for the date of the composition of *Oedipus at Colonus*, see the section on this tragedy under 4. Date).

The sequence in the myth chosen by Sophocles in *Oedipus the King* is tragic par excellence. It illustrates in an exemplary way the rapid passage from fortune to misfortune, as the chorus emphasizes at the end of the tragedy (vv. 1524–30): in a single day, Oedipus, a powerful king who is expert in solving puzzles and is envied by everyone, has become the most miserable of mortals. This reversal of fortune is all the more impressive because the king has tried everything to cope with the tragedy of his city: a plague that is ravaging Thebes and has made it sterile in all the domains of life (plants, animals, humans). But his attempts to save the city, as he had saved it the first time when he came to Thebes to solve the enigma of the Sphinx, gradually leads him to evoke and discover his own past and to look into his origins: he thought he was the son of Polybus, king of Corinth, and his wife Merope, but he turns out to be the murderer of his father Laius, the husband of his mother Jocasta and the brother of his own children, of his two sons Eteocles and Polynices, and of his two daughters, Antigone and Ismene. His discovery of this past leads first to Jocasta's suicide by hanging, and then to Oedipus's self-mutilation by blinding himself.

Oedipus's destiny, given in chronological order, is fabulous: Laius, married to Jocasta, has had a son despite the warning given by Apollo's oracle, who had predicted that he would die by the hand of his own son (vv. 713–14). Out of fear that the oracle might be fulfilled, Laius had the infant abandoned immediately after birth, with his feet pinioned, in an inaccessible place in the mountains (vv. 717–19). The mountain in question is the Cithaeron, which is south of Thebes and north of Corinth, where shepherds from the two cities meet in the summer during the transhumance (v. 1027; vv. 1133–39). Pitying the child (v. 1178), Laius's shepherd, who had been given the infant by Jocasta herself (cf. v. 1173) to abandon him in the mountains, gave him to a Corinthian shepherd so that he might raise him as his own child (v. 1177; vv. 1142–43). The Corinthian shepherd saved the child, removing his bonds (v. 1034), and gave him to the king of Corinth, Polybus (v. 1022), who, desiring to have a child, passed him off as his own son and that of his wife, Merope (vv. 774–75). But one day at a banquet an inebriated man said that Oedipus was Polybus's "supposed child" (v. 780). Concerned, Oedipus secretly consulted the Delphic oracle, who, without replying directly to the question regarding Oedipus's origin, told him that he would marry his mother and kill his father (vv. 787–93); to avoid what the oracle had predicted, Oedipus decided never to return to Corinth, and as he was leaving Delphi, at the intersection of the roads from Delphi and from Daulis (v. 734), he encountered his true father coming from Thebes, riding in a chariot and accompanied by five servants; in a futile dispute about who was to pass first, Oedipus killed Laius without knowing who he was and killed all his servants as well (vv. 800–813). At least Oedipus thought he killed them all, because one of them survived (v. 118; v. 756). Now this servant was none other than the shepherd who had been assigned to abandon the young Oedipus in the mountains (vv. 1051–52). Oedipus continued on his way to Thebes, where he freed the Thebans from the Sphinx by solving its riddle (vv. 35–39). Thanks to his exceptional intelligence, he was thus made king (vv. 383ff.) and married the wife of the former king. In the meantime, Laius's servant had returned and recounted the murder of Laius, departing from the truth somewhat to avoid declaring his coward-ice (vv. 122–23): according to his account, Laius was murdered by a band of brigands. When Oedipus came to power, the servant begged Jocasta to allow him to live in the countryside far from the palace (vv. 758–64). Oedipus reigned peacefully until this new crisis for the city arose: after the ravages of the Sphinx, the Thebans are prey to a second crisis, the rav-ages of the plague.

That is the history of Oedipus as it can be reconstituted on the basis of information given here and there in the tragedy. But the subject of the tragedy is different: it consists in leading the king to look into his past and his origins. All Sophocles' art consists in weaving the plot and mak-ing it advance, with apparent flashbacks, with the help of various bits of information subtly dosed out, whether true or false, properly or improp-erly interpreted, and with the help of various peripeteias. The knot of the tragedy is the reply of the Delphic oracle that Oedipus consulted through the intermediary of his brother-in-law Creon, to find a remedy for the plague. The oracle recommends eliminating the pollution left by the un-avenged murder of the preceding king. This response leads the current king to launch an investigation into Laius's murderers, an investigation that he conducts vigorously at first, for the good of his city. However, he ultimately discovers that he is not only the guilty party but also the son of the victim and thus the husband of his mother and the brother of his sons. This discovery of the truth comes only after Oedipus receives vari-ous bits of information that he misinterprets, thinking himself the victim of a conspiracy (the seer Tiresias's revelations regarding Oedipus's past), or that worry him (Jocasta's revelations regarding the circumstances of Lai-us's murder). The arrival of two messengers causes an alternation of illu-sion and awareness. First, the arrival of a Corinthian messenger who has come to announce officially the death of King Polybus, Oedipus's sup-posed father; this scene ends with Jocasta's recognition of the truth and her silent departure. The second arrival is that of a Theban messenger who provokes, after a confrontation with the Corinthian messenger, Oedipus's own recognition of his true origin.

b) The myth of Oedipus, which had been known since Homer, evolved as it passed from the epic to the tragedy (for the history of the myth and for the growing importance of Delphi, see above). In tragedy, this sequence in the myth had already been dealt with by Aeschylus in his tragedy entitled *Oedipus*, which was the second play in a connected tetralogy including three tragedies, *Laius*, *Oedipus*, and *Seven against Thebes*, along with a satyr play, *The Sphinx*. Of this tetralogy, with which Aeschylus won the prize in 467, only *Seven against Thebes* is extant (see the argument of *Seven against Thebes*). No fragment of Aeschylus's *Oedipus* remains (see S. Radt, *TrGF* 3, 1985, pp. 287ff.). However, in *Seven against Thebes* (vv. 752–56 and vv. 771–91) there a few allusions to "parricidal Oedipus," who dared to seed the sacred field of his mother," to his prestige as king of Thebes when he freed the Thebans from the monster that was ravaging the people (the Sphinx), and to the twofold catastrophe that he caused when he learned the reality of his marriage: putting out his eyes and cursing his two sons. That does not authorize any detailed reconstitution of the lost tragedy. At most we can say that by inserting his tragedy into the whole of the family's destiny over three generations, Aeschylus was able clearly to connect—as Sophocles declined to do in his tragedy—Oedipus's destiny with the hereditary curse laid on the family after Laius's initial offense, "quickly punished but which still endures down to the third generation": Laius had three times disobeyed Apollo's oracle forbidding him to have a child if he wanted to save Thebes (*Seven against Thebes*, vv. 742–50). In his *Oedipus the King*, Sophocles does not emphasize Laius's crime (cf. vv. 707ff.) and does not mention Oedipus's curses against his sons (cf. vv. 1459–61).

This sequence of the myth was also dramatized by Euripides in a tragedy that was also called *Oedipus* and that is very certainly later than that of Sophocles. Like that of Aeschylus, Euripides' tragedy is lost; however, we have a few fragments of it (H. Van Looy, *Euripides*, *Fragments*, vol. 2, CUF, 2000, pp. 429–58, and *TrGF* 5.1, pp. 569–83 Kannicht). Without allowing a certain restitution of the tragedy, these fragments enable us to discern innovations with regard to Sophocles: for example, Oedipus's eyes are put out by Laius's servants when they learn that the "son of Polybus" is the murderer of Laius (see the scholium on *The Phoenician Women*, v. 61). In the fourth century the subject was taken over by several Greek tragic authors and one comic author, and also in the Roman theater, notably by Seneca (see the complete list in S. Radt. *TrGF* 3, 1985, p. 288).

2. Characters and sites of the drama
   a) The chorus consists of Theban citizens (cf. vv. 222–23). They are subject to their king (cf. v. 530), but they advise him (vv. 650ff.). They are not ordinary citizens. Jocasta calls them, deferentially, "Princes of the country" (v. 911). They are elders highly honored in the city (v. 1223). The comparison with the chorus in *Antigone* composed of Theban elders forming the royal council (cf. the section on *Antigone*) suggests that the

chorus in *Oedipus the King* is none other than this royal council, because it was already operating in the time of Oedipus and even of Laius. The members of the chorus in *Antigone* were already called "Princes of Thebes" (*Antigone*, v. 988). Nonetheless, in *Oedipus* there is no explicit reference to the royal council. They are rather chosen representatives of the people (cf. v. 145).

The speaking characters are, in the order in which they speak: Oedipus (vv. 1ff.), a priest of Zeus (vv. 14ff.), Creon, Oedipus's brother-in-law (vv. 87ff.), the seer Tiresias, Jocasta, Oedipus's wife (and mother, vv. 911ff.), a Corinthian messenger (vv. 924ff.), a Theban servant (vv. 1123ff.), and a messenger who comes out of the palace (vv. 1223ff.). Silent characters complete the roster. Here are the ones who are mentioned in the text: at the beginning, a group of children that remains throughout the prologue; one of Oedipus's servants who has been sent to summon the people (v. 144); then, when Theseus enters, two of Oedipus's envoys who have been sent to look for him (cf. vv. 288ff.), and a child to guide the blind old man (cf. v. 444); at the end of the tragedy, Oedipus's two daughters, Antigone and Ismene (vv. 1472ff.).

The protagonist plays only the character of Oedipus, who is present from the beginning of the tragedy to the end, apart from several moments when he has gone into the palace (vv. 146–215; vv. 463–530; vv. 863–949; vv. 1186–296). The deuteragonist plays Creon, Tiresias, and the Corinthian messenger, while the tritagonist plays Zeus's priest, Jocasta, and the Theban shepherd. The messenger who comes from inside the palace might have been played either by the deuteragonist or by the tritagonist.

b) The visible space is in front of the royal palace in Thebes, whose façade is seen at the back of the stage. At the beginning of the tragedy, during the prologue, a group of suppliants composed of children sits on the steps of the altars located in front of the palace, under the guidance of a priest of Zeus (cf. vv. 15–18). Very close to the palace gate is a representation of Apollo, because Jocasta, on emerging from the palace, addresses it (cf. v. 919). The text does not say what kind of representation it is (statue, a conical stone, or an altar?).

The virtual external space is on the one hand the city of Thebes (right-side passage: Creon's first entrance; the entrance and exit of Tiresias; Creon's second entrance and exit; the Theban servant's entrance and exit; Creon's third entrance and exit); on other, it is the foreign (left-side passage: Creon's first entrance coming from Delphi, then the messenger coming from Corinth). The virtual internal space is the palace; Oedipus and Jocasta come out of it and go into it, and it is there that Jocasta commits suicide and Oedipus puts out his eyes. The messenger who comes to announce these two disasters also comes out of the palace.

3. Structure of the tragedy

* **Prologue** (vv. 1ff.): two scenes.
  1. Oedipus and the priest of Zeus (vv. 1–84). This scene presents a great
     spectacle. Oedipus comes out of the royal palace and finds a group of
     children holding branches and seated in the position of suppliants on the
     steps of his altar in front of the palace. Moved by this sight, the king ad-
     dresses a priest of Zeus who is their spokesman. In a long speech, the
     priest first reminds Oedipus of the critical situation of the city, which is
     in the grip of a plague that is killing plants, animals, and humans. Then
     he praises the person whose help he is going to beg, saying that for the
     Thebans, that person is Oedipus: not a god, but the first of men, the one
     who saved the city from the Sphinx's tribute by solving its riddle without
     knowing anything. Finally, he begs him to find a way to save the city
     again. Oedipus replies, addressing the children. After long reflection, the
     king, who is sensitive to his subjects' suffering, has found only one solu-
     tion: sending his brother-in-law Creon, the son of Menoeceus, to consult
     the Delphic oracle.
  2. Oedipus and Creon (vv. 85–146). Oedipus, in a dialogue that provides
     information, questions Creon, who has returned from Delphi, regarding
     the oracle's reply. The oracle demands the cleansing of the pollution
     caused by the unavenged murder of Laius, the king who reigned over
     Thebes before Oedipus's arrival: the murderers still present in the city
     must be driven out or killed. On the occasion of this announcement,
     Oedipus questions Creon concerning the circumstances of Laius's mur-
     der. It is learned that Laius had left to consult the oracle at Delphi and
     that a single survivor returned, saying that Laius had fallen victim to a
     group of brigands. This is the first information about the Theban shep-
     herd, whose arrival toward the end of the tragedy (vv. 1110ff.) will defini-
     tively enlighten Oedipus regarding his origins. Like a good king, Oedipus
     takes charge of the investigation by examining the case from the outset.
     Everything encourages him to do so: the interest of Thebes, the interest
     of the god, and also his own interest, because he could himself become a
     victim of his predecessors' murderers. Oedipus concludes by asking the
     group of children to leave and by commanding the people to assemble.
     This is a way of justifying the entrance of the chorus.
* **Parodos** (vv. 151–215): the chorus, informed of Creon's return, hastens to learn
  the news. The parodos is composed of three strophe/antistrophe pairs (metrical analysis in A. M. Dale, *Metrical Analyses of Tragic Choruses*, fasc. 3: Dactylic, BICS, supp. 21, 3, 1983, pp. 270ff.). It wonders, with concern and hope,
  what the content of the oracle's response might be, and what Apollo might
  demand (str. 1). Then it calls on divinities to come to Thebes's aid: first
  Athena, Artemis, and Apollo (ant. 1). The chorus evokes, like the priest,
  Thebes's sufferings in the grip of the scourge (str. 2 and ant. 2). Then it again

calls on divinities for help: Zeus, Apollo, and Dionysus, the god of Thebes (str. 3 and ant. 3).

* **First episode** (vv. 216–462): two scenes.

1. Oedipus, the chorus. Oedipus comes out of the palace. Once again, he finds himself confronted by a group; but this time it consists of citizens and not children. He has heard the chorus's prayers and has come to make an official proclamation addressed to all the residents of the city founded by Cadmus. In a long, solemn speech of sixty verses, the king issues his instructions for discovering Laius's murderer. He asks those who have knowledge to speak up, promising impunity to the murderer if he admits his guilt, and a reward to anyone who identifies him. On the other hand, he threatens with a severe punishment a murderer who does not accuse himself or anyone who does not accuse another whom he knows to be guilty, and he utters curses against the guilty party, who must be excluded from everything, in accord with the oracle's demand. All through this proclamation, tragic irony is present, because the king, showing severity in the name of praiseworthy principles, promulgates a punishment that will be applied to himself. In a short dialogue following the proclamation, the chorus admits its ignorance and suggests asking the seer Tiresias. This suggestion corresponds to the one Creon made to Oedipus, who had sent two messengers to bring Tiresias to him.

2. Oedipus and Tiresias (vv. 300–462). This scene between the king and the seer repeats, with variants, a scene in *Antigone* between King Creon and the seer Tiresias (vv. 988–1090; see the section on *Antigone*). But whereas Tiresias came spontaneously in *Antigone* to tell the king the truth, here Tiresias comes before Oedipus against his will. The king receives the seer with respect, praising his knowledge, and after reminding him of the city's sickness and the reply of Apollo's oracle, asks him to save the city. But the seer, fearing for his life, refuses to speak and wants to leave. This refusal arouses the king's anger, and he denounces the seer's treachery and lack of concern for the city, even going so far as to accuse him of having ordered the murder, if not of having committed it himself. These accusations arouse the seer's anger, and he replies by accusing Oedipus of being himself the origin of the pollution, and then, faced by the king's redoubled anger, of having shameful relations with his relatives. Two angry men confront one another, as the chorus emphasizes, but their anger differs in nature. The seer's anger pushes him to reveal the truth, whereas the king's anger leads him astray. The king accuses the seer of being the agent of a conspiracy fomented by Creon. The seer, in response, multiplies, in a more or less enigmatic way, his revelations regarding Oedipus's past, present, and future. He leaves, asking the king to go back into the palace and reflect. The king enters the palace without saying a word.

* **First stasimon** (vv. 463–512): left alone, the chorus also reflects on the situation. The stasimon is composed of two strophe/antistrophe pairs; for the metrical analysis see A. M. Dale, *Metrical Analyses of Tragic Choruses*, fasc. 2: Aeolo-Choriambic, BICS, supp. 21, 2, 1981, pp. 36ff. The first pair is devoted to the Delphic oracle, the second to the seer. The chorus wonders about the identity of the culprit designated by the Delphic oracle, imagining him as a fugitive pursued by avenging divinities and seeking to escape the oracles, but in vain, because the oracles are still alive. On the other hand, the chorus, even though it is terribly troubled by the wise seer's revelations, cannot grant him as much credence as it would to the divine clairvoyance of Zeus or Apollo. According to the chorus, the seer's knowledge remains human: so long as the accusations made by the seer against Oedipus have not been verified, the chorus cannot reproach the king, whose knowledge was shown in the episode of the Sphinx.

* **Second episode** (vv. 513–862): four scenes.

   1. Creon and the chorus (vv. 513–31). Learning that Oedipus has charged that he and Tiresias are involved in a conspiracy, Creon has returned to the palace, considering this allegation intolerable. He asks the chorus if this is true and in what state of mind Oedipus has made the allegation.

   2. Oedipus, Creon, the chorus (vv. 532–630). Having come out of the palace, Oedipus is still in the grip of his anger and brutally attacks Creon when he finds him near his palace. He accuses Creon of wanting to assassinate him to seize his throne. The whole scene consists of a confrontation between the two men, and despite Creon's vain efforts to clear himself and the chorus's advice urging moderation, Oedipus remains angry: he wants to sentence Creon to death. The confrontation ends in a violent altercation in which Creon refuses to obey a bad king.

   3. Jocasta, Oedipus, Creon, the chorus (vv. 631–77). To put an end to this quarrel, Jocasta suddenly comes out of the palace and tries to separate the two men, condemning a private quarrel that pointlessly adds to the city's sickness. She is helped by the chorus's intervention in the first part of a commos (strophe, vv. 649–67: lyric iambic rhythm; metrical analysis in A. M. Dale, *Metrical Analyses of Tragic Choruses*, fasc. 3: Iambic, BICS, supp. 21, 3, 1983, p. 213). The chorus persuades Oedipus to let Creon leave. Creon goes away, but Oedipus continues to express his hatred for him.

   4. Oedipus, Jocasta, the chorus (vv. 679–82). In the second part of the commos (antistrophe, vv. 678–97), the chorus intervenes to get Jocasta to make Oedipus go back inside the palace. But first Jocasta wants to know the cause of the quarrel. All the rest of this long scene is a dialogue between the royal couple, in which each of them provides the other with information about the past. Jocasta questions Oedipus regarding the cause of the quarrel and the reasons for his anger. The account Oedipus gives is incorrect: his imagination, to support the claim of a conspiracy,

attributes to Creon the accusation that he is Laius's murderer; he sees
Tiresias as no more than the conspirator's spokesman. In her reply (vv.
707–15), Jocasta tries to reassure Oedipus. She questions the seer's knowledge, arguing that no human can be competent in the art of prophecy. To
prove this, she takes an example from Oedipus's past: the oracle given
Laius by Apollo's interpreters in Delphi, according to which the king was
to die at his son's hand, was not fulfilled, because on the one hand Laius
was killed, according to what is said, by brigands at the intersection of
three roads, and on the other hand, his son was abandoned two days after
his birth in inaccessible mountains. Jocasta's argument produces on Oedipus an effect contrary to the one she expected. One detail, the intersection of three roads, intrigues him and leads him to ask a series of precise
questions concerning the place and the time of the assassination, the description of the victim, and the number of servants accompanying him.
As he receives replies to his questions, Oedipus reveals through indirect
expressions his dread of being Laius's murderer: he fears that he has issued
curses against himself (vv. 744–45), and that the seer might have been
right (v. 747). A final question regarding the informer revives the memory
of the only survivor, the sole witness of the scene (cf. already vv. 118–23).
Jocasta says that he is no longer in the palace, but in the countryside.
Oedipus asks Jocasta to summon him. He will arrive only much later (vv.
1110ff.). Jocasta, after answering Oedipus's questions, inquires in turn
about the reasons for her husband's anxiety. In a long speech, Oedipus in
turn reveals his past (vv. 771–833). The scene between husband and wife
becomes more than ever a moment of revelations concerning a past that
they had both kept buried for many years. But whereas Jocasta had presented this past in an argumentative speech, Oedipus recounts his life in
chronological order, starting with what he believes to be his origins: the
son of Polybus of Corinth and his wife, Merope, Oedipus was considered
the first of citizens when the incident occurred in which an inebriated
man accused him of not really being the king's son, an accusation that led
him to consult the oracle at Delphi, who, without answering his question
about his origins, told him that he would marry his mother and have
children with her, and would kill his father. To prevent the fulfillment of
the oracle, Oedipus left Corinth and arrived at the place where Jocasta
has just told him Laius was killed, the intersection of three roads. Oedipus recounts precisely how he met a man riding on a chariot, like the
man Jocasta described, and preceded by a herald; how he was pushed
aside by these two men and how he took vengeance on them by striking
and killing the old man as well as all those who accompanied him. After
giving this account, Oedipus reflects: he is afraid that there might be a
relation between Laius and the old man on whom he took revenge, that
he might fall victim to his own curses, and that he is polluting the bed of

the man whom he killed. But if he fears that he might be Laius's murderer, he is far from suspecting yet that Laius might be his father, because he still thinks that his father is Polybus. It is not Jocasta who replies to this long speech, but the chorus: it does not conceal its concern but advises Oedipus to remain hopeful so long as he has not yet seen the sole witness who escaped the tragedy. In fact, in his despair, Oedipus clings to this last hope: if the witness says again that Laius was killed by several brigands, Oedipus will be exculpated; on the other hand, if he says that the murderer was alone, the crime will fall on him. Jocasta encourages Oedipus in this hope: the witness gave his version in public, and even if he changed his story, he would not prove the truth of Apollo's oracle, because Laius was supposed to die at his son's hand, whereas this son died before his father. Jocasta ends the scene as she began it, with a declared skepticism with regard to prophecy; but there is a development in her criticism, because she rejects any prophecy whatever, and no longer draws a distinction between Apollo and his interpreters. Oedipus agrees with her but reminds her that what is essential for him is the arrival of the sole witness. Both of them go back into the palace.

* **Second stasimon** (vv. 863–910): consists of two strophe/antistrophe pairs; for the metrical analysis see A. M. Dale, *Metrical Analyses of Tragic Choruses*, fasc. 2: Aeolo-Choriambic, BICS, supp. 21, 2, 1981, pp. 38ff. Faced by the royal couple's impious skepticism, the chorus, which has remained alone, cries out in alarm and declares its reprobation, even though it expresses itself in general terms. It wishes to remain pure in its words and in its conduct by observing the divine laws. On the other hand, it condemns the lack of moderation that gives rise to the tyrant and denounces the behavior of anyone who does not respect justice and does not venerate the gods. For "if such deeds are held in honor, why should we join in the sacred dance?" (v. 896). If such behavior is not blamed, the sanctuaries will be deserted. The chorus calls on Zeus's power and worries that there might be an attempt to abolish Laius's oracles. This is the most precise allusion to Jocasta's position approved by Oedipus. For the chorus, this is tantamount to destroying the divine: "The worship of the gods is perishing!"—those are the chorus's last words in this stasimon (v. 910).

* **Third episode** (vv. 911–1072): four scenes.

1. Jocasta, the chorus (vv. 911–23). Jocasta comes out of the palace and explains to the chorus that she has just made offerings to Apollo Lyceus in his adjacent temple. She fears for Oedipus, who is in turmoil. Unable to reason with him, she addresses the god and begs him to find a remedy.

2. The Corinthian messenger, the chorus, Jocasta (vv. 924–49). The completely unexpected arrival of a messenger bringing what is apparently good news seems to be a response to Jocasta's prayer. However, Jocasta, learning from the messenger who has come from Corinth that Polybus is dead, far from

thanking the god, continues to sink into impiety by stressing the vanity of divine oracles, since Oedipus did not kill his father Polybus.

3. The Corinthian messenger, Oedipus, Jocasta, the chorus (vv. 950–1072). Oedipus, summoned by a servant on Jocasta's orders, comes out of the palace in turn. He learns from Jocasta that his father Polybus is dead and asks the messenger what the circumstances of the death were. Informed of the natural character of the death, he is suddenly freed of his anxiety. He shows this by impiously condemning the oracles of Delphi and the seers' prophecies even more mockingly than Jocasta had. But Oedipus has changed, as Jocasta had suggested. This first wave of fear having passed (the fear of having killed his father, Polybus), a second wave arrives: the fear of having to marry his mother, Merope. Jocasta seeks in vain to rid him of this new fear. Informed of the reason for this fear, namely the Delphic oracle, the Corinthian messenger, wanting to relieve Oedipus of any anxiety, makes new revelations concerning his origin in a long, stichomythic dialogue: Oedipus is not Polybus's natural son but an adoptive son whom Polybus received from one of Laius's shepherds, when his feet were still bound. Oedipus questions the messenger, then the chorus, then Jocasta regarding this shepherd. Jocasta, who has now understood after the messenger's revelations, asks Oedipus to halt the investigation, expresses her pity for him, and then abruptly goes back into the palace without saying anything further.

4. Oedipus, the chorus (vv. 1073–85). The chorus is worried by this hasty, silent exit. But Oedipus, exasperated by Jocasta's temporizing attitude, misinterprets her reaction: he thinks she feels ashamed at the obscurity of his origin. Defiantly, he calls himself the "son of Fortune" (v. 1080).

* **Third stasimon** (vv. 1086–109): composed of a single strophe/antistrophe pair (metrical analysis in A. M. Dale, *Metrical Analyses of Tragic Choruses*, fasc. 1: Dactylo-Epitrite, BICS, supp. 21, 1, 1971, pp. 34ff.). In the presence of Oedipus, who has remained in front of the palace, and of the Corinthian messenger, the chorus, continuing the preceding scene, wonders about its king's origin. First it addresses the Cithaeron and Apollo, then Oedipus himself. It acts as a prophet and envisages a divine origin for Oedipus; it wonders what divinity might have engendered him with a Nymph in the mountains: Pan, Apollo, Hermes, or Dionysus. But the chorus's prophecies are not as good as those of Tiresias. The answer to the question will be given in the following scene, after the arrival of Laius's former servant.

* **Fourth episode** (vv. 1110–85): this episode contains only one scene marked by the arrival of the servant from the countryside. Oedipus suspects that this is the shepherd he has been awaiting for some time (cf. the end of the second episode); this is confirmed by the chorus (it is one of Laius's former servants) and by the Corinthian messenger (the man is the shepherd who gave him the child in the Cithaeron). Oedipus then addresses the servant directly and

subjects him to close interrogation. The servant claims not to remember having seen the Corinthian in the Cithaeron. The Corinthian takes over from Oedipus to refresh the servant's memory. He reminds him of the three summers they spent side by side on Cithaeron. The servant acknowledges this; but when the Corinthian mentions the infant he gave him at that time and triumphantly tells him that he has before his eyes that infant of yesteryear, what the Corinthian expected to be a happy recognition turns into a tragedy for the servant, who wants to make him shut up by threatening him with his stick. Oedipus then resumes his interrogation and gradually forces the servant to confess by threatening him: he is indeed the servant who handed over the child after having received it; he was supposed to be the son of Laius; it was his mother who had given him the child and told him to kill him because of an oracle; but he took pity on the child. The scene ends with Oedipus's definitive recognition of his origin: he is his father's murderer and his mother's husband. All the characters disappear: Oedipus goes into the palace; the servant and the Corinthian leave by the lateral entrances through which they came.

* **Fourth stasimon** (vv. 1186–222): composed of two strophe/antistrophe pairs (metrical analysis in A. M. Dale, *Metrical Analyses of Tragic Choruses*, fasc. 2: Aeolo-Choriambic, BICS, supp. 21, 2, 1981, p. 40 sq.). The chorus contrasts this exemplary man's past happiness and his present unhappiness. Who has been happier and unhappier than he? He had destroyed the Sphinx and saved Thebes; he had become the highly esteemed king of a powerful city. But he shared the same bed as his father. Time, which sees everything, has revealed this "monstrous marriage." The chorus, horrified, would have preferred not to have known the son of Laius. It sees in Oedipus the cause of both its past salvation and its present death.

* **Exodos** (vv. 1223–530): three scenes.

   1. A messenger, who comes out of the palace, and the chorus (vv. 1223–96). The messenger, addressing the chorus, announces the disasters that have occurred inside the palace. First there is Jocasta's suicide, which the messenger announces in a single verse (v. 1235); then comes a detailed account in a long speech. But the surprise arises from the fact that the narrative includes not only what Jocasta did after she rushed back into the palace after becoming aware of the situation (cf. v. 1072), but also what Oedipus has done since he also went back into the palace after having fully understood his tragedy (cf. v. 1185). The messenger's account makes it possible to compare Oedipus's conduct with that of Jocasta. Jocasta takes refuge in the nuptial bedchamber, where she shuts herself up and dies in solitude after having invoked her dead husband Laius. Oedipus, mad with pain, speaks to all his servants, asking them to bring him a weapon. His social pain is contrasted with Jocasta's solitary pain.

The two destinies will intersect one last time. It is Oedipus who discovers Jocasta hanged. And he puts out his eyes with the gold pins of Jocasta's robe, in front of all his servants. It is a "mingled woe for man and wife" (v. 1281). Oedipus wants to go outside to show himself to all the residents of Thebes and to go into exile, since he falls under his own curses by being the murderer of Laius.

2. Oedipus, the chorus (vv. 1297–421). The palace gate is opened. The horrified chorus sees the unbearable sight of Oedipus, his face covered with blood. A dialogue between Oedipus and the chorus is begun, first in recitative (vv. 1297–311), then in the form of a semilyric dialogue (commos) consisting of two strophe/antistrophe pairs (vv. 1313–67), in which Oedipus, in the grip of emotion, sings in an agitated rhythm (dochmiacs; metrical analysis in A. M. Dale, *Metrical Analyses of Tragic Choruses*, fasc. 3: Dochmiac, BICS, supp. 21, 3, 1983, pp. 34ff.), while the chorus speaks. After the commos, Oedipus returns to speech (vv. 1368–415). The rhythm of the scene corresponds to a rise in Oedipus's emotion as he deplores his own fate (with the transition from recitative to song), then a calming in which lamentation is replaced by reflection. In response to a remark made by the chorus, which does not understand why he put out his eyes, Oedipus justifies his act, with a certain irritation. He can no longer look in the face either of his family, after what he has done, or his city, after the curses he has uttered. In conclusion, he lists, in a series of exclamations and emotional questions, the diverse stages in his past (though he no longer mentions the victory over the Sphinx): the Cithaeron where he was abandoned and saved, Corinth, where he spent his youth in the royal palace, the crossroads where he killed his father, and the marriage to his mother. In his despair, he addresses two contradictory wishes to the chorus: to be expelled, and then to be touched. The chorus announces Creon's arrival; he is now the country's sole guardian.

3. Creon, Oedipus, the chorus (vv. 1422–530), with the arrival of Oedipus's two daughters played by silent actors in v. 1472. Creon, the city's new ruler, conducts himself with Oedipus with generosity and wisdom, forgetting past resentments. Oedipus communicates his last wishes to him. Creon has foreseen one of them by having Oedipus's daughters come; Oedipus would like to touch them. This last scene, in which the blind father gropes for his two little girls (v. 1480), makes a striking contrast with the initial scene of the tragedy in which the king appeared in all his "majesty" before a group of suppliant children. The sight emphasizes the reversal of fortune. The tragedy ends with a finale with the change in rhythm (vv. 1515–30): the catalectic trochaic tetrameters divided between Creon and Oedipus correspond to an inversion of the rhythm and to an acceleration of the dialogue. Creon asks Oedipus to go back into the palace. Oedipus is about to obey, but two requests delay his departure.

He wants to leave the country. Creon cannot grant his request before consulting the gods. Oedipus does not want to be separated from his daughters. Creon accuses him of being pretentious in wishing to be master in all things.

The chorus's final speech brings out the contrast between Oedipus's triumphal past as a knowledgeable, powerful man envied by everyone, and the flood of misfortunes that is currently buffeting him. From this emblematic example, the chorus draws a valuable lesson for everyone regarding the fragility of the human destiny: no one can say he is happy before the end of his life. The authenticity of the chorus's reflection has been debated.

4. Date

There is no indication external to the tragedy itself that would allow us to date it. It is traditionally situated between *Antigone* and *Electra*. The presence of the pestilence has been related to the "plague" in Athens. In fact, before Sophocles the pestilence in Thebes does not seem to have been part of the myth of Oedipus. If we agree to see an influence of the plague in Athens on the insertion of the theme of the pestilence in *Oedipus the King*, the consequence is that the tragedy is later than 430, the date of the first attack of the plague of Athens. It has been related more particularly to the second attack in the summer of 426, and the performance of the tragedy has been placed in the spring of 425 (B.M.W. Knox, "The Date of the *Oedipus Tyrannus of Sophocles*," *AJP* 77, 1956, pp. 133–47); see above.

5. Iconography

See L. Séchan (cited in chapter X, "Humans and the Gods"), pp. 143–45; T.B.L. Webster (cited in chapter V, "Happy Sophocles"), p. 150; A. D. Trendall and T.B.L. Webster (cited in chapter X, "Humans and the Gods"), pp. 66–69.

6. Editions with notes; or commentaries

R. C. Jebb, Cambridge, 3rd ed. 1893 (Greek text, English translation, notes in English); rpt. with an introduction by J. Rusten, gen. ed. P. E. Easterling, London, 2004; L. Roussel, Paris, 1940 (Greek text, French translation, notes in French); A. Dain and P. Mazon, Paris: CUF, 1st ed. 1958 (Greek text, French translation, notes in French), and compare, for the French translation, P. Masqueray, Paris: CUF, 1922; J. C. Kamerbeek, Leiden, 1967 (notes in English); R. D. Dawe, Cambridge, 1982, 2nd ed. 2006 (Greek text, notes in English); J. Wilkins and M. Macleod, *Sophocles' Antigone and Oedipus the King*, Bristol Classical, 1987 (commentary in English); J. Bollack, 4 vols., Lille, 1990 (Greek text, French translation, notes in French); H. Lloyd-Jones and N. G. Wilson, *Sophoclea: Studies on the Text of Sophocles*, Oxford, 1990, pp. 79–114 (notes in English); J. C. Hogan, *A Commentary on the Plays of Sophocles*, 1991; H. Lloyd-Jones and N. G. Wilson, *Sophocles: Second Thoughts*, Göttingen, 1997, pp. 48–66 (notes in English).

Oedipus at Colonus

1. Subject of the tragedy and history of the myth
    a) The tragedy is based, like *Oedipus the King* and *Antigone*, on the myth of Oedipus. In the sequence of the myth of Oedipus's family, *Oedipus at Colonus* comes several years after *Oedipus the King*. At the end of *Oedipus the King*, Oedipus wants to go into exile. At the beginning of *Oedipus at Colonus*, after long years spent in exile, Oedipus, guided by his daughter Antigone, arrives at a stage that will prove to be the last, where he will find a heroic death. And since the tragedy of *Oedipus at Colonus* was composed about twenty years after *Oedipus the King* (for the date of *Oedipus at Colonus*, see below, 4. Date), there is a correspondence between the relative chronology of the myth and the relative chronology of composition. Thus in *Oedipus at Colonus* Sophocles sought to establish continuities and to reduce discordances so that the two tragedies could be read as a diptych in which we see in a single view the two sides of Oedipus's destiny, his fall from the summits of power and glory into misfortune and dishonor, and then his rehabilitation after a long exile. This diptych on the fall and rehabilitation of the hero is comparable to the treatment of Ajax's destiny, where the two sides are presented in one and the same tragedy. Nevertheless, the two tragedies of *Oedipus the King* and *Oedipus at Colonus* retain their autonomy, and the secondary characters may differ. There is, in particular, an enormous difference in the conception of the character of Creon, who is singularly degraded in *Oedipus at Colonus* in order to serve as a foil and to highlight Oedipus's rehabilitation; analogously, there is no contrast between Oedipus's two daughters, Antigone and Ismene, as was the case in *Antigone*, the better to bring out here a different opposition, that between Oedipus's daughters and his sons, the former being devoted to their father in his misfortunes, the latter having abandoned him (cf. Oedipus's speech, vv. 421–60).
    b) The sequence begins with the arrival of the blind Oedipus, accompanied by his daughter Antigone. Expelled from Thebes, Oedipus reaches, after a long exile, an unknown sanctuary not far from Athens—a sanctuary devoted to the Eumenides, as he discovers thanks to information provided by a resident of the place, the Athenian deme of Colonus. This detail about the divinities of the sanctuary leads him to realize that the old Delphic oracle concerning the end of his sufferings is about to be realized: Apollo had predicted to Oedipus that after a long exile he would arrive in a last country where he would be received by venerable divinities and where he would become, at a turning point in his destiny, a source of advantages for the country that welcomed him and of disadvantages for the country that had expelled him. Oedipus accordingly establishes himself as a suppliant in the sanctuary. The tragedy, devoted to the gradual

steps in the heroization of Oedipus, thus develops in the context of a supplication in which the suppliant, after an exile, asks to be adopted by the city where he arrives, but where his request encounters obstacles (see above, chapter VIII, "Time and Action," under "The Supplication Trag-edies"). It advances through dramatic turnabouts in which factors that oppose the oracle's fulfillment alternate with others that favor it. After the initially hostile attitude of the chorus formed by the administrators of the deme of Colonus (cf. v. 145), and after Ismene's friendly arrival from The-bes to bring her father information about the situation and about new oracles, the attitude of the king of Athens, Theseus, contrasts with that of the chorus: he feels spontaneous pity for the suppliant and agrees to let him settle in the country. The principal opponent will be Creon, who has come, on behalf of Thebes, to seek Oedipus's support at a time when his city is being besieged by Polynices and the Argive army (in the so-called war of the Seven against Thebes). Creon, who is at first unctuous, ulti-mately resorts to violence and abducts Antigone; he had already seized Ismene (offstage). King Theseus then becomes the protector acting ener-getically against violence and returns Oedipus's daughters to him. An-other dramatic reversal is produced by the arrival of Polynices, who has come, for his part, to obtain his father's help. Oedipus rejects him vio-lently and utters curses against him. Finally, the signs announcing the fulfillment of the oracle occur (Zeus's thunder and lightning). Oedipus, accompanied both by his daughters and by the king of Athens, leaves for his final resting place. A messenger comes to recount the heroized Oedi-pus's miraculous end; he is followed by Oedipus's daughters, mourning their father, and then by King Theseus, who holds the secret bequeathed by Oedipus so that his tomb might protect the Athenian land against any Theban invasion.

c) Oedipus's death in the deme of Colonus is a version of the myth that is contrary to the Homeric version, in which Oedipus dies at Thebes. In fact, according to an allusion in the *Iliad* (23, vv. 679ff.), funeral games were held in Thebes in honor of Oedipus, who probably died in combat. The version of the death of Oedipus in *Oedipus at Colonus* is already at-tested in Euripides' *Phoenician Women* (vv. 1703–7), performed a few years before the composition of *Oedipus at Colonus*. The convergence of the two testimonies indicates that the local version was well known to the Athenians, unless we consider that the allusion at the end of the *Phoeni-cian Women* is a later interpolation due to the success of *Oedipus at Colo-nus*. In any case, this local version was not created by Sophocles. It is also attested by another source (Androtion, a fourth-century BCE historian, in a scholium on *Odyssey* 11, v. 271 [= *FRrHist* 324 F 62 Jacoby]; see above). There are probably other testimonies that have been lost (cf. an ancient scholium on the *Phoenician Women*, v. 1707). The presence of a tomb of

Oedipus on Athenian territory was then attested in the second century
CE, when Pausanias visited Athens. But the tomb is now located *intra
muros* in the sanctuary of the Eumenides (Pausanias 1, 28, 7), whereas in
Colonus Pausanias saw only a sanctuary of Oedipus (Pausanias 1, 30, 4).
Another version situated Oedipus's tomb in Eteonus in Boeotia (scholium on *Oedipus at Colonus*, v. 91, whose source is the Alexandrine historian Lysimachus; for the text of this scholium, see above).

2. The site of the drama and the characters

The site of the drama is the Athenian deme of Colonus, Sophocles' birthplace. The visible space represents a wooded sanctuary along a road. This
sacred space, where nature is simultaneously wild and welcoming, turns out
to be the sanctuary of the venerable goddesses, the Eumenides, a sanctuary
that is forbidden to humans and in which there is no human structure. The
building at the back of the stage is thus masked, as is the central door, probably by painted panels representing the vegetation of the sacred wood,
though the panel in front of the door does not prevent Ismene from leaving
when she goes into the sacred wood (see above chapter VII, "Space and Spectacle"). This sacred place is part of a larger one, the deme of Colonus, which
is itself sacred because of the presence of other gods, in particular the sanctuary of Poseidon located in the virtual space, not far from the visible space. In
this virtual space, we also find the city of Athens, whose ramparts are supposed to be visible in the distance.

The characters enter solely through the lateral entrances, since the sanctuary at the back of the stage is forbidden to humans. Which entrance is used
depends on where the character is coming from. Those who come from
abroad enter on the left: thus, at the beginning, Oedipus and Antigone (v. 1).
On the other hand, those who come from Colonus or Athens enter on the
right: first the resident of the deme (v. 36), then the chorus formed of the
elders responsible for the deme (v. 117). While Oedipus waits for the king of
Athens, Theseus, to enter from the right, it is Ismene who unexpectedly enters from the left, riding on a horse, because she is coming from Thebes; she
exits on foot through the door at the back, making an exception by going
into the wood to make libations on behalf of Oedipus (v. 509). Theseus,
coming from Athens, enters on the right (v. 551) and exits on the right (v.
667). Creon, coming like Ismene from Thebes, enters from the left (v. 847).
Theseus, on whom the chorus has called for help, hurriedly returns through
the right-hand entrance, because he has been making a sacrifice in the sanctuary of Poseidon (v. 887). Thus we see in this part of the tragedy a rather
regular alternation of entrances on the left and on the right. Theseus, taking
Creon with him, leaves by the left entrance to look for Antigone and Ismene,
who have been abducted by Creon's guards (v. 1043). Theseus returns from
the left, having found Oedipus's daughters (v. 1099). He exits on the right (v.

1210). It is from the right that Polynices enters, even though he is coming from the plain of Thebes where his army is camped, because he has passed by the sanctuary of Poseidon, where he had taken refuge as a suppliant (cf. vv. 1156–59). Polynices, not having obtained anything from his father, leaves again by the left to rejoin his army, which is going to attack Thebes (v. 1447). From that moment on, all the entrances and exits take place on the right, because no one will come from a foreign land or leave for one. The most important exit is that of Oedipus, who goes to his last resting place in Colonus (v. 1555). The sight of this departure contrasts with his arrival at the beginning of the tragedy: whereas the blind old man entered guided by his daughter Antigone, he leaves without a human guide, escorted by his two daughters and by the king of Athens, who has hastened back a second time at the summons of the chorus and Oedipus (v. 1500). Those who accompany Oedipus to his last resting place will return one after the other: first the man in Theseus's entourage who plays the role of messenger (v. 1579), then Oedipus's daughters (v. 1670), and finally Theseus (v. 1751).

The constraint of the limitation to three actors is particularly noticeable in this tragedy, where two actors are occupied by the continual presence of Oedipus, played by the protagonist, and that of Antigone, played by the deuteragonist during a large part of the tragedy. These two actors are occupied until Antigone is abducted by Creon's guards (v. 847). Thus during almost half the tragedy, Sophocles has only the tritagonist for the arrival of new characters and thus has to give him time to change costumes and roles. But it is not necessary to bring in a fourth actor (see above, chapter VII, "Space and Spectacle," under "The Constraint of Three Actors in Oedipus at Colonus: The Myth of the Fourth Actor").

3. Structure of the tragedy

* **Prologue** (vv. 1–116): three scenes.

   1. Oedipus, Antigone (vv. 1–32). In a dialogue between Oedipus and Antigone, we learn the essentials of the situation. Oedipus, who has long been blind and exiled, is reduced to begging and being content with little, but always remains noble (v. 8), even in misfortune, asks his daughter precisely where they have come. After a long day's travel, he wants to rest. Antigone sees the ramparts of a city that they know is Athens, but she does not know the name of the place where they are, which seems, however, to be sacred. She has the old man sit down on a rock. Just as she is proposing to go further to inquire about the place, a stranger who is a local resident conveniently arrives.

   2. Oedipus, the resident, and Antigone, who remains silent (vv. 33–80). Oedipus wants to question the resident about the place, but he does not have time to finish his question. The man tells him that he has entered a place forbidden to humans and asks him to leave it. It is a sanctuary of

redoubtable divinities, called by antiphrasis the Eumenides ("the gracious ones"). This indication becomes for Oedipus an abrupt revelation. He refuses to budge and declares himself the suppliant of the divinities. Oedipus asks the resident about the place where he is (the deme of Colonus) and about the person politically responsible for it (King Theseus). He tells the man of his desire to see the king in order to give him a great benefit in exchange for a small one. The resident of Colonus leaves to inform the local authorities, the *demotes*, who will have to decide Oedipus's fate: whether he will be allowed to remain or be driven away. This is an announcement of the chorus's arrival.

3. Oedipus, Antigone (vv. 84–116). After the resident's departure, Oedipus addresses a long prayer to the divinities of the sanctuary, in which he reveals the prophecies of the Delphic oracle that seem to him to be being fulfilled: after a long period of time, Oedipus will find an end to his sufferings by reaching a last country where he will be received by the venerable goddesses and where he will see the course of his life change, bringing advantages to those who receive him and disadvantages to those who drove him away; signs will announce this change: Zeus's earthquake, thunder, or lightning. Sophocles, by adding these indications to the traditional prophecies that we know from *Oedipus the King*, not only increases the continuity with that tragedy but foretells what will ultimately happen in *Oedipus at Colonus*. In this prayer, Oedipus invokes in conclusion not only the Eumenides, but also the city protected by Athena, so that they might take pity on the "ghost of the man Oedipus" (vv. 190ff.). Antigone announces the arrival of the chorus consisting of old men. Oedipus asks his daughter to take him away from the road and into the sacred wood.

* **Parodos** (vv. 118–253): the chorus of the old men who administer the deme (cf. v. 145) hurries in. The resident (cf. vv. 297ff.) has told them that there is a vagabond in the sanctuary of the Eumenides that is forbidden to humans. The parados is composed of two strophe/antistrophe pairs (with an anapaestic epirrhema, except for antistrophe 2) followed by an epode. Within this framework, the parados is extremely flexible. The chorus first seeks the vagabond, with aggressive intentions: it wants to stone him. But it sees nothing. Then Oedipus shows himself. The chorus is frightened by the spectacle; then it is gripped by pity. But it asks him to come out of the forbidden space. Oedipus addresses the chorus (v. 174). The parados is then transformed into a lyric dialogue in the second strophe/antistrophe pair and the epode (vv. 178–237). From a distance, the chorus tells Oedipus, guided by Antigone, how to leave the forbidden space. Then it asks him to introduce himself. And when it learns that he is Oedipus, it wants to drive him away (v. 226). Antigone then intervenes in a monody (vv. 257–54) begging the chorus to have pity.

* **First episode** (vv. 254–509): two scenes.
  1. The chorus, Oedipus, Antigone (vv. 254–323). The beginning of the epi-
     sode is a continuation of the parodos, as in *Electra*. The characters remain
     the same. The only difference is the passage from song to speech. After
     Antigone's prayer, the chorus, while feeling pity, refuses to change its
     view, because it fears the gods. But Oedipus, in a speech that is both pas-
     sionate and closely reasoned, succeeds in convincing the chorus to revise
     its decision. To do so, he appeals to Athens's reputation for piety and
     humanity, which the chorus is endangering through its conduct, because
     it is seeking to expel a suppliant whom it had promised to protect, and
     moreover it is doing so on the basis of a false understanding of his crimes:
     Oedipus merely defended himself and acted without knowing what he
     was doing. Then Oedipus reverses the chorus's line of argument by show-
     ing that it will have to fear the gods' punishment if it acts contrary to re-
     ligion. He, Oedipus, is holy and pious, and is even the bearer of a benefit.
     He asks to see the king of the country. Antigone announces the arrival of
     a woman whom she sees in the distance mounted on a horse and wearing
     a hat to protect her from the sun. After a moment's hesitation, she recog-
     nizes Ismene.
  2. Ismene, Oedipus, the chorus; Antigone is present but does not speak (vv.
     324–509). Ismene enters accompanied by a single servant (cf. v. 334). She
     brings news from Thebes, though the Thebans do not know she is doing
     so (cf. v. 354). First about her brothers, Eteocles and Polynices, telling
     Oedipus about their quarrel for the possession of power: Eteocles has
     driven out his elder brother Polynices, who went into exile in Argos,
     where he mounted an expedition to seize Thebes. Then Ismene gives Oe-
     dipus news that concerns him personally: new Delphic oracles say that
     people from Thebes will come to seek Oedipus to save them. She tells
     him that Creon is coming (v. 396). But when Oedipus learns that his sons
     refuse to bury him on Theban territory, on the pretext that he is a parri-
     cide, he angrily launches into a long speech (vv. 421–60) cursing them
     and promising that their quarrel will end up with neither of them obtain-
     ing satisfaction. He reminds them of his grievances against them: they did
     nothing to prevent his exile when he no longer wanted to leave, because
     they preferred power to their father, whereas his daughters did everything
     they could to help him in his exile. In these new oracles, Oedipus sees a
     confirmation of the old ones: he asks the chorus's protection, and that of
     the sanctuary's divinities, against the potential envoys from Thebes and
     promises them in return to be a powerful savior. The chorus then speaks
     at the end of the scene, advising Oedipus to make libations to the divini-
     ties of the sanctuary whose soil he has trodden on, and describes the rite
     in great detail. Oedipus, too weak and blind, delegates the task to one of
     his daughters. Ismene volunteers. She goes into the sacred wood at the

back of the stage. The actor playing Ismene (the tritagonist) exits through the door in the stage building, which is concealed.

* **First stasimon** (vv. 510–48): this takes the form of a purely lyric dialogue between the chorus and Oedipus (in the presence of Antigone, who remains silent). It consists of two strophe/antistrophe pairs. The chorus wants to question Oedipus to find out if the rumor concerning his past is true, namely the marriage with his mother and the murder of his father. The dialogue is very rapid, including numerous antilabai. The chorus's questions reopen two of Oedipus's past wounds, but they provide him with an opportunity to continue to plead not guilty. These two crimes are not voluntary. He has committed them without knowing what he was doing (cf. v. 525 and v. 548).

* **Second episode** (vv. 549–667): a single scene in dialogue between Theseus and Oedipus, with a comment by the chorus (vv. 629–30). Theseus's arrival has been announced by the coryphaeus (vv. 549–50). Theseus approaches Oedipus with great humanity. His welcome contrasts with that of the chorus in the parodos. Theseus feels a spontaneous pity for Oedipus, because he himself has known the difficulties of exile and the dangers of being on foreign territory. He is coming to ask him the purpose of his supplication. Oedipus offers his body so that Theseus might bury it. If he does so, the king will acquire an advantage for Athens in the coming war against Thebes. But Oedipus does not conceal the immediate dangers: his sons are going to try to make him return to Thebes to obtain his support, in conformity with the oracles (announced by Ismene). After a brief comment made by the chorus in favor of Oedipus (vv. 629–30), Theseus spontaneously honors the supplication: he welcomes into a hospitable land the foreigner who is a suppliant of the gods and who brings, in exchange, a benefit for the country. Before leaving, Theseus reassures Oedipus, who is anxiously awaiting the arrival of emissaries (coming from Thebes).

* **Second stasimon** (vv. 668–719): song by the chorus in the presence of Oedipus and Antigone, who remain silent. It consists of two strophe/antistrophe pairs. Now that Oedipus has been accepted, the chorus addresses him (v. 668) to praise the land where he has been received, the Athenian deme of Colonus. It is a rich country, watered by the Cephissus, where the vegetation is luxuriant (ivy, narcissus, and especially olive trees), full of birds (the nightingale) and animals (horses), and beloved by the gods: Dionysus; the two great goddesses Demeter and Korè; the Muses; Aphrodite; Zeus and Athena, who watch over the olive trees; and Poseidon, both as the god of horses (the inventor of the bit) and of the sea (the inventor of the oar).

* **Third episode** (vv. 720–1043): two scenes.
    1. Antigone, Oedipus, the chorus, Creon (vv. 728–886). The arrival of Creon is announced by Antigone. He is accompanied by an escort. With consummate craftiness, he first addresses the chorus (vv. 728–39) to reassure it and to explain his mission: he has been delegated by the Thebans, be-

cause of his family connection with Oedipus, to convince the latter to return to his homeland. He subsequently addresses Oedipus (vv. 740ff.).

Then begins an agōn between Creon and Oedipus (vv. 740–832). The confrontation takes place in two long speeches: Creon seeks to persuade Oedipus to return to Thebes (vv. 740–60), but Oedipus, in his reply (vv. 761–99), allows his anger to explode and violently refuses, accusing Creon of deceit. The confrontation continues in an accelerated dialogue. Creon, who has not succeeded by persuasion, resorts to violence: he reveals that he has abducted Ismene and tells his guards to abduct Antigone.

The end of the second scene is occupied by a commos corresponding to Oedipus's and the chorus's emotional reaction to Creon's violence. It is composed of a strophe (vv. 833–43) and an antistrophe (vv. 876–86) in an agitated rhythm (dochmiacs: metrical analysis in A. M. Dale, *Metrical Analyses of Tragic Choruses*, fasc. 3: Dochmiac, BICS, supp. 21, 3, 1983, p. 39), separated by thirty-two iambic trimeters. In the strophe, the chorus tries to prevent Creon from leaving with Antigone and calls for help, but in vain. In the antistrophe, it tries to prevent Creon from taking Oedipus away and calls for help; but this time not in vain.

2. Theseus's second entrance (vv. 887–1043). Theseus, alerted by the chorus's cries, hurries in, followed by his guard; he had been sacrificing oxen on the altar of the god of the sea (Poseidon) in his sanctuary at Colonus. Rapidly brought up to date by Oedipus regarding the kidnapping of his two daughters, Theseus instructs a member of his guard to see to it that the people in arms who were attending the sacrifice go to stop the kidnappers. The guard exits (v. 904).

Then Theseus turns to Creon. Two opposed speeches by Theseus to Creon (vv. 909–36) and by Creon to Theseus (vv. 939–59), separated by a brief comment by the chorus, constitute the first part of an agōn scene. Theseus, controlling his anger, accuses Creon of having acted violently in a state ruled by law, denounces his madness, and threatens to hold him prisoner if he does not return the women he has abducted. Creon, in response, tries to justify his conduct. The rapid dialogue expected after the two long speeches is replaced by an unanticipated speech by Oedipus, who draws up, with anger and at great length (vv. 960–1013), an indictment of Creon and defends himself against the accusations he has made against him (parricide and incest): Oedipus acted without knowledge, both in killing his father and in marrying his mother; his acts are the work of the gods, who have long been angry at his family.

Theseus, making Creon precede him, leaves to look for Oedipus's daughters. Oedipus thanks Theseus for his help and remains where he is.

* **Third stasimon** (vv. 1044–95): choral song in the presence of Oedipus, who remains silent. The song is composed of two strophe/antistrophe pairs (metrical analysis in A. M. Dale, *Metrical Analyses of Tragic Choruses*, fasc. 1:

Dactylo-Epitrite, BICS, supp. 21, 1, 1971, pp. 40ff.). The chorus imagines the conflict that will take place between the kidnappers and their pursuers, hopes for the return of Antigone, and invokes the gods (Zeus, Athena, Apollo, and Artemis), asking them to come the Athenians' aid.

* **Fourth episode** (vv. 1906–210): a single scene. The chorus announces the return of Oedipus's daughters. They have been brought back by Theseus, who appears for the third time. Touching reunion of Oedipus with his daughters. Oedipus then expresses his gratitude to Theseus and praises his piety, equity, and loyalty. Theseus tells Oedipus about the arrival of a suppliant who wants to see him. When Oedipus understands that it is his son Polynices, he refuses at first to listen to him but gives in after a vibrant intervention on Antigone's part in favor of her brother.

* **Fourth stasimon** (vv. 1211–48): the chorus's song in the presence of Oedipus and his two daughters. Famous general reflections on human life by the chorus consisting of elderly men. Their view of life is not affectionate. Joys are rare. The best thing is not to be born, or to return as soon as possible to the place one comes from. After careless youth, no misfortune is spared: murders, dissensions, battles, and especially envy! There is nothing worse than execrable old age. These reflections are inspired in the chorus not only by its great age but also by the example of Oedipus, who is compared to a promontory battered by storms. This is probably a way of presenting the arrival of Polynices as another assault that Oedipus must undergo.

* **Fifth episode** (vv. 1249–446): a single scene. Polynices comes as a suppliant to obtain his father's aid in driving his brother Eteocles from power. Sophocles has made Polynices the elder son and Eteocles the younger. The scene takes the form of an agōn. The center is occupied by the long, opposed speeches of Polynices (sixty-two verses) and Oedipus (forty-nine verses), each followed by two verses by the chorus. Oedipus violently rejects his son's request and utters curses against him. After the opposing speeches, we expect the accelerated dialogue ending the agōn scene. It takes place, but it opposes Polynices, not to his father, who has just rejected him, but to his sister. But Oedipus does not yield and resigns himself to his destiny. The touching farewell between the brother and sister contrast with the violent rupture between the father and his son. Polynices' departure.

* **Fifth stasimon** (vv. 1447–99): this is a semilyric dialogue in which the chorus sings (two strophe/antistrophe pairs; metrical analysis in A. M. Dale, *Metrical Analyses of Tragic Choruses*, fasc. 3: Dochmiac, BICS, supp. 21, 3, 1983, p. 40 sq.), and in which two characters, Oedipus and Antigone, regularly speak between the chorus's sung remarks (in three epirrhemas of five iambic trimeters placed after strophe 1, antistrophe 1, and strophe 2, respectively). We hear and then see on three occasions the signs foretelling Oedipus's death. These are the same signs that had been predicted by the oracle (vv. 94–95): Zeus's thunder and lightning. Oedipus, remaining calm, calls for Theseus's

arrival so that he can tell him the benefits that his death will bring to Athens. The chorus, frightened by all these signs, also calls Theseus.

* **Sixth episode** (vv. 1500–55): this episode, like the two preceding ones, is composed of a single scene. Theseus enters for the fourth time. He has been alerted by Oedipus's voice and those of the chorus. Oedipus tells Theseus the meaning of the celestial signs. He will lead him, without a guide, to the secret place where he must die, and once they have arrived there he will reveal to him a secret that will enable his tomb to protect Athens, like a multitude of shields, against a Theban invasion. This secret must be unveiled by Theseus only to his successor. At the god's summons, he asks his daughters to follow him. Oedipus, the blind man who at the beginning of the tragedy was guided by his daughter Antigone, will now serve as a guide for those who exit with him, not only his daughters, but also Theseus, accompanied by his servants. Oedipus is in reality following invisible guides: two divinities, Hermes and the goddess of the Underworld. Before he leaves, he reminds the Athenians not to forget his cult, so that their prosperity endures.

* **Sixth stasimon** (vv. 1556–78): the chorus, left alone, sings. Its song is brief: a single strophe/antistrophe pair (metrical analysis in A. M. Dale, *Metrical Analyses of Tragic Choruses*, fasc. 3: Dochmiac, BICS, supp. 21, 3, 1983, p. 42). The chorus invokes the divinities of the Underworld so that Oedipus can reach "the nether fields of the dead" without suffering. The existence of this stasimon is necessary from a dramaturgical point of view. It allows the necessary time for the action (the miraculous death of Oedipus) to take place in the virtual space.

* **Exodos** (vv. 1579–779): three scenes.

    1. Arrival of the messenger, one of Theseus's servants (vv. 1579–669). In a long report of eighty-one verses, he tells the chorus what happened after the other characters left the stage. The messenger first describes the path they followed, with very precise topographical indications, then Oedipus's purifying ablutions and moving farewells to his daughters. A new celestial signal (the voice of a divinity) reminded Oedipus to return to his mission. He entrusted his daughters' fate to Theseus, ordered them to leave, and asked Theseus to accompany him without his servants. The servants departed in tears, escorting Oedipus's daughters, who were also weeping. For this reason, the messenger did not witness Oedipus's death. The messenger's furtive glance backward provides us with a snapshot: Theseus alone, his hand to his forehead, as if he had seen a frightening and unbearable spectacle. The messenger can only speculate on the manner in which Oedipus died. But he died without feeling pain. What the messenger recalls in conclusion is a miraculous end (v. 1665; cf. v. 1586).

    2. Arrival of Antigone and Ismene (vv. 1670–750). Purely lyric dialogue between Antigone, the chorus, and Ismene (two strophe/antistrophe pairs; lyric iambic rhythm; metrical analysis in A. M. Dale, *Metrical Analyses of*

Tragic Choruses, fasc. 3: Iambic, BICS, supp. 21, 3, 1983, pp. 218–20). This is a commos in the full sense of the term: a funeral lamentation coming from the chorus and the stage. The two sisters mourn, and the chorus tries to console them.

3. Theseus's arrival (vv. 1751–79). Final scene in recitative. Theseus puts an end to Oedipus's daughters' threnody. They want to see their father's tomb. Theseus reminds them that the dead man had forbidden that. Then they ask to return to Thebes to try to prevent the death of their brothers. Thus a link is established between the dramatic sequence of *Oedipus at Colonus* and that of *Antigone*, where the two sisters are in the palace at Thebes, but have not been able to prevent the fratricidal single combat that has taken place during the night preceding the drama.

4. Date

The date of the performance of the tragedy is certain. It took place after Sophocles' death, in 401, and was arranged by his grandson, Sophocles the Younger. This information is given in argument no. 2 (see above). We do not know whether the tragedy was part of a set. We can compare the posthumous performance of three tragedies by Euripides at the Great Dionysia (*Iphigenia in Aulis, Alcmeon, Bacchantes*) arranged by his son of the same name (see the scholium on Aristophanes, *Frogs*, v. 67) or by his nephew (*Suda*, s.v. Euripides). *Oedipus at Colonus* is not only Sophocles' last tragedy, but also the last tragedy preserved from all the Greek theatrical production.

The date of composition, on the other hand, is not known. It has been related to the assault made by Agis, a Lacedemonian king who had come from Decelia in 407 and who tried to take advantage of a moonless night to seize Athens while Alcibiades was away. The hero Oedipus, buried at Colonus, is supposed to have helped repel the assault. But this is only a hypothesis (see above). A scholium on Aelius Aristides mentions an epiphany of Oedipus at Colonus during an attack on the Athenians made by the Thebans: Oedipus is supposed to have urged the Athenians to resist, and they are supposed to have won the battle. However, no indication of the date is given (Aelius Aristides, *To Plato: In Defense of the Four*—viz., Miltiades, Themistocles, Cimon, and Pericles—apropos of the expression "the Oedipus who rests at Colonus," ed. Dindorf, 2, 172, 1ff., for the text, and 3, 560, for the scholium).

5. Iconography

See T.B.L. Webster (cited in chapter V, "Humans and the Gods"), p. 150.

6. Editions with notes; or commentaries

R. C. Jebb, Cambridge, 3rd ed. 1900 (Greek text, English translation, notes in English); rpt. with introduction by R. Rehm, gen. ed. P. E. Easterling, London, 2004; A. Dain and P. Mazon, Paris: CUF, 1st ed. 1960 (Greek text, French translation, notes in French), and compare, for the French translation, P. Masqueray, Paris: CUF, 1942; J. C. Kamerbeek, Leiden, 1984 (commentary in English); H. Lloyd-Jones and N. G. Wilson, *Sophoclea: Studies on the Text of Sophocles*, Oxford, 1990, pp. 214–66 (notes in English); J. C. Hogan, *A Commentary on the Plays of Sophocles*, 1991; H. Lloyd-Jones and N. G. Wilson, *Sophocles: Second Thoughts*, Göttingen, 1997, pp. 114–37 (notes in English); A. Rodighiero, Venice, 1998 (translation and commentary in Italian).

Philoctetes

1. Subject of the tragedy and the site of the action
   a) The tragedy is drawn from a sequence of the Trojan myth, as is *Ajax*. It is also later than Achilles' death, but this time it comes after Ajax's death as well (cf. v. 412, where Neoptolemus tells Philoctetes that Ajax is dead). On the Atreids' orders, Odysseus abandoned Philoctetes on a deserted part of the island of Lemnos when the Achaian expedition left for Troy: Philoctetes was suffering from a cankerous ulcer on his foot as the result of a snakebite, and his cries of pain were disturbing the normal performance of religious ceremonies. Odysseus returns ten years later, along with Neoptolemus, Achilles' son, to bring Philoctetes to Troy; in fact, the Achaians had learned from the Trojan seer Helenus, whom Odysseus had captured, that Troy could not be taken unless Philoctetes came with his bow inherited from Heracles and fought alongside Neoptolemus.
   b) The tragedy's sequence begins with Odysseus's and Neoptolemus's arrival in Lemnos, in front of Philoctetes' grotto, which is for the moment empty. The setting is comparable to that of satyr plays: at the back of the stage there is Philoctetes' grotto, with two entrances, only one of which is visible; there is a spring on the left below.
      Odysseus, who has come from Troy with Neoptolemus, explains the mission of deception that the latter must carry out in order to gain possession of the bow and of Philoctetes himself. After a little resistance to a way of proceeding that is contrary to his nature, Achilles' son allows himself to be persuaded. Odysseus conceals himself so that Philoctetes will not recognize him. Returning from a search for food or for a medicinal plant, Philoctetes, armed with his bow, meets Neoptolemus and the chorus of marines.
      Neoptolemus easily wins Philoctetes' trust by pretending that he is on his way back to his homeland of Skyros, as a victim of the injustice of the Atreids, who have awarded the arms of his father, Achilles, to Odysseus. Philoctetes begs Neoptolemus to take him along so that he, too, might return to his homeland, which is located beyond Skyros, at the foot of Mount Oeta. The plan for trickery is also favored by chance. Philoctetes is struck by an attack of his illness that forces him to hand over his bow to Neoptolemus. But this plan is then compromised by Neoptolemus's

moral crisis: pitying Philoctetes and regretting his deception, Neoptolemus tells him the truth and prepares to return his bow to him. Thus the
plan to trick him fails.

But trickery will be replaced by force. Odysseus intervenes directly,
preventing Neoptolemus from returning the bow. In his subsequent confrontation with Philoctetes, Odysseus resorts to force: he has Philoctetes'
hands tied when he tries to commit suicide and then lets him go, pretending to abandon him, without his bow, probably in the hope that he
will change his mind. But this hope is vain. Philoctetes does not change
his mind, and Neoptolemus's moral crisis ultimately leads him to return
the bow to Philoctetes before Odysseus can stop him again. This is the
failure of the forceful method, marked by Odysseus's definitive departure.

Force will be replaced by persuasion. Neoptolemus tries to persuade
Philoctetes to go to Troy, where, according to the oracle Helenus, he is to
be healed and find glory. Despite a momentary hesitation, Philoctetes'
hatred of the Atreids leads him to refuse. It will take the intervention of
the god Heracles to persuade Philoctetes. Divine persuasion has taken
over from human persuasion for the success of the mission. Philoctetes,
accompanied by Neoptolemus, finally leaves for Troy.

c) This sequence in the myth was dealt with in a poem in the epic cycle, the
Little Iliad. In this epic poem, the sequence in question immediately follows Ajax's suicide (see the section on *Ajax*, 1 c). Here is the summary of
it preserved in Proclus's *Chrestomathy* (ed. Bernabé 74, 6–11): "Next Odysseus lies in wait and catches Helenus, who prophesies as to the taking of
Troy, and Diomedes accordingly brings Philoctetes from Lemnos.
Philoctetes is healed by Machaon, fights in single combat with Alexandrus (Paris) and kills him: the dead body is outraged by Menelaus, but
the Trojans recover and bury it. After this Deiphobus marries Helen, Odysseus brings Neoptolemus from Scyros and gives him his father's arms."
Even though this sequence from the Trojan myth comes later than the
one dealt with in the *Iliad* (the wrath of Achilles up to the death of Patrocles and Hector), the myth of Philoctetes is already mentioned (*Iliad*
2, vv. 716–25: the Achaians' abandonment on Lemnos of the archer
Philoctetes, the leader of contingent from the peninsula of Magnesia; the
announcement of his recall by the Achaians). This abandonment of
Philoctetes was recounted in the epic cycle poem whose subject dealt with
the Trojan myth before the *Iliad*, namely the *Cypria*. Here is the summary
of the episode, also preserved in Proclus's *Chrestomathy* (ed. Bernabé 41,
50ff.): "Then they sail off to Tenedos. During a feast, Philoctetes is stung
by a snake and because of the bad smell is left behind on Lemnos."

The sequence about Philoctetes' return to Troy is mentioned in choral
lyric poetry (Pindar, *Pythian Ode* 1, vv. 50–55). It was dramatized by the
three great tragedians: Aeschylus at an unknown date (but before 456, the

date of his death); Euripides in 431 (at the same time as *Medea*; see Aristophanes the Grammarian's argument [*Hypothesis*] preceding this tragedy). In these two tragedies, which are earlier than Sophocles' *Philoctetes*, which was performed in 409 (see below, 4. Date), we have only a few slender fragments (for Aeschylus, see *TrGF* 3, frag. 249–57 Radt; for Euripides, *TrGF* 5.2, frag. 787–803 Kannicht, and F. Jouan, *Euripides*, vol. 8, 3, Paris: CUF, 2002, pp. 269–312). However, the way in which the subject is treated by the three tragedians is rather well known through a discourse by Dio Chrysostom that compares the three *Philoctetes* (*Disc.* 52, a translation of which is given here in appendix IV; see also *Disc.* 59, which summarizes the prologue to Euripides' *Philoctetes*). Although the subject is identical, the characters, the chorus, and the peripeteias vary from one author to another: whereas the mission is led by Diomedes in the *Little Iliad*, it is led by Odysseus in Aeschylus, by Odysseus and Diomedes in Euripides, and by Odysseus and Neoptolemus in Sophocles (for the details of the comparison, see chapter VI, "The Mythic Imagination").

2. Chorus, characters, and actors

The chorus consists of marines from Neoptolemus's ship who are in the service of their leader; the chorus is thus comparable to the one in Ajax. Sophocles innovates with respect to Aeschylus and Euripides, who had chosen a chorus of residents of Lemnos. This choice increases Philoctetes' solitude. The characters are, in the order that they appear, Odysseus and Neoptolemus, the chorus, Philoctetes, a (false) merchant performing the role of messenger, and Heracles appearing as a deus ex machina. There is no female character in the play. The greatest innovation is the character of Achilles' son, Neoptolemus. To introduce this character, Sophocles inverted the order of the two missions that in the epic model (*Little Iliad*) went to seek first Philoctetes, then Neoptolemus.

The protagonist, who plays the role of Philoctetes, is almost constantly onstage from the moment he enters at v. 219. Neoptolemus, who is also almost constantly present, is played by the deuteragonist. The tritagonist plays the roles of Odysseus and the false merchant, as well as that of Heracles, who appears at the end of the tragedy to complete the denouement.

3. Structure of the tragedy

* **Prologue** (vv. 1–134): this is composed of a single scene between Odysseus and Neoptolemus. They enter through the right-side entrance and reach the place where Odysseus, following the Atreids' orders, had formerly abandoned Philoctetes when he was suffering from an ulcer on his foot and was disturbing libations and sacrifices by his cries of pain. Odysseus now wants to seize Philoctetes by deception. For fear of being recognized by him, Odysseus acts through the intermediary of Achilles' son. He stops before reaching the scene and sends Neoptolemus ahead to scout out the grotto and make sure that Philoctetes has left it. Odysseus sends one of Neoptolemus's servants to

watch the path by which Philoctetes might return, then explains to Neoptolemus the plan of deception he is supposed to put into practice: he is to
win Philoctetes' trust by inventing a story to trick him out of his bow and
seize him. He is to tell Philoctetes that he is returning from Troy to his own
country, revolted by the Achaians who have refused to give him his father,
Achilles', arms, awarding them instead to Odysseus. However, Neoptolemus
is reluctant to use trickery, which is contrary to his nature, and he proposes
to use force or persuasion. Odysseus nonetheless succeeds in persuading him
that deception is the only possible way to successfully carry out a mission
that is vital for the Achaians, because the combined action of Philoctetes'
bow and Neoptolemus's bravery is necessary to conquer Troy. Odysseus withdraws, saying that he will send the sentinel, disguised as a merchant, to complete the ruse, if Neoptolemus is too late returning with the bow and
Philoctetes.

* **Parodos** (vv. 135–218): the chorus, composed of Neoptolemus's marines, has
come from the ship through the right-side entrance and now addresses Neoptolemus in a sung dialogue consisting of three strophe/antistrophe pairs,
with epirrhemas in recitative after strophe 1, antistrophe 1, and antistrophe 2.
The dialogue is thus semilyric: the chorus sings (metrical analysis in A. M.
Dale, *Metrical Analyses of Tragic Choruses*, fasc. 2: Eolo-Choriambic, BICS,
supp. 21, 2, 1981, pp. 44ff.), and the character expresses himself in recitative.
The marines ask their leader what they should do, inform themselves regarding Philoctetes' grotto and the hero himself, and announce his approach,
because they hear his groans.

* **First episode** (vv. 219–675): three scenes.
    1. Philoctetes, Neoptolemus, and the chorus (vv. 219–541): On entering,
    Philoctetes finds the strangers and questions them concerning their ori-
    gin. Neoptolemus introduces himself and begins to implement the plan
    of deception by saying that he is coming from Troy and returning to his
    homeland. He pretends not to know who Philoctetes is, which naturally
    leads Philoctetes to recount, in a long, emotional speech (vv. 254–316) the
    story of his misfortunes: his abandonment on Lemnos by the two leaders
    of the army and by Odysseus while he was sleeping after a serious attack
    of his illness; his awakening in total solitude; his efforts to survive using
    the bow he had and with the fire he had made by rubbing two stones to-
    gether; the passage of a few foreigners who, while feeling pity for him, did
    not agree to take him to his homeland. Philoctetes accuses the Atreids
    and Odysseus of being the cause of all his ills. Neoptolemus uses this ha-
    tred as a springboard for developing the plan of deception conceived by
    Odysseus. He pretends to share Philoctetes' anger at Odysseus and the
    Atreids the better to win his trust and recounts his history in a long
    speech (vv. 343–90) in which he mixes truth and lies: after the death of
    Achilles, an embassy formed of Odysseus and Phoenix went to seek him

on the island of Skyros, where he was born, because his presence was needed to take Troy. When he arrived in Troy, he demanded his father's arms as something due him, but the Atreids refused and awarded them to Odysseus. Angry after an altercation with the Atreids and Odysseus, he left for his homeland.

Neoptolemus's trickery is strengthened by that of the chorus, which intervenes with a sung strophe (vv. 391–402); lyric iambic rhythm with dochmiacs (metrical analysis in A. M. Dale, *Metrical Analyses of Tragic Choruses*, fasc. 3: Iambic, BICS, supp. 21, 3, 1983, pp. 217ff.). In an invocation to the goddess Earth, he denounces the unjust violence of the Atreids, who have deprived him of his father's arms, which are rightly his, in order to award them to Odysseus. For Philoctetes, this feigned hatred is the decisive sign that wins his complete trust. And when Neoptolemus pretends to leave for Skyros, Philoctetes begs him, in a second speech (vv. 468–506) to take him along so that he might also return to his homeland, the country of Mount Oeta.

In a sung antistrophe (vv. 507–18: same rhythm as the strophe of vv. 391–402), the chorus urges its master to grant this request. Neoptolemus, after warning the chorus, ends up agreeing, to Philoctetes' great joy.

2. The (false) merchant, Neoptolemus, Philoctetes (vv. 542–627). The arrival of the false merchant constitutes the first peripeteia. It is expected by the spectators, because it was announced by Odysseus (vv. 127–31). But it causes Philoctetes to move from joy to anxiety, for the false merchant, playing the role of messenger in the plan of deception, begins by announcing that Neoptolemus is being sought by a first expedition from Troy (Phoenix and Theseus's two sons), and then a second expedition (Diomedes and Odysseus, as in Euripides' *Philoctetes*) has left to bring Philoctetes to Troy by persuasion or by force. The false merchant mixes truth and falsity in his report. He is the first character to state explicitly the oracle of the Trojan seer Helenus, who had been captured by Odysseus, and who is the origin of the mission to bring Philoctetes to Troy. After a short moment of joy, Philoctetes is cast back into despair by the false merchant's report, which revives the violence of his hatred for Odysseus and makes his departure even more urgent.

3. Philoctetes and Neoptolemus (vv. 628–75). Facing the threat of Odysseus's imminent arrival, Philoctetes wants to hasten his departure. Neoptolemus, finding a reason to delay (the wind is not favorable), merely increases Philoctetes' desire to leave. Before doing so, Philoctetes returns to his cavern to get the plant that he uses to treat his ulcer, and possibly arrows for his bow. This is an opportunity for Neoptolemus to try get his hands on the bow. Philoctetes has to be deprived of his bow before reaching the ship. But this first attempt, without being a failure—since Philoctetes promises to entrust him with the bow at some time in the

future—leads to nothing in the present. Philoctetes, supported by Neop-
tolomeus, goes back into the cavern.

* **First stasimon** (vv. 676–729): the chorus, which has remained alone in the
  visible space, sings in two strophe/antistrophe pairs in the eolo-choriambic
  rhythm (metrical analysis in A. M. Dale, *Metrical Analyses of Tragic Choruses*,
  fasc. 2: Aeolo-Choriambic, BICS, supp. 21, 2, 1981, pp. 46ff.). It emphasizes
  what is exceptional in Philoctetes' misfortune and expresses its astonishment
  at the resistance of a hero who has succeeded in surviving in total solitude for
  the past ten years. But it opposes to this past of misfortunes a future happiness and grandeur, thanks to Neoptolemus, who is going to take Philoctetes
  back to his homeland.

* **Second episode** (vv. 730–826): Philoctetes and Neoptolemus come out of the
  grotto. The second episode consists of one long scene that continues, moreover, beyond the second stasimon as far as the beginning of the third episode,
  because no new character enters before Odysseus arrives (v. 974). This central
  scene in *Philoctetes* is marked by two further peripeteias. But unlike the first
  peripeteia (the arrival of the false merchant), they are unexpected. The first
  one is Philoctetes' physical crisis, which facilitates the plan of deception,
  because the sick man is forced to entrust his bow to Neoptolemus (v. 776):
  he knows, in fact, that the crisis will end with a phase of sleep during which
  he will not be able to keep his bow. But the spectacle of Philoctetes' pain
  causes Neoptolemus to feel a pity (cf. v. 806) that foretells a moral crisis. At
  the end of the second episode, Philoctetes, after a brief fit of madness, falls
  asleep, overcome by his illness.

* **Second stasimon** (vv. 828–64): this takes place during Philoctetes' sleep. It
  takes the form of a semilyric dialogue between the chorus (which sings; metrical analysis in A. M. Dale, *Metrical Analyses of Tragic Choruses*, fasc. 3:
  Dactylic, BICS, supp. 21, 3, 1983, pp. 277ff.) and Neoptolemus (in recitative).
  It is composed of a triad (strophe, antistrophe, epode). The chorus begins
  with a prayer to Sleep that it might come to heal the sick man, then turns to
  Neoptolemus to urge him not to delay taking advantage of the situation. But
  Neoptolemus refuses to leave with the bow alone, because both Philoctetes
  and his bow must be taken back to Troy. And since the chorus insists at the
  moment when it sees Philoctetes in a deep sleep, Neoptolemus rebuffs it,
  because he sees Philoctetes awakening.

* **Third episode** (vv. 867–1080): two scenes.

  1. The first scene (vv. 867–974) is the continuation of the preceding one.
     First Philoctetes awakens, discovering with relief that the foreigners have
     not left. He gets to his feet and is preparing to leave when a new peripe-
     teia, Neoptolemus's moral crisis, interrupts the departure again (v. 895), as
     Philoctetes' earlier physical crisis had. Neoptolemus's nature is reawak-
     ened and manifests itself in a feeling of shame that causes the plan of de-
     ception to fail. Neoptolemus reveals to Philoctetes the whole truth about

the purpose of the voyage, but he refuses to return the bow, invoking
both justice and self-interest. In a further triad (vv. 927–62), which is simultaneously ardent and pathetic, Philoctetes explodes in indignation
against Neoptolemus and begs him to return his bow, but he is twice met
by silence on the part of the young man—which he misinterprets—and
turns twice to what remains to him, his grotto, to complain about the
harm that the son of Achilles has done him and the fate that will be his
now that he is deprived of his bow. Neoptolemus is already gripped by
pity and is about to return the bow when Odysseus rushes in to prevent
him from doing so.

2. Odysseus, Philoctetes, Neoptolemus, the chorus (vv. 974–1080). This is
the first encounter between Odysseus and Philoctetes. It is very quickly
placed under the sign of threats and violence, whereas Neoptolemus remains silent during the confrontation. Odysseus, who has said he is a
man of words, wastes little time on an attempt to persuade an intractable
Philoctetes, who threatens to commit suicide by throwing himself off a
cliff. Odysseus orders his servants to seize Philoctetes. Now Odysseus's
prisoner, Philoctetes addresses an indictment of forty-two lines full of
hatred against him in a scene of the "agōn scene" type, with two opposed
speeches in which the adversaries confront one another. But Odysseus's
response, which is astonishingly short for an agōn scene, counts on surprise. He does not waste time justifying himself; instead, he orders his
entourage to release the prisoner and pretends that he is about to abandon Philoctetes and leave, taking just the bow with him. Neoptolemus,
who is carrying the bow, is asked to follow him. Philoctetes, deprived of
his bow, remains alone with the chorus.

* **Third stasimon** (vv. 1081–217): the stasimon takes the form of a dialogue between Philoctetes and the chorus. The dialogue is purely lyric, consisting of
two strophe/antistrophe systems (vv. 1081–168) and an epode (vv. 1169–217).
In truth, until the epode there is no dialogue in the strict sense, because although the chorus addresses Philoctetes, the hero himself laments his fate,
addressing external elements (his grotto, his bow, the birds). He sees himself
abandoned a second time, but in a more tragic way, without his bow. The
chorus, which had earlier admired the hero's resistance, accuses him of not
having made a reasonable decision in refusing to go to Troy. Then, in the
epode, a lively and eventful dialogue is established between Philoctetes and
the chorus. Remaining deaf to the chorus's advice, Philoctetes sends it away
and then, seized by panic at the idea of being abandoned, immediately calls
it back, begging it not to leave, and then finally refusing to depart for Troy.
Wishing to die at once, Philoctetes retreats to his grotto.

* **Exodos** (vv. 1218–471): six scenes.
  1. Odysseus, Neoptolemus (vv. 1218–60). Neoptolemus suddenly returns,
  followed by Odysseus. Urged on by remorse, he has decided, offstage, to

go back and restore to Philoctetes the bow he obtained from him by trickery, even though this means disobeying the orders given by Odysseus and the army. Odysseus tries to oppose him in this. The scene ends with a brief but violent confrontation in which the two men threaten to draw their swords. But Odysseus gives in and withdraws, saying that he will report to the whole army so that it will punish Neoptolemus for his insubordination.

2. Neoptolemus, Philoctetes (vv. 1261–92). Neoptolemus calls to Philoctetes, who comes warily out of his grotto. Seeing that Philoctetes has made up his mind to remain and to endure his fate rather than leave, Neoptolemus returns his bow to him. Odysseus rushes forward once again to try to prevent the return of the bow, but he comes too late.

3. Philoctetes, Odysseus, Neoptolemus (vv. 1293–307). This is the shortest and most spectacular scene among the three characters. Hearing Odysseus coming, then seeing him prepared to use violence to take him away by force, Philoctetes draws his bow against him; he would have released the arrow had Neoptolemus not held his arm. The man of words who wanted to act by force finally retreats without saying anything. This is the failure of the attempt to fulfill the mission by force.

4. Neoptolemus, Philoctetes (vv. 1308–408). A long scene constructed as an agōn scene (with two long opposed speeches followed by a stichomythia). Neoptolemus, who has won Philoctetes' trust, not by trickery but by his frankness and nobility of soul in returning his bow, tries as a friend to use true persuasion to convince Philoctetes to go to Troy, where he will not only be healed by Asclepius's son but also win glory, as Helenus's oracle predicted. Philoctetes hesitates for an instant, but his hatred for Odysseus and the Atreids wins out. Neoptolemus finally gives up trying to persuade him, and when Philoctetes reminds him of his promise to take him back to his homeland, he suddenly decides to grant his request. A change in meter and mode of expression (passage from iambic trimeter to trochaic tetrameter, passage from speech to recitative accompanied by the "flute" marks the departure and gives the spectators the sense of an ending).

5. Epiphany of Heracles (vv. 1409–51). This departure is interrupted by the arrival of Heracles, appearing in the air with the help of the mechanè. The god, the spokesman for Zeus's designs, first addresses Philoctetes, the heir to his bow, to forestall his project of going back to his homeland, and to urge him to go to Troy. He promises him glory and healing. Then he addresses Neoptolemus to urge him to fight alongside Philoctetes to conquer Troy. This message from the god confirms the truth of Helenus's oracle, whose content had been partly revealed by the false merchant and partly by Neoptolemus. The god nonetheless corrects them on one point (Philoctetes will not be healed by the son of Asclepius, but by the god Asclepius himself), and he makes additional recommendations, notably concerning the value that is more important than any other in Zeus's

eyes, piety toward the gods. Philoctetes is immediately convinced by the god's words; and the same is true for Neoptolemus. The god asks them to depart and then flies off toward the heavens with the help of the mechanè.

6. Final scene (vv. 1452–68). Before departing, Philoctetes says a heartfelt farewell to the land he is about to leave and prepares to go to "the destination appointed me by mighty Fate and the will of my friends, and by the all-taming god who has brought these things to pass" (vv. 1466–68). The chorus concludes the tragedy with a call to leave and a prayer to the Nymphs of the sea for a safe return.

4. Date

Philoctetes is one of the two tragedies by Sophocles whose date is known with certainty. The clue is found in the *Hypothesis* II given at the head of the manuscripts, a notice that is anonymous but probably goes back to Aristophanes of Byzantium (for the text, see above). In it we read that the tragedy was performed under the archontate of Glaukippos, that is, in 410–409 (for the date, cf. the archon Diodorus of Sicily XIII, 43), and that Sophocles won the competition.

5. Iconography

No indication for Sophocles' *Philoctetes*; on the other hand, for Euripides' *Philoctetes*, see L. Séchan (cited in chapter X, "Humans and the Gods"), pp. 485–93, and T.B.L. Webster (cited in chapter V, "Happy Sophocles"), p. 162.

6. Editions with notes; or commentaries

R. C. Jebb, Cambridge, 4th ed. 1894; rpt. with introduction by F. Budelmann, gen. ed. P. E. Easterling, London, 2004; A. Dain and P. Mazon, Paris: CUF, 1st ed. 1960 (Greek text, French translation, notes in French), and compare, for the French translation, P. Masqueray, Paris: CUF, 1942; T.B.L. Webster, Cambridge, 1970 (Greek text, notes in English); J. C. Kamerbeek 1980 (commentary in English); R. G. Ussher, Warminster, 1990, revised ed. 2001 (Greek text, English translation, notes in English); H. Lloyd-Jones and N. G. Wilson, *Sophoclea: Studies on the Text of Sophocles*, Oxford, 1990, pp. 179–213 (notes in English); J. C. Hogan, *A Commentary on the Plays of Sophocles*, 1991; H. Lloyd-Jones and N. G. Wilson, *Sophocles: Second Thoughts*, Göttingen, 1997, pp. 103–13 (notes in English); P. Pucci, G. Avezzù, and G. Cerri, Fondazione L. Valla, 2003 (Greek text, Italian translation, notes in Italian); S. L. Schein, *Sophocles' Philoctetes*, Newburyport, MA, 2003 (introduction, translation, notes in English); H. M. Roisman, *Sophocles: Philoctetes*, London: Duckworth, 2005 (monograph in English).

The Women of Trachis

1. Subject of the tragedy and the site of the action

a) The subject of the tragedy is part of the myth of Heracles. Heracles, the illustrious son of Zeus and Alcmene (v. 19), belongs to the generation preceding the Trojan War. The site of the action is the city of Trachis (v.

39), at the foot of Mount Oeta (vv. 200, 436, 635, 1191), near the Malian Gulf (v. 636) and not far from the warm springs of Thermopylae (v. 634). The sequence concerns the hero's return after a long absence. He is awaited by his wife Deianira, who is the guest of the king of Trachis (v. 40). The absence has been long for an anxious woman who has had no news of her husband for fifteen months (vv. 44ff.). During this time Heracles has been first the slave of Omphale, queen of Lydia, for a year (v. 252), before returning as a conqueror after the capture of Oechalia, King Eurytus's city in central Euboea, which he conquered out of love for Iole, the king's daughter. Deianira's anxiety is increased by a tablet left behind by Heracles before his departure (v. 47). On the advice of her nurse, Deianira sends her elder son, Hyllus, to look for his father. The news of Heracles' victorious return is announced first by an anonymous messenger, then by Heracles's herald, Laches, who brings back with him the captives, including Iole. Heracles himself has remained at the northern extremity of Euboea, where he is founding a sanctuary in honor of Zeus, his father, to thank him for the victory (vv. 237ff.). Deianira's joy is soon followed by anxiety, then by jealousy when she gradually discovers the identity of the young woman and the real reason for Heracles' expedition. Wanting to win back her husband's love, she then decides to anoint the tunic that she is planning to give him as a present with what she believes to be a love philter: the blood gathered from the wound of the centaur Nessus, mortally wounded by Heracles' arrow, which had already been dipped in the venom of the Lernaean Hydra. This love philter turns out in fact to be a lethal poison. A first sign of this is given to Deianira by what happened to the bit of wool she had used to anoint the tunic. It was destroyed by the heat of the sun's rays. Thus she becomes aware too late that the centaur Nessus had deceived her as he died. This first sign is confirmed by the arrival of Hyllus, who accuses his mother of being his father's murderer. Having witnessed the effect produced by the poison on Heracles' body when he donned the tunic to offer a sacrifice in honor of Zeus, Hyllus describes his father's sufferings and his fit of madness, during which he killed Lichas. After the account of these misfortunes, Deianira departs in silence. Her nurse says that she has committed suicide and that her son, before leaving again to look for Heracles, has understood too late how unjust his accusation of his mother was. Heracles, accompanied by his son Hyllus, returns as an invalid, lying on a stretcher and suffering from unbearable pain. The hero who had triumphed over so many monsters has been brought low by a woman's treachery. That is, at least, what he thinks. But his son Hyllus, who had so violently accused his mother, now defends her by revealing that she had been deceived by the perfidious recommendations of the centaur Nessus. Through these new revelations Heracles abruptly becomes aware that he is reaching the end of his life when he recalls ancient oracles of Zeus that are being fulfilled (he was to die not at the hands of a living being, but of a dead one) and also new oracles of Zeus at Dodona (regarding the end of his misfortunes, which is supposed to occur on this fateful day). Heracles thereupon informs his son of his last wishes: Hyllus must first carry him to the summit of Mount Oeta, where his funeral pyre is to be built, and then marry Iole. At first, Hyllus is horrified by the command to marry Iole, because she is the cause of his mother's death, but he ends up agreeing to obey in order to avoid his father's curse. The tragedy ends with the cortege that accompanies Heracles carried by his son toward his last resting place.

b) This is the oldest extant tragedy about the myth of Heracles if we agree that, as seems very likely, Euripides' *Heracles* is later. The epic had already treated this part of the myth. We know, in fact, the existence of an epic poem entitled *The Capture of Oechalia*, attributed sometimes to Homer, sometimes to his friend (or son-in-law) Creophylus of Samos. The extant fragments are very short (*Poetae Epici Graeci*, ed. Bernabé, pp. 161–64). But as early as this poem, Heracles conquered the city of Oechalia in Euboea out of love for Iole, the king's daughter. And as early as Hesiod, in the *Catalog of Women* (frag. 25, 17–24 Merkelbach-West), we find a reference to Deianira's act of giving Lichas the poisoned tunic so that he might take it to Heracles after the destruction of a city. The gift causes Heracles' death. It seems that Deianira's act was voluntary (due to great wrath), and nothing is said about the origin of the poison. Archaic poetry had also mentioned several elements of this mythic sequence: Archilogus (seventh century BCE) had mentioned the scene in which Heracles kills the centaur Nessus, who tried to rape Deianira as he carried her across the Evenus river (see Dio Chrysostom, *Disc.* 60, 1: Archilochus was accused of delaying too long Heracles' intervention, which left Nessus time to do what he wanted; conversely, Sophocles was reproached for having had Heracles intervene too quickly by killing Nessus as he was crossing the river, which would have led to Deianira's death). Bacchylides (fifth century BCE), in his *Dithyramb* 16, mentions elliptically what is developed in *The Women of Trachis*: after the capture of Oechalia, Heracles made a sacrifice in honor of Zeus Ceneus (compare Bacchylides, 14–15, and Sophocles vv. 238 and 760); but a divinity acted on Deianira: the victim of a violent jealousy when she learned that Heracles brought "white-armed" Iole home with him in order to marry her, she used the magical means she had received from the centaur Nessus. Scholars do not all agree regarding the relative dates of Bacchylides's *Dithyramb* and Sophocles' tragedy.

2. Chorus, characters, and actors

The title of the tragedy, *The Women of Trachis*, comes from the chorus formed of young women living in Trachis. They are associated with Deianira, because they know her past (the combat between Achelous and Heracles for the possession of Deianira); having learned of her anxiety due to Heracles' long absence, they come to reassure her. But they are still young women, who do not know the fears that a woman can have for her husband or for her children. Nonetheless, they serve as confidants for Deianira. Their role recedes into the background after Heracles arrives.

The characters are, in the order that they appear: Deianira, the daughter of Oeneus and Heracles' wife, her nurse, her son Hyllus, and then the chorus. Two messengers announce, successively, Heracles' return, an anonymous messenger (who must be one of Deianira's slaves), and Lichas, Heracles' personal messenger. Heracles arrives only after Deianira's death, accompanied by an old man and Hyllus.

In the *Women of Trachis*, a so-called diptych tragedy like *Ajax*, the protagonist plays two characters who do not encounter one another: Deianira and Heracles. The other roles are played by the deuteragonist (Hyllus and Lichas) and the tritagonist (the nurse, the messenger, and the old man).

3. Structure of the tragedy

* **Prologue** (vv. 1–93): two scenes. In the first, Deianira comes out of the palace accompanied by an elderly female slave, her nurse (vv. 1–60). In a monologue (vv. 1–48), Deianira recounts her past destiny, which has been filled with anxiety ever since her beauty made her an object of desire: fear of a monstrous suitor, the river Achelous, who presented himself in an animal (bull, serpent) or a hybrid form (the body of a man and the head of an ox); fear during Heracles' struggle with this monster to free her; and after a transitory moment of joy in which the victorious Heracles married her, fears of another kind; the incessant fear for her beloved, who did, it is true, give her children, but who has often been absent. This fear is aroused in the present, even though Heracles has completed the cycle of labors imposed on him by Eurystheus. In fact, he has been absent for fifteen months without giving any sign that he is still alive; and a letter that he had given her before his departure makes her fear the worst. After this monologue, the slave advises Deianira to send her son Hyllus to look for his father. At the same moment, Hyllus arrives.

The second scene (vv. 61–93) is a dialogue between Deianira and Hyllus. Approving the advice of her slave, Deianira asks her son to go find out what has happened to his father. An exchange of information between the two characters shows that this day is crucial. Hyllus has just heard a rumor that Heracles has spent a year in Lydia in the service of a woman, and that he is currently in Euboea on an expedition against Eurytus's city. This news coincides with the oracle Heracles communicated to Deianira just before his departure. This is the decisive moment in Heracles' destiny: it will be the end of his life or the end of his travails. After this exchange of information, Hyllus sets out to find his father.

* **Parodos** (vv. 94–140): formed of a triad (metrical analysis in A. M. Dale, *Metrical Analyses of Tragic Choruses*, fasc. 1: Dactylo-Epitrite, BICS, supp. 21, 1, 1971, pp. 22–24). The search for Heracles makes the connection between the prologue and the parodos. When it enters, the chorus begins by invoking the Sun, the god who sees everything, to ask it to indicate where Heracles is. The chorus has heard about Deianira's concern, and that is what motivates its arrival. With respect but also with frankness, the young women urge Deianira not to despair: Zeus does not abandon his own; and in the universal alternation, which is compared to the rotation of the constellation Ursa Major, hardships and joys succeed one another.

* **First episode** (vv. 141–496): five scenes.

    1. The first scene (vv. 141–79) is in reality only a continuation of the preceding scene (begun with the entrance of the chorus, which has addressed Deianira since v. 122); no other characters enter or exit between the parodos and the first episode. In turn, Deianira addresses the chorus in a long speech in which she reveals her fears. This introspection prolongs, completes, and deepens what she had already revealed in her initial speech. At the same time, Deianira presents the chorus indirectly: they are young women who have not experienced the fears of a mother for her husband and her children. Deianira explains above all her present anxiety, which is due to the letter left by Hercules before his departure. The spectator has already heard about this letter and the oracle that it contains, in the two scenes of the prologue (v. 47 and vv. 76ff.) But the present clues provide new information about the content: Heracles has given instructions concerning the distribution of his legacy: as for the oracle, its origin is explained (it is an oracle from Dodona), and the decisive moment of its fulfillment is calculated differently—no longer relatively, by reference to the siege of Eurytus's city, but rather absolutely, by the period of a year and three months, which corresponds exactly to the current length of Heracles' absence. Everything converges to make the moment in the tragedy a decisive stage in Heracles' destiny. The nightmare that has just made Deianira leap out of bed is another sign. It is also a stage direction that justifies a posteriori the appearance of Deianira at the beginning of the tragedy.

    2. The whole first part of the tragedy, dominated by the anxiety of Deianira, who is waiting for news of her husband, is succeeded, in an alternation that seems to confirm the chorus's view, by a moment of pure joy, with the arrival of the first messenger. In this second scene (vv. 180–224), an anonymous messenger, probably one of Deianira's old servants, announces the good news: Heracles is alive and will return victorious. This occasional messenger has learned the news from Heracles' herald Lichas, who is being delayed by the Malian people, who are eager for information. For a brief instant, Deianira gives herself up to joy and asks the

women to join her. The chorus sings and dances a short, astrophic passage (vv. 205–24; lyric iambic rhythm; metrical analysis in A. M. Dale, *Metrical Analyses of Tragic Choruses*, fasc. 3: Iambic, BICS, supp. 21, 3, 1983, pp. 211ff.). This song is interrupted by the arrival of a cortege of women led by Lichas.

3. The third scene (vv. 225–334) is the true messenger scene, including, after a short dialogue, a long speech typical of this kind of scene. In the dialogue, it is confirmed that Heracles is alive and the victor, and it is learned that he is still in Euboea, where he is founding a sanctuary in honor of Zeus to thank him for his victory; and it is also learned that the women accompanying Lichas are choice captives coming from Eurytus's city. According to Lichas, these two facts are connected. Having been insulted by Eurytus, Heracles avenged himself on Eurytus's son Iphitus by taking him by surprise and killing him. Zeus did not accept this murder perpetrated by trickery and condemned Heracles to slavery; and Heracles is supposed to have undertaken his expedition against Eurytus to make him pay for this snub, for which he held him responsible, After the messenger's narrative, we would expect Deianira to show a more unalloyed joy. But the sight of the captives is a new source of fear for her: the fear that her children might fall into a similar misfortune. Deianira's pity is focused on one of these captives, to whom she speaks, but from whom she receives no response. And the questions she asks Lichas regarding the identity of this captive run into a wall of ignorance. Everyone goes into the palace.

4. Nonetheless, at the last moment, the first messenger holds Deianira back. In this fourth scene (vv. 335–92) he accuses Lichas of lying and gives Deianira an entirely different version of the causes of Heracles' expedition that he has heard from Lichas himself in the presence of many witnesses: it was out of love for the young woman noticed by Deianira that Heracles killed Eurytus and destroyed his city, Oechalia. The rest was merely a pretext. This young woman is not nameless: she is noble and beautiful; she is the king's daughter. Deianira's first reaction is stupefaction (v. 386; cf. v. 24).

5. The fifth scene (vv. 393–496) is an exchange between Lichas and Deianira, with a speech by the messenger who accuses Lichas of bearing false witness. In a long speech (vv. 436–69), Deianira, having recovered an apparent calm, begs Lichas to tell her the truth. She shows both wisdom and gentleness: wisdom with regard to those who are victims of Love, a power superior to the gods as well as to humans; gentleness with regard to Lichas, from whom she nonetheless demands honesty. Touched by Deianira's humanity and encouraged by the chorus, Lichas reveals the truth that he had sought to mask out of concern for his mistress, and he ends by advising her to resign herself. Deianira asks him to go into the palace and announces that she is going to give him gifts for Heracles in

exchange for the captives. This is an announcement that heralds all the catastrophes.

* **First stasimon** (vv. 497–530): formed of a triad (metrical analysis in A. M. Dale, *Metrical Analyses of Tragic Choruses*, fasc. 1: Dactylo-Epitrite, BICS, supp. 21, 1, 1971, pp. 25–27). The chorus does not comment directly on the preceding situation but begins with a eulogy of Cypris, the goddess of love, inspired by Deianira's reflections on Eros (vv. 441–44). The eulogy celebrates Cypris's omnipotence, which is exercised on the gods as well as on mortals. It illustrates the goddess's power over humans by the memorable episode in Deianira's past when Heracles won her by defeating the river Achelous transformed into a bull. The chorus evokes, in a lyric and epic register, this combat, which Deianira had mentioned at the beginning of the tragedy but could not describe because she was so paralyzed by fear (vv. 20–24).

* **Second episode** (vv. 531–632): two scenes.

    1. Deianira, having come out of the palace alone carrying a box in her arms, comes to find the chorus to tell it what she has done and what she feels, and to ask its advice (vv. 531–93). Iole's presence in her home has aroused in her heart an unbearable feeling of jealousy. To be sure, her declarations of understanding and wisdom made earlier to Lichas have not completely disappeared. She does not want to get angry at her husband, who is suffering from the disease of love. But she is lucid regarding the effects of the blooming beauty of a young woman compared with the declining beauty of a mature woman. To avoid being left by her husband, she has thought of a remedy, the gift given her by the centaur Nessus, which she has kept hidden in a bronze box. This gift leads her to evoke a scene in her past that took place not long after the battle between Heracles and Achelous mentioned by the chorus in the preceding stasimon. This is a second scene in which Heracles, taking the young bride away, intervenes again to save her from a monstrous being: Nessus, who carried travelers across the River Evenus, tried to rape Deianira on the way; Heracles then wounded him mortally with an arrow already poisoned with the venom of the Lernaean Hydra. Following the dying centaur's recommendations, Deianira collected the blood flowing from his wound, which was mixed with the hydra's venom: this is supposed to be a balm that will allow her to retain Heracles' love. Recalling this ancient gift, Deianira decides to anoint with this balm the tunic that she is going to give Heracles as a gift. Fearful by nature, Deianira nonetheless asks the advice of the chorus, which does not discourage her. The entrance onstage of Lichas, who comes out of the palace to leave again, puts an end to any hesitation.

    2. In the second scene (vv. 598–632), Deianira, after asking the chorus to be discreet, hands Lichas the gift for Heracles and makes recommendations concerning the way Heracles should use it: he should not put the tunic in contact with heat before having put it on for the sacrifice. The reason for

this recommendation is not given. But a little later we learn that Deianira is in fact repeating the instructions of the centaur Nessus (cf. vv. 684–87; cf. already v. 662).

* **Second stasimon** (vv. 633–62): consists of two strophe/antistrophe pairs (metrical analysis in A. M. Dale, *Metrical Analyses of Tragic Choruses*, fasc. 1: Dactylo-Epitrite, BICS, supp. 21, 1, 1971, pp. 28–29). The chorus, which has remained alone after Lichas exits through a side entrance and after Deianira has gone back into the palace, centers its song on Heracles' expected return. After a long absence, his victorious return will restore joy to all the residents of the region. The chorus hopes he will come back full of amorous desire, once the balm has acted.

* **Third episode** (vv. 663–820): two scenes.

    1. The chorus, Deianira (vv. 663–733). Deianira, who has burst out of the palace, comes to express her fears regarding the effect of the balm. In a long narrative (vv. 672–722), she informs the chorus of an unexpected marvel: the bit of wool she had used to anoint the tunic has been reduced to dust. This is a sign foretelling the balm's destructive potential. After announcing this disturbing news, she describes in detail what happened, in a speech comparable to that of a messenger. She recalls the centaur Nessus's recommendations and the scrupulousness with which she followed them, both for the preservation of the balm and for its use: the balm must be protected from light and heat. But the bit of wool, thrown by accident into the sunlight, has been transformed into dust, and a boiling foam has emerged from the soil. Such a sign leads Deianira to become aware, but too late, of the gravity of her act: the centaur Nessus had no reason to wish her well, and his blood threatens to wreak the dead creature's vengeance on the man who struck him. If she is the cause of her husband's death, she has decided to die with him, because living without honor is intolerable.

    2. The second scene (vv. 734–820) will provide the confirmation of Deianira's fear. Hyllus, having returned, comes to tell his mother what happened to his father after he received the gift. The son's message rings like an indictment. He accuses his mother, whom he no longer recognizes as such, of having killed in Heracles a husband and a father. After making this accusation, Hyllus reports, in a long speech (vv. 749–812), the diverse moments in Heracles' tragedy: during the return after the destruction of Eurytus's city in Euboea, he paused at the Cenean Cape before crossing the Malian Gulf and reaching Trachis, in order to found a sanctuary to Zeus, his father, to thank him for his victory. It was at that point that Hyllus saw his father again. While Heracles was getting ready to make the sacrifice connected with the foundation, Lichas came to bring him Deianira's gift, the tunic, which he put on with joy. But the balm heated by the fire of the sacrifices began to produce its effect. Sophocles describes with pre-

cision the symptoms of the illness, the fit of madness during which Heracles killed the innocent Lichas, and his return to consciousness after the crisis. Heracles then perceived his son among the crowd of those present and asked him to take him away as fast as he could so that he did not die on the spot. Thus Heracles has been taken to the continent by boat and will soon appear, dead or alive. Hyllus concludes his speech as he had begun it, by accusing his mother of murder, adding a curse so that she might be punished by the divinities.

The scene ends with the exit of Deianira, who goes back into the palace, despite the chorus's intervention. This exit is greeted with ironic and scornful joy by her son, who also goes back into the palace.

* **Third stasimon** (vv. 821–62): two strophe/antistrophe pairs (metrical analysis in A. M. Dale, *Metrical Analyses of Tragic Choruses*, fasc. 1: Dactylo-Epitrite, BICS, supp. 21, 1, 1971, pp. 30ff.). The chorus, which has remained alone, comments lucidly on what has just happened. This is the fulfillment of what the oracle predicted, long before, regarding the end of Heracles' trials: a man who no longer sees the light no longer has to suffer. After the combined effect of Nessus's blood and the Lernaean hydra's venom, how could Heracles survive another day? As for Deianira, obsessed as she is by the sudden arrival of a new woman, she has not understood and was deceived by the centaur's advice. The chorus sheds tears over Heracles' pitiful illness and sees in all this the work of Cypris. The chorus thus returns to the explanation it gave in the first stasimon: but the image of Cypris, a multiform goddess, is different: she is no longer the referee with her rod at the center of a combat, but the silent servant whose work explodes in the light.

* **Fourth episode** (vv. 863–946): a single scene. The nurse comes out of the palace to announce Deianira's death to the chorus. After a dialogue between the nurse and the chorus in which emotion transforms the spoken exchanges into a brief dialogue whose peculiarity is to be astrophic (commos, vv. 879–95; metrical analysis in A. M. Dale, *Metrical Analyses of Tragic Choruses*, fasc. 1: Dactylo-Epitrite, BICS, supp. 21, 1, 1971, pp. 32ff.), the nurse recounts in a long speech (vv. 899–946) the pathetic and courageous suicide of Deianira, who has stabbed herself, under the liver, in Heracles' bedchamber. She also recounts Hyllus's belated discovery of his mother's body; he feels responsible for her death because in a fit of anger he had made a mad accusation against her. The nurse ends her account with a general reflection on the fragility of human destiny. This reflection echoes the one Deianira uttered at the very beginning of the tragedy (vv. 1–3) and concludes Deianira's tragedy. The nurse goes back into the palace.

* **Fourth stasimon** (vv. 947–70): two very brief strophe/antistrophe pairs (metrical analysis in A. M. Dale, *Metrical Analyses of Tragic Choruses*, fasc. 2: Aeolo-Choriambic, BICS, supp. 21, 2, 1981, p. 34). This stasimon serves as a transition from Deianira's misfortunes, which have already occurred, to those

of Heracles, which the chorus is awaiting. It would like to be carried far away by the wind in order not to witness the spectacle of Heracles' malady. But it spots a group of foreigners approaching in a cortege, transporting Heracles on a stretcher. Heracles is silent. Is he dead or only sleeping?

* **Exodos** (vv. 971–1278): the technical term *exodos*, designating the whole part of the tragedy following the chorus's final song and preceding its exit (see above) risks masking the reality. The beginning of the exodos corresponds to Heracles' arrival. There is a great contrast between the triumphant Heracles who was expected at the beginning of the tragedy, after the first messenger's announcement, and the invalid that the spectators see lying on a litter. The whole of the exodos forms a single scene, because from this point on no characters enter or exit. The three actors are onstage: the protagonist plays the role of Heracles, the deuteragonist that of Hyllus, and the tritagonist that of an old man assigned to take care of Heracles. Nonetheless, even though there is only one scene, several parts can be distinguished if we take into account both the formal characteristics (changes in meter, the rhythm of communication) and the dramatic content.

1. In the first part, in recitative and sometimes in song (vv. 971–1043), Heracles lies on a stretcher sleeping, then wakes, struck by two attacks of his illness that make him wish he were dead. Heracles sings during the two attacks (a strophe/antistrophe pair; for the metrical analysis, see A. M. Dale, *Metrical Analyses of Tragic Choruses*, fasc. 2: Aeolo-Choriambic, BICS, supp. 21, 2, 1981, pp. 34–35; see also J. Irigoin, "Le trio des Trachiniennes de Sophocle vv. 971–1043: Analyse métrique et établissement du texte," cited in the bibliographical guide for *The Women of Trachis*).

2. We then return to the spoken (vv. 1044–258). First, Heracles gives a long speech (vv. 1046–111), framed by two comments made by the chorus. In them Heracles denounces his wife's treachery, which has caused his devouring malady, and asks his son to bring her to him so that he can take revenge; removing his covers, he displays his miserable body to his son and to all those present; then he is struck by a third attack of the illness that makes him desire death once more. In contrast with his present state, he describes his past exploits: the Nemean lion, the Lernaean hydra, the centaurs, the Erymanthian boar, the dog of Hades and the dragon that guarded the Hesperides' golden apples. He ends his speech as he began it, with the desire to punish the woman who has caused his illness. The spoken parts are followed by a dialogue between father and son (vv. 1114–258). First, Hyllus wants to justify his mother, whose offenses were involuntary. Despite Heracles' protests, he informs him not only of her death, but also of the trick played by the centaur Nessus, who persuaded her to use the unguent as a love philter. This detail leads Heracles to understand everything, because he connects this information with Zeus's two oracles concerning his destiny: an old oracle, which has not previously been

mentioned, according to which he is to die not by the hand of a living person, but by a dead one; and a new oracle, which the spectator has already heard mentioned on several occasions, the one from Dodona according to which Heracles will see, on this same day, the end of his travails. So here he is dying from the effects of a dead creature, the centaur Nessus, and finds the end of his travails not in a peaceful life but in death. Sure of his destiny, Heracles imposes his last wishes on his son after making him swear to obey. First, he is to take Heracles to the highest summit of Mount Oeta, where he is to build a funeral pyre and burn his body. The second wish concerns Iole: Heracles bequeaths her to his son as his wife. Hyllus protests still more vigorously, but this time Heracles makes no concession. The son is obliged to obey his father.

3. The final recitative (vv. 1259–78) corresponds to the cortege's departure for Heracles' last resting place. Heracles is now in control of his pain, becoming once again the hero that he once was. His son gives the order to leave, but he despairs at the silence of the gods, who seem not to care about mortals. The chorus, for its part, sees in all this the mark of Zeus.

4. Date

There is no clue at the head of the manuscripts regarding the circumstances of the performance or its date. There is no allusion to the tragedy in comic theater. And attempts to relate the tragedy to contemporary events are arbitrary. Thus there is no evidence external to the tragedy. On the basis of an internal examination, most modern critics classify the tragedy in the group of older plays (*Ajax*, *The Women of Trachis*, *Antigone*), comparing it with *Ajax* and contrasting it with two later, dated tragedies (*Philoctetes* and *Oedipus at Colonus*). Like *Ajax*, the tragedy is a so-called diptych tragedy, that is, the first part is focused primarily on Deianira, while the second part is focused primarily on Heracles. This is confirmed from a dramaturgical point of view, because the protagonist plays the two main roles in succession. However, this technique does not threaten the unity of the tragedy, which is presented as a return tragedy. We have seen the resemblances between Sophocles' *Women of Trachis* and Euripides' *Alcestis*, which dates from 438: the account of Deianira's death (vv. 899ff.) is comparable to that of Alcestis's last moments (vv. 152–98). But it is not possible to infer from these resemblances that *The Women of Trachis* is later than *Alcestis*. *The Women of Trachis* does not have the innovations in the way the sung parts are dealt with that we find starting with *Electra*. In this respect we can contrast the traditional parodos in *The Women of Trachis* with *Electra*'s parodos in dialogue, even though the situation is comparable: the presence of the heroine before the entrance of the chorus (see above).

5. Iconography

See L. Séchan (cited in chapter X, "Humans and the Gods"), pp. 145–47; T.B.L. Webster (cited in chapter V, "Happy Sophocles"), pp. 152ff.; A. D.

Trendall and T.B.L. Webster (cited in chapter X, "Humans and the Gods"), p. 71.

6. Editions with notes; and commentaries

R. C. Jebb, Cambridge, 1892 (Greek text, English translation, notes in English); rpt. with an introduction by B. Goward, gen. ed. P. E. Easterling, London, 2004; A. Dain and P. Mazon, Paris: CUF, 1st ed. 1955 (Greek text, French translation, notes in French), and compare, for the French translation, P. Masqueray, Paris: CUF, 1942; J. C. Kamerbeek, 1970 (commentary in English); P. E. Easterling, Cambridge, 1982 (Greek text, notes in English); H. Lloyd-Jones and N. G. Wilson, *Sophoclea: Studies on the Text of Sophocles*, Oxford, 1990, pp. 150–78 (notes in English); M. Davies, Oxford, 1991 (Greek text, notes); J. C. Hogan, *A Commentary on the Plays of Sophocles*, 1991; H. Lloyd-Jones and N. G. Wilson, *Sophocles: Second Thoughts*, Göttingen, 1997, pp. 87–102 (notes in English); B. Levett, *Sophocles: Women of Trachis*, London: Duckworth, 2002 (monograph in English); A. Rodighiero, *La morte di Eracle (Trachinie)*, Venice, 2004 (introduction, translation, and commentary in Italian).

Appendix II

....

SOPHOCLES, FRAGMENTS: LIST AND PRESENTATION OF THE PLAYS EXTANT IN THE FORM OF FRAGMENTS

For the editions of Sophocles' fragments and the studies on them, see in the bibliographical guide "Particular Studies on Each Tragedy," under "Sophocles' Lost Works." The current basic edition is that of S. Radt, 1977, 2nd ed. 1999 (cited as Radt), which has replaced that of Nauck, and which is complemented, for the satyr plays, by that of R. Krumeich, N. Pechstein, and B. Seidensticker, *Das griechische Satyrspiel*, 1999 (cited as *Das griechische Satyrspiel*). But A. C. Pearson's edition of 1917 (cited as Pearson) remains fundamental for its introductions and commentary on the fragments. H. Lloyd-Jones's edition (Loeb, 1996; cited as Lloyd-Jones) is convenient to use. The old synthesis by F. G. Welcker, *Die Griechischen Tragödien*, 1839–41 (cited as Welcker), has provided the basis for all later research on Sophocles' lost plays in particular and on Greek and Latin theater in general. For the iconography, see L. Séchan, *Études sur la tragédie grecque dans ses rapports avec la céramique*, Paris, 1967 (1926), pp. 139–230 (cited as Séchan); T.B.L. Webster, *Monuments Illustrating Tragedy and Satyr Play*, 2nd ed., London (BICS, supp. 20), 1967 (cited as Webster); A. D. Trendall and T.B.L. Webster, *Illustrations of Greek Drama*, London, 1971, pp. 63–71 (cited as Trendall-Webster), and see the articles in the *Lexicon Iconographicum Mythologiae classicae* (*LIMC*), 1981–99 corresponding to the characters in Sophocles' plays.

All the plays extant in fragments are presented here in the order traditionally adopted by scholars all over the world, that of the titles of the plays in Greek, with their conventional numbers.

Presentation of the plays extant in fragments. The titles are given first in Greek (with a transcription that seeks as far as possible to make the Greek alphabetical order comprehensible), then in English, if the English translation differs from the Greek transcription.

1–2. **Athamas** 1 and 2 (frag. 1–10 Radt). Sophocles wrote two plays on Athamas, king of Boeotia; for the first *Athamas*, see frag. 1; for the second, see frag. 2–3 and also the scholium on Aristophanes, *The Clouds*, v. 257, where the "other" *Athamas* is mentioned. The comic author Aristophanes alludes to one of these two plays in *The Clouds* of 423, when Strepsiades replies to Socrates, who is offering him a chaplet (v. 257), "For what purpose a chaplet? Ah me! Socrates, see that you do not sacrifice me like Athamas!" The scholium, which recalls at length the story of Athamas, explains that this is an allusion to a scene in the tragedy in which Sophocles represented Athamas crowned in front of Zeus's altar, when he was to be sacrificed because he was accused of having caused his son Phrixus's death (cf. no. 113, *Phrixus*); but when Heracles arrived and declared that Phrixus was alive, he was saved.

Such a scene is located in a larger context of the tragedy whose content the scholium reports with rather exceptional precision. Athamas, the son of Aeolus, was first married to a goddess, Nephele (the Cloud), and had two children with her, Phrixus and Helle; then, being jealous, Nephele returned to the sky. Athamas remarried a mortal, Ino, one of the daughters of Cadmus, king of Thebes, with whom he had two sons, Learchus and Melicertes. To avenge herself, Nephele started a drought. To put an end to this scourge, Athamas sent envoys to consult the oracle of Apollo at Delphi. But his new wife, Ino, wanting to rid herself of the children from Athamas's first marriage, bribed the envoys and had them say that the oracle demanded that they be sacrificed. Athamas tried to make the children return from the countryside to be sacrificed. But a goat who could speak warned them. They fled with the goat, and we know what happened then: while crossing the Hellespont on the goat's back, Helle fell in and drowned (whence the name "Hellespont"), while Phrixus reached Colchides, where he was saved. There he sacrificed the goat—who had, thanks to the gods, a golden fleece—to Ares or to Hermes; and he settled in this country, giving his name to the land henceforth known as Phrygia. Nephele wanted to take revenge on Athamas. That is how Athamas was condemned to be sacrificed before he was saved at the last moment, as we have seen, by Heracles. According to the scholium, that is the content of Sophocles' *Athamas*. And the rest of the scholium indicates that this was the second *Athamas*. Thus Sophocles' two *Athamas* are both earlier than Aristophanes' *The Clouds*, a comedy performed in 423. Sophocles chose among the variants of the myth. For the variants, see no. 113, *Phrixus*.

As for the first *Athamas*, it must have dealt with a sequence of the myth that was chronologically later. Athamas is also known for having raised the young Dionysus with his wife, Ino, Semele's sister, after the latter had died as a result of gazing on Zeus in his full radiance. He once again became the victim of a goddess, but this time of Hera, who drove him mad along with his wife. He killed his eldest son born of his second marriage with Ino, Learchus, during a hunting party, when he thought he was striking a stag. As for his wife, Ino, she boiled her second son, Melicertes, in a cauldron and plunged into the sea with her dead child. Changing in status and name—she taking the name of Leucothea, he that of Palaemon—they became two divinities who help sailors during storms (cf. Apollodorus 3, 26–29). A fragment of a Homeric bowl in the collection of the German archeologist L. Curtius (dating from 170–30 BCE) represents a bearded man sitting; an inscription identifies him as Athamas. He is holding out his arms toward a figure that can be identified as the (infant) Dionysus. According to remains of the title of the scene we understand that Athamas is receiving the young Dionysus from Hermes, so that he can raise him, and that he will be the victim of Hera's anger. In addition, the presence of the name Sopho[cles] to the right of the head indicates that the scene is taken from one of Sophocles' tragedies. See H. Fuhrmann, JDAI, 65/66, 1950–51, pp. 103–34 (already p. 130, n. 9); the fragment of the Homeric bowl is reproduced in *LIMC* II, 2 (1984), p. 700, with a commentary in *LIMC* II, 1 (1984), s.v. Athamas (Christine Schwanzar), pp. 950–53 (p. 951 A 2). The inscriptions given by Fuhrmann (p. 105) are reproduced in *TrGF* 4 Radt, p. 100. One of the two *Athamas* was thus centered on Nephele's anger, the other on Hera's anger. Aeschylus had composed an *Athamas* (*TrGF* 3, frag. 1–4a Radt) that was supposed to deal with a sequence in the destiny of Athamas that resulted from Hera's anger. In fact, one of the fragments probably alludes to Melicertes, whom Ino had boiled in a cauldron (frag. 1).

In any case, there is no reason to doubt that Sophocles composed two plays with the same title. This way of proceeding might seem peculiar to a modern reader. But it is well attested in antiquity. It was assuredly the case for Euripides' two *Phrixus*, which are even two variants on the same mythic sequence. See here under no. 113, *Phrixus*. For Sophocles, see also two *Lemnian women* (nos. 63–640), two *Tyros* (nos. 102–3), two *Phineus* (nos. 110–11), and even three *Thyestes* (nos. 41–43).

3. **Aias locros, Ajax the Locrian** (frag. 10a–18 Radt). Sophocles wrote two tragedies on Ajax. But they are not the same Ajax. The extant tragedy is that of Ajax son of Telamon, leader of the Salaminians during the expedition to Troy (see appendix 1). The lost tragedy is that of Ajax son of Oileus, leader of the Locrians during the same expedition to Troy; see above, chapter VI, "The Mythic Imagination." Oileus is known especially for having committed an impious act during the conquest of Troy. This scene was recounted in the epic poem *The Sack of Ilium*, which belongs to the Trojan cycle; see Proclus's summary quoted above; cf. also Apollodorus, *Epitome* 5, 22 and 25, quoted above. It was probably this sequence that was dramatized. There is subject matter for a tragedy with an agōn scene for the trial; cf. the figured representation of the scene of the trial by Polygnotus at the Poecile in Athens (Pausanias 1, 15, 2, cited above). Athena was supposed to appear and be very angry against the man who had abducted Cassandra and torn down her statue (cf. *P. Oxy.* 3152, frag. 2, plausibly attributed by the editor Haslam in 1976 to the play by Sophocles, though there is no reference to it in the papyrus = frag 10 c Radt); see above. If Ajax escapes stoning, he will not escape the gods' punishment. He will die at sea in a storm during his return, cast into the waves by Poseidon when he utters an impious word: see *Odyssey* 4, vv. 499–509; cf. *Nostoi* (*Returns*), where Proclus's summary mentions the storm near the Gyraean Rocks and the death of Ajax the Locrian (ed. Bernabé 94, 12ff.).

For an attempted reconstruction of the tragedy, see D. Fitzpatrick, "Sophocles' Aias Lokros," in A. H. Sommerstein (ed.), *Shards from Kolonos* (2003), pp. 243–59.

For the iconography of the famous scene of Cassandra's abduction, see *LIMC* I, 1 (1981), s.v. Aias II (O. Touchefeu), pp. 336–51, and I, 2 (1981), pp. 253ff. It was painted by Polygnotus in the Lesche of Delphi; see Pausanias 10, 26, 3. For the iconography in general, see Webster, pp. 146–47.

4. ***Aigeus, Aegeus*** (frag. 19–25a Radt). Aegeus was the king of Athens and the father of Theseus (see no. 40, *Theseus*). The son of Pandion, Aegeus's brothers were Lycus, Nisus, and Pallas. They divided Attica in four parts, one for each of them. Regarding this division the geographer Strabo cites precisely the seven verses of Sophocles' *Aegeus* in which it is mentioned (Strabo 9, 1, 6 = frag. 24 Radt). It is Aegeus who speaks in this fragment. Euripides also wrote an *Aegeus*; see H. Van Looy, *Euripide*, vol. 8, *Fragments* l, CUF, 1998, pp. 1–37 and *TrGF* 5.1, pp. 151–57 Kannicht. Aegeus, not being able to have a child, went to consult the Delphic oracle, who advised him not to loosen the mouth of the wineskin before reaching Athens. But when he went to Troezen (in the Peloponnese) to ask the wise King Pittheus's advice as to how to understand the oracle, he slept with the king's daughter Aethra before returning to Athens and asked her, if a son were to be born from their union, not to reveal to him who his father was and to send him in secret to Athens when he was capable of lifting a rock under which Aegeus had hidden his sword and his sandal (see Plutarch, "Life of Theseus," c. 3ff. We think that the two tragedies had a comparable subject, the recognition between Aegeus and his son Theseus who has come from Troezen to Athens overland after having vanquished several monsters or brigands. The sequence is presented this way by Apollodorus, *Epitome* 1, 4–6): "So, having cleared the road, Theseus came to Athens. But Medea, being then wedded to Aegeus, plotted against him and persuaded Aegeus to beware of him as a traitor. And Aegeus, not knowing his own son, was afraid and sent him against the Marathonian bull. And when Theseus had killed it, Aegeus presented to him a poison which he had received the selfsame day from Medea. But just as the draught was about to be administered to him, he gave his father the sword, and on recognizing it Aegeus dashed the cup from his hands. And when Theseus was thus made known to his father and informed of the plot, he expelled Medea." Several fragments of Sophocles' tragedy seem to concern Theseus's journey from Troezen (cf. frag. 19) to Athens, in the course of which he killed monsters (frag. 20–22). Frag. 25 of Sophocles' tragedy is drawn from the context of the preparations for Theseus's struggle to tame the Marathonian bull. Frag. 24 (mentioned above), in which Aegeus speaks about his father's division of the lands among his sons, can be inserted into the recognition scene where the father addresses his son.

See C. Hahnemann, "Zur Rekonstruktion und Interpretation von Sophokles' *Aigeus*," *Hermes* 127, 1999, pp. 385–96; Hahnemann, "Sophokles' *Aigeus*: Plaidoyer for a Methodology of Caution," in A. H. Sommerstein (ed.), *Shards from Kolonos* (2003), pp. 201–18.

5. *Aithopes, The Ethiopians* (frag. 28–33 Radt). Subject unknown. The fragments provide no clues. It is thought, given the title designating the chorus, that it is a tragedy featuring the Ethiopian prince Memnon, the son of Aurora, who took part in the Trojan War on the Trojan side after Hector's death. The chorus was probably formed of the soldiers who accompanied him, like, for example, the chorus of Salaminians in *Ajax*. Memnon's exploit and his death were recounted in the epic that followed the *Iliad*, namely *The Ethiopians*. He killed Antilochus, Nestor's son, and was in turn slain by Achilles. For more details, see *Memnon* (no. 67). Aeschylus had devoted two tragedies to this son of Aurora, one entitled *Memnon* (*TrGF* 3, frag. 127–30 Radt), the other focused on his death and entitled *The Weighing of Souls* (*Psychostasie*) (*TrGF* 3, frag. 279–80a Radt). This play was famous for its scene in which Zeus used a scale to weigh the souls of Memnon and Achilles in the presence of their two mothers, Thetis and Aurora.

6. *Aichmalotides, The Captive Women* (frag. 33a–58 Radt). A tragedy in the Trojan cycle; see the beginning of the argument of *Ajax*: "The drama [sc. *Ajax*] is part of the Trojan myth, like the *Antenorides* [= no. 16], *The Captive Women*, *The Rape of Helen* [= no. 25] and *Memnon* [= no. 67]." Subject unknown. However, the chorus, as the title indicates, consisted of Trojan female captives. The situation is comparable to that of Euripides' *The Trojan Women*. Nothing more can be said about it.

7. *Akrisios* (frag. 60–76 Radt). Acrisius, king of Argos, has learned by an oracle that he will be killed by his grandson. To prevent the oracle from being fulfilled, he has imprisoned his daughter Danaë (cf. no. 21, *Danaë*) with her nurse in a bronze underground chamber in the courtyard of his house. There she was inseminated by Zeus in the form of a shower of gold (cf. Sophocles, *Antigone*, vv. 944–51). After the birth of the child, Perseus, Acrisius put the mother and her son in a chest and threw it into the sea. The chest floated as far as the island of Seriphos, where it was caught in Dictys's nets; both of them were taken in by Dictys, whose mother was also the mother of Polydectes, the king of the island. After achieving celebrated feats—decapitating Medusa and petrifying Polydectes, freeing Andromeda (cf. no. 15, *Andromeda*)—Perseus returned to Argos with Danaë and Andromeda. Acrisius, wanting to escape the oracle, left for Larissa in Thessaly. However, during the funeral games in Larissa, Perseus, who has come to compete in the games, mortally wounds his grandfather by hitting him with the discus he had thrown during the competition. The oracle is fulfilled, as in the case of Oedipus, despite the useless precautions taken by the human being (see no. 62, *The Men of Larissa*). The complete story is reported in detail by Pherecydes of Athens (scholium by Appollonius of Rhodes IV 1091 = *FGrHist* 3 F 10, F 4, F 12 Jacoby); cf. also Apollodorus 2, 4, 1–4 (34–48). The whole problem is to determine what the subject of *Acrisios* is

if, on the one hand, *Danaë*'s subject is Acrisius's discovery of the child Perseus's existence and the expulsion of the mother and her son thrown into the sea in a chest, and if, on the other hand, *The Men of Larissa* deals with the final realization of the oracle through Acrisius's death at his grandson's hands. The few significant fragments of *Acrisios* that are extant fit rather well into the same sequence as *Danaë*. For example, frag. 64 and 67 might correspond to a scene in which Canisius addresses his daughter, whom he asks to speak briefly in her own defense (frag. 64), and in which he reminds her that life is the most precious good (frag. 67)—her life being threatened by the existence of the child who is, according to the oracle, supposed to kill him. Cf. also frag. 66, where it is said that the old man clings to life more than others do; frag. 61, where a cry is heard by the frightened chorus, may correspond to the moment when the presence of the child in the underground prison is about to be discovered. From this we can conclude either that the two plays, *Acrisios* and *Danaë*, are actually one and the same (but the double title designated by two characters in the play is not customary), or that they are variations on the same subject in the same register, tragedy (cf. the example of Euripides' two *Athamas* mentioned apropos of no. 1–2 *Athamas*), or in different registers (tragedy and satyr play). Another tragedy by Sophocles concerning the same family: *Amphitryon* (no. 13); Amphitryon may be one of Perseus's grandsons. For the iconography, see Webster, p. 147.

8. ***Aleadai, The Sons of Aleus*** (frag. 77–91 Radt). Aleus, king of Tegea, received an oracle comparable to Acrisius's. Having consulted the Delphic oracle, he received the reply that if his daughter had a son, he would kill Aleus's own sons. That is Alcidamas's version in *Odysseus*, c. 14: Aleus, to prevent the oracle's fulfillment, made his daughter Auge a priestess of Athena and threatened her with death if she had a child. But she was inseminated by Heracles, who passed by the temple while he was on an expedition against King Augeas of Elis. When Aleus realized that his daughter was pregnant, he rid himself of her by entrusting her to Nauplius, the father of Palamedes (see no. 72, *Nauplius Sails In*, no. 73, *Nauplius Lights a Fire*, no. 78, *The Madness of Odysseus*, and no. 80, *Palamedes*), who was to drown her in the sea. But in the course of the voyage between Tegea and Nauplia, she gave birth to her son Telephus on a mountain (the Parthenon; cf. Euripides, *Telephus*, frag. 696 Kannicht, vv. 5ff.); struck by pity, Nauplius did not follow Aleus's instructions but instead took Auge and the child to Mysia, where he sold them to Teuthras, the king of Mysia; being without a child, Teuthras married Auge and adopted the child, to whom he gave the name Telephus, but he asked Priam to raise him. However, in other versions (cf. Apollodorus 2, 7, 4 [146] and 3, 9, 1 [103–4]; cf. also Hyginus, *Fables*, 99 and 100), the son was separated from his mother and abandoned in his birthplace, where he was fed by a doe (*elaphos*) who suckled him at her breast (*thele*)—whence his name, Telephus—and was taken in by shepherds. It is this version that Sophocles adopted in his tragedy (cf. frag. 89, where the doe is mentioned). After many trials

(cf. Euripides, *Telephus*, frag. 696 Kannicht, vv. 8–11), Telephus went to consult the oracle at Delphi, who sent him to Mysia, where he rejoined his mother and became king of Mysia upon Teuthras's death. Telephus's misfortunes certainly included the murder of his uncles; cf. *Append. prov.* 2, 85: "Telephus, being still young, went into exile from Tegea after killing his mother's brothers," and Hyginus, *Fables*, 244, 2, apropos of those who killed relatives: "Telephus, the son of Heracles, killed Hippothous and Nerea (or Perea), his grandmother's sons." Telephus had grown up in the mountains, and it was precisely his fulfillment of the oracle by killing his uncles in order to make himself recognized in Tegea that must have been the subject of Sophocles' *Sons of Aleus* (see also no. 70, *The Mysians*). Some fragments (frag. 84–87) can be interpreted as coming from a discussion in which Telephus was accused of being a bastard. The tragedy includes a rather long fragment on the power of wealth (frag. 88). Four of Sophocles' tragedies concern the history of this family: in addition to *The Sons of Aleus*, *The Mysians* (no. 70), *Telephus* (no. 96), and *Eurypylus* (no. 34), about Telephus's son; see also *The Gathering of the Achaeans* (no. 18). Sophocles may have written a trilogy (or a tetralogy) on Telephus, a *Telepheia* (cf. *TrGF* 1 Snell DID B 5, 8 inscription from the fourth century BCE, and *TrGF* 4 Radt, p. 434). Thus it has been suggested that there was a connection among these plays. But the interpretation of the inscription is subject to debate; see above (where the inscription is quoted).

9. ***Alexandros, Alexander*** (frag. 91a–100a Radt). The subject is probably analogous to that of Euripides' *Alexander*, performed in 415; see F. Jouan, *Euripide*, vol. 8, 1, CUF, 1998, 39ff., and *TrGF* 5.1, pp. 174–204 Kannicht. Two main mythographic texts set forth the legend with variants (Apollodorus 3, 12, 5 [148–50]; Hyginus, *Fables*, 91: Alexander-Paris) along with the argument of Euripides' tragedy, which has been known since 1974. Paris-Alexander, the son of Priam, king of Troy, and Hecuba, had been exposed in the mountains shortly after his birth because when he was born his mother had a prophetic dream announcing that he would be the ruin of his city. He was taken in by a shepherd and lived as a shepherd; then, during a contest organized at Troy twenty years later, precisely in honor of the child who had disappeared, he won numerous victories and was superior to all of Priam's other sons, who resented him, especially Delphos's. They asked their mother, Hecuba, to put a certain slave to death. Cassandra, in her delirium, recognized him and prophesied the future. Just as she was about to have her son killed, Hecuba recognized him, because the man who had raised him revealed the truth.

Fragments of Euripides' plays are much more numerous than those of Sophocles'. But one fragment of Sophocles' *Alexander* (frag. 90: "A shepherd defeating men from the city! How can that be?") alludes to the indignation provoked by Paris-Alexander's victories in the contest, which leads us to think that Sophocles dramatized the same mythic sequence. Some scholars believe that Sophocles' *Alexander* is later than Euripides', but there is no proof of this. Given the very small number of fragments, it is impossible to know how Sophocles dealt in detail with the mythic sequence.

10. **Alkmeon, Alcmeon** (frag. 108–10 Radt). Alcmeon is one of the tragic heroes par excellence (Aristotle, *Poetics* c. 13, 1453 a 20). In Sophocles' time, his myth was as famous as that of Orestes; see above, chapter VI, "The Mythic Imagination." On the three extant fragments of Sophocles' *Alcmeon*, only one is significant (frag. 108). It concerns a sequence from the myth in which Alcmeon is still in the grip of madness after the murder of his mother, Eriphyle, whom he has killed to avenge his father, Amphiaraus, and in which a character wishes that he be cured. But Alcmeon's wanderings in the grip of madness are long (above, chapter VI, "The Mythic Imagination"). From this period when Alcmeon is pursued by his mother's Erinyes and is seeking to purify his pollution, Euripides drew two tragedies. One is *Alcmeon in Corinth* (performed after Euripides' death along with *Iphigeneia in Aulis* and *The Bacchantes*): Alcmeon had twins, a son and a daughter, with Manto, the daughter of the Theban seer Tiresias, whom he had received as booty after his victory over the Epigoni; he went to Corinth, where he entrusted the children to King Creon, who was to raise them; on the adventures of these two children forming the subject of the tragedy, see Apollodorus 3 7, 7 (94–95), cited above; for Euripides' tragedy, see H. Van Looy, *Euripide*, vol. 8, 1, Paris: CUF, 1998, pp. 81ff., and *TrGF* 5.1, pp. 205–18 Kannicht). The other tragedy is *Alcmeon in Psophis*, performed along with *Alcestis* in 438: Alcmeon, exiled from Argos, goes to Psophis in Arcadia, where the king named Phegeus purified him and gave him in marriage his daughter, who received Eriphyle's necklace, that is, the necklace of Harmony; see Pausanias 8, 24, 8, and Apollodorus 3, 7, 5 (87); for Euripides' tragedy, see H. Van Looy, *Euripide*, vol. 8, and *TrGF* 5.1, pp. 205–18 Kannicht. Concerning Sophocles' *Alcmeon*, it is conjectured (Welcker pp. 278ff., Pierson pp. 68ff.) that the sequence is the same as the one in Euripides' *Alcmeon in Psophis*. The mention of Alphesibea (the name of Phegeus's daughter, according to Pausanias and the Latin poet Accius, whereas in Apollodorus she is called Arsinoe) in a fragment from one of Sophocles' tragedies whose title is not known (frag. 880 Radt) is adduced in support of this conjecture. Nonetheless, this remains merely a conjecture. Another sequence, just as plausible even though it has not been considered by the scholarly tradition, is the third and last stage in Alcmeon's exile (see Thucydides, 2, 102, 5–6, cited above; Pausanias 8, 24, 7–10; Apollodorus 3, 7 5 [88–93]). Still pursued by his mother's Erinyes, despite Phegeus's purgation, Alcmeon left for a new country, the delta of Achelous, the river god who purified him and gave him his daughter Callirrhoe as his wife, with whom he had two sons (Acarnan and Amphoterus). But like Alphisibea, Alcmeon's first wife, Callirrhoe, wanted to have Eriphyle's necklace, and this led to his death. He went to Psophis to take back Harmony's necklace but was treacherously assassinated by Peguses's two sons and thus buried in Psophis (Pausanias 8, 24, 8). For Sophocles' other plays about this family, see *Amphiaraos* (no. 12), *The Epigoni* (no. 27), and *Eriphyle* (no. 30). The

Latin poet Accius composed an *Alcmeon* whose subject was also a sequence from the period of exile, and probably the last period, when Alcmeon returned to Psophis to get back Harmony's collar on a poor pretext and was put to death by Phegeus's sons or by Phegeus himself; see J. Dangel, *Accius, Fragments*, Paris: CUF, 2002, pp. 228–30, and commentary, pp. 365–68.

11. *Amukos saturikos, Amycus* (satyr play) (frag. 111–12 Radt). Athenaeus, *Deipnosophistes* 9, 400 b (cf. frag. 111 Radt) tells us that this is a satyr play. The myth is drawn from the expedition of the Argonauts. The Argonauts, who had left from Mysia, went to the land of the Bebryces, in Bithynia, which was ruled by Amycus, the powerful son of Poseidon who boxed with foreigners coming there and thus got rid of them. He challenged the Argonauts when they landed there, boxed against one of the two Dioscuri, Pollux, the strongest of the Argonauts, and was defeated—killed by him, according to some sources (cf. Apollonius of Rhodes, *Argonautica* 2, vv. 1–97; Apollodorus 1, 9, 20 [119]; Hyginus, *Fables*, 17), spared according to others (Theocritus, 22, *The Dioscuri*, vv. 44–136). A version (known from the scholium on Apollonius of Rhodes 2, 98, where the names of Epicharmus and Pisander are mentioned) says that Pollux, after defeating Amycus, put him in chains. This scene in which Amycus is chained up by Pollux is well represented in the iconography; see *LIMC*, s.v. "Amycos" (G. Beckel) I, 1, 1981, pp. 738–42 (pp. 739–40), and I, 2, 1981, pp. 594–97. Two fragments of one verse tell us nothing about the version Sophocles adopted. See *Das griechische Satyrspiel*, pp. 243–49. For the iconography, see Webster, p. 147.

12. *Amphiareos saturikos, Amphiaraus* (satyr play) (frag. 113–21 Radt). It is again Athenaeus, *Deipnosophistes* 10, 454 a (cf. frag. 121 Radt) that indicates that this is a satyr play. Amphiaraus is the famous seer from Argos, the father of Alcmeon (cf. no. 10), who took part, against his will, in the expedition of the Seven against Thebes, was swallowed up by the earth, along with his chariot, and became a healing hero in Oropos; see above, chapter VII, "The Mythic Imagination," with the reference to P. Sineux's study *Amphiaraos, Guerrier, devin et guérisseur*, Paris, 2007. The play's subject cannot be determined on the basis of the extant fragments. See *Das griechische Satyrspiel*, pp. 236–42.

13. *Amphitruon, Amphitryon* (frag. 122–24 Radt). Nothing is known about the subject, even though the myth has been known since Homer (*Odyssey* 11, vv. 266–68): "And after her I saw Alcmene, wife of Amphitryon, who lay in the arms of great Zeus, and bore Heracles, staunch in fight, the lion-hearted," and in a more detailed way, since Hesiod (*Shield of Heracles*, vv. 1–556); cf. Apollodorus 2, 4, 6–8 (54–62); Hyginus, *Fables*, 29. Exiled to Thebes after having voluntarily or involuntarily killed his father-in-law, Electryon, Amphitryon, the son of Alcaeus, Perseus's grandson (cf. no. 7, *Acrisios*), married Alcmene. The same night when he returned after having avenged the death of his brothers-in-law killed by the Taphians, his wife conceived twins by two different fathers: one was Heracles, the son of Zeus, and the other was Iphicles, the son of Amphitryon. Euripides composed an *Alcmene* in which the sequence revolves around this

twofold conception (see H. Van Looy, *Euripide*, vol. 8, 1, CUF, 1998, p. 117ff., and *TrGF* 5.1, pp. 219–27 Kannicht). Did Sophocles deal with the same sequence in which Amphitryon, despite his victorious return, was received by his wife without enthusiasm and discovered, perhaps through Tiresias's revelations, Zeus's intervention? Amphitryon is also a character in Euripides' *Heracles*, a dramatic sequence that is supposed to take place much later, when he is a weak old man unable to defend Heracles' children, whom the tyrant Lycus, in the absence of their father who had descended into the Underworld, was threatening to kill. In Euripides' play, Amphitryon gives, in particular, the initial speech setting forth the situation (vv. 1ff.). The Latin poet Accius also composed an *Amphitryon* whose content is comparable to that of Euripides' *Heracles* (see J. Dangel, *Accius, Fragments*, Paris: CUF, 2002, pp. 233–36, and commentary, pp. 370–72).

14. ***Andromache*** (frag. 125 Radt). A single fragment giving just one word is attributed to this play. Andromache is Hector's wife, who has become, since the death of her husband and the fall of Troy, the concubine of Neoptolemus, Achilles' son. Euripides wrote a tragedy entitled *Andromache*, which is extant.

15. ***Andromeda*** (frag. 126–36 Radt). The subject of this play is known through Pseudo-Eratosthenes, *Catasterismi*, 16, apropos of Cassiopeia (the wife of Cepheus, king of Ethiopia): "Sophocles, the tragic poet, tells us in his *Andromeda* that having competed with the nymphs in beauty she [sc. Cassiopeia] fell into misfortune and that Poseidon sent a sea monster (*Cetus*) to ravage the region. Through her fault, her daughter [sc. Andromeda] was exposed to the monster." What happened next is recounted in the same work apropos of the sea monster Cetus: "This is the monster that Poseidon sent to Cepheus because Cassiopeia had competed in beauty with the nymphs. Perseus killed the monster; and that is why he was transformed into a star, in memory of this exploit. That is what is what is recounted by Sophocles, the tragic poet, in his *Andromeda*." Euripides also composed an *Andromeda*, which Aristophanes parodied in his *Thesmophoriazusae*, vv. 1015ff. (see H. Van Looy, *Euripide*, vol. 8, 1, CUF, 1998, pp. 147ff., and *TrGF* 5.1, pp. 233–60 Kannicht). On Andromeda in Sophocles, Euripides, and the Latin tradition, see R. Klimek-Winter, *Andromedatragödien: Sophokles, Euripides, Livius Andronikos, Ennius, Accius; Text, Einleitung und Kommentar*, Stuttgart, 1993. For Sophocles' Andromeda and the iconography, see Séchan, pp. 148–55; Webster, p. 147; Trendall and Webster, pp. 163–65.

16. ***Antenoridai, The Sons of Antenor*** (frag. 137–39 Radt). The play is mentioned in the argument of *Ajax* as belonging to the Trojan myth (see already no. 6, *The Captive Women*). The sons of Antenor are the descendants of the Trojan Antenor and his wife, Theano, the priestess of Athena (*Iliad* 6, v. 298). According to Homer, there were eleven sons: five were killed in combat (Coön, Demoleon, Laodamas, and Pedaeus), two brave sons, Archelochus and Acamas, fought alongside Aeneas (*Iliad* 2, vv. 822ff.), and there were four others, Agenor, Helicaon, Laodocus, and Polybus. According to Bacchylides there were fifty of them (scholium T on *Iliad* 24, 496; the indication is supposed to have been given in

the dithyramb 15). In the *Iliad*, Antenor is an elderly Trojan who serves as a counselor to Priam. He had received Odysseus and Menelaus in his palace when they came on an embassy to Troy at the beginning of the hostilities to ask for Helen's return (*Iliad* 3, vv. 205ff.). He was in favor of returning Helen (*Iliad* 7, vv. 345ff.), and he had protected the ambassadors, whereas some Trojans, including Antimachus, wanted to kill them by trickery (*Iliad* 11, vv. 138–40; cf. no. 24, *The Demand for Helen's Return*). Because he had received and protected Odysseus and Menelaus during their embassy, Antenor was spared, along with his family, when Troy was taken. That is what is said in a scholium on *Iliad* 3, v. 205: "When Menelaus and his entourage came as ambassadors from Tenedos, then Antenor, son of Iketaon, received them and saved them when they were going to be killed by trickery. That is why, after the capture of Troy, a panther skin was placed before Antenor's door as a sign that the house should be spared during the pillage, and that Antenor and his sons, along with the surviving Eneti (allies of Paphlagonia; cf. *Iliad* 2, v. 852) found their salvation in Thrace, and from there they reached the region on the shores of the Adriatic known as Venetia." In this summary we see the subject or a part of the subject of the *Sons of Antenor*. The panther's skin was also mentioned in *Ajax the Locrian* (no. 3, frag. 11). This detail was famous. It was painted by Polygnotus in the Lesche of the Cnidians in Delphi when Antenor's family departed (Pausanias 10, 27, 3–4). In the *Little Iliad*, Lesche mentioned how, during the night battle, Odysseus recognized Helicaon, Antenor's son, and saved him when he was wounded (Pausanias 10, 26, 7 = frag. 12 Bernabé). For Antenor's departure with the Eneti, compare Livy, 1, 1. Sophocles is the only known Greek tragic author who did not deal with such a subject. The Latin poet Accius composed a tragedy with the same title; see J. Dangel, *Accius, Fragments*, Paris: CUF, 2002, pp. 156–57, and commentary, pp. 314–16.

17. *Atreus è Mukenaiai*, **Atreus or the Women of Mycenae** (frag. 140–41 Radt). Atreus, son of Pelops, Thyestes' hostile brother (cf. no. 41–43, *Thyestes*), is the father of Agamemnon and Menelaus, the Atreids. He was king of Mycenae. The chorus must have been composed of women from Mycenae (*Mukenaiai*). On this great tragic family, see above, chapter VI, "The Mythic Imagination." The two extant fragments cannot be used to restitute the subject. In an epigram in honor of Sophocles (*Anth. Palat.* 9, 98), Statilius Flaccus (first century BCE) mentions famous plays in his repertory: after the two *Oedipus*es and *Electra*, he quotes, in a periphrasis, "Sun turned away by Atreus's banquet." There is no doubt that the author of the epigram is referring to Sophocles' *Atreus*, whose central element was the famous banquet at which Atreus, to take revenge on his brother who had stolen his power and his wife, had served him his own children to eat, a banquet so horrible that the Sun had reversed its course. A scholium on Euripides, *Orestes*, v. 812, describing the rivalry between the two brothers ends with a reference to the retrograde movement of the Sun and the Pleiades because of this criminal banquet ("the sun, not being able to endure this crime, led his

chariot for one day from west to east; and with him the Pleiades moved in the opposite direction"). This same scholium says that Atreus, according to Sophocles, avenged himself on his wife, Aerope, by throwing her into the sea. But that notion can be found in one of the three *Thyestes* as well as in his *Atreus*. The Latin poet Accius composed a tragedy with the same title; see J. Dangel, *Accius, Fragments*, Paris: CUF, 2002, pp. 115–22, and commentary, pp. 275–83.

18. ***Achaion sullogos, The Gathering of the Achaeans*** (frag. 143–48 Radt). This play belongs to the Trojan cycle. The subject was apparently the gathering of the Greeks before the departure for Troy. In fact, one character addressed another to make a roll call of the participants to see if any were absent among Helen's suitors, who had sworn to come to the aid of the man she chose, if he asked for their help (frag. 144). An allusion to this oath is found in *Philoctetes*, v. 72. It is generally thought that this tragedy is the same as *The Those Who Dine Together* (no. 93). In fact, the two plays are situated neither at the same time nor in the same place. When one character calls the roll of the participants in the expedition (frag. 144), that cannot occur long before the expedition's departure, whereas the banquet explaining the title *Those Who Dine Together* (see no. 93) took place when the expedition arrived on the island of Tenedos, that is, when the crossing of the Aegean Sea was almost over. The tempting comparison made by Wilamowitz in 1907, between a papyrus in Berlin in which Achilles asks Odysseus about the "gathering of friends" and this play by Sophocles (the *Pap. Berol.* 9908 in "Sophokles Achäerversammlung," BKT V 2, 1907, pp. 64–72) had pointed toward a subject that dealt with Telephus (cf. no. 96, *Telephus*), as in Euripides' *Telephus*. But since we now know of a new papyrus fragment that partially fits with the Berlin papyrus (*P. Oxy.* 2460, ed. pr. J. Read in Handley and Rea, BICS, supp. 5, 1957, 1–16), the Berlin papyrus has been taken away from Sophocles and attributed to Euripides' *Telephus*. However, that does not mean that *The Gathering of the Achaeans* did not conclude the episode in which Telephus, after consulting an oracle, comes to be treated by Achilles' sword that had wounded him, and, in exchange, to serve as a guide for the expedition, as had been recounted in the epic *Cypria*; cf. Proclus's summary (ed. Bernabé 41, 41–42): "Achilles . . . heals Telephus, who had been led by an oracle to go to Argos, so that he might be their guide on the voyage to Ilium"; cf. Apollodorus *Epitome*, 3, 19; cf. scholium on *Iliad* 1, v. 59 (cited by A. Severyns, *Le Cycle épique dans l'école d'Aristarque*, p. 293). This gathering of the army might theoretically also be devoted to the other important matter to be settled before the departure, the sacrifice of Iphigeneia by her father, Agamemnon, in order to pacify Artemis, who is withholding favorable winds, and to allow the fleet to depart. However, this theme was dealt with by Sophocles in his *Iphigeneia* (no. 48). For the iconography, see Webster, p. 146.

19. ***Achilleos erastai, The Lovers of Achilles*** (frag. 149–57 Radt). This is a satyr play. The satyrs, forming the chorus, were the lovers of the young Achilles (frag. 153). Two characters in the play can be identified on the basis of frag. 153,

Phoenix, Achilles' tutor (cf. no. 23, *Dolopes*; no. 92, *Scyrians*; no. 112, *Phoenix*) and on the basis of frag. 150, Achilles' father, Peleus (cf. no. 82, *Peleus*). In this play Sophocles says that Thetis, Achilles' mother, had left Peleus because he had insulted her (scholium Apollonius of Rhodes 4, 816 = frag. 151 Radt). In this play, a change in place must have taken place, as in Ajax and as in Aeschylus's *Eumenides* and his *Women of Etna* (see the argument of this play in *P. Oxy.* 2257, frag. 1, 5ff., ed. Lobel = *TrGF* 4, pp. 165ff., and *TrGF* 3, pp. 126ff. Radt); see above. One of these places might be Peleus's palace and the other Mount Pelion (cf. frag. 154), where the grotto of the centaur Chiron was located; Chiron was Achilles' other teacher (cf. *Iliad* 11, v. 832). The rest is conjectural. See *Das griechische Satyrspiel*, pp. 227–35. For the iconography, see Webster, p. 146.

20. **Daidalos, Daedalus** (frag. 158–64a Radt). A famous Athenian engineer and craftsman, the first inventor of statuary. Exiled to Crete after committing a murder (Apollodorus 3, 15, 9 [214–15]; he used his resourcefulness to help Pasiphaë, Minos's wife; see no. 68, *Minos*), to have intercourse with a bull sent by Poseidon, and he constructed the labyrinth in which Minos was obliged, in conformity with oracles, to imprison the monster born of this union, the Minotaur (Apollodorus 3, 1, 4 [9–11]). Daedalus helped Theseus, who was loved by Ariadne, to escape from the labyrinth (the famous Ariadne's thread!) after he had killed the Minotaur. Learning of this escape, Minos angrily confined Daedalus along with his son Icarus. Daedalus then escaped with his son by constructing wings using feathers and wax: but when he flew off he lost his son, who fell because he had come too close to the sun (Apollodorus, *Epitome*, 1, 7–13). To escape from Minos's pursuit, Daedalus took refuge in Sicily, with the king of Camicus (see no. 52, *The Men of Camicus*), where Minos, who had found him, was scalded to death in a bath. The subject of the play entitled *Daedalus* is not known. However, it must have been related to Crete, because Sophocles (scholium on Plato *Republic* 337 a = frag. 160, and scholium on Apollonius of Rhodes 4, 1646–48 = frag. 161) speaks, in this play, of the bronze giant that Hephaestus has made for Minos so that it might protect Crete by making the rounds of the island three times a day (see Apollodorus 1, 9, 26 [140–41]). It is possible that this is a satyr play. See *Das griechische Satyrspiel*, pp. 389–90. For the iconography, see Webster, p. 148.

21. **Danaë** (frag. 165–70 Radt). For the myth, see also *Acrisios* (no. 7) and *The Larissans* (no. 62). Euripides composed a play with the same title. See H. Van Looy, *Euripide*, vol. 8, 2, CUF, 2000, pp. 47–71, and *TrGF* 5.1, pp. 371–80 Kannicht. According to John Malalas, a Byzantine writer of the sixth century CE (2, 34, 19 Dindorf), it was the fact that Danaë had been thrown into the sea in a chest because she had been seduced by Zeus in the form of a shower of gold. It is very likely that Sophocles' *Danaë* dealt with an analogous mythic sequence. Frag. 165 ("I do not know your trial; I know only one thing, if this child lives, I die") can be understood very well in a scene in which Danaë, accompanied by her infant Perseus, pleads for her life and that of her son, while her father

Canisius remains intransigent, because Perseus's life is equivalent to his own death, according to the Delphic oracle, which had predicted that he must die because of his daughter's son (for the oracle, see no. 7, *Acrisios*). This scene inevitably led to the one with the chest in which Danaë and Perseus were cast into the sea. Nonetheless, such a scene, which is familiar in the iconography (see J.-J. Maffre *LIMC*, s.v. "Acrisios" I, 1 [1981], pp. 449–52, and I, 2 [1981], p. 344), could not have been performed in the theater; it must therefore have been presented in the form of a narrative.

22. ***Dionusiskos saturikos, The Infant Dionysus*** (satyr play) (frag. 171–73 Radt). The subject is Dionysus's infancy; he was probably raised by Silenus, who was bald (frag. 171 Radt). This play was about Dionysus's discovery of wine, a remedy against the sorrow that the satyrs who formed the chorus tasted for the first time (frag. 172 Radt). See *Das griechische Satyrspiel*, pp. 250–58. For the iconography, see Webster, p. 148.

23. ***Dolopes, The Dolopians*** (frag. 174–75 Radt). The Dolopians were a Thessalian people whose leader was Phoenix in *Iliad* 9, v. 484; cf. also Pindar, frag. 184 Snell-Maehler (= Strabo 9, 5, 5). Phoenix's destiny is familiar to us, especially from the time when he becomes Achilles' tutor (no. 19, *The Lovers of Achilles*) and when he takes part in the Trojan War (cf. no. 92, *The Scyrians*). But as early as the *Iliad*, the turbulent youth of this hero, who was the victim of his father Amyntor's wrath and who left him to go into exile, is recounted in detail (*Iliad* 9, vv. 448–80): Phoenix, son of Amyntor, king of Eleon in Boeotia, had seduced his father's mistress on the urging of his jealous mother. The object of his father's anger, he decided to leave, despite close surveillance by those close to him, taking refuge with Peleus, Achilles' father, at Phthia in Thessaly. Peleus entrusted him with the education of his son and gave him power over the Dolopes within the confines of Phthia. The myth subsequently evolved insofar as Amnytor punished his son by blinding him before he went into exile. The account given by Apollodorus 3, 13, 8 [175] provides a fairly exact idea of this: "Phoenix had been blinded by his father on the strength of a false accusation of seduction preferred against him by his father's concubine Phthia. But Peleus brought him to Chiron, who restored his sight, and thereupon Peleus made him king of the Dolopians." Sophocles' play, whose subject is unknown, might concern Phoenix, since Dolopians constituted the chorus. One of the two fragments that we have (frag. 174) might allude to Phoenix's exile before his arrival at Peleus's home, but the sequence dealt with can be situated only later on, Phoenix now being king of the Dolopians. Compare no. 112 (*Phoenix*).

24. ***Helenes apaitesis, The Demand for Helen's Return*** (frag. 176–80 a Radt). An episode of the Trojan myth developed toward the end of the *Cypria* (ed. Bernabé 42, 55–57): after he first battles at Troy, in which Protesilas was killed by Hector and Cycnus by Achilles, the dead are retrieved, and an embassy is sent to Troy to demand Helen and her treasures, but it is unsuccessful; so the Achains besiege Troy. Cf. no. 16 (*The Sons of Antenor*), in which, as we have seen, Antenor

received two ambassadors, Odysseus and Menelaus, whom he protected when some Trojans wanted to put them to death. In the chronology of the myth, the sequence of *The Demand for Helen's Return* is earlier than that of *The Sons of Antenor*: one corresponds to the beginning of the Trojan War, the other to its end. The subject of *The Demand for Helen's Return* is also the subject of a dithyramb by Bacchylides (15), partly preserved under the title "The Sons of Antenor or the Demand for Helen's Return" (cf. J. Irigoin, J. Duchemin and L. Bardollet, *Bacchylide*, Paris: CUF, 1993, pp. 5–12). The double title of Bacchylides's dithyramb cannot be applied to Sophocles' tragedies, which are distinct. In Bacchylides' work, Theano, Antenor's wife and priestess of Athena, is mentioned in a beginning full of lacunae, and so are the Greek ambassadors, Odysseus and Menelaus. Then, after a large gap, Antenor is about to present the ambassador's proposals to Priam and his sons. Heralds assemble the Trojan army, in front of which Menelaus makes a speech. Sophocles treated the same sequence in his play, but the very rare fragments attributed expressly to this tragedy do not allow us to reconstitute it in detail (frag. 178, in which Helen speaks, is not attributed to the play by name). Helen or one of her servants recognized Menelaus's Laconian way of speaking (frag. 176). Sophocles mentioned the oracle according to which Calchas, the Achaeans' seer, was to die after having met a seer better than he (Mopsos) and placed the quarrel in Pamphylia, which corresponds in the language of tragedy to Cilicia (frag. 180 = Strabo 14, 1, 27 and 5, 16). This detail, which is of interest to a geographer, was obviously secondary in Sophocles' play. For the iconography connected with the play, see Séchan, pp. 181–84 (cf. Webster, p. 148). More recently, J. D. Beazley, "Helenes apaitesis," *Proceedings of the British Academy* 43, 1957, pp. 233–44, has published for the first time the magnificent Corinthian crater with small columns in the Astarita collection, currently in the Vatican (Gregorian Etruscan Museum, Hall XX: inv. 35525). It represents the scene of the ambassadors coming to demand Helen and dates from the middle of the sixth century CE. Cf. also M. I. Davies' reexamination of this vase compared with the literary testimonies, "The Reclamation of Helena," *Antike Kunst*, 20, 1977, pp. 73–85 and pl. 17 (with the bibliography). Here is the scene on the vase: we see Odysseus and Menelaus, along with Talthybios, sitting on steps (of the altar to Athena, as suppliants?). Standing opposite them is Theano, Antenor's wife and priestess of Athena, accompanied by two female servants, and then her nurse, and followed by a cortege of about fifteen knights with two footmen. This scene corresponds to the beginning of Bacchylides' dithyramb, which refers to Theano and the Greek envoys. This correspondence between the poet and the painter may refer to a single model, the *Cypria*. A comparable scene is not impossible in Sophocles' play.

25. **Helenes harpagè, *The Rape of Helen*** (no fragments). A play based on the Trojan myth cited in the argument of *Ajax* (see already no. 6, *The Captive Women*, and no. 16, *The Sons of Antenor*). The subject is unknown, even though one thinks first of Helen's abduction by Paris, which was the subject of an episode

in the epic *Cypria*: Paris has been received by Menelaus; then, after Menelaus's departure for Crete, "Aphrodite brings Helen and Alexandrus (Paris) together, and they, after their union, put very great treasures on board and sail away by night" (Proclus's argument, ed. Bernabé 39, 16–18).

26. ***Helenes gamos, Helen's Wedding*** (frag. 181–84 Radt). Helen's Wedding took place after her abduction. Here is the continuation of the *Cypria's* summary after their departure by night: "Hera stirs up a storm against them and they are carried to Sidon, where Alexandrus (Paris) takes the city. From there he sailed to Troy and celebrated his marriage with Helen" (Proclus's argument, ed. Bernabé 39, 18–20). But the reference might also be to Helen's wedding to Deiphobus after Paris's death; see the episode in the *Little Iliad*: "After this [Paris's death], Deiphobus marries Helen" (Proclus's argument, ed. Bernabé 74, 10). Some scholars have sought to connect this play with an allusion made by Aelius Aristides (in the *Discourse against Plato for the Defense of the Four* summarized by Photius Bibl. 438 a) to the effect of Helen's irresistible beauty on "Sophocles' Satyrs." Under these conditions, the play would be a satyr play. However, the connection remains hypothetical. See *Das griechische Satyrspiel*, pp. 391–93.

17. ***Epigonoi, The Epigones*** (frag. 185–90 Radt). The Epigoni are the sons of the Seven against Thebes who, following their fathers' disastrous expedition, mounted a victorious expedition to avenge them. In particular, Alcmeon, Amphiaraus's son (cf. no. 10, *Alcmeon*, and no. 12, *Amphiaraus*), participated in this expedition, and upon his return he avenged his father by killing his mother, Eriphyle, the sister of Adrastus, the king of Argos (cf. no. 30, *Eriphyle*). See above, chapter VI, "The Mythic Imagination," under "The Two Theban Wars and the Two Trojan Wars." The myth is set forth in a synthetic way in the scholium on Homer II, v. 326, whose source is the historian Asclepiades of Tragilus (*FGrHist* 12 frag. 29 Jacoby): "Amphiaraus, the son of Oecles, having married Eriphyle, the daughter of Talaus, having quarreled with Adrastus about something, then reconciled, agreed, under oath, that in their future disagreements he and Adrastus would rely on Eriphyle to settle the argument and follow her advice. After that, during the expedition against Thebes, Amphiaraus wanted to discourage the Argives [from making the expedition] and predicted his own death. Eriphyle, having received Harmony's necklace from Polynices, took the side of Adrastus and of his entourage, which wanted to force Amphiaraus to do their will. Seeing that Eriphyle had accepted the gift, Amphiaraus made her many reproaches. Of course, he had to take part in the expedition, but he ordered his son not to leave with the epigones against Thebes before having killed his mother. It is said that Alcmeon carried out all these orders, and that he was struck by madness because of the murder of his mother. But the gods delivered him from his illness because he had piously avenged his father by killing his mother. The account is in Asclepiades." See also Apollodorus 3, 6, 2 (60–62). Aeschylus had already composed a tragedy bearing the same name (see *TrGF* 3 frag. 55–56 Radt). The fragments attributed by name to Sophocles' *Epigoni* are rare (frag. 188–90) and are not very

significant. Some add testimonies from the Roman period that speak of the *Epigoni* without giving the author's name (Athenaeus, Cicero), on the ground that Sophocles' theater was at that time more famous than that of Aeschylus. From the whole of the testimonies thus collected, it emerges that the sequence must have been that of the son's vengeance, in which he invokes his father before killing his mother (frag. 186), of the confrontation between the mother and the son before the murder (frag. 185), of the consequences of this murder with an altercation between Adrastus and Alcmeon, Alcmeon accusing Adrastus of being the brother of the woman who killed her husband, and Adrastus accusing Alcmeon of being his mother's murderer (frag. 187), and probably of the announcement of Alcmeon's exile pursued by his mother's Erinyes (frag. 190 with Casaubon's conjecture). This play is mentioned by Philodemus, *De musica* (1, 35, 31 Rispoli, cited by Radt p. 183). Thus there is no reason to conflate it with *Eriphle* (no. 30) as was proposed by Welcker (p. 269) and others after him; recently, for instance, by A. Kiso, "Notes on Sophocles' Epigoni," *GRBS*, 18, 1977, pp. 207–26 (pp. 212–13). The Latin author Accius had also composed two different plays, one entitled *Epigoni* and the other *Eriphyla*; see J. Dangel, *Accius, Fragments*, Paris: CUF, 2002, pp. 18 and 223–27 with the notes p. 358 and pp. 363–65. For the iconography, see Webster, p. 148.

28. **Epi Tainaro Saturoi, *The Satyrs at Taenarum*** (frag. 198a–198e Radt). Subject unknown. Since Cape Tainaron in Laconia is an entrance to the Underworld, it must be about a descent into Hades in the context of a satyr drama. It is through this entrance that Heracles, one of the satyr play genre's favorite characters, descended to complete his last labor, namely, bringing back Cerberus, the dog that guards the Underworld: cf. Strabo 8, 5, 1 (363): "In the bend of the seaboard one comes, first, to a headland that projects into the sea, Taenarum, with its temple of Poseidon situated in a grove; and secondly, nearby, to the cavern through which, according to the myth writers, Cerberus was brought up from Hades by Heracles"; cf. Pausanias 3, 25, 5. The myth of Heracles' descent into the Underworld is already well attested in Homer (*Iliad* 8, vv. 367–69; *Odyssey* 11, vv. 623–26), but Taenarum is not mentioned; Taenarum is mentioned by Euripides, *Heracles*, vv. 23–25; cf. also Apollodorus 2, 5, 12 (123–26), where Heracles descended through Taenarum but comes back up with Theseus through Troezen. Compare no. 37 (*Heracles*) and no. 53 (*Cerberus*). See *Das griechische Satyrspiel*, pp. 261–65.

29. **Eris (*Strife*)** (frag. 199–201 Radt). Subject unknown. However, we do know that the goddess Eris (Strife) plays an important role at the beginning of the *Cypria*, during the marriage of Peleus and Thetis. Here is Proclus's summary (ed. Bernabé 38ff., 4–8): "Zeus plans with Themis to bring about the Trojan War. Strife (*Eris*) arrives while the gods are feasting at the marriage of Peleus, and starts a dispute between Hera, Athena, and Aphrodite, as to which of them is fairest. The three are led by Hermes at the command of Zeus to Alexandrus on Mount Ida for his decision, and Alexandrus, lured by his promised marriage with Helen,

decides in favor of Aphrodite." For this marriage, see no. 25, *The Rape of Helen*, no. 26, *Helen's Wedding*, and no. 24, *The Demand for Helen's Return*. The tone of frag. 199 ("I, being starved, look toward the cake") seems to be that of a satyr play. See *Das griechische Satyrspiel*, pp. 390–91.

30. **Eriphule, Eriphyle** (frag. 201a–201h Radt). This is the sister of Adrastus, king of Argos, the wife of the seer Amphiaraus (see no. 12, *Amphiaraus*), and the mother of Alcmeon (see no. 10, *Alcmeon*, and no. 27, *Epigoni*) and of Amphilocus. On Eriphyle, see above, chapter VI, "The Mythic Imagination." Seduced by Harmony's necklace given by Polynices, Eriphyle forced Amphiaraus to participate against his will in the expedition of the Seven against Thebes, even though he knew its disastrous outcome: Amphiaraus asked his sons to avenge him, which Alcmeon did by killing his mother ten years later, after the expedition of the Epigoni that he led (cf. no. 27, *Epigoni*). If the *Epigoni* deal with Alcmeon's revenge by killing his mother ten years later, and if *Eriphyle* is distinct from the *Epigoni* (see no. 27, end), we can conclude that in Sophocles, as in Accius, Eriphyle is about the departure of the first expedition against Thebes: cf. Apollodorus 3, 6, 2 (60–62), and Hyginus, *Fables*, 73. On the iconography, see G. Schwarz, "Der Abschied des Amphiaraos: Zwei Tragödienszenen auf dem Volutenkrater T 19 C in Ferrara?," *Jahreshefte des Österreichischen Archäologischen Instituts* 57, 1986–87, pp. 39–54, according to whom the Chicago painter was probably inspired by Sophocles' *Eriphyle*.

31. **Ermione, Hermione** (frag. 202–3 Radt). The subject is known through Eustathius, *Commentary on the Odyssey* 1479, 10: "It is said that Sophocles states in *Hermione* that Menelaus still being in Troy, Hermione [his daughter] was given by Tyndareus [Menelaus's father] to Orestes, because she had been captured to give to Neoptolemus [Achilles' son] in accord with the promise made at Troy [cf. Homer, *Odyssey* 4, vv. 6ff.], but that when Neoptolemus was killed at Delphi by Marchaereus when he was trying to punish Apollo to avenge his father's murder, she was given instead to Orestes, and they had a son, Tisamenus"; cf. the scholium on Euripides, *Orestes*, v. 1655. The mythic sequence is thus comparable to that in Euripides's *Andromache*, but with variants. For example, in Euripides, Neoptolemus is killed at the instigation of Orestes, whereas Neoptolemus was coming to ask the god's pardon for having dared first to demand vengeance for the death of his father; in Sophocles, he comes to ask vengeance and is killed by the Delphic priest Machaereus; cf. Pindar, *Paeans* 6, vv. 117–20, where Neoptolemus is killed by the god during a quarrel with his servants regarding the sharing of the victims. The version adopted by Sophocles is taken up again by Strabo 9, 3, 9. These two different versions are mentioned conjointly by Apollodorus, *Epitome* 6, 14. Philocles, Aeschylus's nephew, had also written a tragedy in which Hermione was first given by Tyndareus to Orestes. See the scholium on Euripides, *Andromache*, v. 32 (= *TrGF* 1, 24, frag. 2 Snell). Also compare no. 108, *The Women of Phthia*. On the play, see recently A. H. Sommerstein, et al., *Sophocles: Selected Fragmentary Plays* I, Oxford, 2006, pp. 1–40.

32. **Eumelos, Eumelus** (frag. 204–5 Radt). The son of Admetus and Alcestis, Eumelus commanded a Thessalian contingent at Troy (*Iliad* 2, v. 711ff.); he was famous for his horses (*Iliad* 2, vv. 763ff.), took part in the chariot race in the funeral games in honor of Patroclus (*Iliad* 23, vv. 288ff.) and won the chariot race during the games in honor of Achilles (Apollodorus, *Epitome*, 5, 5). In the theater, Eumelus, while still a boy, sings a monody in Euripides' *Alcestis* at the time of his mother's death (vv. 393ff.). The subject of the play is not known.

33. **Eurualos, Euryalis** (no fragments). The play is cited by Eustathius, *Commentary on the Odyssey*, 1796, 52 (= p. 194 Radt): "According to Lysimachus, Odysseus had a son by Euippe of Thesprotia, Leontophron, whom others call Doryclus. Sophocles recounts that the same woman gave birth to Euryalis, who killed Telemachus (Odysseus's son)." The subject of the play is known from a summary in Parthenius, *Narrationes amatoriae* 3 (= p. 194 Radt): after murdering the suitors, certain oracles led Odysseus to go to Epirus, where he was received by Tyrimmas. He seduced the latter's daughter, Euippe, and had a son with her, Euryalis. When her son had reached maturity, Euippe sent him to Ithaca with signs that would allow him to be recognized. But since Odysseus was absent, Penelope, informed of the situation and having already learned about the relationship between Odysseus and Euippe, got Odysseus to commit himself, upon his return and before he knew the situation, to kill Euryalis, saying that he was weaving a conspiracy against him. Odysseus killed his own son without recognizing him. Odysseus was to die at the hand of another of his sons, Telegonus, whose mother was Circé; see the *Telegony*, the last poem in the cycle, and no. 77, *Odysseus Wounded by the Spine*. These two testimonies are not in complete accord: according to Parthenius, Euryalis is killed by Odysseus, while according to Eustathius he is killed by Odysseus's son Telemachus.

34. **Eurupulos, Eurypylus** (frag. 206–22b Radt). A tragedy in Trojan cycle. It is on the list of plays cited by Aristotle (*Poetics*, 23 (1459 b)) as derived from the epic poem the *Little Iliad*, but Aristotle does not attribute it by name to Sophocles; see above chapter VI, "The Mythic Imagination." It was Plutarch's testimony (De cohibenda ira c. 10, 458 d), quoting two verses of Sophocles relating to the absence of boasting and insults in the confrontation between Eurypylus and Neoptolemus, that caused the Eurypylus to be attributed to Sophocles as early as the thirteenth century (Tyrwhitt, 1794). Eurypylus is the son of the king of Mysia, Telephus (see no. 8, *The Sons of Aleus*, no. 70, *The Mysians*, and no. 96, *Telephus*) and his wife, Astyoche, Priam's sister. He must not have participated in the Trojan War, because his father, wounded by Achilles' lance, and healed by it as well, had promised that no member of his family would come to the aid of the Trojans. But after the death of Telephus, Priam, seducing his sister by giving her a prestigious gift, the golden grapevine Zeus had given Laomedon, Priam's father, in exchange for Ganymede, persuaded Eurypylus to take part, and he distinguished himself before being killed by Neoptolemus; see the scholium on Juvenal, *Satires* 6, v. 655 (cited by Radt, p. 195), where, however, the gift

is made to Eurypylus's wife. As early as *Odyssey* 11, vv. 519–21, Eurypylus's death at Neoptolemus's hands "because of presents given to women" alludes to the gift Priam made to his sister; the gift of the golden grapevine is mentioned in the *Little Iliad*, frag. 29 Bernabé (= scholium on Euripides, *The Trojan Women* 822). Sophocles' tragedy must have returned to the epic sequence in the *Little Iliad* summed up this way by Proclus (ed. Bernabé 74, 12–14): "Eurypylus the son of Telephus arrives to aid the Trojans, shows his prowess and is killed by Neoptolemus." Cf. Apollodorus, *Epitome* 5.12. Fragments on papyrus that have been known since 1912 but whose reading has been considerably improved (cf. R. Carden, *The Papyrus Fragments of Sophocles*, Berlin, 1974, pp. 1–51), can be reasonably attributed to this tragedy (*P. Oxy.* 1175 + 2081 b = frag. 206–22b Radt with the correspondence between Plutarch's quotation of Sophocles in *De cohibenda ira* and frag. 210, v. 9). If we trust this papyrus, the messenger came to inform Astyoche, Eriphyle's mother, of the death of her son, over whom Priam lamented as if he had been his own son, regretting his death even more than that of Memnon (cf. no. 67, *Memnon*) or that of Sarpedon. Astyoche recognized her mistake in allowing herself to be seduced by a gift that had led to the death of her son (frag. 210). The tragedy must have taken place in Priam's palace at Troy.

35. **Eurusakes, Eurysaces** (frag. 223 Radt). This is the son of Ajax who appears in the extant tragedy *Ajax* (see appendix I), but does not speak (vv. 545ff.; vv. 1168ff.). Before committing suicide, Ajax bequeaths to Eurysaces his shield, which has given him his name: *Eurysakès* means "with a large shield" (v. 575). After Ajax's death, he stands near his father's body with his mother, Tecmessa, and at the end of the tragedy, Teucer (cf. no. 95, *Teucer*) asks him to help with the burial (vv. 1409–11). After the Trojan War, Eurysaces returned to Salamis, his father's homeland, and succeeded Telamon, his grandfather, as king, while Teucer, driven away by Telamon, went into exile in Cyprus, where he founded Salamis in Cyprus. Eurysaces (or his son Philaius) gave the island of Salamis to Athens and settled in Attica (cf. Plutarch, "Life of Solon" 10, 3 (83 d), and Pausanias 1, 35, 2). There was a cult of Eurysaces and one of Ajax in Athens (cf. Pausanias 1, 35, 3). Only one word of the tragedy has been preserved, by Hesychius (frag. 223). The precise subject is unknown. The Latin poet Accius (second to first century BCE) composed a tragedy of the same name; see J. Dangel, *Accius, Fragments*, Paris: CUF, 2002, pp. 172–80 and pp. 328–32.

36. **Erakleiskos, Young Heracles** (satyr play) (frag. 223a–223b Radt). Subject unknown. However, the exploit carried out by Heracles, the son of Zeus and Alcmene, when he was still a child, consisted in strangling two serpents that Hera had sent, out of jealousy, to kill him and his twin brother Iphicles, born from Amphitryon (cf. no. 13, *Amphitryon*). His courage contrasted with the fear felt by his brother, who ran away. Concerning this feat by the young Heracles, see Pindar, *Nemean Ode* 1, vv. 33ff., and *Paean* 20 (fragmentary); Theocritus 24 (*Young Hercules*), Apollodorus 2, 4, 8 (62). See *Das griechische Satyrspiel*, pp. 266–69.

38. **Erigone** (frag. 235–36 Radt). The mythographers know two persons named Erigone, both related to the Athenian festival called the *aiōra* (Latin *oscillatio*): on the one hand, the daughter of Clytemnestra and Aegisthus, according to one version, she and her grandfather Tyndareus brought Orestes before the court of the Areopagus; after Orestes was acquitted, she hanged herself, demanding vengeance, and a festival called the *aiōra* was established in Athens in her honor, in conformity with an oracle (*Etymologicum Magnum*, s.v. *aiōra* 42, 3–9; cf. Apollodorus, *Epitome* 6, 25, where the trial of Orestes was instituted by the Erinyes, by Tyndareus, or by Erigone, the daughter of Aegisthus and Clytemnestra). The second person named Erigone is the daughter of the Athenian Icarius. Dionysus, when he came to Athens, had given Icarius a vine stock and taught him how to make wine; Icarius had shepherds try the beverage, but they got drunk and killed him. His daughter, having discovered his body thanks to a dog, hanged herself in despair (Apollodorus 3, 14, 7 [192]); the festival of the *oscillatio* was instituted in her honor (Hyginus, *Fables*, 130: Icarius and Erigone). In favor of the first Erigone, we can adduce the *Erigone* by the Latin poet Accius, which mentions Aegisthus (frag. 4) and Orestes (frag. 5); on Accius's tragedy, see J. Dangel, *Accius, Fragments*, Paris: CUF, 2002, pp. 170–71 and pp. 326–28. The character in *Erigone* had a certain success in the Greek theater. In addition to Sophocles' play, we know three other plays entitled *Erigone*: one by Philocles I, Sophocles' rival, who won the prize when *Oedipus the King* was performed (see above; the other by Cleophon, and still another by Phrynicus II; see *TrGF* I, 24 T 1 (= *Suda* φ 378); 77 T 1 (*Suda* κ 1730), and 212 T 1 (= *Suda* φ 765). But we know only the titles.

39. **Thamuras, Thamyras** (frag. 236a–245 Radt). The Thracian musician and singer Thamyras, the son of Philammon (scholium on Euripides, *Rhesos*, v. 916 = frag. 236 a), king of the shore at the foot of Mount Athos (Eustathius, *Commentary on the Iliad* 299, 5; cf. frag. 237), had boasted that with his songs he could outdo the Muses, Zeus's daughters. The myth is already known from the *Iliad* 2, vv. 594–600. The Muses were enraged, and when he came to Eurytus's home in Dorion, in Oechalia, they disabled him (blinded him?), deprived him of his divine song, and made him forget how to play the cithara; see also Euripides, *Rhesos*, vv. 915–25, where the Muses, after a contest with Thamyras in the region of the Pangaion hills, blinded him; cf. Apollodorus, 1, 3, 3 (17). One detail of Thamyras's face (one eye was clouded and the other black; cf. the scholium on *Iliad* 2, v. 595) must have been represented by the mask; see Pollux, 4, 141. Sophocles himself played the cithara in the performance of the tragedy; see above, chapter I, "The Young Sophocles," with the translation of *Iliad* 2, vv. 594–600. Angered, Thamyras broke his lyre (frag. 244). Compare no. 69, *The Muses*. For the iconography connected with the play, see Séchan, pp. 193–98, Webster, p. 152, and Trendall and Webster, pp. 69ff.

40. **Theseus** (frag. 246 Radt; cf. also frag. 730 a–g, and 905 Radt). We have only one reference to this tragedy. Some scholars doubt its existence and prefer

to see in it a quotation from the tragedy *Aegeus* (no. 4), about Theseus's father. But why would Sophocles not have composed both a *Theseus* and an *Aegeus*, as Euripides did? For Euripides' *Theseus*, see H. Van Looy, *Euripide*, vol. 8, 2, CUF, 2000, pp. 145ff., and *TrGF* 5.1, pp. 426–36 Kannicht.

41–43. ***Thuestes, Thyestes*** 1, 2, and 3 (frag. 247–69 Radt). Sophocles composed three plays entitled *Thyestes*, because "Sophocles' third" *Thyestes* is mentioned (*P. Lond. Inv.* 2110, cited by Radt, p. 239). Thyestes, son of Pelops and brother of Atreus (see no. 17, *Atreus*) belongs to the great tragic family known especially through the branch of Atreus, the Atreids, Agamemnon and Menelaus. To the branch of Thyestes belong his son Aegisthus, who seduced Clytemnestra wife of Agamemnon, as his father Thyestes had seduced Atreus's wife, Aerope. On this tragic family, see chapter VI, "The Mythic Imagination." One of these three *Thyestes* was entitled *Thyestes in Sicyon* (mentioned by Hesychius = frag. 248–52). It deals with a sequence about Thyestes' vengeance after the meal Atreus served him, in which he had devoured his own children (see no. 17, *Atreus*). Having learned by an oracle that the child that he was to have with his own daughter Pelopia would be his avenger, he went to Sicyon where his daughter was. He had with her, without her knowledge, a son, Aegisthus, who ended up killing Atreus and restoring the throne to Thyestes. Hyginus, *Fables*, 87 and 88 (with numerous fantastic peripeteias); cf. Apollodorus, *Epitome* 2, 14. Euripides also composed a *Thyestes*; see H. Van Looy, *Euripide*, vol. 8, 2, CUF, 2000, pp. 167ff., and *TrGF* 5.1, pp. 437–41 Kannicht. For the iconography connected with the play, see Séchan, pp. 199–213.

44. ***Inachos, Inachus*** (frag. 269a–295a). Inachus, the son of Ocean (cf. frag. 270) and Tethys, is the first mythical king of Argos; he gave his name to Argolis's river. He is the father of Io (frag. 284), priestess of Hera, whom Zeus seduced and transformed into a heifer when Hera found out about it (or perhaps it was Hera who transformed Io into a heifer). The myth appears for the first time in Hesiod, in the *Catalog of Women* (frag. 124–25 Merkelbach-West) and the Aigimos (294–96 Merkelbach-West), and it is attested in Aeschylus's *The Suppliants* (vv. 291ff.) and in *Prometheus Bound* (vv. 562ff.); cf. also Apollodorus 2, 1, 3 (5). Pursued by Hera's jealousy, the heifer was watched over by Argos "who sees everything" (frag. 281), but he was killed by Hermes. Then the heifer was pursued by a horsefly that made her wander until she reached Egypt, where she gave birth to Epaphus, the ancestor of several important family lineages, including that of Danaus and that of Egyptus (cf. Aeschylus, *The Suppliants*, vv. 291–305), which was the origin of the royalty of Argos (marriage of Egyptus's son Lynceus to Danaus's daughter Hypermnestra); cf. Canisius, king of Argos, the grandson of Lynceus and Hypermnestra, in *Canisius* (no. 7), and his brother Proetus, king of Tirynthia, in *Iobates* (no. 46). The play seems to deal with the initial sequence in the myth. Among the characters there were Inachus (frag. 270, where the chorus addresses Inachus), Argos (frag. 281 a), Hermes (frag. 272; cf. 269 c 22) and Iris (frag. 272). Io's metamorphosis is mentioned in a narrative (frag. 269 a

36ff.). Although there are a rather large number of fragments with which two papyruses have been connected (*P. Tebtunis* 692 published in 1933 and *P. Oxy.* 2369 published in 1956, with the new edition by R. Carden, *The Papyrus Fragments of Sophocles*, Berlin, 1974, pp. 52–109), many uncertainties remain, even regarding the nature of the play (a satyr play as most scholars think, or a tragedy?). See S. West, "Io and the Dark Stranger (Sophocles, *Inachus* F 269 a)," *CQ* 34, 1984, pp. 292–302; A. L. Allan "Cattle-Stealing Satyrs in Sophocles' *Inachos*," in A. H. Sommerstein (ed.), *Shards from Kolonos* (2003), pp. 309–28; *Das griechische Satyrspiel*, pp. 313–43. For the iconography, see Webster, pp. 148ff.

45. **Ixion** (frag. 296 Radt). We have only one fragment, giving just one word, and the existence of this play has been doubted; but an inscription found in the agora in Athens and published in 1938, relating to the actors' competition in the third century BCE, confirms the existence of Sophocles' *Ixion* (B. D. Meritt, *Hesperia* 7, 1938, 116–18 = *TrGF* 1 Snell DID A 4 b 6ff.). The other two great tragic authors, Aeschylus and Euripides, also composed an *Ixion* (for Aeschylus, see *TrGF* 3, frag. 89–93 Radt, and for Euripides. H. Van Looy, *Euripide*, vol. 8, 2, CUF, 2000, pp. 211ff., and *TrGF* 5.1, pp. 456–58 Kannicht). The source on the myth is Pindar, *Pythian Ode* 2, vv. 21–48 (with the scholium on v. 40 b = *TrGF* 3, frag. 89 Radt). Ixion, king of the Lapiths, committed two crimes: he became "the first mortal to shed his race's blood" by throwing his father-in-law, Eioneus, who had come to claim the wedding presents he had promised him, into a ditch full of red-hot coals, to avenge himself for a theft of mares; and he tried to rape Hera, the wife of his benefactor, Zeus, who had agreed to purify him of the murder. In reality, Ixion had intercourse with a cloud shaped to look like Hera. From this union was born a centaur, who, mating with mares at the foot of Mount Pelion, gave birth the race of centaurs resembling their mother in their lower bodies and their father by their upper bodies. For his crimes, Ixion was condemned to an eternal punishment, attached to a wheel that never ceases to turn. We do not know if this tragedy dealt with the first crime or the second; however, it is more likely to be about the second, because in stasimon 1 of Sophocles' *Philoctetes* (vv. 677–80) the chorus alludes, without naming him, to the destiny of Ixion, whom Zeus has condemned to punishment on the wheel for having tried to have intercourse with his wife, Hera.

46. **Iobates** (frag. 297–99 Radt). Iobates is not well known by his name. But he is connected with a very famous myth, that of Bellerophon, which is already well attested in Homer (*Iliad* 6, vv. 160ff.). Iobates is the king of Lycia (not designated by name in Homer), whose daughter (Antea in Homer, Stheneboea in tragic poets; cf. Euripides' *Stheneboea*) was married to Proetus, king of Tirynthia and the brother of Canisius, king of Argos (cf. no. 7, *Canisius*). Proetus's wife fell in love with Bellerophon, but when she was rejected by him she falsely told her husband that he had tried to rape her. Proetus sent Bellerophon to his father-in-law in Lycia, along with a letter to give him. In the letter, Proetus asked Iobates to put Bellerophon to death. Iobates subjected Bellerophon to a series

of tests (the Chimera, the Solymes, the Amazons) and finally set an ambush for him; but Bellerophon triumphed over all these. Iobates understood his nobility and gave him his daughter Cassandra as his wife; they had two sons and a daughter together. Iobates also shared power with Bellerophon. Then Bellerophon, the object of all the gods' hatred, lost one of his sons, as a victim of Ares, and his daughter, as a victim of Artemis. Homer does not mention Pegasus, the winged horse that allowed Bellerophon to achieve his exploits; his existence is nonetheless attested very early on, in the seventh century, in both literature (Hesiod) and iconography. Three small fragments do not enable us to determine which sequence of the myth Sophocles dealt with, but the action must have been situated in Lycia, in Iobates' palace, as the title indicates. Hypothetically, we might think of the sequence of the myth that goes from Bellerophon's arrival in Lycia to his marriage with Iobates' daughter. Euripides composed two plays on this myth, *Stheneboea* (whose subject is well known through a summary in which we see that Euripides deviates considerably from Homer: see F. Jouan, *Euripide*, vol. 8, 3, CUF, 2002, pp. 1ff.) and *Bellérophon* (F. Jouan, *Euripide*, vol. 8, 2, CUF, 2000, 1ff.).

47. **Hipponous** (frag. 300–304 Radt). Hipponous is the king of Olenus; his daughter Periboea married Oeneus, the king of Calydon in Aetolia (of the king of Pleuron; *The Women of Trachis*, v. 7), after the death of his first wife, Althea. We are well acquainted with Oeneus's children from his first marriage, notably his daughter Deianira, the heroine of the extant tragedy *The Women of Trachis* (v. 6) and his son Meleager (cf. no. 66, *Meleager*). We also know a son of Oeneus born of his second marriage with Periboea: Tydeus, one of the seven leaders of the expedition against Thebes (cf. *Oedipus at Colonus*, v. 1315: "the son of Oeneus, Aetolian Tydeus"). Sophocles nonetheless mentions only the father of Deianira and Tydeus, without mentioning the mother. That presupposes a rather exceptional mythical culture on the part of the spectators. The versions on the way in which Oeneus obtained Hipponous's daughter in marriage differ: according to the *Thebiad* (frag. 5 Bernabé = Apollodorus 1, 8, 4 [74–75]), he obtained her as his share of the honor after the conquest of Olenus; according to Hesiod (frag. 12 Merkelbach-West = Apollodorus ibid.), Hipponous, after learning that his son had been seduced by Hippostratos, sent her far from Olenus, to Oeneus, so that he could put her to death; the same version is found, with a variant, in Diodorus (4, 35: Periboea is said to be pregnant by Ares). In addition to these two versions, Apollodorus mentions a third one: "Some say that Hipponous discovered that his daughter had been debauched by Oeneus, and therefore he sent her away to him when she was with child. By her Oeneus begat Tydeus." The variants are further complicated by the fact that there are two cities named Olenus, one in Aetolia, the other in Achaia. It is possible that frag. 300 is uttered by Periboea, coming from Oeneus's palace in Olenus, and that frag. 301 is part of a dialogue in which Oeneus was questioning Periboea, asking her not to hide the truth. We would thus have Sophocles' use of a version in which Periboea is sent to Oeneus

by Hipponous. But nothing is certain here. Pollux (4, 111) refers to the tragedy, saying that in one song the chorus speaks for the author.

48. **Iphigeneia** (frag. 305–12 Radt). Iphigeneia is the daughter of Agamemnon and Clytemnestra (cf. no. 55, *Clytemnestra*). According to one of the eight extant fragments (frag. 305), in which Odysseus addresses Clytemnestra apropos of Achilles, saying that in him she is acquiring a very great son-in-law, it is clear that Agamemnon has sent Odysseus to Clytemnestra to fetch Iphigeneia on the pretext that she is to marry Achilles, whereas in reality she is to be sacrificed. The sequence is thus comparable to the one Euripides dramatized in his *Iphigeneia in Aulis*. The sacrifice was already mentioned in Hesiod's *Catalog of Women*, but the name of Agamemnon's and Clytemnestra's daughter was Iphimede (see above). The tragic sequence was used in the *Cypria*, a poem in the Trojan cycle. Here is the sequence in Proclus's summary (ed. Bernabé 41, 42–49): "When the expedition had mustered a second time at Aulis, Agamemnon, while at the chase, shot a stag and boasted that he surpassed even Artemis. At this the goddess was so angry that she sent stormy winds and prevented them from sailing. Calchas then told them of the anger of the goddess and bade them sacrifice Iphigeneia to Artemis. This they attempt to do, sending to fetch Iphigeneia as though for marriage with Achilles. Artemis, however, snatched her away and transported her to the Tauri, making her immortal, and putting a doe [translation modified] in place of the girl upon the altar." Cf. Hyginus, *Fables*, 98 (Iphigeneia), and Apollodorus, *Epitome* 3, 21 and 22. We do not know whether Sophocles adopted the substitution of the doe for Iphigeneia. Hyginus seems to refer primarily to Euripides.

49. **Iphicles** (frag. 313). We have only one attestation to this play, in a scholium on *Oedipus at Colonus*, v. 793, where we read that Apollo received his oracles from Zeus. Iphicles is Heracles' twin brother, born of the same mother, Alcmene, but not of the same father. Whereas Heracles is a demigod, the son of Zeus, Iphicles is a mortal, the son of Amphitryon (Hesiod, *Shield*, vv. 48–56); cf. no. 13, *Amphitryon*, and no. 36, *Young Heracles*. By his first wife, Automedusa, Iphicles had a son Iolaus, who helped Heracles with most of his labors (Apollodorus 2, 4, 11 [70]; Pausanias 8, 14, 9). Iphicles himself took part in battles at Heracles' side, for example in the Thebans' war against the Minyans, where he received as his reward the youngest daughter of the king of Thebes, Creon, who became his second wife (Apollodorus 2, 4, 11 [70]), and in the first expedition against Troy, with Telamon (Diodorus 4, 49, 3). He lost two children killed by Heracles during his fit of madness (Apollodorus 2, 4. 12 [72]). He died during an expedition with Heracles against Lacedemonia to punish the sons of Hippocoön (Apollodorus 2, 7, 3 [143–45]); or after a battle against the Aelians and Augias; he was mortally wounded and was buried in Pheneus in Arcadia, where he received a heroic cult (Pausanias 8, 14, 9–10). The subject is unknown.

50. **Ichneutai Saturoi, Ichneutae** (satyr play) (frag. 314–18 Radt). This is the only one of Sophocles' plays for which we have enough fragments to follow the

plot, at least in the first part, thanks to two papyruses published starting in 1912 (*P. Oxy.* 1174 + 2081 a). The satyr play owes its title to the chorus consisting of satyrs leaving to track down (in Greek, *ichneutai* means "trackers") a herd of cattle stolen from Apollo. The subject is taken from the Hymn to Hermes; cf. vv. 17–19 ("Born with the dawning, at mid-day he [Hermes] played on the lyre, and in the evening he stole the cattle of far-shooting Apollo on the fourth day of the month"). Sophocles uses both these exploits, but he reverses them, because the heifer's skin is necessary to invent the lyre (the skin is used to make the lyre's strings). The play begins with Apollo's to reward with gold anyone who finds his cattle, which he has sought everywhere in Thrace, Thessaly, and Boeotia before finally coming to Mount Cyllene in Arcadia. The old Silenus appears at Apollo's summons, attracted by the reward. He promises to leave with his children, the satyrs, to track down the cattle. Apollo promises him a twofold reward, gold and freedom. Thereupon enters the chorus of satyrs who will leave with their father on this mission. They find the cattle's tracks, but everything becomes confused because the tracks go in opposite directions. This quest is abruptly interrupted by the sound of the lyre, which frightens the satyrs because they have never heard it before. Admonished by their father, they resume their search. They hear the sound of the lyre again. This time it is Silenus who is frightened. And despite the satyrs' admonishments, he gives up and leaves. The chorus, which has come to the door of a cavern in which it believes the thief is hiding, makes noise to get him to come out. It is Cyllene, the mountain's eponymous nymph, who appears. It is learned that she is the nurse of Hermes, who was born six days earlier to Maia, the daughter of Atlas, and Zeus, who came to visit her at night, without his wife, Hera's, knowledge. In a dialogue with the satyrs, Cyllene explains to them the sources of the astonishing sound they heard: an instrument invented in one day by Hermes, using the shell of a dead animal, the tortoise. The satyrs then suggest that it is Hermes who stole Apollo's cattle, because he needed a skin to make his invention. Cyllene protests and accuses them of insulting Zeus's son. The end of the play is missing. The cattle found by the satyrs must have been returned to Apollo, and the god must have given them the promised reward: gold and freedom. For the French translation (with a presentation and the Greek text), see P. Masqueray, *Sophocle* II, 2nd revised and corrected ed., Paris: CUF, 1942, pp. 227–50. For an edition with commentary, see *Ichneutai: Introd., testo critico, interpretazione & comm.*, ed. E. V. Maltese, Florence, 1982; R. Krumeich, N. Pechstein, and B. Seidensticker (eds.), *Das griechische Satyrspiel*, Darmstadt, 1999, pp. 280–312 (with the bibliography); see also N. Zagagi, "Comic Patterns in Sophocles' *Ichneutae*," in J. Griffin (ed.), *Sophocles Revisited: Essays Presented to Sir Hugh Lloyd-Jones*, Oxford, 1999, pp. 177–218; E. OKell, "The 'Effeminacy' of the Clever Speaker and the 'Impotency' Jokes of *Ichneutai*," in A. H. Sommerstein (ed.), *Shards from Kolonos* (2003), pp. 283–307.

51. **Ion** (frag. 319–22 Radt). The subject of Sophocles' play, whose existence is attested by four fragments, is not known, but the myth is famous, even though there are many variants. Ion, the eponymous hero of the Ionians, is the son of Xouthus (Herodotus 7, 94). His mother is Creusa, the daughter of Erectheus, king of Athens. She had two sons; the second, Achaius, is eponymous of the Achaeans just as Ion is eponymous of the Ionians (Pausanias 7, 1, 2; Strabo 8, 7, 1; Apollodorus 1, 7, 3). According to Pausanias's version (7, 1, 4), he was king of the region called Aigialus (= Achaia), following Selinous, who had given him his daughter Helice as his wife, and he gave his own name to the residents of this country. Summoned to help the Athenians in their war against Eleusis, he fought at their head (Pausanias 1, 31, 3). He died in Attica; his tomb is in the deme of Potamoi (Pausanias 1, 31, 3 and 7, 1, 5). The Athenians also draw from him their name as Ionians (Herodotus 8, 44). According to Strabo's version (8, 7, 1), Ion had more political influence in Athens. Through his victory over Eumolpus's Thracians he won such renown that the Athenians entrusted him with the management of their affairs (cf. Aristotle, *Constitution of Athens* 41, 2). He divided the population into four tribes designated by the names of his four children (cf. Herodotus 5, 66), and into four categories; at his death, he left the Athenians the name of Ionians. On the other hand, Strabo does not mention an important role for Ion in Aigialus, where there was a colony of Ionians who had come from Athens. Euripides composed an extant tragedy also entitled *Ion*. This tragic author innovates a great deal with regard to the mythic fund collected by the prose writers (Herodotus, Strabo, Pausanias) by making Ion the son of Creusa and Apollo (and not Xouthus); however, there are traces of this version of the myth in Pausanias 1, 28, 4 (Apollo's grotto where Erectheus's daughter is supposed to have had intercourse with the god); cf. also the scholia on Aristophanes, *The Clouds*, v. 1468, and *The Birds*, v. 1527. Nothing indicates that Sophocles' play *Ion* should be conflated with *Creusa* (no. 57), or that in *Ion* Sophocles dramatized the same sequence of the myth that Euripides did, even if that hypothesis is the most plausible one. Ion's destiny is rich enough to provide another sequence for Sophocles' play; one suggestion is the war against Eleusis. For the iconography, see Webster, p. 149.

52. **Kamikoi, The Men of Camicus** (frag. 323–27 Radt). The play's subject is a sequence from the myth of Daedalus (cf. no. 20, *Daedalus*) pursued by Minos (cf. no. 68, *Minos*) when he took refuge in Sicily with the king of Camicus, an ancient city in the territory of Agrigentum. Cf. Herodotus 7, 170, 1: "Minos, it is said, went to Sicania, which is now called Sicily, in search for Daedalus, and perished there by a violent death." Apollodorus (*Epitome* 1, 13–15; cf. Zenobius 4 92) gives details: Daedalus had taken refuge with the king of Camicus, Cocalus (cf. Aristophanes' comedy *Cocalus*, PCG II, 2, pp. 201–7 Kassel and Austin). Minos, searching for him everywhere, brought with him a spiral seashell, promising a great reward to anyone who could pass a thread through it (cf. frag. 324),

convinced that only Daedalus would be able to do so. When Minos arrived in Camicus, Cocalus accepted his challenge. He took the shell to Daedalus, who attached a thread to an ant and made it pass through the hole in the shell. Thus Minos concluded that Daedalus was hidden in the palace and demanded that the fugitive be handed over. Cocalus pretended to agree and welcomed Minos as a guest. But his daughters scalded the guest in his bath by sprinkling him with pitch (Zenobius) or with boiling water (Apollodorus). The chorus must have consisted, as the title indicates, of residents of Camicus.

53. ***Kerberos, Cerberus*** (frag. 327 a). The subject of this play, of which only one fragment is extant, is unknown. Cerberus is the name of Hades' dog who guards the Underworld. He is attested in the oldest epic poetry. He is a monstrous creature born of Typhon and Echidna and has fifty heads (Hesiod, *Theogony*, v. 311, vv. 769ff.) or three heads (cf. Sophocles, *The Women of Trachis*, v. 1098: "the three-headed whelp of Hades, a resistless terror, offspring of the fierce Echidna"). We already find in Homer the most famous episode concerning Cerberus: among the labors Eurystheus imposes on Heracles is to "to bring from out of Erebus the hound of loathed Hades," with Athena and Hermes as his guides (*Iliad* 8, vv. 366ff.; cf. *Odyssey* 11, vv. 623ff.). It is thought that the play entitled *Cerberus* could only be devoted to this episode; cf. the parody of this descent into the Underworld in Aristophanes' *The Frogs*, where Dionysus, wanting to go down into the Underworld to look for Euripides, asks the advice of Heracles, who had gone there to get Cerberus. Compare no. 28 (*The Satyrs at Taenarum*) and no. 37 (*Heracles*). See *Das griechische Satyrspiel*, pp. 275–76.

54. ***Kedalion satsurikos, Cedalion*** (satyr play) (frag. 328–33 Radt). Celdalion is a blacksmith connected with the myth of Hephaestus, the son of Zeus and Hera. Two versions are attested: Cedalion is a smith from Naxos to whom Hera entrusted Hephaestus so that he might learn the smith's trade, in memory of which there was a monument on Naxos (scholium on Homer, *Iliad* 14, v. 296; Eustathius, *Commentary on the Iliad* 987, 8). In that case, this is a satyr play on Hephaestus's youth. But there is another, better-known Cedalion who is probably the subject of this play. He is one of Hephaestus's servants on Lemnos who plays a role in the famous myth of Orion, the son of Poseidon and Minos's daughter Euryalis. Orion's father had given him the power of walking on water. But he was blinded on Chios by Oenopion, the son of Dionysus, when, being drunk, he tried to rape Oenopion's mother. In his wanderings, Orion reached Lemnos, where Hephaestus took pity on him and gave him his own servant Cedalion to serve as his guide. Orion carried Cedalion on his shoulders, and the servant told him where to go. Thus he went toward the east, met the sun, and recovered his eyesight. He sought to take revenge on Oenopion but died while hunting, stung by a scorpion. Orion was transformed into a constellation. The myth is already attested in Hesiod, in the *Catalog of Women* (frag. 148 Merkelbach-West = Ps. Eratosthenes, Catasterismi, 32). Little known to moderns, the myth was famous in antiquity. Lucian (*The Hall* 28–29) describes, among the paintings

in a magnificent home, at least some of which were inspired by the tragic poets, a picture in which the blind Orion carries on his shoulders Cedalion, who is directing him toward the light, and where the sun is rising and heals him, while Hephaestus observes the action from Lemnos. The painter might have taken his inspiration from Sophocles' play. We know of no play other than Sophocles' that is entitled *Cedalion*. See *Das griechische Satyrspiel*, pp. 344–48.

55. ***Klutaimnestra, Clytemnestra*** (frag. 334 Radt). This is one of Sophocles' plays devoted to the great tragic family of the Pelopids well-represented in the fragments. See above, chapter VI, "The Mythic Imagination," under "The Wealth of the Mythic Tradition: The Great Tragic Families in Sophocles' Lost Plays." Clytemnestra, the wife of Agamemnon, with whom she had a son, Orestes, and several daughters, including Iphigeneia (see no. 48, *Iphigeneia*), Electra (see appendix I, *Electra*), and Chrysothemis, killed her husband with the help of her lover Aegisthus and died under the blows of her son who had returned, after a long exile, to avenge his father. The subject of this tragedy is not known. But there is no reason, on the ground that there is only one fragment, to doubt its existence and to identify it with no. 48, *Iphigeneia*. In the great parallel family in which Alcmeon kills his mother to avenge his father, there are also three tragedies that take their names from three of the main characters, including the mother *Eriphyle* (no. 30), the father Amphiarius (no. 12), and the son Alcmeon (no. 10). Why wouldn't there be a *Clytemnestra* alongside an *Electra* and an *Iphigeneia*? Accius composed a *Clytemnestra* (ed. Dangel, pp. 165–67).

56. ***Kolchides, The Women of Colchis*** (frag. 337–49 Radt). This is one Sophocles' rare fragmentary plays about which we have a little precise information. This play is designated by its chorus formed of women from Colchis, friends or servants of Medea. The setting was Colchis, on the extreme eastern shores of the Black Sea, which the Argonauts' expedition reached via Phasis. The subject was the sequence that occurs when Jason's expedition lands in Colchis to win the golden fleece held by Aeëtes, Medea's father (cf. Pindar, *Pythian Ode* 4, vv. 211ff.; Apollonius of Rhodes, Argonautica, 3 and 4, vv. 1–521; Apollodorus 1, 9, 23–24 [127–33]). Sophocles is the only one of the three great tragic authors who dramatized this sequence. Before obtaining the fleece, Jason had to pass tests set by Aeëtes: yoking two fire-breathing bulls (frag. 336 Pierson = 1135 Radt), and then plowing and sowing the dragon's teeth that were supposed to give birth to armed men (frag. 341). Medea, who had fallen in love with Jason, told him, in a scene in dialogue, how to pass the tests (scholium on Apollonius of Rhodes 3, 1040 c: "In *The Women of Colchis* Sophocles represents Medea giving Jason advice in a dialogue for his test"; cf. Pindar, *Pythian Ode* 4, vv. 220–22). In the course of this dialogue, she had to obtain a promise in exchange (frag. 339); cf. Pindar, *Pythian Ode* 4, vv. 222–23): "They agreed to be united with each other in sweet wedlock." We also know that a messenger came to tell Aeëtes how Jason had passed his tests (frag. 341 = scholium on Apollonius of Rhodes 3, 1354–56 a, where the birth of armed men is mentioned). Medea's young brother, Apsyrtus, was killed in

Aeëtes' palace (scholium on Apollonius of Rhodes 4, v. 223 = frag. 343; cf. Euripides, *Medea*, v. 1334: "You killed your own brother at the hearth and then stepped aboard the fair-prowed Argo"). We also know that the myth of Prometheus was mentioned in a secondary way (the argument of Aeschylus's *Prometheus Bound*: "The myth (sc. of Prometheus) is found in an ancillary way in Sophocles, in *The Women of Colchis*; in Euripides it does not appear at all"); cf. also frag. 340. For the iconography, see Webster, p. 149.

57. **Kreousa, Creusa** (frag. 350–59 Radt). Several women in Greek mythology are named Creusa. In addition to Xouthus's wife and Ion's mother (see no. 51, *Ion*), Creusa was also the name of Priam's daughter, the wife of Aeneas (cf. no. 61, *Laocoön*); and also of Creon's daughter who was Medea's rival (also called Glauce; cf. Euripides' *Medea*; Hyginus, *Fables*, 25, where Creon's daughter is called first Glauce, then Creusa). The fragments, which consist mainly of general maxims taken from Stobaeus, do not allow us to decide, even though the scholarly tradition since Brunck favors Ion's mother. Frag. 356, which refers to a maxim from the Letoön in Delphi, would fit the situation. But the speculations drawn from this tragedy, when we are not even sure what it is about, continue to nourish Euripides criticism in an astonishing way, some people having sought to see in Sophocles' Creusa a model from which Euripides distinguished himself; see, for instance, A. Pippin Burnett, *Catastrophe Survived: Euripides' Plays of Mixed Reversal*, Oxford, 1971, p. 103 (following H. Grégoire, *Euripide* III, Paris, 1923, pp. 161–63).

58. **Krisis saturike, The Judgment** (satyr play) (frag. 360 Radt). This is a play drawn from the Trojan cycle. The subject is Paris's judgment of the three goddesses that follows the sequence that was probably dealt with in *Strife* (no. 29). The subject is known through a testimony by Athenaeus (15, 687 c = frag. 361 Radt): "The poet Sophocles, on the other hand, in his play *The Judgment*, brings Aphrodite onstage in the guise of a deity named Pleasure, putting perfume on herself and looking at herself in a mirror, but brings on Athena, who represents insight and Intelligence as well as Virtue, rubbing olive oil on her skin and exercising." The subject, already mentioned in the *Iliad* (24, vv. 27–30), is inspired by the sequence in the *Cypria*, Proclus's summary of which has already been cited apropos of no. 29 (*Eris* or *Strife*); see also Apollodorus, *Epitome*, 3, 2. The theme of the judgment was often taken up by Euripides, notably in five extant tragedies: *Hecuba*, vv. 644–49; *Andromache*, vv. 274–92; *The Trojan Women*, vv. 924–31 and 971–81; and especially *Helen*, vv. 23–31 (etc.) and *Iphigeneia in Aulis*, vv. 1291–309 (among other passages); see T.W.C. Stinton, "Euripides and the Judgement of Paris," *JHS Supp.* 11, 1965, rpt. in *Collected Papers on Greek Tragedy*, Oxford, 1990, pp. 17–75; F. Jouan, *Euripide et les légendes des chants cypriens*, Paris, 1966, pp. 95–109. See *Das griechische Satyrspiel*, pp. 356–62.

59. **Kophoi saturikoi, The Fools** (satyr play). The "fools" must designate the chorus consisting of stupid characters, probably satyrs (cf. frag. 364). The subject is unknown, but several scholia or testimonies of various origins concern this

play. A scholium on Nicander, *Theriaca*, v. 343 (= frag. 362), indicates that it included a myth in connection with Prometheus (cf. also Aelian, *On the Nature of Animals* 6, 51): Prometheus had stolen Zeus's fire in order to give it to humans; the latter, in their ingratitude, told Zeus what he had done; to reward them, Zeus gave them a remedy for old age; those who received it carried it on an ass; dying of thirst, the ass headed for a spring that was guarded by a serpent; to obtain permission to drink, the ass gave the serpent the remedy against old age: that is why serpents are rejuvenated every year by changing their skins; in exchange, the serpent received thirst, which explains why this serpent (called in Greek *dipsas*) causes thirst (*dipsa*) in those it bites. The play also mentions the myth of the Dactyls of Mount Ida in Phrygia (scholium on Apollonius of Rhodes 1, 1126 = frag. 364): "In *The Foolish Satyrs* Sophocles calls them [sc. the Dactyls] Phrygians." Without citing the title of the play, Strabo (10, 3, 22 = frag. 366) clarifies what Sophocles said about the Dactyls: "Sophocles thinks that the first male Dactyli were five in number, who were the first to discover and to work iron, as well as many other things which are useful for the purposes of life, and that their sisters were five in number, and that they were called Dactyli from their number. But different writers tell the myth in different ways, joining difficulty to difficulty; and both the names and numbers they use are different; and they name one of them 'Celmis.'" Sophocles must have mentioned the story of Kelmis in this play, according to Zenobius (4, 80 = frag. 365): his character was severe, and he acted violently toward the mother (of the gods) Rhea; in punishment, he was transformed into iron. The connection between these two myths may be the gift of fire to humans with its maleficent or beneficial consequences, which Sophocles could deal with in an amusing way. Finally, the play seems to be mentioned in the papyrus noting that Sophocles came in second when Aeschylus won with his trilogy beginning with *The Suppliants* (*P. Oxy.* 2256 frag. 3 = *TrGF* 3, test. 70 Radt). The play would thus be ancient and probably date from 463; but the end of the papyrus is very uncertain; on this document, see above, chapter IV, "Sophocles and Dionysus: The Theatrical Career." See *Das griechische Satyrspiel*, pp. 349–55.

   60. ***Lakainai, The Laconian Women*** (frag. 367–69 a Radt). The play was on Aristotle's list, in the *Poetics* 23 (1459 b), of the tragedies inspired by the *Little Iliad*; see above, chapter VI, "The Mythic Imagination." The tragedy owes its title to the chorus formed of Helen's servants who originally came from Lacedemonia and traveled with her to Troy. As can be deduced from frag. 367, the tragedy deals with the mission of Odysseus and Diomedes, who sneaked into Troy through a sewer and stole the wooden statue called the *Palladium*; cf. Aristophanes, scholium on *The Wasps* 351, and Servius on Virgil, *Aeneid* 2, v. 166. Here is the sequence from the *Little Iliad* in Proclus's summary (ed. Bernabé 74, 15ff.): "Odysseus disfigures himself and goes in to Ilium as a spy, and there being recognized by Helen, plots with her for the taking of the city; after killing certain of the Trojans, he returns to the ships. Next he carries the Palladium out of Troy

with help of Diomedes." The two separate episodes (for the first episode, see the detailed description in *Odyssey* 4, vv. 244–58) are combined in Apollodorus, *Epitome* 5, 13: "Ulysses went with Diomedes by night to the city, and there he let Diomedes wait, and after disfiguring himself and putting on mean attire he entered unknown into the city as a beggar. And being recognized by Helen, he with her help stole away the Palladium, and after killing many of the guards, brought it to the ships with the aid of Diomedes." One of the problems is to tell whether Sophocles dealt with only the second expedition with Diomedes, or instead joined the two expeditions in a single one, as Apollodorus did. The list of tragedies cited by Aristotle seems to plead in favor of the first solution, because *The Laconian Women* is mentioned after *The Begging* (*Ptōkeia*), a tragedy that must be about the first episode in which Odysseus disguised as a beggar (cf. *Odyssey* 4, v. 245) is recognized by Helen. *The Laconian Women* thus corresponds to the following sequence, that of Odysseus's expedition with Diomedes to bring back the statue of Pallas Athena. For the iconography connected with the play, see Séchan, pp. 156–59; Webster, p. 149.

61. ***Laocoon, Laocoön*** (frag. 370–77 Radt). The tragedy belongs to the plays on the Trojan myth (see above, chapter VI, "The Mythic Imagination"). Part of its content is given by Dionysius of Halicarnassus (*Roman Antiquities* 1, 48, 2): "Sophocles, the tragic poet, in his drama *Laocoön* represents Aeneas, just before the taking of the city, as removing his household to Mount Ida in obedience to the orders of his father Anchises, who recalled the injunctions of Aphrodite and from the omens that had lately happened in the case of Laocoön's family conjectured the approaching destruction of the city." Dionysius also cites six verses (frag. 373) spoken by another character, certainly a messenger, recounting Aeneas's departure when he was at the gates of the city, carrying his father on his back and surrounded by all his servants and a crowd that wanted to leave to found a colony of Phrygians elsewhere. But since the historian is interested only in Aeneas's flight, he does not mention what must, given the tragedy's title, have been central in the play, namely the death of Laocoön, the priest of Apollo in Troy, with his son (or his two sons). The epic poem *The Sack of Ilium* (*Iliupersis*) already dealt with this episode, which was summed up this way by Proclus (ed. Bernabé, 88, 6–9): "Then they turned to mirth and feasting believing the war was at an end. But at this very time two serpents appeared and destroyed Laocoon and one of his two sons, a portent which so alarmed the followers of Aeneas that they withdrew to Ida." Cf. Apollodorus *Epitome* 5, 17–18, and Hyginus, *Fables*, 135. Sophocles gave the names of the two serpents in his tragedy (Servius on Virgil, *Aeneid* 2, v. 204 = frag. 372). For the iconography connected with the play, see Séchan, pp. 160–66; Webster, p. 149.

62. ***Larisaioi, The Men of Larissa*** (frag. 378–83 Radt). The tragedy was set in Larissa. As the title indicates, the chorus consisted of citizens of Larissa. The subject was the final destiny of Canisius, the father of Danaë and grandfather of Perseus (see no. 7, *Canisius*; cf. also no. 21, *Danaë*). It is the moment when the

oracle predicting that he would die at his grandson's hand is about to be fulfilled. The precautions he had taken by leaving for Larissa at the time of his grandson's return to Argos proved fruitless. See Pherecydes of Athens (scholium on Apollonius of Rhodes 4, v. 1901 = *FGrHist* 3 F 12 Jacoby); cf. also Apollodorus 2, 4, 4 (47–48): during a contest in Larissa to which foreigners were invited and that offered numerous prizes (frag. 378), a contest organized by Canisius himself or by the king of Larissa, Teutamidas, Perseus wounded his grandfather when he threw a discus that accidentally rolled on his foot. In Sophocles' play, Perseus himself must have recounted what happened during the discus competition (frag. 380). The wound proved mortal. Before leaving, Perseus buried Canisius at the gates of Larissa, and the residents of the city worshipped him as a hero.

63–64. *Lemnai, The Lemnian Women* 1 and 2 (frag. 384–89 Radt). There seem to have been two versions of this tragedy, because Stephanus of Byzantium (257, 5 Meineke = frag. 386) mentions the title "The first Lemnians." The subject is drawn from the myth of the Argonauts' expedition (cf. no. 56, *The Women of Colchis*). When the Argonauts left for Colchis, their first stop was the island of Lemnos. The women of Lemnos, who, in an act of collective murder, had killed their husbands and fathers under the leadership of their queen, Hypsipyle (who nonetheless spared her father Thoas), prevented the Argonauts from landing so long as they did not agree to have intercourse with them. The Lemnian episode was known to Homer, who mentions a son of Jason and Hypsipyle, Euneus (*Iliad* 7, vv. 468–69). In 462 Pindar, in his *Pythian Ode* 4, v. 252, mentions the Lemnian episode, but he situates it during the expedition's return. The myth was dramatized by Aeschylus in his *Hypsipyle* (*TrGF* 3 frag. 247–48 Radt) and perhaps his in his *The Lemnian Women* or *Lemnians* (ibid., frag. 123a–123b). A scholium on Apollonius of Rhodes 1, 769–73 indicates that the episode of the Lemnian women was the subject of Aeschylus's *Hypsipyle* and Sophocles' *The Lemnian Women*: "In his *Argonautics* Herodorus [c. 400 BCE] says that the Argonauts had intercourse with the Lemnian women (*FGrHist* 31 F 6 Jacoby). In his *Hypsipyle* Aeschylus says that the Lemnian women came armed to repel them, and that the Argonauts endured a storm at sea before the Lemnian women obtained from them a promise of intercourse once they had landed. In his *Lemnian Women* Sophocles says that they even fought a violent battle against them." In his play, Sophocles listed all those who took part in the expedition (scholium on Pindar, *Pythian Ode* 4, v. 303 b = frag. 385; cf. frag. 386). The sequence dealt with by Aeschylus and Sophocles was developed in the Hellenistic period by Apollonius of Rhodes, *Argonautica* 1, vv. 609ff., but there is no battle as in Sophocles: on the other hand, the tradition of the battle was taken up by Statius, *Thebiad*, vv. 376–97. Euripides also composed a *Hypsipyle*. However, although he chose the same title as Aeschylus did, his play deals with a different, and later, sequence. Because she had spared her father Thoas during the general androcide, Hypsipyle was sold as a slave when the Lemnian women learned what she had done, and she was made a slave of the king of Nemea. For this sequence, which took place

at the time of the expedition of the Seven against Thebes and the foundation of
the Nemean games, see H. Van Looy, *Euripide*, vol. 8, part 3, Paris: CUF, 2002,
pp. 155ff., and *TrGF* 5. 2, pp. 736–97 Kannicht.

65. ***Manteis è Poluidos, The Seers* or *Polyidus*** (frag. 389a–400 Radt). The
myth concerns Glaucus, the son of Minos (no. 68, *Minos*) and the seer of
Corinth, Polyidus. The story is recounted by Hyginus, *Fables*, 136, under the title
"Polyidus" and by Apollodorus 3, 3 (17–20). The two accounts are identical apart
from a few details. When he was a child, Glaucus, the son of Minos and Pasiphaë, fell into a jug of honey. His father, who had gone to look for him, consulted the oracle of Apollo (or, according to Apollodorus, the Curetes). The reply
was that the man who would solve a riddle would return his son to him. The
riddle was to find the most accurate comparison with a wonder that had been
born in Minos's herd, a calf that changed color in the course of the day: it was
green in the morning, red in the afternoon, and black in the evening. None of
the seers was capable of solving the riddle, except for a seer from Corinth, Polyidus, son of Coiranus (frag. 390). He compared the calf to a blackberry, which is
first green, then, red, and finally black (frag. 395). Minos then asked the seer who
had solved the riddle to find the child. Thanks to his powers of divination,
Polyidus found Glaucus dead. Minos thereupon begged Polyidus to resuscitate
the child. When Polyidus said he could not do that, Minos imprisoned him in
a tomb with the body of his child. A serpent penetrated the tomb. Polyidus killed
it. Another serpent came. Seeing that the first serpent was dead, the second went
to find an herb that it used to resuscitate the first. Seeing that, Polyidus applied
the herb to the child's body and resuscitated him. A passerby heard cries coming
from the tomb and told Minos. According to Hyginus, Minos rewarded the seer
for having restored his child to life. According to Apollodorus, Minos also demanded that Polyidus give Glaucus the gift of prophecy. Against his will, Polyidus gave it to him but then took it back, asking him to spit into his mouth. For
the iconography, see Webster, p. 149.

Before Sophocles, Aeschylus had dramatized this scene in his *Cretan Women*
(*TrGF* 3, frag. 116–20 Radt), and Euripides composed a *Polyidus* (see H. Van
Looy, *Euripide*, vol. 8, part 2, Paris: CUF, 2000, pp. 549ff., and *TrGF* 5.2, pp.
623–32 Kannicht).

66. ***Meleagros, Meleager*** (frag. 401–6 Radt). The family of Meleager is mentioned in Aristotle, *Poetics* 12 (1453 a), among the tragic families par excellence,
along with those of Alcmeon, Oedipus, Orestes, Thyestes, and Telephus. Meleager was the son of the king of Calydon, Oeneus (cf. no. 47, *Hipponous*) and his
first wife, Althea, the daughter of Thestius. Deianira was his sister (see appendix
I, *The Women of Trachis*). In Homer, the myth of Meleager is already recounted
at length by Phoenix during the embassy sent to Achilles to persuade him not
to act like Meleager and to agree to return to the battle before the ships are set
on fire (*Iliad* 9, vv. 529–99); see above, chapter VI, "The Mythic Imagination."
The city of the king of Calydon was at war, besieged by the Curetes. The cause

of the conflict was the body of the giant boar that Meleager had killed with the help of the Curetes and other heroes. This boar had been sent by Artemis to ravage Oeneus's fields (cf. frag 401); Artemis had been angered that she had not received the expected sacrifice from Oeneus. So long as Meleager took part in the battle, the enemy was kept at bay. But scandalized by the attitude of his mother, who had cursed him for the death of his (two) brothers (whom Meleager had probably killed in combat), Meleager withdrew and remained with his wife, Cleopatra, in their bedroom, remaining deaf to the supplications of the elders, who sent priests as envoys, and deaf to the supplications of his father, Oeneus, and his friends, until the Curetes crossed the ramparts and began to burn the city. Meleager's wife then begged him to act. He returned to the fray and routed the enemy. That is what Homer says, drawing a parallel between Meleager and Achilles. Meleager is also mentioned by Hesiod in the *Catalog of Women* (or *Ehoiai*) apropos of the descendants of Althea and Oeneus (frag. 25, 10–13 Merkelbach-West) and in an epic poem (*The Descent of Pirithous* or *Mynias*?), in which Meleager enters into dialogue with Theseus, who has descended into the Underworld (frag. 280 Merkelbach-West—frag. 7 Bernabé). In these two passages, Meleager's death is attributed to the god Apollo fighting on the side of the Curetes, and not to Althea's anger, involving the Erinyes, as is implicit in Homer. The agreement between the *Catalog of Women* and the *Mynias* regarding this version of Meleager's death is mentioned by Pausanias (10, 31, 3) when he describes the paintings in the Lesche of Delphi, where Meleager was represented. In lyric poetry, the myth appears in Bacchylides in his *Epinicia* 5 (476 BCE), in which the dead Meleager talks with Heracles, who has descended into the Underworld to get Cerberus (cf. no. 53, *Cerberus*), and recounts his destiny to him. This time the death of Meleager is explained by the magic firebrand that his mother extinguished when he was born, and then relit to make him die. This is the first time this innovation in the myth appears in an extant text (on the final version of the myth, see Apollodorus 1, 8, 2–3 [65–71]; cf. also Hyginus, *Fables*, 174). However, according to Pausanias (10, 31, 4), this version appears for the first time in a tragedy by Phrynichus (sixth to fifth centuries BCE), *Pleuron's Wives* (*TrGF* 1 frag. 6 Snell), without Phyrnicus presenting it as an innovation. The same tradition concerning Meleager's death is adopted by Aeschylus in *The Libation Bearers*, vv. 602–12.

The extant fragments of Sophocles' play are too slender to allow us to determine which version of Meleager's death he adopted. Neither do we know whether Atalanta played a role in the tragedy. The role of Atalanta, the virgin huntress loved by Meleager (cf. Diodorus 4, 34, the accounts given by Apollodorus and Hyginus cited above, and others, such as Ovid, *Metamorphoses* 8, vv. 317ff.) could not have yet existed in the time of Homer, in whose work Meleager withdraws from combat to stay with his wife Cleopatra. On the other hand, Atalanta seems to have played a role in Euripides' *Meleager*; see H. Van Looy, *Euripide*, vol. 8, part 2, Paris: CUF, 2000, pp. 397–425, and *TrGF* 5.1, pp.

554–68 Kannicht. Aeschylus had already composed an *Atalanta*, but we do not know its subject. It is thought that Apollodorus's second version (1, 8, 3 [72–73]), which is close to that of Homer (without the role given to Atalanta and without death by igniting the firebrand) but ends, after Meleager's death in combat, with the suicides of Althea and Cleopatra, and with the transformation of the mourners into birds (the "Meleagrids"), reflects the version chosen by Sophocles. In fact, Pliny, *Hist. Nat.* 37, 11, 40 (= test. 15 Radt + frag. 830 a Radt), says that Sophocles explained the formation of yellow amber outside India by the tears of the meleagrid birds, that is, of the weeping Meleager. Sophocles must therefore be alluding to his *Meleager*. Radt, while recognizing that this is the opinion of most scholars, prefers to place this fragment in the category of fragments of uncertain origin, basing himself on a remark made by Wilamowitrz (frag. 830 a Radt). Pliny cites Sophocles' explanation of yellow amber as the most egregious example of Greek foolishness among those that he has just listed on this subject. The whole passage deserves to be quoted, because it is exceptional for Sophocles to be criticized so severely: "The one that has surpassed them all is Sophocles, the tragic poet; a thing that indeed surprises me, when I only consider the surpassing gravity of his lofty style, the high repute that he enjoyed in life, his elevated position by birth at Athens, his various exploits, and his high military command. According to him, amber is produced in the countries beyond India, from the tears that are shed for Meleager, by the birds called 'meleagrides!' Who can be otherwise than surprised that he should have believed such a thing as this, or have hoped to persuade others to believe it? What child, too, could possibly be found in such a state of ignorance as to believe that birds weep once a year, that their tears are so prolific as this, or that they go all the way from Greece, where Meleager died, to India to weep? 'But then,' it will be said, 'do not the poets tell many other stories that are quite as fabulous?' Such is the fact, no doubt, but for a person seriously to advance such an absurdity with reference to a thing so common as amber, which is imported every day and so easily proves the mendacity of this assertion, is neither more nor less than to evince a supreme contempt for the opinions of mankind, and to assert with impunity an intolerable falsehood."

A single source provides a precise indication regarding Sophocles' tragedy, namely regarding the composition of the chorus. This is a scholium on Homer apropos of the passage in the *Iliad* in which the elders send priests as envoys to beg Meleager (scholium on the *Iliad* 9, v. 575): "It is from there," says the scholium, "that Sophocles drew his chorus formed of priests in his *Meleager*." The Latin poet Accius composed a *Meleager* (ed. Dangel, pp. 207–11).

67. **Memnon** (no fragments). This tragedy is cited in the argument of *Ajax* as a tragedy belonging to the Trojan cycle, like the *Sons of Antenor* (= no. 16), *The Captive Women* (= no. 6), and *The Rape of Helen* (= no. 25). We have no fragments of it. The subject was probably taken from the sequence in the *Aethiopis* (an epic whose subject continues the subject of the *Iliad*), in which Memnon comes to

the aid of the Trojans. Here is that sequence in Proclus's summary (ed. Bernabé 68, 10–15): "Memnon, the son of Eos, wearing armour made by Hephaestus, comes to help the Trojans, and Thetis tells her son about Memnon. A battle takes place in which Antilochus is slain by Memnon and Memnon by Achilles. Eos then obtains of Zeus and bestows upon her son immortality." Compare Apollodorus, *Epitome* 5, 3: "Memnon, the son of Tithonus and the Dawn, came with a great force of Ethiopians to Troy against the Greeks, and having slain many of the Greeks, including Antilochus, he was himself slain by Achilles." Following this tendency that consists in simplifying the tradition, attempts have been made to identify this tragedy with *The Ethiopians* (no. 5). But Aeschylus wrote two tragedies on Memnon, as we have seen apropos of *The Ethiopians*. Why would Sophocles not also have composed two tragedies about the same character?

68. *Minos* (frag 407 Radt). The title of *Minos* is attested only once, with a single verse cited by Clement of Alexandria, *Stromata* 6, 2, 10, 7. It is a general maxim: "To those who act not, fortune is no ally." Thus we can say nothing about the sequence Sophocles chose from the rich destiny of this son of Zeus and Europa (*Iliad* 14, vv. 321ff.), whose brother was Rhadamanthus, and who after his death was the judge of the Underworld (*Odyssey* 11, vv. 567ff.). The king of Crete's wife is Pasiphaë, the daughter of Helios. One of the best-known episodes concerns the love affair between his wife and the bull sent by Poseidon. This affair was, in fact, instigated by Poseidon to avenge himself on Minos. To have intercourse with the bull, Pasiphaë resorted to Daedalus's ingeniousness (cf. no. 20, *Daedalus*). With Pasiphaë, Minos had two notable daughters, Phaedra and Ariadne. The second known episode connects Ariadne and Theseus. Sent as an Athenian tribute to the Minotaur, Theseus succeeded in killing the monster, who lived in the center of the labyrinth, and to escape, thanks to the thread that Ariadne had given him out of love, on Daedalus's suggestion. When Minos learned of this, he blamed Daedalus and imprisoned him in the labyrinth, from which he escaped by flying (see no. 20, *Daedalus*). Minos pursued him everywhere until he found him in Sicily, where he died as the victim of a trick by Daedalus (see no. 52, *The Men of Camicus*). On Minos and his son Glaucus, see no. 65, *The Seers* or *Polyidus*. The Latin poet Accius composed a tragedy entitled *Minos* or *The Minotaur* (ed. Dangel, p. 187).

69. *Mousai, The Muses* (frag. 407a–408 Radt). The subject of this play, attested by an inscription found in Piraeus that provides, notably, a catalog of Sophocles' works (IG II2 2363, col. 1, 25 = *TrGF* 1 CAT B 1, 25 Snell), and by two fragments, is not known. Some have proposed connecting it with no. 29 (*Thamyras*).

70. *Musoi, The Mysians* (frag. 409–18 Radt). It has been suggested that this play was part of a trilogy or a tetralogy on Telephus, with *The Mysians* coming after *The Sons of Aleus* (no. 8) and before *Telephus* (no. 96). This obviously remains hypothetical; see no. 8 (*the Sons of Aleus*) for the myth of Telephus and *The Telepheia*. As the title indicates, the tragedy's chorus consisted of Mysians,

that is, the residents of the city called Mysia, the site of the tragedy's action (frag. 411). A stranger arrived (frag. 411), to whom a character indicated the place where he had come. In his *Poetics* 24 (1460 a 32) Aristotle mentions a tragedy entitled *The Mysians*, in which the character who arrives in Tegea in Mysia remains silent. This refers to the silence of Telephus, who had been exiled after the murder of his uncles (cf. the comic authors' allusions to this silence: *PGC* II Alexis, frag. 183, 3, and Amphis, frag. 30, 6). Since Aeschylus composed a tragedy with the same name that was also part of a trilogy on Telephus (*TrGF* 3, frag. 143–45 Radt), it is generally thought that Aristotle is referring instead to Aeschylus's tragedy, because the silence of characters entering the stage is a characteristic of Aeschylus's theater that is mocked by Aristophanes' Euripides (cf. *The Frogs*, vv. 913ff.). Nonetheless, if we think that Sophocles' *The Mysians* followed *The Sons of Aleus* in the trilogy, we can agree, on the basis of frag. 111, that in Sophocles' play Telephus also came to Mysia for the first time, without for all that being silent. In that case the tragedy must have ended, after reversals among which was the victory over Idas, King Teuthras's enemy, with a recognition scene between Telephus and his mother; cf. Hyginus, *Fables*, 100 (Teuthras) and also *Anth. Pal.* 3, 2. However, these variants of the myth are too numerous to allow us to determine the choices made by Sophocles in dealing with the sequence. In particular, was Auge King Teuthras's wife (cf. Alcidamas, *Odysseus*, c. 14) or was she considered his daughter (cf. Hyginus, *Fables*, 99 and 100)? And we cannot exclude the possibility that *The Mysians* was devoted to another sequence connected with the Trojan myth. Couldn't the stranger who arrives (frag. 111) be an Achaean emissary during the Achaeans' first attempt to conquer Troy, which we know went astray in Mysia, thinking it had arrived at Troy? During this first expedition, Telephus, king of the Mysians, defending his territory, killed Thersander, the son of Polynices, and was himself wounded by Achilles, before the expedition retreated. This sequence of the myth was dealt with in the epic *Cypria*; see also Proclus's summary, ed. Bernabé 40, 36ff.; cf. Apollodorus, *Epitome* 3, 17. For the iconography, see Webster, p. 149.

71. ***Momos saturikos, Momus*** (satyr play). (frag. 419–24 Radt). In Greek, *momos* means "blame," "reproach." In Hesiod's *Theogony* (v. 214), Momus is a son of Night. According to a scholium on the *Iliad* I v. 5, he appealed to Zeus when he decided to relieve the Earth, which was being crushed under the weight of humans. Zeus first started the war of the Seven against Thebes, and then, when he intended to completely destroy humanity by lightning and floods, he was dissuaded him from doing so by Momus, who advised him to arrange two things: Thetis's marriage to a mortal (Peleus) and the birth of a beautiful girl (Helen), which led to the Trojan War, and once again relieved the Earth by causing a new series of deaths. This myth was found, according to the scholium, in the epic *Cypria*. The name Momus does not, however, appear in Proclus's summary, where it is said simply that Zeus made his decision with Themis to provoke the Trojan War (ed. Bernabé 38, 4). But the summary is very general. Another

act of Momus's is known through Lucian, *Hermotimus* 20, according to which Momus, in a judgment analogous to that of Paris, blamed Hephaestus for having made a model of a human without windows in his chest to show his thoughts and reveal whether or not he is telling the truth. See *Das griechische Satyrspiel*, pp. 363–67.

72. ***Nauplios katapleon, Nauplius Sails In*** (frag. 425–28 Radt). Sophocles composed two plays on Nauplius. They are distinguished by different complements: *Nauplius Sails In* and *Nauplius Lights a Fire*. However, some fragments (frag. 432 to 438 Radt) are attributed to *Nauplius* without further specification and may therefore theoretically belong to one or the other of the plays. Nauplius, the son of Poseidon, a redoubtable sailor (see no. 8, *The Sons of Aleus*), is the father of Palamedes. During the Trojan War, Odysseus unjustly accused Nauplius's son of high treason, and he is stoned to death (no. 80, *Palamedes*). When Nauplius learned of his son's death, he went to Troy and demanded reparations. He did not succeed and decided to avenge himself: he traveled along the Greek coast to ask the warriors' wives to deceive their husbands—Agamemnon's wife, Diomedes', Idomeneus's, and others. Then he seized ten cities in Crete where he made himself tyrant; cf. Apollodorus, *Epitome* 6, 8–10, and John Tzetzes, commentary "On Lycophron," v. 384. Nauplius's praise of his son's discoveries (frag. 432: eleven verses) can reasonably be attributed to this tragedy. It was probably when he went to plead his son's case before the leaders of the expedition to Troy that he delivered such a eulogy.

73. ***Naupliuos purkaeus, Nauplius Lights a Fire*** (frag. 429–31 Radt). Nauplius sought vengeance during the storm that assailed the Achaeans' expedition, south of Euboea as they were returning after the Trojan War; see above, chapter VI, "The Mythic Imagination." By night he lit fires at places where the coast was rocky (the Gyraean Rocks). Pilots, thinking they could land, wrecked their ships against the rocks. Nauplius killed the survivors; see Apollodorus, *Epitome* 6, 7, and 11; Hyginus, *Fables*, 116 (Nauplius). This was the subject of Sophocles' tragedy; cf. Pollux 9, 156, according to whom Aeschylus had composed a *Prometheus's Fires* and Sophocles a *Nauplius Lights a Fire*. In his *Helen*, vv. 767 and 1126ff., Euripides alludes to these fires lit by Nauplius. In his *Automata* (22, 3–6), Hero of Alexandria describes an animated tableau corresponding to the myth of Nauplius and his fires, with marionettes in a succession of several scenes: the preparation of the Achaeans' fleet (for the return from Troy), the ships setting out to sea, the crossing with the appearance of dolphins, the arrival of the storm, Nauplius the lighter of fires with Athena at his side, the wreck of the fleet, Ajax (the Locrian) swimming, struck by lightning, then his marionette disappearing. The artist was able, in a way, to take his inspiration from Sophocles' tragedy. See C. W. Marshall, "Sophocles' Nauplius and Heron of Alexandria's mechanical theater," in A. H. Sommerstein (ed.), *Shards from Kolonos* (2003), pp. 261–79.

74. ***Nausikaa è plunteriai, Nausicaa* or *The Women Washing Clothes*** (frag. 439–41 Radt). This play has two titles. It was designated either by the name of

the main character or by the chorus. It is one of Sophocles' plays drawn from the *Odyssey*; cf. *Life of Sophocles* 20 (test. 1 Radt = appendix V): "He takes the *Odyssey* as his model in several plays"; cf. also no. 76, *The Bath*, and no. 106, *The Phaeacians*. The subject is drawn from *Odyssey* 6, vv. 99ff., where Odysseus, having landed on the coast after his shipwreck, encounters Nausicaa, the daughter of the king of the Phaeacians, Alcinous. She has come to wash clothing with her servants, following the suggestion of Athena, who appeared to her in a dream. Once the clothes are washed and spread out to dry, Nausicaa eats and then plays ball with her servants, who form the play's chorus. When all their clothes fall in the river, the girls' cries awaken Odysseus, who approaches them naked and makes all the young girls flee except Nausicaa, to whom Athena lends courage. Tradition reports that Sophocles himself played the role of Nausicaa throwing the ball to her servants and that his dexterity was admired (Athenaeus, 1, 20 3; Eustathius, Comm. *Iliad* 381, 8, and *Odyssey* 1553, 63; see above, chapter I, "The Young Sophocles." For this reason, the play is dated to the first period of Sophocles' production. Among the paintings on the left side of the Propylaea (in the *Pinakotheke*) there was a picture by Polygnotus showing "Odysseus coming upon the women washing clothes with Nausicaa at the river, just like the description in Homer" (Pausanias 1, 22, 6). The subjects of the painting and the play are, to be sure, identical; but the discussions of the relations between the picture and the play remain speculative. On the nature of the play, whether a tragedy or a satyr play, see *Das griechische Satyrspiel*, pp. 394–95. For the iconography connected with the play, see Séchan, pp. 167–72, Webster, pp. 149ff., and Trendall and Webster, pp., 66ff.

75. **Niobe** (frag. 441a–451 Radt and frag. 441 aa in *Addenda et Corrigenda* in vol. 3, pp. 575–76 Radt, and in vol. 4, 2nd ed., p. 758). The story of Niobe is famous. It was well known to Homer, who gives the oldest extant version (*Iliad* 24, vv. 602–17). Her fate is mentioned in two of Sophocles' extant tragedies, *Antigone* (vv. 823–33) and *Electra* (vv. 150–53). See M. Hopman, "Une déesse en pleurs," *Revue des Études Grecques* 117, 2004, pp. 447–67. What is mentioned in these tragedies is her eternal sorrow. Niobe was petrified on Mount Sipylus in Asia Minor, where she constantly weeps over the death of her children. Sophocles' two heroines, Antigone and Electra, compare their destiny with hers. Aeschylus had already composed a tragedy entitled *Niobe*, in which she mourned the death of her children (*TrGF* 3, frag. 154a–167 Radt). We know that Niobe boasted of being a mother more fortunate than Leto because she had more children (twelve, according to Homer, six boys and six girls, whereas Leto had only two, Apollo and Artemis). Apollo killed her sons, and Artemis killed her daughters. The gods turned her to stone, and her tears are eternal. In Aeschylus, the murders had taken place before the time of the action, which began with a long silence on the part of Niobe, who was veiled and overwhelmed by sorrow (see Aristophanes, *The Frogs*, vv. 911–13). In Sophocles, on the contrary, the murder of the sons and daughters took place during the time of the tragedy, if

it is true that *P. Oxy.* no. 2805, published in 1971 (frag. 441 a Radt), and *P. Oxy.* no. 3653, published in 1984, giving a fragment and the argument of a *Niobe* (= frag. 441 aa), do in fact correspond to Sophocles' play. The setting was Thebes. Niobe, the daughter of the Lydian Tantalus (no. 94, *Tantalus*), was the wife of Amphion, who built, with his brother Zethus, Thebes' ramparts. According to Sophocles, Niobe had seven sons and seven daughters (frag. 446). Apollo killed the sons during a hunt, and when Amphion found out about it he challenged the god, but he was also killed (frag. 441 aa). Apollo, who appeared in the tragedy, urged his sister to kill the daughters, who had remained at home (frag. 441 aa). After the death of her children, Niobe left for Lydia (scholium T Hom. *Iliad* 24, v. 602: "Sophocles says that her children died in Thebes, and that she went to Lydia").

76. **Niptra, *The Bath*** (frag. 451 a Radt). A play drawn from the *Odyssey* like no. 74 (*Nausicaa*); see also no. 106, *The Phaeacians*. The central scene must have been the recognition of Odysseus by his nurse when she saw his scar as she washed his feet (cf. *Odyssey* 19, vv. 357ff.); see chapter VI, "The Mythic Imagination." Pacuvius wrote a tragedy with the same title that included not only the bath, but also represented Odysseus wounded. Since Cicero (*Tusculan Disputations* 2, 48–50) considers the attitude of the wounded Odysseus more heroic in Pacuvius's *The Bath* than in Sophocles (without specifying the title of the tragedy), many scholars have concluded, since Brunck, that Sophocles' play entitled *The Bath* was not different from the one that is entitled *Odysseus Wounded by the Spine* (above, no. 77). But as has been pointed out by a minority of scholars, if Sophocles followed the epic poems faithfully, he could hardly have combined two sequences that are very far apart in the epic model, the recognition of Odysseus when he returns, which occurs in *Odyssey* 19, and his death, which occurs much later, at the end of the *Telegony*. Thus it can be argued that Pacuvius combined two of Sophocles' plays in a single tragedy; cf. Séchan, p. 178, and P. Venini, "Sui Niptra di Pacuvio," *Rendiconti dell'Istituto Lombardo*, 87, 1954, pp. 175–87. For the iconography, see Séchan, pp. 173–80; Webster, p. 150.

77. **Odusseus akanthoplex, *Odysseus Wounded by the Spine*** (frag. 453–61a Radt). The subject is taken from the final episode of the epic dealing with the sequence that comes after the *Odyssey*, namely the *Telegony* (see chapter VI, "The Mythic Imagination," where Proclus's summary is quoted). After learning the identity of his father, Telegonus, the son Odysseus had with Circé, sets out to find him. He lands on the island of Ithaca and ravages it. Having come to the aid of the people of Ithaca, Odysseus is killed by his son, who does not recognize him; cf. also Apollodorus, *Epitome* 7, 16 and 36–37, and Hyginus, *Fables*, 127 (Telegonus); cf. also the argument of the *Odyssey* in the *Palatinus* (scholia on the *Odyssey*, ed. Dindorf, vol. 1, pp. 6, 13–23). In his *Poetics* 14 (1453 b 33ff.), Aristotle mentions Telegonus as an example of a character who in the course of the tragedy's action kills someone without realizing what he has done. Aristotle gives the tragedy's title: *The Wounded Odysseus*, but not the author's name. It is generally

thought that this refers to Sophocles' tragedy. The qualifier in the title that has come down to us, "wounded by the spine," comes from the fact that Telegonus's sword was made with the spine of a fish, a kind of ray (see Apollodorus, *Epitome* 7, 36; scholium on the *Odyssey* 11, v. 134). The fragments in which the oracle of Dodona is mentioned (frag. 455, 456, 461) must be related to the fact that an oracle had told Odysseus that he would die by his son's hand (cf. Hyginus, *Fables*, 127, and the argument of the *Odyssey* cited above, in which the origin of the oracle is not, however, specified). The oracle of Dodona thus played a role in this tragedy, as it did in *The Women of Trachis*. Sophocles must have combined this prediction with the one that Tiresias made to Odysseus regarding his future destiny when he spoke with the dead during his homeward journey: after the massacre of the suitors, he was to leave again with his oar over his shoulder until he met a stranger who would mistake his oar for a winnowing fan (*Odyssey* 11, vv. 121–37). Toward the end of the tragedy, Odysseus was to appear on a litter, mortally wounded, like Heracles in *The Women of Trachis*, lamenting and weeping unrestrainedly; the scene was adopted by the Latin tragic dramatist Pacuvius in his play entitled *The Bath* (see above, no. 76).

78. ***Odusseus mainomenos, The Madness of Odysseus*** (frag. 462–69 Radt). Odysseus pretended to be mad when he did not want to participate in the expedition against Troy, even though he had sworn, like all of Helen's suitors, to come to the aid of the man she married (cf. the allusion to this oath in *Philoctetes*, v. 72); see above, chapter VI, "The Mythic Imagination." His madness was unmasked by Palamedes (no. 80, *Palamedes*). This episode was found in the epic *Cypria*. Here is Proclus's summary (ed. Bernabé 40, 30–33): "Then they travel round Greece assembling the leaders. Odysseus feigned insanity, as he did not want to take part in the expedition, but they found him out by acting on a suggestion of Palamedes and snatching his son Telemachus for a beating." Apollodorus's *Epitome* (3, 7) says much the same: "When Ulysses pretended to rave, Palamedes followed him, and snatching Telemachus from Penelope's bosom, drew his sword as if he would kill him. And in his fear for the child Ulysses confessed that his madness was pretended, and he went to the war." A variant is given by Hyginus, *Fables*, 95: "He put on a cap, pretending madness, and yoked a horse and an ox to the plow. Palamedes felt he was pretending when he saw this, and taking his son Telemachus from the cradle, put him in front of the plow with the words: 'Give up your pretense and come and join the allies.' Then Ulysses promised that he would come; from that time he was hostile to Palamedes." Same variant in Philostratus, *Heroicus* (*On Heroes*) 33, 4 de Lannoy. Lucien (second century) describes a picture (*The Hall* 30) whose subject is the same as Sophocles' tragedy: it shows the Greek ambassadors sent to fetch Odysseus, who is simulating madness with a bizarre outfit, Palamedes drawing his sword as if to kill Telemachus, Odysseus's son, and Odysseus, faced by his son's peril, putting an end to his dissimulation. Compare no. 54 (*Cedalion*), end.

79, **Oinomaos, Oenomaus** (frag. 471–77 Radt). Stobaeus 3, 27, 6 designates this play under the name of *Hippodamia* (= frag. 472). Even though the fragments are too few to allow us to reconstitute the action, the chariot race, which must have been central to the tragedy and the object of a messenger's narrative analogous that that of the tutor in *Electra*, is famous. This race had already been represented on Cypelus's chest, an offering to Olympia described by Pausanias, *Description of Greece*, 5, 17, 7: "Oenomaus is pursuing Pelops, who has Hippodamia: each of them has two horses, but the horses of Pelops are winged." The chorus in Sophocles' *Electra* (v. 505) alludes to this race. Before the tragedy, this myth was already present in Pindar's *Olympian Ode* dating from 476 BCE. Oenomaus, king of Pisa (in Elis) forced all suitors to undergo a test, a chariot race; the suitor started, carrying Hippodamia on his chariot, and if Oenamaus, whose horses had been given him by Ares, caught him, he killed him. Oenomaus had already killed thirteen suitors in this way (*Ol.* 1, v. 79) when Pelops, Tantalus's son, set out in the race; according to Pindar, Pelops won, thanks to a golden chariot and winged horses, a gift from Poseidon (*Ol.* 1, v. 87). In the tragic myth, Pelops won his victory by trickery, by bribing Myrtilus, Oenomaus's coachman. The wheel of Oenomaus's chariot fell off, and his chariot was smashed to pieces. Then the victorious Pelops, taking Hippodamia and Myrtilus with him on his winged chariot, threw Myrtilus into the sea, and this was the source of the curses on the tragic family of the Pelopids (Sophocles, *Electra*, v. 509; Euripides, *Orestes*, v. 900 with a long scholium on the passage). Oenomaus was one of the tragedies that dealt with a hero's passage from good fortune to ill. Hippodamia, his daughter, was one of the play's characters (frag. 474). The tragedy is earlier than 414, because three verses are cited by Aristophanes in his *The Birds* (vv. 1337–39, with scholium). Euripides also composed a tragedy with the same title, but the fragments are no more explicit. See H. Van Looy, *Euripide*, vol. 8, 2, Paris: CUF, 2000, pp. 477ff. (with the main sources of the myth, p. 477, n. 1), and *TrGF* 5.2, pp. 591–95 Kannicht. The Latin poet Accius composed a tragedy entitled *Oenomaus* (ed. Dangel 110–13). For the iconography, see Webster, p. 150.

80. **Palamedes** (frag. 478–81 Radt). Compare no. 72 (*Nauplius Sails In*) and no. 78 (*The Madness of Odysseus*). Palamedes, son of Nauplius, famous for his inventive mind, had unmasked the madness Odysseus simulated, and the latter never forgave him and took revenge on him. The myth, which Homer does not discuss, is attested in the epic *Cypria*, where Odysseus, aided by Diomedes, drowned Palamedes during a fishing trip (Pausanias 10, 31, 2 = frag. 30 Bernabé). The version used in the tragedies is different (cf. Polyaenus 1, Preamble 12): Odysseus, after fabricating two proofs (a false letter and gold placed in Palamedes' home and alleged to proceed from the enemy), accuses Palamedes of high treason. Palamedes was condemned and stoned to death by the army. The main testimonies on this sequence contain variations in detail (Apollodorus, *Epitome* 3, 7–8; Hyginus, *Fables*, 105; scholium on Euripides, *Orestes*, v. 452; Alcidamas,

Odysseus). But it is pointless to try to connect Sophocles' tragedy with Hyginus's version rather than with another one. In a famous fragment of the tragedy (frag. 479), a character mentions that among Palamedes' inventions was the game of checkers and ice to forget hunger and while away the time (compare no. 72, *Nauplius Sails In*, frag. 432). The sequence Sophocles chose cannot be determined with certainty. It is likely that it was devoted to the preparations for Odysseus's vengeance (cf. frag 478: a servant who is ordered to silently carry the gold into Palamedes' tent?) and the accusation against Palamedes (cf. frag. 479, words uttered by a defender of Palamedes, perhaps in an agōn scene). If we situate the tragedies Sophocles wrote about Nauplius and his son Palamedes in the chronology of the myth, we have the following plausible order: no. 8, *The Sons of Aleus* (birth of Telephus); no. 78, *The Madness of Odysseus*; no. 80, *Palamedes*; no. 72, *Nauplius Sails In*; and no. 73, *Nauplius Lights a Fire*.

Aeschylus had already written a *Palamedes* (*TrGF* 3, frag. 181–82a Radt), and Euripides also had a *Palamedes* performed in 415; it is mentioned by Aristophanes in the *Thesmophoriazusae* (F. Jouan, *Euripide*, vol. 8, 2, Paris: CUF, 2000, pp. 487ff., and *TrGF* 5.2, pp. 596–605 Kannicht). The three tragic poets praised Palamedes' discoveries, which included the science of numbers, and Plato (*Republic* 7, 522 d) mocks the tragedians on this point. The myth of Palamedes was not used solely by the tragic authors; it was also used in rhetorical exercises: cf. Gorgias's *Defense of Palamedes* (Diels and Kranz 82 B 11 a).

81. ***Pandora è sphurokopoi, Pandora* or *The Hammerers*** (frag. 482–86 Radt). It is assumed, on the basis of the title, that the subject is the creation of Pandora, the first woman, and the misfortunes she brings to mortals. The myth is attested in Hesiod, especially in *Works and Days*, vv. 54ff. (see also *Theogony*, vv. 570ff.): angry at Prometheus, who had stolen fire to give it to humans, Zeus gives humans a gift named "Pandora" because it is a gift from all the gods (*Works and Days*, vv. 81ff.). He has Hephaestus make, with the help of Athena, Aphrodite, and Hermes, a woman in the image of the immortal goddesses. Hermes gives the present to Epimetheus, Prometheus's thoughtless brother. The woman opens a jar from which escape all misfortunes, and especially illnesses. Only hope remains inside the jar. The chorus, as the second title indicates, must have been composed of blacksmiths (literally, "those who strike with the hammer"), perhaps satyrs working in the forge of Hephaestus, who was assigned to create Pandora. The mention of a chamber pot (frag. 485) also suggests that this was a satyr play. In frag. 482, a character (an envoy from Zeus?) addresses another (Hephaestus?) asking him to make Pandora out of clay thinned with water, exactly as in Hesiod (*Works and Days*, v. 61). See *Das griechische Satyrspiel*, pp. 375–80. For the iconography, see Webster, pp. 150ff.

82. ***Peleus*** (frag. 487–91 Radt). In this play, Peleus, the father of Achilles, is very old. He appears accompanied by a woman who is the only one caring for him, like a child (frag. 487). The tragedy must have dealt with the elderly Peleus's misfortunes after the death of his son, when his grandson Neoptolemus had not

yet returned from Troy. Peleus had been deprived of power. There is already an indirect allusion to this in Homer: Achilles' ghost in the *Odyssey* 11, vv. 494–97, asks Odysseus if his aged father was able to keep his power. According to some, he was in reality dethroned by Acastus, son of Pelias, king of Iolcos; according to others, by Acastus's two sons. The first version is found in Euripides, in *The Trojan Women* (vv. 1126–28): Neoptolemus, Peleus's grandson, having left Troy with Andromache, hastened his departure because he learned that his grandfather, the king of Phthia, had been expelled by Acastus. The second variant is attested in Apollodorus (*Epitome* 6, 13): Peleus was driven from power by the sons of Acastus, and after Peleus's death, Neoptolemus reconquered the kingdom he had received from his father. Details regarding Peleus's exile are given by two scholia (a scholium on Euripides' *The Trojan Women*, v. 1128, and a scholium on Pindar's *Pythian Ode* 3, v. 166 = Callimachus, frag. 178, 24 Pfeiffer): having left to find Neoptolemus, he is supposed to have gone aground, because of a storm, on the small island of Icos, north of Euboea, where he was received by an Abantian named Molon and died pitifully. Peleus's misfortunes and the vengeance Neoptolemus took on Acastus and his sons are recounted differently and in a more fantastic fashion by Dictys of Crete, *Journal of the Trojan War* 6, 7–9 (see English translation by R. M. Frazer, *The Trojan War: The Chronicles of Dictys of Crete and Dares the Phrygian*, Bloomington: University of Indiana Press, 1966): Peleus, to escape Acastus's violence, took refuge in a seaside cavern in the region of Cape Sepias in Thessaly; Neoptolemus, after weathering a storm in which he lost most of his fleet, lands by accident at this place, finds his grandfather there, and learns of his misfortunes. He takes advantage of a hunt to which Acastus's sons happen to have come to introduce himself to them, in disguise. Then he kills them one after the other, and when their father arrives, kills him as well. Some scholars have tried to see in this story a reflection of Sophocles' *Peleus*, but that is merely a hypothesis. The play is earlier than 414, because it was known to Aristophanes in his *The Birds* (frag. 489–91). In his *Poetics* (c. 18 (1456 a 1ff.)) Aristotle cites *Peleus* as an example of a tragedy of character on the model of *The Women of Phthia*. To be sure, Aristotle does not mention the author's name. But since *The Women of Phthia* is by Sophocles (= no. 108), we can infer that this also refers to his *Peleus*, even though Euripides also composed a tragedy with this title; see H. Van Looy, *Euripide*, vol. 8, 2, Paris: CUF, 2000, pp. 531–40, and *TrGF* 5.2, pp. 615–17 Kannicht. The fragments of Euripides' *Peleus* are too general to allow us to determine the subject. However, it is thought that Euripides chose a sequence from the life of Peleus earlier than the one Sophocles chose.

83. **Poimenes, *The Shepherds*** (frag. 497–521 Radt). "In his *Shepherds*, Sophocles says that Protesilaus was killed by Hector" (scholium on Lycophron 530 = frag. 497). This is a sequence from the Trojan myth inspired by the epic *Cypria*, summed up this way by Proclus (ed. Bernabé 42, 53–55): "Then the Greeks try to land at Ilium, but the Trojans prevent them, and Protesilaus is killed by Hector. Achilles then kills Cycnus, the son of Poseidon, and drives the Trojans back.

And the Greeks take up their dead." Cf. Apollodorus, *Epitome* 3, 29. Thus this is the sequence in which the Greeks land at Troy and engage in the first battles. In the chronology of the myth, the sequence dealt with in *The Shepherds* follows *Those Who Dine Together* (no. 93) and precedes *The Demand for Helen's Return* (no. 24). The action is seen from the Trojan point of view. Hector is one of the characters (frag. 498, where we can read a verse from the passage in which Hector expresses his desire to fight against the Achaeans). The chorus consists of Trojan shepherds (cf. frag. 515). One character, presumably a messenger, has seen the army land (frag. 502). The sequence included not only the death of Protesilaus killed by Hector, but also that of Cygnus, the son of Poseidon, whose white skin had won him his name (*Cycnus*, "the Swan"); cf. Hesiod, frag. 237 Merkelbach-West. In Sophocles' play, he must have already been invulnerable by bronze or iron (frag. 500 and 508). But as he retreated, he struck his head against a stone and was strangled by Achilles (cf. Ovid, *Metamorphoses* 12, vv. 64–145, where the combat between Achilles and Cygnus is described at length). The play is mentioned in the fragment of a document concerning the contest in which Sophocles came in second, whereas Aeschylus won first prize with his trilogy containing *The Suppliants* (*P. Oxy.* 2256 frag. 3 = *TrGF* 1 Snell DID C 6, 7 = *TrGF* 3, test. 70 Radt); see above, chapter IV, "Sophocles and Dionysus: The Theatrical Career." If this does in fact refer to Sophocles' play, it belongs to his oldest production (probably 463 BCE); but the end of the papyrus is very uncertain. Regarding the nature of the play, whether a tragedy or a satyr play, see recently R. M. Rosen, "Revisiting Sophocles' *Poimenes*: Tragedy or Satyr Play?," in A. H. Sommerstein (ed.), *Shards from Kolonos* (2003), pp. 373–86.

84. **Poluxene, Polyxena** (frag. 522–28 Radt). This is another play based on the Trojan myth. See above chapter VI, "The Mythic Imagination." Like Euripides' *Hecuba*, Sophocles' *Polyxena* is set at the time of the Greeks' departure after sacking Troy. It deals with a mythic sequence that appears in the epic poems of the Trojan cycle, both at the end of the *Sack of Ilium* (*Iliupersis*) and at the beginning of *Returns from Troy* (*Nostoi*). Here is Proclus's summary (ed. Bernabé 94, 9–11): "When Agamemnon and his followers were sailing away, the ghost of Achilles appeared and tried to prevent them by foretelling what should befall them." The sacrifice of Polyxena was dealt with by Euripides in his *Hecuba*—where she was sacrificed by Neoptolemus—and before Euripides by the lyric poet Ibycus (scholium on Euripides, *Hecuba*, v. 41 = *PMG* frag. 307 Page). But a scholium on the beginning of *Hecuba* (v. 1) explains that "what concerns Polyxena can also be found in Sophocles' *Polyxena*." The scene was set in the Troad (frag. 522). In Sophocles' play, Achilles' ghost appears on his tomb, probably at the beginning of the tragedy, just as Polydorus's ghost appeared at the beginning of Euripides' *Hecuba*. The first three verses that he speaks are extant (frag. 523). They are comparable to the first two verses of Euripides' *Hecuba*, which are spoken by Polydorus's ghost. This apparition was impressive (*On the Sublime*, 15, 7). Achilles must have asked the Achaean to compensate him by granting him

part of the honor. Another theme of the tragedy was the dispute between the two Atreids, Agamemnon and Menelaus. Here is Proclus's summary of this sequence (ed. Bernabé 94, 3–4): "Athena causes a quarrel between Agamemnon and Menelaus about the voyage from Troy. Agamemnon then stays on to appease the anger of Athena." Nestor had already told Telemachus about this quarrel in *Odyssey* 3 (vv. 130–58). A scene in *Polyxena* opposed Menelaus to Agamemnon. We have a fragment (frag. 522) in which Menelaus says to Agamemnon: "So you, living here on the land of Ida itself, gather together Olympia's flocks and make a sacrifice." The sequence of the myth dealt with by Sophocles in his *Polyxena* and by Euripides in *The Trojan Women* was to be taken up by Seneca in his tragedy also entitled *The Trojan Women*. For an attempted reconstruction of Sophocles' tragedy, see W. M. Calder III, "A Reconstruction of Sophocles' *Polyxena*," *GRBS* 7, 1966, pp. 31–56. For the apparition of Achilles' ghost, see R. Bardel, "Spectral Traces: Ghosts in Tragic Fragments," in F. MacHardy et al., *Lost Dramas of Classical Athens* (2005), pp. 83–112 (pp. 92–100). For the play, see recently A. H. Sommerstein et al., *Sophocles: Selected Fragmentary Plays* I, Oxford, 2006, pp. 41–83. For the iconography, see Webster, p. 151.

85. ***Priamos, Priam*** (frag. 528a–532 Radt). The king of Troy was a character that Athenians were used to seeing in tragedies (see Aristophanes, *The Birds*, vv. 511ff.). The very slender fragments (four words!) offer hardly any clues to the subject. We might think of the famous episode of the death of Priam, killed by Neoptolemus on the altar of Zeus during the capture of Troy, a theme dealt with in *The Sack of Ilium*. Here is the episode in Proclus's summary (ed. Bernabé 88, vv. 13–14): "Neoptolemus kills Priam who had fled to the altar of Zeus Herceius"; cf. also *Little Iliad*, frag. 16 Bernabé; Pindar, *Paeans*, 6, vv. 113–15; Apollodorus, *Epitome* 4, 21. Some point, however, to a preceding episode recounted in *Iliad* 24: "Priam visits Achilles to ask him to return, in exchange for ransom, the body of his son Hector." In that case, *Priam* would be another title of the tragedy entitled *The Phrygians* (no. 114).

86. ***Procris*** (frag. 533 Radt). Procris, the daughter of Erectheus, the king of Athens, was married to Cephalus. Before wedding Procris, Cephalus was abducted by Aurora, with whom he had a son, Phaeton (Hesiod, *Theogony*, vv. 986ff.). The relations between Procris and Cephalus gave rise to fantastic variants. According to one rather ancient source (the genealogy of the gods written by the historian Pherecydes of Athens, book 7, scholium on Homer's *Odyssey* 11, v. 321 = *FGrHist* 3 F 34 Jacoby), Cephalus put his young wife, who was still a virgin, to the test by declaring that he was leaving to travel abroad for eight years, but he came back having changed his appearance and succeeded in seducing Procris and having sex with her. He then revealed his identity to her and showed his anger by reproaching her for allowing herself to be seduced. They reconciled. Then it was Procris's turn to feel jealous. Since Cephalus often went hunting, she questioned a servant who told her that her husband went to a mountain peak and cried: "O Cloud, come!" Procris went to this peak, hid, and when she heard

her husband utter these words, showed herself. Outraged, Cephalus killed her on the spot with an arrow. "The story of Procris is told by all men," Pausanias declares (10, 29, 6). For variants and later versions of the myth, see for instance Apollodorus 3, 15 (197–98), Hyginus, *Fables*, 189, and Ovid, *Metamorphoses* 7, vv. 690ff. This was probably the subject of Sophocles' tragedy, but we have no precise evidence regarding the way he dealt with the myth. Cephalus was put on trial for homicide in Athens, before the Areopagus, six generations before the trial of Orestes, and he was sentenced to exile, according to Hellanicus of Lesbos, a historian of the fifth century BCE (see the scholium on Euripides, *Orestes*, v. 1648, which gives a long quotation from Hellanicus = *FGrHist* 4 F 169 Jacoby). Sophocles surely did not fail to include this trial so well known to Athenians, as Pearson notes (II, p. 171); in the sole extant fragment he sees a possible reference to the judges of the Areopagus (frag. 533). For the iconography, see Webster, p. 151.

87. ***Rhizotomoi, Root-Cutters*** (frag. 534–36 Radt; cf. frag. 648). In this play, "Sophocles describes Medea cutting noxious plants, but turning her head away to avoid dying by the power of the odor, and pouring the sap into brazen vessels" (Macrobius, *Saturnalia*, 5, 19, 8, also giving frag. 534). This is the only reliable information we have on this play. We can presume, on the basis of the title, that the chorus was formed of men or women (the Greek word *rhizotomoi* can be either masculine or feminine) cutting roots, that is, plants with harmful or beneficial properties, probably Medea's servants. A female chorus may be more likely. The chorus's invocation of the Sun and Hecate (frag. 535) has been preserved. The play is one in a series of plays about Medea and the expedition of the Argonauts: *The Women of Colchis* (no. 56) and *The Scythians* (no. 91). Its subject remains undetermined. Nevertheless, just as *The Women of Colchis* deals with the magician Medea in Colchis, when she is helping Jason meet the tests that are imposed on him to win the golden fleece, it is thought that *The Root-Cutters* is located in Iolcos (now Volos, in Thessaly), after the return of the Argonauts, when Medea helped Jason take revenge on Pelias, king of Iolcus. She persuaded the king's daughters to boil him in a cauldron to rejuvenate him. He was scalded (see Pindar, *Pythian Ode* 4 v. 251, which dates from 462; in this ode, Medea is called "the murderer of Pelias"). Its subject would thus be analogous to that of Euripides' *Peliades*, a tragedy performed in 455 BCE; for the variants of the myth and Euripides' tragedy, see H. Van Looy, *Euripide*, vol. 8, 2, Paris: CUF, 2000, pp. 515–30, and *TrGF* 5.2, pp. 607–14 Kannicht. An indication confirming the hypothesis that the subject had to do with Medea as the murderer of Pelias is that Erotian, a scholiast on Hippocrates who was a contemporary of Nero's, attributes an expression (frag. 648 Radt) to a *Pelias* composed by Sophocles that would be the same play under a different title—*Pelias* or *The Root Cutters*—depending on whether it takes its name from the chorus or from a character in the play (Welcker, pp. 340–44). However, this reasonable hypothesis is not a certitude, as is too often thought.

88. **Salmoneus** (satyr play) (frag. 537–41a Radt). Salmoneus, less well known than his brother Sisyphus (no. 90, *Sisyphus*), is one of the three sons of Aeolus, king of Thessaly (who gave his name to the Aeolians) and his wife, Enarete. He is the perfect example of a man suffering from proud madness. Here is what Apollodorus says about him in his *Library* 1, 9, 7 (89): "Salmoneus at first dwelt in Thessaly, but afterwards he came to Elis and there founded a city. And being arrogant and wishful to put himself on an equality with Zeus, he was punished for his impiety; for he said that he was himself Zeus, and he took away the sacrifices of the god and ordered them to be offered to himself; and by dragging dried hides, with bronze kettles, at his chariot, he said that he thundered, and by flinging lighted torches at the sky he said that he lightened. But Zeus struck him with a thunderbolt, and wiped out the city he had founded with all its inhabitants"; cf. Hyginus, *Fables*, 61; Virgil, *Aeneid* 6, vv. 586–94. Such a myth can easily give rise to a satyr drama. Salmoneus is also mentioned as having "the voice of the wineskin" in Sophocles' lost play *Ajax the Locrian* (no. 3, frag. 10 c.v. 6 Radt). The myth of Salmoneus is supposed to extend over several generations before the Trojan War, because his daughter Tyro (cf. no. 102–3 *Tyro*) is the mother of Neleus, whose son Nestor is oldest figure involved in the Trojan War. See *Das griechische Satyrspiel*, pp. 381–87.

89. **Sinon** (frag. 542–44 Radt). This is one of the tragedies in the Trojan cycle mentioned by Aristotle as being taken from the epic poem the *Little Iliad* (*Poetics*, c. 23 (1459 b 7)); see above, chapter VI, "The Mythic Imagination." However, Aristotle does not give the author's name. It is Hesychius, the source of our four extant fragments, who attributes it to Sophocles. The character who gives his name to the tragedy, Sinon, is not mentioned in the *Iliad*. It was during the capture of Troy that he played a crucial role. Although the tragedy is, according to Aristotle, drawn from the *Little Iliad*, Proclus's summary of this epic by Lesches ends with the Trojans celebrating after the wooden horse has been brought inside the walls but does not mention Sinon. However, a summary cannot say everything. Through a scholium, we know that Lesches mentioned the ruses Sinon used to persuade the Trojans to accept the wooden horse, and then the fires that he lit during the night as an agreed-on signal to alert the Greeks (scholium on Lycophron, *Alexandra*, v. 344 = frag. 9 Bernabé); also see Apollodorus, *Epitome* 5, 15, according to which the Greeks, pretending to leave and burning their camp, "leaving Sinon, who was to light a beacon as a signal to them." On the other hand, Sinon appears in the summary of the epic poem that followed the *Little Iliad*, namely *The Sack of Ilium* (*Iliupersis*) (ed. Bernabé 88, 10ff.): "Sinon then raised the fire-signal to the Achaeans, having previously got into the city by pretence"; cf. Apollodorus, *Epitome* 5, 19.

These fires were a signal given at night for joint attack by the Achaeans returning from Tenedos and those who were inside the wooden horse. According to Hyginus (*Fables*, 108, 3), Sinon opened the Trojan Horse. The very slender extant fragments of the tragedy (four words mentioned in Hesychius's dictionary) provide no information regarding the way Sophocles dealt with this mythic sequence. However, it is thought that Virgil's very beautiful description (*Aeneid* 2, vv. 57–197), with a long, crafty speech by Sinon, might have been inspired by Sophocles' tragedy. See above, chapter VI, "The Mythic Imagination," where the role played by Sinon in persuading the Trojans to bring the wooden horse into Troy (with reference to Virgil) is already indicated, and where Sophocles' originality is emphasized; he appears to be the only one to have composed a tragedy on this sequence of the myth.

90. **Sisuphos, Sisyphus** (frag. 545 Radt). Sisyphus, the son of Aeolus, described as crafty, is already mentioned in the *Iliad* 6, v. 153, as the fourth-generation ancestor of a warrior on the Trojan side in the Trojan War, Glaucus. Aeschylus had composed two plays with the same title (*TrGF* 3 frag. 225–34 Radt). One is *Sisyphus the Runaway*, the other *Sisyphus the Stone-Roller*, alluding to Sisyphus's punishment in the Underworld, which had been known since Homer (*Odyssey* 11, vv. 593–600); Sisyphus had to roll up a hill a stone that fell back as soon as he had reached the summit. The first play, as the title also indicates, must have dealt with Sisyphus when by ruse he managed to escape the Underworld after an initial death that Zeus had inflicted on him to punish him for having revealed the rape of Aegina to her father, the River Asopus; when the fugitive dead man later returned to the Underworld, he was condemned to his eternal punishment (see scholium on the *Iliad* 6, v. 153 = Pherecydes in *FGrHist* 3 F 119; cf. also Theognis, vv. 703–4). Euripides had also written a satyr play entitled *Sisyphus*, performed in 415, at the same time as *The Trojan Women*; his subject cannot be determined with certainty, despite the presence of Heracles; see H. Van Looy, *Euripide*, vol. 8, 3, Paris: CUF, 2002, pp. 29ff., and *TrGF* 5.2, pp. 657–59 Kannicht. Even though Sophocles' play is attested by only one author (Hesychius), there is no ground for doubting its existence. Since Sophocles composed a play on Sisyphus's brother Salmoneus, who is less famous (no. 88, *Salmoneus*), why wouldn't he have composed a tragedy about Sisyphus? Obviously, this is not the only time when the three tragic poets composed a play with the same title, the most famous case being that of *Philoctetes*. The name of Sisyphus, the king of Ephyre (the ancient name of Corinth) who was famous for being crafty, appears in Sophocles' extant tragedies as Odysseus's father, instead of Laertes, when the characters want, in a scornful way, to emphasize his deceptiveness (*Ajax*, v. 190; *Philoctetes*, v. 417 and v. 1311); see above. This version of the myth, though well attested in tragedy, mixes up the chronology of the generations clearly distinguished in Homer. See *Das griechische Satyrspiel*, pp. 395–96.

91. **Skuthai, The Scythians** (frag. 546–52 Radt). Like *The Women of Colchis* (no. 56), this play belongs to the myth of Medea and the expedition of the Argonauts. In fragment 546 (= scholium on Apollonius of Rhodes 4, v. 223), it is said that Apsyrtus, Medea's brother (by the same father, Aietes), was not born of the same mother. His mother was a Nereid, whereas her mother was Idyia. We know that Medea, after helping Jason win the golden fleece, killed this younger

brother to protect Jason's return when he was being pursued by Aietes, either in the latter's palace, according to Sophocles in *The Women of Colchis* (frag. 343 = scholium on Apollonius of Rhodes 4, v. 228), or in the ship, before throwing him into the river (sc. the river of Colchis, the Phasis), according to Pherecydes, a historian contemporary with Sophocles (scholium ibid., v. 223 and v. 228 = *FGrHist* 3, frag. 33 a–b Jacoby; cf. Apollodorus 1, 9, 24 [133]). *The Scythians* also mention the route of the Argonauts who returned by the same route and did not sail north on the Tanais, a river of Scythia that was the border between Europe and Asia (frag. 547 = scholium on Apollonius of Rhodes 4, v. 282; frag. 548 = scholium on Dionysius Periegetes 10). However, the title of the play supposes that the chorus consisted of Scythians. This is open to doubt, and thus the title cannot be determined with certainty.

92. **Skurioi è Skuriai, The Scyrians** (frag. 553–61 Radt). The fragments hesitate between a masculine, *Skurioi* (frag. 554, 559, 560), and a feminine, *Skuriai* (frag. 558, 561). Thus there is a possible hesitation between a male and a female chorus. The argument advanced for the male chorus, namely the Piraeus inscription (IG II2 2363 = *TrGF* 1, CAT B 1, 39 Snell) giving a catalog of tragedies in which we find the title *Skurioi*, does not hold for Sophocles, because the piece belonging to the catalog is by Euripides, not Sophocles. Of course, because in Euripides there is a comparable division of the testimonies between masculine and feminine, it has been inferred by analogy that the same must be true in Sophocles. But an argument by analogy is in no way conclusive. The Scyrians, whether male or female, are residents of Scyrus, an island in the Sporades east of Euboea, which Sophocles says is windy (frag. 553; but which play is involved?). Scyros is mentioned several times in *Philoctetes*: Neoptolemus, son of Achilles and Deidamia, the daughter of Lycomedes, the king of Scyrus, was born on Scyros (vv. 240–43, 326 and 381); they pretend to return to Scyros (vv. 459, 970, and 368). Given the play's title, the chorus is formed of residents of Scyrus. Theoretically, the subject might be Achilles (see below, Euripides' *Scyrians*) or his son, Neoptolemus. Fragment 557 points toward the second solution, because it seems to be drawn from a scene in which Neoptolemus addresses an old man and talks about the death of his father, Achilles. The play would thus be about the sequence in the myth earlier than Sophocles' *Philoctetes*, where, after Achilles' death Odysseus, accompanied Phoenix, Achilles' tutor, came to Scyros on a mission to find Neoptolemus and make him go to Troy, where he would receive his father's arms and where his presence is necessary to win the war. This mission assigned to Odysseus and Phoenix is alluded to in *Philoctetes*, v. 344, but it is in Neoptolemus's deceptive speech where lying is mixed with reality (vv. 343ff.). This sequence had already been dealt with in the epic poem the *Little Iliad* (but after Philoctetes was called back). Here is Proclus's summary (ed. Bernabé 74, 10–12): "Odysseus brings Neoptolemus from Scyros and gives him his father's arms, and the ghost of Achilles appears to him"; cf. Rylands Papyrus 22 (= Arg. 2 ed. Bernabé 75, 7–9), where it is noted that Odysseus was accompanied by

Phoenix; cf. Apollodorus, *Epitome* 5, 11, where Phoenix is mentioned along with Odysseus. For a later testimony regarding this sequence, see Quintus of Smyrna 7, vv. 169ff. (with, in particular, the comparison of vv. 297–311 on the dangers of sailing with frag. 555). As we have just seen, Euripides composed a play with the same title, but the subject was different: see F. Jouan, *Euripide*, vol. 8, 3, Paris: 2002, pp. 51ff., and *TrGF* 5.2, pp. 665–70 Kannicht. Euripides' play was not about Neoptolemus but about Achilles, whom Thetis had hidden in Scyros at the palace of King Lycomedes, disguising him as a girl so that he would not have to take part in the expedition against Troy, because she knew that he was supposed to die there; however, an oracle having announced to the Achaeans that the presence of Achilles was indispensable, Odysseus went to find him and discovered him with the help of a ruse (cf. argument in *PSI* 1286 frag. A, col. 2, 1, 9–27, p. 63, Jouan pp. 665ff. Kannicht, and cf. Apollodorus 3, 13, 8 [174], and Hyginus, *Fables*, 96). For the iconography connected with the play, see Séchan, pp. 185–92; Webster, pp. 151ff.

93. ***Sundeipnoi è Sundeipnon, Those Who Dine Together*** (frag. 562–71 Radt). The play belongs to the Trojan cycle. The subject is taken from the *Cypria*. Having landed on Tenedos during their expedition against Troy, the Achaeans held a banquet. Here is Proclus's summary (ed. Bernabé 41, 50–52): "Next they sail as far as Tenedos: and while they are feasting, Philoctetes is bitten by a snake and is left behind in Lemnos because of the stench of his sore. Here, too, Achilles quarrels with Agamemnon because he is invited late." According to Aristotle (*Rhetoric* 2, 24 (1401 b)), Achilles quarreled with Agamemnon when the Achaeans were on Tenedos because he had not been invited to the banquet. Sophocles' Achilles was probably angered by the lack of respect shown him during the invitations to the banquet (cf. Philodemus, *On Anger*, col. 18, 14). In the tragedy, Odysseus is one of the characters and is contrasted with Achilles, claiming that his anger was not due to the meal but to the fear of confronting Hector, now that they are approaching Troy (frag. 566). Achilles scornfully points out that Odysseus is the son and grandson of two great scoundrels, Sisyphus and Autolycus (frag. 567). The goddess Thetis, Achilles' mother, appears to her son (frag. 562), perhaps as a deus ex machina. For the discussions on the nature of the play, see *Das griechische Satyrspiel* (1999), pp. 396–98; see also A. H. Sommerstein, "The Anger of Achilles, Mark One: Sophocles' *Syndeipnoi*," in *Shards from Kolonos* (2003), pp. 355–86. For a more recent discussion of the play, see A. H. Sommerstein et al., *Sophocles: Selected Fragmentary Plays* I, Oxford, 2006, pp. 84–140.

94. ***Tantalos, Tantalus*** (frag. 572–73 Radt). The son of Zeus and the nymph Plout, and king of the region of Mount Sipylus in Lydia, Tantalus is the father of Niobe (cf. *Antigone*, v. 825, and no. 75, *Niobe*) and Pelops (cf. no. 79, *Oenomaus*). He is the ancestor of the great tragic family of the Pelopids (see no. 17, *Atreus*; no. 41–43, *Thyestes*; no. 55, *Clytemnestra*; no. 48, *Iphigeneia*; appendix I, *Electra*). On this tragic family in Sophocles, see above, chapter VI, "The Mythic

Imagination," under "The Wealth of the Mythic Tradition: The Great Tragic Families in Sophocles' Lost Plays." Tantalus is known for having committed a grave offense against the gods and being given an eternal punishment. But the versions differ considerably regarding his crime and even his punishment. The most famous punishment is described in the *Odyssey* 11, vv. 582–92: in the Underworld, he is tormented by thirst and hunger, because everything slips away from him when he tries to grasp it. His most serious crime is having served Pelops his own son's flesh during a banquet in honor of the gods (scholium on Pindar, *Olympian Ode* 1, v. 40 a; scholium on Lycophron v. 152). Pindar, writing about the myth of Tantalus in his *Olympian Ode* 1, knows this crime but challenges it. He chooses a version of the punishment different from the one in Homer, attested in lyric poetry: a rock hangs over his head, constantly threatening him. But another punishment and another crime are also attested: the Milesian Pandarus stole the dog that Zeus had made the guardian of his sanctuary in Crete and gave it to Tantalus. Zeus sent Hermes to Tantalus, who swore he did not have the dog. To punish him, Zeus put him under Mount Sipylus (scholium on Pindar, *Olympic Ode* 1, v. 91 a). Since Hermes is mentioned in one of the two extant fragments of the play (frag. 572), Pearson (II, 209ff.) thinks this version of the myth constitutes the subject of Sophocles' play. He sees this as confirmed by the second extant fragment (frag. 572), which is a maxim on the brevity of life and the length of time spent under the earth. According to him, this fragment is in agreement with the punishment of Tantalus imprisoned under Mount Sipylus. This proposal remains hypothetical.

95. ***Teukros, Teucer*** (frag. 576–79 Radt). In *Ajax*, Teucer, Ajax's half brother, after learning of the hero's death, fears that he will be badly received by their father when he returns alone (vv. 1008–11). This is a fear that foreshadows what will happen. The sequence of the tragedy entitled *Teucer* must have been centered on Teucer's return to Salamis, the announcement of Ajax's death, which casts Telamon into despair (cf. frag. 577), and the rejection of Teucer, who goes into exile, where he was to found Salamis in Cyprus. This foundation myth was already known to Pindar (*Nemean Ode* 4, vv. 46ff.) and Aeschylus, *The Persians*, v. 897. One fragment (frag. 578). mentions a storm that strikes the fleet as it is returning from Troy. A few other bits of information regarding the characters or scenes can be drawn from testimonies that are not expressly attributed to Sophocles' *Teucer*. Cicero says that in Sophocles' play Oileus, the father of the other Ajax (cf. no. 3, *Ajax the Locrian*) consoled Telamon for the loss of his son before learning of the death of his own son and mourning in his turn (*Tusculan Disputations* 3, 71; cf. frag. 576, of uncertain attribution). This situation fits well after the scene in which Telamon, learning of his son's death, despaired. Aristotle mentions the presence of Odysseus in *Teucer* (without giving the author's name); Odysseus emphasized Teucer's kinship with Priam through his mother Hesione, Priam's sister, whereas his interlocutor objected that his father, Telamon, was Priam's enemy (*Rhetoric*, 3, 15 (1416 b 1–3) = frag. 579 a; another reference to

Teucer, ibid. 2, 23 (1398 a 4)). This is probably Sophocles' *Teucer*. There is no possible confusion with the other two great tragic poets, who did not write plays entitled *Teucer*. It is true that Sophocles' contemporary Ion also wrote a *Teucer* (*TrGF* 1, 19 frag. 34–35 Snell). But if Aristotle feels no need to cite the author, that is because his is the most famous one. Sophocles' tragedy is earlier than Aristophanes' comedy *The Clouds* of 421, because v. 583 contains a paratragic reminiscence of Sophocles' *Teucer*, as in indicated by the scholium on this verse (frag. 578). Aeschylus had composed a tragedy entitled *The Salaminians* (*TrGF* 3, frag. 216–20 Radt) that might have already dealt with the same subject, but the fragments, which are even more slender and less significant than those of Sophocles' play, provide no clues. Pacuvius had composed a *Teucer* that some scholars believe was inspired by Sophocles.

96. **Telephos, Telephus** (frag. 580 Radt). See no. 8, *The Sons of Aleus*, and no. 70, *The Mysians*, for the myth of Telephus and the question of the Telepheia; cf. also no. 34, *Eurypalus*, and no. 18, *The Gathering of the Achaeans*. Aeschylus had composed a tragedy that had the same title and was part of a trilogy (Aeschylus, *TrGF* 3, frag. 238–40 Radt). Euripides also composed a Telephus, the extant fragments of which are more numerous: see Cl. Preiser, *Euripides' Telephos: Einleitung, Text, Kommentar*, in *Spoudasmata*, 78, 2000; F. Jouan, *Euripide*, vol. 8, part 3, Paris: CUF, 2002, pp. 91ff.; and *TrGF* 5.2, pp. 680–718 Kannicht. The sequence dealt with in Euripides' *Telephus* is well known through Aristophanes' parodies in *The Acharnians* and the *Thesmophoriazusae*. It corresponds to a sequence in the *Cypria* that comes after Telephus was wounded during the first expedition (see no. 70, *Les Mysians*, end). Here is Proclus's brief summary (ed. Bernabé 41, 41ff.): "Achilles . . . then heals Telephus, who had been led by an oracle to go to Argos, so that he might be their guide on the voyage to Ilium"; cf. Apollodorus, *Epitome* 3, 19, which gives further details. Two scenes were famous: the speech given to the army by Telephus, disguised as a beggar, and the abduction of the young Orestes, once the beggar is unmasked. The wound is healed by bits of the lance that caused it, on the principle of "like cures like" (Euripides, *Telephus*, frag. 724 Kannicht). In his tragedy, Sophocles might have dealt with a sequence analogous to that used by Euripides, which would constitute the third part of Telephus's destiny after *The Sons of Aleus* and *The Mysians*, but a single testimony bearing on a single word in the play, whose form remains moreover debatable, does not allow us to arrive at an assured conclusion. Furthermore, if the play entitled *The Gathering of the Achaeans* (no. 18) dealt with this episode in Telephus's life, we can ask whether this is not another name for the same play: *Telephus* or *The Gathering of the Achaeans*. Scholars have long sought to determine whether *Telephus* was a tragedy or a satyr play, basing themselves particularly on an inscription found in Rome (IG XII 1, 125 = *TrGF* 1 DID A 5 Snell), where the name of Sophocles appears in fragment a, and a "Telephus satyr play" in fragment g. But the connection between of two words so distant in the inscription is in no way certain; see Radt, p. 434, and *Das griechische Sa-*

tyrspiel, p. 398, n. 73. The Latin poet Accius composed a tragedy entitled *Telephus* (ed. Dangel 124–27).

97. ***Tereus*** (frag. 581–95 b Radt). Among Sophocles' lost tragedies, this is one of those for which we have the most information and a few fairly extensive fragments. "In his *Tereus*, Sophocles created Tereus transformed into a bird, like Procne; in this play he made great fun of Tereus." That is the scholiast's commentary on the passage in Aristophanes' *The Birds* (v. 100) that alludes expressly to the way Sophocles' mistreated Tereus "in his tragedies." The tragedy is thus earlier than 414, the date of Aristophanes' comedy. The tragedy's argument is indirectly preserved in Tzetze's commentary on Hesiod, *Works and Days*, v. 566, where he sets forth the myth, making explicit reference to Sophocles' play in concluding his presentation: "Sophocles wrote on that in his play *Tereus*." A comparable account is given by the scholium on Aristophanes' *The Birds*, v. 212, but without any indication of the source. In addition to these testimonies that have long been known, there is the argument of a *Tereus* preserved in a papyrus published in 1974 (*P. Oxy.* 3013, s. II/III, ed. Parsons 1974, reproduced in Radt pp. 435ff.). Insofar as it corresponds to Tzetzes' presentation, this should be considered a summary of Sophocles *Tereus*. These three very similar texts derive from one another or have a common source. Here are the data that can be reconstituted on the basis of these texts: Pandion, king of Athens, having two daughters, Procne and Philomela, married the elder, Procne, to Tereus, king of the Thracians, who had with her a son named Itys. After some time had passed, Procne, desiring to see her sister again, asked Tereus to go to Athens to bring her to Thrace. Tereus, having arrived in Athens and received the young woman from Pandion, fell in love with her as he was returning (according to Tzetzes, at Aulis in Boeotia). Not keeping the promises he had made to Pandion, he deflowered her, and to prevent her from revealing this to her sister, he cut out her tongue. When she arrived in Thrace, Philomela, who could not tell what had been done to her, revealed it to her sister by weaving a tapestry. Procne, understanding and driven by extreme jealousy, killed Itys, had him boiled, and offered his flesh to Tereus to eat; he, suspecting nothing, ate it. Then when he understood what he had eaten, he pursued the two sisters with his sword, and as he was preparing to kill them, the gods, taking pity on them, transformed them into birds. Procne was transformed into a nightingale mourning Itys, and Philomela into a swallow saying "Tereus violated me"; whereas Tereus himself was transformed into a hoopoe saying "Where, where are those who cut up my son to serve him to me at supper?" In his *Poetics* 16 (1454 b 30 = frag. 586), Aristotle cites Sophocles' *Tereus* for its famous recognition scene in which the sign is "the voice of the shuttle," that is, the tapestry revealing Tereus's crime (cf. frag. 586). The setting of the tragedy was Thrace (frag. 582). In a long speech Procne—like Deianira in *The Women of Trachis*—reflects on the hard condition of women (frag. 583), in her case adding exile in a barbarian land (frag. 583, v. 9, and frag. 584; cf. frag. 587). A character (or the chorus) consoles her, urging her to accept what is im-

posed on mortals by the gods, despite her pain (frag. 585). Toward the end of the tragedy, a character denounces Tereus's folly, but also the greater folly of Procne and Philomela, who, driven by anger, used a remedy worse than the disease (frag. 589). The chorus's conclusion is much the same: "Mortal nature must have mortal thoughts" (frag. 590; cf. frag. 585). Obviously, the transformation of the three main characters into birds was mentioned only at the end of the tragedy, in an account given by a messenger or a deus ex machina.

For a recent attempt to reconstruct the play, see D. Fitzpatrick, "Sophocles' Tereus," *Classical Quarterly* 51, 2001, pp. 90–101 (with the bibliography). But any enterprise of this kind necessarily remains aleatory. See also J. March, "Sophocles' *Tereus* and Euripides' *Medea*," pp. 139–61, in A. H. Sommerstein (ed.), *Shards from Kolonos* (2003). On the play, see A. H. Sommerstein et al., *Sophocles: Selected Fragmentary Plays* I, Oxford, 2006, pp. 141–95. For the iconography, see Webster, p. 152.

The Latin poet Accius composed a tragedy entitled *Tereus* (ed. Dangel 197–99).

98. ***Triptolemos, Triptolemus*** (frag. 596–617 Radt). Triptolemus is an Eleusinian hero connected with Demeter in the Homeric hymn *To Demeter*. He is one of the Eleusinian kings who dispensed justice and to whom Demeter, after finding her daughter Kore/Persephone and making wheat grow, taught the rites. Triptolemus was familiar to Athenian audiences because he had a temple in Athens that contained a statue of him, and that was adjacent to the temple of Demeter and Kore. Pausanias (l, 14, 1ff.) saw it and discusses in this connection the differing Argive and Athenian versions of Triptolemus and his ancestry, though he does not reveal everything. For Athenians, Triptolemus is the son of Celeus and was the first to cultivate wheat. Demeter sent him around the world in a chariot drawn by winged dragons to spread the benefits of cultivating wheat. In Sophocles' play, this chariot is mentioned (frag. 596). Demeter herself appeared and addressed Triptolemus to give him directions regarding his journey; see Dionysius of Halicarnassus, *Roman Antiquities* 1, 12, 2: "[In his *Triptolemus*] Sophocles represents Demeter telling Triptolemus all the lands that he must travel through to sow there the seeds she has given him." Demeter listed the countries and the peoples. The historian cites three verses from Demeter's speech (= frag. 598). According to Strabo (1, 2, 20), Homer is superior to Sophocles in his *Triptolemus* so far as the geographical order of the enumeration of the places and peoples is concerned. These instructions given by Demeter to Triptolemus have been compared with the instructions of the same kind given by Prometheus to Io in *Prometheus Bound* (vv. 786ff.), with an analogous recommendation to be sure to retain the instructions in the "tablets of the mind" (Aeschylus, *Prometheus Bound*, v. 789, and Sophocles, *Tripotelmus* frag. 597). This comparison has given rise to endless discussions that have produced little fruit (cf. the bibliography in Radt, p. 446). According to Pliny, *Natural History* 18, 65 (cf. frag. 600 Radt), Sophocles' *Triptolemus* was performed around 145 years before the death

of Alexander (= 323); that brings us to 468, the date of Sophocles' first participation in a contest and his first victory. On the iconography, see Webster, p. 153.

99. **Troïlos, Troilus** (frag. 618–35 Radt). Troilus is one of the sons of Priam and Hecuba. He is mentioned in the *Iliad* (24, v. 257) among the valiant sons of Priam who died in the Trojan War (Mestor, Troilus, and Hector). The two scholia on this passage from Homer, where Troilus is described as "the warrior charioteer," are interesting. One (scholium A) notes the contrast between the conception of the character in Homer, where Troilus is a mature man, and in later poets, where Troilus is still very young. In Sophocles' tragedy, Troilus is described as a "child-man" (frag. 619). The other (scholium T) gives the subject of Sophocles' tragedy: "That is why in his Troilus Sophocles says that he was the victim of an ambush laid by Achilles while he [Troilus] was exercising his horses near the temple of Apollo Thumbraios, and died." This sequence of the Trojan myth had already been dealt with in the epic poem *Cypria*, where, according to Proclus's summary (ed. Bernabé 42, 63), Achilles, having devastated the cities around Troy, including Lyrnessus and Pedasus, "kills Troilus." The summary is rather short; but Apollodorus, in his *Epitome* 3, 32, gives a few more details that agree with the scholium on Homer: "Achilles, laying an ambush, kills Troilus in the sanctuary of Apollo Thumbraios"; cf. also Dio Chrysostom, 11, 77. A fragment of Sophocles' tragedy speaks of a spring where several characters went (frag. 621). Many vases from various periods of Greek ceramics also present Polyxena who has come to get water at the spring outside the walls. Polyxena could thus be a character in the tragedy. After Troilus's death, a eunuch slave came to announce his master's death (frag. 619–20). Was the theme of love already present in the encounter between Achilles and Troilus? This theme is older than Sophocles. We recall that Sophocles, during the famous banquet reported by Ion of Chios, where he dazzled everywhere (see above), quotes the verse of one of his predecessors, Phrynicus: "The light of love shines in scarlet cheeks." Now we know that this verse is spoken regarding the young Troilus (*TrGF* 1, 3 Phrynicus frag. 13 Snell = Athenaeus 13, 564 F). The love theme was developed in Hellenistic poetry (Lycophron, *Alexandra*, vv. 307–13), with the scholium on v. 307). Achilles, who is in love with Troilus, is said to have killed him because he rejected his advances. Nothing allows us to assert, or for that matter to deny, that this version was developed by Sophocles in his Troilus. For the iconography connected with the play, see Séchan, pp. 214–18; Webster, p. 153. On the play, see A. H. Sommerstein et al., *Sophocles: Selected Fragmentary Plays* I, Oxford, 2006, pp. 196–247.

100. **Tumpanistai, The Drummers** (frag. 636–45 Radt). The play is named after the chorus formed of tambourine players, very probably followers of Dionysus or Cybele, the mother goddess (cf. Euripides, *Bacchantes*, v. 58). The subject of this play is probably the myth of the Phineids, the two sons of the king of Thrace, Phineus (cf. no. 110–11 *Phineus*), and his first wife, Cleopatra, who were blinded and imprisoned. This myth was mentioned by the chorus in *Antigone* after the heroine's departure for her underground prison (vv. 968–87); see

above, chapter VI, "The Mythic Imagination." It is precisely a scholium on this passage in *Antigone* that points to this subject (scholium on *Antigone*, v. 981 = frag. 645). Here is part of that scholium: "After the death of Cleopatra (sc. the daughter of Boreas and the granddaughter, on the side of her mother Orithyia, of the king of Athens, Erectheus), Phineus then married Idaia, the daughter of Dardanos, or according to others, the sister of Cadmus, whom Sophocles himself mentions in his *Drummers*, she who deliberately blinded Cleopatra's sons and imprisoned them in a tomb; according to some, it was because she [Idaia] had accused them [Cleopatra's sons] of trying to kill her that Phineus, deceived, blinded both of them. That is what Apollodorus says in his *Library* (3, 15, 3 [200]). Some say that Phineus repudiated Cleopatra when she was still alive and then married Idaia, and that Cleopatra blinded her own sons out of anger." Several extant fragments of the play say much the same. In particular, the grotto where Boreas abducted Orithyia, Cleopatra's mother, and where her daughter had been raised (compare *Antigone*, v. 983, and *The Drummers* frag. 637) is mentioned. Whereas in *Antigone* the poet limits himself to noting that this grotto is far away, in *The Drummers* he specifies that it is located near a rocky hill in Thrace. The verse "We in the grotto where the Sarpedon rock is" (frag. 637) is spoken by Cleopatra with reference to her mother and herself. The site of the tragedy must have been Salmydessus in Thrace (cf. *Antigone*, v. 970). The myths, as the scholium on *Antigone* shows us, had several versions. The children were blinded and poisoned either by their stepmother, their father, or their mother. It is the first version, that of the criminal stepmother (supposing that Cleopatra is not dead), that is adopted in *The Drummers*; the stepmother chosen is Idothea, Cadmus's sister. That is also the version used in *Antigone*, where, nonetheless, the stepmother is allusively designated by the expression "his [Phineus's] savage wife," without giving her name (v. 973). On the other hand, the second version, the one in which Phineus kills the children of his first marriage, is adopted by Sophocles in *Phineus* or, at least, in one of the two plays with that title (see no. 110–11, *Phineus* frag. 704 and 705). The tragedy *The Drummers* was performed again in Tibur before 199 CE by an actor who won first prize; the title is inscribed on an altar erected in his honor along with those of five other tragedies, all by Euripides (see DID B 14 a in *TrGF* 2, p. 327 Kannicht-Snell). Moreover, the disproportion between the plays by Sophocles and those by Euripides testifies to the success of Euripides' theater as compared with that of Sophocles at that time.

　　101. ***Tundareos, Tyndareus*** (frag. 646–47 Radt). Tyndareus, the son of Oebalus, was born in Sparta and driven from power by his brother Hippocoön. In exile, he married Leda, the daughter of the king of Aetolia, Thestius. He was reinstated by Heracles, who expelled Hippocoön. Tyndareus had the honor of sharing his bed with Zeus. Leda had two sons, the Dioscuri, Castor and Pollux (*Odyssey* 11, vv. 298ff.), and two daughters, Clytemnestra and Helen, who were married to the two sons of Atreus: Clytemnestra became Agamemnon's wife, and

Helen Menelaus's. Tyndareus, one of the characters in Euripides' *Orestes*, said he was happy until he experienced misfortune as a result of his daughters' actions (vv. 540–41). One of them killed her husband; the other abandoned hers. In the *Odyssey* 24, v. 199, Clytemnestra, "the daughter of Tyndareus" and the murderer of her husband, Agamemnon, was already contrasted with Odysseus's faithful wife, Penelope. Clytemnestra is a character in an extant tragedy by Sophocles (*Electra*; see appendix I) and of two lost tragedies (*Clytemnestra*, no. 55; *Iphigeneia*, no. 48). As for Helen, also called "the daughter of Tyndareus" in Euripides' *Helen* (v. 17)—even though the passage alludes to the story of Leda's seduction by Zeus in the form of a swan, which is considered not very credible—she was the subject of several plays by Sophocles, but it happens that none of them is extant; see in particular *Momus* (no. 71), *Strife* (no. 29), *The Judgment* (no. 58), *The Rape of Helen* (no. 25), *The Demand for Helen's Return* (no. 24), *Helen's Wedding* (no. 26), and *The Laconian Women* (no. 60). Although the only two extant fragments of *Tyndareus* do not allow us to determine its subject, the sequence chosen must have been the one about old age (frag. 647), when Tyndareus was experiencing unhappiness because of his daughters after a period of happiness (frag. 646). Thus it was a period comparable to that in which Euripides, in his *Orestes*, represents Tyndareus dressed in black and his head shaved as a sign of mourning after the death of his daughter Clytemnestra, murdered by Orestes.

102–3. **Turo, Tyro** 1 and 2 (frag. 648–55 Radt). Tyro is the daughter of Salmoneus, the son of Aeolus (see no. 88, *Salmoneus*), and his first wife, Alcidice. Her destiny is known as early as the *Odyssey* 11, vv. 235–59. She fell in love with the god of the River Enipeus in Thessaly; Poseidon, taking advantage of the situation and using a ruse, made himself look like Enipeus and slept with the beautiful Tyro; from this union were born two twins, Pelias, who settled in Iolcos, in Thessaly (cf. no. 82, *Pelias*, and no. 87, *Root-Cutters*), and Neleus, who left for Pylos in Messinia. Since Neleus is the father of Nestor, a character who is very old in the *Iliad*, the myth of Tyro is earlier than the Trojan War. Sophocles composed two distinct tragedies with the same title, because three testimonies speak of "the second *Tyro*"; cf. frag. 654, which gives the beginning of the second *Tyro*; cf. also frag. 653 and 656. But it is impossible to determine whether the two subjects were different or whether we are dealing with two versions of the same tragedy, as is the case for the two plays by Euripides entitled *Hippolytus* (only one of which is extant). Any attempt to reconstruct each of the two plays is aleatory. Apollodorus's account (1, 9, 8 [90–92]) sheds light on the subject, because it mentions a recognition that is not mentioned in the *Odyssey*: Tyro, after her union with Poseidon, secretly gave birth to the twins, whom she abandoned in a basket; they were found by a herdsman. When they had grown up, the two sons recognized their mother and killed her stepmother, Sidero, who was tormenting her. Now, in Sophocles there was a recognition scene that took place toward the end of the play (scholium on Euripides, *Orestes*, v. 1691); it happened through the intermediary of an external sign, the basket (cf. Aristotle, *Poetics*,

c. 16 (1454 b 25), where, nonetheless, the name of the play's author is not mentioned). It was the basket in which Tyro's two sons, Pelias and Neleus, had been abandoned. In Sophocles' work, as in Apollodorus's account, Tyro was the victim of the violence of Sidero, Salmoneus's second wife. In fact, Tyro wore a bluish mask to suggest the bruises resulting from beatings by her violent stepmother (Pollux 4, 141). This "iron woman" (*sideros* = iron) was well named (frag. 658 = Aristotle, *Rhetoric*, 2, 23 (1400 b 16)). In a moving scene, Tyro compares herself to a mare whose mane has been cut by herdsmen and discovers in a mirror the ravages done to her hair (frag. 6549 = Aelian, *De natura animialium* 11, 18). On two occasions, Aristophanes alludes to one or the other of Sophocles' two plays entitled *Tyro*:

> 1. In v. 275 of *The Birds* (a comedy performed in 414), Aristophanes imitates the beginning of the second *Tyro* (frag. 654 = scholium ad loc.); this implies that both *Tyros* are earlier than 414.
> 2. In *Lysistrata*, which dates from 411 (frag. 657 = scholium on *Lysistrata*, v. 138), the eponymous heroine declares, when she sees that women cannot do without men: "We're no more than Poseidon and the basket." This is an allusion to Tyro seduced by Poseidon and obliged to abandon her two children in a basket to escape the wrath of her father, Salmoneus.

During a meal, serpents appear and come onto the table to eat and drink (frag. 660). After a recognition scene, the tragedy ended with the punishment of Sidero. The sons, having understood the situation, pursued Sidero, who sought refuge as a suppliant at the altar of Hera. There she was killed by Pelias (frag. 669 a = Apollodorus 1, 9, 8, 3 [92]). For the iconography connected with this play, see Séchan, pp. 219–30); Webster, p. 153.

On *Tyro*, recent studies include, in A. H. Sommerstein (ed.), *Shards from Kolonos* (2003); A. C. Clark, "*Tyro Keiromene*," pp. 79–116; and G. Moodie, "Sophocles' *Tyro* and Late Euripidean Tragedy," pp. 117–38.

104. **Hubris, Hybris** (satyr play) (frag. 670–71 Radt). Here, Hybris must designate a personification like *Eris* (no. 29) or *Momus* (no. 71). The only known personification bearing the name Hybris is Pan's mother, according to Apollodorus 1, 4, 1 (22) (text of the manuscripts chosen by P. Scarpi, 1996, against the earlier editions giving "Thymbris") and according to Tzetzes, commentary "On Lycophron," 772, where Pan is the son of Zeus and Hybris. Such a subject dealing with Pan's mother and probably the birth or youth of her son, comparable to the birth of Hermes in *Ichneutae* or those of Heracles in *Infant Heracles* (no. 36) or Dionysus in *Infant Dionysus* (no. 22), are very suitable for a satyr play: cf. Pearson II, p. 291, and Lloyd-Jones, pp. 320–21. See *Das griechische Satyrspiel*, pp. 277–79.

105. **Hudrophoroi, The Water Carriers** (frag. 672–74 Radt). The subject of this play, designated the composition of the chorus, is not known. Aeschylus had entitled *Semele* or *The Water Carriers* (*TrGF* 3 frag. 221–24 Radt) one of his trag-

edies whose subject was probably the tragic destiny of Semele thunderstruck by Zeus when she was pregnant with Dionysus. Making the comparison with Aeschylus's title, Welcker (p. 286) proposed an analogous subject for Sophocles' play. To be sure, Dionysus was a character in Sophocles (frag. 674), but he does not seem to have been an infant. For infant Dionysus, see *Infant Dionysus*, no. 22.

106. **Phaiakes, The Phaeacians** (frag. 675–76 Radt). Subject unknown, even though one might naturally think of a sequence taken from the *Odyssey*, like *Nausicaa* (no. 74) and more precisely of the reception of Odysseus by the Phaeacians.

107. **Phaidra, Phaedra** (frag. 677–93 Radt). The tragedy must correspond to the same mythic sequence as the one dealt with by Euripides in his two plays entitled *Hippolytus* (of which only the second is extant). See an essay comparing these three tragedies in W. S. Barrett, *Euripides, Hippolytos*, Oxford, 1964, pp. 10–45 (with the examination of the fragments of Sophocles' *Phaedra*, pp. 22–26). If one is not willing to indulge in gratuitous conjectures, one is incapable of situating Sophocles' *Phaedra* chronologically with respect to Euripides' two tragedies. On the basis of the slender fragments of Sophocles' play we can establish the following facts: Phaedra, the daughter of Minos and the wife of Theseus (cf. no. 40, *Theseus*), the son of Aegeus (cf. no. 4, *Aegeus*), could not control her love for Hippolytus, the son of Theseus and an Amazon, and she tells this to the chorus composed of women (frag. 679 and 680; cf. also frag. 684 on the power of love). Hippolytus disdainfully rejected this love when he learned of it (frag. 678). Theseus, who had long been away on his descent into the Underworld, returned in the course of the tragedy (frag. 686 and 687). This return, comparable to that of Theseus in Euripides' *Hippolytus*, involves inevitable themes that are not attested in the fragments: Phaedra's false accusations against Hippolytus, the father's curses that led to the son's death and probably to Phaedra's suicide. But it is pointless to multiply hypotheses on the basis of variants of the myth: cf. Aclepiades of Tragilus. *The Subjects of Tragedy* (*FGrHist* 12 F 28 Jacoby = scholium V Homer *Od.* 11, v. 321), Apollodorus, *Epitome* 1, 18–19, and Hyginus, *Fables*, 47 (Hippolytus), and also Seneca's *Phaedra*. Sophocles' choices remain unknown.

In A. H. Sommerstein (ed.), *Shards from Kolonos* (2003), see S. Mills, "Sophocles' *Aegeus* and *Phaidra*," pp. 219–32, and Th. Talboy, "A Tell-Tale Tail: Sophocles' *Phaidra* fr. 687 and 687 a," pp. 233–40. On the play, see A. H. Sommerstein et al., *Sophocles: Selected Fragmentary Plays* I, Oxford, 2006, pp. 248–317. For the iconography see Webster, p. 151.

108. **Phtiotides, The Women of Phthia** (frag. 694–96 Radt). The title of the play indicates not only that the chorus was composed of women, but also that the setting was Phthia, a city in Thessaly. It was the homeland of Peleus, king of Phthia (no. 82, *Peleus*), of his son Achilles (no. 19, *The Lovers of Achilles*), and also of Achilles' son, Neoptolemus, after his return from Troy with the captive

Andromache, with whom he had a son, Molossus, before marrying Hermione (no. 31, *Hermione*; cf. also Euripides, *Andromache*, which is also set in Phthia). The tragedy is mentioned by Aristotle (*Poetics*, c. 18 (1456 a 1)) as an example of a tragedy of character, along with *Peleus* (see no. 82, end). The rare extant fragments do not allow us to specify the subject. One fragment is from a dialogue in which a person addresses a young man who has much to learn (frag. 694): is it Achilles? Or rather Molossus, the son of Neoptolemus and Andromache? Another fragment indicates that two old men enter the stage and one of them is guiding the other (frag. 695 = Euripides *Bacchantes*, v. 193): is one of these old men Peleus? Finally, a trial for the murder of a father is mentioned (frag. 696): is this the trial of Orestes, who murdered his father Agamemnon, or rather the complaint that Neoptolemus sought to bring against the god of Delphi whom he accused of having killed his father? Cf. no. 31, *Hermione*, and also Euripides *Andromache*, vv. 53 and 1108, and *Orestes*, v. 193. Is it a second title of the tragedy entitled *Hermione*? For this hypothesis, following Vater, Pearson II, p. 306 and n. 1.

109. **Philoktetes ho en Troia, Philoctetes at Troy** (frag. 697–701 Radt). As its title indicates, this tragedy deals with the sequence of the myth following the one that is staged in the extant tragedy entitled *Philoctetes* (see appendix I). That does not mean, obviously, that Sophocles composed *Philoctetes at Troy* after his *Philoctetes*. In the epic, the sequence was part of the *Little Iliad*. Here is the part of Proclus's summary (ed. Bernabé 74, 7–8) concerning Philoctetes after his arrival in Troy: "Philoctetes is healed by Machaon [one of Asclepius's two sons], fights in single combat with Alexandrus [Paris] and kills him." The healing of Philoctetes and his military exploit must have been two important elements of the tragedy. This is confirmed by the prophetic announcement made by Heracles when he appears at the end of *Philoctetes* (vv. 1423–33 and 1437ff.). Three of the fragments of *Philoctetes at Troy* are related to his malady that is now over or has not yet been cured (vv. 697–99). The rest gives no indication regarding what happens in the tragedy. *Philoctetes* did not follow exactly the tradition of the *Little Iliad* concerning the healing. Helenus's oracle mentioned as healers the two sons of Asclepius (v. 1333), that is, not Machaon alone, but also Podalirius. However, when Heracles appeared at the end of *Philoctetes*, he announced the intervention of the god Asclepius in person (vv. 1437ff.). For the significance of this difference, see above, chapter III, "Sophocles the Religious Man," under "The Presence of Asclepius in Sophocles' Theater." What was the solution Sophocles chose to carry out the healing of Philoctetes in his *Philoctetes at Troy*? Asclepius's two sons or Asclepius himself?

110–11. *Phineus* 1 and 2 (frag. 704–17 a Radt). On the basis of several testimonies that cite sometimes the first *Phineus* (frag. 706, 707, 717 a), sometimes the second *Phineus* (frag. 707 a, 708, 709), and sometimes both (frag. 705), we cannot doubt the existence of two different plays about the same character. But none of these fragments provide reliable information regarding the difference in content between the two plays. For the myth in Sophocles, see no. 100, *The Drummers*, and *Antigone*, vv. 968–87. Cf. above, chapter VI, "The Mythic Imagination." Phineus is the king of Salmydessus, a Thracian city on the west coast of the Black Sea. In *Phineus* Sophocles says that Phineus was blinded because he had killed his own sons (frag. 705 = *Etym. gen.* A, s.v. *opizesthai*); or, more plausibly, because he had blinded them (frag. 704 = scholium on Apollonius of Rhodes 2, 178–82b; cf. Apollodorus 3, 15, 3 [200]). These are the two sons he had had from his first marriage to Cleopatra, the daughter of Boreas and Orithyia, the daughter of the king of Athens, Erectheus. Phineus had been persuaded by his second wife's calumnies (frag. 704). The version of the myth is thus different from the one in *The Drummers*, on the one hand because the second wife was Eidothea and not Idaea, and on the other hand because the two sons from the first marriage were blinded by their stepmother and not by their father. According to another fragment that is attributed to Sophocles' *Phineus* without making a distinction between the two plays, a blind man recovered his sight thanks to Asclepius (frag. 710 = Aristophanes, *Plutus*, v. 633, and scholium ad loc.); see above chapter III, "Sophocles the Religious Man." It is possible that in the second *Phineus* the two sons took revenge by scalping their stepmother (frag. 707 a). Phineus, for his part, was blinded by the Argonauts with Boreas, the children's grandfather, according to Apollodorus (3, 15, 3 [200] and 1, 9, 21 [120]). Once he had been blinded, the Harpies (frag. 714) starved him by stealing away his food before fleeing (cf. frag. 713), so that he must have looked like a dried-up skeleton (cf. frag. 712). Aeschylus had also composed a *Phineus* (*TrGF* 3 frag. 258–59 a Radt), performed in 472 at the same time as *The Persians* (cf. argument of *The Persians*), where the blind Phineus was tormented by the Harpies who came to take away his food (frag. 258). For the iconography, see Webster, p. 151.

112. **Phoenix** (frag 718–20 Radt). Phoenix, king of the Dolopians, is already the main character in *The Dolopians* (see no. 23, for the myth); he is also a character in *The Lovers of Achilles* (no. 19) and *The Scyrians* (no. 92). Euripides is also the author of a play entitled *Phoenix* (*TrGF* 5.2, frag. 803a–817a Kannicht; see F. Jouan, *Euripide*, vol. 8, 3, CUF, 2002, pp. 313–38). In Euripides' play, Phoenix's conflict with his father, Amyntor, over women is central. Whereas in the *Iliad* (9, v. 458) the son, quarreling with his father, considers for a moment killing him with his sword, in Euripides it is the father who blinds his son. Euripides' blind Phoenix is mentioned in Aristophanes' *Acharnians* (v. 421); the tragedy is thus later than 425, the date of the comedy. On the other hand, the three slender fragments of Sophocles' tragedy that have been preserved do not allow us to say whether it dealt with the same sequence. One wonders whether *Phoenix* and *The Dolopians* are not two titles for the same tragedy, designated either by the main character or by the chorus.

113. **Phrixos**, **Phrixus** (frag. 721–23 Radt). Phrixus is the son that Athamas (cf. no. 1–2, *Athamas*) had from a first marriage with the goddess Nephele. When Athamas remarried with a mortal, Ino, the daughter of Cadmus, Phrixus was

persecuted by his stepmother, who wanted to get rid of him. Euripides is also the author of two plays entitled *Phrixus*, which do not begin in the same way and of whose arguments we have remnants on papyrus (see H. Van Looy, *Eurip-ide*, vol. 8, 3, CUF, 2002, pp. 339–71, and *TrGF* 5.2, pp. 856–76 Kannicht). What is central in Euripides' two plays entitled *Phrixus* is the sacrifice of Phrixus that Ino caused by her scheming, triggering a famine and falsifying the Delphic or-acle's response. But one of the differences between the two versions is that the sacrifice of Phrixus in the second version is voluntary. Euripides' first *Phrixus* can be compared to Sophocles' second *Athamas* (no. 2, *Athamas*), with the difference that in Euripides the drought is caused not by Nephele, as in Sophocles, but by Ino, who has made the women of the land roast the seed before plating it (cf. the argument of the first *Phrixus*, frag. 822 b Kannicht, and Apollodorus, *Library* 1, 80–82). What about Sophocles' *Phrixus*? The fragments provide no evidence on this point. Since Welcker (pp. 317–19), scholars imagine a different version in which Phrixus is a victim, not of his stepmother Ino, but of his aunt De-modice, the second wife of Cretheus, Athamas's brother (Hyginus, *Astron.* 2, 20). The schema is analogous to that of Phaedra and Hippolytus (cf. no. 107, *Phae-dra*). Having fallen in love with Phrixus, Demodice, not obtaining what she desired, slandered Phrixus, whom his father Athamas wanted to chastise, but who was saved by his mother, Nephele. This solution, presented as possible by H. Van Looy (*Euripide* VIII, 3, p. 345, n. 5), is only a hypothesis, as Pearson al-ready emphasized (II, p. 323). To be sure, Demodice is mentioned in a scholium on Pindar, *Pythian Ode* 4, v. 288. Since Pindar says that Phrixus did not have "the impious traits of his stepmother," without giving her name, the scholiast suggests two names: Demodice in Pindar's *Hymns* (= frag. 49 Snell-Mähler), and Nephele for *Athamas* (= frag. 4 a Radt). But Demodice does not concern Soph-ocles, and the reference to the latter apropos of *Athamas* reveals the mediocre quality of the scholium, since it confuses the mother (Nephele) and the step-mother (Ino), as Pearson already noted (II, p. 323). What is the point of inserting as a new fragment of *Athanas* (= frag. 4 a Radt) what is obviously an error? In the end, there is no certainty regarding the sequence used by Sophocles in his *Phrixus*. However, it is likely that *Phrixus* is another name for one of the two plays entitled *Athamas*, as Lloyd-Jones suggests (p. 338).

114. **Phruges, *The Phrygians*** (frag. 724–25 Radt). Aeschylus had composed a play with the same title; its second title was *The Ransom of Hector* (*TrGF* 3 frag. 263–72 Radt). Aeschylus's tragedy was thus about the sequence corresponding to book 24 of the *Iliad*, in which Priam, on the advice of the goddess Iris, Zeus's messenger, goes alone to the Achaeans' camp, bearing presents, to persuade Achilles to return the body of his son, and returns with the corpse, which all the Trojans then weep over. The subject dealt with by Sophocles could be the same, as Welcker already suggested (pp. 135–36). In any case, Achilles appeared in Sophocles' *Phrygians* as a character who remained silent—out of self-importance, according to the scholium on *Prometheus Bound*, v. 436: "In the poets, characters

are silent either out of self-importance, like Achilles in Sophocles' *The Phrygians*, or because of misfortunes, like Niobe in Aeschylus, or because they are thinking, like Zeus in the Poet [= Homer] faced by Thetis's request (=*Iliad* 1, v. 512)." Such a haughty silence would be easily comprehensible when faced by Priam's request for the body of his son. Cf. also no. 85, *Priam*.

115. **Chruses, Chryses** (frag. 726–30 Radt). The play appears to be earlier than 414, because a paratragic expression from Aristophanes' *The Birds*, v. 1240, is said to come from Sophocles' *Chryses* (scholium on this passage = frag. 727). Contrary to what H. Grégoire says in his presentation of Sophocles' *Chryses* (Euripides, *Iphigeneia in Tauris*, CUF, Paris, 1st ed. 1925, pp. 97–99), the subject of the tragedy is not known with certainty. This alleged subject, thought it was proposed as early as the middle of the nineteenth century (Naecke 1842), is only a possible hypothesis based on giving priority to two of Hyginus's fables (120, 5 and 121). The subject is supposed to be, not the priest of Apollo who comes at the beginning of the *Iliad* to ransom his daughter Chryseis, but his grandson in a later version of the myth. When Agamemnon returned the girl to Chryses the Elder, she was already pregnant with Chryses the Younger, to whom she gave birth claiming that he was the son of Apollo. This myth was connected with that of Orestes and Iphigeneia returning from Tauris, from which they brought back with them the statue of Artemis (cf. Euripides' *Iphigeneia in Tauris*). Having escaped from Thoas, king of the Taurians, Orestes and Iphigeneia landed, during their return, on the island of Sminthe where the priest of Apollo, Chryses, lived with his daughter and his grandson. Chryses almost compromised Orestes and Iphigeneia's return to Mycenae because he wanted to return them to Thoas. But when he learned that they were Agamemnon's children, he revealed to his grandson that he, too, was a son of Agamemnon. After the recognition scene, the two brothers went to kill Thoas and arrived safe and sound in Mycenae with the statue of Artemis. This sequence of the myth could certainly provide the subject matter for a tragedy with a recognition scene. But it has been objected that this state of the myth's development presupposed Euripides' *Iphigeneia in Tauris*, which is earlier than *Chryses*: see Wilamowitz (*Hermes* 18, 1883, pp. 256–57); he points instead to other versions that had circulated regarding Chryses the Younger in relation to the city of Chrysopolis: this city owed its name to this son of Chryseis and Agamemnon, who is supposed to have died of illness and to be buried there, when he was fleeting Clytemnestra and Aegisthus and trying to join his sister Iphigeneia, priestess of Artemis in Tauris (Dionysius of Byzantium [second century CE], *Per Bosporum navigatio* 109; cf. also Tzetzes in his *Commentary* on Lycophron).

Nonetheless, the name "Chryses" makes us think first of the priest of Apollo in the first book of the *Iliad*: having come to ransom his daughter Chryseis, who is Agamemnon's war captive, he meets with a flat refusal on the part of the Achaean leader. He addresses a prayer to Apollo, who unleashes a pestilence. To put an end to the scourge, Agamemnon agrees to give Chryseis back but demands in compensation Briseis, Achilles' captive, and this triggers the wrath of Achilles, the subject of the *Iliad*, and his withdrawal from the fighting. Sophocles, whose inspiration accorded so much importance to the Trojan cycle, might have taken his play from book 1 of the *Iliad*, just as he drew another play from book 24 (cf. no. 114, *The Phrygians*). In any case, nothing is certain. None of the slender extant fragments provides clues to the subject. Pacuvius composed a *Chryses*.

116. ***Aleites* or *Aletes*** (frag. 97–103 Nauck[2] frag. 101–7 Pearson). Stobaeus cites seven passages from a play by Sophocles entitled *Aleites* (*The Culprit*), which has often been corrected to read *Aletes* (son of Aegisthus). This play is not attested by other testimonies. If we follow the text of the manuscripts, the title *The Culprit* gives us no hint about the subject. If it is corrected to *Aletes*, we can see in it a play whose title character is the son of Aegisthus, and we can try to reconstitute the subject using Hyginus's fable 122 (*Aletes*); see Welcker, 1839, pp. 215–19, and Pearson I, p. 62. Hyginus's fable could correspond, in fact, to a tragedy with recognition. But can a reconstruction of the subject be based on a correction? Besides, the style of the fragments Stobaeus gives has been judged unworthy of the great Sophocles by Wilamowitz (*Kleine Schriften* 4, 291, n. 1, and 483ff.) The consequence is that the play has been removed from the modern corpus of the fragments of the Greek tragic poets (*TrGF* 4) and placed in the *Adespota*, that is, among the plays whose author is unknown (= *TrGF* 2 frag. 1 b Kannicht-Snell). It is also absent from the fragments of Sophocles by H. Lloyd-Jones, 1996. Wouldn't it be better to respect the tradition, and simply indicate a doubt regarding authenticity?

117. **Frag. 941 Radt (unknown tragedy): Eulogy of Cypris, goddess of love**. In addition to the fragments belonging to Sophocles' identified plays, many fragments have been preserved without the title of the original tragedy (= frag. 739a–1154 Radt). The most important fragment (Stobaeus 4, 20, 6 = frag. 941 Radt) is a eulogy on the power of Cypris, goddess of love (comparable to the hymn to Eros by the chorus in *Antigone*, vv. 781ff.):

O children, Cypris is not just Cypris,
she is called by many names.
She is the Invisible [Hades], she is indestructible power,
she is mad rage, she is desire
in the pure state, she is lamentation. In her, all is
lively, calm, bearing violence.
For she insinuates herself into all those into whom the lungs
breathe life. What path is forbidden to this divinity?
She enters into the species of fish who swim,
and she is present, on land, in the race of quadrupeds;
her wing is the guide of birds; . . .
among wild animals, humans, the gods on high.

Which of the gods does she not defeat in three-fall wrestling?
If I am permitted—but it is permitted—to tell the truth,
she reigns over Zeus's lungs, without a lance,
without a sword. All plans, assuredly, Cypris
upsets, those of mortals and those of the gods.

Appendix III

·················

THE IDENTIFICATION OF SOPHOCLES
AS A HELLENOTAMIAS

There has been debate regarding the identification of both Sophocles' name and that of his deme in list 12 of the tributes (443/2 BCE).[1]

The Identification of Sophocles' Name

Pittakis, the first editor, did not read the name as [S]OPHOKLÈS but as [H]EROKLÈS (K. S. Pittakis, *L'Ancienne Athènes*, Athens, 1835, p. 437). The second editor (A. R. Rangabé, *Antiquités helléniques*, Athens, 1842, no. 165, p. 260) was the first to read the name as Sophocles but did not think of the tragic poet, because he was led astray by his restitution of the geographical place Colo[phon] and wondered who this Sophocles of Colophon, a foreigner who had received citizenship rights in Athens, might be. In an article published in the *Éphèméris Archaiologikè* for 1853 (no. 1189, pp. 729 and 733), Pittakis returned to Rangabé's reading, accepted the name "Sophocles," and restituted for the first time "Sophocles of the deme of Colonus"—but without commenting on the identification. This restitution was later adopted in the corpus of inscriptions until the standard publication of the tribute lists (B. D. Meritt, H. T. Wade-Gery, and M. F. MacGregor, *The Athenian Tribute Lists*, vol. 2, Princeton, 1949, p. 18, list 12), where SOPHOKLÈS KOLONÈTHEN ([Σ]οφοκλὲς κολο[νέθεν]) is restituted.

The restitution of the name of Sophocles seemed definitive. However, it was later the subject of a heated exchange between two scholars concerning the second preserved letter of the proper name: should it be read as a φ (= *ph*)? This question is clearly of capital importance, because if it is not read as φ, the name "Sophocles" disappears. In a 1955 article, "Notes on Attic Inscriptions" (*Annual of the British School at Athens*, 50, 1955, pp. 1–36), the British epigraphist David Malcolm Lewis remarks, regarding the end of list 12, that the reading of the φ may not be correct "since no trace of a chisel remains." He therefore suggests that the name be read TH[E]OKLÈS or [CH]O[R]OKLÈS. A few years later, in 1959, this incidental suggestion elicited a response from one of the three American editors of the Corpus of the Attic tribute lists. After reading Lewis's article, B.

D. Meritt went to verify the reading on the stone itself. In a one-page article entitled "The Name of Sophocles" (*American Journal of Philology*, 80, 1959, p. 189), he notes that the examination of the stone leaves no doubt regarding the presence of the φ: "Each stroke of the letter φ is certain," he concludes. Thus it is in fact Sophocles' name that must be read, and all speculation on other restitutions seems idle. The name of "Sophocles," who seemed for a moment in danger of being thrown out, now seems definitively established in his office as a hellenotamias. But is he also the poet?

The Identification of the Deme

Like the name "Sophocles," the name of the deme was not immediately established, and its identification has recently been challenged.

Pittakis (1835) restituted nothing beyond κοLO-, and Rangabé, as we have seen, went astray by restituting "of Colophon."

It was D. M. Lewis's article cited above that brought new life the debate regarding the deme of Colonos (XXIV. "The Deme Colonos," pp. 12–17). In this study, he tried to dispel the ambiguities of the root *Kolo-* among the three demes: one, the deme Kolonos (a masculine noun; literally, "the mound"), an urban deme of the Aegeid tribe that is Sophocles' deme (Kolonos Agoraios is said not to be a deme, but a district); and two other demes named Kolonai (a feminine noun; literally "the hills"), demes of Mesogeia belonging to two other tribes, the tribe Leontis and the tribe Antiochis, and later on, the tribe of the Ptolemaïds; cf. also W. E. Thompson, "Notes on Attic Demes," *Hesperia* 39, 1970, pp. 64ff. (*Kolonai*). To partially distinguish between these demes, when people wanted to indicate the origin of a person in the expression "so-and-so from such-and-such a deme," Lewis thinks they said *ek Kolonou* (ἐκ Κολωνοῦ) or *Kolonothen* (Κολωνόθεν) to designate Colonus, Sophocles' deme, and *Kolonèthen* (Κολωνηθεν) to designate the other two *Kolonai*. This distinction is in fact in conformity with the regular form of the Greek language.

Reexamining the reference to Sophocles the hellenotamias in the light of this distinction, Lewis considers four possibilities (p. 15):

(a) We can read TH[E]OKLÈS or [CH]O[R]OKLÈS (a possibility that Meritt dismisses; see first paragraph above).

(b) If we adopt the traditional restitution *Sophoklès kolonèthen* (Σοφοκλης κολονηθεν), then we have to imagine a Sophocles different from the tragic poet, one belonging to one of the two demes called *Kolonai* ("the hills").

(c) The distinction traditionally drawn between *Kolonothèn* (κολωνοθεν) and *Kolonèthen* (κολωνηθεν) does not exist, and even if we adopt *Sophoklès kolonèthen* (Σοφοκλης κολωνηθεν), it might refer to our poet.

(d) If it does in fact refer to the poet Sophocles, we should read Σοφοκλης κολωνοθεν, "Sophocles of the deme of Colonus" ("the mound").

If we accept the name "Sophocles," Lewis favors possibility (d), that is, restoring *Kolonothen* (Κολωνοθεν). This is the solution B. D. Meritt adopts in his article "The Name of Sophocles," cited above.

However, almost twenty years later another British scholar, H. C. Avery, drew on Lewis's analyses to cast doubt on the solution Lewis favored (in "Sophocles' Political Career," *Historia* 22, 1973, pp. 509–14, esp. pp. 509ff.). According to Avery, the existence of the adverb *Kolonothen*, which Lewis sought to restitute, was uncertain, because it was attested only once in a single manuscript; then he adds that the members of Sophocles the tragedian's family are reliably known only through the expression *ek Kolonou*, "from Colonus." Thus he concludes that the most prudent solution to be drawn from Lewis's argument is that the hellenotamias named Sophocles was not from the deme of Colonus ("the Mound") but from one of the two demes named *Kolonai* ("the Hills"), to which the demotic *Kolonethen* corresponds. This amounts to choosing Lewis's possibility (b) and depriving the poet Sophocles of the office of hellenotamias.

If Avery is right to doubt the form *Kolonothen* attested as a variant in a single manuscript (argument of *Oedipus at Colonus* no. 1: Κολωνηθεν LRQ: Κολωνοθεν A), it is not true that the members of Sophocles' family are reliably known only through the expression *ek Kolonou*, "from Colonus." To remain with literary passages where Sophocles and his deme of Colonus are mentioned, we can note that although we find *ek Kolonou* once (scholium on Aristides p. 485, 28 Dinsdorf = test. 19 Radt, confirmed by the inscription on the Marble of Paros A 56 *FGrHist* 239 Jacoby = test. 33 Radt), all the other literary testimonies where Sophocles the poet's deme of origin is mentioned have the adverb *Kolonèthen*: in addition to the argument of *Oedipus at Colonus* cited above, see the *Life of Sophocles*, c. 1 (= test. 1, 1. 10 Radt); *Suda* (= test. 2, 1. 1 Radt); Eustathius, who, in explaining the feminine κολωνη, "the hill," in *Iliad* 2, v. 811, also mentions Sophocles and his deme (= test. 13 Radt). This last testimony, not cited by Lewis, is important for the question. Here is a translation of it: "To say Κολωνός ('the mound') and here Κολωνη ('the hill') is to say the same thing. However, the Homeric word wins out, a word that Sophocles adopted when he said 'the summit of the [funeral] mound (Κολωνη)' (= *Electra*, v. 894); he must have been well aware of the synonymy, since his Athenian deme was Colonus ('the mound') and a resident of that deme, like him, was called a native *Kolonèthen* (Κολωνθεν) and not a *Kolonothen* (Κολωνόθεν)." It would be impossible to say more clearly that the usual form for designating the residents of Sophocles the tragic poet's deme was *Kolonèthen* (Κολωνθεν). Given that fact, how would it be possible to maintain a theoretical distinction like Lewis's between *ek Kolonou* and *Kolonèthen* as designating different demes? It is Lewis's possibility (c) that must be adopted. The restitution *Kolonèthen* (Κολωνθεν) in the list of Attic tributes remains the most plausible one. Thus we would have *Sophokles Kolonèthen* (Σοφοκλης Κολονηθεν) in the inscription of the tributes, as in the *Life of Sophocles*, the *Suda*, and Eustathius.

Nothing prevents us from thinking that the tragic poet Sophocles was a hellenotamias.

This identification is generally accepted: see V. Blumenthal, "Sophokles," in RE 15 Halfband, 1927, col. 1043: "Das nächste sichere Nachricht zeigt ihn politischer Tätigkeit: nach der Beamten liste IG I 237 war er im J. 443/2 Hellenotamias" ("The closest reliable report shows him engaging in political activity: according to the list of officials IG I 237, he was a Hellenotamias in 443–442"); cf. also T.B.L. Webster, *An Introduction to Sophocles*, London, 1936, p. 11: "It is usually assumed that this Sophocles was the poet, and there is no reason to doubt the identification, although the fact is not mentioned in any literary source." It as a fact is also acknowledged by V. Ehrenberg, *Sophocles and Pericles*, Oxford, 1954, pp. 117 and 120ff. More recently, see two studies on Sophocles' career that appeared at the same time but independently: L. Woodbury, "Sophocles among the Generals," *Phoenix* 24, 1970, p. 217 (despite his skepticism regarding Sophocles' political career, he considers Sophocles' tenure of the office of hellenotamias a fact), and J. H. Jameson, "Sophocles and the Four Hundred," *Historia* 20, 1971, 3 pp. 541ff. See G. Ugolini's recent *Sofocle e Atene*, 2000, pp. 35–42.

Appendix IV

·················

DIO CHRYSOSTOM, *Discourse* 52: ON AESCHYLUS, EURIPIDES, AND SOPHOCLES; OR, THE BOW OF PHILOCTETES

1. Having risen about the first hour of the day, both on account of the feeble state of my health and also on account of the air, which was rather chilly because of the early hour and very much like autumn, though it was mid-summer, I made my toilet and performed my devotions. I next got into my carriage and made the round of the race-course several times, my team moving along as gently and comfortably as possible. After that I took a stroll and then rested a bit. Next, after a rub-down and bath and a light breakfast, I fell to reading certain tragedies.

2. These tragedies were the work of topmost artists, I may say, Aeschylus and Sophocles and Euripides, all dealing with the same theme, which was the theft—or should I say the seizure?—of the bow of Philoctetes. However that may be, Philoctetes was portrayed as being deprived of his weapons by Odysseus and as being carried off to Troy along with them, for the most part willingly, though in some measure also yielding to the persuasion of necessity, since he had been deprived of the weapons which furnished him with not only a living on his island, but courage in his sore affliction, and at the same time fame.

3. So I was feasting my eyes on the spectacle portrayed by these dramas and figuring to myself that, even if I had been in Athens in those days, I could not have witnessed such a contest as this of those distinguished poets. On the contrary, while there were some who did witness contests between the youthful Sophocles and the aged Aeschylus and some who saw the older Sophocles compete with Euripides, his junior, yet the career of Euripides fell quite outside the period of Aeschylus; and besides, probably the tragic poets seldom or never competed against one another with plays on the same theme. And so I was evidently having a rare treat and a novel solace for my illness. 4. Accordingly, I

played choregus for myself in very brilliant style and tried to pay close attention, as if I were a judge passing judgement on the premier tragic choruses.

Yet I could not on oath have produced a single reason why any one of those great poets could have been defeated. For both the nobility of character and the antique flavour of Aeschylus, as well as the ruggedness of his thought and diction, seemed suited to tragedy and to the old-time manners of the heroes, nor was there aught of premeditation or prating or humility in their bearing. 5. For example, even his Odysseus he brought upon the scene as a shrewd and crafty person, as men were in those days, yet far removed from the rascality of to-day, in consequence of which he might seem truly ancient as compared with those who to-day lay claim to simplicity and nobility of character. And again, Aeschylus had no need to add Athena for the purpose of transforming Odysseus so as not to be recognized by Philoctetes for the man he was, as Homer has handled the problem, and also Euripides in imitation of Homer. So possibly one of those who do not like Aeschylus might complain that he was not at all concerned to make his Odysseus convincing in the scene where he is not recognized by Philoctetes. 6. But in my opinion the poet would have a defence against such a criticism; for while the lapse of time was perhaps not sufficient to explain his not recalling the lineaments of Odysseus since only ten years had passed, yet the affliction and distress of Philoctetes and the lonely life he had led in the interval made this lapse of memory not impossible. For many in the past, either from illness or from misfortune, have had that experience.

Furthermore, the chorus of Aeschylus had no need for special pleading, as did that of Euripides. 7. For both poets made their choruses to consist of Lemnians; yet, while Euripides has represented them as immediately apologizing for their former neglect, admitting that during so many years they had neither come near Philoctetes nor rendered him any aid, Aeschylus simply brought his chorus on the scene, a course which is altogether more in keeping with a tragedy and more natural, whereas the other course is more courteous and more strictly correct. Of course, if poets, were able to avoid all violations of logic in their tragedies, perhaps there might be reason for refusing to gloss over even this instance; but as the truth is, the poets often cause their heralds to complete in a single day a journey which calls for several days. 8. Again, it was quite impossible to conceive that not a single Lemnian had come near Philoctetes or given him any attention at all, for in my opinion he could not even have survived those ten years without receiving some aid; no, it is reasonable to suppose that he did get some aid, though but rarely and of no great importance, and, furthermore, that no one chose to take him into his house and give him medical attention because of the disgusting nature of his ailment. At any rate Euripides himself does bring upon the scene one Lemnian, Actor, who approaches Philoctetes as being already known to him and as having often met him.

9. Furthermore, I do not feel that one could justly find fault with Aeschylus for this either—that his hero narrates to the chorus, as if they were in ignorance, the details concerning his desertion by the Achaeans and his experiences in general. The reason is that the victims of misfortune are wont to recall their trials repeatedly, and by their constant rehearsing of details they bore those who know every detail already and have no need to be told. Then again, the deception which Odysseus practised upon Philoctetes and the arguments by which he won him over are not merely more becoming and suited to a hero—though not the words of a Eurybates or a Pataecion—but in my opinion they are even more plausible. 10. For what need was there for subtle craft and scheming in dealing with a sick man and, what is more, an archer, whose means of defence had lost its power the moment you merely got close to him? Besides, the device of having Odysseus report that the Achaeans had met with disaster, that Agamemnon had died, that Odysseus had been charged with an act that was utterly disgraceful, and that in general the expedition had gone to rack and ruin, was not merely serviceable toward cheering Philoctetes and making the discourse of Odysseus more acceptable; no, in a way it was not without plausibility even, because of the length of the campaign and because of what had happened not so long before in consequence of the wrath of Achilles, at the time when Hector barely missed burning the naval station.

11. Again, the sagacity of Euripides and his careful attention to every detail, as a result of which not only does he not tolerate anything which lacks plausibility or is marred by carelessness, but also he handles the action, not in artless style, but with entire mastery in the telling—all this forms, as it were, an antithesis to the nature of Aeschylus, being to a high degree characteristic of the citizen and the orator and capable of proving most useful to those who read him. At the very outset of Euripides' play, for instance, Odysseus is introduced as speaker of the prologue and as not only inwardly debating questions of civic nature in general, but first and foremost expressing embarrassment on his own account, lest, while generally reputed to be wise and distinguished for sagacity, he may really be the opposite. 12. For, though he might live free from care and trouble, he is ever being involved in troubles and perils of his own volition. But the cause of this, he claims, is the ambition which actuates gifted men of noble birth. For, in aiming at a fine reputation and general acclaim, they voluntarily undertake very great and difficult labours.

> For nothing quite so proud as man
> exists.

Odysseus then reveals clearly and precisely the plot of the drama and why he has come to Lemnos. 13. And he says he has been disguised by Athena, so that when he meets Philoctetes he may not be recognized by him, Euripides having imitated Homer in this detail. For Homer has represented Odysseus, in his sundry encounters with Eumaeus and Penelopē and the others, as having been disguised by Athena. Odysseus goes on to say that an embassy from the Trojans will soon visit Philoctetes for the purpose of entreating him to place at their disposal both himself and their weapons, offering the throne of Troy as his reward; thus he complicates the plot and invents occasions for debate, in the course of which he shows himself most resourceful and most proficient in combating the opposing arguments, no matter with whom he is compared. 14. Again, Euripides causes Odysseus to arrive not unattended but in company with Diomedes, another Homeric touch. Thus all in all, as I was saying, throughout the whole play he displays the greatest dexterity and plausibility in the action; an irresistible, yes, amazing, power of language; a dialogue that is clear and natural and urbane; and lyrics that not only are delightful but also contain a strong incentive toward virtue.

15. As for Sophocles, he seems to stand midway between the two others, since he has neither the ruggedness and simplicity of Aeschylus nor the precision and shrewdness and urbanity of Euripides, yet he produces a poetry that is august and majestic, highly tragic and euphonious in its phrasing, so that there is the fullest pleasure coupled with sublimity and stateliness. In his management of the action he is most excellent and convincing; for instance, he causes Odysseus to arrive in company with Neoptolemus—since it was ordained that Troy should be taken by Neoptolemus and Philoctetes together, Philoctetes wielding the bow of Heracles—and he makes Odysseus conceal himself but send Neoptolemus to Philoctetes, suggesting to him what he must do. Furthermore, he has composed his chorus not of the natives of Lemnos, as Aeschylus and Euripides do, but of those who sailed in the ship along with Odysseus and Neoptolemus.

16. Again, as Sophocles portrays them, the characters in the drama are wonderfully dignified and noble, his Odysseus being much more gentle and frank than Euripides has depicted him, and his Neoptolemus surpassing all in artlessness and good breeding—at first he aims to get the better of Philoctetes, not by craft and deception, but by strength and without disguise; then, after he has been prevailed upon by Odysseus and has tricked Philoctetes and gained possession of the bow, when Philoctetes becomes aware of what had happened, is indignant at the deception which has been practised upon him, and demands the return of his weapons, Neoptolemus does not try to retain possession of them but is prepared to return them—though Odysseus appears on the scene and tries to prevent this—and he finally does return them; yet after he has handed them over he tries by argument to persuade Philoctetes to accompany him voluntarily to Troy. But when Philoctetes will by no means yield or be persuaded, but entreats Neoptolemus to take him back to Greece, as he had promised to do, Neoptolemus once more gives his promise, and he is prepared to keep his word, until Heracles comes upon the scene and persuades Philoctetes to sail to Troy of his own free will.

The lyrics of Sophocles do not contain the didactic element to any great extent, nor any incentive to virtue such as we find in the lyrics of Euripides, but a marvellous sweetness and magnificence, such that Aristophanes could say of him not without reason words like these:

But he in turn the lips of Sophocles,
With honey smeared, did lick as if as a jar.

Appendix V

....

Life of Sophocles

The *Life of Sophocles* is found at the beginning of several medieval manuscripts that reproduce the tragic author's works.[2] Anonymous, it is an abbreviated version of a *Life* probably composed in the first century BCE and uses testimonies ranging from the fourth century BCE to the second century BCE. It constitutes our main source of information about Sophocles' life, along with the brief article in the Byzantine encyclopedia known as the *Suda* (tenth century CE), given below, under "The *Suda*'s Article on Sophocles."

[Test. 1 Radt]. 1. Sophocles was by origin an Athenian, the son of Sophillos, who was not, as Aristoxenes [fourth century BCE] says, a carpenter or a smith, nor, as Istros [third century BCE] says, a dagger maker by trade, but he did have slaves who were smiths or carpenters. For it is not likely that the man, if he was born of such a father of such humble station, would have been deemed worthy of the office of strategos along with Pericles and Thucydides, the city's most prominent men. And neither would he have escaped the raillery of the comedians, who did not spare even Themistocles. We must also be wary of Istros when he says that he [Sophocles] was not from Athens but from Phlius [a city in Argolis]. Even if he was from Phlius by ancestry, in any case, with the exception of Istros, it is impossible to find anyone else who mentions it. Sophocles was thus Athenian by origin, from the deme of Colonus. He was famed for his life and for his poetry. He received a good education and was brought up in a well-off household. He proved his ability in governmental administration and in his embassies.

2. He was born, it is said, in the second year of the seventy-first Olympiad, under the archontate of Philippos in Athens [= 495–494]. He was younger than Aeschylus and twenty-four years older than Euripides.

3. As a child, he was trained in wrestling and music, and won prizes in both these domains, as Istros says. He studied music with Lampros. And after the naval battle at Salamis, when the Athenians had gathered around the trophy, his body naked and anointed with oil, he sang a prelude, accompanying himself on his lyre, to the chorus that was singing the paean to the victory.

4. It was from Aeschylus that he learned [the art of] tragedy. And he made several innovations in the contests: first of all, he put an end to the role played by the author, because of the weakness of his own voice (earlier, the author was

himself an actor); he increased the number of choreuts from twelve to fifteen, and he introduced the third actor.

5. It is said that taking his cithara, he played it a single time in his *Thamyris*. That is why, it is said, he is represented with his cithara in the Poecile's pictures.

6. Satyros [third century BCE] says that he [Sophocles] had the idea of the curved stick. Istros also says that he invented the white buskins that are worn by both the actors and the choreuts; that he wrote his dramas in conformity with the natural qualities [of his actors and choreuts]; and that he assembled for the Muses a *thiase* [religious association] consisting of educated people.

7. And in short, there was so much grace in his character that he received everyone's affection under all circumstances.

8. He won the contest twenty times, as Carystios [second century BCE] says, often took second prize, and never came in third.

9. And the Athenians chose him as strategos at the age of sixty-five [or seventy-nine] in the war against the Anaioi [= the Samians] seven years before the Peloponnesian War.

10. He was so attached to Athens that despite being invited by several kings he refused to leave his homeland.

11. He was also the priest for Halo, who was an [elevated] hero, along with Asclepius for Chiron. [A statue?] was erected by Iophon, his son, after his death.

12. Sophocles was loved by the gods more than any other, according to what Hieronymus [third century BCE] said about the golden crown. When the latter had been stolen from the Acropolis, Heracles revealed to Sophocles, in a dream, the place where it had been hidden, telling him the house where he should look for it, entering on the right. Sophocles made a "revelation" to the people regarding this crown and received a talent. That was in fact the reward that had been promised. Receiving this talent, he founded the sanctuary of Heracles "Revealer."

13. Several sources report the lawsuit he filed against his son Iophon. Since he had with Iophon with Nicostrata and Ariston with the Siconyian Theoris, he was fonder of the latter's son, who was also named Sophocles. One he even introduced into a drama <the name of Theoris. It is said that> Iophon was jealous of this son and, before members of the phratry, he accused his father of being senile. They sentenced Iophon to pay a fine. According to what Satyros says, Sophocles declared: "If I am Sophocles, I am not mad; if I am mad, I am not Sophocles," and then recited his *Oedipus*.

14. He died, according to Istros and Neanthes [third century BCE], in the following way: the actor Callipides, who had returned from Oponte after a performance, sent him [Sophocles] grapes on the occasion of the Conges [shell-like vases] festival; Sophocles put in his mouth a grape that was still green and choked to death because of his great age. But according to Satyros, it was while reciting *Antigone* and coming toward the end to a long thought that had neither

period nor comma for a pause, he overstressed his voice and lost both his voice and his life. Others say that when he was proclaimed the winner after the performance of his tragedy, he died overcome by joy.

15. He was buried in the cemetery of his ancestors, which is located on the road to Decelea, eleven stadia from the rampart. It is said that on his tombstone a siren had been erected, or according to some, a bronze nightingale. And when the Lacedemonians had fortified this place in the war against the Athenians, Dionysus, having appeared to Lysander in a dream, ordered him to allow the man to be interred in his tomb. Since Lysander had paid him no attention, Dionysus appeared to him a second time, repeating his order. Lysander, asking the exiles about the identity of the dead man and having learned that it was Sophocles, sent a herald to indicate that he granted the authorization to bury him.

16. Lobo [third century BCE] says that the epitaph engraved on his [Sophocles'] tomb was this:

> "In this tomb, I conceal Sophocles, who won first prize in the tragic art, a very venerable figure."

17. Istros says that the Athenians, because of the man's merit, established by decree an annual sacrifice in his honor.

18. His plays, as Aristophanes [of Byzantium, third-to-second century BCE] are 130 in number. Among these, seventeen are not authentic.

19. He competed with Aeschylus, Euripides, Choirilus, Aristias, and many others as well, in particular his son Iophon.

20. In every way he expressed himself in Homer's fashion: for his subjects, he follows in the poet's footsteps; in particular, he takes the *Odyssey* as his model in several plays. He also establishes, in the Homeric way [*Odyssey* 19, vv. 407–9], the etymology of Odysseus's name:

> "I am rightly called Odysseus [*Odusseus*] because of my misfortunes;
>   because many enemies are angry [*ōdusanto*] at me" [= frag. 965 Radt].

He creates characters, introduces variety, and uses ideas with art, preserving the imprint of Homeric grace. That is why an Ionian [?] said that only Sophocles is a disciple of Homer. Many others have imitated one of their predecessors or their contemporaries, but only Sophocles selects from each of them what is most luminous. That is why he was also called "the bee." He produced a mixture of suitability, sweetness, audacity, and variety.

21. He knows how to make aptness proportionate to actions, so that he characterizes character or state of mind in a short hemistich or a single word. That is the most important thing in poetry, knowing how to show character or state of mind.

22. Aristophanes says "Honey was laid [on his lips]" [*PCG* III 2 frag. 679], and in another passage, "Sophocles, whose lips are coated with honey" [cf. above, appendix IV = *PCG* III 2 frag. 598].

23. Aristoxenes says that he was the first of the Athenian poets to introduce the Phrygian mode in his own songs and to mix with it the dithyrambic genre.

The *Suda*'s Article on Sophocles

[Ed. Adler S 815 = test. 2 Radt]. Sophocles, son of Sophilos, of Colonus, Athenian, author of tragedies, born during the seventy-third Olympiad [488–485], so that he is seventeen years older than Socrates.[3] It is he who was the first to use three actors and the actor who is called the tritagonist. And he was the first to have the chorus enter composed of fifteen young people, whereas earlier twelve entered. He was nicknamed "the Bee" because of his sweetness. It is also he who began to compete with subjects play by play, and no longer with a [single] subject for the tetralogy. He wrote an elegy and paeans, and a prose treatise on the chorus, opposing Thespis and Choirilus. The children he had are: Iophon, Leosthenes, Stephanos, and Menecleides. He died after Euripides, at the age of ninety. He had 130 plays performed, and according to some, many more. He won twenty-four victories.

NOTES

·················

Prelude to Part I: A Snapshot of Sophocles

1. Athenaeus, *Deipnosophistes*, 13, 603f–604d (= test. 75 Radt).

Chapter I. The Young Sophocles

1. All the testimonies from antiquity regarding the life and works of Sophocles have been conveniently assembled by S. Radt, *Tragicorum Graecorum Fragmenta*, vol. 4, Sophocles, Göttingen, 1977, pp. 27–95; now see the editio correctior et addendis aucta published in 1999. The main testimonies on Sophocles' life are a *Life of Sophocles* that has been dated to the first century BCE (= test. 1 Radt; French translation given in appendix V) and an article from the encyclopedia called the *Suda*, which dates from the tenth century CE (= test. 2 Radt; French translation also given in appendix V). For testimonies concerning Sophocles' life and death, see test. sect. B Radt. Although the date of his death is certain (archontate of Callias 406/405; see below), the exact date of his birth is still debatable, because all the testimonies are not entirely concordant. The *Life of Sophocles* says that he was born in the second year of the seventy-first Olympiad, under the archontate of Philippos. The *Chronicle of Paros* A64 (*FGrHist* 239 Jacoby = test. 3 Radt) gives the date of his death under the archontate of Callias (406/405) and adds that he was ninety-two years old (= 497/496 for the date of birth, according to the inclusive mode of calculation); cf. also A 56 (*FGrHist* 239 with Jacoby's commentary = test. 33 Radt). The historian Diodorus Siculus's *Bibliotheca historica*, 13, 103, 4 (referring to Apollodorus's chronicle = *FGrHist* 244 F 35 Jacoby = test. 85 Radt) gives the same date for the poet's death but differs by two years regarding his age: ninety (= 495/494 for the birth date, like the *Life of Sophocles*). We can therefore hesitate between the dates of 497–496 and 495/494. According to Pseudo-Lucian, *Examples of Longevity*, c. 24 (= test. 90 Radt), Sophocles died at the age of ninety-five, which would push his date of birth back to 500/499. This isolated testimony is less plausible. The date given by the *Suda* is also isolated: the seventy-third Olympiad (= 488/485) instead of the seventieth (= 496/493).

2. See *Life of Sophocles*, c. 1 (= test. 1 Radt = appendix V): "Sophocles, Athenian by origin, of the deme of Kolonos"; cf. argument no. 1 of *Oedipus at Colonus* (= test. 12 Radt); *Chronicle of Paros* A56 (*FGrHist* 239 Jacoby = test. 33 Radt). For the distinction between the two demes of Colonos, see argument no. 2 of *Oedipus at Colonus* (with a quotation from the fifth-century comic poet Pherecrates, also given by Harpokration = PCG 7, frag. 142 Kassel and Austin). The sanctuary of Poseidon and the eponymous hero Kolonos are mentioned in Sophocles, *Oedipus at Colonus*, vv. 54–55 and 59–61. Modern writers doubt the existence of a deme of Kolonos Agoraios. It is supposed to be not a deme but a district. See D. M. Lewis, "Notes on Attic Inscriptions (II)," *Annual of the British School at Athens* 50, 1955, p. 16 (in its

development XIV, "The Deme Kolonos"). On the Attic demes and their names, see D. Whitehead, *The Demes of Attica 508/7–ca. 250 BC: A Political and Social Study*, Princeton, 1986.

3. On the membership of Sophocles and his family in the tribe of the Aegeis, see D. M. Lewis (quoted above), pp. 14ff.: "The tribal affiliation is demonstrably Aegeis. Sophocles himself stands second on the generals' list of 441–0 (= Androtion *FGrHist* 324 F 38 Jacoby). His grandson stands second on the list of tamaii of 402–401 (= IG II2 1374, l. 3)." On Androtion's list of strategoi and Sophocles' tenure of the office of strategos, see above.

4. Sophocles, *Oedipus at Colonus*, vv. 14–18.

5. Ibid., vv. 53–63.

6. Ibid., vv. 668–93. The ancient critic's remark is to be found in argument no. 1 of *Oedipus at Colonus* (= test. 12 Radt): "The play is one of the admirable ones. Sophocles composed it when he was already old, wanting to please not only his homeland, but also his deme. For he was from Colonus."

7. Sophocles, *Oedipus at Colonus*, v. 40.

8. Ibid., vv. 130–33.

9. The evidence indicating that Sophocles was the son of Sophillos is extensive: see test. C nomen patris Radt. Cf. in particular *Life of Sophocles* c. 1 (= test. 1 Radt = appendix V); *Suda*, s.v. Sophocles (= test. 2 Radt = appendix V); *Chronicle of Paros* A56 (*FGrHist* 239 Jacoby); *Palatine Anthology,* 7, 21 (= test. 177 Radt). Both spellings are attested; but the form Sophillos (with two *l*s), attested in antiquity in the inscription on the Marble of Paros, is the *lectio difficilior*. Grammarians classified this name in the series of words with two *l*s (Arcadius, *De accentibus*, 61, 5 Schmidt; *Theognostos*, Canones 336 in *Anecd. Ox.* 2, 62, 10 Cramer). On the examination of the two forms in the manuscript tradition, see E. Villari, "Due Note sulla Vita Sophoclis § 1 (*TGrF* 429–30 Radt," in A. F. Belleza, *Un Incontro con la Storia nel centenario della nascita di Luca de Regibus 1895–1995*, Genoa, 1996, pp. 165–73), but her conclusion regarding her preference for the form "Sophilos" (with a single "l") is not convincing; she takes into account neither the inscription on the Marble of Paros or the testimony of the grammarians.

10. The reference here is not to the historian but to the politician, Thucydides son of Melesias; it has been suggested that this should be corrected to read "Andocides"; on the discussion of this passage see below.

11. *Life of Sophocles*, c. 1 (= test. 1 Radt = appendix V). The manuscripts give "Themistocles," usually changed to "Pericles." The reading given in the manuscripts is defended by E. Villari (cited above).

12. Istros, a pupil of Callimachus, was an Alexandrian historian of the third century BCE (*FGrHist* 334 Jacoby).

13. Pliny, *Nat. Hist.* 37, 40: principi loco genito Athenis (= test. 15 Radt).

14. Aristophanes, *Acharnians*, v. 457 and scholium; v. 478; *Knights*, v. 19 and scholium; *Thesmophoriazusae*, v. 456; *Frogs*, vv. 840 and 947.

15. See below, chapter II, "Sophocles the Politician."

16. See above, prelude to part I, "A Snapshot of Sophocles."

17. *Life of Sophocles*, c. 4 (= test. 1 Radt = appendix V).

18. For all this, see *Life of Sophocles* c. 3 (= test. 1 Radt = appendix V) and Athenaeus, *Deipnosophistes* 1 20 e (= test. 28 Radt). Lampros, who is mentioned in both these

documents, was a famous music teacher of the fifth century BCE; see Plato, *Menexenus* 236 a (where Socrates mentions Lampros as the Athenian music teacher par excellence, along with the Athenian rhetoric teacher par excellence, Antiphon of Rhamnus). Also see Pseudo-Plutarch, *On Music*, c. 31, 1142 b (VI 3, p. 27, 2 Ziegler = Aristoxène frag. 76 Wehrli). Some scholars think that the reference is actually to Lamprocles, the author of hymns and dithyrambs (evidence and fragments in D. Page, *Poetae Melici Graeci*, Oxford, 1962, pp. 379–80).

19. Herodotus, *Histories*, 6, 109.

20. See Pausanias, *Description of Greece*, trans. W.H.S. Jones and H. A. Ormerod, 1, 14, 5: "This is the victory of which I am of the opinion the Athenians were proudest; while Aeschylus, who had won such renown for his poetry and for his share in the naval battles before Artemisium and at Salamis, recorded at the prospect of death nothing else, and merely wrote his name, his father's name, and the name of his city, and added that he had witnesses to his valor in the grove at Marathon and in the Persians who landed there." Aeschylus died at Gela in Sicily in 456/455. The following epitaph has been preserved in the *Life of Aeschylus*, c. 11 (= *TrGF* 3, test. F b Radt = Page, *Further Greek Epigrams* 476ff.): "This tomb holds Aeschylus, son of Euphorion, Athenian, who died in Gela rich in wheat. His famous valor can be told by the sacred wood at Marathon, as well as by the long-haired Persian who knows it well." Herodotus notes that Aeschylus's brother Cynegirus also fought at Marathon, where he died, "his hand cut off" (*Histories* 6, 114 = Aeschylus test. 16 Radt); cf. also the testimonies *TrGF* 3, test. F b Radt.

21. See the preceding note. At Salamis, Aeschylus fought with his young brother Ameinas: see *Life of Aeschylus*, c. 4 (= *TrGF* 3, test. 16 Radt); cf. also the testimonies in *TrGF* 3, test. F c Radt.

22. Aeschylus, *The Persians*, vv. 402–5.

23. Athenaeus, *Deipnosophistes* 1, 20 f (= test. 28 Radt); cf. *Life of Sophocles*, c. 3 (test. 1 Radt).

24. *Iliad* 2, vv. 594–600.

25. For the fragments of the lost tragedy, see Radt, pp. 234–38, and here appendix II no. 39. On the role he played in his *Thamyris*, also see *Life of Sophocles*, c. 5 (= test. 1 Radt = appendix V) and Anonymous, *On Tragedy*, c. 12 (= test. 99 b Radt). It is debatable whether Sophocles was then a character who did not speak (because *Life* c. 4 says that because of his hoarse voice, Sophocles departed from the tradition according to which the author should also be an actor) or whether he played the role of Thamyris; see the bibliography in test. H a Radt. It is hard to see how he could have played the cithara in his *Tamyris* or played ball in his *Nausicaa* without taking the role of the title character; see the very reasonable note in A. Pickard-Cambridge, *The Dramatic Festivals of Athens*, 2nd ed., revised by J. Gould and D. M. Lewis, reissued with supplement and corrections, Oxford, 1988, p. 130, n. 4.

26. For the evidence, apart from Athenaeus (cited above), see Eustathius of Thessalonica, *Commentary on the Iliad* 381, 8 (= test. 29 Radt); *Commentary on the Odyssey*, 1553, 63 (= test. 30 Radt). On this play, see appendix II, no. 74.

27. Homer, *Odyssey* 6, vv. 99ff.

28. For the three short fragments of this play, which is either a tragedy or a satyr play, see Radt, pp. 361–62, and here appendix II, no. 74.

29. See Victor Hugo, *La Légende des siècles*, "Les Trois Cents," vv. 27–30.

Chapter II. Sophocles the Politician

1. On Sophocles' political career, see R. Develin, *Athenian Officials 684–321 BC*, Cambridge, 1989, p. 503, no. 2766; G. Ugolini, *Sofocle e Atene: Vita politica e attività teatrale nella Grecia classica*, Rome, Carocci, 2000, 275 pp.

2. For a recent study on the *hellenotamiae*, see Loren J. Samons II, "Empire of the Owl: Athenian Imperial Finance," in *Historia*, Einzelschriften 142, Stuttgart, 2000, pp. 70ff.

3. Xerxes on Mount Aigaleos: Herodotus, 8, 90; Xerxes rending his garments: Aeschylus, *The Persians*, vv. 466–68.

4. Thucydides, *The Peloponnesian War*, 1, 96.

5. B. D. Meritt, H. T. Wade-Gery, and M. F. MacGregor, *The Athenian Tribute Lists*, vol. 2, Princeton, 1949, p. 18 (= list 12, l. 36): Σ]οφοκλῆς Κολο[νῆθεν ἑλλενοταμί] ασ ἕν (= test. 18 Radt).

6. The Greek curator of Antiquities, Pittakis, who succeeded the Dane Ross, was the first to reassemble the fragments he had found in 1835 near the gateways and to read them. He recognized immediately that they were all part of a single inscription giving "a catalogue of the contribution made annually to the Athenians by the cities" (K. S. Pittakis, *L'Ancienne Athènes*, Athens, 1835, p. 410); cf. also his article in *Ephèméris Arkaiologikè*, 1853, p. 693, where he recapitulates his discovery of the fragments "near the angle formed by the north wing of the gateways." In this work of 1835, he published for the first time, on pages 410–38, the text of almost seventy fragments that have not yet been numbered.

7. B. D. Meritt, H. T. Wade-Gery, and M. F. MacGregor (cited above).

8. First the Ionian cities (31); then the cities of the Hellespont (26); the cities of Thrace (40), the cities of Caria (42), and finally the cities of the islands (23).

9. The last part is preserved on fragment no. 139 in B. D. Meritt, H. T. Wade-Gery, and M. F. MacGregor, *The Athenian Tribute Lists*, vol. 1, Cambridge, MA, 1939, pp. 59–60; see the photo of the fragment (taken before the reconstruction of the stele), p. 59 (fig. 79) and the drawing (pl. XIII).

10. For the history of the reading of the inscription and the technical debate regarding the identification of the name of Sophocles and the name of the deme, see appendix III, "The Identification of Sophocles as a Hellenotamias."

11. On the question of the chairmanship of the hellenotamiae, see M. H. Jameson, "Seniority in the Stratēgia," *Transactions and Proceedings of the American Philological Association* 86, 1955, pp. 63–87 (pp. 72–77).

12. For evidence concerning the deposit of tribute at the theater during the Great Dionysia, see below, chapter VII, "Space and Spectacle." Sophocles first participated in the tragedy competition in 468 and won it that year; see below, chapter IV, "The Theatrical Career."

13. Thucydides, 1, chap. 97, 1. For this whole section, the references to Thucydides are found in book 1, chaps. 97 to 101.

14. On the problem of the date of this revolt, see É. Lévy, *Athènes devant la défaite de 404*, Bibliothèque des Ecoles françaises d'Athènes et de Rome 225, Athens, 1976, p. 278.

15. Plutarch, "Life of Pericles," 23, 4.

16. Aristophanes, *The Clouds*, vv. 211–13 (staged in 423); cf. also Xenophon, *Hellenica* 2,

3, where we find an allusion to the punishments inflicted on the people of Histiaea, among others.

17. Aristotle, *Constitution of Athens*, 24, 2.

18. See Thucydides, 1, 115; cf. Diodorus, 12, 27, and Plutarch, "Life of Pericles," 25, 14.

19. Thucydides, 8, 76, 4: "Having a city in Samos which, so far from wanting strength, had when at war been within an ace of depriving the Athenians of the command of the sea."

20. Thucydides, 1, 116, 1.

21. On the successive reinforcements, see Thucydides, 1, 115–17; cf. Diodorus 12, 28.

22. The strategoi were recruited, at least initially, from the wealthiest class; see Aristotle, *Constitution of Athens*, 4, 2.

23. During the expedition in the Gulf of Corinth; see Thucydides, 1, 111, 2.

24. Ostracism was a banishment for ten years, voted by the people, of a man judged potentially dangerous for democracy. For Thucydides' ostracism, see Plutarch, "Life of Pericles" 14, 3: "Finally he ventured to undergo with Thucydides the contest of the ostracism, wherein he secured his rival's banishment, and the dissolution of the faction which had been arrayed against him."

25. Thucydides, 2, 65, 9 (trans. Perrin).

26. Strabo, *Geography*, 14, 1, 18, p. 638 C (= test. 21 Radt), trans. H. C. Hamilton and W. Falconer. See also Aristodemos, *FGrHist*. 104 F 1, 15, 4 Jacoby (= test. 21 Radt): "During the fourteenth year [of the thirty-year truce] the Athenians, having besieged Samos, seized it when Pericles and Sophocles were generals." We have to note, however, that the word "Sophocles" is a correction of the manuscript, which reads "Themistocles" (= Par. supp. Greek 607). This correction was made based on the scholium on Hermogenes, ed. Walz, Rhet. gr. 5, 388, 24 (= test. 22 Radt): "During the fourteenth year, the Athenians broke the thirty-year truce, having taken Samos by siege, while Pericles and Sophocles were generals"; cf. also Justin, 3, 6, 12 (= test. 23 Radt).

27. Androtion's text is not known directly, but only through the intermediary of a scholium on Aristides (p. 485, 28 Dind.: a text edited following the *Marc. graecus* 423 by F. Lenz, *Transactions of the American Philological Association*, 72, 1941, pp. 266ff. = *Opuscula selecta*, Amsterdam, 1972, 68ff. = *FGrHist* 324 F 38 Jacoby with the commentary = test. 19 Radt). Androtion's list is introduced into the scholium this way: "In Samos, he himself (sc. Pericles) was the tenth general. The names of the ten generals at Samos, according to Androtion, [are the following.]"

28. For the statues of the eponymous heroes in the agora, see Pausanias 1, 5, 2–4 (with F. Chamoux's commentary in Pausanias, *Description of Greece*, Livre 1, Paris: CUF, 1992, pp. 158ff.).

29. See above, chapter I, "The Young Sophocles," for Sophocles' membership in the Aigeis tribe. This list raises a technical problem debated by historians. It includes in fact eleven names. Some scholars think there is an error in the list handed down to us (the repetition of a name, for instance). Others maintain that there were ten strategoi elected by each tribe and one strategos elected by all the tribes; since two strategoi on the list come from demes belonging to the same tribe (Pericles of Cholargès and Glaucon of Kerameies belong to the same tribe, the Akamantis), it is supposed to be Pericles who was elected by all the tribes (*ex hapantōn*). This double representation of one tribe has been seen as reflecting the desire not to penalize the

other members of a tribe in the event of the regular reelection of one of their members (which was in fact the case for Pericles), or perhaps the desire to elect, in addition to the strategos representing the tribe, a prestigious strategos whether he was de jure or de facto the leader of the college of strategoi. For the recent bibliography on this question, see G. Ugolini (2000), p. 43, n. 1, and p. 45, n. 5. If there were in fact eleven strategoi that year, ten left on the expedition, and one remained in Athens. We will return to this problem apropos of the Soplocles' and Nicias's terms as strategoi below.

30. This information is absolutely certain, because it is his grandson himself, Andocides, who mentions it in his speech "On the Peace," 6: "Ten citizens chosen among all the Athenians were sent to Lacedaemonia with full powers to negotiate the peace treaty: among them was Andocides, my grandfather."

31. *Life of Sophocles*, c. 1 (= test. 1 Radt, p. 30, l. 1ff. = appendix V): text cited above. In order to be elected as a strategos, one had in fact to be able to show an unencumbered property of not less than a hundred minas. On the question of his tenure as a strategos along with Thucydides, and regarding the proposed replacement of Thucydides by Androcides, see below.

32. For more details on this presentation by Aristophanes of Byzantium, see below.

33. Thucydides, 1, 116–17.

34. Diodorus Siculus, *Bibliotheca historica*, 12, 27–28.

35. Plutarch, "Life of Pericles," 24–28.

36. Ibid., 26, 2.

37. On the testimonies to and fragments of Melissus's work in Greek, see H. Diels and W. Kranz, *Die Fragmente der Vorsokratiker*, 10th ed., I, Berlin, 1952, pp. 258–75 (30 A and B).

38. Diogenes Laertius, *Lives of the Eminent Philosophers*, book 9, chap. 4.

39. Plutarch, "Life of Themistocles," 2, 5.

40. *Suda*, s.v. "Meletus," no. 496 Adler (= test. 24 Radt). This is the article on Meletus, the accuser, along with Anytos, of Socrates. The end of the article has nothing to do with Meletus but instead concerns Melissus. It is strange that the author of the *Suda* did not dissociate the end of the article by a specific numbering (no. 496 b).

41. The Olympiad dating the naval battle in the article in the *Suda* is the same as that designating the philosopher's floruit in Diogenes Laertius.

42. Plutarch, "Life of Pericles" 26, 2.

43. Ibid., 8, 8. See also Stobaeus, 3, 17, 18 (= test. 74 e Radt), which contributes nothing new. Pericles' witticism was later erroneously attributed to Isocrates in Pseudo-Plutarch, "Lives of the Ten Orators" 838 f (= test. 74 e Radt).

44. See the explanation of Pericles' witticism by the Roman historian Valerius Maximus (first century CE), 4. 3, ext. 1 (= test. 74 d Radt): "Pericles, the leader of the Athenians, when Sophocles, the author of tragedies, was his colleague as a praetor [strategos], and the latter, restrained as he was by his public office, had praised the beauty of a noble boy too enthusiastically, Pericles, reproaching him for his lack of moderation, declared that a general ought to keep not only his hands away from the attraction of money, but also his eyes away from the spectacle of love."

45. Cicero, *De Officiis*, 1, 144 (= test. 74 c Radt).

46. See above, prelude to part I, "A Snapshot of Sophocles."

47. For this interpretation, cf. F. Jacoby, *FGrHist*. III b (no. 392 T 5), p. 194.

48. The reinforcement of twenty-five ships from Chios and Lesbos is mentioned by both Thucydides (1, 116, 2) and Diodorus Siculus (12, 27, 4).

49. Strabo, *Geography*, 14, 1, 35: "Famous natives of Chios are: Ion the tragic poet, and Theopompus the historian, and Theocritus the sophist."

50. Plutarch, "Life of Cimon," 9, 1 (for the banquet episode) and "Life of Pericles," 5, 3 (for the judgment on Pericles).

51. Whereas Sophocles was born in 495/494 (or 497/496), Ion was born in the 480s; and whereas Sophocles' theatrical career began in 469/468 (see below), that of Ion began during the eighty-second Olympiad (451/448); see *Suda*, s.v. Ion of Chios.

52. According to the *Suda* (ibid.), some authorities said he wrote twelve tragedies, while others said he wrote thirty; or according to still others, forty.

53. We do not know the exact date of this victory. Regarding the victory itself, see the scholium on Aristophanes' *Peace*, v. 835 (s.v. Ion of Chios): "It is said that having competed for both the dithyramb and the tragedy in Attica, he won the prize and as a gesture of good will sent each of the Athenians a glass of wine from Chios." In 429/428, he won third prize, behind Euripides (with his *Hippolytus*) and Iophon, Sophocles' son; see the "argument" of Euripides' *Hippolytus*.

54. Aristophanes, *Peace*, v. 835.

55. Longinus, *On the Sublime*, 33, 5.

56. See Aristophanes, *Peace*, vv. 834–37, with the scholium RV on v. 835; see also *Suda*, s.v. dithyrambodidaskaloi.

57. Isocrates, *Antidosis* ("Exchange"), 268.

58. Plutarch, "Life of Pericles," 28, 1, 6.

59. Plutarch, "Whether an Old Man Should Engage in Public Affairs," c. 2 (784 d). In Plutarch, *Moralia*, trans. F. C. Babbitt, Cambridge, MA: Harvard University Press, Loeb Classical Library, 193.

60. Thucydides, *Peloponnesian War*, trans. Warner, 2, 16, 2.

61. On the ramparts of Athens being visible from the deme of Colonus, see Sophocles, *Oedipus at Colonus*, vv. 14–15 (quoted above).

62. Aristophanes, *Acharnians*, v. 32.

63. See Thucydides, 2, 47, 3–54, 5; cf. also Diodorus Siculus, 12, 45, and esp. 58. For the return of the epidemic after a short remission, there is a difference in date between Thucycides and Diodorus: whereas Thucydides gives the year 427/426, Diodorus places it a year later (426/425).

64. See G. Daux, "Œdipe et le fléau (Sophocle, *Œdipe Roi*, 1–275)," *Revue des études greques* 53, 1940 pp. 97–122.

65. Sophocles, *Oedipus the King*, vv. 22–30.

66. Ibid., vv. 168–86.

67. According to Thucydides (3, 87), forty-four hundred hoplites and three hundred horses; and according to Diodorus Siculus (12, 58, 2), more than four thousand hoplites and four hundred horses.

68. It seems that the term Thucydides used (*anexeuretos*) echoes the one Sophocles used (*anarithmos*, v. 179). We must not forget that Thucydides' narrative was composed after the tragedy. Diodorus, for his part, gives a figure for the civilian population as well: more than ten thousand men, both free and slave. It has been estimated that

the city lost more than a quarter of its adult male citizens. On the calculation of the Athenian population at the beginning of the Peloponnesian War, see É. Lévy, *La Grèce au Ve siècle de Clisthène à Socrate*, Paris, Le Seuil, 1995, pp. 122–34.

69. Thucydides, 2, 48, 3: "I had the disease myself."

70. Thucydides, 2, 51, 4–5, and 52, 2–4.

71. Thucydides, 2, 47, 4.

72. Thucydides, 2, 50. [Translation modified.]

73. Sophocles, *Oedipus the King*, vv. 170–71.

74. Thucydides, 2, 47, 4. [Translation modified.]

75. Plutarch, "Life of Sophocles," 34, 5.

76. For the comparison of Oedipus with Pericles, see Jebb, *The Oedipus Tyrannus*, Cambridge, 3rd ed., 1893, p. xxx, who mentions this comparison, while at the same time distancing himself from it: "Modern ingenuity has recognized Pericles in Oedipus,—the stain of the Alcmaeonid lineage in his guilt as the slayer of Laïus"; see also V. Ehrenberg, *Sophocles and Pericles*, Oxford, 1954, pp. 114–16. Pericles has even been compared with Creon in *Antigone*; see ibid., pp. 145–49, and C. G. Thomas, "Sophocles, Pericles and Creon," *Classical World* 69, 1975, pp. 120–22.

77. For the attempt to relate the tragedy to the two successive epidemics of "plague" in Athens, see B.M.W. Knox, "The Date of the Oedipus Tyrannus," *American Journal of Philology* 77, 1956, pp. 133–47. In its plea to the divinities to spare them, the chorus alludes to an earlier disaster (vv. 164–66). But is that sufficient reason to see in this distinction between an ancient scourge and a new one a reference to two attacks of the plague in Athens, in 429/428 and 427–426? Though he mentions a return of the plague in Athens in 427–426, Thucydides recognizes that the epidemic had never completely ended (3, 87). Moreover, this reference to the past takes place in a ritual formula invoking the divinities (cf. for example Homer, *Iliad* 5, v. 116). In such a context, an allusion to reality is hardly perceptible.

78. Homer, *Iliad* 1, vv. 50–52: the plague that strikes the Achaeans at the beginning of the *Iliad* affects first the animals, mules and dogs, then men. Hesiod, *Works and Days*, vv. 242–45: the scourge that strikes the unjust king's city is both a plague and a famine, as is also the case in Sophocles. For the influence of the epic model on Sophocles, see J. Jouanna, "Médecine hippocratique et tragédie grecque," in P. Ghiron-Bistagne and B. Schouler (eds.), *Anthropologie et théâtre antique*, Cahiers du Gita 3, Montpellier, pp. 109–31 (particularly pp. 110–14).

79. The plague is mentioned neither in testimonies before Sophocles (*Odyssey* 11, vv. 271–80; *Oedipodie* in Pausanias 9, 5, 10–11; Pindar, *Olympics* 2, vv. 42–47; Aeschylus, *Seven against Thebes*, vv. 778–80), nor in the later testimonies (Euripides, *The Phoenician Women*, v. 59; Androtion, *FGrHist* 324 F 62 Jacoby = scholium on the *Odyssey* 11, v. 271; Diodorus Siculus, *Bibliotheca historica* 4, 64–65; Apollodorus, *Bibliotheca*, 3, 8–9).

80. *Antigone*, v. 1015.

81. Plutarch, "Life of Pericles," 38, 1.

82. Ibid., 36, 6–8.

83. Thucydides, 2, 65, 9–10.

84. Sophocles plays on the meaning of the Greek word *presbutatos*, which means "the oldest," but also "the most respected."

85. Plutarch, "Life of Nicias," 15, 2 (= test. 26 Radt).

86. Historians have taken a great interest in this passage from the "Life of Nicias." See M. H. Jameson (cited above), pp. 70ff., and H. D. Westlake, "Sophocles and Nicias as colleagues," *Hermes* 84, 1956, pp. 110–16. These two articles, written independently, arrive at convergent conclusions regarding the importance of this passage not only for Sophocles' life but also for the office of strategos (the question of the chairmanship of the college of strategoi and of the strategos called ex hapantōn). These two articles, which can be considered as foundational, have served as the basis for the subsequent discussions that have borne chiefly on the existence of an annual chairmanship of the college: see K. J. Dover, "DEKATOS AUTOS," *Journal of Hellenic Studies* 80, 1960, pp. 61–77 (pp. 62ff.) and N.G.L. Hammond, "Strategia and Hegemonia in Fifth-Century Athens," *Classical Quarterly*, n.s., 19, 1969, pp. 111–44 (p. 132, n. 1); L. Woodbury, "Sophocles among the Generals," *Phoenix* 24, 1970, pp. 209–24 (pp. 211–15).

87. We do not know Nicias's exact date of birth; we know only that he was older than Socrates, who was born in 469 (Plato, *Laches*, 186 c): "They (sc. Nicias and Laches) are older," says Socrates.

88. Plato, *Gorgias*, 472 a. On the office of choregos, see below, chapter VII, "Space and Spectacle," under "The Role of the Choregos."

89. Plutarch, "Life of Nicias," 3, 3.

90. For Nicias, see Plutarch, "Life of Nicias," 3, 3: "He was often victorious with choruses, and was never defeated." For Sophocles, see below.

91. On this Sophocles, son of Sostratidès, see Thucydides 3, 115, and 4, 65. It is said that this argument goes back to F. Schultz, *De vita Sophoclis poetae*, Berolini, 1836, pp. 48ff. It was taken up again, with a question mark, by Schmidt-Stählin, *Gr. Literatur Gesch.* I, 2, Munich, 1934, p. 319, n. 1.

92. For this argument, see M. H. Jameson (cited above) p. 71; H. D. Westlake (cited above), p. 111.

93. The council of strategoi that decided on the general strategy to be adopted when the expedition, which had reached Rhegion, at the southern tip of Italy, was across from Sicily is a sign of Alcibiades' preeminence. At this council, which is recounted in detail by Thucydides (6, 47–50), Nicias, Alcibiades, and Lamachos set forth their plans one after the other. The plan that won out was Alcibiades, because Lamachos threw his support to him. In practice, Lamachos's support for Alcibiades deprived Nicias of any power and gave Lamachos himself a relative power.

94. Thucydides, 6, 62.

95. Plutarch, "Life of Nicias," 14, 4, and 15, 1.

96. Thucydides, 6, 53 and 61.

97. Thucydides, 6, 101.

98. The change in the tense of the verbs (from a past tense to an atemporal present tense, *legetai*) and the distinction of temporal adverbs (*pote/tote*) makes it clear that the event recounted in the anecdote did not take place at the time when Nicias was in Sicilia.

99. On Nicias's career as a strategos, see A. Gugenheim, "Chronologie des stratégies de Nicias de la mort de Périclès à la paix de 421," *Bull. Fac. Lettres de Strasbourg* 42, 1964, pp. 251–56; see also H. D. Westlake, "Nicias in Thucydides," *Classical Quarterly* 35, 1941, pp. 58–65 (very skeptical regarding Sophocles' career as a general, except for his performance on Samos).

100. Plutarch, "Life of Nicias," 2, 2.
101. See D. M. Lewis, "Double Representation in the Strategia," *Journal of Hellenic Studies* 81, 1961, pp. 118–23 (p. 121: "Against Plutarch's vague statement [Nikias 2, 2] that Nikias was a general with Perikles and carried on many expeditions with him, we must set the silence of our other sources and the certainty that he was not general for Aigeis in 441/440, 439/438, 432/431 or 431/430").
102. Thucydides, 3, 51.
103. In 426/425, Nicias was once again the general leading an expedition of sixty ships that operated on the island of Melos in Boeotia and then on the coast of Locris (Thucydides 3, 91); for the strategia of the years 427/426 and 426/425, see D. M. Lewis (cited above), pp. 119–21. The following year (425/424, Nicias was strategos at Pylos, assigned to blockade the island of Sphacteria, where four hundred Spartan hoplites were trapped; but he yielded his command to his rival, the demagogue Cleon, who had accused him of being unwilling to take prompt action (Thucydides 4, 27–28); and Nicias led an expedition of eighty ships against Corinth, where he won a victory (Thucydides 4, 42–44). Reelected strategos in 424/423, he led, with two other strategoi, the successful expedition that seized the island of Cythera, a Lacedaemonian possession situated across from Laconia (Thucydides 4, 129–32). The following year (423/422) he was one of the three Athenian generals who signed the one-year peace treaty between Sparta and Athens (Thucydides 4, 119), and one of the leaders of the expedition of fifty ships the Athenians sent to bring back into the Athenian alliance two cities in Thracian Chalcidice, Mende and Skione (Thucydides 4, 129–32). In 422/421 Nicias, who had up to that point always been successful in leading operations, was the principal architect in Athens of the peace, and he was one of the seventeen Athenians who swore the five-year peace treaty and the treaty of alliance with Sparta (Thucydides 5, 19 and 24); he was certainly a strategos that year as well, because Thucydides presents him as the one "who had done better in his military commands than anyone else of his time" (5, 16, 1).
104. Plutarch, "Life of Nicias," 9, 8–9.
105. Thucydides 5, 46.
106. Thucydides, 5, 52.
107. In his account of the year 417/416, Thucydides (5, 83) refers to Nicias's activity as a strategos: an expedition under his command was supposed to move against the Chalcidians in Thrace and against Amphipolis, but it was cancelled after the defection of the king of Macedonia, Perdiccas, who did not provide the aid he had promised; this incident occurred before the winter of 417/416.
108. Like Colonus, Sophocles' deme (see above), Nicias's deme, Cydantidae (cf. IG I3 370, 50), belonged to the Aïgeis tribe (cf. IG II2 1749 20). This fact was noted in passing by A. B. West, "Notes on Certain Athenian Generals of the Year 424–3 B.C.," *American Journal of Philology* 45, 1924, p. 156, n. 53; it was used by M. H. Jameson (cited above), p. 70, and H. D. Westlake (cited above), pp. 111ff.
109. See above for the year 441/440. This is the first attestation of a double representation of the Akamantis tribe, to which Pericles belonged. This occurred five more times for Pericles in the space of ten years; see the list in M. H. Jameson (cited above), pp. 65ff.
110. This technical expression (*strategos ex hapantōn*) is customarily employed by histo-

rians to refer to the strategoi in Athens, although Aristotle does not mention them in his *Constitution of Athens*.

111. In fact, in 426/425 we note a case of double strategia when Nicias was strategos, but this case does not concern the Aïgeis tribe, so that the strategos ex hapantōn cannot be Nicias; see D. H. Lewis (cited above), pp. 119–21.

112. H. D. Westlake (cited above), pp. 114ff., proposes 423/422, suggesting that the presence of the "conservative" Sophocles might have been useful for Nicias in the negotiations for the armistice and the peace treaty.

113. Plutarch, "Life of Phocion," 24, 5; cf. *Moralia*, 791 e–f and 819 a: Dio Chrysostom, 73, 7.

114. See below.

115. Plutarch, "Life of Nicias," 5, 1.

116. Scholium on Aristophanes' *Peace*, v. 697 (extract): "Simonides was accused of loving money; Sophocles therefore resembles Simonides because of their love of money; it is said that after his strategia on Samos he had grown rich."

117. Cf. Jameson (cited above), pp. 70ff., and Westlake (cited above), p. 115. See also T.B.L. Webster, *An Introduction to Sophocles*, London, 1969, pp. 12ff. Contrast Woodbury's skepticism (cited above), p. 215, n. 30.

118. *Life of Sophocles*, c. 1 (= test. 1 Radt = appendix V). Already cited above.

119. On Sophocles' strategia with Thucydides, son of Melesias, see Webster (cited above), p. 12; A. E. Raubitschek, "Theopompos on Thucydides the son of Melesias," *Phoenix* 14, 1960, pp. 81–95 (pp. 85ff.).

120. The expression is V. Ehrenberg's in his *Sophocles and Pericles*, Oxford, 1954, p. 116, n. 1.

121. Elected in 440/439, this Thucydides came from Athens to Samos with his colleagues Hagnon and Phormion at the head of forty ships of reinforcements. This information is provided by the historian Thucydides, 1, 117.

122. V. Leutsch, *Philol. Anz.* 7, 1875/1876, p. 204 (cf. test. 1 Radt, app. crit. ad loc.).

123. *Life of Sophocles*, c. 9 (= test. 1 Radt). On the city of Anaia, see R. E. s.v., Zweite Halbband 1894 (Hirschfeld); on the topography of the region, see Louis Robert, *Philologie et géographie, Anatolia* 4, 1959, pp. 15–24.

124. Thucydides, 4, 75, 1.

125. Thucydides, 3, 32.

126. Thucydides, 3, 19. Other references to Anaia in Thucydides: 8, 19; 8, 61.

127. Webster (cited above), p. 12, considers both hypotheses.

128. The replacement of "Anaians" by "Samians" was proposed by Seidler in Hermann, *Antigona*, Lipsiae, 1823, p. xxiv (cf. test. 1 Radt. app. crit. ad loc.). That is the hypothesis adopted by Westlake (cited above), p. 110, n. (he gives no arguments for his choice). But is it plausible that the "Samians," who were well known, disappeared in the transmission of the text in favor of the much less well-known Anaians? Besides, neither of the two chronological indications given by the *Life of Sophocles* allows us to go back as far as 441/440. Both of them would have to be modified. The solution that consists in trying to assimilate Sophocles' strategia during the "war" against the Anaians to the one in which he took part in the expedition against Samos is thus implausible.

129. This modification is owed to G. Perotta, *Sofocle*, Messina-Milan, 1935, p. 42, n. 1. It was taken up by Ugolini (2000, cited above), pp. 59–64. Ugolini calls Perotta's cor-

rection a "geniale intuizione" (p. 59). However, this correction is far from being generally accepted. The expression *ta Peloponnsiaka* usually means "the Peloponnesian War," whereas the corrected expression *ai Peloponnesiakai spondai* is unparalleled. This remark was already made by Woodbury (cited above), p. 14, n. 29. Moreover, the correction does not solve every problem, as Perotta and Ugolini think. Certainly, Sophocles' age corresponds, more or less; certainly, in 428/427 the Anaians made a surprise attack on an Athenian strategos. But can we speak of a war? In addition, saying that Nicias was a strategos in 428/427, based on Thucydides 3, 51, 1 (Perotta, p. 42, no. 1, and Ugolini, p. 61), is problematic: Nicias was a strategos in the summer of 427, but we do not know to what Athenian year this period of the summer corresponded (end of 428/427 or the beginning of 427/426?). Finally, the date 428/427 is too early in Nicias's career to allow us to envisage a strategia ex hapantōn.

130. Thucydides, 4, 75, 1.

131. The fact that Thucydides does not speak of this war against the Anians at the time when it took place is not an objection. The history of the revolt of Samos is part of the history of the Pentekontaetia, that is, the period of fifty years separating the Persian Wars from the Peloponnesian War. But Thucydides did not deal in detail with the period. In this interpretation Sophocles' age has to be modified. It is pointless to recall that in the manuscripts errors in figures are not rare when the figures are notated by letters, as is the case here.

132. Thucydides, 7, 86, 5.

133. Thucydides, 8, 1, 3–4.

134. Aristotle, *Constitution of Athens*, 29, 2.

135. *Lexica Segueriana* (e cod. Coislin 345) = Becker, *Anecd.*, p. 128: "Probouloi: ten magistrates, at the rate of one per tribe, whose function is to bring together the Council and the popular assembly." The evidence is given by P. Foucart, "Le poète Sophocle et l'oligarchie des Quatre Cents," *Revue de Philologie* 17, 1893, pp. 1–10 (p. 4, n. 1).

136. Aristotle, *Constitution of Athens*, 32, 2.

137. Aristotle, *Rhetoric*, 3, 18 (1419 a 23–31).

138. The two obscure candidates are Sophocles, son of Sostratides, who had been sent to Sicily in 425 and had been banished upon his return (see above), or another Sophocles who was part of the second oligarchic regime, that of the Thirty Tyrants in 404 (see the list of the names of these Thirty Tyrants in Xenophon, *Hellenica*, 2, 3, 2). These candidates had been already proposed by nineteenth-century scholars (for example, Curtius and Dindorf, cited by P. Foucart [cited above], p. 2, n. 1); as for the twentieth century, see for example Woodbury (cited above), p. 216, who considers the second of the obscure Sophocles. For the identification of the poet Sophocles as a *proboulos*, in the nineteenth century see the short but excellent article by P. Foucart (cited above); and in the twentieth century, see especially M. H. Jameson, "Sophocles and the Four Hundred," *Historia* 20, 1971, pp. 541–68; and recently, Ugolini (cited above), pp. 80–82.

139. Aristotle, *Rhetoric*, 3, 17 (1418 b, 31–34).

140. Thus we can also conclude that the two other passages in the *Rhetoric* where Sophocles is mentioned without reference to one of his works also concern the tragic poet. Here are those two passages: *Rhetoric*, 3, 15 (1416 a 14–17): "Another method consists in saying that it was a case of error, misfortune, or necessity; as, for example,

Sophocles said that he trembled, not, as the accuser said, in order to appear old, but from necessity, for it was against his wish that he was eighty years of age"; and *Rhetoric*, I, 14 (1374 b 35–1375 a 2), regarding the seriousness of the offense, judged in relation to the significance of the damage done: "And if the sufferer, having been wronged, has inflicted some terrible injury upon himself, the guilty person deserves greater punishment; wherefore Sophocles, . . . when pleading on behalf of Euctemon, who had committed suicide after the outrage he had suffered, declared that he would not assess the punishment at less than the victim had assessed it for himself."

141. P. Foucart (cited above), p. 2.

142. Lysias ("Against Eratosthenes," c. 65) mentions that the father of Theramenes was one of the *probouloi*; and Thucydides (8, 77, 4) gives the name of this father when he presents Theramenes for the first time: "Theramenes, son of Hagnon"; cf. also Thucydides, 8, 89, and Xenophon, *Hellenica*, 2, 3, 30.

143. For his descent, see Thucydides 2, 58, 1; for the deme of Steiria, see the scholium on Aristophanes, *The Frogs*, v. 541. For both at once, see Cratinos, *Ploutoi*, PGC IV, frag. 171 Kassel and Austin p. 208, vv. 67–68, and p. 209, v. 73: the son of Nicias of Steira who is called Hagnon.

144. Thucydides, 1, 117 (see above). He was also the founder, in 437/436 of the colony of Amphipolis (Thucydides, 4, 102; 5, 11).

145. Thucydides, 2, 58. He also played a stabilizing role during the conflicts between the people and Pericles (Plutarch, "Life of Pericles," c. 32).

146. Thucydides, 2, 95, 3.

147. Thucydides, 5, 19 and 24. Since Hagnon was the son of a certain Nicias (cf. Thucydides, 4, 102, 3; cf. Cratinos, cited above), it has been asked whether there was a family tie between Hagnon and Nicias. However, they did not come from the same deme.

148. Xenophon, *Hellenica*, 2, 3, 30, says that Theramenes was "initially highly esteemed by the popular party because of the merits of his father Hagnon."

149. Aristophanes, *Lysistrata*, vv. 599–613.

150. Aristotle, *Rhetoric*, 3, 15 (passage cited above).

151. Aristophanes, *Lysistrata*, vv. 421–22.

152. Thucydides, 8, 1, 3; passage cited above.

153. Thucydides, 8, 4, and 5, 1.

154. Thucydides 8, 8, 4.

155. Thucydides 8, 10, 2 and 3.

156. Thucydides 8, 15, 1.

157. Aristophanes, *Lysistrata*, vv. 422ff. and v. 496.

158. Aristophanes, *Lysistrata*, vv. 488ff.

159. Thucydides 8, 14 to 19.

160. Thucydides 8, 79, 6.

161. Thucydides 8, 68, 4.

162. Thucydides 8, 68, 4.

163. In Aristophanes' comedy *The Thesmophoriazusae*, performed like *Lysistrata* in 411, it is said (vv. 808ff.) that the preceding year (= 413/412) the members of the council had handed over their offices to others. This clearly alludes to the election of the *probouloi*.

164. See above.
165. Thucydides 8, 66, 5.
166. See Lysias, "Against Eratosthenes" c. 45: "He (sc. Theramenes) at first contributed more than anyone to the establishment of the first oligarchy, by pesuading you to adopt the regime of the Four Hundred. His father, who was a *proboulos* (already) followed the same policy."
167. Xenophon, *Hellenica*, 2, 3, 30: "It is he (Theramenes) who, esteemed at first by the popular party because of his father Hagnon's merits, was the most disposed to transform the democracy to make it the regime of the Four Hundred, and he was a major figure among the latter. But when he perceived that a certain opposition was being constituted against the oligarchy, he was the first to lead the people against the Four Hundred: and that is what earned him his nickname of 'buskin.'"
168. In the institutional history of the formation of the oligarchic government of the Four Hundred, historians have great difficulties, because there are significant differences between Aristotle's *Constitution of Athens* and Thucydides' account. Whereas Aristotle, citing Pythocles' decree, speaks of the enlargement of the commission of the ten *probouloi* by an additional twenty members to make better proposals in the city's interest, Thucydides (8, 67, 1) mentions a committee of ten members given full powers to propose the best regime for the city. This opposition was already noted in antiquity by Harpocration (s.v. *suggrapheis*), who tells us that Aristotle's version was also that of Androtion and Philocorus in their history of Attica. See also the scholium on Aristophanes, *Lysistrata*, v. 421 for the thirty-member enlarged commission.
169. Thucydides 8, 67, 2.
170. M. H. Jameson (cited above), p. 561: "Did his name secure the compliance of the balky?"
171. Thucydides 8, 70, 2.
172. In the last popular assembly held in Colonus, it was proposed to put an end to all the old order's magistracies (Thucydides 8, 67, 3).
173. Aristotle, *Constitution of Athens*, 32, 3.
174. Thucydides, 8, 76, 1.
175. Thucydides 8, 70, 2; 71, 3.
176. Thucydides 8, 75, 1.
177. Thucydides 8, 82, 2.
178. Thucydides 8, 89, 2–4.
179. Thucydides 8, 92, 7 sq.
180. Thucydides 8, 93, 3.
181. Thucydides 8, 97, 2; Aristotle, *Constitution of Athens* 33, 2.
182. M. Lebeau le cadet, "Mémoires sur les tragiques grecs," Mém. de lit., taken from the records of the Académie royale des inscriptions et belles-lettres, Paris XXXV (1770), 441–43. The discussions that inaugurated the question at the end of the eighteenth and the beginning of the nineteenth century remain exemplary of the three possible positions. When Lebeau le cadet prudently advanced the hypothesis of a possible relation between Philoctetes' return and that of Alcibidades, M. Patin, in his *Étude sur les Tragiques grecs*, absolutely condemned it, whereas Charles Lenormand, in a long article in the *Correspondant* for 1855 devoted to *Philoctetes* on the occasion of a performance of the tragedy by the pupils of the little chapel seminary

in the episcopal palace of Orléans, finds that Lebeau le cadet's sole error is the "lack of development and confidence" regarding the political allusions that can be found in *Philoctetes*. Jebb (*Philoctetes*, 1898, p. xl, n. 5) alludes to this debate and, while recognizing the analogy between the political situation and the mythical subject that might have justified Sophocles' choice, does not see the influence of current events in the general development of the tragedy. For modern views concerning an analogy between Alcibiades and Philoctetes, see for example L. Canfora, *Histoire de la littérature grecque d'Homère à Aristote*, Paris, 1995, p. 225. On the criticism of this analogy in the context of an attentive comparison of the historical situation and the tragedy, see M. H. Jameson, "Politics and the Philoctetes," *Classical Philology* 51, 1956, pp. 217–27 (p. 219 sq.). On the connections between current events and *Philoctetes*, see also W. M. Calder III, "Sophoclean Apologia: Philoctetes," *Greek, Roman and Byzantine Studies* 12, 1971, pp. 153–74.

183. This is Thucydides' version (8, 97, 3). Diodorus Siculus (13, 38, 41, and 42) does not disagree, because he attributes the decree recalling Alcibiades to the initiative of Theramenes, who was the head of state; this clearly alludes to a decree issued by the government of the Five Thousand. According to Plutarch ("Life of Alcibiades," 33), the decree was proposed by Critias, a politician and poet who in any case boasted, in his elegies, that he had proposed and written the decree. Plutarch quotes three of Critias's verses relative to this decree.

184. Thucydides 8, 81–82.

185. Thucydides 8, 108.

186. Plutarch, "Life of Alcibiades," 27, 1.

187. Diodorus Siculus, *Bibliotheca historica* 13, 41–42. Diodorus's version can be traced back to the historian Ephorus.

188. Thucydides 8, 89.

189. Thucydides 8, 70, 1.

190. Xenophon, *Hellenica* 1, 4, 18; Plutarch, "Life of Alcibiades," 32, 2.

191. Thucydides 8, 53, 2. These families were the Eumolpides and the Kerykes. The family of the Eumolpides provided the *hierophant* ("priest displaying the sacred objects") and that of the Kerykes provided the *dadouchos* ("torch-bearer").

192. Thucydides 8, 47–48.

193. Thucydides 8, 81.

194. Thucydides 8, 65, 2.

195. Xenophon, *Hellenica*, trans. C. L. Brown, Cambridge, MA: Harvard University Press, Loeb Classical Library, 1918, 1, 1, 23.

196. Homer, *Iliad* 2, vv. 724ff.

197. For details, see the presentation of *Philoctetes* in appendix I.

198. Pindar, *Pythian* 1, vv. 54ff.

199. Thucydides, 8, 53, 1.

200. Sophocles, *Philoctetes*, vv. 1340ff.

201. Jameson (cited above) uses such differences on pp. 219ff. to contest any analogy between Alcibiades and Philoctetes.

202. Thucydides 8, 81, 2.

203. Sophocles, *Philoctetes*, vv. 254–316.

204. L. Canfora (cited above), p. 225 ("The analogy with Alcibiades—who several times declined the offer to return to Athens, despite the unanimous wish and the guaran-

tee offered by his former adversaries, like Theramenes—is clear. For Philoctetes as for Alcibiades, all the conditions for a return have been met except the will of the person concerned").

205. The conviction that there is a political allusion here is ancient. It already existed in antiquity, as is shown by the scholium on Sophocles' *Philoctetes*, v. 99: "The poet criticizes the orators of his time, accusing them of doing everything by means of the word."

206. M. Lebeau le cadet (cited above), p. 442.

207. See Dio Chrysostom, *Orations*, 42, c. 13 (cf. appendix IV): "And he (sc. Euripides) says that an embassy must come from the Trojans to Philoctetes to ask him to hand over to them his own person and his weapon in exchange for the throne of Troy."

208. Even among the relatively rare modern scholars who agree to see a connection between contemporary events and the Philoctetes, interpretations may vary or even diverge. M. H. Jameson (cited above), pp. 221–24, does not believe in the analogy between Philoctetes and Alcibiades but draws an interesting parallel between Achilles' young son and the young son of Pericles (and Aspasia) at the dawn of a political career that began with an appointment as a hellenotamia in 410 and ended tragically after the battle of Arginusae; see below. For his part, W. M. Calder III (cited above), pp. 153–74, also thinks, contrary to Wilamowitz, that the tragedy is "intimately related to the events preceding March 409" and establishes a connection between Philoctetes and Sophocles himself. A man of honor like Philoctetes, and abused like him by an unscrupulous entourage, Sophocles voted for an oligarchic government that betrayed his principles. The tragedy would be a kind of "apology" offered by the old man to justify his behavior.

Chapter III. Sophocles the Religious Man

1. *Life of Sophocles*, c 12 (= test. Radt). Cf. also Libanios, Letters, 9: Libanios speaks of a man "more chaste than Peleus and no less loved by the gods than Sophocles."

2. On Sophocles' piety, see the scholium on Sophocles, *Electra*, v. 831: "It is absolutely impossible that Sophocles blasphemed against the gods; in fact, he was one of the most pious men."

3. *Life of Sophocles*, c. 12 (= Hieronymus frag. 31 Wehrli = test. 1 Radt = appendix V).

4. Strabo, 14, 2, 13 mentions Hieronymus as one of the famous men of the island of Rhodes. His work *On the Poets* consisted of at least five books, the fifth dealing with the poets of Cithara (cf. Athenaeus, 14, 635ff.); one book was devoted to the tragic poets (cf. *Suda*, s.v. Anagyrasios). The anecdote might also come from Hieronymous's *Historical Memoirs*, because Athenaeus preserved another anecdote concerning Sophocles that he found in Hieronymus of Rhodes (Athenaeus 13, 604 d–e = fr. 35 Wehrli = test. 75 Radt); and there, Athenaeus explains that it is found in the *Historical Memoirs*. This other anecdote concerns Sophocles' love life. On Hieronymus the disciple of Aristotle, see for example Athenaeus 10, 424ff.; cf. Diogenes Laertius 4, 41; 5, 68, and 9, 112.

5. See the list of the works of Aristotle in Diogenes Laertius 5, 22 (*On the Poets*, I–II–III).

6. Cicero, *De divinatione* ("On divination"), trans. W. A. Falconer, 25, 54.

7. Contrast H. Dettmer, "De Hercule attico" (diss., Bonn, 1869, p. 14): "videtur . . . Cicero liberius rem ex graecis fontibus depromptam tractare" and L. Radermacher

(*Sophokles . . .* 1 *Aias* 10 Berlin, 1913, 3*): "Das Richtige steht bei Cicero; die Vita berichtet falsch nach Hieronymus." Median position in E. Hiller, "Hieronymi Rhodii peripatetici fragmenta," in *Satura Philologa H. Sauppio . . .* , Berolini 1878, pp. 85–118 (pp. 112ff.): like Dettmer, Hiller attributes the differences to Cicero's free adaptation of a model; however, he gives preference to Cicero on an important point: the existence of the sanctuary of Heracles before Sophocles. According to him, the legend of the sanctuary's foundation was transferred to Sophocles, who was known for his piety.

8. As F. Wehrli points out in *Die Schule des Aristoteles* X, p. 38 (commentary on frag. 31): "Gold crowns were in fact kept on the Acropolis" (IG II 699–701 = IG II2 1437, 1441, 1443); their theft was punished as a sacrilege (cf. Goran-Zimec RE XI, 1601). Thus the legend at least contains Athenian elements."

9. Tertullian, *De anima*, 46, 9 (= test. 167 c Radt).

10. See U. Köller, "Der Südabhang der Akropolis in Athen," *Mitteilungen des Deutschen Archäologischen Instituts (Athenische Abteilung)* 2, 1877, pp. 249–51 (four votive inscriptions to Heracles), and C. Watzinger, "Herakles ΜΗΝΥΤΗΣ," ibid., 29, 1904, pp. 237–43 (the statuette of Heracles). According to Watzinger, Sophocles founded a sanctuary of Heracles Ménutes. F. Kutsch, "Attische Heilgötter und Heilheroen," diss., Giessen, 1913, pp. 22ff., approves Watzinger's position; but he deforms it somewhat: according to Watzinger, as presented by Kutsch, Sophocles reestablished the cult of Heracles in the Asclepieion.

11. Plutarch, "Life of Numa," 4, 8 (= test. 67 Radt). The god who obtained a tomb for Sophocles is Dionysus (see below). On this passage, see R. Flacelière, "Sur quelques passages des *Vies* de Plutarque," *Revue des Etudes Grecques* 61, 1948, pp. 391–429 (14. "Sophocle aimé des dieux: *Numa* IV, 10," pp. 412–17).

12. Plutarch, "That Epicurus Actually Makes a Pleasant Life Impossible," 22 (1103 a) (= test. 68 Radt).

13. Philostratus the Younger (third century CE), *Images* 13 (= test. 174 Radt). For a description of the painting as a whole, see below.

14. For Sophocles' paean in honor of Asclepius, see below.

15. Cf. Pausanias 2, 26, 8, and Philostratus, *Vita Apollonii* 4, 18, 3.

16. Pausanias 2, 10, 3.

17. Livy, *History of Rome*, 11, summary, trans. B. O. Foster, Loeb Classical Library.

18. See also the foundation of Epidauros Limera in Laconia (Pausanias 3, 23, 6).

19. *Life of Sophocles*, c 11 (= test. 1 Radt = appendix V).

20. On the proposed modifications (Alcon, or Aulon, or Amynos), see test. 1 app. crit. pp. 33ff. Radt. The question of the name of the healer-hero of whom Sophocles was the priest is the subject of an extensive bibliography. Current scholarship, having abandoned the corrections "Alcon" and "Aulon," is now divided between two solutions: 1. "Amynos": a correction proposed by A. Körte; see below. "Halon": the reading given by the manuscripts and defended against Körte's correction by E. Schmidt, "Halon," *Mitteilungen des Deutschen Archäologischen Instituts (Athenische Abteilung)* 38, 1913, pp. 73–77.

21. See the Arcadian decree IG V 2, 265, 21ff.: "(The priestess) received the divinity (Korè) in her own home as was the custom for priests who succeeded one another"; a decree mentioned by W. S. Ferguson, "The Attic Orgeones," *Harvard Theological Review* 37, 1944, pp. 61–140 (p. 90).

22. *Etymologicum genuinum* (ninth century CE), s.v. Dexion (= test. 69 Radt).

23. It is probably in relation to the foundation of this altar that we should situated Sophocles' offering preserved as a votive epigram in the *Palatine Anthology*, 6, 145 (= test. 182 Radt): "The first to raise these altars to the gods was Sophocles, who had obtained the greatest glory from the tragic muse." But the motif indicated seems to be an emendation. See D. L. Page, *Further Greek Epigrams*, Oxford, 1981.

24. See J. Jouanna, *Hippocrate*, Paris, Fayard, 1992, p. 59 and n. 56.

25. Despite the contribution made by epigraphic documents regarding Dexion (dating from the fourth century BCE), which have convinced almost all scholars since their discovery at the end of the nineteenth century, skepticism is now becoming the fashion, a century later, among those for whom the biographical data on ancient authors can be nothing other than inventions of the Hellenistic period; see M. R. Lefkowitz, *The Lives of the Greek Poets*, Baltimore, 1981, p. 84 (speaking, following an astonishing shift, of inscriptions of the second and third centuries CE). Criticized by E. Kearns, "The Heroes of Attica," *Bulletin of the Institute of Classical Studies*, supp. 57, 1989, pp. 154ff., M. R. Lefkowitz has just received support from an article by A. Connoly, "Was Sophocles Heroised as Dexion?," *Journal of Hellenic Studies* 118, 1998, pp. 1–21. This article, though very well informed, is not very convincing.

26. For the first reports on the excavations begun in 1892, A. Körte, "Bezirk eines Heilgottes," *Mitteilungen des Deutschen Archäologischen Instituts (Athenische Abteilung)* 18, 1893, pp. 231–56; W. Dörpfeld, "Die Ausgrabungen am Westabhange der Akropolis I," *Mitteilungen des Deutschen Archäologischen Instituts (Athenische Abteilung)* 19, 1894, pp. 496–509 (p. 508). The excavation was continued until 1895; for a complete account, see A. Körte, "Die Ausgrabungen am Westabhange der Akropolis: IV. Das Heiligtum des Amynos," *Mitteilungen des Deutschen Archäologischen Instituts (Athenische Abteilung)* 21, 1896, pp. 287–332 (with table 11).

27. Körte (1896, above), pp. 298–302 = IG II/III21252 = Syll. 3 1096 (= test. 70 Radt).

28. It is certain that the sanctuary of Dexion had an administrative relationship with that of Amynos, but it is likely that it was not contiguous with it, because then there would have been no need to make two different steles bearing the same decree to put one in each of the two sanctuaries. Apart from that negative conclusion, any effort to localize the sanctuary of Dexion must remain hypothetical.

29. The orgeons of Amynos, Asclepius, and Dexion appear in another, entirely comparable inscription (IG II/III2 1253 = test. 71 Radt). This is a decree issued by the same orgeons to reward two benefactors. The only difference is that there is no mention of erecting a stele in the sanctuary, that is, the sanctuary of Amynnos and Asclepius. The stone bearing this decree was at the French School of Athens at the time that the German Institute was excavating the west slope of the Acropolis; the decree was first published by E. Bourguet, "Décret des orgéons d'Amynos," *Bulletin de Correspondance hellénique* 18, 1894, pp. 491–92, and reproduced by Körte (1896, cited above), pp. 302–3.

30. The correction of "Halon" to read "Amynos," which in Greek capital letters is rather easy, was proposed in 1896 by A. Körte (cited above), p. 312. This correction was criticized by E. Schmidt (cited above). Subsequently, scholars are divided between the two solutions. For Körte's correction, see for example W. S. Ferguson (cited above), p. 86, n. 34, and S. B. Aleshire, *The Athenian Asklepieion: The People, Their Dedications, and the Inventories*, Amsterdam, 1989, p. 425 and n. 5 (with the bibliography). But do we have to choose between Amynos and Halon?

31. Pausanias I, 21, 4.

32. On the Asclepieion in Athens, the most recent summary of the scholarship is by S. B. Aleshire (cited above).

33. The most recent summary of scholarship on the paean is L. Käppel, *Paian: Studien zur Geschichte einer Gattung, dans Untersuchungen zur antiken Literatur und Geschichte*, Berlin, 1992, vol. 37; see also I. Rutherford, *Pindar's Paeans*, Oxford, 2001, pp. 3–136 ("The Paian: A Survey of the Genre").

34. On Paean, the gods' physician in Homer, see *Iliad* 5, vv. 401 and 899ff.; *Odyssey* 4, v. 232.

35. Hesiod, frag. 307 Merkelbach-West: "Apollo Phoibos . . . or Paean himself, who knows the remedies for all ills."

36. Homer, *Iliad* I, v. 473.

37. *Suda*, s.v. Sophocles (= test. 2 Radt): "He composed . . . paeans."

38. Philostratus, *Life of Apollonius of Tyana*, 3, 17 (cf. test. 73 a Radt).

39. Another testimony to the fame of Sophocles' paean to Asclepius is found in Pseudo-Lucian, "Eulogy of Demonsthenes" 27 (cf. test. 73 b Radt). The author, to praise Demosthenes, is going to reproduce word for word a book he has obtained from a friend; and to justify his decision to reproduce it without change, he declares: "For even for Asclepius the honor is no less great if the paean of those who come to visit him is not of their own composition, but instead that of the Trezenian Isodemos or that of Sophocles that is sung."

40. The discoverer, unfortunately too often forgotten, was S. A. Koumanoudis, "Supplément d'inscriptions," *Athenaion* 5, 1876, pp. 323–40 (p. 340).

41. F. Buecheler, "Sophoclis paian eis Asclepion," *Rhein. Mus.* 32, 1877, p. 318 (with emendations to Koumanoudis's text).

42. A. Wilhelm, *Beiträge zur griechischen Inschrifterkunde*, Vienna, 1909, pp. 102–4 (with a photo of the three fragments, p. 103). See the critical edition of these three fragments in IG II2 4510 (Kirchner 1935).

43. J. H. Oliver, "The Sarapion Monument and the Paean of Sophocles," *Hesperia* 5, 1936, pp. 91–122. For the Greek text of the paean (with photo and a drawing of the fragments), see ibid., pp. 110–12. Oliver's text, with his critical notes, remains fundamental, because it is the result of a direct examination of all the available fragments. There are numerous reprintings of the text in the lyric corpuses (Diehl, ALG³ 1, 1949, pp. 80–81; Page, PMG, 1962 no. 737, etc.). But there is no genuine critical edition that takes into account the history of the diverse restitutions proposed since the discovery. The text of *SEG* 28 (1978), 225, p. 96, reproduces Oliver's. The most recent editions are not necessarily better. See finally L. Käppel (cited above), pp. 366ff., and W. D. Furley and J. M. Bremer, *Greek Hymns*, Tübingen, 2001, vol. 1, pp. 261ff. (introduction and translation in English), and vol. 2, pp. 219–21 (partial Greek text and notes), with the recent bibliography.

44. The fundamental article is by J. H. Oliver (cited above). For the indispensable complements, see *SEG* 28 (1978), 225, with the text of the three sides. On the history of the reconstruction of the monument begun by the Belgian Paul Graindor in 1927 and continued by the American School, see the very lively clues provided by J. H. Oliver, "An Ancient Poem on the Duties of a Physician," *Bulletin of the History of Medicine* 7, 1939, pp. 315–23.

45. The identification of Sarapion (side A) was first made by J. H. Oliver, "Two Athenian Poets," *Hesperia*, supp. 8, 1949, pp. 243–58 (p. 245). For Sarapion's medical

poem on the physician's duties, see J. H. Oliver 1939 (cited above), where he adds a new fragment and reproduces the Greek text by Paul Maas: see also *SEG* 28 (1978), 225 Front l. 8–34. This poem is situated in the enclosure of a medical god; see a French translation of the poem in R. Flacelière, "Le poète stoïcien Sarapion d'Athènes, ami de Plutarque," *Revue des Études Grecques* 64, 1951, pp. 325–27 (p. 326). Sarapion's paean, which follows, is too fragmented to be reconstituted.

46. For side B on the singers of paeans, see J. H. Oliver "Paeanistae," *Transactions and Proceedings of the American Philological Association* 71, 1940, pp. 302–14 (pp. 306–11), where he takes into account the discovery of a new fragment published by Pritchett in 1938. This new fragment makes it possible to reconstruct the name of the archon Mounatios Themison and to date the list to the beginning of the third century CE (cf. S. Follet, *Athènes au IIe et au IIIe siècle*, Paris, 1976, p. 517: the first decade of the third century).

47. We will not enter into these debates, which do not directly concern Sophocles. See D. J. Geagan, "The Sarapion Monument and the quest for Status in Roman Athens," *Zeitschrit für Papyrologie und Epigraphik* 85, 1991, pp. 145–65 (with a new edition of side A and side B, without any commentary on side C), and S. B. Aleshire, *Asklepios at Athens: Epigraphic and Prosopographic Essays on the Athenian Healing Cults*, Amsterdam, 1991, pp. 49–74.

48. Sarapion's grandson, Quintus Statius Glaucon, the author of the dedication to his grandfather, is said on side A to be a priest of Asclepius Savior (cf. IG II2 3704, l. 4ff., where he is said to be priest for life of Asclepius Savior). On this family, see J. H. Oliver 1949 (cited above) and more recently S. B. Aleshire (cited above).

49. That is what J. H. Oliver already thought in 1940 (cited above), pp. 309–11. The inscriptions on sides B and C are supposed to be later than A, but contemporary. Since the list of the singers of paeans (side B) is datable approximately by the archon Mounatios Themison (see above), Sophocles' paean would have been inscribed at the same date, that is, at the beginning of the third century CE.

50. At the beginning of this paean we do not find the Greek adjective *klutométis*, "Illustrious for wisdom," which, according to Philostratus the Younger's description of the painting (see above), was characteristic of Sophocles' paean to Asclepius. In addition, some scholars have expressed doubts regarding the object of Sophocles' paean; see first Th. Bergk, *Poetae lyrici Graeci*, Leipzig, 1882, pp. 248ff.: "ambigo utrum nobilis ille paean fuerit, . . . an peculiare carmen in honorem matris Coronidis, siquidem Sophocles plures paeanes condidisse fertur"; he was followed by J. H. Oliver 1936 (cited above), pp. 119ff., and J. H. Oliver 1940 (cited above), p. 309, n. 13. But this is not the general opinion; see for example Aleshire (cited above), p. 10, n. 1.

51. Compare the so-called Erythrean paean to Apollo and Aesclepius (Furley/Bremer, cited above, vol. 1, pp. 211–14, and vol. 2, p 161–67), which enjoyed great fame for a long time (from the fourth century BCE to the second century CE) and in the various sanctuaries of Asclepius, as is indicated by the four versions preserved on stone that originated in Asia Minor (sanctuary of Asclepius in Erythrea), continental Greece (sanctuary of Asclepius in Athens; Dion in Macedonia) and Egypt (Ptolemais Hermion).

52. O. Walter ("Ein neugewonnenes Athener Doppelrelief," *Öst. Jahresheft* 26, 1930, pp. 75–104) has the merit of having reconstituted in its general outlines this votive

monument to Asclepius by fitting together Pentelic marble fragments proceeding
from the Athens museum, but also from the London museum. L. Beschi reexamined
the monument in a long study entitled "Il monumento di Telemachos, fondatore
dell'Asklepieion Ateniese," *Annuario della scuola archeologica di Atene* 45/46 (n.s.
29/30), 1967/1968, pp. 381–436. The monument is reconstituted on p. 411, and the
text of the inscription is given on pp. 412–13; the text is reproduced in *SEG* 25 (1971),
226. For the bibliographical complements concerning this monument after Beschi's
study, see *SEG* 32 (1982), 266 (with a new fragment published by L. Beschi the same
year), and Aleshire (cited above), p. 7, n. 3.

53. This beginning, translated here, corresponds to IG II2 4961 (EM 8821). The two
fragments are not adjoining. The equivalent of two lines is missing between the two
fragments. The text has recently been republished after a new examination of the
stone and with a critical apparatus and commentary by K. Clinton, "The Epidauria
and the Arrival of Asclepius," in R. Hägg, *Ancient Greek Cult Practice from the Epigraphical Evidence* (Acta Instituti Atheniensis Regni Sueciae, series in 8, 13), Stockholm, 1994, pp. 17–34 (pp. 21–25, with a photo of EM 8821, p. 22).

54. Despite the details provided by the inscription, everything is not clear. First, we
must not forget that the restitutions are rather numerous, from diverse periods, and
that certain readings are not entirely certain. The text on which the historians rely
(*SEG* 25 [1971] 226) has no critical apparatus. It has also been forgotten that the
Greek word *zeothen* (not attested elsewhere), meaning "from Zea" (one of the har-
bors at Piraeus) is based on a reading of a zeta proposed, with hesitations, by
S. N. Dragoumis, "Asclépios à Ahènes," *Ephémeris Archaiologikè* 3, 1901, pp. 98–111
(he put the zeta between parentheses), whereas earlier it was read as a delta. Körte
had read *de opse* "having arrive late," thus relating the inscription to Philostratus
(cited above). K. Clinton's republication (cited above) is much more precise, because
it restores bracketed letters where the reading is not certain. Moreover, even where
the reading is clear, the restitutions are debatable. Since Körte, we have understood
that Telemachus transported in his chariot a serpent (*drakonta*) to represent the god.
But as Clinton reminds us, the word to be restituted begins with *dia-* and not *dra-*.
However, Dragoumis's restitution of *diakonon* ("servant") and Clinton's restitution
of *diakonous* ("servants") do not make much sense. And the abandonment of Körte's
correction does not mean that the serpent was not involved in the introduction of
the cult of Asclepius in Athens, as Clinton thinks (p. 24). Telemachus took the god
in his chariot, but nothing tells us what represented the god (a statue or a serpent?
Both are possible, and are not incompatible). Besides, the epigraphists do not often
try to translate. Many difficulties thus remain latent. For example, what must we
understand by *oikothen* (lit., "of the house")? Does the word mean "at his own cost,"
as it is often understood, or concretely, "of the house"? And in that case, is the reference to the god's home in Epidaurus, from which Telemachus is supposed to have
had the serpent brought? Or is it rather to the house of Telemachus himself in
Athens, where he would have received the representation of the god, as we have seen
for Sophocles?

55. Asclepius is supposed to have arrived from Epidaurus belatedly for the Great Myster-
ies and to have been initiated into the Eleusinion before being installed in Athens.
In commemoration of this new arrival of the god, there was each year, during the
Great Mysteries, a day reserved for Asclepius, the festival of the Epidauria, clearly

recalling by its name the place from which the god had come (see Pausanias 2, 26, 8). A procession was organized on that day by the eponymous archon (Aristotle, *Constitution of Athens*, 56, 4). On the date of that festival (17 Boedromion) commemorating the arrival of Asclepius, on its denomination and its progress, on the role played by the Epidaurian clergy in the introduction of the cult of Asclepius in Athena, and on the reexamination of the role of Telemachus and Sophocles in the reception of the god, see the recent very valuable article by K. Clinton (cited above) which is based, notably, on epigraphic evidence. From P. Foucart, *Les Grands Mystères d'Eleusis*, Paris, 1900, pp. 115–21, to Clinton, the numerous studies on the introduction of the cult of Asclepius in Athens encounter the question of the respective roles of Sophocles and Telemachus; see, for instance, O. Walter, "Das Priestertum von Sophocles," *Geras A. Keramopoullou*, Athens, 1953, pp. 469–79, and Aleshire (cited above), pp. 9–11. More recently, see R. Parker, *Athenian Religion: A History*, Oxford, 1996, pp. 175–85.

56. For the date of the monument (first decade of the fourth century), see L. Beschi (cited above), pp. 428ff.; Beschi (pp. 422–28) also proposes to add a new element on the presence of Sophocles in the Asclepieion. The shaft of the monument where Telemachus's inscription is engraved is topped by a relief block that supports the amphiglyphic stele. On the four sides of the relief block four scenes are represented. On the back, Beschi reconstitutes the depiction of a diner lying on a couch at a funeral banquet; its particularity is the presence of a lyre (and a mask?). He identifies the person lying on the couch as the heroized Sophocles under the name of Dexion. This identification has been accepted by J.-M. Dentzer, *Le Motif du banquet couché dans le Proche-Orient et le monde grec du VIIe au IVe siècle avant J.-C.*, Bibliothèque des Ecoles françaises d'Athènes et de Rome 246, 1982, p. 467 ("The demonstration attributing to Dexion the banquet scene on the Telemachus monument is acceptable"). S. B. Aleshire (cited above), p. 10, n. 4, is much more skeptical. We can add to Aleshire's arguments that it is difficult to see how Telemachus, who claims to be the sole founder of the sanctuary of Asclepius, could represent on his monument the very person that the Athenians had heroized precisely because he had received the god. See also, for other reasons, A. Connoly's criticism (cited above), pp. 14ff.

57. Marinos, *Vie de Proclos*, 29 (= test. 72 Radt).

58. See R. Martin and H. Metzger, *La Religion grecque*, Paris, 1976 (chap. 2, "L'évolution du culte d'Asclépios en Grèce des origines à l'époque romaine," pp. 62–109). Cf. also B. Holtzmann, *LIMC*, s.v. Asklepios, pp. 863–65.

59. See Strabo, *Geography* 9, 5, 17: "Trikka, where the oldest and most famous sanctuary of Asclepius is found."

60. For Hesiod, see frag. 50 Merkelbach-West (= Pausanias 2, 26, 7: Asclepius son of Apollo and Arsinoé from Messenia) and frag. 51 (Zeus struck down Asclepius); Pindar, *Pythians* 3, vv. 14–60.

61. Aristophanes, *The Wasps*, v. 123.

62. See above, the plague in Athens and the plague in *Oedipus the King*.

63. For Athena as the protector of health, in the period of Pericles, see Plutarch, "Pericles," c. 13 (160 c).

64. For the distinction between the sanctuary in Piraeus and the one in the city, see the scholium on Aristophanes, *Ploutos*, v. 621. Some scholars have tried to situate the foundation of this sanctuary in Piraeus in 421, one year before the divinity's arrival

in Athens, while others situate it during the arrival of the god in 420. It is normal to think of a creation in Piraeus before Athens, given the progression of the cult established earlier in Aegina. But we do not have any testimony to this. In any case, there was no Asclepieion in Athens in 422, the date of Aristophanes' *The Wasps*.

65. According to the scholiast (*Ploutos*, v. 621), it was the sanctuary in the city. But since the blind man was first taken *epi thalassan*, "toward the sea," (v. 656) before going to the sanctuary of the god (v. 659), some modern scholars think the reference is to the sanctuary in Piraeus. See F. Robert, "Le Plutus d'Aristophane et l'Asclépiéion du Pirée," *Revue de Philologie* 57, 1931, pp. 132–39, according to which it could be only the sanctuary in the port because the bath takes place outside the sanctuary; cf. also F. Sartori, "Aristofane e il culto attico di Asclepio," *Atti e memorie dell' Accademia Patavina di Scienze, lettere ed arti: Classe di Scienze morali*, 85, 1972/1973, pp. 363–78. To avoid contradiction, some modern scholars think that *epi thalassan* means "toward a salt spring." The scholiast, for his part, sees no contradiction between a bath in the sea and an incubation in the sanctuary in the city. On this problem, see for example S. B. Aleshire (cited above), p. 13 (with the bibliography).

66. On the date of *Philoctetes*, see below.

67. Sophocles, *Philoctetes*, trans. T. Francklin, vv. 1437–38.

68. *Little Iliad*: summary by Proclus in his *Chrestomathia* (ed. Bernabé, 74, 6–8). For more details about the *Little Iliad* see chapter VI, "The Mythical Imagination," below.

69. Sophocles, *Philoctetes*, v. 1333.

70. See the inscription on the monument of Telemachus cited above. Also see, at about the same date (before the middle of the fourth century), an inscription on three fragments of Hymettan marble found on the south flank of the Acropolis (EM 9005. 8810. 8809) and reassembled by Koehler, where the names of Machaon and Podalire can be reconstituted (IG II2 4353 ed. Kirchner 1935).

71. There is another passage in Sophocles' tragic work in which Asclepius appears: in a fragment of one of his two plays about Phineus (frag. 710 Radt), where a blind man (probably one of Phineus's sons, Phylarchus, *FGrHist* 81 frag. 18 Jacoby = Sextus Empiricus, *Against the Mathematicians*, 1, 260, where it is said that Asclepius restored the sight of Phineus's two sons) recovers his sight thanks to "Asclepius Healer," exactly as in Aristophanes' *Ploutos*. This passage is preserved precisely by Aristophanes' pastiche of it in his comedy, which is pointed out by the scholiast (scholium on *Ploutos*, v. 635). Thus Sophocles had introduced the new healing divinity into the myth of Phineus, as he had into the myth of Philoctetes. On the two plays about Phineus, see appendix II, nos. 110–11.

Chapter IV. Sophocles and Dionysus: The Theatrical Career

1. Pausanias 1, 21, 1 (cited below).

2. Plutarch, "Life of Cimon," 8, 7 (= *TrGF* 3, test. 57 Radt; *TrGF* 4, test. 36 Radt).

3. *Chronicle of Paros* A56 (*FGrHist*. 239 Jacoby = test. 33 Radt).

4. However, it should be noted that Plutarch's manuscripts give Aphepsion instead of Apsephion.

5. To be sure, the *Chronicle of Paros* does not expressly state that this was Sophocles'

first victory. But that is what we have to understand based on a comparison with the way in which Aeschylus and Euripides are mentioned. It is the only victory of Sophocles' that is mentioned; for Aeschylus and Euripides, the chronicle also mentions only one victory, but it indicates that it was the first. *Chronicle of Paros* A50: "Aeschylus the poet won the victory in the tragedy competition for the first time . . . under the archontate of Philocrates in Athens" (= 485/484); ibid., A 60: "Euripides won the victory in the tragedy competition for the first time under the archontate of Diphilus in Athens" (= 442–441).

6. On Aeschylus as Sophocles' teacher, see above.

7. See also the *Life of Aeschylus* c. 8 (= *TrGF* 4, test. 37 Radt): "Aeschylus left to go to Hieron, according to some because he had been the victim of the Athenians' ardor against him and because he had been defeated by Sophocles, who was young." Nonetheless, this explanation of the facts is not unanimously accepted. Other explanations are mentioned in the *Life of Aeschylus*: his defeat by Simonides for the elegy in honor of the soldiers who died at Marathon; the terror of the spectators faced with the chorus of the Furies during the performance of *The Eumenides*.

8. See the argument of *Seven against Thebes* and *P. Oxy.* 2256, fr. 2 (= *TrGF* 3, test. 58 a and b Radt): "The play was performed under Theagenes in the first year of the seventy-eighth Olympiad (= 467). Aeschylus was the winner, with *Laïus, Oedipus, Seven against Thebes,* and *The Sphinx* as the satyr play. Second: Aristias with *Perseus, Tantalus,* . . . and *The Wrestlers* as the satyr play, plays by his father Pratinus. Third, Polyphrasmon with his tetralogy on Lycurgus."

9. See below.

10. See the argument to *Agamemnon*: "The play was performed under the Archontate of Philocles, the second year of the eightieth Olympiad (458 BCE). Aeschylus was first with *Agamemnon, The Libation Bearers,* and *The Eumenides,* with *Proteus* as the satyr play."

11. For more details regarding the performance of the plays during the festival of Dionysus and the composition of the audience, see below, chapter VII, "Space and Spectacle."

12. The existence of judges is clearly attested by Aristophanes' comedies, in which he alludes to them several times. See *Acharnians,* v. 1224; *Clouds,* vv. 1115–16; *Birds,* vv. 445–47, vv. 1101–4; vv. 1114–15; *The Assembly Women,* vv. 1154–62. The main other testimonies, apart from the passage in Plutarch's "Life of Cimon" in question here, are Lysias, *On a Wound by Premeditation,* 3; Isocrates, *Trapeziticus,* 33–34; Demosthenes, *Against Midias,* 17. They are conveniently collected in A. Pickard-Cambridge, *The Dramatic Festivals of Athens,* 2nd ed., revised by J. Gould and D. M. Lewis, reissued with supplement and corrections, Oxford, 1988, pp. 95–99. The details of the final procedure for the ranking are still a matter of debate, because the ancient testimonies are not very explicit and may diverge (on the one hand Zenob. III, 64: "The decision lies in the lap of five judges"; cf. Hesychius, s.v. five judges; and on the other Lucian, *Harmonides* 2: "In the competitions, although the mass of the spectators is able to applaud or whistle, the judges are seven or five or of that order of grandeur"). Does this refer to the last five judges drawn by lots who were the only ones who put their votes in the urn, or to the earlier drawings of lots until a candidate had five votes (cf. M. Pope, "Athenian Festival Judges: 'Seven, Five, or However Many,'" *Classical Quarterly* 36, 1986, 322–26), or to successive drawings of five, and

then, if the result was not achieved, of seven, etc. (cf. C. W. Marshall and Stephanie Van Willigenburg, "Judging Athenian Dramatic Competitions," *Journal of Hellenic Studies* 124, 2004, pp. 90–107)? In any case, the essence of the procedure, by respecting the democratic equality among the tribes and within the tribes by the drawing of lots, and also by leaving open, in the people's mind, the possibility that the gods would intervene by this mode of selection, must also have ensured against risks of corruption.

13. The most explicit testimony concerning the risks of the audience influencing the judges is Plato, *Laws*, 2, 659 a: "The true judge should not take his verdicts from the dictation of the audience, nor yield weakly to the uproar of the crowd."

14. Plutarch, "Life of Cimon" 7, 1–2 and 8, 7.

15. Scholium on Aeschines, *Against Ctesiphon*, 67: "A few days before the Great Dionysia Festival, there took place in what is called the Odeon a competition among tragic authors and a presentation of plays that were to be performed in the theater in the contexts of the competition; whence the name Proagon ('Prelude to the competition,' or 'preliminary competition'). The actors enter without their masks and their costumes." Cf. also the scholium on Aristophanes, *The Wasps*, v. 1109: "The Odeon is a place in the form of a theater where it is the custom to present plays before their performance in the theater." On the Proagon, see Pickard-Cambridge (cited above), pp. 67ff.; J.-Ch. Moretti, *Théâtre et société en Grèce ancienne*, Paris, 2001, p. 84.

16. Plato, *Symposium*, 194 ab.

17. See above.

18. *Life of Sophocles* 4 (= test. 1 Radt = appendix V).

19. Eusebius, *Chronicle of the Seventy-Seventh Olympiad*, 2 (= test. 32 a and b Radt). See especially W. Luppe, "Zur Datierung einiger Dramatiker in der Eusebios/Hienonymus-Chronik," *Philologus* 114, 1970, pp. 1–8 (pp. 7ff.).

20. See *Life of Aeschylus*, c. 13 (*TrGF* 3, test. 1 Radt): "In all, he won thirteen victories; but after his death he also won a great many"; cf. also *Suda*, s.v. Aeschylus (= *TrGF* 3, test. 2 Radt), where the figures twenty-eight and thirteen are given for the victories. We understand this to mean thirteen victories during his lifetime; and by adding the victories after his death, a total of twenty-eight; see B. Snell, *TrGF* 1, p. 28 (note to DID A 3 a, col. 1, 11). Aeschylus thus won fifteen victories after his death.

21. On Aeschylus's first victory in 464, see *Chronicle of Paros* A50 (*FGrHist* 239 Jacoby = *TrGF* 3, test. 54 a Radt). Born in 525, he had already competed against Pratinas in the Olympiad of 500–496; see *Suda*, s.v. Pratinas (= *TrGF* 3, test. 52 Radt): "Pratinas was opposed to Aeschylus and to Choirilos in the competitions on the occasion of the seventieth Olympiad (500–496)."

22. According to the *Chronicle of Paros* A56 (*FGrHist* 239 Jacoby = test. 33 Radt), quoted above, Sophocles was then twenty-eight.

23. The figure of eighteen victories at the Great Dionysia is given by the inscription known as the "inscription of the victors" (see below), IG II2 2325 (= *TrGF* 1 Snell DID A3a = Pickard-Cambridge, cited above), which begins with a list of the tragic poets who were victors at the Dionysia with the total number of their victories: col. 1, l. 15 Sophokles ΔΙΙΙΙ (= 18). This number of eighteen is also given by Diodorus Siculus 13, 103, 4 (= test. 85 Radt) when he is dealing with the year in which Callias was archon (407/406), and he presents Sophocles on the occasion of his death: "It is at this same time that Sophocles son of Sophilos died. He was the author of trag-

edies, had lived ninety years, and had won eighteen victories." Thus this must refer to eighteen victories won at the Great Dionysia. On the other hand, the *Suda*, s.v. Sophocles (test. 2 Radt), gives the figure of twenty-four victories. This difference has been interpreted as being due to the fact that the *Suda* gives the total number of Sophocles' victories. The six additional victories are supposed to be victories won at the Lenaia which, starting in the 440s, opposed two tragic authors (and not three), with two tragedies (and not three), and without a satyr play. A different (and less plausible) explanation is that of C. W. Mueller, "Die Zahl der Siege des älteren und des jüngeren Sophokles," *Rheinisches Museum* 128, 1985, pp. 93–95: the six additional victories would come, according to the author of this study, not from the participation in the Lenaia, a competition too humble for a confirmed dramaturge like Sophocles, but from victories won after his death, as in the case of Aeschylus. However, the comparison with Aeschylus appears to be fallacious, because the Athenians had granted by decree, after Aeschylus's death, the authorization to revive his tragedies in the competitions, whereas we have nothing comparable for Sophocles. A final source, the *Life of Sophocles*, cited below, speaks of twenty victories. The total figure of 123 for Sophocles' plays is taken from the *Suda*, s.v. Sophocles (= test. 2 Radt). The *Life of Sophocles*, c. 18 (= test. 1 Radt = appendix V) gives the figure of 130.

24. *Life of Sophocles* c. 8 (= test. 1 Radt = appendix V): "He won twenty victories, as Carystios says (= Carystios of Pergamum, second century BCE), often won second place, but was never third."

25. *Life of Euripides*, c. 2 (1, 2, 14–3, 1 Schwartz): "He began to present plays under the archontate of Callias during the first year of the eighty-first Olympiad (= 455); he presented first the Peliades, when he was ranked third." For the fragments of the Peliades, see H. Van Looy, *Euripide*, vol. 8, 2, Paris: CUF, 2000, pp. 515–30, and *TrGF* 5.2, pp. 607–14 Kannicht.

26. This information is provided by the *Chronicle of Paros* A60 (*FGrHist* 239 Jacoby = *TrGF* 1 Snell DID D 1).

27. *Suda*, s.v. Euripides: "He won five victories, four during his lifetime and one after his death, the performance having been arranged by his nephew Euripides." The *Suda* alludes here to Euripides' posthumous victory that is also mentioned in the scholium to Aristophanes, *The Frogs*, v. 67 (= *TrGF* 1, Snell, DID C 22): "According to the didascaliae, at the death of Euripides his son, who had the same name as he, presented at the city (= at the Great Dionysia) *Iphigeneia at Aulis*, *Alcmaeon*, and *The Bacchae*." The date of the performance cannot be determined with precision (between 405 and 400).

28. See below.

29. Argument 2 of *Hippolytus*: "The play was performed under the archontate of Epameinon, the fourth year of the eighty-seventh Olympiad (= 428). Euripides won first place, Iophon second, and Ion third." We know that Iophon was the son of Sophocles; see below.

30. Plutarch, "Life of Nicias" 29, 3–4.

31. *Life of Euripides* 2 (1, 3, 11–14 Schwartz = test. 54 Radt).

32. *Gnomologium Vaticanum* (e codice Vaticano graeco 743) 517 Sternbach (= test. 57 Radt). The same remark is applied to two other comic authors in another collection of maxims (*Gnomologium Vindobonense* 130 Wachsmuth apud test. 57 Radt).

33. Aelius Aristides, *Oration 46, Against Plato for the Defense of the Four*, 256, 11 (II, p.

334 Dindorf = *TrGF* 1 Snell, 24 test. 3 b = test. 40 Radt). See also the argument 2 for *Oedipus the King* cited below. Compare Euripides' analogous misadventure: in 415, with the trilogy that included *The Trojan Women*, he won second prize behind Xenocles, son of Carcinos (*TrGF* 1, no. 33); the source is Aelian (*Varia Historia*, 2, 8), who is scandalized by this ranking and questions the judges: "Either those responsible for the vote were mad, ignorant, and incapable of making an equitable judgment, or they had been bribed. In one case as in the other, it is very strange and absolutely unworthy of the Athenians."

34. The testimonies regarding Philocles have been collected by B. Snell in *TrGF*1, 24 (Philoclès I), pp. 139–42. On Philocles' place in Aeschylus's lineage, see below.

35. Aristophanes, *Thesmophoriazusae* (year 411), v. 168. Other passages in which Philoclès is mocked by Aristophanes: *The Wasps*, v. 461 (year 422); *The Birds*, vv. 279 and 1291 (year 414).

36. The figure of one hundred is given by the *Suda*, s.v. Philocles, son of Polypeithes, Athenian. This encyclopedia cites the titles of seven tragedies by Philocles, including an *Oedipus* and a *Philoctetes*.

37. On the office of choregos see below, chapter VII, "Space and Spectacle," under "The Role of the Choregos."

38. Plato, *Laws*, 7, 817 d.

39. Athenaeus 14, 638 f (= test. 31 Radt = *TrGF* 1 Snell 27 Gnesippus T 1 = PCG Kassel and Austin 4, Cratinus, frag. 17).

40. The only information regarding this Gnesippus comes from this single passage in Athenaeus in which several quotations from the comic poets concerning him are collected.

41. It is Aristophanes, in his *Peace*, v. 802 (year 421) who is delighted that Morsimos did not obtain a chorus.

42. Aristophanes, *Frogs*, vv. 89–91 (year 405).

43. These two works are mentioned by Diogenes Laertius (5, 26) in his list of Aristotle's works. The philosopher had also written a work entitled *On the Tragedies*, mentioned in the same list. These three works are lost. For the fragments of the *Didascaliae*, see V. Rose, *Aristot. Fragm.*, Leipzig, 1886, nos. 618–30; see also G. Jachmann, *De Aristotelis Didascaliis*, Göttingen, 1908. On these three works by Aristotle, see P. Moraux, *Les Listes anciennes des ouvrages d'Aristote*, Louvain, 1951, pp. 126–28, and Pickard-Cambridge (cited above), p. 71.

44. Pickard-Cambridge (cited above) gives, in an appendix to his chapter 2 (pp. 101–25) the text of these three inscriptions with an introduction and notes; see also *TrGF* 1 Snell DID A 1, 2 and 3. The first list (Fasti) is IG II2 2318: it contains, in fragmentary form, the results in thirteen columns going from a victory by Aeschylus in 473–472 to 329–328. The second list (*Didascaliae*) is IG II2 2319–23: so far as tragedy is concerned, it gives only very meager information on two years at the end of the fifth century, for the Lenaia (years 419–418) and on three years of the fourth century for the Great Dionysia (years from 341 to 339). The third list is IG II2 2325: on the tragic authors victorious at the Great Dionysia, it gives eleven names, including those of Aeschylus and Sophocles (but not Euripides); and for the Lenaia seven names can be identified. The last two lists come from a single hexagonal votive monument. See also P. Ghiron-Bistagne, *Recherches sur les acteurs dans la Grèce antique*, Paris, 1976, pp. 7ff. (with a partial French translation of the lists).

45. IG II2 2318, col. III, l. 2 *Sophokles edidasken* = Pickard-Cambridge (cited above), p. 104 = *TrGF* 1 Snell DID A 1, 69.

46. See above.

47. U. Köhler, "Documente zur Geschichte des athenischen Theater," *Mitteilungen des deutschen Arkäologischen Instituts: Athenische Abteilung* (A), 3, 1878, pp. 229–58 (p. 247), gives the transcription of the fragment (EM 8188 = no. 9 in his article = no. a Wilhelm), but he was far from thinking about Sophocles, even though he had restored four lines earlier "Aeschylus," because he assumed from the outset that the list gave only the names of comic authors victorious at the Great Dionysia (p. 253) and regretted not being able to find a place for the aforesaid fragment. The only discussion he had with his Greek colleague S. A. Koumanoudis, who was the first to mention, in 1861, the first fragment on the list and had just published an initial series of twenty-two fragments (*Athenaion* 7, 1878, pp. 74–97) concerned the question whether the list included not only comic authors but actors. The list, with its thirty-nine fragments, was first published by A. Wilhelm in 1906 (*Urkunden dramatischer Aufführungen in Athen*, Vienna, 1906, pp. 89ff., with a photograph of the fragment a on which the names of Aeschylus and Sophocles appear, p. 101). On the history of fitting the fragments back together, see the materials in IG II2 2325 (ed. I. Kirchner 1931).

48. See in chapter V under "Sophocles and the Family Heritage: A Family of Authors of Tragedies."

49. IG II2 3090 = *TrGF* 1 Snell DID B 3; cf. Pickard-Cambridge (cited above), pp. 47ff. (with the commentary).

50. A second dedication by two choregoi found in Attica near Axisonè, a coastal deme of Attica, also includes Sophocles' name IG II2 3091 = *TrGF* 1 Snell DID B 5, 8; cf. Pickard-Cambridge (cited above), pp. 54–56, with bibliography, p. 54, n. 6, and commentary pp. 55ff.; and W. Luppe, "Zur einer Choregeninschrift aus Aixōnai (IG II/III2 3091)," *Archiv für Papyrusforschung* 19, 1963, pp. 147–51. It dates, judging by the form of the letters, from the beginning of the fourth century (the 380s). It ends this way: "Epicharès, being choregos, won the tragedy competition; Sophocles presented his *Telephus*." The interpretation of this inscription has been much debated since its publication in 1929. According to some scholars, it refers to the great Sophocles (cf. Pickard-Cambridge, p. 55, and *TrGF* 4 Radt, p. 434); according to others, it refers to his grandson (cf. W. Luppe, "Nochmals zur Choregeninschrift IG II/III2 3091," *Archiv für Papyrusforschung* 22, 1974, pp. 211–12; *TrGF* 1 Snell p. 17 and p. 39). If it referred to the grandfather, we would have the attestation of a trilogy on Telephus.

51. The information on the first revival of an old tragedy is given by the list of the *Fasti* (IG II2 2318, cited above), for the year 387–386. The three notations regarding the revival of an old tragedy are given by the list of the *Didascaliae* (also cited above): in 341, it is Euripides' *Iphigeneia*; in 340, Euripides' *Orestes*; in 339, another tragedy by Euripides whose title has not been preserved.

52. The fragment in which Sophocles' name appears (= B) was published by B. D. Meritt, "Greek Inscriptions," *Hesperia* 73, 1938, pp. 77–160 (pp. 116–18) (after another fragment = A). The text is available in Pickard-Cambridge (cited above), p. 123, and in *TrGF* 1 Snell DID A 4 b 8: [S]ofo(kleous); see also P. Ghiron-Bistagne (cited above), pp. 77ff. (with a photo of the two fragments, p. 76). The inscription is also

important for the history of the theater, as A. Körte rightly emphasizes ("Bruch-stücke einer Didaskalischen Inschrift," *Hermes* 73, 1938, pp. 123–27). It was known as early as 387/386 BCE that an old tragedy had been performed hors coucours at the Great Dionysia (see the preceding note). Thanks to this inscription, we learn that toward the middle of the third century three old tragedies were performed on the occasion of an actors' competition. The same was true for the old comedies and the old satyr plays.

53. On Mestos, see *TrGF* I Snell II Mesatus, pp. 87ff. Mesatos won his first victory shortly after that of Sophocles. He won at least two first places, but not more than four. All that can be inferred from the fragment a of the list of Victors (= *TrGF* I Snell DID A 3a 11–17; photograph of the fragment in Wilhelm (cited above, p. 101). Just under Sophocles' name, with the complete number of his victories (= 1. 16), appears the restored name of MESATOS followed by two vertical lines visible before a scratch on the stone (l. 17). The restitution of the name of Mesatos, proposed by Capps, with doubts, in the *American Journal of Philology* 20, 1899, p. 401, and con-tested by Wilhelm (cited above), p. 103 ("The fact that no poet of the time is known whose name ended in "-to" is not a reason to immediately add something"), is brilliantly confirmed by the papyrus, which gives in full the name of Mesatos, a tragic poet contemporary with Sophocles.

54. *P. Oxy.* 2256 frag. 3 (first publication: E. Lobel, *The Oxyrhynchus Papyri* 20, 1952, 30 = *TrGF* I Snell DID C 6 = *TrGF* 3 test. 70 Radt). The bibliography on this fragment is immense. See, after the fundamental study by F.A.F. Garvie (*Aeschylus' Supplices: Play and Trilogy*, London, Cambridge University Press, 1969), the very concise as-sessment by H. F. Johansen and E. W. Whittle, *Aeschylus: The Suppliants*, vol. 1, Copenhagen, 1980, pp. 1–23. These works give preference to the date of 463. Some scholars, basing themselves on Eusebius's testimony (see above), have proposed a later date (470, 469, or 466; cf. E. C. Yorke, "The Date of the *Supplices* of Aeschylus," *Classical Review*, n.s., 4, 1954, pp. 10–11). We have the remains of other papyruses giving information on the subject of Sophocles' tragedies, both preserved and lost. But none contains information about his theatrical career. For these papyruses, see M. Van Rossum-Steenbeek, *Greek Readers' Digests? Studies on a Selection of Subliter-ary Papyri*, Leiden: Brill, 1998, pp. 21ff. and pp. 34ff. (= pap. nos. 17–19).

55. On Aeschylus's victory in 472 with *The Persians*, see the argument for this tragedy; cf. also the list of the *Fasti* (quoted in n. 44).

56. See above. However, let us remember that some scholars want to make Sophocles' career begin in 470.

57. See above.

58. On Aeschylus's victory in 458 with the *Oresteia*, see the argument for Aeschylus's *Agamemnon*, cited above; cf. also the list of the Fastes (*TrGF* I Snell DID A 1, 41–51).

59. Sophocles, *Oedipus the King*, argument 2.

60. See above.

61. Aristophanes of Byzantium refers expressly to Sophocles only in this preface to *Antigone*. For his edition of Aeschylus, see A. Wartelle, *Histoire du texte d'Eschyle dans l'Antiquité*, Paris, 1971 (chap. 9: "L'édition d'Aristophane de Byzance," pp. 143–61). For his edition of Euripides, see A. Tuilier, *Recherches critiques sur la tradi-tion du texte d'Euripide*, Paris, 1968, pp. 53–61. For his edition of the poet Pindar, cf.

the excellent development in J. Irigoin, *Histoire du texte de Pindare*, Paris, 1952, pp. 35–50.

62. On Euripides' *Antigone*, see H. Van Looy, *Euripide*, vol. 8, 1, Paris: CUF, 1998, pp. 191–212, and *TrGF* 5.1, pp. 261–312 Kannicht.

63. See above.

64. *Chronicle of Paros* A60 (*FGrHist.* 239 Jacoby). In any case, the election of the strategoi for the year 441/440 (= July 441–July 440) must have been held the preceding year (442/441), in the *prytany* that followed the sixth, if the sacrifices were favorable (Aristotle, *Constitution of Athens*, 44), thus in principle in January 441, for a term of office to begin in July 441, whereas the Great Dionysia of 442/441 did not take place until the end of March 441. During the elections in January 441, the members of the popular assembly remembered the performance of *Antigone* in March of the preceding year (July 443–July 442).

65. This same figure is given at the end of the second argument of the same tragedy, where it is said more clearly that it is an order relative to the performance (*Didascalia*). This order number must include only the tragedies, not the satyr plays, because a count with the satyr plays would make it the last play of the eighth competition, that is, a satyr play, which is clearly impossible for *Antigone*. We can compare the order number in the argument for Euripides' *Alcestis*, which also goes back to Aristophanes of Byzantium (rank 17). But this figure cannot be explained in the same way. There are also indications of an ancient classification of Aristophanes' comedies. See P. Boudreaux, *Le Texte d'Aristophane*, Paris, 1919, pp. 20–21.

66. This calculation presupposes that the tragic competitions at the festival of the Lenaia had not yet begun at that date; on this problem, see below.

67. The reference is to argument no. 2. It is not attributed to Aristophanes of Byzantium by name, but its structure leaves no doubt as to its origin.

68. These plays, listed in the order of performance, are: *The Cretans, Alcmaeon at Psophis, Telephus, Alcestis.* Mentioned in fourth position, *Alcestis* occupies the place of the satyr play.

69. The reference is to argument no. 2, attributed by name to Aristophanes the Grammarian.

70. Dictys is the name of the fisherman on the island of Seriphos who found the chest containing Danaë and her son Perseus that had been thrown into sea. We have only a few fragments of Euripides' *Dictys* that do not allow us to arrive at a reliable reconstitution of the text, but the myth is well known; see H. Van Looy, *Euripide, Fragments*, vol. 8, 2, Paris: CUF, 2000, pp. 73–92, and *TrGF* 5.1, pp. 381–89 Kannicht.

71. See *Suda*, s.v. Euphorion: "Euphorion, son of Aeschylus the tragic poet, Athenian; he was also a tragic author. With the tragedies of his father that had not yet been performed, he won first prize four times. He also wrote tragedies himself." The *Suda* does not mention any victory won by Euphorion with is own tragedies. But since we know that after Aeschylus's death the Athenians had decreed that anyone who wished could compete using Aeschylus's plays (*Life of Aeschylus* 12 = *TrGF* 3, test. 1 Radt = *TrGF* 1 Snell DID C 8 a; cf. also b and c), Euphorion could have also competed using tragedies by his father that had already been performed during his lifetime. See Snell in *TrGF* 1, p. 88 (quoting H. Hoffmann, "Chronologie der attischen Tragödie" (diss., Hambourg, 1951, p. 56); see also C. W. Müller, "Der Sieg

des Euphorion, die Zurücksetzung des Sophokles und die Niederlage des Euripides im Tragödienagon des Jahres 431," *Rheinisches Museum*, n.f., 145, 2002, pp. 61–67.

72. This preface comes second, after an initial preface in verse. It is introduced by the vague word "otherwise."

73. See Diodorus Siculus, *Bibliotheca historica*, 13, 43.

74. This is argument no. 2 in the editions. In the manuscripts we find nothing concerning this Saloustios. But since erudition abhors a vacuum, in Jebb's edition this Saloustious is presented in the following way: "An orator of the fifth century A.D. to whom Suidas devotes a short note. A Syrian by birth who lived first in Athens, then in Alexandria, where he devoted himself to the life of a sophist. His argument for *Antigone* is also preserved. Among these other writings are commentaries on Demosthenes and Herotodus" (Jebb, *Oedipus at Colonus*, p. 6). In reality, in the *Suda* (Jebb's *Suidas*) there is no reference to a study by Saloustios on Sophocles, and Jebb's presentation of Saloustios results from the contamination of two different Saloustios in the *Suda* (= ed. Adler S60 and S62). It is not useless to form hypotheses, but it is dangerous to present them as facts. Saloustios's argument for *Oedipus at Colonus* is partly preserved on a papyrus dating from the fourth to fifth century CE in Vienna (*P. Vindob.* G. 29779, frag. 3 b, ed. W. Luppe, *WS*, n.f., 19, 1985, pp. 89–104).

75. In the editions that give the prefaces—they are not found in the two most recent editions, those of Dawe and Lloyd Jones-Wilson; we have to go back to Jebb's old edition or to the more recent editions of Dainand Mazon or Colonna—the two prefaces nos. 1 and 2 appear one after the other. But this order does not correspond to their place in the manuscript tradition. They never appeared side by side. The first preface is placed at the head of several manuscripts. But the only manuscript that presents both prefaces is the Florence manuscript (Laurentianus 32, 9; eleventh century; initial L). If the first preface appears at the head of the tragedy (fol. 96 r), the second is placed after the tragedy.

76. The performance of plays left behind by a great tragic poet was not exceptional. It had already happened in the case of Aeschylus: see above. It was also the case for Euripides. His son arranged to have the trilogy Euripides left behind at his death in Macedonia (*Iphigeneia at Aulis, Alcmaeon, the Bacchae*) performed in Athens (cf. the scholium on Aristophanes, *The Frogs*, v. 97) and also by his nephew (*Suda*, s.v. Euripides).

Chapter V. Happy Sophocles

1. This is the most extensive fragment we have concerning this lost comedy by this poet of old comedy, a rival of Aristophanes. For other testimonies and fragments, see R. Kassel and C. Austin, *Poetae comici graeci*, vol. 7, Berlin, 1989, pp. 393–430.

2. Plato, *Republic* 1, 329 c–d.

3. See above.

4. Sophocles, *Oedipus at Colonus*, vv. 1236–38.

5. For the death of Agathon, which occurred before 405, see Aristophanes, *Frogs*, v. 83, with the scholium ad loc. (= *TrGF* 1 Snell 39 *Agathon* T 7 a and b).

6. To explain the small part played by Sophocles in this comedy, some have wondered whether he was not dead at the time when Aristophanes was finishing his comedy. But in any case, only Euripides could represent "the new tragedy" against Aeschylus.

7. Aristophanes, *Frogs*, vv. 71–82.

8. Ibid., vv. 771–94.

9. Ibid., vv. 1515–23.

10. These indications regarding the ranking in the Lenaia competition of 405 and on the success of *The Frogs* can be read at the end of argument no. 1 of Aristophanes' comedy.

11. Diodorus Siculus (Diodorus of Sicily), *Bibliotheca historica*, trans. C. H. Oldfather, Loeb Classical Library, 13, 103, 4. On this death by joy and the two other versions of the death of Sophocles, see J. Labarbe, "La mort tragique de Sophocle," *Bull. Classe Lettres Acad. Belgique* 55, 1969, pp. 265–92.

12. According to the *Chronicle of Paros* A63 (*FGrHist* 239 Jacoby), Euripides died in 407/406, under the archontate of Antigènes, and Sophocles in 406/405, under the archontate of Callias (A 64, *FGrHist* 239 Jacoby = test. 3 Radt).

13. *Life of Euripides* 2 (1, 3, 11–14 Schwartz = test. 54 Radt); French translation in L. Méridier, *Euripide* I, Paris: CUF, 1926, pp. 2, 45–49). See the reference to this testimony above, in chapter IV, "Sophocles and Dionysus: The Theatrical Career."

14. See also *Life of Sophocles*, c. 14 (= test. 1 Radt = appendix V). This anecdote is also attested in the Latin tradition: Pliny, *Natural History*, 7, 180 (= test. 87 Radt), and Valerius Maximus 9, 12 (= test. 86 Radt).

15. To restore coherence to Diodorus's report citing Apollodorus, it has been thought that Apollodorus, badly transcribed by Diodorus, placed the deaths of Euripides and Sophocles under the archontate of Antigenes (407/406) and not under that of Callias (406/405). In this case, Euripides would have died just before the Great Dionysia in 406, and Sophocles just after the competition, which he won. See C. W. Müller, "Der Tod des Sophokles: Datierung und Folgerungen," *Rheinisches Museum für Philologie*, n.f., 138, 1995, pp. 97–114.

16. *Life of Sophocles*, c. 14 (= test. 1 Radt = appendix V). The source mentioned is Satyros. He was a biographer of the third to second centuries BCE who lived in Egypt, notably at Oxyrhynchos. In that city a papyrus was found that contained remains of his *Life of Euripides* (*P. Oxy.* 9, 1176 published in 1912; ed. G. Arrighetti 1964).

17. *Life of Sophocles*, c. 14 (= test. 1 Radt = appendix V). Two sources are mentioned: Istros of the third century BCE (see above), and Neanthes of Cyzicus (fourth to third centuries BCE), an orator and historian trained by the disciple of Isocrates, Philiscos of Miletus (*FGrHist* 84 Jacoby). Cf. also, on this version of Sophocles' death, Pseudo-Lucian, *Examples of Longevity*, c. 24 (= test. 90 Radt); the *Palatine Anthology*, 7, 20 (= test. 88 Radt) and Sotades, cited below. The details regarding the festival of the Conges (the second day of the festival of the Anthesteria in honor of Dionysus) would place Sophocles' death in February 405 (corresponding to the Greek month *anthesterion*) if Sophocles did indeed die under the archontate of Callias (406/405). But that date is too late, since Sophocles was already dead before the Lenaia of 405, a festival that took place the month before the Anthesteria.

18. These verses are attributed to Sotades, a lyric poet of the third century BCE. They were preserved by Stobaeus 4, 34, 8 (= Sotadès frag. 15, 13–15 Powell = test. 89 Radt). Another example of this passion for the extraordinary deaths of famous men is Ptolemy son of Hephaestion, the author of a *New History* who lived, according to the *Suda* (s.v. 3036 "Ptolemaios"), in the time of Trajan and Hadrian. A specialist

in extraordinary stories, he discussed at the beginning of his book 1 on the death of Sophocles, among others. That is what Photius tells us in his summary of this work (*Bibl.* 146 b 1726; ed. Henry, III, p. 52). Sophocles' death was in second place. Unfortunately, Photius does not give any details regarding this version of Sophocles' death. Was it by swallowing a grapeseed? In any case, a little further on Ptolemy recounts an analogous death: the courtesan Laïs is supposed to have died by swallowing an olive pit!

19. Xenophon, *Hellenica* 1, 4, 20–23; cf. Plutarch, "Life of Alcibiades," 34, 4–35, 1.
20. Diodorus Siculus, *Bibliotheca historica*, 13, 72–73.
21. Sophocles, *Oedipus at Colonus*, vv. 1524–25 and vv. 1533–34.
22. Ibid., vv. 668ff. and v. 711.
23. Xenophon *Hellenica*, 1, 5, 11–17; cf. Plutarch, "Life of Alcibiades," 35, 3–36, 5; cf. also Diodorus Siculus, *Bibliotheca historica*, 13, 73, 3–74 (with variants); 13, 79: the account of Conon's and Callicratidas's operations at Mytilene belongs to the year 406/405, when the eponymous archon was Callias (13, 97).
24. See Diodorus's account in his *Bibliotheca historica*, 13, 99.
25. Aristophanes, *Frogs*, v. 191 (the ancient scholia on this verse had already noticed the allusion to the Battle of the Arginusae) and vv. 693ff. (with the scholium on v. 694).
26. See Xenophon, *Hellenica* 1, 7, 15, and Plato, *Apology* 32 b–c.
27. See Diodorus, *Bibliotheca historica* 13, 79: the account of the operations of Conon's and Callicratidas's operations at Mytilene belongs to the end of the year 407/406, when the Athenian eponymous archon was Antigenes; whereas the account of the help sent by Athens to the Argisunae islands belongs to the year 406/405, when the eponymous archon was Callias (13, 97). From one scholium on Aristophanes' *Frogs* it emerges that Hellanikos (fifth century BCE) discussed the Battle of the Argisunae in what belonged to the year of Antigenes, preceding that of Callias. If we follow that chronology, Sophocles would have still been alive at the time of the Battle of the Argisunae.
28. Information about the tomb and the funeral are given especially by the *Life of Sophocles*, c. 15 (test. 1 Radt = appendix V). For other testimonies, see the following note.
29. The *Life of Sophocles* offers the following details: Dionysus appeared twice to Lysander in a dream to enjoin him to let the dead man be buried, and when Lysander learned from fugitives that the deceased was Sophocles, he sent a messenger to say that he authorized the funeral. See also the anecdote in the Latin literature (Pliny, *Natural History* 7, 109 = test. 92 Radt). It has been pointed out that Lysander must not have been at Decelea; it was probably Agis who gave the authorization (cf. Xenophon, *Hellenica* 2, 2, 7). A comparable version is given by Pausanias (second century CE), but the leader who saw Dionysus in a dream is not identified, and the content of the dream is not exactly the same. Here is the passage in Pausanias (*Description of Greece* 1, 21, 1 = test. 94 Radt): "After Sophocles' death, it is said, the Lacedaemonians invaded Attica; their leader saw Dionysus in a dream and ordered him to pay homage, in accord with the honors due to the dead, to the new Siren, and he understood that the dream concerned Sophocles and his poetry."
30. *Life of Sophocles* c. 17 (test. 1 Radt = appendix V). The source cited is Istros, an Alexandrian historian of the third century BCE, already mentioned (see n. 17).
31. For details on the heroization, see above, chapter III, "Sophocles the Religious Man."

32. *Life of Sophocles*, c. 1 (test. 1 Radt = appendix V). According to others, it was a bronze swallow.

33. *Palatine Anthology*, 7, 37. Dioscorides dates the from the second half of the third century BCE. The satyr has come from Phlius, because Pratinas of Phlius, in the Peloponnese, is considered the foremost author of satyr plays; see *Suda*, s.v. Pratinas, 34.

34. The Danish official, L. Münter, published his discovery in *Das Grab des Sophokles*, Athens, 1893, 12 pp. See the very interesting assessment by G. Grmek concerning the history of this skull said to be Sophocles' in *Les Maladies à l'aube de la civilisation occidentale*, Paris: Payot, 1983, pp. 104–7.

35. Sophocles, frag. 765 Radt.

36. Testimonies on these two sons of Sophocles are unanimous: *Life of Sophocles* c. 13 (test. 1 Radt = appendix V); *Suda*, s.v. Iophon (test. 17 Radt); cf. also the scholium on Aristophanes, *Frogs*, v. 78 (test. 16 Radt). The article on Sophocles in the *Suda* (= test. 2 Radt = appendix V) mentions five sons in all: in addition to Iophon and Ariston, three sons about whom we have no precise knowledge: Leosthenes, Stephanos, and Menecleides. On the courtesan Theoris of Sicyone, see, in addition to the *Life of Sophocles*, c. 13, Athenaeus, *Deipnosophistes* 13, 592 a (= test. 77 Radt) and Hesychius, s.v. Theoris (test. 76 Radt). On Sophocles' family, we must add to the literary documents a body of epigraphic material that has not been recorded in Radt's testimonies. It was collected by D. M. Lewis (cited above), pp. 14ff. It consists of four inscriptions: (1) An inscription about a Sophocles of Colonus, one of the ten stewards of the treasury of the goddess Athena in 402/401, representing the Ageis tribe (= IG II2 1374, l. 3). He must be one of Sophocles' grandsons, very probably Iophon's son. (2) An inscription about a Sophocles, son of Iophon, from Colonus in 376/375 (= IG II2 1445, l. 37). This is the same person as the preceding. (3) Iophon son of Sophocles, from Colonus, the assistant secretary of a college of ten members representing the ten tribes toward the middle of the fourth century (IG II2 2825, 1, 2). This is the son of the preceding, that is, Sophocles' great-grandson. (4) The last representative of the family attested epigraphically is Iophon son of Sophocles, in the list of the ephebes who participated in the official procession of the Athenians to Delphi (Pythaïde of 138 BCE = *Fouilles de Delphes* III, 2, 23, col. I, l. 28 Colin).

37. The main information is given in the *Life of Sophocles*, c. 13 (test. 1 Radt = appendix V), but the text is not certain in all its details. It has given rise to innumerable debates regarding the nature of the dispute and its causes. For the bibliography, see test. O 81–84 a Radt: "Lis cum filiis (vel cum Iophonte solo)." The *Life* cites, as the source for the words uttered by Sophocles, a biographer of the Hellenistic period, Satyros (already mentioned). Other testimonies confirm the notoriety of this quarrel: Cicero (*On Old Age*, c. 22 = test. 82 Radt), Plutarch ("Whether an Old Man Should Engage in Public Affairs," c. 3 (785 a–b) = test. 82 Radt), Apuleius, *Apology*, c. 37 (= test. 83 Radt), and Pseudo-Lucian (*Examples of Longevity*, c. 24 = test. 84 Radt). In the *Life of Sophocles*, it is not indicated which Oedipus is referred to. But Cicero, Plutarch, Apuleius, and Pseudo-Lucian all agree that the reference is to *Oedipus at Colonus*. Plutarch is the only one who specifies the passage: he says it is the chorus's song celebrating "white Colonus" (vv. 668ff.). All these testimonies are not entirely consistent. Some, like the *Life*, speak of a trial instigated by a single son, whether Iophon is mentioned by name or not (Apuleius, Pseudo-Lucian), while

others speak of a trial instigated by the sons of Sophocles (Cicero, Plutarch). The *Life of Sophocles* is the only testimony that speaks of an appearance before the phratry, which would in that case seem to exclude a trial; see P. Mazon, "Sophocles devant ses juges," *Revue des Etudes Anciennes* 47, 1945, pp. 82–96.

38. Aristophanes, *Frogs*, vv. 74–79.

39. For the testimonies on Iophon, see *TrGF* 1 Snell, 22 Iophon, pp. 132–34. The victory in 435 is attested by an inscription (*Fasti* year 435 = *TrGF* 1 Snell DID A 1, 84), and the second place in 428 by argument no. 2 for Euripides' *Hippolytus* (= *TrGF* 1 Snell DID C 13). These two successes were won during his father's lifetime. We do not have enough information about his career to know what became of his work after his father's death. It is the *Suda* (s.v. "Iophon") that gives us the total number of the tragedies he composed. This encyclopedia also cites eight titles out of fifty: *Achilles*, *Actaeon*, *Aulodoi* (*The Flute-Singers*), *Bacchae*, *Dexamenos*, *The Destruction of Troy*, *Pentheus*, and *Telephus*. Unfortunately it does not indicate the total number of victories. The only two clues we have regarding his success are certain, but they probably do not correspond to the total of the victories he won, because our documentation on the *Didascalia* is very fragmentary.

40. *Life of Sophocles*, c. 19 (= test. Radt = appendix V). The text does not allow us to say whether this situation happened once or several times.

41. For the references to Iophon's son and grandson, see above.

42. *Life of Sophocles* c. 13 (= test. 1 Radt = appendix V).

43. For the testimonies on Sophocles the Younger, see *TrGF* 1 Snell, 62 Sophocles II, p. 208. The main information is given by the *Suda*, s.v. Sophocles, son of Ariston (S 816 Adler = test. 1 Snell): "Sophocles, son of Ariston, grandson of the earlier Sophocles, Athenian, tragic author. He presented forty dramas, according to others eleven; he won seven victories; he also composed elegies." The date of the beginning of his career is given by Diodorus Siculus 14, 53, 6: "(Under the archontate of Souniades = 397–396) in Athens, Sophocles, grandson of Sophocles, began to present tragedies and won twelve victories." Regarding the number of victories there is a difference between Diodorus and the *Suda*. Attempts have been made to reconcile the figures by saying that he won seven victories at the Great Dionysia and five at the Lenaia. The two victories at the Great Dionysias in 387 and 375 are certain, because they are attested by the inscription of the *Fasti* (= *TrGF* 1 Snell, DID A 1, 199 and 244). Of the content of his work, we know only that he dealt with the Dioscuri (Clement of Alexandria, *Protrepticus* 2, 30, 4 = 62 frag. 1 Snell).

44. For the testimonies on Sophocles III, see *TrGF* 1 Snell, 147 Sophocles III, p. 307. The *Suda* also devotes an article to this third Sophocles (S 817 Adler = test. 3 Snell): "Sophocles, Athenian, tragic and lyric poet, descendent of the Ancient. He lived after the Pleiades, that is, after the seven tragic authors who were also called the Pleiades. These plays are fifteen in number." His victory at the *Charitesia* of Orchomenus around 100 BCE is attested by an inscription giving the list of victors in the competition (IG VII 3197, l. 28 sq. = *TrGF* 1 Snell, DID A 10 [b], and 147 Sophocles III test. 2): "Author of tragedy, Sophocles son of Sophocles, Athenian."

45. See D. F. Sutton, "The Theatrical Families of Athens," *American Journal of Philology* 108, 1987, pp. 9–26.

46. For the testimonies (few in number) on Aeschylus's two sons, see *TrGF* 1 Snell, 12 Euphorion and 13 Euæon, pp. 88–89.

47. Argument of *Medea* owed to Aristophanes of Byzantium (= *TrGF* I Snell, 12 test. 2). See above.
48. See above.
49. For the testimonies on Philocles, see above.
50. For Aeschylus's family tree, see *TrGF* I Snell, p. 88. The testimonies on all these tragic authors are given in the same volume: Morsimos no. 29, Astydamas no. 59, Philocles the Younger no. 61, and Astydamas the Younger no. 60. See also a more recent Astydamas (third century BCE), who was also a tragic author (no. 96). However, the attribution of the testimonies to Astydamas the Elder and Astydamas the Younger is not obvious, even if the *Suda* clearly distinguishes between them. Some modern scholars think there is in this ancient source a confusion between two articles: see the bibliography to *TrGF* I Snell, 59 T I, p. 198; and in particular E. Capps, "III.—Chronological Studies in the Greek Tragic and Comic Poets," *American Journal of Philology* 21, 1900, pp. 38–61 (pp. 41–45).
51. Astydamas the Elder began his career in 398, that is, just two years before Sophocles the Younger, whose career began, as we have seen, in 396. The source of this information is the same: Diodorus Siculus, *Bibliotheca historica* 14, 43, 5 (= *TrGF* I Snell, DID D 2, and 59 Astydamas I test. 2): "(Under the archontate of Aristocrates = 398) the author of tragedy Astydamas presented his first play; he lived sixty years"; ibid., 14, 53, 6, for Sophocles the Younger (see above).
52. Thanks to inscriptions, we can follow the performances of new plays until the first century BCE: see A. Pickard-Cambridge, *The Dramatic Festivals*, p. 82, n. 2.
53. Of the seven victories at least in the Great Dionysia (cf. the List of Victors = *TrGF* I Snell, DID A 3 a 44), three are known: the first victory in 372 (see above); in 347 (List of the *Fasti* for the year 347 = *TrGF* I Snell, DID A 1, 281); in 341 (List of the *Didascalia* = *TrGF* I Snell, DID A 2 a), in 340 (List of the *Didascalia* = *TrGF* I Snell, DID A 2 a). In 341, he won with three tragedies (*Achilles, Athamas, Antigone*); in 340 with only two tragedies (*Parthenopeia* and *Lycaon*).
54. See Pausanias, *Atticistarum fragmenta*, s 6, ed. Erbse 208, 18–27, where the testimony is falsely attributed to Astydamas the Elder (= *TrGF* I Snell, 60 Astydamas II, T 2 a); cf. Zenob. 5, 100 (= *TrGF* I Snell, 60 Astydamas II, T 2 b).
55. For the testimonies on Astydamas the Younger on which this development is based, see *TrGF* I Snell, 60 Astydamas II test. 2 a, 2 b, 4, 5, 6, 8 a, and 8 b. The fragment of the marble base is the IG II2 3775 from the fourth century, giving "Asty[damas]."
56. See Pseudo-Plutarch, *Lives of Ten Orators*, 841 f (= test. 156 Radt). The second measure mentioned by the same testimony is more important, but it concerns the destiny of works and not of men. It was decided to copy the text of the tragedies of the three great tragic authors to preserve an official copy in the archives in order to stabilize the text and to serve as a reference for future performances. See below.
57. For the portraits of Sophocles, see G.M.A. Richter, *The Portraits of the Greeks*, 1, London, 1965, pp. 124ff. (revised and simplified edition by R.R.R. Smith, Ithaca, NY: Cornell University Press, 1984), and also J. D. Breckenridge, "Multiple Portrait Types," *Acta ad archaeologian et artium historian pertinentia* 2, 1965, 9–22 (ancient portraits of Socrates, Sophocles, and Euripides); cf. K. Schefold et al., *Die Bildnisse der antiken Dichter, Redner und Denker*, 2nd ed. 1997 (see "Sophocles" in the index). The portraits that have been preserved carrying the name of Sophocles are very rare. The only portrait about which we are totally certain (because the name of Sophocles

is complete) is a herm in the Vatican, in the Hall of the Muses, inv. 326 (= figs. 611–12 Richter). The face, before being restored, was very damaged. It nonetheless made it possible, with a medallion from the Orsini collection that had an inscription of Sophocles—a medallion now lost, but of which we have a very precise drawing made by Th. Gallaeus in the sixteenth century and preserved in a manuscript in the Vatican, the Capponianus 228 (and not Coppianus 228 p. 125 Richter)—to bring together a series of portraits representing Sophocles in a group that specialists call the Farnese type (type I). It is the rather realistic head of an old man with a full head of hair, a mustache, and a beard. A second herm in the Hall of the Muses, inv. 322 (= Fig. 678–79 Richter; photo on the cover of the present work) also has an inscription, partially preserved. Only the end, . . .]OKLES is perfectly legible. The reading of the preceding letter (probably a *phi*) has been the subject of bitter debates. This herm has been used as a basis for defining a second group of portraits called Latran type (type II), in which the portrait is more idealized and younger. And it is to this second group that the famous draped marble statue of the Latran, coming from the city of Terracina south of Rome and given in 1839 by a family of this Italian port to Pope Gregory XVI (figs. 675–77, 680 Richter), is assigned. At the feet of the figure is a box containing papyrus scrolls (but this box was added by the sculptor, Pietro Tenerani, who restored the statue!). As soon as it was revealed to the scholarly world, the statue made an impression and was identified as Sophocles (first by the Marquis Melchiorri, on December 9, 1839, in Rome, followed by others). In this scholarly consensus, a single discordant voice made itself heard in 1922, that of Theodore Reinach, in a very well documented article in the *Journal of Hellenic Studies* 42,1922, "Poet or Law-Giver?," pp. 50–69. Reinach questioned the resemblance between the face of the herm and that of the statue from Terracina, arguing that the two faces could not derive from the same original. Then, comparing the statue with the documents, including the inscription by Sophocles, which gave rise to the Farnese type (type I), he arrived at the conclusion that the statue was of a person other than Sophocles. The statue's posture seemed to him that of a good old-time orator—or one behaving as in the good old times—with his arm folded under his cloak in a dignified posture. Ultimately, he saw in it a copy of the bronze statue of Solon erected in Salamina in the early fourth century BCE, mentioned by Aeschines in his oration *Against Timarch* 25, saying that Solon put his arm under his cloak when he addressed the Athenian people. This article led to a dispute between the French scholar and a German scholar in this same journal. The following year, Franz Studniczka of Leipzig, in an article entitled "The Sophocles Statues" (*Journal of Hellenic Studies* 43, 1, 1923, pp. 57–67), criticized Reinach's thesis and defended the traditional position. According to the German scholar (and others), the type I Sophocles derives from a statue erected by Iophon after Sophocles' death (cf. a fragmentary and debated passage of the *Life of Sophocles* 11 = test. 1, 40 Radt = appendix V), whereas the Latran's type II, and especially the statue from Terracina, derives from the statue of Sophocles that Lycurgus had erected in the theater of Athens. The types I and II thus would both derive from two original statues of Sophocles. This explains the plural in the title of F. Studniczka's article ("The Statues of Sophocles"!). Reinach responded in the second fascicule of the same year ("The 'Sophocles' Statue: A Reply," *Journal of Hellenic Studies* 43, 2, 1923, pp. 149–55), maintaining his position and finding an important ally in the person of Léon Heuzey, speaking of "the alleged statue of Sophocles" in his *Histoire du costume antique*, Paris, 1922, p. 100. The polemic continued the next year in the same journal (F. Studniczka, "One More Sophocles and Not Solon," *Journal of Hellenic Studies* 44, 1924, pp. 281–85; and W. Amelung, "Note on J.H.S. XLIII, 1923, p. 150," ibid., p. 54); cf. also aussi W. Amelung, "Il ritratto di Sofocle," *Atti della Pontificia Accademia romana di archeologia* (series III), *Memorie*, vol. 1, part 2, Rome, 1924, pp. 119–27; Th. Reinach's last reply in the *Journal of Hellenic Studies* 45, 1925, p. 131. The position taken by Th. Reinach is not mentioned in G. Richter's classic work. However, it deserves to be recalled, because it is not without interest in its nonconformism based on an intelligent comparison, insofar as concerns the drapery, between the texts and the images. The statue's posture is rather that of an orator than that of a poet. In any case, when visitors to the remarkable Villa Kerylos, of which Theodore Reinach was the founder, see the cast of the famous statue in question they will know that in the mind of its owner it is not the poet Sophocles who has entered this villa, but the orator Solon! On this quarrel, see J. Jouanna, "Le poète Sophocle est-il entré à la villa Kérylos?," *Comptes rendus de l'Académie des Inscriptions et Belles Lettres* (= CRAI), 2007. In addition to the two types mentioned above, G. Richter distinguishes two other types (pp. 130–32), but unlike the two earlier ones, they have not been authenticated by inscriptions. The bronze portrait of Sophocles in the British Museum proceeding from Constantinople (figs. 708–10 Richter) belongs to type IV (IV, 1 Richert p. 131). A good reproduction will be found in J. R. Green and E. W. Handley, *Images of the Greek Theatre*, London, 1995, p. 105 (fig. 78). But is it really Sophocles?

58. See above.

59. Pausanias, *Description of Greece*, 1, 15–16.

60. However, some say that it is the words that create the painting.

61. A periphrasis designating Homer, a member of the sect of Calliope, the Muse of epic poetry. This is a reference to Homer, *Iliad* 3, v. 65, where Alexander-Paris says to his brother, to justify his love for Helen, that she was given him by Aphrodite: "Not to be flung aside, look you, are the glorious gifts of the gods."

62. Probably a qualification of Asclepius in Sophocles' Paean; see D. Page, *PMG* no. 737 a.

63. Philostratus the Younger (third century CE), *Imagines*, 13 (= test. 174 Radt). On the hospitable relations Asclepius accorded Sophocles, cf. Plutarch, "Life of Numa" 4, 10 (= test. 67 Radt), cited above. Moderns say that it was Sophocles who received Asclepius in his home. But the ancients had a more ambiguous view: the god honored the man by being received in his home. This change in perspective leads to inexactitudes of translation in the "Life of Numa" and in Philostratus as well. The god consents to be received by Sophocles as he consents to be sung by him.

64. See *Life of Sophocles*, c. 20 (= test. Radt = appendix V); cf. c. 22; Hesychius of Miletus, *De viris illustribus*, 61 (= test. 109 Radt); *Suda*, s.v. Sophocles (= test. 2 Radt = appendix V); two scholia on Aristophanes, *Wasps* 462 (= test. 112 Radt); cf. also the Hellenistic poet Hermesianax (cited by Athenaeus 13, 598 c = test. 78 Radt), where Sophocles is called "the bee of Attica." In 421, when Sophocles was still alive, Aristophanes recognized the sweetness of Sophocles' songs (*Peace*, v. 531 with the scholium). In a fragment whose date is not known, Aristophanes even speaks of "Sophocles anointed with honey (on his mouth)" (Dion of Prusa Or. 35, 17 = frag. 598

Kassel and Austin = test. 108 Radt). On this theme, see Ch. Mauduit, "Sophocle, l'abeille et le miel," in A. Billult and Ch. Mauduit (eds.), *Lectures antiques de la tragédie grecque*, Lyon, 2001, pp. 27–41, and F. Conti Bizzarro, "Due testimonianze su Sofocle nella commedia attica," in *Rendiconti della Accademia di Archeologia, Lettere e belle arti*, Napoli (= *RAAN*), 70, 2001, pp. 319–27.

65. On this whole aspect of his work, see above, chapter III, "Sophocles the Religious Man."

Prelude to Part II: A Tragic Disaster

1. As we have already seen in the chapter on Sophocles' theatrical career, only three of the tragedies can be dated: *Antigone* (shortly before 441), *Philoctetes* (409), and *Oedipus at Colonus* (performed in 401, after Sophocles' death).

2. These two figures of 123 or 130, already mentioned in chapter IV, "Sophocles and Dionysus: The Theatrical Career," are found, respectively, in the *Suda* (= test. 2 Radt = appendix V) and in the *Life of Sophocles*, c. 18 (= test. 1 Radt = appendix V). But seventeen of the 130 plays counted by the *Life of Sophocles* are not authentic, and the *Suda* acknowledges that some writers count more than 123 plays. On scholars' attempts to reconcile these two figures, see S. Radt, "Sophocles in seinen Fragmenten," in J. de Romilly (ed.), *Sophocle*, Entretiens de la Fondation Hardt 29, Vandoeuvres-Geneva, 1983, p. 186.

3. Each time he competed in the Great Dionysia, Sophocles wrote one satyr play and three tragedies. But in the Lenaia, there was no satyr play. If Sophocles participated in the Lenaia (and he probably did; see chapter IV, "Sophocles and Dionysus: The Theatrical Career"), the proportion of satyr plays as compared with tragedies is less than a quarter. We know of only ten titles expressly described as satyr plays, not very many compared to the total of 115 known titles. But some titles might correspond to satyr plays without that fact being explicitly mentioned: see S. Radt (cited above), p. 193; more recently, see R. Krumeich, N. Pechstein, and B. Seidensticker (eds.), *Das griechische Satyrspiel*, Texte zur Forschung 72, Darmstadt: Wissenschaftliche Buchgesellschaft, 1999, pp. 224–398 (with the bibliography, pp. 643–60).

4. The first order of the plays is given by the oldest manuscript, the Florence manuscript from the tenth century, 31, 9 (= L). The second order is given by the Paris manuscript 2712 from the thirteenth century (= A) and its family. The editors vary a great deal in the order they give. The editio princeps (1502; see below) followed the order of the A family. The most recent English editor, H. Lloyd-Jones (with the collaboration of N. Wilson), in the Oxford Collection (1990) and then in the Loeb Classical Library (1994), followed the L order. The order adopted in the CUF edition by Dain and Mazon (vol. 1, *les Trachiniennes*, *Antigone*; vol. 2, *Ajax*, *Œdipe Roi*, *Electr*; vol. 3, *Philoctète*, *Œdipe à Colone*) must have corresponded in the mind of the authors to a chronological order (cf. the beginning of the preface to vol. 2, p. v: "Sophocles' three plays collected in this volume, *Ajax*, *Oedipus the King*, and *Electra*, which were all produced during the poet's maturity, are, by a curious coincidence, the same ones that the Middle Ages chose in the way we call 'Byzantine,' placing the true *Electra* before *Oedipus the King*"). But such statements, made without any demonstration, are not convincing. It would have been preferable to follow the tradition. It is rather piquant to note that respect for the textual tradition that the

French editors rightly claim to have (cf. J. Irigoin's remark regarding Dain, vol. 1, 1994, p. lxx) is so little shown in the order of the tragedies.

5. On the Byzantine choice, see below. The two standard works on Sophocles' manuscripts are A. Turyn, *Studies in the Manuscript Tradition of the Tragedies of Sophocles*, Urbana: University of Illinois Press, 1952; R. D. Dawe, *Studies on the Text of Sophocles*, 3 vol., Leiden: Brill, 1973–78.

6. For further details, see below, in "Deus ex Machina: Time and Nature."

7. The figure of nineteen includes a tragedy whose attribution is debated, the *Rhesos* (see for example F. Jouan, *Euripides, Tragédies, Rhésos*, Paris: CUF, 2004, pp. ix–xvi), and a satyr play, *The Cyclops: Alcestis*, was also performed in the position of a satyr play (see above, chapter IV, "Sophocles and Dionysus: The Theatrical Career").

8. The fragments on papyrus (except *Ikhneutaí*, "The Searchers") have been collected by R. Carden, *The Papyrus Fragments of Sophocles*, Berlin, 1974. For a complete inventory of the papyruses relating to Sophocles, see Mertens-Pack³ (accessible on the Internet).

9. Archeologists use the term "Homeric bowl" to designate a series of Hellenistic ceramic bowls with reliefs representing literary scenes, notably from Homer (hence "Homeric") or from epic poetry, but also from tragedy, notably Euripides. The fragment, which belongs to the German archeologist L. Curtius's collection, represents a scene from one of Sophocles' plays entitled *Athamas*. See the excellent publication by H. Fuhrmann, "*Athamas*: Nachklang einer verlorenen Tragödie des Sophokles auf dem Bruchstück eines 'homerischen' Bechers," *Jahrbuch des Deutschen Archäologischen Instituts* 65/66, 1950/1951, pp. 103–34.

10. The standard edition is S. Radt, *Tragicorum graecorum fragmenta*, vol. 4. Sophocles, Göttingen, 1977 (= Radt); see also the *Addenda et corrigenda* in his vol. 3, *Aeschylus*, published in 1985 (pp. 561–92); now see the "editio correctior et addendis aucta" published in 1999. For the presentation of the fragments, see S. Radt (cited above), pp. 185–231. H. Lloyd-Jones, *Sophocles: Fragments* (with an English translation) in the Loeb collection, 1996, is also useful. However, the fundamental edition remains that of A. C. Pearson, *The Fragments of Sophocles*, 3 vols., 1917. For more recent partial editions, see appendix II (beginning) and in the bibliographic guide, "Particular Studies on Each Tragedy," under "Sophocles' Lost Works."

11. The information on Sophocles' works other than his plays derives primarily from the *Suda* (s.v. Sophocles = test. 2 Radt = appendix V): "He wrote an elegy and paeans, as well as a discourse in prose on the chorus, arguing against Thespis and Choirilos." Of Sophocles' elegies, there remains practically nothing; for the testimonies and the fragments on the elegies and the epigrams, see M. L. West, *Iambi et elegi graeci*, 2nd ed., vol. 2, Oxford, 1992, pp. 145ff., and B. Gentili and C. Prato, *Poetae elegiaci: Testimonia et fragmenta*, 2nd ed., pars altera, Teubner, 2002, pp. 58ff. According to an epigram quoted by Plutarch ("Whether an Old Man Should Engage in Public Affairs," c. 3 (785 b) = frag. 5 West), at the age of fifty-five Sophocles composed an ode in honor of Herodotus. For the paean to Asclepius, see above, chapter III, "Sophocles the Religious Man," under "The Rediscovery of Sophocles' Paean." The treatise *On the Chorus* was directed against Thespis and Choirilos, two of Sophocles' most ancient predecessors. For testimonies on Thespis and Choirilos, see *TrGF* 1, 1 and 2 Snell. According to the *Life of Sophocles*, c. 19 (= test. 1, Radt = appendix V), Sophocles was in competition with Choirilos. On Sophocles' works

outside the theater, see F. de Martino, "Sofocle 'stravagante,'" in A. H. Sommerstein (ed.), *Shards from Kolonos: Studies in Sophoclean Fragments*, Bari, 2003, pp. 435–64 (pp. 441–64).

12. Sophocles' remarks on the development of his art are preserved by Plutarch, "How a Man May Become Aware of His Progress in Virtue," c. 7 (79 b) (= test. 100 Radt).

Chapter VI. The Mythic Imagination

1. Herodotus 6, 21.
2. Aeschylus, *The Persians*, v. 713.
3. Thucydides, 1, 21, 1.
4. Ibid., 1, 20, 1.
5. In a study on tragedy, myth should be resituated in the reception that spectators gave it during the performance before proposing modern interpretations that are necessarily rereadings. On the conception of Greek myth among the ancients and among the moderns, see R. Buxton, *Imaginary Greece: The Contexts of Mythology*, Cambridge: Cambridge University Press, 1994.
6. Aristotle, *Poetics*, c. 13 (1453 a 18–22).
7. Ibid., c. 14 (1454 a 9–10).
8. For this designation in Sophocles, see *Antigone*, vv. 593 and 861; *Oedipus the King*, vv. 489 and 495; cf. also v. 1226; *Oedipus at Colonus*, v. 221. Oedipus is the son of Laius, who is Labdacus's son. This royal family of Thebes, despite the name chosen to designate it, does not begin with Labdacus. Labdacus is the son of Polydorus, who is the son of Cadmus, the founder of Thebes; cf. *Oedipus the King*, vv. 267ff.
9. For the Pelopids, see Sophocles, *Electra*, vv. 10 and 1498. On Pelops and his descendents in the lost tragedies of Sophocles, see below. The denomination "Atreids" is much more frequent in Sophocles' theater: it occurs about forty times in three tragedies (*Ajax, Electra, Philoctetes*). It designates, in fact, a branch of the family of the Pelopids, the descendants of Atreus (cf. *Electra*, v. 1508: "the seed of Atreus"). In the strict sense, the Atreids designate the two sons of Atreus, Agamemnon and Menelaus. That is the case for all the uses of the term in *Ajax* and in *Philoctetes*.
10. Aristotle, *Poetics*, c. 14 (1453 b).
11. Antiphanes, *Poetry*, frag. 189 (PCG II pp. 418ff. Kassel and Austin).
12. Sophocles, *Oedipus the King*, vv. 634ff.
13. Ibid., vv. 1472ff.,
14. See also Euripides' *Iphigeneia in Tauris* and *Orestes*.
15. On these two tragedies, see appendix II, *Clytemnestra* (no. 55) and *Iphigeneia* (no. 48).
16. The analogy between the myth of Orestes and that of Alcmeon is also found in the Platonist corpus (*Second Alcibiades*, 143 c). See M. Delcourt, *Oreste et Alcméon*, Paris, 1959.
17. See appendix II, *Alcmeon* (no. 10); *Amphiaros* was a satyr play.
18. One of these plays is entitled *Alcmeon in Psophis*. It was performed in 438, at the same time as his *Alcestis*; see the argument of *Alcestis*. The other play is entitled *Alcmeon in Corinth* and was performed after Euripides' death, at the same time as *Iphigeneia in Aulis* and the *Bacchae*. For the fragments of these two tragedies, see Euripides *TrGF* 5.1, frag. 65087 a Kannicht, and H. Van Looy, *Euripide*, vol. 8, 1,

Paris: CUF, 1998, pp. 81–116. For a comparison between these two tragedies by Euripides and Sophocles' *Alcmeon*, see appendix II, no. 10 (*Alcmeon*). For the subject of *Alcmeon in Corinth* as summarized by Apollodorus, see below, the discussion of the children of Alcmeon.

19. *TrGF* 1 Snell 39 Frag 2. In the fifth century, another play entitled *Alcmeon* was composed by a younger contemporary of Sophocles, Achaios of Eretria, but it was a satyr play (*TrGF* 1 Snell 20 frag. 12–15).

20. Homer, *Odyssey* 11, v. 326 and 15, vv. 244–48. It is said that Amphiaraus died in Thebes because of presents given to his wife (an allusion to the gold necklace given to Eriphyle by Polynices); and his two sons, Alcmeon and Amphilochus, are also mentioned. The myth was dealt with in two lost epics, one from the seventh century, entitled *The Epigoni* and attributed to Antimachus of Teos, the other from the sixth century, by an unknown author, that derived its title from Alcmeon, the *Alcmeonids*. For the testimonies and the few fragments of these two epic poems, see A. Bernabé, *Poetarum Epicorum graecorum* I, coll. Teubner, 1967, pp. 29–36; M. Davies, *Epicorum Graecorum Fragmenta*, Göttingen, 1988, pp. 26ff.; 139ff.; and H. L. West, *Greek Epic Fragments*, Loeb Classical Library, 2003, pp. 54–63. To avoid excessive length, the references will henceforth be given to Bernabé's edition, which remains the *editio maior*, and secondarily to West's, which is the most recent and the most accessible.

21. For the mythographers, see especially Apollodorus, 3, 6–7 (60–95) and Hyginus, *Fables*, 68–73. For the historians, see Thucydides, 2, 68, 3 and 102, 5–6; Diodorus 4, 66, and Pausanias 8, 24, 7–10 (on the tomb of Alcmeon in Psophis in Arcadia; a parallel account is found in Apollodorus 3, 7, 5 (87–90 with variants); cf. also 6, 17, 6 and 9, 33, 2. We must not neglect the iconography, which attests to the existence of concrete scenes, certain representations of which are earlier than tragedy; for example, the very famous scene of Amphiaraus's departure for the expedition of the *Seven against Thebes* represented on chest of Cypselos, an offering of Olympia described by Pausanias (5, 17, 7–8, with the commentary by A. Jacquemin in Pausanias, *Description of Greece*, 5, Paris: CUF, 2002, p. 212) and on a Corinthian krater from the 560s BCE (see I. Krauskopf, s.v. Amphiaraos, *LIMC* I, 1, 1981, pp. 691–717, and I, 2, 1981, pp. 555–69).

22. Aeschylus's tragedy dates from 467 BCE (see above). The myth was to be taken up again by Euripides in his *Phoenician Women*.

23. Sophocles, *Electra*, vv. 837–48.

24. Apollodorus, *Library*, 3, 7, 7 (94–95). This is the subject of Euripides' second tragedy, *Alcmeon in Corinth*.

25. Pausanias 6, 17, 6 (inscription concerning Eperastus, of the family of the Clytids, who won the *Hoplitodromos*—a soldier's race—in Olympia).

26. See above.

27. Thucydides, 2, 68, 3–4.

28. Ibid., 2, 102, 5–6. See also Pausanias 8, 24, 8–10, and Apollodorus 3, 7, 5 (88–93).

29. Aeschylus, *Seven against Thebes*, vv. 568ff.

30. See the description of the sanctuary, and in particular the altar, in Pausanias 1, 34.

31. Ibid., 1, 34, 3: "Amphilochus has an altar in Athens, in the city."

32. Astydamas's *Alcmeon* is mentioned by Aristotle in his *Poetics*, c. 14 (1453 b) = *TrGF* 1 Snell 60 Astydamas II F 1 b.

33. Aeschylus, *Eumenides*, vv. 482ff.; Euripides, *Electra*, vv. 1250–72; cf. also *Iphigeneia in Tauris*, vv. 940ff.; *Orestes*, vv. 1648ff. The Athenian version of the myth of Orestes has variants. Whereas in Aeschylus the tribunal of the hill of Ares was created by Athena to judge Orestes' bloody crime, and then the analogous crimes that were to follow, Euripides returns to a more traditional version of the foundation of the tribunal, preceding the judgment of Orestes: as the name "Areopagus" indicates, it is the hill where Ares was put on trial for having killed Halirrothios, Poseidon's son, who had raped his daughter Alcippe near a spring on the Acropolis; see the scholium on Euripides, *Orestes*, v. 1648, citing the historian Hellanicus of Lesbos, who was a contemporary of the tragic dramatists (= *FGrHist.* 321 a frag. 22 Jacoby).

34. Sophocles, *Electra*, vv. 1508–10. In the chorus's last words Orestes' vengeance is seen as the end of misfortunes and the return to freedom after the usurper's tyranny. The tragedy ends, significantly, with a word meaning "accomplishment," as if the tragic destiny of the race of the Atreids ended there. This end is opposed to that of Aeschylus's play dealing with the same sequence of the myth, *The Libation Bearers*, in which Orestes, after taking his revenge, is struck by madness and flees, while the chorus (vv. 1065–76) sees the breaking of a third storm over the tragic family. In Aeschylus, this foreshadows the third play in the trilogy, the *Eumenides*, in which the Athenian version of the myth of Orestes is central. By choosing to ignore the Athenian version, Sophocles could adopt the oldest version, that of Homer, where the act of the divine Orestes killing "his hateful mother and the craven Aegisthus" is cited with high praise (Homer, *Odyssey* 3, vv. 306–10), and where there is no mention of Orestes being mad or pursued by the Erinyes.

35. Homer, *Iliad* 23, vv. 679ff.: during boxing competition in the funeral games in honor of Patroclus, one of the fighters is Euryalus, whose father, Mecisteus, is said to have excelled in Thebes at the funeral games in honor of Oedipus, "when he had fallen" (that is, in all likelihood, "fallen in battle").

36. Pausanias 1, 28, 7.

37. Ibid., 1, 30, 4.

38. Sophocles, *Oedipus at Colonus*, vv. 1520–29ff.

39. Ibid., vv. 39–43; also see above (the sanctuary of the Venerables).

40. Euripides, *Phoenician Women*, vv. 1703–7. See the ancient scholium on this passage: "In another place we have dealt in detail the tomb of Oedipus at Colonos Hippios."

41. Analogously, Euripides foreshadows the Athenian version of the myth of Orestes (see above) at the end of *Electra* and the end of *Iphigeneia in Tauris*. On the bibliographical references relating to the discussion of the passage from the *Phoenician Women*, see recently Ch. Amiech, *Les Phéniciennes d'Euripide: Commentaire et traduction*, Paris, 2004, pp. 594ff.

42. On the burial of Oedipus in Colonus, see also the testimony of Androtion, a politician and historian of the fourth century BCE who wrote a history of Attica (scholium on the *Odyssey* 11, v. 271 = *FGrHist* 324 F 62 Jacoby with notes ad loc.): "Oedipus, exiled by Creon, reached Attica and settled at the place called Colonos Hippios. He established himself as a suppliant in the sanctuary of the goddesses Demeter and Athena, protectress of the city. Whereas Creon had driven him away by force, he had in Theseus a protector. When he was about to die of old age, Oedipus asked Theseus not to show his tomb to any Thebans; for, he said, the Thebans

wanted to mistreat him, even dead. The story is found in Androtion." Androtion's source can hardly have been Sophocles' tragedy alone, because of the differences. Here are the main ones: in *Oedipus at Colonus*, Oedipus is a supplicant in the sanctuary of the Venerables, and not in that of Demeter and Athena; and in Sophocles' tragedy, Oedipus does not fear that his body will be mistreated by the Thebans, but instead, confident in the oracle of Delphi (*Oedipus at Colonus*, vv. 92ff.), he sees his body lying in Colonus as a way of protecting the Athenians against the Thebans. Androtion, although he knew Sophocles' tragedy, may have used another source or other sources; cf. the scholium on *The Phoenician Women* cited above: a detailed development on the subject seems to indicate the existence of several sources.

43. See the scholium on *Oedipus at Colonus*, v. 91, whose source is the Alexandrian historian Lysimachus (c. 200 BCE), in book 13 of his work on Thebes, citing Arizelos, an author not known elsewhere (= *FGrHist.* 382 F 2 Jacoby): "Oedipus being dead and the members of his family intending to bury him in Thebes, the Thebans forbade it, deeming it impious because of the events that had occurred. They then took his body to a place in Boeotia called Cos and buried it. Since certain misfortunes had befallen the residents of the town, they, thinking that Oedipus's tomb was the cause, ordered the members of the family to take the body out of the country. They, perplexed by the situation, carried away the body and took it to Eteonos. Wanting to bury it without being seen, they buried it during the night in the sanctuary of Demeter, without knowing the place. Once the thing was known, the residents of Eteonos asked the god what they should do. The god told them not to touch the supplicant of the goddess. That is why Oedipus is buried in that place. The sanctuary, it is said, is called the 'sanctuary of Oedipus.'" This variant of the myth is obviously incompatible with that of Sophocles. It belongs to the tradition that has Oedipus die in Thebes. However, it presents a few analogies with the tragedy: 1. in *Oedipus at Colonus* the Thebans, while wanting to bring Oedipus home to gain his protection, do not want to bury him on the territory of Thebes, but only nearby, because of his parricide (*Oedipus at Colonus*, vv. 309, 404ff.). 2. In Sophocles' play, Oedipus is a supplicant in a sanctuary where he has stopped without recognizing it. Similarly, in the version preserved by the scholium on v. 91, the body of Oedipus is that of a supplicant in a sanctuary where he has been buried, although his family does not know where. Did Sophocles know this variant of the myth and use it indirectly? That is not impossible. See L. Edmunds, "The Cults and the Legend of Oedipus," *Harvard Studies in Classical Philology* 85, 1981, pp. 221–38 (pp. 223–25).

44. Hesiod, *Works and Days*, trans. H. G. Evelyn-White, Cambridge, MA: Harvard University Press, Loeb Classical Library, 1914, vv. 161–66.

45. Homer, *Iliad* 23, vv. 679ff.

46. See above.

47. See, for example, Aeschylus, *Seven Against Thebes*, vv. 377ff.

48. Homer, *Iliad* 6, vv. 222ff.

49. Ibid., 4, vv. 374ff.

50. We have already seen that Alcmeon, the son of Amphiaraus, took part in this expedition; see above.

51. Homer, *Iliad* 2, v. 564.

52. Ibid., 4, vv. 406–10.

53. Ibid., 5, vv. 638–42 and 649–51. For further details, see Apollodorus, *Library* 2, 103–4 and 134–36; cf. Hellanicos, *FGrHist.* 4 F 26 b Jacoby, and Diodorus Siculus 4, 42, 6–7.

54. Ibid., 5, v. 637.

55. Ibid., 1, vv. 260ff.

56. The severe judgment made by one of the Epigoni, Sthenelus, son of Capaneus, regarding the war of the Seven against Thebes—which ended with a defeat, whereas the Epigoni won a victory (Homer, *Iliad* 4, vv. 406–10)—is an exception that confirms the rule. It is the sign of Sthenelus's lack of wisdom.

57. Sophocles, *Ajax*, vv. 433–48.

58. For Telamon's bravery during the first expedition against Troy and for the reward given by Heracles, see Diodorus Siculus 4, 32, 5: "Heracles crowned Telamon with the first prize, giving him Laomedon's daughter Hesione; because during the siege he was the first to rush forward, forcing his way through into the city." Cf. also Apollodorus 2, 135–36.eHer

59. Sophocles explains this in a speech by Oedipus in *Oedipus at Colonus*, vv. 765–70: when Oedipus wanted to go into exile (cf. *Oedipus the King*, v. 1518), Creon opposed his desire, and now, when he no longer wants to leave, Creon drives him away. On the relations between the two tragedies, see B. Seidensticker, "Beziehungen zwischen den beiden Œdipusdramen des Sophokles," *Hermes* 100, 1972, pp. 255–74.

60. Sophocles, *Oedipus at Colonus*, vv. 1484ff., where the seven leaders are enumerated.

61. The tragic authors retained a certain freedom concerning the chronological sequence of certain elements of the myth. Euripides, in the *Phoenician Women*, had made Oedipus go into exile accompanied by Antigone right after the war of the Seven against Thebes and the death of Eteocles and Polynices. Sophocles, in *Oedipus at Colonus*, has Oedipus arrive at the end of his exile just before the war of the Seven.

62. Sophocles, *Oedipus at Colonus*, vv. 1769–72.

63. Ibid., vv. 1409ff.; cf. vv. 1435ff.

64. For example, the character of Creon, who is reasonable and level-headed at the end of *Oedipus the King*, is a hypocritical and violent old man in *Oedipus at Colonus*. See below, chapter IX, "The Characters."

65. Sophocles, *Antigone*, v. 50.

66. Ibid., vv. 986–91. The death of Oedipus in Thebes is the oldest tradition; see above.

67. See above.

68. Eurystheus, king of Argos, is mentioned only once in *Women of Trachis*, at line 1049. The rivalry between Eurystheus and Heracles dates from their birth (see below). Eurystheus forced on Heracles the "labors" already known from Homer (*Iliad* 19, v. 133), some of which are mentioned by Heracles himself in the tragedy (vv. 1092–100).

69. Sophocles, *Women of Trachis*, vv. 31–35.

70. Homer, *Iliad* 18, vv. 117–19.

71. On Hera's jealousy, which dates from Heracles' birth, see *Iliad* 19, vv. 136ff.: Hera, using trickery, has delayed Heracles' birth and hastened Eurystheus's, so that power over Argos will belong not to Heracles, as Zeus desired, but to another of his descendents, Eurystheus, son of Sthenelus, whose father was Perseus, who himself was already one of Zeus's bastards, born from Zeus in the form of a shower of gold and Danaë, who was imprisoned. Hera's hatred for Heracles appears only once in Soph-

ocles' tragedy, at line 1048, to increase Heracles' anger against his wife, whom he accuses of having caused him, through her trickery, more suffering than Zeus's wife.

72. On this version of the myth, see the preface to *Women of Trachis* in appendix I.

73. Aeschylus, *Agamemnon*, vv. 1035ff.; Sophocles, *Women of Trachis*, vv. 307ff.

74. Aeschylus, *Agamemnon*, vv. 1372ff.

75. Sophocles, *Women of Trachis*, vv. 813ff.

76. Homer, *Odyssey* 11, vv. 602–4.

77. On the other hand, when Heracles appears at the end of *Philoctetes*, he is coming from his "divine seat" (vv. 1413ff.): this is a reference to his life as an Immortal. Nonetheless, it is not impossible that at the end of *Women of Trachis* Sophocles cleverly left an empty place for the divinization of Heracles (v. 1270); see below, chapter IX, "The Characters."

78. Sophocles, *Women of Trachis*, v. 1211.

79. On the intrigues between the two leaders, see Sophocles, *Ajax*, vv. 445ff.

80. For the discovery of Athena's intervention, see Sophocles, *Ajax*, vv. 401ff.

81. For the death of Achilles, see Sophocles, *Philoctetes*, vv. 333ff.; and for that of Ajax, vv. 411ff. The myth of Philoctetes and Sophocles' tragedy have already been presented above in chapter II, "Sophocles the Politician," but from a different perspective, in order to raise the question of the relations between myth and reality (the return of Alcibiades).

82. Sophocles, *Philoctetes*, vv. 6–11.

83. Philoctetes had received Heracles' bow for having lit his pyre on the summit of Mount Oeta. Reminders are discreetly scattered throughout the tragedy: v. 670, vv. 726ff., v. 943, v. 1406, and v. 1427.

84. Odysseus alludes to this prophecy at the beginning of the tragedy when he explains his mission to Neoptolemus (vv. 50–122), but its source is not mentioned. The first express indication of the content of the prophecy is given by the false merchant (vv. 604–13). The second indication is provided by Neoptolemus in his final effort to convince Philoctetes to go to Troy (vv. 1326–42).

85. Sophocles, *Electra*, vv. 98ff.

86. Ibid., vv. 185–92.

87. Homer, *Iliad* 23, vv. 679ff. See above.

88. Homer, *Odyssey* 11, vv. 271–80. In Homer, Oedipus's wife is named Epicaste, not Jocasta.

89. This was already stressed in a scholium on Homer (at *Odyssey* 11, v. 275): "He [sc. Homer] does not know Oedipus's blindness and exile." There is no mention of children in this passage. But Eteocles and Polynices are already mentioned in *Iliad* 4, v. 450 and v. 439.

90. Oedipus's self-mutilation is already attested in Aeschylus, *Seven against Thebes*, vv. 783–84: "With the hand that killed his father he struck out his eyes, which were dearer to him than his children." Thus it must also have been mentioned in his lost tragedy entitled *Oedipus* that preceded the *Seven* in the trilogy.

91. For the testimonies on these two epics and for the fragments, see A. Bernabé (cited above), pp. 17–28, and M. L. West (cited above), pp. 38–54. The two extant verses of the *Oedipodea* (scholium on Euripides, *The Phoenician Women*, v. 1760 = frag. 1 Bernabé 3 West) provides us with an interesting detail concerning Hemon, Creon's son, who was one of the Sphinx's victims. In the epic, Hemon thus died before Oedipus took power in Thebes. That is not the case in the tragedy. In the works of

both Sophocles (*Antigone*) and Euripides (a lost tragedy with the same title), Hemon is Antigone's fiancé. The fragments of the *Thebaid* inform us mainly about Oedipus's curses on his two sons (frag. 2 and 3 Bernabé West). Let us also note that there was a third epic entitled *The Epigoni*, which dealt with the second expedition against Thebes (on this expedition, see above).

92. On Aeschylus's *Oedipus*, clues are give indirectly in a refrain sung by the chorus in *Seven against Thebes*, vv. 721–26, 751–56, and especially 771–91: first he is a king honored by gods and men for having freed Thebes from the Sphinx; then he becomes aware that he has murdered his father and married his mother, and finally, in his mad pain, he does two things: he mutilates himself (cf. above) and curses his sons. For the bibliography on Aeschylus's Oedipus, see *TrGF* 3, pp. 287ff. Radt. Euripides had also composed an *Oedipus* that was probably after *Oedipus the King*; this tragedy is lost, but there remain a few fragments of it: see H. Van Looy, *Euripide, Fragments*, vol. 8, 2, Paris: CUF, 2000, pp. 429–58, and *TrGF* 5.1, pp. 569–83 Kannicht.

93. The *editio princeps* of the Lille papyrus 76 a (+ 73) we owe to G. Ancher and C. Meillier, in *Cahiers de Recherches de l'Institut de papyrologie et d'égyptologie de Lille*, III (1976), pp. 287ff.

94. The bibliography is immense. For my part, I have offered a comparison of the compositional technique of *The Libation Bearers* with that of Sophocles' *Electra* in a study entitled "L'Electre de Sophocle, tragédie du retour" (in A. Machin and L. Pernée, *Sophocle: Le texte, les personnages*, Aix-en-Provence, 1993, pp. 173–87), a drop of water in the ocean of publications.

95. Homer, *Odyssey* 3, vv. 303–11; cf. also 1, vv. 40–41, vv. 298–300, and 4, vv. 546ff.

96. Ibid., 1, 298–300: the goddess Athena, disguised as Mentor, cites the example of Orestes killing his father's murderer as a model of bravery for Odysseus's son Telemachus, to encourage him to set out in search of news about his father, who has not yet returned from Troy. The parallel is justified in the context of the heroes' return from Troy.

97. For Orestes as liberator, see the end of *Electra*, v. 1509, Some critics have sought to see an allusion to Orestes' future misfortunes in Aegisthus's last words (v. 1498). For the discussion of this passage, see below, chapter X, "Humans and the Gods."

98. *Returns* (*Nostoi*), summary by Proclus (ed. Bernabé 94–95, l. 17–19; ed. West 156, l. 7–9).

99. Aeschylus's tragedy takes its name from the chorus: the "libation bearers" are the women who pour libations on the deceased's tomb; but the main character is Orestes. By giving the same title, *Electra*, to their tragedies, Sophocles and Euripides shifted the emphasis from Orestes to his sister.

100. Homer, *Iliad* 9, v. 145.

101. However, this mention of Iphianassa, made by the chorus (v. 157) is the only one. The character plays no role in the tragedy.

102. Frag. 23 (a), 13–30 Merkelbach-West (= *P. Oxy.* 2075 frag. 4 and 9; 2481 frag. 5, col. 1; 2482; P. Michigan inv. 6234 frag. 2).

103. This identification, already proposed by Aristarchus (scholium on the *Iliad* 9, v. 145), assumes that the sequence of the sacrifice of Iphianassa/Iphigeneia was not known to Homer, because Agamemnon alludes to his three daughters left at home, while he is in Troy.

104. This is the most ancient testimony regarding the sacrifice of the daughter of

Agamemnon and Clytemnestra, along with the version in the *Chants Cypriens* (ed. Bernabé 41, 42–49; ed. West 74, 8–23). Sophocles composed an *Iphigeneia* on this sacrifice (see appendix II, no. 48) whose mythic sequence must have been comparable to that of Euripides' *Iphigeneia in Aulis*, and Aeschylus had earlier represented an *Iphigeneia* (*TrGF* 3, frag. 94 Radt). There are also indirect clues in the extant tragedies. For Sophocles, see in particular the discussion between Clytemnestra and Electra in *Electra*, vv. 530ff. and vv. 563ff.

105. For the testimonies and fragments of Stesichorus's *Oresteia*, see D. L. Page, *Poetae Melici Graeci*, Oxford, 1962, frag. 210–19, and M. Davies (cited above), frag. 210–19. On the place of Stesichorus's *Oresteia* in the myth before tragedy, see for example A. Neschke, "L'Orestie de Stésichore et la tradition littéraire du mythe des Atrides avant Eschyle," *Antiquité classique* 55, 1986, pp. 283–301.

106. See Athenaeus, 12, 513 a (= PMG 699 Page): "Stesichorus borrowed a great deal from the works of Xanthos, for example what is called the Oresteia." Of Xanthos's *Oresteia* we know only one detail concerning the name of Electra (Aelianus, *Varia Historia*, 4, 26 = PMG 700 Page). She was first called "Laodice" (as in the *Iliad*), and then is supposed to have been called "Electra" (= "without a bed," "unmarried") after the death of her father and during Aegisthus's reign, because she was getting old without having married. Xanthos already tried to reconcile the two different traditions by seeing in them an evolution that he justified by a folk etymology of "Electra."

107. For these three elements in Stesichorus, see frag. 217, 22–24 (= *P. Oxy.* XXIX *comm. in melicos*): the role played by Apollo in the vengeance; frag. 219 (= Plutarch, "On the delay of the divine justice," 10): Clytemnestra's dream; frag. 217, 11–13 (= *P. Oxy.* cited above): recognition by the lock of hair. Here we cannot enter into the debates regarding the interpretation of these testimonies on the use or transformation of these elements in the three tragic poets; see for example, A. F. Garvie, *Aeschylus, Choephori*, Oxford, 1986, pp. xix–xxi. On the role of Apollo and on the dream, see below.

108. Pindar, *Pythian* 11, vv. 15–37. This testimony to the myth of Orestes has often been analyzed and compared with that of Aeschylus. On the recent bibliography, see B. Gentili et al., *Pindaro, Le Pitiche*, Fond. Lorenzo Valla, 1995, pp. 293–95. The date of this ode is not entirely clear (the earliest date of 474 is accepted by most scholars; the latest date of 454 has been adopted by some, including J. Herington, "Pindar's Eleventh Pythian Ode and Aeschylus' *Agamemnon*," in D. E. Gerber, *Greek Poetry and Philosophy: Studies in Honour of Leonard Woodbury*, Chico, CA: Scholars Press, 1984, pp. 137–46). Aeschylus's *Agamemnon* dates from 468. The choice of the date of Pindar's ode is obviously related to the explanation of the relations between Pindar and Aeschylus. On the other hand, Sophocles' *Electra* is later than Pindar's ode. On the myth of Orestes in Pythian XI, see the recent article by P. Angeli Bernardini, "Il mito di Oreste nella Pitica 11 di Pindaro," in R. Pretagostini (ed.), *Tradizione e innovazione nella cultura greca da Omero all' età ellenistica: Scritti in onore di Bruno Gentili* II, Rome, 1993, pp. 413–26.

109. That is how Pindar describes Clytemnestra in his *Pythian* 11, v. 22. The sacrifice of Iphigeneia is also mentioned at the point where Pindar is wondering about the motivations of Clytemnestra's act: was her murder of Agamemnon the result of her resentment of the sacrifice of Iphigeneia or her love for another man, Aegisthus?

110. In Homer, Orestes comes from Mycenae; in Greek tragedy, from Argos, except for

Sophocles, who returns to Myceneae in his *Electra* (see below). On the other hand, Orestes' Dorian (i.e., Lacedaemonian) origin is already attested in Stesichorus and Simonides, according to a scholium on Euripides (scholium on *Orestes*, v. 46 = Stesichorus frag. 216 and Simonides frag. 44); cf. also Herodotus 7, 159.

111. Homer, *Iliad* 9, vv. 404ff.

112. Homer, *Odyssey* 8, vv. 79–81.

113. Hesiod, *Theogony*, vv. 497–500.

114. On the history of the oracle of Delphi, see the classic work by H. W. Parke and D.E.W. Wormell, *The Delphic Oracle* I–II: *The History; The Oracular Responses*, Oxford, 1956. See also the synthesizing article by H. Lloyd-Jones, "The Delphic Oracle," *Greece and Rome* 23, 1976, pp. 60–73.

115. Homer, *Odyssey* 3, vv. 306ff.

116. Sophocles, *Electra*, vv. 32–37.

117. *Phoibos* means either "the brilliant" or "the pure." From the epic onward, it is one of Apollo's epithets, and then a name replacing "Apollo."

118. Sophocles, *Electra*, v. 1424.

119. Aeschylus, *The Libation Bearers*, vv. 269ff. The name "Loxias" designating Apollo means "the Oblique" and seems to allude to the ambiguity of his oracles. The term, unknown in the epic, first appears in lyric poetry (Pindar, Bacchylides) and in tragic poetry (Aeschylus). But the use of "Loxias" in tragedy does not necessarily refer to the ambiguity of oracles. On the role of the oracle of Apollo in the *Oresteia*, see D. H. Roberts, "Apollo and His Oracle in the *Oresteia*," in *Hypomnemata* 78, Göttingen, 1984, 136 pp.

120. Sophocles, *Oedipus the King*, vv. 69–71.

121. Ibid., vv. 95–98.

122. Ibid., vv. 135–36.

123. Ibid., vv. 244–45.

124. Ibid., vv. 711–19.

125. Ibid., vv. 787–93.

126. Ibid., vv. 1435–45.

127. Ibid., v. 1518.

128. Homer, *Odyssey* 11, vv. 271–80.

129. For Aeschylus's *Oedipodea*, see above.

130. Aeschylus, *Seven against Thebes*, vv. 742–57.

131. Ibid., v. 844.

132. For the Athenian variant of the myth, see above.

133. Sophocles, *Oedipus at Colonus*, vv. 87–95.

134. Sophocles, *Oedipus the King*, vv. 789–93.

135. For the questions that have been raised about the presence of the Athenian version of Oedipus's death in Euripides' *The Phoenician Women*, see above.

136. On the responses of the oracle of Delphi, see J. Fontenrose, *The Delphic Oracle: Its Responses and Operations, with a Catalogue of Responses*, University of California Press, 1978. The author distinguishes four categories of responses (historical, quasi-historical, legendary, and fictive). The oracle of *Oedipus at Colonus* is counted among the legendary oracles.

137. On this pure hypothesis, formulated by Wilamowitz-Moellendorf in his *Aischylos Orestie II. Das Opfer am Grabe*, Berlin, 1896, pp. 246–56 ("Die delphische Orestie"),

see for example J. Defradas, *Les Thèmes de la propagande delphique*, Paris, 1972, pp. 175ff.

138. On the presentation of the *Oresteia* in Stesichorus, see above.

139. Euripides, *Orestes*, vv. 268–70.

140. Scholium on Euripides, *Orestes*, v. 279: "Euripides says that Orestes received the bow from Apollo by following Stesichorus."

141. On the presentation of Pindar's testimony in *Pythian* 11, vv. 15–37, see above.

142. Nonetheless, there are limits to the Delphic oracle's penetration into tragic myth. The tragedies that are set outside continental Greece, those that are directly related to the expedition to Troy (*Ajax, Philoctetes*), do not involve action by Apollo of Delphi any more than Homer does. And in the tragedies set in continental Greece, there may be rivalry between the oracle of Apollo at Delphi and the oracle of Zeus at Dodona. In the myth of Heracles (*Women of Trachis*), it is the oracle at Dodona that plays the role played by the oracle of Elphi in the myths of Oedipus and Orestes.

143. Homer, *Iliad* 2, vv. 484–759.

144. Homer, *Iliad*, Cambridge, MA: Harvard University Press, Loeb Classical Library, 1924, 2, v. 648 (*poleis*) and v. 649 (*hekatonpolin*).

145. Homer, *Iliad* 2, vv. 501, 505, 546 (Athens), 569 (Mycenae).

146. For Thebes and the myth of Oedipus, see Homer, *Iliad* 23, vv. 679ff.; *Odyssey* 11, v. 275; for the expedition of the Seven against Thebes, see *Iliad* 4, v. 378; v. 6, 223; 10, v. 286; and for that of the Epigoni against the same city, *Iliad* 4, 406. See E. Cingano, "Tradizioni su Tebe nell'epica e nella lirica greca arcaica," in P. Angeli Bernardini (ed.), *Presenza e funzione della citta' di Tebe nella cultura greca*, Urbino, 2000, pp. 127–61.

147. Hesiod, *Works and Days*, v. 162.

148. Homer, *Iliad* 4, v. 406; *Odyssey* 11, v. 263; Hesiod, *Works and Days*, v. 162; *Shield of Heracles*, v. 49; *Catalogue of Women*, frag. 195, 49 Merkelbach-West.

149. Sophocles, *Antigone*, vv. 101 and 119. Aeschylus, *Seven against Thebes*, v. 165; cf. Euripides, *Heracles*, v. 543; *The Phoenician Women*, v. 79. In lyric poetry see Pindar, *Pythian* 11, v. 11, among many other examples; Bacchylides, *Dithyrambs* 5, v. 47.

150. Pausanias, *Description of Greece*, 9, 8, 4: "Coming from Plataea you enter Thebes by the Electran gate." Pausanias's testimony was oddly challenged by some philologists or historians (since Wilamowitz) who see in these seven gates a "poetic invention"; see the recent article by E. Cingano (cited above), pp. 142ff. (with the bibliography). However the latest archeological discoveries (with new Mycenaean tablets in Linear B) continue to confirm the importance of this city in the Mycenaean period. See V. L. Aravantinos, "Le scoperte archeologiche ed epigrafiche micenee a Tebe: Un bilancio riassuntivo di un quinquennio (1993–97) di scavi," in P. Angeli Bernardini (cited above), pp. 27–59 (with the map, p. 55, on which the seven gates are indicated, and with the reminder, p. 56, no. 8, of the excavations of Kermaopoullos in 1915 of the Proïtides gate and the uncovering of part of the Mycenaean ramparts). For the publication of the Mycenaean tables, see V. L. Aravantinos, Louis Godart, and Anna Sacconi, *Thèbes, fouilles de la Cadmée I*, Pisa, 2001. If the seven gates were a poetic invention, it would also be hard to understand why Pindar, who came from Thebes, would mention even more frequently than other poets a characteristic of his city that was imaginary.

151. See, for example, Paul Wathelet, "Thèbes de Béotie, vue par Homère et par Eschyle, ou le reflet de deux sensibilités différentes," *Serta Leodiensa secunda*, Liège, 1992, pp. 451–62; and see especially the various contributions in P. Angeli Bernardini (cited above).

152. Sophocles, *Antigone*, vv. 100–140.

153. Thucydides 2, 2–6; 71–78; cf. 20–24; cf. 52–68.

154. Thucydides 4, 76–77; 89–101.

155. In particular, the meeting of the heralds in Thucydides 4, 97, 2 has been connected with their meeting in *The Suppliants*, vv. 381ff. With respect to this event, *The Suppliants* is dated 423 or 422. For the image of Thebes in the scene between the Theban herald and Theseus (vv. 399–584), see L. Pepe, "L'agone tra Teseo e l'araldo tebano nelle Supplici di Euripide," in P. Angeli Bernardini (ed.), cited above, pp. 203–18. Taking into account the diversity of the images of Thebes in Greek tragedy and the historical dimension qualifies the structuralist vision of tragic Thebes that functions as a corrupt city, as a kind of "anti-Athens" (F. Zeitlin, "Thebes: Theater of Self and Society in Athenian Drama," in J. J. Winkler and F. I. Zeitlin, eds., *Nothing to Do with Dionysos?*, Princeton, 1989, pp. 130–67).

156. For a comparison of these two scenes regarding the image of Athens incarnated by Theseus, see below.

157. *Oedipus at Colonus*, 919–23.

158. Another explanation is found in P. Vidal-Naquet, "Oedipe entre les deux cités: Essai sur l'*Oedipe à Colone*," in J.-P. Vernant and P. Vidal-Naquet, *Mythe et tragédie II*, Paris, 1986, pp. 175–211: the negative image of Thebes is explained by the application of the principle of the "tragic Thebes as a paradigm of the divided city" (pp. 182ff.).

159. Homer, *Iliad* 2, 557.

160. Sophocles, vv. 596–99.

161. Homer, *Iliad* 2, vv. 557ff.: "And Aias led from Salamis twelve ships, and stationed them where the battalions of the Athenians stood." For the use made of this testimony by the Athenians, see Aristotle, *Rhetoric*, 1, 15 (1378 b 29ff.); cf. Plutarch, "Life of Solon," c. 10; Diogenes Laertius, 1, 48 (Solon), and Strabo 9, 1, 10; cf. also the scholium B L on the *Iliad* 2, v. 494.

162. Sophocles, *Ajax*, vv. 201–2; cf. also v. 861.

163. Ibid., vv. 1216–22.

164. This was already noted by the scholiast on v. 1221.

165. Additional reasons can be found for Sophocles' effort to relate the epic myth of the Salaminian Ajax to Athens. Among the audience composed of Athenian citizens, those who were particularly concerned by Ajax's tragedy were the members of the tribe of Aiantis, which took its name precisely from the Salaminian hero, and this is a unique exception in the choice of names made by the ten Cleisthenian tribes, the nine other heroes being from Attica. Because of this name, the Athenians must have considered the Salaminian hero an Athenian hero. In addition, it is worth pointing out that Ajax was the object of a heroic cult in Athens itself; see Pausanias 1, 35, 3.

166. In the *Iliad*, Agamemon is said to be the king of Mycenae; see 7, v. 180; 11, v. 46.

167. Homer, *Odyssey* 3, vv. 303–10.

168. Schliemann's excavations in 1876 were the true starting point for Mycenaean archeol-

ogy. See R. Laffineur, "Un siècle de fouilles à Mycènes," *Revue belge de philologie et d'histoire* 55, 1977, pp. 5–20.

169. For Mycenae "rich in gold," see *Iliad* 7, v. 180; 11, v. 46; *Odyssey* 3, v. 305. For "broad-wayed Mycenae" see *Iliad* 4, v. 52.

170. See the *Kleine Pauly* 3, Stuttgart, 1969, s.v. "Mykenai," col. 1584.

171. At Thermopylae, the Mycenaean contingent numbered eighty (Herodotus 7, 202) and at Plataea, four hundred (ibid., 9, 28 and 31).

172. The principal source is Diodorus Siculus 11, 65; cf. Strabo 8, 6, 10, and 19, and Pausanias 2, 16, 5; 7, 27, 5–6; 8, 27, 1; and 33, 2. On the history of Mycenae in the fifth century, see M. Piérart, "Deux notes sur l'histoire de Mycène (Ve, III/IIe s.)," in *erta Leodiensia secunda*, Liège, 1992, pp. 377–87. The date of 468 is given by Diodorus. Some historians, including Piérart, are inclined to give a somewhat more recent date if the Messinians' revolt and the destruction of Mycenae are assumed to be simultaneous. However, the earthquake, which was the occasion of this revolt, is situated in 464–463; see J. Ducat, "Le tremblement de terre de 464 et l'histoire de Sparte," *Tremblements de terre: Histoire et Archéologie, 4e rencontre internationale d'histoire et d'archéologie d'Antibes*, 1984, pp. 73–85.

173. Aeschylus, *Agamemnon*, v. 24; *Libation Bearers*, vv. 676 and 680; cf. *Eumenides*, v. 654.

174. Homer, *Iliad* 2, vv. 559 and 567 (Catalog of Ships). The two cities are also distinct in 4, v. 52, or 4, v. 376 (Mycenae did not participate in the expedition of the Seven against Thebes, which was led by Argos). On the other hand, in 2, v. 108, Agamemnon's kingdom is said to extend to all Argos (= Argolis), and in 1, v. 30, Agamemnon himself speaks of his palace "in Argos" (= in Argolis); cf. *Odyssey* 3, vv. 305–7: Aegisthus reigned over Mycenae, but Orestes, after killing him and killing his mother, gave a funeral feast for the "Argives." On this delicate problem, see G. S. Kirk, *The Iliad: A Commentary*, vol. 1, books 1–4, Cambridge, 1985, pp. 180ff.

175. Aeschylus, *Eumenides*, 757ff.

176. At the beginning of his *Electra*, Euripides situates the tragedy in Argos and makes Argos the point of departure for Agamemnon's fleet (v. 1 and 6; cf. v. 48, etc.) In *Orestes*, Electra clearly indicates in her initial speech that they are in Argos (v. 46). Regarding this passage, the scholiast remarks: "It is obvious that the site of the drama is Argos. Homer says that Agamemnon's palace is in Mycenae, Stesichorus and Simonides [say that it is] in Lacedaemnia." For this scholium, see above.

177. For Mycenae in Euripides' *Electra*, see v. 963 (where it is obviously a synonym of Argos). But if that is so, why do the commentators repeat that in the tragedy the adjective "Mycenaean" (vv. 35, 170, 248, 674, 708, 761, 776) always refers to an ancient lineage? It is a simple substitute for "Argive," as "Mycenae" is a simple substitute for Argos. Is the Mycenaean mountain man (v. 170) of an ancient lineage? We find the same synonymy in *Heracleides*, vv. 289 (Argives) and 290 (Mycenaeans): vv. 759–60 (Mycenae) and v. 765 (Argos). Cf. Strabo, 8, 6, 19: "The tragic writers, on account of the proximity of the two cities, speak of them as one, and use the name of one for the other. Euripides in the same play calls the same city in one place Mycenæ, and in another Argos, as in the Iphigeneia, and in the Orestes."

178. Sophocles, *Electra*, vv. 160–62.

179. Ibid., vv. 160–62.

180. *Iliad* 2, v. 108, and *Odyssey* 3, vv. 305–7, passages already mentioned above.

181. Sophocles, *Electra*, v. 1459.

182. Athenaeus, *Deipnosophistes* 15, 695 b (no. 13; cf. no. 10).

183. Athenaeus, ibid., no. 11. Cf. Aristophanes, *Acharnians*, scholia on vv. 980 and 1093.

184. On the image of Theseus in tragedy, see C. Calame, *Thésée et l'imaginaire athénien*, Lausanne, 1990; H. J. Walker, *Theseus and Athens*, New York, 1995, and S. Mills, *Theseus, Tragedy and the Athenian Empire*, Oxford, 1997. See also *LIMC* VII, s.v. "Theseus" (J. Neils and S. Woodford).

185. Already in antiquity, these two heroes, Heracles the Dorian and Theseus the Athenian, were often compared. The most famous comparison is that of Isocrates, in his *Encomium on Helen*, 23ff.

186. *Iliad* 1, v. 265.

187. On Menestheus, king of Athens, see the Catalog of Ships in Homer, *Iliad* 2, vv. 552–54; cf. 4, vv. 327 and 338; 12, v. 331; 13, vv. 195 and 690. Theseus's two sons, Demophon and Acamas, although they are not mentioned in the *Iliad*, had participated in the expedition, from which they brought back Aethra, Theseus's mother (cf. the epic poem *The Little Iliad*, frag. 20 Bernabé, frag. 17 West = Pausanias 10, 25, 8, and *The Sack of Troy* in his summary at the end, and his frag. 6 Bernabé and West = scholia on Euripides' *The Trojan Women*, v. 31). The two sons appear in Euripides' *Children of Heracles*, where Demophon, the son of the noble Theseus (v. 115) is the king of Athens. He enters accompanied by his brother Acamas, played by a silent actor. Demophon has the role of the Athenian king who protects suppliants, as his father Theseus had in Euripides' *The Suppliants*.

188. See Aristotle, *Poetics*, 8 (1451 a 20), where those who had composed poems on Heracles or on Theseus are mentioned (= Theseus test. 1 Bernabé). There are few other testimonies on these poems in honor of Theseus; see test. 2 Bernabé and frag. 1 and 2 Bernabé and West. On *The Thesiad*, see A. Bernabé, "El mito de Teseo en la poesia arcaica y clásica," in R. Olmos (ed.), *Coloquio sobre Teseo y la copa de Aison*, Madrid, 1992, pp. 97–118.

189. Bacchylides, *Dithyrambs* 17 and 18.

190. Herodotus, 9, 27. Plutarch, "Life of Aristides" 12, says that this speech was given by Aristides, but the content of the speech reported by Plutarch, which is much shorter, does not cite the exploits of the ancients.

191. It is Plutarch, "Life of Theseus" 29, 5, that mentions the opposition between the choices made by Aeschylus and Euripides. Plutarch favors the peaceful version, which he considered more widespread. Originally from Boeotia, Plutarch has a natural sympathy for the Thebans: he must not have liked Euripides' hostile view of the Thebans.

192. In the course of his career, a fourth-century orator, Isocrates, maintained both versions. *Panegyric* 54–58 (warlike version); *Panathenaic* 168–72 (peaceful version). In the latter speech, Isocrates tries to justify the contradiction; for the warlike version, see also Lysias, "Epitaphios," 2, 8, and Plato, *Menexenus*, 239 b.

193. Homer, *Iliad* 14, v. 114.

194. Sophocles also wrote a play entitled *Theseus*, whose subject is unknown (frag. 246 Radt; cf. frag. 730 a–g and 905 Radt); see appendix II, no. 40. He also composed a tragedy about Theseus's father, entitled *Aegeus* (frag. 19 to 25 a Radt); see appendix II, no. 4.

195. On the tragedy of supplication, see below, chapter VIII, "Time and Action."

196. Aeschylus's *The Suppliants* dates from around 463 BCE; see above.

197. Aeschylus, *The Suppliants*, vv. 911–53.

198. Ibid., vv. 942–49.

199. For the date of Euripides *The Suppliants* around 423–422, see above.

200. Euripides, *Suppliants*, vv. 399–584. For the image of Thebes in this scene, see above.

201. Euripides, *The Suppliants*, vv. 403–8.

202. Thucydides, 2, 15.

203. Aristotle, *Constitution of Athens*, 41, 2.

204. Menestheus, son of Peteus; see below. Menestheus is a fourth-generation descendant of Erectheus; see Plutarch, "Life of Theseus," 32.

205. Pausanias, *Description of Greece*, 1, 3, 3.

206. Isocrates is very tempted to see Theseus as the founder of democracy; however, he restrains himself by declaring that Theseus tried to hand power over to the people, but the citizens preferred to leave it in his hands, thinking that "his sole rule was more to be trusted and more equitable than their democracy" (*Helen*, 36).

207. Aeschylus, *The Suppliant Women*, v. 913.

208. Sophocles, *Oedipus at Colonus*, v. 917.

209. In Sophocles, the king of Athens recovers the title of "ruler" (*Oedipus at Colonus*, v. 884), just as the king of Argos does in Aeschylus (*The Suppliant Women*, v. 905).

210. Sophocles, *Oedipus at Colonus*, vv. 636ff. (contrast with Aeschylus, *The Suppliant Women*, vv. 368ff.).

211. Sophocles, ibid., v. 897.

212. Ibid., vv. 66ff.

213. For the fragments' contribution to our knowledge of Sophocles' work, see the convenient and well-informed study by S. Radt, "Sophocles in seinen Fragmenten" (cited above), pp. 185–231. For the richness of the mythic imagination in the plays, see the analyses of each of these plays in appendix I.

214. See above.

215. Sophocles, *Oedipus the King*, vv. 267–68; cf. v. 224 for Laius, son of Labdacus.

216. See also the reference to the past in *Ajax* vv. 1291–97; but this is in a polemical context: Teucrus goes so far as to call Pelops, the founder of the family, a "barbarian," because he came from Phrygia.

217. Sophocles, *Electra*, vv. 9–10.

218. Ibid., vv. 505–15.

219. The myth of Pelops, son of Tantalus, was treated at length by Pindar in a personal manner in his *Olympian 1* (dating from 476), vv. 38ff. Pindar's version of Pelops's chariot race is quite different from that of the tragic poets. Pelops defeated Oenomaos, not by ruse but thanks to the golden chariot and the winged horses given him by the god Poseidon, who loved him. There is no mention of the coachman Myrtilus. With his wife, Hippodamia, Pelops had six noble sons. There again there is no reference to the internal conflicts in the family. Pelops is an honored hero buried in the Olympian enclosure.

220. Compare Euripides, *Orestes* (dating from 408 BCE), vv. 988ff. In a monody, Electra speaks of the family's past, tracing its misfortunes back to Pelops's murder of the coachman Myrtilus. A son of Hermes, Myrtilus asks his father to avenge him. Hermes causes to be born in the flock a golden ram, which is the origin of the quarrel between Atreus and Thyestes; on this quarrel, also see in the same tragedy the

chorus's song, vv. 811ff. (with the scholia on v. 812 describing the quarrel between Atreus and Thyestes); and see, already in Euripides' *Electra*, the chorus's song vv. 699ff. For a summary of the whole of the tragic version of the myth, see Apollodorus, *Epitome*, 2, 3–16.

221. See, for example, Sophocles, *Ajax*, vv. 1293–94.

222. For the tragedy *Atreus*, see appendix II, no. 17, and for the three *Thyestes*, ibid., no. 41–43. *Atreus* must have included the famous banquet, which was so horrific that the sun altered its course (*Anth. Palat.* 9, 98). It is impossible to determine the subject of the three *Thyestes*. However, we know that according to Sophocles, Atreus, in order to punish his wife Aerope, who had slept with his brother Thyestes and given him the golden sheep, the token of royalty, threw her into the sea (scholium on Euripides *Orestes*, v. 812). One of the three plays entitled *Thyestes* was called *Thyestes at Sicyon* (see frag. 249–52 Radt). This title alludes to an episode in Thyestes' life after the banquet at which he ate his children. Seeking to take revenge on his brother, he learned from an oracle that the child he would have from his own daughter Pelopia would be the avenger. He went to Sicyon, where his daughter was living, and he had with her, without her knowing it, a child, Aegisthus, who in fact became the avenger; see Hyginus, *Fables*, 87 and 88, where there is a profusion of perepeteias. However, we cannot determine exactly what Sophocles' version of the myth was.

223. This overview of the families as a whole is sometimes neglected. Curiously, at the very time when Aristotle said in his *Poetics*, 13 (1453 a, 19–21) that tragic authors concentrated their subjects on a few houses, he enumerates the examples in a strange order: "Alcmeon, Oedipus, Orestes, Meleager, Thyestes, and Telephus." Why did he separate Orestes from Thyestes? They both belong to the Pelopid family.

224. See above, in this same chapter, the section "The Difference between the Mythic Culture of the Spectators in Sophocles' Time and Our Own: The Myth of Alcmeon."

225. This summary comes from Proclus's *Chrestomathy*, which is a short literary manual in four volumes, of which the first two are known through a summary made by Photius (*Bibliotheca*, codex no. 239, ed. Henry, vol. 5, pp. 155ff.). Modern scholarship does not consider the author of this work to be Proclus, a fifth-century neo-Platonist, but rather an earlier grammarian. The Greek text and a French translation are found in A. Severyns, *Recherches sur la Chrestomathie de Proclos*, vol. 4: *La Vita Homeri et les Sommaires du cycle*, Paris: Les Belles Lettres, 1963, 110 pp. The Greek text of the summaries of each poem is reproduced in the editions of the fragments of epic poems (A. Bernabé [1987], M. Davies [1988], M. L. West [2003] cited above). For the knowledge of the lost works, Proclus's summary must be completed by iconographic documents of diverse provenance and date. The Greco-Roman tables known as the *Iliadic Tables*, illustrating the various poems in the Trojan cycle in the form of a series of images, are an indispensable complement to Proclus's summary. They have been published in A. Sadurska, *Les Tables iliaques*, Warsaw, 1964. The editions of the fragments of epic poems give references to the *Iliadic Tables*, but since they do not give the illustrations corresponding to the legends, these references cannot be used, which is all the more unfortunate because Sadurska's work is not easy to consult. Going further back in time, there are the Homeric bowls with reliefs from the Hellenistic period. The most ancient vase paintings (sixth to fifth centuries BCE)

do not give the same overall views. Nonetheless, we can note that the oldest representation, a large (1.34 meters tall) *pithos* with a relief, found on Mykonos in 1961 and dating from the second quarter of the seventh century, has on its neck a representation of the Trojan Horse, and on its body scenes relating to the taking of Troy, already in a series of images, as in the *Iliadic Tables*, but without inscriptions (ed. princeps M. Ervin, "A Relief Pithos from Mykonos," *Archeologikon Deltion* 18, 1963, pp. 37–75; with additions by the author, M. Ervin-Caskey, in *American Journal of Archeology* 80, 1976, pp. 19–41). On the contribution of archaic iconography to the knowledge of epics based on the Trojan myth, see, for example, K. Schefold, *Frühgriechischen Sagenbilder*, Munich, 1964 (English translation, London, 1966). For the iconography of the *Iliupersis* (*The Sack of Troy*), see M. J. Anderson, *The Fall of Troy in Early Greek Poetry and Art*, Oxford, 1997.

226. For the testimonies and the fragments from this period, see A. Bernabé (cited above), pp. 36–64, and M. L. West (cited above), pp. 64–107. The epic was traditionally attributed to Homer (see *Suda*, s.v. "Homer") or to an unknown poet (Herodotus 2, 117), or to Stasinos of Cyrpus, a son-in-law of Homer, or to Hegesinus of Salamis (cf. Proclus *apud* Photius, *Bibliotheca*, codex no. 239, ed. Henry, vol. 5, p. 157). It is dated to the seventh century BCE. Here are the main episodes in the *Cyprian Songs*: the deliberation between Zeus and Themis regarding how to bring about the Trojan War; during Thetis's wedding banquet, a quarrel among the three goddesses Athena, Hera, and Aphrodite for the beauty prize; the judgment of Paris on Mount Ida, when he awards the prize to the goddess of love because she promised him Helen, Menelaus's wife; the voyage made by Paris who, taking advantage of Menelaus's absence, takes Helen to Troy; preparations for the Greek expedition; a first, unsuccessful expedition that gets lost in Mysia, where the king of Mysia, Telephus, kills Thersander, Polynices' son, and where he is wounded by Achilles; a second expedition that leaves from Aulis, where Agamemnon is obliged to sacrifice his daughter Iphigeneia to obtain favorable winds; the arrival at Troy after leaving Philoctetes behind on Lemnos, where he was bitten by a serpent; the first battles; the failure of negotiations with the Trojans to get Helen back; the siege of Troy and the devastation of the surrounding area, with the sharing of the booty, notably captives: Briseis for Achilles, Chryseis for Agamemnon; this will be the subject of the quarrel with which the *Iliad* opens, when Agamemnon is forced to give Chryseis back and takes Briseis away from Achilles.

227. On the testimonies and the fragments of the *Aethiopis*, see A. Bernabé (cited above), pp. 65–69, and M. L. West (cited above), pp. 108–17. This epic in five books is attributed to Arctinus of Miletus, a disciple of Homer's (see *Suda*, s.v.). It is dated to the end of the eighth century BCE. It owes its title to the homeland of one of Achilles' most famous adversaries, Memnon, king of the Ethiopians, the son of Aurora, who has come to the aid of the Trojans and whom Achilles kills to avenge the death of Antilochus, Nestor's son, just as he had killed Hector to avenge the death of Patroclus. Here are the main episodes in the *Aetheopis*, most of which are devoted to Achilles' exploits in combat and then to his death: Achilles kills the Amazon Pentheselea, the daughter of Ares, who has come from Thrace as an ally of the Trojans, and in his own camp he kills Thersitus, who had mocked him by accusing him of being in love with his enemy (contrast Sophocles, *Philoctetes*, vv. 442–45). Then he kills Memnon, after Memnon had killed Antilochus, the son of Nestor (cf.

Sophocles, *Philoctetes*, v. 425). Finally, Achilles himself, after routing the Trojans, is killed by Paris, with the help of Apollo, at the moment that he is entering the city. A fight ensues over the possession of the body. Ajax succeeds in carrying it off, while Odysseus keeps the enemies at bay. Achilles is buried with funeral games. Then begins the quarrel between Odysseus and Ajax for the possession of Achilles' arms.

228. On the testimonies and fragments of the *Little Iliad*, see A. Bernabé (cited above), pp. 71–86, and M. L. West (cited above), pp. 118–43. The epic, in four books, is attributed to Lesches of Mytilene and dated to the seventh century BCE. Here are the main episodes: 1. The attribution of Achilles' arms and its consequences; in accord with the will of Athena, they are given to Odysseus. Ajax goes mad and massacres the herds of the Achaeans' captured livestock and then commits suicide. 2. Philoctetes' arrival and his exploit: brought back from Lemnos by Diomedes, in accord with the oracle of the Trojan seer Helenus captured by Odysseus, Philoctetes is healed by the physician Machaon and kills Paris-Alexander in a single combat. 3. The arrival and exploits of Neoptolemus, son of Achilles (compare Neoptolemus's *aristeia* in the *Odyssey* 11, vv. 508ff.): brought back from Scyros by Odysseus, who gives him his father's arms, Neoptolemus sees his father appear to him above his tomb, and he kills Eurypylus, the son of Telephus. 3. The siege of Troy and preparations for taking the city. At Athena's suggestion, Epeius constructs the wooden horse; Odysseus's nocturnal spying mission inside Troy, where he is recognized by Helen and seizes the statue of Athena (Palladion), which he carries back to the Achaean camp; the best warriors get inside the wooden horse, while the rest of the expedition, after burning their camp, make a tactical retreat to the island of Tenedos; the Trojans, thinking the invaders have left, bring the wooden horse into Troy and celebrate a feast.

229. On the testimonies and fragments of the *Sack of Troy*, A. Bernabé (cited above), pp. 86–92, and M. L. West (cited above), pp. 142–52. Composed of two books attributed to Actinus of Miletus, the author of the *Aetheopis*, the *Sack of Troy* presents the following main episodes: during the banquet of the Trojans, who think themselves saved, two serpents appear and kill Laocoon and one of his two sons; disquieted by this portentous event, Aeneas and his men surreptitiously leave for Ida. A concerted attack when Sinon gives the signal: the fleet returns from Tenedos and the warriors emerge from the wooden horse. They seize the city. Several scenes stand out once the city has been taken: 1. Neoptolemus kills Priam on an altar. 2. Menelaus finds Helen and takes her back to the ships, after having killed Deiphobus. 3. Ajax, son of Oileus, seeking to take Cassandra away, pulls down the statue of Athena to which she is clinging as a suppliant; angered by this impious act, the Hellenes want to stone him, but Ajax saves himself by taking refuge at the altar of Athena; then come the preparations for departure, with the sharing out of the captives: Neoptolemus receives Andromache, but Odysseus kills her son Astyanax; finally, after burning the city, they sacrifice Polyxena on Achilles' tomb.

230. On the testimonies and fragments of the poem on the *Returns*, see A. Bernabé (cited above), pp. 93–99, and M. L. West (cited above), pp. 152–63. This poem, dated to the middle of the seventh century BCE, is composed of five books. It is attributed to Agias of Troezen. Here are the principal episodes: a quarrel inspired by Athena arises between Agamemnon and Menelaus at the moment of departure. Agamemnon wants to stay to calm Athena's anger (owing to the impious act committed by

Ajax son of Oileus, Ajax the Locrian, who tore down her statue). Some of the war-riors leave by sea, others by land. 1. Departure of Diomedes and Nestor by sea; they get home safe and sound. 2. Then it is Menelaus who leaves; he reaches Egypt with five ships after having survived a storm that destroyed the rest of his fleet. 3. The return of the seer Calchas, Leonteus, and Polypoetes by land, by the southern route. When they arrive in Colophon, Calchas (and not Tiresias; cf. Apollodorus, *Epitome* 6, 2) dies, and they bury him. 4. When Agamemon embarks, Achilles' ghost appears to him and tries to hold him back by predicting his future. 5. The storm near the promontory of Capharea and the death of Ajax, son of Oileus. 6. At Thetis's sug-gestion, Neoptolemus travels north by land. When he arrives in Thrace, he meets Odysseus at Maronea. He continues on his way; at one point he buries Phoenix, Achilles' tutor. Neoptolemus himself reaches the Molossians and is recognized by Peleus, Achilles' father. 7. Then, after Agamemnon has been killed by Aegisthus and Clytemnestra, there is the vengeance taken by Orestes and Pylades, and Menelaus's return to his home.

231. On the testimonies and fragments of the *Telegony*, see A. Bernabé (cited above), pp. 103–5, and M. L. West (cited above), pp. 164–71. The *Telegony*, attributed to Eugam-mon of Cyrene, consists of two books; it is the most recent epic based on the Trojan myth (sixth century BCE). It begins with the burial of the suitors and a journey Odysseus takes to Elis. A second journey takes him to the Thesprotians, where he marries the Queen, Callidice. After the latter's death, Odysseus leaves the kingdom to his son Polypoetes (born of Callidice; cf. Apollodorus, *Epitome* 7, 34), and he returns to Ithaca. It is there that the most important episode takes place, summa-rized this way by Proclus (ed. Bernabé 102, 14ff.): "At that time, traveling in search of his father, Telegonus [son of Odysseus and Circé; cf. Apollodorus, *Epitome* 7, 16 and 36–37], sailing to look for his father, lands at Ithaca and ravages the island; Odysseus, having gone out to help, is killed by his son, who does not recognize him. Telegonus, becoming aware of his mistake, takes his father's body, Telemachus, and Penelope to his mother. Circé makes them immortal. Telegonus marries Penelope, and Telemachus marries Circé."

232. Aristotle, *Poetics*, c. 23 (1459 b, 2–7).

233. For a comparison of the three tragedies, see below.

234. See appendix II, no. 109.

235. See appendix II, no. 34 (*Eurypylus*), no. 60 (*The Laconian Women*), no. 89 (*Sinon*).

236. On Eurypylus and his companions who die "because of the gifts given to women," see *Odyssey* 11, vv. 519–21. Eurypylus wanted to honor the commitments made by his father Telephus—who, once he was cured of the wound dealt him by Achilles, had promised that neither he nor his family would come to the aid of the Trojans—and initially refused to be Priam's ally. But Priam, by giving Astyoche, Eurypylus's mother, a golden vine, forced him to come. See the scholium on *Odyssey* 11, v. 520.

237. In his essay "On the Absence of Anger" (458 d = frag. 768 Nauck 2) Plutarch quotes two of Sophocles' verses in which a messenger relates a single combat between Eu-rypylus and Neoptolemus, who fought each other without anger. This quotation takes its place in the fragments of the tragedy that have been found in part on pa-pyrus (cf. frag. 210, vv. 8 and 9 Radt).

238. Compare *Odyssey* 4, vv. 244–58 (especially v. 250).

239. Virgil, *Aeneid* 2, vv. 57–198.

240. Compare in particular the same charge made against Odysseus to make the wily speech more persuasive. The hypothesis of Sophocles' influence on Virgil was formulated long ago.

241. See appendix II, no. 61 (*Laocoon*), no. 3 (*Ajax the Locrian*), no. 84 (*Polyxena*). On these three tragedies by Sophocles taken from *The Sack of Troy*, see M. J. Anderson (cited above), pp. 174–81 (chap. 1: "The Lost *Iliupersis Dramas of Sophokles*").

242. Dionysius of Halicarnassus, *Roman Antiquities*, 1, 48, 2 (ed. Fromentin 146–47) with a quotation of six verses (= frag. 373 Radt).

243. Compare Apollodorus, *Epitome* 5, 22: "When he sees Cassandra clinging to the statue of Athena, Ajax the Locrian does her violence. For that reason the statue's eyes are turned toward the heavens"; and 25: "As they were about to leave by sea after having sacked Troy, they [sc. the Hellenes] were held back by Calchas, who said that Athena was angry with them because of Ajax's impious act. Thus they were going to kill him, when Ajax took refuge on an altar so that they left him." On Ajax the Locrian in this epic poem, see W. Rösler, "Der Frevel des Aias in der 'Iliupersis,' " *Zeitschrift für Papyrologie und Epigraphik* 69, 1987, pp. 1–8; cf. Rösler, "Formes narratives d'un mythe dans la poésie épique, la poésie lyrique et les arts plastiques: Ajax de Locres et les Achéens," in C. Calame (ed.), *Métamorphoses du mythe en Grèce antique*, Geneva, 1988, pp. 202–9.

244. *Ajax the Locrian*, frag. 10 c Radt (the fragment is not, however, attributed by name to the tragedy). The sole extant literary testimony preceding Sophocles is Alcaeus, frag. 298 Voigt, Liberman. It concerns the scene in which Ajax tears Helen away, but it is fragmentary. Nonetheless, we grasp one detail: Athena, faced by Ajax's impiety, "pales" (with anger). The judgment scene was known to the Athenians through Polygnotus's painting in the Painted Porch (*Stoa Poikile*; cf. Pausanias 1, 15, 2: "After the Amazons come the Greeks when they have taken Troy, and the kings assembled on account of the outrage committed by Ajax against Cassandra. The picture includes Ajax himself, Cassandra and other captive women"). On *Ajax the Locrian*, see appendix II, no. 3.

245. See above. Compare Apollodorus, *Epitome* 5, 23: "After killing the Trojans, they [the Hellenes] burned the city and divided the spoils among themselves. Having sacrificed to all the gods, they threw Astyanax off the ramparts. Then they killed Polyxena on Achilles' tomb."

246. See the scholium on Euripides, *Hecuba*, v. 1 (ed. E. Schwartz, vol. 1, p. 10). For the presentation of Polyxena, see appendix II, no. 84. We have no testimony regarding the sacrifice of Polyxena itself.

247. Sophocles, *Polyxena*, frag. 523 Radt. In Euripides, the appearance of Achilles demanding a share of the honor before the Greeks depart is simply announced by the chorus when it enters the stage (vv. 109–15); but the appearance of Achilles is replaced by that of Polydorus at the beginning of the tragedy, with an allusion to the first words uttered by Achilles; see R. Goossens, *Euripide et Athènes*, Brussels, 1962, pp. 311–13.

248. The comparison is in the treatise *On the Sublime* 15, 7: "Sophocles too describes with superb visualization the dying Oedipus conducting his own burial amid strange portents in the sky, and Achilles at the departure of the Greeks, when he appears above his tomb to those embarking."

249. See *The Phrygians* (appendix II, no. 114), whose subject is drawn from book 24 of

the *Iliad*. Priam goes to Achilles' camp to obtain the restitution of his son Hector's body; cf. *Priam* (appendix II, no. 85). See also *Chriseis* (appendix II, no. 115, at the end), which might be inspired by book I of the *Iliad*; but the determination of the subject of this play remains hypothetical. That does not mean that Sophocles was not indirectly inspired by scenes from the *Iliad* that he transposed; see below.

250. On Sophocles' plays drawn from the *Cyprian Songs*, see F. Jouan, "Sophocle et les chants cypriens," in J. A. López-Férez (ed.), *La Epica griega y su influencia en la literatura espanola*, Madrid, 1993, pp. 189–212.

251. On *Iphigeneia*, see above and appendix II, no. 48. On *The Madness of Odysseus*, see appendix II, no. 78.

252. Sophocles, *Philoctetes*, vv. 1025–26.

253. Aeschylus, *Agamemnon*, v. 841.

254. Two variants of the episode are reported by the mythographers. According to Apollodorus, *Epitome* 3, 7, Palamedes seized Telemachus, who was in the arms of his mother, and drew his sword to kill him. Odysseus, out of concern for his son, acknowledged his pretense and took part in the expedition. According to Hyginus, *Fables*, 95, Odysseus simulated madness by yoking a horse and an ox; Palamedes, seeing that he was pretending, placed Telemachus in front of the plow.

255. See appendix II, no. 80 (*Palamedes*).

256. Pausanias 10, 31, 2.

257. Polyaenus, *Stratagems in War*, I. Prol. 12. The stratagem of the letter is mentioned by the mythographers, with variants in the details; see Apollodrous, *Epitome*, 3, 7–8; Hyginus, *Fables*, 105; scholium on Euripides *Orestes*, v. 432; see also Gorgias, *Defense of Palamedes*; Ps. Alkidamas, *Odysseus*; Philostratus, *Heroicus*. On Aeschylus's *Palamedes*, see *TrGF* 3, frag. 181–82 a (Radt); on that of Sophocles, *TrGF* 4, frag. 478–81; on that of Euripides, see F. Jouan, *Euripide Fragments*, vol. 8, 2, Paris, 200, pp. 487–513, and *TrGF* 5.2, pp. 596–605 Kannicht.

258. See appendix II, no. 73 (*Nauplius Lights a Fire*). In reality, Sophocles wrote two tragedies on this vengeance. See also *Nauplius Sails In* (appendix II, no. 72), which is placed, from the point of view of the myth's chronology, between *Palamedes* and *Nauplius Lights a Fire*. Even before awaiting the return of the fleet, Nauplius, after his son's condemnation to death, had gone to Troy by sea to try to obtain reparation. Not have been able to do so, he tried to avenge himself by sailing to the different regions of Greece to convince the warriors' wives to deceive their husbands; cf. Apollodorus, *Epitome*, 6, 8–10. Whence the title of the tragedy *Nauplius Sails In* (*Nauplius Katapleon*).

259. Euripides, *Helen*, v. 767.

260. See especially Apollodorus, *Epitome*, 6, 7, and 11; Hyginus, *Fables*, 116. On the title of the tragedy, see Pollux 9, 156.

261. See above, pp. 185–87.

262. See the *Life of Sophocles* 20 (test. 1, 20 Radt = appendix V). In several plays, he borrowed from the *Odyssey*.

263. See above, chapter I, "The Young Sophocles," and appendix II, no. 74 (*Nausicaa* or *The Laundresses*). Another play entitled *The Phaeacians* might also be drawn from book 6 of the *Odyssey*; see appendix II, no. 106.

264. *Odyssey* 19, vv. 357ff. For Sophocles' play, see appendix II, no. 76 (*The Footwashing*).

265. See appendix II, no. 77 (*Odysseus Wounded by the Spine*).

266. For the episode in the epic poem, see Proclus's summary, above, n. 231. On this mythical sequence, compare also Apollodorus, *Epitome*, 7, 36–37, and Hyginus, *Fables*, 127. For the scene in which Odysseus laments, see Cicero, *Tusculan Disputations*, 2, 49 (= frag. 461 a Radt). It was reworked by Pacuvius in his tragedy entitled *Niptra*. The comparison with *Women of Trachis* can be pursued for the second major character. Telegonus is involuntarily responsible for the death of his father, whom he wanted to find, just as Deianira is involuntarily responsible for the death of her husband Heracles, whom she wanted to win back.

267. Athenaeus, *Deipnosophistes* 7, 277 e (= test. 136 Radt). The reference is to Zoilus. His general observation is an extension of a particular comparison apropos of a rare expression used by Sophocles in *Ajax* (v. 1297), which he finds in a poem in the cycle, the *Titanomachia*. The example reminds us that the epic cycle is not limited to the Trojan cycle.

268. The use of secondary myths is obviously not peculiar to Sophocles' theater. For this kind of evocation of the myth by analogy in Greek tragedy, see the brief but suggestive remarks in D. Lanza, "Redondances de mythes dans la tragédie," in C. Calame (cited above), pp. 141–49.

269. Homer, *Iliad* 9, v. 527. Phoenix's account runs from v. 529 to v. 599. Sophocles' tragedy is entitled *Meleager* (frag. 401–6 Radt); see appendix II, no. 66 (for the myth and the presentation of the tragedy). On the myth as an example in the *Iliad*, see M. M. Willcock, "Mythological Paradeigma in the Iliad," *Classical Quarterly*, n.s., 14, 1964, pp. 141–54. On the myth of Meleager in the *Iliad*, see J. M. Renaud, *Le Mythe de Méléagre: Essai d'interprétation*, Liège, 1993. For the iconography of the myth, see *LIMC* VII, s.v. "Meleagros" (S. Woodford).

270. See above.

271. Sophocles, *Antigone*, vv. 944–87 (4th stasimon). This song by the chorus has very often been commented on in general studies on Sophocles or in more specific studies on the chorus. Two articles are devoted entirely to it: I. Errandonea, "Das 4. Stasimon der "Antigone" von Sophocles (944–87)," *Symbolae Osloenses* 30, 1953, pp. 16–26; Chr. Sourvinou-Inwood, "Le mythe dans la tragédie, la tragédie à travers le mythe: Sophocle, *Antigone* vv. 944–987," in C. Calame (cited above), pp. 167–83; taken up again and developed in "The Fourth Stasimon of Sophocles' Antigone," *Bulletin of the Institute of Classical Studies* 36, 1989, pp. 141–65 (with the bibliography).

272. Heracles, who was of the same generation as the heroes of the war of the Seven against Thebes, is a fourth-generation descendant of Danaë (Danaë—Perseus, son of Danaë—Electryon, son of Perseus—Alcmene daughter of Electryon—Heracles son of Alcmene and Zeus); see Diodorus 4, 9, 1.

273. *Iliad* 14, vv. 319ff.

274. For a literary testimony on the golden rain before Sophocles, see Pindar, *Pythians* 12, v. 17 (490 BCE). For the underground prison of bronze, see Pausanias 2, 23, 7. For the myth as a whole, see especially the very precise testimony of Pherecydes of Athens, a historian contemporary with Sophocles (*FGrHist* 3F. 4, 10, and 11 Jacoby = scholia on Apollonius of Rhodes 4, vv. 1091 and 1515); cf. also Apollodorus 2, 4, 1ff. On the myth of Danaë, see F. Lissarrague, "Danaé, métamorphoses d'un mythe," m S. Georgoudi and J.-P. Vernant (eds.), *Mythes grecs au figuré*, Paris, 1996, pp. 105–33; on the iconography, see *LIMC* III, s.v. (J.-J. Maffre).

275. For *Acrisius* (frag. 60–76 Radt), see appendix II, no. 7; for *Danaë* (frag. 165–70

Radt), see appendix II, no. 21; for *The Larissans* or *The Inhabitants de Larissa* (frag. 378–83 Radt), see appendix II, no. 62. J. M. Lucas, "Le mythe de Danaé et de Persée chez Sophocle," in A. Machin and L. Pernée, *Sophocle: Le texte, les personnages*, Aix-en-Provence, 1993, pp. 35–48, proposes seeing in this a trilogy, *Acrisius, Danaë, The Larissans* (and perhaps with Andromeda as a satyr play); but the solution of a trilogy, already proposed by T. Zielinski in 1925 (*Tragodumenon libri tres*, Cracow, p. 289, n. 1), remains very hypothetical. Aeschylus had composed a satyr play, *The Net Draggers* (*Diktyyoulkoi*), on part of this myth (*TrGF* 3, frag. 46a–47c Radt): at the birth of Perseus, Acrisius had put the child and the mother in a wooden casket that he threw into the sea, but Dictys caught it in his nets on the island of Seriphos; see Strabo, 10, 5, 10, and especially Phrerecydes cited above. Euripides had also dramatized the myth in two tragedies, *Danaë* (*TrGF* 5, 1, frag. 316–30 a Kannicht) and *Dictys* (ibid., frag. 331–48 Kannicht), performed at the same time as his *Medea* and his *Philoctetes* in 432 BCE (cf. the argument of *Medea*); on Euripides' two tragedies, see H. Van Looy, *Euripide*, vol. 8, 2, *Fragments*, Paris, 2000, pp. 47–71.

276. Sophocles, *Antigone*, vv. 955–65.

277. *Iliad* 6, vv. 130–40. See also the scholium on 131 (= Eumélos, frag. 11 Bernabé frag. 27 West).

278. This tetralogy of the *Licurgeia* comprised a tragic trilogy including *The Edoni, The Bassarides*, and *The Youths*, and a satyr play entitled *Lycurgus* (*TrGF* 3, test. 68 Radt = scholium on Aristophanes, *Thesmophoriazusae*, v. 135). For the extant fragments of these plays, see *Edoni* frag. 7–67 Radt; Bassarides (= Bacchantes dressed in foxes' skins), frag. 23–25 Radt; *The Youths* frag. 146–49 Radt; *Lycurgus* frag. 124–26 Radt.

279. Information provided by the didascalia of Aeschylus's *Seven against Thebes*: the reference is to Polyphrasmon, who came in third (*TrGF* 3, test. 58 a Radt; cf. test. 58 b). He was the son of Phrynichus; see *Suda*, s.v. Phrynichus (= *TrGF* 1, p. 69 Snell).

280. Aristophanes, *Thesmophoriazusae*, vv. 134ff. (411 BCE).

281. The punishment of Lycurgus took various forms, if we refer to the testimonies later than Sophocles. See Diodorus of Sicily 3, 65, 4–5 and 4, 3–4; Apollodorus 3, 5, 1, and Hyginus, *Fables*, 132.

282. Compare *Antigone*, v. 774.

283. *Antigone*, v. 943.

284. See the scholium on *Antigone*, v. 955: "Let us not interpret this to mean that Antigone, being impious, undergoes the same punishment as the impious Lycurgus, but simply that it consoles the young woman by comparing analogous misfortunes."

285. See *Antigone*, vv. 381–83 (cf. v. 603); vv. 471ff.; v. 875; vv. 929ff. For further details on the chorus's attitude toward Antigone and on the analogy between Antigone and Lycurgus, see J. Jouanna, "Lyrisme et drame: Le choeur dans l'*Antigone* de Sophocle," in *Le Théâtre antique: La tragédie*, Cahiers de la villa "Kérylos" 8, Paris, 1998, pp. 101–28 (p. 126, n. 54). Some modern readers see in the choice of King Lycurgus a deliberate ambiguity on Sophocles' part, an indirect way of warning Creon who has remained onstage. But could be only an involuntary tragic irony, because the chorus's thoughts have been focused on Antigone from the beginning to the end of the stasimon.

286. Boreas's abduction of Cleopatra's mother, whose name was Orythia, took place in the Athenian countryside on the banks of the River Ilissus. The Athenians were well acquainted with the place where she had been abducted; it is marked by the presence

of an altar to Boreas, which Socrates mentions at the beginning of Plato's *Phaedrus* (229 c).

287. Sophocles had mentioned Cleopatra's misfortunes in his play *The Drummers* (*Tympanistai*), where the cruel stepmother had in fact blinded Phineus's children and put them in an underground prison. See appendix II, no. 100. No testimony on this lost tragedy speaks of Cleopatra's fate; but according to Diodorus 4, 43, 3, the mother was also imprisoned. In addition, Sophocles wrote two plays on Phineus in which he blinds (or kills) his own sons and was punished by being blinded himself; see appendix II, nos. 110–11. Thus Sophocles did not necessarily adopt the same variants in the several tragedies in which he mentions or deals with the same myth; in *Antigone* and *The Drummers*, it is the stepmother who is responsible, while in *Phineus* it is the father. A third variant is attested (scholium on *Antigone*, v. 981): it is the mother who blinds her own sons out of anger at her unfaithful husband, who had repudiated her. Thus we can see why the historian Diodorus (4, 44, 5ff.), discussing this subject, mentions that the ancient myths did not have a single tradition and that it is hardly surprising if his judgment does not agree on certain points with that of the poets or prose writers. Aeschylus had also composed a *Phineus* performed at the same time as his *Persians* in 472 (see appendix II, nos. 110–11, at the end).

288. *Antigone*, vv. 986ff.

289. Ibid., vv. 823–33. Sophocles also wrote a tragedy entitled *Niobe* on this secondary myth; see above (where the tragedy is mentioned in the context of the family of Pelops and Tantalus), and see appendix II, no. 75.

290. Aristotle, *Poetics*, 14 (1454 a).

291. For the history of the mythic subject of *Women of Trachis* before Sophocles, see appendix I, "*Women of Trachis*," 1b.

292. That depends on the solution that we adopt for the end of Aeschylus's *Seven against Thebes* (vv. 1005–78). Antigone appears there and announces her intention of burying Polynices despite the fact that this is prohibited by a Cadmean herald. It is generally thought that this ending is not by Aeschylus, but was later than Sophocles' *Antigone* and even than Euripides' *The Phoenician Women*; see G. O. Hutchinson, *Aeschylus, Septem contra Thebas*, Oxford, 1985, pp. 209–11 (with the bibliography, p. 209).

293. See above, in this same chapter, "Tragic Myth and Athenian Reality: The Myths of Orestes and Oedipus."

294. For *Oedipus the King* reworking the central play in Aeschylus's *Oedipodeis*, namely the lost tragedy *Oedipus*, see above in this same chapter, "The Gaps in the Prehistory of the Tragic Myth: The Myth of Oedipus Again," n. 92. For *Electra* reworking the central play in Aeschylus's *Oresteia*, namely the extant tragedy *The Libation Bearers*, see above in this same chapter "A Prehistory of a Tragic Myth with Fewer Gaps: The Myth of Orestes."

295. *TrGF* 3, frag. 83–85 Radt.

296. See above.

297. For Oedipus and Orestes, see above, in this same chapter.

298. See above in this same chapter "A Prehistory of a Tragic Myth with Fewer Gaps: The Myth of Orestes"; also in that section, compare the Pindaric version.

299. Scholium on *Ajax*, v. 833 (= frag. 83 Radt); cf. also the scholium on Lycophron v. 455 (where the place on the body where Ajax is vulnerable varies: according to some

it is the collarbone, according to others the armpit, like Aeschylus in *The Thracian Women*), and the scholium on Homer, *Iliad* 14, v. 404.

300. Homer, *Iliad* 14, v. 404. It is regarding this passage that a scholium on Homer mentions the difference between the myth of Ajax in Homer and in Aeschylus: "Ajax is vulnerable all over his body, and not only in the region of the armpit, as in Aeschylus and others."

301. J. Jouanna, "La lecture de Sophocle dans les scholies: Remarques sur les scholies anciennes d'Ajax," in A. Billault and Ch. Mauduit (eds.), *Lectures antiques de la tragédie grecque*, Lyon 2001, pp. 9–26 (p. 19).

302. Aeschylus's *Philoctètes* was necessarily performed before 456 (the date of Aeschylus's death). Euripides' *Philoctetes* was performed in 431 (along with *Medea*; see the argument of *Medea* by Aristophanes of Byzantium.

303. Dio Chrysostom, *Discourse* 52 (as a whole). See also the *Discourse* 59, entitled *Philoctetes*, which is a paraphrase of the beginning of Euripides' *Philoctetes* (Odysseus's monologue; the encounter between Odysseus and Philoctetes).

304. For the fragments and testimonies on Aeschylus's *Philoctetes*, see *TrGF* 3, frag. 249–57 Radt (with the bibliography). For Euripides' *Philoctetes*, see *TrGF* 5.2, frag. 787–803 Kannicht; see also C. W. Müller, *Euripides, Philoktet: Testimonien und Fragmente*, Berlin, 2000, and F. Jouan, *Euripide*, vol. 8, 3, Paris: CUF, 2002, pp. 269–312 (with the preface and the bibliography). We also have a papyrus fragment (*P. Oxy.* 2256 frag. 5 = frag. 451 w Radt) that may correspond to the subject of Aeschylus's *Philoctetes*; but the text is very mutilated and does not contribute anything new. A more important papyrus fragment (*P. Oxy.* 2455 frag. 17 = C. Austin, *Nova Fragmenta Euripidea*, 1968, p. 100) gives the subject of Euripides' play, but nothing certain or important in comparison with Dio's testimony.

305. See above in this same chapter "The Wealth of the Mythic Tradition: The Trojan Cycle in Sophocles' Lost Plays."

306. In the choice of the chorus, Sophocles deviated from Aeschylus in his *Ajax* as well as in his *Philoctetes*. He chose a chorus closer to his characters. In *Ajax*, instead of the chorus of Thracian women that had given its name to Aeschylus's tragedy, he introduced the chorus of Ajax's sailors. Analogously, in his *Philoctetes*, instead of the chorus of Lemnians chosen by Aeschylus (and adopted by Euripides), Sophocles introduced the chorus of Neoptolemus's sailors. The innovation is comparable, insofar as a chorus close to a character can participate more closely in the action. But these two innovations, while comparable, do not have the same impact in the two tragedies. In the *Philoctetes*, the chorus is close, not to the protagonist, as in *Ajax*, but to the secondary hero, which reinforces the Sophoclean Philoctetes' isolation in comparison to Aeschylus and Euripides.

Chapter VII. Space and Spectacle

1. A. R. Rangabé, I, 1840, p. 120.

2. For an overview of Dörpfeld's excavations, see W. Dörpfeld and E. Reisch, *Das griechische Theater*, Athens, 1896; see also Dörpfeld, "Grabungen im Dionysos-Theater in Athen," *Praktika* 1925/1926, pp. 25–32. On more recent excavations and the interpretation of the earlier ones, see especially E. Pöhlmann (ed.), *Studien zur Bühnendichtung und zum Theaterbau der Antike, mit Beiträgen von R. Bees,*

H. R. Götte, O. Lendle, P. von Möllendorff, U. Wagner, Frankfurt am Main: P. Lang, 1995, pp. 9–48 (with the bibliography); cf. J.-Ch. Moretti, "Le théâtre du sanctuaire de Dionysos Éleuthéros à Athènes, au Ve s. av. J.-C.," *Revue des Etudes Grecques* 113, 2000, pp. 275–98.

3. Aristophanes, *Thesmophoriazusae*, v. 395. On the *ikria*, see also Cratinos, *PCG* IV, frag. 360 Kassel and Austin.

4. See Pausanias 1, 20, 3: "The oldest sanctuary of Dionysus is near the theater. Within the precincts are two temples and two statues of Dionysus, the Eleuthereus Deliverer and the one Alcamenes made of ivory and gold." Both temples existed in Sophocles' time; the older and smaller, situated nearer the theater, dated from the sixth century and held an ancient wooden statue of Dionysus (an *xoanon*) that Pegasus had brought from Eleutherai when he introduced the cult of Dionysus in Athens; see Pausanias 1, 2, 5 and 38, 8. The second dates from the fifth century and holds a colossal statue of Dionysus in gold and ivory, created by the sculptor Alcamenes. It also held painting depicting the life of Dionysus that Pausanias described.

5. See Pausanias 1, 20, 3 (cited above): "The oldest sanctuary of Dionysus is near the theater."

6. See below (the problem of the form of the orchestra). The beginning of the extant inscription consists of four letters, ιερε[. It is arbitrary to attribute this seat to the priest of Dionysus, as has been generally done; for example, E. Pöhlmann (cited above), p. 22. Since there were numerous priests occupying the first row, this seat may have been assigned to any one of them.

7. See, for example, Euripides, *Bacchantes*, vv. 274–83.

8. See, among many other testimonies, Aristophanes, *The Birds*, v. 794 (with the scholium: "*Bouleutikos* is the theatrical space reserved for the *bouleutes* [council members], just as the *ephebikos* is the place reserved for the ephebes").

9. Demosthenes, *Against Midias* 127: the judges must take vengeance on Midias, basing the penalty "on the ground that all alike are victims of the same wrong—the laws, the gods, the city of Athens."

10. See Hesychius "*Lenai*: Bacchantes; that is the name the Arcadians give them." The explanation of the word "Lenaians" by the substantive *lenos*, meaning "winepress" is less probable. The Lenaian festivals, which took place in the winter, are not a wine-pressing festival. Nonetheless, in people's minds, the link between the winepress and the Lenaian festival was not impossible.

11. See in particular Aristotle, *Constitution of Athens* 57, 1: "Next the Dionysia in Lenaeon; this festival consists of a procession and a competition, the former conducted by the King and the Superintendents jointly, the latter organized by the King and the Superintendents jointly." For the presentation of all the testimonies concerning the Lenaian festivals and their discussion, see A. Pickard-Cambridge, *The Dramatic Festivals of Athens*, 2nd revised ed., supplement et corrections, Oxford, 1988, pp. 25ff.

12. That is what emerges from the inscription on the didaskalia, IG II2 2319 col. 2 (419–418 BCE); text given by Pickard-Cambridge (cited above), p. 109 (= *TrGF* 1 DID A 2 b 70–83 Snell).

13. See above.

14. The banquet at Agathon's home brought together guests speaking about love, including the philosopher Socrates, the comic author Aristophanes, and the physician

Erymachus, and took place the day after Agathon, accompanied by his choreutes, made his sacrifice in honor of the victory (*Symposium* 173 a). The victory took place in winter, because the nights are long (*Symposium* 223 c). It was Athenaeus (*Deipnosophistes* 5 217 a) who gave the precise circumstances and date of Agathon's victory: "Aristion, under whose archonship Xenophon's symposium is supposed to be held, was archon four years before Euphemus, in whose year Plato has placed the celebration of Agathon's victory." See the inscription on the didaskalia IG II2 2319 col. 2 (Pickard-Cambridge, cited above, p. 109 = *TrGF* 1 DID A 2b 70–83 Snell), which begins with the remains of results of the Lenaian tragedy contest of 421–20.

15. See the inscription on the didaskalia IG II2 2319 col. 2 (Pickard-Cambridge, cited above, p. 109 = *TrGF* 1 DID A 2b 70–83 Snell), which begins with the remains of the results of the tragedy contest at the Lenaian festival of 421–20.

16. On the problem of the location of the Lenaion, see Hesychius, s.v. *epi Lenaiō agōn*: "Contest in the Lenaion: in the city there is a Lenaion surrounded by a large peribolos and including the sanctuary of Dionysos Lenaios; it was there that the Athenians' contests took place before the theater was built" (test. no. 25 on the Lenaian festival in Pickard-Cambridge, cited above, p. 28). It was adjacent to the agora or was considered part of the agora; see Schol. Patm. on Demosthenes, *On the Crown*, 129 (test. no. 24 on the Lenaian Festival in Pickard-Cambridge, cited above, p. 28). There was a dance space (the orchestra), where the performances took place before the theater was built; see Photius, s.v. *orchestra* and Lenaion (= test. no. 27 and 25 on the Lenaian festival in Pickard-Cambridge, cited above, pp. 28ff.). The seating tiers were temporary wooden structures; see Photius, s.v. *ikria*; cf. Pollux, *Onomasticon*, 7, 125 (= test. no. 26 on the Lenaian festival in Pickard-Cambridge, cited above, p. 29). However, no vestige has been found. The location of the Lenaion remains a subject of debate.

17. The expression is preserved in Aristophanes, *Acharnians*, v. 504 (cited below) and in Plato, *Protagoras* 327 d 4.

18. We have already seen that the name of "Dionysos Eleuthereus" was on the inscription of the throne of the priest of Dionysus in the theater (above). This name comes from the fact that when the cult was introduced in Athens, the god's statue was brought from Eleutherai; see Pausanias 1, 20, 3, cited above. This festival of Dionysus is also called the City Dionysia (as opposed to the Rural Dionysia or the Little Dionysia), or simply Dionysia. For testimonies on the Great Dionysia, see Pickard-Cambridge (cited above), pp. 57–101; see also S. Goldhill, "The Great Dionysia and Civic Ideology," *Journal of Hellenic Studies* 107, 1987, pp. 58–76.

19. He organized the procession with ten *epimeletai*, and he organized or supervised the various competitions; see Aristotle, *Constitution of Athens*, 66, 2.

20. See the Marble of Paros A43 (*FGrHist* 239 Jacoby); cf. *Suda*, s.v. Thespis (= *TrGF* 1, 1 test. 1 and 2 Snell).

21. This is the inscription of the "Fasti," IG II2 2318 col. 1 (text in Pickard-Cambridge, cited above = *TrGF* 1, DID A 1, 11 Snell). The inscription records Aeschylus's victory without giving the names of the plays. The list is known through the argument of *The Persians*.

22. Demosthenes, *Against Midias* 10 (text of a law whose authenticity is not known).

23. This is the inscription cited above.

24. Aristophanes, *The Birds*, vv. 785–89.

25. The price of a seat was two oboles. An equivalent indemnity was established for the most indigent citizens. But this arrangement, attributed by some to Pericles (Plutarch, "Life of Pericles," 9, 1), may not yet have existed in Sophocles' time; see Harpocration, s.v. *theorikon*, where this arrangement is attributed to Agyrrhios, a demagogue of the early fourth century BCE.

26. Aristophanes, *Acharnians*, 504–8.

27. See the scholium on Aristophanes, *Acharnians*, v. 504: "During the Dionysia, the cities were ordered to bring the tribute, as Eupolis says in [his comedy] *The Cities*" (= Eupolis PCG V, ed. Kassel and Austin, frag. 254); cf. also the scholium on v. 378 ("the festival of the Dionysia, which is in the spring, during which the allies brought the tribute"); see Isocrates, *On the Peace*, 82: the Athenians had voted to have the tribute brought "into the orchestra at the Dionysia when the theater was full." Pickard-Cambridge (cited above), pp. 58ff.; J.-Ch. Moretti, *Théâtre et société en Grèce ancienne*, Paris, 2001, pp. 83ff.

28. See the opposed points of view of J. Henderson, "Women and the Athenian Dramatic Festivals," *Transactions and Proceedings of the American Philological Association* 121, 1991, pp. 133–47 (women present), and S. Goldhill, "Representing Democracy: Women at the Great Dionysia," in R. Osborne and S. Hornblower (eds.), *Ritual, Finance, Politics: Athenian Democratic Accounts Presented to David Lewis*, Oxford, 1994, pp. 347–70 (women absent).

29. See *Women of Trachis*, v. 225 (Deianira addressing the chorus of "women friends" for the first time).

30. See *Electra*, v. 129 (for the noble origin of the women in the chorus) and v. 134 (for the friendship between the chorus and the heroine).

31. Aristophanes, *Peace*, vv. 50–53; Menander, *Dyscolos*, vv. 965–67.

32. Plato, *Gorgias*, 502 d–e. See also *Laws*, 7, 817 c; cf. *Laws*, 2, 658 d.

33. The reference must be to "pedagogue" slaves accompanying the children; see Theophrastus, *Characters* 9, 5 ("The Shameless Man"): "When he has taken places at the theatre for his foreign visitors, he will see the performance without paying his own share; and will bring his sons, too, and their attendants the next day."

34. This is a passage in the *Thesmophoriazusae* (vv. 395–97) already cited apropos of the existence of wooden benches in the fifth-century theater; see above.

35. Alexis in Pollux, *Onomasticon*, 9, 44 (= PCG II, Alexis, frag. 42 Kassel and Austin); cf. also the scholium on Aristophanes, *Assemblywomen*, v. 22.

36. Aeschines, *Against Ctesiphon* 41–43. Demosthenes had wanted to proclaim in the theater, during the Great Dionysia, the people's decree that awarded him a crown for having made donations during his exercise of a magistracy. Aeschines initiated a lawsuit against the author of the decree, pleading notably on the basis of this law forbidding the proclamation of popular decrees in the theater.

37. Plutarch, "Life of Nicias," 3, 3.

38. Plato, *Apology*, 26 c–e.

39. Plato (*Symposium* 175 e) estimates the audience for Agathon's victory at the Lenaia in 416 at more than thirty thousand people, which seems clearly excessive to modern scholars who are inclined to reduce the number by half. For the discussion of Plato's testimony, see Pickard-Cambridge, cited above, p. 263.

40. The designation of three choregoi for the Great Dionysia was one of the archon's first tasks once he had taken office; see Aristotle, *Constitution of Athens*, 56, 3.

41. Demosthenes, *Against Midias* 16.

42. See the inscription known as the "Fasti" IG II2 2318 (= Pickard-Cambridge, cited above, pp. 104ff. = *TrGF* I, DIDA A I, pp. 22–25 Snell). Similarly, on the amphora from the middle of the fifth century representing, on a three-step base, the tripod of a victory in the choral contest won by the Acamantis tribe (A.R.V. 2 1581, no. 20 = Pickard-Cambridge, cited above, fig. 31), only the name of the choregos Glaucon is mentioned below the name of the tribe. Nonetheless, on the choregic monuments, the name of the author might appear. That is the case for the monument of Aristides in the sanctuary of Dionysus (Plutarch, "Life of Aristides," 1, 3), for that of Lysicrates (334 BCE), and for that of Thrasyllos (319 BCE). However, in the hierarchical order, the author naturally appears after the choregos (cf. the inscription on the monument of Aristides preserved by Plutarch: "The tribe Antiochis was victorious; Aristides was Choregus; Archestratus was Poet" [Plutarch, "Life of Aristides," 1, 3]); on the monuments of Lysicrates and Thrasyllos the author even appears after the *aulos* player (IG II2 3042 = Pickard-Cambridge, cited above, p. 78, n. 1, "Lysicrates, son of Lysithides, of the deme of Kikinna, was choregos; the Akamantis tribe won in the chorus of children; Theon was the *aulos* player; Lysiades the Athenian was the author, Euaenetos was the archon"; IG II2 3056 = Pickard-Cambridge, cited above: "Thrasyllos son of Thrasyllos of Decelea dedicated this monument having won the victory as choregos for men's chorus with the Hippothontis tribe; Euios of Chalcis was the *aulos* player; Neaechmos was the archon; Karkidamos Sotios [?] was the author"). The presence of the aulos player before the author on fourth-century monuments reflected a reality: whereas at first, in the time of Simonides, Pindar, and Bacchylides, music was subordinated to the text, in a second period it became the essential element to the detriment of the text, and the aulos player's performance was decisive. In the fourth century, Demosthenes recognizes that when he proposed himself as the choregos for his tribe in the men's choral contest, he was favored by the drawing of lots that gave him the opportunity to have first choice of the aulos player (*Against Midias*, 13).

43. IG II2 2318, col. 3 (= *TrGF* I, DID A I, 67–68 Snell). All we know about the choregos is the name of the deme from which he came, Lamptres.

44. See Pausanias 1, 20.

45. Plato, *Gorgias*, 472 a: "Nicias, son of Niceratus, with his brothers, whose tripods are standing in a row in the Dionysium"; Plutarch, "Life of Nicias," 3, 3, "the temple surmounted by choregic tripods." On Nicias as choregos and his relations with Sophocles, see above.

46. Plutarch, "On the Glory of the Athenians" 6 (348c–349b).

47. On the *choregia*, see P. Wilson, *The Athenian Institution of the Khoregia: The Chorus, the City and the Stage*, Cambridge, 2000, 435 pp.

48. The procedure of drawing lots can be indirectly deduced from the testimonies that we have on what happened in the *Thargelia* (Athenian festivals in honor of Apollo) with regard to the *choregia* of the choruses; see Antiphon, *On the Choreutes*, 11: "When I was appointed Choregus for the Thargelia, Pantacles falling to me as poet." The festival of the Thargelia, like that of the Great Dionysia, was organized by the eponymous archon; see Aristotle, *Constitution of Athens*, 56, 3. Thus it was he who presided over the drawing of lots mentioned by Antiphon.

49. On the increase in the number of choreutes, which was twelve under Aeschylus, to

fifteen starting with Sophocles, see *The Life of Sophocles*, c. 4 (= test. 1, 22ff. Radt = appendix V) and *Suda*, s.v. "Sophocles" (= test. 2, 4 Radt = appendix V).

50. Xenophon, *Memorabilia*, 3, 4, 4 and 4, 5.

51. Demosthenes, *Against Midias* 60. The remark refers to a tribal chorus.

52. See Athenaeus 1, 21 d–f (Aeschylus), 22 a (Thespis, Pratinas, Phrynichus).

53. See above.

54. Athenaeus, *Deipnosophistai*.

55. See Pollux, *Onomasticon*, 7, 78: "those who rent clothing to the choregoi."

56. Plutarch, "Life of Phocion," 19, 2–3 (750 c–d).

57. See Lysias, "On the Refusal of a Pension to the Invalid," 24, 13.

58. Lysias, "Defense against a Charge of Taking Bribes," 21, 1 and 5. *Philoctetes* was performed under the archontate of Theopompus (411/410). A few years later, another of Lysias's clients spent, for two tragic *choregia*, the total sum of five thousand drachmas (Lysias, "On the Property of Aristophanes," 19, 29 and 4), that is, for each of them slightly less than the first client had paid.

59. Lysias, "Defense against a Charge of Taking Bribes," 21, 4.

60. See the scholium on Aeschines, *Against Timarchus* 10: "Traditionally, the Athenians established a chorus of fifty children or fifty men per tribe, so that there were ten choruses, since there were ten tribes." Greek text quoted by Pickard-Cambridge (cited above), p. 75, n. 1.

61. Allusions to how much the state allotted the author as a salary for his participation in the contest are rare; see Aristophanes, *The Frogs*, v. 367, which referring to comedy at the Dionysia, mentions "the pay of poets," which a politician has reduced.

62. Aristotle, *Poetics*, 6 (1450 b, 16–20).

63. Aristophanes, *The Knights*, vv. 231ff.

64. Aristotle, *Poetics*, 1453 b.

65. See Antiphon, *On the Choreutes* 13.

66. For the literary sources, in addition to Aristotle's *Poetics*, see a valuable source that is unfortunately much later, Julius Pollux of Naucratis in Egypt (second century CE), in his *Onomasticon* (4, 106–54); on the occasion of his explanation of words grouped by subject, he gives valuable information concerning the chorus (106–12), the actors (113–14), the costumes (115–20), the theater and its machines (121–32), and the masks (133–54). See also the scholia, that is, the marginal notes in the manuscripts, which are the remains of commentaries the oldest of which go back to the Hellenistic period, and more precisely to the great scholars of the Library of Alexandria. As for the iconographic sources, they are essentially painted vases from Greece or southern Italy representing actors or theatrical scenes; see A. D. Trendall and T.B.L. Webster, *Illustrations of Greek Drama*, London, 1971.

67. I will employ the usual terms of flute player and flute, even though they are imprecise. The wind instrument designated by the Greek word *aulos* differed from the flute, in the sense that it consisted of two pipes pierced with holes and fitted with reeds that the breath caused to vibrate. On the aulos, A. Belis, *Bulletin de Correspondance hellénique* 108, 1984, pp. 111–22; 110, 1986, pp. 205–18; I, 1988, pp. 109–18. In the text, I have preferred to use the words "flute" and "flute player" reserving for the notes the technical terms *aulos* and *aulete*.

68. On the use of the theater in Athens for gladiatorial combats and aquatic spectacles, see J.-Ch. Moretti, cited above, pp. 108–17 (with the bibliography, pp. 310–11).

69. Dio Chrysostom, *Discourses* ("The Rhodian Oration"), 31, 101.

70. The term *eisodos* is already found in Aristophanes; see *The Clouds*, v. 326, and *The Birds*, v. 293.

71. Letter from W. Dörpfeld to Albert Müller, April 19, 1886, reproduced in A. Müller, *Lehrbuch der griechischen Bühnenaltertümer*, Freiburg, 1886, pp. 415ff.

72. U. von Wilamowitz-Moellendorff, "Die Bühne des Aischylos," *Hermes* 21, 1886, pp. 597–622, especially pp. 603–5.

73. On this altar of Dionysus sometimes called *thymele*, see Pollux, *Onomasticon*, 4, 123: "in the orchestra, there is the *thymele*, which is either a rostrum or an altar"; *Suda*, s.v. S = *skene*: "after the *orchestra* there is the altar of Dionysus, which is called *thymele*"; cf. *Etymologicum magnum*, s.v. *skene*, which gives the same note as in the *Suda* but adds a detail on the altar of Dionysus: "after the *orchestra* there is the altar of Dionysus, a quadrangular structure empty in the middle (sc., of the *orchestra*), which is called *thymele*." These recent testimonies (second century CE for Pollux, tenth century CE for the *Suda* and twelfth century for the *Etymologicum magnum*) are not necessarily valid for the theater of the fifth century BCE. However, we have a much older testimony, a quotation in Athenaeus from a hyporchema by Pratinas of Phlius, who was a tragic dramatist contemporary with Aeschylus and older than Sophocles, since he competed against Aeschylus at the very beginning of the fifth century (Olympiad 70 = 499–496). Pratinas complains about a development in which the auletes, rather than accompanying the choruses' songs, took precedence over the choruses. Here is the beginning of the hyporchema (*TrGF* 1, 4. Pratinas frag. 3 Snell = Athenaeus 14, 617 c): "What is all this noise? What are these choruses? What violence has struck the altar (*thymele*) of Dionysus, which resounds so often?" The testimony attests to the existence of an altar of Dionysus as early as the fifth century but does not tell us exactly where it was. The reference may be to the altar in the sanctuary of Dionysus, near the theater, where sacrifices were made, in accord with the etymological meaning of thymele, and not to a small altar in the center of the dance floor that would limit the movements of a tragic chorus formed in a rectangle. In other theaters in the Attica of the classical period (Thorikos, Icarion; see the maps in J.-Ch. Moretti, cited above, pp. 277 and 279), there is no altar in the middle of the orchestra. In Thorikos, the altar protrudes into the orchestra, on the left side with respect to the spectators; in Ikarion, it is outside the orchestra and also on the left side with respect to the spectators. These examples suggest that room was left for the movements of the choral dances in the center of the orchestra. But the question is delicate.

74. See above.

75. K. Lehmann-Hartleben, "Steinerne Proedrieschwelle," in H. Bulle, *Untersuchungen an griechischen Theatern*, Munich, 1928, pp. 61–63, table 6/7.

76. Still, in 1947 C. Anti (*Teatri greci arcaici da Minosse a Pericle*, Padua, 1947) postulated the layout of an archaic theater with straight tiers, of which Thorikos was an important example; cf. also C. Anti and L. Polacco, *Nuove ricerche sui teatri arcaici*, Padua, 1969.

77. R. Ginouvès, *Le théâtron à gradins droits et l'odéon d'Argos*, Études péloponnésiennes 6, Paris, 1972.

78. E. Gebhard, *The Theater at Isthmia*, Chicago, 1973.

79. E. Gebhard, "The Form of the Orchestra in the Early Greek Theater," *Hesperia* 43, 1974, pp. 428–40.

80. See *Bulletin de Correspondance hellénique* 101, 1977 ("Chronique des fouilles en 1976," by G. Touchais), p. 531.

81. See in E. Pöhlmann (cited above), the article by H. R. Goette, "Griechische Theaterbauten der Klassik-Forschungsstand und Fragestellungen," pp. 9–48, and that of E. Pöhlmann, "Die Proedrie des Dionysostheaters im 5. Jh. und das Bühnenspiel der Klassik," pp. 49–62; see also, for the theater in Athens, J.-Ch. Moretti (cited above) and, for other theaters in Greece in the classical period, J.-Ch. Moretti (cited above), pp. 121ff.

82. On the cyclical dances of the dithyrambic choruses, see, for example, Aristophanes, *The Birds*, v. 1403 (with the scholium). Aristophanes calls the author of dithyrambs an author of "cyclical choruses."

83. See *Life of Sophocles*, c. 4 (test. 1 Radt = appendix V): "He increased the list of *choreutes* from twelve to fifteen."

84. On the position of the aulete at the head of the chorus when he leaves at the end of the tragedy, see the scholium on Aristophanes, *The Wasps*, v. 582: "It is the custom that at the end of tragedies the aulete precedes the members of the chorus, so as to play the *aulos* as he leads the cortege." We can infer from this that he must have also preceded the chorus when it made its entrance. On the vases where an aulete appears making a chorus of satyrs dance, the choreutes are masked, but not the aulete (see for example Berlin F 1697, Attic amphora with black figures: a chorus of four masked knights is accompanied by an aulete; around 540–530 BCE = fig. 10 de Moretti cited above; see also the "Pandora Vase" from the middle of the fifth century = fig. 28 in A. E. Haigh, *The Attic Theatre*, 3rd ed. revised and in part rewritten by Pickard-Cambridge, Oxford, 1907).

85. On the formation of the chorus, see Pollux, *Onomasticon*, 4, 108–9+: "The parts of the chorus are the file and rank. For a tragic chorus, there are five ranks of three, and three files of five. They were fifteen in a chorus. They advanced by threes, if the entrance was made by files, and by fives if the entrance was made by ranks; sometimes they entered in a single file." For other testimonies regarding the quadrangular formation of the tragic chorus, see Pickard-Cambridge (cited above), p. 239, n. 1. The less talented choreutes were in the middle file, because they were never facing the audience.

86. Photius, s.v. *tritos aristerou* ("the third in the left-hand file"): "In the tragic choruses ... the left-hand file faced the audience ...; the one [choreute] who was in the middle of the left-hand file had the most esteemed place."

87. Sophocles, *Ajax*, vv. 134–71. These verses are "anapaestic dimeters." The basic unit is the anapaest, consisting of two short syllables followed by a long syllable on which the rhythmic emphasis falls, corresponding to the foot striking the floor (=⌣-). Since a meter consists of two basic units, the verse formed of two basic units respectively, the caesura being median. The verse including four basic units in all has four stresses. When there is no substitution, the verse has twelve syllables. It is generally thought that the parts in recitative were spoken by the coryphaeus alone, whereas the sung parts were sung by the whole chorus. But this common opinion is not based on any ancient testimony. The manuscripts of the tragic poets make no distinction and assign everything to the chorus.

88. See above, prelude to part II, "A Tragic Disaster."

89. Nevertheless, the arguments that are based on the evolution of the structure of Greek

tragedy remain fragile. At the same time, the same author was able to choose to vary the chorus's entrance. This is the case for Aeschylus in his *Oresteia*. *Agamemnon*, the first play in the linked trilogy, includes a choral entrance with a recitative preceding the part that is sung and danced; on the other hand, in the second play, *The Libation Bearers*, the choral entrance begins directly with the system of strophes/antistrophes.

90. Sophocles, *Ajax*, v. 701.

91. Sophocles, *Oedipus the King*, vv. 895ff.

92. For details on this change of place, see below.

93. Sophocles, *Ajax*, vv. 803–14.

94. Ibid., vv. 866–78.

95. The technical term is *epiparodos*; see Pollux, *Onomasticon*, 4, 108.

96. See the scholium on Aristophanes, *The Wasps*, v. 582 (cited above).

97. See above.

98. Sophocles, *Ajax*, vv. 349ff.

99. Sophocles, *Electra*, vv. 121ff.

100. Sophocles, *Antigone*, vv. 806ff. As in the two preceding examples, this is a dialogue between the character and the chorus; and we see at the beginning of the dialogue a gap that is comparable, from the point of view of the mode of expression, to that of *Ajax*; although Antigone sings, the chorus does not. Nonetheless, the chorus does not speak as it does in *Ajax* but instead expresses itself in a mode intermediary between the spoken and the sung, that is, in recitative (anapaestic dimeters). On the modes of expression in Greek tragedy (spoken-recitative-sung), see below, chapter VIII, "Time and Action."

101. [Plutarch], *Life of the Ten Orators*, 848 b.

102. Pollux, *Onomasticon*, 4, 113–14 (discussion of the actors); cf. 2, 111–18 (discussion of the voice).

103. See C. D. Buck and W. Petersen, *A Reverse Index of Greek Nouns and Adjectives*, Chicago, 1945 (rpt. Olms 1945), pp. 287ff.

104. Sophocles, *Ajax*, vv. 16ff.

105. *The Life of Sophocles* 4 test. 1, 21ff. Radt = appendix V.

106. See Pickard-Cambridge (cited above), p. 72: "In 447 B.C. the name of the tragic actor who won the prize is added, and considerations of spacing suggest that it appeared in two previous years." It is impossible to be as certain as P. Ghiron-Bistagne (*Recherches sur les acteurs dans la Grèce antique*, Paris: Belles Lettres, 1976) when she declares, p. 1, that 450/449 is "the date when a prize for acting was first awarded at the Great Dionysia's tragedy contest in Athens."

107. The inscription on the didaskalia giving the results of the tragic contest at the Lenaia begins with the remains of the year 421/420 (see above). But the last line is already reserved for the results of the actors' contest. For the names of the actors who won at the Lenaia, see also the inscription of the "List of the winners" IG II2 2325 (Pickard-Cambridge [cited above], p. 113).

108. Scholium on Aristophanes, *The Clouds*, v. 1266 (= test. 42 Radt). Another possible name of one of Sophocles' actors: Clidemides (scholium on Aristophanes, *The Frogs*, v. 791 = test. 43 Radt). Aeschylus also chose his actors; see *The Life of Aeschylus* 15 (*TrGF* 3, test. 1, 57ff. Radt), where Aeschylus, who played the role of the protagonist,

chose Cleandros as the second actor, and then, when there was a third actor, Myn-niscos of Chalcis.

109. Epictetus, *Dissertationes*, frag. 11 (= test. 47 Radt).

110. Aristotle, *Poetics*, 4 (1449 a 15–19). For Sophocles, who introduced the third actor, see also *Suda*, s.v. "Sophocles" (= test. 2 Radt = appendix V); *Life of Sophocles* 4 (= test. 4 Radt = appendix V).

111. This criterion allows us to divide Aeschylus's work into old tragedies that could be performed by two actors (*The Persians, Seven against Thebes,* and *The Suppliants*) and more recent tragedies that required a third actor (*Prometheus,* whose attribution to Aeschylus is debated, and the trilogy of the *Oresteia: Agamemnon, The Libation Bearers, The Eumenides*). The introduction of the third actor thus took place between 463 (the probable date of *The Suppliants*) and 458 (the certain date of the *Oresteia*).

112. Horace, *Art of Poetry*, v. 122.

113. In *Women of Trachis*, there are eight characters, but one of them is silent (Iole, not mentioned in the list of characters); in *Electra*, there are seven characters, one of which is silent (Pylades, Orestes' companion).

114. Demosthenes, *On the Crown*, 129, 209, 267; Demosthenes, *On the Embassy*, 247; cf. also the verb "to be a tritagonist" in *On the Crown*, 262 and 265, and in *On the Embassy*, 200 and 337.

115. He was tritagonist in famous troupes of actors such as Theodorus and Aristodemus when they revived Sophocles' *Antigone* (*On the Embassy*, 246); or less admired actors, known as "wailers," such as Simyccas and Socrates (*On the Crown*, 262).

116. Demosthenes, *On the Crown*, 265 and 262; cf. also *On the Embassy*, 337.

117. The criterion of song is not usually taken into account in the discussion of the distribution of roles among the actors; see, for example, the presentation on the distribution of roles among the actors in Sophocles' work in Pickard-Cambridge (cited above), pp. 140–42.

118. The part sung by Ajax in his dialogue with the chorus, then with Tecmessa (vv. 349–427 with a system of three strophes/antistrophes).

119. The chorus's entrance gives rise to a sung dialogue between the chorus and Electra (vv. 121–232). Electra also sings after she recognizes Orestes in a dialogue with (vv. 1232–87 with a triadic system: strophe/antistrophe/epode).

120. Part sung by Oedipus in a dialogue with the chorus when he appears with bloodied eyes toward the end of the tragedy (vv. 1313–65 with a system of two strophes/antistrophes).

121. In the parodos, part sung by Oedipus in a dialogue with the chorus (vv. 178–236); commos, vv. 510–48; scene in which he is the victim of Creon's violence (v. 833 and v. 876).

122. Long sung dialogue between Philoctetes and the chorus, when he believes he has been abandoned without his bow (vv. 1081–17 with a system of two strophes/antistrophes and an astrophic continuation). Thus we cannot leave open, as does Pickard-Cambridge (cited above), p. 142, the possibility that the protagonist played the role of Neoptolemus, because this role does not include any sung part.

123. Part sung by Antigone as she is leaving, in a lyric dialogue with the chorus (vv. 806–82); the final part sung by Creon in a dialogue with the chorus (vv. 1261–346).

124. This is the commos (vv. 1670–750) between Antigone, the chorus, and Ismene. For more information on the distribution of roles in *Oedipus at Colonus*, see below.
125. See above.
126. Demosthenes, *On the Embassy*, 246–47. The verses cited from *Antigone* are vv. 175–90.
127. This is the explanation given by Pickard-Cambridge (cited above), p. 141, n. 2.
128. Aristotle, *Politics*, 7, 17 (1336 b 27–31).
129. Hippocrates, *Lex*, 1, 1.
130. Sophocles, *Ajax*, vv. 1223ff.
131. Sophocles, *Oedipus at Colonus*, v. 1250.
132. Sophocles, *Antigone*, v. 491; v. 578; v. 885.
133. Ibid., vv. 1108–10.
134. The existence of these extras is mentioned in the text itself. Creon addresses them at v. 1320.
135. Sophocles, *Antigone*, vv. 988ff.; v. 1012; v. 1087. *Oedipus the King*, v. 444.
136. Sophocles, *Ajax*, vv. 541ff. The child, who does not speak, is brought by another silent character, a servant. He will return with Tecmessa (cf. v. 578). But unlike other children, his presence exceeds the length of a scene. In fact, he reappears in the second part of the tragedy (cf. v. 1169) and remains until the end (cf. v. 1409).
137. Sophocles, *Oedipus the King*, vv. 1480–521.
138. This is the Sophoclean version of the Aeschylean Pylades who, in *The Libation Bearers*, is also constantly present and almost constantly silent (a role limited to three verses: vv. 900–902.
139. Sophocles, *Electra*, vv. 15–16. Orestes will be constantly accompanied by Pylades in his entrances and exits (cf. v. 75, v. 1104; v. 1367; v. 1373; v. 1422; v. 1430).
140. Sophocles, *Ajax*, vv. 985–89.
141. Ibid., vv. 1168–70.
142. Ibid., v. 293.
143. Antigone remains until v. 846, when Creon's servants lead her away by force. She will be brought back, thanks to Theseus's intervention, with her sister Ismene, in vv. 1096ff. Oedipus remains longer, until his final exit (v. 1555).
144. Resident of Colonus: arrival v. 33; departure, v. 80. Ismene: arrival v. 324; departure v. 509. Theseus: arrival v. 551; departure v. 667. Creon: arrival v. 728; departure v. 1043. For further details regarding the modalities of the arrivals and departures of the characters, as well as on the changes of costumes and masks made by the tritagonist, see below.
145. Theseus's first arrival: v. 551. Second arrival: v. 887. Departure of Antigone: v. 846. On the rapidity of this change, see below.
146. The second return of Antigone and Ismene vv. 1670ff.
147. Sophocles, *Ajax*, vv. 89–117.
148. Ibid., vv. 1318–73.
149. Ibid., v. 1321.
150. In *Women of Trachis*, the same can be said of the scene with three characters involving the messenger, Lichas and Deianira (vv. 393–496), which consists of a series of dialogues between two characters (first Lichas and Deianira, then the messenger and Lichas, and finally Deianira and Lichas again).
151. Sophocles, *Antigone*, vv. 531–81.

152. Ibid., v. 549.

153. Similarly, in *Ajax* Agamemnon, after his violent quarrel with Teucer, has broken off all communication with him when Odysseus arrives (vv. 1318ff.).

154. Sophocles, *Antigone*, v. 523.

155. Ibid., vv. 883ff.

156. Ibid., vv. 935ff.

157. Sophocles, *Philoctetes*, vv. 974–1065.

158. Ibid., vv. 1291–307.

159. Sophocles has deliberately contrived analogies between Odysseus's two unexpected interventions; compare the first (vv. 976–77) with the second (vv. 1295–96).

160. Aristotle, *Poetics*, 18 (1456 a 25).

161. See above, n. 87.

162. The sole exception is *Philoctetes*. There is no spoken dialogue, because the chorus's entrance, in the form of a lyric dialogue with Neoptolemus, is immediately followed by the entrance of the second character, Philoctetes.

163. The inscription of Phaidros is found in C.I.A. III 239 (Haigh, cited above, p. 88): "For you, you who love festivals, this beautiful theater stage has been built by Phaidros, son of Zoilus giver of life, archon of Attica."

164. P. G. Kalligas, *Arch. Delt.* 18, 1963 [1965], *Chron.*, pp. 12–18. See also Moretti (cited above), p. 296.

165. Thus it is natural to postulate, in accord with this change in the movement of the characters, that the stage building did not yet exist when Aeschylus's first plays were performed; see Wilamowitz (*Kleine Schriften* I, pp. 148ff. = 1886), taken up again with a good argument in O. Taplin, *The Stagecraft of Aeschylus*, Oxford, 1977, pp. 452–59. And we may ask whether the appearance of the third actor was not contemporaneous with the appearance of the stage building. In any case, it was in the *Oresteia* that these two new resources were used for the first time in the extant tragedies. Some scholars nonetheless think that the stage building existed, if only for acoustic reasons; see E. Pöhlmann (cited above), "Bühne und Handlung im Aias des Sophokles," pp. 108ff.; other references in Moretti, "Les entrées en scène dans le théâtre grec: L'apport de l'archéologie," *Pallas* 38, 1992, pp. 79–107 (p. 103, n. 10). But the stage building was not included as a virtual interior space before the *Oresteia*.

166. On the integration of the stage building in dramatic fiction, see below.

167. The question of the number of doors in the facade of the stage building is one of the dilemmas that feed debates on the material organization of the theater. Pollux (4, 123) speaks of three doors but acknowledges the possibility that one of them, the left door, was masked for the performance of tragedy. Without going into the detail of debates that bear as much on comedy as on tragedy in the fifth century, it suffices to note that Sophocles' seven extant tragedies require no more than one door for their performance.

168. A door behind the building is not possible, at least in the fourth century, because the stage building was constructed directly against a portico located between the stage building and the old temple. The long side of a stage building opposite the façade was thus completely blind. Even if we cannot infer the state of the structure in the fifth century from the fourth-century vestiges, it remains that the hypothesis of a central rear door lengthens the distance an actor had to cover to exit by the

lateral passageways; but some changes of role had to be made rapidly: see the example of *Oedipus at Colonus* analyzed a little further on.

169. See above.

170. Sophocles, *Oedipus at Colonus*, vv. 886–90.

171. Ibid., vv. 847b–886.

172. Before the stage building existed, costume changes must have been made in the little archaic temple nearby.

173. The term *logeion* means literally the place where the actors speak. It is attested rather late, especially in the lexicographers and commentators; in addition to Pollux, *Onomasticon*, 4, 123, see Hesychius, s.v. *logion* ("the place of the stage where the actors speak"); *Etymologicum Magnum* 569.25; but see a third-century CE inscription from Delos (*Bulletin de Correspondance hellénique* 14, 401) and Vitruvius, *On Architecture* 5, 6, 8 (quoted here in the text).

174. Pollux, *Onomasticon*, 4, 123.

175. Pollux *Onomasticon*, 4, 127.

176. Vitruvius, *On Architecture*, 5, 7, 2.

177. Aristotle, *Poetics*, 12 (1452 b).

178. See Höpken, *De theatro attico saeculi a. C. quinti*, Bonn 1884. For a scene in Sophocles' theater where the chorus is in contact with the characters, see *Oedipus at Colonus*, vv. 856–57, with the analysis below.

179. L. Bodin and P. Mazon, *Extraits d'Aristophane et de Ménandre*, Classiques Hachette, 1st ed. 1902, 2nd ed. 1908 (frequently reprinted). See also the role played by O. Navarre, *Le Théâtre grec*, Paris, 1925.

180. See A. E. Haigh, *The Attic Theatre*, Oxford, 1st ed. 1889 (cited above in its third edition).

181. Euripides, *Electra*, vv. 489–92. *Ion*, vv. 727ff., *The Phoenician Women*, vv. 845–48; see for example J. Jouanna, "Remarques sur le texte et la mise en scène de deux passages des Phéniciennes d'Euripide (vv. 103–26 and 834–51)," *Revue des Etudes Grecques* 89, 1976, pp. 46–56.

182. See R. Weil, "Dans les bras d'Ajax? (Sophocle, Ajax, 545 sq.)," *Revue de Philologie* 51, 1977, pp. 202–6. This interpretation has been adopted by J. Irigoin in the new edition of Sophocles in the CUF series, 1994, p. 28 ("She takes the child from the slave's hands and places it on the *logeion*"), and p. 29, n. 1.

183. Sophocles, *Ajax*, vv. 538–51.

184. This fear is not groundless if one knows that Heracles killed his children in a fit of madness. The myth was dramatized by Euripides.

185. The Greek expression *chersi euthunon* (v. 542) indicates that the servant guides the child "with his hand," that is, he leads him by holding his hand, rather than carrying him.

186. The dramaturgical question is even more complex than that. At that moment, is Ajax on the *eccyclema*? See below.

187. Sophocles, *Ajax*, v. 578.

188. Sophocles, *Oedipus at Colonus*, vv. 192–96.

189. Sophocles, *Philoctetes*, vv. 999–1003.

190. Sophocles, *Oedipus at Colonus*, vv. 856–57.

191. Cf. Aristophanes, *Peace*, vv. 426ff.

192. See A. E. Haigh (cited above), pp. 170ff. (in the criticism of Dörpfeld's thesis).

193. Sophocles, *Women of Trachis*, v. 40.
194. Aristotle, *Poetics*, 4 (1449 a 18). Another, more recent source, Vitruvius (first century BCE) attributes the invention of sets to the painter Agatharchus, on the occasion of the performance of a tragedy by Aeschylus; see *On Architecture*, 7, preface 11: "In the first place Agatharcus, in Athens, when Aeschylus was bringing out a tragedy, painted a scene, and left a commentary about it." See also *Life of Aeschylus* 14 (*TrGF* 3, test. 1, 54 Radt).
195. Sophocles, *Oedipus at Colonus*, v. 39.
196. Ibid., vv. 503–6.
197. Ibid., vv. 113ff.
198. A similar change in setting may have been made by Aeschylus and Sophocles in two other plays that have been lost: in Aeschylus's *The Women of Aetna*, and a satyr play by Sophocles, *Lovers of Achilles*; see the argument of *The Women of Aetna*, which has been partially preserved on a papyrus (Lobel, *P. Oxy.* 2257, frag. 1, 5ff. = *TrGF* 3, pp. 126ff. Radt); this argument presupposes several changes of place, which is wholly extraordinary; see O. Taplin (cited above), pp. 416–18; for *Lovers of Achilles*, see appendix II, no. 19.
199. The presence of the statue and Orestes' suppliant attitude are indicated in the text itself by two stage directions, one progressive and given by Apollo (Aeschylus, *The Eumenides*, v. 80), the other regressive and given by Athena (Aeschylus, *The Eumenides*, v. 409).
200. For these painted panels, according to the vestiges of the theaters and inscriptions from the Hellenistic period, see J.-Ch. Moretti, "Formes et destinations du proskènion dans les théâtres hellénistiques de la Grèce," *Pallas* 47, 1997, pp. 13–39 (pp. 17–25).
201. See Pollux, *Onomasticon*, 4, 126; cf. also Vitruvius 5, 6, 8.
202. Thus it does not seem plausible to imagine, with E. Pöhlmann (cited above), pp. 110ff., a production that divided the scenic space into two juxtaposed settings, one corresponding to the first part of the tragedy, the other to the second; this would presuppose the use (which would be, to say the least, exceptional in tragedy) of two doors in the stage building.
203. See above, chapter VI, "The Mythic Imagination," under "The Elaboration of the Mythic Tradition in Sophoclean Tragedy: Tradition and Innovation."
204. Sophocles, *Ajax*, vv. 815ff.
205. See Hesychius, s.v. *suspaston*: "So was called a little dagger of the tragedians, as Polemon says, with a retractable blade to play the role of Ajax."
206. Sophocles, *Ajax*, vv. 654–59.
207. Ibid., vv. 815–22.
208. Ibid., vv. 833–34.
209. Ibid., v. 892.
210. Sophocles, *Oedipus the King*, vv. 91–94.
211. Except in cases in which the theatrical machine known as an *eccyclema* was used; see below.
212. Sophocles, *Antigone*, vv. 18ff.
213. The conventional aspect of this beginning was criticized by G. Kaibel in his commentary on *Electra* (1896), p. 65 ("The sisters come and speak solely because the play has begun"). It has been pointed out that it is not implausible that young women

might go outside to avoid being overheard by people in the palace; see W. M. Calder III, "Sophokles' Political Tragedy, Antigone," *Greek, Roman and Byzantine Studies* 9, 1968, pp. 389–407 (p. 392, n. 18 citing R. C. Flickinger, *The Greek Theater and Its Drama*, 4th ed., Chicago, 1936, pp. 240–41), taken up by D. Bain, *Actors and Audience*, Oxford, 1977, p. 10. We must also take the moment into account.

214. Pollux, *Onomasticon*, 4, 126–27.

215. Sophocles, *Oedipus at Colonus*, vv. 887–90.

216. The six tragedies in which a messenger appears in the list of characters are *Ajax*, *Women of Trachis*, *Antigone*, *Oedipus the King*, *Philoctetes*, and *Oedipus at Colonus*.

217. Aeschylus, *The Persians*, vv. 353–432. Obviously, other tragedies by Aeschylus also include accounts given by messengers (*Seven against Thebes*, *Agamemnon*).

218. See above in this same chapter, "The Stage Building and the Movement of the Actors."

219. Sophocles, *Electra*, v. 1406.

220. Sophocles, *Antigone*, vv. 1183–91.

221. Sophocles, *Women of Trachis*, vv. 813ff.; *Antigone*, vv. 1244ff.; *Oedipus the King*, vv. 1073–75.

222. Sophocles, *Women of Trachis*, vv. 871ff.; *Antigone*, vv. 1277ff.; *Oedipus the King*, vv. 1223ff.

223. For the altar in the account of Eurydice's suicide, see Sophocles, *Antigone*, v. 1301; and in the account of Deianira's suicide, see Sophocles, *Women of Trachis*, v. 904.

224. Compare Sophocles, *Women of Trachis*, v. 913, and *Antigone*, vv. 804 and 946.

225. In *Women of Trachis*, the nurse and Deianira's son Hyllos arrive too late; here Haemon, who has nonetheless come before Creon, is already too late.

226. Sophocles, *Antigone*, vv. 1234–41.

227. Sophocles, *Oedipus the King*, vv. 1287–89.

228. The words "pity" and "terror" are present in the text; for pity, see v. 1296; for the shiver of fear, v. 1306.

229. Ancient testimonies on the *eccyclema*: Pollux, *Onomasticon*, 4, 127–29; Eustathius, commentary on the *Iliad* 976, 15; several scholia on the tragic dramatists (Aeschylus, *The Libation Bearers*, v. 973, and *Eumenides*, v. 64; Sophocles, *Ajax*, vv. 346–47; Euripides, *Hippolytus*, v. 171) or the comic dramatists (Aristophanes, *Acharnians*, v. 408; *The Clouds*, v. 184; *Thesmophoriazusae*, v. 96); cf. also the scholium on Clement of Alexandria 4, 97. There is no reason to examine here the discussions concerning the practical construction (a platform on wheels that was pushed through the open door or that turned on an axis). What matters is the purpose of such a machine, on which all the ancient testimonies are in agreement: "it shows the forbidden acts that have occurred in the houses" (Pollux 4, 128); "it showed what was supposed to have taken place inside the house even to those outside it, that is, to the spectators" (scholium on *The Acharnians*, v. 108); "what was inside seemed visible to those outside" (scholium on Clement of Alexandria).

230. Aristophanes, *Acharnians*, vv. 408ff. et *Thesmophoriazusae*, v. 96. The very remarkable use of the verb "roll outside" (*ekkuklein*) in these two passages suggests that the word *eccyclema* already existed in Sophocles time as a name for this theatrical machine.

231. Aeschylus, *Agamemnon*, v. 1372; *The Libation Bearers*, v. 973 (with the scholium ad loc.); *Eumenides*, v. 64 (with the scholium ad loc.)

232. Sophocles, *Ajax*, vv. 91ff.

233. Ibid., vv. 301–5.

234. Ibid., vv. 346ff.

235. Scholium on *Ajax*, v. 346: "There the *eccyclema* is used so Ajax can appear amid the livestock.

236. It is not surprising that such a tableau has inspired painters. In antiquity there was a famous picture by Timomachus of Byzantium that was described by Philostratus (*Life of Apollonius of Tyana*, 2, 22) and brought from Cyzicus (cf. Cicero, *Against Verres* 2, 4, 60) to the temple of Venus Genitrix in Rome (Pliny, *Natural History* 7, 38 § 126).

237. This inverse maneuver consisted in "rolling inside" (*eiskuklein*); see Aristophanes, *Thesmophoriazusae*, v. 265; cf. also Pollux, *Onomasticon*, 4, 128.

238. Aristophanes, *Acharnians*, v. 409.

239. Aristophanes, *Acharnians*, v. 479. In the *Thesmophoriazusae*, the closing of the door is not indicated. It is implicit in the order Agathon gives to "roll inside" (v. 265).

240. Sophocles, *Ajax*, vv. 578–82.

241. Ibid., vv. 348–595.

242. On the discussion of this passage, which has been cited to show the difference in level between the orchestra and the stage, see above in this same chapter, "The Stage and the Orchestra: The Limits of Dramaturgical Analysis."

243. Sophocles, *Ajax*, vv. 430ff.

244. Sophocles, *Electra*, v. 1458.

245. Aeschylus, *The Libation Bearers*, v. 973.

246. To recreate the magnitude of the spectacle, we must not forget all the extras, the palace's servants who had hurried off following Creon with axes to free Antigone, and who slowly return behind Creon in a long funeral procession. See above, in this same chapter, "The Silent Characters and the Spectacle."

247. Sophocles, *Antigone*, 1293–300.

248. Scholium on *Antigone* v. 1293: "the woman is brought by the *eccyclema*."

249. Sophocles, *Antigone*, v. 1293.

250. The position presented here agrees with that in M. Griffith, ed., *Antigone*, Cambridge, 1999, pp. 349ff.

251. Ajax, when he asks Tecmessa to close the door, indirectly reminds the audience that she is outside, because he asks her to stop moaning "in front of the house" (v. 579 *episkenous*).

252. Sophocles, *Electra*, vv. 1491–96.

253. Pollux, *Onomasticon*, 4, 128.

254. Aristophanes, *The Clouds*, vv. 173ff.

255. Pollux, *Onomasticon*, 4, 130. *The Weighing of Souls* is a lost play by Aeschylus (*TrGF* 3 frag. 279–80 a Radt). However, the scene in which Zeus appears on the theologeion, using his scale to weigh the fates of Achilles, son of Thetis, and Memnon, son of Aurora, had remained famous. The two divinities who appeared on either side of Zeus were the mothers of the two warriors; see Plutarch, "How a Young Man Should Study Poetry," c. 2 (17 a).

256. Pollux, *Onomasticon*, 4, 129–30.

257. Unlike the divinities appearing at the end of the tragedy, which regularly address human characters. This is a sort of law in Euripides' theater. It holds true even in the exceptional cases where two divinities appear in a single tragedy, one to begin

it, the other to end it: thus to Cypris's initial monologue in Euripides' *Hippolytus* corresponds the dialogue between Artemis and the dying Hippolytus in the final scene of the same tragedy.

258. Sophocles, *Ajax*, vv. 1–7 and 14–17.

259. Ibid., vv. 36ff.

260. On the divinity's omnipotence, see below, chapter X, "Humans and the Gods."

261. Sophocles, *Ajax*, vv. 91–93.

262. For the philosophers, see Plato, *Cratylus* 425 d: Plato mocks tragic authors who, when they get into difficulties, resort to the mechane by elevating the gods; Aristotle, *Poetics*, 15 (1454 b 1ff.): he criticizes the denouements of tragedies that result, not from the subject, but from the apparition of a god with the help of the mechane, as in Euripides' *Medea*. For the comic authors, see Antiphanes, *Poetry*, frag. 189 (*PCG* II, pp. 418ff. Kassel and Austin), vv. 13–16 (already cited). The Greek expression *apo mechanes* had already become proverbial by that time. See Demosthenes, *Against Boeotos* 2, c. 59: a character has arrived "as if by machine," that is, in a dramatic turn of events; cf. also Menander *apud* Scholia on Plato (Bekk. 381): "You've appeared like a god with the help of the mechane." The expression was later adopted by the Romans in the form, better known in English, of "deus ex machina."

263. In Euripides, see *Andromache* (Thetis), *Bacchantes* (Dionysus), *Electra* (the Dioscuri), *Helen* (the Dioscuri), *Hippolytus* (Artemis), *Ion* (Athena), *Iphigeneia in Tauris* (Athena), *Medea* (Medea), *Orestes* (Apollo), *Suppliants* (Athena). To be sure, we have to take into account the fact that Euripides' extant tragedies (seventeen) are more numerous than those of Sophocles (seven). But the proportion is much larger in Euripides. Several apparitions of divinities are known in Sophocles' tragedies preserved in the form of fragments; see below, chapter X, "Humans and the Gods."

264. Sophocles, *Philoctetes*, v. 1409.

265. Ibid., vv. 1409–17.

266. Cf. Sophocles, *Ajax*, v. 14, and *Philoctetes*, v. 1445.

267. Contrast Sophocles, *Ajax*, v. 15, and *Philoctetes*, vv. 1411ff.

268. Euripides, *Hippolytus*, vv. 84–86.

269. Euripides, *Andromache*, vv. 1226–30.

270. We see the same absence of explanations concerning the way in which the divinity appears at the end of certain tragedies by Euripides: Athena at the end of *The Suppliants* (v. 1183) and *Iphigeneia in Tauris* (v. 1435); the Dioscuri at the end of *Helen* (v. 1642).

271. The references are given above.

272. On the apparition of the gods in the tragedies of Sophocles and Euripides, see A. Spira, *Untersuchungen zum Deus ex machina bei Sophokles und Euripides*, Frankfurt, 1950.

Chapter VIII. Time and Action

1. For Aristotle's position regarding spectacle, see above, chapter VII, "Space and Spectacle."

2. Aristotle, *Poetics*, 6 (1449 b 24–31).

3. Ibid., 6 (1450 a): "Every tragedy has six constituent parts, and on these its quality depends. These are plot, character, diction, thought, spectacle, and song."

4. Ibid., 6 (1450 a 4ff.).

5. Ibid., 6 (1450 a 22ff.).

6. Ibid., 6 (1450 a 38ff.).

7. Ibid., 6 (1450 b 1–3).

8. Ibid., 7 (1451 a 6–9).

9. *Suda*, s.v. Aristarchos (E 3893 Adler = *TrGF* 1, 14 test. 1 Snell). This Aristarchus had written seventy tragedies and had won the competition twice.

10. *Women of Trachis*: 1,278 verses, *Oedipus at Colonus*: 1,779 verses. The comparison of the number of verses involves a certain inexactitude because the verses in the lyric parts are not of the same length. This remark applies to all the following calculations.

11. *Agamemnon*: 1,673 verses; *Eumenides*: 1,047 verses. The central play in the trilogy, *The Libation Bearers*, currently consists of 1,076 verses, but it was longer, because part of the beginning of the prologue was lost as a result of an accident that affected the only manuscript that transcribed the text.

12. Euripides, *Cyclops*: 709 verses.

13. Euripides, *Alcestis*: 1,163 verses. Performed under the archontate of Glaukinos in 438, in a competition in which Sophocles won first prize (see above), *Alcestis* was performed after a tragic trilogy (*The Cretan Women, Alcmeon in Psophis, Telephus*); see argument 2 for this play.

14. They were also free to vary, within each play, the length of the episodes; see below.

15. The only one of Aeschylus's tragedies that exceeds 1,100 verses is *Agamemnon*. The only one of Euripides' tragedies that is shorter than 1,100 verses (if we do not count *Rhesus*) is *Heracleidae* (1,055 verses).

16. Euripides' *Phoenician Women* (performed between 411 and 406; cf. scholium on Aristophanes, *Frogs*, v. 53) has 1,766 verses. Sophocles' *Oedipus at Colonus* (performed in 401; cf. argument 2) has 1,779 verses.

17. See above, chapter VIII, "Space and Spectacle."

18. See J. Irigoin, "Structure et composition des tragédies de Sophocle," in J. de Romilly (ed.), *Sophocle*, Entretiens sur l'Antiquité classique 29, Vandoeuvres-Genève, 1983, pp. 39–76; with the complements in two articles, one on Sophocles' *Electra* compared with Euripides' *Electra*, in 1993 (see bibliography), and the other on *Philoctetes* (see bibliography).

19. Aristotle, *Poetics*, 7 (1450 b 37).

20. This definition reminds us that a tragic action does not always end tragically. Unlike the four oldest tragedies, the three most recent tragedies of Sophocles show instead the passage from unhappiness to happiness (*Electra, Philoctetes*, and also, to a certain extent, *Oedipus at Colonus*).

21. Aristotle, *Poetics*, 5 (1449 b 12ff.).

22. Sophocles, *Women of Trachis* vv. 175ff.; *Electra*, vv. 410ff.

23. Rising sun: *Antigone*, v. 100; noonday sun: *Antigone*, v. 416.

24. Sophocles, *Ajax*, vv. 756ff. and 778ff.

25. Sophocles, *Women of Trachis*, vv. 79–85; cf. vv. 805ff. and vv. 1169ff.

26. Sophocles, *Oedipus at Colonus*, vv. 44ff. and vv. 84ff. For his realization, see below.

27. Sophocles, *Oedipus at Colonus*, v. 91.

28. Aristotle, *Poetics*, 12 (1452 b 15–25). [Translation modified.]

29. On the structure of Greek tragedy, see a study that remains fundamental, W. Jens

(ed.), *Die Bauformen der griechischen Tragödie*, Munich, 1971. It includes in particular studies on each of the different parts of tragedy distinguished by Aristotle (prologue, episode, exodos, choral song, the last being divided into parode and stasimon). To these parts common to all tragedies we must add amoebaean songs (or commoi) and monodies (or songs coming from the stage), parts that appear in certain tragedies.

30. For a tabular comparison of the choral parts in the three great tragic poets, see W. Kranz, Stasimon: *Untersuchungen zu Form und Gehalt der griechischen Tragödie*, Berlin, 1933, pp. 124–25; compare with the table of episodes given by K. Aichele, "Das Epeisodion," in W. Jens (cited above), pp. 50–51. See also the structure of Sophocles' tragedies given here in appendix I. The possible divergences in the number of episodes and stasima proceed from the apparent ambiguity of the function of lyric dialogues between the chorus and a character, some of which replace stasima, while others are inserted into the spoken parts. For the criteria allowing us to determine the lyric dialogues that replace choral songs, see J. Jouanna, cited below. The most important divergences bear on the structure of Sophocles' last tragedy, *Oedipus at Colonus* (from four stasima and four episodes according to Kranz to five according to Aichele, and six according to Jouanna).

31. Aristotle, *Poetics*, 4 (1449 a 10–18). Here, we will not go into the numerous discussions of Aristotle's thesis concerning the origin of tragedy. They have no impact on our understanding of Sophocles' theater. Let us say simply that Aristotle's thesis does not account for even the name of "tragedy," whose etymological meaning is "goat's song," interpreted by some as the song in a contest in which the prize is a goat, and by others as the song on the occasion of the sacrifice of a goat; see P. Chantraine, *Dictionnaire étymologique de la langue grecque*, s.v. *tragōdos*. All we know for sure is that song was primordial in what gave rise to tragedy. Tragedy may not have been originally connected with the cult of Dionysus. Some cite the case of Sicyon (Herodotus, *Histories*, 5, 67), where "tragic choruses" in honor of a hero, Adrastus, were transferred to Dionysus by Clisthenes the Elder. This passage, in which the adjective "tragic" appears for the first time, is pointed up by those who see primitive tragedy as consisting of songs performed during the sacrifice of a goat in the context of the worship of a hero or a dead man; see for example F. Robert, *Thymélè: Recherches sur la signification et la destination des monuments circulaires dans l'architecture religieuse de la Grèce*, Paris, 1939, pp. 287–89. But from this transfer, which was an exceptional measure, we cannot draw excessively general conclusions.

32. *The Persians* (472 BCE) does not have a prologue; *Seven against Thebes* (468) has a prologue; *The Suppliants* (after 468) does not have a prologue.

33. This development was already perceptible for the Greeks at the end of the fifth century. In his comedy *The Frogs*, Aristophanes represents Euripides accusing Aeschylus of aligning four series of choral songs one after the other, whereas the characters remain silent (vv. 914ff.).

34. Aeschylus's tragedies had only three stasima. On the other hand, tragedies with three stasima are the exception in Sophocles (one tragedy out of seven, *Philoctetes*) and Euripides (one play out of seventeen, *The Trojan Women*).

35. Aristotle, *Poetics*, 12 (1452 b 18, cited above). Among the parts peculiar to tragedy he distinguishes songs coming from the stage, that is, the characters' songs, without

the participation of the chorus, and the commoi, defined as threnodies common to the chorus and the characters. For these parts peculiar to tragedy, see below.

36. In the manuscripts, the sole indication that it is intervening, whether in speech or in song, is the notation "the chorus" (*choros*). This fact needs to be recalled, because it is systematically neglected.

37. However, the word "melodrama" in this technical sense is archaic. It should be replaced by that of "recitative." The corresponding Greek word is *parakatalogè*; see Aristotle, *Problemata* 19, 6; Pseudo-Plutarch, *De musica* 1141 a. According to *De musica*, recitative accompanied by a musical instrument was invented by Archilochus.

38. The criterion for distinguishing these parts in recitative is the meter. They are essentially systems of anapaestic dimeters (whose basic foot is the anapaest, composed of two short syllables followed by a long syllable). They are used quite freely by the poet and are generally assigned to the chorus, when it enters the orchestra (it is, in fact, a march rhythm; example, *Ajax*, vv. 134–71) or when it introduces a character (example, *Antigone*, 155–61). They also appear in the semilyrical dialogues between the chorus and a character. The flexibility of their use is such that these anapaestic systems can be treated, exceptionally, as a lyrical piece when there is a strophic symmetry; example, Electra's song (*Electra* vv. 86–120, divided into two strophes: vv. 86–102 and vv. 103–20). It is not impossible that the tetrameters (catalectic trochaics) used occasionally by Sophocles (see below) were also delivered in recitative. They correspond to increasing emotion. Nonetheless, unlike anapaestic systems, they appear only in the choral parts. Accompaniment by an aulos must have been an innovation (cf. Xenophon, *Symposium* 6, 2).

39. However, this Dorian coloration is not systematic in the manuscripts. It has been reestablished in a more coherent way by the editors.

40. Pindar (sixth/fifth centuries BCE) was born near Thebes (Aeolian dialect), and Bacchylides, his contemporary, was born on the island of Ceos (Ionian dialect).

41. In ancient Greek, the rhythm of the verse is based not on the number of syllables (as in French) but rather on the regular alternation of the length of the syllables (short or long) forming, on the basis of units having a distinct rhythm corresponding to the tapping of the foot (whence the term "foot") during the dance, rhythms that varied, either ascending or descending.

42. For the term *iambeion*, see Aristotle, *Poetics*, 4 (1449 a 21). This verse is composed of three measures (trimeter) each with two feet. The basic foot (iamb) is constituted by the succession of one short syllable and one long syllable, with a few possible substitutions.

43. Aristotle, *Poetics*, 4 (1449 a 21–28): "The iambic meter was used instead of the trochaic tetrameter. At first they used the tetrameter because its poetry suited the satyrs and was better for dancing, but when dialogue was introduced, Nature herself discovered the proper meter. The iambic is indeed the most conversational of the meters, and the proof is that in talking to each other we most often use iambic lines but very rarely hexameters and only when we rise above the ordinary pitch of conversation." This evolution of the rhythm of the spoken parts can be verified by comparing the spoken parts in Aeschylus and Sophocles. Aeschylus's work constituted a transition, because his oldest tragedies continued to have passages in trochaic tetrameters. But after *Agamemnon* (458) the tetrameter is no longer regularly used.

It reappears rarely in Sophocles (in addition to *Oedipus the King*, vv. 1515–30, see *Philoctetes*, vv. 1402–7, and *Oedipus at Colonus*, vv. 887–90). It is found more often in Euripides, starting with *The Trojan Women* (415 BCE).

44. This term, now so frequently used, is attested only once in antiquity, in the second century CE, in Pollux's *Onomasticon*, 4, 1123: "Exchanging iambic verse for iambic verse was called *stichomythein* and the action was called *stichomythia*." Two sorts of stichomythia were to be distinguished: the stichomythia of information (in which a character informs himself through a series of one-verse questions with his informer replying to each question with one verse), and the stichomythia of opposition in which two characters confront each other, verse for verse. On stichomythia of opposition, see recently S. Pfeiffer-Petersen, *Konfliktstichomythien bei Sophokles: Funktion und Gestaltung*, Wiesbaden, 1996, p. 186.

45. The term and its definition are found in Hesychius's *Lexicon* (sixth century CE), s.v. *antilabai*: "dialogic exchanges called 'by semi-verses' in the tragic poets."

46. See A. Dain, *Traité de métrique grecque*, Paris, 1965, p. 237: "Chose non moins curieuse, Sophocle évite de couper ainsi le vers iambique en différentes répliques dans les premières scènes de ses tragédies."

47. In the other tragedies, for which we have no criterion permitting us to date them on the basis of external evidence, *Women of Trachis* (six verses) and *Ajax* (eight verses) make discreet use of antilabai; *Oedipus the King* has a few more (thirteen verses); *Electra* many more (twenty-six verses).

48. Sophocles, *Electra*, v. 1502.

49. Sophocles, *Philoctetes*, vv. 751–54.

50. On the meters of choral lyric and tragedy, see A. M. Dale, *The Lyric Metres of Greek Drama*, 2nd ed., Cambridge, 1968; *Metrical Analyses of Tragic Choruses*, fasc. 1, Dactylo-epitrite, *Bulletin of the Institute of Classical Studies*, supp. 21, 1, 1971; fasc. 2, Aeolo-Choriambic, ibid., 21, 2, 1981; fasc. 3, Dochmiac-Iambic-Dactylic-Ionic, ibid., 21, 3, 1983. In appendix I on the presentation of each tragedy, I have referred for convenience to Dale's analyses, because the scansion is clearly applied to the Greek text. This does not allow us to avoid coping with the metric analyses in the most recent editions. For a historical view of the metrics of tragedy, see M. L. West, *Greek Metre*, Oxford, 1982, pp. 77–137. For an intelligent presentation of the different rhythms, see D. Korzeniewski, *Griechische Metrik*, Darmstadt, 1968. For an analysis of the metrical architecture of the lyric parts of tragedy on the basis of stresses, see the studies by J. Irigoin. On Sophocles, see Irigoin's 1983 article "Le trio des *Trachiniennes* de Sophocle (vv. 971–1043)" (cited in the bibliographical guide).

51. See above the discussion in the first part of this book on the familial transmission of the tragic craft.

52. This correspondence was no longer felt by the scribes who recopied our medieval manuscripts, and it has sometimes been restituted by modern editors at the price of drastic corrections which ultimately alter in dangerous ways the meaning of the text transmitted.

53. *Ajax*, vv. 172–200; *Philoctetes*, vv. 878–64; *Oedipus at Colonus*, vv. 1211–48.

54. The longest extant series is Pindar's *Fourth Pythian*, which has thirteen triads in all.

55. The dochmiac is a syncopated iambic tripody - (◡——◡-), whose two short syllables can be replaced by two long ones, and each long one by two short ones.

56. See A. Dain (cited above), p. 231: "Sophocle n'emploie jamais de dochmies dans la première partie de ses tragédies" ("Sophocles never uses dochmiacs in the first part of his tragedies"). Nonetheless, the assertion has to be qualified, because in *Ajax* dochmiacs appear in vv. 349–50; see the following note.

57. Sophocles, *Ajax*, vv. 349–50 (= vv. 357–58); vv. 364–66 (= vv. 379–81); vv. 394–96 (= vv. 412–14); vv. 879–90 (= 925–36) and vv. 900–903 (= 946–49). Sophocles, *Antigone*, vv. 1261–76 = 1284–1300 and 1306–25 = 1328–46. For the use of the dochmiac in the other tragedies, see *Women of Trachis*, vv. 1041–43 (Heracles, overcome by pain, despairs); *Oedipus the King*, vv. 1313–68 (Oedipus's despair in the exodos); *Electra*, vv. 1232–87 (Electra's joy when she recognizes Orestes); *Oedipus at Colonus*, vv. 833–43 = 876–86 (the chorus's emotional reaction to Creon's violence); vv. 1447–99 (the chorus's emotion when signs announce Oedipus's death); vv. 1556–79 (the chorus's emotion after Oedipus leaves for his last resting place). For the metric analysis of most of these passages, see A. M. Dale, *Metrical Analyses of Tragic Choruses*, fasc. 3, Dochmiac-Iambic-Dactylic-Ionic (cited above), pp. 30–42.

58. See O. Taplin, "Lyric Dialogue and Dramatic Construction in Later Sophocles," *Dioniso*, 55, 1984–85, pp. 115–22. Nonetheless, we need to draw a distinction in kind between lyric dialogues that are inside the spoken parts and those that replace the stasima; see J. Jouanna, "Riflessioni sui dialoghi lirici sostitutivi dei canti corali nelle tragedie di Sofocle (*Elettra*, 823–870 e Edipo a Colono, 510–548 e 1447–1499)," *Aion*, 28, 2006, pp. 77–89.

59. Sophocles, *Electra*, vv. 121–250 (parodos). In other tragic authors, there are also dialogic *parodoi*, as O. Taplin notes (cited above), p. 118. The dialogic parodos in the *Prometheus Bound* attributed to Aeschylus (a semilyric dialogue between the chorus and Prometheus) is a composition *sui generis* in Aeschylus. Eight of Euripides' tragedies have a dialogic prologue, including *Medea* (431 BCE; a semilyric dialogue between the chorus and the nurse), not counting *Rhesus*. In Euripides' *Electra*, which deals with same mythic sequence as Sophocles' play, the parodos also takes the form of a purely lyrical dialogue between the chorus and Electra. Some scholars have seen in this evidence of Euripides' influence on Sophocles.

60. Sophocles, *Electra*, vv. 823–70 (second stasimon).

61. The first sung dialogue is composed of three strophe/antistrophe pairs, followed by a single epode; the second consists of two strophe/antistrophe pairs without an epode.

62. In the first sung dialogue, each strophe or antistrophe is composed of a speech by the chorus followed by Electra's reply; and within each strophe/antistrophe pair, the part reserved for each of the characters is exactly the same. Only the two final speeches of the chorus and of Electra lack a correspondent, because they are situated in the epode, which does not itself have a correspondent.

63. Eriphyle had been won over by the gold necklace Polynices gave her. For this myth of Alcmeon, which parallels that of Orestes, see above, chapter VI, "The Mythic Imagination."

64. Sophocles, *Electra*, vv. 823–48.

65. The first choral part (or parodos: vv. 135–218) and the third choral part (or the second stasimon: 827–64) in dialogue with Neoptolemus. Fourth choral part (or third stasimon: vv. 1081–217) in dialogue with Philoctetes.

66. This is the case for the parodos and the second stasimon. The presence of recitative

in the song is brought about technically by inserting *epirrhemata* (addresses) at the end of (sung) strophes. The epirrhematic element thus also lends flexibility to the exchanges, because the correspondences are not as strict in the epirrhematic pieces as they are in the strophic elements (either in the number of verses or in the distribution of the speeches among the interlocutors. For example, in the first strophe/antistrophe pair, the epirrhematic element (vv. 144–49), which follows strophe 1 (vv. 135–43) is shorter than the element of the same kind (vv. 159–68) that follows the antistrophe (vv. 150–58); six anapaestic dimeters as compared with ten anapaestic dimeters; and while the six verses of the first epirrhema are spoken by Neoptolemus, the ten verses of the second epirrhema are shared between Neoptolemus and the chorus.

67. The example of Aeschylus's *The Suppliants* reminds us how dangerous it is to try to establish the date—even a relative date—of a tragedy on the basis of the analysis of its choral parts alone.

68. Sophocles, *Oedipus at Colonus*, vv. 117–253 (semilyrical parodos); vv. 510–48 (first stasimon purely lyrical); vv. 1447–99 (fifth stasimon semilyrical).

69. As an example, we will take the first strophe/antistrophe parodos pair in *Oedipus at Colonus*. The first strophe (vv. 117–37) is sung by the chorus. It is followed by an epirrhema of ten verses (vv. 138–48) in recitative with exchanges between the chorus and Oedipus. The antistrophe (vv. 149–69) is sung by the chorus. It is followed by an epirrhema of eight verses (170–77) with dialogue between Oedipus and Antigone, then Oedipus and the chorus enter. In the semilyrical dialogue of the fourth stasimon (1447–99), the chorus and the same two characters also speak. In this way, the lyrical part in dialogue is inserted even more naturally into the course of the drama, because the characters speak. However, the three sets of spoken verses between the chorus's spoken speeches preserve a remarkable symmetry: two verses spoken by Oedipus, one verse by Antigone, two verses by Oedipus.

70. The alternation between the spoken parts and the sung parts was also made subtler by inserting into the spoken parts passages in which a character, at the height of emotion, sings either alone or in dialogue with the chorus or with another character; see below.

71. See also *Women of Trachis*, v. 102 ("I learn"); *Ajax*, vv. 148–50; *Oedipus at Colonus*, vv. 118ff. (cf. vv. 77–80).

72. Antigone's first burial of Polynices is supposed to have taken place during the chorus's first song (or parodos, vv. 100–161) and the scene that follows (vv. 162–222). Antigone has left just before the chorus's arrival, and the guard has just announced the news of the burial, in v. 223. Antigone's second burial of Polynices takes place during the second choral song (or the first stasimon, vv. 331–83). The guard who had left just before this choral song returns immediately afterward, dragging Antigone behind him.

73. This is the sixth choral song (= fifth stasimon, vv. 1115–52).

74. Deianira's suicide in *Women of Trachis* occurs during the fourth choral song (or the third stasimon, vv. 821–61); that of Jocasta occurs during the fifth choral song (or the fourth stasimon, vv. 1186–221).

75. This negative dramatic function of the chorus is related to its dramaturgical function, which is also negative. We have seen that the choral songs allowed the tragic dramatist to provide the time required for actors to change masks and costumes so

that they could play different characters. See above, chapter VII, "Space and Spectacle."

76. The lateral entrance to the theater is also sometimes referred to by the same word, *parodos*; see Pollux 4, 126ff. Post-Aristotle writers added a variant of *parodos*, namely *epiparodos* (see Pollux 4, 108), to refer to the chorus' second entrance after it has gone away for a time (*Ajax*, v. 866).

77. The chorus, even though it has taken its position in the orchestra, dances during stasima. See the self-reference to the chorus's dancing in the second stasimon of *Ajax*, vv. 693–701 ("I shiver with rapture. . . . Now I want to dance"). See also the chorus's song of joy in *Women of Trachis*, v. 205 (with v. 216); however, this very brief song is not unanimously considered a stasimon; some post-Aristotle commentators have drawn the unjustified conclusion that the chorus remained immobile; see in particular *Suda*, s.v. stasimon: "a kind of song that the choreutes sang while remaining immobile": cf. also the scholium on Sophocles, *Women of Trachis*, v. 216, and Euripides, *Phoenician Women*, v. 202. Consequently, they wrongly opposed to the stasima the *hyporchemas* in which the chorus sang and danced; see Tzetzès, *Versus de differentiis poematorum: De tragoedia*, vv. 97 and 115–18. On the errors of these commentators, see A. M. Dale, "Stasimon and Hyporcheme," *Eranos* 48, 1950, pp. 14–20. The definition Aristotle gives for parodos and stasima (cited above) is less clear, because it does not begin from the meaning of the words. Moreover, it lacks coherence, since the criteria of definition are not the same for each of the two parts. Aristotle defines the parodos by its place in the chronological unfolding of the performance, saying that it is "the whole first part where the chorus expresses itself," which corresponds both to recitative and to song. On the other hand, he defines the stasima by rhythm. According to him, "A stasimon is a choral song without anapaests or trochaics" (*Poetics*, 12 (1452 b 2)). For an explanation of this second technical definition, see A. M. Dale (cited above), p. 15. By anapaests, we must understand anapaestic dimeters, and by trochees, catalectic trochaic tetrameters. Now, these two verses are of the order of recitative and not of song. By stasimon, Aristotle thus delimits the chorus's parts that are truly sung, to the exclusion of recitative.

78. The relation is personal when the chorus is close to the hero or the heroine; and in this case the chorus is of the same sex as the character. In *Ajax* and in *Philoctetes*, the chorus is formed of sailors who have made the voyage with the hero, Ajax in one case, Neoptolemus in the other. A heroine, for her part, is accompanied by a chorus of women friends, sometimes younger, sometimes older; this is the case for Deianira in *Women of Trachis* and for Electra in the tragedy that bears her name. The relation is more political in the three other tragedies; and in this case, the chorus is necessarily composed of elderly citizens. In *Antigone*, the old men of Thebes play an eminent role in the city, because they form the traditional royal council. In *Oedipus the King*, the chorus is once again composed of elderly Thebans, but they have a less precise function: they represent more generally the people of the city. Without being as prestigious as the chorus in *Antigone*, the chorus in *Oedipus at Colonus* is formed of the elders who administer the deme of Colonus (cf. v. 78).

79. In *Ajax*, *Women of Trachis*, and *Electra*, where the relations are rather personal, the choruses come on their own initiative to find the hero or heroine and to learn the news (*Ajax*, vv. 141ff.; *Women of Trachis*, vv. 141ff.; *Electra*, vv. 129ff.); whereas in *Antigone* and in *Oedipus the King*, where the relations are more political, the choruses

are convoked by the king of the city (*Antigone*, v. 161; *Oedipus the King*, v. 144). In *Oedipus at Colonus*, the deme's administrators have been summoned by the resident of Colonus (cf. vv. 78–80).

80. In exceptional cases the chorus's arrival is preceded by a separate announcement. This can happen only when the chorus, having a political role, is convoked or summoned: *Oedipus the King*, v. 144, and *Oedipus at Colonus*, v. 78–80.

81. *Antigone*, vv. 100–109.

82. Ibid., v. 16.

83. Ibid., vv. 332–41.

84. Ibid., vv. 330ff.

85. Similar remarks could be made regarding the hymn to Love chanted by the chorus after the third episode (vv. 781ff.). When the altercation between the father and the son has led to a break and the son's hatred of the father, when this quarrel has simply increased Creon's hatred of Antigone, whom he describes precisely as an object of hatred (v. 760), when Creon, in his last words, has determined Antigone's final punishment: she will be imprisoned alive underground, in the realm of Hades (vv. 777 and 780), and when, immediately afterward, the spectator hears a hymn to Eros the invincible, who reigns from the earth to the heavens, his imagination is transported, without any visible transition—here again, from the lower to the higher, but in a different sense, from the world below, from the realm of the dead and of Hades to that of the world above, the realm of Love.

86. The terms used in the singular, at the beginning of the stasima in Sophocles, are not the expression of the particular, but the sign of the universal: here, "man" does not refer to an individual but to humanity.

87. *Antigone*, v. 382; cf. v. 367.

88. On the negative dramatic function of the stasima, see above in this same chapter.

89. The only exception seems to be *Women of Trachis*, which begins with a long speech by Deianira that is not addressed to anyone (vv. 1–48). However, Deianira has probably just come out of the palace, accompanied by her nurse who has listened to her and speaks, naturally, after she has heard her out. In any event, Deianira's initial speech is very different from Euripides' introductory monologues. She does not make an objective presentation to inform the audience regarding the characters and the details of the situation—her information is very incomplete, and she does not even name herself—but she does recount, with feeling, her own destiny, which has consisted of a series of fears that culminate in a present fear occasioned by Heracles' prolonged absence. Deianira merely alludes to what Sophocles wants to reveal gradually, in particular the tablet Heracles left when he departed (v. 47).

90. Electra's entrance is distinguished from all the other entrances of characters who arrive in the course of the prologue. Ordinarily, the new arrival joins the characters already present. But in *Electra* she is alone on the stage, because at the point when she comes in, the characters who had already been present, Orestes and the tutor (accompanied by Pylades played by a silent actor) go away. This structure of the prologue in which characters succeed one another without meeting is explained in the framework of the return tragedies with a recognition scene (for this type of tragedy, see below); the same technique is found in the prologue of Euripides' *Electra*.

91. *Art of Poetry*, vv. 189ff.: "Let a play which would be inquired after, and though seen, represented anew, be neither shorter nor longer than the fifth act."

92. Regarding the flexibility in the number of stasima, see above.

93. First episode: vv. 201–595 (= 395 verses). Second episode: vv. 646–92 (= 47 verses); this latter is the shortest episode in all of Sophocles' tragedies.

94. The metaphor is inspired by Sophocles' text; see *Ajax*, v. 786.

95. First episode: 170 verses; second episode: 198 verses; third episode: 155 verses; fourth episode: 138 verses. The equilibrium is even clearer if we add that the exodos has 199 verses.

96. Third episode: 324 verses (vv. 720–1043); fourth episode: 215 verses (vv. 1096–210); fifth episode: 198 verses (vv. 1249–446); sixth episode: 58 verses (vv. 1500–1555).

97. On the basis of this meaning, we can explain the definition of "episode" given in Pollux 4, 108 ("an episode in tragedies is an action connected with the action"). But it does not seem to refer to the same reality as Aristotle's definition.

98. Sophocles, *Oedipus at Colonus*.

99. This interpretation is coherent with the designation of most of the other parts of tragedy, which can also be understood by reference to the movement of the chorus and the characters: parodos, stasima, exodos.

100. The first critic to introduce the image of complicating and resolving the plot is Aristotle, in his *Poetics*, 18 (1455 b 24ff.): "In every tragedy there is a complication (*desis*) and a denouement (*lusis*). . . . I mean this, that the complication is the part from the beginning up to the point which immediately precedes the occurrence of a change from bad to good fortune or from good fortune to bad; the denouement is from the beginning of the change down to the end."

101. The arrival follows the parodos if the stage is empty when the chorus enters (*Ajax, Antigone, Oedipus the King*). It is generally deferred if a character in the prologue has remained when the chorus enters (*Women of Trachis, Electra, Oedipus at Colonus*). However, in *Oedipus at Colonus*, the situation is slightly different from that in *Women of Trachis* and *Electra*. Whereas Deianira and Electra are present when the chorus comes in, Oedipus has hidden when the chorus arrives, then shows himself in the course of the parodos. In *Philoctetes*, even though the chorus in the parodos has joined Neoptolemus, the new character—in this case, Philoctetes—arrives immediately after the parodos, which is possible because the parodos is in dialogue form.

102. His arrival can be compared with that of Creon (in *Oedipus the King*), who also wears a crown on his head, which the priest, playing the role of presenter in the absence of the chorus, says is a sign of good news. Cf. *Women of Trachis*, vv. 178ff., and *Oedipus the King*, vv. 82ff. These two arrivals have analogous functions, even though Creon's arrival is situated in the prologue, as we have seen (above), and not in the first episode.

103. Sophocles, *Women of Trachis*, vv. 229ff.

104. Sophocles, *Electra*, vv. 378–82. The following verse quoted is v. 387.

105. Sophocles, *Oedipus at Colonus*, vv. 353–60.

106. Sophocles, *Antigone*, vv. 223ff.

107. Sophocles, *Philoctetes*, vv. 542ff.; *Oedipus at Colonus*, vv. 324ff.

108. Sophocles, *Philoctetes*, vv. 628–38.

109. See above in this same chapter, "The Spoken Parts: The Middle of the Tragedy or the Episodes."

110. Sophocles, *Oedipus the King*, vv. 513–862.

111. Sophocles, *Women of Trachis*, vv. 813ff., and *Antigone*, vv. 766–67.

112. Sophocles, *Oedipus the King*, vv. 1073–75. For the discussions of this silence mentioned by the chorus, see below, chapter IX, "The Characters," under "Women's Silence."

113. Sophocles, *Antigone*, v. 1175.

114. Sophocles, *Oedipus the King*, v. 1235.

115. Three of these four silent exits concern women who are about to commit suicide. See below, chapter IX, "The Characters," under "Women's Silence."

116. Cf. Sophocles, *Oedipus at Colonus*, vv. 1579ff. ("Oedipus is dead"), *Antigone*, v. 1175 ("Haemon is dead") and *Oedipus the King*, v. 1235 ("the divine Jocasta is dead").

117. Cf. Sophocles, *Oedipus at Colonus*, vv. 1586–666 (= eighty-one verses), *Antigone*, vv. 1192–243 (= fifty-two verses), and *Oedipus the King*, vv. 1237–85 (= forty-eight verses).

118. *Women of Trachis*, v. 1275; *Philoctetes*, v. 1469.

119. *Women of Trachis*, vv. 1276ff.; *Oedipus the King*, vv. 1524–27.

120. *Ajax*, vv. 1418–20; *Oedipus the King*, vv. 1524–27.

121. *Women of Trachis*, v. 1278 ("And in all of them there is nothing that is not Zeus").

122. *Antigone*, v. 1349.

123. *Electra*, *Philoctetes*, *Oedipus at Colonus*. In *Electra*, there is still a reflection on the fate of the tragic family that has finally gained freedom through suffering, but it does not include the broader perspective on the human condition. Finally, in *Philoctetes* and *Oedipus at Colonus*, there is not even a reference to the play. In *Philoctetes*, vv. 1469–71, the only subject is the departure, and in *Oedipus at Colonus*, vv. 1677–79, the final formula ("These things are established firm and fixed") would be suitable for any tragedy.

124. On the end of tragedies, see D. H. Roberts, "Parting Words: Final Lines in Sophocles and Euripides," *Classical Quarterly* 37, 1987, pp. 51–64. For the allusions to the future at the end of tragedies, see *Women of Trachis*, vv. 1270–71; *Electra*, vv. 1497–98; *Philoctetes*, vv. 1440–44; *Oedipus at Colonus*, vv. 1769–72. On these allusions to the future, see for example D. H. Roberts, "Sophoclean Endings: Another Story," *Arethusa* 21, 1988, pp. 177–96, with the clarification by M. Lloyd, *Sophocles: Electra*, London, 2005, p. 109: "Some of the allusions which she discusses are not merely to 'another story' but are highly relevant to prominent themes in the plays themselves." For the discussion of the meaning of the end of *Women of Trachis*, see chapter XI, "Seeing, Hearing, and Understanding"; for the end of *Electra*, see chapter X, "Humans and the Gods."

125. See above in this same chapter.

126. The only tragedy in which the passage from speech to recitative occurs is *Electra*, in the chorus's final lines.

127. In six out of seven of Sophocles' tragedies, we pass from iambic rhythm (iambic trimeter) to anapaestic rhythm (anapaestic dimeter). *Oedipus the King*, where we move to a trochaic rhythm (catalectic trochaic tetrameter), is an exception.

128. On recitative, see above.

129. Sophocles, *Ajax*, vv. 1402ff.

130. Sophocles, *Women of Trachis*, vv. 1259ff.

131. The heading for this section is from Sophocles, *Oedipus the King*, v. 1515.

132. Sophocles, *Philoctetes*, vv. 1402–7.

133. Change of rhythm starting at v. 1445 (the passage from iambic trimeter to anapaestic dimeter) and the chorus's speech at vv. 1469–71. For more details on the double end of *Philoctetes*, see J. Jouanna, "La double fin du Philoctète de Sophocle: Rythme et spectacle," *Revue des Etudes Grecques* 114, 2001, pp. 359–82.

134. Aristotle, *Poetics*, 9 (1452 a 15), cited above.

135. Euripides, *Helen*, vv. 625–97 (recognition of a wife and a husband: Helen and Menelaus); *Iphigeneia in Tauris*, vv. 827–99 (recognition of a sister and a brother: Iphigeneia and Orestes); *Ion*, vv. 1437–509 (recognition of a mother and her son: Creusa and Ion); cf. also, for the recognition of a mother and her sons, the tragedy *Hypsipyle*, extant in the form of fragments (H. Van Looy, *Euripide*, vol. 8, 3, CUF, 2002, pp. 212–14 = *TrGF* 5.2, frag. 759 a, pp. 786–88 Kannicht: semilyrical dialogue between Hypsipyle and her son Euneos).

136. Sophocles, *Electra*, vv. 1232–87. Strophe vv. 1232–52; antistrophe: vv. 1253–72; epode: vv. 1273–87. For the use of dochmiacs, see above. In the epode, two short replies by Orestes are part of two lyrical verses he shares with Electra (vv. 1276 and 1280). Thus he must sing these two brief replies. But his only complete verse in the epode (v. 1278) is an iambic trimeter that has no lyrical character. It must have been spoken.

137. For the term "monody," see Aristophanes, *Frogs*, v. 1330 (on Euripides' monodies); see also the definition in *Suda*, s.v. *monodia*: "the song coming from the stage in plays. . . . When a single person utters the song and the chorus does not sing at the same time, we call it a monody." On monody in Greek tragedy, see W. Barner, "Die Monodie," in W. Jens (ed.), cited above, pp. 277–320. However, W. Barner gives a broader definition of monody than the one adopted here, because it includes in monody some songs sung by characters in dialogues with the chorus. Thus it includes as monodies (see the table on p. 279) the songs of Ajax (*Ajax*, vv. 394–427), Heracles (*Women of Trachis*, vv. 983–1043), and Philoctetes (*Philoctetes*, vv. 1081–162). But these songs are part of a broader strophic system in which the chorus and sometimes other characters participate. Thus they are not, strictly speaking, monodies. According to Aristotle's distinction, they belong instead to the category of commoi.

138. Sophocles, *Oedipus at Colonus*, vv. 237–54.

139. Aristotle, *Problemata*, 19, 15 (918 b 22–29). In the same passage, it is said that the presence of strophes/antistrophes (whose rhythm is simpler with the echoing repetitions) was better suited to a chorus of citizens who were less skilled at imitating than specialists.

140. Sophocles, *Electra*, vv. 86–91.

141. From a formal point of view, the lyrical character is marked by the presence of catalectic anapaestic dimeters, with a predominance of spondees (vv. 88–89 and vv. 105–6): see G. Kaibel, *Sophokles Electra* (1896), rpt. Stuttgart: Teubner, 1967, pp. 82ff. It is also marked by the rather frequent absence of a central caesura in the verse between the two meters (vv. 94, 201, 203, 221, and 223): see D. Korzeniewski (cited above), p. 95. It has also been seen as a strophic composition (strophe: vv. 86–102; antistrophe: vv. 103–20): see P. Mazon and A. Dain (*Sophocle* II, p. 141, n. 1). However, these latter editors conclude, rather surprisingly, that this expository piece was not sung but recited. On the other hand, the linguistic criterion is not very clear.

In theory, in the sung anapaests, the coloring of the language is Dorian, whereas the anapaests in recitative are Ionian-Attic. The Dorian coloring is very discreet here (solely in v. 90); the rest is in Ionian-Attic. For a convenient list of the criteria for distinguishing between the anapaestic lyric and the recited anapaests, see M. L. West, *Greek Metre* (cited above), p. 121.

142. Sophocles, *Electra*, v. 107.

143. Euripides, *Electra*, vv. 112–66. In Euripides, the monody includes a system of two strophe/antistrophe pairs and a more varied lyrical rhythm (with a predominance of aeolo-choriambic verses).

144. We do not have the didaskalia for either of the two tragedies. For the question of the relative chronology of the two tragedies, see the presentation in the editions of Euripides' *Electra* with commentaries: J. D. Denniston, Oxford, 1939, pp. xxxiv–xxxix; M. J. Cropp, 1988, pp. xlviii–l; cf. also K. Mathiessen, *Die Tragödien des Euripides*, in *Zetemata* 114, Munich, 2002, pp. 125ff.

145. They occur in the final lyric dialogue between the chorus and Xerxes (*Persians*, vv. 931ff.) They reappear not only in Sophocles' *Electra*, but also in Euripides' monodies, the oldest of which are those of *Hecuba*, dating from around 425 (Hecuba, vv. 153ff., and Polymestor, vv. 1056ff.).

146. Sophocles, *Electra*, 89ff.: "the thudding blows against this bloodied breast."

147. Aeschylus, *Libation Bearers*, v. 423 (*ekopsa kommon Arion*), where the etymology of the word is clearly felt.

148. The Greek word *thren*, which serves to define *commos* in Aristotle, is used by Theseus (v. 1751) to describe the song of mourning sung by Antigone and Ismene.

149. Sophocles, *Oedipus at Colonus*, vv. 1705–23.

150. The present definition deviates from both a limited and a broad use of the term *commos*. The limited use is the one that reserves the term *commos* for dialogues between the chorus and the character that are sung, and whose subject is mourning; see C. Pirozzi, *Il commo nella tragedia greca*, Naples, 2003. But it is hard to see how Aristotle, who defined the particular parts of tragedy by distinguishing between songs coming solely from the stage and those coming from the stage and the chorus, could limit the second category by its thematic content. In that case, what happens to songs sung by the chorus and a character that have a different content? The broad use of the term—which is the more frequent—designates by *commos* any sung dialogue between a character and the chorus, whether it is inserted into a spoken part or replaces a stasimon. But it does not seem that Aristotle conflated commoi with stasima in dialogue form. According to him, from the moment that the commoi are connected with particular parts of certain tragedies, they must not be confused with a general part, like a stasimon. In any case, the sung dialogues inserted into the spoken parts must not be confused with the sung dialogues that were substituted, in the course of the evolution of tragedy, for a sung part; on this substitution, see above. There is, in fact, a difference between the song that has been added to the dialogue (in the spoken parts) and the dialogue which has been added to a song (in the sung parts). The distinction is justified by the chronology of their appearance in Sophocles' work. Sung dialogues inserted into the spoken parts are found even in Sophocles' earliest extant tragedy, *Ajax*. On the other hand, it is only starting with *Electra* that the traditional choral song was replaced by sung dialogues (see above).

This distinction is also justified by the chorus's mode of expression: the chorus always expresses itself through song in the sung dialogues that replace the traditional choral songs, because that is its traditional mode of expression, whereas in the spoken part the author is free to choose the mode of expression in relation to the degree of emotion of the chorus or the characters reacting to a given situation. The distinction between sung dialogues that take the place of stasima and those that are inserted into spoken parts is sometimes a subject of debate. That is the case for a sung dialogue in *Electra* (vv. 823–70) and another in *Oedipus at Colonus* (vv. 510–50). Some scholars (including Jebb) consider both as commoi inserted into a spoken part. In reality, they have the function of stasima: they are preceded by the exit of a character and followed by the entrance of another, so that they separate two spoken parts; moreover, from the dramaturgical point of view, they allow an actor the necessary time to change costume. Finally, these are purely lyrical dialogues that are suited to replace a choral song. See J. Jouanna (cited above). In the second half of the twentieth century, the difficulties involved in determining exactly Aristotle's use of the word *commos* led scholars to choose another Greek term to designate lyrical dialogues in tragedy, the term *amoiboion*; see H. Popp, "Das Amoiboion," in W. Jens (ed.), cited above, pp. 221–75. By *amoiboion* is meant any dialogue in a tragedy in which there is a lyrical element. This notion is thus broader than the Aristotelian notion of commos, because it also covers the sung dialogues coming from the stage. But this new term has the disadvantage that it is based on a Greek word—*amoibè*—whose usage does not correspond to the modern definition.

151. In Sophocles, there is one exception: the commos in *Women of Trachis*, vv. 879–95, which is astrophic.

152. In Sophocles, two commoi are purely lyrical (that is, both the chorus and the characters sing): the threnody at the end of *Oedipus at Colonus*, which is, as we have seen a ritual song; and the commos in *Women of Trachis* (cited above), where the nurse and the chorus, with shared emotion, lament the death of Deianira.

153. Sophocles, *Ajax*, vv. 221–62.

154. Sophocles, *Electra*, vv. 1407ff.

155. Other short commoi in which the chorus sings under the impact of emotion: *Oedipus the King* (strophe: vv. 649–67; antistrophe: vv. 678–97); *Oedipus at Colonus* (strophe: vv. 833–43; antistrophe: vv. 876–86). In both cases, the antistrophe is separated from the strophe. This is a good example of the flexibility with which tragic authors used lyrical frameworks.

156. *Antigone*, vv. 806–16.

157. Ibid., vv. 883–86.

158. Ibid., vv. 806–82. The commos is formed of two strophe/antistrophe pairs (first pair: vv. 806–38; second par: vv. 839–75) and ends with an epode (876–82). Each strophe or antistrophe includes a speech by Antigone and by the chorus. Everything Antigone says is sung. The chorus's first two remarks are in recitative (anapaestic dimeters), and the last two are sung (iambic dimeters).

159. Sophocles, *Ajax*, vv. 348–429. This commos has three strophe/antistrophe pairs.

160. Tecmessa speaks starting in the second pair (from v. 368 on). Like the chorus, she speaks. Her few remarks are inserted into the strophic scheme in place of those of the chorus, even though one might hesitate in one case, at verse 371, between as-

signing the speech to the chorus (as in the manuscripts followed by the Dawe edition; cf. also the scholium) or to Tecmessa (as in Dain's and Lloyd Jones-Wilson's
editions based on O. Müller).

161. Sophocles, *Women of Trachis*, vv. 983–87 and 993–1003.

162. Ibid., vv. 1004–17 and vv. 1023–43. According to most scholars today, these two songs
constitute a strophe and an antistrophe; see J. Irigoin, "Le trio des Trachiniennes de
Sophocle (vvv. 971–1043). Analyse métrique et établissement du texte," in *Théâtre et
spectacles dans l'Antiquité: Actes du Coll. de Strasbourg (5–7 novembre 1981)*, Centre de
recherche sur le Proche-Orient et la Grèce antique 7, Leiden, 1983, pp. 181–91.

163. Sophocles, *Women of Trachis*, vv. 1044ff. This chorus of young women never addresses Heracles. It simply witnesses a tragedy among men.

164. Ibid., vv. 1018–22.

165. The two men express themselves in dactylic hexameters. This verse form, which is
very rare in tragedy, does not in itself signify a specific register. In theory, they could
be sung, recited, or spoken: see M. L. West, *Greek Metre* (cited above), p. 98. Here,
they were probably recited (cf. *Philoctetes*, vv. 839–42) to contrast with Heracles'
song, in which the dactylic hexameters were surely sung.

166. Sophocles, *Ajax*, vv. 430ff.

167. Sophocles, *Women of Trachis*, vv. 1046–111.

168. Ibid., v. 1011 ("in my death, as in my life, I punished the guilty!").

169. Ibid., v. 1081 (cries and laments: "Ah, misery!"; vv. 1085–86, two anapaestic trimeters:
"King Hades, receive me! Strike me, O fire of Zeus! Hurl down your thunderbolt,
ruler, dash it, Father, upon my head!").

170. Aristotle, *Poetics*, 7 (1451 a 13ff).

171. Sophocles, *Oedipus the King*, vv. 1313–67. The commos is composed of two strophe/
antistrophe pairs.

172. The chorus expresses itself in two iambic trimeters spoken at the end of each strophe
and each antistrophe of the two pairs. However, it also sings two iambic dimeters
in the middle of the strophe and the antistrophe of the second pair (vv. 1336 and
1356). Thus there is an increase in the chorus's emotion in the second part of the
commos. This can be compared with rise of the chorus's emotion in the commos in
Antigone (see above), but here it is manifested only in two brief instants.

173. Thus what is comparable in *Ajax* and in *Oedipus the King* is not only the commos
organized in strophes/antistrophes shared between the hero and the chorus (*Ajax*,
vv. 349–429: three strophes/antistrophes; *Oedipus the King*, vv. 1313–67: two strophes/
antistrophes), but also the hero's lengthy speech that follows them (*Ajax*, vv. 430–80;
Oedipus the King, vv. 1369–415), with three or four verses by the chorus providing a
conclusion or transition (*Ajax*, vv. 481–84; *Oedipus the King*, vv. 1416–18) before a
new character speaks (Tecmessa in *Ajax* and Creon in *Oedipus the King*).

174. Sophocles, *Antigone*, vv. 1261–353.

175. Ibid., v. 1316.

176. A. Dain (quoted above), p. 206.

177. The commos is composed of two strophe/antistrophe pairs with the addition of
spoken iambic trimeters (= *epirrhemata*) at the end of the first strophe and the first
antistrophe (vv. 1277–83 and vv. 1301–5 without exact correspondence) and the insertion of spoken iambic trimeters within the strophe and antistrophe of the second

pair (vv. 1312–16 and vv. 1334–38 with exact correspondence). The first *epirrhema* (vv. 1277–83) allows the messenger from inside the palace to make his entrance and tell Creon that his wife is dead, while the second *epirrhema* (1301–5) allows him to give details regarding her death.

178. Sophocles, *Antigone*, vv. 1281, 1314, 1336.

179. In his song dochmiacs are dominant; as we have seen, in tragedy, this is the lyrical verse that expresses the greatest agitation (see above).

180. Sophocles, *Antigone*, vv. 1339–46. The lyrical verses are all dochmiacs. Creon's preceding spoken verse is v. 1336.

181. Sophocles, *Oedipus at Colonus*, v. 1751.

182. So far as the lyric framework is concerned: variations in the number of strophe/antistrophe pairs, occasionally with an epode (Antigone's commos in *Antigone*); variations in the choice of rhythms and, consequently, diverse registers of diction (song, recitative, speech). Insofar as dialogue is concerned, alongside the normal type in which the hero engages in dialogue with the chorus, the hero may enter into dialogue successively with the chorus and with another character (Tecmessa in Ajax's commos, the messenger in Creon's commos in *Antigone*); and even in an exceptional case (Heracles' commos in *Women of Trachis*), the chorus does not intervene in the dialogue but is replaced by two characters (the old man and Hyllus).

183. On the importance of analyzing the entrance and exit of characters in Greek theater, see O. Taplin, *The Stagecraft of Aeschylus: The Dramatic Use of Exits and Entrances in Greek Tragedy*, Oxford, 1977, and *Greek Tragedy in Action*, London, 1978, pp. 31–57 (chap. 4: "Exits and Entrances").

184. In Aeschylus, a character already sometimes remains present during the chorus's song. In *The Persians* (vv. 623ff.), Queen Atossa remains during the chorus's song, but her presence is explicitly mentioned and justified for ritual reasons (vv. 619–22): she pours the libations on Darius's tomb while the chorus sings hymns in memory of the deceased. Similarly, in *The Suppliants*, Danaus remains present during the Danaids' song of thanks (vv. 625–709); cf. also *Eumenides*, vv. 255ff. See O. Taplin (1977, cited above), pp. 108 and 209.

185. The scene between Deianira and the chorus thus includes the parodos and the first thirty-nine verses of the first episode (vv. 94–179). The entrance of the first messenger announcing Heracles' return is separated from the beginning of the first episode by about forty verses.

186. On the insertion of a dialogic stasimon into tragedy, see J. Jouanna, "L'insertion du lyrisme dans le drame chez Sophocle: L'exemple d'un dialogue lyrique (*Philoctète*, vv. 1081–217)," in J. Jouanna-J. Leclant (ed.), *La Poésie grecque antique*, Paris, 2003, pp. 151–68.

187. Sophocles, *Electra*, vv. 1–85.

188. The voluntary withdrawal of the characters who have just arrived is a new version of Aeschylus's *Libation Bearers* dealing with the same sequence in the myth. But in Aeschylus this withdrawal took place at the "Aristotelian" suture, at the end of the prologue, and not at the middle. Orestes and Pylades left the stage empty before the entrance of the chorus of captive women and Electra. Moreover, this withdrawal does not have the same meaning, because the scene is presented differently. In Sophocles' *Electra*, Agamemnon's tomb is in the virtual space: Orestes leaves with

the tutor to go there. In *The Libation Bearers*, the tomb is in the visible space: Orestes hides with Pylades to see the cortege's arrival (vv. 20ff.), but in Sophocles' *Electra* the tutor does not allow Orestes to do the same.

189. On this change, see above, chapter VII, "Space and Spectacle," under "A Bold Change in Setting: An Inhabited Residence."

190. Sophocles, *Ajax*, vv. 485–595.

191. Homer, *Iliad* 6, vv. 407–96.

192. See the scholia on *Ajax*, v. 501 (compared with *Iliad* 6, vv. 476ff.).

193. See above, chapter VII, "Space and Spectacle" (a suicide presented live, simultaneously visible and hidden; or Heracles' appearance at the end of *Philoctetes*).

194. See J. Barrett, *Staged Narrative: Poetics and the Messenger in Greek Tragedy*, Berkeley: University of California Press, 2002, 250 pp. (including two chapters devoted to messengers in Sophocles, one on *Electra*, the other on *Oedipus the King*). On the messenger scene in Euripides, see I. de Jong, *Narrative in Drama: The Art of the Euripidean Messenger-Speech*, Leiden: Brill, 1991.

195. For the first category, see above, chapter VII, "Space and Spectacle."

196. Or again, in *Oedipus the King* the Corinthian messenger enters from the side to announce the death of Polybus, the King of Corinth and the supposed father of Oedipus, whereas a messenger comes from inside the palace to recount both Jocasta's suicide and Oedipus's self-mutilation.

197. Sophocles, *Women of Trachis*, vv. 739ff.

198. Ibid., vv. 874ff.

199. Ibid., vv. 746ff.

200. Ibid., v. 889.

201. Aeschylus, *Persians*, vv. 353–432, vv. 447–71; vv. 480–514.

202. Just as in *Philoctetes* Neoptolemus develops, in a framework suggested by Odysseus (vv. 58ff.), a story about himself (vv. 343–90) in which fiction is mixed with reality in order to deceive Philoctetes and win his confidence. There too, the spectator knows that the story is false. A falsified narrative of another kind is found in *Women of Trachis* (vv. 248–90), where the herald Lichas, out of respect for his mistress Deianira, does not reveal the whole truth about the causes of the expedition against Eurytus, king of Oechalia, from which Heracles returned victorious. Lichas does not mention the main cause, Heracles' love for Iole, the king's daughter, even though she is part of the cortege of captives accompanying the messenger. This time, the audience does not know that the herald's narrative is false. It learns this only later on, when Lichas is confounded by the first messenger.

203. Aeschylus, *Libation Bearers*, v. 682.

204. Homer, *Odyssey* 13, vv. 256–86 (deceptive report) and vv. 287ff. (Athena's reaction).

205. Sophocles, *Women of Trachis*, vv. 200–224.

206. A woman in a messenger scene in *Antigone* also departs in silence: Eurydice goes back into the palace after hearing the messenger recount the death of her son Haemon. In both cases, the silent departure is a portent of suicide.

207. Sophocles, *Women of Trachis*, vv. 947–70.

208. On tragic irony, see below, chapter XI, "Seeing, Hearing, and Understanding."

209. On the agōn scene in tragedy, see in particular J. Duchemin, *L'agōn dans la tragédie grecque*, 2nd ed., Paris: Les Belles Lettres, 1968, 247 pp. (on Sophocles, see esp. pp. 56–72, pp. 112–17 and passim).

210. Sophocles, *Ajax*, vv. 1047–162.

211. After the chorus's critical judgment of Menelaus's speech, Teucer addresses it (v. 1093); but he does not reply to the chorus after its critical judgment on his own speech (vv. 1018–19).

212. Sophocles, *Antigone*, vv. 631–765. First exchange of two sets of four verses: Creon vv. 631–34; Haemon vv. 635–38. Creon's speech: vv. 639–80; Haemon's speech: vv. 683–723. Two verses by the chorus punctuate each speech: vv. 681ff. and vv. 724ff. Stichomythia: vv. 730–57. Final exchange of two sets of four verses: Creon vv. 758–61; Haemon vv. 762–65. Exchange of two sets of two verses before the stichomythia: Creon vv. 726ff.; Haemon vv. 728ff.

213. Sophocles, *Oedipus the King*, vv. 300–462.

214. Oedipus's speech: vv. 380–403; the chorus's comment: vv. 404–7; Tiresias's speech: vv. 408–28. Rapid dialogue: vv. 429–46.

215. Sophocles, *Oedipus the King*, vv. 300–315.

216. Ibid., vv. 316–79.

217. Sophocles, *Women of Trachis*, vv. 813ff.

218. Sophocles, *Ajax*, vv. 1316ff.

219. This is a technique that Sophocles also used in a lyrical context. Within the final commos of *Antigone* (vv. 1261–346), consisting of two strophe/antistrophe pairs, Sophocles has a messenger enter to tell Creon that his wife is dead (vv. 1278ff.).

220. On the Greek supplication tragedies, see J. Kopperschmidt, "Hikesie als dramatische Form," in W. Jens (1971, cited above), pp. 321–46; cf. also J. Gould, "Hiketeia," *Journal of Hellenic Studies* 93, 1973, pp. 74–103; more recently, R. Bernek, *Dramaturgie und ideologie: Der politische Mythos in den Hikesiedramen des Aischylos, Sophokles und Euripides*, in *Beiträge zur Altertumskunde* 188, Munich: Saur, 2004, 347 pp. For *Oedipus at Colonus* as a supplication tragedy, see, in addition to J. Kopperschmidt, pp. 329–35, P. Burian, "Suppliant and Saviour: *Œdipus at Colonus*," *Phoenix* 28, 1974, pp. 408–29 (the author was not aware of Kopperschmidt's dissertation); J. Jouanna, "Espaces sacrés, rites et oracles dans l'*Œdipe à Colone* de Sophocle," *Revue des Etudes Grecques* 108, 1995, pp. 38–58 (esp. pp. 51–58), and P. Cassella, *La supplica all'altare nella tragedia greca*, Naples, 1999 (esp. II 8, Sofocle, *Edipo a Colono*, pp. 151–74).

221. Euripides had used the schema earlier, in his *Heracleidae* and in his tragedy *The Suppliants*, which has the same title as Aeschylus's tragedy, but deals with a different myth.

222. For the reminiscences of the corresponding scene in Aeschylus's *The Suppliants*, see above, chapter VI, "The Mythic Imagination."

223. Euripides' play is a tragedy that is still related to the Heracles myth and connected with the first type: *Heracles* (or *The Madness of Heracles*). *The Persians* can also be assigned to this first large group. But the latter might be said to constitute a new subgroup, because the return is that of a prince who is defeated and not victorious.

224. The period of waiting is much longer in *Women of Trachis* than it is in *Agamemnon*.

225. However, in *Women of Trachis* there are two messenger scenes. For the technique of doubling in Sophocles, see the end of this chapter.

226. *Agamemnon*, vv. 1035ff.; *Women of Trachis*, vv. 307–34.

227. Euripides' *Electra* obviously also belongs to this group. For more details on the

comparison between the structure Aeschylus's *Libation Bearers* and that of Sophocles' *Electra*, both of which are return tragedies, see Jacques Jouanna, "L'Electre de Sophocle, tragédie du retour," in A. Machin and L. Pernée, *Sophocle: Le texte, les personnages*, Aix-en-Provence, 1993, pp. 173–87.

228. This schema is not peculiar to tragedy. Scenes of recognition and murder are already found in the *Odyssey*: Odysseus, back in his homeland after the Trojan War, is recognized by his niece before he massacres the suitors.

229. Here I will not linger over more specific variations in structure that are well known, such as the order of the murders: the murder first of Aegisthus, then of Clytemnestra in Aeschylus; the murder of Clytemnestra, and then of Aegisthus (outside the time of the tragedy) in Sophocles. It is less well known that this inversion allows the technique of transfer. Aesgisthus's cries (heard from inside the palace) during his murder in Aeschylus are transferred to Clytemnestra in Sophocles. The tense dialogue between Orestes and Clytemnestra before her murder in Aeschylus becomes, in Sophocles, a tense dialogue between Orestes and Aegisthus before Aegisthus's murder. For other examples of transfers made by Sophocles in his *Electra*, see J. Jouanna (1993, cited above).

230. It is replaced by a face-to-face encounter with Aegisthus before his murder; see the preceding note.

231. Aeschylus, *The Libation Bearers*, vv. 900–902.

232. See above.

Chapter IX. The Characters

1. Aristotle, *Poetics*, 6 (1449b–1450a).

2. Since the beginning of the twentieth century, especially after the unfinished thesis of Tycho von Wilamowitz, the young son of Ulrich Wilamowitz, who perished in the First World War (*Die dramatische Technik des Sophokles*, dans *Philologische Untersuchungen* 22, 1917; cf. H. Lloyd-Jones, "Tycho von Wilamowitz-Moellendorf on the Dramatic Technique of Sophocles," *Classical Quarterly*, n.s., 22, 1972, pp. 214–28), scholars have rightly warned against a purely psychological analysis of Sophocles' theater. A tragic poet's goal was not to sketch in the abstract characters that he would put in a given conflictual situation. It was on the basis of situations in which characters act and speak that their ethos is revealed. To judge the author's choices and the effects he seeks to produce, we need to take into account the constraints on performance and the major effects on the audience sought in each scene. But it would be arbitrary to give priority to contradictions in details between one scene and another (some of which are explained by the characters' subjective perspective) in order to put in question Sophocles' desire to present coherent and lifelike characters—not only heroes, but also the many minor characters admirably sketched by the author with precision and subtlety, and sometimes with an affectionate irony.

3. Aristotle, *Poetics*, 25 (1460 b 33ff.) The manuscripts contain an error that excludes Sophocles from what is said about Euripides. This error has been corrected (since Heinsius) in all editions except that of R. Dupont-Roc and J. Lallot (Paris, 1980), probably out of respect for the direct manuscript tradition. But the indirect tradition (*Gnomologium Vaticanum* cited below) confirms the correction.

4. Jean de La Bruyère, *The Characters*, trans. H. van Laun, London: John C. Nimmo,

1885. It remains to explain the role played by the *Parallèle de M. De Corneille et de M. Racine* by Hilaire-Bernard Longepierre, which appeared in the edition of his play *Médée* (1686), as an intermediary between Aristotle and La Bruyère (1st ed. of *Les Caractères*, 1688).

5. Aristotle, *Poetics*, 25 (1460 b 8).

6. This remark of Sophocles is quoted in direct discourse in the *Gnomologium Vaticanum* 518 Sternbach (ed. Luschnat, p. 190 = test. 53 b Radt), but in a different context that is no longer critical: "The same (viz., Sophocles), asked why he made characters of good men and Euripides of bad men, declared: 'it's because I represent men as they should be and Euripides represents them as they are.'" This new presentation was itself transposed in a comparison between Sophocles and another author, Philoxenus, concerning a category of characters, namely women: "The poet Philoxenus, asked why Sophocles presented good women and he himself presented bad women, declared: 'it's because Sophocles introduces women as they should be, and I as they are'" (Maximus the Confessor, *Serm.* 39 = Antonios Melissa 2, 34 = *Gnomol. Vindob.* 132 Wachsmuth = test. 172 Radt).

7. Aristophanes, *Frogs*, vv. 949ff. and vv. 959–61.

8. Aristotle, *Poetics*, 15 (1454 b 8ff.).

9. Ibid., 15 (1454 a 28–33): three examples of flaws in the conception of character are taken from Euripides: for a base character, Menelaus in *Orestes*; for the lack of a character's conformity to the norms of her sex, Melanippe, a learned woman, in *Melanippe the Wise*; for the lack of the character's coherence in the course of the tragedy, Iphigeneia in *Iphigeneia in Aulis*.

10. Aelius Aristides, *Oration* 46, "Against Plato for the Defense of the Four" (sc. Miltiades, Themistocles, Pericles, Cimon") 133, 2 (II, p. 179 Dindorf = test. 135 Radt).

11. Aristotle, *Poetics*, 25 (1461 a 4–9).

12. Cf. Aristotle, *Poetics*, 25 (1460 b 13–15): "The standard of what is correct is not the same in the art of poetry as it is in the art of social conduct or any other art."

13. Aristotle, *Poetics*, 25 (1461 a 4–9).

14. Sophocles, *Women of Trachis*, vv. 49–57.

15. Ibid., vv. 61–63.

16. Aristotle, *Rhetoric*, 3, 17 (1418 b 13–15).

17. Sophocles, *Antigone*, vv. 694–700.

18. Ibid., vv. 718–23.

19. Aristotle, *Poetics*, 18 (1456 a 25–28): "The chorus too must be regarded as one of the actors. It must be part of the whole and share in the action, not as in Euripides but as in Sophocles."

20. Sophocles, *Ajax*, v. 14; *Philoctetes*, v. 1445. For the apparition of the gods on high, see above, chapter VII, "Space and Spectacle." For the voice of the gods, see below, chapter X, "Humans and Gods."

21. Sophocles, *Ajax*, vv. 154–61.

22. Plato, *Laws*, 10, 902 e.

23. Sophocles, *Ajax*, vv. 349–52.

24. The expression is Paul Mazon's in his *Sophocle (Ajax, Œdipe Roi, Electre)*, Paris, 1958, p. 16, n. 1.

25. See, as soon as the chorus enters, the passage from "we" (v. 165) to "me" (v. 200); and there had already been a passage from "I" (vv. 136, 139) to "us" (v. 142).

26. Sophocles, *Ajax*, vv. 134–40.
27. Ibid., vv. 165ff.
28. Ibid., v. 201.
29. For the tragedy's reshaping of the image of Salamis in the *Iliad*, see above, chapter VI, "The Mythic Imagination."
30. Homer, *Iliad* 2, v. 557.
31. Sophocles, *Ajax*, v. 203.
32. Ibid., vv. 282–84.
33. Ibid., v. 330.
34. Ibid., vv. 811–13.
35. Ibid., v. 896.
36. Ibid., vv. 942–43.
37. Ibid., vv. 485–524.
38. Ibid., vv. 600–606.
39. Ibid., vv. 1199–210.
40. Ibid., vv. 1216–22. For a commentary on this passage, see above, chapter VI, "The Mythic Imagination."
41. Sophocles, *Ajax*, vv. 1182–84.
42. Ibid., vv. 693–715.
43. Ibid., vv. 719ff.
44. Ibid., vv. 812–13 and 866ff.
45. Ibid., vv. 912–14.
46. Scholium on Sophocles, *Ajax*, v. 134.
47. Sophocles, *Ajax*, vv. 866–69.
48. Sophocles, *Antigone*, vv. 223–32.
49. Ibid., v. 238. Cf., for example, the entrance of the messenger in *Ajax* addressing the chorus: "Friends, my first news is this" (v. 719).
50. The reversal comes from the difference between the chorus's and a character's normal modes of expression: the chorus sings, the character speaks.
51. Sophocles, *Ajax*, vv. 693–701.
52. Sophocles, *Antigone*, vv. 388–400.
53. Ibid., v. 441.
54. Ibid., vv. 435–40.
55. On *Women of Trachis* as a return tragedy, see above, chapter VIII, "Time and Action," under "The Return Tragedies."
56. On the technique of doubling in Sophocles, cf. above, chapter VIII, "Time and Action," under "The Technique of Doubling and New Developments in the Plot."
57. Sophocles, *Women of Trachis*, vv. 393–496.
58. Ibid., v. 402.
59. Ibid., v. 191.
60. Ibid., vv. 453–54 (cited above).
61. Ibid., vv. 188–89.
62. Ibid., v. 414.
63. Ibid., vv. 429ff.
64. Ibid., 434ff.
65. Ibid., 779–84.
66. Sophocles, *Oedipus the King*, vv. 1110–85.

67. Ibid., vv. 1005–6; cf. *Women of Trachis*, vv. 189–91.
68. Compare *Oedipus the King*, vv. 1132–46, with *Women of Trachis*, vv. 401–35.
69. Sophocles, *Oedipus the King*, vv. 1142–48.
70. Ibid., vv. 118–23; cf. vv. 753–56.
71. Ibid., vv. 758–64.
72. Ibid., vv. 836ff.
73. Ibid., vv. 1157; 1178–81.
74. Ibid., v. 1030.
75. Ibid., vv. 1177–81.
76. Sophocles, *Ajax*, vv. 1093–96.
77. Ibid., vv. 721ff.
78. See above in this same chapter.
79. See above.
80. Sophocles, *Women of Trachis*, vv. 453–54.
81. This scene has been analyzed in this same chapter, above.
82. Sophocles, *Oedipus the King*, v. 1123.
83. Jocasta had granted him his wish when he asked to leave the palace (vv. 763–64).
84. We have seen the importance Sophocles accorded to this question in *Ajax* as a reflection of reality. See F. Robert, "Sophocle, Périclès, Hérodote et la date d'Ajax," *Revue de Philologie* 38, 1964, pp. 213–27. According to Robert, *Ajax*, which dates from 445, is directed against Pericles' law of 451/450 that denied nobility to citizens whose parents were not Athenians.
85. For Telamon's exploits, see Sophocles, *Ajax*, vv. 434–36; for Telamon father of Teucer and Ajax, see v. 1008.
86. Sophocles, *Ajax*, v. 569.
87. Compare Sophocles, *Ajax*, vv. 460–66 (Ajax and Telamon) and vv. 1006–20 (Teucer and Telamon).
88. Sophocles, *Ajax*, vv. 1012–15; cf. v. 1020.
89. Ibid., vv. 1228, 1235, 1263 (with Teucer's indignant repetition of these insults, v. 1289: "I, the slave, the son of the barbarian mother").
90. Sophocles, *Ajax*, v. 190; *Philoctetes*, vv. 417 and 1311.
91. Scholium on Sophocles, *Ajax*, v. 190; cf. Hyginus, *Fables*, 201.
92. Sophocles, *Ajax*, v. 1393.
93. Sophocles, *Antigone*, vv. 582–92.
94. See above, chapter VI, "The Mythic Imagination," and below, chapter X, "Humans and the Gods."
95. Sophocles, *Antigone*, vv. 471–72. See below the analysis of the character of Antigone.
96. On the young women's heroism, see in particular below.
97. The character of the tutor is designated by his social function. However, it is not certain that this designation, given by the manuscripts in the list of *dramatis personae*, goes back to Sophocles himself. In the text, Orestes introduces this character by saying simply, "True friend and follower" (v. 23).
98. Sophocles, *Electra*, vv. 11–13.
99. Sophocles, *Oedipus the King*, vv. 1175 and 1178.
100. Sophocles, *Electra*, vv. 82–85, contrast with vv. 15–16.
101. Ibid., v. 1326.

102. Ibid., vv. 1346ff.
103. Sophocles, *Ajax*, vv. 666–68.
104. Ibid., v. 1045 and vv. 1223ff.
105. Ibid., v. 1050.
106. Ibid., vv. 445ff.
107. Sophocles, *Philoctetes*, vv. 263–65.
108. On Tecmessa as a silent character in the second part of the tragedy, see chapter VII, "Space and Spectacle."
109. Sophocles, *Antigone*, vv. 164ff.
110. Sophocles, *Oedipus the King*, vv. 408–11.
111. Sophocles, *The Women of Trachis*, vv. 749–812.
112. We might add that the image of the absent father remains for the hero a paradigm, especially in moments of crisis; see above the discussion of *Ajax*.
113. Cf. *Ajax*, vv. 749ff., and *Philoctetes*, vv. 603ff.
114. On the other hand, the corpse that is the stake in the same problem in *Ajax* remains visible all during the end of the tragedy.
115. Sophocles, *Electra*, vv. 1419–21. These words remind us of Aeschylus *The Libation Bearers*, v. 886: "I tell you the dead are killing the living." The presence of the dead was more crushing in Aeschylus, notably in the very long prayer to the dead Agamemnon (vv. 315–509). On the dead who kill the living in Sophocles, see for example H.D.F. Kitto, *Form and Meaning in Drama: A Study of Six Greek Plays and of Hamlet*, London: Methuen, 1956, pp. 193ff.
116. Sophocles, *Oedipus the King*, v. 101: "It is this blood [sc. that of Laius] which brings the tempest on our city."
117. The first reason Oedipus gives the chorus to justify his self-mutilation is the desire not to see his father again in Hades after his death (vv. 1371ff.).
118. Sophocles, *Women of Trachis*, v. 1163.
119. See above, chapter VII, "Space and Spectacle," under "The *Eccyclema* and the Exposition of Corpses."
120. Sophocles, *Ajax*, v. 1026.
121. Some scholars have connected this presence of the dead in Greek tragedy with the origin of tragedy, which they claim was originally a choral song in honor of a hero or a dead person on the occasion of the sacrifice of a goat (*trag-ōdia*). See for example F. Robert, "Les origines de la tragédie grecque," in J. Jacquot, *Le Théâtre tragique*, Paris, 1962, pp. 9–18. He sees tragedy as linked with the cult of the dead and understands in this perspective the evolution of tragedy "among the great classical poets since Aeschylus, whose whole theater is in revolt against the very origins of the tragic and puts on trial this cult of the dead from which tragedy arose: Aeschylus exalts human power, human justice, in opposition to the old conceptions. Then comes Sophocles' theater, a reaction of the common people, almost superstitious, and it shows us (apropos of the burial of Ajax or—and this its most sublime moment—apropos of Antigone's burial of Polynices, and even in *Oedipus the King*, where it is Laius who finally gets his vengeance at the same time that Apollo's oracle is fulfilled) the value of these old cults; Sophocles glorifies them, associates them with images and noble ideas and rehabilitates them" (pp. 17ff.).
122. See above.
123. Sophocles, *Ajax*, vv. 134 and 184.

124. Mentioned by Ajax: *Ajax*, vv. 434–40 and 462–65; v. 570. Mentioned by Teucer: vv. 1008–20; vv. 1299–305. Cf. the reference to Telamon in Homer, *Iliad* 8, vv. 267 and 281–85; and for Heracles expedition to Troy, see *Iliad* 5, vv. 640–42.

125. Sophocles, *Ajax*, vv. 434–40. This passage was cited in chapter VI, "The Mythic Imagination" (from a different point of view, the comparison of the generations in epic and in tragedy).

126. Sophocles, *Ajax*, vv. 462–65.

127. Sophocles, *Ajax*, v. 549.

128. Sophocles, *Ajax*, vv. 550–51.

129. Homer, *Iliad* 11, vv. 8ff.

130. Sophocles, *Ajax*, 3 17–20. The rejection of tears is a constant of the heroic nature; but heroes have moments when they are overcome by psychological or physical pain; cf. Heracles in *The Women of Trachis*, vv. 1071–75 (cited below) and in Euripides' *Heracles*.

131. Sophocles, *Ajax*, v. 326.

132. Ibid., vv. 470–72.

133. Ibid., vv. 479–80.

134. Ibid., vv. 481–82.

135. Ibid., vv. 483–84.

136. Ibid., vv. 523–24.

137. Ibid., vv. 548–49.

138. See above, chapter VIII, "Time and Action," under "Scenes, from Epic to Tragedy."

139. Homer, *Iliad* 6, vv. 484–93.

140. Sophocles, *Ajax*, vv. 594–95.

141. Ibid., vv. 650–53.

142. Ibid., v. 864.

143. Sophocles, *Philoctetes*, vv. 193ff.; vv. 265–67; vv. 1326–28.

144. Ibid., vv. 271ff.; cf. vv. 5–11.

145. Ibid., vv. 276–84.

146. Ibid., vv. 169–218.

147. Ibid., vv. 533–38.

148. Cf. *Ajax*, v. 364, and *Philoctetes*, v. 535.

149. Sophocles, *Philoctetes*, v. 226.

150. Ibid., v. 1321.

151. Ibid., v. 492.

152. For a detailed study of Philoctetes' realizations, see below, chapter XI, "Seeing, Hearing, and Understanding."

153. Cf. *Ajax*, vv. 356–59, and *Philoctetes*, vv. 1204–17.

154. Sophocles, *Philoctetes*, vv. 993–96.

155. Ibid., v. 1007.

156. For the enemies' laughter, cf. *Ajax*, v. 367, v. 382, and *Philoctetes*, v. 1023. On this theme, see B. Knox, *The Heroic Temper*, Berkeley, 1964, pp. 30–32; cf. also D. Mastronarde, *Euripides' Medea*, Cambridge, 2002 (introduction and commentary on v. 383). For curses cast on Odysseus and the Atreids, cf. *Ajax*, vv. 387–91, and *Philoctetes*, vv. 1113–15; vv. 1200–1202.

157. Compare *Ajax*, v. 386, and *Philoctetes*, v. 1387.

158. Sophocles, *Philoctetes*, vv. 1350ff.

159. See above, chapter VI, "The Mythic Imagination," under "Innovation and Creation: The Myth in Sophocles' *Philoctetes*."
160. Sophocles, *Philoctetes*, vv. 3–4.
161. The periphrasis "son of Achilles" is used fourteen times in the tragedy. All the characters refer to him this way: Odysseus (vv. 4, 50, 57, 1237–98), Philoctetes (vv. 260, 940, 1066), the chorus (v. 1220), the false merchant (vv. 542, 582), Heracles (v. 1433); cf. also v. 364 (words spoken by the Atreids reported by Neoptolemus in his speech of deception).
162. Sophocles, *Philoctetes*, v. 260.
163. Ibid., vv. 357–58.
164. Ibid., vv. 50–53.
165. Ibid., vv. 79–80.
166. Ibid., vv. 88–95.
167. Ibid., vv. 119–20.
168. Ibid., vv. 1006–12.
169. Ibid., v. 806; cf. vv. 965–66.
170. Ibid., v. 906.
171. Ibid., vv. 902–3.
172. Ibid., vv. 1310–13.
173. Ibid., vv. 94–95.
174. However, we must note a slight difference with Menelaus's view with regard to burying an enemy; see below, chapter X, "Humans and the Gods," under "The Dead, the Gods Below, and the Gods Above."
175. On this twofold origin, see above, in this same chapter, "The Fundamental Components of a Dramatic Character: Nature."
176. On Odysseus, the classic study is that of W. B. Standford, *The Ulysses Theme: A Study in the Adaptability of a Traditional Hero*, Oxford, 1954; see also J. Boulogne, "Ulysse: Deux figures de la démocratie chez Sophocle," *Revue de Philologie* 62, 1988, pp. 99–107.
177. *Ajax*, vv. 1374–75 (the chorus's laudatory judgment), and 1381–85 (Teucer's laudatory judgment). For further details regarding Odysseus's wisdom, see chapter X, "Humans and the Gods," under "The Voice of the Gods: Athena at the Beginning of *Ajax*."
178. Sophocles, *Philoctetes*, vv. 96–99.
179. Ibid., vv. 1049–52.
180. Ibid., v. 1307.
181. Ibid., vv. 1116–22 and vv. 1140–45.
182. On this partial rehabilitation, see J. Jouanna, "L'insertion du lyrisme dans le drame chez Sophocle: L'exemple d'un dialogue lyrique (Philoctète, vv. 1081–1217)," in J. Jouanna and J. Leclant (eds.), *La Poésie grecque antique*, Cahiers de la Villa "Kérylos" 14, Paris: De Boccard, 2003, pp. 151–68 (pp. 164–65).
183. For example, in 423 spectators also attended Aristophanes' comedy *The Clouds*, which ridiculed the excesses to which the sophists' new techniques led.
184. Sophocles, *Ajax*, vv. 1374–75.
185. Sophocles, *Philoctetes*, vv. 431–32. The word *sophos* is used in conjunction with *deinos* in v. 440, which confirms the meaning "clever."
186. Sophocles, *Philoctetes*, vv. 1244–49. [Translation modified.]

187. Ibid., vv. 1259–60. [Translation modified.]

188. I quote J. de Romilly, "L'actualité intellectuelle du Ve siècle: Le Philoctète de Sopho-cle," in J. de Romilly, *Tragédies grecques au fil des ans*, Paris: Les Belles Lettres, 1996, pp. 97–109 (p. 104). Also see P. W. Rose, "Sophocles' *Philoctetes* and the Teachings of the Sophists," *Harvard Studies in Classical Philology* 80, 1976, pp. 49–105.

189. In Euripides, we also see a deterioration of the image of Odysseus. Starting with *Hecuba* (424 BCE), Odysseus became the very type of the demagogue; cf. vv. 254ff., Hecuba to Odysseus: "A thankless race! all you who covet honor from the mob for your oratory." Sophocles' Odysseus is not the representative of a category as clearly shaped by contemporary reality.

190. See above in this same chapter, "The Fundamental Components of a Dramatic Character: The Social Function."

191. Sophocles, *Antigone*, vv. 173–74.

192. Ibid., vv. 178–91. See Demosthenes, *On the False Embassy*, 247, which cites Creon's declaration of principles (vv. 175–90) as a model of the conduct to be followed by a politician.

193. Sophocles, *Antigone*, vv. 192ff.

194. On this prohibition, see below, chapter X, "Humans and the Gods," under "The Dead, the Gods Below, and the Gods Above." On this line of argument as applied to Antigone, see W. Vischer, "Zu Sophokles Antigone," *Rheinisches Museum* 20, 1865, pp. 444–52, discussed by D. A. Hester, "Sophocles the Unphilosophical: A Study in the *Antigone*," *Mnemosyne*, ser. 4, 24, 1971, pp. 11–59, and V. J. Rosivach, "On Creon, Antigone and Not Burying the Dead," *Rheinisches Museum* 126, 1983, pp. 193–211.

195. Sophocles, *Antigone*, vv. 175–77.

196. Aristotle, *Nicomachean Ethics* 5, 1 (1130 a), attributes the maxim "Office will show a man" to Bias; cf. also the scholium on v. 175: "Some attribute to Chilon, others to Bias, the maxim saying that office will reveal a man"; see also Harpocration, s.v. *archè*.

197. On involuntary tragic irony in Sophocles, see below, chapter XI, "Seeing, Hearing, and Understanding."

198. This is where the word "anger" first appears in *Antigone*.

199. Herodotus, 3, 80 (criticism of monarchy by Otanes, who praises democracy). In Herodotus two feelings explain this transformation of the monarch into a tyrant: the feeling of *hubris* (pride) connected with the position of king, and the feeling of *phthonos* (envy) innate in every human being.

200. Sophocles, *Antigone*, v. 1261.

201. Contrast Sophocles, *Antigone*, vv. 1271–75, with v. 278. On Creon's realization of his mistakes, see chapter XI, "Seeing, Hearing, and Understanding."

202. On this plague, see above, chapter II, "Sophocles the Politician," under "The Plague in Athens and the Plague in *Oedipus the King*."

203. Sophocles, *Oedipus the King*, vv. 63–64.

204. Sophocles, *Antigone*, vv. 988–1090; cf. Homer, *Iliad* 1, vv. 68–120.

205. Sophocles, *Oedipus at Colonus*, vv. 656–67; vv. 904–31, etc. On the character of The-seus, see above, chapter VI, "The Mythic Imagination," under "The Image of Theseus, King of Athens, in Aeschylus, Euripides, and Sophocles: A Comparison."

206. Sophocles, *Oedipus the King*, vv. 523–24. [Translation modified.]

207. Thucydides 2, 22, 1: "He [Pericles], meanwhile, seeing anger and infatuation just

now in the ascendant, and confident of his wisdom in refusing a sally, would not call either assembly or meeting of the people, fearing the fatal results of a debate inspired by passion [*orgè*] and not by prudence [*gnomè*]." This comparison is not mentioned in the standard annotated editions. However, the antithesis is still not very frequent in the fifth century. The passage in Sophocles is, in fact, the oldest attestation of its use. In the fifth century, the two terms are compared four times by Thucydides and twice by Antiphon (*The Murder of Herod*). Hence it is implausible to say, with V. Ehrenberg, *Sophocles and Pericles*, Oxford, 1954, pp. 141ff., that the character of Oedipus reflects that of Pericles.

208. Sophocles, *Oedipus the King*, v. 398.

209. Ibid., v. 629.

210. Ibid., v. 738. Some scholars have thought that this verse was parodied by Aristophanes in his play *Peace*, v. 62 and v. 106, in the same way that the cry "Hear him, O city, O city of Thebes!" (v. 629) had been parodied in *The Acharnians*, v. 27.

211. For a detailed study of these phases in which Oedipus goes from lucidity to blindness and error before he realizes the truth, see below, chapter XI, "Seeing, Hearing, and Understanding," under "From Ignorance to Blindness and Distraction: The Prism of Feelings"; on becoming aware, see chapter XI, under "Coming to Awareness in *Oedipus the King*: Doubling and Orchestration"; and on the effects of awareness, chapter XI.

212. It is expressions such as "humans" and "mortals" that we encounter; see, for example, Sophocles, *Oedipus the King*, vv. 1288 and 1359.

213. Cf. ibid., v. 1288 and v. 1359.

214. Ibid., v. 1345.

215. Ibid., vv. 427–28.

216. Sophocles, *Ajax*, v. 293.

217. Sophocles, frag. 64, 4, and Euripides, *Heracleides*, v. 474.

218. Democritus, frag. 274.

219. Aristophanes, *Lysistrata*, vv. 507ff. (esp. v. 515).

220. Aristotle, *Politics*, 1 (1260 a 30).

221. On the place of these scenes in the action, see above, chapter VIII, "Time and Action," under "The Action in the Other Episodes: The Preparation and Accomplishment of Catastrophes."

222. For a dramaturgical commentary on this, see chapter VII, "Space and Spectacle."

223. Sophocles, *Antigone*, vv. 1246–50.

224. Ibid., vv. 1251–52.

225. Ibid., v. 1191.

226. Ibid., v. 1303.

227. Ibid., v. 1282. The use of the Greek adjective *pammètōr* ("totally a mother") is noteworthy. It is usually used to qualify the Earth goddess; cf. Aeschylus, *Prometheus Bound*, v. 90. The scholium on this passage clearly indicates what is emphatic in the choice of this adjective.

228. Sophocles, *Oedipus the King*, vv. 1073–75. There is, of course, a difference between Eurydice's departure and that of Jocasta. Whereas Eurydice says nothing at all, Jocasta expresses herself before leaving, twice crying out in despair and pitying Oedipus. But the silence when she goes out is of the same kind as that of Eurydice. She does not mention that she is leaving, and she does not explain why. This silence also

has the same meaning, which is discovered after the fact: she has decided to go back into the palace to commit suicide. Modern scholars are strangely perplexed by this silence mentioned by the chorus, which bothers them because Jocasta has just cried out, twice. Some of them want to transform the silence into a cry (Nauck, who emends the text), while others attenuate the meaning of the word "silence" by translating it as "reticence" (Jebb, Kamerbeek), and still others suppress the cries "theatrically" by arguing that they are asides and are not perceived by the chorus (L. Roussel's solution, mentioned by D. Bain, *Actors and Audience*, Oxford, 1977, p. 76). But the chorus's remark bears very precisely on the way Jocasta has just left, stunned by a terrible sorrow and remaining silent as she goes out. These are stage directions. Jocasta's wordless reaction contrasts with her cries of pain. It is a powerful additional dramatic effect that makes the silence of her departure even more impressive. Sophocles does not need advocates to defend an excellent cause.

229. Sophocles, *Oedipus the King*, vv. 634–36.
230. Ibid., v. 700 and v. 862.
231. Ibid., v. 716.
232. See her last words before she leaves in silence: ibid., vv. 1071–72.
233. Sophocles, *Oedipus the King*, vv. 1076–79.
234. Sophocles, *Women of Trachis*, vv. 813–20.
235. Ibid., vv. 464–67.
236. Ibid., v. 25.
237. Ibid., vv. 490–92.
238. Ibid., v. 543 (cf. v. 1233) and vv. 552–53.
239. Ibid., vv. 582–83.
240. On the comparison between Clytemnestra and Deianira, see chapter VI, "The Mythic Imagination," under "The Tragedies Whose Subjects Precede the Trojan War: The Myth of Heracles."
241. On Deianira's coming to awareness, see chapter XI, "Seeing, Hearing, and Understanding."
242. Sophocles, *Women of Trachis*, vv. 719–22.
243. Sophocles, *Ajax*, vv. 479–80, quoted above in this same chapter, under "Epic Heroes in Tragedy: Ajax and Philoctetes."
244. Sophocles also used a sudden, unjustified departure for a young man, Haemon, at the end of his quarrel with his father in *Antigone*. The presentation is analogous to that of other scenes in which a woman suddenly leaves, and particularly to Jocasta's departure. The chorus notes the departure and emphasizes it with concern (*Antigone*, vv. 766–67; compare with *Oedipus the King*, vv. 1073–75). The character who remains onstage expresses his anger by issuing one or several orders in the third person (*Antigone*, v. 768; compare with *Oedipus the King*, v. 1076). But unlike the women, the young man does not leave with the intention of committing suicide, even if in the end, after a further confrontation with his father in the virtual space, Antigone's prison, he commits suicide (vv. 1226ff.).
245. On the commos, see chapter VIII, "Time and Action," under "Women's Song in the Commoi."
246. Sophocles, *Antigone*, vv. 806–16. Already cited above; repeated here to show the parallel between the beginning and the end.
247. Sophocles, *Antigone*, vv. 937–43.

248. Ibid., v. 441.

249. Ibid., vv. 449–57.

250. They will be analyzed below in the context of relations between humans and the gods in chapter XI, "Humans and the Gods," under "The Dead, the Gods Below, and the Gods Above."

251. Sophocles, *Antigone*, vv. 1070–72; cf. v. 451 and v. 519.

252. Ibid., vv. 937–43 (cited above).

253. Ibid., v. 74. Cf. also v. 924.

254. Ibid., v. 72.

255. Ibid., vv. 502–4.

256. Sophocles, *Ajax*, v. 769; *Philoctetes*, vv. 251 and 1347; Electra, v. 60 (Orestes' *kléos*).

257. Sophocles, *Antigone*, 502; *Electra*, v. 985.

258. Sophocles, *Antigone*, vv. 61–64.

259. Ibid., v. 73.

260. Ibid., vv. 897–903.

261. Ibid., v. 523.

262. This verse was imitated by Euripides in *Iphigeneia in Aulis*, v. 407; and Plutarch cited it, using it to define the true friend: "He shares with him his loves, but not his hates" (53 c).

263. Sophocles, *Antigone*, vv. 643–44.

264. Ibid., vv. 688–700.

265. Aristotle, *Rhetoric*, 3, 17 (1418 b) (quoted above, chapter II, "Sophocles the Politician"): "Sophocles, also, introduces Haemon, when defending Antigone against his father, as if quoting the opinion of others."

266. Sophocles, *Antigone*, vv. 791–94.

267. Ibid., vv. 469–70. On this traditional morality, see for example M. Whitlock Blundell, *Helping Friends and Harming Enemies*, Cambridge, 1989.

268. Sophocles, *Antigone*, vv. 471–72.

269. Ibid., vv. 583–603.

270. On the family of the Labdacids, see chapter VI, "The Mythic Imagination."

271. Sophocles, *Antigone*, vv. 853–56.

272. Ibid., vv. 857–71.

273. On this theme of the presence of the dead, see above, in this same chapter, "The Dramatic Presence of Virtual Characters."

274. Sophocles, *Antigone*, vv. 929–30.

275. Ibid., vv. 905–12.

276. Herodotus, *Histories*, 3, 119. The parallel between the two passages does not necessarily indicate a direct influence of Herodotus on Sophocles.

277. J. W. Goethe, *Gespräch mit Eckermann*, March 28, 1826.

278. Aristotle, *Rhetoric*, 3 16 (1417 a 32–33).

279. Sophocles, *Antigone*, vv. 568–72.

280. Ibid., vv. 1240–41.

281. Ibid., v. 899. Antigone was not able to carry out Eteocles' burial rites; he had already been buried by Creon before the tragedy began (cf. v. 25). It is to Polynices that she addresses this vocative, as in v. 870.

282. Ibid., v. 517.

283. To these two silences on Antigone's part that make the character so enigmatic, we

must add Sophocles' silence regarding Antigone, which makes the treatment of the character enigmatic as well, the absence of any reference to her in the concluding scene of the tragedy; see chapter XI, "Seeing, Hearing, and Understanding."

284. Sophocles, *Antigone*, vv. 93–94; cf. already v. 86.

285. Ibid., v. 555.

286. In *The Libation Bearers*, Electra disappears at v. 580, when the revenge is carried out, on the orders of Orestes, who sends her into the palace to keep watch (the tragedy has 1,047 verses).

287. For a comparison between Sophocles' *Electra* and Aeschylus's *The Libation Bearers* from the point of view of structure, see chapter VIII, "Time and Action," under "The Return Tragedies." This preeminence of Electra also appears, but to a lesser degree, in Euripides' tragedy, also entitled *Electra*, though we do not know with certainty whether Euripides' tragedy is later than that of Sophocles.

288. Sophocles, *Electra*, vv. 32–37 (consultation of oracle of Apollo at Delphi) and vv. 69–70 (Orestes addressing himself to the palace): "I come by divine mandate to cleanse you as justice demands." Concerning the problem of the oracle's justness in *Electra*, see chapter X, "Humans and the Gods."

289. After describing his plan for deception to the tutor, Orestes hears a cry of lamentation (v. 77) inside the palace. He suggests that they remain to listen, but the tutor reminds him of his duty to take vengeance. See chapter X quoted in the preceding note.

290. Pity for his sister: for example, v. 1199. In the recognition scene duet, Electra's emotion is stronger than Orestes', at least at first, since in the strophe and antistrophe Electra sings whereas Orestes speaks; see chapter VIII, "Time and Action."

291. Sophocles, *Electra*, vv. 1424–27. For a discussion of the meaning of v. 1425, on which partisans of an ironic interpretation of *Electra* base themselves, see chapter XI, "Humans and the Gods."

292. Sophocles, *Electra*, vv. 680–763. On this narrative, see chapter VIII, "Time and Action."

293. See chapter VIII, "Time and Action," under "The Technique of Doubling and New Developments in the Plot" (doubling not only of the two sisters by introducing Chrysothemis, but also of the active element of the vengeance by introducing the tutor).

294. See Sophocles, *Electra*, v. 325; cf. *Antigone*, v. 1.

295. First scene: *Antigone*, vv. 1–99; *Electra*, vv. 328–471. Second scene: *Antigone*, vv. 531–81; *Electra* vv. 871–1057.

296. Sophocles, *Antigone*, vv. 471–72; see above.

297. Sophocles, *Electra*, vv. 341–44 and vv. 365–67.

298. See above, in this same chapter.

299. Compare Ismene's argument (*Antigone*, vv. 61–62) and that of Chrysothemis (*Electra*, vv. 997–98).

300. Compare Ismene's argument (*Antigone*, vv. 63–64) with that of Chrysothemis (*Electra*, v. 396 and v. 1014).

301. Compare Ismene's argument (*Antigone*, v. 68) with that of Chrysothemis (*Electra*, vv. 335–36).

302. Compare Ismene (*Antigone*, vv. 65–66) and Chrysothemis (*Electra*, v. 400).

303. For Antigone's piety, see *Antigone*, v. 943 (above). For Electra's piety, see *Electra*, v.

250, v. 464, v. 968, v. 1097; this is Sophocles' tragedy in which the word "piety" (*eusebeia*) is the most frequently used.

304. Compare Antigone (*Antigone*, v. 38) and Electra (*Electra*, v. 257).

305. Compare Antigone (*Antigone*, v. 72) and Electra (*Electra*, vv. 1320–21; cf. also v. 989). See also Deianira in *Women of Trachis*, vv. 721–22 (in the form of understatement).

306. Sophocles, *Electra*, vv. 990–91 and vv. 1015–16.

307. Ibid., vv. 1082–89. The chorus's admiration for Electra should be compared with Thebes's admiration for Antigone reported by Haemon (*Antigone*, vv. 694ff.).

308. Sophocles, *Electra*, vv. 189–91.

309. Ibid., vv. 217–20.

310. Ibid., v. 191.

311. Ibid., vv. 217–20.

312. Ibid., vv. 374–82.

313. Compare Sophocles, *Electra*, vv. 380–83, and *Antigone*, vv. 773–75 and vv. 885–86. Verbal reminiscences are obvious.

314. It is confirmed by Clytemnestra (Sophocles, *Electra*, vv. 626–27).

315. Sophocles, *Electra*, vv. 516–659. For Electra's hatred, see vv. 261–62.

316. The goddess Justice is first mentioned by Clytemnestra (especially v. 528; cf. also v. 551), who is then refuted by Electra (v. 561). This antilogy, in which Justice is predominant, takes on all its meaning in the broader context in which it is situated. The chorus, in the stasimon immediately preceding Clytemnestra's arrival, has predicted Justice's arrival (v. 477), basing itself on an interpretation of Clytemnestra's dream. For this dream, see chapter X, "Humans and the Gods," under "The Dream, a Message from Elsewhere." For Justice as the goddess of vengeance, see chapter X.

317. For the vocabulary of dishonor in Electra's speech, see especially v. 593; cf. also v. 559.

318. For the reaction of the powerful opponent, compare Sophocles, *Electra*, vv. 612–15, and *Antigone*, vv. 473–85: the same accusation of insolence (*hubris*). For the chorus's reaction, compare Sophocles, *Antigone*, vv. 471–72, and *Electra*, vv. 610–11: "I see her breathing fury"; the Greek term *menos*, meaning "fury," is extremely strong and has a pejorative connotation; the second part of the chorus's remark on justice (*dikè*) is the subject of much debate; see for example J. Bollack, "Une question de mot: Dikè dans Sophocle, *Electre*, v. 610 sq.," *Revue des Etudes Grecques* 101, 1988, pp. 173–80.

319. Compare Sophocles, *Electra*, vv. 938–1057, and *Antigone*, vv. 1–99.

320. Compare Sophocles, *Electra*, vv. 1091–20, and *Antigone*, vv. 71–72.

321. See Euripides, *Electra*, vv. 1177–232.

322. On these double entendres, see chapter XI, "Seeing, Hearing, and Understanding," under "The Signs of Tragic Irony: Consciously Ambivalent Language."

323. Sophocles, *Electra*, v. 1490.

324. Ibid., v. 1509.

325. Agamemnon and Menelaus, who usually form a pair in the Trojan plays (*Ajax* and *Philoctetes*), appear separately as characters at the end of *Ajax*, but they are only mentioned in *Philoctetes*. Agamemnon is also mentioned in *Electra*, as the father of Orestes (v. 2 and v. 695) and Electra (v. 125) and the possessor of the palace that his son saves (v. 1354).

326. For the two scenes in which the seer Tiresias appears, see chapter X, "Humans and

the Gods." For the repetition of the character of Oedipus, see below in this same chapter, "Oedipus Ten Years Later: Evolution and Continuity."

327. They have not yet reached the age of reason; see Sophocles, *Oedipus the King*, v. 1508. If we follow the chronology of the myth, they next appear in *Oedipus at Colonus*. Antigone has followed her father in his exile, whereas Ismene has remained in Thebes. But Ismene continues to be the link between Thebes and her father in exile. If she appears in the tragedy, it is out of concern about her father (v. 332). There is perfect harmony between the two sisters and their father (cf. vv. 324–25). Oedipus praises his two daughters' devotion, which he contrasts with the ignoble behavior of his sons (vv. 337–43). Antigone and Ismene are united at the end of the tragedy in a song of mourning after the death of their father. For Antigone in *Oedipus at Colonus*, see A. Machin, "L'autre Antigone," *Pallas* 44, 1996, pp. 47–56. Having set out for Thebes after Oedipus's death (cf. *Oedipus at Colonus*, vv. 1769–70), they quarrel in *Antigone* regarding the burial of Polynices. For Antigone and Ismene in that tragedy, see above, in the same chapter. Following the chronology of the myth, there is no incoherence in the presentation of the two sisters. But Sophocles wrote *Antigone*, the tragedy in which they quarrel, before the two others.

328. For *The Madness of Odysseus*, see chapter VI, "The Mythic Imagination." On these two tragedies, see appendix II, nos. 77 and 78.

329. On *Philoctetes at Troy*, see above chapter VI, "The Mythic Imagination," and appendix II, no. 109.

330. Odysseus's two-sidedness was studied above in this same chapter.

331. Sophocles, *Oedipus at Colonus*, vv. 728–1043.

332. For the absence of political ambition, see Sophocles, *Oedipus the King*, vv. 584ff.; for the absence of bitterness, see ibid., vv. 1422ff.

333. For the Creon of *Antigone*, see above.

334. There is a great contrast between the dialogue between Oedipus and Creon at the end of *Oedipus the King*, in which Oedipus declares that Creon is "noble" (*aristos*) and describes himself as "most vile" (*kakiston*) (v. 1433), and their dialogue in *Oedipus at Colonus*, where Oedipus describes Creon as the "most evil of men" (*kakiste*) (v. 866).

335. Creon mentions his age in his first words (v. 733). He is an old man addressing an old man, Oedipus (v. 744). Oedipus calls Creon an old man "barren of sense" (v. 931). Old age is, moreover, very present in *Oedipus at Colonus*. The expression "old man" is used sixteen times in this tragedy alone, whereas it is used only thirty-one times in all the extant tragedies. We also recall the chorus song (fourth stasimon, vv. 1236–38), where he refers to old age as the crowning misfortune of life, "wherein dwells every misery among miseries."

336. For Oedipus in *Oedipus the King*, see above.

337. We have seen that both Odysseus and Philoctetes are also title characters in two tragedies (see above, in this same chapter).

338. Sophocles, *Oedipus at Colonus*, vv. 1–8.

339. Ibid., v. 208.

340. Ibid., vv. 109–10.

341. Ibid, vv. 1258–61.

342. Sophocles, *Oedipus the King*, v. 1522.

343. Sophocles, *Oedipus at Colonus*, v. 8. The Greek word used here is *gennaion*, that is,

"what comes from the family." These are natural inherited qualities. The word is not used carelessly in the tragedy. It qualifies either *Oedipus* (v. 8 and v. 76) or the ideal king, Theseus (v. 569, v. 1042, v. 1636), or Oedipus's daughters (1640).

344. Compare Sophocles, *Philoctetes*, vv. 535–38 (with *stergein*, v. 538), and *Oedipus at Colonus*, vv. 5–8 (with *stergein*, v. 7).

345. Sophocles, *Philoctetes*, v. 538 and v. 535.

346. Compare Philoctetes' speeches when he is confronting Odysseus (*Philoctetes*, vv. 1004–44) and those of Oedipus when he is confronting Creon (*Oedipus at Colonus*, vv. 761–99), and then his son Polynices (*Oedipus at Colonus*, vv. 1348–96).

347. The later version of Oedipus is thus treated differently than the later versions of Creon or Odysseus.

348. Sophocles, *Oedipus at Colonus*, v. 394.

349. On Heracles at the end of *The Women of Trachis*, see also P. Holt, "The End of the *Trachiniae* and the Fate of Heracles," *Journal of Hellenic Studies* 109, 1989, pp. 69–80.

350. Sophocles, *Women of Trachis*, v. 1030 and v. 1084.

351. Ibid., vv. 1071–75. Compare Ajax's groans reported by Tecmessa in *Ajax*, vv. 317–22.

352. Ibid., vv. 1107–11.

353. Ibid., vv. 1112–13.

354. The expression "best of mortals" (or "of men") to designate Heracles has already been used by Deianira (v. 177) and by her son Hyllus (v. 811).

355. Sophocles, *The Women of Trachis*, vv. 1175–90.

356. Ibid., v. 1239; compare with v. 1202.

357. Ibid., vv. 1250–52.

358. Compare and contrast Sophocles, *Antigone*, vv. 631–765.

359. Sophocles, *Women of Trachis*, v. 1175.

360. Ibid., vv. 1259–63.

361. Sophocles, *Philoctetes*, vv. 1409–22.

362. See *LIMC*, 4, 1 and 2, s.v. Herakles.

363. The same use of the word "pyre" in *Philoctetes*, v. 1432 (and not "tomb"), and in *Women of Trachis*, vv. 1213 and 1254.

364. Ibid., vv. 1191–92.

365. Ibid., vv. 1210–11.

366. See Diodorus of Sicily, 4, 38, 4; Lucian, "On the Death of Peregrinus" 21; Ovid, *Metamorphoses*, 9, vv. 233ff.; Hyginus, Fab. 36; Seneca, *Hercules on Oetna*, vv. 1648ff. According to another variant, it was his father Poeas who lighted the pyre and received the bow, which he gave to his son; see Apollodorus, 2, 7, 7.

367. See Herodotus 9, 26; on the marriage of Hyllus and Iole, cf. Apollodorus 2, 7, 7 and 2, 8, 2.

368. See Diodorus 4, 38, 4; cf. Apollodorus 2, 7, 7. As for the connection between the pyre and the heroization, fragments of a bell-shaped krater from the villa Giulia (11688, provenance Conca) dating from the 460s, on which the presence of Athena near the pyre seems to indicate heroization. For a description and reproduction of these fragments, see Ch. Clairmont, "Studies in Greek Mythology and Vase-Painting: 1. Heracles on the Pyre," *American Journal of Archaeology* 57, 1953, pp. 85–89 (with plate 45).

369. Diodorus 4, 39, 1. For the sanctuaries of Heracles at Marathon and at the Cyno-sarges, see Herodotus, 7, 108 and 116; cf. Pausanias 1, 15, 3.

370. On the cult of Heracles on the summit of Mount Oeta, see in antiquity Livy, 36, 30: "Manilius Acilius climbed Mt. Oeta and made a sacrifice to Heracles at the place called Pyra, because it was there that the mortal body of the god was cremated"; cf. scholium T on *Iliad* 22, v. 159. Archeological discoveries were made there in August 1920 by N. Pappadakis, not on the highest summit but in a place called "Marmara" on the southeast flank of the mountain. Among these discoveries was a pyre with shards of black-figured vases, a few of which bore archaic dedications to Heracles, and two archaic bronze statues of Heracles. The shards indicate that the sacrifices continued from the archaic period down to Roman times. See *Bulletin de Correspon-dance hellénique* 44, 1920, *Chronique des fouilles*, pp. 392–93. On the publication of the excavations, see N. Pappadakis in *Deltion* 5, 1919, pp. 25ff. See also Y. Béquignon, *La vallée du Spercheios*, Paris, 1937, pp. 206ff. (with maps). On taking these cultural realities into account in interpreting Sophocles, see P. Holt, "The End of the *Tra-chiniai* and the Fate of Herakles," *Journal of Hellenic Studies* 109, 1989, pp. 69–80 (pp. 73–74).

371. Sophocles, *Women of Trachis*, v. 1270.

372. On Hyllus's indignation at Zeus's indifference, see chapter XI, "Seeing, Hearing, and Understanding," under "The Gods' View and Humans' Indignation."

Chapter X. Humans and the Gods

1. Sophocles, *Philoctetes*, v. 1415. On the problem of the god's apparition in the scenic space, see chapter VII, "Space and Spectacle," under "The Elevated Apparitions: The *Mechane* and the *Theologeion*." In Sophocles' extant tragedies, only two divinities appear before the spectators: Heracles at the end of *Philoctetes* and Athena at the beginning of *Ajax*. In the lost work, Athena must have also appeared in *Ajax the Locrian* (frag. 10 c Radt): she was furious with the Achaeans because of the abduc-tion of Cassandra; see appendix II, no. 3. Other divinities appear: Demeter in *Trip-tolemus* (frag. 598 Radt), one of Sophocles' oldest plays (see appendix II, no. 98); Thetis in *Those Who Dine Together* (frag. 562 Radt); see appendix II, no. 93; Apollo in *Niobe* (frag. 441 a Radt); see appendix II, no. 75. On the apparitions of the gods in Sophocles' tragedies, see R. Parker, "Through a Glass Darkly: Sophocles and the Divine," in J. Griffin (ed.), *Sophocles Revisited: Essays Presented to Sir Hugh Lloyd-Jones*, Oxford, 1999, pp. 11–30 (pp. 11–13).

2. *Iliad* 1, vv. 194ff.

3. Sophocles, *Philoctetes*, vv. 1440–44.

4. Ibid., vv. 1445–47.

5. Ibid., vv. 1350–51.

6. *Iliad* 24, v. 5, and *Odyssey* 9, v. 373.

7. Sophocles, *Antigone*, vv. 605–8.

8. The Greek noun denoting piety is not very frequently used in Sophocles' theater (eight times). But its distribution is significant. In addition to this message from Zeus, it is the value that guides both Antigone (twice) and Electra (four times); see chapter IX, "The Characters," under "The Heroism of Young Women: Antigone and Electra."

9. The oldest attestation is in the argument of *The Sack of Troy* (*Iliupersis*), ed. Bernabé 88, 13 (= ed. West 144, 25ff.): "Neoptolemus kills Priam who has taken refuge on the altar of Zeus Protector of the Hearth."

10. Sophocles, *Philoctetes*, v. 85 and v. 1051.

11. Compare *Philoctetes*, v. 1445, and *Ajax*, v. 14.

12. The elective affinities between Athena and Odysseus in book 13 of the *Odyssey*, where Athena inspects a grotto so Odysseus can deposit there his riches, have disappeared in the tragedy. The distance between humans and gods has grown. This distance is also visible in the mise en scène, where the gods appear at a level different from that of humans.

13. Euripides, *Hippolytus*, v. 1391: he recognizes her by her scent.

14. Sophocles, *Ajax*, vv. 51–52 and vv. 59–60.

15. See chapter VII, "Space and Spectacle," under "The Apparition of Athena at the Beginning of *Ajax*."

16. Sophocles, *Ajax*, vv. 118–20.

17. On Odysseus's double-sidedness in Sophocles' extant works, see chapter IX, "The Characters."

18. Sophocles, *Ajax*, vv. 121–26.

19. See ibid., v. 79, On this code, see M. Whitlock Blundell, *Helping Friends and Harming Enemies*, Cambridge, 1989.

20. Sophocles, *Oedipus the King*, vv. 1295–96; cf. *Ajax*, v. 924.

21. Sophocles, *Philoctetes*, v. 318.

22. Sophocles, *Oedipus the King*, v. 1422.

23. Ibid., v. 1473.

24. Ibid., v. 1477.

25. Aristotle, *Poetics*, 6 (1449 b 27), etc.

26. Sophocles, *Ajax*, vv. 127–33.

27. Pindar, *Pythian* 8, vv. 76–78 and vv. 92–96.

28. Since Pindar's *Pythian Ode* 8 is dated by the scholia to 446 BCE, Sophocles' *Ajax* must be later than that date.

29. See, for example, Plato, *Protagoras*, 343 a–b.

30. On the conclusion of Sophocles' tragedies, see chapter VIII, "Time and Action," under "The Final Ritual of the Exodos."

31. Sophocles, *Antigone*, vv. 1347–53.

32. Sophocles, *Ajax*, vv. 1418–20.

33. Ibid., v. 1348.

34. Ibid., vv. 1332 and 1343.

35. Ibid., v. 1365.

36. Ibid., v. 124.

37. Ibid., v. 1366.

38. Ibid., vv. 1374–75.

39. Ibid., v. 75 and v. 79. Verse 79 must not be taken literally as Athena's suggestion that he mock his enemy. It is an ironic provocation.

40. On the deliberate tragic irony in this scene, see chapter XI, "Seeing, Hearing, and Understanding," under "The Signs of Tragic Irony: Consciously Ambivalent Language."

41. Scholium on Sophocles, *Ajax*, v. 112.
42. For the explanation of Athena's wrath, see Sophocles, *Ajax*, vv. 758–77; the messenger's speech as a whole runs to thirty-six verses.
43. Sophocles, *Ajax*, vv. 758–61.
44. Ibid., vv. 764–69.
45. Ibid., vv. 434–40. See chapter IX, "The Characters," under "Epic Heroes in Tragedy: Ajax and Philoctetes."
46. Homer, *Iliad* 17, vv. 629–33.
47. Homer, *Odyssey* 4, v. 504.
48. Sophocles, *Ajax*, vv. 770–75.
49. Ibid., vv. 455–56. Compare *Electra*, vv. 696ff.: "When a god sends harm, not even the strong man can escape."
50. Sophocles, *Ajax*, vv. 666ff.
51. Sophocles, *Philoctetes*, vv. 603–19.
52. Ibid., vv. 1337–42.
53. The echoes between vv. 611ff. and v. 1334 are obvious. However, the second mention adds a collaboration between Philoctetes and Neoptolemus in destroying Troy.
54. It also reveals when Troy will fall: the same summer (v. 1340).
55. Sophocles, *Philoctetes*, v. 1338 and vv. 1341–42.
56. Ibid., vv. 54–120.
57. Ibid., vv. 1423ff.; see below, in the present chapter, "The Voice of the Gods: Heracles at the End of *Philoctetes*." A single shift: in the god's message Asclepius is mentioned instead of Asclepius's sons, the Asclepiads Machaon and Podaleirios, in the seer's prophecy. On the significance of this shift, see chapter III, "Sophocles the Religious Man," under "The Presence of Asclepius in Sophocles' Theater."
58. Sophocles, *Antigone*, vv. 988–1090; *Oedipus the King*, vv. 316–462.
59. Sophocles, *Antigone*, vv. 1035ff.; *Oedipus the King*, vv. 388ff.
60. Sophocles, *Antigone*, v. 1055.
61. Ibid., v. 1059: "You are a wise seer, but fond of doing injustice."
62. Sophocles, *Oedipus the King*, vv. 388ff.
63. In Sophocles, this accusation of venality against the seer can also be justified by a reference to the social reality of his time. The proliferation of mendicant seers had led to a deterioration of the profession's image. In fact, a testimony contemporary with Sophocles, that of Hippocrates in *On the Sacred Disease* (c. 1, Littré VI, 354, 13ff. = Grensemann 60, 20ff. = Jouanna 3, 20–24, 1ff.), gives, before Plato, an analogous image of the cupidity of this shady world formed by magi, purifiers, mendicant priests, and charlatans.
64. Sophocles, *Oedipus the King*, v. 709.
65. Ibid., vv. 711ff.
66. Ibid., v. 946.
67. Ibid., vv. 964–66.
68. Homer, *Iliad* 1, vv. 68ff.
69. Ibid., v. 106.
70. Ibid., v. 122.
71. Sophocles, *Antigone*, vv. 1033–36; cf. vv. 289ff., where the idea of a conspiracy and the connection with venality is mentioned for the first time. Sophocles, *Oedipus the*

King, vv. 380–89. In Sophocles, the challenge to seers is always made by the powerful and is not without a political dimension, whereas in Euripides' *Helen* (vv. 744ff.) a simple soldier complains of Calchas's and Helenus's charlatanism.

72. Homer, *Iliad* 12, vv. 237–40.

73. However, there is still an important difference. Hector's criticism of divination does not in any way put in question the gods. If the Trojan hero makes this criticism, it is in the name of his trust in Zeus's intentions (*Iliad* 12, vv. 235–36 and v. 241).

74. In any case, the ambiguity of the oracles' answers resulted in their being in fact debated. We can take as an example the two successive oracles issued by the Pythia at Delphi regarding Salamis at the time of the Persian invasion; concerning the second oracle, Themistocles had an interpretation different from that of the chresmologists (Herodotus 7 140–43).

75. Cicero, *De divinatione* 1, c. 3, 5.

76. Hippocrates, *Régime dans les maladies aiguës*, c. 3 Littré VI, 242, 3–7 (= c. 8 Joly 39, 15–20).

77. Sophocles, *Oedipus the King*, vv. 906–10.

78. Sophocles, *Antigone*, v. 1178.

79. Sophocles, *Oedipus the King*, vv. 1182–85.

80. Ibid., v. 747.

81. Ibid., v. 1011.

82. Sophocles, *Antigone*, vv. 998–1022.

83. Ibid., vv. 1064ff.

84. Sophocles, *Oedipus the King*, vv. 298ff.

85. Ibid., v. 410.

86. Homer, *Iliad* 1, v. 72. The seer Calchas knows the present.

87. Sophocles, *Women of Trachis*, vv. 1159–73. Zeus's oracle at Dodona is mentioned here allusively: the sanctuary is designated by the periphrasis "the grove of the Selli" (the Selli were the priests of the sanctuary, the oracle's interpreters, and subject to ritual obligations such as sleeping on the ground; cf. Homer, *Iliad* 16, vv. 234ff.). The oracle is designated by "my father's oak of many tongues." This is Zeus's great oak; the rustling of its leaves in the wind was interpreted (cf. Homer, *Odyssey* 14, vv. 327–28, and 19, vv. 296–97). Here Sophocles combines and adapts the information given in the *Iliad* and the *Odyssey*. On the sanctuary and the oracle of Dodona, in addition to H. W. Parke's classic study, *The Oracles of Zeus: Dodona, Olympia, Ammon*, Oxford, 1967, see A. Gartziou-Tatti, "L'oracle de Dodone, mythe et rituel," *Kernos* 3, 1990, pp. 175–84; on Dodona in the theater, see D. Marotta, "Dodona nel teatro ateniese del V secolo a. C.," *Hormos* 3–4, 2001–2, pp. 119–48.

88. Sophocles, *Women of Trachis*, vv. 46ff.; vv. 76–85; vv. 164–74.

89. Heracles left fifteen months earlier (vv. 44ff.). That is the length of time indicated on the oracular tablet (vv. 164ff.) for the fulfillment of the oracle. Speaking to the chorus, Deianira emphasizes this temporal concordance (vv. 173ff.).

90. This is already the case in *Ajax*, where we learn from the messenger reporting the seer Calchas's prophecy that Athena will pursue Ajax with her vengeful anger only for this single day, leaving some hope for escape if Ajax manages to get through it (vv. 756ff. and 778ff.).

91. Sophocles, *Electra*, vv. 32–37.

92. The tutor's arrival: vv. 660ff. Orestes' arrival: v. 1098. The tutor's emergence to inform Orestes as to what is happening in the palace: vv. 1326ff.

93. Sophocles, *Electra*, vv. 82–85.

94. Euripides, *Electra*, vv. 1190–91.

95. Ibid., vv. 1245ff.

96. Sophocles, *Electra*, v. 70.

97. Ibid., vv. 1424ff. For a comparable conditional clause expressing confidence in the veracity of Apollo's oracles, cf. *Oedipus at Colonus*, v. 623: "My slumbering and buried corpse, cold in death, will drink their warm blood, if Zeus is still Zeus, and Phoebus, the son of Zeus, speaks clear."

98. On the different interpretations of the tragedy by modern critics, see the clear and convenient discussion in J. H. Kells, *Electra*, Cambridge University Press, 1973, pp. 2–5. The ironic interpretation, which Kells follows, goes back to J. Sheppard, "A Defense of Sophocles," *Classical Review* 41, 1927, pp. 2–9 and 163–65. Scholars continue to differ regarding the final interpretation. More recently, see M. Lloyd, *Sophocles*: Electra, Duckworth, 2005. In his chapter 6 ("Matricide," pp. 99–115), Lloyd reviews the traditional interpretation, which he calls "affirmative," and the ironic interpretation, which he tries to justify.

99. On the Erinyes in Aeschylus, see *Libation Bearers*, vv. 1047ff.; and in Euripides, *Electra*, vv. 1252ff. For the chorus's explicit reference to Justice and to the Erinyes in Sophocles' *Electra* in the vengeance of Agamemnon, see the first stasimon, vv. 477 and 491; cf. also, for the Erinyes, the fourth stasimon, v. 1388. See below, in this same chapter.

100. Sophocles, *Electra*, vv. 1376–83. Conversely, Clytemnestra's prayer to Apollo (vv. 634ff.) was followed by an effect that seemed at first to be favorable, but was in reality contrary; see chapter XI, "Seeing, Hearing, and Understanding."

101. Sophocles, *Electra*, v. 1423. In Euripides' *Electra* (vv. 1203–5) the chorus, on the contrary, reproaches Electra for having involved her brother in an impious crime. The two passages are related. But which author is distinguishing himself from the other?

102. Sophocles, *Electra*, vv. 1426ff.

103. In Aeschylus, as in Euripides, Aegisthus's murder precedes that of Clytemnestra.

104. Sophocles, *Electra*, vv. 1505–7. The use of the adjective *panourgo* (lawbreaking) to designate the despised group to which Aegisthus belongs (v. 1507 *panourgon*) was already used by Aeschylus's Orestes in his long prayer to the dead (*Libation Bearers*, v. 384), but the term did not have the crucial place that it has in Sophocles in Orestes' last words.

105. Sophocles, *Electra*, v. 1498. This verse is the second (and last!) in the passage cited by the partisans of the ironic interpretation of Sophocles' *Electra*. M. Lloyd (quoted above) calls it "the jewel in the crown of the ironic interpretation, since it seems to refer to the imminent pursuit of Orestes by the Furies," and "the target of attempts by advocates of the affirmative interpretation to play down its significance." The matter is presented as if it were an amusing match between two teams of scholars arguing over two verses. But where is the spectator . . . of Sophocles' tragedy?

106. Aegisthus is a criminal without remorse, because he makes a sarcastic joke about his victim, Agamemnon, whom he calls a bad seer because he was incapable of predict-

ing his own death (v. 1500). This possible allusion to Aeschylus is part of the wider play of intertextuality between Sophocles' *Electra* and Aeschylus's *Libation Bearers*.

107. Sophocles, *Electra*, vv. 1508–10. This closure at the end of Sophocles' *Electra* contrasts with the end of Aeschylus's *Libation Bearers*, where the chorus wonders when all this will cease (vv. 1074–76).

108. See chapter VI, "The Mythic Imagination."

109. Sophocles, *Oedipus the King*, vv. 1329–30.

110. Ibid., vv. 1366ff. and vv. 1522ff.

111. Sophocles, *Oedipus at Colonus*, vv. 87–95. On this addition of the second part of the oracle, see chapter VI, "The Mythic Imagination," under "The Death of Oedipus in *Oedipus at Colonus* and the Apollo of Delphi."

112. Sophocles, *Oedipus at Colonus*, vv. 41–45. This realization of the fulfillment of an oracle is comparable to that of Heracles in *The Women of Trachis*, v. 1143. For a fully developed comparison, see chapter XI, "Seeing, Hearing, and Understanding."

113. Sophocles, *Oedipus at Colonus*, v. 273.

114. Ibid., vv. 387ff. From that point on, Oedipus can draw on the combined teachings of these oracles, which he knows through Ismene, and the "old oracles" of Apollo that he knew by himself (vv. 452–54). These old oracles are the one that Oedipus earlier announced in person (vv. 87ff.). They concern not only "Oedipus's parricide and incest" (ed. Dain and Mazon, p. 97, n. 1) but also and especially the predicted end of his misfortunes. With these two categories of oracles, we find ourselves back in a configuration analogous to that of *The Women of Trachis*, in which new oracles are added to old ones (see above). However, in *The Women of Trachis*, the new oracles were earlier than the time of the tragedy, whereas in *Oedipus at Colonus* they are announced in the course of the tragedy.

115. Sophocles, *Oedipus at Colonus*, v. 394.

116. When she announced the new oracles to Oedipus, Ismene also announced the arrival of Creon (*Oedipus at Colonus*, vv. 396ff.). Oedipus himself announces these new oracles to Theseus (vv. 603–5), interpreting what Ismene had said (v. 411), probably in light of the old oracle, to adapt it to his interlocutor. Creon, diplomatically, does not mention them in front of Oedipus. But Polynices clearly refers to them (*Oedipus at Colonus*, vv. 1331–32: "For if anything trustworthy comes from oracles, they said that whoever you join with in alliance will have victorious strength"). This presentation is entirely comparable to what Ismene said (v. 392). These new oracles proceeding from Apollo of Delphi must not be confused with the prophecies of the "seers" (probably Argives) mentioned by Polynices in v. 1300 (*pace* Kamerbeek *ad* 1300: "This can only refer, but in vague way, to the *manteumata* mentioned by Ismene 387"). The plural "seers" (*manteōn*) in v. 1300 (not to be translated by "oracles," as Mazon does; Masqueray had correctly translated this as *devins* ("seers") excludes any confusion, because Sophocles never uses this plural to designate the Apollo of Delphi.

117. Sophocles, *Oedipus at Colonus*, vv. 1456ff.

118. Ibid., vv. 1460ff.

119. Ibid., vv. 1623–30.

120. See J. Jouanna, "Homme d'exception et homme d'élection chez Pindare et Sophocle," in *Signes et destins d'élection dans l'Antiquité*, Besançon, 2006, pp. 137–54.

121. The standard work on this subject is G. Devereux, *Dreams in Greek Tragedy: An*

Ethno-psycho-analytical Study, Berkeley: University of California Press, 1976. Well-informed and bursting with ideas, this work proposes a philological and psychoanalytic reading that must be used critically. The bibliography on dreams in antiquity is abundant, but there is no study devoted to Sophocles in particular. The most recent synthetic study is that of Chr. Walde, *Die Traumdarstellungen in der griechisch-römischen Dichtung*, Munich: K. G. Saur, 2001.

122. Aeschylus, *Persians*, vv. 159–200.

123. Sophocles, *Women of Trachis*, vv. 175–76. The comparison with *The Persians* is all the less arbitrary because in fact we find a comparable effect of alliteration; cf. Aeschylus, *Persians*, v. 205 (Atossa addressing a male chorus): *Phoibou: phobō. . . philoi*, and Sophocles, *Women of Trachis*, v. 176 (Deianira addressing a female chorus): *phobō, philai*.

124. On the dream in Sophocles' *Electra*, see recently Chr. Walde (cited above), pp. 125–44 (with the bibliography).

125. Sophocles, *Electra*, vv. 417–25.

126. Ibid., vv. 459ff.

127. Ibid., vv. 474–501 (first stasimon).

128. Sophocles, *Oedipus the King*, vv. 980–83.

129. This is involuntary tragic irony. On this type of tragic irony in Sophocles, see chapter XI, "Seeing, Hearing, and Understanding."

130. For the critique of psychoanalytic interpretations of *Oedipus the King*, see J. P. Vernant, "Œdipe sans complexe," in J.-P. Vernant and P. Vidal-Naquet, *Mythe et tragédie en Grèce ancienne*, Paris: Maspero, 1972, pp. 77–98 (pp. 97–98), with supplements by J. Bollack, *L'Œdipe-Roi*, vol. 3, Lille, 1990, pp. 636ff. (commentary on vv. 981ff.). The content of the dream (the son sleeping with his mother) is found in Herodotus (6, 107) and also in Plato (*Republic* 9, 571 c–d). Contrary to what Jocasta thinks, these dreams are considered significant in Herodotus and Plato. But they are interpreted differently. In Herodotus, it is a metaphorical interpretation: for the exiled tyrant Hippias, who wants to return to Athens with the Persians at Marathon, it is a favorable omen for his possession of the mother-earth; in Plato, it is a physiological interpretation (the domination of the animal part of the soul during the night). HH

131. Compare above chapter III, "Sophocles the Religious Man."

132. On Stesichorus's *Oresteia*, see chapter VI, "The Mythic Imagination," and n. 107. The presence of Clytemnestra's dream as early as Stesichorus is proven by a quotation Plutarch makes in "On the Delays of Divine Vengeance," c 10 (555a): "So that Stesichorus may seem to have composed the dream of Clytemnestra, to set forth the event and truth of things:

> Then seemed a dragon to draw near,
> With mattery blood all on his head besmeared;
> Therefrom the king Plisthenides appeared."

But the interpretation of the dream is subject to debate. The serpent definitely represents Agamemnon, who head has been wounded by Clytemnestra. But who is the king who descends from Plisthenes? Probably Orestes, being born from the serpent's head to avenge his father (see for example G. Devereux, cited above); other scholars think it is Agamemnon appearing in his human form (see A. F. Garvie, *Aeschylus, Choephori*, Oxford, 1986, p. xix–xxi)

133. Aeschylus, *Libation Bearers*, vv. 514–52.

134. Ibid., vv. 527–34.

135. Ibid., vv. 549ff.

136. The content of the dream in Sophocles has long been compared with the content of Astyage's dream in Herodotus 1, 108 ("He dreamed that a vine grew out of the genitals of this daughter, and that the vine covered the whole of Asia"). This is a dream announcing the birth of Cyrus (the Great), who ended up reigning over all Asia and thus founding the Persian Empire that succeeded that of the Medes. In Sophocles the dream does not conflate, as in Herodotus, the two orders of birth, animal and vegetal.

137. Sophocles, *Electra*, vv. 644ff.: "That vision which I saw last night [645] in ambiguous dreams."

138. On the reestablishment of freedom, see Sophocles, *Electra*, vv. 1509ff. For the absence of the consequences of the matricide, see above, in this same chapter, "Is Apollo's Oracle Advising Orestes to Take Revenge Just?"

139. For libations and sacrifices in Greek tragedy, see J. Jouanna, "Libations et sacrifices dans la tragédie grecque," *Revue des Études Grecques* 105, 1992, pp. 406–34. I shall not repeat here what was said in this article on perverted sacrifice in *The Women of Trachis*, vv. 756ff. (= pp. 429–30). See also Jouanna, "Espaces sacrés, rites et oracles dans l'Œdipe à Colone de Sophocle," *Revue des Études Grecques* 108, 1995, pp. 38–58. Neither shall I return to the rite of libations in *Oedipus at Colonus*, vv. 469–92 (= pp. 44–48), which I commented on in detail in the same article.

140. Sophocles, *Electra*, vv. 431–37.

141. Aeschylus, *Libation Bearers*, vv. 22–164.

142. As for Orestes' libations on his father's tomb, they are mentioned at the beginning of the tragedy (v. 84); as for the young women's offerings, they are locks of hair and a girdle (vv. 449–52). Orestes' offerings are discovered by Chrysothemis when she goes to put offerings on the tomb, and when she returns she tells Electra about what she discovered (vv. 893ff.): libations of milk, flowers, and a lock of hair.

143. Sophocles, *Electra*, vv. 431–37.

144. Orestes' libations on his father's tomb are mentioned at the beginning of the tragedy (v. 84); the young women's offerings are locks of hair and a girdle (vv. 449–52); Orestes' offerings are discovered by Chrysothemis when she takes offerings to the tomb, and when she returns she recounts this discovery to Electra (vv. 893ff.): libations of milk, flowers, and a lock of hair.

145. Sophocles, *Electra*, vv. 472–77 and 489–91.

146. Sophocles, *Women of Trachis*, 807–9.

147. Sophocles, *Ajax*, vv. 1389–92; cf. vv. 835–44. For the conjunction of Justice and Erinys, compare Aeschylus, *Agamemnon*, vv. 1432ff., where Justice is also the one who fulfills; Euripides, *Medea*, vv. 1389–90. Beyond the tragedy, see Heraclitus DK 22 B 94 (= Plutarch, "On Exile," 11 (604 a): "'The Sun will not transgress his bounds,' says Heracleitus; 'else the Erinyes, ministers of Justice, will find him out'"; see also the discussion of the Erinyes in the Papyrus of Derveni (col. 1ff. = ed. G. Betegh, 2004, pp. 4ff.); in col. 4 the passage from Heraclitus is cited more extensively than it is in Plutarch.

148. Sophocles, *Electra*, vv. 110–17.

149. In Homer, we already find an alternation between *Erinys* in the singular (*Iliad* 9, v. 571; 19, v. 87; *Odyssey* 15, v. 234) and *Erinyes* in the plural (*Iliad* 9, v. 454; 15, v. 204;

19, v. 259 and v. 418; 21, v. 412; *Odyssey* 2, v. 135; 11, v. 280; 17, v. 475; 20, v. 78). In Hesiod, the Erinyes are the daughters of the Earth splashed with the bloody seed of Uranos (*Theogony*, v. 185). In Sophocles (*Oedipus at Colonus*, v. 40), they are the daughters of Earth and Skotos (= the obscure). On the Erinyes in general, see E. Wüst, *RE* supp. 8, 1956, pp. 82–166; M. A. Visser, *The Erinyes: Their Character and Function in Classical Greek Literature and Thought*, University of Toronto Press, 1980; *LIMC*, s.v. "Erinys" (H. Sarian-P. Delev). On the Erinyes in Greek tragedy, see H. Lloyd-Jones, "Les Erinyes dans la tragédie grecque," *Revue des Études Grecques* 102, 1989, p. 19 (= "Erinyes, semnai theai, Eumenides," in E. Craik [ed.], *Owls to Athens: Essays on Classical Subjects Presented to Sir Kenneth Dover*, Oxford, 1990, pp. 203–11).

150. For an invocation to Hades and Persephone, compare, for example, Homer, *Iliad* 9, v. 569.

151. Compare *Oedipus at Colonus*, v. 1548: Hermes pompos guides the blind Oedipus to his last home.

152. Sophocles, *Electra*, v. 1419. The deification of *Ara* or *Arai* already appears in Aeschylus; for the singular, see *Seven against Thebes*, v. 70 (where *Ara* is already cited with *Erinys*) and, for the plural, *The Eumenides*, v. 417 (where *Arai* is a denomination of the Erinyes). In Sophocles, the divinities are distinct. There was probably a temple of Ara in Athens (Aristophanes, *Horai* [*Seasons*], PCG III 2, frag. 585 Kassel and Austin = Hesychius, s.v. *Aras hieron*): "There is a sanctuary of Ara in Athens. Aristophanes in his *Horai*." On the nature and function of the ara, see D. Aubriot-Sevin, *Prière et conceptions religieuses en Grèce ancienne jusqu'à la fin du Ve siècle av. J.-C.*, Lyon, 1992, pp. 350ff. (with the bibliography).

153. Sophocles, *Electra*, vv. 1384–97.

154. Aeschylus, *Libation Bearers*, v. 924 and v. 1054, "the hounds of wrath"; see also Euripides, *Electra*, v. 1252, "the dread goddesses of death, the ones who glare like hounds."

155. See for example Apollodorus, *Library* 1, 1, 4: "From the drops of the flowing blood were born Furies, to wit, Alecto, Tisiphone, and Megaera"; cf. *Argonautica Orphica*, v. 968, and Hymn 69, v. 2. Photius, *Lexicon*, s.v. *semnai theai*: "The venerable deities: by euphemism, the Erinyes; the same are also called the Eumenides. There are three of them."

156. In Euripides' *Electra*, the Erinyes play no role at all in the course of the tragedy, but they are referred to as "the dread goddesses of death" (*Keres*) in the final message where the Dioscuri announce the fate of Orestes after the tragedy (vv. 1252ff.). This announcement corresponds more or less to what happens in Aeschylus's *The Eumenides* (with the variants). Orestes is persecuted by the goddesses, who drive him mad; he will be judged and acquitted by the tribunal of the Areopagus, by tie vote; the "dreadful deities" will disappear underground, where they will have an oracle. In Euripides, even more than in Aeschylus, there is a strong opposition between the goddesses of vengeance, on the one hand, and Apollo and Athena on the other hand. The theme of Orestes and the Erinyes is taken up by Euripides in two other tragedies, *Iphigeneia in Tauris* and *Orestes*.

157. Sophocles uses it twice, in addition to *Electra*, see *Ajax*, v. 837 (*semnas Erinys*): Ajax's invocation in his monologue before committing suicide (v. 837). The context is analogous: a prayer to the Erinyes to avenge a dead man.

158. The Athenian usage is reflected in *Oedipus at Colonus* in referring to their sanctuary

at Colonus. They are never referred to in the tragedy by the term "Erinyes." The local residents call them the "Eumenides" (v. 42). We also find other euphemisms: vv. 89–90, "venerable Goddesses," and v. 127, "invincible Virgins." For the Athenian use of the euphemisms "Eumenides" and "venerable Goddesses," see Pausanias, *Description of Greece*, 1, 28, 6 ("the goddesses which the Athenians call the August, but Hesiod in the Theogony calls them Erinyes") and Harpocration, *Lexicon*, s.v. *semnai theai* (venerable goddesses): "the Athenians call the Erinyes by this name" (definition repeated in Photius, *Lexicon*). It is significant that at the end of *Oedipus at Colonus* the word "Erinys" is used in a different context, that of the Erinys or the Erinyes of Oedipus (v. 1299 and v. 1434).

159. Sophocles, *Electra*, v. 276 (concerning Clytemnestra): "fearing no Erinys."

160. Ibid., v. 37.

161. Electra's prayer to Apollo (vv. 1376–83) precedes the chorus's song (vv. 1384–97).

162. Sophocles, *Ajax*, vv. 1057–63.

163. Ibid., vv. 1125–32.

164. On this law concerning traitors and sacrileges, see Xenophon, *Hellenica* 1, 7, 22 ("if anyone shall be a traitor to the state or shall steal sacred property . . . he shall not be buried in Attica") and Pseudo-Plutarch, *Life of Antiphon*, 23–24 (the burial of Antiphon, accused of treason, was forbidden in Athens and on the territory of the Athenian Empire). In his *Laws* (9, 873b–874b, 960b) Plato continued to recommend forbidding burial for those who had stolen sacred objects, sorcerers, and certain murderers. For the necessity of burying a dead person and the exceptions to this rule, see R. Parker, *Miasma, Pollution and Purification in Early Greek Religion*, Oxford, 1983, pp. 43–48 (with reference to Sophocles' theater, and especially to *Antigone*).

165. Thucydides 1, 138, 6.

166. Sophocles, *Ajax*, v. 1305.

167. On Odysseus's wisdom, see chapter IX, "The Characters," and especially the present chapter.

168. Sophocles, *Ajax*, vv. 1342–45.

169. Ibid., vv. 1563–64.

170. Sophocles, *Antigone*, vv. 26ff.

171. Ibid., vv. 198–206.

172. Ibid., vv. 282–89.

173. Aeschylus, *Persians*, v. 810; cf. here v. 286.

174. Sophocles, *Antigone*, v. 77.

175. Ibid., vv. 449–60. The passage has already been quoted in part in the study of the character of Antigone in chapter IX, "The Characters," under "The Heroism of Young Women: Antigone and Electra."

176. Aristotle, *Rhetoric*, 1, 13 (1373 b 2–13), with the quotation of verses 456–57.

177. The fact that the first occurrence of the expression "unwritten law" in the extant literature is found in Sophocles does not mean that he was its creator. In fact, the philosopher Socrates used this expression, while discussing justice with the sophist Hippias, as if it were well-known (Xenophon, *Memorabilia*, 4, 4, 19). Socrates refers, as does Sophocles, to the divine laws that are incumbent on all humans in all countries. This especially suggests that Sophocles was not the creator of the expression is that it implies the written laws of the city, which did not exist in the time of the

myth. Creon's laws are proclaimed by a herald. This is one of the numerous anachronisms that result from the insertion of contemporary reality into myth, anachronisms to which the public was not sensitive. The classification of laws into two categories, general laws common to all people and particular laws that vary according to the states, was usually expressed by the distinction between written and unwritten laws; cf. for example Aristotle, *Rhetoric*, I, 13 (1373 b), quoted above (there are also unwritten laws peculiar to states, the ancestral laws). On written and unwritten laws, the bibliography is vast. After R. Hirzel's fundamental work in German, *Agraphos Nomos* (1900), see in English M. Ostwald, *Nomos and the Beginning of the Athenian Democracy*, Oxford, 1969, and in French J. de Romilly, *La Loi dans la pensée grecque des origines à Aristote*, Paris, 1971, pp. 25–49.

178. Sophocles, *Antigone*, vv. 471–72. The passage is quoted and commented on in chapter IX, "The Characters."

179. Creon was not the only one who considered his decree a law (v. 449). At the outset, this legitimate king (v. 174) is in no way presented as a tyrant. The royal council, constituted by the chorus, does not contest the king's right to declare laws for all citizens, living or dead (vv. 213ff.). Ismene, for her part, had refused to follow Antigone in her revolt against established authority, not wanting and not being able to oppose the law (v. 59). Later on, even Antigone uses the term "law" (v. 847) to designate Creon's decision to send her to her underground prison.

180. Sophocles, *Antigone*, v. 487 (the Zeus of the hearth) and vv. 658–59 (the Zeus of blood ties).

181. Ibid., vv. 1039–44.

182. For the sophistic origin of the theory of the impossibility of contaminating the gods, see W. Schmid, *Philologus* 62, 1903, p. 9; cf. also G. W. Bond, *Euripides: Heracles*, Oxford, 1981, p. 376 (n. on vv. 1232–34).

183. Euripides, *Heracles*, v. 1232.

184. Sophocles, *Antigone*, vv. 1068–76.

185. Ibid., v. 519.

186. In his last tragedy, *Oedipus at Colonus*, Sophocles returned to the problem of the interdiction on burying an exile in his homeland, but there the theme plays a secondary role, because the central problem is that of the reception of the exile in a foreign land. The Thebans want to bring Oedipus back close to Thebes, without however burying him on Theban territory, because he has shed his family's blood by killing his father (v. 407; cf. v. 785). The pollution excludes burial in the homeland.

187. On hymns in general in Sophocles' work, see W. D. Furley and J. M. Bremer, *Greek Hymns*, vol. 1, Tübingen, 2001, pp. 297–309 (with a convenient table of these hymns, p. 299), and vol. 2, pp. 269–93 (a study of each hymn with bibliography, critical text, and commentary). The hymn to Dionysus in *Antigone* is a prayer by the chorus to keep the illness outside the city of Thebes. In *Oedipus the King*, where the theme of the illness of Thebes is developed much more fully, one of the chorus's songs has the same function. This is the hymn of the parodos (vv. 158–215), in which the chorus of Theban elders invokes in succession two triads of divinities, first Athena, Artemis, and Apollo, and then Zeus, Apollo, and finally Dionysus, asking them to come to deliver Thebes from the plague that is ravaging the city. A comparison of these two

hymns would be pertinent, especially the invocation to Dionysus, who is also called Bacchus in *Oedipus the King* (v. 211).

188. Composed of two strophe/antistrophe pairs, it takes in reality the form of two hymns that succeed and reinforce one another. The first hymn, the longer of the two, occupies strophe 1, antistrophe 1, and strophe 2. It includes the two conventional parts, first the invocation to the god (vv. 1115–39), then the prayer (vv. 1140–45). The second hymn, constructed in the same way, occupies antistrophe 2. [The English translation of the text has been modified for the needs of this analysis.—Translator.]

189. This is not the first time that the chorus mentions the god in the tragedy. Already in the parodos, the chorus, celebrating the victory of Thebes, which has just repelled the Argive enemy during the night, naturally turns at the end toward the gods, in order to thank them. Amid the anonymity of all the gods of the city, Dionysus is distinguished under the name of Bacchus (vv. 153–54). Thus the god returns at the end of the tragedy in a sort of annular composition (= with a symmetry between the beginning and the end). The god that the chorus wished to see come in a moment of joy is now called on for help at a critical juncture. Between these two evocations, initial and final, the chorus mentions the god under the name of Dionysus in its fourth stasimon (v. 957); but not as the god of Thebes.

190. J. Roux, *Euripide: Les Bacchantes* II, Paris, 1972, p. 355 (note on v. 307) interprets this as the two crests of Parnassus, and not the twin peaks of the Phedriades. But if it refers to the crests of Parnassus, it is hard to understand the preposition *hyper* ("over")! For criticism of this interpretation, see R. Seaford, *Euripides: Bacchae*, Warminster, 1996, p. 178 (note on v. 307).

191. Stephanus of Byzantium, s.v. *Nysai*: "There are several cities called Nysa. The first in the Helicon, the second in Thrace, the third in Caria, the fourth in Arabia, the fifth in Egypt, the sixth on Naxos, the seventh in India, the eight in the mountains of the Caucasus, the ninth in Libya, the tenth in Euboea, where it is said that the vine blooms and the grape matures in a single day."

192. Sophocles, frag. 255 Radt.

193. This is the traditional interpretation. Quite recently, it has been criticized by S. Scullion, "Dionysos and Katharsis in Antigone," *Classical Antiquity* 17, 1998, pp. 96–122. The article is well informed, and is not without interest in showing the importance of this stasimon. It is entirely possible that the expression "come . . . with purifying feet" might also involve the dance, which is in fact a recurrent theme in this stasimon. But it seems impossible to eliminate the reference to the sickness of "the whole city" that the seer had explained by the pollution of the altars, in order to give priority to human madness. The chorus, which has heard the seer's lesson, first weighed on the action by urging Creon to eliminate the causes of the pollution (by burying Polynices and freeing Antigone), and it now calls on a god for help in purifying the whole of the city of the already established contamination and thus to reestablish the relation between humans and the gods. The fact that Dionysus is otherwise unknown in this role as purifier of the illness of a city due to a pollution does not encourage us to modify on these grounds an interpretation that is imposed by the relation between the text (vv. 1140–41) and its context (vv. 1015–22).

194. The name "Thyiads" means "those who dash." It is particularly apt in the context in which the servants of the god dash in a frenetic dance. The name "Thyiads" is already found in Aeschylus (*Seven against Thebes*, v. 498 and v. 836).

195. See J. Jouanna, "Lyrisme et drame: Le choeur dans l'Antigone de Sophocle," in J. Jouanna and J. Leclant (eds.), *Le théâtre antique: La tragédie*, Cahiers de la Villa "Kérylos" 8, Paris, 1998, pp. 101–28 (pp. 121–22).

196. Sophocles, *Antigone*, vv. 1155ff.

197. The prayers addressed to the gods during the burial of Polynices (vv. 1199–200) will have just as little effect, as we learn from the messenger's account.

198. This discussion repeats the essence of part of my article "L'hymne chez Sophocle," in G. Freyburger-L. Pernot (ed.), *L'Hymne antique et son public* (Actes du colloque de Strasbourg, October 18–20, 2004), Turnhout: Brepols, 2007, pp. 109–32 (pp. 117–32). For details and discussions of the bibliography, see the article.

Chapter XI. Seeing, Hearing, and Understanding

1. Sophocles, *Women of Trachis*, vv. 1264–74.

2. Ibid., vv. 1275–78.

3. Ibid., v. 1269 (Hyllus) and v. 1277 (the chorus).

4. As soon as he appears alongside Heracles sleeping on his litter, he is unable to conceal his suffering upon seeing his father's fate (vv. 971–73).

5. Sophocles, *Women of Trachis*, vv. 250ff.

6. Ibid., vv. 995ff.

7. Ibid., vv. 1020–22.

8. This is one of the allusions to the future that are found at the end of Sophocles' tragedies; see chapter VIII, "Time and Action," under "The Final Ritual of the Exodos."

9. See the end of the development on Heracles in chapter IX, "The Characters," under "Heracles in *The Women of Trachis* and in *Philoctetes*."

10. Sophocles, *Electra*, vv. 173–77.

11. Homer, *Iliad* 3, v. 277. Cf. also *Odyssey* 11, v. 109 and 12, v. 323. On this transposition see J. Jouanna, " 'Soleil, toi qui vois tout': Variations tragiques d'une formule homérique et nouvelle étymologie de *aktis*," in L. Villard (ed.), *Études sur la vision dans l'Antiquité classique*, Publications des Universités de Rouen, 2005, pp. 39–56. For Zeus who sees everything in Sophocles, see also *Antigone*, v. 184; *Oedipus at Colonus*, vv. 1085ff. Already in Aeschylus, Zeus is the god who sees everything: *Suppliants*, v. 139; *Eumenides*, v. 1045. Before tragedy, see Hesiod, *Works and Days*, v. 267.

12. Sophocles, *Electra*, vv. 823–36. This is the first strophe of the second stasimon.

13. Scholium on *Electra*, v. 823 (ed. Papageorgius 137ff.).

14. Sophocles, *Electra*, vv. 657–59.

15. The concept of tragic irony is difficult to handle, because it cannot be defined unambivalently. See S. Dresden, "Remarques sur l'ironie tragique," in *Misc. Trag. in Hon. Kamerbeek*, Amsterdam, 1976, pp. 55–69; A. Garzya, *La parola e la scena*, Naples, 1997 (II. "L'ironia tragica nel teatro greco del V secolo a. C.," pp. 31–45); T. G. Rosenmeyer, "Irony and Tragic Choruses," *Essays in Honor of G. F. Else*, Ann Arbor, 1977, pp. 31–44; G. Markantonatos, "On the Concept of the Term Tragic Irony," *Platon* 32–33, 1980–81, pp. 367–73. For Sophocles, see G. M. Kirkwood (*A Study of Sophoclean Drama*, Ithaca, NY: Cornell University Press, 1st ed. 1958; 2nd ed. 1994), who devoted the last chapter of his synthetic study to Sophocles' irony ("The Irony of Sophocles," pp. 247–87). In the absence of a single definition of irony, we can define it in this precise case as connected with the situation: the audience

knows what the characters and the choreutes (except the tutor) do not know. Taking into account the degree of the spectators' knowledge, which varies depending on the tragedy or the scene, is an essential part of interpreting Sophocles' theater. This variable is nonetheless much neglected, whereas Sophocles never ceases to play on the spectator's status in a subtle spectrum ranging from omniscience to ignorance, in order to vary the nature and intensity of his emotions during the performance. See below, "The Perception of Tragic Irony: The Different Statuses of the Spectator."

16. The prayer Clytemnestra addresses directly to Apollo in Sophocles' *Electra* is an innovation with respect to Aeschylus's *The Libation Bearers*. This innovation is at the same time a reworking of the prayer Jocasta addresses directly to Apollo in *Oedipus the King* (vv. 918–23). Both prayers result from anxiety and are followed by the same effect: the arrival of a messenger. The news he brings seems to free the woman from her fears, but in the end it turns against her. This comparison of the two sequences has been made for a long time: see for example G. Kaibel, *Sophokles Elektra*, Stuttgart, 1967 (rpt. 1896), p. 174. The same tragic irony elicits an illusory and reprehensible joy in the person praying, before she becomes aware of her blindness in a tragic ending.

17. Compare the two invocations to Apollo Lyceus in *Oedipus the King*, v. 919, and in *Electra*, v. 655. They are identical and occupy the same place in the verse.

18. Compare *Oedipus the King*, vv. 924–25, and *Electra*, vv. 660–61.

19. On tragic irony in this scene, see A. Salmon, "L'ironie tragique dans l'exodos de l'*Electre* de Sophocle," *Les Etudes Classiques* 29, 1961, pp. 241–70.

20. The technique is different from that of Aeschylus in *The Libation Bearers*, where the plan for deception is set forth only after the recognition scene. In Aeschylus, the spectator's omniscience thus comes later. But while he announces the plan for deception earlier, and gives more details in doing so, Sophocles adds an extreme sophistication in its implementation, which is twofold.

21. The scenes announced in *Electra*: (1) the tutor's arrival with the scenario for the deceptive speech given by Orestes (announcement: vv. 39–50; scene: vv. 660–803); (2) Orestes' visit to his father's tomb to deposit offerings there (announcement: vv. 51–53; cf. the scene where Chrysothemis has just announced the signs of Orestes' return that she has seen on the tomb: vv. 871–937); (3) Orestes' arrival with the urn (announcement: vv. 53–58; scene: vv. 1098ff.). Announced scenes in *Philoctetes*: (1) Neoptolemus is supposed to win Philoctetes' trust by means of a deceptive speech whose scenario is provided by Odysseus (announcement: v. 54–v. 65; scene: vv. 219ff.); (2) arrival of the (false) merchant (announcement: vv. 126–31; scene: vv. 542–627). However, the announcement does not exclude surprise. Nothing makes it possible to foresee the magnitude of these scenes or the richness of the "literary" exploitation of the deception.

22. Sophocles, *Ajax*, v. 186.

23. In a seminal article, "Ambiguïté et renversement: Sur la structure énigmatique d' 'Œdipe-Roi' " (in *Mythe et tragédie*, Paris: Maspero, 1972, pp. 101–31), J.-P. Vernant mentions in passing the status of the spectators, but he is a little too quick to compare it to that of the gods.

24. Sophocles, *Ajax*, vv. 690–92. The ambiguity of the quotation does not bear only on the last word. The expression "where my journey inexorably leads" is understood by

the chorus as the place where he is going to purify himself and bury his sword (cf. vv. 654–60) and by Ajax as the place where he will be able to thrust his sword into the earth in order to commit suicide.

25. Aeschylus, *Agamemnon*, vv. 855–913.

26. See above, "The Perception of Tragic Irony: The Different Statuses of the Spectator."

27. Sophocles, *Electra*, vv. 1439–41 for the chorus's advice; and vv. 1442–57 for the dialogue between Aegisthus and Electra.

28. The hunting metaphor is made explicit when Aegisthus realizes that he has fallen into Orestes' nets (v. 1376).

29. Sophocles, *Ajax*, 89–117.

30. See for example, in the same tragedy, the exchange of ironic remarks at the end of the discussion between Menelaus and Teucer, vv. 1142–58.

31. For the initial congratulations, see *Ajax*, v. 94; for the encouragement at the end, see *Ajax*, v. 115. [Translation modified.]

32. See chapter X, "Humans and the Gods," under "The Voice of the Gods: Athena at the Beginning of *Ajax*."

33. Sophocles, *Ajax*, v. 93.

34. Sophocles, *Electra*, v. 1445–1447. [Translation modified.]

35. See in particular J.-P. Vernant (cited above).

36. Sophocles, *Oedipus the King*, v. 105.

37. Ibid., vv. 219–23.

38. Ibid., vv. 236–48.

39. Ibid., vv. 249–51. For the various interpretations of the edict, see E. Carawan, "The Edict of Oedipus (*Oedipus Tyrannus* 223–251)," *American Journal of Philology* 120, 1999, pp. 187–222.

40. For Oedipus's final recognition of his identity, see Sophocles, *Oedipus the King*, v. 1182. For his recognition of the aggravating circumstances provoked by his edict, see vv. 1381–85.

41. Ibid., vv. 258–66. Jebb's commentary on this passage remains, in its sobriety, the best: "The language of this passage is carefully framed so as to bear a second meaning, of which the speaker is unconscious, but which the spectators can feel."

42. Compare what Oedipus says when he learns the truth, v. 1405: "You gave me birth, and when you had brought me forth, you again bore children to your child, you created an incestuous kinship of fathers, brothers, sons, brides, wives, and mothers."

43. Sophocles, *Women of Trachis*, v. 1168.

44. Sophocles, *Antigone*, v. 1001.

45. Sophocles, *Oedipus the King*, v. 723 ("the prophetic voices").

46. Pausanias, *Description of Greece*, 7, 22, 2–3 (Cf. Casevitz-Lafond edition, CUF, 2000, with the note ad loc.; and M. Moggi edition, Fondazione Lorenzo Valla, 2000, with the note ad loc.). See J. J. Peradotto, "Cledonomancy in the Oresteia," *American Journal of Philology* 90, 1969, pp. 1–21, which discusses the widespread use of *cledones*, unintentional declarations that others take to be omens, in *Agamemnon* and *The Libation Bearers*. There are none in *The Eumenides*, most of the characters being gods.

47. For Tiresias's seat in Thebes, see Sophocles, *Antigone*, v. 999.

48. Homer, *Odyssey* 19, vv. 98–121.

49. Aeschylus, *Prometheus Bound*, vv. 486ff.

50. In the *Odyssey* 18, vv. 112–17, we already find an example of involuntary tragic irony. After Odysseus, disguised as a beggar, has chastised the beggar Iros, the suitors congratulate him and express the wish that Zeus and the other gods might accord Odysseus all he desires. The suitors' wish will turn against them, because what Odysseus desires is their death.

51. Sophocles, *Ajax*, v. 90 ("ally" used by Athena) and v. 117 ("ally" used by Ajax).

52. Sophocles, *Oedipus the King*, vv. 788–93.

53. Ibid., vv. 280–81.

54. Scholium on Sophocles, *Oedipus the King*, v. 264.

55. Scholium on Sophocles, *Oedipus the King*, v. 251.

56. However, a sharp criticism of this device is found in L. Roussel, *Sophocle, Œdipe, Texte, traduction, commentaire*, Montpellier, 1940, p. 77, note on v. 264: "It was absolutely necessary that this Oedipus not compare him with his father: psychologically, such an idea could never occur to him. There is something indecent about it. If Oedipus expresses it, it is because Sophocles arbitrarily desires it, for melodramatic reasons, to make the spectator shiver, even though he also knows the truth, and is indulgent. It is surprising that on the evidence of a scholiast people continue to find these rather crude speeches admirable, and the author who resorts to them clever." It is rather surprising that Roussel traces moderns' admiration back to the scholiast, whereas the scholiast largely agrees with him, though with much more level-headed judgment.

57. He left for the countryside before the tragedy begins (v. 313) and does not return until just after Clytemnestra's murder (v. 1142). However, during his absence, he is present indirectly through a rather large number allusions to him. In the past, he helped Clytemnestra kill Agamemnon with an axe (vv. 97–99). Since then he has taken the king's place, his throne, his scepter, his bed, and even his clothes (vv. 267ff.). He treats Electra with severity: she is not allowed to go out of the palace when he is there. She takes advantage of his absence to go out. But she learns that he even intends to confine her to an underground prison when he returns (vv. 376–86; cf. 626ff.), which is an innovation on Sophocles' part with respect to Aeschylus, and it makes the character's absence dramatically significant. In Aeschylus's *The Libation Bearers*, Aegisthus was already absent. He returned, warned by the nurse (vv. 838ff.). But the meeting with Electra and then with Orestes is one of Sophocles' innovations. In Aeschylus, Aegisthus went back into the palace, where he was executed before Clytemnestra was.

58. In Aeschylus's *The Libation Bearers*, the length of time Aegisthus is present is still shorter (but the spectators had already seen him at the end of *Agamemnon*). He says only a few words in front of the chorus (vv. 838–47 and vv. 851–54) before going back into the palace to receive confirmation of the news; then a cry is heard coming from the interior when he is killed (v. 869). In Aeschylus the murder of Aegisthus, as we know, precedes that of Clytemnestra. In Sophocles, Aegisthus first encounters Electra, then Orestes. In Euripides' *Electra*, Aegisthus does not appear before the spectators as a character; only his body is seen, but his absence is all the more remarkable because he does not play a major role in the tragedy.

59. Sophocles, *Electra*, v. 1479. Sophocles transposed to Aegisthus the words that Aeschylus had put in the mouth of Clytemnestra (*Libation Bearers*, v. 887).

60. Ibid., v. 1500. Aegisthus's irony echoes that of Orestes (v. 1481). The echo is clear, because in both cases the irony bears on the pretension to be a seer.
61. Sophocles, *Women of Trachis*, vv. 841–51.
62. Ibid., v. 862.
63. Sophocles, *Oedipus the King*, v. 324: "I see" (*horō*).
64. Ibid., v. 371.
65. Ibid., vv. 388ff. These verses are cited and commented on in chapter X, "Humans and the Gods," under "When Humans Challenge the Gods' Interpreters."
66. Ibid., vv. 412–13.
67. Ibid., v. 419.
68. Ibid., vv. 404–5.
69. See chapter IX, "The Characters," under "Political Heroes in Tragedy: Creon in *Antigone* and Oedipus in *Oedipus the King*."
70. Sophocles, *Oedipus the King*, v. 910. On Oedipus's (and Jocasta's) criticism of the oracles and on the chorus's indignation, see chapter X, "Humans and the Gods."
71. For a comparison between Oedipus and Creon, see chapter IX, "The Characters," under "Political Heroes in Tragedy: Creon in *Antigone* and Oedipus in *Oedipus the King*."
72. Sophocles, *Oedipus the King*, vv. 726ff.
73. Aeschylus, *Prometheus Bound*, v. 828.
74. Sophocles, *Oedipus the King*, vv. 914–23.
75. On the importance of the interval separating two episodes in the psychological development of the characters and in their decisions, see chapter IX, "The Characters," under "Women's Silence" (the example of Deianira; comparison with Ajax and Neoptolemus). Here Oedipus's development moves toward indecisiveness and anxiety. In that respect, Oedipus's development contrasts with the other examples.
76. Sophocles, *Oedipus the King*, vv. 834–45.
77. See already chapter X, "Humans and the Gods," under "The Dream, a Message from Elsewhere."
78. Aristotle, *Poetics*, 11 (1452 a 24–26).
79. Ibid., 11 (1452 a 32–33).
80. Sophocles, *Oedipus the King*, vv. 1182–85.
81. Ibid., vv. 1186–95.
82. Ibid., vv. 1216–21.
83. See chapter X, "Humans and the Gods," under "Old Oracles and New Oracles."
84. For this silent departure, see chapter IX, "The Characters," under "Women's Silence."
85. See chapter X, "Humans and the Gods," under "Old Oracles and New Oracles."
86. Sophocles, *Women of Trachis*, vv. 932–35.
87. Sophocles, *Oedipus the King*, vv. 1182–85, cited above. The repetition of the quotation seemed necessary to emphasize the formal parallel between the discoveries made by Sophocles' characters.
88. In addition to Oedipus and Heracles, see also Jocasta (*Oedipus the King*, v. 1071). The discovery does not concern the main characters alone. The messenger in *Ajax* also cries "Oh! Oh!" (*Iou! Iou!*) when he realizes that he has come too late.
89. Sophocles, *Women of Trachis*, vv. 932–35.
90. Ibid., vv. 706–11.

91. Just after the first stage in her coming to awareness, Deianira had decided that if the facts confirmed her fears, she would die heroically (vv. 719–22). See chapter IX, "The Characters," under "Women's Silence."

92. Sophocles, *Women of Trachis*, vv. 1136–42.

93. Ibid., vv. 1159–63. The last verse was cited in chapter X, "The Characters," apropos of the role of the dead, in "The Dramatic Presence of Virtual Characters."

94. Aegisthus: *Electra*, v. 1482: "Oh, I am destroyed, undone! (*olōla*)." Heracles: *Women of Trachis*, v. 1144: "Oh oh! Wretch that I am! Oh, I am dying!" (cited above).

95. Sophocles, *Ajax*, v. 896: "I am lost, destroyed (olōla), razed to the ground, my friends!"

96. Sophocles, *Oedipus the King*, v. 1071. On the cry *Iou! Iou!*, see above.

97. For Deianira, see *Women of Trachis*, vv. 904 and 909; for Eurydice, *Antigone*, v. 1302; for Jocasta, *Oedipus the King*, v. 1249.

98. Sophocles, *Oedipus the King*, vv. 1252, 1258, 1260, 1275, 1287. There is a great contrast between Jocasta's groans when she has taken refuge in the marriage chamber (v. 1249) and Oedipus's cries in what might be called the public space inside the palace (v. 1252).

99. Sophocles, *Antigone*, vv. 1261–46. C. H. Whitman (*Sophocles*, Cambridge, MA, 1951) aptly titled his study on *The Women of Trachis* (pp. 103–21) "Late Learning."

100. Sophocles, *Antigone*, vv. 1261–76. This is the first strophe of the semilyrical dialogue.

101. The dochmiac meter; on the effects produced by this meter, see chapter VIII, "Time and Action," under "Speech and Song in the Greek Theater: The Criterion of Versification."

102. Out of a total of twenty-four uses of the verb "commit errors" (*hamartanō*) in Sophocles, seven are in *Antigone*, four in *The Women of Trachis*, four in *Oedipus at Colonus*, three in *Ajax*, two in *Oedipus the King*, two in *Electra*, two in *Philoctetes*. The noun *harmatèma* present here (v. 1261) is not attested elsewhere in Sophocles' extant tragedies.

103. Sophocles, *Antigone*, vv. 1113–14.

104. Ibid., vv. 743–45.

105. Ibid., vv. 1023–28.

106. Ibid., v. 996.

107. Sophocles, *Oedipus the King*, v. 341.

108. Sophocles, *Antigone*, vv. 1257–60.

109. Ibid., v. 1270. The use of the adverb "late" in the context of a discovery is also found in *Oedipus at Colonus*, v. 1264 (Polynices): cf. also *Women of Trachis*, v. 934, where, nonetheless, the discovery is not expressed by the character (Hyllus) but reported in the narrative (that of the nurse).

110. This is a maxim that is already found in Aeschylus's *Agamemnon* (v. 1425): "You shall learn discretion though taught the lesson late."

111. Sophocles, *Antigone*, vv. 1324–25.

112. See chapter IX, "The Characters," under "Political Heroes in Tragedy: Creon in *Antigone* and Oedipus in *Oedipus the King*."

113. In *Antigone*, the end of the fifth episode (vv. 988–1114); in *Oedipus the King*, the end of the fourth episode (vv. 1110–85).

114. Oedipus's discovery: *Oedipus the King*, vv. 1182–85 (quoted above); Creon's discovery: *Antigone* vv. 1113–14 (quoted above).

115. In Antigone, in the fifth stasimon, vv. 1115–54; in *Oedipus the King*, the fourth stasimon, vv. 1186–221. The two stasima are very different in their themes, but their negative dramatic function is the same: they allow the development of tragic events that the two heroes experience after their departure from the visible space.

116. *Antigone*, vv. 1155ff.; *Oedipus the King*, vv. 1223ff. In both cases, the messengers arrive immediately after the stasimon, without being announced, and they address the chorus. They begin their speeches with general reflections before announcing a death, one Haemon's suicide, the other Jocasta's suicide.

117. Semilyrical dialogue in *Antigone*, vv. 1261–346; in *Oedipus the King*, vv. 1313–67.

118. Sophocles, *Antigone*, vv. 1324–25; *Oedipus the King*, vv. 1340–41. This punctual comparison is noted in the annotated editions (see for example Jebb on *Antigone*).

119. Sophocles, *Oedipus the King*, vv. 1327–32.

120. For the seer Tiresias's prediction, see vv. 376ff.; for Oedipus's denial of the oracles, see vv. 964ff.

121. Sophocles, *Antigone*, v. 1339.

122. Sophocles, *Oedipus the King*, vv. 1366ff.

123. Ibid., v. 1522.

124. See above, in this same chapter, "Discoveries in Sophocles' Theater: The Example of *The Women of Trachis*."

125. Sophocles, *Women of Trachis*, vv. 719–22. Passage already cited in chapter IX, "The Characters," under "Women's Silence."

126. In that case, we would have the example of a second decision made by Deianira in the virtual space of the palace, between two episodes. For the first decision, that to smear the gift intended for Heracles with the ointment she thought was a love philter, see chapter IX, "The Characters," under "Women's Silence."

127. In Greek, the expression "I am resolved" (*dedoktai*) is in the perfect, a tense of irreversibility. The same expression is used by Electra when she has decided to avenge all by herself her father after the (fictive) death of Orestes (*Electra*, v. 1049: "My resolve is not new, but long since fixed").

128. Sophocles, *Ajax*, v. 259: "And now in his right mind he has new pain."

129. See chapter IX, "The Characters," under "Epic Heroes in Tragedy: Ajax and Philoctetes."

130. Sophocles, *Ajax*, vv. 349ff.

131. The rhythm is particularly agitated. We find dochmiacs, for example in the two other commoi in *Antigone* and *Oedipus the King* (cf. n. 117). Each strophe and antistrophe begins with a series of dochmiacs.

132. Sophocles, *Ajax*, vv. 394–403.

133. Ibid., vv. 450–56.

134. Ibid., vv. 51–65. In these parallel passages, we can savor the variations in expression: the same illness, a furious madness, is sent by the goddess but is qualified with two different adjectives (v. 59 and v. 452).

135. See above, in this same chapter, "Discoveries in Sophocles' Theater: The Example of *The Women of Trachis*."

136. Sophocles, *Women of Trachis*, vv. 1259–63.

137. Ibid., v. 1040.

138. Ibid., vv. 1004–43.

139. Aristotle, *Poetics*, 18 (1455 b 28).

140. For an overall comparison of *Antigone* and *Electra*, see chapter IX, "The Characters," under "The Heroism of Young Women: Antigone and Electra."

141. Sophocles, *Antigone*, vv. 806–82 (commos in which Antigone sings); vv. 891–928 (Antigone's speech). There is, however, a slight technical difference: the speech immediately follows the commos in *Ajax* (and also in *Oedipus the King*), whereas Antigone's song is interrupted by Creon's abrupt departure (vv. 883–90).

142. This is the second lyrical dialogue with the chorus (vv. 813–70 = second stasimon). The first dialogue was the parados (vv. 121–250). From a technical point of view, there is also an innovation with respect to the semilyrical dialogues after the discovery in the old tragedies. This is a lyrical dialogue replacing a stasimon, and not a commos within an episode; see chapter VIII, "Time and Action," under "Speech and Song in the Greek Theater: The Criterion of Versification."

143. The expression of the decision is comparable; see above. However, the sequence is not continuous in *Electra*, as it is in *The Women of Trachis*. Between the lamentation and the decision, an interlude is inserted: the arrival of Chrysothemis, who thinks she is bringing good news: the signs left on the tomb indicating Orestes' return.

144. Aristotle, *Poetics*, 11 (1452 a 29–32).

145. Sophocles, *Electra*, vv. 1108ff. and 1115ff.

146. Orestes recognizes his sister from the moment that Electra, lamenting over the urn that is supposed to contain Orestes' ashes, has uttered the word "brother" (v. 1164). Electra recognizes her brother only a few moments later (vv. 1222–24), when Orestes is willing to be recognized after making sure that the chorus will be discreet and after showing a sign of recognition, their father's seal.

147. For this semilyrical duet, see chapter VIII, "Time and Action," under "The Parts Peculiar to Certain Tragedies: Songs Proceeding from the Stage."

148. In Aeschylus, *Libation Bearers*, v. 232, Orestes cuts Electra's joy short: "Control yourself! Do not go mad with joy!"

149. The tutor's deceptive speech: *Electra*, vv. 680ff.; the false merchant's deceptive speech: *Philoctetes*, v. 542.

150. Sophocles, *Philoctetes*, v. 530.

151. Ibid., v. 622.

152. Ibid., vv. 276ff. For the quotation of the beginning of the passage and the comparison with Ajax's discovery, see chapter IX, "The Characters," under "Epic Heroes in Tragedy: Ajax and Philoctetes."

153. Ibid., vv. 872ff.

154. Ibid., v. 923.

155. Ibid., v. 978. In both cases, the expression "I am destroyed" translates the first person perfect of the Greek verb, with the preverb *apolōla*. This cry is characteristic of Philoctetes (five times), whereas it is not used by Sophocles' other characters. Philoctetes uses it either when he is suffering from his illness (v. 742 and 745; cf. Euripides, *Hippolytus*, v. 1350), or when he becomes aware of the tragedy of the situation. The two values are probably combined in v. 1187. We will also find once the first person of the simple verb *olōla*, but the word is uttered not by Philoctetes but by Odysseus (v. 76). On the theme of Philoctetes' deaths see C. Mauduit, "Les morts de Philoctète," *Revue des Etudes Grecques* 108, 1995, pp. 339–70.

156. This lyrical dialogue takes the place of the third stasimon.

157. For a detailed comparison of these two parallel lamentations in a different register,

see J. Jouanna, "L'insertion du lyrisme dans le drame chez Sophocle: L'exemple d'un dialogue lyrique (*Philoctète*, vv. 1081–217)," in J. Jouanna and J. Leclant (eds.), *La Poésie grecque antique*, Cahiers de la Villa "Kérylos" 14, Paris: De Boccard, 2003, pp. 151–68.

158. Sophocles, *Philoctetes*, vv. 1194–95. Cf. *Antigone*, vv. 563–64.

159. Ibid., v. 1217. the end of this lyrical dialogue can be compared with the one that concludes *Antigone*: a hero's desire for death reduced to nothing. But what was a definitive end in *Antigone* is a provisional end in *Philoctetes*. Two new developments are still to come.

160. Sophocles, *Philoctetes*, vv. 1307–12.

161. On this, see above in this same chapter "Coming to Awareness in *Oedipus the King*: Doubling and Orchestration."

162. Sophocles, *Oedipus at Colonus*, vv. 44ff.

163. Ibid., vv. 84–98.

164. On this modification of the oracle, see chapter VI, "The Mythic Imagination," under "The Death of Oedipus in *Oedipus at Colonus* and the Apollo of Delphi," and chapter X, "Humans and the Gods," under "Oracles That Destroy and Oracles That Save."

165. This comparison develops what was first stated in chapter X, "Humans and the Gods," under "Oracles That Destroy and Oracles That Save." For Heracles' discovery in *Women of Trachis* (vv. 1143–45), see above in this same chapter, "Discoveries in Sophocles' Theater: The Example of *The Women of Trachis*." In both cases, the surprise depends on the fact that the character has knowledge concerning the oracles that the spectator does not possess.

166. See chapter X, "Humans and the Gods," under "Oracles That Destroy and Oracles That Save."

167. Sophocles, *Oedipus at Colonus*, vv. 265–74.

168. Sophocles, *Oedipus the King*, vv. 1331–32.

169. Sophocles, *Oedipus at Colonus*, vv. 7–8.

170. Cf. the account of the murder in *Oedipus the King*, vv. 808–9: "The old man, when he saw this, watched for the moment I was passing, and from his carriage, brought his double goad straight down on my head." The Greek verb used in *Oedipus at Colonus* to say that he was merely "requiting a wrong," responding to a provocation (*antidrān*, v. 271), is characteristic of that play, where it is used four times (cf. 953, 959, 1191), whereas it does not appear in any of Sophocles' other extant tragedies.

171. Sophocles, *Oedipus at Colonus*, v. 512.

172. Ibid., vv. 510–48. The lyric dialogue formed by two strophe/antistrophe pairs is devoted first to incest (vv. 510–41 = strophe 1, antistrophe 2), and then to the murder of his father (vv. 542–48 = antistrophe 2).

173. This law, which consists in exonerating some who kills to repel an aggressor, is attributed to Rhadamanthus in Apollodorus, *Library* (2, 4, 9 [64]). This passage in Sophocles has been rightly related to Plato's legislation in *The Laws*, 9 (869 c): "If a brother kill a brother in fight during a civil war, or in any such way, acting in self-defence against the other, who first started the brawl, he shall be counted as one who has slain an enemy, and be held guiltless." The comparison is made by Jebb, ad loc.

174. A.W.H. Adkins, *Merit and Responsibility*, Oxford, 1960, pp. 105ff., rightly empha-

sizes the importance of these two passages. He sees in them a new line of argument that he relates to Antiphon's *Tetralogies* and to a passage in Euripides' *Orestes* (vv. 75ff.). This new kind of justification, which attenuates the excessive absoluteness of the notion of corruption due to a murder and insists instead on individual responsibility, emerged, according to Adkins, between *Oedipus the King* and *Oedipus at Colonus*. That is not impossible. But the subjective temporal dimension must not be neglected, even if the two characters of Oedipus apparently do not belong to the same tragedy and do not coincide with each other. The Oedipus of *Oedipus at Colonus* is indeed still the Oedipus who committed the acts of which he became aware in *Oedipus the King*. But in the meantime, time has done its work. Just as corruption fades away during a long exile, the view of the act committed changes subjectively in the perpetrator of the act himself after a long exile. Crushed by the horror of the act at the moment that he discovers it in *Oedipus the King*, Oedipus can now, in *Oedipus at Colonus*, react against the chorus, which discovers him, by insisting on the involuntary nature of his act.

175. Sophocles, *Oedipus at Colonus*, vv. 960–1002. Oedipus responds at length to the accusations Creon made briefly (vv. 944–46).

176. The Greek adjective *akon*, "involuntary," is the key word at the beginning of the speech (v. 964, v. 977, v. 987 a). Antigone had already been used it at the beginning of the tragedy in her plea to the chorus, where she spoke of her father's "involuntary" acts.

177. Sophocles, *Oedipus at Colonus*, vv. 964–65 and v. 998.

178. Ibid., v. 72.

179. Ibid., v. 92.

180. Ibid., vv. 287–88.

181. Ibid., v. 16 and v. 54.

182. Ibid., vv. 1542–46.

183. Ibid., vv. 1760–65.

Deus ex Machina: Time and Nature

1. Antiphanes, *Poems*, fr. 189 (PCG II Kassel and Austin), cited in chapter VI, "The Mythic Imagination," under "Tragic Invention and Comic Invention."

2. Sophocles, *Ajax*, vv. 646–47. [Translation modified.]

3. Aristophanes, *The Frogs*, vv. 907ff. Tragic poetry, like all poetry, must be useful for educating the audience. That idea is implicit in the speeches of the two adversaries; but the whole problem is what is meant by education.

4. Sophocles, *Antigone*, vv. 1115–54. See chapter X, "Humans and the Gods," under "Human Prayer and the Silence of the Gods: The Chorus's Hymn to Dionysus in *Antigone*."

5. On the history of the text of the tragic dramatists in antiquity, the study by U. von Wilamowitz-Moellendorff, *Einleitung in die Griechische Tragödie*, Berlin, 1907, pp. 120–19 (3. "Geschichte des Tragikertextes") remains fundamental. Chapter 2 of this work ("Was ist eine attische Tragödie?") has recently been translated into French (U. von Wilamowitz-Moellendorff, *Qu'est-ce qu'une tragédie attique? Introduction à la tragédie attique*, Paris: Belles Lettres, 2001, 153 pp.). In France, in the twentieth century there have been two dissertations on the history the tragic

dramatists: Aeschylus (A. Wartelle, *Histoire du texte d'Eschyle*, Paris, 1971, 396 pp.) and Euripides (A. Tuilier, *Recherches critiques sur la tradition du texte d'Euripide*, Paris: Klinksieck, 1968, 304 pp., with the first supplements of 1972). An equivalent study on Sophocles is lacking. For a recent synthesis on the destiny of Greek tragedy in general in antiquity, see P. E. Easterling, "From Repertoire to Canon," in P. E. Easterling (ed.), *The Cambridge Companion to Greek Tragedy*, Cambridge, 1997, pp. 211–27.

6. [Plutarch], "Lives of the Ten Orators," 7. Lycurgus, 15, 841ff. On the statues of the three great tragedians, see chapter V, "Happy Sophocles," under "The Portraits of Sophocles."

7. See R. Hamilton, "Objective Evidence for Actors' Interpolations in Greek Tragedy," *Greek, Roman and Byzantine Studies* 15, 1974, pp. 387–402. For a discussion of interpolations in Sophocles, see M. D. Reeve, "Some Interpolations in Sophocles," *Greek, Roman and Byzantine Studies* 11, 1970, pp. 283–93, and R. D. Dawe, "On Interpolations in the Two Oedipus Plays of Sophocles," *Rheinisches Museum* 144, 2001, pp. 1–21.

8. See chapter IV, "Sophocles and Dionysus: The Theatrical Career," under "The Inscriptions and Sophocles' Theatrical Career." Aeschylus's tragedies might have already been reperformed in the fifth century, but in the context of a traditional contest.

9. Demosthenes, *On the Crown*, 180. Aeschines also played, in Euripides' dramas, the roles of Chresphontes and Oenomaus (ibid., 180 and 272).

10. Demosthenes, *On the Embassy*, 247.

11. Aristotle, *Poetics*, 9 (1451 b 21) = *TGrF* 1, 19 frag. 2 a Snell (his tragedy entitled *Antheus*); 15 (1454 b 14) (Achilles is a character represented by Agathon); 18 (1456 a 18); 18 (1456 a 24); 18 (1456 a 29) (Agathon as the creator of choral interludes that no longer have any relation to the plot of the tragedy).

12. *On the Sublime*, 33, 5 (= *TrGF* 1, 39 test. 6 Snell).

13. On Ion of Chios, see chapter II, "Sophocles the Politician," under "Who Was Ion of Chios?"

14. Plutarch, "Life of Alexander" 8, 3. (= test. 169 Radt). The order "Euripides, Sophocles, Aeschylus" may not be accidental. Euripides had finished his career and his life in Pella. Thus he must have been the best known of the three Athenian tragedians. The Athenian archive created by Lycurgus was certainly not the only library in the Greek world that included the tragedies of the three Athenian tragedians.

15. The physician Galen is the source of this information; see Hippocrates, *Epidemics* 2, 4, ed. Wenkebach CMG, 10, 2. 1, pp. 79, 23–80, 6 (= test. 157 Radt). This important text is worth citing: "To show that this Ptolemy [Ptolemy III Euergetes] showed such zeal in acquiring old books, people cite as non-negligible evidence his conduct toward the Athenians. Having given them a security deposit of fifteen silver talents and having received the books of Sophocles, Euripides, and Aeschylus solely to make a copy, and then to immediately return them intact, Ptolemy made at great cost a copy on very fine leaves. But he kept what he had received from the Athenians, and sent them what he had had made, asking them to keep the fifteen talents and to accept, instead of the old works, the new ones. For the Athenians, even if Ptolemy had not sent the new books but had kept the old ones, they could not have acted differently, given that they had received the money under such conditions, namely

to keep the money if he, for his part, kept the books. That is why they accepted the new books and also kept the money."

16. See Tzetzes, Proleg. de comoed. XI a I 1 (= test. 158 a Radt); cf. also test. 158 b and c Radt. On the testimonies and fragments concerning Alexander of Aetolia, see *TrGF* 1, 101, pp. 278–79 Snell.

17. For the plan of these introductions, see chapter IV, "Sophocles and Dionysus: The Theatrical Career," under "A Preface to Sophocles' *Antigone*, Written by an Alexandrian Librarian."

18. A. Tuilier (cited above), p. 69, basing himself on C. Wendel's thesis. For criticism of the claim regarding the burning of the Museum's library, see B. Hemmerdinger, "Que César n'a pas brûlé la bibliothèque d'Alexandrie," *Bollettino dei classici* 3, 6, 1985, pp. 76–77, and L. Canfora, *La Véritable histoire de la bibliothèque d'Alexandrie*, Paris, 1986, pp. 151–58.

19. Suetonius, *Life of Caesar*, 44.

20. These tragic authors are Livius Andronicus and Cn. Naevius (third century BCE), Ennius and Pacuvius (third/second century BCE), and then Accius (second/first century BCE). The titles of Livius Andronicus's tragedies that we find already in Sophocles are: *Ajax*; *Andromeda* (appendix II, no. 15); *Danaè* (no. 21); *Hermione* (no. 31); *Tereus* (no. 97). Those of Naevius are: *Danaè* (no. 21); *Iphigeneia* (no. 48). Those of Ennius: *Ajax*; *Alcmeon* (no. 10); *Alexander* (no. 9). *Andromache* (no. 14); *Andromeda* (no. 15); *Athamas* (no. 12); *Iphigeneia* (no. 48); *Phoenix* (no. 112); *Telephus* (no. 96). Those of Pacuvius: *Chryseis* (no. 115); *Hermione* (no. 31); *Niptra* (no. 76); *Teucer* (no. 95). Finally, those of Accius: *Alcmeon* (no. 10); *Amphitryon* (no. 13); *Andromeda* (no. 15); *Antenorides* (no. 16); *Antigone*; *Athamas* (no. 1–2); *Atreus* (no. 17), *Clytemnestra* (no. 55); *Epigones* (no. 27); *Erigone* (no. 38); *Eriphyle* (no. 30); *Eurysakes* (no. 35); *Meleager* (no. 66); *Minos* (no. 68); *Oenomaos* (no. 79); *Philoctetes*; *Telephus* (no. 96); *Tereus* (no. 97). For the fragments of Roman tragedies, see O. Ribbeck, *TRF3* (1897), and A. Klotz, *Scaenicorum Romanorum fragmenta I: Tragicorum fragmenta*, Munich: Oldenbourg, 1953, 376 pp. For Accius, see the annotated edition by J. Dangel, *Accius, Fragments*, Paris: CUF, 2002. Information concerning Sophocles' influence on these Latin authors will be found in A. Wartelle (cited above), pp. 197ff. (although he deals chiefly with Aeschylus). On Pacuvius's Greek models (Euripides and Sophocles), see I. Lana, "Pacuvio e i modelli greci," *Atti della Accademia delle Scienze di Torino: Classe di Scienze morali* 81–83, 1947–49, pp. 26–62, and more recently on Pacuvius, see G. Manuwald, *Pacuvius, summus tragicus poeta: Zum dramatischen Profil seiner Tragödien*, Munich: Saur, 2003, 189 pp. (with the bibliography, pp. 149–58).

21. Modern criticism attributes eight of these tragedies to Seneca himself: *Hercules furens, The Trojan Women, The Phoenician Women, Medea, Phaedra, Oedipus, Agamemnon, Thyestes.* On the other hand, there is debate about the authenticity of *Hercules on Oeta.* For the Latin theater, see F. Dupont, *Le Théâtre latin*, Paris: Armand Colin, 1988; J. Christian Dumont and M.-H. François-Garelli, *Le Théâtre à Rome*, Paris: Le Livre de poche, 1998.

22. Euripides' influence bears on four tragedies: *Hercules furens, Medea, Phaedra, and The Trojan Women.*

23. Many scenes of themes from Sophocles' *Oedipus* are taken up again, for example the chorus's reference to the plague (Seneca, vv. 110–200; Sophocles vv. 168–86); the

return of Creon coming to report the Delphic oracle's reply (Seneca vv. 201–87; Sophocles, vv. 85–146); the scene in *Oedipus* with the seer Tiresias (vv. 288–402); Oedipus's altercation with Creon, whom he accuses of conspiracy (Seneca vv. 659– 708; Sophocles vv. 532–630); the scene with the elderly Corinthian who has come to tell Oedipus of the death of his supposed father Polybus and who reveals to him that Merope, Polybus's wife, is not his mother (Seneca vv. 784–837; Sophocles vv. 950–1072); the arrival of the Theban shepherd bringing the final revelation (Seneca vv. 838–81; Sophocles vv. 1110–85); the account of Oedipus's self-mutilation (Seneca vv. 915–79; Sophocles vv. 1223–96). However, the content of the scenes may be very different. For example, the scene with Tiresias conflates two scenes treated by Sophocles in his *Oedipus* and in his *Antigone*. Moreover, Seneca adds to it, imitating Homer, an evocation of the dead in which Laius appears. The memory of *Antigone* also explains the presence of the hymn to Bacchus (Seneca, vv. 403–509; Sophocles, *Antigone*, vv. 1115–54). One of the important innovations in the development of tragedy in Seneca is the inversion of the suicide of Jocasta and Oedipus's self-mutilation. From the theatrical point of view, we no longer find in Seneca the precision of stage directions, the dramatic progression with the subtle, delayed revelation of the oracles, the intensity of the pathos with the alternation of joy and despair, the refinement of the characterization of the minor characters, the power emotional effect produced by the exit or entrance of characters (Jocasta's silent departure; the appearance of the blind Oedipus), the evocative power of narratives offering a spectacle within the spectacle, or, finally, the sobriety of the mythological allusions. In short, comparison brings out the eminent theatrical qualities of Sophocles' play and its modernity. On Seneca's *Oedipus*, see K. Töchterle, *Lucius Annaeus Seneca: Œdipus; Kommentar mit Einleitung, Text und Übersetzung*, Heidelberg, 1994, and F.-R. Chaumartin, *Œdipe, Agamemnon, Thyeste*, Paris: CUF, 1999. On the comparison of the two tragedies, see especially E. Thummer, "Vergleichende Untersuchungen zum König Oedipus des Seneca und Sophokles," in R. Muth (ed.), *Serta philologica Aenipontana*, Innsbruck, 1972, pp. 151–95; cf. aussi W. Poetscher, "Beobachtungen zu Sophokles und Seneca," in J. Dalfen et al. (eds.), *Symmicta philologica Salisburgensia G. Pfligsdorffer . . . oblata*, Rome: Ed. dell'Ateneo, 1980, pp. 105–23, and H. M. Roisman, "Teiresias, the Seer of 'Œdipus the King': Sophocles' and Seneca's Versions," *Leeds International Classical Studies* (*LICS*), 2, 5,2003, 20 pp. Another play attributed to Seneca has a sequence comparable to that of another tragedy of Sophocles: *Hercules on Oeta* deals with the death of Hercules as a victim of his wife Deianira's jealousy, as in *The Women of Trachis*. There the influence of Sophocles is also clear, even though the dramatic structure is very different—the composition in diptych has disappeared—and even though the character of Deianira is at the outset considerably modified: she is presented at first not as a women worried about her husband's fate, but as a woman mad with jealousy and wanting to kill him. Without being able to make a detailed comparison, we will note passages and scenes where reminiscences of Sophocles are manifest: Deianira's announcement of her plan to use Nessus's blood as a love philter to anoint a tunic that she will give Hercules as a gift (Seneca vv. 485–538; Sophocles vv. 531–87); the scene where she puts the gift in a box and gives it to Lichas, Hercules' herald (Seneca vv. 567–82; Sophocles vv. 598–632); Deianira's account of a sinister omen, the destruction by heat of a bit of wool that was used to smear the supposed philter on the tunic (Seneca vv. 716–39;

Sophocles vv. 672–704); Hyllus's account to his mother Deianira of the destructive effects of the poison on Hercules, who kills Lichas during a sacrifice to Zeus Ceneus (Seneca, vv. 775–841; Sophocles vv. 749–812); Deianira's suicide, with an important difference concerning her exit: whereas in Sophocles she leaves silently, in Seneca she addresses her nurse, then Hyllus (Seneca vv. 842–1030; Sophocles vv. 813–20 and 871ff.); Hercules' return suffering from the effects of the poison, also with a theatrically important difference: in Seneca's tragedy Hercules walks in, whereas in Sophocles *The Women of Trachis* he is carried in on a litter (Seneca vv. 1131ff.; Sophocles vv. 971ff.); the last part in common: the dialogue between Hyllus and Hercules, where Hercules becomes aware of the fulfillment of the oracles and gives his son his final instructions (Seneca vv. 1448–96; Sophocles vv. 1114–258). Whereas Sophocles' tragedy ends with the departure of Hercules, Seneca's continues with the arrival of two characters: Philoctetes, carrying Hercules' bow, comes to recount Hercules' heroic death on the funeral pyre, which he (Philoctetes) had been assigned to light; then Alcmena, Hercules' mother, returns bearing the urn containing her son's ashes. On models in Seneca's theater in general, see R. J. Tarrant, "Senecan Drama and Its Antecedents," *Harvard Studies in Classical Philology* 82, 1978, pp. 213–63, and J. Dangel, "Devanciers grecs et romains de Sénèque le Tragique," in M. Billerbeck and E. A. Schmidt (eds.), *Sénèque le tragique*, Entretiens sur l'Antiquité classique, Vandoeuvres-Geneva: Fondation Hardt, 2004, pp. 63–105 (pp. 68ff.). A synthesis on the presence of Sophocles in Seneca's theater remains to be produced.

24. Dio Chrysostom, *Discourse* 52. This comparison is given in appendix IV.

25. We refer here to the authority of Wilamowitz in his *Einleitung in die griechische Tragödie*, Berlin, 1907 (rpt. 1889), p. 195. The date of the choice is approved by J. Irigoin, "La tragédie grecque, de l'auteur à l'éditeur et au traducteur," in *I venerdì delle Accademie Napoletane nell' anno accademico 2003–2004*, Naples: Giannini editore, 2005, pp. 47–64 (p. 56). It is accepted, with reservations, by A. Wartelle (cited above), p. 340. It is contested by A. Tuilier (cited above), p. 89.

26. The seven plays by Aeschylus chosen are: *Prometheus Bound*, *Seven against Thebes*, *The Persians*, *The Suppliants*, and the *Oresteia* trilogy composed of *Agamemnon*, *The Libation Bearers*, and *The Eumenides*. The seven plays by Sophocles chosen are: *Ajax*, *Electra*, *Oedipus the King*, *Antigone*, *The Women of Trachis*, *Philoctetes*, *Oedipus at Colonus*. The ten plays by Euripides are: *Hecuba*, *Orestes*, *The Phoenician Women*, *Hippolytus*, *Medea*, *Alcestis*, *Andromache*, *Rhesus*, *The Trojan Women*, *The Bacchantes*.

27. These are the figures given by the Mertens-Pack[3] database, which can be consulted on the internet (CEDOPAL).

28. *On the Sublime*, 15, 3 (Euripides) and 33, 5 (Pindar and Sophocles). On Sophocles, see also 15, 7, where the author cites, as an example of a gripping spectacle, the death of Oedipus (in *Oedipus at Colonus*) and the apparition of Achilles (in Sophocles' *Polyxena*; cf. appendix II, no. 84).

29. In the case of Euripides, an extraordinary accident resulted in an early fourteenth-century scholar having at his disposition, in addition to the chosen ten tragedies, the remains of an ancient edition in which the plays were arranged by the alphabetical order of their titles, from E to K. Thus we have recovered nine additional plays that were preserved in two fourteenth-century manuscripts: (*H*)*elen*, *Electra*,

(H)ercules, (H)erakleidae, Ion, Iphigeneia in Aulis, Iphigeneia in Tauris, (H)iketides (The Suppliants), Cyclops (the only ancient satyr play preserved in its entirety).

30. See J. Irigoin, "Les éditions de textes," in F. Montanari (ed.), La Philologie grecque à l'époque hellénistique et romaine, Entretiens sur l'Antiquité classique 40, Vandoeuvres-Geneva, 1994, pp. 39–93; J. Irigoin, Le Livre grec des origines à la Renaissance, Paris: BNF, 2001, pp. 71ff.; and especially J. Irigoin, "La tragédie grecque, de l'auteur à l'éditeur et au traducteur" (cited above), pp. 47–64 (p. 56). He places the choice in the time of Marcus Aurelius.

31. A. Dain, Sophocle I, Paris: CUF, 1955, p. xxiv, considering that the choice may have been made in the age of Hadrian, says that "l'édition (du choix) était encore présentée sous forme de volumen"; see also A. Dain, Les Manuscrits, 2nd ed. Paris, 1963, p. 115, where he emphasizes more clearly our ignorance regarding the circumstances in which the choice was made. Nonetheless, he thinks it likely that it was made in the time of Hadrian. But we cannot exclude the possibility that the choice was made later, when the transition from scroll to codex had already taken place. Our ignorance concerning the date of the choice is too great for us to be able to establish with certainty a relation between the transition from volumes to the codex and the choice of the tragedians' plays.

32. See chapter IV, "The Theatrical Career," under "A Disappointment When a Masterpiece Was Produced."

33. Aristotle, Poetics, 11 (1452 a 32–33): "A discovery is most effective when it coincides with reversals, such as that involved by the discovery in the Oedipus" (= Oedipus the King).

34. See chapter IV, "The Theatrical Career," under "A Disappointment When a Masterpiece Was Produced."

35. See J. Irigoin, "La tragédie grecque, de l'auteur à l'éditeur et au traducteur" (cited above), p. 57: "L'influence du choix a été rapide." He bases his view on the proportion of the plays chosen and the plays not chosen in the papyruses of Euripides' plays found in Egypt; cf. also J. Irigoin, "Les éditions de textes" (cited above), p. 76 ("Wherever the choice of nine tragedies by Euripides plus the Rhesus was made, in Egypt it is as if the plays that were excluded had been rapidly withdrawn from the book trade").

36. Lucian, The Hall, 23 (= ed. Bompaire, Lucien Œuvres I, Paris: CUF, 1993, p. 169). The painting depicts the murder of Aegisthus, whereas Clytemnestra is already dead. This order of the murders is peculiar to Sophocles, because in Euripides, as in Aeschylus, Aegisthus dies before Clytemnestra (see above). The model of the painting is thus Sophocles rather than Euripides. However, the painter innovates with respect to the poet because the picture is centered on the murder of Aegisthus, whereas Sophocles' tragedy ends just before this murder.

37. Lucian, Symposium 25 (ed. Bompaire, cited above, p. 215 = TrGF 4 frag. 401 Radt). For Meleager, see appendix II, no. 66.

38. Sophocles is mentioned one hundred times; Euripides eighty-six times, and Aeschylus sixty times. This precise figure (obtained by computer) is very different from the one A. Wartelle (cited above) drew from the index of Kaibel's edition of Athenaeus (Euripides eighty, Sophocles seventy-eight, and Aeschylus forty-seven). Such divergences little affect Aeschylus, who remains in third place. On the other hand, the conclusions are reversed for Euripides and Sophocles. Athenaeus does not provide,

as A. Wartelle says (p. 282), "a confirmation of the popularity of Euripides." On Aeschylus in Athenaeus, see A. Marchiori, "Ateneo testimone di Eschilo," *Lexis* 22, 2004, pp. 173–90. As in Sophocles' case, Athenaeus informs us not only regarding the plays chosen from Aeschylus (*Prometheus Bound*, vv. 293ff., and *Agamemnon*, v. 284), but also regarding the lost plays (frag. 57, 124, 135, 180, 258 Radt).

39. Here are the titles of Sophocles' plays that we find mentioned in Athenaeus's *Deipnosophistae*: *Ajax*, *Lovers of Achilles* (no. 19 in appendix II); *Amphiaraos satyrikos* (no. 12); *Amycos* (no. 11); *Andromeda* (no. 15); *The Sons of Antenor* (no. 16); *Antigone*; *The Gathering of the Achaeans* (no. 93); *The Shepherds* (no. 83); *Cedalion* (no. 54); *Women of Colchis* (no. 56); *Aegeus* (no. 4); *The Ethiopians* (no. 5); *Eris* (no. 29); *Iphigeneia* (no. 48); *Men of Camicus* (no. 52); *Heracles* (no. 37); *Hybris* (no. 104); *Inachus* (no. 44); *Judgment* (no. 70); *Niobe* (no. 75); *Oedipus*; *Oenomaus* (no. 79); *Pandora* (no. 81); *Phineus* (no. 110–11); *Phoenix* (no. 112); *Salmoneus* (no. 88); *The Satyrs at Taenarum* (no. 28); *The Scythians* (no. 91); *Thamyras* (no. 39); *The Women of Trachis*; *Triptolemus* (no. 98); *Tyro* (no. 102–3); *Drummers* (*Tympanistai*) (no. 100).

40. He does not even cite all the plays chosen. We also have to take into account quotations of Sophocles that Athenaeus makes without specifying the name of the play.

41. See prelude to part II: "A Tragic Disaster."

42. Among the references to the three tragic poets in Stobaeus, Euripides clearly comes in first (715 times), ahead of Sophocles (216 times) and Aeschylus (41 times). For Sophocles, Stobaeus cites, in addition to the seven chosen tragedies, thirty-three titles of plays that were not chosen. Here is a list of them: *Acrisius* (no. 7), *Ajax the Locrian* (no. 3), *The Sons of Aleus* (no. 8), *Lovers of Achilles* (no. 19), *Those Who Dine Together* (no. 93), *Women of Colchis* (no. 56), *Creusa* (no. 57), *The Prophets* (no. 65), *Epigoni* (no. 27), *Eriphyle* (no. 30), *Women of Phthia* (no. 108), *Hippodamia* (no. 79), *Hybris* (no. 104), *Inachus* (no. 44), *Ion* (no. 51), *Iphigeneia* (no. 48), *Laocoön* (no. 61), *Men of Larissa* (no. 62), *Mysians* (no. 70), *Nauplius* (no. 73), *Peleus* (no. 82), *Phaedra* (no. 107), *Phrygians* (no. 114), *Polyxena* (no. 84), *Men of Scyros* (no. 92), *Tantalus* (no. 14), *Tereus* (no. 97), *Teucer* (no. 95), *Thyestes* (nos. 41–43), *Drummers* (no. 100), *Tyndareus* (no. 101), *Tyro* (nos. 102–3). Stobaeus cites several times another play entitled *Aleitès* (*The Culprit*) which is sometimes corrected to read *Alétès* ("son of Aegisthus") (no. 116).

43. Sophocles is, by far, the tragic author most often cited by Hesychius (254 times). This is exceptional, since Euripides does not even come in second, but in third place (76 times), whereas Aeschyluls is mentioned 107 times. This ranking does not correspond at all to that of Stobaeus. It is true that the point of view is different. Stobaeus is attached to content, while Hesychius is more interested in expression. Nonetheless, Hesychius's interest in Sophocles is clear. The number of tragedies cited (in addition to those chosen) is 72. Here is a list: *Acrisius* (no. 7 in appendix II), *Alcmeon* (no. 10), *Sons of Aleus* (no. 8), *Alexander* (no. 9), *Amphiaraus* (no. 12), *Amphitryon* (no. 13), *Andromeda* (no. 15), *Sons of Antenor* (no. 16), *Athamas* 1 and 2 (nos. 1–2), *Atreus* or *The Mycenaean Women* (no. 17), *Those Who Dine Together* (no. 93), *Shepherds* (no. 83), *Cedalion* (no. 54), *Women of Colchis* (no. 56), *Root-Cutters* (no. 87), *Creusa* (no. 57), *Danaë* (no. 21), *Daedalus* (no. 20), *Dolopes* (no. 23), *Aegeus* (no. 4), *Eris* (no. 29), *Ethiopians* (no. 5), *Eumelus* (no. 32), *Eurysakes* (no. 35), *Men of Camicus* (no. 52), *Heracles* (no. 37), *Hipponous* (no. 47), *Inachus* (no. 44), *Iobates* (no. 46), *Ion* (no. 51), Iphigeneia (no. 48), *Men of Larissa* (no. 62), *Women of Lemnos*, *Men of Scyros* (no. 63–64), *Mysians* (no. 70), *Meleager* (no. 66), *Momus* (no.

71), *Nauplius* (no. 72 or 73, including *Nauplius Sails In* and *Nauplius Lights a Fire*), *Nausicaa* (no. 74), *Oenomaus* (no. 79); *Palamedes* (no. 80), *Pandora* (no. 81), *Dionysiacus* (no. 22), *Phineus* (nos. 110–11 including *Phineus 2*), *Phaedra* (no. 107), *Philoctetes at Troy* (no. 109), *Polyidos* (no. 65), *Polyxena* (no. 84), *Water Carriers* (no. 105), *The Captive Women* (no. 6), *The Gathering of the Achaeans* (no. 18), *The Demand for Helen's Return* (no. 24), *Salmoneus* (no. 88), *The Satyrs at Taenarum* (no. 28), *Men of Scyros* (no. 92), *Scythians* (no. 91), *Sinon* (no. 89), *Sisyphus* (no. 90), *Telephus* (no. 96), *Tereus* (no. 97), *Thyestes* (nos. 41–43 including *Thyestes at Sicyone* and *Thyestes 2*), *Triptolemus* (no. 98), *Troilus* (no. 99), *Drummers* (no. 100), *Tyro 1* and *2* (nos. 102–3), *Odysseus Wounded by the Spine* (no. 77), *The Madness of Odysseus* (no. 78).

44. Concerning Stobaeus, we have irrefutable proof through Photius. This ninth-century scholar could still read the complete version of Stobaeus's work and gives a marvelous review of it in his *Bibliotheca*: first the author's intention (to produce an anthology of texts for his son Septimus), next the detailed content of the four books, which proves that we have only extracts, and then the incredibly long list of the three categories of authors cited by Stobaeus: ([1] philosophers; [2] poets; [3] orators and historians). This list, in which authors are cited in each of the three categories by alphabetical order, occupies four pages in the edition of Photius published by the CUF (ed. R. Henry II, pp. 155–59). For the poets, the list includes more than a hundred and fifty names! The names of the three great tragedians appear in their place in the alphabetical list, but they are lost in the crowd. They are not the only authors of tragedies listed among the poets. Ten other tragic authors of the fifth century are also on the list (Thespis, Choerilus, Phrynichus, Euphorion son of Aeschylus. Neophron, Ion, Carcinos, Iophon son of Sophocles, Agathon, Critias), as well as an author of the fourth century (Astydamas). Our view of the survival of the tragic authors thus risks being oddly skewed if we do not take these clues into account: tragic authors who were not included in the first choice made by Lycurgus in the fourth century BCE were still known seven to eight centuries later.

45. This is Laurentian 32, 9 (L), which we have already mentioned in connection with the order of the seven tragedies; see prelude to part II: "A Tragic Disaster." This manuscript is difficult to access, but it can be consulted in an excellent facsimile (*Facsimile of the Laurentian Manuscript of Sophocles*, with an Introduction by E. M. Thompson and R. C. Jebb, London, 1885). It is, moreover, this facsimile that has served as the basis for most editors. For the text of the ancient scholia given by the manuscript, see P. N. Papageorgius, *Scholia in Sophoclis tragoedias vetera e codice Laurentiano denuo collato*, Leipzig: Teubner, 1888. The Florence manuscript is the most important of the first family of manuscripts used by present-day editors. This family also includes the palimpsest of Leyden from the tenth century, Lugd. Bat. BPG 60 A (= P in Dain and Mazon and L in Lloyd-Jones and Wilson), as well as the Florence manuscript, Laur. 31 10 from the twelfth century (= K according to Lloyd-Jones-Wilson). A second family, called the Roman family, consists of four manuscripts from southern Italy, the oldest of which is the Laurentianus CS 152 (= G), which dates from 1282, and the most complete is the Vaticanus gr. 2291 from the fifteenth century, including the seven tragedies (= R). The first family was earlier than Byzantine scholarship, the second seems to have remained at a distance from it. The third family, the oldest representative of which is the Parisinus gr. 2712 from the thirteenth century (= A) is assessed differently by editors depending the propor-

tional importance they accord to old readings and to Byzantine innovations. Here we cannot enter into too technical discussions of the other groups. On the manuscript tradition of Sophocles' works, the two main studies (which are very different) are those of A. Turyn and R. D. Dawe mentioned above). For the presentation of the major groups of manuscripts used by editors, see the introduction to Dain and Mazon's edition in the CUF, with the supplements by Jean Irigoin (1994) and the prefaces to R. D. Dawe's editions in the Teubner collection (2 vols., 3rd corrected ed., 1996) and to H. Lloyd-Jones and Wilson in the Oxford *Scriptorum classicorum bibliotheca* (1990). The critical edition that gives the most information regarding the variants of the manuscripts is R. D. Dawe's.

46. An analogous selection was made for the other two tragic poets, Aeschylus (*Prometheus Bound, Seven against Thebes, The Persians*) and Euripides (*Hecuba, Orestes, The Phoenician Women*), as well as for Aristophanes.

47. It is the manuscripts of Maximus Planudes, Manuel Moschopoulos, Thomas Magister, and Demetrius Triclinius that have scholia. But modern scholars debate the role played by these scholars in the establishment of the text. Only Triclinius seems to have systematically corrected the text (Par. gr. 2711 and Marc. gr. 470). He was the first to recognize the strophic construction. He was of great importance in the constitution of the printed vulgate of Sophocles from the middle of the sixteenth century to the end of the eighteenth (see below). For the work of Demetrius Triclinius on Sophocles, see R. Aubreton, *Démétrius Triclinius et les recensions médiévales de Sophocle*, Paris: Les Belles Lettres, 1949, 289 pp.; A. Turyn (cited above), pp. 69–86, R. D. Dawe (cited above), pp. 80ff., and more recently J. Irigoin, *Tradition et critique des textes grecs*, Paris, 1997, pp. 123–28 (not only on Sophocles, but also on Aeschylus and Euripides). For an edition of the Byzantine scholia on a tragedy by Sophocles, see O. Longo, *Scholia byzantina in Sophoclis Œdipum Tyrannum*, Padua, 1971.

48. The title page ("Sophoclis Tragaediae septem cum commentariis") bravely announces commentaries in addition to the text. But the text alone is given! The edition was dedicated to an illustrious Greek who had come to the West, Janus Lascaris, who had inaugurated the publication of the Greek tragedians with four tragedies by Euripides in 1494 or 1495, when he was teaching Greek in Florence, and he was also the first to publish the commentaries announced on the title page of the first edition of Sophocles, namely the ancient scholia, when he was in Rome in 1518. The Aldine edition was based on the Petropolitanus gr. 731 for the three plays selected (*Ajax, Electra, Oedipus the King*); see W. Beneševič, "Das Original der Ausgabe 'Sophoclis tragoedie septem' 1502 von Aldus Manutius," *Philologische Wochenschrift* 46, 1926, col. 1145–52, and B. L. Fonkič in *Vizant. Vremmenik* 24, 1964, pp. 109–20. For the other plays, the Aldine edition used a manuscript from the A family, as is indicated by the order of the tragedies (for the order *Antigone, Oedipus at Colonus, The Women of Trachis, Philoctetes* in family A, see above). This manuscript may be the Vindobonensis phil. gr. 48 (Y) or rather a lost copy, because the Vienna manuscript does not bear traces of having been used for printing. The model of the princeps edition of the ancient scholia produced by Lascaris is probably the Parisinus gr. 2799 that belonged to him; see J. Irigoin (cited above), pp. 115–17.

49. After the first edition of 1502 and the first edition of the scholia in 1518, in the first half of the sixteenth century there were four other complete editions: Florence,

Juntes, 1522 (rpt. 1547); Paris, 1528; Haguenau, 1535; and Frankfurt, 1544. The second half of the sixteenth century: the editions by Adrien Turnèbe, Paris, 1553 (on Turnèbe, see J. Lewis, *Adrien Turnèbe, 1512–1565: A Humanist Observed*, Geneva: Droz, 1998); Henri Estienne, 1568; the Dutch scholar Guillaume Canter in the Officina Plantiniana in Antwerp in 1579, and then in Leyden in 1593, then in Heidelberg in 1597. There were thus eight complete editions in the sixteenth century, not counting the reprintings and separate editions. On the Greek editions of Sophocles from the sixteenth century to the beginning of the nineteenth century, see R. Aubreton (cited above), pp. 239–74 (with precise references giving the classification marks in the French National Library).

50. The first Latin translation of the whole of Sophocles' extant theater that appeared in France described him as "the prince of the ancient tragedians" and was produced by Jean Lalemant (Paris, 1557). The title suggests that it is the first translation of Sophocles into Latin (*Sophoclis tragicorum veterum facile principis tragoediae, quotquot extant, septem. Nunc primum latinae factae et in lucem emissae per Joannem Lalamantium*, apud F. Morellum, Lutetiae, 1557). In reality, a Latin translation of all of Sophocles' extant theater had already appeared in Venice in 1543 (*Sophoclis Tragoediae omnes, nunc primum Latinae ad verbum factae, ac scholiis quibusdam illustratae, Ioanne Baptista Gabia Veronensi interprete*, Venetiis: apud Io. Baptistam a Burgofrancho Papiensem, 1543). This Latin translation was widely read in Italy, as is shown by the large number of Italian libraries that still have this edition (sixteen to eighteen, according to the site EDIT 16-ICCU). Lalemant's ignorance of the existence of the Latin translation of his Italian predecessor is astonishing. A third Latin version of the extant works was published in Basel by Oporinus in 1588, translated by Thomas Neogeorgus, a Protestant scholar who was not only a translator but also the author of neo-Latin tragedies.

51. Here is the title: *Tragédie de Sophocles intitulée Electra, contenant la vengence de l'inhumaine et piteuse mort d'Agamemnon roi de Mycènes . . . Ladicte tragédie traduicte du grec dudit Sophocles en rythme françois, vers pour vers . . .* , Paris: E. Roffet, 1537. The translator's name is not given on the cover, but it can be read in acrostic in the preface to the reader (see the digitized copy on the GALLICA site). On Lazare de Baïf the translator, see B. Garnier, "Guillaume Bochetel et Lazare de Baïf, traducteurs-conseillers de Francois Ier," in Jean Delisle (ed.), *Portraits de traducteurs*, Ottawa: Presses de l'Université d'Ottawa; Arras: Artois Presses Université, 1999, pp. 33–67. For the translations into Latin and French of the Greek tragic authors, see M. Delcourt, *Etude sur les traductions des tragiques grecs et latins en France depuis la Renaissance*, Bruxelles, 1925. For translations into modern languages, see R. R. Bolgar, *The Classical Heritage and Its Beneficiaries*, Cambridge, 1954, pp. 508–25.

52. *Euvres [sic] en rime*, vol. 2, Paris, 1573 (contains the books of *Jeux*, dedicated to Monseigneur the Duke of Alençon, Paris, 1572, where the translation is found); the text is now available in E. Balmas and M. Dassonville (eds.), *La Tragédie à l'époque d'Henri II et de Charles IX*, vol. 5 (1573–75), Paris-Florence: PUF-Olschki, 1993, pp. 1–69. There is another French translation in verse of *Antigone* that remained unpublished. It was done by Calvy de La Fontaine and is preserved in a manuscript in Soissons (B. M. 201 [189 A]. It has recently been published: Calvy de La Fontaine, *L'Antigone de Sophocle*, ed. M. Mastroianni, Alexandria: edizioni dell'Orso, 2000. On these two French translations and the Latin translations of *Antigone* published

in the sixteenth century, see M. Mastroianni, *Le Antigoni sofoclee del Cinquecento francese*, Florence: Olschki, 2004 (list of dramatic texts of the sixteenth century that rework Sophocles' *Antigone*, p. 239).

53. A. Dacier translated both *Oedipus the King* and *Electra*, as the title indicates: *L'Œdipe et l'Electre de Sophocle, tragédies grecques: Traduites en français avec des remarques*, Paris: Cl. Barbin, 1692. On Dacier's translation, see P. Vidal-Naquet, "Œdipe à Vicence et à Paris: Deux moments d'une histoire," in J.-P. Vernant and P. Vidal-Naquet, *Mythe et tragédie* II, Paris: La Découverte, 1986, pp. 213–35 (pp. 225–35). In his article, P. Vidal-Naquet used (cf. p. 227, n. 51) Christian Biet's doctoral thesis (*Les Transcriptions théâtrales d'Œdipe Roi au XVIIIe siècle*, Paris, 1980); Biet has since published *Œdipe en monarchie, tragédie et théorie juridique à l'âge classique*, Paris: Klincksieck, 1994.

54. See P. Burian, "Tragedy Adapted for Stages and Screens: The Renaissance to the Present," in P. E. Easterling (cited above), pp. 228–85. This reception includes four major, interconnected domains: translation, interpretation, performance, creation. Synthetic works are beginning to appear in France, written by specialists in French literature or comparative literature. For the classical period, see Ch. Biet, *Œdipe en monarchie*, 491 pp.; for the end of the nineteenth century and the beginning of the twentieth, see Sylvie Humbert-Mougin, *Dionysos revisité: Les tragiques grecs en France de Leconte de Lisle à Claudel*, Paris: Belin, 2003. The problem of translation and the history of translations has begun to attract a great deal of attention: the two syntheses mentioned above begin there. See also, even though it is not about Sophocles, C. Lechevalier's *L'Invention d'une origine: Traduire Eschyle en France de Lefranc de Pompignan à Mazon; Le Prométhée enchaîné*, Paris: Honoré Champion, 2007.

55. In the history of the editions of Sophocles, the transition from the traditional editions to a scholarly edition based on the collation of several manuscripts took place at the end of the eighteenth century, with the edition produced by Richard François Philippe Brunck (1729–1803, a French Hellenist born in Strasbourg who published Sophocles' works in his native city in 1786. Brunck put an end to the vulgate based, since Turnèbe's edition (1553, cited above), on the recension of the Byzantine scholar Triclinius (cited above). Brunck proposed a return to the Aldine edition (cited above), relying on the collation of several manuscripts that he properly identified. In particular, he knew the Paris manuscript (Parisinus gr. 2712, thirteenth century = A), which still constitutes one of the bases for the constitution of the text. However, he did not yet know the oldest manuscript, the Florence manuscript 31, 9 from the tenth century (= L). Nonetheless, Brunck's vulgate remained the model for the numbering of the verses, with all the difficulties that involves for the numbering of the lyrical parts, because in modern editions the arrangement of the *cola* differs from that in Brunck's. The Florence manuscript, which was already known in the Aeschylus tradition, was not used in the Sophocles tradition until the beginning of the nineteenth century, when the German scholar Karl Wilhelm Dindorf (1802–83), a professor at Leipzig, produced an edition that was published in Oxford in 1832 and was reissued in subsequent editions. At the end of the nineteenth century, the edition produced by Sir Richard Claverhouse Jebb (1841–1905), consisting of seven volumes published from 1883 to 1896, brilliantly concluded the century and remained fundamental for its sobriety and the pertinence of its commentaries. The recent reprinting of this edition by P. Easterling, with new introductions, testifies

to that fact. On R. C. Jebb, see P. Easterling in the reprint of R. C. Jebb's edition of *Antigone*, London: Bristol Classical, 2004, pp. 7–30 (with the bibliography). In the twentieth century, advances in the history of the text have been based on taking into account new documents (the Leyden palimpsest identified by Vürtheim in 1926 and the papyruses edited by R. Carden in 1974), the classification of manuscripts (the identification of the family called "Roman" by V. De Marco in 1936), on overall syntheses dealing with the manuscript tradition (A. Turyn, in 1952, and R. D. Dawe, in 1973–78, already cited above). All this led at the end of the twentieth century to the two most recent critical editions (including only the Greek text): R. D. Dawe in the Bibliotheca Teubneriana (1975–79), with the subsequent editions, and H. Lloyd-Jones and N. G. Wilson in the Oxford Classical Texts series (1990). In France, the edition of Sophocles in the Collection des Universités de France was initially the work of P. Masqueray in the first half of the twentieth century (1922), and then of A. Dain and P. Mazon in the second half of the century (1955–60), with numerous editions revised by Jean Irigoin. At the end of the century, J. Bollack published a monumental edition of *Oedipus the King* (4 vols., Lille, 1990). His lively history of "le texte dans la modernité: les éditions depuis Brunck," vol. 1, pp. 7–42, is well worth reading.

56. For Hegel, Sophocles' tragedies, and especially *Antigone*, mark a crucial advance in the conception of destiny; in this regard they are exemplary through the appearance of moral justice that supersedes blind fate. Here is what Hegel says in one of his lectures on the philosophy of religion: "Fate is what is devoid of thought, of the Notion, something in which justice and injustice disappear in abstraction; in tragedy, on the other hand, destiny moves within a certain sphere of moral justice. We find this truth expressed in the noblest form in the Tragedies of Sophocles. Fate and necessity are both referred to there. The destiny of individuals is represented as something incomprehensible, but necessity is not a blind justice; on the contrary, it is recognized as the true justice. And just because of this these Tragedies are the immortal spiritual productions of moral understanding and comprehension, the eternal patterns or models of the moral Notion. Blind destiny is something unsatisfying. In these Tragedies justice is grasped by thought. The collision between the two highest moral powers is set forth in a plastic fashion in that supreme and absolute example of tragedy, 'Antigone.' In this case, family love, what is holy, what belongs to the inner life and to inner feeling, and which because of this is also called the law of the nether gods, comes into collision with the law of the State. Creon is not a tyrant, but really a moral power; Creon is not in the wrong; he maintains that the law of the State, the authority of government, is to be held in respect, and that punishment follows the infraction of the law. Each of these two sides realizes only one of the moral powers, and has only one of these as its content; this is the element of one-sidedness here, and the meaning of eternal justice is shown in this, that both end in injustice just because they are one-sided, though at the same time both obtain justice too." G.W.F. Hegel, *Sämtliche Werke*, ed. H. Glockner, vol. 16. *Vorlesungen über die Philosophiie der Religion*, part 2, Stuttgart: Fromann, 1928, 11. *Die Religion der geistigen Individualität*, pp. 133ff. English translation by E. B. Speirs and J. Burdon Sanderson, in *Hegel on Tragedy*, New York: Doubleday/Anchor, 1962, p. 325.

57. Freud's first allusion to the myth of Oedipus goes back to a letter from Fliess dating from October 15, 1897, in which one passage has remained famous: "Greek legend

was able to grasp the feelings that all humans recognize because they have all felt them. Every spectator was once an Oedipus in germ, in imagination, and he is scared of seeing the realization of his dream transported into life. He trembles in proportion to the repression that separates his infantile state from his current state." This letter, which contains in germ the theory of the Oedipus complex that Freud developed a little later (the son's love for the mother and hatred of the father), offers a reinterpretation of Sophocles' play, or, one might say, an exploitation of a detail in the tragedy. The dream of the son who sleeps with his mother does exist in the tragedy; moreover, its frequency is noted: "Many men before now have slept with their mothers in dreams" (vv. 981ff.) This observation is made by Jocasta. However, Jocasta attaches no significance to such dreams. The Freudian interpretation is not in the Greek tragedy, but Freud could find a confirmation of his own theory in a verse of from the tragedy taken out of its context. On the other hand, the other aspect of the Oedipus complex (the hatred of the father) has no foundation in the tragedy. Oedipus kills his father without knowing it, and there is no question of dreams in which the son would like to kill his father. On the criticism of psychoanalytic interpretations of *Oedipus the King*, see Ch. Segal, "Freud, Language, and the Unconscious," in *Sophocles' Tragic World*, Cambridge, MA, 1995, pp. 161–79.

58. See S. Goldhill, "Modern critical approaches to Greek tragedy," in P. E. Easterling (cited above), pp. 324–47. This is a very suggestive synthetic essay on the different twentieth-century approaches considered in the following order: (1) philology (which is studied starting with the emblematic quarrel at the end of the nineteenth century between Nietzsche, *The Birth of Tragedy*, 1872, defining tragedy as the product of the Apollonian and the Dionysian, and Wilamowitz, presenting as soon as Nietzsche's book appeared a sharp criticism of this alleged "philology of the future"); (2) anthropology and structuralism; (3) theatrical criticism; (4) psychoanalysis and Greek tragedy.

59. On this first performance, see L. Schraden, *La Représentation d'Edipo Tiranno au Teatro Olimpico (Vicence 1595)*, Paris, 1960; A. Gallo, *La prima rappresentazione al teatro Olimpico*, Milan, 1973; and P. Vidal-Naquet (cited above), pp. 217–25.

60. The amplest study in this domain is that of H. Flashar, *Inszenierung der Antike: Das griechische Drama auf der Bühne der Neuzeit 1585–1990*, Munich, 1991. It is no accident that his study begins in 1585: it is the first performance, that of Sophocles' *Oedipus* in Vicenza. See also F. Macintosh, "Tragedy in Performance: Nineteenth- and Twentieth-Century productions," in P. E. Easterling (cited above), pp. 284–323. For Sophocles' tragedies performed in France from 1870 to 1922, see S. Humbert-Mougin (cited above), pp. 267–72 (among the other Greek tragedians). The list is firsthand work, established especially on the basis of the Rondel collection in the Bibliothèque de l'Arsenal. It turns out that "the modern trilogy" was performed at the Comédie-Française: *Oedipus the King* from 1881 to 1917, in a verse translation by Jules Lacroix; *Antigone* from 1893 to 1909 in a verse translation by Paul Meurice and Auguste Vacquerie; *Electra*, a tragedy based on Sophocles in three acts and in verse by Alfred Poizat, in 1907 with a few revivals until 1932. In other theaters, directors ventured beyond this choice (*Philoctetes, Oedipus at Colonus*, and an adaptation of *The Women of Trachis* entitled *Deianira*). On the other hand, *Ajax* is totally absent.

61. He presented it again twice, in 1971 (at the Nanterre-Amandiers Theater) and in 1986; see *Electra de Sophocle*, trans. Antoine Vitez, Arles: Actes Sud, 1986.

62. J. and M. Bollack, *Sophocle, Antigone*, Paris: Les Éditions de Minuit, 1999. See also J. Bollack, M. Bollack, M. Bozonnet, P. Guyomard, Ph. Porret, and V. Porret, *Antigone: Enjeux d'une traduction*, Paris: Ed. Campagne première, 2004, 123 pp. In Véronique Porret's interview with Marcel Bozonnet (pp. 99–122), we find valuable information about the collaboration between the translators and the director (M. Bozonnet) concerning the final touches on the translation. The same year a translation of *Antigone* by Marie-Claire Boutan appeared, with a preface by George Steiner (Paris: Hermann), but it does not seem to have been made for performance. Before doing their translation of *Antigone*, J. and M. Bollack had already published in 1985, with the Éditions de Minuit, a translation of *Oedipus the King* written for the stage (produced by the Théâtre de la Salamandre in Lille, with a revival in Paris in 1985).

63. Ph. Lacoue-Labarthe's two French translations were published with the German text (it is fine to have the German text, but in order to judge the interpretive value of the translation it would be desirable to have the source as well, that is, the Greek text of Juntes's edition): Hölderlin, *Antigone de Sophocle*, trans. from the German by Ph. Lacoue-Labarthe, Paris: Christian Bourgois, 1978; Hölderlin, *Œdipe le tyran de Sophocle*, trans. from the German by Ph. Lacoue-Labarthe, Paris: Christian Bourgois, 1998. For a philologist, it seems very surprising that Hölderlin chose as the point of departure for his translation the second edition that appeared in the sixteenth century, as if philology had made no progress in editing Sophocles from the sixteenth century to the beginning of nineteenth century. When these translations by Hölderlin appeared in 1804, opinions were very reserved. People saw in them the first signs of his madness. Since then, they have been rehabilitated "in a spectacular resurrection" (the expression is George Steiner's, cited above), p. 74. Thus we have a paradoxical phenomenon, to say the least: a regression in the establishment of the text that is supposed to be accompanied by progress in understanding, the translation becoming "a fundamental text for modern hermeneutics."

64. *Electre de Hugo von Hofmannsthal*, directed by Stanislas Nordey, trans. by Jacqueline Verdaux, in *L'Avant-scène*, no. 1220, March 2007.

65. R. Garnier, *Œuvres complètes: La Troade, Antigone*, ed. R. Lebègue, Paris: Belles Lettres, 1952; R. Garnier, *Antigone*, critical ed. by J.-D. Beaudin, Paris: Champion, 1987. Garnier's play is inspired by several models, Sophocles (acts 4 and 5), but also Seneca's *The Phoenician Women* (acts 1 and 2) and song 11 in Statius's *Thebaid* (act 3); see also M. Mastroianni (cited above).

66. George Steiner, *Antigones*, Oxford, 1984. Steiner's essay is less a history of interpretations, which he does not study in the chronological order, than a reflection on the reasons for the obsessive permanence of Greek myth in the Western imagination, among poets, philosophers, anthropologists, and psychologists, with many subtle and suggestive analyses not only of the different interpretations or re-creations but also of the great problems related to comprehending Sophocles' work itself. See also S. Fraisse, *Le Mythe d'Antigone*, Paris: Armand Colin, 1974; C. Molinari, *Storia di Antigone: Un mito nel teatro occidentale*, Bari: De Donato, 1977; M. Mastroianni (cited above).

67. Bertolt Brecht, *Théâtre complet*, vol. 7, Paris: L'Arche, 1979, pp. 7–56 (French trans. by Maurice Regnaut). The model Brecht chose was not Sophocles himself, but Hölderlin's translation. This fact alone testifies to the success of Hölderlin's translation in the twentieth century. Brecht reinserted the Sophoclean model into the

contemporary state of war in 1945, as is clearly indicated by the added initial dialogue, in which two sisters, a modern Ismene and Antigone, emerge from an air-raid
shelter to return to their house: they discover the body of their brother, a deserter
who has been hanged; and the modern Antigone takes a knife to cut him down,
risking her life, because an S.S. man is coming (pp. 9–12). The first performance
dates from 1948. In 1951, this prologue was replaced by a presentation of the situation
and the characters by the seer Tiresias, who is the author's spokesman (p. 56). Tiresias
suggests that the spectator see in these events a revolt of the humane Antigone
against the inhumane Creon, and he implicitly refers to the heroic acts of women's
resistance against the order established during the Second World War. To reinforce
this interpretation and the better to adapt it to the contemporary situation, Tiresias
presents Creon as conducting a war of plunder against distant Argos. This is clearly
contrary to the situation in Sophocles' play, where the Argives led by Polynices are
the aggressors and where the war was conducted by Eteocles before the fratricidal
single combat forced Creon to take power.

68. See Jean Cocteau, *Théâtre complet*, Paris: Gallimard, Bibliothèque de la Pléiade,
2003, pp. 303–28. This contraction of Sophocles' *Antigone* was performed for the
first time at L'Atelier on December 20, 1922 (sets by Picasso, music by A. Honegger,
costumes by G. Chanel). Cocteau chose Antigone because "Antigone is [his] saint"
(p. 325). For the music at the first performance, here is what Cocteau, who was a
pianist, said about it: "Honegger's music is so beautiful and so modest that it does
not superpose itself on the words but plays the role of a gesture or an accessory. That
is why I asked him to use a single instrument" (p. 328).

69. Anouilh's *Antigone* was performed for the first time on February 4, 1944, in Paris, at
the L'Atelier theater. See Jean Anouilh, *Antigone*, Paris: La Table Ronde, 1946, 127
pp. Anouilh borrowed from Sophocles the idea of several scenes: (1) the confrontation between the two sisters, Ismene and Antigone; (2) the first entrance of the guard
who tells Creon, after equivocations, that Polynices has been buried; (3) the second
entrance of the guard, who has caught Antigone burying Polynices again; (4) the
long confrontation between Creon and Antigone (which occupies a much greater
part of Anouilh's play than it does of Sophocles': almost a third of the tragedy); (5)
the entrance of Ismene, who wants to share Antigone's fate and is rejected (this is
one of the passages where Anouilh's play is very close to Sophocles'); (6) the encounter between Creon and his son Haemon (much shorter than in Sophocles); (7) the
entrance of the messenger coming to announce that Antigone has hanged herself in
her prison and that Haemon has committed suicide over Antigone's body. However,
Anouilh added a scene between two characters who already exist in Sophocles but
who do not meet in his play: Antigone and her fiancé Haemon. Anouilh had earlier
added an initial scene between Antigone and her nurse, a character who does not
exist in Sophocles' play. On the other hand, she is an important character in the
play. Anouilh eliminated an important character in Sophocles' play, the seer Tiresias.
His absent is very significant. Despite being largely faithful to the sequence of scenes
in the Sophoclean model, and also to the depiction of minor characters (the guard),
the tone of the tragedy changes considerably, less as a result of its familiarity and the
insertion of the drama into the modern world than as a result of the destruction of
the political, moral, and religious values that underlie Sophocles' tragedy. Antigone
is still Oedipus's inflexible daughter, but her rebellion is reduced to a young person's

refusal to compromise. The character of Creon is completely transformed by his skepticism, so that the indifference of the modern Creon at the end of the tragedy, when he is faced by the deaths of his son and his wife, stands in stark contrast to the pathos of the lament of Sophoclean Creon, who has passed in the space of a single day from holding power to utter annihilation, from his mistakes to painful awareness. The conception of the tragic has also changed. Paradoxically, the modern saw in the Greek tragedy the fulfillment of a blind fate: as in Cocteau's *La Machine Infernal*, Anouilh's prologue, as well as the chorus, present a tragedy that has been played out in advance, without hope. This contrasts with the spectator's feelings during the performance of Sophocles' tragedy, where the author skillfully makes hope spring up again after fear, creating the illusion that it is still possible that Antigone might be saved, before plunging the spectator into despair again. Anouilh's *Antigone*, like Brecht's, was born in the circumstances of the Second World War (here is what Anouilh himself said about it: "Sophocles' *Antigone*, which I read and reread, and had known by heart forever, was a sudden shock for me during the war, on the day of the little red posters. I rewrote it in my own way, with the resonance of the tragedy that we were then living through").

70. Obviously, these are not the only plays entitled *Oedipe* that were written the seventeenth and eighteenth centuries. A list of these productions (from 1614 to 1818) is given by Ch. Biet in his *Oedipe en monarchie* (cited above), pp. 16–17 (add for 1614 Nicolas de Sainte Marthe's *Oedipe*, a tragedy that appeared in the same year as Jean Prévost's). Ch. Biet's work is fundamental for the history of the afterlife of Sophocles' *Oedipus* (and also of Seneca's) during the French classical period. In addition to the tragedies, there were also tragicomedies. We can read in a modern edition Dominique's *Oedipe travesti*, which appeared one year after Voltaire's *Oedipe* (*Oedipe, tragédie de Voltaire, suivie de Œdipe travesti, parodie de Dominique*, Éd. Espaces 34, 2002). There were also lyrical tragedies, for example the *Oedipus at Colonus* performed at the court of Versailles in 1786 (music by Antonio Sacchini with a libretto by Nicolas Guillard). In his list, Ch. Biet also mentions a tragedy in English by John Dryden (1672), which he presents on pp. 223–35.

71. In Corneille's career, *Œdipe* (Corneille, Œuvres complètes, ed. G. Couton, Paris: Gallimard, Bibliothèque de la Pléiade, 1987, vol. 3, pp. 17–93) came after a long silence occasioned by the failure of his play *Pertharite* (1651). It was at the instigation of Fouquet, the superintendant of finances and a protector of men of letters, that Corneille chose Oedipus among three subjects that Fouquet had proposed to him. This commissioned work was rapidly written, in two months. It met with approval when it was performed at the Hôtel de Bourgogne. It was Corneille's last success; he was soon to be eclipsed by Racine. In his preface to the reader and in his *Examen* of the play, Corneille put Sophocles' *Oedipus* and Seneca's on the same level. His ambition was initially to translate these great geniuses who had preceded him. But he could not make up his mind to follow them, because the ancient tragedies were too likely to shock or disappoint the taste of the audience of his time, either because of what they had too much of (the description of bloodshed) or too little of (love). So he eliminated the excessively realistic description of Oedipus's self-blinding and "reduced the number of oracles, which might be unseemly"; and he did not include the chorus. The character of Creon disappeared (without Corneille talking about it in his *Examen*). On the other hand, he introduced the "happy episode of Theseus

and Dircé." For this purpose, he invented the character of Dircé (the daughter of Laius and Jocasta, named after one of the rivers in Thebes), and he added the character of Theseus, whom he might have found in *Oedipus at Colonus*, but whom he made into an amorous hero. "The different path I have taken," he declares in his *Examen*, "prevented me from following them (sc. Sophocles and Seneca) and adorning myself with their work: but in recompense I have been fortunate enough to make people admit that I have written no plays in which as much art is found as in this one." A precise study of the way sources are used and conflated remains to be written. The "shade of great Laius" invoked by Tiresias when he delivers a message (act 2, scene 3, v. 181 and vv. 191ff.; cf. Seneca, *Oedipus*, vv. 623ff.) comes from Seneca, not from Sophocles. In Sophocles, the two Theban and Corinthian shepherds who saved the infant Oedipus when he was abandoned by his parents remain anonymous. In Corneille, they have names, Phorbas and Iphicrates. The name "Phorbas" comes from Seneca; that of Iphicrates was invented by Corneille, because the old Corinthian remains nameless in Seneca, as he did in Sophocles. For the political and religious stakes involved in Corneille's *Oedipe*, see C. Biet, *Oedipe en monarchie* (cited above), pp. 203–21 (Corneille or the legitimation of the future king). Also see P. A. Ogundele, "The Oidipus Story in the Hands of Sophocles, Seneca, and Corneille," *Nigeria and the Classics* 12, 1970, pp. 31–51.

72. Letter written in 1719 about the criticism of Sophocles' *Oedipus*. Voltaire's *Oedipe* is the first play in a body of theatrical work that would eventually be very large (fifty-seven plays!). Voltaire was nineteen years old at the time. His *Oedipe* was performed in 1718 and was very successful (forty-five consecutive performances). As Voltaire himself admits in the letter cited above, several scenes are borrowed from Sophocles. After saying that he would not have undertaken his *Oedipe* without Sophocles, he goes on: "First I translated the first scene of my fourth act; the one in which the high priest accuses the king is entirely his [Sophocles']; the scene with the two old men is his as well." Voltaire borrowed from Corneille "the shade of great Laius" (act 1, scene 3) and the name of the old Theban, Phorbas; he changed the name of the old man from Corinth, from the "Iphicrates" invented by Corneille to "Icarus." Above all, he transposed Corneille's main innovation, the introduction of a love interest. Just as Corneille had added a love story by replacing Creon with Theseus (see above), Voltaire replaced Creon with a Philoctetes in love with Jocasta before her marriage to Laius. The role of Jocasta would have been insipid, Voltaire says, "had she not had at least the memory of a legitimate love." Granted! But the choice of Philoctetes is strange. Unlike Corneille, Voltaire blithely conflates generations that the ancients, who since Homer had been so careful with the generational history of their heroes, would never have confused. Theseus, introduced by Corneille, is actually of Oedipus's generation. But Philoctetes belongs to the following generation, that of the Trojan War, when Oedipus was already dead. How are we to imagine Philoctetes being in love with Jocasta before her marriage to Laius? Jocasta belongs, in fact, to the generation of Philoctetes' grandmother! Thus we fall into a cheap mythology. Unlike Corneille, who had done away with the chorus, Voltaire reintroduces the chorus of Theban men. But its role is in no way comparable to that of Sophocles' chorus.

73. See Jean Cocteau (cited above), pp. 209–31. The Latin translation of Cocteau's libretto was made by Jean Danielou, the future cardinal. The opera-oratorio in two

acts retains from Sophocles' *Oedipus the King* only "a certain monumental aspect." A voice, called "The Speaker," intervenes in French in a prologue and in the course of action to remind the audience "of Sophocles' play as the action proceeds" (p. 211). The first stage performance took place in Vienna (Staatsoper, February 23, 1928). The opera met with a worldwide success, and, thirty years after its performance in 1928, there was another performance in Vienna (under the direction of Herbert von Karajan) in which Cocteau played the role of The Speaker. After Stravinsky's opera, Oedipus inspired another composer, Georg Enescu (1881–1955), who wrote an opera with a libretto by Edmond Fleg that combines *Oedipus the King* with *Oedipus at Colonus*, replacing Oedipus's destiny in chronological order from his birth to his death at Colonus.

74. See Jean Cocteau (cited above), pp. 425–43. Cocteau completed his *Oedipe Roi* in 1925. It was published by Plon in 1928 and first performed at the Nouveau Théâtre Antoine in June 1937. In the preface to the 1928 edition, Cocteau declares that "Oedipe, c'est la méthode d'Antigone après l'expérience du théâtre. Je le tire du premier travail de l'opéra-oratorio en latin Œdipus Rex, en collaboration avec Igor Strawinsky" (p. 443).

75. This play in four acts was first performed at Louis Jouvet's theater (Comédie des Champs-Élysées) on April 10, 1934. At the beginning, a voice, using the technique adopted in *Oedipus Rex*, summarizes the basics of Oedipus's destiny as it can be reconstructed from flashbacks in Sophocles' play by putting it in a chronological order from the abandonment of the infant in the mountains after the first oracle down to Jocasta's suicide and Oedipus's self-mutilation; then the voice extracts the meaning Cocteau gave to the myth: "one of the most perfect machines constructed by the infernal gods for the mathematical annihilation of a mortal." The play no longer respects the unity of time; before Oedipus's arrival in Thebes, the shade of Laius tries to warn Jocasta (act 1); during this time, the encounter between Oedipus and the Sphinx takes place (act 2); Oedipus's and Jocasta's wedding night (act 3); seventeen years later, comes the sequence that corresponds to Sophocles' *Oedipus* (act 4). The idea of Laius's shade appearing in act 1 goes back, in principle, to Seneca, and not to Sophocles. Had Cocteau read Seneca? In any case, he did not adopt the name of Phorbas that Seneca had given to the Theban shepherd. We have seen that the shade of Laius was also mentioned in Corneille and in Voltaire (see above). But Cocteau might have taken the idea of a ghost from Shakespeare's *Hamlet*.

76. Published in 1930, Gide's play in three acts was performed by Georges Pitoëff at the Théâtre de L'Oeuvre. See André Gide, *Oedipe, suivi de Brouillons et textes inédits, édition critique établie, présentée et annotée par Clara Debard*, Paris: Honoré Champion, 2007, 324 pp. Despite the merits of this edition, which collects interesting documents concerning the genesis of the work and its reception, a precise study of the rewriting of Sophocles' play remains to be written.

77. Anouilh, *Œdipe ou le roi boiteux*, Paris: La Table Ronde, 1986; rpt. 1996. Here is what Anouilh himself said about it: "*Oedipus the King*, reread not long ago by accident, like all the classics, when I walk in front of my bookshelves and pick one out, dazzled me once again—I who have never been able to read a detective novel all the way through. What was beautiful in the time of the Greeks is still beautiful, it's knowing the outcome in advance. That's the real 'suspense' . . . and I slipped into Sophocles' tragedy like a thief—but a scrupulous thief in love with his booty."

78. J. Harpmann, *Mes Oedipe*, Éd. Luc Pire, 2006. The first part is entitled "Eyes Blind-folded," the second "Oedipus Illuminated," and the third "The Last Generation."

79. Henri Bauchau, *Œdipe sur la route*, Arles: Actes Sud, 1990. This was followed by another novel on Antigone, Arles: Actes Sud, 1997.

80. *Œdipe Roi, traduit du mythe par Didier Lamaison*, Paris: Gallimard, 1994; rpt. 2006, with the addition of Sophocles, *Œdipe roi*, translated from the Greek, presented and annotated by Didier Lamaison.

81. The list presented here is far from being exhaustive, even for the French theater. For a more complete list, see P. Brunel, *Le Mythe d'Electre* (3rd ed.), Paris: Honoré Champion, 1995, 212 pp. (with an appendix on three modern plays: André Suarès, *La Tragédie d'Elektre et Oreste*, 1907; Marguerite Yourcenar, *Electre ou la chute des masques*; Jean Anouilh, *Tu étais si gentil quand tu étais petit*). See the chronological list given by P. Brunel, pp. 197–200.

82. Pasolini also wrote plays. He wrote a play inspired by the myth of Orestes and Electra, entitled *Pilade* (Pylades), in eight episodes. Original edition: *Pilade*, Milan: Aldo Garzanti, 1997.

83. For *The Women of Trachis*, we may mention Haendel's musical drama *Hercules*, with a libretto by Thomas Broughton (1745), based on Sophocles' *The Women of Trachis* and Ovid's *Metamorphoses*. The complete libretto with a French translation by Marie-Thérèse Fauquet has recently been published in *Avant-Scène Opéra*, no. 221, 2004, 102 pp.

84. On the Byzantine triad, see above. See A. Dain and P. Mazon, *Sophocle I*, CUF, 1st ed. 1955, p. xlviii, n. 2: "At the end of the Byzantine era, the academic choice included only *Ajax*, the only play by Sophocles that had never ceased to be read."

85. This would be a vast domain of study, indispensable for gauging Sophocles' afterlife in all its breadth. Sophocles served, in particular, as a subject for the Prix de Rome competitions in painting and sculpture. Two themes in his life were proposed as subjects: the young Sophocles after the victory at Salamis (see above) and Sophocles at the end of his life, accused by his son or sons (see above). For the theme on Sophocles' old age, see the pictures entitled *Sophocles Accused by his Sons*, by E. Michel (Prix de Rome for painting, 1860; Paris, École nationale supérieure des Beaux-Arts: inv. PRP 110) and V. Giraud (project for the picture presented in 1860 for the Prix de Rome competition; Musée du Louvre, department of graphic arts; inv. RF 38532, recto). For the theme on his youth, see the sculptures entitled *The Young Sophocles after the Victory at Salamis* by C. Crenier (Prix de Rome for sculpture in 1908; Paris, École nationale supérieure des Beaux-Arts: inv. PRS 97) and by M. Gaumont (Prix de Rome for sculpture in 1908; Paris, École nationale supérieure des Beaux-Arts: inv. PRS 96). Concerning Sophocles' works, we find in the subjects for the Prix de Rome what I have called the modern trilogy (*Electra, Oedipus the King, Antigone*). For *Electra*, the Prix de Rome for painting in 1823 is entitled *Aegisthus, Thinking to Discover the Body of the Dead Orestes, Recognizes That of Clytemnestra* (= Sophocles, *Electra*, v. 1475: "What do I see?"): pictures by F. Bouchot (Paris, École nationale supérieure des Beaux-Arts: inv. PRP 63) and by A. Debay (Paris, ibid.: inv. PRP 62). For Antigone, the Prix de Rome in 1825 is entitled *Antigone Burying Poly-nices*, a painting by S. Norblin de La Gourdaine (Paris, École nationale supérieure des Beaux-Arts: inv. PRP 65). With *Oedipus the King*, we can attach the Prix de Rome for painting in 1843, *Oedipus and Antigone Going into Exile from Thebes*, even

though Sophocles' play does not end, as is too often believed, with exile, since Oedipus in fact goes back into the palace: picture by E. Damery (Paris, École nationale supérieure des Beaux-Arts: inv. PRP 88). For the Prix de Rome, see Ph. Grunchec, *Le Grand Prix de peinture, les concours des prix de Rome de 1797 à 1863*, Paris, 1983.

86. Sophocles, *Oedipus at Colonus*, vv. 1549–55.

87. I would like to thank all those who have helped me during the composition of this biography of Sophocles, which follows my study of Hippocrates, which appears in the same collection and which was written in the same spirit of openness to a broad audience without for all that yielding to facileness. I thank first of all Madame Jacqueline de Romilly, to whom I owe so much, from her courses at the Sorbonne to her activity in the Academy. It is thanks to her that I became acquainted with the director of the present collection, Denis Maraval, to whom I would like to pay homage for his friendly confidence in me and his infinite patience, without which the work would never have seen the light of day. Heinrich von Staden, to whom this work is dedicated, welcomed me with his friendly attention during the semester I spent at Princeton in 2001–2, as a member of the Institute for Advanced Study, where I conducted an intense bibliographical investigation and where I wrote part of the chapters in this book. He shared with me a passion for the "minor characters" in Sophocles. The generations of students at the Sorbonne who have participated in my seminar on Greek tragedy, whose subject changed each year, will recognize here and there the pieces of a puzzle presented here for the first time as a whole. My gratitude also goes to those who, especially in the final stages, reread the manuscript in whole or in part: Danielle Jouanna, who wrote her *Aspasie* (published by Fayard in 2005) at Princeton while I was writing my *Sophocles*; Edmond Lévy, my former colleague and a professor of history at the University of Strasbourg, who reread the first part; Anne Lebeau, my colleague at the Sorbonne, whom I thank for her attentive reading of the whole and for her spontaneous and perceptive reactions; then those of my students whom I relied on for a final reading: Michel Fartzoff, professor at the University of Besancon, and the trio formed by three professors or researchers already known by their works published on Greek tragedy: Christine Mauduit, professor at the University of Lyon III, Alessia Guardasole, a researcher at the CNRS who came from the Neopolitan school of Antonio Garzya, and Diane Cuny, lecturer at the University of Tours. Finally, I thank Nathalie Reignier, who helped with competence and devotion in the correction of the proofs and the preparation of the book.

The author joins the [original French] publisher in thanking Christelle Derda.

Appendix III. The Identification of Sophocles as a Hellenotamias

1. Complement to note 10, chapter II.
2. [Retranslated from the French.]
3. [Retranslated from the French.]

BIBLIOGRAPHICAL GUIDE

....

General Bibliographical Tools on Socrates

For 1939–59: H. Friis Johansen, *Lustrum* 7, 1962, pp. 94–342.

In all, A. Lesky, and then H. Strohm have produced twelve bibliographical syntheses on Sophocles in *Anzeiger für die Altertumswissenschaft*, the oldest being that of A. Lesky in vol. 2 (1949), col. 1–11, and the most recent is that of H. Strohm: 12. Fortsetzung (Sophokles) 30 (1977), col. 129–44.

The details of these bibliographical syntheses, as well as the bibliographical tools for older periods, are conveniently given under the rubric *Bibliographica* by H. Lloyd-Jones and N. G. Wilson, *Studies on the Text of Sophocles*, Oxford, 1990, p. 8.

S. Saïd, "Travaux récents sur la tragédie grecque (1960–1980: Un essai de mise au point," *Information littéraire* 33, 2, 1981, pp. 69–77.

———, "Cinq ans de recherches sur la tragédie grecque (1980–1984)," *Revue des Etudes Anciennes* 86, 1984, pp. 259–94.

Ch. Jacob, "Bibliographie sélective concernant Eschyle, Sophocle et Euripide (1500–1900)," *Métis* 3, 1988, pp. 363–407.

S. Saïd, "Bibliographie tragique (1900–1988): Quelques orientations," *Métis* 3, 1988, pp. 402–512.

J. R. Green, "Theatre Production (1971–1986)," *Lustrum* 31, 1989, pp. 7–71.

———, "Theatre Production (1987–1995)," *Lustrum* 37, 1995, pp. 7–202.

The bibliographical tools online are now the easiest to consult, in particular the *Année philologique* (with subscription) or *Gnomon* (direct access). For the papyruses concerning Sophocles and their bibliography, see Mertens-Pack online with direct access (CEDO-PAL). For the history of the reception of ancient theater, see the site "Archive of Performances of Greek and Roman Drama," University of Oxford (APGRD), and the site DIDASKALIA, University of Warwick.

Recent Introductions to Greek Tragedy

P. E. Easterling and B.M.W. Knox, *Greek Drama*, in *The Cambridge History of Classical Literature*, I, 2, Cambridge, 1989, 217 pp. (for Sophocles, pp. 43–64).

P. E. Easterling (ed.), *The Cambridge Companion to Greek Tragedy*, Cambridge, 1997.

J. Gregory (ed.), *A Companion to Greek Tragedy*, Oxford: Blackwell, 2006 (pp. 233–50 for Sophocles, by Ruth Scodel).

In France, see J. de Romilly, *La Tragédie grecque*, Paris: PUF, 1970 (with new editions); see also P. Demont and A. Lebeau, *Introduction au théâtre grec antique*, Le Livre de poche, 1996 (2nd ed. 2003).

Recent Editions of the Greek Text of Sophocles' Theater

A. Dain and P. Mazon, *Sophocle*, 3 vols., Paris: Les Belles Lettres, 1st ed., 1955 (Greek text by A. Dain, French translation by P. Mazon, many reprintings, some of which have revisions and corrections by J. Irigoin; the most recent reprints corrected by J. Irigoin are: vol. 1, 7th printing, 1994; vol. 2, 8th printing, 1994; vol. 3, 5th printing, 1999; printings after 2002 are without changes).

R. D. Dawe, *Sophocles Tragoediae*, Bibliotheca Teubneriana, 2 vols., Teubner Verlagsgesellschaft, 1975–79; 2nd ed. 1984–85; 3rd ed. 1996 (Greek text only).

A. Colonna, *Sophoclis Fabulae*, 3 vols., in *Corpus Scriptorum Graecorum Paravianum*, Turin: Paravia, 1975–83.

For editions with commentaries and separate editions of each tragedy, see the end of the section on each tragedy presented in appendix I.

For the Greek text of the fragments, the standard edition is S. Radt, *Tragicorum graecorum fragmenta* (*TrGF*), vol. 4, *Sophocles*, Göttingen, 1977 (including also the *Testimonia* on Sophocles) with the addenda and corrigenda in S. Radt *TrGF* 3, *Aeschylus*, Göttingen, 1985, pp. 561–92. A new edition appeared in 1999 ("editio correctior et addendis aucta"), 791 pp. For the presentation of the fragments, see appendix II, and for the bibliography of the fragments, see below in this bibliographical guide.

For the Greek text of the ancient scholia (in the margin of the tenth-century Florence manuscript), the standard reference is P. N. Papageorgius, *Scholia in Sophoclis Tragoedias vetera* (e codice Laurentiano denuo colloto), Lipsiae, in aedibus Teubneri, 1888.

Dictionaries and Concordances

F. Ellendt, *Lexicon Sophocleum*, Berlin, 1872, rpt. Hildesheim: Olms, 1958.

M. Papathomopoulos, *Concordantia Sophoclea*, 2 vols., Hildesheim: Olms-Weidmann, 2006, 958 pp.

General Studies on Sophocles (or on Greek Tragedy with a Discussion of Sophocles)

S. M. Adams, *Sophocles The Playwright*, Toronto, 1957, *Phoenix.*, supp. 3, 182 pp. (studies of the tragedies in this order: *Ajax, Antigone, Électra, Oedipus the King, The Women of Trachis, Philoctetes, Oedipus at Colonus*).

J. Alaux, *Le Liège et le filet: Filiation et lien familial dans la tragédie athénienne du Ve siècle*, Paris: Belin, 1995, 319 pp.

F. Allègre, *Sophocle: Étude sur les ressorts dramatiques de son théâtre et de la composition de ses tragédies*, Lyon, 1905 (study of the tragedies in this order: *The Women of Trachis, Ajax, Philoctetes, Électra, Oedipus at Colonus, Oedipus the King, Antigone*).

M. Altmeyer, *Unzeitgemässes Denken bei Sophokles*, in *Hermes Einzelschriften* 85, 2001, 330 pp.

G. Avezzù (ed.), *Il dramma sofocleo: Testo, lingua, interpretazione*, Drama, *Beiträge zum antiken Drama und seiner Rezeption*, vol. 13, Stuttgart, 2003, 404 pp.

A. Bagordo, *Reminiszenzen früher Lyrik bei den attischen Tragikern*, Zetemata 118, Munich, 2003, 286 pp.

E. S. Belfiore, *Murder among Friends: Violation of Philia in Greek Tragedy*, Oxford, University, 2000, 282 pp.

A. Bierl, *Dionysos und die griechische Tragödie: Politische und "metatheatralische" Aspekte im Text*, Tübingen: Narr, 1991, 298 pp.

M. W. Blundell, *Helping Friends and Harming Enemies: A Study in Sophocles and Greek Ethics*, Cambridge, 1989, 298 pp. (particularly *Ajax, Antigone, Electra, Philoctetes, Oedipus at Colonus*).

————, "Sophocles: An Ethical Approach; A Study of *Electra, Philoctetes* and *Oedipus at Colonus*," diss. University of California, Berkeley, 1984, 377 pp.

C. M. Bowra, *Sophoclean Tragedy*, Oxford, 1944, 384 pp. (general study of the tragedies in this order: *Ajax, Antigone, The Women of Trachis, Oedipus the King, Electra, Philoctetes, Oedipus at Colonus*).

F. Budelmann, *The Language of Sophocles: Communality, Communication and Involvement*, Cambridge, 2000, 297 pp.

R.G.A. Buxton, *Sophocles*, Greece and Rome: New Surveys in the Classics 16, Oxford, 1984, 38 pp.

M. Coray, *Wissen und erkennen bei Sophokles*, Schweizerische Beiträge zur Altertumswissenschaft 24, Berlin, 1993, 457 pp.

D. Cuny, *Une leçon de vie: Les réflexions générales chez Sophocle*, Paris: Les Belles Lettres, 2007, 419 pp.

J. de Romilly, *L'Évolution du pathétique d'Eschyle à Euripide*, Paris: PUF, 1961, 148 pp.

————, *Le Temps dans la tragédie grecque*, Paris: Vrin, 1971, 160 pp.

———— (ed.), *Sophocle*, Entretiens sur l'Antiquité classique 29, Vandoeuvres-Genève: Fondation Hardt, 1982, 274 pp.

V. Di Benedetto, *Sofocle*, Florence, 1983, 264 pp.

V. Di Benedetto and E. Medda, *La tragedia sulla scena*, Turin: Einaudi, 1997, 422 pp.

H. Diller, *Sophokles*, Wege der Forschung 95, Darmstadt, 1967, 546 pp. (selection of articles on Sophocles).

J. Duchemin, *L'agôn dans la tragédie grecque*, 2nd ed., Paris: Les Belles Lettres, 1968, 247 pp.

F. R. Earp, *The Style of Sophocles*, Cambridge, 1944, 177 pp.

P. Easterling, "Repetition in Sophocles," *Hermes* 101, 1973, pp. 14–34.

V. Ehrenberg, *Sophocles and Pericles*, Oxford, 1954, 187 pp.

H. Flashar, *Sophokles: Dichter im demokratischen Athen*, Munich, 2000, 220 pp. (general study of the plays in the following order: *Ajax, Antigone, The Women of Trachis, Oedipus the King, Electra, Philoctetes, Oedipus at Colonus, Ichneutae*, with introductory chapters on the theater and on Sophocles' life, and a conclusion on the tragic).

R. C. Flickinger, *The Greek Theater and Its Drama*, 4th ed., Chicago, 1936.

A. F. Garvie, *The Plays of Sophocles*, Bristol Classical Press, 2005, 94 pp. (brief study of each tragedy).

G. H. Gellie, *Sophocles: A Reading*, Melbourne, 1972, 307 pp.

J. Griffin (ed.), *Sophocles Revisited: Essays Presented to Sir Hugh Lloyd-Jones*, Oxford University Press, 1999, 343 pp.

H.-Ch. Günther, *Exercitationes Sophocleae*, Hypomnemata 109, 1996, 158 pp.

J. C. Hogan, *A Commentary on the Plays of Sophocles*, Carbondale: Southern Illinois University Press, 1991, 386 pp.

I.J.F. de Jong and A. Rijksbaron, *Sophocles and the Greek Language: Aspects of Diction, Syntax and Pragmatics, Mnemosyne*, supp. 269, Leiden: Brill, 2005, 300 pp.

J. Jouanna, "Fiction poétique et contraintes théâtrales chez Sophocle," in *La Poétique, théorie et pratique* (XVe Congrès de l'Association Guillaume Budé: Orléans, August 25–28, 2003), Paris: Les Belles Lettres, 2007, pp. 240–65.

G. M. Kirkwood, *A Study of Sophoclean Drama*, Ithaca, NY: Cornell University Press, 1994 (1st ed. 1958), 308 pp. (general study by themes: construction; character portrayal; the role of the chorus; some notes on diction; the irony of Sophocles); rpt. 1994 with a new preface and an enlarged bibliography.

H.D.F. Kitto, *Form and Meaning in Drama: A Study of Six Greek Plays and of Hamlet*, London: Methuen, 1956, 341 pp. (On Sophocles: "Philoctetes, Antigone, Ajax," pp. 87–198).

———, *Sophocles Dramatist and Philosopher*, Oxford University Press, 1958, 64 pp.

B.M.W. Knox, *The Heroic Temper: Studies in Sophoclean Tragedy*, Berkeley: University of California Press, 1964, 210 pp. (two general chapters on the character traits shared by Sophocles' heroes, two chapters on *Antigone*, one chapter on *Philoctetes*, one chapter on *Oedipus at Colonus*).

———, *Word and Action: Essays on Ancient Theater*, Baltimore, 1986 (1979), 378 pp.

J. Kott, *Manger les dieux: Essais sur la tragédie grecque et la modernité*, Paris: Payot, 1975, 262 pp.

J. Lacarrière, *Sophocle: Essai*, L'Arche, 1960, 2nd ed. 1978, 132 pp.

E. Lefèvre, *Die Unfähigkeit sich zu erkennen: Sophokles' Tragödien*, Leiden: Brill, 2001, 320 pp.

F.J.H. Letters, *The Life and Work of Sophocles*, London, 1953, 310 pp.

H. Lloyd-Jones and N. G. Wilson, *Sophoclea: Studies on the Text of Sophocles*, Oxford, 1990, 282 pp.

———, *Sophocles: Second Thoughts, Hypomnemata* 100, 1997, 146 pp.

A. A. Long, *Language and Thought in Sophocles*, London, 1968, 186 pp.

N. Loraux, *La Voix endeuillée: Essai sur la tragédie grecque*, Paris: Gallimard, 1999, 185 pp.

A. Machin, *Cohérence et continuité dans le théa^tre de Sophocle*, Québec, 1981, 542 pp.

A. Maddalena, *Sofocle*, 2nd ed., Turin, 1963 (1st ed. 1959), 391 pp. (study of each tragedy: *Ajax, Antigone, The Women of Trachis, Electra, Philoctetes, Oedipus the King, Oedipus at Colonus*).

G. Méautis, *Sophocle: Essai sur le héros tragique*, Paris, 1957, 292 pp. (study of each tragedy *Ajax, Philoctetes, Oedipus the King, Oedipus at Colonus, Antigone, Electra, The Women of Trachis*).

A. C. Moorhouse, *The Syntax of Sophocles*, Leiden, 1982, 353 pp.

H. Musurillo, *The Light and the Darkness: Studies in the Dramatic Poetry of Sophocles*, Leiden, 1967, 165 pp.

W. Nicolai, *Zu Sophokles' Wirkungsabsichten*, Heidelberg, 1992, 128 pp.

"Patience, mon coeur! . . .": L'essor de la psychologie dans la littérature grecque classique, Paris, 1984 (Sophocles, pp. 71–92).

A. Pérez Jiménez, C. Alcalde Martin, and R. Caballero Sanchez (eds.), *Sofocles el hombre, Sofocles el poeta*, Malaga, 2004, 512 pp.

G. Perrotta, *Sofocle*, Milan, 1935, rpt. Rome: L'Erma, 1963, 646 pp.

S. Pfeiffer-Petersen, *Konfliktstichomythien bei Sophokles: Funktion und Gestaltung*, Wiesbaden: Reichert, 1996, 186 pp.

M. D. Reeve, "Some Interpolations in Sophocles," *Greek, Roman and Byzantine Studies* 11, 1970, pp. 283–93.

R. Rehm, *Greek Tragic Theater*, London: Routledge 1992, 168 pp.

K. Reinhardt, *Sophokles*, Frankfurt am Main, 3rd ed., 1947 (1st ed. 1933), 291 pp. (study of each tragedy in the "canonical order," with a last chapter on the fragments).

M. Ringer, *Electra and the Empty Urn: Metatheater and Role Playing in Sophocles*, Chapel Hill: University of North Carolina Press, 1998, 253 pp. (application of modern theories of metatheater to Sophocles' tragedies: *Ajax, The Women of Trachis*, the Theban plays, *Antigone, Oedipus the King, Oedipus at Colonus*, then *Philoctetes* and *Electra*).

G. Ronnet, *Sophocle, poète tragique*, Paris, 1969, 346 pp. (first part is a synthetic study on dramatic structure, the characters, the chorus, and lyricism, and finally destiny and the gods; the second part studies three tragedies: *Electra, Philoctetes, Oedipus at Colonus*). See B.M.W. Knox's review in *American Journal of Philology* 92, 1971, pp. 692–701.

S. Saïd, *La Faute tragique*, Paris, 1978, 536 pp.

M. Schauer, *Tragisches Klagen: Form und Funktion der Klagedarstellung bei Aischylos, Sophokles und Euripides*, *Classica Monacensia* 26, 2002, Tübingen: Narr, 381 pp.

R. Scodel, *Sophocles*, Boston, 1984, 155 pp. (study of *Ajax, The Women of Trachis, Antigone, Oedipus the King, Electra, Philoctetes, Oedipus at Colonus*); see also his study on Sophocles in J. Gregory (ed.), cited above in "Recent Introductions to Greek Tragedy."

L. Séchan, *Études sur la tragédie grecque dans ses rapports avec la céramique*, Paris, 1967 (1926), 642 pp. (Sophocles, pp. 139–230).

Ch. Segal, *Sophocles' Tragic World: Divinity, Nature, Society*, Cambridge, MA: Harvard University Press, 1995, 276 pp.

————, *Tragedy and Civilization: An Interpretation of Sophocles*, Cambridge, MA: Harvard University Press, 1981, 506 pp. (after three general chapters, including one entitled "A Structural Approach to Greek Myth and Tragedy," a tragedy-by-tragedy study: *The Women of Trachis, Ajax, Antigone, Oedipus the King, Electra, Philoctetes, Oedipus at Colonus*).

O. Taplin, *Greek Tragedy in Action*, London, 1978, 203 pp. (particularly *Ajax, Oedipus the King, Philoctetes*).

A. D. Trendall and T.B.L. Webster, *Illustrations of Greek Drama*, London, 1971 (Sophocles pp. 63–71).

E. Ugolini, *Sofocle e Atene: Vita politica e attività teatrale nella Grecia classica*, Rome, 2000, 275 pp.

A.J.A. Waldock, *Sophocles the Dramatist*, Cambridge, 1951, 234 pp.

T.B.L. Webster, *An Introduction to Sophocles*, 2nd ed., London, 1969, 220 pp.

————, *Monuments Illustrating Tragedy and Satyr Play*, 2nd ed., *Bulletin of the Institute of Classical Studies of the University of London*, supp. 20, 1967 (Sophocles, pp. 146–53).

C. H. Whitman, *Sophocles: A Study of Heroic Humanism*, Cambridge, MA: Harvard University Press, 1951, 292 pp. (general study by work following the chronological order adopted by the author: *Ajax, Antigone, The Women of Trachis, Oedipus the King, Electra, Philoctetes, Oedipus at Colonus*, with an introductory part, notably on *Hamartia* and a concluding part entitled "The Heroic World," in which Sophocles is resituated in his time).

T. von Wilamowitz-Moellendorff, *Die dramatische Technik des Sophokles*, in *Philologische Untersuchungen* 22, Berlin, 1917, 379 pp.; cf. H. Lloyd-Jones, "Tycho von Wilamowitz-Moellendorf on the Dramatic Technique of Sophocles," *Classical Quarterly*, n.s., 22, 1972, pp. 214–28 (*Greek Epic, Lyric and Tragedy: The Academic Papers of Sir Hugh Lloyd-Jones*, Oxford, 1990, pp. 401–18).

R. P. Winnington-Ingram, *Sophocles: An Interpretation*, Cambridge, 1980, 346 pp. (study by tragedy in the order *Ajax, Women of Trachis, Antigone, Oedipus the King, Electra, Oedipus at Colonus, Philoctetes*, with the insertion of more general chapters, particularly chap. 7, "Fate in Sophocles"; chap. 9, "Furies in Sophocles," and chap. 13, "Heroes and Gods").

Particular Studies on Each Tragedy

I. *AJAX*

a. Annotated Editions or Commentaries That Are Fundamental and/or Recent
See appendix I, section on *Ajax* (end).

b. Articles

For a bibliography of Sophocles' *Ajax*, see Alain Moreau, "Bibliographie de l'*Ajax* de Sophocle," *Supp. aux cahiers du Gita*, no. 10, Université de Montpellier, 1997, 45 pp.

S. M. Adams, "The *Ajax* of Sophocles," *Phoenix* 9, 1955, pp. 93–110.

J. Alaux, "Éponymie et paternité dans *Ajax*: Sophocle dans l'ombre d'Homère," *Gaia* 4, 2000, pp. 45–59.

E. Barker, "The Fall-Out from Dissent: Hero and Audience in Sophocles' *Ajax*," *Greece and Rome*, ser. 2, 51, 2004, pp. 1–20.

S. H. Barlow, "Sophocles' *Ajax* and Euripides' *Heracles*," *Ramus* 10, 1981, pp. 112–28.

L. Bergson, "Der *Aias* des Sophokles als 'Trilogie': Versuch einer Bilanz," *Hermes* 114, 1986, pp. 36–50.

P. Biggs, "The Disease Theme in Sophocles' *Ajax, Philoctetes* and *Trachiniae*," *Classical Philology* 61, 1966, pp. 223–35.

W. E. Brown, "Sophocles' Ajax and Homer's Hector," *Classical Journal* 61, 1965–66, pp. 118–21.

W. M. Calder III, "The Entrance of Athena in *Ajax*," *Classical Philology* 60, 1965, pp. 114–16.

M. G. Ciani, "*Aiace* tra epos e tragedia," *Studi Italiani di Filologia Classica* 15, 1997, pp. 176–87.

L. F. Coraluppi, "Interpretazione dell' *Aiace* di Sofocle," *Dioniso* 42, 1968, pp. 115–42.

L. R. Cresci, "Il prologo dell' *Aiace*," *Maia* 26, 1974, pp. 217–25.

J. F. Davidson, "Sophocles, *Ajax* 192–200," *Mnemosyne* 29, 1976, pp. 129–35.

———, "Sophocles, *Ajax* 172–79," *American Journal of Philology* 104, 1983, pp. 192–98.

———, "Sophocles, *Ajax* 148–150," *Mnemosyne* 37, 1984, pp. 438–40.

M. I. Davies, "Ajax and Tekmessa: A Cup by the Brygos Painter in the Bareiss Collection," *Antike Kunst* 16, 1973, 1, pp. 60–70 (+ plates 9–11).

B. Deforge, "Le glaive d'Ajax," *Kentron* 11, 1995, pp. 59–70.

P. Demont, "Remarques sur la folie d'Ajax," in J. M. Galy and M.-R. Guelfucci, *L'Homme grec: Hommage à Antoine Thivel*, Nice, 2000, pp. 140–56.

R. Ebeling, "Missverständnisse um den *Aias* des Sophokles," *Hermes* 76, 1941, pp. 283–314.

I. Errandonea, "Les quatre monologues d'*Ajax* et leur signification dramatique," *Les Études Classiques* 26, 1958, pp. 21–40.

Ch. Eucken, "Die thematische Einheit des sophokleischen 'Aias,' " *Würzburger Jahrbücher für die Altertumswissenschaft*, n.f., 17, 1991, pp. 119–33.

E. Fraenkel, *Due seminari romani di Eduard Fraenkel. Aiace e Filottete di Sofocle*. Introduction by L. E. Rossi, Rome, 1977, 82 pp.

———, "Sophokles *Aias* 68–70," *Museum Helveticum*, 20, 1963, pp. 103–6.

K. von Fritz, "Zu Sophokles' *Aias* 51/52," *Hermes* 93, 1965, pp. 129–30.

R. Grütter, "Untersuchungen zur Structur des Sophokleischen Aias," diss., Kiel, 1971, 160 pp.

A. Heinrichs, "The Tomb of Aias and the Prospect of Hero Cult in Sophokles," *Classical Antiquity* 12, 1993, pp. 165–80.

Ph. Holt, "The Debate-Scenes in the *Ajax*," *American Journal of Philology* 102, 1981, pp. 275–88.

Th. K. Hubbard, "The Architecture of Sophocles 'Ajax,' " *Hermes* 131, 2003, pp. 158–71.

Ch. Josserand, "Note sur un passage de l'*Ajax* (v. 32–33)," in *Mélanges E. Boisacq*, Université de Bruxelles, Annuaire de l'Institut de philologie et d'histoire orientales et slaves, 6, 1938, pp. 5–10.

F. Jouan, "Ajax, d'Homère à Sophocle," *Information littéraire* 39, 1987, pp. 67–73.

J. Jouanna, "La lecture de Sophocle dans les scholies: Remarques sur les scholies anciennes d'*Ajax*," in A. Billault and Ch. Mauduit (eds.), *Lectures antiques de la tragédie grecque*, Lyon 2001, pp. 9–26.

———, "La métaphore de la chasse dans l'*Ajax* de Sophocle," *Bulletin Association Guillaume Budé*, 1977, pp. 168–86.

G. M. Kirkwood, "Homer and Sophocles' Ajax," in M. J. Anderson (ed.), *Classical Drama and Its Influence* (essays presented to H.D.F. Kitto), London: Methuen, 1965 pp. 53–70.

B.M.W. Knox, "The *Ajax* of Sophocles," *Harvard Studies in Classical Philology* 65, 1961, pp. 1–37 (rpt. in *Word and Action*, Baltimore, 1986 [1979], pp. 125–60).

E. Lefèvre, "Die Unfähigkeit, sich zu erkennen: Sophokles' *Aias*," *Würzburger Jahrbücher für die Altertumswissenschaft*, n.f., 17, 1991, pp. 91–117.

G. Ley, "A Scenic Plot of Sophocles' *Ajax* and *Philoctetes*," *Eranos* 86, 1988, pp. 85–115.

I. M. Linforth, "Three Scenes in Sophocles' *Ajax*," *University of California Publications in Classical Philology* 15, no. 1, 1954, pp. 1–28.

A. A. Long, "Sophocles, *Ajax* 68–70: A Reply to Professor E. Fraenkel," *Museum Helveticum* 21, 1964, pp. 228–31.

A. Machin, "Ajax, ses ennemis et les dieux," (Sophocles, *Ajax*, part. 970, 646–92), *Les Études Classiques* 68, 2000, pp. 3–26.

J. R. March, "Sophocles' *Ajax*: The Death and Burial of a Hero," *Bulletin of the Institute of Classical Studies of the University of London* 38, 1991–93, pp. 1–36 (+ plate 4).

J. Moore, "The Dissembling-Speech Ajax," *Yale Classical Studies* 25, 1977, pp. 47–66.

K. Ormand, "Silent by Convention? Sophocles' Tekmessa," *American Journal of Philology* 117, 1996, pp. 37–64.

A. J. Podlecki, "Ajax's Gods and the Gods of Sophocles," *Antiquité classique* 49, 1980, pp. 45–86.

J. P. Poe, *Genre and Meaning in Sophocle' Ajax*, in *Beiträge zur Klassischen Philologie* 172, Frankfurt-am-Main, 1987, 102 pp.

E. Pöhlmann, "Bühne und Handlung im *Aias* des Sophokles," *Antike und Abendland* 32, 1986, pp. 20–32.

F. Robert, "Sophocle, Périclès et la date d'*Ajax*," *Revue de Philologie* 38, 1964, pp. 213–27.

K. Schefold, "Sophokles' Aias auf einer Lekythos," *Antike Kunst* 19, 1976, pp. 71–78 + plates 15 and 16 (lekythos in the Basel Museum representing Ajax before his suicide).

J. Scodel, "The Politics of Sophocles 'Ajax," *Scripta Classica Israelica* 22, 2003, pp. 31–42.

Ch. Segal, "Drama, Narrative, and Perspective in Sophocles' *Ajax*," *Sacris erudiri* 31, 1989–90, pp. 395–404.

M. Sicherl, "The Tragic Issue in Sophocles' *Ajax*," *Yale Classical Studies* 25, 1977, pp. 67–98.

M. Simpson, "Sophocles' *Ajax*: His Madness and Transformation," *Arethusa* 2, 1969, pp. 88–103.

Ch. E. Sorum, "Sophocles' *Ajax* in Context," *Classical World* 79, 1985–86, pp. 361–77.

J. Starobinski, "L'épée d'Ajax," in *Trois fureurs: Essais*, Gallimard, 1974, pp. 11–71.

P. T. Stevens, "Ajax in the Trugrede," *Classical Quarterly* 36, 1986, pp. 327–36.

O. Taplin, "Yielding to Forethought: Sophocles' Ajax," in G. W. Bowersock, W. Burkert, and M.C.J. Putnam, *Arktouros: Hellenic Studies Presented to Bernard M. W. Knox*, Berlin, 1979, pp. 122–29.

R. M. Torrance, "Sophocles: Some Bearings," *Harvard Studies in Classical Philology* 69, 1965, pp. 269–327 (for *Ajax*, pp. 273–81).

J. Tyler, "Sophocles' *Ajax* and Sophoclean Plot Construction," *American Journal of Philology* 95, 1974, pp. 24–42.

P. Vidal-Naquet, "Ajax ou la mort du héros," *Bulletin de la classe des Lettres de l'Académie royale de Belgique* 74, 1988, pp. 463–86.

R. Weil, "Dans les bras d'Ajax? (Sophocle, *Ajax*, 545 sq.)," *Revue de philologie* 51, 1977, pp. 202–6.

M. L. West, "Tragica II," *Bulletin of the Institute of Classical Studies of the University of London* 25, 1978, pp. 106–22.

W. Whallon, "The Shield of Ajax," *Yale Classical Studies* 19, 1966, pp. 5–36.

M. M. Wigodsky, "The Salvation of *Ajax*," *Hermes* 90, 1962, pp. 149–58.

D. Williams, "Ajax, Odysseus and the Arms of Achilles," *Antike Kunst* 23, 1980, no. 2, pp. 137–45 (+ plates 33 to 36).

C. W. Willink, "Critical Studies in the Cantica of Sophocles: II. *Ajax, Trachiniae, Oedipus Tyrannus*," *Classical Quarterly*, n.s., 52, 2002, pp. 50–80 (on *Ajax*, pp. 50–63).

G. Zanker, "Sophocles' *Ajax* and the Heroic Values of the *Iliad*," *Classical Quarterly* 42, 1992, pp. 20–25.

B. Zimmermann, "Der tragische Homer: Zum 'Aias' des Sophokles," in *Festschrift für W. Kullmann*, Stuttgart, 2002, pp. 239–46.

2. *ANTIGONE*

a. Annotated Editions or Commentaries That Are Fundamental and/or Recent
See appendix I, section on *Antigone* (end).

b. Articles and Monographs

S. M. Adams, "The *Antigone* of Sophocles," *Phoenix* 9, 1955, pp. 47–62.

J. Alaux, "Remarques sur la *philia* labdacide dans *Antigone* et *Œdipe à Colone*," *Metis* 7, 1992, pp. 209–29.

B. Alexanderson, "Die Stellung des Chors in der *Antigone*," *Eranos* 64, 1966, pp. 85–105.

S. Benardete, "A Reading of Sophocles' *Antigone*," *Interpretation: A Journal of Political Philosophy* 4, 1975, pp. 148–96; 5, 1975, pp. 1–55 and pp. 148–84.

D. Bertolaso, "Emone parricida mancato?," *Annali dell'Università di Ferrara*, n.s., 1, 2000, pp. 43–63.

A. Bierl, "Was hat die Tragödie mit Dionysos zu tun? Rolle und Funktion des Dionysos am Beispiel der 'Antigone' des Sophokles," *Würzburger Jahrbücher für die Altertumswissenschaft*, n.f., 15, 1989, pp. 43–58.

J. Bollack, "Le garde de l'Antigone et son message," in A. Bierl and P. von Möllendorff, *Orchestra: Drama, Mythos, Bühne* (Mélanges Flashar), Stuttgart, 1994, pp. 119–28.

W. M. Calder III, "Sophokles' Political Tragedy, *Antigone*," *Greek, Roman and Byzantine Studies* 9, 1968, pp. 389–407.

R. Coleman, "The Role of the Chorus in Sophocles' *Antigone*," *Proceedings of the Cambridge Philological Society*, n.s., 18, 1972, pp. 4–27.

E. Craik, "Significant Language in Sophocles 'Antigone' 1192–1243," *Quaderni Urbinati di Cultura Classica*, n.s., 70, 2002, pp. 89–94.

M. Cropp, "Antigone's Final Speech (Sophocles, *Antigone* 891–928)," *Greece and Rome* 44, 1997, pp. 137–60.

D. Cuny, "Du discours du trône au plaidoyer contre l'anarchie: Les réflexions politiques de Créon dans 'Antigone,'" in *Fondements et crises du pouvoir*, Bordeaux: Ausonius, 2003, pp. 173–88.

J. Dalfen, "Gesetz ist nicht Gesetz und fromm ist nicht fromm: Die Sprache der Personen in der sophokleischen Antigone," *Wiener Studien* 90, 1977, pp. 5–26.

J. F. Davidson, "The Parodos of the *Antigone*: A Poetic Study," *Bulletin of the Institute of Classical Studies of the University of London* 30, 1983, pp. 41–51.

P. Demont, "Autour du vers 899 de l'*Antigone* de Sophocle," in A. Machin and L. Pernée, *Sophocle: Le texte, les personnages*, Aix-en-Provence, 1993, pp. 111–23.

J. de Romilly, "Les débats dans l'*Antigone* de Sophocle," *Atti della Accademia delle Scienze di Torino* 127, no. 1, 1993, pp. 17–24.

———, "La prévison et la surprise dans l'*Antigone* de Sophocle," *KTERISMATA*, Mélanges Kambitsis, 2000, pp. 1–10.

P. E. Easterling, "The Second Stasimon of Antigone," in *Dionysiaca* (nine studies in Greek poetry by former pupils, presented to Sir Denys Page on seventieth birthday), Cambridge, 1978, pp. 141–58.

E. Eberlein, "Über die verschiedenen Deutungen des tragischen Konflikt in der Tragödie 'Antigone' des Sophokles," *Gymnasium* 68, 1961, pp. 16–34.

I. Errandonea, "Das 4. Stasimon der 'Antigone' von Sophocles (944–87)," *Symbolae Osloenses* 30, 1953, pp. 16–26.

A. Etman, "A Light from Thucydides on the Problem of Sophocles' 'Antigone' and Its Tragic Meaning," *Antiquité Classique* 70, 2001, pp. 147–53.

Ch. Eucken, "Das Drama zwischen Kreon und dem Chor in der 'Antigone,' " *Würzburger Jahrbücher für die Altertumswissenschaft*, n.f., 18, 1992, pp. 77–87.

H. P. Foley, "Antigone as Moral Agent," in M. S. Silk, *Tragedy and the Tragic: Greek Theatre and Beyond*, Oxford, 1966, pp. 49–73.

B. H. Fowler, "Plot and Prosody in Sophocles' *Antigone*," *Classica et Mediaevalia* 28, 1967, pp. 143–71.

R. F. Goheen, *The Imagery of Sophocles' Antigone: A Study of Poetic Language and Structure*, Princeton, 1951.

G. Greve (ed.), *Sophokles: Antigone*, Tübingen, 2002, 125 pp. (includes four studies: W. Jens, "Nachdenken über 'Antigone,' " pp. 9–24; K. Heinrich, "Der Staub und das Denken," pp. 25–58; H. Beland, "Todesbereitschaft und die Rettung des Menschen: Antigones Verarbeitung ihrer Herkunft," pp. 59–92; H. Böhme, "Götter, Gräber, und Menschen in der 'Antigone' des Sophokles," pp. 93–123).

M. Griffith, "The Subject of Desire in Sophocles' *Antigone*," in V. Pedrick and S. M. Oberhelman (eds.), *The Soul of Tragedy: Essays on Athenian Drama*, University of Chicago Press, 2005, pp. 91–135 (psychoanalytic interpretation).

H. Gundert, "Grösse und Gefährdung des Menschen: Ein sophokleisches Chorlied und seine Stellung im Drama (Sophokles, *Antigone* 332–375)," *Antike und Abendland* 22, 1976, pp. 21–39.

C. E. Hadjistephanou, "Sophocles Antigone 179ff.," *Mnemosyne* 46, 1993, pp. 227–28.

D. A. Hester, "Sophocles the Unphilosophical: A Study in the *Antigone*," *Mnemosyne*, ser. 4, 24, 1971, pp. 11–59.

Ph. Holt, "Polis and Tragedy in the *Antigone*," *Mnemosyne* 52, 1999, pp. 658–90.

M. Hopman, "Une déesse en pleurs: Niobé et la sémantique du mot *théos* chez Sophocle," *Revue des Études Grecques* 117, 2004, pp. 447–67.

M. H. Jameson, "Sophocles, Antigone 1005–1022: An Illustration," in M. Cropp, E. Fantham, and S. E. Scully, *Greek Tragedy and Its Legacy: Essays Presented to D. J. Conacher*, Calgary, 1986, pp. 59–65.

J. Jouanna, "Lyrisme et drame: Le choeur dans l'*Antigone* de Sophocle," in J. Jouanna and J. Leclant (eds.), *Le Théâtre antique: La tragédie*, Cahiers de la villa "Kérylos" 8, Paris, 1998, pp. 101–28.

E. Lefèvre, "Die Unfähigkeit, sich zu erkennen: Sophokles' *Antigone*," *Würzburger Jahrbücher für die Altertumswissenschaft*, n.f., 18, 1992, pp. 89–123.

R. G. Lewis, "An Alternative Date for Sophocles' *Antigone*," *Greek, Roman and Byzantine Studies* 29, 1988, pp. 35–50.

I. M. Linforth, *Antigone and Creon*, University of California Publications in Classical Philology 15, 5, Berkeley, 1961, pp. 153–259.

H. Lloyd-Jones, "Notes on Sophocles' *Antigone*," *Classical Quarterly*, n.s., 7, 1957, pp. 12–27.

A. S. McDevitt, "Sophocles' Praise of Man in the *Antigone*," *Ramus* 1, 1972, pp. 152–64.

H. J. Mette, "Die Antigone des Sophokles," *Hermes* 84, 1956, pp. 129–34.

E. Mogyoródi, "Tragic Freedom and Fate in Sophocles' *Antigone*: Notes on the Role of the 'Ancient Evils' in 'the Tragic,' " in M. S. Silk, *Tragedy and the Tragic: Greek Theatre and Beyond*, Oxford, 1996, pp. 358–76.

G. Müller, *Sophokles: Antigone*, Heidelberg, 1967, 287 pp.

S. Murnaghan, "*Antigone* 904–20 and the Institution of Marriage," *American Journal of Philology* 107, 1986, pp. 192–207.

M. Neuburg, "How Like a Woman: Antigone's 'Inconsistency,' " *Classical Quarterly*, n.s., 40, 1990, pp. 54–76.

R. M. Newton, "Sophocles, *Antigone* 40," *American Journal of Philology* 96, 1975, pp. 128–30.

M. C. Nussbaum, *The Fragility of Goodness: Luck and Ethics in Greek Tragedy and Philosophy*, Cambridge, 1986, 544 pp. (3. "Sophocles' *Antigone*: Conflict, Vision and Simplification," pp. 51–82).

M. Oswald, *From Popular Sovereignty to the Sovereignty of the Law*, University of California Press, 1986, pp. 148–61 ("Sophocles' *Antigone*: The Family Collides with the State").

Th. C. W. Oudemans and A.P.M.H. Lardinois, *Tragic Ambiguity: Anthropology, Philosophy and Sophocles' Antigone*, Leiden: Brill, 1987, 263 pp.

A. C. Pearson, "Sophocles' *Antigone*," *Classical Quarterly* 22, 1928, pp. 179–90.

H. Petersmann, "Die Haltung des Chores in der Sophokleischen *Antigone*," *Wiener Studien*, n.f., 16, 1982, pp. 56–70.

———, "Mythos und Gestaltung in Sophokes' *Antigone*," *Wiener Studien*, n.f., 12, 1978, pp. 67–96.

A. J. Podlecki, "Creon and Herodotus," *Transactions and Proceedings of the American Philological Association* 97, 1966, pp. 359–71.

P. Riemer, *Sophokles, Antigone: Götterwille und menschliche Freiheit*, Akademie der Wissenschaften und der Literatur, Mainz: Abhandlungen der Geistes- und Sozialwissenschaftlichen Klasse, 1991, 12, 59 pp.

H. Rohdich, *Antigone: Beitrag zu einer Theorie des sophokleischen Helden*, Heidelberg, 1980, 242 pp.

V. J. Rosivach, "On Creon, *Antigone* and Not Burying the Dead," *Rheinisches Museum* 126, 1983, pp. 193–211.

W. Rösler, "Der Chor als Mitspieler: Beobachtungen zur 'Antigone,' " *Antike und Abendland* 29, 1983, pp. 107–24.

M.-A. Sabiani, "Le roi et le serment dans les pièces thébaines de Sophocle" (*Antigone*, *Oedipus the King* and *Oedipus at Colonus*), in *Fondements et crises du pouvoir*, Bordeaux, Ausonius, 2003, pp. 147–59.

J.-U. Schmidt, "Grösse und Grenze der *Antigone*," *Saeculum* 31, 1980, pp. 345–79.

A. Schmitt, "Bemerkungen zu Charakter und Schicksal der tragischen Hauptpersonen in der *Antigone*," *Antike und Abendland* 34, 1988, pp. 1–16.

E.-R. Schwinge, "Die Rolle des Chors in der sophokleischen 'Antigone,' " *Gymnasium* 78, 1971, pp. 294–321.

S. Scullion, "Dionysos and Katharsis in *Antigone*, *Classical Antiquity* 17, 1998, pp. 96–122.

Ch. Segal, "Sophocles' Praise of Man and the Conflicts of the *Antigone*," *Arion* 3, 1964, pp. 46–66.

Chr. Sourvinou-Inwood, "Assumptions and the Creation of Meaning: Reading Sophocles' *Antigone*," *Journal of Hellenic Studies* 109, 1989, pp. 134–48.

————, "The Fourth Stasimon of Sophocles' *Antigone*," *Bulletin of the Institute of Classical Studies of the University of London* 36, 1989, pp. 141–65.

————, "Sophocles' *Antigone* 904–920: A Reading," *AION (filol.)* 9–10, 1987–88, pp. 19–35.

Th. A. Szlezák, "Bemerkungen zur Diskussion um Sophocles, *Antigone* 904–920," *Rheinisches Museum* 124, 1981, pp. 108–42.

Ch. Théâtre and L. Delatte, "Sophocle, Eschyle, Protagoras et les autres," *Les études classiques* 59, 1991, pp. 109–21.

C. G. Thomas, "Sophocles, Pericles and Creon," *Classical World* 69, 1975, pp. 120–22.

R. M. Torrance, "Sophocles: Some Bearings," *Harvard Studies in Classical Philology* 69, 1965, pp. 269–327 (on *Antigone*, pp. 297–300).

M. Trapp, "Tragedy and the Fragility of Moral Reasoning: Response to Foley," in M. S. Silk, *Tragedy and the Tragic: Greek Theatre and Beyond*, Oxford, 1966, pp. 74–84.

W. B. Tyrrell and L. J. Bennett, *Recapturing Sophocles' Antigone*, Lanham, 1998, 176 pp.

Ch. Utzinger, *Periphrades Aner: Untersuchungen zum ersten Stasimon der Sophokleischen "Antigone" und zu den antiken Kulturentstehungstheorien*, Hypomnemata 146, Göttingen, 2003, 324 pp.

E. Van Nes Ditmars, *Sophocles' Antigone: Lyric Shape and Meaning*, Pisa: Giardini, 1992, 195 pp.

P. Vidal-Naquet, "Le chant du cygne d'Antigone: À propos des vers 883–84 de la tragédie de Sophocle," in A. Machin and L. Pernée, *Sophocle: Le texte, les personnages*, Aix-en-Provence, 1993, pp. 285–97.

E. Viketos, "Sophocles, *Antigone* 411–12," *Hermes* 125, 1997, pp. 379–80.

W. Vischer, "Zu Sophokles *Antigone*," *Rheinisches Museum* 20, 1865, pp. 444–54.

K. von Fritz, "Haimons Liebe zu Antigone," *Philologus* 89, 1934, pp. 19–34 (rpt. in *Antike und moderne Tragödie*, Berlin, 1962, pp. 227–40).

A. T. von S. Bradschaw, "The Watchman Scenes in the *Antigone*," *Classical Quarterly*, n.s., 12, 1962, pp. 200–211.

S. West, "Sophocles' *Antigone* and Herodotus Book Three," in J. Griffin (ed.), *Sophocles Revisited: Essays Presented to Sir Hugh Lloyd-Jones*, Oxford, 1999, pp. 109–36.

C. W. Willink, "Critical Studies in the *Cantica* of Sophocles: I. *Antigone*," *Classical Quarterly*, n.s., 51, 2001, pp. 65–89.

————, "The Opening Speech of Sophocles' *Antigone*," *Mnemosyne*, ser. 4, 53, 2000, pp. 662–71.

H. M. Zellner, "Antigone and the Wife of Intaphrenes," *Classical World* 90, 1997, pp. 315–18.

3. *ELECTRA*

a. Annotated Editions or Commentaries That Are Fundamental and/or Recent

See appendix I, section on *Electra* (end).

b. Articles or Studies

S. M. Adams, "The Sophoclean Orestes," *Classical Review* 47, 1933, pp. 209–10.

B. Alexanderson, "On Sophocles' *Electra*," *Classica et Mediaevalia* 27, 1966, pp. 79–98.

H. C. Baldry, *Le Théâtre tragique des grecs*, Paris: Maspero, 1975, pp. 141–63 (8. "La vengeance d'Oreste").

F. Bechet, "Electra, the Father's Daughter" (Sophocles, *Electra*, 1st episode, duo, 328–471), *Studii Clasice* 31–33, 1995–97, pp. 17–25.

J. Bollack, "Une question de mot: *Dikè* dans Sophocle, *Électre*, v. 610 *sq.*," *Revue des Études Grecques* 101, 1988, pp. 173–80.

J. M. Bremer, "Exit Electra," *Gymnasium* 98, 1991, pp. 325–42.

A. P. Burnet, *Revenge in Attic and Later Tragedy* (chap. 5: "Delphic Matricide: Sophokles' *Electra*," pp. 119–41), Sather Classical Lectures 62, Berkeley, 1998.

W. M. Calder III, "The End of Sophocles' *Electra*," *Greek, Roman and Byzantine Studies* 4, 1963, pp. 213–16.

U. Criscuolo, *Lettura dell'Elettra di Sofocle*, Naples, 2000, 221 pp.

B. Deforge, "Le modèle des *Choéphores*: Contribution à la réflexion sur les trois 'Électre,'" *Cahiers du Gita* 10, 1997, pp. 213–30.

F. M. Dunn (ed.), "Orestes and the Urn (Sophocles, *Electra* 54–55)," *Mnemosyne* 51, 1998, pp. 438–41.

———, *Sophocles' Electra in Performance*, Beiträge zum antiken Drama und seiner Rezeption 4, Stuttgart, 1996, 170 pp.

F. Dupont, *L'Insignifiance tragique*, Paris: Le Promeneur, 2001, 219 pp. (chap. 4, "L'*Électre* de Sophocle, tragédie à trois temps," pp. 91–128).

H. Erbse, "Zur *Electra* des Sophokles," *Hermes* 106, 1978, pp. 284–300.

M. A. Harder, "Right and Wrong in the *Electra*'s," *Hermathena* 159, 1995, pp. 15–31.

M. Hopman, "Une déesse en pleurs: Niobé et la sémantique du mot *théos* chez Sophocle," *Revue des Études Grecques* 117, 2004, pp. 447–67.

G.H.R. Horsley, "Apollo in Sophokles' *Elektra*," *Antichthon* 14, 1980, pp. 18–29.

J. Irigoin, "Les deux Électres et les deux *Électres*," in A. Machin and L. Pernée, *Sophocle: Le texte, les personnages*, Aix-en-Provence, 1993, pp. 163–72.

H. F. Johansen, "Die Elektra des Sophocles: Versuch einer neuen Deutung," *Classica et Mediaevalia* 25, 1964, pp. 8–32.

J. Jouanna, "L'*Électre* de Sophocle, tragédie du retour," in A. Machin and L. Pernée, *Sophocle: Le texte, les personnages*, Aix-en-Provence, 1993, pp. 173–87.

D. M. Juffras, "Sophocles' *Electra* 973–85 and Tyrannicide," *Transactions and Proceedings of the American Philological Association* 121, 1991, pp. 99–108.

J. H. Kells, "Sophocles, *Electra* 1243–1257," *Classical Review*, n.s., 16, 1966, pp. 255–59.

P. Klimpe, "Die *Elektra* des Sophokes und Euripides' *Iphigenie bei den Taurern*: Ein Beitrag zur Diskussion über das Aufführungsjahr von Sophokles' Elektra," *Göppinger Akademische Beiträge* 9, Göppingen, 1970, 174 pp.

E. Lefèvre, "Die Unfähigkeit, sich zu erkennen: Sophokles' *Electra*," *Würzburger Jahrbücher für die Altertumswissenschaft*, n.f., 19, 1993, pp. 19–46.

I. M. Linforth, "Electra's Day in the Tragedy of Sophocles," *University of California Publications in Classical Philology* 19, no. 2, 1963, pp. 89–126.

G. A. Longman, "Sophocles, *Electra* 1478" (review), *Classical Review*, n.s., 4, 1954, pp. 192–94.

A. Machin, "Électre ou le triomphe maîtrisé (Sophocle, *Électre*, 1483–1490)," *Pallas* 37, 1991, pp. 25–37.

L. MacLeod, *Dolos and Dike in Sophocles' Electra*, in *Mnemosyne*, supp. 219, Brill, 2001, 207 pp.

G. Markantonatos, "Dramatic Irony in the *Electra* of Sophocles," *Platon* 28, 1976, pp. 147–50.

G. W. Most, "Sophocles, *Electra* 1086–87," in A. Bierl and P. von Möllendorff, *Orchestra: Drama, Mythos, Bühne* (Mélanges Flashar), Stuttgart, 1994, pp. 129–38.

A. Salmon, "L'ironie tragique dans l'exodos de l'*Électre* de Sophocle," *Les Études Classiques* 29, 1961, pp. 241–70.

S. L. Schein, "*Electra*: A Sophoclean Problem Play," *Antike und Abendland* 28, 1982, pp. 69–80.

E.-R. Schwinge, "Abermals: Die Elektren," *Rheinisches Museum*, n.s., 112, 1969, pp. 1–13.

Ch. P. Segal, "The *Electra* of Sophocles," *Transactions and Proceedings of the American Philological Association* 97, 1966, pp. 473–545.

J. T. Sheppard, "*Electra*: A Defence of Sophocles," *Classical Review* 41, 1927, pp. 2–9.

———, "Electra Again," *Classical Review* 41, 1927, pp. 163–65.

F. Solmsen, "Electra and Orestes: Three Recognitions in Greek Tragedy," *Mededelingen der Koninklijke Nederlandse Akademie Van Wetenschappen*, Afd. Letterkunde, NR 30, 2, Amsterdam, 1967, pp. 31–62.

M. C. Stokes, "Sophocles, *Electra* 1087: Text and Context," in G. W. Bowersock, W. Burkert, and M.C.J. Putnam, *Arktouros: Hellenic Studies Presented to Bernard M. W. Knox*, Berlin, 1979, pp. 134–43.

G. Swart, "Dramatic Function of the 'Agon' Scene in the *Electra* of Sophocles," *Acta Classica* 27, 1984, pp. 23–29.

Th. A. Szlezák, "Sophokles' *Electra* und das Problem des ironischen Dramas," *Museum Helveticum* 38, 1981, pp. 1–21.

R. M. Torrance, "Sophocles: Some Bearings," *Harvard Studies in Classical Philology* 69, 1965, pp. 269–327 (on *Électre*, pp. 307–14).

M. Trédé, "Kairos dans le théâtre de Sophocle et son rôle dans l'action dans l'*Électre* et le *Philoctète*," in A. Machin and L. Pernée, *Sophocle: Le texte, les personnages*, Aix-en-Provence, 1993, pp. 201–17.

A. Vögler, *Vergleichende Studien zur sophokleischen und euripideischen Elektra*, Heidelberg, 1967, 194 pp.

S. Vogt, "Das Delphische Orakel in den Orestes-Dramen," in A. Bierl and P. von Möllendorff, *Orchestra: Drama, Mythos, Bühne* (Mélanges Flashar), Stuttgart, 1994, pp. 97–104.

U. von Wilamowitz-Möllendorff, "Die beiden Elektren," *Hermes* 18, 1883, pp. 214–63.

B. X. de Wet, "The Electra of Sophocles: A Study in Social Values," *Acta Classica* 20, 1977, pp. 23–36.

G. Wheeler, "Gender and Transgression in Sophocles' *Electra*," *Classical Quarterly*, n.s., 53, 2003, pp. 377–88.

C. W. Willink, "Critical Studies in the *Cantica* of Sophocles: III. Electra, Philoctetes, Oedipus at Colonus," *Classical Quarterly*, n.s., 53, 2003, pp. 75–110 (On *Électre*, pp. 75–84).

R. P. Winnington-Ingram, "The *Electra* of Sophocles: Prolegomena to an Interpretation," *Proceedings of the Cambridge Philological Society* 183, 1954–55, pp. 20–26 (rpt. in German translation in H. Diller [ed.], *Sophokles*, Darmstadt, 1967, pp. 400–411).

Th. M. Woodard, "*Electra* by Sophocles: The Dialectical Design," *Harvard Studies in Classical Philology* 68, 1964, pp. 163–203, and 70, 1965, pp. 195–233 and 276–79.

4. *OEDIPUS THE KING*

a. Annotated Editions or Commentaries That Are Fundamental and/or Recent
See appendix I, section on *Oedipus the King* (end).

b. Articles and Studies

F. Ahl, *Sophocles' Oedipus: Evidence and Self-Contradiction*, Ithaca, NY: Cornell University Press, 1991, 297 pp.

J. Alsina, "Hippocrate, Sophocle et la description de la peste chez Thucydide," in G. Baader and R. Winau, *Die hippokratischen Epidemien: Theorie-Praxis-Tradition*, Verhandlungen des V. Colloque international hippocratique (Berlin, September 10–15, 1984), Stuttgart, 1989, pp. 213–21.

W. Burkert, *Oedipus, Oracles, and Meaning: From Sophocles to Umberto Eco*, Toronto, 1991, 31 pp.

R. Buxton, "What Can You Rely On in *Oedipus Rex*? Response to Calame," in M. S. Silk, *Tragedy and the Tragic: Greek Theatre and Beyond*, Oxford, 1966, pp. 38–48.

C. Calame, "Vision, Blindness, and Mask: The Radicalization of the Emotions in Sophocles' *Oedipus Rex*," in M. S. Silk, *Tragedy and the Tragic: Greek Theatre and Beyond*, Oxford, 1966, pp. 17–37.

A. Cameron, *The Identity of Oedipus the King: Five Essays on the Oedipus Tyrannus*, New York, 1968, 165 pp.

D. A. Campbell, "Ship Imagery in the *Oedipus Tyrannus*," in M. Cropp, E. Fantham, and S. E. Scully, *Greek Tragedy and Its Legacy: Essays Presented to D. J. Conacher*, Calgary, 1986, pp. 115–20.

E. Carawan, "The Edict of Oedipus (*Oedipus Tyrannus* 223–51)," *American Journal of Philology* 120, 1999, pp. 187–222.

C. Carey, "The Second Stasimon of Sophocles' *Oedipus Tyrannus*," *Journal of Hellenic Studies* 106, 1986, pp. 175–79.

C. Catenacci, "Edipo in Sofocle e le *storie* di Erodoto," in P. Angeli Bernardini, *Presenza e funzione della città di Tebe nella cultura greca*, Pisa, 2000, pp. 195–202.

G. Daux, "Œdipe et le fléau (Sophocle, *Œdipe-roi*, 1–275)," *Revue des Études Grecques* 53, 1940, pp. 97–122.

M. Davies, "The End of Sophocles' *O. T.*," *Hermes* 110, 1982, pp. 268–77.

———, "The End of Sophocles' *O. T.* Revisited," *Prometheus* 17, 1991, pp. 1–18.

R. Dawe, "On the Interpolations in the Two Oedipus Plays of Sophocles," *Rheinisches Museum für Philologie*, n.f., 144, 2001, pp. 1–21.

E. R. Dodds, "On Misunderstanding the *Oedipus Rex*," *Greece and Rome*, ser. 2, 13, 1966, pp. 37–49.

H. Drexler, "Die Tiresias-Szene des König Oedipus," *Maia* 8, 1956, pp. 3–26.

M. Dyson, "Oracle, Edict, and Curse in Oedipus Tyrannus," *Classical Quarterly* 23, 1973, pp. 202–12.

E. Flaig, *Ödipus: Tragischer Vatermord im klassischen Athen*, Munich: Beck, 1998, 151 pp.

H. Flashar, "*König Ödipus*. Drama und Theorie," *Gymnasium* 84, 1977, pp. 120–36.

G. Gellie, "The Last Scene of the *Oedipus Tyrannus*," *Ramus* 15, 1986, pp. 35–42.

R. D. Griffith, *The Theater of Apollo: Divine Justice and Sophocles'* Oedipus the King," Montreal: McGill-Queen's University Press, 1996, 147 pp.

A. Heinrichs, "'Why Should I Dance?': Choral Self-Referentiality in Greek Tragedy," *Arion*, n.s., 3, 1994–95, pp. 56–111.

A. Hug, "Der Doppelsinn in Sophokes *Oedipus König*," *Philologus* 31, 1872, pp. 66–84.

R. L. Kane, "Prophecy and Perception in the *Oedipus Rex*," *Transactions and Proceedings of the American Philological Association* 105, 1975, pp. 189–208.

B. W. Knox, "The Date of the *Oedipus Tyrannus* of Sophocles," *American Journal of Philology* 77, 1956, pp. 133–47 (rpt. in *Word and Action*, pp. 112–24).

———, *Oedipus at Thebes*, New Haven: Yale University Press, 1957 (2nd ed. 1998), 280 pp. (5 chapters: "Hero," "Athens," "Man," "God," "Hero").

———, "Sophocles' Oedipus," in C. Brooks, *Tragic Themes in Western Literature*, New Haven, 1955 (rpt. in *Word and Action*, Baltimore, 1986 [1979], pp. 96–111).

———, "Why Is Oedipus Called Tyrannos?" *Classical Journal* 50, 1954, pp. 97–102 (rpt. in *Word and Action*, Baltimore, 1979, pp. 87–95).

E. L. de Kock, "The Sophoklean Oidipus and Its Antecedents," *Acta classica* 4, 1961, pp. 7–28.

M. Kraus, "Erzählzeit und erzählte Zeit im *König Ödipus* des Sophokles," in A. Bierl and P. von Möllendorff, *Orchestra: Drama, Mythos, Bühne* (Mélanges Flashar), Stuttgart, 1994, pp. 289–99.

W. Kullmann, "Die Reaktionen auf die Orakel und ihre Erfüllung im *König Ödipus* des Sophokles," in A. Bierl and P. von Möllendorff, *Orchestra: Drama, Mythos, Bühne* (Mélanges Flashar), Stuttgart, 1994, pp. 105–18.

S. Lattimore, "Oedipus and Teiresias," *Californian Studies in Classical Antiquity* 8, 1975, pp. 105–11.

E. Lefèvre, "Die Unfähigkeit, sich zu erkennen: Unzeitgemässe Bemerkungen zu Sophokles' *Oidipus Tyrannos*," *Würzburger Jahrbücher für die Altertumswissenschaft*, n.f., 13, 1987, pp. 37–58.

R. G. Lewis, "The Procedural Basis of Sophocles' *Œdipus Tyrannus*," *Greek, Roman and Byzantine Studies* 30, 1989, pp. 41–66.

I. M. Linforth, *Antigone and Creon*, Berkeley and Los Angeles, *University of California Publications in Classical Philology* 15, no. 5, 1961, pp. 183–259.

B. Manuwald, "Oidipus und Adrastos: Bemerkungen zur neueren Diskussion um die Schuldfrage in Sophokles' 'König Oidipus,'" *Rheinisches Museum* 135, 1992, pp. 1–43.

P. G. Maxwell-Stuart, "Interpretations of the Name Oedipus," *Maia* 27, 1975, pp. 37–43.

A. S. McDevitt, "The Dramatic Integration of the Chorus in *Oedipus Tyrannus*," *Classica et Mediaevalia* 30, 1969, pp. 78–101.

C. W. Müller, *Zur Datierung des sophokleischen Ödipus*, in *Akademie der Wissenschaften und der Literatur, Abhlandlungen der Geistes- und Sozialwissenschaftlichen Klasse, Mainz*. Wiesbaden, 1984, 85 pp.

R. M. Newton, "*Hippolytus* and the Dating of *Œdipus Tyrannus*," *Greek, Roman and Byzantine Studies* 21, 1980, pp. 5–22.

J. Peradotto, "Disauthorizing Prophecy: The Ideological Mapping of *Oedipus Tyrannus*," *Transactions and Proceedings of the American Philological Association* 122, 1992, pp. 1–15.

A. J. Podlecki, "The Hybris of Oedipus: Sophocles, *Oedipus Tyrannos* 873 and the Genealogy of Tyranny," *Eirene* 29, 1993, pp. 7–30.

P. Pucci, "On the 'Eye' and the 'Phallos' and Other Permutabilities in *Oedipus Rex*," in

G. W. Bowersock, W. Burkert, and M.C.J. Putnam, *Arktouros: Hellenic Studies Presented to Bernard M. W. Knox*, Berlin, 1979, pp. 130–33.

A. Schmitt, "Menschliches Fehlen und tragisches Scheitern: Zur Handlungsmotivation im Sophokleischen 'König Ödipus,'" *Rheinisches Museum* 131, 1988, pp. 8–30.

R. Scodel, "Hybris in the Second Stasimon of the *Oedipus Rex*," *Classical Philology* 77, 1982, pp. 214–23.

W. C. Scott, "Musical Design in Sophocles' *Oedipus Tyrannus*," *Arion*, 3rd ser., 4, 1996, pp. 33–44.

Ch. Segal, "The Chorus and the Gods in *Oedipus Tyrannus*," *Arion*, 3rd ser., 4, 1996, pp. 20–32.

———, *Oedipus Tyrannus: Tragic Heroism and the Limits of Knowledge*, 2nd ed., Oxford, Oxford University Press. 2001 (1st ed. 1993), 196 pp.

B. Seidensticker, "Beziehungen zwischen den beiden Oidipusdramen des Sophokles," *Hermes* 100, 1972, pp. 255–74.

K. Sidwell, "The Argument of the Second Stasimon of *Oedipus Tyrannus*," *Journal of Hellenic Studies* 112, 1992, pp. 106–22.

R. G. Tanner, "Sophocles, *O. T.* 236–41," *Classical Review*, n.s., 16, 1966, pp. 259–61.

R. M. Torrance, "Sophocles: Some Bearings," *Harvard Studies in Classical Philology* 69, 1965, pp. 269–327 (on *Oedipus the King*, pp. 304–7).

P. H. Vellacott, "The Chorus in *Oedipus Tyrannus*, *Greece and Rome* 14, 1967, pp. 109–25.

J.-P. Vernant, "Ambiguïté et renversement: Sur la structure énigmatique d'*Œdipe-Roi*," in J.-P. Vernant and P. Vidal-Naquet, *Mythe et tragédie en Grèce ancienne*, Paris: Maspero, 1972, pp. 101–31.

———, "'Œdipe' sans complexe," in J.-P. Vernant and P. Vidal-Naquet, *Mythe et tragédie en Grèce ancienne*, Paris: Maspero, 1972, pp. 77–98.

U. von Wilamowitz-Möllendorff, "Excurse zum Oedipus des Sophokles," *Hermes* 34, 1899, pp. 55–80.

C. W. Willink, "Critical Studies in the Cantica of Sophocles: II. *Ajax, Trachiniae, Oedipus Tyrannus*," *Classical Quarterly*, n.s., 52, 2002, pp. 50–80 (on *Oedipus the King*, pp. 72–80).

R. P. Winnington-Ingram, "The Second Stasimon of the *Oedipus Tyrannus*," *Journal of Hellenic Studies* 91, 1971, pp. 119–35.

5. *OEDIPUS AT COLONUS*

a. Annotated Editions or Commentaries That Are Fundamental and/or Recent
See appendix I, section on *Oedipus at Colonus* (end).

b. Articles

S. M. Adams, "Unity of Plot in the *Oedipus Coloneus*," *Phoenix* 7, 1953, pp. 136–47.

J. Alaux, "Remarques sur la *philia* labdacide dans *Antigone* et *Œdipe à Colone*," *Metis* 7, 1992, pp. 209–29.

U. Albini, "L'ultimo atto dell'*Edipo a Colono*," *Parola del Passato* 29, 1974, pp. 225–31.

R. H. Allison, "'This Is the Place': Why Is Oidipous at Kolonos?," *Prudentia* 16, 1984, pp. 67–91.

W. Bernard, *Das Ende des Ödipus bei Sophokles: Untersuchungen zur Interpretation des "Ödipus auf Kolonos," Zetemata* 107, Munich, 2001, 278 pp.

E. A. Bernidaki-Aldous, *Blindness in a Culture of Light: Especially the Case of Oedipus at Colonus of Sophocles*, American University Studies, ser. 17, Classical Languages and Literature, vol. 8, New York, 1990, 243 pp.

M. W. Blundell, "The Ideal of Athens in *Oedipus at Colonus*," in A. H. Sommerstein (ed.), *Tragedy, Comedy and the Polis*, Bari, 1993, pp. 287–306.

P. Burian, "Suppliant and Savior: Oedipus at Colonus," *Phoenix* 28, 1974, pp. 408–29.

W. Burkert, *Oedipus, Oracles, and Meaning: From Sophocles to Umberto Eco*, Toronto 1991, 31 pp.

E. B. Ceadel, "The Division of Parts among the Actors in Sophocles' *Oedipus Coloneus*," *Classical Quarterly* 35, 1941, pp. 139–47.

L. S. Colchester, "Justice and Death in Sophocles," *Classical Quarterly* 36, 1942, pp. 21–28.

J. Dalfen, "Philoktet und Oedipus auf Kolonos, Das Spätwerk des Sophokles und sein zeitgeschichtlicher Hintergrund," in *Studia Grassi*, Munich: Fink, 1973, pp. 43–62.

R. Dawe, "On the Interpolations in the Two Oedipus Plays of Sophocles," *Rheinisches Museum für Philologie*, n.f., 144, 2001, pp. 1–21.

V. Di Benedetto, "Da Odisseo a Edipo: Soph. *O.C.* 1231," *Rivista di Filologia Classica* 107, 1979, pp. 15–22.

———, "L'emarginazione di Edipo," *Annali della Scuola Normale Superiore di Pisa*, ser. 3, vol. 9, 1, 1979, pp. 919–57.

H. Dietz, "Sophokles, Oed. Col. 1583ff.," *Gymnasium* 79, 1972, pp. 239–42.

J. Dittmer, "Die Katharsis des Oidipus: Überlegungen zur religiöspolitischen Funktion von Sophocles' 'Oidipus auf Kolonos,'" in *Abschied von der Schuld?* Stuttgart, 1996, pp. 26–50.

F. M. Dunn, "Introduction: Beginning at Colonus," *Yale Classical Studies* 29, 1992, pp. 1–12.

P. E. Easterling, "Oedipus and Polynices," *Proceedings of the Cambridge Philological Society* 13, 1967, pp. 1–13.

———, "Plain Words in Sophocles," in J. Griffin (ed.), *Sophocles Revisited: Essays Presented to Sir Hugh Lloyd-Jones*, Oxford, 1999, pp. 95–107.

L. Edmunds, *Theatrical Space and Historical Place in Sophocles'* Oedipus at Colonus, Lanham, 1996, 191 pp.

E. Garcia Novo, *Estructura composicional de Edipo en Colono*, Madrid, Universidad Complutense, 1978, 304 pp.

A. Heinrichs, "The 'Sobriety' of Oedipus: Sophocles *OC* 100 Misunderstood," *Harvard Studies in Classical Philology* 87, 1983, pp. 87–100.

D. A. Hester, "To Help One's Friends and Harm One's Enemies: A Study in the *Oedipus at Colonus*," *Antichthon* 11, 1977, pp. 22–41.

J. Jouanna, "Espaces sacrés, rites et oracles dans l'*Œdipe à Colone* de Sophocle," *Revue des Études Grecques* 108, 1995, pp. 38–58.

B. Knox, "Sophocles' Oedipus" (cited in the bibliographical guide on *Oedipus the King*); see also chapter 6 of *The Heroic Temper*, Berkeley, University of California Press, 1964, pp. 143–62 (cited in the bibliographical guide, under "General Studies on Sophocles").

D.-A. Kukofka, "Sophokles: *Oidipus auf Kolonos*: Eine Interpretation vor dem Hintergrund der Polis Athen am Ende des fünften Jahrhunderts," *Gymnasium* 99, 1992, pp. 101–18.

A. Lardinois, "Greek Myths for Athenian Rituals: Religion and Politics in Aeschylus' *Eumenides* and Sophocles' *Oedipus Coloneus*," *Greek, Roman and Byzantine Studies* 33, 1992, pp. 313–27.

I. M. Linforth, "Religion and Drama in *Oedipus at Colonus*," *University of California Publications in Classical Philology* 14, no. 4, 1951, pp. 75–191.

A. Machin, "L'autre Antigone," *Pallas* 44, 1996, pp. 47–56.

A. Markantonatos, *Oedipus at Colonus: Sophocles, Athens, and the World*, Berlin: de Gruyter, 2007, 360 pp.

———, *Tragic Narrative: A Narratological Study of Sophocles'* Oedipus at Colonus, Untersuchungen zur antiken Literatur und Geschichte 63, Berlin: de Gruyter, 2002, 296 pp.

G. Méautis, *L'Œdipe à Colone et le culte des héros*, Neuchâtel, 1940.

R. Meridor, "Sophocles *O.C.* 217." *Classical Quarterly*, n.s., 22, 1972, pp. 214–28.

S. Mills, *Theseus, Tragedy and the Athenian Empire*, Oxford, Clarendon, 1997, 293 pp. (5. "Theseus at Colonus," pp. 160–85).

W. Pötscher, "Der Tod des Oidipus (Sophokles, *Oid. Kol.* 1583ff.)," *Emerita* 40, 1972, pp. 151–56.

M. P. Pattoni, "Sofocle, *Edipo a Colono* 1293," *Rivista di Filologia* 127, 1999, pp. 257–62.

H. W. Schmidt, *Das Spätwerk des Sophokles: Eine Strukturanalyse des Oidipus auf Kolonos*, Tübingen, 1961, 208 pp.

B. Seidensticker, "Beziehungen zwischen den beiden Oidipusdramen des Sophokles," *Hermes* 100, 1972, pp. 255–74.

R. M. Torrance, "Sophocles: Some Bearings," *Harvard Studies in Classical Philology* 69, 1965, pp. 269–327 (on *Oedipus at Colonus*, pp. 281–97).

G. Ugolini, "L'immagine di Atene e Tebe nell'*Edipo a Colono* di Sofocle," *Quaderni Urbinati di cultura classica* 60, 1998, pp. 35–53.

P. Vidal-Naquet, "Œdipe entre deux cités: Essai sur l'*Œdipe à Colone*," in *Mythe et tragédie en Grèce ancienne* II, Paris, 1986, pp. 175–211.

C. W. Willink, "Critical Studies in the *Cantica* of Sophocles: III. *Electra, Philoctetes, Oedipus at Colonus*," *Classical Quarterly*, n.s., 53, 2003, pp. 75–110 (on *Oedipus at Colonus*, pp. 95–110).

6. *PHILOCTETES*

a. Annotated Editions or Commentaries That Are Fundamental and/or Recent

See appendix I, section on *Philoctetes* (end).

b. Articles or Studies

K. Alt, "Schicksal und *Physis* im *Philoktet* des Sophokles," *Hermes* 89, 1961, pp. 141–74.

L.W.J. Aultman-Moore, "Moral Pain and the Choice of Neoptolemus: *Philoctetes* 894," *Classical World* 87, 1994, pp. 309–10.

H. C. Avery, "Heracles, Philoctetes, Neoptolemus," *Hermes* 93, 1965, pp. 279–97.

V. Bers, "The Perjured Chorus in Sophocles' 'Philoctetes,'" *Hermes* 1909, 1981, pp. 500–504.

Ch. R. Beye, "Sophocles' *Philoctetes* and the Homeric Embassy," *Transactions and Proceedings of the American Philological Association* 101, 1970, pp. 63–75.

P. Biggs, "The Disease Theme in Sophocles' *Ajax*, *Philoctetes* and *Trachiniae*," *Classical Philology* 61, 1966, pp. 223–35.

M. W. Blundell, "The Moral Character of Odysseus in *Philoctetes*," *Greek, Roman and Byzantine Studies* 28, 1987, pp. 307–29.

———, "The *Phusis* of Neoptolemus in Sophocles' *Philoctetes*," *Greece and Rome* 35, 1988, pp. 137–48.

G. W. Bowersock, *Fiction as History: Nero to Julian* (chap. 3: "The Wounded Savior," pp. 55–76), Sather Classical Lectures, Berkeley: University of California Press, 1994.

A. M. Bowie, "Tragic Filters for History: Euripides' *Supplices* and Sophocles' *Philoctetes*," in Ch. Pelling (ed.), *Greek Tragedy and the Historian*, Oxford, 1997, pp. 39–62.

W. M. Calder III, "Sophoclean Apologia: *Philoctetes Greek, Roman and Byzantine Studies* 12, 1971, pp. 153–74.

A. Cook, "The Patterning of Effect in Sophocles' *Philoctetes*," *Arethusa* 1, 1968, pp. 82–93.

E. M. Craik, "Philoktetes: Sophoklean Melodrama," *L'Antiquité classique* 48, 1979, pp. 15–29.

U. Criscuolo, "Lettura del *Filottete* di Sofocle," *Atti della Accademia Pontaniana*, n.s., 46, 1997, pp. 19–38.

J. Daly, "The Name of Philoctetes: *Philoctetes 670–73*," *American Journal of Philology* 103, 1982, pp. 440–42.

J. Davidson, "Homer and Sophocles' *Philoctetes*," in A. Griffiths, *Stage Directions: Essays in Ancient Drama in Honour of E. W. Handley*, *Bulletin of the Institute of Classical Studies of the University of London*, supp. 66, 1995, pp. 25–35.

———, "The *Philoctetes* Stasimon," *Liverpool Classical Monthly* 16, 8, 1991, pp. 125–28.

M. Davies, "The Stasimon of Sophocles' Philoktetes and the Limits of Mythological Allusion," *Studi italiani di filologia classica* 19, 2001, pp. 53–58.

W. Deicke, "Zur Interpretation des Sophokleischen Philoktet," *Hermes* 127, 1999, pp. 172–88.

Jesus de la Villa, "El concepto de *aristeia* y la interpretación de Sófocles, *Phil.* 128–33," *Emerita* 58, 1990, pp. 205–15.

J. de Romilly, "L'actualité intellectuelle du Ve siècle: Le *Philoctète* de Sophocle," in J. de Romilly, *Tragédies grecques au fil des ans*, Paris: Les Belles Lettres, 1996, pp. 97–109.

P. E. Easterling, "*Philoctetes* and Modern Criticism," *Illinois Classical Studies* 3, 1978, pp. 27–39.

H. Erbse, "Neoptolemos und Philoktet bei Sophokles," *Hermes* 94, 1966, pp. 177–201.

Th. M. Falkner, "Containing Tragedy: Rhetoric and Self-Representation in Sophocles' *Philoctetes*," *Classical Antiquity* 17, 1998, pp. 25–58.

E. Fraenkel, *Due Seminari romani (Aiace e Filottete di Sofocle)*, Rome, 1977, pp. 43–76 (on *Philoctetes*).

Ch. Fuqua, "Studies in the Use of Myth in Sophocles' *Philoctetes* and the *Orestes* of Euripides," *Traditio* 32, 1976, pp. 29–95 (pp. 29–62 on *Philoctetes*).

A. F. Garvie, "Deceit, Violence and Persuasion in the Philoctetes," in *Studi Classici in onore di Quintino Cataudella*, vol. 1, Catania, 1972, pp. 213–26.

C. Gill, "Bow, Oracle, and Epiphany in Sophocles' *Philoctetes*," *Greece and Rome* 27, 1980, pp. 137–46.

J. A. Haldane, "A Paean in the Philoctetes," *Classical Quarterly* 13, 1963, pp. 53–56.

R. Hamilton, "Neoptolemos' Story in the *Philoctetes*," *American Journal of Philology* 96, 1975, pp. 131–37.

S. J. Harrison, "Sophocles and the Cult of Philoctetes," *Journal of Hellenic Studies* 109, 1989, pp. 173–75.

Ph. W. Harsh, "The Role of the Bow in the *Philoctetes* of Sophocles," *American Journal of Philology* 81, 1960, pp. 408–14.

A. H. Hawkins, "Ethical Tragedy and Sophocles' *Philoctetes*," *Classical Word* 92, 1999, pp. 337–57.

M. Heath, "Sophocles' *Philoctetes*: A Problem Play?," in J. Griffin (ed.), *Sophocles Revisited: Essays Presented to Sir Hugh Lloyd-Jones*, Oxford, 1999, pp. 137–60.

A. E. Hinds, "The Prophecy of Helenus in Sophocles' *Philoctetes*," *Classical Quarterly* 17, 1967, pp. 169–80.

M. C. Hoppin, "Metrical Effects, Dramatic Illusion, and the Two Endings of Sophocles' *Philoctetes*," *Arethusa* 23, 2, 1990, pp. 141–82.

———, "What Happens in Sophocles 'Philoctetes,'" *Traditio* 37, 1981, pp. 1–30.

E. Inoue, "Sight, Sound and Rhetoric: *Philoctetes* 29ff.," *American Journal of Philology* 100, 1979, pp. 217–27.

J. Irigoin, "La composition architecturale du *Philoctète* de Sophocle," *Revue des Études anciennes* 100, 1998, pp. 509–24.

M. H. Jameson, "Politics and the *Philoctetes*," *Classical Philology* 51, 1956, pp. 217–27.

J. A. Johnson, "Sophocles' *Philoctetes*: Deictic Language and the Claims of Odysseus," *Eranos* 86, 1988, pp. 117–21.

D. M. Jones, "The Sleep of Philoctetes," *Classical Review* 63, 1949, pp. 83–85.

J. Jouanna, "La double fin du *Philoctète* de Sophocle: Rythme et spectacle," *Revue des Études Grecques* 114, 2001, pp. 359–82.

———, "Le sommeil médecin (Sophocle, *Philoctète*, v. 859)," in *Théâtre et spectacles dans l'Antiquité*. Actes du Coll. de Strasbourg (November 5–7, 1981). Centre de Recherche sur le Proche-Orient et la Grèce antique 7, Leiden, 1983, pp. 49–62.

———, "L'insertion du lyrisme dans le drame chez Sophocle: L'exemple d'un dialogue lyrique (*Philoctète*, v. 1081–1217)," in J. Jouanna and J. Leclant (eds.), *La Poésie grecque antique*, Cahiers de la Villa "Kérylos" 14, Paris: De Boccard, 2003, pp. 151–68.

———, "Sémantique et temporalité tragique = remarques sur le sens de *palaios* et de *palai* à partir du *Philoctète* de Sophocle," *Revue des Études Grecques* 117, 2004, pp. 21–36.

J. C. Kamerbeek, "Sophoclea VIII: Notes on the *Philoctetes*," *Mnemosyne*, ser. 4, 32, 1979, pp. 70–74.

G. M. Kirkwood, "Persuasion and Allusion in Sophocles' 'Philoctetes,'" *Hermes* 122, 1994, pp. 425–36.

J. C. Kosak, "Therapeutic Touch and Sophokles' *Philoktetes*," *Harvard Studies in Classical Philology* 99, 1999, pp. 93–134.

W. Lameere, "L'ode au sommeil du *Philoctète* de Sophocle (vv. 827–864)," *Antiquité classique* 54, 1985, pp. 159–79.

Ch. Lenormant, "Du Philoctète de Sophocle, à propos de la représentation de cette tragédie à Orléans," *Le Correspondant* 36, July 25, 1855, pp. 583–610.

G. Ley, "A Scenic Plot of Sophocles' *Ajax* and *Philoctetes*," *Eranos* 86, 1988, pp. 85–115.

I. M. Linforth, *Philoctetes: The Play and the Man*, University of California Publications in Classical Philology, Berkeley, 15, 3, 1956, 62 pp.

W. Luppe, "Nochmals zur 'Philoctetes'—Hypothesis," *Würzburger Jahrbücher für die Altertumswissenschaft*, n.f., 19, 1993, pp. 47–53.

P. Masqueray, *Philoctète*, Paris, 1942.

K. Mathiessen, "Philoktet oder die Resozialisierung," *Würzburger Jahrbücher für die Altertumswissenschaft*, n.f., 7, 1981, pp. 11–26.

C. Mauduit, "Les morts de Philoctète," *Revue des Études Grecques* 108, 1995, pp. 339–70.

R. Neuberger-Donath, "Die Pfeile des Philoktetes," *Eranos* 77, 1979, pp. 163–65.

D. O'Higgins, "Narrators and Narrative in the *Philoctetes* of Sophocles," *Ramus* 20, 1991, pp. 37–52.

F. Picco, "L'autorité dans le *Philoctète* de Sophocle ou l'émergence d'une troisième voie," in *Fondements et crises du pouvoir*, Bordeaux: Ausonius, 2003, pp. 161–71.

A. J. Podlecki, "The Power of the Word in Sophocles' *Philoctetes*," *Greek, Roman and Byzantine Studies* 7, 1966, pp. 233–50.

J. P. Poe, *Heroism and Divine Justice in Sophocles' Philoctetes*, Mnemosyne, supp. 34, 1974, 51 pp.

N. T. Pratt Jr., "'Sophoclean Orthodoxy' in the *Philoctetes*," *American Journal of Philology* 70, 1949, pp. 273–89.

J. Psichari, "Sophocle et Hippocrate: À propos du Philoctète à Lemnos," *Revue de philologie* 32, 1908, pp. 95–128.

P. Pucci, "Gods' Intervention and Epiphany in Sophocles," *American Journal of Philology* 115, 1994, pp. 15–46.

D. B. Robinson, "Topics in Sophocles' *Philoctetes*," *Classical Quarterly* 19, 1969, pp. 34–56.

H. M. Roisman, "The Appropriation of a Son: Sophocles' *Philoctetes*," *Greek, Roman and Byzantine Studies* 38, 1977, pp. 127–71.

———, "The Ever-Present Odysseus: Eavesdropping and Disguise in Sophocles' *Philoctetes*," *Eranos* 99, 2001, pp. 38–53.

P. W. Rose, "Sophocles' *Philoctetes* and the Teachings of the Sophists," *Harvard Studies in Classical Philology* 80, 1976, pp. 49–105.

M. Ryzman, "Neoptolemus' Psychological Crisis and the Development of Physis in Sophocles' *Philoctetes*," *Eranos* 89, 1991, pp. 35–41.

S. L. Schein, "Divine and Human in Sophocles' *Philoctetes*," in V. Pedrick and S. M. Oberhelman (eds.), *The Soul of Tragedy: Essays on Athenian Drama*, University of Chicago Press, 2005, pp. 27–47.

———, "Herakles and the Ending of Sophokles' *Philoktetes*," *Studi italiani di Filologia Classica* 94, 3rd ser., 19, 2001, pp. 38–52.

E. Schlesinger, "Die Intrige im Aufbau von Sophokles' Philoctetes," *Rheinisches Museum für Philologie*, n.s., III, 1968, pp. 97–156.

J.-U. Schmidt, *Sophokles: Philoktet; Eine Strukturanalyse*, Heidelberg, 1973, 255 pp.

A. Schnebele, "Die epischen Quellen des Sophokleischen Philoktet: Die Postiliaca im frühgrichischen Epos," diss., Tübingen, 1988, 194 pp.

D. Seale, "The Element of Surprise in Sophocles' *Philoctetes*," *Bulletin of the Institute of Classical Studies of the University of London* 19, 1972, pp. 94–102.

Ch. Segal, "Divino e umano nel Filottete di Sofocle," *Quaderni Urbinati di Cultura Classica* 23, 1976, pp. 67–89.

———, "Philoctetes and the Imperishable Piety," *Hermes* 105, 1977, pp. 133–58.

A. Spira, *Untersuchungen zum Deus ex machina bei Sophokles und Euripides*, Kallmünz über Regensburg, 1960, 167 pp. (on *Philoctetes*, pp. 12–32).

J. C. Stephens, "The Wound of Philoctetes," *Mnemosyne* 48, 1995, pp. 153–68.

H. Strohm, "Zum Trug- und Täuschungsmotiv im sophokleischen *Philoktetes*," *Wiener Studien*, n.f., 20, 1986, p 109–22.

O. Taplin, "The Mapping of Sophocles' *Philoctetes*," in B. Gredley (ed.), *Essays on Greek Drama, Bulletin of the Institute of Classical Studies of the University of London* 34, 1987, pp. 69–77.

———, "Significant Actions in Sophocles' *Philoctetes*," *Greek, Roman and Byzantine Studies* 12, 1971, pp. 25–44.

R. J. Tarrant, "Sophocles, *Philoctetes* 676–729: Directions and Indirections," in M. Cropp, E. Fantham, and S. E. Scully, *Greek Tragedy and Its Legacy: Essays Presented to D. J. Conacher*, Calgary, 1986, pp. 121–34.

R. M. Torrance, "Sophocles: Some Bearings," *Harvard Studies in Classical Philology* 69, 1965, pp. 269–327 (on *Philoctetes*, pp. 314–20).

M. Trédé, "Kairos dans le théâtre de Sophocle et son rôle dans l'action dans l'*Électre* et le Philoctète," in A. Machin and L. Pernée, *Sophocle: Le texte, les personnages*, Aix-en-Provence, 1993, pp. 201–17.

P. Vidal-Naquet, "Le *Philoctète* de Sophocle et l'éphébie," in J.-P. Vernant and P. Vidal-Naquet, *Mythe et tragédie en Grèce ancienne*, Paris, 1972, pp. 161–84.

T. Visser, *Untersuchungen zum sophokleischen Philoktet*, Leipzig: Teubner, 1998, 289 pp.

M. Whitby, "Telemachus Transformed? The Origins of Neoptolemus in Sophocles' *Philoctetes*," *Greece and Rome* 43, 1996, pp. 31–42.

C. W. Willink, "Critical Studies in the *Cantica* of Sophocles: III: *Electra, Philoctetes, Oedipus at Colonus*," *Classical Quarterly*, n.s., 53, 2003, pp. 75–110 (on *Philoctetes*, pp. 84–95).

R. P. Winnington-Ingram, "Tragica (3. Sophocles' *Philoctetes* 839–42)," *Bulletin of the Institute of Classical Studies of the University of London* 16, 1969, pp. 48–50.

Ch. Wolff, "A Note on Lions and Sophocles, *Philoctetes* 1436," in G. W. Bowersock, W. Burkert, M.C.J. Putnam, *Arktouros: Hellenic Studies Presented to Bernard M. W. Knox*, Berlin, 1979, pp. 144–50.

N. Worman, "Infection in the Sentence: The Discourse of Disease in Sophocles' *Philoctetes*," *Arethusa* 33, 2000, pp. 1–36.

7. THE WOMEN OF TRACHIS

a. Annotated Editions or Commentaries That Are Fundamental and/or Recent

See appendix I, section on *The Women of Trachis* (end).

b. Articles

A. Beck, "Der Empfang Ioles," *Hermes* 81, 1953, pp. 10–21.

P. Biggs, "The Disease Theme in Sophocles' *Ajax, Philoctetes* and *Trachiniae*," *Classical Philology* 61, 1966, pp. 223–35.

N. Blössner, "Deianeiras Entscheidung: Zur poetischen Funktion von Sophokles' *Tra-chinierinnen* 582–597," *Philologus* 146, 2002, pp. 217–51.

J. Boardman, "Herakles, Peisistratos and Sons," *Revue Archéologique*, ser. 8, 1972, pp. 57–72.

J. Bollack, "Meurtre et suicide: De l'emploi d'une métaphore guerrière; Le kommos des *Trachiniennes* (vers 874–897)," *Sileno* 10, 1984, pp. 83–91.

L. Bowman, "Prophecy and Authority in *The Trachiniai*," *American Journal of Philology* 120, 1999, pp. 335–50.

E. Carawan, "Deianira's Guilt," *Transactions and Proceedings of the American Philological Association* 130, 2000, pp. 189–237.

Chronique des fouilles (La Direction), *Bulletin de Correspondance hellénique* 44, 1920, pp. 392–93 (Mount Oeta).

Ch. Clairmont, "Studies in Greek Mythology and Vase-Painting: 1. Heracles on the Pyre." *American Journal of Archaeology* 57, 1953, pp. 85–89 (with plates 45–48).

D. J. Conacher, "Sophocles' *Trachiniae*: Some Observations," *American Journal of Philology* 118, 1997, pp. 21–34.

J. de Romilly, "L'excuse de l'invincible amour dans la tragédie grecque," in *Tragédies grecques au fil des ans*, Paris: Les Belles Lettres, 1996, pp. 129–42 (Misc. studies of tragedies, in honor of Kamerbeek, 1976, pp. 309–21).

J.-R. Dumanoir, "Les semailles et la peine Héraklès et les femmes dans les *Trachiniennes*," in A. Moreau, *Panorama du théâtre antique*, Cahier du Gita 9, Montpellier, 1996, pp. 53–68.

P. E. Easterling, "The End of the *Trachiniae*," *Illinois Classical Study* 6, 1981, pp. 56–74.

———, "Sophocles, *Trachiniae*," *Bulletin of the Institute of Classical Studies of the University of London* 15, 1968, pp. 58–69.

M. Finkelberg, "The Second Stasimon of the *Trachiniae* and Heracles' Festival on Mount Oeta," *Mnemosyne* 49, 1996, pp. 129–43.

———, "Sophocles *Tr.* 634–639 and Herodotus," *Mnemosyne* 48, 1995, pp. 146–52.

R. L. Fowler, "Three Places of the *Trachiniae*," in J. Griffin (ed.), *Sophocles Revisited: Essays Presented to Sir Hugh Lloyd-Jones*, Oxford, 1999, pp. 161–75.

C. E. Hadjistephanou, "Sophocles, *Trachiniae* 526," *Hermes* 127, 1999, pp. 495ff.

J. Heinz, "Zur Datierung des Trachinierinnen," *Hermes* 72, 1937, pp. 270–300.

Ph. Holt, "The End of the *Trachiniai* and the Fate of Heracles," *Journal of Hellenic Studies* 109, 1989, pp. 69–80.

J. Irigoin, "Le trio des *Trachiniennes* de Sophocle (vv. 971–1043): Analyse métrique et établissement du texte," in H. Zehnacker (ed.), *Théâtre et spectacles dans l'Antiquité*. Actes du Colloque de Strasbourg (November 5–7, 1981). Centre de Recherche sur le Proche-Orient et la Grèce antique 7, Leiden, 1983, pp. 181–91.

H. F. Johansen, "Heracles in Sophocles' *Trachiniae*," *Classica et Mediaevalia* 37, 1986, pp. 47–61.

F. Jouan, "Déjanire, Héraclès et le centaure Nessos: Le cheminement d'un mythe," in H. Limet and J. Ries (eds.), *Le Mythe, son langage et son message*, Louvain-la-Neuve, 1983, pp. 225–43.

J. Jouanna, "La solitude de Déjanire (Sophocle, *Trachiniennes*, v. 904–905)," in J. Champeaux and M. Chassignet (eds.), *Aere Perennius: Hommage à Hubert Zehnacker*, Paris: PUPS, 2006, pp. 503–14.

S. G. Kapsomenos, *Sophokles' Trachinierinnen und ihr Vorbild*, Athens, 1963, 123 pp.

G. M. Kirkwood, "The Dramatic Unity of Sophocles' *Trachiniae*," *Transactions and Proceedings of the American Philological Association* 72, 1941, pp. 203–11.

Ch. S. Kraus, " '*Logos me'n est' archaios*': Stories and Storytelling in Sophocles' *Trachiniae*," *Transactions and Proceedings of the American Philological Association* 121, 1991, pp. 75–98.

S. E. Lawrence, "The Dramatic Epistemology of Sophocles' *Trachiniae*," *Phoenix* 32, 1978, pp. 288–304.

I. M. Linforth, "The Pyre on Mount Oeta in Sophocles' 'Trachiniae,' " *University of California Publications in Classical Philology* 14, 1950–12, pp. 255–67.

J. K. MacKinnon, "Heracles' Intention in His Second Request of Hyllus: *Trach.* 1216–51," *Classical Quarterly*, n.s., 21, 1971, pp. 33–41.

J. R. March, "Deianeira and Heracles," in *The Creative Poet: Studies on the Treatment of Myths in Greek Poetry, Bulletin of the Institute of Classical Studies of the University of London*, supp. 49, 1987, pp. 49–77.

M. McCall, "The *Trachiniae*: Structure, Focus, and Heracles," *American Journal of Philology* 93, 1972, pp. 142–63.

H.-G. Nesselrath, "Der Flammentod des Herakles auf dem Oite," *Archiv für Religionswissenschaft* 21, 1922, pp. 310–16.

———, "Herakles als tragischer Held in und seit der Antike," in H. Flashar (ed.), *Tragödie: Idee und Transformation, Colloquim Rauricum*, vol. 5, Stuttgart, 1997, pp. 307–31.

M. P. Nilsson, "Fire-Festivals in Ancient Greece," *Journal of Hellenic Studies* 43, 1923, pp. 144–48.

K. Ormand, "More Wedding Imagery: *Trachiniae* 1053ff.," *Mnemosyne*, ser. 4, 46, 1993, pp. 224–26.

H. Parry, "Aphrodite and the Furies in Sophocles' *Trachiniae*," in M. Cropp, E. Fantham, and S. E. Scully, *Greek Tragedy and Its Legacy: Essays Presented to D. J. Conacher*, Calgary, 1986, pp. 103–14.

A. Roselli, "Livelli del conoscere nelle *Trachinie* di Sofocle," in *Materiali e discussioni per l'analisi dei testi classici* 7, Pisa, 1982, pp. 9–38.

M. Ryzman, "Deianeira's Moral Behaviour in the Context of the Natural Laws in Sophocles' '*Trachiniae*,' " *Hermes* 119, 1991, pp. 385–98.

E.-R. Schwinge, *Die Stellung der Trachinierinnen im Werk des Sophokles*, in *Hypomnemata* 1, Göttingen, 1962, 139 pp.

R. Seaford, "Wedding Ritual and Textual Criticism in Sophocles' 'Women of Trachis,' " *Hermes* 114, 1986, pp. 50–59.

Ch. Segal, "The Oracles of Sophocles' *Trachiniae*: Convergence or Confusion?," *Harvard Studies in Classical Philology* 100, 2000, pp. 151–71.

———, "Sophocles' *Trachiniae*: Myth, Poetry, and Heroic Values," *Yale Classical Studies* 25, 1977, pp. 99–158.

M. S. Silk, "Heracles and Greek Tragedy," *Greece and Rome* 32, 1985, pp. 1–22.

A. H. Sommerstein, "Sophocles, *Trachiniai* 809," *Hermes* 120, 1992, sp. 115–17.

Ch. E. Sorum, "Monsters and the Family: The Exodos of Sophocles' *Trachiniae*," *Greek, Roman and Byzantine Studies* 19, 1978, pp. 59–73.

T.C.W. Stinton, "The Apotheosis of Heracles from the Pyre," *Journal of Hellenic Studies*, supp. 15, 1987, pp. 1–16 (= *Collected Papers on Greek Tragedy*, Oxford, 1990, pp. 493–507).

————, "Heracles' Homecoming and Related Topics: The Second Stasimon of Sophocles' *Trachiniae*," *Papers of the Liverpool Latin Seminar* 5, 1985, pp. 403–32 (= *Collected Papers on Greek Tragedy*, Oxford, 1990, pp. 402–29).

————, "Sophocles, *Trachiniae* 94–102," *Classical Quarterly*, n.s., 36, 1986, pp. 337–42 (= *Collected Papers on Greek Tragedy*, Oxford, 1990, pp. 446–53).

S. Tilg, "Die Symbolik chthonischer Götter in Sophokles' *Ödipus auf Kolonos*," *Mnemosyne* 57, 2004, 2, pp. 407–20.

R. M. Torrance, "Sophocles: Some Bearing," *Harvard Studies in Classical Philology* 69, 1965, pp. 269–327 (on *The Women of Trachis*, pp. 301–4).

E. Viketos, "Sophocles, *Trachiniae* 389 Again," *Hermes* 118, 1990, p. 128.

————, "Sophocles, *Trachiniae* 777–782," *Hermes* 119, 1991, p. 467.

————, "Sophocles, *Trachiniae* 94–102," *Hermes* 120, 1992, p. 377.

D. Wender, "The Will of the Beast: Sexual Imagery in the *Trachiniae*," *Ramus* 3, 1974, pp. 1–17.

C. W. Willink, "Critical Studies in the Cantica of Sophocles: II. *Ajax, Trachiniae, Oedipus Tyrannus*," *Classical Quarterly*, n.s., 52, 2002, pp. 50–80 (on *The Women of Trachis*, pp. 63–72).

R. P. Winnington-Ingram, "Tragica (1. The Entry of Hyllus: Sophocles *Trachiniae* 947–1043; 2. Sophocles *Trachiniae* 1206–9)," *Bulletin of the Institute of Classical Studies of the University of London* 16, 1969, pp. 44–48.

Th. Zielinski, "Excurse zu den *Trachinierinnen*," *Philologus*, n.f., 9, 1896, pp. 491–540 and pp. 577–633.

8. SOPHOCLES' LOST WORKS

a. Editions

A. C. Pearson (3 vols. Cambridge, 1917); R. Carden, *The Papyrus Fragments of Sophocles* (1974); S. Radt (*TrGF* 4, Göttingen, 1977, 731 pp.; rpt. 1999 with corrections and additions, 791 pp.); H. Lloyd-Jones (Loeb, 1996); J. Diggle, *Tragicorum graecorum fragmenta selecta* (Oxford, 1998); A. H. Sommerstein, D. Fitzpatrick, and Th. Talboy, *Sophocles: Selected Fragmentary Plays* I (*Hermione, Polyxene, The Diners, Tereus, Troilus, Phaedra*), Oxford: Oxbow Books, 2006, 317 pp. (with introductions, translations, and commentaries).

b. General Studies

Particular studies on plays are mentioned in appendix II on the fragments.

M. J. Anderson, *The Fall of Troy in Early Greek Poetry and Art*, Oxford, 1997, pp. 174–76 (10. "The Lost Ilioupersis Dramas of Sophokles").

F. Jouan, "Sophocle et le drame satyrique," *Pallas* 37, 1991, pp. 7–23.

J. J. Keaney, "A New Fragment of Sophocles and Its Schedographic Context," *American Journal of Philology* 122, 2001, pp. 173–77.

A. Kiso, *The Lost Sophocles*, New York, 1984, 161 pp.

R. Krumeich, N. Pechstein, and B. Seidensticker (eds.), *Das griechische Satyrspiel*, Texte zur Forschung 72, Darmstadt: Wissenschaftliche Buchgesellschaft, 1999, pp. 224–398 on Sophocles (with the bibliography pp. 643–60).

H. Lloyd-Jones, "Notes on Fragments of Sophocles," *Studi italiani di filologia classica*, 3rd ser., 12, 1994, pp. 129–48 (= *Further Academic Papers of Sir Hugh Lloyd-Jones*, Oxford, 2005, pp. 115–35).

J. M. Lucas de Dios, *Sofocles: Fragmentos*, Madrid, 1983, 459 pp.

F. MacHardy, J. Robson, and D. Harvey, *Lost Dramas of Classical Athens: Greek Tragic Fragments*, Exeter, 2005, 248 pp.

S. Radt, "Sophokles in seinen Fragmenten," in J. de Romilly (ed.), *Sophocle*, Entretiens sur l'Antiquité classique 29, Vandoeuvres-Geneva: Fondation Hardt, 1983, pp. 185–231.

A. H. Sommerstein (ed.), *Shards from Kolonos: Studies in Sophoclean Fragments* (Atti del convegno di Nottingham, July 17–19, 2000), Bari: Levante, 2003, 573 pp.

D. F. Sutton, *The Lost Sophocles*, Lanham, MD: University Press of America, 1984, 190 pp.

M. E. Van Rossum-Steenbeek, *Greek Readers' Digests? Studies on a Selection of Subliterary Papyri*, Leiden: Brill, 1998, pp. 21ff., and pp. 34ff. (= pap. no. 17–19).

F. G. Welcker, *Die Griechischen Tragödien mit Rücksicht auf den epischen Cyclus*, Bonn, 3 vols., 1839–41 (*Rh. Mus.* supp. 2, 1–3). Sophocles: I, pp. 59–436, and III, pp. 1526–81.

Other Studies concerning Each Chapter More Particularly

CHAPTER I. THE YOUNG SOPHOCLES

M. R. Lefkowitz, *The Lives of the Greek Poets*, Baltimore, 1981, 187 pp. (8. "Sophocles," pp. 75–87; appendix 4, "The Life of Sophocles," pp. 160–63).

G. E. Lessing, *Sofocle: Introduzione, traduzione e note a cura di G. Ugolini*, Naples: Bibliopolis, 2003, pp. 178.

D. M. Lewis, "Notes on Attic Inscriptions (II)," *Annual of the British School at Athens* 50, 1955, pp. 1–36 (24. "The Deme Colonos," pp. 12–17).

S. Radt, *Tragicorum Graecorum Fragmenta*, vol. 4., *Sophocles*, Göttingen, 1977 (2nd ed. 1999), pp. 27–95 (in which almost all the ancient testimonies regarding Sophocles' life are collected).

G. Ugolini, *Sofocle e Atene: Vita politica e attività teatrale nella Grecia classica*, Rome: Carocci, 2000, 275 pp.

CHAPTER II. SOPHOCLES THE POLITICIAN

H. C. Avery, "Sophocles' Political Career," *Historia* 22, 1973, pp. 509–14.

R. Develin, *Athenian Officials 684–321 BC*, Cambridge, 1989.

P. Foucart, "Le poète Sophocle et l'oligarchie des Quatre Cents," *Revue de philologie* 17, 1893, pp. 1–10.

M. H. Jameson, "Seniority in the Stratêgia," *Transactions and Proceedings of the American Philological Association* 86, 1955, pp. 63–87.

———, "Sophocles and the Four Hundred," *Historia* 20, 1971, pp. 541–68.

P. Karavites, "Tradition, Skepticism, and Sophocles' Political Career," *Klio* 58, 1976, pp. 359–65.

M. Lebeau le cadet, "Mémoires sur les tragiques grecs," *Mém. de lit., tirés des registres de l'Académie royale des Inscriptions et Belles-Lettres* 35, 1770, pp. 441–43.

B. D. Meritt, "The Name of Sophocles," *American Journal of Philology* 80, 1959, pp. 189.

F. Schachermeyr, "Sophokles und die Perikleische Politik," *Wiener Studien* 79, 1996, pp. 45–63.

H. D. Westlake, "Sophocles and Nicias as Colleagues," *Hermes* 84, 1956, pp. 110–16.

L. Woodbury, "Sophocles among the Generals," *Phoenix* 24, 1970, pp. 209–24.

CHAPTER III. SOPHOCLES THE RELIGIOUS MAN

S. B. Aleshire, *Asklepios at Athens: Epigraphic and Prosopographic Essays on the Athenian Healing Cults*, Amsterdam, 1991, 256 pp.

———, *The Athenian Asklepieion: The People, Their Dedications, and the Inventories*, Amsterdam, 1989.

L. Beschi, "Il monumento di Telemachos, fondatore dell' Asklepieion Ateniese," *Annuario della scuola archeologica di Atene* 45/46 (n.s., 29/30), 1967/1968, pp. 381–436.

K. Clinton, "The Epidauria and the Arrival of Asclepius," in R. Hägg, *Ancient Greek Cult Practice from the Epigraphical Evidence*, Acta Instituti Atheniensis Regni Sueciae, ser. in 8, 13, Stockholm, 1994, pp. 17–34.

A. Connoly, "Was Sophocles Heroised as Dexion?," *Journal of Hellenic Studies* 118, 1998, pp. 1–21.

J.-M. Dentzer, *Le Motif du banquet couché dans le Proche-Orient et le monde grec du VIIe au IVe siècle avant J.-C.*, in *Bibliothèque des Écoles françaises d'Athènes et de Rome* 246, 1982, pp. 462–68.

W. S. Ferguson, "The Attic Orgeones," *Harvard Theological Review* 37, 1944, pp. 61–140 (A 7: "Orgéons of Amynos, Asclepios and Dexion," pp. 86–95).

R. Flacelière, "Sur quelques passages des *Vies* de Plutarque," *Revue des Études grecques* 61, 1948, pp. 391–429 (14. "Sophocles *theophilès* [beloved by the gods]: *Numa* IV, 10," pp. 412–17).

D. J. Geagan, "The Sarapion Monument and the Quest for Status in Roman Athens," *Zeischrift für Papyrology und Epigraphik* 85, 1991, pp. 145–65.

E. Kearns, "The Heroes of Attica," *Bulletin of the Institute of Classical Studies of the University of London*, supp. 57, 1989, 212 pp. (pp. 154 sq.).

A. Körte, "Die Ausgrabungen am Westabhange der Akropolis: IV. Das Heiligtum des Amynos," *Mitteilungen des deutschen Arkäologischen Instituts: Athenische Abteilung* 21, 1896, pp. 287–332 (with table 9).

F. Kutsch, "Attische Heilgötter und Heilheroen," diss., Giessen, 1913.

R. Martin and H. Metzger, *La Religion grecque*, Paris, 1976 (chap. 2, "L'évolution du culte d'Asclépios en Grèce des origines à l'époque romaine," pp. 62–109).

M. P. Nilsson, *Geschichte der griechischen Religion*, I, Munich, 1967 (4. Sophokles, pp. 754–59).

J. H. Oliver, "An Ancient Poem on the Duties of a Physician," *Bulletin of the History of Medicine* 7, 1939, pp. 315–23.

———, "The Sarapion Monument and the Paean of Sophocles," *Hesperia* 5, 1936, pp. 91–122.

R. Parker, *Athenian Religion: A History*, Oxford, 1996, 370 pp. (pp. 175–85).

O. Walter, "Das Priestertum von Sophokles," *Geras A. Keramopoullou*, Athens, 1953, pp. 469–79.

C. Watzinger, "Heraclès mènutès," *Mitteilungen des deutschen Arkäologischen Instituts: Athenische Abteilung* 29, 1904, pp. 237–43.

CHAPTER IV. SOPHOCLES AND DIONYSUS: THE THEATRICAL CAREER

L. Canfora, *Histoire de la littérature grecque d'Homère à Aristote* (trans. D. Fourgous), Paris, 1994, 705 pp.

E. Capps, "Greek Inscriptions: A New Fragment of the List of Victors at the City Dionysia," *Hesperia* 12, 1943, pp. 1–11.

F.A.F. Garvie, *Aeschylus' Supplices: Play and Trilogy*, Cambridge University Press, 1969, 279 pp.

P. Ghiron-Bistagne, *Recherches sur les acteurs dans la Grèce antique*, Paris, 1976, 442 pp.

H. F. Johansen and E. W. Whittle, *Aeschylus: The Suppliants*, vol. 1, Copenhagen, 1980, 120 pp. (pp. 1–23).

A. Körte, "Bruchstücke einer Didaskalischen Inschrift," *Hermes* 73, 1938, pp. 123–27.

W. Luppe, "Die Sophokles—Titel im Bibliotheks—Katalog IG II/III2 2363," *Zeitschrift für Papyrologie und Epigraphik* 67, 1981, pp. 1–4 (table 1).

———, "Nochmals zur Choregeninschrift IG II/III2 3091," *Archiv für Papyrusforschung* 22–23, 1973–74, pp. 211–12.

———, "Zu einer Choregeninschrift aus *Aixônai* (IG II/III2 3091)," *Archiv für Papyrusforschung* 19, 1969, pp. 147–51.

———, "Zur Datierung einiger Dramatiker in der Eusebios/Hienonymus-Chronik," *Philologus* 114, 1970, pp. 1–8.

B. D. Meritt, "Greek Inscriptions," *Hesperia* 73, 1938, pp. 77–160 (pp. 116–18).

H. J. Mette, *Urkunden dramatischer Aufführungen in Griechenland*, Berlin, 1977, 247 pp.

C. W. Müller, "Der Sieg des Euphorion, die Zurücksetzung des Sophokles und die Niederlage des Euripides im Tragödienagon des Jahres 431," *Rheinisches Museum*, n.f., 145, 2002, pp. 61–67.

———, "Die Zahl der Siege des älteren und des jüngeren Sophokles," *Rheinisches Museum*, n.f., 128, 1985, pp. 93–95.

A. W. Pickard-Cambridge, *The Dramatic Festivals of Athens*, 2nd ed. revised by J. Gould and D. M. Lewis, with supplements and corrections. Oxford, 1988, 365 pp. (including inscriptions on the didaskalia in the appendix to chap. 2, pp. 101–25).

B. Snell, *Tragicorum Graecorum fragmenta*, vol. 1 (= *TrGF* 1), 2nd ed. revised by R. Kannicht, Göttingen, 1986, pp. 1–58 (including the testimonies regarding the didaskalia [= DID] and the Catalogs [= CAT] of the tragic authors or the tragedies), pp. 132–35 (no. 22: "Testimonies and Fragments about Iophon, Sophocles' Son"), pp. 208–9 (no. 62: "Testimonies and Fragments about Sophocles II, Sophocles' Grandson"), and pp. 307 (no. 147: "Sophocles III, a Descendant of Sophocles in the Hellenistic Period").

D. F. Sutton, "The Theatrical Families of Athens," *American Journal of Philology* 108, 1987, pp. 9–26.

A. Wilhelm, *Urkunden dramatischer Aufführungen in Athen*, Vienna, 1906, 278 pp. (pp. 89ff. with the photograph of fragment a where Aeschylus and Sophocles are found, pp. 101).

CHAPTER V. HAPPY SOPHOCLES

W. Amelung, "Il ritratto di Sofocle," *Atti della Pontificia Accademia romana di archeologia* (ser. 3), *Memorie*, vol. I, part 2, Rome, 1924, pp. 119–27.

———, "Note on J.H.S. XLIII, 1923, pp. 150," *Journal of Hellenic Studies* 44, 1924, pp. 54.

D. Breckenridge, "Multiple Portrait Types," *Acta ad archaeologiam et artium historiam pertinentia* 2, 1965, pp. 9–22 (ancient portraits of Socrates, Sophocles, and Euripides).

J. R. Green and E. W. Handley, *Images of the Greek Theatre*, London, 1995, 127 pp. (p. 105, fig. 78: portrait of Sophocles).

M. Grmek, *Les Maladies à l'aube de la civilisation occidentale*, Paris: Payot, 1983, pp. 104–7 (Sophocles' skull).

J. Jouanna, "Sophocle est-il entré à la villa Kérylos?," Colloque "Les Reinach," Académie des inscriptions et belles-lettres, 2007 (to appear in Actes).

J. Labarbe, "La mort tragique de Sophocle," *Bull. Classe Lettres Acad. Belgique* 55, 1969, pp. 265–92.

Ch. Mauduit, "Sophocle, l'abeille et le miel," in A. Billault and Ch. Mauduit (ed.), *Lectures antiques de la tragédie grecque*, Lyon, 2001, pp. 27–41.

P. Mazon, "Sophocle devant ses juges," *Revue des Études anciennes* 47, 1945, pp. 82–96.

C. W. Müller, "Der Tod des Sophokles: Datierung und Folgerungen," *Rheinisches Museum* n.f., 138, 1995, pp. 97–114.

G. Németh, "On Dating Sophocles' Death," *Homonoia* 5, 1983, pp. 115–28.

Th. Reinach, "Poet or Lawgiver?," *Journal of Hellenic Studies* 42, 1, 1922, pp. 50–69 (about the statue in the Vatican traditionally attributed to the poet Sophocles and that Reinach wants to attribute to the legislator Solon).

———, "The 'Sophocles' Statue: A Reply," *Journal of Hellenic Studies* 43, 2, 1923, pp. 149–55 (reaffirmation, a criticism of Studniczka, of his position regarding the attribution of the statue in the Vatican to Solon); cf. *Journal of Hellenic Studies* 45, 1925, pp. 54.

G.M.A. Richter, *The Portraits of the Greeks*, vol. I, London, 1965, pp. 124ff. (portraits of Sophocles); cf. G.M.A. Richter, *The Portraits of the Greeks*, revised by R.R.R. Smith, Ithaca, NY: Cornell University Press, 1984, 256 pp.

K. Schefold et al., *Die Bildnisse der antiken Dichter, Redner und Denker*, prepared and revised, Basel, 1997, 180 sq. (illustration 86).

F. Studniczka, "Once More Sophocles and Not Solon," *Journal of Hellenic Studies* 44, 1924, pp. 281–85 (new critique of Reinach's position).

———, "The Sophocles Statues," *Journal of Hellenic Studies* 43, 1, 1923, pp. 57–67 (critique of Reinach's position regarding the attribution of the statue in the Vatican to Solon).

PRELUDE TO PART II: A TRAGIC DISASTER

R. D. Dawe, *Studies on the Text of Sophocles*, 3 vols., Leiden: Brill, 1973–78.

A. Turyn, *Studies in the Manuscript Tradition of the Tragedies of Sophocles*, Urbana: University of Illinois Press, 1952, 217 pp.

CHAPTER VI. THE MYTHIC IMAGINATION

R. Aélion, *Euripide héritier d'Eschyle*, vols. 1–2, Paris: Belles Lettres, 1983.

———, *Quelques grands mythes héroïques dans l'oeuvre d'Euripide*, Paris: Belles Lettres, 1986, 263 pp.

P. Angeli Bernardini, "Il mito di Oreste nella *Pitica* II di Pindaro," in R. Pretagostini (ed.), *Tradizione e innovazione nella cultura greca da Omero all' età ellenistica: Scritti in onore di Bruno Gentili*, II, Rome, 1993, pp. 413–26.

——— (ed.), *Presenza e funzione della città di Tebe nella cultura greca*, Pisa, 2000, 378 pp.

A. Bernabé, "El mito de Teseo en la poesia arcaica y clásica," in R. Olmos (ed.), *Coloquio sobre Teseo y la copa de Aison*, Madrid, 1992, pp. 97–118.

J. Bollack, P. Judet de la Combe, and H. Wismann, "La réplique de Jocaste," *Cahiers de philologie de Lille* 2, 1977, 108 pp.

W. Burkert, "Mythos: Begriff, Struktur, Funktionen," in F. Graf (ed.), *Mythos in mythenloser Gesellschaft: Das Paradigma Roms. Coll. Rauricum* 3, Stuttgart, 1993, pp. 9–24.

———, *Structure and History in Greek Mythology and Ritual*, Sather Classical Lectures 47, Berkeley, 1979, 226 pp.

R. Buxton, *Imaginary Greece: The Contexts of Mythology*, Cambridge: Cambridge University Press, 1994.

C. Calame (ed.), *Métamorphoses du mythe en Grèce antique*, Geneva, 1988, 247 pp.

———, *Thésée et l'imaginaire athénien*, 2nd ed., Lausanne, 1996, 496 pp.

R. Cantarella, "Imitazioni e reminiscenze omeriche in Sofocle secondo la critica antica," in *Scritti minori sul teatro greco*, Brescia, 1970, pp. 307–19.

Th. H. Carpenter, *Art and Myth in Ancient Greece*, London: Thames and Hudson, 1991, 256 pp.

E. Cingano, "Tradizioni su Tebe nell'epica e nella lirica greca arcaica," in P. Angeli Bernardini (ed.), *Presenza e funzione della città di Tebe nella cultura greca*, Pisa, 2000, pp. 127–61.

J. Defradas, *Les Thèmes de la propagande delphique*, Paris, 1972 (1954), 305 pp.

M. Delcourt, *Oreste et Alcméon*, Paris, 1959.

P. E. Easterling, "The Tragic Homer," *Bulletin of the Institute of Classical Studies of the University of London* 31, 1984, pp. 1–8.

L. Edmunds, "The Cults and the Legend of Oedipus," *Harvard Studies in Classical Philology* 85, 1981, pp. 221–38.

———, *Oedipus*, London: Routledge, 2006, 177 pp.

R. Engelmann, *Archäologische Studien zu den Tragikern*, Berlin, 1900.

J. Fontenrose, *The Delphic Oracle: Its Responses and Operations, with a Catalogue of Responses*, Berkeley: University of California Press, 1978, 476 pp.

R. Garner, *From Homer to Tragedy: The Art of Allusion in Greek Poetry*, London: Routledge, 1990, 269 pp.

R. Goossens, *Euripide et Athènes*, Bruxelles, 1962, 772 pp.

M. Lacore, "Traces homériques et hésiodiques du mythe d'Œdipe," *Kentron* 15, 1999, pp. 7–26.

F. Lissarrague, "Danaé, métamorphoses d'un mythe," in S. Georgoudi and J.-P. Vernant (eds.), *Mythes grecs au figuré*, Paris, 1996, pp. 105–33.

F. Jouan, *Euripide et les légendes des Chants cypriens*, Paris: Belles Lettres, 1966, 511 pp.

———, "Sophocle et les *Chants cypriens*," in Juan Antonio López Férez (ed.), *La Épica griega y su influencia en la literatura española*, Madrid, 1994, pp. 189–212.

W. Kullmann, *Die Quellen der Ilias (Troischer Sagenkreis)*, 1960, 407 pp.

D. Lanza, "Redondances de mythes dans la tragédie," in C. Calame, *Métamorphoses du mythe en Grèce antique*, Geneva, 1988, pp. 141–49.

H. Lloyd-Jones, "The Delphic Oracle," *Greece and Rome* 23, 1976, pp. 60–73.

J. M. Lucas, "Le mythe de Danaé et de Persée chez Sophocle," in A. Machin and L. Pernée, *Sophocle: Le Texte, les personnages*, Aix-en-Provence, 1993, pp. 35–48.

C. Meillier, "La succession d'Œdipe d'après le P. Lille 76a + 73, poème lyrique probablement de Stésichore," *Revue des Études grecques*, 91, 1978, pp. 12–43.

A. Moreau, *La Fabrique des mythes*, Paris: Belles Lettres, 2006, 253 pp.

A. Neschke, "L'*Orestie* de Stésichore et la tradition littéraire du mythe des Atrides avant Eschyle," *Antiquité classique* 55, 1986, pp. 283–301.

H. W. Parke and D.E.W. Wormell, *The Delphic Oracle* I–II: *The History; The Oracular Responses*, Oxford, 1956, 436 pp.

P. J. Parsons, "The Lille Stesichorus," *Zeitschrift für Papyrologie und Epigraphik* 26, 1977, pp. 7–36.

M. Piérart, "Deux notes sur l'histoire de Mycènes (Ve, III/IIe s.)," in *Serta Leodiensia secunda*, Liège, 1992, pp. 377–87.

J. M. Renaud, *Le Mythe de Méléagre: Essai d'interprétation*, Liège, 1993, 173 pp.

C. Robert, *Die griechische Heldensage*, Berlin, 1920–26.

D. H. Roberts, *Apollo and His Oracle in the Oresteia*, Hypomnemata 78, Göttingen, 1984, 136 pp.

A. Sadurska, *Les Tables iliaques*, Warsaw, 1964, 108 pp., 19 plates.

K. Schefold, *Frühgriechischen Sagenbilder*, Munich, 1964 (English translation: London, 1966), 110 pp.

A. Severyns, *Le Cycle épique dans l'école d'Aristarque*, Liège, 1928, 455 pp.

———, *Recherches sur la Chrestomathie de Proclos* IV. *La Vita Homeri et les sommaires du Cycle*, Paris: Belles Lettres, 1963, 110 pp.

P. Sineux, *Amphiaraos: Guerrier, devin et guérisseur*, Paris, 2007, 276 pp.

H. J. Walker, *Theseus and Athens*, Oxford, 1995, 224 pp.

F. Zeitlin, "Thebes: Theater of Self and Society in Athenian Drama," in J. P. Euben, *Greek Tragedy and Political Theory*, Berkeley, 1986, pp. 101–41.

CHAPTER VII. SPACE AND SPECTACLE

P. Arnott, *Greek Scenic Conventions in the Fifth Century B.C.*, Oxford, Oxford University Press, 1962, 147 pp.

D. Bain, *Actors and Audience: A Study of Asides and Related Conventions in Greek Drama*, Oxford, 1977, 230 pp.

———, "Some Reflections on the Illusion in Greek Tragedy," in B. Gredley (ed.), *Essays on Greek Drama, Bulletin of the Institute of Classical Studies of the University of London* 34, 1977, pp. 1–14.

H. C. Baldry, *Le Théâtre tragique des Grecs*, Paris: Maspero, 1975, 182 pp.

P. Burian, "The Play before the Prologue: Initial Tableaux on the Greek Stage," in J. H. D'Arms and J. W. Eadie, *Ancient and Modern: Essays in Honor of Gerald F. Else*, Ann Arbor, 1977, pp. 79–94.

E. Csapo and W. J. Slater, *The Context of Ancient Drama*, Ann Arbor, 1995, 435 pp.

Ch. Dedoussi, "Greek Drama and Its Spectators: Conventions and Relationships," in A. Griffiths, *Stage Directions: Essays in Ancient Drama in Honour of E. W. Handley*, *Bulletin of the Institute of Classical Studies of the University of London*, supp. 66, 1995, pp. 123–32.

B. Deforge, *Le Festival des cadavres: Morts et mises à mort dans la tragédie grecque*, Paris: Les Belles Lettres, 1997, 144 pp.

V. Di Benedetto and E. Medda, *La tragedia sulla scena*, Turin: Einaudi, 1997, 422 pp.

J.-Rh. Dumanoir, "Les mondes virtuels de Sophocle," in J. Leclant and J. Jouanna (eds.), *Le Théâtre grec antique: La tragédie*, Cahiers de la Villa "Kérylos" 8, Paris, 1998, pp. 59–84.

R. C. Flickinger, *The Greek Theater and Its Drama*, 4th ed., Chicago, 1936.

E. Garcia Novo, *La entrada de los personajes y su anuncio en la tragedia griega: Un estudio de técnica theatral*, Madrid: Facultad de Filologia, Universidad complutense, 1981, 784 pp.

E. R. Gebhard, "The Form of the Orchestra in the Early Greek Theater," *Hesperia* 43, 1974, pp. 428–40.

S. Goldhill, "The Great Dionysia and Civic Ideology," *Journal of Hellenic Studies* 107, 1987, pp. 58–76.

———, "Representing Democracy: Women at the Great Dionysia," in R. Osborne and S. Hornblower (eds.), *Ritual, Finance, Politics: Athenian Democratic Accounts Presented to David Lewis*, Oxford, 1994, pp. 347–69.

J. R. Green, *Theatre in Ancient Greek Society*, London, 1994, 234 pp.

A. E. Haigh, *The Attic Theatre*, 1st ed., Oxford, 1889; 3rd ed. revised and in part rewritten by Pickard-Cambridge, Oxford, 1907, 396 pp.

R. Hamilton, "Announced Entrances in Greek Tragedy," *Harvard Studies in Classical Philology* 82, 1978, pp. 63–82.

J. Henderson, "Women and the Athenian Dramatic Festivals," *Transactions and Proceedings of the American Philological Association* 121, 1991, pp. 133–47.

U. Hölscher, "Schrecken und Lachen: Über Ekkyklema-Szenen im attischen Drama," in A. Bierl and P. von Möllendorff, *Orchestra: Drama, Mythos, Bühne* (Mélanges Flashar), Stuttgart, 1994, pp. 84–96.

F. Jouan, "Réflexions sur le rôle du protagoniste tragique," in H. Zehnacker (ed.), *Théâtre et spectacles dans l'Antiquité*, Actes du Coll. de Strasbourg (November 5–7, 1981), Centre de Recherche sur le Proche-Orient et la Grèce antique 7, Leiden, 1983, pp. 63–80.

J. Jouanna, "Remarques sur le texte et la mise en scène de deux passages des *Phéniciennes* d'Euripide" (vv. 103–26 et 834–51), *Revue des Études Grecques* 89, 1976, pp. 40–56.

A. Lebeau, "Le camp des Grecs en Troade dans la tragédie grecque," in J. Leclant and J. Jouanna (eds.), *Le Théâtre grec antique: La tragédie*, Cahiers de la Villa "Kérylos" 8, Paris, 1998, pp. 167–78.

K. Lehmann-Hartleben, "Steinerne Proedrieschwelle," in H. Bulle, *Untersuchungen an griechischen Theatern*, Munich, 1928, pp. 61–63.

G. Ley, *The Theatricality of Greek Tragedy: Playing Space and Chorus*, Chicago: University of Chicago Press, 2007, 226 pp.

D. J. Mastronarde, "Actors on High: The Skene Roof, the Crane, and the Gods in Attic Drama," *Classical Antiquity* 9, 1990, pp. 247–94.

Ch. Mauduit, "Les murs auraient-ils des oreilles? Contribution à l'étude du palais dans les tragédies de Sophocle," in J. Leclant and J. Jouanna (eds.), *Le Théâtre grec antique: La tragédie*, Cahiers de la Villa "Kérylos" 8, Paris, 1998, pp. 43–58.

J.-C. Moretti, "Formes et destinations du proskènion dans les théâtres hellénistiques de la Grèce," *Pallas* 47, 1997, pp. 13–39.

———, "Les entrées en scène dans le théâtre grec: L'apport de l'archéologie," *Pallas* 38, 1992, pp. 79–107.

———, "Le théâtre du sanctuaire de Dionysos Éleuthéreus à Athènes au Ve s. av. J.-C.," *Revue des Études Grecques* 113, 2000, pp. 275–98.

———, *Théâtre et société dans la Grèce antique*, Paris: Le Livre de poche, 2001, 322 pp.

H.-J. Newiger, "Ekkyklema und Mechanè in der Inszenierung des Griechischen Dramas," *Würzburger Jahrbücher für die Altertumswissenschaft*, n.f., 16, 1990, pp. 33–42.

E. Pöhlmann (ed.), *Studien zur Bühnendichtung und zum Theaterbau der Antike*, with contributions by R. Bees, H. R. Götte, O. Lendle, P. von Möllendorff, U. Wagner, Frankfurt am Main: P. Lang, 1995, 264 pp.

R. Rehm, *The Play of Space: Spatial Transformation in Greek Tragedy*, Princeton, 2002, 448 pp.

D. Seale, *Vision and Stagecraft in Sophocles*, Chicago, 1982, 269 pp.

A. Spira, *Untersuchungen zum Deus ex machina bei Sophokles und Euripides*, Mainz, 1960, 167 pp.

O. Taplin, "Did Greek Dramatists Write Stage Directions?," *Proceedings of the Cambridge Philological Society* 23, 1977, pp. 121–32.

———, "Sophocles in His Theatre," in J. de Romilly (ed.), *Sophocle*, Entretiens sur l'Antiquité classique 19, Vandoeuvres-Geneva: Fondation Hardt, 1982, pp. 155–83.

———, *The Stagecraft of Aeschylus*, Oxford, 1977, 508 pp.

U. von Wilamowitz-Moellendorff, "Die Bühne des Aischylos," *Hermes* 21, 1886, pp. 597–622.

D. Wiles, *Tragedy in Athens: Performance Space and Theatrical Meaning*, Cambridge: Cambridge University Press, 1997, 230 pp.

P. J. Wilson, *The Athenian Institution of the Khoregia: The Chorus, the City and the Stage*, Cambridge, 2000, 435 pp.

CHAPTER VIII. TIME AND ACTION

J. Barrett, *Staged Narrative: Poetics and the Messenger in Greek Tragedy*, Berkeley: University of California Press, 2002, 250 pp. (including two chapters devoted to messengers in Sophocles' work, one on *Electra*, the other on *Oedipus the King*).

A. Bélis, "Aristophane, *Grenouilles*, v. 1249–1364: Eschyle et Euripide *melopoioi*," *Revue des Études Grecques* 104, 1991, pp. 31–51.

R. Bernek, *Dramaturgie und ideologie: Der politische Mythos in den Hikesiedramen des Aischylos, Sophokles und Euripides*, Beiträge zur Altertumskunde 188, Munich: Saur, 2004, 347 pp.

P. Cassella, *La supplica all'altare nella tragedia greca*, Naples, 1999, 257 pp. (on *Oedipus at Colonus*, pp. 151–74).

A. M. Dale, *The Lyric Metres of Greek Drama*, 2nd ed., Cambridge, 1968, 228 pp.

———, *Metrical Analyses of Tragic Choruses*, fasc. 1, *Dactylo-epitrite*, in *Bulletin of the Institute of Classical Studies of the University of London*, supp. 21, 1, 1971; fasc. 2, *Aeolo-*

choriambic in *Bulletin of the Institute of Classical Studies of the University of London*, supp. 21, 2, 1981; fasc. 3, *Dochmiac-iambic-dactylic-ionic* in *Bulletin of the Institute of Classical Studies of the University of London*, supp. 21, 3, 1983.

———, "Stasimon and Hyporcheme," *Eranos* 48, 1950, pp. 14–20.

I. de Jong, *Narrative in Drama: The Art of the Euripidean Messenger-Speech*, Leiden: Brill, 1991, 214 pp.

G. O. Hutchinson, "Sophocles and Time," in J. Griffin (ed.), *Sophocles Revisited: Essays Presented to Sir Hugh Lloyd-Jones*, Oxford, 1999, pp. 47–72.

J. Irigoin, "Structure et composition des tragédies de Sophocle," in J. de Romilly (ed.), *Sophocle*, Entretiens sur l'Antiquité classique 29, Vandoeuvres-Geneva: Fondation Hardt, 1982, pp. 39–76.

W. Jens (ed.), *Die Bauformen der griechischen Tragödie*, Munich, 1971, 450 pp.

J. Jones, *On Aristotle and Greek Tragedy*, New York, 1962 (Sophocles, pp. 141–235).

J. Jouanna, "Riflessioni sui dialoghi lirici sostitutivi dei canti corali nelle tragedie di Sofocle (*Elettra*, 823–870 e *Edipo a Colono*, 510–548 e 1447–1499)," *Aion* 28, 2006, pp. 77–89.

J. Kopperschmidt, "Hikesie als dramatische Form," in W. Jens (ed.), *Die Bauformen der griechischen Tragödie*, Munich, 1971, pp. 321–46.

W. Kranz, *Stasimon: Untersuchungen zu Form und Gehalt der griechischen Tragödie*, Berlin, 1933, 325 pp.

C. Pirozzi, *Il commo nella tragedia greca*, Naples, 2003, 196 pp.

J. P. Poe, "The Determination of Episodes in Greek Tragedy," *American Journal of Philology* 114, 1993, pp. 343–96.

D. H. Roberts, "Parting Words: Final Lines in Sophocles and Euripides," *Classical Quarterly* 37, 1987, pp. 51–64.

———, "Sophoclean Endings: Another Story," *Arethusa* 21, 1988, pp. 177–96.

O. Taplin, *Greek Tragedy in Action*, London, 1978, 203 pp.

———, "Lyric Dialogue and Dramatic Construction in Later Sophocles," *Dioniso* 55, 1984–85, pp. 115–22.

CHAPTER IX. THE CHARACTERS

a. The Chorus: General Studies

(Particular studies are listed in the bibliography for each tragedy.)

R. W. Burton, *The Chorus in Sophocles' Tragedies*, Oxford, 1980.

J. F. Davidson, "Chorus, theatre, text and Sophocles," *Studies in Honour of T.B.L. Webster*, Bristol, 1986, pp. 69–78.

S. Esposito, "The Changing Roles of the Sophoclean Chorus," *Arion*, 3rd ser., 4, 1996–97, pp. 85–114.

C. P. Gardiner, *The Sophoclean Chorus: A Study of Character and Function*, University of Iowa, 1987, 205 pp.

G. M. Kirkwood, "The Dramatic Role of the Chorus in Sophocles," *Phoenix* 8, 1954, pp. 1–22.

D. Korzeniewski, "Interpretationen zu Sophokleischen Chorliedern," *Rheinisches Museum* 104, 1961, pp. 193–201.

Th. Paulsen, *Die Rolle des Chors in den späten Sophokles-Tragödien: Untersuchungen zu Elektra, Philoktet und Oidipus auf Kolonos*, Bari: Levante, 1989, 175 pp.

b. The Characters

R. Aélion, "Quelques jalons pour une étude structurale des personnages de la tragédie grecque," *Lalies* 6, 1987, pp. 231–47.

D. Bain, *Masters, Servants, and Orders in Greek Tragedy: A Study of Some Aspects of Dramatic Technique and Convention*, Manchester, 1982, 73 pp.

R. Bernard-Moulin, *L'élément homérique chez les personnages de Sophocle*, Aix-en-Provence, 1966, 251 pp.

J. Boulogne, "Ulysse: Deux figures de la démocratie chez Sophocle," *Revue de Philologie* 62, 1988, pp. 99–107.

D. M. Carter, "The Co-operative Temper: A Third Dramatic Role in Sophoclean Tragedy," *Mnemosyne*, ser. 4, 58, 2005, pp. 161–82.

J. de Romilly, "Les conflits intérieurs chez Sophocle," in *Tragédies grecques au fil des ans*, Paris: Les Belles Lettres, 1996, pp. 79–95.

H. Diller, "Über das Selbstbewusstsein der sophokleischen Personen," *Wiener Studien* 69, 1956, pp. 70–85.

P. E. Easterling, "Character in Sophocles," *Greece and Rome* 24, 1977, pp. 121–29.

———, "Constructing Character in Greek Tragedy," Ch. Pelling (ed.), *Characterization and Individuality in Greek Literature*, Oxford, 1990, pp. 83–99.

———, "Constructing the Heroic," in Ch. Pelling (ed.), *Greek Tragedy and the Historian*, Oxford, 1997, pp. 21–37.

———, "Women in Tragic Space," in B. Gredley (ed.), *Essays on Greek Drama, Bulletin of the Institute of Classical Studies of the University of London* 34, 1977, pp. 15–26.

M. Fartzoff, "Le roi et l'armée chez Sophocle," in S. Franchet d'Espèrey et al. (eds.), *Fondements et crises du pouvoir*, Bordeaux: Ausonius, 2003, pp. 135–45.

———, "Les Agamemnons de Sophocle," in A. Machin and L. Pernée, *Sophocle: Le texte, les personnages*, Aix-en-Provence, 1993, pp. 343–64.

Ch. Gill, "The Character-Personality Distinction," in Ch. Pelling (ed.), *Characterization and Individuality in Greek Literature*, Oxford, 1990, pp. 1–31.

S. Goldhill, "Character and Action, Representation and Reading: Greek Tragedy and Its Critics," in Ch. Pelling (ed.), *Characterization and Individuality in Greek Literature*, Oxford, 1990, pp. 100–127.

J. Gould, "Dramatic Character and 'Human Intelligibility' in Greek Tragedy," *Proceedings of the Cambridge Philological Society* 24, 1978, pp. 43–67.

———, "Law, Custom and Myth: Aspects of the Social Position of Women in Classical Athens," *Journal of Hellenic Studies* 100, 1980, pp. 38–59.

M. Hose, "Hauptpersonen und Gegenspieler: Zu den Verwendungsweisen von Figurenperspektiven bei Sophokles," *Philologus* 144, 2000, pp. 29–44.

F. Jouan, "Trois contre-héros chez Sophocle: Chrysotémis, Teucer, Créon," in A. Machin and L. Pernée, *Sophocle: Le texte, les personnages*, Aix-en-Provence, 1993, pp. 269–84.

J. C. Kamerbeek, "Individu et norme dans Sophocle," in J. Jacquot, *Le Théâtre tragique*, Paris, 1962, pp. 29–36.

G. Karsai, "Oedipe et Créon, Thésée et Hippolyte," in A. Machin and L. Pernée, *Sophocle: Le texte, les personnages*, Aix-en-Provence, 1993, pp. 329–42.

N. Loraux, *Façons tragiques de tuer une femme*, Paris: Hachette, 1985, 127 pp.

———, *Les Expériences de Tirésias: Le féminin et l'homme grec*, Paris: Gallimard, 1989, 400 pp.

A. Machin, "L'autre Antigone," *Pallas* 44, 1996, pp. 47–56.

P. Michelakis, *Achilles in Greek Tragedy*, Cambridge Classical Studies, Cambridge University Press, 2002, 218 pp.

K. Ormand, *Exchange and the Maiden: Marriage in Sophoclean Tragedy*, Austin: University of Texas Press, 1999 (especially the epilogue: "Exit to Silence," pp. 153–61).

Th. Papadopoulou, *Heracles and Euripidean Tragedy*, Cambridge Classical Studies, Cambridge University Press, 2005, 229 pp.

A. Podlecki, "Another Look at Character in Sophocles," in R. F. Sutton Jr. (ed.), *Daidalikon: Studies in Memory of Raymond V. Schoder*, Wauconda, 1989, pp. 279–84.

F. Robert, "Les origines de la tragédie grecque," in J. Jacquot, *Le Théâtre tragique*, Paris, 1962, pp. 9–18.

S. Saïd, "Couples fraternels chez Sophocle," in A. Machin and L. Pernée, *Sophocle: Le texte, les personnages*, Aix-en-Provence, 1993, pp. 299–328.

R. Seaford, "The Imprisonment of Women in Greek Tragedy," *Journal of Hellenic Studies* 110, 1990, pp. 76–90.

———, "The Tragic Wedding," *Journal of Hellenic Studies* 107, 1987, pp. 106–30.

B. Seidensticker, "Beobachtungen zur sophokleischen Kunst der Charakterzeichnung," in A. Bier and P. von Möllendorff (eds.), *Orchestra: Drama, Mythos, Bühne* (Festschrift H. Flashar), Stuttgart, 1994, pp. 276–88.

W. B. Standford, *The Ulysses Theme: A Study in the Adaptability of a Traditional Hero*, Oxford, 1954, 292 pp.

R. P. Winnington-Ingram, "Sophocles and Women," in J. de Romilly (ed.), *Sophocle*, Entretiens de la Fondation Hardt 29, Vandoeuvres-Geneva, 1982, pp. 233–57.

CHAPTER X. HUMANS AND THE GODS

A.W.H. Adkins, *Merit and Responsibility: A Study in Greek Values*, Oxford: Clarendon, 1960, 380 pp.

———, *Moral Values and Political Behaviour in Ancient Greece: From Homer to the End of the Fifth Century*, New York: Norton, 1972, 160 pp.

D. Aubriot-Sevin, *Prière et conceptions religieuses en Grèce ancienne jusqu'à la fin du Ve siècle av. J.-C.*, Lyon, 1992, 604 pp.

H. Bowden, *Classical Athens and the Delphic Oracle: Divination and Democracy*, Cambridge: Cambridge University Press, 2005, 188 pp.

W. Burkert, "Greek Tragedy and Sacrificial Ritual," *Greek, Roman and Byzantine Studies* 7, 1966, pp. 87–121.

———, "Opferritual bei Sophokles: Pragmatik, Symbolik, Theater," *Der altsprachliche Unterricht* 28, 1985, pp. 5–20.

J. M. Bremer, *Hamartia: Tragic Error in the Poetics of Aristotle and in Greek Tragedy*, Amsterdam, 1969 (Sophocles, pp. 135–72).

D. L. Cairns, *Aidos: The Psychology and Ethics of Honour and Shame in Ancient Greek Literature*, Oxford, 1993, 474 pp.

H. Diller, "Göttliches und menschliches Wissen bei Sophokles" (1950), in H. Diller, W. Schadewalt, and A. Lesky, *Gottheit und Mensch in der Tragödie des Sophokles*, Darmstadt, 1963, pp. 1–28.

K. J. Dover, *Greek Popular Morality in the Time of Plato and Aristotle*, Oxford, 1974, 330 pp. (pp. 14–18: special characteristics of tragedy).

P. E. Easterling, "Gods on Stage in Greek Tragedy," *Grazer Beiträge*, supp. 5 (Religio Graeco-Romana: Festschrift für Walter Pötscher), 1993, pp. 77–86.

N.R.E. Fischer, *Hybris: A Study in the Values of Honour and Shame in Ancient Greece*, Warminster: Aris and Phillips, 1992, 526 pp.

J. Griffin, "The Social Function of Attic Tragedy," *Classical Quarterly* 48, 1998, pp. 39–61.

———, "Sophocles and the Democratic City," in J. Griffin (ed.), *Sophocles Revisited: Essays Presented to Sir Hugh Lloyd-Jones*, Oxford, 1999, pp. 73–94.

J. Jouanna, "Libations et sacrifices dans la tragédie grecque," *Revue des Études grecques* 105, 1992, pp. 406–34.

———, "'Soleil, toi qui vois tout': Variations tragiques d'une formule homérique et nouvelle étymologie de *aktis*," in L. Villard (ed.), *Études sur la vision dans l'Antiquité classique*, Publications des Universités de Rouen, 2005, pp. 39–56.

M. Landfester, "Über Sinn und Sinnlosigkeit menschlichen Leids in den Tragödien des Sophokles," *Antike und Abendland* 36, 1990, pp. 53–66.

A. Lesky, "Sophokles und das Human" (1951), in H. Diller, W. Schadewalt, and A. Lesky, *Gottheit und Mensch in der Tragödie des Sophokles*, Darmstadt, 1963, pp. 61–85.

H. Lloyd-Jones, "Erinyes, Semnai Theai, Eumenides," in E. M. Craik (ed.), *Owls to Athens: Essays on Classical Subjects Presented to Sir Kenneth Dover*, Oxford, 1990, pp. 203–11 (=*Further Academic Papers of Sir Hugh Lloyd-Jones*, Oxford, 2005, pp. 90–99).

———, "Ritual and Tragedy," in F. Graf, *Ansichten griechischer Rituale: Geburtstag-Symposium für W. Burkert*, Stuttgart, 1998, pp. 271–95 (=*Further Academic Papers of Sir Hugh Lloyd-Jones*, Oxford, 2005, pp. 141–62).

J. D. Mikalson, *Honor Thy Gods: Popular Religion in Greek Tragedy*, Chapel Hill, 1991, 359 pp. (Sophocles, pp. 217–25).

J. C. Opstelten, *Sophocles and Greek Pessimism* (translated from the Dutch by J. A. Ross), Amsterdam, 1952, 250 pp.

R. Parker, *Miasma, Pollution and Purification in Early Greek Religion*, Oxford, 1983, 413 pp.

———, *Polytheism and Society at Athens*, Oxford, 2005, 544 pp. (7. "Religion in the Theatre," pp. 136–52).

———, "Through a Glass Darkly: Sophocles and the Divine," in J. Griffin (ed.), *Sophocles Revisited: Essays Presented to Sir Hugh Lloyd-Jones*, Oxford, 1999, pp. 11–30.

V. Parker, "The Semantics of a Political Concept from Archilochus to Aristotle," *Hermes* 126, 1998, pp. 145–72.

W. Schadewaldt, "Sophokles und das Leid" (1947), in H. Diller, W. Schadewalt, and A. Lesky, *Gottheit und Mensch in der Tragödie des Sophokles*, Darmstadt, 1963, pp. 31–57.

T.C.W. Stinton, "Hamartia in Aristotle and Greek Tragedy," *Classical Quarterly*, n.s., 25, 1975, pp. 221–54.

Chr. Walde, *Die Traumdarstellungen in der griechisch-römischen Dichtung*, Munich: Saur, 2001, 487 pp.

M. West, "Ancestral Curses," in J. Griffin (ed.), *Sophocles Revisited: Essays Presented to Sir Hugh Lloyd-Jones*, Oxford, 1999, pp. 31–45.

R. P. Winnington-Ingram, "Tragedy and Greek Archaic Thought," in M. J. Anderson (ed.), *Classical Drama and Its Influence* (essays presented to H.D.F. Kitto), London: Methuen, 1965, pp. 31–50.

M. Woronoff, "Ville natale et cité chez Sophocle," *Ktema* 8, 1983, pp. 85–94.

CHAPTER XI. SEEING, HEARING, AND UNDERSTANDING

M. Coray, *Wissen und erkennen bei Sophokles*, in *Schweizerische Beiträge zur Altertumswissenschaft* 24, Basel/Berlin, 1993, 457 pp.

J. de Romilly, "Indulgence et pardon dans la tragédie grecque," in J. de Romilly, *Tragédies grecques au fil des ans*, Paris: Les Belles Lettres, 1996, pp. 61–77.

———, "La prévision et la surprise dans la tragédie grecque," in J. Leclant and J. Jouanna (eds.), *Le Théâtre grec antique: La tragédie*, Cahiers de la Villa "Kérylos" 8, Paris, 1998, pp. 1–9.

———, "Les réflexions générales dans la tragédie grecque," in J. de Romilly, *Tragédies grecques au fil des ans*, Paris: Les Belles Lettres, 1996, pp. 45–60.

———, "Le thème de la liberté et l'évolution de la tragédie grecque," in H. Zehnacker (ed.), *Théâtre et spectacles dans l'Antiquité*, Leiden: Brill, 1983, pp. 215–26.

S. Dresden, "Remarques sur l'ironie tragique," in *Misc. Trag. in Hon. Kamerbeek*, Amsterdam, 1976, pp. 55–69.

M. Fartzoff, "Pouvoir, destin et légitimité chez Sophocle: D'*Œdipe Roi* à *Œdipe à Colone*," in J. Leclant and J. Jouanna (eds.), *Le Théâtre grec antique: La tragédie*, Cahiers de la Villa "Kérylos" 8, Paris, 1998, pp. 85–99.

A. Garzya, *La parola e la scena*, Naples: Bibliopolis, 1997, 410 pp. (II. "L'ironia tragica nel teatro greco del V secolo a. C.," pp. 31–45).

G. M. Kirkwood, *A Study of Sophoclean Drama*, Ithaca, NY: Cornell University Press, 1st ed. 1958; 2nd ed. 1994, pp. 247–87 ("The Irony of Sophocles").

H. Lloyd-Jones, *The Justice of Zeus* (chap. 5, "Sophocles," pp. 104–28), Sather Classical Lectures, Berkeley, 1971 (2nd ed. 1983).

G. Markantonatos, "On the Concept of the Term Tragic Irony," *Platon* 32–33, 1980–81, pp. 367–73.

F. Robert, "Exigences du public et ressorts de la tragédie chez les Grecs," in J. Jacquot, *Le Théâtre tragique*, Paris, 1962, pp. 55–62.

T. G. Rosenmeyer, "Irony and Tragic Choruses," in J. H. D'Arms and J. W. Eadie, *Ancient and Modern: Essays in Honor of Gerald F. Else*, Ann Arbor, 1977, pp. 31–44.

C. H. Whitman, *Sophocles*, Cambridge, MA, 1951, pp. 103–21 ("Late Learning").

DEUS EX MACHINA: TIME AND NATURE

R. Aubreton, *Démétrius Triclinius et les recensions médiévales de Sophocle*, Paris: Les Belles Lettres, 1949, 289 pp.

A. Bagordo, *Die antiken Traktate über das Drama* (with a collection of fragments), Stuttgart: Teubner, 1998, Beiträge zum Altertumskunde III, 181 pp.

Ch. Biet, *Œdipe en monarchie en France: Tragédie et théorie juridique à l'âge classique*, Paris: Klincksieck, 1999, 491 pp.

A. Billault, "Les romanciers grecs et la tragédie," in J. Leclant and J. Jouanna (eds.), *Le Théâtre grec antique: La tragédie*, Cahiers de la Villa "Kérylos" 8, Paris, 1998, pp. 179–94.

P. Brunel, *Le Mythe d'Électre* (3rd ed.), Paris: Honoré Champion, 1995, 212 pp. (with an appendix of the three modern plays).

P. Burian, "Tragedy Adapted for Stages and Screens: The Renaissance to the Present," in P. E. Easterling (ed.), *The Cambridge Companion to Greek Tragedy*, Cambridge, 1997, pp. 228–83.

W. Burkert, *Oedipus, Oracles, and Meaning: From Sophocles to Umberto Eco*, Toronto 1991, 31 pp.

L. Canfora, *La Véritable histoire de la bibliothèque d'Alexandrie*, Paris, 1988.

P. J. Conradie, "Recent Criticism and Hegel's Interpretation of Sophocles' 'Antigone,'" in *Studies . . . in Honour of W. J. Henderson*, Frankfurt-am-Main: Lang, 2003, pp. 197–210.

C. Constans, "Scènes de la tragédie grecque chez les peintres romantiques philhellènes," in J. Leclant and J. Jouanna (ed.), *Le Théâtre grec antique: La tragédie*, Cahiers de la Villa "Kérylos" 8, Paris, 1998, pp. 229–46.

A. Daskarolis, *Die Wiedergeburt des Sophokles aus dem Geist des Humanismus: Studien zur Sophokles-Rezeption in Deutschland vom Beginn des 16. bis zur Mitte des 17. Jahrhunderts*, Tübingen: Niermeyer, 2000, 394 pp.

J. de Romilly, "Les traductions du théâtre antique depuis le XVIIIe siècle," in *Tragédies au fil des ans*, Paris: Les Belles Lettres, 1995, pp. 207–18.

F. Dupont, "Le temps dans les transpositions modernes des tragédies grecques," *Dioniso* 45, 1971–74, pp. 69–81.

———, *Le Théâtre latin*, Paris: Armand Colin, 1988, 156 pp.

P. E. Easterling, "From Repertoire to Canon," in P. E. Easterling (ed.), *The Cambridge Companion to Greek Tragedy*, Cambridge, 1997, pp. 211–27.

H. Flashar, "Die Poetik des Aristoteles und die griechische Tragödie," in H. Flashar (ed.), *Tragödie: Idee und transformation, Colloquim Rauricum*, vol. 5, Stuttgart, 1997, pp. 50–64.

———, *Inszenierung der Antike: Das griechische Drama auf der Bühne der Neuzeit 1585–1990*, Munich, 1991, 407 pp.

S. Goldhill, "Modern Critical Approaches to Greek Tragedy," in P. E. Easterling (ed.), *The Cambridge Companion to Greek Tragedy*, Cambridge, 1997, pp. 324–47.

S. Halliwell, *Aristotle's Poetics*, Chapel Hill: University of North Carolina Press, 1986, 369 pp.

Th. Halter, *König Oedipus: Von Sophokes zu Cocteau*, Stuttgart: Steiner, 1998, 169 pp.

L. Holford-Strevens, "Sophocle à Rome," in J. Griffin (ed.), *Sophocles Revisited: Essays Presented to Sir Hugh Lloyd-Jones*, Oxford, 1999, pp. 219–59.

S. Humbert-Mougin, *Dionysos revisité: Les tragiques grecs en France de Leconte de Lisle à Claudel*, Paris: Belin, 2003, 298 pp.

J. Irigoin, "La tragédie grecque, de l'auteur à l'éditeur et au traducteur," in *I venerdi delle Accademie Napoletane nelle anno accademico* 2003–4, Naples: Giannini editore, 2005, pp. 47–64.

———, *Tradition et critique des textes grecs*, Paris: Belles Lettres, 1997 (Lectures given on the Greek tragic authors at the École pratique des hautes études: the contribution of the papyruses, pp. 105–10; the first printed editions, pp. 111–21; under the first paleologists, pp. 123–37. Lectures given at the Collège de France: "La tradition des tragiques grecs," pp. 237–71).

F. Jouan, "Quelques réflexions sur Plutarque et la tragédie," *Studi Italiani di Filologia Classica*, 3rd ser., 20, 1–2, 2002, pp. 186–96.

J. Jouanna, "La lecture de Sophocle dans les scholies: Remarques sur les scholies anciennes de l'*Ajax*," in A. Billault and Ch. Mauduit (eds.), *Lectures antiques de la tragédie grecque*, Lyon, 2001, pp. 10–26.

C. W. Kallendorf, *A Companion to the Classical Tradition*, Oxford: Blackwell, 2007, 491 pp.

O. Karavas, *Lucien et la tragédie*, Berlin: De Gruyter, 2005, 374 pp.

M. Kasper, "'Das Gesetz von allen der König': Hölderlins Anmerkungen zum Oedipus und zur Antigonä," *Epistemata* 265, Würzburg 2000, 219 pp.

E. Koczisky, "Der Verklärte Sünder: Zur Rezeption des Oedipus-Mythos im 18. Jahrhundert," *Acta Antiqua Academiae Scientiarum Hungaricae* 40, 2000, pp. 227–37.

U. Korzeniewski, "*Sophokles! Die Alten! Philoktet!": Lessing und die antiken Dramatiker*, Konstanz: Universitäts-Verlag, 2003, 585 pp.

B. Le Guen (ed.), *De la scène aux gradins: Théâtre et représentations dramatiques après Alexandre le Grand*, Toulouse: Presses universitaires du Mirail, 1998, 281 pp.

———, "Théâtre et cités à l'époque hellénistique," *Revue des Études Grecques* 108, 1995, pp. 59–90.

M. Lurje, *Die Suche nach der Schuld: Sophokles' Oedipus Rex, Aristoteles' Poetik und das Tragödieverständnis der Neuzeit*, Munich: Saur, 2004, 505 pp.

F. Macintosh, "Tragedy in Performance: Nineteenth- and Twentieth-Century productions," in P. E. Easterling (ed.), *The Cambridge Companion to Greek Tragedy*, Cambridge, 1997, pp. 284–323.

M. Mastroianni, *Le Antigoni sofoclee del Cinquecento francese*, Florence: L. S. Olschki, 2004, 258 pp.

L. Moretti, "Sulle didascaliae del teatro attico rinvenute a Roma," *Athenaeum*, n.s., 38, 1960, pp. 263–82.

C. W. Müller, "Die Thebanische Trilogie des Sophokles und ihre Aufführung im Jahre 401: Zur Frühgeschichte der antiken Sophoklesrezeption und der Überlieferung des Textes," *Rheinisches Museum* 139, 1996, pp. 193–224.

H.-G. Nesselrath, "Herakles als tragischer Held in und seit der Antike," in H. Flashar (ed.), *Tragödie: Idee und transformation, Colloquium Rauricum*, vol. 5, Stuttgart, 1997, pp. 307–31.

M. J. O' Brien (ed.), *Twentieth-Century Interpretations of Oedipus Rex: A Collection of Critical Essays*, Englewood Cliffs, NJ, 1968, 119 pp.

Ch. Pelling, *Greek Tragedy and the Historian*, Oxford, 1997 (conclusion by Ch. Pelling: "Tragedy as Evidence: Tragedy and Ideology").

S. Perlman, "Quotations from Poetry in Attic Orators of the Fourth Century B.C.," *American Journal of Philology* 85, 1964, pp. 155–72.

M. Pinnoy, "Plutarch's Comment on Sophocles' Style," *Quaderni Urbinati di Cultura Classica*, n.s., 16, 1, 1984, pp. 159–64.

R. Renehan, "The New Oxford Sophocles," *Classical Philology* 87, 1992, pp. 335–75.

S. Saïd and Ch. Biet, "L'enjeu des notes: Les traductions de l'*Antigone* de Sophocle au XVIIIe siècle," *Poétique* 58, 1984, pp. 155–69.

P. Sauzeau (ed.), *La Tradition créatrice du Théâtre antique I. En Grèce ancienne*, Cahiers du Gita 11, 1998, 228 pp.

————, *La Tradition créatrice du Théâtre antique II. De Rome à nos jours*, Cahiers du Gita 12, 1999, 308 pp.

E.-R. Schwinge, "Griechische Tragödie: Das Problem ihrer Zeitlichkeit," *Antike und Abendland* 38, 1992, pp. 48–66.

Ch. Segal, "Catharsis, Audience, and Closure in Greek Tragedy," in M. S. Silk, *Tragedy and the Tragic Greek Theatre and Beyond*, Oxford, 1966, pp. 149–72.

————, "Freud, Language, and the Unconscious," in *Sophocles' Tragic World*, Cambridge, MA, 1995, pp. 161–79.

G. Steiner, *Les Antigones*, Paris: Gallimard, 1986, 347 pp.

W. McC. Stewart, "Racine's Response to the Stagecraft of Attic Tragedy as Seen in his Annotations," in M. J. Anderson (ed.), *Classical Drama and Its Influence*, London: Methuen, 1965 (essays presented to H.D.F. Kitto), pp. 177–90.

E. Thummer, "Vergleichende Untersuchungen zum 'König Oedipus' des Seneca und Sophokles," in R. Muth (ed.), *Serta philologica Aenipontana*, Innsbruck, 1972, pp. 151–95.

M. Trédé, "Le théâtre comme métaphore au IIe siècle ap. J.-C.: survivances et métamorphoses," *Comptes rendus de l'Académie des inscriptions et belles-lettres*, 2002 (2), pp. 581–605.

P. Vidal-Naquet, "Œdipe à Vicence et à Paris: Deux moments d'une histoire," in J.-P. Vernant and P. Vidal-Naquet, *Mythe et tragédie II*, Paris: La Découverte, 1986, pp. 213–35.

U. von Wilamowitz-Moellendorff, *Einleitung in die attische Tragödie*, Berlin, 1907 (rpt. of chaps. 1–4 of *Euripides, Herakles*, 1889).

————, *Qu'est-ce qu'une tragédie attique? Introduction à la tragédie attique*, Paris: Belles Lettres, 2001, 153 pp. (=trans. of the second chapter of the work cited above). Introduction by Caroline Noirot, French translation by Alexandre Hasnaoui.

G. Xanthakis-Karamanos, *Studies in Fourth Century Tragedy*, Athens, 1980, 246 pp.

LIST OF TRANSLATIONS USED
IN THE ENGLISH EDITION

....

Unless otherwise noted, all references cite the Loeb Classical Library editions (first series), most of which are available on the Tufts University "Perseus" website: http://www.perseus.tufts.edu/hopper/.

Aeschines, *Against Ctesiphon*, trans. C. D. Adams, 1919.

Aeschylus, *Prometheus Bound*, trans. H. W. Smyth, Cambridge, MA: Harvard University Press, 1926.

———, *Seven against Thebes*, trans. H. W. Smyth, Cambridge, MA: Harvard University Press, 1926.

———, *The Suppliant Women*, trans. H. W. Smyth, Cambridge, MA: Harvard University Press, 1926.

Antiphon, *On the Choreutes*, trans. K. J. Maidment, 1941 (Minor Attic Orators).

Apollodorus, *Epitome*, trans. J. G. Frazer, 1921.

———, *Library*, trans. J. G. Frazer, 1921.

Aristophanes, *The Birds*, trans. J. Henderson, 2000.

———, *Frogs*, trans. M. Dillon.

Aristotle, *Poetics*, trans. W. H. Fyfe, Cambridge, MA: Harvard University Press, 1927.

Athenaeus, *The Deipnosophists*, trans. C. D. Jonge, London: H. G. Bohn, 1854; trans. C. B. Gulick, 1927; *The Learned Banqueters*, trans. S. D. Olson, 2012.

Cicero, *De Officiis, On Moral Duties*, trans. W. Miller, Cambridge, MA: Harvard University Press, 1913.

De divinatione ("On divination," trans. W. A. Falconer).

Demosthenes, trans. A. T. Murray, 1939.

———, *The Public Orations of Demosthenes*, trans. A. W. Pickard-Cambridge, Oxford: Clarendon, 1912.

Dio Chrysostom, *Discourses*, trans. J. W. Cohoon and H. L. Crosby, 1932–.

Diogenes Laertius, *Lives of the Eminent Philosophers*, trans. R. D. Hicks, Cambridge, MA: Harvard University Press, 1972.

Euripides, *The Complete Greek Drama*, edited by Whitney J. Oates and Eugene O'Neill Jr., in two volumes. 2. *The Phoenissae*, translated by E. P. Coleridge, New York: Random House, 1938.

———, *Hecuba*, trans. E. P. Coleridge. In *Complete Greek Drama*, ed. Whitney J. Oates and Eugene O'Neill Jr. 2 vols., New York: Random House, 1938.

———, *Medea*, trans. D. Kovacs, 1994.

Hegel, G.W.F., *Hegel on Tragedy*, New York: Doubleday/Anchor, 1962.

Herodotus, *The Histories*, trans. A. D. Godfrey 1920.

Hesiod, *Works and Days*, trans. H. G. Evelyn-White, Cambridge, MA: Harvard University Press, 1914.

Hippocrates, *Lex*, trans. C. D. Adams, 1868.

Homer, *Iliad*, trans. A. T. Murray, Cambridge, MA: Harvard University Press, 1924.

The Homeric Hymns and Homerica, trans. H. G. Evelyn-White, 1914 (Hymn to Hermes).

Horace, *Satires, Epistles, and Ars Poetica*, trans. H. Rushton Fairclough, 1929.

Livy, *History of Rome*, trans. B. O. Foster.

Longinus, *On the Sublime*, trans. W. Rhys Roberts.

Pausanias, *Description of Greece*, trans. W.H.S. Jones and H. A. Ormerod, Cambridge, MA: Harvard University Press; London: William Heinemann, 1918.

Pindar, *Odes*, trans. Diane Arnson Svarlien, 1990.

Plato, *Apology*, trans. H. N. Fowler, 1966.

———, *Laws*, trans. R. G. Bury.

———, *Symposium*, trans. H. N. Fowler

Plutarch, trans. B. Perrin, in Plutarch, *The Parallel Lives*, Cambridge, MA: Harvard University Press, 1916. (Moral Essays.)

Plutarch, *Life of Aristides*, trans. B. Perrin, 1914.

———, *Lives of the Ten Orators*, trans. C. Bancroft. In *Plutarch's Lives and Writings*, ed. A. H. Clough and William W. Goodwin. London: Simpkin, Hamilton, Kent, 1914, vol. 5.

———, *On the Glory of the Athenians*, trans. F. C. Babbit, 1936.

Proclus, *Lives of Homer, Chrestomathy*, trans. H. G. Evelyn-White, 1914 (includes summaries of the Trojan cycle; cf. http://www.maicar.com/GML/TCSummaries.html).

Sophocles, *The Ajax of Sophocles*, edited with introduction and notes by Sir Richard Jebb, Cambridge: Cambridge University Press, 1893.

———, *Antigone*, trans. R. Jebb, Cambridge University Press, 1891.

———, *Electra*, trans. R. Jebb, Cambridge, MA: Harvard University Press, 1894.

———, *Oedipus at Colonus*, trans. R. Jebb, Cambridge, MA: Harvard University Press, 1889.

———, *Oedipus Tyrannus*, trans. R. Jebb, Cambridge University Press, 1887.

———, *Philoctetes*, trans. R. Jebb, Cambridge University Press 1898.

———, *The Women of Trachis*, trans. R. Jebb, Cambridge, MA: Harvard University Press, 1892.

Strabo, *Geography*, trans. H. C. Hamilton and W. Falconer, 1917ff.

Theophrastus, *Characters*, trans. R. C. Jebb, 1870.

Thucydides, *Peloponnesian War*, trans. C. F. Smith, 1919–1923.

....

INDEX LOCORUM

·················